WHITE-COLLAR CRIME

SAGE Text/Reader Series in Criminology and Criminal Justice

Craig Hemmens, Series Editor

Other Titles of Related Interest

WHITE-COLLAR CRIME A Text/Reader

Brian K. Payne
Georgia State University

Los Angeles | London | New Delhi
Singapore | Washington DC

Los Angeles | London | New Delhi
Singapore | Washington DC

FOR INFORMATION:

SAGE Publications, Inc.
2455 Teller Road
Thousand Oaks, California 91320
E-mail: order@sagepub.com

SAGE Publications Ltd.
1 Oliver's Yard
55 City Road
London EC1Y 1SP
United Kingdom

SAGE Publications India Pvt. Ltd.
B 1/I 1 Mohan Cooperative Industrial Area
Mathura Road, New Delhi 110 044
India

SAGE Publications Asia-Pacific Pte. Ltd.
33 Pekin Street #02-01
Far East Square
Singapore 048763

Acquisitions Editor: Jerry Westby
Editorial Assistant: Erim Sarbuland
Production Editor: Catherine M. Chilton
Copy Editor: Kris Bergstad
Typesetter: C&M Digitals (P) Ltd.
Proofreader: Tracy Villano
Indexer: Diggs Publication Services
Cover Designer: Janet Kiesel
Marketing Manager: Erica DeLuca
Permissions: Karen Ehrmann

Printed in the United States of America

Library of Congress Cataloging-in-Publication Data

White-collar crime : a text/reader / editor, Brian K. Payne.

p. cm.
Includes bibliographical references and index.

ISBN 978-1-4129-8749-3 (pbk. : alk. paper)

1. White collar crimes. 2. Criminal justice, Administration of.
I. Payne, Brian K.

HV6768.W492 2012
364.16'8—dc23   2011029056

This book is printed on acid-free paper.

11 12 13 14 15 10 9 8 7 6 5 4 3 2 1

Brief Contents

Detailed Contents

Section XIV The Corrections Subsystem and White-Collar Crime 591

READINGS 622

Foreword

You hold in your hands a book that is part of a series we have created at Sage and that we think represents an innovative approach to criminology and criminal justice pedagogy. It is a "text/reader." What that means is that we have attempted to blend the two most commonly used types of books, the textbook and the reader, in a way that will appeal to both students and faculty.

Our experience as teachers and scholars has been that textbooks for the core classes in criminal justice and criminology (or any other social science discipline) leave many students and professors cold. The textbooks are huge, crammed with photographs, charts, highlighted material, and all sorts of pedagogical devices intended to increase student interest. Too often, though, these books end up creating a sort of sensory overload for students; they suffer from a focus on "bells and whistles," such as fancy graphics, at the expense of coverage of the most current research on the subject matter.

The reader-type book, on the other hand, typically comprises recent and classic research articles on the subject matter. These books generally suffer from an absence of meaningful textual material. Articles are simply lined up and presented to the students, with little or no context or explanation. Students, particularly undergraduate students, are often confused and overwhelmed by the jargon and detailed statistical analysis presented in the articles.

This text/reader represents our attempt to take the best of both the textbook and reader approaches. It includes many research articles on white-collar crime and is intended to serve either as a supplement to a core textbook or as a stand-alone text. The book includes a combination of previously published articles and textual material that introduces and provides some structure and context for the selected readings. The book is divided into a number of sections. The sections follow the typical content and structure of a textbook on the subject. Each section of the book has an overview of the topic that serves to introduce, explain, and provide context for the readings that follow. The readings are a selection of the best recent research that has appeared in academic journals, as well as some essential older readings. The articles have been edited as necessary. This variety of research and perspectives provides students with an understanding of both the development of research and the current status of research on white-collar crime. This approach gives the student the opportunity to learn the basics (in the text portion of each section) and to read some of the most interesting research on the subject.

There are also a preface and an introductory chapter. The preface explains the organization and content of the book. The introductory chapter provides a framework for the text and articles that follow and introduces relevant themes, issues, and concepts. This will assist the student in understanding the articles.

Each section also includes a summary of the material covered and a selection of discussion questions. These summaries and discussion questions should facilitate student thought and class discussion of the material.

We acknowledge that this approach may be viewed by some as more challenging than the traditional textbook. To that we say, "Yes! It is!" But we believe that if we raise the bar, our students will rise to the challenge. Research shows that students and faculty often find textbooks boring to read. It is our belief that many criminology and criminal justice instructors welcome the opportunity to teach without having to rely on a standard textbook that covers only the most basic information and that lacks both depth of coverage and attention to current research.

This book provides an alternative for instructors who want to get more out of the basic criminal justice courses or curriculum than one can get from a basic textbook that is aimed at the lowest common denominator and is filled with flashy but often useless features that merely serve to drive up the cost of the textbook. This book is intended for instructors who want to go beyond the ordinary, basic coverage provided in textbooks.

We also believe students will find this approach more interesting. They are given the opportunity to read current, cutting-edge research on the subject, while also being provided with background and context for this research. We hope that this unconventional approach will make learning and teaching more fun. Crime and criminal justice are fascinating subjects, and they deserve to be presented in an interesting manner. We hope you will agree.

Craig Hemmens, JD, PhD, Series Editor
Department of Criminology & Criminal Justice
Missouri State University

Preface

Compared to other subjects in the social sciences, relatively few white-collar crime texts are available for use in criminal justice, criminology, and sociology courses. Those that are available have done a great job introducing students to the topic. One thing I found missing among available texts, however, was a book that approached the topic as a crime problem, a criminal justice problem, and a social problem. In effect, my intent has been to create a work that examines the many facets of white-collar crime by focusing on different crimes committed during the course of work as well as the various systems that are given the task of responding to white-collar misconduct.

In addition, I have addressed white-collar crime by balancing consensus and conflict perspectives. The need to objectively understand white-collar offending and the most appropriate response to white-collar offending is central to my approach in this text/reader. All too often, white-collar crimes and white-collar criminals are vilified with little thought given to the intricacies surrounding the event or the system's response to the event. This vilification limits our understanding of the topic.

To demonstrate why it is important to address white-collar crime objectively, consider a book we can call *Introduction to Criminal Justice* as an example. If the author presented crime and criminals as inherently evil, readers would not be given an accurate picture of criminal justice (or crime, for that matter). The same can be said of a white-collar crime book—if authors discuss white-collar crime or white-collar criminals as inherently evil, an inaccurate foundation from which readers can understand the criminal justice response to white-collar crime is created.

Of course, I am not saying that white-collar crime is not bad or that white-collar criminals do not harm society. Instead, I am suggesting that we need to go beyond these emotions and perceptions in order to fully understand white-collar crime. Indeed, throughout *White-Collar Crime: A Text/Reader* readers will learn about the various consequences stemming from white-collar misconduct. Readers will also be exposed to the different systems involved in both perpetrating and responding to white-collar crime.

Following the format of the SAGE Criminology and Criminal Justice Text/Reader series, this book includes original textual material and a collection of scholarly journal articles addressing white-collar crime. The articles were chosen to help increase understanding about this type of behavior and the criminal justice system's response to the behavior. The textual material summarizes each relevant topic and creates a foundation from which readers will be able to understand and critically analyze the articles in each section. The book is intended as either a standalone or a supplemental book for undergraduate and graduate classes focusing on white-collar crime.

The book will be of value to criminal justice, criminology, and sociology courses focusing on white-collar crime. Criminal justice and criminological topics related to white-collar crime are integrated throughout the text. Because many white-collar crime texts fail to address either criminal justice or criminological themes, integrating these topics together should make the text more appealing to a wider audience.

This book is divided into 14 sections that represent the topics covered in most white-collar crime courses. They include the following:

- Introduction and Overview of White-Collar Crime
- Understanding White-Collar Crime
- Crimes in Sales-Related Occupations
- Crimes in the Health Care System
- Crime in Systems of Social Control
- Crimes in the Educational System
- Crime in the Economic and Technological Systems
- Crimes in the Housing System
- Crimes by the Corporate System
- Environmental Crime
- Explaining White-Collar Crime
- Policing White-Collar Crime
- Judicial Proceedings and White-Collar Crime
- The Corrections Subsystem and White-Collar Crime

Several features have been included to make the book more user friendly for students and professors. These features include:

1. Each section concludes with a bulleted summary statement.

2. A list of 5 to 10 critical thinking questions is included after the summary statements.

3. After each introductory chapter, two or three readings addressing the topic covered in the section are included. These readings include both classic articles on white-collar crime as well as more recent articles. Additional readings are also available on SAGE's website: www.sagepub.com/payne

4. Before each reading, a one-paragraph summary of the reading is included to help transitions between the readings.

5. Each reading is followed by three critical thinking questions.

6. Each section includes between two and four photographs that are appropriate to the topic.

7. The book includes a "How to Read a Research Article" essay similar to those in other SAGE text/ readers, advising students how to get the most out of journal articles and research papers.

8. A list of key terms is included at the end of each section and defined in the Glossary.

9. Recent examples, particularly those that are interesting to college students, are integrated throughout the work.

10. Inserts called "In Focus" are included in Sections III through XIV to further describe real examples of white-collar crimes and issues related to each specific section.

A number of different ancillaries are available for students and professors using *White-Collar Crime: A Text/Reader*. Visit www.sagepub.com/payne to access these valuable instructor and student resources:

- The password-protected Instructor Teaching Site includes a test bank, PowerPoint slides, and sample syllabi
- The free, open-access Student Study Site

It is my hope that this text/reader and the accompanying ancillaries will help readers to fully appreciate and understand white-collar crime and the justice system's response to this misconduct.

Acknowledgments

This work would not have been completed without the guidance, direction, and support of many different individuals. I am indebted to Craig Hemmens (Boise State University) for calling me one Thursday afternoon and asking if I would be interested in authoring the work. Also, SAGE Executive Editor Jerry Westby had a way of making it seem like deadlines really meant something and his excitement about this project helped me to move along. I very much appreciate the efforts of Jerry's development editors, Erim Sarbuland and Leah Mori, in helping to keep the project running along as smoothly as possible. In addition, I am indebted to Catherine Chilton, production editor, and to Kristin Bergstad for her helpful and amazing skills as a copy editor. Thanks also to Erica Deluca for her careful attention given to marketing this work. As well, the rest of the SAGE team has been a pleasure to work with.

I am also indebted to a small army of graduate assistants who helped with different parts of the project. Tatum Asante, Andrea Barber, Erin Marsh, Susannah Tapp, and Johnnie Cain spent countless hours locating references for me. Danielle Gentile and Katie Taber created the Glossary and performed numerous other tasks that I often assigned at the last minute. A white-collar crime professor could not ask for a better group of graduate assistants!

Several friends and colleagues also helped in different ways. Randy Gainey and Ruth Triplett (both at Old Dominion University) read different parts of the book and provided valuable feedback. Leah Daigle (Georgia State University) was an invaluable sounding board for those moments when I felt like whining about workload. It was particularly enjoyable to write the book at the same time that Randy and Leah were working on their own separate text/readers. Just as I would not want to be stranded in the desert by myself, it was refreshing to have friends plowing through this sort of project at the same time.

I cannot say enough about the invaluable feedback provided by reviewers throughout this process. The final product looks nothing like the original proposal. The feedback from the reviewers helped me to shape a book that best meets the needs of the discipline. Those who reviewed different parts of drafts of the book included: George Burrus, Southern Illinois University Carbondale; William Calathes, New Jersey City University; John Casten, Old Dominion University; William Cleveland, Sam Houston State University; Heith Copes, University of Alabama at Birmingham; Dean Dabney, Georgia State University; Lisa Eargle, Francis Marion University; Robert Handy, Arizona State University; Patrick Hegarty, Stonehill College; Roy Janisch, Pittsburg State University; Shayne Jones, University of South Florida; Kent Kerly, University of Alabama at Birmingham; Jiletta Kubena, Sam Houston State University; Tom O'Connor, Austin Peay University; Paul Leighton, Eastern Michigan University; Nicole Leeper Piquero, University of Texas at Dallas; Jerome Randall, University of Central Florida; Dawn Rothe, Old Dominion University; Rashi Shukla, University of Central Oklahoma; Christopher Warburton, John Jay College; and Bruce Zucker, California State University, Northridge.

I want to thank my family—Kathleen, Chloe, Charles, and Claire. Kathleen is the perfect soul mate and mother to our children. Some say that marriage is a contract. If that's the case, I got the better end of that deal. At age 10, Chloe is the most precious ballerina I have ever watched dance. Of course, when she's on stage, she's the only one I see. At age 8, Charles—who told me he wants to be an author—has a sense of wonder that makes me proud and a sense of humor that keeps me giggling. As my favorite chess opponent, he talks smack to his dad better than any other 8-year-old I know. At just under 5, Claire has a smile that opens my heart and my mind to all that is possible. She inspires me to see the many ways that messages can be sent between individuals. If you watch closely, thanks to the photojournalist I married, you'll see photos of each of my kids scattered throughout this book. To my family—I love you all very much.

—bkp

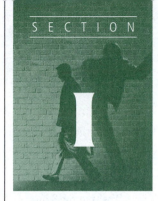

Introduction and Overview of White-Collar Crime

A Systems Perspective

Not long ago an employee of a Netherlands-based McDonald's was fired after she gave a coworker an extra piece of cheese on a hamburger ordered by the coworker. The worker then filed a lawsuit arguing that the firing was unjust. The court eventually decided that the worker should not have been fired for doling out an extra piece of cheese and ordered the restaurant to pay several months in back pay to the worker. In the words of the court, "The dismissal was too severe a measure. It is just a slice of cheese" ("McDonald's Wrong to Fire Worker," 2010).

This case raises several questions relevant to crime in the workplace. Did the worker commit a crime by breaking the restaurant's rules? Did the restaurant commit a crime by firing the worker for giving away an extra piece of cheese? Why did the worker give out the extra piece of cheese? Would the case have been handled differently if it occurred in the United States or another country? Have we committed similar acts during the course of our own jobs?

Rule breaking in the workplace is common. Consider the following examples as they were described verbatim in press reports:

- A practicing attorney in Orange County, California, was arrested today on charges that include one count of conspiracy to commit grand theft, and 97 felony counts of grand theft by false pretenses, with sentencing enhancements for white collar crime and excessive taking. ("OC Lawyer Arrested for Defrauding 400 Homeowners," 2010)
- This conviction is based upon [the denturist's] conduct involving five Washington State Medicaid clients across three counties for whom she was supposed to have provided dentures and related services to and then billed the program for services she did not render. (*Medicaid Fraud Reports*, 2009)
- ***** played a leadership role in the underlying conspiracy which involved at least 32 residential properties in the greater Phoenix area. The objective of the conspiracy was to recruit unqualified borrowers as straw buyers, submit fraudulent loan applications on their behalf, obtain mortgage loans in excess of the selling price of the property and then take the excess amount of the loans out through escrow in what is known as a "cash back" scheme. (Norman, 2009)
- Dr. ***** pleaded guilty . . . for submitting a false claim to the state's Medicaid program. ***** specialized in treating drug addiction patients. . . . The charge was based on evidence that he double billed for initial consultations, by collecting the full fee from the patient and also billing Medicaid. ***** was sentenced to pay a $2,000 fine, $1,600 in restitution to Medicaid, and serve 30 days in the county jail. (*Medicaid Fraud Reports*, 2009)
- The California Department of Insurance announced that ***** of Huntington Park, Calif., was arrested Dec. 22 and faces one felony count of grand theft after allegedly taking a premium payment and failing to purchase a policy for the victim. ("Huntington Park Insurance Agent Arrested," 2009)
- Attorney General Abbott announced on August 13 that licensed vocational nurse ***** was indicted on two counts of injury to an elderly person by exploitation. ***** allegedly diverted hydrocodone in April 2008 from four elderly residents of the Good Samaritan Society, Denton Village, for her personal use. (*Medicaid Fraud Reports*, 2009)
- A teacher was arrested on suspicion of putting a hit on one of his students. *****, a 10th-grade teacher at Mundy's Mill High School in Clayton County, is accused of trying to persuade another student to kill a 16-year-old boy. ("Teacher Accused of Putting Hit on Student," 2009)

Three similarities exist across each of these examples: (1) in terms of time, they were committed during the course of work; (2) in terms of location, they occurred in a work setting; (3) in terms of offender role, the offender was serving as a worker. At the most general level, one might be tempted to refer to these behaviors as workplace offenses. On another level, one could argue that each of these examples helps us to understand what is meant by the concept of white-collar crime.

Edwin Sutherland first introduced the concept of white-collar crime in 1939 during a presentation to the American Sociological Association. A decade later in his now classic book, *White-Collar Crime*, he defined the concept as "crime committed by a person of respectability and high social status in the course of his occupation" (Sutherland, 1949). Sutherland was calling attention to the fact that criminal acts were committed by individuals from all social and economic classes. He used the phrase *white-collar* to emphasize the occupational status assigned to individuals.

In Section II, more attention will be given to how white-collar crime is conceptualized. As a brief introduction to the concept, three factors are typically used to distinguish white-collar crimes from other crimes. First, white-collar crimes are committed during the course of one's job. Second, the offender's occupational role plays a central feature in the perpetration of the crime. Third, the offender's occupation is viewed as a legitimate occupation by society (e.g., a drug dealer's occupation is illegitimate, but a pharmacist's occupation is legitimate).

Perhaps an example can help to clarify what is meant by crime committed as a part of one's employment. Believe it or not—some professors have committed crimes. Consider a case in which a psychology professor was charged for hiring actors to pretend that they had participated in his research study as part of an investigation that alleged that the professor had committed scientific fraud. The actors were interviewed by investigators, but they did not realize that the interviews were actual official interviews because the professor had told them the interviews were part of a mock trial he was conducting for his research study (Office of New York State Attorney General, 2010). This would be a white-collar crime—the offender's employment role was central to the act. Alternatively, consider a case where a criminal justice professor was charged with sexually assaulting students (Elofson, 2010). This would not typically be considered a white-collar crime unless the offender's employment role was central to the commission of the act.

▲ **Photo 1.1** White-collar crimes typically occur where offenders work. Wall Street has been heralded as the location of many white-collar crimes. In reality, white-collar misconduct occurs in all types of workplace settings.

Distinguishing between white-collar crime and traditional crimes is not meant to suggest that one form of crime is worse than the other. Instead, the intent is to note that different forms of crime exist and a full understanding of crime, explanations of crime, and responses to crime will not occur unless the differences between these forms of crime are understood.

Why Study White-Collar Crime?

Six reasons support the need to study white-collar crime. First, and perhaps foremost, white-collar crime is a serious problem in our society. Estimates provided by the Federal Bureau of Investigation (FBI) routinely suggest that far more is lost to white-collar crimes than to traditional property crimes such as larceny, robbery, and burglary. Beyond these economic costs, and as will be shown later in this text, white-collar offenses have the potential to cause serious physical and emotional damage to victims.

Second, unlike some offense types, it is important to recognize that white-collar offenses affect everyone. While a specific street offense might have just one or two victims, white-collar offenses tend to have a large number of victims, and on a certain level, some white-collar offenses are so traumatic that they actually may influence all members of society. For instance, Bernie Madoff's transgressions duped thousands of individuals and organizations out of billions of dollars. It was not just these individuals, however, who were victims. Members of society who then felt distrust for financial institutions and their employees were also affected by Madoff's behaviors. Members of society may also experience what one social scientist calls demoralization costs (Coffee, 1980). In this context, demoralization means that individuals have less faith in societal values, and this reduction in faith may actually create a situation where individuals justify their own future misdeeds based on the illicit behaviors of those white-collar and corporate organizations we have been socialized to trust. As one author team wrote, "Because most white-collar offenses violate trust, they breed distrust" (Moore & Mills, 1990, p. 413).

A third reason it is important to study white-collar offending is that by studying white-collar offending we can learn more about all types of crime. Just as medical researchers might learn more about all forms of diseases by studying one form of disease, the study of white-collar crime allows criminologists, students, members of the public, and policy makers greater insight into all variations of criminal behavior and types of criminal offenders.

Fourth, it is important to study white-collar crime so that effective prevention and intervention systems and policies can be developed. It cannot be assumed that prevention and intervention policies and strategies developed for, and used for, traditional forms of crime are appropriate for responding to offenses committed during the course of one's occupation. The underlying dynamics of different forms of white-collar crime need to be understood so that response strategies and policies based on those dynamics can be developed.

▲ **Photo 1.2**   Many careers exist that target white-collar offending. In this photo, EPA workers are responding to a specific form of white-collar crime, environmental white-collar crime.

Fifth, and as will be discussed in more detail below, studying white-collar crime provides important information about potential careers related to white-collar crime. This is not meant to suggest that you can learn how to be a white-collar criminal by studying white-collar crime; rather, a number of occupations exist that are designed to help the criminal and civil justice systems respond to white-collar crimes. These occupations typically require college degrees and many are more lucrative than traditional criminal justice occupations. To actually enter one of those careers, one would need a keen understanding of white-collar crime. Thus, we study white-collar crime in order to develop the critical thinking skills and base of awareness needed to understand white-collar crime.

Finally, studying white-collar crime allows additional insight into a particular culture and various subcultures. On the one hand, the study of white-collar crime provides an insider's view into the American workforce and the cultural underpinnings that are the foundation of values driving the activities of the workforce. On the other hand, the study of white-collar crime provides all of us additional insight into specific occupational subcultures, with all of which we have some degree of familiarity—whether accurate or inaccurate. Many individuals assume that a trip to the auto mechanic has the potential to result in unnecessary repairs and outrageous bills. Few, however, assume that trips to the doctor or pharmacist might result in similar outcomes. As will be shown later in this text, however, white-collar crime research shows that misconduct occurs in all occupations. By understanding misconduct in these occupations, we better understand the occupational subcultures where the misconduct occurs.

Researching White-Collar Crime

Several different research strategies are used to study white-collar crime and white-collar criminals. For the most part, these research strategies are similar to those used to study other social problems. The way that these strategies apply to white-collar crime, however, is somewhat different from how they might be applied to research studies of other topics. Strategies that can be used to research white-collar crime include but are not limited to:

- Surveys
- Archival research
- Field research
- Experiments
- Case studies

Survey Research and White-Collar Crime

Surveys are perhaps among the more common research strategies used to study white-collar crime. Survey methods include on-site administration surveys, face-to-face interviews, telephone interviews, and mail surveys. Strengths and weaknesses exist for each of these strategies (see Table 1.1). The aim of surveys is to gather information from a group of individuals and use that information to paint a picture of the topic under consideration.

Table 1.1   Strengths and Weaknesses of Different Survey Methods

Survey Method	Strengths	Weaknesses
On-site administration	<ul><li>Surveys occur in one setting</li><li>Large sample is possible</li><li>Does not take long to gather</li><li>Convenient</li></ul>	<ul><li>Difficult to give surveys on site to both offenders and victims</li><li>No database of white-collar offenders</li><li>Educational differences make it hard to use the same surveys for everyone</li><li>Hard for some to recall incidents</li><li>Gaining entrance and trust of victims hard</li></ul>
Face-to-face interviews	<ul><li>Can watch respondent's reactions</li><li>Probing is an option</li><li>Rapport is easier to develop</li></ul>	<ul><li>More time consuming</li><li>More expensive</li><li>Difficulty in finding participants and place to conduct interviews</li><li>Trust and rapport is important</li><li>Must gain access and permission of businesses</li></ul>
Telephone interviews	<ul><li>Most comprehensive studies have been conducted using telephone interviews</li><li>Respondents seem more open answering questions over the phone</li></ul>	<ul><li>People without home phones are excluded from the study</li><li>Some do not answer their phones due to increase in telemarketing</li></ul>
Mail surveys	<ul><li>Less costly</li><li>Able to survey a large number of respondents.</li></ul>	<ul><li>May not fully understand the questions</li><li>No opportunity to develop rapport</li><li>Takes time to develop a comprehensive list of residents</li><li>Certain subjects are excluded from mailing list</li></ul>

Groups who are surveyed in white-collar crime research studies include criminal justice officials, members of the public, victims of white-collar crime, and white-collar offenders. Each of these groups has the potential to provide important information about various issues related to white-collar crime.

Surveys of criminal justice officials in the white-collar crime literature tend to focus on the strategies used to identify and respond to white-collar offenses, the kinds of offenses encountered by the officials, and the barriers that must be overcome to successfully respond to the cases. One author interviewed probation officers to determine how white-collar offenders were supervised by community corrections officials (Mason, 2007). Another author described a survey of 1,142 fraud examiners conducted by the Association of Certified Fraud Examiners (Holtfreter, 2005). As will be demonstrated later in this text, this research provided important insight about the types of offenders, offenses, and organizations involved in occupational fraud cases.

White-collar crime researchers have also surveyed members of the public to assess attitudes about, and experiences with, white-collar crime. Such research is useful for at least five reasons. First, determining what members of the public think about white-collar crime provides a baseline that helps to paint a picture about a culture at a given moment of time. For example, if surveys of the public show that the public is tolerant of white-collar offending, this would tell us something about the culture at that moment in time. Second, focusing on citizens' attitudes about white-collar crime provides an indication of the likelihood that individuals might engage in white-collar criminal activity. Third, surveying members of the public potentially allows researchers access to a larger group of white-collar offenders than they might otherwise get, particularly in self-report studies. Fourth, and in a similar way, surveys of members of the public could provide researchers access to a large group of white-collar crime victims. A survey of 400 residents of Tennessee, for example, found that 227 (58%) reported being victimized by fraud in the prior 5 years (Mason & Benson, 1996). Fifth, surveys of the public could provide policy makers with information they can use to develop policies and laws designed to prevent white-collar crime.

Researchers have also surveyed white-collar crime victims to increase our understanding about the victimization experiences of this group. In this context, victims could be (1) individuals, (2) businesses and nongovernmental institutions, or (3) "government as a buyer, giver, and protector-gatekeeper" (Edelhertz, 1983, p. 117). One of the issues that arises in such studies is the ability to identify a sample of white-collar crime victims. An early study on appliance "repairman" fraud used a sample of 88 victims of one offender, "Frank Hanks" (not his real name) (Vaughan & Carlo, 1975). Victims were identified through press reports, prosecutors' files, and public files. Incidentally, the researchers identified 133 victims who had complained about the repairman to various consumer agencies. Through this survey, the researchers were able to identify complaint patterns, provide insight into the victims' interactions with Hanks, and delineate the experience of victimization. The authors also drew attention to the plight of victims trying to formally resolve the cases. They noted that "pursuing justice became more expensive than being a victim and they [often] dropped the matter" (p. 158).

Another issue that arises when surveying white-collar crime victims is that victims may be reluctant to discuss their experiences. Survey respondents may not trust researchers who ask about fraud victimization, perhaps partly because they are on guard about having been scammed in the first place (Mason & Benson, 1996). Despite these issues, the need to study white-collar crime victims continues because they have been ignored historically in victimization studies and the victims movement (Moore & Mills, 1990).

Surveys of white-collar offenders are equally difficult to conduct. Sutherland (1941) recognized this as a barrier in white-collar crime research shortly after introducing the concept. White-collar offenders simply do not want to participate in research studies. As noted above, general self-report surveys of members of the public might help to develop samples of white-collar offenders. Other times, researchers have surveyed members of a specific occupational group with the aim of identifying attitudes about white-collar offending among members of that occupational group. Criminologist Dean Dabney, for example, interviewed nurses (1995) and pharmacists (2001) to shed light on the types of crimes occurring in those fields. After he built up rapport over time, participants in his study were willing to open up about crimes in their occupations, particularly those crimes committed by their coworkers.

Other researchers have confronted barriers in their efforts to interview convicted white-collar offenders. This group of offenders experiences a significant amount of stigma and that stigma may keep them from wanting to talk about their experiences with researchers. One journalist tried contacting 30 different convicted white-collar offenders who had been released from prison in an effort to try to get them to contribute to a story she was writing. She described their resistance to talking with her the following way: "Understandably, most of them told me to get lost. They had done their time and that part of their life was a closed chapter. They had made new lives and did not want to remind anyone of their pasts" (Loane, 2000, n.p.).

Across each of these survey types, a number of problems potentially call into question the validity and reliability of white-collar crime surveys. First, as one research team noted, the field of criminology has not yet developed "comprehensive measures . . . that tap into the concepts of white-collar and street crime" (Holtfreter, Van Slyke, Bratton, & Gertz, 2008, p. 57). The lack of comprehensive measures makes it difficult to compare results across studies and generalize findings to various occupational settings. Second, difficulties developing representative samples are inherent within white-collar crime studies. It is particularly difficult to develop a random sample of white-collar crime victims or offenders. Third, questions about white-collar crime on surveys are potentially influenced by other items on the survey, meaning the findings might actually reflect methodological influences as opposed to actual patterns. Fourth, the scarcity of certain types of white-collar crime surveys (like those focusing on offenders) has made it even more difficult to develop and conduct these sorts of studies—if more researchers were able to do these surveys, others would learn how to follow in their path. Despite these potential problems, surveys are useful tools to empirically assess various issues related to white-collar offending.

Archival Research and White-Collar Crime

Archival research is also relatively common in the white-collar crime literature. In this context, archival research refers to studies that use some form of record (or archive) as a database in the study (Berg, 2009). Archives commonly used in white-collar crime studies include official case records, pre-sentence reports, media reports, and case descriptions of specific white-collar offenses.

Case records are official records that are housed in an agency that has formal social control duties. One problem that arises with using case records is locating a sample that would include the types of offenders that criminologists would label as white-collar offenders (Wheeler, Wiesburd, & Bode, 1988). Still, with a concerted effort, researchers have been able to use case records to develop databases from which a great deal of valuable information about white-collar crime will flow. Crofts (2003), for example, reviewed 182 case files of larcenies by employees. Of those 182 cases, she found that gambling was a direct cause of the larceny in 36 cases. Of those 36 cases, Crofts found that 27 offenders were responsible for 1,616 charges of larceny by employee. Note that there is absolutely no other way Crofts could have found these findings other than by reviewing case records.

Researchers have also used pre-sentence reports to study different topics related to white-collar crime. **Pre-sentence reports** are developed by probation officers and include a wealth of information about offenders, their life histories, their criminal careers, and the sentences they received. In one of the most cited white-collar crime studies, criminologist Stanton Wheeler and his colleagues (Wheeler, Weisburd, & Bode, 1988) used the pre-sentence reports of convicted white-collar offenders from seven federal judicial circuits to gain insight into the dynamics of offenders, offenses, and sentencing practices. The authors focused on eight offenses: securities fraud, anti-trust violations, bribery, tax offenses, bank embezzlement, post and wire fraud, false claims and statements, and credit and lending institution fraud. Their research provided groundbreaking information about how white-collar offenders compared to traditional offenders as well as information about the way offenders are sentenced in federal court. The findings are discussed in more detail in later sections of this text.

Researchers have also used **media reports** to study white-collar crime. Using news articles, press reports, and television depictions of white-collar crimes helps researchers (a) demonstrate what kind of information members of the public are likely to receive about white-collar crime and (b) uncover possible patterns guiding white-collar offenses that may not be studied through other means. With regard to studies focusing on what information the public receives about white-collar offenders, criminologist Michael Levi (2006) focused on how financial white-collar crimes were reported in various media outlets. His results suggested that these offenses were portrayed as "infotainment" rather than serious crimes, suggesting that the cases were sensationalized to provide somewhat inaccurate portrayals of the offenses. Another researcher who used newspaper articles to study the portrayal of white-collar crime found that the cases tended to be reported in business or law sections rather than the crime sections of newspapers, suggesting that the behaviors are not real crimes (Stephenson-Burton, 1995).

With regard to the use of press reports to describe patterns surrounding specific forms of white-collar crimes, a recent dissertation by Philip Stinson (2009) focused on 2,119 cases of police misconduct committed by 1,746 police officers that were reported in the national media between 2005 and 2007. In using media reports, Stinson was able to access a larger number of police misconduct cases than he would have been able to access through other methods. His findings provide useful fodder for those interested in generating awareness about police misconduct.

Another archive that may be of use to white-collar crime researchers involves **case descriptions of specific white-collar offenses** that may be provided by some agencies. In some states, for example, the state bar association publishes misdeeds committed by attorneys. Researchers have used these case descriptions to examine how lawyers are sanctioned in Alabama (Payne & Stevens, 1999) and Virginia (Payne, Time, & Raper, 2005). Some national agencies provide reports of white-collar crimes committed by occupations they are charged with regulating. The National Association of Medicaid Fraud Control Units, for instance, describes cases prosecuted by Medicaid Fraud Control Units in a publication titled *Medicaid Fraud Reports*. This publication has served as a database for studies on crimes by doctors (Payne, 1995), crimes in nursing homes (Payne & Cikovic, 1995), crimes in the home health care field (Payne & Gray, 2001), and theft by employees (Payne & Strasser, 2010). Table 1.2 shows the kinds of information available in the fraud reports for these offense types.

With each of these types of archival research, researchers often develop a coding scheme and use that scheme much like they would use a survey instrument. Instead of interviewing an individual, the researcher "asks" the archive a set of questions. Several advantages exist with the use of case records for white-collar crime research (see Payne, 2005). For example, such strategies provide white-collar crime researchers access to a large group of subjects that they would not be able to otherwise access. It would have been impossible,

Table 1.2   Types of Information Available in Fraud Reports

Type of Crime	Case Description Example
Financial abuse by workers against patients	Attorney General Sorrell announced on October 6 that Heather Whitehouse, a former caregiver who provided care to seniors with Alzheimer's disease, has been sentenced to jail for financial exploitation of a vulnerable adult, fraud and other crimes of dishonesty. The charges stemmed from her employment as a caregiver at The Arbors, a residential care community dedicated to serving the needs of seniors with Alzheimer's disease and related memory impairments.
Physical abuse against patients	Attorney General Abbott announced on August 6 that home living staff member Brandon Eugene Crow was indicted by a state grand jury for injury to a disabled individual. This case alleges that Crow, while employed with D & S Residential, gave a resident a cold shower, shaved him with a loose razor causing multiple scratches on his face and threw him against a bathroom door causing a bruise on his back.
Fraud by doctors	Attorney General Abbott announced on December 2, 2005 that Dr. Sanford Rosensweig, a podiatrist, was sentenced by Judge Sam Sparks in United States Federal District Court, Western District of Texas, to serve 24 months incarceration, ordered to pay full restitution, fined $25,000 and to surrender his medical license. . . .Rosensweig was convicted of utilizing unlicensed persons to perform routine foot care and billing Medicare and Medicaid for physician services.
Fraud by pharmacists	Attorney General McMaster announced on April 30 that Christopher L. Alderman, the owner of Alderman Pharmacy, a pharmacy, was convicted on April 30, 2009 of two counts of Filing a False Claim. . . . Alderman was sentenced to three years and a $1,000 fine, both suspended.
Corporate offending by medical company	Attorney General Charlie Christ announced on November 18 that Alexis Vincent Robinson was arrested and charged with one count of Organized Fraud and two counts of Criminal Use of Personal Identification Information. Robinson, president of A&S Respiratory Home Medical, Inc., was accused of stealing more than $500,000 from the state's Medicaid program in a scheme that included the fraudulent use of the identities of numerous Medicaid recipients. . . . Robinson filed the claims in the names of Medicaid recipients without their knowledge, seeking reimbursement for durable medical equipment that the patients never received and in most cases did not request.
Drug theft by nurses	Attorney General Abbott announced on May 14 that licensed vocational nurses John Vanecek and Dara Dabelgott were indicted by a state grand jury for obtaining a controlled substance by fraud, a third-degree felony. The two allegedly diverted patient narcotics on February 27, 2008, from Woolridge Nursing Home, where they were employed as LVNs. Both admitted to taking the narcotics.

for example, for Stinson to locate and interview more than 1,700 police officers who had been arrested for misconduct. Another benefit is that these strategies allow white-collar crime researchers to explore changes over long periods of time, particularly if the researchers have access to case records that cover an extended period of time. A third benefit is that the research subject, in this case the white-collar offender or victim described in the case record, will not react to being studied simply because there are no interactions between the researcher and the subject.

As with any research strategy, a number of limitations arise when using archives to study white-collar crime. The saying, "you get what you get" comes to mind. The case files are inflexible and white-collar crime researchers will not be able to probe as they would with interview strategies. Also, the way that records are coded or saved over time may change, which will create problems when researchers try to study white-collar crimes over longer periods of time. Perhaps the most significant problem that arises is that these cases typically represent only those that have come to the attention of the authorities. In effect, unreported white-collar crimes would not be included in most types of archival research. Common reasons that victims will not report white-collar crimes include: (a) a belief that there is not enough evidence, (b) the offense is not seen as that serious, (c) concerns that reporting would be futile, (d) concerns that reporting the victimization could be costly, particularly for businesses that are victims of white-collar crimes, (e) shame, (f) businesses may want to handle it on their own, and (g) realization that it may take more time than it seems worth taking to respond to the case (Crofts, 2003). If nobody reports the white-collar crime, it will not be a part of an official record.

Indeed, Sutherland (1940) recognized decades ago that official statistics (and records) typically exclude many white-collar crimes.

Field Research

Field research involves strategies where researchers enter a particular setting and gather data through their observations in those settings (Berg, 2009). In some instances, researchers will share their identity as a researcher with those in the setting, while in other instances researchers may choose to be anonymous. These strategies can be quite time consuming and are conducted much less frequently than other white-collar crime studies, but they have the potential to offer valuable information about behavior in the workplace. For example, Stannard (1973) entered a nursing home as a janitor and worked there for several months. While the staff knew that he was a researcher, they seemed to forget this over time and their actions included various types of misconduct (ranging from minor offenses to more serious ones that could have resulted in one resident's death).

In many white-collar crime studies, field research methods are combined with other research strategies. As an illustration, Croall (1989) conducted court observations as part of a broader study focusing on crimes against consumers. She observed 50 cases and used the time she spent doing those observations to develop rapport with the justice officials involved in handling the cases. Over time, the officials later granted Croall access to their case files. Had she not "put in her time," so to speak, she probably would have been denied access to the case files.

Experiments

Experiments are studies where researchers examine how the presence of one variable (the causal or independent variable) produces an outcome (the effect or dependent variable). The classic experimental design entails using two groups—an experimental group and a control group. Subjects are randomly selected and assigned to one of the groups. Members of the experimental group receive the independent variable (or the treatment) and members of the control group do not. The researcher conducts observations before and after the independent variable is introduced to the experimental group to determine whether the presence of the independent variable produced observable or significant changes.

Consider a situation where we are interested in whether a certain treatment program would be useful for reintegrating white-collar offenders into the community. The researcher would develop a measurement for assessing white-collar offenders' reintegration values. As well, a sample of white-collar offenders would be randomly assigned to two groups—an experimental group and a control group. The researcher would ask members of both groups to complete the reintegration values survey. Then, the experimental group would be exposed to the treatment program and the control group would receive traditional responses. At some point after the treatment has been completed, the researcher would ask members of both groups to complete a similar (or even the same) reintegration values survey. Any differences between the two groups of offenders could then potentially be attributed to the treatment (or independent variable) received by the experimental group.

Because of difficulties in recruiting white-collar individuals to participate in these studies, very few white-collar crime studies have actually used a classic experimental design. Some, however, have used what are called **quasi-experimental designs.** Quasi-experiments are studies that mimic experimental designs but lack certain elements of the classic experimental design. One author team, for example, compared two similar businesses (health care offices) to determine whether an "ethical work climate" contributed to employee theft (Weber, Kurke, & Pentico, 2003). The two organizations included one in which an internal audit revealed that workers were stealing and one in which an audit did not reveal theft. The authors surveyed workers from both businesses and found that an ethical work climate appeared to influence theft. In this case, the authors did not randomly select the comparison groups and they did not manipulate the independent variable (ethical work climate). Still, their design mimicked what would be found in an experimental design.

While some criminologists have used quasi-experiments to study white-collar crime issues, the use of experiments in the broader body of white-collar crime research remains rare. This may change in the future, however, as experimental research is becoming much more common in criminology and criminal justice. In 1998, for example, a group of criminologists created the Academy of Experimental Criminology (AEC) to recognize those criminologists who conduct experimental research. Part of AEC's current mission is to support the *Journal of Experimental Criminology*, which was created in 2005 as an outlet for promoting experimental research on crime and criminal justice issues. According to the journal's website, the *Journal of Experimental Criminology* "focuses on high quality experimental and quasi-experimental research in the development of evidence based crime and justice policy. The journal is committed to the advancement of the science of systematic reviews and experimental methods in criminology and criminal justice." Incidentally, the current editor of the journal (David Weisburd) has a long history of conducting prominent white-collar crime research studies.

Case Studies

Case studies entail researchers selecting a particular crime, criminal, event, or other phenomena and studying features surrounding the causes and consequences of those phenomena. Typically, the sample size is "one" in case studies. Researchers might use a variety of other research strategies (like field research, archival research, and interviews) in conducting their case study. Case studies are relatively frequent in the white-collar crime literature. An early case study was conducted by Frank Cullen and his colleagues (Cullen, Maakestad, & Cavender, 1987), who focused on what is now known as the "Ford Pinto Case." In the mid- to late-1970s, Ford Motor Company had come under intense scrutiny over a series of high profile crashes. Eventually, prosecutor Michael Cosentino filed criminal charges against Ford Motor Company after three teenage girls—Judy, Lin, and Donna Ulrich—driving a Ford Pinto, were killed in an August 1978 collision.

The authors chronicled the situational and structural factors that led to Cosentino's decision to pursue criminal penalties against the large automaker. While the details of this case will be described in more detail later, as Cullen and his coauthors note, this case "signified the social and legal changes that had placed corporations under attack and made them vulnerable to criminal intervention in an unprecedented way" (p. 147).

Different criminologists and social scientists have also studied the role of white-collar and corporate crime in the U.S. savings and loan crisis, which occurred in the 1980s and 1990s. Perhaps the most comprehensive case study of this crisis was conducted by criminologists Kitty Calavita, Henry Pontell, and Robert Tillmann (1997). The research team, through a grant funded by the National Institute of Justice, explored those crimongenic factors contributing to the collapse of the savings and loan institutions in the late 1980s and 1990s. The authors relied on public records, Congressional testimony, media reports, and interviews with key informants to demonstrate how white-collar offending contributed to a significant proportion of the bank failures. While Calavita and her colleagues focused on the crisis from a national perspective, other researchers used a more specific case study approach to consider specific instances where a bank failed. One author team, for example, conducted a case study on the Columbia Savings and Loan Association of Beverly Hills (Glasberg & Skidmore, 1998b). Using Congressional testimony, interviews, and media reports, their research drew attention to the way that structural changes in economic policies (deregulation and federal deposit insurance policies) promoted individual greed.

Case studies are advantageous in that they allow criminologists an insider's view into specific white-collar and corporate crimes. As well, these studies have provided a great deal of insight into the dynamics, causes, and consequences of various types of white-collar crimes. In many ways, because case studies use multiple strategies to gather data, the potential strengths of those strategies (e.g., non-reactivity for archival research, etc.) exist with case studies. At the same time, though, the same disadvantages that arise with these other strategies also manifest themselves in case studies. In addition, it is important to note that case studies can take an enormous amount of time to complete.

Studying White-Collar Crime From a Scientific Perspective

Almost everyone has heard about crimes committed by individuals in the workplace or by white-collar offenders. In recent times, a great deal of media attention has focused on infamous white-collar offenders such as Bernie Madoff, Martha Stewart, and Ken Lay. The reality is, however, that these media depictions—while providing a glimpse into the lives and experiences of a select few high profile white-collar offenders—provide a superficial, and somewhat confusing, introduction to white-collar crime. To fully understand white-collar crime, it is best to approach the topic from a scientific perspective.

Studying white-collar crime from a scientific perspective requires that students understand how the principles of science relate to white-collar crime. In 1970, Robert Bierstedt described how various principles of science were related to the study of human behavior. Fitzgerald and Cox (1994) used these same principles to demonstrate how social research methods adhered to traditional principles of science. Taking this a step farther, one can use these principles as a framework for understanding why, and how, the principles of science relate to the study of white-collar crime. The principles include:

- Objectivity
- Parsimony

- Determinism
- Skepticism
- Relativism

Objectivity and White-Collar Crime

Objectivity as a principle of science suggests that researchers must be value-free in doing their research. The importance of objectivity is tied to the research findings. Researchers who allow their values to influence the research process will be more apt to have findings that are value-laden rather than objective.

With regard to white-collar crime, the challenge is to approach the behaviors and the offenders objectively. In many cases, white-collar offenders are vilified and portrayed as evil actors who have done great harm to society. While the harm they create is clearly significant, demonizing white-collar offenders and white-collar offenses runs the risk of (a) ignoring actual causes of white-collar crime, (b) relying on ineffective intervention strategies, (c) failing to develop appropriate prevention strategies, and (d) making it virtually impossible for convicted white-collar offenders to reintegrate into society.

Consider that many individuals attribute the causes of white-collar crime to greed on the part of the offender. Intuitively, it makes sense that individuals who already seem to be making a good living are greedy if they commit crime in order to further their economic interests. However, as Benson and Moore (1992) note, "self-reports from white-collar offenders suggest that they often are motivated not so much by greed as by a desire to merely hang on to what they already had" (p. 267). Inadequately identifying the causes of behavior will make it more difficult to respond appropriately to these cases.

Furthermore, in promoting understanding about the criminal justice system's response to white-collar offenders, it cannot be automatically assumed that the justice system is doing a bad job or treating these offenders more leniently than other offenders. An objective approach requires an open mind in assessing the ties between white-collar crime and the criminal justice system. As will be seen later, for example, several studies show that convicted white-collar offenders are more likely than other convicted offenders to be sentenced to jail, albeit for shorter periods of time (Payne, 2003b). The lack of an objective approach might force some to automatically assume that white-collar offenders are treated more leniently than conventional offenders. This is problematic because a lack of objectivity may create faulty assumptions about the criminal justice system's handling of white-collar crime cases, which in turn could reduce the actual deterrent power of the efforts of criminal justice practices.

On another level, some criminologists have argued that a lack of objectivity among criminologists has resulted in some researchers overextending the concept of white-collar crime. According to Ruggiero (2007):

> Given the increasing variety of white-collar criminal offenses being committed, and the avalanche of crime committed by states and other powerful actors, scholars are faced with a fuzzy analytical framework, with the result that some may be tempted to describe as crime everything they, understandably, find disturbing . . . the word nasty is not synonymous with criminal, and the concept of crime may be useless if it is indiscriminately applied to anything objectionable by whoever uses the term. (p. 174)

In terms of objectivity and the study of white-collar crime, researchers should not define white-collar crimes simply as those things that are "nasty" or as behaviors that offend them. Instead, white-collar crime must be objectively defined, measured, researched, and explained.

Parsimony and White-Collar Crime

The principle of **parsimony** suggests that researchers and scientists keep their levels of explanation as simple as possible. For explanations and theories to be of use to scientists, practitioners, and the public, it is imperative that the explanations are reduced to as few variables as possible, and explained in simple terms. In explaining white-collar crime, for instance, explanations must be described as simply as possible. One issue that arises, however, is that many white-collar crimes are, in fact, very complex in nature and design. As will be shown later in this text, this complexity often creates obstacles for criminal justice officials responding to these cases.

While many types of white-collar crimes may be complex, and it may be difficult to explain the causes of these offenses in simple terms, this does not mean that the offenses cannot be understood through relatively simple explanations. Consider fraud by physicians, misconduct by lawyers, or misdeeds by stockbrokers. One does not need to be a doctor, attorney, or financial investor to understand the nature of these offenses, ways to respond to these offenses, or the underlying dynamics contributing to these behaviors. By understanding relatively simple descriptions of these behaviors, readers will be able to recognize parallels between the offenses and will develop a foundation from which they can begin to expand their understanding of white-collar crime.

Determinism and White-Collar Crime

Determinism means that behavior is caused or influenced by preceding events or factors. With regard to crimes in the workplace, a great deal of research has focused on trying to explain (or "determine") why these offenses occur. Understanding the causes of white-collar crime is important because such information would help in developing both prevention and intervention strategies. In terms of prevention, if researchers are able to isolate certain factors that seem to contribute to white-collar misconduct, then policy makers and practitioners can use that information to develop policies and implement practices that would reduce the amount of crime in the workplace. Consider a study on student cheating that finds that the cheating is the result of the nature of the assignments given. With this information, professors could redo the assignment so that cheating is more difficult and less likely.

Understanding the causes of white-collar crime also helps to develop appropriate intervention strategies. If, for example, a study shows that certain types of white-collar offenses are caused by a lack of formal oversight, then strategies could be developed that provide for such oversight. One study, for example, found that patient abuse in nursing homes was at least partially attributed to the fact that workers were often alone with nursing home residents (Payne & Cikovic, 1995). To address this, the authors recommended that workers be required to work in teams with more vulnerable patients and video cameras be added where feasible.

To some, the principle of determinism is in contrast to the idea of free will, or rational decision making. However, it is not necessary, at least in this context, to separate the two phenomena. Whether individuals support deterministic ideals or free-will ideals, with white-collar offenses it seems safe to suggest that understanding why these offenses occur is informative and useful. For those adhering to deterministic ideals, explaining the source of workplace misconduct helps to develop appropriate response systems. For those adhering to free-will ideals, the same can be said: By figuring out what makes individuals "choose" to commit white-collar offenses, strategies can be developed that would influence the offender's decision making. In other words, choices are caused by, and can be controlled by, external factors. Put another way, by understanding *why* individuals commit crime in the workplace, officials are in a better position to know *how* to respond to those crimes.

Skepticism and White-Collar Crime

Skepticism simply means that social scientists must question and re-question their findings. We must never accept our conclusions as facts! Applying this notion to the study of white-collar crime is fairly straightforward and simple. On the one hand, it is imperative that we continue to question past research on white-collar crime in an effort to develop and conduct future white-collar crime studies. On the other hand, in following this principle, it may be difficult for some to think differently about the occupations covered in this book. Put simply, crime and deviance occur in all occupations.

Sociologist Emile Durkheim noted that deviance occurs in all cultures and subcultures. He used the example of a "society of saints" to illustrate this point. Even a group of nuns or priests would have someone committing deviant behavior. So, as readers, when we think of any occupation, we must question and re-question how and why crime is committed in that occupation. We cannot assume that because the occupation is "trustworthy," that crime does not occur in that occupation. Doing so would provide an inaccurate and incomplete picture of white-collar crime.

Relativism and White-Collar Crime

Relativism means that all things are related. If all things are related, then, this principle implies that changes in one area will lead to changes in other areas. A simple example helps to highlight this principle. Think of a time when you were driving your car, listening to your favorite Lady Gaga, Eminem, or Taylor Swift song with the music turned up loudly, and you suddenly smell something that makes you think that your engine is failing. What's the first thing you do? For many of us, the first thing we do is turn the music down so we can smell better. Think about that—we do not smell with our ears, we smell with our noses. But we turn the music down because it helps us to smell. Changes in one area (smelling) led to changes in other areas (hearing).

White-collar crime is related to the ideal of relativism in three ways: (1) how white-collar crime is defined, (2) the nature of white-collar crime, and (3) how the criminal justice system responds to white-collar crime. First, the notion of "white-collar" is a relative concept in and of itself. What makes someone a white-collar worker? Is it the clothes worn to work? Are your professors "white-collar" workers? Do they all wear "white collars" to work? Are you a "white-collar" worker? Will you ever be a "white-collar" worker? In using the concept of white-collar to describe these offense types, Sutherland was highlighting the importance of status. However, the very concept of status is relative in nature. What is high status to one individual might actually be low status to another person. What one group defines as a "white-collar" occupation may be different than what another groups defines as "white-collar." A basic understanding of white-collar crime requires an appreciation for the relative nature of status and occupations.

Second, the principle of relativism also highlights the need to recognize how changes in society have resulted in changes in white-collar offending. Throughout history, as society changed, and workplace structures changed, the nature of, and types of, workplace offenses changed. Describing this pattern from a historical review of the 1800s, one author team commented:

> During this time period, large scale changes within the business environment brought new opportunities for acts or workplace taking, particularly those associated with "respectable" echelons of staff hierarchies. Such acts were labeled as illegitimate and criminalized . . . the representation of fraud and embezzlement as activities that were criminal was bolstered through a reconceptualization of the nature of property rights and, in particular, the relationship between staff and the property worked with. (Locker & Godfrey, 2006, p. 977)

In effect, changes in the occupational arena create new opportunities for, and strategies for, white-collar crime. In our modern society, note that globalization has created worldwide opportunities for white-collar offending (Johnstone, 1999). As an example of the way that changes in society result in changes in misbehavior that may hit home with some students, "studies by the Center for Academic Integrity show a decline in traditional peeking over someone's shoulder cheating, but a steady increase in Internet plagiarism" (Zernike, 2003). Changes in society resulted in changes in the way some students cheat.

Third, the notion of relativism relates to white-collar crime in considering how the criminal justice system responds to white-collar crimes, and the interactions between the criminal justice system and other societal systems. John Van Gigch's *applied general systems theory* helps to illustrate this point. Van Gigch noted that society is made up of a number of different types of systems and that these systems operate independently, and in conjunction with, other systems (see Figure 1.1). At a minimum, systems that are related to white-collar crime include those shown in Figure 1.1. These systems include the following:

Figure 1.1   The Systems Perspective

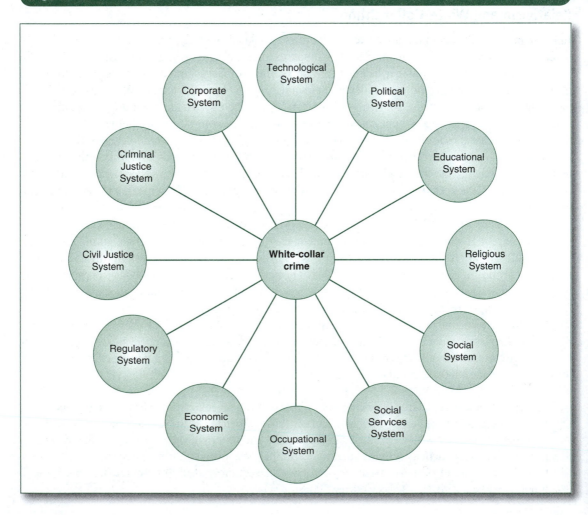

Political/government system

Educational system

Religious system

Technological system

Social system

Social services system

Occupational system

Economic system

Corporate system

Regulatory system

Civil justice system

Criminal justice system

At the most basic level, the political system is involved in defining laws and regulations defining all forms of crime, including white-collar crimes. Three levels of the political system include local, state, and federal systems of government. Each of these levels plays a role in defining various white-collar offenses, detecting offenders, adjudicating cases, and punishing offenders. On a separate level, one section of this book will focus on crimes committed in the political system. Note also that the political system plays a central role in developing and implementing policies designed to prevent and respond to white-collar crime. Throughout this text, significant attention is given to the interplay among white-collar crime policies, the occurrence of white-collar crimes, and the actions of various systems assigned the tasks of preventing and responding to white-collar crime.

The **educational system** relates to white-collar crime inasmuch as white-collar careers typically come out of this system. From preschool through higher education, one can see that the educational system prepares individuals for their future careers and lives. Some research has focused on how the educational system might promote certain forms of white-collar offending, with students potentially learning how to commit crimes as part of their training (Keenan, Brown, Pontell, & Geis, 1985). At the same time, the educational system provides opportunities to increase understanding about white-collar crime through college coursework and advanced training for criminal justice professionals. As with the political system, white-collar crimes also occur in the educational system.

The **religious system** relates to white-collar crime (and other crimes) in that this system has been seen as providing institutions that have the potential to prevent misconduct. Many studies have focused on the ties between religion and crime, and while few have focused on how religion relates to white-collar crime, the underlying assumption is that religion has the potential to prevent these behaviors, or at least provide a setting where definitions of appropriate and inappropriate misconduct can be developed. Interestingly, white-collar crime pioneer Edwin Sutherland's father "was a religious fundamentalist who believed in strict adherence to the Baptist faith" (Martin, Mutchnick, & Austin, 1990). While Sutherland eventually parted ways with his father's church, it has been noted that "a prominent and overt expression of his moralistic side appears in *White Collar Crime* (1949) where Sutherland calls for something other than a strict legal definition of

▲ **Photo 1.3**   The political system develops laws to guard against white-collar crime, provides funding to respond to white-collar crime, and is a setting where different types of white-collar crime occur.

acceptable behavior" (Martin et al., 1990, p. 141). As an aside, in the same way that crime is found in the political and educational systems, white-collar offenses also occur in the religious system.

The **technological system** has evolved greatly over the past few decades. This system is related to white-collar crime in at least two distinct ways. First, and as was noted earlier, changes in the technological system have led to changes in the way that some white-collar offenders commit their crimes. Second, the technological system has provided additional tools that government officials can use in their pursuit of identifying and responding to white-collar crimes.

The **social system** represents a setting where individuals have various needs fulfilled and learn how to do certain things, as well as reasons for doing those behaviors. In terms of white-collar crime, some individuals may learn how to commit white-collar offenses, and why to commit those offenses, as part of the social systems in which they exist. Research, for example, shows that nurses learn from their peers how to rationalize their workplace misdeeds (Dabney, 1995).

The **social services system** includes numerous agencies involved in providing services to members of the public. In some cases, the services they provide might be in direct response to white-collar crime victimization. For example, individuals who lose their life savings to fraudulent investors may need to seek assistance from the social service system to deal with their victimization. As with the other systems, white-collar crimes could also be committed by workers in the social services system.

The **occupational system** is, for the purposes of this discussion, that system where the bulk of professions are found. This system is composed of other systems, which at the broadest level can be characterized as lower-class and upper-class occupational systems. Within the lower-class and upper-class occupational systems, specific subsystems exist. White-collar offenses are found in each of these subsystems. As outlined in this text, these subsystems include the legal system, the health care system, the higher education system, the religious system, the technological system, the housing system, the insurance system, and the **economic system.**

The **economic system** represents the system that drives our economy. This system is influenced by, and has an influence on, each of the other types of systems. In recent times, problems in the economic system have had far-reaching and serious effects on countries across the world. Many of the white-collar crimes discussed in this text originate in the economic system.

The **corporate system** includes the businesses and corporations that carry out business activity as part of our capitalist system. These corporations strive to make profits and grow in strength and numbers. Various types of white-collar crimes have been uncovered in the corporate system. As well, the corporate system is sometimes given the power to regulate itself.

The **regulatory system** describes those local, state, and federal agencies that have been charged with regulating various businesses. This system is different from the criminal and civil justice systems in many different ways. For example, the formal source of rules comes from administrative regulations in the regulatory system. As well, the rights of offenders, corporations, and victims are different in the three types of systems (e.g., offenders have one set of rights in the criminal justice system, another set of rights in the civil justice system, and another set of rights in the regulatory system). Procedures and guidelines used to process the cases also vary in the three types of systems.

The **civil justice system** represents that system of justice where individuals (plaintiffs) seek recourse for offenses by way of a civil lawsuit. The accused (defendant) could be an individual or a company. In cases of white-collar crime, for example, it is common for lawsuits to be filed by victims in order to recover their losses. Note that the victim, in many cases, may actually be an individual, company, or governmental agency.

The **criminal justice system** is that system of justice where violations of the criminal law are handled. The criminal law is the branch of law dealing with crimes against the state. Like each of these systems, our criminal justice system is composed of various subsystems: the police, courts, and corrections. On one level, the criminal justice system operates independently from other agencies when white-collar offenses are investigated, prosecuted, and sentenced. On another level, it is imperative to note that the system's responses to white-collar crimes, and behaviors of actors in the criminal justice system, are influenced by changes in other societal systems. Changes in the technological system (brought about by advances in the educational system) led to the development of the Internet. The Internet, in turn, created new ways for criminal offending. These new strategies, then, meant that the criminal justice system had to alter its practices. As society changes, criminal justice and other systems of formal control are forced to change how they respond to white-collar offenses (Edelhertz, 1983). As one author put it several years ago, "an emerging area of difficulty is the challenge of devising powers of investigation that are responsive to the needs of enforcement in a modern corporate society" (Fisse, 1991, p. 7). Two decades later, this same challenge remains "an emerging area of difficulty."

A full understanding of white-collar crime requires an understanding of (a) the changing nature of crime occurring in various systems; (b) how the criminal justice, civil justice, and regulatory systems respond to white-collar crimes; and (c) how interactions between the systems influence criminal behavior as well as response systems. To promote broad insight into white-collar crime, this text relies on the systems perspective to guide the discussion about white-collar crime. In doing so, it is argued that students (a part of the educational system) have a significant role in white-collar crime.

The Student Role in White-Collar Crime

Some readers may have given very little thought to their role in white-collar crime. In reading this text, students are encouraged to think about how white-collar crime relates to their lives—their past, their current lives, and their future. In effect, students have at least ten potential roles in white-collar crime. These roles include (1) past victims, (2) past offenders, (3) current offenders, (4) current victims, (5) future offenders, (6) future victims, (7) future crime fighters, (8) future policy makers, (9) current research subjects, and (10) future white-collar crime researchers.

First, most students have been victimized by white-collar crimes in the past, though many likely may not have realized they were victimized at the time. From being overcharged for services to being a victim of corporate misconduct, students—like the rest of society—are not immune from victimization by white-collar or corporate offenders.

Second, some students may have actually been past offenders, particularly if broader definitions of occupational offending are used. These definitions will be addressed in Section II. For now, several questions could be asked to determine whether students have broken the rules in their past jobs. Did they take breaks for too long? Did they give away company food or merchandise? Did they skip work and lie to their boss about the reason? Did they, like the example in the beginning of this chapter, give someone an extra piece of cheese? One of the exercises I use in my white-collar crime classes is to have students write about occupational offenses they have committed in past jobs. Very few of my students ever had a problem identifying past misdeeds. Some even described actions that would have resulted in felony convictions had they been caught for their transgressions!

Third, another role that students may have in white-collar crime is that some may be current victims of white-collar crime. In Section IX, attention will be given to the way that colleges and universities sometimes break rules in recruiting students and providing financial aid. (Some have even argued that ineffective instruction by college professors victimizes students, but that can be saved for another text.) Students might also be victims of white-collar and corporate misconduct in their roles as consumers of various goods and services that extend beyond the college boundaries.

Fourth, some students can also be seen as current occupational offenders if they are violating the rules of their jobs or the rules set by their educational institution. This will be discussed in more detail in Section VI. At this point, it is sufficient to suggest that college students can be seen as "pre-white-collar" professionals. In this context, then, some misdeeds that college students commit could technically be seen as versions of white-collar offending.

Fifth, some college students may have the role of future white-collar offenders. Note that most white-collar offenders have at least some college education. While most readers of this text will not (hopefully) go on to careers of white-collar offending, the fact remains that some college graduates eventually graduate into these criminal careers.

Sixth, all college students will be future victims of white-collar and corporate misconduct at least on some level. There is no reason to expect that these offenses will end. Because the consequences of white-collar offenses are so far reaching, none of us will be completely immune from future misdeeds—though we may not always know when we have been victimized.

Seventh, some college students will also have a future role of white-collar crime fighters or white-collar criminal defense lawyers. At first blush, a career battling white-collar offenders may not seem as exhilarating as other law enforcement careers. However, nothing could be farther from the truth. A major focus of this text will be on how the criminal justice system, and criminal justice professionals, responds to white-collar offenses. In addressing the mechanics of the response to these offenses, it is hoped that readers will see just how important, and exciting, these careers are. From going undercover in a doctor's office to sifting through complex computer programs, the search for misconduct and clues of wrongdoing can far outweigh more mundane or routine criminal justice practices.

Eighth, some college students will go on to employment positions where they will play a role in developing and implementing various crime policies. As future policy makers, college students will be better prepared to develop policies addressing white-collar crime if they have a full understanding of the dynamics of white-collar crime, the causes of the behavior, and the most effective response systems. Without an understanding of these issues, future (and current) policy makers run the risk of relying on crime prevention policies and strategies that might work for traditional forms of crime, but not necessarily for white-collar crimes.

Ninth, some college students will also assume the role of research subjects. Many researchers have used college student samples to generate understanding about white-collar offending. One researcher used a sample of college students to learn about the kinds of crimes committed in fast food restaurants (O'Connor, 1991). Another research team surveyed students to learn about digital piracy and illegal downloading (Higgins, et al., 2007). The same research team surveyed college students to test the ability of criminological theories to explain different forms of occupational misconduct. Another study of 784 undergraduate students found that question item sequencing influences attitudes about white-collar crime (Evans & Scott, 1984). The simple fact of the matter is that we have a great deal to learn from you, just as you have a great deal to learn from your professors! Indeed, many of the studies cited in this book will come from studies involving college students on some level.

Tenth, as you read about the studies discussed in this text, and read the articles in each section, one thing to bear in mind is that the authors of these studies and articles were students themselves in the not-so-distant past (well, maybe the more distant past for some of us). Edwin Sutherland, once a college student at Grand Island College, went on to create the study of white-collar crime. His students, his students' students, and their students have created a field of study that has significantly evolved over the past 70 years. Thus, the tenth role that students have in white-collar crime is that the discipline of criminology and crimi-

▲ **Photo 1.4**   While many careers exist to respond to white-collar crime, most of those careers require employees to have a college degree. It is important that college students have an understanding of white-collar crime so they are better able to enter those careers.

nal justice is counting on some of you to take the torch and become future white-collar crime researchers. This text provides a foundation to understanding white-collar crime. Hopefully, this foundation will spark your interest so that you will want to learn more about this important criminological issue and one day go on to help generate future empirical and scientific awareness about white-collar crime.

Plan for the Book

This text uses the systems perspective as a guide for understanding white-collar crime. Each section provides readers an introduction to topics related to white-collar crime. The text is divided into the following sections:

- Understanding White-Collar Crime
- Crimes in Sales-Oriented Occupations
- Crimes in the Health Care System
- Crimes in Systems of Social Control
- Crimes in the Educational System
- Crime in the Economic and Technological Systems
- Crimes in the Housing System
- Crimes by the Corporate System
- Environmental Crime
- Explaining White-Collar Crime
- Policing White-Collar Crime
- Judicial Proceedings and White-Collar Crime
- The Corrections Subsystem and White-Collar Crime

Throughout each section, both criminological and criminal justice themes are covered. White-collar crime has been addressed with little or no attention given to "white-collar criminal justice." Pulling together criminological and theoretically driven issues with criminal justice-oriented discussions will help to provide a full picture of white-collar crime and the responses to white-collar crime.

After each section, a few readings that build on the information presented in that section are included. The readings come from the scholarly literature on white-collar crime. Included are studies using those methodologies highlighted above as well as theoretical or conceptual pieces. Readers are encouraged to think critically about issues presented in each section as they read the works accompanying each section. In doing so, it is hoped that readers will recognize the interactions between various systems involved in preventing and responding to white-collar crime as well as the way that white-collar crime influences their lives.

◩ Summary

- According to Edwin Sutherland, white-collar crime is "crime committed by a person of respectability and high social status in the course of his occupation." The distinguishing features of white-collar crime are that the crime was committed (a) during work, (b) when the offender was in the role of worker, and (c) as part of the employment duties of the offender.
- We study white-collar crime because (a) it is an enormous problem, (b) it affects everyone, (c) to learn more about all forms of crime, (d) to develop prevention and intervention systems, (e) to learn about careers, and (f) to learn about subcultures.
- Survey research with white-collar offenders tends to include surveys of offenders, victims, criminal justice officials, and members of the public.
- Archival research on white-collar offenders includes reviews of case records, pre-sentence reports, media reports, and case descriptions of specific white-collar offenses.
- Field research involves situations where researchers enter a particular setting to study phenomena. While relatively rare in the white-collar crime literature, these studies provide direct insight into issues related to the behaviors of offenders, criminal justice officials, and other members of society.
- Experiments involve studies where researchers assess the influence of a particular variable on an experimental group (which receives the "treatment" or the variable) and a control group (which does not receive the treatment or the variable). It is expected that white-collar crime experiments will increase in the future as experimental criminology grows as a research strategy.
- Case studies entail researchers selecting a particular crime, criminal, event, or other phenomenon and studying features surrounding the causes and consequences of those phenomena.
- It is important that those studying white-collar crime be objective in conducting research on the topic. As well, readers are encouraged to keep an open mind about the topic to help as they critically assess issues related to white-collar crime and the study of the topic.
- Researchers are encouraged to keep their explanations as simple as possible. For white-collar crime researchers, this means that one does not need to understand everything about a career in order to understand issues related to crime in that career.
- The aim of many white-collar crime studies is to explain why white-collar crime occurs. Determinism suggests that behavior can be explained. By explaining why white-collar crimes occur, appropriate prevention and intervention remedies can be developed.

- Skepticism as a principle of science means that scientists question and re-question everything. For students of white-collar crime, this means that we must question and re-question all of our assumptions about various careers and recognize that crime occurs in all careers.
- Relativism means that all things are related. From a systems perspective, this means that all societal systems are influenced by, and have an influence on, white-collar crime. Those systems considered in this section included the (1) political/government system, (2) educational system, (3) religious system, (4) technological system, (5) social system, (6) social services system, (7) occupational systems, (8) economic system, (9) corporate systems, (10) regulatory system, (11) civil justice system, and (12) criminal justice system.
- Students have at least ten potential roles in white-collar crime. These roles include (1) past victims, (2) past offenders, (3) current offenders, (4) current victims, (5) future offenders, (6) future victims, (7) future crime fighters, (8) future policy makers, (9) current research subjects, and (10) future white-collar crime researchers.

KEY TERMS

Applied general systems theory	Educational system	Pre-sentence reports
Archival research	Experimental group	Quasi-experimental designs
Case records	Experiments	Regulatory system
Case studies	Field research	Relativism
Civil justice system	Media reports	Skepticism
Corporate system	Objectivity	Social services system
Criminal justice system	Occupational system	Social system
Determinism	Parsimony	Technological system
Economic system	Political system	White-collar crime victims

DISCUSSION QUESTIONS

1. Below are examples of misdeeds committed by celebrities. Read each of them and classify them according to whether the acts are crimes or, to borrow Ruggiero's concept, just "nasty." Also identify those actions that you think are white-collar crimes and those that would be traditional crimes.

   a. Former boy-band manager Lou Pearlman (former manager of N' Sync and Backstreet Boys) was convicted of defrauding more than $300 million from investors as part of a Ponzi scheme.

   b. In January 2010, Mark McGuire admitted using steroids while he was a professional baseball player.

   c. In January 2009, crooner Chris Brown was arrested and accused of assaulting his then-girlfriend Rhianna.

   d. L'il Kim was convicted of perjury after it was found that she lied during the course of a criminal investigation.

   e. Kanye West interrupted the MTV music awards while Taylor Swift was giving an acceptance speech.

   f. In January 2009, Dane Cook's manager was charged with embezzling $10 million from Cook. The manager, Darryl J. McCauley, was Cook's half-brother.

g. Actor Zac Efron told a reporter that he has stolen costumes from movie sets after the filming was completed. He said: "I think I stole some of the stuff. Always, on the last day, they try and get it out of your trailer really quick. Always steal some of your wardrobe. You never know what you're going to need."

h. Actress Winona Ryder was arrested for shoplifting in 2001.

i. Hugh Grant was arrested for having sexual relations with a prostitute.

j. Martha Stewart was convicted of perjury after it was found that she lied to investigators about some of her stock purchases.

2. Why does it matter how you classify these behaviors?

3. How are the behaviors you labeled "white-collar crime" different from those you labeled "traditional crimes"?

4. Why do we study white-collar crime?

5. What is your role in white-collar crime?

WEB RESOURCES

National White Collar Crime Center, White Collar Crime Research Consortium WCCRC: http://www.nw3c.org/research/white_collar_crime_consortium.cfm

Fraud Watchers: http://www.fraudwatchers.org/

U.S. Department of the Treasury: http://www.treasury.gov/Pages/default.aspx

How to Read a Research Article

As you travel through your criminal justice/criminology studies, you will soon learn that some of the best known and/or emerging explanations of crime and criminal behavior come from research articles in academic journals. Research articles are included throughout this book, but you may be asking yourself, "How do I read a research article?" It is my hope to answer this question with a quick summary of the key elements of any research article, followed by the questions you should be answering as you read through the assigned sections.

Every research article published in a social science journal will have the following elements: (1) introduction, (2) literature review, (3) methodology, (4) results, and (5) discussion/conclusion.

In the introduction, you will find an overview of the purpose of the research. Within the introduction, you will also find the hypothesis or hypotheses. A hypothesis is most easily defined as an educated statement or guess. In most hypotheses, you will find that the format usually followed is: If X, Y will occur. For example, a simple hypothesis may be: "If the price of gas increases, more people will ride bikes." This is a testable statement that the researcher wants to address in his or her study. Usually, authors will state the hypothesis directly, but not always. Therefore, you must be aware of what the author is actually testing in the research project. If you are unable to find the hypothesis, ask yourself what is being tested and/or manipulated, and what are the expected results?

The next section of the research article is the literature review. At times the literature review will be separated from the text in its own section, and at other times it will be found within the introduction. In any case, the literature review is an examination of what other researchers have already produced in terms of the research question or hypothesis. For example, returning to my hypothesis on the relationship between gas prices and bike riding, we may find that five researchers have previously conducted studies on the increase of gas prices. In the literature review, I would discuss their findings, and then discuss what my study will add to the existing research. The literature review may also be used as a platform of support for my hypothesis. For example, one researcher may have already determined that an increase in gas causes more people to head to work on in-line skates. I can use this study as evidence to support my hypothesis that increased gas prices will lead to more bike riding.

The methods used in the research design are found in the next section of the research article. In the methodology section you will find the following: who/what was studied, how many subjects were studied, the research tool (e.g., interview, survey, observation), how long the subjects were studied, and how the data that were collected was processed. The methods section is usually very concise, with every step of the research project recorded. This is important because a major goal of the researcher is "reliability," or, if the research is done over again the same way, will the results be the same?

The results section is an analysis of the researcher's findings. If the researcher conducted a quantitative study (using numbers or statistics to explain the research), you will find statistical tables and analyses that explain whether or not the researcher's hypothesis is supported. If the researcher conducted a qualitative study (non-numerical research for the purpose of theory construction), the results will usually be displayed as a theoretical analysis or interpretation of the research question.

Finally, the research article will conclude with a discussion and summary of the study. In the discussion, you will find that the hypothesis is usually restated, and perhaps a small discussion of why this hypothesis was chosen. You will also find a brief overview of the methodology and results. Finally, the discussion section will end with a discussion of the implications of the research, and what future research is still needed.

Now that you know the key elements of a research article, let us examine a sample article from your text.

Crime and Business

By Edwin H. Sutherland

1. What is the thesis or main idea of this article?

   - The first sentence of the article describes the main idea of the article. Sutherland notes that the articles "is concerned with crimes committed by businessmen rather than crimes committed against businessmen." He goes on to explain that these crimes are called white-collar crime.

2. What is the hypothesis?

   - Sutherland highlights two hypotheses in this article. His first hypothesis appears at end of the "Poverty and Crime" section. In particular, he suggests that white-collar crime is learned. His second hypothesis appears in the third paragraph of the "Methods of Study" section. He suggests that crime rates in various occupations are tied to the degree of organization for and against crime in those occupations.

3. Is there any prior literature related to the hypothesis?

   - Perhaps because of the time it was written, Sutherland does not actually cite prior literature related to his hypotheses. In fact, his arguments are the foundation for future studies.

4. What methods are used to support the hypothesis?

   - Sutherland does not actually test his hypotheses, but he suggests possible strategies that can be used to study white-collar crime. In particular, he notes that case studies and historical studies are methods that can be used to study various types of white-collar crime.

5. Is this a qualitative study or quantitative study?

   - Sutherland does not actually present any statistics or numbers to support his findings. In fact, he does not present any data at all. As a result, this article is technically not a qualitative or quantitative study. It is probably best characterized as a descriptive article rather than a study.

6. Do you believe that the author or authors provided a persuasive argument? Why or why not?

   - Given the influence that Sutherland has had on the field of criminology and criminal justice, it is safe to suggest that he has made a persuasive argument about the existence and source of white-collar crime.

8. Who is the intended audience of this article?

   - A final question that will be useful for the reader deals with the intended audience. As you read the article, ask yourself, to whom is the author wanting to speak? After you read this article, you will see that Sutherland is writing for not only students, but also professors, criminologists, policy makers, historians, and/or criminal justice personnel. The target audience may most easily be identified if you ask yourself, "who will benefit from reading this article?"

9. What does the article add to your knowledge of the subject?

- This answer is best left up to the reader, because the question is asking how the article improved your knowledge. However, one way to answer the question is as follows: This article helps the reader to understand the source of the concept white-collar crime. Readers also better understand the ways to study white-collar crime and the way the political and justice systems need to be organized to respond effectively to white-collar crime.

10. What are the implications for criminal justice policy that can be derived from this article?

- Implications for criminal justice policy are most likely to be found in the conclusion or the discussion sections of the article. In this article, those implications appear in the last two paragraphs. Sutherland points to the need to have an organized response to white-collar crime. He also draws attention to the way legal changes can reduce white-collar crime.

Now that we have gone through the elements of a research article, it is your turn to continue through your text, reading the various articles and answering the same questions. You may find that some articles are easier to follow than others, but do not be dissuaded. Remember that many of the articles will follow the same format: introduction, literature review, methods, results, and discussion. If you have any problems, refer to this introduction for guidance.

READING

As a follow up to his address to the American Sociological Association, which was subsequently published in *American Sociological Review* in 1940, in this reading Sutherland provides further details regarding his description of the white-collar crime concept. Particular attention is given to the level of respectability given to upper class workers, and the way that trust violations are what separate white-collar crimes from other crimes. Sutherland notes that the trust given to upper class workers provides a mechanism by which offenders can use that trust to commit criminal acts. As a result, the violations of trust result in distrust and create a host of consequences for victims and society. Sutherland also stresses that while it is difficult to determine how often these crimes occur, their consequences can be devastating. He further discusses why white-collar crimes cannot be defined simply by the presence of a conviction in criminal court and brings attention to civil courts (or the civil justice system). After considering how traditional explanations of crime (like poverty) do not explain white-collar crime, Sutherland provides an overview of strategies to study white-collar crime.

Crime and Business

Edwin H. Sutherland

This analysis is concerned with crimes committed by businessmen rather than crimes committed against businessmen. The crimes committed against businessmen would make an interesting study, as would also the crimes committed by professional men, farmers, and certain other occupational groups. These other aspects of crime are not included here because of lack of space. While attention is concentrated on the crimes of businessmen, this is not done as an attack on business but as an attack on the current theories of criminal behavior. The crimes committed by businessmen will be generally designated "white-collar crimes."

Definition of White-Collar Crime

A white-collar crime is defined as a violation of the criminal law by a person of the upper socioeconomic class in the course of his occupational activities. The upper socioeconomic class is defined not only by its wealth but also by its respectability and prestige in the general society. A fraud committed by a wealthy confidence man of the underworld or a murder committed by a businessman in a love triangle would not be a white-collar crime. On the other hand, a fraud committed by a realtor in the sale of a house or a murder committed by a manufacturer in strike-breaking activities would be a white-collar crime.

This definition is arbitrary and not very precise. It is not necessary that it be precise, for the hypothesis is that white-collar crime is identical in its general characteristics with other crime rather than different from it. The purpose of the concept of white-collar crime is to call attention to a vast area of criminal behavior which is generally overlooked as criminal behavior, which is seldom brought within the scope of the theories of criminal behavior, and which, when included, calls for modifications in the usual theories of criminal behavior.

SOURCE: Sutherland, E. (1941). Crime and business. *Annals of the American Academy of Political and Social Science, 217,* 112–118.

The most general, although not universal, characteristic of white-collar crime is violation of trust. The trust may be delegated or may be implied in the relationship, and in both cases the violation of the trust is generally accompanied and consummated by misrepresentation. The behavior is criminal in that it consists of obtainment of money under false pretenses. These misrepresentations occur in the financial statements of corporations, in the advertising and other sales methods, in manipulations on the stock exchange, in short weights and measures and in the misgrading of commodities, in embezzlement and misapplication of funds, in commercial bribery, in the bribery of public officials, in tax frauds, and in the misapplication of funds in receiverships and bankruptcies. Embezzlement is usually a violation of trust by an employee at the expense of the employer, while most other white-collar crimes are violations of trust by businessmen at the expense of consumers, investors, and the state. Many white-collar crimes are made possible because a businessman holds two or more incompatible and conflicting positions of trust, and is analogous to a football coach who umpires a game in which his own team is playing. This duplicity cannot be altogether avoided in the complexities of modern business, but white-collar criminals strive mightily to secure such positions because of the opportunities they offer for criminal behavior in relative secrecy and security.

 ## Prevalence of White-Collar Crimes

White-collar crimes are very prevalent in present American society. No index or rate of white-collar crimes has been officially constructed, but their prevalence has been shown abundantly in many industries by congressional and other investigations of banking, insurance, investment trusts, the stock market, receiverships and bankruptcies, public utilities, railways, shipping, munitions, oil, lumber, milk, meat, tobacco, and flour milling. The prevalence of white-collar crimes can be readily appreciated by anyone who reads a few of the current annual reports of the Federal Trade Commission and other commissions which have the responsibility of regulating business. Moreover, it is easy for a person to learn a good deal about white-collar crime merely by asking intimate friends, "What crooked practices are prevalent in your business or in the industries with which you deal in your business?" The manufacturers of practically every class of articles used by human beings have been involved in legal difficulties with these commissions with more or less frequency during the last thirty years, including the manufacturers of the surgical instruments with which an infant may be assisted into the world, the bottle and nipple from which he may secure his food, the milk in his bottle, the blanket in which he is wrapped, the scales on which he is weighed, the flag which the father displays in celebration of the event, and so on throughout life until he is finally laid away in a casket which was manufactured and sold under conditions which violated the law.

The financial loss to society from white-collar crimes is probably greater than the financial loss from burglaries, robberies, and larcenies committed by persons of the lower socioeconomic class. The average loss per burglary is less than one hundred dollars, a burglary which yields as much as fifty thousand dollars is exceedingly rare, and a million-dollar burglary is practically unknown. On the other hand, there may be several million-dollar embezzlements reported in one year. Embezzlements, however, are peccadilloes compared with the large-scale crimes committed by corporations, investment trusts, and public utility holding companies; reports of fifty-million-dollar losses from such criminal behavior are by no means uncommon.

The financial losses from white-collar crimes, however, are the least important of their consequences. Ordinary crimes cause some inconvenience to the victims and occasionally, in flagrant cases of bodily attack or when repeated in quick succession, cause a general community disturbance. When a community becomes disturbed it usually gathers its forces under the leadership of men of the upper socioeconomic class for more adequate enforcement of the criminal law according to conventional methods. In that directed conflict the morale of the society is increased, just as in military conflict patriotism is heightened, and the society is strengthened. White-collar crimes, on the other hand, destroy morale and promote social disorganization. Since the crimes are generally violations of trust, they create and extend feelings of distrust. Leadership against white-collar crime is generally lacking since most leaders come from the upper socioeconomic class and since the persons in this class who do not participate in white-collar crimes are generally reluctant to attack other members of their own class. Consequently there is no directed and effective program for enforcement of the criminal law against white-collar criminals, and morale does not develop as it does in campaigns against lower-class criminals. Finally, the white-collar criminals resist efforts to enforce the criminal law against themselves by attacks, through the agencies of public opinion which they control, on the integrity of public officials and private parties who object to white-collar crime. These attacks result in further disintegration of the society.

 ## Convictions in Criminal Courts

Although white-collar crimes are very prevalent and very costly, few of the perpetrators are prosecuted or convicted in the criminal courts. The relative absence of convictions under the criminal law is not evidence that the behavior is not criminal. First, the criminal courts have been very lenient toward white-collar criminals. This leniency is not so much in the form of mild penalties in case of conviction as in the form of failure of conviction due to the personal appreciation of and sympathy with the practices of the white-collar criminals and due to the precedents which the skilled attorneys for white-collar criminals argue with great ability. Pickpockets and confidence men, also, are seldom convicted in the criminal courts. While their relative immunity is due to technical considerations and to political and financial connections they have made with the criminal courts through their "fixers," the white-collar criminals secure immunity largely

because of their social prestige. In neither case does the immunity from punishment prove that their behavior is not criminal.

Second, many of the white-collar crimes are committed by corporations. No effective method of dealing with corporations under the criminal law has yet been devised. While the theory of Blackstone that a corporation cannot commit a crime has now been abandoned in American law, no satisfactory penal sanction for corporate crimes has been found. It is not possible to put a corporation to death, or whip it, or commit it to prison, except in a figurative sense. The only penalty that has been used is the fine, and the fine is paid by innocent stockholders in the form of reduced dividends. It has been suggested that since the officers and directors of corporations are men of respectability, greatly interested in preserving the prestige of themselves and of the corporation, they can be punished most effectively by some method of social degradation. Because of the absence of effective penal sanctions for corporate crimes, relatively few of the crimes of corporations are prosecuted under the criminal law.

Action in the Civil Courts

Third, other methods than prosecution in the criminal courts are used to protect society against white-collar crime. One of these is action in the civil courts. While civil fraud may differ in some respects from criminal fraud, a great many frauds can be dealt with under either the criminal law or the civil law. The relative lack of prosecutions of fraud under the criminal law is due, in part, to the fact that many frauds are dealt with under the civil law. For that reason the small number of prosecutions of white-collar criminals is not evidence that their behavior is not criminal. Even more important than the civil law is the regulation of business by boards and commissions. The reports of these boards and commissions provide abundant evidence of the prevalence of white-collar crimes. The crimes flourish in spite of the boards, just as some other crimes flourish in spite of the police and the criminal courts. The personnel of these boards has been inefficient in many cases and they have often been affected by bribery or by personal considerations; their funds have been limited; and they have been restrained by political considerations from active initiative in preventing white-collar crimes.

When efforts have been made to perfect the implements for enforcement of the criminal law as it applies to white-collar offenders, the business interests which would be affected have been energetic in preventing such action. Burglars do not send strong lobbies to the municipal, state, or Federal legislatures to prevent the enactment of bills designed to equip the police with squad cars carrying two-way radio sets, but business groups use exactly that method of preventing the implementation of the criminal law as it applies to themselves. They succeed in this because of their power and prestige in the general society.

White-collar crime is real crime. If it is not a violation of the criminal law it is not white-collar crime or any other kind of crime. But differences in administrative procedures do not justify the designation of this behavior as something different from crime. Any definition, of course, is somewhat arbitrary. If we desired, we could say that behavior which resulted in arrest by the municipal police was crime and that which resulted in arrest by the state police was not crime, or that certain behavior of blue-eyed persons was crime and the same behavior by brown-eyed persons was not crime. Such definitions are analogous to the definition of certain behavior by a poor man as a crime and of the same behavior by a well-to-do man as not a crime. Instead of such arbitrarily limited definitions, the definition here presented is designed to include the entire area of homogeneous behavior. This is desirable for reasons of logic, economy, and simplicity. By this definition behavior which is fraudulent when committed by poor persons is fraudulent when committed by persons of the upper class, regardless of differences in the administrative procedures used. It is possible, indeed certain, that criminal acts are homogeneous only with reference to a small number of abstract characteristics. But if all criminal behavior is to be broken up into elements or classes, the divisions will cut across class lines, so that some crimes of some white-collar offenders will be in the same class as some crimes of some persons of the lower socioeconomic class.

The preceding description is designed to give an understanding of the nature, extent, and consequences of white-collar crimes. The purpose in this is not to reform white-collar criminals or devise plans for immediate prevention of such crimes. Possibly we should extend the methods of the criminal law to white-collar criminals, and possibly we should extend to ordinary criminals the more lenient methods which have been reserved for white-collar criminals. Any policy regarding crime should issue from an understanding and demonstration of the genetic processes involved in the behavior. If we can secure a more adequate understanding of the genesis of criminal behavior, both lower class and upper class, we can develop wiser and more effective policies for control of that behavior. The concept of white-collar crime is significant principally from the point of view of theoretical understanding of criminal behavior and is therefore designed to reform the criminologists rather than the white-collar criminals.

Poverty and Crime

The theories of criminal behavior which are held by most scholars working in this field have been based on studies of the criminals who are arrested, tried in the criminal courts, and, if convicted, fined, placed on probation, or committed to penal and reformatory institutions. Such criminals have their origin in a very large proportion of cases in the lower socioeconomic class. Because the criminologists who have attempted to explain criminal behavior have based their studies on criminals from the lower class, they have emphasized as the cause of crime either poverty or the sociopathic and psychopathic characteristics which are associated statistically with poverty, such as poor houses, lack of recreational facilities, broken and deteriorated families, lack of academic education, feeblemindedness, frustration, and other emotional disturbances. The conclusions derived from studies of criminals of the lower socioeconomic class have then been generalized for all criminals without realization that the sample from which the conclusions were derived was grossly biased from the point of view of class status.

It is obvious, however, that white-collar criminals do not suffer from poverty in the conventional sense of that word or from the sociopathic and psychopathic conditions which are statistically associated with poverty. On the contrary, they are well adjusted to other persons in their personal relations. Consequently these theories do not explain the criminal behavior of the upper socioeconomic class since the factors are seldom found in that class.

Nor do these theories explain the criminal behavior of the lower socioeconomic class. The association between crime and poverty, or the variants of poverty, is a spurious association due to the bias in the sample of criminals which has been studied. The procedure which has been used is logically similar to that of an investigator who might select only blue-eyed criminals and then conclude that blue eyes were the cause of crime since that was the only common characteristic found among the criminals. This conclusion is patently absurd, but the logic is the same as that used in drawing general conclusions regarding criminal behavior from a sample which is selected on the basis of economic status.

The factor or process which is here suggested hypothetically as the explanation of both upper class and lower class crime is that the criminal behavior is learned in direct and indirect association with persons who had practiced the same behavior previously and in relative isolation from those who opposed such behavior. In both classes a person begins his career free from criminality, learns something about the legal code which prohibits certain kinds of behavior, and also learns in variant groups that other kinds of behavior which conflict with the general code may be practiced. Through contact with these variant cultures he learns the techniques, rationalizations, and the specific drives and motives necessary for the successful accomplishment of crimes. If he is reared in the lower socioeconomic class he learns the techniques, rationalizations, and drives to be used in petty larceny, burglary, and robbery; while if he is reared in the upper socioeconomic class and engaged in an occupation of the kind characteristic of that class he learns the techniques, rationalizations, and drives to be used in frauds and false pretenses. The process of acquiring criminal behavior is identical in the two situations although the contents of the patterns which are transmitted in communication differ. It is obvious that no general motive or drive, such as the profit motive or frustration, will explain criminal behavior since those general motives and drives are characteristic of both criminal and lawful behavior.

 ## Methods of Study

Relatively few concrete studies of the genesis of white-collar crime have been made. Two methods may be used in the future in studies of this kind. One is the case history method, especially of the autobiographical type. Few studies of that nature have been made. We do, to be sure, have a few autobiographical descriptions, such as the confessions of a bond salesman, but we have very few directed investigations of the genesis of white-collar crimes of the more important business leaders. It is extremely difficult to secure the co-operation of these leaders in such investigations because they wish to maintain their respectability.

A second method of study is the observation of white-collar crimes in the mass. While this method, if used alone, is inadequate, it does throw light on the genesis of white-collar crime. Historical studies have shown that certain criminal practices have developed and been diffused in the same manner as fashions and fads. The history of the holding company in the public utility industry, which is confined almost entirely to the period since 1905, is a case in point. While the holding company itself has not been a violation of the criminal law, almost all of the holding companies have developed practices which were in violation of the criminal law, as shown in the recent report on utility corporations by the Federal Trade Commission. They have "milked" the subsidiary operating companies of all surplus funds that might have been used for a reduction of rates to consumers, and they have achieved this by misrepresentations of their asset values and their net incomes in the statements made to regulatory commissions and to prospective investors. One holding company made a profit of more than one million dollars a year for ten years on its Federal income tax, and that is no mean achievement. It made this profit by collecting money from the subsidiary companies for payment of the income tax on an individual-corporation basis, making a return to the Bureau of Internal Revenue on a consolidated-system basis, and keeping the balance in its own account. The utility corporations have obtained money under false pretenses as certainly as have the confidence men of the underworld. The various techniques employed have been developed and diffused in the utility industry almost entirely since 1905 under the control and direction of many of the most important and respected men of the financial world. Many of these practices were abruptly discontinued as soon as they received publicity.

A second hypothesis regarding white-collar crime is that a crime rate in any culture area, such as the public utility industry or the medical profession, is a function of the ratio between organization for and organization against criminal behavior in that area. This differs from the preceding hypothesis in that it refers to a crime rate rather than the criminal behavior of a particular person. The two hypotheses must be consistent with each other, if both are valid, since a crime rate is merely a summation of criminal acts of persons.

Organization for criminal behavior is apparent in various industries. It has been revealed in such investigations as those of the Federal Trade Commission in the utility corporations or the flour-milling industry. The organization includes working arrangements, division of labor, and consensus.

In comparison with a developed organization for conducting criminal practices in certain industries, the organization against criminal practices in those industries has been relatively weak and the crime rate therefore has been relatively high. This has been illustrated again and again in the descriptions of the failure of the antitrust law. The law was passed, but until recently there was no implementation of the law that made its enforcement possible. The antitrust division of the Department of Justice until recently has been similar to the pickpocket division in many city police departments, being in sympathy with the violators of the law rather than the victims, and doing the minimum in the enforcement of the law. It is probable that the organization which has developed against white-collar crime during the last decade is resulting in a significant reduction in the rate of this type of crime.

DISCUSSION QUESTIONS

1. Does Sutherland think someone needs to be convicted to be a criminal? Explain.

2. What "systems" does Sutherland refer to either directly or indirectly?

3. What methods does Sutherland suggest for studying white-collar crime? How would these methods vary in studying white-collar crimes rather than traditional crimes?

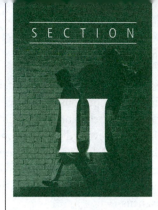

II

Understanding White-Collar Crime

Definitions, Extent, and Consequences

Section Highlights

- White-Collar Crime: An Evolving Concept
- Modern Conceptualizations of White-Collar Crime
- Extent of White-Collar Crime
- Consequences of White-Collar Crime
- Public Attitudes About White-Collar Crime
- Characteristics of White-Collar Offenders

A s noted in the introduction, Edwin Sutherland created the concept of **white-collar crime** more than 70 years ago to draw attention to the fact that crimes are committed by individuals in all social classes. As will be seen in this section, one of the largest difficulties in understanding white-collar crime has centered on an ongoing debate about how to define white-collar crime. After discussing various ways that white-collar crime can be defined, attention will be given to the extent of white-collar crime, the consequences of this illicit behavior, public attitudes about white-collar crime, and patterns describing the characteristics of white-collar offenders.

As a backdrop to this discussion, consider the following recent white-collar crimes described in the media:

- A jury convicted [then-Baltimore mayor Sheila] Dixon . . . of embezzling about $500 worth of gift cards donated to the city for needy families. Dixon then pleaded guilty last month to lying about thousands of dollars in gifts from her former boyfriend, a prominent developer. (Nuckols, 2010)
- The money manager and technology investor convicted of stealing some $22 million from clients and using his gains to support charitable causes in Colorado and elsewhere was sentenced in New York Friday to nine years in federal prison. (Harden, 2010)
- The secretary of a St. Peters business has been indicted in connection with the embezzlement of $573,388 from her employer. ("Secretary Charged With Embezzling," 2010)
- A former Redondo Beach police officer accused of taking more than $75,000 from a law enforcement officers' association pleaded guilty . . . to one count of grand theft by embezzlement, authorities said. (Lopez, 2010)
- An employee at Goldman Sachs from May 2007 to June 2009 was arrested in July of 2009 and charged with illegally transferring and downloading hundreds of thousands of lines of source code for Goldman's high-frequency trading system on his last day at the firm. (Heires, 2010)

In reviewing these cases, five questions come to mind. First, are each of these cases white-collar crimes? Second, how often do these kinds of crimes occur? Third, what are the consequences of these crimes? Fourth, how serious do you think these crimes are? Finally, who are the offenders in these cases? While the questions are simple in nature, as will be shown in this section, the answers to these questions are not necessarily quite so simple.

White-Collar Crime: An Evolving Concept

While Edwin Sutherland is the pioneer of the study of white-collar crime, the development of the field, and the introduction of the concept of white-collar crime, did not occur in a vacuum. Indeed, prior academic work and societal changes influenced Sutherland's scholarship, and his scholarship, in turn, has had an enormous influence on criminology and criminal justice. Tracing the source of the concept of white-collar crime and describing its subsequent variations helps to demonstrate the importance of conceptualizing various forms of white-collar misconduct.

Sutherland was not the first social scientist to write about crimes by those in the upper class. In his 1934 *Criminology* text, Sutherland used the term "white-collar criminaloid," in reference to the **"criminaloid concept"** initially used by E. A. Ross (1907) in *Sin and Society*. Focusing on businessmen who engaged in harmful acts under the mask of respectability, Ross further wrote that the criminaloid is "society's most dangerous foe, more redoubtable by far than the plain criminal, because he sports the livery of virtue and operates on a titanic scale." Building on these ideas, Sutherland called attention to the fact that crimes were not committed only by members of the lower class. As noted in the introduction, Sutherland (1949) defined white-collar crime as "crime committed by a person of respectability and high social status in the course of his occupation."

Sutherland's appeal to social scientists to expand their focus to include crimes by upper class offenders was both applauded and criticized. On the one hand, Sutherland was lauded for expanding the focus of the social sciences. On the other hand, the way that Sutherland defined and studied white-collar crime was widely criticized by a host of social scientists and legal experts. Much of the criticism centered around five concerns that scholars had about Sutherland's use of the white-collar crime concept. These concerns included (1) conceptual ambiguity, (2) empirical ambiguity, (3) methodological ambiguity, (4) legal ambiguity, and (5) policy ambiguity.

In terms of **conceptual ambiguity,** critics have noted that white-collar crime was vaguely and loosely defined by Sutherland (Robin, 1974). Robin further argued that the vagueness surrounding the definition fostered ambiguous use of the term and vague interpretations by scholars and practitioners alike. Focusing on the link between scholarship and practice, one author suggested that the concept was "totally inadequate" to characterize the kinds of behavior that are at the root of the phenomena (Edelhertz, 1983). Further describing the reactions to this conceptual ambiguity, white-collar crime scholar David Friedrichs (2002) wrote, "perhaps no other area of criminological theory has been more plagued by conceptual confusion than that of white-collar crime" (p. 243).

Criticism about Sutherland's work also focused on the **empirical ambiguity** surrounding the concept. In effect, some argued that the concept only minimally reflected reality. For example, one author said that Sutherland's definition underestimated the influence of poverty on other forms of crime (Mannheim, 1949). Another author argued that by focusing on the offender (in terms of status) and the location (the workplace) rather than the offense, the concept did not accurately reflect the behaviors that needed to be addressed (Edelhertz, 1983). Edelhertz went as far as to suggest that this vague empirical conceptualization created barriers with practitioners and resulted in a lack of research on white-collar crime between the 1950s and 1970s. Shapiro (1990) also recognized the problems that the conceptualization of white-collar crime created for future researchers. She wrote:

> The concept has done its own cognitive mischief. It . . . is founded on a spurious correlation that causes sociologists to misunderstand the structural impetus for these offenses, the problems the offenses create for systems of social control, and the sources and consequences of class bias in the legal system. (p. 346)

The consequences of this empirical ambiguity are such that findings from white-collar crime studies sometimes call into question the nature of white-collar offenders. One study of white-collar offenders convicted in seven federal districts between 1976 and 1978, for example, found that most offenses described as white-collar were actually "committed by those who fall in the middle classes of our society" (Weisburd, Chayet, & Waring, 1990, p. 353).

Sutherland was also criticized for **methodological ambiguity.** He defined white-collar crime as behaviors committed by members of the upper class, but his research focused on all sorts of offenses including workplace theft, fraud by mechanics, deception by shoe sales persons, and crimes by corporations (see Robin, 1974). One might say that Sutherland committed a "bait and switch" in defining one type of crime, but actually researching another variety.

A fourth criticism of Sutherland's white-collar crime scholarship can be termed **legal ambiguity.** Some legal scholars contended that the concept was too sociological at the expense of legal definitions of white-collar offending (Tappan, 1947). To some, white-collar crimes should be narrowly defined to include those behaviors that are criminally illegal. Some even take it a step farther and suggest that white-collar criminals are those individuals convicted of white-collar crimes (suggesting that if one were not caught for a white-collar crime one actually committed, then one would not be a white-collar criminal). Sutherland, and others, have countered this argument by suggesting that conviction is irrelevant in determining whether behaviors constitute white-collar crimes (Geis, 1978).

A final criticism of the white-collar crime concept is related to the **policy ambiguity** surrounding the concept. In particular, some have argued that the vagueness of the definition, and its purely academic focus, created a disconnect between those developing policies and practices responding to white-collar crime and those studying white-collar crime (Edelhertz, 1983). Over the past decade or so, criminologists have become more vocal about the need for evidence-based practices to guide criminal justice policies and activities. In terms of white-collar crime, an issue that has been cited is that unclear definitions about white-collar crime make it extremely difficult for policy makers and practitioners to use criminological information to guide policy development and criminal justice practices. In effect, how can criminologists call for evidence-based practices for certain types of crime when they have not adequately provided the evidence needed to develop subsequent practices?

Sutherland was aware of the concerns about the concept potentially being vague. He noted that his point was not precision, but to note how white-collar crime is "identical in its general characteristics with other crime rather than different from it" (Sutherland, 1941, p. 112). He wrote:

> The purpose of the concept of white-collar crime is to call attention to a vast area of criminal behavior which is generally overlooked as criminal behavior, which is seldom brought within the score of the theories of criminal behavior, and which, when included, call for modifications in the usual theories of criminal behavior. (p. 112)

Thus, Sutherland conceded that the concept was vague in nature, but it was necessarily vague in order to promote further discussion about the concept.

Sutherland was successful in promoting further discussion about the phenomena, though the topic received very little attention in the 1950s and 1960s. This began to change in the early 1970s when criminologists Marshall Clinard and Richard Quinney published *Criminal Behavior Systems*. Building on Sutherland's work, Clinard and Quinney (1973) argued that white-collar crime can be divided into two types: corporate crime and occupational crime. They focused their definition of **corporate crime** on illegal behaviors that are committed by employees of a corporation to benefit the corporation, company, or business. In contrast, they defined **occupational crime** as "violations of legal codes in the course of activity in a legitimate occupation." By distinguishing between crimes by corporations and crimes against corporations, Clinard and Quinney took an important step in addressing some of the ambiguity surrounding the white-collar crime concept. Indeed, corporate crime and occupational crime are viewed as "the two principal or 'pure' forms of white-collar crime" (Friedrichs, 2002, p. 245).

After Clinard and Quinney's work, white-collar crime research by criminologists escalated in the 1970s and 1980s. Much of this research focused on ways to conceptualize and define the phenomenon in ways that addressed the criticisms surrounding Sutherland's definition. Table 2.1 shows eight different concepts and definitions that criminologists have used to describe these behaviors. Just as Sutherland's definition was criticized, each of the concepts provided in Table 2.1 are imperfect. Still, they illustrate the impact that Sutherland's white-collar crime scholarship has had on criminology and criminal justice.

A definition of white-collar crime acceptable to all groups is yet to be developed. This is troublesome for at least five reasons. First, the lack of a sound definition of white-collar crime has hindered detection efforts. Second, without a concrete definition of white-collar crime, the most effective responses to the problem cannot be gauged. Third, varying definitions among researchers have made it difficult to draw comparisons between different white-collar crime studies. Fourth, vague conceptualizations have made it more difficult to

Table 2.1 Evolution of the White-Collar Crime Concept

Concept	Definition	Reference
Criminaloid	The immunity enjoyed by the perpetrator of new sins has brought into being a class for which we may coin the term *criminaloid*. By this we designate such as prosper by flagitious practices which have not yet come under the effective ban of public opinion. Often, indeed, they are guilty in the eyes of the law; but since they are not culpable in the eyes of the public and in their own eyes, their spiritual attitude is not that of the criminal. The lawmaker may make their misdeeds crimes, but, so long as morality stands stock-still in the old tracks, they escape both punishment and ignominy.	E.A. Ross (Sin and Society, 1907, p. 48)
White-collar crime	Crime committed by a person of respectability and high social status in the course of his occupation.	Sutherland (1949)
Corporate crime	Offenses committed by corporate officials for their corporation and the offenses of the corporation itself.	Clinard and Yeager (1980, p. 189)
Occupational crime	Offenses committed by individuals in the course of their occupations and the offenses of employees against their employers.	Clinard and Yeager (1980, p. 189).
Organizational deviance	Actions contrary to norms maintained by others outside the organization . . . [but] supported by the internal operating norms of the organization.	Ermann and Lundman (1978, p. 7)
Elite deviance	Acts committed by persons from the highest strata of society . . . some acts are crimes . . . may be criminal or noncriminal in nature.	Simon (2006, p. 12)
Organizational crime	Illegal acts of omission or commission of an individual or a group of individuals in a formal organization in accordance with the operative goals of the organization, which have serious physical or economic impact on employees, consumers, or the general public.	Schrager and Short, (1978, p. 408)
Occupational crime	Any act punishable by law which is committed through opportunity created in the course of an occupation that is legitimate.	Green (1990)

identify the causes of the behavior. Finally, varied definitions of white-collar crime have made it difficult to determine with great accuracy the true extent of white-collar crime.

⊠ Modern Conceptualizations of White-Collar Crime

Today, criminologists and social scientists offer various ways to define white-collar crime (see Figure 2.1). These variations tend to overlap with one another and include the following:

- White-collar crime as moral or ethical violations
- White-collar crime as social harm
- White-collar crime as violations of criminal law

- White-collar crime as violations of civil law
- White-collar crime as violations of regulatory laws
- White-collar crime as workplace deviance
- White-collar crime as definitions socially constructed by businesses
- White-collar crime as research definitions
- White-collar crime as official government definitions
- White-collar crime as violations of trust
- White-collar crime as occupational crimes
- White-collar crime as violations occurring in occupational systems

Figure 2.1   Defining White-Collar Crime

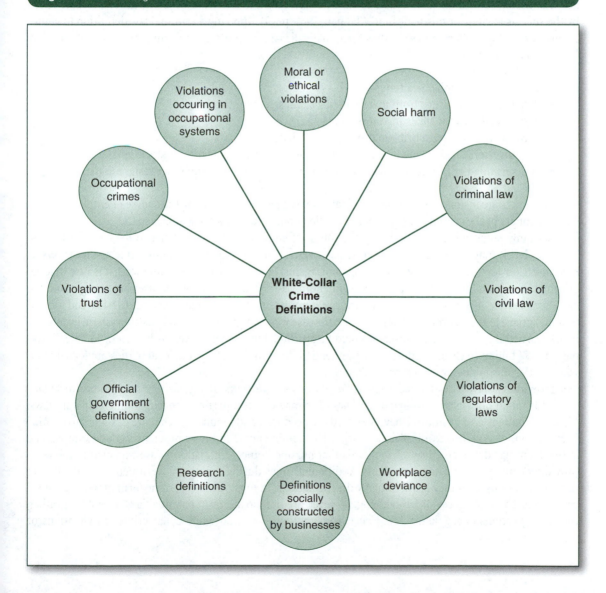

Defining *white-collar crime as moral or ethical violations* follows ideals inherent within principles of what is known as natural law. **Natural law** focuses on behaviors or activities that are defined as wrong because they violate the ethical principles of a particular culture, subculture, or group. The immoral nature of the activities is seen as the foundation for defining certain types of white-collar activities as criminal. Some individuals, for example, define any business activities that destroy animal life or plant life as immoral and unethical. To those individuals, the behaviors of individuals and businesses participating in those activities would be defined as white-collar crimes.

Some prefer to define *white-collar crime as violations of criminal law*. From this framework, white-collar crimes are criminally illegal behaviors committed by upper class individuals during the course of their occupation. From a systems perspective, those working in the criminal justice system would likely define white-collar crime as criminally illegal behaviors. Crime, in this context, is defined as "an intentional act or omission committed in violation of the criminal law without defense or justification and sanctioned by the state as a felony or misdemeanor" (Tappan, 1960, p. 10). Applying a criminal law definition to white-collar crime, white-collar crimes are those criminally illegal acts committed during the course of one's job. Here are a few examples:

- An accountant embezzles funds from his employer.
- Two nurses steal drugs from their workplace and sell them to addicts.
- A financial investor steals investors' money.
- A prosecutor accepts a bribe to drop criminal charges.
- Two investors share inside information that allow them to redirect their stock purchases.
- A disgruntled employee destroys the computer records of a firm upon her resignation.

These acts are instances where the criminal law has been violated during the course of employment. As such, members of the criminal justice could be called upon to address those misdeeds.

Certainly, some rule breaking during the course of employment does not rise to the level of criminal behavior, but it may violate civil laws. Consequently, some may define *white-collar crime as **violations of civil law.*** Consider cases of corporate wrongdoing against consumers. In those situations, it is rare that the criminal law would be used to respond to the offending corporation. More often, cases are brought into the civil justice system. When the *Exxon Valdez* ran aground in Prince William Sound, Alaska, and caused untold damage to the environment, for example, the case was brought into the civil justice system. Eventually it was learned that the cause of the crash could be attributed to the ship's overworked crew. To date, Exxon has paid $2 billion in cleanup efforts and another $1 billion in fines. Ongoing legal battles are focusing on whether Exxon should pay even more in damages.

Individuals have also defined *white-collar crime* as ***violations of regulatory law.*** Some workplace misdeeds might not violate criminal or civil laws, but may violate a particular occupation's regulatory laws. Most occupations and businesses have standards, procedures, and regulations that are designed to administratively guide and direct workplace activities. The nursing home industry provides a good example. The government has developed a set of standards that nursing home administrators are expected to follow in providing care to nursing home residents. At different times during the year, government officials inspect nursing homes to see if they are abiding by the regulations. In most instances, some form of wrongdoing is uncovered. These instances of wrongdoing, however, are not violations of criminal law or civil law; rather, they are violations of regulatory law. Hence, some authors focus on white-collar crimes as violations of regulatory laws.

Sometimes behaviors performed as part of an occupational routine might be wrong, but not necessarily illegal by criminal, civil, or regulatory definitions. As a result, some prefer to follow definitions of *white-collar crime as **workplace deviance.*** This is a broader way to define white-collar crime, and such an approach would include all of those workplace acts that violate the norms or standards of the workplace, regardless of whether they are formally defined as illegal or not. Violations of criminal, civil, and regulatory laws would be included, as would those violations that are set by the workplace itself. Beyond those formal violations of the law, consider the following situations as examples of workplace deviance:

- Professors cancel class simply because they don't feel like going to class.
- A worker takes a 30-minute break when she was only supposed to take a 15-minute break.
- A worker calls his boss and says he is too sick to come to work when in fact he is not actually sick (but he uses that "fake sick voice" as part of his ploy).
- A wedding photographer gets drunk at a client's wedding, takes horrible pictures, and hits on the groom.
- An author uses silly examples to try to get his point across.

In each of these cases, no laws have necessarily been broken; however, one could argue that workplace or occupational norms may have been violated.

Somewhat related, one can also define *white-collar crime as **definitions socially constructed by businesses.*** What this means is that a particular company or business might define behaviors that it believes to be improper. What is wrong in one company might not necessarily be wrong in another company. Some businesses might have formal dress codes while others might have casual Fridays. Some companies might tolerate workers taking small quantities of the goods it produces home each night, while other companies might define that behavior as inappropriate and criminal. The expectations for workplace behavior, then, are defined by the workplace. Incidentally, some experts have suggested that expectations be defined in such a way as to accept at least minor forms of wrongdoing (see Mars, 1983, for a description of the rewards individuals perceive from workplace misconduct). The basis for this suggestion is that individuals are more satisfied with their jobs if they are able to break the rules of their job at least every now and then. As a simple example, where would you rather work: (1) in a workplace that lets you get away with longer breaks every now and then or (2) in a workplace where you are docked double pay for every minute you take over the allotted break?

In some cases, workplace behaviors might not be illegal or deviant, but might actually create forms of harm for various individuals. As a result, some prefer to define *white-collar crime as **social harm.*** Those defining white-collar crime from this perspective are more concerned with the harm done by occupational activities than whether behavior is defined either formally or informally as illegal or deviant. According to one author, "by concentrating on what is defined as illegal or criminal, a more serious threat to society is left out" (Passas, 2005, p. 771). Galbraith (2005, p. 731) offers the following examples: "The common practices of tobacco companies, hog farmers, gun makers and merchants are legal. But this is only because of the political nature of the perpetrators; in a democracy free of their money and influence, they would be crimes." Additional examples of white-collar crimes that are examples of this social harm perspective have been noted by Passas (2005), who highlighted the following "crimes" that occur without lawbreaking occurring: cross-border malpractices, asymmetrical environmental regulations, corrupt practices, child labor in impoverished communities, and pharmaceutical practices such as those allowing testing of drugs in third world countries. Passas emphasized that lawbreaking does not occur when these actions are performed, but argues the actions are, in fact, criminal.

Another way to define these behaviors is to consider *white-collar crime as **research definitions.*** When researchers study and gather data about white-collar crime, they must operationalize or define white-collar crime in a way that allows them to reliably and validly measure the behavior. As an example, in 2005, the National White-Collar Crime Center conducted its second national survey on white-collar crime. The results of this survey will be discussed later. For now, the way that the researchers defined white-collar crime illustrates what is meant by research-generated white-collar crime definitions. The researchers defined white-collar crime as: "illegal or unethical acts that violate fiduciary responsibility or public trust for personal or organizational gain" (Kane & Wall, 2006). Using this definition as their foundation, the researchers were able to conduct a study that measured the characteristics of white-collar crime, its consequences, and contributing factors. Note that had they chosen a different definition, their results may have been different. The way that we define phenomena will influence the observations we make about those phenomena.

Another way to define these behaviors is to consider *white-collar crime as official **government definitions.*** Government agencies, and employees of those agencies, will have definitions of white-collar crime that may or may not parallel the way others define white-collar crime. The Federal Bureau of Investigation (FBI), for example, has used an offense-based perspective to define white-collar crime as part of its Uniform Crime Reporting program. The FBI defines white-collar crime as:

> Those illegal acts which are characterized by deceit, concealment, or violation of trust and which are not dependent upon the application or threat of physical force or violence. Individuals and organizations commit these acts to obtain money, property, or services; to avoid payment or loss of money or services; or to secure personal or business advantage. (United States Department of Justice, 1989, p. 3; as cited in Barnett, no date)

In following this definition, the FBI tends to take a broader definition of white-collar crime than many white-collar crime scholars and researchers do. Identity theft offers a case in point. The FBI includes identity theft as a white-collar crime type. Some academics, however, believe that such a classification is inappropriate. One research team conducted interviews with 59 convicted identity thieves and found that offenses and offenders did not meet the traditional characteristics of white-collar crimes or white-collar offenders. Many offenders were unemployed and working independently, meaning their offenses were not committed as part of a legitimate occupation, or in the course of their occupation (Copes & Vieraitis, 2009).

Another way to define white-collar crime is to focus on *white-collar crime as **violations of trust*** that occur during the course of legitimate employment. To some authors, offenders use their positions of trust to promote the misconduct (Reiss & Biderman, 1980). Criminologist Susan Shapiro (1990) has argued for the need to view white-collar crime as abuses of trust and she suggests that researchers should focus on the *act* rather than the *actor.* She wrote:

> Offenders clothed in very different wardrobes lie, steal, falsify, fabricate, exaggerate, omit, deceive, dissemble, shirk, embezzle, misappropriate, self-deal, and engage in corruption or incompliance by misusing their positions of trust. It turns out most of them are not upper class. (p. 358)

In effect, Shapiro was calling for a broader definition of white-collar crime that was not limited to the collar of the offender's shirts.

Others have also called for broader conceptualizations that are not limited to wardrobes or occupational statuses. Following Clinard and Quinney's 1973 conceptualization, some have suggested that these behaviors be classified as *white-collar crimes as occupational crimes.* One author defines occupational crimes as "violations that occur during the course of occupational activity and are related to employment" (Robin, 1974). Robin argued vehemently for the broader conceptualization of white-collar crime. He noted that various forms of lower class workplace offenses "are more similar to white-collar crime methodologically than behaviorally," suggesting that many occupational offenders tend to use the same methods to commit their transgressions. He further stated that the failure of scholars to broadly conceive white-collar crime "results in underestimating the amount of crime, distorts relative frequencies of the typology of crimes, produces a biased profile of the personal and social characteristics of the violators, and thus affects our theory of criminality" (p. 261).

Criminologist Gary Green (1990) has been a strong advocate of focusing on occupational crime rather than a limited conceptualization of white-collar crime. He defined occupational crime as "any act punishable by law which is committed through opportunity created in the course of an occupation that is legal" (p. 13). Green described four varieties of occupational crime: (1) organizational occupational crimes, which include crimes by corporations, (2) state authority occupational crimes, which include crimes by governments, (3) professional occupational crimes, which include those crimes by individuals in upper class jobs, and (4) individual occupational crimes, which include those crimes committed by individuals in lower class jobs. The strength of his conceptualization is that it expands white-collar crime to consider all forms of misdeeds committed by employees and businesses during the course of employment.

Using each of the above definitions as a framework, white-collar crime can also be defined as *violations occurring in occupational systems.* This text uses such a framework to provide broad systems perspective about white-collar crime. White-collar crime can therefore be defined as "any violation of criminal, civil, or regulatory laws—or deviant, harmful, or unethical actions—committed during the course of employment in various occupational systems." This definition allows us to consider numerous types of workplace misconduct and the interactions between these behaviors and broader systems involved in preventing and responding to white-collar crimes. As will be shown in the following paragraphs, the extent of these crimes is enormous.

Extent of White-Collar Crime

Determining the extent of white-collar crime is no simple task. Two factors make it particularly difficult to accurately determine how often white-collar crimes occur. First, many white-collar crimes are not reported to formal response agencies. One study found that just one third of white-collar crime victims notify the authorities about their victimization (Kane & Wall, 2006). When individuals are victims of white-collar crimes, they may not report the victimization because of shame, concerns that reporting will be futile, or a general denial that the victimization was actually criminal. When businesses or companies are victims, they may refrain from reporting out of concern about the negative publicity that comes along with "being duped" by an employee. If victims are not willing to report their victimization, their victimization experiences will not be included in official statistics.

A second factor that makes it difficult to determine the extent of white-collar crime has to do with the conceptual ambiguity surrounding the concept (and discussed above). Depending on how one defines white-collar crime, one would find different estimates about the extent of white-collar crime. The federal government, and other government agencies, offer different definitions of white-collar crime than many scholars and researchers might use. The result is that white-collar crime researchers typically observe caution when relying on official statistics or **victimization surveys** to determine the extent of white-collar crime victimization. Despite this caution, the three main ways that we learn about the extent of white-collar crime are from official statistics provided by government agencies, victimization surveys, and research studies focusing on specific types of white-collar crime.

With regard to official statistics and white-collar crime, the FBI's Uniform Crime Reports (UCR) and National Incident Based Reporting System (NIBRS) provide at least a starting point from which we can begin to question how often certain forms of white-collar crime occur. These data reflect crimes known to the police. The UCR includes eight Part I (or index offenses: homicide, robbery, rape, aggravated assault, motor vehicle theft, larceny, arson, and burglary) and 29 Part II offenses, which are typically defined as "less serious" crimes. With regard to white-collar crime, Part II offenses have been regarded as possible white-collar crimes. Table 2.2 shows the number of times these crimes occurred between 1990 and 2008. As shown in the table, the number of forgery/counterfeiting and embezzlement cases increased somewhat dramatically between 1990 and 2009, while the number of fraud cases was lower in 2009 than in 1992, though the number of fraud cases fluctuated significantly over this time frame. Also, note the increase in all arrests for all three offense types between 2008 and 2009.

A word of caution is needed in reviewing these estimates. Not all criminologists agree that these offenses are appropriate indicators of white-collar crimes. Many of these offenses may have occurred outside of the scope of employment. Also, because the UCR does not capture information about offender status, it is not possible to classify the crimes according to the occupational systems where the offenses occurred.

Limitations in the UCR prompted the federal government to expand its efforts in reporting crime data through the National Incident Based Reporting System. NIBRS data provide more contextual information surrounding the crimes reported to the police. For example, this reporting system provides information about where the crime occurred, the victim-offender relationship, victim characteristics, and so on. While more contextual information is provided from NIBRS data, the same limitations that plague the UCR data with regard to the measurement of white-collar crime surface: (1) not everyone would agree these are white-collar crimes, (2) the database was created for law enforcement and not for researchers, (3) many cases are reported to regulatory agencies rather than law enforcement, (4) some white-collar crime victims are unaware of their victimization, and (5) shame may keep some victims from reporting their victimization (Barnett, no date). Also, the NIBRS data are not as "user friendly" as UCR data at this point.

▲ **Photo 2.1**   Most victims of white-collar crime do not call the police. As a result, using police-based data to examine white-collar crime offers a limited picture of white-collar crime.

Victimization surveys offer an opportunity to overcome some of these problems. These surveys sample residents and estimate the extent of victimization from the survey findings. The 2005 National White-Collar Crime Center (NW3C) Victimization

Table 2.2 Arrests Reported in UCR for Three "White-Collar" Offenses, 1990–2009, U.S. Department of Justice, Available online.

Year	Forgery/Counterfeiting	Embezzlement	Fraud
1990	50403	7708	182752
1991	53853	7458	188100
1992	66608	8860	279682
1993	69063	8886	246127
1994	71322	9155	233234
1995	84068	10832	295584
1996	81319	11763	248370
1997	77773	10935	298713
1998	70678	10585	220262
1999	56813	9692	166413
2000	58493	10730	155231
2001	77692	13836	211177
2002	83111	13416	233087
2003	79188	11986	208469
2004	73082	9164	235412
2005	87346	14097	231721
2006	79477	14769	197722
2007	78005	17015	185229
2008	68976	16458	174598
2009	85844	17920	210255

Survey is the most recent, and most comprehensive, white-collar crime victimization survey available. The results of this survey, a phone interview with 1,605 adults in the United States, found that 46.5% of households and 36% of individuals reported experiencing forms of white-collar crime in the prior year (Kane & Wall, 2006). Nearly two thirds of the respondents reported experiencing some form of white-collar victimization (as measured by the researchers) in their life time.

Table 2.3 Household Victimization Trends (12 months)	
False stockbrocker info	4.4%
Illegitimate e-mail	5.5%
Business venture	5.9%
New account fraud	8.1%
Unnecessary repair (home)	11.7%
Monetary loss (Internet)	12.4%
Existing account fraud	12.6%
Unnecessary repair (object)	20.8%
Affected by national corporate scandal	21.4%
Credit card fraud	24.5%
Price lie	35.9%

Table 2.4 Household Victimization Reporting Trends	
Internet crime complaint center	2.6%
Consumer Protection Agency	4.5%
Personal lawyer	4.9%
District attorney or state attorney general	7.7%
Better Business Bureau	14.2%
Police/law enforcement	19.3%
Entity involved	31.8%
Other	32.1%
Credit card company	34.9%

Table 2.3 shows the types of victimization reported by respondents in the NW3C victimization survey. As shown in the table, more than a third of the respondents indicated that they had been lied to about prices in the prior year, and one fourth reported being victims of credit card fraud. Also, about one fifth reported being victimized by unnecessary object repairs and corporate scandals.

The NW3C also asked victims about their decisions to report their victimization to various agencies. Table 2.4 shows the formal agencies that respondents reported their victimization to (among those who did report the victimization). As shown in the table, respondents tended to report their victimization either to their credit card company or the entity involved. Perhaps most interesting is how infrequently respondents reported their victimization to formal governmental agencies of social control. Less than one fifth of respondents reported their victimization to the police, one seventh of them notified the Better Business Bureau, one in 14 notified the district attorney, and about one in 20 notified a personal lawyer or the consumer protection agency.

Researchers have also used specific studies to gauge the extent of various forms of white-collar crime. One author, for example, cites a study by the Government Accountability Office that found fraud in "every single case" of the Savings and Loan institutions included in the study (Galbraith, 2005). Another study found that one in 30 employees (out of 2.1 million employees) was caught stealing from his or her employer in 2007 ("Record Number of Shoplifters," 2008). A Federal Trade Commission (FTC) survey of 2,500 adults in the United States found that consumer fraud was rampant (Anderson, 2004). Based on the survey findings, Anderson estimates that "nearly 25 million adults in the United States—11.2% of the adult population— were victims of one or more of the consumer frauds covered in the survey during the previous year" (p. ES-2). Anderson further estimated that 35 million cases of consumer fraud occur each year.

Figure 2.2 shows the extent of the types of consumer fraud considered in the FTC survey. As shown in the figure, the most common frauds were paying an advanced fee for a loan/credit card, fraudulent billing for buyers' club memberships, and purchasing credit card insurance. Note that these are only estimates about the extent of victimization. Accurately determining the extent of white-collar crime remains a difficult task.

Figure 2.2   Common Types of Consumer Fraud

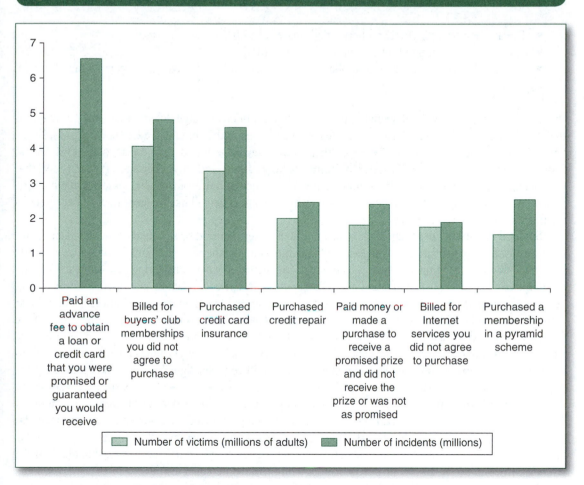

Number of victims (millions of adults)   Number of incidents (millions)

While it is difficult to gauge the extent of white-collar crime, all indications are that these offenses occur with great regularity. The regularity of these offenses exacerbates their consequences.

Consequences of White-Collar Crime

Crime, by its very nature, has consequences for individuals and communities. White-collar crime, in particular, has a set of consequences that may be significantly different from the kinds of consequences that arise from street crimes. In particular, the consequences can be characterized as (1) individual economic losses, (2) societal economic losses, (3) emotional consequences, (4) physical harm, and (5) "positive" consequences.

Individual economic losses refer to the losses that individual victims or business lose due to white-collar crimes. One way that criminologists have captured these losses is to compare them to losses experienced by victims of conventional crimes. By some estimates, the average amount lost to embezzlement, for example, is about $1,000,000 ("The Marquette Report," 2009). By comparison, consider the following:

- The average street/highway robbery entails losses of $1,032
- The average gas station robbery entails losses of $1,007
- The average convenience store robbery entails losses of $712 (Federal Bureau of Investigation, 2009b).

It is important to note that a small group of offenders can create large dollar losses. One study found that 27 white-collar offenders were responsible for dollar losses in the amount of $2,494,309 (Crofts, 2003). Each offender stole an average of $95,935. Other studies have also found large dollar losses as a central feature of white-collar crimes (Wheeler, Weisburd, & Bode, 1988). In fact, Sutherland (1949) argued that white-collar crimes cost several times more than street crimes in terms of financial losses. While his estimate may be a little dated, the fact remains that a white-collar crime will likely cause larger dollar losses to victims than a street crime would.

Societal economic losses entail the total amount of losses incurred by society from white-collar crime. Kane and Wall (2006) cite estimates suggesting that white-collar crime costs the United States between $300 and $600 billion a year in financial losses. These costs are increased when considering the secondary societal economic costs such as business failures and recovery costs. In terms of business failures, one estimate suggests that one third to one half of business failures are attributed to employee theft (National White Collar Crime Center, 2009). With regard to recovery costs, taxpayers pay billions of dollars to support the efforts of the criminal, civil, and regulatory justice systems. As an illustration of how these costs can quickly add up, one white-collar criminal involved in a $7 million Ponzi scheme eventually lost everything and was unable to afford his own attorney. In this case, the federal public defender's office was assigned the task of representing the accused (Henning, 2010). Attorney costs in white-collar crime cases are believed to be particularly exorbitant.

Emotional consequences are also experienced by victims of white-collar crime and all members of society exposed to this misconduct. These emotional consequences include stress from victimization, violation of trust, and damage to public morale. With regard to stress, any experience of victimization is stressful, but the experience of white-collar crime victimization is believed to be particularly stressful. Much of the stress stems from the violation of trust that comes along with white-collar crimes.

According to Sutherland (1941), the violation of trust can be defined as the "most general" characteristic of white-collar crime. Victims of a street robbery didn't trust the stranger who robbed them in the first place. Victims of a white-collar crime, in addition to the other losses incurred from the victimization, have their trust violated by the offender. There is reason to believe that the level of trust may be tied to the specific level of trust given to different types of white-collar offenders (e.g., we trust doctors and pharmacists at a certain level, but auto mechanics on another level).

Researchers have used various strategies to consider how these trust violations manifest themselves in white-collar crimes. Spalek (2001) interviewed 25 individuals who lost some of their pension funds to a fraudulent scheme by Robert Maxwell. She focused on the degree to which victimization bred distrust. She found that many of the victims already distrusted their offender before the victimization came to light. The victims said that they felt forced or coerced into trusting the offender as part of his investment scheme. In terms of trust, they placed their trust in outside agencies to protect them from the offender. The following comments from Spalek's participants highlight this pattern:

- I've always mistrusted Maxwell. But I felt that because pensioners were, to a large extent, the province of the state . . . that there was very little Maxwell could do to make off with the money.
- I suppose at the time I actually thought that the law would actually safeguard against anything that was mine so I wasn't too worried about it, although I thought that Maxwell would do his best to get his hands on the money (n.p.).

With regard to public alienation, violations of trust potentially do damage to the economy and social relationships. According to Frankel (2006), "with few exceptions, trust is essential to economic prosperity" (p. 49). If individuals do not trust financial institutions, they are not likely to invest their funds in the economy. Sutherland (1941) recognized this relationship between trust, the economy, and social relationships. He wrote:

The financial loss from white-collar crime, great as it is, is less important than the damage to social relations. White-collar crime violates trust and therefore creates distrust; this lowers social morale and produces disorganization. Many white-collar crimes attack the fundamental principles of the American institutions. Ordinary crimes, on the other hand, produce little effect on social institutions or social organization. (p. 13)

Building on Sutherland's ideas, Moore and Mills (1990) described the following consequences of white-collar crime:

- Diminished faith in a free economy and in business leaders
- Erosion of public morality
- Loss of confidence in political institutions, processes, and leaders

Physical harm may also result from white-collar crime victimization. Sometimes, physical harm may be a direct result of the white-collar offense. For example, cases of physical or sexual patient abuse will result in physical harm for victims. Other times, experiencing financial harm can lead to physical problems. The loss of one's entire retirement savings, for example, has been found to contribute to health problems for white-collar crime victims (Payne, 2005).

Death or serious physical injury is also a possible consequence of white-collar crimes. In one case, for instance, seven people died after a doctor "used lemon juice instead of antiseptic on patients' operation wounds" (Ninemsn Staff, 2010). In another case, Reinaldo Silvestre was running a medical clinic in

▲ **Photo 2.2**   In the aftermath of the *Exxon Valdez* grounding, workers worked tirelessly to eradicate harmful effects of the white-collar offense. Researchers have not yet been able to identify the full extent of the consequences of this disaster.

Miami Beach when it was discovered that he was practicing without a license, using animal tranquilizers as sedatives for humans, and performing botched surgeries. In a widely publicized case, a male body builder was given female C-cup breast implants—he had requested pectoral implants to make his chest look bigger ("Fugitive Phony Doctor Nabbed," 2004).

It is possible to more generally highlight the physical harm stemming from white-collar crime. Consider the following estimates, quoted verbatim from their sources:

- Research from the U.S. Consumer Product Safety Commission indicates that defective or unsafe products cause 29.4 million injuries and 21,400 deaths each year. (Ria, 2009)
- As many as 231,000 people have died from asbestos-related diseases in the U.S. since 1980; an equal number could die by 2040 according to testimony given at the [Senate] hearing. Dr. David Weissman, from the National Institute for Occupational Safety and Health, informed the Senate Committee that deaths from the asbestos cancer mesothelioma are increasing. (Kazen-Allen, 2007)
- At least 12,000 Americans die each year from unnecessary surgery, according to a *Journal of the American Medical Association* report. And tens of thousands more suffer complications. (Black, 2005)
- An estimated 7.5 million unnecessary medical and surgical procedures are performed each year, writes Gary Null, PhD, in *Death by Medicine.* (Black, 2005)
- An average of 195,000 people in the USA died due to potentially preventable, in-hospital medical errors in each of the years 2000, 2001 and 2002. (Loughran, 2004)
- The National-Scale Air Toxics Assessment . . . study is used by the EPA to identify parts of the country where residents could face the greatest health threats from air pollution. . . . Almost 2.2 million people lived in neighborhoods where pollution raised the risk of developing cancer to levels the government generally considers to be unacceptable. (Heath & Morrison, 2009)

In line with the objective approach presented in Section I, it is important to stress that not all consequences of white-collar crime are necessarily bad. Sociologist Emile Durkheim has highlighted four functions of crime that illustrate how crime in some ways has positive influences on individuals and communities (see Martin et al., 2009). These four functions can also be applied to white-collar crime. They include: warning light syndrome, boundary maintenance, social change, and community integration.

The **warning light syndrome** refers to the fact that outbreaks of white-collar crime could potentially send a message to individuals, businesses, or communities that something is wrong in a particular workplace system. If an outbreak of employee theft occurs in a hospital, for example, the administrators would be warned that they need to address those aspects of the occupational routines that allowed the misconduct to occur.

In terms of **boundary maintenance,** it is plausible to suggest that individuals learn the rules of the workplace when some individuals are caught breaking those rules. In effect, they learn the boundaries of appropriate and acceptable behaviors by seeing some individuals step over those boundaries. Some even recommend that white-collar offenders, when caught, be arrested at times when the vast majority of workers would be able to see the arrests (Payne & Gray, 2001). This recommendation is promoting a strategy to promote boundary maintenance.

With regard to **social change**, our society has changed significantly because of white-collar misdeeds. Some people have talked about how survivors of violent crime actually become stronger because of their experience with violence. Following this same line of thinking, those who survive white-collar crime victimization might actually become stronger. As well, when cultures and societies survive corporate victimization, they too may actually grow stronger.

Community integration is a fourth function of white-collar crime. In particular, groups of individuals who otherwise would not have become acquainted with one another may come together in their response to white-collar crime. When there is a crime outbreak in a neighborhood, those neighbors come together to share their experiences and make their neighborhood stronger (Martin et al., 2009). A crime outbreak in a business could have the same result. Coworkers who never talked with one another might suddenly become lunch buddies simply because they want to get together to talk about the crimes that occurred in their workplace. As well, at the societal level, new groups have been formed to prevent and respond to white-collar crime.

Consider the National White Collar Crime Center (NW3C). Formed in 1992, the center includes professionals, academics, and researchers interested in addressing white-collar crime on different levels. The NW3C's mission is: "to provide training, investigative support, and research to agencies and entities involved in the prevention, investigation, and prosecution of economic and high tech crime" (National White Collar Crime Center, 2009). Without the problem of white-collar crime, this center would never have been created and its members would never have been brought together (or integrated as a community).

Other possible positive consequences of white-collar crime can be cited. For example, some criminologists have noted that occasional forms of deviance might be enjoyable or pleasurable to commit. The 2010 Conan O'Brien/Jay Leno debacle comes to mind. It was announced in January 2010 that O'Brien was to be replaced by Leno after he had been promised a long-term contract to host *The Tonight Show*. In the last several episodes of his NBC show, O'Brien spent much of his show trashing his bosses at NBC. He even had skits suggesting that he was blowing NBC's money on pointless props for his show. The studio and home audiences raved about these skits. Who wouldn't want to go on national television every now and then and blow their company's money while trashing their bosses? (For the record, the thought never entered my mind.) In a similar way, some cases of workplace deviance might have the positive benefit of making the worker a more satisfied worker (see Mars, 1983). Authors have talked about "the joy of violence" (Kerbs & Jolley, 2007). In some ways, there might also be "the joy of white-collar deviance."

▲ **Photo 2.3** After his dispute with NBC, Conan O'Brien mocked his employer, joking about ways he could waste the company's money.

For some students, the numerous careers available to respond to white-collar crime might also be seen as a positive. Whenever I teach my criminal justice classes, I always ask my students if they would make crime go away if they could. Seldom do any students indicate that they would make crime disappear. In their minds, if they made crime disappear, they'd have to change their majors! So, in some ways, white-collar crime helps keep some criminal justice officials employed. A few of these careers can be particularly lucrative—one defense attorney was recently paid $50,000 simply for providing counsel to a white-collar worker who had to testify in a grand jury proceeding (Nelson, 2010).

Of course, this brief overview of the "functions of white-collar crime" should not be interpreted as an endorsement of white-collar criminal behavior. In fact, the seriousness of many white-collar crimes means that the offenses cannot be taken lightly. The question that arises is whether members of the public view the offenses seriously.

Public Attitudes About White-Collar Crime

A large body of criminological research has focused on public attitudes about crime and different crime policies. Unfortunately, of the hundreds of criminological studies focusing on attitudes about crime, only a handful have focused on what the public thinks about white-collar crime. Yet research on white-collar crime attitudes is important for empirical, cultural, and policy-driven reasons (Piquero, Carmichael, & Piquero, 2008). In terms of empirical reasons, because so few studies have considered what the public thinks about white-collar crime, research on this topic will shed some light on how members of the public actually perceive this offense type. As well, such research will provide interesting, and important, insight into a particular culture or subculture. Perhaps most important, such research provides policy makers information they can use to implement prevention, response, and sentencing strategies.

In one of the first studies on public attitudes about white-collar crime, Cullen and his colleagues (Cullen, Clark, Mathers, & Cullen, 1983) surveyed a sample of 240 adults and assessed various perceptions about this behavior. The researchers found that the sample (1) supported criminal sanctions for white-collar offenders, (2) viewed white-collar crimes as having greater moral and economic costs than street crimes, and (3) did not define the offenses as violent. They also found that perceptions of seriousness of white-collar crime increased more than any other offense type in the 1970s and that physically harmful offenses were viewed as the most serious forms of white-collar crime.

Other studies have shown similar results. A study of 268 students found that perceptions of the seriousness of white-collar crime have increased over time and that these perceptions were tied to wrongfulness and harmfulness (Rosenmerkel, 2001). The NW3C National Victimization Survey also included items assessing perceptions of seriousness. The researchers found that the sample of 1,605 adults viewed (1) white-collar crime as serious as conventional crime, (2) physically harmful white-collar offenses as more serious than other white-collar crimes, (3) organizational offenses as more serious than individual offenses, and (4) offenses by higher status offenders as more serious than offenses by lower status offenders (Kane & Wall, 2006).

More recent research has built on these findings. A telephone survey of 402 residents of the United States focused on perceptions about white-collar crime and the punishment of white-collar offenders (Holtfreter, Van Slyke, Bratton, & Gertz, 2008). The authors found that one third of the respondents said that white-collar offenders should be punished more severely than street criminals. They also found that two thirds of the respondents believed that the government should "devote equal or more resources towards white-collar crime control" (p. 56).

Around the same time, telephone interviews with 1,169 respondents found that the majority of respondents defined white-collar crime as equally serious as, if not more serious than, street crime (Piquero, Carmichael, & Piquero, 2008). They also found that the presence of a college education impacted perceptions of seriousness. Those with a college education were more likely to define street crime and white-collar crime as equally serious. Another study using the same dataset found that respondents believed that street criminals were more likely than white-collar offenders to be caught and to receive stiffer sentences (Schoepfer, Carmichael, & Piquero, 2007). Respondents also believed that robbery and fraud should be treated similarly. Another way to suggest this is that the respondents believed that robbers and occupational offenders committing fraud should be handled the same way. In addressing this point, it is important to call attention to similarities and differences between conventional criminals and white-collar criminals.

Characteristics of White-Collar Offenders

Because white-collar offenses are viewed as equally serious as street crimes, there may be a tendency among some to view white-collar criminals as similar to street criminals (Payne, 2003b). Such an assumption, however, is misguided and represents an inaccurate portrait of "the white-collar criminal." As well, focusing narrowly on white-collar offenders may result in individuals failing to recognize the interactions between the offenders' background characteristics and their offensive behavior (Wheeler et al., 1988).

Criminologists have devoted significant attention to describing the characteristics of various types of white-collar offenders. Comparing records of street offenders and white-collar offenders, Benson and Moore (1992) concluded: "Those who commit even run-of-the-mill garden variety white-collar offenses can, as a group, be clearly distinguished from those who commit ordinary street offenses" (p. 252). In one of the most comprehensive white-collar crime studies, Wheeler and his colleagues (1988) found that white-collar offenders were more likely than conventional offenders to (1) have a college education, (2) be white males, (3) be older, (4) have a job, (5) commit fewer offenses, (6) start their criminal careers later in life, and (7) be Jewish. Focusing on the interactions between offender characteristics and offense characteristics, the same research demonstrated that white-collar crime was more likely than street crime to:

- Be national or international in scope
- Involve a large number of victims
- Have organizations as victims
- Follow demonstrated patterns
- Be committed for more than a year
- Be committed in groups

Recognizing the differences between white-collar crime/white-collar offenders and street crimes/street offenders is significant for theoretical and policy reasons. In terms of theory, as will be demonstrated later in this text, if one of the criminological theories can explain both types of crimes, then that theory would be seen as having strong explanatory power. In terms of policy, it is important to recognize that different criminal justice strategies may be needed for the two types of offenses and that street offenders and white-collar offenders may respond differently to the criminal justice process.

Consider efforts to prevent crime. Strategies to prevent street crimes might focus on community building and poverty reduction; preventing white-collar crime is much "more complex" (Johnstone, 1999, p. 116). The impact of convictions and incarceration is also different between street offenders and white-collar offenders (Payne, 2003b). While such events may actually allow street offenders to gain "peer group status," the white-collar offender would not experience the same increase in status as the result of a conviction (Johnstone, 1999; Payne, 2003b). At the most basic level, recognizing the differences between street offenders and white-collar offenders helps to promote more useful prevention and intervention strategies. On a more complex level, recognizing these differences fosters a more objective and accurate understanding about the dynamics, causes, and consequences of the two types of behavior.

⊠ Summary

- Sutherland (1949) defined white-collar crime as "crime committed by a person of respectability and high social status in the course of his occupation."
- Criticism of the concept centered around (1) conceptual ambiguity, (2) empirical ambiguity, (3) methodological ambiguity, (4) legal ambiguity, and (5) policy ambiguity.
- Corporate crime and occupational crime are viewed as "the two principal or 'pure' forms of white-collar crime" (Friedrichs, 2002, p. 245).
- Criminologists and social scientists offer various ways to define white-collar crime. These variations tend to overlap with one another and include the following: (1) white-collar crime as moral or ethical violations, (2) white-collar crime as social harm, (3) white-collar crime as violations of criminal law, (4) white-collar crime as violations of civil law, (5) white-collar crime as violations of regulatory laws, (6) white-collar crime as workplace deviance, (7) white-collar crime as definitions socially constructed by businesses, (8) white-collar crime as research definitions, (9) white-collar crime as official government definitions, (10) white-collar crime as violations of trust, (11) white-collar crime as occupational crimes, and (12) white-collar crime as violations occurring in occupational systems.
- Determining the extent of white-collar crime is no simple task. Two factors make it particularly difficult to accurately determine how often white-collar crimes occur: unreported crimes and conceptual ambiguity.
- With regard to official statistics and white-collar crime, the FBI's Uniform Crime Reports (UCR) and National Incident Based Reporting System (NIBRS) provide at least a starting point from which we can begin to question how often certain forms of white-collar crime occur.
- The consequences of white-collar crime can be characterized as (1) individual economic losses, (2) societal economic losses, (3) emotional consequences, (4) physical harm, and (5) "positive" consequences.
- Research on white-collar crime attitudes is important for empirical, cultural, and policy-driven reasons (Piquero, Carmichael, & Piquero, 2008).
- Because white-collar offenses are viewed as equally serious as street crimes, there may be a tendency among some to view white-collar criminals as similar to street criminals (Payne, 2003b). Such an assumption is misguided and represents an inaccurate portrait of "the white-collar criminal."
- Wheeler and his colleagues (1988) found that white-collar offenders were more likely than conventional offenders to (1) have a college education, (2) be white males, (3) be older, (4) have a job, (5) commit fewer offenses, (6) start their criminal careers later in life, and (7) be Jewish.

KEY TERMS

Boundary maintenance	Definitions socially constructed by businesses	Individual economic losses
Community integration		Natural law
Conceptual ambiguity	Emotional consequences	Occupational crime
Corporate crime	Empirical ambiguity	Physical harm
Criminaloid concept	Government definitions	Research definitions

Social change	Violations-of-occupation crimes	Warning light syndrome
Social harm	Violations of criminal law	White-collar crime
Societal economic losses	Violations of regulatory law	Workplace deviance
Victimization surveys	Violations of trust	

DISCUSSION QUESTIONS

1. Review the five white-collar crimes described in the beginning of this chapter. Answer the following questions for each offense description:
   a. Is it a white-collar crime?
   b. How often do these crimes occur?
   c. What would the consequences of this crime be?
   d. How serious do you think this crime is?
   e. Who is the offender in each case?
   f. How does that offender vary from street offenders?

2. Why does it matter how we define white-collar crime?

3. How serious is white-collar crime in comparison to street crimes?

4. What are the negative and positive consequences of white-collar crime?

WEB RESOURCES

FBI White-Collar Crime: http://www.fbi.gov/about-us/investigate/white_collar/whitecollarcrime

10 Biggest White-Collar Crimes in History: http://www.businesspundit.com/white-collar-crimes-history-and-how-they-were-unravelled/

Protect yourself online: http://stlouis.jobing.com/protectagainstfraud.asp

READING

Edelhertz, a legal scholar, provides a different look at the concept of white-collar crime. He calls for a more specific way to define the phenomenon so that it will have utility to both practitioners and academics alike. Edelhertz suggests that the conceptual ambiguity surrounding the concept made officials from different areas define the concept within their own domains. Part of the conceptual confusion, he notes, relates to the fact that it is not always clear how white-collar crimes (and criminals) should be processed in the justice system. Edelhertz summarizes categories of white-collar crime including personal crimes, abuses of trust, offenders who deny or rationalize their crimes are legitimate business activities, and crimes that are a central part of the business activity. Edelhertz also highlights the various kinds of victims of white-collar crime. Edelhertz concludes with strategies to improve the response to these crimes.

White-Collar and Professional Crime

The Challenge for the 1980s

Herbert Edelhertz

This article addresses a very broad range of anti-social behavior that, literally, cries out for a new and descriptive title that conveys some sense of who does what and to whom. The term "white-collar crime" is totally inadequate for this purpose, as is the descriptor "economic crime" that is increasingly used in the United States and is the prevailing term abroad. The very word "crime" is out of place here because we are dealing with behaviors and activities that, spectrum-like, merge imperceptibly into one another, with the legitimate and laudable on one end and the dishonest and disreputable on the other.

Sutherland (1940) coined the term "white-collar" relatively recently, only a little more than forty years ago. Already distinguished for his contributions in the field of criminology, he turned with populist gusto to upper-class crime, particularly in the business sector (Geis and Edelhertz, 1973). Sutherland was not the one to discover the crimes of business and the upper

classes; law enforcement and regulatory agencies were already active in the field. Before the turn of the century, the federal mail fraud statute was already a key part of an extensive law enforcement arsenal against business fraud; powerful legislative weapons against financial frauds had been deployed in the early 1930s with the passage of the first federal securities act, and bankers and government officials had been prosecuted for abuses of trust. Even a president of the New York Stock Exchange had been convicted before Sutherland focused a spotlight on white-collar crime. He did, however, place white-collar crime on the agenda of American criminologists. It has been a part of that agenda these past forty years, though relatively dormant until this past decade.

Sutherland's perspective, whatever its merits, was responsible for a barrier between academic, or research investigators, and practitioners, or legislators in the field. He defined white-collar crime as "an illegal act committed in the course of one's business or profession," thus focusing attention on who the offender was and where the offense was committed, rather than on the nature of the antisocial behavior that we are concerned with. Such a perspective made it difficult for the researcher to meet on common ground with the practitioner. No prosecutor could accept, as a basis for a criminal charge, that embezzlement by a bank president was white-collar crime, and that the same act by a low-paid bank teller was not. It is fair to speculate that the long hiatus in research in white-collar crime—extending from the early 1950s to the early 1970s (there were of course occasional and isolated studies during this period)—stemmed in part from this gulf. Criminological research in other areas—juvenile justice, delinquency, deterrence, and rehabilitation—flourished during this same period.

Starting in the mid-1970s, there was a new burst of research activity in the white-collar crime area. This occurred at the same time that thought was being given to the definition of white-collar crime. The new view was that the focus should be on the behavior rather than the character of the offender, a view taken by this writer (Edelhertz, 1970), the American Bar Association (ABA, 1977), and the U.S. Department of Justice's Criminal Division (Civiletti, 1978). If there was a link between these two developments, it probably did not lie in any departure from Sutherland's conceptions by the research community. Rather, it may have stemmed from the ability of those outside the research community to perceive the potential of the social sciences to contribute to law enforcement agency and other governmental agency goals, because practitioners were able to identify with these new definitional approaches. A broad range of studies were launched in the white-collar crime area that included extensive examinations of corporate crime (Clinard et al., 1979), fraud against government programs (Lange, 1979), prosecutive policies (Edelhertz and Hoff, 1980), organized crime (Blakely and Gettings, 1980), operation of prosecutive units (Blakely et al., 1978), federal data sources reflecting white-collar criminal activity (Reiss and Biderman, 1980), relationships between federal, state, and local efforts (Edelhertz and Rogovin, 1980), definitional

issues (Shagiro, 1980; Saxon, 1980), the impact of white-collar crime (Schrager and Short, 1978; Meier and Short, 1981), and a host of other issues.[1] There have been numerous symposia held and journal articles published dealing with operational issues, measurement, and evaluation.

Finally, in explaining the burst of public and research interest in white-collar crime in the latter half of this decade, one must suspect that the Watergate drama was also a major factor in focusing attention on the problem.

 ## White-Collar Criminal Behavior

The term "white-collar crime" means so many things to so many people that it will be rarely "out of fashion" as an attractive area for the attention of parts of the public, government, business, and the research or academic community. Each will, of course, concentrate on that aspect of this very broad area that particularly concerns it. Thus, many will concentrate, for ideological or political reasons, on the antisocial behavior of the business community and the wealthy, while at the same time finding it quite difficult to give serious attention to frauds committed by the poor, to frauds that exploit institutions that serve the disadvantaged, or even to the activities of con artists who make a business of fraud.

The business community lines up its concerns with its economic interests. Those who extend credit cry out for attention to bankruptcy frauds or to those who deliberately misuse credit cards; telephone companies are concerned with those who use technical devices to make long distance calls without leaving footprints that are necessary for billing; and electric utilities seek the prosecution of those who divert power by tapping wires before electricity gets to the user's meter. Merchants concerned with the thefts of merchandise have come to the startling conclusion that this is a form of white-collar crime, or at least they did when white-collar crime enforcement appeared to be a more popular enforcement vehicle than it is now (Chamber of Commerce, 1974). The business community has a more difficult time, however, placing antitrust or price-fixing violations under the same umbrella.

Government is not a monolith, but rather a conglomeration of interests, each of which competes with others. It speaks with many voices and its allocation of enforcement resources also responds to political and economic interests. At one time, or in one place, the stress will be on curbing abusive or deceptive behavior by the business community. At another time, the emphasis will be on seeking out and acting on frauds against government programs and frauds against entitlement programs—all of which add to the costs of government. At all times, there is an ambivalence as to the issue of tax fraud because every segment of our society has some stake in the weakness of the tax collection function.

This brief mention of divergent views of white-collar crime only scratches the surface. Even where there is some consensus as to what general behavior constitutes white-collar crime, there is not likely to be agreement on what is to be done in individual cases. For example, it is unlawful to use fraud and deception in offering to sell stock, bonds, or other securities. Yet one part of the same statute that proscribes this behavior and makes it punishable as a felony, also provides alternative remedies and gives the U.S. Securities and Exchange Commission the power to refer for criminal prosecution or to refrain from doing so. What "crime" is, therefore, depends on whether the cognizant agency chooses to see it as crime, which in turn will depend on the quantum of available proof and also on how the agency balances its many, often conflicting enforcement objectives (Steir, 1981).

What is being suggested here is that in the area of white-collar crime, there is more of a gap between legal proscriptions and enforcement than in other areas of the criminal law. Murder and theft are violations of criminal law. When such crimes are committed, and we know how and by whom, we expect to see a prosecution though we recognize that juries may acquit or lesser charges may be traded for guilty pleas in order to ease burdens on the criminal justice system. But in the white-collar crime area, it is often

difficult to know whether or not there is a prosecutable case, even when we have persuasive and uncontrovertible evidence as to who did what and how it was done. The wild card here is that most white-collar crimes involve wrongful behaviors in what appear to be thoroughly legitimate contexts. For example, it is legitimate to sell stocks, but not to deliberately misrepresent what is being sold. It is legitimate for a scientist to use grant money for a trip to a professional meeting, but certainly more questionable for two scientists to use that money for a Caribbean cruise with their secretaries to discuss their work. If you are mugged, the intent of the mugger can rather clearly be inferred from his behavior. But if competing contractors' bids for public road construction work just happen to fall into a pattern that results in their sharing available contracts by alternative successful bids, can we make a parallel inference that the coincidence of bids demonstrates intent to unlawfully collude in the same way as the mugger's act evidences his intent? Certainly we would need much more than this in order to make a case (Maltz and Pollock, 1980).

We make a mistake if we think that victims can be relied on to report these crimes, even if they know they have been defrauded. Offenders are far more likely to escape prosecution, if only because their behavior is less likely to be reported. Top corporate management may hesitate to report the white-collar crimes of middle- or high-level management for fear that this will hurt the corporate image. Top management often fears that its own position will be jeopardized because it failed to prevent or detect earlier such crimes, or because it will be subject to financial liability if stockholders sue them for negligence on behalf of their corporations. Corporate offenders are also members of "old boy" networks; one does not call for the arrest of a bridge partner whose wife shops with yours. Finally, some such offenders are valued executives with real track records for producing high profits; one motion picture production company resisted firing its chief executive even after he admitted stealing from his own company. On a lower, more personal level, one elderly victim was most concerned about possible harm to the dance studio instructor who had exploited her loneliness to take many thousands of dollars from her.

Categories of White-Collar Crime

There are a number of lenses through which we can observe white-collar criminality. We can examine these behaviors in terms of motivations, victims, or the schemes that are employed. For the purposes of this paper, it may be helpful first to consider the objectives of white-collar offenders and to simultaneously consider classes of victims and the schemes that are used against them.

This writer has previously suggested a four-part typology of white-collar schemes that may serve to illustrate the range of criminal purposes in this crime area (Edelhertz, 1970). These four parts are not necessarily mutually exclusive; many schemes will fall into more than one category, and may even involve common crimes.

The first category is that of personal, or ad hoc crimes. The offender here is pursuing some individual objective and usually has no face-to-face relationship with the victim. Examples would be personal income tax violations, frauds against government entitlement programs, and credit card frauds. The motives here are usually simple greed, or very serious real or perceived need. Schemes are facilitated and prevention or detection hampered by the fact that the offender is usually part of a sea of anonymous faces dealt with by government and corporate victims.

The second category involves abuses of trust. Criminal or abusive behavior falling in this category usually involves an offender who has been given custody of the assets of another, or power to make decisions that bind another. Embezzlements by employees or fiduciaries, accepting bribes or other favors to grant contracts on behalf of one's government or business employer, misuse of an employer's property or information for private profit, misuse of labor union pension funds, creating "ghosts" on payrolls or fictitious accounts payable—all of these are typical examples in this category. Here the offender has power to cause harm by virtue of his or her position and, through

control and manipulation of paper or computer records, to temporarily or permanently bury evidence of crime.

The third category is, in many ways, the most troublesome of white-collar behaviors since it involves offenders who rarely think of themselves as criminals or abusers of society. These offenders usually have very real status in their communities. Theirs are crimes incidental to and in furtherance of organizational operations, but crimes that are not the central purpose of the organization. Typical examples would be: antitrust violations; collusive bidding for public contracts; violations of the federal Corrupt Practices Act to assemble a pool of monies to influence the political process to support a business interest or create or save a tax loophole; or bribing a contracting officer domestically or abroad to contract for goods or services. On a smaller scale, such violations may involve fraudulent medicare or medicaid claims, the thumb on the butcher's scale, or the submission of a misleading financial statement to obtain more credit for a business than it would otherwise be entitled to. There have been cases involving government defense contracts (and I am sure in many a research grant area) where funds from one contract or grant are used to support another effort that is in trouble. These crimes or abuses are difficult to deal with because they are submerged in a mass of legitimate activities. They are both well hidden and extensively rationalized.

The final category is white-collar crime as a business, or as the central activity of a venture. Here we are talking about the con man and the con game. It is the easiest one to visualize because we are dealing with the business of cheating. There is no way to put a nice face on, or find any justification for the swindler who is in business only to get something for nothing. For these swindlers, the provision of goods, services, or property is only an excuse to grasp monies that bear no recognizable relationship to what is provided. Sometimes the scheme may be close to picking a victim's pocket, as in the case of the street "pigeon drop" that victimizes any vulnerable passerby. At other times the scheme will involve sale of worthless desert land or investment securities at high prices, based on fraudulent descriptions. These schemes can victimize a business and government, as well as individuals. The IRS pays out millions every year to schemers who claim many refunds under phony names and who submit fabricated W-2 forms to support these claims. Businesses lose many millions of dollars by selling on credit to bankruptcy fraud artists who buy or set up a business, establish credit, then resell the merchandise and pocket the proceeds while leaving business creditors with an empty, bankrupt shell. Simply because these swindlers are the easiest to understand they receive disproportionate public, and perhaps law enforcement, attention, and are even romanticized in films such as *The Sting* and *The Producers*.

Victims, Schemes, and Harm

It is helpful to consider what kinds of schemes are directed against different categories of victims. There is little reliable data here, but reasoning and experience in the area can take us at least some distance. Developing a structure for consideration of the scheme-victim-harm relationship can be a starting point for policy analysis, action priority development, and marshalling the tools of social sciences for valuable and helpful research on white-color crime. As a starting point, it would appear that white-collar assaults are mounted against three general categories of victims: (1) individuals; (2) businesses and non-government institutions; and (3) government as buyer, giver, and protector-gatekeeper.

In considering these categories, one should also keep in mind the relationships of victims to the offender(s). There are at least three such relationships, which we can call "assault categories." There are external assaults, which are externally conceived and executed with no knowing collaboration by the victim or the victim organization. Examples would be a fraudulent claim for a tax refund, or the sale of worthless stock to an investor. There are internal assaults, that involve no knowing collaborators outside a victimized organization. Embezzlement would be the classic example. Finally, there are mixed assaults which involve inside-outside collaboration. The classic example would be commercial bribery in which an outside organization bribes the trusted employee of the victim organization to grant a contract.

Crimes against individuals fall into five broad groups. These are (1) street con games such as the "pigeon drop," (2) consumer frauds that include personal improvement schemes involving work-at-home schemes, trade schools, vanity publishing, modeling schools, and the marketing of inventions, (3) charity and religious frauds, (4) investment frauds, and (5) fiduciary frauds, such as thefts from estates or attorneys' embezzlements of escrow funds. Some crimes against business will have very direct impact on individuals, for example where an uninsured financial institution is looted, wiping out the savings of many (often small) investors.

Crimes against business fall into seven very general groups. These are (1) internal thefts through embezzlements and misapplications, (2) commercial bribery (that may well be the major desert area of detection and enforcement), (3) conflicts of interest and exploitation of inside information for personal gain, (4) external swindles, such as advance fee schemes, bankruptcy frauds, and use of phony security or false financial statements as a basis for loans or credit, (5) false entitlement claims, such as internal expense accounts, external fraudulent insurance claims, or billing for goods or services not supplied, (6) business investment fraud, such as mergers or business purchases induced by false financial statements, and (7) unlawful competition due to market domination by competitors. Though the examples offered relate to businesses, other private institutions are similarly vulnerable. Universities have suffered from embezzlements, and admissions to at least one medical school were sold.

The list of white-collar crimes that have been committed against government and government functions is an exceedingly lengthy one, and very difficult to divide into categories. As a starting point, we can consider the following: (1) frauds arising out of procurement of goods and services, such as collusive bidding, billing for "phantom" goods or services, commingling of contract costs, and commercial bribery; (2) program frauds that involve false entitlement claims, fraudulent exploitation of public programs to promote housing, agriculture, small business development, and foreign aid; and (3) frauds against the revenue. In addition there is a broad range of white-collar violations against government as gatekeeper or protector of the public. Examples in the gatekeeper-protector area would be fraudulent abuse of the zoning function, fraudulent information supplied to regulators to obtain permission to establish a bank or insurance company or to sell securities, unlicensed export of arms, soliciting for charities in violation of state registration laws, environmental offenses, fraudulent immigration applications, and fraudulent test result submissions to get permission to market a prescription drug.

 ## Conclusion

White-collar crimes and related abuses are not adversaries that can be targeted, met, attacked, and defeated once and for all. They are, rather, forms of group behavior that can be expected to surface again and again in response to new opportunities, or to avoid the loss of money, property, markets, or personal advantages. Since total victory and perpetual safety are not attainable, society's general objective in this area should be to marshal and deploy its public and private administrative, research, and law enforcement resources to contain white-collar crime, that is, to deter, detect, investigate, and prosecute (criminally and civilly) these crimes and related abuses.

Many resources exist that have not been fully brought to bear on this area. In the academic community, schools of business have totally ignored the problem of white-collar crime; law schools, with rare exceptions, treat the problem as a very minor part of courses in criminal law and regulatory law; social scientists have noted the problems in this field but have not yet developed methods to gather, organize, and describe white-collar criminal behavior or measure the effectiveness of remedies (all of which may not be achievable). Only in the area of policy analysis—and there in but a few instances—has there been a systematic effort to relate agency organization and functions, and to consider the pros and cons of alternative approaches. Within law enforcement agencies, the stress has been on day-to-day operations and defense of white-collar crime containment resources against competing programmatic demands, such as the clamor for resources by those combating violent crimes and common theft.

In a few instances—in such places as the policy analysis branch of the Criminal Division of the U.S. Department of Justice, the New Jersey Division of Criminal Justice (Stein, 1981), and the Arizona Attorney General's Office (Edelhertz et al., 1981)—there has been systematic consideration of strategies to deal with white-collar and organized crime that take into account the complex issues of enforcement tools, remedies, and criminal behaviors to be contained. Law enforcement agencies must adjust their planning to exploit the total arsenal of weapons available to them, particularly in the area of civil prosecution that has been made more promising by the enactment of relatively new federal and state anti-racketeering statutes (Blakely and Gettings, 1980). Professions such as law and accounting will have to reconsider their reluctance to assume any responsibility for containment of white-collar crime, or to report such crimes. Such a reconsideration may be encouraged by successful criminal prosecutions and massive civil judgments against major public accounting firms.[2]

In reacting to white-collar crime challenges, we will have to distinguish more carefully between sociological and economic impacts. Doing so should help to set enforcement priorities and allocate resources. For example, welfare frauds may be insignificant in economic terms as compared to antitrust violations, but welfare programs are most vulnerable to attack whenever frauds are exposed. Conversely, swindles and con games may bulk large in terms of public consciousness and individual victim injuries, but the economic injury to the body politic caused by the hemorrhaging costs of procurement fraud and abuses could suggest greater emphasis and use of enforcement resources in the latter area.

Finally, all those concerned with white-collar crime and related abuses must consider what contribution they can make to the development of a rational method of marshaling and deploying those containment resources that are available (Edelhertz and Rogovin, 1980). These resources are currently divided among numerous federal, state, local, and private agencies that are, in turn, divided by function: police departments, investigative agencies, compliance offices within agencies that procure goods and services or distribute program benefits, regulatory agencies, pros-ecutors, and the courts. Groups in private industry perform many of these same functions. There is no reason to believe that decisions as to which agency responds to a white-collar crime challenge are in any way related to the resources or other capabilities of that agency. Rather, who becomes involved is likely to reflect which agency moved first, or which has greater clout or resources. Agencies have overlapping jurisdictions, and there is little to prevent dysfunctional duplication of effort or significant matters falling between the cracks.

In this high-altitude pass over the world of white-collar crime, it has been necessary to omit many issues of importance which some would consider more sig-nificant than those discussed here. To carry the space analogy further, however, the major task in the 1980s for those concerned with white-collar crime is to develop high-resolution lenses with which to better survey the terrain.

 Notes

1. For a bibliography of the more recent work in the field of white-collar crime, see Edemertt and Overeast (1981). For exam-ples of more recent research in the field, see Geis and Stotland (1980).

2. There is already considerable concern in the accounting profession. See Elliot and Willingham (1980).

 References

American Bar Association Commission on Criminal Law (1977) Report, Committee on Economic Offenses 31. Washington, DC, March.

BLAKEY, C. R. and B. GETTINGS (1980) "Racketeer influenced and corrupt organizations (RICO): basic concepts—criminal and civil remedies." Temple Law Q. 53: 1009–1048. S3:1009-1048.

BLAKEY, G. R., R. GOLDSTOCK, and C. H, ROGOVIN (1978) Rackets Bureaus: Investigation and Prosecution of Organized Crime. Washington, DC; U.S. Department of Justice, March.

Chamber of Commerce of the United States (1974) A Handbook of White-Collar Crime: Everyone's Loss. Washington, DC: Author.

CIVILETTI, B. R. (1978) Statement, pp. 64-65 in White-Collar Crime. House Committee on the Judiciary, Subcommittee on Crime, 95th Congress, Second Session.

CLINARD, M. B. et al. (1979) Illegal Corporate Behavior. Washington, DC: U.S. Department of Justice, October.

EDELHERTZ, H. (1980) "Transnational white-collar crime: a developing challenge and need for response." Temple Law Q. 53:1114-1126.

_____ (1970) The Nature, Impact and Prosecution of White-Collar Crime, Report No. ICR 70-1. Washington, DC: U.S. Department of Justice, May.

_____ and B. HOFF (1980) Report to the National District Attorney Association Economic Crime Project Battelle Memorial Institute, Seattle, WA., December.

EDELHERTZ, H. and T. D. OVERCAST [eds.] (1981) White-Collar Crime: An Agenda for Research. Lexington, MA: D. C. Heath.

EDELHERTZ, H. and C ROGOVIN (1980) A National Strategy for Containing White-Collar Crime. Lexington, MA: D. C. Heath.

EDELHERTZ, H. et al. (1981) The Containment of Organized Crime: A Report to the Arizona Legislative Council. Report No, BHARC 300/81/043. Battelle Human Affairs Research Centers, Seattle, WA., December.

ELLIOTT, R. K. and J. J. WILLINGHAM (1980) Management Fraud: Detection and Deterrence. New York: Petrocelli.

ERMANN, M. D. and R. J. LUNDMAN (1981) "Corporate violations of the Corrupt Practices Act," pp. 51-68 in H. Edelhertz and T. Overcast (eds.) White-Collar Crime: An Agenda for Research. Lexington, MA: D. C. Heath.

GEIS, G. and E. STOTLAND [eds.] (1980) White-Collar Crime. Sage Criminal Justice System Annuals, Vol. 13. Beverly Hills, CA: Sage.

GEIS, G. and H. EDELHERTZ (1973) "Criminal law and consumer fraud: a sociolegal view." Amer. Criminal Law Rev. 11 (Summer): 989-1010.

GEIS, G. (1967) "The heavy electrical equipment antitrust cases of 1961," pp. 139-150 in M. B. Clinard and R. Quinney (eds.) Criminal Behavior Systems: A Typology. New York: Holt, Rinehart & Winston.

GROSS, E. (1980) "Organizational Structure and organizational crime," pp. 52-76 in G. Geis and E. Scotland (eds.) White-Collar Crime. Beverly Hills, CA: Sage.

LANGE, A. G. (1979) Fraud and Abuse in Government Benefit Programs. Washington, DC: U.S. Department of Justice, October.

MALTZ, M. D. and S. M. POLLOCK (1980) "Analyzing suspected collusion among bidders," pp. 174-198 in G. Geis and E. Stotland (eds.) White-Collar Crime. Beverly Hills, CA: Sage.

MEIER, R. F. and J. F. SHORT, JR. (1981) "The consequences of white-collar crime," pp. 23-49 in H. Edelhertz and T. D. Overcast (eds.) White-Collar Crime: An Agenda for Research. Lexington, MA: D. C. Heath.

REISS, A. J., Jr. and A. D. BIDERMAN (1980) Data Sources on White-Collar Law-Breaking. Washington, DC: U.S. Department of Justice, September.

SAXON, M. S. (1980) White-Collar Crime: The Problem and the Federal Response. Report No. 80-84 EPW. Washington, DC: Library of Congress, Congressional Research Service, April 14.

SCHRAGER, L. S, and J. F. SHORT, Jr. (1978) "Toward a sociology of organi-zational crime." Social Problems 25:407-419.

SHAPIRO, S. P. (1980) Thinking About White-Collar Crime: Matters of Conceptualization and Research. Washington, DC: U.S. Department of Justice, December.

STEIR, E. H. (1981) "The interrelationships among remedies for white-collar criminal behavior," pp. 153–173 in H. Edelhertz and T. D. Overcast (eds.) White-Collar Crime: An Agenda for Research. Lexington, MA: D. C Heath.

SUTHERLAND, E. H. (1949) White-Collar Crime. New York: Holt, Rinehart & Winston.

_____ (1940) "White-collar criminality." Amer. Soc Rev. 5:1-12.

DISCUSSION QUESTIONS

1. Who are the victims of white-collar crime?

2. How does the way Edelhertz defines white-collar crime vary from Sutherland's approach?

3. Given that Edelhertz wrote this article a quarter of a century ago, how might he change his views about these concepts given today's technologically oriented society?

READING

David Friedrichs is regarded as one of the top criminologists currently studying white-collar crime. In this article, Friedrichs directly addresses all of the issues that arise when academics use different concepts to describe white-collar crime. One major part of his argument is that these new concepts create additional confusion, rather than limit it. He provides a summary of the history of the white-collar crime concept. Friedrichs then reviews the concepts of occupational crime, occupational deviance, and workplace crime. The occupational crime concept, Friedrichs argues, distorts what Sutherland meant by "white-collar crime" by including occupations with less status, power, and wealth. The occupational deviance concept is also viewed as too vague by Friedrichs, who sees the concept as describing behaviors (like child abuse in day care centers) as outside of the scope of white-collar crime. In a similar way, Friedrichs argues that many of the behaviors included under the heading of "workplace crime" are more similar to street crime than white-collar crime.

Occupational Crime, Occupational Deviance, and Workplace Crime

Sorting Out the Difference

David O. Friedrichs

 Introduction

Perhaps no other area of criminological inquiry has been more plagued by conceptual confusion than that of white collar crime. Many attempts have been made

to resolve the definitional conundrums that arise in this realm (e.g. Friedrichs, 1992, 1996a, 1996b; Geis, 1992; Helmkamp et al., 1996; Meier, 2001). At least some of those who write about white collar crime choose to address the definitional question very

SOURCE: Friedrichs, David O. (2002). Occupational Crime, Occupational Deviance, and Workplace Crime. *Criminal Justice, 2*(3): 243-256.

briefly—if at all—and then move on to other substantive issues or empirical research findings. Although a certain level of impatience with the definitional and conceptual debates may be understandable, a premise adopted here is that theoretical advancement, meaningful analysis of empirical research, and the development of effective policy responses in the realm of white collar crime is only possible if it is grounded in optimal conceptual clarity (Helmkamp et al., 1996; Gerring, 1999). This claim should not be confused with a failure to recognize that consequential disputes about the best way to define key terms are inevitable, or that for some purposes intentionally ambiguous definitions are desirable. On the first point, one can agree with John Braithwaite's observation that 'It is an enormously valuable type of scholarship to study the struggle between those with an interest in clarifying and those with an interest in muddying the criminal-non-criminal distinction' (2001: 23). On the second point, one can agree with Vilhelm Aubert's (1952) call for adopting a deliberately ambiguous definition of white collar crime itself. The specific concern here, however, is with explicit or implicit claims that key terms have discrete, coherent meaning, when any such claims enhance rather than diminish conceptual confusion. Accordingly, further engagement with definitional and conceptual issues is called for, however tedious it may seem to some.

The present article was inspired by a long-standing dissatisfaction with Gary Green's (1997 [1990], 2001) solution to the definitional challenge, and more immediately by a review of several new encyclopedia entries, on: occupational crime, occupational deviance, and workplace crime.

 ## A Brief Review of the History of the White Collar Crime and Occupational Crime Concepts

It is well known that Edwin Sutherland (1940) introduced the concept of white collar crime in his 1939 American Sociological Society address in Philadelphia.

In the present context only two observations need to be made. First, Sutherland has also been faulted with having contributed to the long history of conceptual confusion in this realm both because he defined white collar crime in somewhat different ways at different points, and because these definitions themselves were intrinsically problematic; second, Sutherland's (1949) own major work on white collar crime focused on the crimes of corporations.

In their influential *Criminal Behavior Systems: A Typology*, Clinard and Quinney (1973 [1967]: 131), building on earlier work by Quinney (1964), discriminated between corporate crime and occupational crime, or 'violation of the legal codes in the course of activity in a legitimate occupation.' This typological distinction has been widely accepted, along with the recognition that the term 'white collar crime' encompasses an exceptionally broad range of activities that can only be analyzed and discussed in a coherent manner when broken down into types. Indeed, the usefulness of typologies within criminology generally is quite established, despite some criticisms of limitations or distortions inherent in existing criminological typologies (Gibbons, 1983; Miethe and McCorkle, 2001). Gilbert Geis, the most respected active white collar crime scholar over a period of more than four decades, has long favored a typological approach to white collar crime (Geis, 1962, 1982, 1992, 2002; Meier, 2001). In my own approach to typologies of white collar crime I have argued for recognition of the term itself as relativistic and heuristic (Friedrichs, 1996a). While corporate crime and occupational crime are the two principal, or 'pure,' forms of white collar crime, I make the case for recognition of cognate, hybrid, and marginal forms of white collar crime, including: governmental crime; state-corporate crime; finance crime; technocrime; enterprise crime; contrepreneurial crime; and avocational crime (Friedrichs, 1996a). Each of these activities has a fundamental link with the core concept of white collar crime. But in the present context I will only address the conceptual confusion that has arisen in relation to the invocation of the terms 'occupational crime', 'occupational deviance', and 'workplace crime'. The concept of occupational deviance—or deviance in an occupational setting—was especially influenced by Clifton Bryant's (1974) reader, *Deviant Behavior: Occupational and Organizational Bases.* The term 'workplace crime' seems to derive principally from some recent attention to workplace violence (e.g. Southerland et al., 1997). On the one hand, occupational crime, occupational deviance, and workplace crime—as invoked today—are often used quite interchangeably, although I will argue that it makes more sense to differentiate quite clearly between them. On the other hand, although traditional white collar crimes are frequently encompassed by these terms, many of the other activities subsumed within these categories have nothing to do with white collar crime. This inevitably produces great conceptual confusion, and hinders both empirical and policy-related work.

 ## Occupational Crime

Gary Green (1997 [1990], 2001) has promoted the case for replacing the term 'white collar crime'—which he regards as conceptually incoherent—with his particular conception of occupational crime. He defines such crime as 'any act punishable by law that is committed through opportunity created in the course of an occupation that is legal' (Green, 1997 [1990]: 15). The core argument here is that it is the structuring of crime opportunities, as a consequence of having a legitimate occupation, that most fully and effectively distinguishes what has traditionally been characterized as white collar crime from other forms of criminal behavior, and most especially conventional crime. Gerald Robin (1974) is credited with first having called for replacement of the term 'white collar crime' with 'occupational crime'. As Green puts it, 'The concept of occupational crime seeks only to identify a general type of opportunity' (2001: 406).

Certainly opportunity is a highly significant variable in the occurrence of crime, and arguably it has not been adequately emphasized in some criminological theories and typologies. But the claim is made here that the opportunity factor can also be overstated in the formulation of viable criminological theories and typologies. If occupations structure or facilitate the commission of certain forms of crime it does not necessarily follow that this dimension is the most significant element of the crime. All truly useful typologies of crime use multiple criteria, and attempt to group together activities that most logically belong together (Gibbons, 1983; Miethe and McCorkle, 2001). I hope to demonstrate here that the typological groupings emerging out of Green's approach are fundamentally flawed, and distorting.

Green breaks down occupational crime into four types. The first of these, 'Organizational Occupational Crime,' is essentially the equivalent of corporate crime. But Green loses more than he gains in this translation, and not only by virtue of the awkwardness of the term itself. It is the corporate structure, resources, environment, mission, and so on, that are the key elements for understanding crime in this category—e.g. environmental pollution; unsafe products; unsafe working conditions; price-fixing; contractual fraud; etc.—not the fact that company executives and managers have legitimate occupations. It is not so much the occupation as the organization that structures the opportunities in this realm. Indeed, corporate crime such as environmental pollution typically involves corporate personnel on various different levels for purposes of implementation, from CEOs to lowly workers.

Green's second type, 'State Authority Occupational Crime,' is arguably an even more awkward term for what I have chosen to characterize as governmental crime (with state crime and political white collar crime as the major types). This term is applied to abuses and illegal applications of state power by those holding some official position. In relation to this term an unusually broad array of activities is encompassed, ranging from a notary public who takes a bribe to genocide. In my own approach state crime is the public sector equivalent of corporate crime, and political white collar crime is the public sector equivalent of occupational crime. In the case of genocide, the fact that those carrying it out—from the high command to killing squads or concentration camp guards—may have 'legitimate' occupations in some sense is far less significant than the role of the apparatus, resources, and ideology of the state.

Green's third type is 'Professional Occupational Crime,' the equivalent of crimes of professionals in other typologies. As an example under this heading we have unnecessary treatment and fraud by physicians. Green characterizes unnecessary surgery as a form of aggravated assault uniquely available to physicians. Certainly the injury to patients is real, but unnecessary surgery typically differs in a fundamental way from aggravated assault, insofar as the intent is not to do physical harm but rather to realize a financial gain. Green also includes sexual assault by physicians, and misappropriation of drugs, under this heading. It makes more sense to recognize that physicians may have special opportunities to commit sexual assaults, and to shield their actions from prosecution, but that such offenders are basically rapists/molesters or drug abusers simply utilizing the enhanced opportunity they have as physicians, and the dynamic and motivation for such offenses is fundamentally at odds with that of white collar crime, or financially driven crimes of professionals.

Green's fourth and final category is 'Individual Occupational Crime,' which is conceded to be a catch-all term for all other forms of occupational crime. Personal income tax evasion is given as one example of this type of crime. But one's personal income tax obligation is not linked to one's occupation; rather, it is linked to one's having income, from whatever source. Accordingly, I characterize it as a form of avocational crime, parallel to white collar and occupational crime, but in definitional terms outside the boundaries of such crime because it does not specifically occur within an occupational context.

Under this heading, as well, Green includes offenses ranging from thrifts fraudsters to nonprofessionals molesting children at day care centers. While the former example certainly fits under the traditional heading of white collar crime, the latter clearly does not. Again, as in the case of physicians, while it may be true that day care workers who molest have unusual opportunities to carry out this type of crime, they are best classified as molesters, not as occupational offenders. We do not characterize conventional crime as 'neighborhood crime,' despite the fact that in many respects the neighborhood structures the opportunity for such crime. The offenders identified here have far more in common with others with tendencies promoting pedophilia than they do with financially oriented occupational offenders, such as the crooked thrift executives, or employees who steal.

In noting the dissension on the meaning of white collar crime, Green claims that 'some scholars include among white collar crimes those offenses committed in the course of occupations that are illegal themselves' (2001: 406). Mafioso, contract killers, bookies, burglars, and the like might be said to occupy illegal occupations, but I am not aware of white collar crime scholars who would label those occupying such positions as white collar offenders. However, it should be recognized that the legality (or legitimacy) of a particular occupation is not always entirely clear-cut, and occupations could be ranged along a continuum of legitimacy and legality. For example, real estate agent is a fully legitimate/legal occupation, con artist is not, but what about a time share entrepreneur who is using high-pressure sales tactics and some forms of misrepresentation? In my book *Trusted Criminals* I adopted a term formulated by Francis, 'contrepreneur,' to encompass a wide range of activities (and related occupations) that incorporate in varying degree elements of both legitimacy and illegitimacy, legality and illegality (Friedrichs, 1996a). A 'fence' who deals in stolen goods is obviously engaged in illegal activity, so fence is not a legitimate occupation, but fences are invariably legitimate businessmen (e.g. pawnbrokers) who engage in much legitimate and legal activity along with their illegal and illegitimate activity. Accordingly, if we address actual cases, it is not necessarily accurate to characterize someone as either engaged in a legal or an illegal occupation, as opposed to elements of both. 'Enterprise crime' is another term I have used to characterize activities involving the intersection of legitimate businesses with syndicated (organized) crime. Again, what level of engagement with illegal enterprises is required for a businessman to no longer be legitimate?

Green argues that '. . . the concept of occupational crime can be equally as useful as "white collar crime" in seeking an understanding of the ways in which wealth and political powers affect the making of law and their application' (2001: 406). But many legal occupations are essentially devoid of real wealth and political power. White collar crime, in its traditional use, incorporating corporations and the professions, does in fact highlight the disproportionate political clout of organizations and occupations in the elite or at least upper middle class realm.

In sum, Green fails to make the case that the benefits of replacing the concept of white collar crime with occupational crime outweigh the costs. What Green gains—the emphasis on how occupations can structure criminal opportunities—is more than offset by what he loses, through wholly abandoning the important social class dimension of the traditional concept of white collar crime, and by conflating activities that may occur within a single occupational framework but are fundamentally different in terms of motivation and form. Those who adopt the white collar crime concept typically only make heuristic claims for it; Green claims a fundamentally analytical coherence for his concept of occupational crime that simply cannot be demonstrated. The Clinard and Quinney conception of occupational crime as a subtype of a broader category of white collar crime remains more valid, in this view.

Occupational Deviance

The term 'occupational deviance' has also been invoked. Nathan W. Pino (2001: 260) defines it as 'any self-serving deviant act that occurs during the course of one's occupation,' broken down into deviant occupational behaviors (e.g. extramarital relations with a co-worker; consuming alcohol in the workplace; whistle-blowing) and occupational crime (e.g. embezzlement; sexual harassment; accepting kickbacks). Pino cites Clifton D. Bryant's (1974) reader *Deviant Behavior* as one basic source of inspiration for this conception. Readings in this volume addressed such matters as work-norm violations in the factory, drug addiction among physicians, lesbian behavior among strippers, fortunetelling, and abortion clinic ethnography, as well as some forms of white collar crime. Deviant occupational behavior is characterized as activity undertaken for one's own gain, or to cope with workplace stress, and not for the benefit of one's employer or organization. However, there are obviously fundamental differences between extramarital relations with a co-worker and whistle-blowing; the latter activity can be exceptionally selfless, for example. It is also important to differentiate between the workplace norms established by employers (often quite formally, in employee manuals) and the norms of co-workers, typically informal but often quite potent. 'Rate-busting,' or exceeding employer quotas and expectations, is likely to be viewed positively by the employer, and may well be rewarded; from the point of view of co-workers, however, it is more likely to be viewed negatively. Professionals must also orient themselves in relation to the norms of their professional associations (e.g. the American Medical Association; the American Bar Association), and such professional association norms may be at odds with the norms and expectations of both employers and co-workers.

Some of those who write about white collar crime—or at least certain forms of white collar crime—have opted to use the term 'deviance', instead of 'crime' (e.g. Douglas and Johnson, 1977; Ermann and Lundman, 1996; Simon, 1999). But the application of deviance in the realm of white collar generates several fundamental problems. First, 'deviance' as a term is powerfully associated with those who are fundamentally (and sometimes visibly) different from mainstream members of society—e.g. prostitutes; homosexuals; drug addicts; the mentally ill; and so on. One of the striking dimensions of white collar crime (and occupational crime) is that the offenders are typically quite fully integrated into the mainstream of society, and are widely so perceived. Second, for certain significant forms of white collar crime offenders are in fact conforming to prevailing organizational or occupational norms, rather than deviating. Of course many traditional forms of deviance are characterized by peer group conformity—e.g. gang members—but in the case of white collar crime or occupational crime the deviance from mainstream norms may be more ambiguous, or less clear-cut. Finally, any invocation of the term 'deviance' in this context has to clarify whether deviance from formal or informal societal norms, from formal or informal organizational norms, from formal or informal professional peer association norms, or from informal norms of workgroup peers, is involved.

In discussing occupational crime (as a subtype of occupational deviance), Pino (2001) basically adopts Green's approach, and accordingly includes such phenomena as child molesting in a day care center, along with embezzlement and accepting kickbacks, but expands on Green to include workplace violence. Occupational crime, then, has been conceived of as financially driven crimes committed by middle and upper class individuals within the context of their legitimate occupation; financially driven crimes committed within the context of any legitimate occupation, regardless of socioeconomic status; financial and non-financial forms of crime and deviance committed within the context of any legitimate occupation; and conventional criminal behavior committed in the setting of the workplace. Occupational crime can range from that which conforms to widely held norms within the occupation (e.g. taking kickbacks; favoring some suppliers; tax evasion) to that which is wholly at odds with occupational norms (e.g. sexual molestation; violence against co-workers). Occupational crime, as

defined here, incorporates violations of society's laws and regulations (e.g. fraud and embezzlement); violation of the norms of professional associations (e.g. ambulance chasing); violations of the rules or norms of employers (e.g. misappropriating trade secrets); and violations of coworkers' norms (e.g. rate-busting). All of this tends to contribute to and enhance conceptual confusion. In my view it would make more sense to restrict the term 'occupational deviance' to non-criminal violations of norms within a legitimate occupational setting, with differentiation between violations of the norms of the employer, of professional or occupational associations, and of co-workers. See Table 2.5.

Workplace Crime

Finally, we have the concept of 'workplace crime,' defined as 'any harmful act committed by a person or group of persons during the course of a legitimate occupation' (Ismaili, 2001: 530). It is taken to be harm specifically generated by the workplace, and accordingly is broken down into: occupational crime; corporate (organizational) crime; and workplace violence.

Table 2.5 Comparing Forms of White Collar and Conventional Crime

White Collar Crime		Conventional Crime	
Corporate/Occ. (C&Q)	Organ. Occ. (Green)	Occupational (Green)	Conventional
HMO defrauds Medicaid	MD defrauds Medicaid	MD steals patient's wallet	Pickpocket steals stranger's wallet
Pharmaceutical corporation sells dangerous product (e.g. Dalkon shield)	Surgeon performs unnecessary surgery	MD molests patient	Uncle molests niece
Corporation defrauds consumers	Employee steals from employer	Maid steals from guest	Burglar steals from homeowner

NOTES: Examples in the two columns to the left would be uniformly defined as white collar crime, either in Clinard and Quinney's (C & Q) typology of Corporate Crime and Occupational Crime, or Green's Typology of Organizational Occupational Crime and Individual Occupational Crime. Examples in the right-hand column would be uniformly defined as forms of conventional crime. In the remaining column we have examples of illegal acts that could be regarded as fitting Green's conception of occupational crime. The question here is this: do they have a closer generic relation to white collar crime or to conventional crime? I would argue, with the latter.

In my view, however, the concept so defined simply confuses our understanding of the range of illegalities that can occur in the context of the workplace. As an 'umbrella' term for a range of different offenses it is quite inferior to the white collar crime concept, which at a minimum offers a fundamental contrast to conventional crime. By analogy, it would not seem to be either theoretically or conceptually useful to put forth a concept of 'home-based crime.' The home can be the locus of a broad range of illegalities that have nothing important in common: burglaries; domestic violence; and even some forms of occupational crime—e.g. investment fraud—in an era when growing numbers are working out of their homes. It is one thing to say that an organizational structure (e.g. an asbestos-producing corporation) can generate a particular form of crime, or a specific occupation (e.g. medicine) can generate a particular form of crime. However, the workplace per se is merely a setting, and has much less to offer toward an understanding of how specific forms of crime are generated. Quite different forms of violence are linked with the workplace: e.g. the violence of unsafe working conditions; the violence of unnecessary surgery; the violence of homicide by a disgruntled worker, or sexual assault by a co-worker. To conflate such different violence under the heading of workplace violence confuses violence that is financially driven (and typically indirect or incremental), with violence that is emotionally driven (and typically direct and immediate).

The notion of 'workplace' is implicit in the concepts of corporate crime and occupational crime: i.e. they occur by definition in the context of the workplace. When this concept is then extended to the activities of state institutions even greater confusion arises. We are informed by Ismaeli (2001: 532), in his encyclopedia entry, that workplace crime occurs in the public sector 'when public officials violently victimize citizens on the basis of either formal or informal policies.' As stated, this definition encompasses genocide, CIA assassinations, and budgetary cutbacks for prenatal care, or inadequate funding for addressing AIDS. Lax enforcement (or non-enforcement) of building codes can produce victims in the context of earthquakes. This concept might also include sexual exploitation of subordinates by a public official.

But if we are informed that some two million Americans are victims of violence at the workplace—including homicides, assaults, rapes, and robberies—how shall we treat this information in relation to the broader concept of workplace violence? First, on homicide, such statistics may include crimes committed by aggrieved, disgruntled, and dismissed employees, and crimes that arise out of the intrinsic dangers of the workplace—e.g. a prison inmate murdering a guard—but also may incorporate victims of violence in the workplace for reasons wholly independent of the work setting itself (e.g. homicides committed by estranged husbands and jilted boyfriends), and by conventional offenders who have invaded the workplace for specifically criminal purposes. Assaults and rapes occur in the workplace, but it seems useful to discriminate between sexual exploitation of a subordinate by a supervising manager (through direct or indirect threats relating to employment status, promotion, and salary bonuses), an employee taking advantage of special access in the workplace (e.g. a janitor raping a doctor, or vice versa), and an assault by an outsider (entering an office where a secretary is working alone, late at night). Official theft statistics relating to the workplace are highly unlikely to include systematic thefts of workers by owners and managers (e.g. looting of a pension fund; illegal underpayment in violation of minimum wage law), but could include theft by a co-worker, or by an outsider.

Although it may be useful for some purposes to recognize that a significant number of crimes occur at the workplace, it is not conceptually or theoretically useful to classify criminal offenses together on that basis. If a convenient market night clerk is robbed and murdered on the job by a stranger at 3 a.m., in an inner city location, this may be 'workplace crime' in the broad sense of the term, but it is best classified as conventional felony robbery and murder. Certainly this crime—as well as many other offenses provided as examples—is about as far removed from what Sutherland meant by white collar crime as one could possibly imagine.

If the term 'workplace crime' has any conceptual and theoretical value it seems that it should be restricted to conventional forms of crime that occur at the workplace, further differentiated in terms of whether they involve insiders or outsiders.

 References

Aubert, Vilhelm (1952) 'White-Collar Crime and Social Structure', *American Journal of Sociology* 58(November): 263-71.

Braithwaite, John (2001) 'Conceptualizing Organizational Crime in a World of Plural Cultures', in Henry Pontell and David Shichor (eds) *Contemporary Issues in Crime and Criminal Justice: Essays in Honor of Gilbert Geis,* pp. 17-32. Upper Saddle River, NJ: Prentice Hall.

Bryant, Clifton D. (1974) *Deviant Behavior: Occupational and Organizational Bases.* Chicago, IL: Rand McNally.

Clinard, Marshall B. and Richard Quinney (1973 [1967]) *Criminal Behavior Systems: A Typology.* New York: Holt, Rinehart & Winston.

Douglas, Jack D. and John M. Johnson (eds) (1977) *Official Deviance.* New York: J.B. Lippincott Co.

Ermann, M. David and Richard J. Lundman (eds) (1996) *Corporate and Governmental Deviance,* 5th edn. New York: Oxford University Press.

Friedrichs, David O. (1992) 'White Collar Crime and the Definitional Quagmire: A Provisional Solution', *Journal of Human Justice* 3(3): 5-21.

Friedrichs, David O. (1996a) *Trusted Criminals: White Collar Crime in Contemporary Society.* Belmont, CA: ITP/Wadsworth Publishing Co.

Friedrichs, David O. (1996b) 'Defining White Collar Crime: In Defense of an Inclusive Approach', in James Helmkamp, Richard Ball and Kitty Townsend (eds) *Definitional Dilemma: Can and Should There Be a Universal Definition of White Collar Crime?,* pp. 263-74. Morgantown, WV: National White Collar Crime Center.

Geis, Gilbert (1962) 'Toward a Delineation of White-Collar Offenses', *Sociological Inquiry* 32(Spring): 160-71.

Geis, Gilbert (1982) *On White-Collar Crime.* Lexington, MA: Lexington Books.

Geis, Gilbert (1992) 'White-Collar Crime: What Is It?', in Kip Schlegel and David Weisburd (eds) *White-Collar Crime Reconsidered,* pp. 31-52. Boston, MA: Northeastern University Press.

Geis, Gilbert (2002) 'White-Collar Crime', in Gary W. Potter (ed.) *Controversies in White Collar Crime,* pp. 37-52. Cincinnati, OH: Anderson Publishing Co.

Gerring, John (1999) 'What Makes a Concept Good? A Criterial Framework for Understanding Concept Formation in the Social Sciences', *Polity* 31(3): 357-93.

Gibbons, Don C. (1983) 'Typologies of Criminal Behavior', in Sanford H. Kadish (ed.) *Encyclopedia of Crime and Justice,* pp. 1572-6. New York: The Free Press.

Green, Gary (1997 [1990]) *Occupational Crime.* Chicago, IL: Nelson-Hall Publishers.

Green, Gary (2001) 'Occupational Crime', in David Luckenbill and Dennis Peck (eds) *Encyclopedia of Criminology and Deviant Behavior. Volume II, Crime and Juvenile Delinquency,* pp. 404-9. Philadelphia, PA: Brunner-Routledge.

Helmkamp, James, Richard Ball and Kitty Townsend (eds) (1996) *White Collar Crime: Definitional Dilemma: Can and Should There Be a Universal Definition of White Collar Crime?* Morgantown, WV: National White Collar Crime Center.

Ismaili, Karim (2001) 'Workplace Crime', in David Luckenbill and Dennis Peck (eds) *Encyclopedia of Criminology and Deviant Behavior. Volume II: Crime and Juvenile Delinquency,* pp. 530-3. Philadelphia, PA: Brunner-Routledge.

Meier, Robert F. (2001) 'Geis, Sutherland, and White-Collar Crime', in Henry N. Pontell and David Shichor (eds) *Contemporary Issues in Crime and Criminal Justice: Essays in Honor of Gilbert Geis,* pp. 1-16. Upper Saddle River, NJ: Prentice Hall.

Miethe, Terance D. and Richard C. McCorkle (2001) 'Typologies of Crime', in David Luckenbill and Dennis Peck (eds) *Encyclopedia of Criminology and Deviant Behavior,* pp. 508-11. Philadelphia, PA: Taylor & Francis.

Pino, Nathan W. (2001) 'Occupational Deviance', in Patricia A. Adler, Peter Adler and Jay Corzine (eds) *Encyclopedia of Criminology and Deviant Behavior. Volume I: Historical, Conceptual, and Theoretical Issues,* pp. 260-5. Philadelphia, PA: Brunner-Routledge.

Quinney, Richard (1964) 'The Study of White Collar Crime: Toward a Reorientation in Theory and Research', *Journal of Criminal Law, Criminology and Police Science* 55(June): 208-14.

Robin, Gerald (1974) 'White-Collar Crime and Employee Theft', *Crime and Delinquency* 20(3): 251-62.

Simon, David R. (1999) *Elite Deviance,* 6th edn. Boston, MA: Allyn & Bacon.

Southerland, Mittie D., Pamela A. Collins and Kathryn E. Scarborough (1997) *Workplace Violence: A Continuum from Threat to Death.* Cincinnati, OH: Anderson.

Sutherland, Edwin H. (1940) 'White-Collar Criminality', *American Sociological Review* 5(February): 1-12.

Sutherland, Edwin H. (1949) *White Collar Crime.* New York: Holt, Rinehart & Winston.

DISCUSSION QUESTIONS

1. How is occupational crime different from occupational deviance?

2. What policy implications arise from the way that white-collar crime is defined?

3. Is workplace violence a form of white-collar crime? Explain.

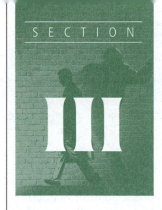

Crimes in Sales-Related Occupations

A Systems Perspective

Not long ago, three student workers were caught stealing textbooks from their university book store. One of the culprits was actually hired to sit at the front of the store and watch the entrance of the store in an effort to keep shoppers from stealing books. Instead, conspiring with two coworkers, he stole textbooks and sold them to fellow students at reduced prices. The bookstore manager told a reporter, "It's always shocking when someone you trust steals from you" (DeJesus, 2007, n.p.).

While shocking to victims of employee theft, to those who study workplace crimes it is not surprising when workers are caught stealing from their workplace or committing other types of crime in the workplace. In sales-oriented occupations, in particular, the likelihood of theft is high. In retail settings, for example, employees are often younger, part-time workers who do not feel attached to the business, and many workplace environments have an assortment of items (including goods and money) that can be targeted for theft. In other sales-oriented occupations, the aim of making profits through the provision of different services may foster misconduct. There is a long-standing perception that salespersons cannot be trusted as they are seen as simply trying to sell goods or services that may not be worth the asking price. From this perspective, it should not be shocking when sales-oriented officials engage in wrongdoing.

As an illustration of the breadth of offenses occurring in sales-oriented occupations, consider the examples in the following quotations from various press reports:

- Unlicensed contractors are preying on Gulf Coast residents whose homes were ravaged by Hurricane Katrina and are in dire need of repair, state and FBI officials say.... Phony contractors are collecting down payments for work and then disappearing, Marceaux says. One scam involves workmen who take down payments and even drop materials off at work sites, only to return in the night to retrieve the materials and sneak away. (Konigsmark, 2006, 3A)
- [The defendant], 48, is accused of stealing nearly $55,000 by running a virtual car lot via eBay but not always following through on his sales. He has been charged with three counts of grand theft, two counts of passing bad checks, six counts of prohibited acts involving certificate of title and one count of selling a car without a title. (Sowinski, 2009, no pagination)
- [The defendant], the owner of 22 Midas auto repair shops, agreed ... to pay $1.8 million to settle allegations from the California attorney general's office that his shops charged some customers hundreds of dollars for repairs they didn't need. (Olivarez-Giles, 2010, p. 7)
- [A student was arrested because it was alleged that he] continuously disrupted his classroom environment by intentionally passing gas and shutting off computers that other students were using. ("Florida Student Arrested," 2008)
- [One consumer] said "just about everything" including his odometer broke down on his 1990 Cadillac Sedan de Ville at about 47,000 miles. He would soon find out why: the actual mileage was 80,000 miles. (Lucchetti, 1996, B1)

As with all white-collar crimes, these offenses have four things in common: (1) they occurred during the course of the offender's work, (2) the offender was engaged in the role of a worker, (3) in terms of setting, the offenses occurred in a workplace setting, and (4) on one level or another, each of them involved occupations where employees were selling goods or services. Literally hundreds of different types of sales-oriented occupations exist. It would be impossible to address the way crime occurs in each of those occupations, but I attempt here to introduce students to the nature of crime in these sales-oriented occupations. In this section, attention will be given to the crimes occurring in the following systems: employee theft in the retail system, crimes in the entertainment and service systems, fraud in sales and service systems, and crimes in the insurance system.

These systems were selected because they capture the kinds of occupational systems about which students likely already have some awareness and a degree of interest. Some of these areas are possibly fields where students have already worked, others are fields they may one day work in, others are service occupations that students have encountered or will encounter in the future. It is important to stress that other sales-oriented occupations, while not covered here, are not immune from crime.

Employee Theft in the Retail System

The **retail system** is the setting where consumers purchase various types of products. As shown in recent times, the success of our economic system is tied to the success of the retail system. When individuals buy more in the retail system, our economic system is stronger. While consumers drive the success of the retail system, employees steer the direction of the retail system. The key to success for retail stores lies in having employees able to perform assigned tasks. One problem that retail outlets face is employee theft. Indeed, internal theft has been "linked to 30% of U.S. business failures" (Mullen, 1999).

Experts use the concept of shrinkage to refer to the theft of goods in the retail industry. Estimates suggest that retailers lost $36.5 billion to shrinkage in 2008, and employees are believed "to be the number one shrinkage offenders" (Friedman, 2009, p. 17). Friedman estimates that retailers lost $15.9 million to employee theft in 2008. Employee theft increased at the end of the 2000s. In line with the idea that changes in one system lead to changes in other systems, some have attributed this increase to the economic changes, such as changes in the economic system that resulted in changes in the extent of employee theft in retail settings ("Record Number of Shoplifters," 2008; Rosenbaum, 2009). Explaining this increase in employee theft, loss prevention expert Richard Hollinger has suggested that more workers being alone in stores (because so many workers have been fired or laid off) means that workers will have more opportunities to steal (Goodchild, 2008).

While it is believed that employee theft has increased, it is difficult to determine with any degree of precision how often employees steal in retail settings. Surveys in these settings would probably underestimate the extent of employee theft (Oliphant & Oliphant, 2001). One study found that 1 in 30 employees (out of 2.1 million) was caught stealing from their employer in 2008 ("Record Number of Shoplifters," 2008). Regardless of the number of employees who steal, and the fact that most employees in retail settings do not steal, Daniel Butler, the former vice president of the National Retail Federation, notes, "a habitual internal thief can cost a lot of dollars" (Pratt, 2001, p. 37).

Several different varieties of employee theft in retail settings occur. Here are some examples.

- **Overcharging:** employees charge customers more than they should have
- **Shortchanging:** employees do not give customers all of their change and pocket the difference
- **Coupon stuffing:** employees steal coupons and use them later
- **Credits for nonexistent returns:** employees give credit for returns to collaborators
- **Theft of production supplies and raw materials:** employees steal items used to produce goods in retail settings
- **Embezzlement:** employees steal money from an account to which they have access
- **Over-ordering supplies:** employees order more supplies than are needed and keep the supplies that were not needed
- **Theft of credit card information:** employees steal customers' credit card information
- **Theft of goods:** employees steal the items the retail setting is trying to sell
- **Theft of money from the cash register:** employees take money out of the register
- **Sweetheart deals:** employees give friends and family members unauthorized discounts (Albright, 2007; Belser, 2008; Mishra & Prasad, 2006).

Explaining why these offenses occur is no simple task. Some have attributed certain types of employee theft to organized crime on the notion that organized crime families have conspired with employees to develop widespread and lucrative employee theft schemes (Albright, 2007). Others have focused on individual motivations among employees and have highlighted the employees' perceived needs, drug problems, and sense of entitlement as causes of employee theft (Leap, 2007). Still others contend that some instances of employee theft (like stealing from the cash register) are not planned events, but impulsive ones that offenders commit when the opportunity presents itself (Anderson, 2007). Some have suggested that retail settings with more turnover will have more employee theft (Belser, 2008). Still others have noted that organizational culture contributes to employee theft (Leap, 2007). Much more attention will be given to explaining all forms of white-collar crime in a later section in this text. For now, it is sufficient to suggest that these offenses are caused by multiple factors.

Because so many different factors potentially contribute to employee theft in the retail system, it should not be surprising that many different types of prevention strategies have been cited as ways to limit the extent of employee theft. These prevention strategies include: (a) importation strategies, (b) internal strategies, (c) technological strategies, (d) organizational culture strategies, and (e) awareness strategies. Importation strategies are those strategies that aim to import only the best types of employees, who are less likely to engage in employee theft. Strategies would include background checks, drug tests, employee screening instruments, and credit checks (Friedman, 2009).

Internal strategies include policies and practices performed within the retail setting in an effort to prevent employee theft. Random inspections, audits, developing rules that guide returns, and developing internal control policies are examples (Mishra & Prasad, 2006). Random inspections include checking cash registers, employee lockers, and other locations for evidence of wrongdoing. Audits are strategies in which supervisors review cash distribution patterns of employees. Rules guiding returns focus on ways to limit the possibility that employees misuse return policies. Internal control policies refer to a "set of policies and procedures that provide reasonable assurance that an organization's assets and information are protected" (Mishra & Prasad, 2006, p. 819).

Technological strategies entail the use of various forms of technology to prevent employee theft in retail settings. The use of video cameras, for example, can be preventive in nature, assuming employees know that they are being "watched." If the cameras don't prevent an employee from stealing, the video will provide direct evidence of the employee "in action" (Holtz, 2009). With color and digital cameras now available, the pictures provided by the videos are even clearer and security officials can store the video longer than they were able to in the past (Pratt, 2001). Closed-circuit television, in particular, has been hailed as the most effective deterrent in retail settings (Anderson, 2007).

Organizational culture strategies aim to promote a sense of organizational culture that would inhibit theft. Most business and management experts agree that the way bosses treat their employees will influence the workers' behavior (Kresevich, 2007). The task at hand is for supervisors and managers to promote an organizational culture that values honesty and loyalty. One expert advises, "from the start, employees should know company values and feel a part of a team committed to eliminating theft" (Mullen, 1999, p. 12). Along this line, Davies (2003) recommends that supervisors (a) provide advice to employers about the organization's culture, (b) build loyalty between the employee and the employer, (c) establish a trusting relationship between workers, and (d) eliminate temptations. Echoing these themes, Mazur (2001) calls for the building of a "strong integrity program" as a strategy to prevent retail theft. Such a program would entail four elements. First, managers would be held accountable for employees' behavior and provided incentives as part of this accountability. Second, managers would ensure that all employees are aware of the rules of conduct in the retail setting. Third, an effort would be made to give employees a "sense of authority." Fourth, managers would provide employees an outlet for reporting misconduct (Mazur, 2001). Anonymous reporting systems have been found to be particularly useful in detecting wrongdoing (Holtfreter, 2005).

Awareness strategies focus on increasing awareness among employees about various issues related to employee theft. In particular, it is recommended that employees be told about or exposed to the following:

- Anonymous tip lines
- New hire orientation

- Formal codes of conduct
- Bulletin board posters related to theft prevention
- Periodic lectures on theft and the consequences of theft
- Loss prevention compensation programs (Korolishin, 2003).

A loss prevention compensation program would provide employees with monetary rewards for reporting and substantiating employee theft by their coworkers.

⬚ Crimes in the Entertainment Service System

While the retail system encompasses the setting where retail goods are sold to consumers, the **entertainment service system** describes those settings where consumers consume or purchase various forms of services designed at least partially for entertainment or pleasure. Many different occupations exist in the entertainment service system. For purposes of simplicity, in this text attention will be given to just two types of industries in this system: the restaurant industry and the hotel industry.

In considering crimes in the restaurant industry, two broad categories of crime can be highlighted: crimes by the restaurant against consumers and crimes by workers against the restaurant. In her review of crimes by businesses, Hazel Croall (1989) identified four types of crimes committed by restaurants against consumers: (1) adulterating food, (2) failing to keep the restaurant as clean as required by standards, (3) using false advertising to describe goods and prices, and (4) selling food at a smaller amount than advertised (short weighting). Restaurants appeared to be over-represented in "hygiene" offenses in her study. Croall studied 118 businesses and uncovered 37 hygiene offenses; restaurants accounted for 29 of the 37 offenses. Croall also calls attention to instances where restaurants short-measure items. She writes, "fiddles, including the sale of short-measure drinks, are so institutionalized that they represent part of an 'informal reward structure'" (p. 160). As Croall notes, while one person being ripped off over a drink may not be significant, when one adds up the number of short-measures, the total sum can be especially significant.

In terms of crimes by workers against the restaurant, patterns similar to those of employee theft in retail settings are found. Surveys of 103 restaurant employees found that their most common offenses included eating the restaurant's food without paying for it, giving food and/or beverages away, selling food at a lower price than it was supposed to be sold for, and taking items for personal use (Ghiselli & Ismail, 1998). In this same study, three fourths of respondents admitted committing some type of employee deviance. Stealing from the cash register is an additional type of crime that can occur in restaurants. In one case, a waitress/manager stole $60,000 from her restaurant's cash register over a 2-year time span (Schaefer, 2003).

A combination of factors is believed to foster theft by workers in restaurants. Restaurants tend to hire younger workers, and younger people in general have

▲ **Photo 3.1** A study by Ghiselli and Ismail (1998) found that three fourths of restaurant employees reported committing some variety of employee deviance.

been found to be more prone toward deviance than older people. Also, the low wages paid to workers may create settings where workers feel they are underpaid and underappreciated. The nature of the work is also part-time, meaning that workers will be less invested in their employer. Also, the erratic hours of restaurant work may contribute to various opportunities for misconduct (Ghiselli & Ismail, 1998). To address these offenses, Ghiselli and Ismail cite the following policies as strategies to reduce theft in restaurants: (a) inventory control, (b) controlled exits so managers know when workers are leaving, (c) inspections of employees' belongings, (d) video cameras, (e) locks on goods and items, and (f) restricted access to the cash register.

White-collar crime also occurs in the hotel industry. Crime types include theft of hotel food, theft of items owned by the hotel, and theft of hotel guests' items. These crimes are particularly difficult to detect (Bloomquist, 2006). When offenders are caught, it is usually because they did something that made the case truly easy to solve. Consider, for example, a case in which two security guards were arrested for stealing three cellular phones and two wallets from a hotel room. They were caught because they used one of the cell phones (Nammour, 2009). Certainly, some of the crimes committed in the hotel industry might be committed by hotel guests. However, there is reason to believe that most hotel crimes are committed by workers. One early estimate suggested that 90% of all crimes committed in hotels were due to employee theft (Worcester, 1998). According to Worcester, employee theft in hotels is believed to be particularly problematic during summer months when temporary employees are hired.

Few studies have focused specifically on white-collar crimes in the hotel industry. Nonetheless, anecdotal evidence suggests that these crimes are somewhat pervasive. Recall that I mentioned that I have students enrolled in my white-collar crime classes write about crimes they committed on their jobs. One of my students worked in a hotel, and described his typical work day as beginning when his manager told him the going rates for that evening. The manager would say something like, "The rate tonight is $90.00 a night. If customers ask for the rate, tell them it is $100.00 a night. If they don't like the rate, tell them you will lower it to $90.00 to get them to stay." The student then shared that he would tell customers that the rate was $120 a night. If customers paid that rate in cash, he would pocket $30 each night and tell his boss that the customer paid $90.00. If the customer said the price was too high, he would offer to reduce it a little and still keep the difference if it was higher than $90.00. Just to be clear, this was not a student at my current university. One can't help but wonder, though, where this student is now working. Hopefully, he's not working anywhere that we will be vacationing!

◪ Fraud in the Sales/Service System

Whereas the entertainment service system sells goods and services that are designed to provide some form of entertainment to consumers, the **sales/service system** entails businesses that sell basic goods and services to consumers. These "basic" goods and services are those that most individuals need in order to function in their communities. The home and the automobile are two examples of basic goods many individuals need in order to carry out their daily routines. When considering fraud in this system, one can draw attention to automotive repair/sales fraud and home repair fraud. While few studies have empirically demonstrated how often these types of fraud occur, they are believed to be particularly pervasive. In Focus 3.1 shows the top 10 consumer complaints made to state attorneys general in 2008. As shown in the box, complaints about auto sales ranked number 2, complaints about home repairs ranked number 3, and complaints about auto repairs ranked number 9. In the following paragraphs, more attention is given to the dynamics surrounding home repair fraud and auto repair/sales fraud.

In Focus 3.1

Top Ten Consumer Complaints
Made to State Attorneys General, 2008

1. Debt collection

2. Auto sales

3. Home repair/construction

4. Credit cards (tie)

5. Internet goods and services (tie)

6. Predatory lending/mortgages

7. Telemarketing/do not call

8. Auto repair

9. Auto warranties (tie)

10. Telecom/slamming/cramming (tie)

Home Repair Fraud

Home repair fraud occurs when contractors and repair persons rip off individuals for various types of repairs. One police department cites the following offenses as the most common types of home repair fraud: roof repair, asphalt paving/driveway sealing fraud, house painting fraud, termite and pest control fraud, and tree pruning and landscaping fraud (St. Louis Police Department, 2006). In most of these cases, the fraud begins as part of a door-to-door scam initiated by the offender. Experts believe that the door-to-door scams target older persons more often, partly because they are more likely to be home during the day (Coffey, 2000), and partly because they are seen as more vulnerable (Davila, Marquart, & Mullings, 2005).

Scammers are able to profit significantly from their offenses. Estimates suggest, for example, that those involved in driveway paving scams make $10,000 a day from their schemes. Typically, they underestimate the repair costs and then try to charge more once they are done (Sambides, 2009).

To be sure, while some of the frauds result from aggressive door-to-door targeting by offenders, others occur as a result of consumers seeking repairs. Consumers are particularly vulnerable to repair frauds when considering the underlying dynamics of repair seeking. When individuals seek repairs, they already must admit to the repairer—at least indirectly—that they do not know how to fix the item themselves. If the contractor commits fraud, the consumer may not even know it. Even when consumers are aware of the fraud, they are often unsure who they should report the offense to (Vaughan & Carlo, 1975).

The consequences of home repair fraud can be particularly problematic. If items are not fixed appropriately, further damage to the home can result. Additional expenses will be incurred by homeowners seeking to repair their homes. Such an experience can cause significant stress to those dealing with the fraud. Family relationships can also be negatively influenced for those living in homes in need of repair as a result of contractor fraud (Burnstein, 2008a, 2008b). Perhaps recognizing the seriousness of these

▲ **Photo 3.2** Concerns about home repair fraud escalate in the wake of disasters. After Hurricane Katrina, reports of home repair fraud soared in Louisiana and Mississippi.

consequences, one police officer made the following comments to a reporter: "Some of the contractors that we arrest, I think of them as worse than armed robbers. At least when it's an armed robbery, you know you're being robbed" (Lee, 2009).

Allegations of home repair frauds appear to increase after natural disasters, likely because many homeowners are in need of labor to fix their damaged homes. In the wake of Hurricane Katrina, authorities investigated more than 400 cases of contractor fraud. Said one official, "there's not enough skilled labor out there, and it's causing chaos" (Konigsmark, 2006). In Mississippi, 87 contractors were arrested after Katrina, and 60 additional contractors were in mediation with homeowners for allegations that they committed fraud against residents of Mississippi whose homes were damaged in the hurricane (Lee, 2009).

In the wake of home repair fraud scandals, many states have passed criminal laws specifically targeting home repair fraud. In Maine, for example, the home repair fraud law states:

§908. Home repair fraud

1. A home repair seller is guilty of home repair fraud if the seller knowingly enters into an agreement or contract, written or oral, with any person for home repair services and the seller, at the time of entering into that agreement or contract:

   A. Intentionally misrepresents a material fact relating to the terms of the agreement or contract or misrepresents a preexisting or existing condition of any portion of the property that is the subject of the home repair services. Violation of this paragraph is a Class D crime; [2001, c. 383, §110 (AMD); 2001, c. 383, §156 (AFF).]

   B. Intentionally creates or reinforces an impression relating to the terms of the agreement or contract that is false and that the seller does not believe to be true or fails to correct such an impression that the seller had previously created or reinforced. Violation of this paragraph is a Class D crime; [2001, c. 383, §110 (AMD); 2001, c. 383, §156 (AFF).]

   C. Intentionally promises performance under the terms of the agreement or contract that the seller does not intend to perform or that the seller knows will not be performed. Violation of this paragraph is a Class D crime; [2001, c. 383, §110 (AMD); 2001, c. 383, §156 (AFF).]

   D. Intentionally uses or employs deception, false pretense or false promise in securing the agreement or contract . . . (Maine Law §908. Home repair fraud).

The advantage of criminal laws (and policies) directed toward home repair fraud is that officials have clear guidance on how these cases should be processed. Whereas these wrongs would have been handled as civil wrongdoings in the past, if they were handled at all, the criminal laws create additional formal policies that can be used to respond to this group of offenders.

In addition to formal policies to respond to home repair fraud, experts urge homeowners to use various prevention strategies to try to avoid fraud in the first place. Common suggestions to prevent home repair fraud include the following practices: obtaining references, relying on local businesses, verifying licensure, obtaining multiple estimates, and using written contracts (Riggs, 2007).

Auto Repair/Sales Fraud

At the broadest level, one can distinguish between auto repair fraud and auto sales fraud. In the early 1990s, auto repair rip-offs were "the most frequently reported consumer complaint" (Munroe, 1992, p. C3). An early estimate suggested that "consumers lose $20 billion annually on faulty auto repairs" (Brown, 1995, p. 21). Automotive industry insiders counter that "faulty" repairs are not the same as "fraudulent" repairs. Recall the discussion in Section I about white-collar crime being defined differently by various groups. To those in the automotive repair industry, faulty repairs would not be a white-collar crime. To those following a broader approach to defining white-collar crime, such repairs can be conceptualized as white-collar crime.

Auto repair fraud includes *billing for services not provided, unnecessary repairs, airbag fraud,* and *insurance fraud.* **Billing for services not provided** occurs when auto mechanics bill consumers (or insurance companies) for services not provided. Consider a study by the California Department of Consumer Affairs/Bureau of Automotive Repair (BAR) that found "42% of collision repair work done in California to be fraudulent" (Sramcik, 2004, p. 16). In this study, the Bureau inspected 1,315 vehicles that received collision repairs and found that on 551 of the vehicles, "parts or labor listed on the invoice ... were not actually supplied or performed" (Thrall, 2003, p. 6). Industry insiders critiqued the BAR study for being methodologically flawed and for using vague definitions of fraud, which included billing mistakes (Grady, 2003). Again, the importance of how one defines white-collar crime surfaces. Critics also suggested that the BAR study was politically driven as a strategy to suggest that the Bureau's existence was justified in a time of tough budgets in order to protect consumers from fraud (Thrall, 2003).

Unnecessary auto repairs occur when mechanics perform mechanical services that are not necessary and bill the consumer for those services. Such practices are believed to be well planned out by those who perform them. These actions are particularly difficult for consumers to detect. Said one assistant attorney general to a reporter, "Most consumers are not knowledgeable enough about auto repairs to know if their cars have been subjected to unneeded repairs" (Munroe, 1992, p. C3). Presumably, an automotive repair shop will advertise cheap specials as a way to get consumers into the shop and then convince consumers that they need certain repairs. One owner of 22 repair shops recently agreed to pay $1.8 million in fines in response to allegations that he engaged in this type of scam (Olivarez-Giles, 2010, p. 7).

Airbag fraud occurs when mechanics fraudulently repair airbags. In general, two types of airbag fraud exist (Adams & Guyette, 2009). The first type involves outright fraud in which mechanics clearly intend not to fix the airbag appropriately. Adams and Guyette (2009) provide the example of situations where "old rags or foam are shoved into dashboard cavities." The second type of airbag fraud is inaccurate repair. This entails situations in which mechanics simply fail to repair the airbag correctly.

Auto insurance fraud occurs when mechanics dupe the insurance company into paying for unnecessary or nonexistent repairs. Types of auto insurance fraud include enhancing damages, substituting parts, and creating damage. Enhancing damages involves situations where mechanics cause further damage to a damaged car in order to collect more from the insurance company. Substituting parts includes situations where mechanics put used parts in the repaired car, but bill the insurance company for new parts (Seibel, 2009). Creating damage occurs when mechanics work with car owners to damage a car so that the owner can file a claim with the insurance company (Bertrand, 2003). This would include stripping and vandalizing cars so that they will be paid to repair the damage they created.

Very few academic studies have focused on auto repair fraud. In one of the first studies done on the subject, Paul Jesilow and his colleagues (Jesilow, Geis, & O'Brien, 1985) conducted a field experiment in which they sought battery testing services from 313 auto shops in California. The researchers found that honesty was related to the size of the shop, with smaller shops exhibiting more honesty than larger shops. How workers were paid (commission vs. hourly rate) was also related to honesty. As might be expected, commissioned workers tended to be less honest than hourly workers.

Building on this study, the authors (Jesilow, Geis, & O'Brien, 1986) introduced a publicity campaign to see if publicity and awareness would influence mechanics' honesty levels. The public awareness campaign included letters from formal regulatory agencies, a major lawsuit, and press announcements. After the campaign, the authors revisited the shops for battery testing. They found that honesty rates were the same among the shops exposed to the public awareness campaigns and the shops that were not exposed to the campaign. In other words, the campaign had no effect.

Automotive sales fraud is another type of fraud in the automotive industry. Varieties of auto sales fraud include turning odometers back, selling unsafe cars, and selling stolen cars (Smith, 1997). Odometer fraud, also known as clocking (see Croall, 1989), is sometimes part of a broader scheme. In those situations, mechanics work as part of a larger scheme in collaboration with dealers in an effort to maximize a particular car sale. It is estimated that changing the odometer may increase the price of a car by $3,000-$4,000, which can add up to losses to consumers of $4 billion a year across the United States (Lucchetti, 1996).

States use a variety of tactics to respond to fraudulent auto dealers. Some states, for example, penalize fraudulent or unregistered dealers by seeking payment of unpaid taxes. Under the idea that dealers did not collect or pay taxes for their sales, state officials recoup losses through these aggressive enforcement efforts. In California, officials collected $2.8 million as a result of these efforts in 2007 (McIntosh, 2008).

Crimes in the Insurance System

The insurance system includes the wide range of agencies and institutions responsible for providing insurance to consumers. Many different types of insurance exist, including homeowners, rental insurance, auto insurance, property insurance, and more. The topic is rarely studied for two reasons: (1) it is hard to understand and (2) people don't typically know when they have been victimized by insurance crimes (Ericson & Doyle, 2006). Of the research that has been done, much of it has focused on crimes by consumers against insurance companies, including overstating losses, arson for profit, bogus insurance claims, and understating property value to get lower insurance rates (Litton, 1998). Crimes by consumers, however, encompass just one portion of the types of crimes committed in the insurance system. As with other occupations, a wide range of offenses are committed by those working in the insurance system. In the following paragraphs attention is given to the types of crimes in this system, the consequences of insurance crimes, and the patterns surrounding these offenses.

Types of Insurance Crimes by Professionals

Four different categories of insurance crimes by workers in the insurance system exist: (1) crimes by agents against the insurance company, (2) investment-focused crimes, (3) theft crimes against consumers, and (4) sales-directed crimes against consumers. With regard to **crimes by agents against the insurance company,** some agents or brokers engage in activities that ultimately defraud the insurance company. Examples include lying about a potential client's income and unauthorized entity fraud (lying about assets). By lying about these items to the company, the agent is able to provide benefits to the consumer and thereby get the consumer to purchase the insurance.

Investment-focused crimes occur when insurance agents commit crimes that are designed to get consumers to invest in various insurance products. These include viatical settlement fraud, promissory note fraud, and annuities fraud. **Viatical settlement fraud** occurs when agents conceal information on viatical settlement policies, which allow individuals to invest in other people's life insurance policies (meaning they collect money when the other person dies). Fraud occurs when agents lie about the income, health of the insured individual, or other matters the investors should know about (Brasner, 2010; Federal Bureau of Investigation [FBI], 2010a).

Promissory note fraud refers to situations where agents get clients to invest in promissory notes that ultimately are scams. A promissory note is basically an IOU. Consumers are told that if they invest in a particular business, after a certain amount of time they will get their entire investment back plus interest. While promissory notes are legitimate investment strategies, here is how investment strategy fraud schemes work:

> A life insurance agent . . . calls with an intriguing investment opportunity. A company is looking to expand its business and needs to raise capital. But instead of borrowing money from a traditional lender such as a bank, it is offering investors an opportunity to purchase "promissory notes," typically with a maturity of nine months and an annual interest rate between 12 percent and 18 percent. Investors are sometimes told the promissory notes, which are like IOUs, are "guaranteed" by a bond from an offshore bonding company. Investors lose money either because fake promissory notes that look authentic are issued on behalf of fraudulent companies, or the crooks abscond with people's money before the notes mature. (Singletary, 2000)

In some cases, insurance agents are not aware that they are selling fraudulent promissory notes because they too have fallen to the scam. In other cases, they are knowing conspirators who profit from the crimes. A series of investigations in the late 1990s found 800 incidents of promissory note fraud costing investors $500 million (Knox, 2000).

Annuities fraud occurs when insurance agents misrepresent the types of returns that their clients would get from investing in annuities. Annuities are "insurance contracts that offer a guaranteed series of payments over time" (Jenkins, 2008). Insurance agents get a 3%–8% commission for selling annuities, giving them incentive to get clients to invest in annuities (Haiken, 2011). However, annuities can sometimes be quite risky investments and agents have been known to convince investors, particularly older individuals, to take their investments out of safe investment portfolios and place them in annuities which could eventually result in the investor losing their savings. One victim described his experiences with annuities fraud in this way:

> The first scam started when the agent showed up and did not tell us he was from Salt Lake City, Utah. . . . His sales pitch convinced me I could use the immediate monthly income from an annuity, it was not disclosed he was selling "life insurance" or that Mr. Smiley was actually an insurance salesman. I was misled into thinking I was investing into a . . . mutual fund program. The instructions he gave me about the contract details such as "single life contract", "no guarantee", "no beneficiary", "no joint annuitant", and "no IRA disclosure statement was presented", these details were all misleading and coordinated in favor of [the insurance company]. Now I understand, the more

I was defrauded, the bigger the commission for the insurance agent, they are trained to deceive. I have now ultimately lost the entire $57,779.00 IRA savings and I have nothing for my years of work and no retirement nest egg. (Adam, 2008)

These scams have increased in recent years. In Florida, 37 investigations for annuities fraud were conducted in fiscal year 2004. In fiscal year 2008, 276 investigations were conducted (Jenkins, 2008).

Theft crimes against consumers occur when agents steal directly from insurance clients. Examples include broker embezzlement, forgery, and falsifying account information (FBI, 2010a). In broker embezzlement cases, agents steal funds from a client's account that the agents have access to. In forgery cases, also called **clean sheeting,** agents sign clients' names on documents and forms and benefit financially from the deception. **Falsifying account information** refers to instances when agents or brokers change account information without the client's knowledge. In these crimes, no actual sale, or even effort to make a sale, occurs and agents are not trying to get clients to invest in anything—they are simply stealing from consumers.

Sales-directed crimes against consumers occur when agents or brokers steal from consumers by using fraudulent sales tactics. Premium diversion theft is the most common form of sales-directed insurance crime (FBI, 2010a). In these situations, brokers or agents convince clients to purchase insurance, but they never actually forward the payment from the client to the insurance company; instead they pocket the payment. This means that clients don't actually have insurance when they think they do.

Other forms of sales-directed insurance crimes are more institutionalized in the insurance sales process. For instance, **churning** refers to situations where agents and brokers introduce new products and services simply to get policy holders to change their policies so the agents/brokers can collect commissions (Eriscon & Doyle, 2006). Such practices are often called "good business" among officials in the insurance agency; the practice certainly is distinguished from cases of direct theft, which are not institutionalized as part of sales strategies. Other sales-directed insurance crimes include the following:

- **Stacking:** persuading persons to buy more policies than are needed
- **Rolling over:** persuading customers to cancel an old policy and replace it with a more expensive "better" policy
- **Misrepresentation:** deliberately misinforming the customer about the coverage of the insurance policy
- **Switching:** the sales person switches the consumer's policy so that the coverage and the premiums are different from what the victim was told
- **Sliding:** agents include insurance coverage that was not requested by customers (Payne, 2005).

Beyond the deception that is tied to these offenses, consumers and the rest of society experience a number of different consequences from crimes committed in the insurance system.

Consequences of Insurance Crimes

Estimates suggest that insurance fraud collectively "raises the yearly cost of premiums by $300 for the average household" (FBI, 2010a). For individuals victimized by these offenses, the consequences of insurance crimes can be particularly devastating. Consider cases of premium diversion thefts—where individuals pay for insurance they don't actually receive. One woman didn't realize she didn't have insurance until after an automobile accident. Her garage called and told her that the insurance company had no policy in her name.

She had thought for more than 2 years that she had insurance. The investigation revealed that the agent did the same thing with 80 other clients. In another scheme, an agent who sold fake policies "left dozens of customers without coverage during hurricane seasons [in Florida] in 2003, 2004, and 2005 during which eight hurricanes struck the neighborhood" ("Insurance Agent Accused," 2007, p. 1).

Many of the insurance crimes target elderly persons, making the consequences of lost income particularly significant. One Florida insurance agent defrauded 60 victims, but only 37 of them participated in the trial. Many of the others "died before the trial took place" (Varian, 2000, p. 1). The agent had asked them "to invest in expansions of his insurance business or for short-term loans to book entertainers from the former Lawrence Welk program." In another case, 75-year-old Martha Cunningham "owned a $417,000 home in Prince George's County and held $61,000 in annuities before she met Edward Hanson [an insurance agent] . . . today the widow is essentially broke and inundated with debt" (Wiggins, 2009, B02). Hanson stole everything the elderly woman owned. The breadth of these schemes is but one pattern surrounding insurance crimes.

Insurance Crime Patterns

In addressing the dynamics of crimes in the insurance system, industry insiders attribute the offenses to either rotten apple explanations or they engage in victim blaming (Ericson & Doyle, 2006). The rotten apple explanations suggest that a few rogue agents and brokers commit the vast majority of insurance crimes, while the victim blaming explanations suggest that failures on the part of victims (and greed) make them potential targets for the few rogue insurance employees that exist. Ericson and Doyle point out that these explanations are shortsighted and argue that insurance crimes are institutionalized in the industry by the practices and strategies encouraged among insurance employees. Aspects of the insurance industry that they discuss as evidence of the way that these crimes are institutionalized in the insurance system include:

- The complex products sold by insurance companies
- The construction of risk as calculable
- The commission structure
- A revolving door of agents
- Mixed messages about an aggressive sales culture
- Limited regulation of market misconduct

As will be discussed later, sometimes white-collar crimes are rationalized by offenders as "sharp business practices." This is particularly the case in insurance crime cases. One former life insurance agent is quoted as saying, "You have to understand, everything is crooked" (Ericson & Doyle, 2006, p. 993). Ericson and Doyle pro-

▲ **Photo 3.3** Researchers suggest that fraudulent insurance agents try to paint the worst scenario possible to get clients to purchase as much insurance as possible. Is this sales tactic a good business practice, or is it criminal? What do you think?

vide an example that describes how "deceptive sales are rife and institutionalized in the life insurance industry" and point to the scare tactics used by agents and brokers that are euphemistically called "backing the hearse up to the door" by insurance insiders. Good business practices, or crime? You can decide for yourself.

▧ Summary

- To introduce students to the nature of crime in lower class occupations, in this section attention was given to the crimes occurring in the following systems: (1) employee theft in the retail system, (2) crimes in the entertainment service system, (3) fraud in the sales/service system and, (4) crimes in the insurance system.
- Several different varieties of employee theft in retail settings occur. Here are some examples: overcharging, shortchanging, coupon stuffing, credits for nonexistent returns, theft of production supplies and raw materials, embezzlement, over-ordering supplies, theft of credit card information, theft of goods, theft of money from the cash register, and sweetheart deals.
- Employee theft prevention strategies include: (a) importation strategies, (b) internal strategies, (c) technological strategies, (d) organizational culture strategies, and (e) awareness strategies.
- In considering crimes in the restaurant industry, two broad categories can be highlighted: crimes by the restaurant against consumers and crimes by workers against the restaurant.
- The most common types of home repair fraud are believed to be: roof repair, asphalt paving/driveway sealing fraud, house painting fraud, termite and pest control fraud, and tree pruning and landscaping fraud.
- Auto repair fraud includes billing for services not provided, unnecessary repairs, airbag fraud, and insurance fraud.
- Insurance crimes are rarely studied for two reasons: (1) they are hard to understand and (2) people don't typically know when they have been victimized by insurance crimes (Ericson & Doyle, 2006).
- Four different categories of insurance crimes by workers in the insurance system exist: (1) crimes by agents against the insurance company, (2) investment-focused crimes, (3) theft crimes against consumers, and (4) sales-directed crimes against consumers.
- Estimates suggest that insurance fraud collectively "raises the yearly cost of premiums by $300 for the average household" (FBI, 2010a).
- For individuals victimized by these offenses, the consequences of insurance crimes can be particularly devastating.
- Industry insiders attribute the insurance offenses to either rotten apple explanations or they engage in victim blaming (Ericson & Doyle, 2006).
- Ericson and Doyle (2006) point out that insurance crimes are institutionalized in the industry by the practices and strategies encouraged among insurance employees.

KEY TERMS

Airbag fraud	Churning	Home repair fraud
Annuities fraud	Clean sheeting	Internal strategies
Auto insurance fraud	Coupon stuffing	Misrepresentation
Auto repair fraud	Credits for nonexistent returns	Organizational culture strategies
Automotive sales fraud	Embezzlement	Over-ordering supplies
Awareness strategies	Entertainment service system	Overcharging
Billing for services not provided	Falsifying account information	Promissory note fraud

Retail system	Stacking	Theft of goods
Rolling over	Sweetheart deals	Theft of money from the cash register
Sales-directed crimes	Switching	
Sales/service system	Technological strategies	Theft of production supplies and raw materials
Shortchanging	Theft crimes against consumers	Unnecessary auto repairs
Sliding	Theft of credit card information	Viatical settlement fraud

DISCUSSION QUESTIONS

1. What types of employee theft do you think are most serious? Why?

2. Should employees always be fired if they are caught engaging in crime in a restaurant? Explain.

3. How are home repair frauds and auto repair frauds similar to one another?

4. Why do you think insurance crimes occur?

5. Do you think you have ever been overcharged by an auto mechanic? If so, why do you think the offense occurred?

6. Do you know anyone who has committed retail theft? Why do you think they committed the offense?

WEB RESOURCES

Prevent Home Repair Fraud: http://www.hbaa.org/remodeling/prevent-home-repair-fraud.html

Coalition Against Insurance Fraud: http://www.insurancefraud.org/scam_alerts.htm

Avoid Student Insurance Scams: http://www.studentfinancedomain.com/budgets/avoid_student_insurance_scams.aspx

READING

In this article, Diane Vaughan and Giovanna Carlo describe the results of a study they did involving interviews with 157 victims of a fraudulent appliance repair person. The authors provide a general overview of the white-collar offender and briefly describe how the case was resolved. Dividing their sample of victims into those who reported the victimization and those who did not, Vaughan and Carlo focused on the dynamics surrounding the business transaction, the complaint patterns, the experiences of the victims, and victim responsiveness. Particular attention was given to the fact that several victims reported their victimization on multiple occasions to the authorities. The authors note how the notion of "trust" related to the offenses, and attention is given to factors that make it difficult for victims to follow through with their complaints. The authors also highlight the need for official agencies to maintain contact with victims in order to build the public's faith in those formal agencies of social control charged with responding to white-collar crime.

The Appliance Repairman

A Study of Victim-Responsiveness and Fraud

Diane Vaughan and Giovanna Carlo

In mid-1973, Frank Hanks (not his true name), an appliance repairman, was indicted on four counts of larceny by trick. Larceny by trick, 2907.21, Ohio Rev. Code (1953), is defined as follows:

No person shall obtain possession of, or title to anything of value with the consent of the person from whom he obtained it, provided he induced such consent by false or fraudulent representation, pretense, token, or writing.

Whoever violates this section is guilty of larceny by trick, and, if the value of the thing so obtained is sixty dollars or more, shall be imprisoned not less than one nor more than seven years. If the value is less than sixty dollars, such person shall be fined not more than three hundred dollars or imprisoned not more than ninety days, or both.

The case against Hanks was developed by the Economic Crime Unit of the County Prosecutor's office,[1] on the basis of four customer complaints turned over to that unit by the Better Business Bureau. In the Court of Common Pleas, Frank Hanks later pled guilty to one misdemeanor. Three felony charges were dropped. He was sentenced to be imprisoned in the county jail for 90 days and was fined $300. Both were suspended conditionally, upon good behavior for one year. Restitution was to be made on all four counts within eight weeks.

The background and modus operandi of the offender show a unique biography. Frank Hanks is about forty-nine years old, white, married, and the father of eight children. He has an eleventh-grade education. He operates Frank's Appliance Repair Service out of the small family home, which is readily identified by a backyard filled with used washers. His quarter-page ad in the yellow pages emphasizes service to all brands of machines, sale of used appliances, low service charges, and service calls on Sunday. He has also advertised in the neighborhood newspaper. The name of the business has been changed four times since Hanks started the appliance repair service in 1969.

Hanks makes his calls in an old station wagon, frequently with one or two of his sons accompanying him as helpers. He invariably requests money in advance, usually saying that it is needed to buy parts. He overcharges for parts and several complaints allege that he was supposed to install new parts but failed to do so. Frequently he either replaced nothing or the replacement part was old but painted to look new. Occasionally he has been reported to have taken a deposit or removed a part and never been heard from again.

SOURCE: Vaughan, Diane & Carlo, Giovanna. (1975). The Appliance Repairman: A Study of Victim-Responsiveness and Fraud. *Journal of Research in Crime and Delinquency, 12*, 153–161. Copyright © SAGE, Inc.

[1]The Economic Crime Unit referred to here is a part of the National District Attorneys' Association Economic Crime Project, which created special units for the prosecution of economic crime in fifteen cities across the country. Financial support for this project came from the Law Enforcement Assistant Administration of the United States Department of Justice.

He sells used appliances, offers guarantees, and many complaints allege that these used appliances do not work and that he does not honor his guarantees. One complaint states he represented a used washer as being only two years old, when it was, in fact, six years old. He presents his victims with a small print contract, which he variously represents as a bill, a receipt, or a work contract. In signing it, the customer agrees to:

1. leave it to the discretion of the repairman whether new, used, rebuilt, or any parts are to be used, unless the customer states preference beforehand,

2. give said company a surety deposit upon request when ordering parts or before work is done,

3. not stop payment on any checks or money made payable to the company,

4. not complain to the Better Business Bureau or any other agency; also, not to sue the company or bring said company to a court of law for judgment or try to retrieve any money for any reason.

Hanks's techniques are anything but subtle. Yet he has managed to operate a business in this manner for five years. Who are the people who become his victims, how have the business transactions occurred, and what have been the effects?

⊠ The Study

Though victimology is a rapidly expanding interest area, the subject of victims of economic crime has scarcely been addressed. A notable exception is Gilbert Geis, who suggests that extensive study of victims may reveal regularities which could increase our understanding of victimization by white-collar criminals and possibly then be related to programs of social action. Such victim studies could explore the possibility of the existence of "victim-responsiveness"[2]—sociodemographic and personality variables that characterize victims particularly susceptible to economic exploitation.

The prosecution of Frank Hanks on four counts of larceny by trick was followed by a newspaper article about the indictment and the restitution due the victims. Twenty more victims, having seen the article, notified the Economic Crime Unit, bringing the total known to 24.

The sample of four victims who had formally complained and the twenty who complained only after seeing the newspaper article presented an opportunity for an in-depth study of complaining and non-complaining victims of consumer fraud. At the outset, the four existing consumer complaint agencies in the city were contacted to see whether other victims of the appliance repairman could be identified.[3] An additional 133 were found to have complained about Hanks to consumer agencies over a five-year period.

The research design was enlarged to include interviews of all victims (n = 157) and a comparison sample, drawn from ten houses away from each victim's address, to control for socioeconomic status. Some of the victims could not be located. The final sample consisted of 88 victims who had identified themselves to some agency, and a comparison group of 92.

The intent of the research was to gather descriptive details concerning the interaction between the offender and his victims. Further, the victim and comparison groups were examined to investigate the possible existence of victim-responsiveness. Finally, the two groups were compared on past victimization, reporting, and attitudes toward crime.[4]

---

[2]Geis, Gilbert, "White-Collar Crime," in *Victimology*, Volume V, Exploiters and Exploited: Dynamics of Victimization, I. Drapkin and E. Viano, eds. (Lexington, Mass.: Lexington Books, D. C. Heath, 1975), pp. 89-105.

[3]The consumer complaint agencies in this city are: the Better Business Bureau, the State Division of Consumer Protection, the Economic Crime Unit of the County Prosecutor's Office, and the Division of Weights and Measures.

[4]To clarify the area under study, the appliance repair fraud discussed here falls into the category of consumer fraud, as delineated in Herbert Edelhertz, *The Nature, Impact and Prosecution of White-Collar Crime* (National Institute of Law Enforcement and Criminal Justice, Washington, D.C.: U.S. Government Printing Office, May, 1970): "Crimes incidental to and in furtherance of business operations, but not the central purpose of the business" (p. 20).

⊠ The Victims

The Business Transaction

Typically, the transactions with Hanks were customer-initiated. Of the eighty-eight victims interviewed, seventy-seven contacted Hanks for service because they saw his advertisement, in either the newspaper or the yellow pages. A few called him at the recommendation of a friend, a matter which would seem to indicate either that Hanks occasionally does an acceptable job or that the individuals who recommended him did not realize they had been cheated. Reasons given for calling this particular serviceman were that he had a low service charge, that he could come immediately, or that the customer preferred to deal with someone in his own neighborhood rather than with a large company. Most frequently, the customer believed he was in desperate need for immediate service.

Seventy-three of the victim group, 83 per cent, were female. Thirty-four of these women were housewives, the rest being employed outside the home. Seventy-nine and one-half per cent of the victim sample were married. The largest percentage of the group was in the 31-to-40 age category, with 78 per cent of the victims having a high school education or better. Family social status, based on the occupation of the head of the house, was 55 per cent white collar and 45 per cent blue collar.[5]

In more than half the cases, the customer was alone in the house when the service call was made. Of those who were alone, 41 per cent stated that they felt the result would have been different had someone been with them. All expressing this sentiment were women.

Most of the victims told us that they had either a negative impression or were uncertain about Hanks from the time he first came to the door. He was not dressed in a uniform, but wore old clothes that were usually soiled. Frequently, he was reported to be unshaven, and occasionally he had alcohol on his breath. The fact that he brought a child with him to help

service the appliances was disturbing to many, but nevertheless, few of the victims even questioned the situation at the time. In some cases, the victims reported Hanks's young teen-age son (estimated to be from thirteen to seventeen years old) went to the basement to service the appliance while Hanks himself remained upstairs talking to the customer.

When in the customers' homes, Hanks variously was reported to be either friendly and folksy, or outspoken and rude. One woman said he had alluded several times to the attractiveness of her 83-year-old mother's legs. He also was reported to have made personal calls from the customers' phones without asking their permission.

Realization that they had been cheated came to the victims in all cases only after the fact. For many, recognition came upon reading the signed work contract after Hanks had gone. For others, it came when they later tried their appliance and found it did not work.

Complaint Patterns

There were four ways in which the victims complained: phone inquiry, verbal complaint, written complaint, or legal action. A phone inquiry meant the consumer contacted an agency to inquire about the repairman's business practices. A verbal complaint meant the consumer described his complaint over the phone and requested some assistance from the agency to deal with the matter. If a verbal complaint was made, the caller was mailed a form to be completed. If the form was returned, the complaint was classified as a written complaint. If the victim took his complaint to the Small Claims Court or Common Pleas Court, the complaint was classed as taking a legal action.

Within the victim sample, forty-four (51.2%) made a phone inquiry. Twelve (14%) made a verbal complaint, twenty-two (25.6%) completed a written complaint, and eight (9.3%) took legal action.[6] Tabular analysis of type of victim complaint by relevant variables was limited by sample size. Nevertheless, some

---

[5]Index used was Alba M. Edwards' *Social-Economic Grouping of Occupations*.

[6]These percentages do not add to 100 per cent because in two cases there was no information obtained about type of victim complaint.

surprising facts appeared. The total loss of the victim group was $4,389.00 ($\overline{X}$ = $49.88). However, total amount of individual loss had no clear association with the type of complaint action taken.

As expected, those victims with the least amount of loss (none to $25) predominantly complained by phone inquiry (61.8%) and took no legal action. However, those falling in the highest loss category (greater than $76) also more frequently complained by phone inquiry than any other type. Analysis of type of victim complaint by sociodemographic variables revealed no associations greater than those which would occur by chance alone.

Victims were asked what they hoped would result from their complaint. Most said they complained to an official agency in order to protect others from the offender. Only 2 per cent said they complained in the hope the offender would be punished. Of those who complained to protect others from the offender, 58 per cent made phone inquiries. If getting their money back was the desired result, 79 per cent either filed a written complaint or took legal action. If the statements that most of the victims complained in order to "protect others from this man" are true, they indicate that moral responses took priority over financial loss.

"Getting Taken"

Amount of loss to the individual, however, remains an insufficient measure of the impact of the fraud upon the victims. Only the description of individual victim-offender interactions can begin to convey the effect of this appliance repairman.

In one case the victims were mother and daughter. The daughter had visited Hanks's home, inspected the used washers in the back yard, and was given a demonstration. She selected a washer to be delivered to her home. On her advice, her mother did the same. Neither received the washer they picked out, and neither of the washers that were delivered worked.

Still another victim reported that Hanks had delivered a used washer to her kitchen when she was not home. She was unable to reach him to move it to the basement. In testing it, oil from the machine ruined her clothes and water flowed all over the floor. She had paid Hanks in cash before the delivery. She called an attorney to garnishee Hanks's wages, but found he was self-employed. The attorney filed a lien against Hanks's property, but found all his property was in his wife's name. In frustration, the victim sent Hanks a notice she was charging him two dollars a day for storage of the machine. A year later she had received no payment and still had the idle washer in her kitchen.

One victim stated that he himself completed the repairs Hanks had started. In his written complaint, he noted the following conditions existed:

1. Motor on dryer was loose and two of four bolts holding the motor were missing.

2. Back of dryer was loose and six of ten screws holding the back were missing.

3. Electric wires were exposed. Safety plate to cover electric wires was lying on the floor.

4. Dryer vent was not on dryer. It was lying on the floor.

5. There was questionable evidence of a new blower. Hanks's charge for the blower was $48.85 (estimated price at local supply company was $9.68).

Unethical personal practices are:

1. Hanks brought a small child (four years old) and let him run loose in the house. I witnessed the child put screws from the dryer into the washer.

2. Hanks brought a dog which he let loose on my property. It urinated in the garage and had to be cleaned up by my wife.

3. Refrigerator next to the dryer was left unplugged. The food in the refrigerator thawed.

4. When Hanks told my wife he wanted $58.35 in addition to the $10.00 deposit, she called me at work. I talked to Hanks and told him the bill was too high, more than our agreement, and

refused to O.K. payment until I could inspect the repairs. He hung up fast and told my wife that I said for her to pay him the additional $58.35, which she did. When I arrived home and saw the unfinished repair, I attempted to call Hanks with no results. I further attempted to stop payment on the check. My bank informed me the check was cashed within an hour from the time of writing.

Clearly, the efforts of the appliance repairman to deceive his victims were matched at times by some degree of self-deception, carelessness, and desire for gain on the part of the victims themselves. Nearly two-thirds of those interviewed admitted there were steps they could have taken to prevent the fraud.

Despite the cues from Hanks's personal appearance and behavior that warned of disreputability, victims stated they were reassured of his legitimacy by the printed word. His large ad in the yellow pages, his printed business cards, and his work contract all increased his credibility in the face of sometimes overwhelming evidence to the contrary. Many victims expressed the feeling that their lack of knowledge about appliances gave them no grounds on which to challenge Hanks or his work.

One of Hanks's customers was an attorney whose wife worked for the Division of Consumer Protection. When the service call was made, only the housekeeper was present. The attorney tried to stop payment on his check, but it already had been cashed. Finally contacting Hanks by phone, the attorney threatened him with legal action. Hanks then filed formal charges of malicious prosecution (using the profession for personal gain) against the attorney, who was forced to defend himself before the bar association.

In open-ended questions in the victim interviews, the respondents repeatedly expressed their indignation at being cheated and their frustration at being unable to get satisfaction from the offender, or from any place else. One family complained many times to the offender and got no satisfaction. They complained to the Better Business Bureau, and the Division of Consumer Protection, and finally took their case to the Small Claims Court. They received judgment but it was not honored. Garnishment was futile.

They then took the judgment to the debtor's court, and acting as their own attorneys, confronted the offender before a judge. Hanks claimed no money and no assets. The victims had to pay court costs, which then doubled the amount of their loss. Pursuing justice became more expensive than being a victim and they dropped the matter. This family expended every possible effort to get a settlement from the offender, short of hiring a lawyer. Yet they received no satisfaction.

Victim-Responsiveness

To explore the possible existence of victim-responsiveness, as suggested by Geis, victim and comparison groups were compared on all relevant variables. The findings revealed no significant differences in sociodemographic or personality variables.[7] Both groups were compared to assess impact of the victimization by measuring attitudes toward seriousness of white-collar crime and street crime. Again, no significant differences between groups appeared. Finally, both groups

---

[7]In examining personality dimensions of the victim sample, we tried to be sensitive to the feelings of the interviewees. We were interviewing them in their homes about a topic which was embarrassing to them. We wanted some simple measures that would be neither time-consuming nor offensive. Srole's Anomia Scale and a self-perception test were used. The Self-Perception test was patterned after Osgood's Semantic Differential. The respondents were presented with ten sets of adjectives, opposite in meaning, that indicated personal characteristics, such as "quiet-active, dominant-submissive, spender-saver, suspicious-trusting, careless-precise." The adjectives chosen were meant to provide extremes of choice in victim and non-victim characteristics. The interviewees were asked to check a point between each pair of words that they felt best described them as they saw themselves, on a seven-point scale. The higher the score, the greater the victim-responsiveness. On the Self-Perception test, the victim group scores showed a normal distribution on the seven point continuum. On the Srole Anomia Scale, the victim sample scores were evenly distributed, except for the highest alienation category which described only six of the 88 respondents. These measures were used for exploratory purposes and are admittedly simplistic.

were compared on the frequency of past victimization and reporting of crime. Both samples showed similar histories of victimization by consumer fraud and by street crime.

The findings showed the only differences between the two groups were in the extent to which formal complaints had been made for past victimizations. The victim group reported with greater frequency for both types of crime than did the comparison group, street crime being reported more frequently than fraud (71% to 32% of the incidents reported). Since the victim sample was composed entirely of people who had identified themselves by complaining to official agencies, the fact that they had a previous history of reporting was not surprising.[8]

✗ Implications

The findings from this case study are limited by the fact that the information gained applies to one type of fraud, perpetrated by one offender, in one particular neighborhood. The sample is small, making generalizations hazardous. These data should be compared with another victim group available in the same section of town, or a victim group in a similar section for an entirely different type of fraud. Comparison of the victim group with a randomly selected sample also would be informative.

The major limitation is the uniqueness of the victim sample. All were individuals who made official complaints about their victimization. To attempt any more definitive conclusions pertaining to the victim-selection process in this particular case would necessitate a sample consisting not only of complaining victims, but of those who were cheated and did not make a complaint, those who were cheated and didn't

realize they were victims, plus those who actually had legitimate dealings with the offender. Therefore, even though no characteristics indicating victim-responsiveness were found, the relevance of personality and sociodemographic variables for identifying victim-proneness cannot yet be discounted. Victims may exist who would evidence characteristics of victim-responsiveness, as Geis suggested.

The fact that the victims in this study admitted insufficient knowledge with which to challenge the appliance repairman suggests the importance of structural elements in understanding victim-responsiveness in cases of fraud. In a rapidly diversifying, specialized world, we are forced to trust strangers to meet many of our needs. The consumer must buy knowledge, and accurately assessing the value of the information he receives would necessitate further cost—in time, energy, and money. In the case of appliance repair, the consumer purchases information and service from the same source. The quality of the information cannot be judged until after the repair. Darby and Karni state, "fraud and related practices follow from significant costs in the determination of quality of a particular good or service."[9] As the victim relies on the expert knowledge of the perpetrator, so the offender relies on the ignorance and acquiescence of the victim.[10]

The similarity between victim and comparison groups on past victimization by consumer fraud seems to offer support for a structural explanation. The necessity of trusting strangers makes us all susceptible to economic exploitation. In a society where everyone is a potential victim, the findings of this study have serious implications for the issue of prevention of white-collar crime victimization.

Though over three-quarters of the complaining victims had a high school education or better, very few

[8]For detailed information on previous consumer fraud victimization and past reporting history of both the victim and the comparison groups in this study, see Vaughan, Diane, and Giovanna Carlo, "Victims of Fraud: Victim-Responsiveness, Incidence, and Reporting," in Viano, Emilio, ed., *Victims, Criminals and Society* (A. W. Sijthoff, Leiden, The Netherlands: forthcoming, 1976).

[9]Darby, Michael R., and Karni, Edi, "Free Competition and the Optimal Amount of Fraud," *Journal of Law and Economics*, Volume 16, Number 1, April, 1973, pp. 67-87.

[10]Edelhertz, op. cit., pp. 12-18.

took legal action. For most, the complaint action seemed to be an end in itself, rather than a means to an end. Furthermore, it must be noted that complaints were made primarily to agencies with no legal clout. Victims who tried actively to get satisfaction themselves met with repeated failure. Of the 157 victims who identified themselves to official agencies over a five-year period, only eight are known to have taken legal action against the offender.

The victims in this study failed to make a strong response to fraud victimization. This fact gains significance in view of the outcome of the appliance repairman's prosecution. Frank Hanks was given a suspended sentence, which was conditional upon good behavior and restitution in all four counts. He failed to make restitution by the prescribed date. His case was never followed up. Ironically, restitution was made three months after the deadline, a result not of the court's sentence but of this study. One of the complaining victims who was interviewed happened to be the wife of a friend of Hanks. Apparently he got word that he was being investigated, because within three days of that interview, restitution had been made to all four victims.

Frank Hanks has an eleventh-grade education. He does not fit Sutherland's definition of a white-collar criminal as a person of high social status.[11] Nevertheless, he has been cheating people in business dealings in the most obvious ways for many years, without the aid of a college degree, a New York lawyer, or a shredding machine. In addition, he is being investigated by a major department store chain for misrepresenting himself in advertising as one of their authorized servicemen. He is being pursued by the zoning board for operating a commercial business in a residential area. He is being investigated for welfare fraud. He has never filed a sales tax return. Since the prosecution, he has opened a store where he sells used appliances.

These facts have relevance not only for the security and integrity of the victims, but for the ongoing efforts of criminologists, prosecutors, consumer protection and regulatory agencies. The diffusion of complaints among several complaint agencies, the ineffective methods by which these victims chose to complain, and the difficulty of law enforcement in this type of crime serve to encourage its continuance. The mechanisms in existence for protecting the public against the type of white-collar crime victimization studied here seem to operate in a self-defeating manner. For many victims in this study, the contact with the interviewer was the only response their complaint received. Considering that many do not recognize their own victimization, it appears essential that complaints that do emerge receive official recognition. Public belief in the effectiveness of complaint agencies and law enforcement efficiency seems a necessary prerequisite to control of white-collar crime victimization.

DISCUSSION QUESTIONS

1. How might these offenses be different in today's world?

2. How were various systems involved in the response to Frank Hanks?

3. What criminal justice penalties do you think would have been appropriate for Hanks?

4. In what ways are fraud victims different from victims of traditional crimes?

---

[11]Sutherland, Edwin H., *White Collar Crime* (Dryden Press, 1949), p. 9.

READING

In this article, Richard Ghiselli and Joseph Ismail describe a study they conducted that focused on crimes committed in commercial food service occupations. The authors point to several factors that potentially increase the amount of crime that occurs in the restaurant industry and discuss these offenses within the framework of employee deviance. The authors surveyed 103 restaurant workers to examine the types of crimes committed by the employees, the characteristics of offenders, and the types of prevention strategies that appear to be most effective. They found that theft of food was the most common type of theft and that males and younger employees were more likely to engage in employee deviance.

Employee Theft and Efficacy of Certain Control Procedures in Commercial Food Service Operations

Richard Ghiselli and Joseph A. Ismail

The importance of reducing or eliminating aberrant employee behavior in the restaurant industry cannot be understated. Many restaurants are relatively small, independent operations, and profit margins are oftentimes meager (Chapdelaine, 1995; National Restaurant Association [NRA] 1990, 1991, 1992, 1993, 1994, 1995, 1996). Theft alone has been estimated to cost the industry as much as $0.04 per dollar in sales (Sherer, 1989; see also Ghiselli & Ismail, 1995; "44% of Foodservice," 1996). At this level, theft certainly would be crippling, if not fatal, to most restaurants.

Studies have shown that, generally, men are more likely to engage in deviant or delinquent behavior, that this type of conduct peaks as individuals approach (legal) adulthood, and that an erratic work history indicates a greater likelihood in young individuals/employees to behave inappropriately (Farrington, 1988; Hirschi & Gottfredson, 1988). In the workplace, studies have linked three factors with employee deviance: the employee's age, the length of tenure with the firm, and the perceptions of employer fairness/unfairness (Hefter, 1986; Hollinger, Slora, & Terns, 1992; Pauly, 1983). Specifically, younger employees are more likely to display certain aberrant behaviors or become involved in certain types of unacceptable activities, employees who have not been with an organization long and have not developed a satisfying relationship or commitment to the organization may engage in certain deviant acts, and employees who perceive inequitable treatment may engage in certain inappropriate acts. Other factors that may also contribute to employee deviance or unreliability include the organizational climate and the opportunities that are available

SOURCE: Ghiselli, Richard, & Ismail, Joseph A. (1998). Employee Theft and Efficacy of Certain Control Procedures in Commercial Food Service Operations. *Journal of Hospitality and Tourism Research, 22*(2), 174-187. Published by SAGE, Inc., on behalf of the International Council on Hotel, Restaurant, and Institutional Education.

(Caudill, 1988; Geller, 1991; Hefter, 1986; Kamp & Brooks, 1991; Sherer, 1989; Slora, 1989). Given these relationships, the food service industry, in particular the restaurant segment, is clearly ripe for employee malfeasance.

Restaurateurs and food service operators rely heavily on young workers for their labor supply: 29% of the workforce is between 16 and 20 years of age, and almost 60% is 29 years or younger (Bureau of Labor Statistics [BLS], 1992a). Not only is the labor force young; it is oftentimes unskilled: According to the BLS (1992a), "very few jobs . . . require any education or formal training after high school" (see also BLS, 1992b). Perhaps as a result, wages in the industry are relatively low: In 1996, workers in eating and drinking places (SIC 58) earned on average $5.79 per hour, whereas the average for all private industry (nonfarm) employees was $11.76 per hour (BLS, 1996). There are also a number of situational factors or conditions that may not promote commitment to, and/or dependability on, an organization. For example, many food service workers are part-time employees who may not become involved in the organization and develop some sense of attachment to it—their primary focus and/or sense of responsibility being elsewhere, such as home, school, a full-time job. In 1990, 36% of the labor force in food service worked less than 30 hours per week (BLS, 1992a). Also, work schedules may be undesirable—often including evenings, weekends, and holidays. There are other factors intrinsic to the industry and the jobs that may drive employee deviance as well. Perhaps the most important of these is that employees have ready access to cash and/or merchandise.

Because of its nature, the effects of employee deviance are difficult to measure. Nevertheless, employee deviance and, in particular, employee theft have been presumed to be a substantial cost of doing business and have been blamed for close to one third of business failures (Caudill, 1988; Hefter, 1986; Madlin, 1986; Pauly, 1983; Sherer, 1989). Employee deviance and theft seem to be quite prevalent in many industries. In manufacturing, 26% to 28% of employees admitted to stealing from their employers (Hollinger & Clark, 1983; Sherer, 1989). In other settings, the situation was as follows:

- One third of office and plant workers have stolen from their employers (Madlin, 1986).
- One third of hospital employees admitted that they have been involved in some type of property theft (Hollinger & Clark, 1983).
- The most common form of theft was to remove hospital supplies: 27% admitted to this behavior.
- In retail, the number of employees reportedly engaging in theft has ranged from 30% (Kamp & Brooks, 1991) to 42% (Sherer, 1989). Hollinger and Clark (1983) reported that 35% of retail employees were involved in theft-related activities.

Kamp and Brooks (1991) found that 30% of retail employees admitted to taking merchandise or property without permission, and 9% admitted to removing cash; in all, about one third of the respondents admitted to stealing from their employer.

- In supermarkets, 27% of the employees admitted to removing cash or property, and 39% indicated they had indirectly supported theft by knowingly not reacting to theft by others (Slora, 1989).

In fast-food restaurants, base rates for certain types of unacceptable employee behavior have been determined (Slora, 1989). In this setting, 62% of all respondents indicated they had stolen either cash or property—including eating food that had not been provided by management (Slora, 1989). Also, 53% indicated they had indirectly supported theft by knowingly not reacting to theft by others, and more than 75% of all respondents admitted they had wasted or misused their employers' time or were counterproductive in some other way (Slora, 1989).

In a study of theft by waiters in "dinner house" restaurants, as many as 45% were involved in activities such as providing free food to friends and taking home restaurant items (Hawkins, 1984). In addition, a majority of waiters indicated they knew of others who were involved in other unacceptable activities.

More recently, 44% of restaurant employees admitted to stealing supplies, merchandise, or cash—including food—on a regular basis ("44% of foodservice," 1996).

Annually, this behavior has been estimated to cost $113.46 (per employee). This quantity is considerably less than the NRA's estimate of 4 cents per dollar in sales (Sherer, 1989) and is about 1½ × higher than the amount based on owners' and managers' estimates (Ghiselli & Ismail, 1995).

There have been a limited number of research studies that have examined employee theft in food service settings. One reason for this may be the difficulties associated with collecting incidence data based on self-reports (see Murphy, 1993). Another may be peculiar to food service; namely, the inability to determine amounts. This is due to the difficulty of separating "losses" ascribable to employee error, waste, and spoilage from those related to theft. The purpose of this study was to further explore employee deviance and theft in food service operations, and to examine in a limited number of settings the efficacy of certain managerial policies and procedures in reducing or preventing the incidence of theft as reported by employees.

 Methodology

In a previous study, food service operators in Indiana were asked to identify company policies regarding unacceptable employee behaviors and about operational practices being used to reduce the opportunity for employee deviance (Ghiselli & Ismail, 1995). They were also asked about the dismissals resulting from inappropriate workplace behaviors and about losses resulting from employee theft. From this pool of respondents potential participants for this (second) study were identified. Except for one, the potential participants were selected from those who estimated their losses to be in the upper quartile.

Ten food service companies were sent a letter explaining the study and requesting their participation; these companies were also contacted by phone. Further conversations explained the purpose and details more fully. Eight of the 10 companies that were contacted agreed to participate; eventually, 7 were included. Four of the 7 were independent food service operations; the other 3 were part of multiunit corporations. All but 1 of the participants had two or more units. In two of the multiunit corporations the stores were company-owned, and the other multiunit corporation was a franchise-independent food service operation. In total, 18 restaurants were involved, and enough questionnaires provided for all of the employees. The restaurants were located in Indiana.

The managers were asked to distribute the questionnaires and post a notice from the researchers on the employee bulletin board explaining the study. A description of the study was also included with the questionnaires to the employees. Postage-paid return envelopes were provided with the questionnaires, and the participants were asked to return the completed questionnaire directly to the researchers. The managers were asked to post another notice about 10 days later. Because some of the information that was requested was of a very personal nature, efforts were made to safeguard the privacy and anonymity of the respondents. (Although follow-up interviews with the respondents would have enriched the data, the researchers felt the respondents would have been reluctant to participate if complete anonymity was not guaranteed.)

The employees were asked to quantify their behaviors. Specifically, they were asked to be as precise as possible when indicating the frequency of their actions. They were also asked to indicate the extent that other employees engaged in certain activities. The data were analyzed primarily by gender, age, and position within the operation (front of the house, back of the house). Statistical analyses were performed using Excel© and SAS© statistical software.

 Results

Altogether, 103 surveys were returned. Assuming the managers distributed all of the questionnaires, this represents a response rate of 11.4% (105/924). On a per store basis, the response rate varied from a low of 6.7% to a high of 30%.

Profile of Respondents

Overall, 65.7% of the respondents were female and 34.3% were male. The age of the respondents ranged from 15 to 62 years; the average was 25.5 years. By gender, men were slightly older than women: The average age for men was 26.5 years; for women, 23.5 years. Almost one third of the respondents were 20 years old or younger (31.3%), and 73.7% were younger than 29.

More than half of the respondents (53%) had worked for their employer less than a year, with 35% having worked 6 months or less. Conversely, almost one quarter of the respondents had been employed for more than 2 years, with over half of these more than 3 years. Whereas the majority of respondents (55.1%) worked more than 30 hours per week, 44.9% worked 30 hours or less.

Theft of Property

The most prevalent type of theft was eating company food. After that, the most prevalent form was providing food and beverage to friends free of charge—almost 40% of the employees indicated they had done this. The next most common methods were selling merchandise at reduced prices and removing property for personal use.

More than half (53.5%) of the respondents indicated they had engaged in some type of property theft. That is, they either removed money or property for personal consumption or gain or provided property to others that was not theirs to administer. When eating company food is included, almost three fourths (73.5%) indicated they were involved in some form of (property) theft.

Theft by Gender

Generally, a greater percentage of men admitted involvement in theft-related activities or behaviors. Nevertheless, a slightly larger percentage of women indicated they took tips that belonged to other employees, added extra amounts to a customer's bill, and added or increased tips on credit sales. None of these three behaviors, however, were widespread (see Table 3.1).

Table 3.1   Incidence Data for Certain Theft Activities by Gender

Percentage of Respondents Who Admitted That They	Overall	Male	Female
Provided food and beverage free of charge to friends	38.8	50.0*	32.8
Sold merchandise at reduced prices to friends	20.2	32.3	13.8
Helped others to take merchandise or property	6.1	14.7*	1.5
Issued refunds for items not purchased	1.1	2.9	0.0
Took or sold company supplies or equipment	6.1	11.8	3.1
Removed food or beverage items from inventory for personal use	15.2	32.4*	6.2
Took money from the register	2.0	5.9	0.0
Took tips or money that belonged to other employees	4.1	3.0	4.6
Took money by not reporting or ringing all sales on the register	13.1	23.5	7.7
Took money by adding extra amounts to a customer's bill	3.0	2.9	3.1
Took money by shortchanging customers	4.0	5.9	3.1
Took money by adding or increasing tips on credit sales	1.0	0.0	1.5
Ate company food without permission	55.1	64.7*	50.0

*Significant differences were detected in the frequencies between male and female respondents at the $\alpha = .05$ level.

When the frequencies of male and female participation were compared, differences were detected. In particular, men were significantly more likely to provide food and beverages free of charge to friends ($\chi^2_{(3)} = 10.22, p < .05$), to help others take merchandise or property ($\chi^2_{(3)} = 6.95, p < .05$), to remove food and/or beverage items from inventory for personal use ($\chi^2_{(3)} = 13.64, p < .05$), and to eat company food without permission ($\chi^2_{(3)} = 11.52, p < .05$).

Theft by Age

Aside from eating company food, the most prevalent form of theft regardless of age was providing food and beverage items free of charge to friends. As a group, however, the oldest employees were least likely to engage in most theft-related activities. The youngest employees were more likely to help others to take merchandise or property, and to engage in activities that represented theft directly from the customer or other employees (as opposed to the business). The middle group participated at a higher rate in all other theft-related activities but was not inclined to engage in activities that involved other employees or customers (see Table 3.2).

A composite value was calculated for each employee indicating the frequency that he or she was likely to engage in the theft-related activities. The value was computed by summing the values that were assigned to the frequencies whereby the respondents indicated their involvement: the greater the frequency, the higher the value. All activities *except* eating company food without permission were included. This behavior was not included because of its prevalence and because food service managers were not definitive in their sentiment or response to it (see Ghiselli &

Table 3.2 Incidence Data for Certain Theft-Related Activities by Age

Percentage of Respondents Who Admitted That They	Age		
	≤ 20	21–29	> 29
Ate company food without permission	54.6	66.7	40.0
Provided food and beverage free of charge to friends	36.4	53.5	16.7
Sold merchandise at reduced prices to friends	18.2	30.2	4.0
Helped others to take merchandise or property	9.1	7.0	0.0
Issued refunds for items not purchased	0.0	2.3	0.0
Took or sold company supplies or equipment	6.1	7.0	8.0
Removed food or beverage items from inventory for personal use	18.2	20.9	4.0
Took money from the register	0.0	4.7	0.0
Took money by not reporting or ringing all sales on the register	9.1	23.3	0.0
Took tips or money that belonged to other employees	9.4	2.3	0.0
Took money by adding extra amounts to a customer's bill	6.1	2.3	0.0
Took money by shortchanging customers	12.2	0.0	0.0
Took money by adding or increasing tips on credit sales	3.0	0.0	0.0

Ismail, 1995). When correlated with age, the relationship was significant and negative, indicating that younger employees tended to engage in these activities more often than older employees ($r = -.20, p < .05$). Moreover, when the data were analyzed by gender, the relationship between age and theft remained the same for women ($r = -.26, p < .05$), but not for men, suggesting that participation in theft-related activities diminished for women as they got older, but not for men. The strength of these relationships, however, was relatively low.

Theft by Opportunity

The respondents were asked to indicate whether they were front-of-the-house (server, host, cashier) or back-of-the-house (cook, dishwasher, maintenance)

employees. Two thirds (66.3%) of the respondents were front-of-the-house employees, 15.8% were back-of-the-house employees, and 17.8% indicated they worked in both areas.

As might be expected, the employees tended to engage in theft-related activities that were more likely to be within the context of their job. That is, they were more likely to commit a form of theft where they perceived, from their vantage point, an opportunity. For example, front-of-the-house employees were more likely to provide food and beverage free of charge to friends, sell merchandise at reduced prices, and take money by not reporting or ringing sales on the register. Back-of-the-house employees, on the other hand, were more likely to take company supplies and remove food and beverage items from inventory (see Table 3.3).

Table 3.3   Incidence Data for Certain Theft Activities by Employee Location

Percentage of Respondents Who Admitted That They	Front of the House	Back of the House	Both
Provided food and beverage free of charge to friends	37.8	25.0	55.6
Sold merchandise at reduced prices to friends	19.4	6.3	33.3
Helped others to take merchandise or property	3.0	12.5	11.1
Issued refunds for items not purchased	1.5	0.0	0.0
Took or sold company supplies or equipment	1.5	31.25*	5.6
Removed food or beverage items from inventory for personal use	11.9	37.5*	11.9
Took money from the register	3.0	0.0	0.0
Took tips or money that belonged to other employees	3.0	0.0	11.8
Took money by not reporting or ringing all sales on the register	17.9	0.0	5.6
Took money by adding extra amounts to a customer's bill	3.0	0.0	5.6
Took money by shortchanging customers	4.5	0.0	5.6
Took money by adding or increasing tips on credit sales	1.5	0.0	0.0
Ate company food without permission	55.2	73.3	44.4

*Significant differences were detected in the frequencies between front-of-the-house and back-of-the-house employees at the $\alpha = .05$ level.

When employees who worked in both areas were eliminated from the analysis, significant differences were detected. In particular, back-of-the-house employees were more likely to take company supplies ($\chi^2_{(1)} = 17.05$, $p < .05$) and remove food and beverage items from inventory ($\chi^2_{(3)} = 8.48$, $p < .05$) than were front-of-the-house employees.

Theft by Others

The respondents were asked to indicate the prevalence of theft-related activities by other employees. Previous studies have suggested that there may be a tendency by respondents/employees to indicate that others are more actively involved than they are (Hawkins, 1984; Hollinger et al., 1992; Slora, 1989). This study had similar findings. *In every activity,* the respondents

indicated that other employees were more involved than they were. The extent to which other employees were perceived to be involved is shown in Table 3.4.

When just incidence is considered—regardless of frequency—others engaged in theft-related activities at a much higher rate than the respondents—in many cases 4 to 5 times the rate. Just as noteworthy, however, is the acknowledgment by many respondents that they do not know whether others are involved in these activities much of the time.

Discussion

In many instances the correlates of deviant behavior are based on, or relate to, the individual. For example, younger individuals/employees are more likely to engage in deviant behavior than older ones. There are

Table 3.4   Extent to Which Other Employees Were Perceived to Engage in Certain Theft-Related Activities by Respondents (in percentages)

Theft-Related Activities	Frequency				
	All the Time	Quite Often	Once in a While	Hardly Ever	Not Sure
Provided food and beverage free of charge to friends	5.4	10.9	35.9	8.7	39.1
Sold merchandise at reduced prices to friends	3.3	9.9	25.3	8.8	52.7
Helped others to take merchandise or property	1.1	4.4	6.7	20.0	67.8
Issued refunds for items not purchased	1.0	1.1	3.3	19.8	74.7
Took or sold company supplies or equipment	1.1	5.5	13.2	18.7	61.5
Removed food or beverage items from inventory for personal use	6.6	5.5	15.4	15.4	57.1
Took money from the register	0.0	2.2	4.4	24.2	69.2
Took tips or money that belonged to other employees	0.0	3.3	15.4	23.1	58.2
Took money by not reporting or ringing all sales on the register	1.1	2.2	12.2	12.2	72.2
Took money by adding extra amounts to a customer's bill	0.0	2.2	2.2	18.9	76.7
Took money by shortchanging customers	0.0	1.1	7.8	16.7	74.4
Took money by adding or increasing tips on credit sales	0.0	1.1	5.6	17.8	75.6
Ate company food without permission	29.7	17.6	11.0	5.5	36.3

other factors, however, that have been blamed or may contribute to employee deviance, most notably the bond between the individual and the organization, and the opportunities that are available. Although there were some minor differences, the findings of this study corroborated what had been found in previous studies. Some refinements, such as the target of employee theft, were detected.

Some of the policies and procedures designed to control and safeguard the assets of food service operations do not appear to be having the desired effect. This may be because the food service environment makes it difficult to follow company procedures exactly, because management has been lax in its efforts to control the problem, or because the costs exceed the benefits— that is, the perceived amounts are not large enough to trouble over.

Although much of the internal thievery in food service appears to be petty in nature when viewed individually or compared to other industries, it must be examined cumulatively and in context. In this light, it could undermine the overall goals of the business. Consequently, management must attempt to control it.

Yet, not all undesirable behaviors are malicious and may not need to be controlled—merely managed. Eating (company) food, for example, may be acceptable in many food service settings. As a result, applying a standard that does not match a (perceived) industry norm may be counterproductive if it prompts employees to express their displeasure in inappropriate ways. In this instance, operators may find it more useful to accept that food service employees will be eating (company) food, and they may use it as a marketing tool. Two possible approaches include developing an employee menu or giving employees a credit toward food for each hour worked. Regardless of the arrangement, employers must clearly define the parameters of the "perk."

Due, in part, to the nature of the work, the age of those who are likely to seek employment in food service is similar to the age of those who are likely to be involved in deviant or delinquent behaviors. These relatively young and/or adolescent unskilled workers provide the industry with a much-needed supply of labor.

Unfortunately, many of the jobs and conditions of employment neither may spur interest in the profession nor warrant loyalty to an organization. All too often these jobs are viewed as temporary. Moreover, profit margins are often too low to support wages at which employees do not feel underpaid or exploited, and feelings of servitude or indenture persist in the industry. Theft or other deviant behavior is easier to rationalize when these feelings linger.

Although relatively young and/or adolescent applicants/employees are more of a risk, they also offer many benefits. One is their youth: They are strong and vibrant—both very agreeable attributes in a labor-intensive and physically demanding industry. They are also malleable. Oftentimes they are entering the workforce for the first time. This experience may be one that helps temper or reduces the tendency to commit acts that employers and society deem unacceptable. Employers may want to consider ways in which they can be more involved in this process.

Employee theft can be devastating to a business. The effect may be more pronounced in food service where profit margins have averaged, depending on the segment, between 4% and 8% before taxes and in some years have been as low as 2.3%. At this time, unfortunately, the competitive environment may be too stringent to allow food service operators much flexibility with regard to pay and labor. Alas, the job requirements and skills as frequently structured may not warrant higher wages. Hence, employee theft that results from these deficiencies will persist.

Nevertheless, employers do not have to accept employee theft: The amount reportedly stolen by employees overall was more than twice that estimated by owners and managers. Even though they may not be able to eliminate it, they certainly may be able to reduce it. The selective use of security cameras is one approach. Another that was borne out in this study is the need for greater attention to order-processing procedures and tighter cash-handling procedures. Also, management must regularly review and revise the implementation of policies and procedures designed to reduce the opportunities for employee malfeasance. Finally, diligence and resolve will make it possible for management to safeguard the assets with which it has been entrusted and, at length, to generate the desired return on investment.

 # References

44% of foodservice employees stealing. (1996, May 15). *FoodService Director,* pp. 34, 36.

Bureau of Labor Statistics. (1992a). *Career guide to industries.* Washington, DC: Government Printing Office.

Bureau of Labor Statistics. (1992b). *Occupational outlook handbook* (Bulletin 2400). Baton Rouge, LA: Claitor's Publishing Division.

Bureau of Labor Statistics. (1996). Service occupations: Cleaning, food, health, and personal (Bulletin 2400-15). *Employment and Earnings, 43*(10), 10-13.

Caudill, D. W. (1988). How to recognize and deter employee theft. *Personnel Administrator, 33*(7), 86-88.

Chapdelaine, S. (1995). A road to the American Dream. *Restaurants USA, 15*(6), 42-45.

Farrington, D. P. (1988). Social, psychological, and biological influences on juvenile delinquency and adult crime. In W. Buikhusen & S. A. Mednick (Eds.), *Explaining criminal behavior* (pp. 68-88). Leiden, the Netherlands: E. J. Brill.

Geller, N, (1991). Rule out fraud and theft: Controlling your food-service operation. *The Cornell H.R.A. Quarterly, 32*(4), 55-65.

Ghiselli, R., & Ismail, J. (1995). Gauging employee theft and other unacceptable behaviors in food service operations. *FIU Hospitality Review, 13*(2), 15-24.

Hawkins, R. (1984). Forms of ripping off by waiters at work. *Deviant Behavior, 5,* 47-69.

Hefter, R. (1986). Employee theft: The crippling crime. *Security World,* March, 36-38.

Hirschi, T., & Gottfredson, M. (1988). Towards a general theory of crime. In W. Buikhusen & S. A. Mednick (Eds.), *Explaining criminal behavior* (pp. 8-26). Leiden, the Netherlands: E. J. Brill.

Hollinger, R. C., & Clark, J. P. (1983). *Theft by employees.* Lexington, MA: Lexington Books.

Hollinger, R. C., Slora, K. B., & Terns, W. (1992). Deviance in the fast-food restaurant: Correlates of employee theft, altruism, and counterproductivity. *Deviant Behavior, 13,* 155-184.

Kamp, J., & Brooks, P. (1991). Perceived organizational climate and employee counterproductivity. *Journal of Business and Psychology, 5*(4), 447-458.

Madlin, N. (1986, February). Crime and your business. *Venture,* p. 26.

Murphy, K. R. (1993). *Honesty in the workplace.* Pacific Grove, CA: Brooks/ Cole.

National Restaurant Association and Deloitte & Touche. (1991). *Restaurant industry operations report 1991.* Washington, DC: National Restaurant Association.

National Restaurant Association and Deloitte & Touche. (1992). *Restaurant industry operations report 1992.* Washington, DC: National Restaurant Association.

National Restaurant Association and Deloitte & Touche. (1993). *Restaurant industry operations report 1993.* Washington, DC: National Restaurant Association.

National Restaurant Association and Deloitte & Touche. (1994). *Restaurant industry operations report 1994.* Washington, DC: National Restaurant Association.

National Restaurant Association and Deloitte & Touche LLP. (1995). *Restaurant industry operations report 1995.* Washington, DC: National Restaurant Association.

National Restaurant Association and Deloitte & Touche LLP. (1996). *Restaurant industry operations report 1996.* Washington, DC: National Restaurant Association.

National Restaurant Association and Laventhol & Horwath. (1990). *Restaurant industry operations Report '90.* Washington, DC: National Restaurant Association.

Pauly, D. (1983, December 26). Stealing from the boss. *Newsweek, 102*(26), p. 78.

Sherer, M. (1989, April 3). Inside job. *Restaurants & Institutions, 99,* 38+.

Slora, K. B. (1989). An empirical approach to determining employee deviance base rates. *Journal of Business and Psychology, 4*(2), 199-219.

Sudman, S., & Bradburn, N. M. (1988). *Asking questions: A practical guide to questionnaire design.* San Francisco: Jossey-Bass.

DISCUSSION QUESTIONS

1. What do you think about the demographic (age and gender) differences described by the authors?

2. What does opportunity have to do with theft in the restaurant industry?

3. What can be done to reduce these crimes?

4. What do these crimes have to do with your own lives?

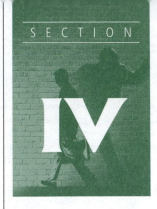

SECTION

IV

Crimes in the Health Care System

┌─────────────────────────────────┐
│ **Section Highlights**

- Fraud by Doctors
- Unnecessary Surgery
- Medication Errors
- General Offending by Doctors
- Fraud by Pharmacists
- Drug Use by Pharmacists
- Sexual Abuse
- Elder Abuse by Health Care Workers
- Home Health Care Fraud
- Medical Malpractice

Introduction

On June 25, 2009, the Internet collapsed momentarily as surfers searched for news about the death of Michael Jackson—an iconic pop star that many loved and many hated. While Jackson's death, on the surface, may seem to relate very little to white-collar crime, at the time of the writing of this book, it is significant that his doctor, Conrad Murray, was charged with involuntary manslaughter for giving Jackson a lethal dose of Propofol. Conrad administered the drug to Jackson to help him sleep. Instead, investigators believe that the drug killed the pop star. As will be shown later in this section, hundreds of thousands of others have died from medication errors.

It is not just Michael Jackson's doctor, however, who has been accused of misconduct in performing health care services. Consider the following cases as they were described verbatim from their original sources:

- Jeffrey H. Sloman, Acting United States Attorney for the Southern District of Florida, and Bill McCollum, Florida Attorney General, announced that two Miami doctors have been convicted of Medicare and Medicaid fraud.... [The defendants] were convicted for their involvement in a scheme with Diagnostic Medical Choice, a Southwest Miami clinic that billed the Medicaid and Medicare programs for expensive infusion medications intended to treat a rare illness suffered by a small portion of those inflicted with HIV/AIDS. The physicians wrote prescriptions for large quantities of these medications and sought federal and state reimbursement, but the clinic had little if any of the medications in stock and rarely if ever provided infusions to patients ("Two Miami Doctors," 2009).

▲ **Photo 4.1** Do you think Michael Jackson's death was caused by a white-collar crime?

- The Tennessee Bureau of Investigation announced on May 20 that ... a health care aide, pleaded guilty in district criminal court to one count of TennCare Fraud. Austin was given a two year suspended sentence and four years probation. Additionally, [the defendant] was ordered to pay restitution in the amount of $3,075 to the Bureau of TennCare. . . [The defendant], a personal assistant employed by United Cerebral Palsy, billed TennCare for services not rendered between June 2006 and June 2007. [She] submitted to her employer contact notes for services and upon investigation, it was discovered that the majority of these contacts never occurred (*Medicaid Fraud Reports*, 2009).

As this brief synopsis shows, health care employees from a range of health care occupations have been accused of wrongdoing. To shed some light on white-collar crime among these employees, in this section, attention is given to crimes committed by offenders working in the health care system. Five points about the health care system help to create a foundation from which insight about health care crimes will evolve:

- Most offenders in the health care system have specific training related to their occupations and some have advanced degrees.
- Individuals seek services from those in the health care system when they are in need of some form of medical care. This may create vulnerability for those seeking services.
- The health care system interacts with other systems. For example, changes in the educational and technological systems influence the type of health care provided. These broader changes also impact the types of crimes committed in the health care system.
- For the most part, citizens place a great deal of trust in health care providers, with a significant respect given to upper class members of both groups.
- The health care profession tends to self-regulate itself in an effort to promote appropriate conduct.

When we go to see our doctors, dentists, pharmacists, or other health care providers, most of us likely give little thought to the possibility that these professionals would engage in criminal actions. In fact, most of us likely assume that our health care providers would never even consider breaking their ethical code or the criminal law. For the most part, we are correct in this assumption because most health care providers do not commit occupational crimes. Some, however, do.

⬛ Fraud by Doctors

As Paul Jesilow and his colleagues (Jesilow, Pontell, & Geis, 1985) note, few criminal justice and criminology textbooks give a great deal of attention to crimes by doctors, "probably because of the respect, power, and trust that the profession engenders" (p. 151). Even Sutherland implied that doctors were unlikely to engage in white-collar crime, and as a result, Sutherland gave "only scant attention to doctors [and] maintained that physicians were probably more honest than other professionals" (Wilson, Lincoln, R., Chappell, D., & Fraser, 1986).

The level of trust that individuals place in doctors cannot be understated. Illustrating the trust that we have in the profession, one author team quoted an FBI agent who said to them, "What other stranger would you go in and take your clothes off in front of? It's that kind of trust?" (Pontell, Jesilow, & Geis, 1984, p. 406). While readers might be able to think of at least one other profession where "clients" remove all of their clothes in front of strangers, the other profession is an illegal profession in most places in the United States (except parts of Nevada). The medical profession is a legal profession that is plagued by illegal acts.

The most pervasive form of fraud committed by doctors entails the commission of Medicare and Medicaid fraud and abuse. Both medical programs were created in the mid-1960s. **Medicare** was created as a federal program to serve elderly citizens, while **Medicaid** operates at the state level to serve the poor. When Medicare and Medicaid were first created, there was no concern about fraud; instead, the concern was whether doctors would actually participate in the programs because Medicare and Medicaid faced opposition from the American Medical Association (Pontell et al., 1984).

In time, doctors increasingly participated in the insurance programs, and by the mid-1970s, authorities recognized that fraud was pervasive in Medicare and Medicaid. This pervasiveness continues today. It is estimated that between three and ten percent of health care spending is lost to fraud. This means that in the United States between $68 and 226 billion is lost to fraud each year (National Health Care Anti-Fraud Association, 2010). The NHCAA points out that the lower limit of these estimates is still "more than the gross domestic product of 120 different countries including Iceland, Ecuador, and Kenya." Incidentally, by 2019, it is expected that one fifth of the gross domestic product in the U.S. will entail health care spending (Center for Medicare and Medicaid Services, 2011).

Several varieties of misconduct are committed by doctors. At the broadest level, legal experts make a distinction between fraud and abuse. **Medical fraud** refers to intentionally criminal behaviors by physicians, whereas abuse focuses on unintentional misuse of program funds. If a doctor intentionally steals from Medicaid, this would be fraud. Alternatively, if a doctor accidentally over utilizes Medicaid services, this would be abuse. Note that authorities will respond to abuse cases as well in an effort to recoup lost funds. The distinction is significant because it predicts the types of justice systems that are likely to respond to the cases. In fraud cases, the criminal justice system will be involved, and criminal penalties such as incarceration, probation, and fines will be applied. In abuse cases, the civil justice system or other regulatory system will respond, and penalties will be monetary in nature. See In Focus 4.1, When Physicians Go Bad, for an overview of the way that a justice system got involved in a case involving a doctor who clearly and intentionally committed fraud, though he tried to blame his actions on others.

In Focus 4.1

When Physicians Go Bad

Physicians: District of Columbia

The District of Columbia Medicaid Fraud Control Unit announced on December 18 that Dr. *****, a medical doctor licensed in the District of Columbia, who practiced medicine under the name of *****, was found guilty on December 17 by a federal jury of one count of Health Care Fraud and sixteen counts of False Statements in Health Care Matters. ***** was already ordered to forfeit $133,418 of proceeds derived from the health care fraud conviction.

According to the government's evidence at trial, during the period between December 2002 and May 2005, ***** repeatedly submitted false claims to Amerigroup Corporation (Amerigroup), which contracted with the District of Columbia Medicaid Program to provide health care services to low income D.C. residents. *****, who prepared and submitted his own billing to Amerigroup, repeatedly submitted false claims in which he purported to have performed invasive surgical procedures on D.C. Medicaid patients that were never performed, billed for "ghost office" visits that never occurred, and continued to bill for a period of time after a minor or major procedure during which no additional bills could be submitted, in violation of global billing rules. To substantiate the false billing, ***** created false progress notes indicating the dates, times, and surgical procedures that he claimed to have performed, and inserted the false progress notes into his patients' medical files.

During the trial, the defense claimed that a now deceased individual was responsible for preparing and submitting the false claims to Amerigroup. The defense called two individuals currently employed by *****, who testified that the deceased individual was responsible for the false billing. In rebuttal, the government was able to establish that neither the deceased individual nor the defense witnesses worked for the defendant during the relevant time.

For further information contact Special Assistant U.S. Attorney Jacqueline Schesnol (202) 727-8008.

Within these broader categories, several specific forms of fraud and abuse exist (FBI, 2010b; Payne, 1995; Pontell, Jesilow, & Geis, 1984). **Phantom treatment** occurs when providers bill Medicare, Medicaid, or other insurance agencies for services they never actually provided. This is also known as fee-for-service reimbursement. **Substitute providers** occur when the medical services were performed by an employee who is not authorized to perform the services. **Upcoding** (or upgrading) refers to situations where providers bill for services that are more expensive than the services that were actually provided. The **provision of unnecessary services** occurs when health care providers perform and bill for tests or procedures that were not needed (just as auto mechanics might perform unnecessary repairs to our cars, so too do some doctors). **Misrepresenting services** occurs when providers describe the service differently on medical forms in an effort to gain payment for the services (e.g., elective surgeries might be defined as medically necessary). **Falsifying records** occurs when providers change medical forms in an effort to be reimbursed by the insurance provider. **Overcharging** patients refers to situations where providers charge patients more than regulations permit. **Unbundling** refers to instances when the provider bills separately for tests and procedures that are supposed to be billed as one procedure (imagine if you ordered a package meal and the restaurant tried to bill you for each type of food separately). **Pingponging** occurs when patients are unnecessarily referred to other providers and "bounced around" various medical providers. **Ganging** refers to situations where providers bill for multiple family members though they treated only one of them. **Kickbacks** occur when providers direct patients to other providers in exchange for a pecuniary response for the other provider. **Co-pay waivers** occur when providers waive the patient's co-pay but still bill the insurance company. **Medical snowballing** occurs when providers bill for several related services though only one service was provided.

These types of fraud occur with different degrees of regularity. Figure 4.1 shows the relative frequency of various types of Medicaid fraud by health care providers that were criminally prosecuted in a study of 572 cases of fraud by health care professionals. As shown in the figure, fee-for-service reimbursement cases were prosecuted most often, followed by upgrading. Unnecessary surgery cases were rarely prosecuted.

Several studies have considered different aspects of fraud by physicians. One consistent finding from these studies is that psychiatrists and psychologists are accused of fraud more often than other providers (Payne, 1995; Geis, Jesilow, Pontell, & O'Brien, 1982). Figure 4.2 shows the types of providers accused of fraud in the

Figure 4.1   Types of Fraudulent Acts Committed by Health Care Providers in Payne's (1995) Study

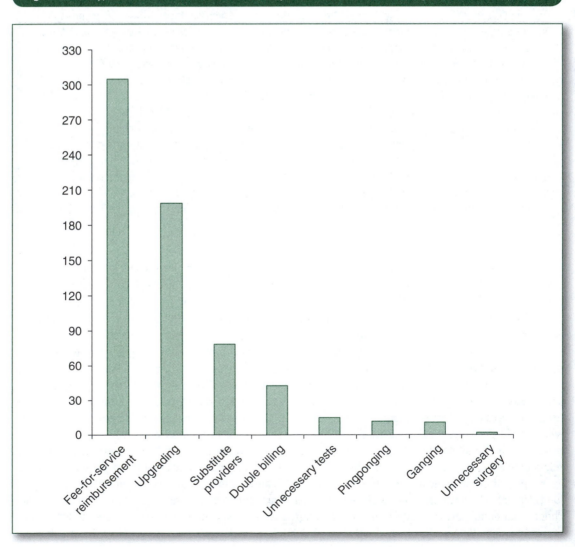

Payne (1995) study. It is striking that so many of the cases involved psychiatrists and psychologists—as compared to the number of psychiatrists and psychologists in the medical profession. Before assuming that their overrepresentation stems from levels of honesty, it is important to consider the nature of billing practices for psychiatrists and psychologists as compared to other health care professionals (Geis et al., 1982). Briefly, mental health professionals often bill for time, whereas other professionals bill for more complicated medical procedures. For investigators, it is much easier to prove "time violations" than "treatment violations." Investigators can ask patients how long they spent with their provider and compare the patient's statement with the providers' bill submitted to the insurance company. If investigators ask about the treatment they received from physicians, it is likely that the patient would be able to identify the services with the same degree of precision. As an illustration of the way that "time violations" are easy to identify, see In Focus 4.2, When Psychologists Go Bad Billing for Time.

Figure 4.2 Types of Providers Accused of Fraud and Abuse in Payne's (1995) Study

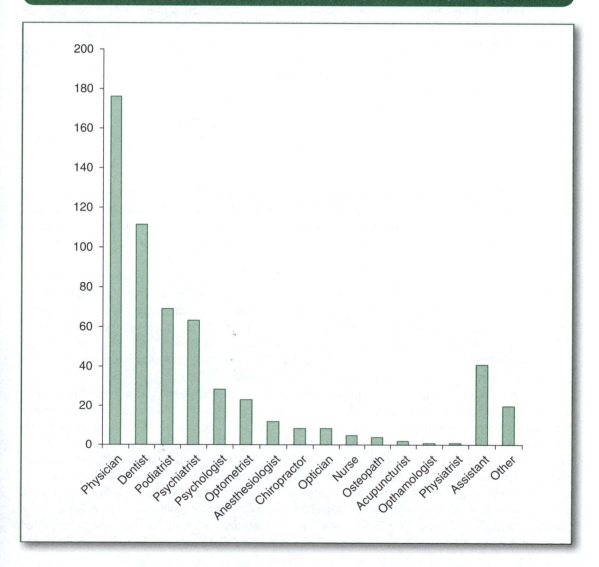

In Focus 4.2

When Psychologists Go Bad Billing for Time

The Tennessee Bureau of Investigation announced on April 20 that *****, a clinical psychologist, pleaded guilty in United States District Court of Middle Tennessee to one count of health care fraud. ***** was sentenced to serve 18 months in the custody of the United States Bureau of Prisons, to be followed by three years probation upon his release. Additionally, ***** was ordered to pay restitution in the amounts of $44,825.95 to the Centers for Medicare and Medicaid Services and $32,264.75 to the Bureau of TennCare. This case was opened on September 29, 2005 based upon a referral from the Department of Health and Human Services, Office of Inspector General. It was alleged that Dr. *****, a provider of psychological services for nursing homes and rehabilitation facilities, billed for services not rendered and overbilled for individual psychotherapy services. *An initial review of the data indicated that ***** billed 139 days in which the total time spent with the beneficiaries exceeded 24 hours per day.* Further investigation showed that over a 90 day period in 2005, ***** billed for 14 days on which he did not travel to a facility or perform psychotherapy services. ***** did travel to facilities on 28 of those days, however in many cases the amount of time billed exceeded the actual amount of time he was present at the facility. On January 27, 2007, Dr. ***** was charged with one count of health care fraud. (emphasis added)

For more information contact Special Agent Ramona Smith (615) 744-4229.

Other patterns characterizing health care fraud have also been identified in prior research. For example, research shows that when females are accused of health care fraud, they tend to be accused along with other providers more so than male offenders are (Payne, 1995). It is plausible that females are prosecuted along with more powerful providers in an effort to get female providers to testify against their colleagues, or in some cases, their bosses.

Another pattern surrounding health care fraud is related to the systems approach—changes in the broader system have influenced the distribution and characteristics of health care fraud (Payne, 2005). For example, as the nature of health care changes, so too does the nature of health care fraud. As the technological system changed, opportunities for health care fraud changed. As the number of doctors changed in the 1970s and 1980s (a period in which the number of doctors increased 66%), allegations of fraud and convictions for health care fraud also increased (Bucy, 1989). In fact, "convictions of health care providers increased almost 234 percent between 1979 and 1986" (Bucy, 1989, p. 870).

Explanations for fraud have focused on structural explanations, socialization factors, and enforcement dynamics. In terms of structural explanations, some have argued that the structure of the Medicare and Medicaid systems is believed to "invite fraud and abuse" (Pontell, Jesilow, & Geis, 1982). Low reimbursement rates, complex red tape, and bureaucratic confusion make participation in the programs difficult for health care providers. In order to get paid the same amount they get paid for treating patients with private insurance, some physicians and other health care providers have fraudulently billed Medicare and Medicaid.

Socialization explanations focus on how medical students perceive Medicaid and Medicare. In general, research shows that students have less than favorable attitudes toward the programs (Byars & Payne, 2000; Keenan, Brown, Pontell, & Geis, 1985). Surveys of 144 medical students found that the students supported tougher penalties for fraudulent providers, but they also believed that structural changes in Medicare and

Medicaid were warranted (Keenan et al., 1985). In effect, there is a possibility that medical students are learning to perceive the insurance programs negatively during their medical training.

Enforcement explanations suggest that the pervasiveness of fraud is attributed to the historical lack of criminal justice enforcement activities against health care providers. This changed in the 1990s when state and federal enforcement efforts in this area increased. Legislative changes also occurred. For example, the **Health Insurance Portability Act of 1996** was passed to make health care fraud a federal offense, with penalties ranging from 10 years to life (if the fraud leads to a death). Note that while physicians are held in high regard, when they violate their codes of conduct, the public reaction is more severe than when some one of lower status breaks the rules. Rosoff (1989) refers to this dynamic as status liability.

Unnecessary Surgery

As noted in the introduction of this text when the consequences of white-collar crime were addressed, it is estimated that 7.5 million unnecessary surgeries and medical procedures occur annually, and 12,000 Americans are killed each year by these unnecessary surgeries (Black, 2005). This estimate, if accurate, means that these unnecessary medical surgeries and procedures occur once every four seconds or so. Put another way, by the time you finish this paragraph, someone has had an unnecessary surgery/procedure. Describing the overuse of screening methods and treatments for prostate cancer, Otis Brawley (2009), chief medical officer for the American Cancer Society, recently commented, "Every treatment looks good, when *more than* 90% of men getting it *do not* need it."

At least six overlapping reasons help to explain the pervasiveness of unnecessary surgeries. First, differing opinions among medical providers will likely result in some providers recommending surgery and other providers recommending a different course of action. Medicine is not an exact science, and those providing unnecessary services would likely justify the services on various medical grounds.

Second, the stigma of various forms of disease is such that patients are willing to expose themselves to procedures in order to battle and overcome the disease. Consider prostate cancer. While Brawley notes that many prostate cancer treatments are not needed, he recognizes that the very concept creates fear in individuals who have long assumed that all forms of cancers must be eradicated in order to live a full life. Most of us would never assume that we can live with cancer or that it would go away on its own. Brawley suggests that we are misinformed in that sense.

Third, the degree of trust that individuals have for their health care providers is such that patients tend to assume that procedures ordered by doctors are necessary. Assuming otherwise opens us up to the risk of the consequences of whatever ailment we are battling. The adage "better safe than sorry" comes to mind. In general, we trust our doctors and will follow their surgical and procedural advice as a matter of protecting ourselves from harm. The irony is that unnecessary procedures may create harm.

Fourth, while we are socialized to trust our health care providers, we have at the same time been socialized not to trust insurance companies. Regularly, we hear of situations where insurance companies deny coverage on the grounds that procedures are not needed. The typical reaction is to assume that the medical provider's recommendation is correct and any suggestion otherwise, particularly those offered by representatives of the insurance industry, are cast aside.

Fifth, and somewhat related to the above explanations, one can draw attention to what can be coined the medicalized socialization that we experience in our lives. In effect, we are socialized to turn to the health care system to fix our illnesses, diseases, and ailments. Although more attention has recently been given to preventing diseases in the first place, as consumers we have an expectation that our health care needs will be met by health care providers. In effect, we have long played a passive role in receiving health care rather

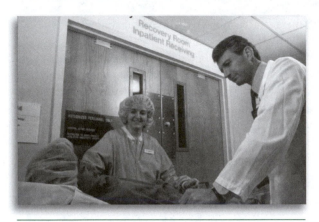

▲ **Photo 4.2**   The doctor-patient relationship is a trusting relationship. Most doctors adhere to these ethical codes. A few, however, do not.

than administering our own health care. As a result, we pass our health care decisions off to our providers.

Finally, one can point to conflict explanations to address the persistence of unnecessary surgeries. Conflict explanations point to the economic gains of health care for those with power. Consider that the United States spends 53% more on health care per person than other countries spend (Anderson, Hussey, Frogner, & Waters, 2005). Anderson and his coauthors argue that it is not over-utilization that is causing these high expenditures, but high prices in the first place. From a conflict perspective, those with power control the pricing of health care. Moreover, by pricing surgeries and procedures at a high price, an even stronger incentive may exist to commit unnecessary surgeries. It's one thing to perform an unnecessary wart removal, which would be a low-cost surgery; it's quite another to perform unnecessary coronary bypass, which is the most common unnecessary surgery in the United States (Black, 2005). As another example, consider that women in the United States have four times more hysterectomies than women in Sweden (Parker, 2009). According to Black (2005), "the only people who seem to really benefit from these unnecessary medical procedures are the medical professionals who stand to make exorbitant amounts of money from performing them" (n.p.).

Many severe consequences may arise from unnecessary surgeries. Jesilow and his colleagues (1985) suggest that unnecessary surgeries are analogous to assaults. They cite a case where an ophthalmologist performed several unnecessary eye surgeries that left patients with either impaired vision or blindness. The doctor performed the procedures simply so he could bill Medicaid for them. Also note that unnecessary surgeries deprive poor individuals of the health care they need (Pontell et al., 1984). Another irony arises— by doling out health care procedures to people who don't need them, those who need the health care services are deprived of the care they do need.

Other consequences also surface. For example, the element of time is relevant. Think about how long a visit to the doctor takes. Individuals need to take off from work, drive to the office or clinic, wait in the waiting room, get moved back to the exam room only to wait some more, and then they experience the procedure/ surgery. Then they are sent to the pharmacist where they will have to spend more time to complete that particular transaction. In the end, if the procedure or surgery was unnecessary, all of this time was wasted (Payne & Berg, 1997). Somewhat related, being told that one needs surgery or a procedure is sure to create some sort of mental anguish or stress for individuals who are told they need the surgery or procedure. That the surgeries or procedures are unnecessary suggests that providers are basically bullying patients mentally.

Medication Errors

Medication errors occur when health care providers deliver or prescribe the wrong medications to patients. These errors can be harmful in two ways: (1) the patient is given a drug he or she does not need, and this drug could cause harm, or (2) the patient could experience harm from not getting the drug that is actually needed. Cox (2010) notes that doctors have long said, "Do not let your friends and family schedule hospital visits in July." The basis for this "warning" is the increase in medication errors that seem to occur each July. Cox describes a study by sociologists David Phillips and Gwendolyn Parker that addressed why this spike in errors seems to occur.

Phillips and Parker, sociologists from the University of San Diego, examined 244,388 deaths occurring from medication errors between 1979 and 2006. They found that deaths at a high number of teaching hospitals increased by 10 percent in July each year. This finding supported previous speculation that the "July effect" could be attributed to the fact that new doctors and residents begin practicing in July. Thus, their lack of experience is believed to contribute to medication errors.

Phillips shared an interesting exchange with another reporter: "One physician—not knowing I was studying this issue—referred to the issue and said to me: 'It's possible, you should probably avoid going in [being hospitalized] during July'" (Raloff, 2010). As noted in the beginning of this section, it is believed that medication errors led to the death of Michael Jackson. Incidentally, his death occurred 5 days before the beginning of July, and his doctor had several years of experience practicing medicine.

General Offending by Doctors

A number of other types of misconduct are committed by malfeasant doctors during the course of their occupational routines. These other types can be characterized as general offending by doctors. The nonprofit group Public Citizen collects data on physicians involved in misconduct and has published a report and database called **Questionable Doctors.** The report includes information about doctors, their violations, and sanctions given to doctors (Lim, 2002). According to Public Citizen, the types of physician misconduct are wide ranging. From most serious to least serious, the general types of offending by doctors include:

- Conviction of a crime
- Practicing without a license or issuing/writing prescriptions without a license
- Losing hospital privileges
- Failing to comply with an order from a medical board
- Deceiving a medical board
- Proving substandard or incompetent care
- Sexually abusing a patient
- Drug/alcohol abuse
- Over prescribing drugs
- Practicing medicine with a mental illness that inhibits service delivery
- Committing insurance fraud
- Falsifying patient records
- Overcharging
- Professional misconduct (e.g., unprofessional behavior)
- Failure to comply with a professional rule (e.g., child abuse reporting) (Lim, 2002)

Lim (2002) used the Questionable Doctors database to review the types of violations and crimes committed by women doctors in California between 1990 and 1994. Of the 425 violations she reviewed, just 30 were committed by female physicians. Most frequently, female physicians were sanctioned for being convicted of a crime, providing substandard care, and failing to comply with a professional rule. Lim noted that the violations committed by women doctors were usually "self-inflicted" (p. 163).

Public Citizen also collects data on the rates of sanctions against physicians by state medical boards for "serious violations" (Wolfe, Kahn, & Resnevic, 2010). Between 2007 and 2009, the 10 states with the lowest rates of violations and violation rates per 1,000 physicians included the following:

- Minnesota (1.07)
- South Carolina (1.09)
- Wisconsin (1.59)
- New Hampshire (1.65)
- Connecticut (1.80)
- Massachusetts (1.93)
- Mississippi (2.17)
- Florida (2.25)
- Maryland (2.30)
- Vermont (2.34)

In reviewing these states, some might assume that lower rates means a lower rate of offending by physicians. While this might be the case, Public Citizen points to another possibility—these may be states where medical boards are allowing physicians to get away with more violations than other states. This is likely a more plausible suggestion as there is nothing to suggest why certain states would have a higher number of malfeasant physicians. It is plausible, though, to suggest that sanctioning behaviors are a product of state medical boards.

Fraud by Pharmacists

Doctors are not the only upper-class members of the health care profession to engage in fraudulent activities. Pharmacists have also been implicated in numerous frauds and abuses against the insurance systems. Interestingly, pharmacists have long been rated among the top most trusted professions on trust surveys of the public. That some of them commit fraud is not a reason to lower the profession's trust ratings, but one must be careful not to assume that all pharmacists are playing by the rules that guide their occupational activities.

Because pharmacists have long been viewed as so trustworthy, few criminologists have focused on deviant action in this profession. One researcher, Dean Dabney, conducted several studies examining illicit drug use by pharmacists. Interviewing dozens of pharmacists, Dabney's research suggests that proximity to drugs that are readily available and beliefs that they know enough about the drugs to self-medicate contribute to their decisions to use, and subsequently abuse, drugs.

In one of his pharmacist studies, Payne and Dabney (1997) (that's me, by the way) examined 292 cases of **prescription fraud** prosecuted by fraud control units across the United States. Our research uncovered eight types of fraud among the prosecuted cases. **Generic drug substitution** involved cases where the pharmacist gave the consumer a generic drug, but billed the insurance company for a more expensive drug (imagine if you bought a box of your favorite cereal made by one of the top cereal makers and generic cereal was in the box, but the box was branded with the more expensive cereal). **Short counting** occurs when pharmacists dispense fewer pills than prescribed, but bill the insurance company as if they had dispensed all of the pills (do you count the pills to make sure you got them all?). Similar to fraud by doctors, **double billing** occurs when pharmacists bill more than two parties for the same prescription. **Billing for nonexistent prescriptions** occurs when pharmacists bill for prescriptions that never actually existed. **Forgery** occurs when pharmacists forge the signature of the doctor or the consumer, or they forge the name of a more expensive drug on the prescription. **Mislabeling drugs** occurs when pharmacists label drugs incorrectly in an effort to hide the fact that the pharmacist did not provide the prescribed drug to the patient. **Delivery of a controlled substance** is more of a legal term and a reference to instances when the pharmacist wrongfully, perhaps without a prescription, provides controlled substances to consumers. Finally, **illegally buying prescriptions** involves situations where pharmacists buy prescriptions from patients, and then bill the insurance company without filling the prescription.

This last variety of prescription fraud typically involves schemes were pharmacists work with drug addicts to carry out the offense. The pharmacist instructs the addict to go to different doctors and get prescriptions filled. The addict is instructed to fake an illness (one that the pharmacist suggests) so that the doctor writes an expensive prescription for the addict. The addict gives the pharmacist the prescription. The pharmacist gives the addict some drugs (usually something addictive like pain killers) and then the pharmacist bills the insurance agency for the prescription that was never actually filled. As will be shown in the policing section, to respond to these cases, sometimes undercover law enforcement officers pose as drug addicts to establish a case against the pharmacist.

Past research has demonstrated difficulty convicting pharmacists. Excluding those schemes where pharmacists illegally buy prescriptions, a common defense used by pharmacists is that they must have misread the doctor's handwriting. If you have ever tried to read a prescription, you will likely be inclined to accept this claim. After all, the handwriting of doctors does, in fact, seem to be very difficult to read. However, pharmacists are trained to read their shorthand, and if they are unable to read it, regulations stipulate that they are supposed to call the doctor's office for clarification.

My research with Dabney identified six patterns of prescription fraud by pharmacists. First, offenders tended to be male. Second, the cases rarely resulted in incarceration, except for egregious cases. Third, in some cases assistants were convicted, presumably in an effort to sustain a conviction against the pharmacist. Fourth, the vast majority of convictions were obtained through guilty pleas, with 95% of the convicted pharmacists entering guilty pleas. Fifth, the cases of misconduct were hard to detect, with forgery being the hardest to detect. Finally, when cases were identified, convicted pharmacists tended to have committed several cases of misconduct. Consider the following case:

▲ **Photo 4.3** Pharmacists accused of prescription fraud often try to blame their misconduct on an error and state they could not read the doctor's handwriting. Such defenses may occasionally work, but pharmacists are expected to contact the doctor's office if they have problems reading a prescription.

[Defendant] submitted false claims for 9,042 prescriptions for 43 patients whose physician never issued the prescriptions and for patients who never received the prescriptions. On some occasions, it is alleged that [the defendant] billed for as many as 37 fraudulent prescriptions for a single patient on the same day.... [The defendant] was paid a total of $220,588 to which he was not entitled by the Medicaid program for these fraudulent claims. (*Medicaid Fraud Reports,* 1991, March, p. 18)

Certainly, the case demonstrates how some instances of prescription fraud can be particularly egregious.

Drug Use by Pharmacists

Illicit drug use by pharmacists is another area of concern in the pharmacy industry. Estimates suggest that up to 65% of practicing pharmacists have engaged in "some form of illicit drug use at least once during their career" and approximately one fifth "used drugs regularly enough that they experienced negative life outcomes" (Dabney & Hollinger, 2002, p. 182). It appears that, compared to other professionals, pharmacists have higher rates of substance abuse problems.

To determine how pharmacists initiated their drug use, Dabney and Hollinger (2002) interviewed 50 drug-addicted pharmacists who were in recovery. They identified two distinct pathways to drug use among addicted pharmacists. Twenty-three of the pharmacists followed a **"recreational path"** to their addiction. These pharmacists began by using illegal street drugs and then after entering pharmacy training they expanded their drug use to include prescription drugs. Experimentation and social acceptability themes (by fellow pharmacy students) were common patterns found in the pharmacists' recreational drug use.

The second type of pharmacist addict was labeled **therapeutic self-medicators** by Dabney and Hollinger (2002). These pharmacists had little exposure to recreational drug use in their pre-employment lives. Their involvement in drug use typically "focused on specific therapeutic goals" (p. 196) and was often the result of health problems (such as insomnia, arthritis, etc.) or trauma (from car accidents, broken bones, or other traumatic incidents). The authors suggested that in the early stages of use, these pharmacists appeared to be "model pharmacists." They defined their drug use in noble terms, suggesting, for example, that they did not want to miss work as a result of their ailment and the drug use allowed them to go to work and help consumers who needed their own prescriptions filled. Eventually, these pharmacists began to create illnesses in order to convince themselves that they needed more drugs. Calling these pharmacists "drug-thirsty pharmacists," the research team quoted one pharmacist who said, "I had a symptom for everything I took" (p. 199).

Elsewhere, the same research team focused on how opportunity, awareness about drugs, and technical knowledge interacted to promote drug use by pharmacists (Dabney & Hollinger, 1999). They wrote, "In the absence of proper appreciation of the risks of substance abuse, [technical knowledge and opportunity] can delude pharmacists into believing that they are immune to prescription drug use" (p. 77). The authors characterized 40 of the 50 pharmacists as poly-drug users, meaning that the pharmacists used more than one type of drug. Thirty of the pharmacists were referred to as "garbage heads," alluding to a drug treatment term that describes those who use whatever drug they can get their hands on. The authors also highlighted the process of "titrating," where pharmacists used "their pharmaceutical knowledge to manage their personal drug use, enhancing or neutralizing specific drug effects by ingesting counteractive drugs" (p. 90).

Dabney and Hollinger (1999) described the "paradox of familiarity" that characterized pharmacists' drug using patterns. Pharmacists were exposed to positive aspects of the substances through aggressive marketing campaigns by pharmaceutical representatives, and their routine exposure to prescription drugs was such that drugs were defined as positive substances designed to help consumers. As the authors wrote, "they believed that these drugs could only improve lives; and therefore, they dismissed or minimized the dangers. Self-medication became a viable and attractive form of medicating every problem" (p. 95). In other words, pharmacists believed they knew enough about drugs that they would not succumb to the dangers of drug use.

Note that drug use by pharmacists is not in and of itself a white-collar crime. One of two conditions must be present for the substance abusing behavior to be considered a white-collar crime. First, if drugs are stolen from the workplace in order to feed the pharmacist's habit, then a white-collar crime has been committed. Second, if the pharmacist is under the influence of illicit substances while at work, one can argue that a white-collar crime has occurred.

Sexual Abuse

In this context, **sexual abuse** refers to situations where health care providers (doctors, dentists, psychologists, psychiatrists, etc.) engage in sexual relationships with their patients. Four types of health care provider-patient sexual relationships exist: (1) power/prestige relationships, (2) mental health controlling relationships, (3) drug-induced relationships, and (4) sexual assault. First, in terms of power/prestige relationships, in some situations, patients may become enamored with their health care provider and open themselves up to the relationship based on the prestige/power that the provider has over the patient. Such relationships run counter to the provider's ethical codes and can do a great deal of emotional harm to patients.

Second, mental health controlling relationships occur in situations where individuals have sexual relationships with the mental health provider (psychiatrist, psychologist, counselor, etc.). It is impossible to know how often these relationships occur, but note that those who seek mental health counseling are in vulnerable states. Surveys of 30 adult incest survivors found that the survivors sought professional therapy from 113 different professionals. Seven of those 30 survivors had a sexual relationship with their helping professional (Armsworth, 1989).

Third, drug-induced relationships occur when health care providers get their patients addicted to drugs so they can have sex with the patients in exchange for access to drugs. These actions are clearly illegal on several different levels. In addition, besides feeding a chemical addiction and harming the victim physically, the health care provider is harming the victim emotionally as well. In one recent case, Dr. Leonard Hudson, of the University of Washington, had his license suspended after it was alleged that he had provided a "pain-killer addicted woman drugs in exchange for sex" (Pulkkinen, 2010). In another case, it was alleged that Dr. Michael Rusling, a doctor in Britain, "threatened to withhold drugs from a depressed patient if she refused to have sexual intercourse with him" ("Doctor Threatened to 'Withhold,'" 2009). Three patients said they had sexual relationships with Rusling, with one of them having sex with him at her home so often that one of her neighbors thought she had a serious health condition.

Fourth, sexual assault occurs when the provider sexually abuses (e.g., rapes) a patient during the course of providing care. One dentist, for example, was convicted of "feeling up" women as part of their dental treatment. In all, 27 women claimed that dentist Mark Anderson groped their breasts during dental examinations. Anderson defended his actions on the grounds that he was providing medical therapy in an effort to treat temporo-mandibular joint disorder, better known as TMJ ("Accused Dentist," 2007). The dentist was eventually convicted and sentenced to 6 years in prison.

Some of these cases can be quite brazen. One case that stands out in my mind involved a psychiatrist I read about during my dissertation work several years ago. In this case, the psychiatrist had sex with his patient, and then he billed Medicaid for the time he spent having sex with the patient. In fact, not only did he bill Medicaid for having sex with his patient, but he billed Medicaid for more time than he actually took having sex with her!

 Elder Abuse by Health Care Workers

Elder abuse can be defined as "any criminal, physical, or emotional harm or unethical taking advantage that negatively affects the physical, financial, or general well being of an elderly person" (Payne, Berg, & Byars, 1999, p. 81). In terms of crimes by workers in the health care field, the following types of elder abuse are relevant: (1) elder physical abuse, (2) elder financial abuse, (3) elder neglect, (4) elder sexual abuse, and (5) failure to report crimes.

In this context, **elder physical abuse** entails instances where workers hit, slap, kick, or otherwise physically harm an older person for whom they are being paid to provide care. **Pacification** (or over medicating) and restraining are also included as forms of elder physical abuse. In one of the earliest studies on physical patient abuse, Pillemer and Moore (1990) conducted phone interviews with 577 nurses' aides and nurses working in nursing homes in Massachusetts. In all, more than a third of the workers said they had seen instances where a resident was abused in the previous year and one tenth of the respondents indicated they had been abusive themselves in the prior year. In another study, researchers suggested that 8 out of 10 nurses and aides saw elder abuse cases in the prior year (Crumb & Jennings, 1998).

Payne and Cikovic (1995) examined 488 cases of patient abuse prosecuted by Medicaid Fraud Control Units across the United States. They found that the offenses typically occurred in isolation, and aides seemed to be overrepresented in allegations of abuse. They also found that the victim-offender relationship followed gender patterns: males were more likely to abuse males and females were more likely to abuse females. More recently, a study of 801 cases of patient abuse identified three types of offenders: (1) stressed offenders who committed the offense as a result of a stressful interaction with the patient, (2) serial abusers who committed multiple offenses at work, and (3) pathological tormentors who committed heinous offenses designed to humiliate or control victims (Payne & Gainey, 2006).

Elder financial abuse is a second type of elder abuse committed by care providers. The National Center on Elder Abuse offers the following definition of elder financial abuse:

> **Financial or material exploitation** is defined as the illegal or improper use of an elder's funds, property, or assets. Examples include, but are not limited to, cashing an elderly person's checks without authorization or permission; forging an older person's signature; misusing or stealing an older person's money or possessions; coercing or deceiving an older person into signing any document (e.g., contracts or will); and the improper use of conservatorship, guardianship, or power of attorney. (National Center on Elder Abuse, 2008)

Researchers have suggested that elder financial abuse can be distinguished from elder physical abuse in the following ways: financial abuse occurs more often, it has different causes, different response systems are used to address the crimes, and the consequences of elder financial abuse have different consequences than other forms of elder abuse (Payne & Strasser, 2010).

In one of the largest studies on theft in nursing homes, criminologists Diane Harris and Michael Benson (1999) surveyed 1,116 nursing home employees and 517 family members of nursing home residents. Their results showed that one fifth of the workers suspected that their colleagues had stolen something from residents, and one fifth of the family members believed that a staff member had stolen something from their relative.

In another study, Harris and Benson (1996) interviewed employees, relatives, and nursing home residents to gain insight into the patterns surrounding theft in nursing homes. They found that the items stolen most often tended to be items of value that could be easily concealed, such as jewelry and money. They also found that theft increased around the holidays and that new workers and dissatisfied workers were more apt to engage in theft. Other research suggests that theft in nursing homes is related to aggressive behaviors by nursing home residents—workers who experienced abuse at the hands of residents were suggested to be more likely to steal from residents (Van Wyk, Benson, & Harris, 2000). Harris and Benson (1999) argue that theft is even less socially acceptable than physical patient abuse on the grounds that the behaviors are intentional and not simply a reaction to a stressful working situation.

In a recent study, Payne and Strasser (2010) compared cases of elder physical abuse ($n = 314$) and elder financial abuse ($n = 242$) provided in the *Medicaid Fraud Reports* (described in the Introduction). Financial abusers were more likely to be directors or employees in another category, while physical abusers tended to be aides. The authors also found that "physical abusers were more likely to be sentenced to jail than financial abusers were, but financial abusers were more likely to be sentenced to prison" (n.p.). Comparing sentence lengths, financial abusers received longer probation sentences, shorter prison sanctions, and higher fines than physical abusers did. The authors identified four patterns that characterized the financial exploitation cases: (1) victims often had serious health issues, (2) multiple victims were frequently targeted by specific offenders, (3) offenses occurred on multiple occasions, and (4) a lack of witnesses made it difficult to investigate the cases.

Elder neglect is a third type of elder abuse. Elder neglect occurs when workers fail to provide the appropriate level of care required by the patient. Experts distinguish between active (intentional) and passive (unintentional) neglect. In cases of active neglect, offenders know the type of care that an individual requires—they simply choose not to provide that care. In cases of passive neglect, offenders are not aware of the most appropriate care—their neglect stems from ignorance. In terms of workplace offenses, neglect is more likely to be active than passive in nature. Workers typically know the type of care the patient needs. In some situations, workplace demands may foster neglect inasmuch as administrators expect workers to provide care to a higher number of patients than is actually possible.

Elder sexual abuse is another variety of elder abuse. One expert cites three types of elder sexual abuse: (1) hands-on offenses where the offender inappropriately touches victims, (2) hands-off offenses such as voyeurism and exhibitionism, and (3) harmful genital practices where genital contact is made between the offender and the victim (Ramsey-Klawsnik, 1999). Sexual abuse is believed to be particularly common against disabled residents of long-term care institutions. One study of 58 subjects found that 27% of the respondents said they had been sexually assaulted by a staff member at the institution (Nibert, Cooper, & Crossmaker, 1989).

A study of 126 elder sexual abuse cases and 314 elder physical abuse cases committed as part of the offender's workplace activities and prosecuted by criminal justice officials found that elder sexual abuse cases were more likely to involve: (1) male offenders, (2) cognitively impaired victims, and (3) instances without witnesses (Payne, 2010). Payne highlighted the element of control involved in elder sexual abuse cases. He described the following three case scenarios as illustrations of this control:

- The sexual assault involved inserting a banana into the rectum of a patient who suffered from left side paralysis and mental confusion. [They] put the soiled banana into another patient's mouth. Not only did the defendants commit these acts while laughing with amusement, but they bragged and laughed about the assault to their friends (*Medicaid Fraud Report*, March 1994, p. 1).
- [He] is accused of hitting a 78-year-old patient in the face with a diaper and pretending to kiss and simulate sexual intercourse with a 92-year-old resident (*Medicaid Fraud Report*, September 1995).
- [The defendant] agitated an 83-year-old dementia patient at least nine times by telling the man that he was having sex with his own daughter (*Medicaid Fraud Report*, July 1995).

A final type of elder abuse by workers in the health care field is the **failure to report** suspected cases of elder abuse. The vast majority of states have laws stipulating that certain types of workers are mandated to report elder abuse cases to the authorities if they suspect an elder abuse incident has occurred. These laws are known as mandatory reporting laws. Several criticisms surround the use of mandatory reporting laws. These criticisms include:

- A lack of empirical basis supporting the need for the laws
- Questions about the effectiveness of the laws
- Concerns that the laws are based on ageist assumptions
- Concerns about patient/health care worker confidentiality
- The likelihood that revictimization will occur from reporting
- A belief that discretion results in inconsistent reporting (Payne, 2011).

In a recent study focusing on mandatory reporting laws, three patterns were found. First, mandatory reporting violations tend to involve multiple collaborators who work together to cover up a case of elder abuse. Second, mandatory reporting violators come from a wider range of health care occupations than is found in other types of elder abuse. Third, fines were commonly used as a sentencing tool in these cases (Payne, 2011). Based on these patterns, Payne suggests policy implications that center on broadening investigations to capture multiple offenders and increasing awareness about the laws.

Health care administrators use a number of different practices and follow various policies in an effort to prevent elder abuse in the workplace. Surveys of 76 nursing home directors identified four broad types of measures commonly used to prevent crimes against nursing home residents (Payne & Burke-Fletcher, 2005). First, facility-based measures are those strategies that directors choose to implement that are driven by facility policies, like background checks, drug tests, and safety committees. Second, educational strategies focus on increasing awareness among workers and residents about strategies to prevent abuse. Third, community outreach efforts entail strategies where crime prevention officials from outside the nursing home are called upon to provide information and resources to protect residents. Finally, building security strategies include measures designed to make the actual physical structure safer (e.g., locked doors, security alarms, and video cameras). The results of this survey showed that the conceptual ambiguity surrounding elder abuse laws made it more difficult to prevent elder abuse. Also, the results showed that the lack of clear and consistent elder abuse response policies created an obstacle to identifying and responding to cases of elder abuse occurring in nursing homes.

Home Health Care Fraud

Home health care entails the provision of health care services at home. In recent years, there has been an increase in the use of home health care due to demographic changes, changes in patient preferences, technological advancements, legislative changes, and cost containment strategies (Payne, 2003a). Along with these changes, there has been evidence of an increase of crimes committed by home health care workers. In *Crime in the Home Health Care Field*, Payne (2003a) describes the way that the following crimes occur in the home health industry: (a) murder, (b) physical abuse, (c) sexual abuse, (d) neglect, (e) drug-related offenses, (f) emotional abuse, (g) theft from patients, and (h) theft from Medicare/Medicaid.

Payne argues that fraud against the Medicare and Medicaid systems is particularly pervasive. He describes eight different types of fraud that home health care workers have committed. These include:

1. Providing unnecessary services to clients and billing the system for those services

2. Billing the system for services that were not provided to the client

3. Overcharging either the system or client for services

4. Forging signatures on medical documents

5. Negative charting (changing the client's medical records so clients seem sicker than they are, thereby convincing the insurance provider to pay for services that may not have been necessary)

6. Having unlicensed (or substitute) workers provide medical care and billing the insurance company as if the services were provided by a licensed professional

7. Double billing the client and one or more insurance companies

8. Providing kickbacks to other service providers in exchange for client referrals

Reviewing hundreds of home health care fraud cases, Payne identified three patterns that were common in the cases. First, he noted that many of the cases involved offenders who had past criminal histories. Second, the offenses were described as occurring over time. Whereas a robbery occurs in one moment in time, fraudulent acts may be more spread out over time. Third, Payne called attention to the fact that many home health care frauds were committed in groups, and the groups sometimes included workers and clients conspiring together to defraud the system. Based on these patterns, the following three policy implications were suggested: (1) the need for background checks in hiring home health care workers, (2) the need to conduct lengthy investigations to substantiate cases, and (3) the practice of investigating multiple offenders simultaneously in an effort to build a case against a specific offender (Payne, 2003a).

🔀 Medical Malpractice

Medical malpractice refers to situations where health care providers "accidentally" injure patients while delivering health care. These cases will almost never be treated as crimes. As a result, they do not enter the criminal justice system. Strategies for recourse for victims of medical malpractice include (1) filing a lawsuit against the health care provider and (2) filing an insurance claim with the provider's insurance company.

Table 4.1 shows the number of medical malpractice trials in U.S. district courts between 1990 and 2003 and the median amount of damages awarded. As shown in the table, fewer trials were held in more recent years, and with the exception of 2003, the amount of damages awarded decreased over the years.

Table 4.1 Medical Malpractice Trials in U.S. District Courts, 1990–2003

Fiscal Year	Medical Malpractice Trials	Trials With Plaintiff Award Winners	
		Number	Estimated Median Award
1990	164	50	$1,565,000
1991	151	40	2,072,000
1992	143	43	354,000
1993	137	37	419,000
1994	151	38	306,000
1995	132	38	805,000
1996	115	35	401,000
1997	108	26	476,000
1998	117	33	748,000
1999	109	37	580,000
2000	98	23	535,000
2001	97	22	454,000
2002	75	25	510,000
2003	88	24	1,350,000

With regard to filing an insurance claim with the provider's insurance company, it may be useful to compare medical malpractice with automobile "accidents." If driver A runs into driver B and is clearly responsible for an accident, then driver B's insurance company will file a claim with driver A's insurance company. In the end, driver A's insurance company will be responsible for paying the claim. In medical malpractice insurance cases, a similar process is followed: the "accident" victim or his or her representative files a claim with the provider's insurance company.

A review of 43,000 medical malpractice insurance claims in seven states between 2000 and 2004 found that "most medical malpractice claims were closed without any compensation provided to those claiming a medical injury" (Cohen & Hughes, 2007, p. 1). Payouts were higher for those who suffered "lifelong major or grave permanent injuries" and lower in cases with temporary or emotional injuries. Other patterns found in the medical malpractice insurance claims included the following:

- Claims were typically filed 15–18 months after the injuries.
- It generally took about 2–2.5 years to close the claims.
- In some states, less than 10% of the claims resulted in payouts. In other states, payouts were given in about a third of the cases.
- When injuries occurred, they were more likely to occur in hospitals.
- Females were claimants in 54%–56% of the cases.
- Approximately 95% of the claims were settled without going to trial.
- The amount of payouts to claimants increased as the case progressed through the justice system.
- Medical malpractice insurance payouts increased from 1990 to 2004.

In Focus 4.3

What Is a Medical Malpractice Insurance Claim?

A medical malpractice insurance claim arises when a person (the claimant) alleges that negligent medical treatment resulted in an injury. The treatment may have been provided by a physician, surgeon, or other health care professional or an organization, such as a hospital, clinic, or nursing home.

In a typical medical malpractice claim, the person claiming an injury or a related family member retains an attorney to file a claim with the medical provider's insurance carrier requesting compensation for the injury. After a claim is filed, the insurance carrier may settle, negotiate with the claimant over the amount of compensation, or refuse to compensate the claimant. If the parties do not come to an agreement, the claimant's attorney may file a lawsuit in the appropriate court or abandon the claim.

Some states require review of medical malpractice claims before a panel of experts prior to a lawsuit, while other states mandate arbitration or alternative dispute resolution as a means of resolving medical malpractice claims. The filing of a lawsuit may produce several outcomes. These include the settlement of the case prior to or during trial, a trial decision in favor of the claimant or the defendant, or the dismissal of the case by the court. Claims may also be abandoned or withdrawn after a lawsuit.

Table 4.2 shows the different types of injuries in medical malpractice cases in Nevada between 2000 and 2004 and how often damages were awarded in those cases. Interestingly, damages were rarely awarded in death cases. They were most often awarded in diminished life expectancy cases.

Table 4.2 Types of Injuries in Medical Malpractice Claims in Nevada, 2000-2004

Type of Injury	Total Number of Claims	Received Payment (%)
Total	1,226	38.0
Death	331	36.9
Diminished life expectancy	30	66.7
Disfigurement	55	54.5
Nervous system damage	108	53.7
Reproductive system damage	12	50.0
Foreign body left after surgery	34	47.1
Birth injury	32	46.9
Organ injury	54	46.3
Diminished use of limbs	52	46.2
Loss of limb/organ	38	42.1
Optical/sensory injury	34	41.2
Circulatory injury	27	40.7
Disease	31	38.7
Prolonged care or recovery	137	30,7
Infection	60	26.7
Side effects	38	18.4
Bone damage	23	17.4
Pain	41	14.6
Other*	26	53.8

*Includes dental injuries, dermal injuries, muscular/limb injuries, and cases where the wrong organ was removed.

 Summary

- In general, categories of crimes committed by health care providers include fraud by doctors, fraud by pharmacists, drug use, unnecessary surgery, medication errors, sexual abuse, elder abuse, home health care fraud, and medical malpractice.
- Sutherland implied that doctors were unlikely to engage in white-collar crime, and as a result, Sutherland gave "only scant attention to doctors [and] maintained that physicians were probably more honest than other professionals" (Wilson et al., 1986).

- The most pervasive form of fraud committed by doctors entails the commission of Medicare and Medicaid fraud and abuse.
- *Fraud* refers to intentionally criminal behaviors by physicians, whereas *abuse* focuses on unintentional misuse of program funds.
- Several specific forms of fraud and abuse exist, including phantom treatment, substitute providers, upcoding, provision of unnecessary services, misrepresenting services, falsifying records, overcharging patients, unbundling, pingponging, ganging, kickbacks, co-pay waivers, and medical snowballing.
- Briefly, mental health professionals often bill for time, whereas other professionals bill for more complicated medical procedures. For investigators, it is much easier to prove "time violations" than "treatment violations."
- Research shows that when females are accused of health care fraud, they tend to be accused along with other providers more so than male offenders are (Payne, 1995). Explanations for fraud have focused on structural explanations, socialization factors, and enforcement dynamics.
- It is estimated that 7.5 million unnecessary surgeries and medical procedures occur annually, and 12,000 Americans are killed each year from these unnecessary surgeries (Black, 2005).
- At least six overlapping reasons help to explain the pervasiveness of unnecessary surgeries: differing opinions, stigma, trust of health care, lack of trust of insurance companies, medicalized socialization, and conflict explanations.
- Many severe consequences may arise from unnecessary surgeries.
- Medication errors occur when health care providers deliver or prescribe the wrong medications to patients.
- Public Citizen has identified 16 varieties of misconduct by physicians. The group believes that variations in sanctions for violations across states can be attributed to differences in the way state medical boards sanction offenders.
- Eight types of prescription fraud include generic drug substitution, overbilling, double billing, billing for nonexistent prescriptions, short counting, mislabeling, delivery of a controlled substance, and illegally buying prescriptions.
- The following types of elder abuse can be seen as white-collar crimes: (1) elder physical abuse, (2) elder financial abuse, (3) elder neglect, (4) elder sexual abuse, and (5) failure to report crimes.
- Types of home health care fraud include providing unnecessary services, billing the system for services that were not provided to the client, overcharging, forgery, negative charting, substitute workers, double billing, and kickbacks.
- Medical malpractice refers to situations where health care providers perform negligent care and/or injure patients. Patients can seek recourse by filing medical malpractice insurance claims against the provider's insurance company or by filing a lawsuit against the provider.

KEY TERMS

Billing for nonexistent prescriptions	Double billing	Elder physical abuse
	Elder abuse	Elder sexual abuse
Co-pay waivers	Elder financial abuse	Failure to report
Delivery of a controlled substance	Elder neglect	Falsifying records

Ganging

Generic drug substitution

Health Insurance Portability Act of 1996

Home health care

Illegally buying prescriptions

Kickbacks

Medicaid

Medical fraud

Medical malpractice

Medical snowballing

Medicare

Medication errors

Mislabeling drugs

Overcharging

Pacification

Phantom treatment

Pingponging

Prescription fraud

Provision of unnecessary services

Questionable doctors

Recreational path

Sexual abuse

Short counting

Substitute providers

Unbundling

DISCUSSION QUESTIONS

1. What's worse—retail theft or health care fraud? Explain.

2. What can be done to limit crimes by health care professionals?

3. Why do doctors engage in inappropriate conduct?

4. What are the similarities between misconduct by pharmacists and crimes by doctors? What about the differences?

5. Why do unnecessary surgeries occur? Do you know anyone who has had a potentially unnecessary surgery? What can be done to prevent them?

6. How do television shows portray misconduct by doctors?

7. How is drug use a white-collar crime? What can be done to prevent drug use by health care providers?

WEB RESOURCES

Medicare Fraud: http://www.medicare.gov/navigation/help-and-support/fraud-and-abuse/fraud-and-abuse-overview.aspx

FBI Healthcare Fraud: http://www.fbi.gov/news/stories/2010/june/health-care-fraud/health-care-trends

Stop Medicare Fraud: http://www.stopmedicarefraud.gov/

Pharmacist Drug Abuse: http://www.ashp.org/menu/News/PharmacyNews/NewsArticle.aspx?id=1446

Prescription Fraud: http://www.popcenter.org/problems/prescription_fraud/

READING

This reading describes the testimony of James Frogue, vice president of the Center for Health Transformation before the U.S. House of Representatives Committee on the Judiciary. Particularly relevant are the ties between the political system and crimes in the health care system. Among other things, it should become evident that the political system plays a central role in defining types of white-collar crimes and the need to respond to various types of white-collar crimes, which in this case includes crimes in the health care system. Frogue draws attention to the enormity of fraud and abuse in the health care system and briefly addresses the regional variation that exists in terms of the extent of fraud by health care professionals. Much of his discussion focuses on the need to improve the justice system's response to these offenses. Frogue suggests that the lack of resources for responding to these crimes contributes to the pervasiveness of the offenses. He concludes with nine recommendations for reducing fraud and abuse in the health care system.

The Enforcement of Criminal Laws Against Medicare and Medicaid Fraud

Testimony to the House of Representatives Committee on the Judiciary Subcommittee on Crime, Terrorism and Homeland Security

James Frogue

Chairman Scott, Ranking Member Gohmert and Members of the Subcommittee, thank you for holding this hearing today and inviting me to share a few thoughts. This is a topic of great importance that affects access to healthcare services for every American. I want to emphasize my willingness to work with all of you following this hearing to develop and implement policies that will ensure our precious healthcare dollars do not end up in the hands of criminals.

I must begin by emphasizing that my oral and written remarks are solely my own. They do not necessarily reflect the views of my employer the Center for Health Transformation or any of its staff or members.

The problem of healthcare fraud is far bigger than most Americans can imagine. But fortunately leaders from both political parties have started speaking up on this critical topic. That is the first step toward creating a climate where real solutions can be offered and implemented.

During his address to a joint session of Congress on September 9, 2009, President Barack Obama accurately spoke of the "hundreds of billions of dollars of

SOURCE: Frogue, James. (2010, March 4). The enforcement of criminal laws against Medicare and Medicaid fraud. Testimony to the House of Representatives Committee on the Judiciary. Subcommittee on Crime, Terrorism, and Homeland Security. Available online at http://judiciary.house.gov/hearings/pdf/Frogue100304.pdf

waste and fraud" in our healthcare system. This was surprising news to a lot of people.

Health and Human Services Secretary Kathleen Sebelius said at the "National Summit on Health Care Fraud" on January 28, 2010, "We believe the problem of healthcare fraud is bigger than government, law enforcement or private industry can handle alone." She was correct about that. Later in her speech she said, "Today, Medicare, Medicaid and private insurance companies pay out billions of dollars in fraudulent claims, and charge taxpayers higher premiums for it."

Congressman Ron Klein of South Florida, a hot spot for healthcare fraud, also spoke at the "National Summit on Health Care Fraud." He said, "Constituents come to me repeatedly with fake billings and stories of solicitations for their Medicare ID number."

Senator Tom Coburn suggested that, "Twenty percent of the cost of government healthcare is fraud," at the White House Health Summit on February 25, 2010. Senator Charles Schumer later associated himself with those comments, "I was glad to hear my friend Tom Coburn's remarks. I think we agree with most of them, and particularly the point that about a third of all of the spending that's done in Medicare and Medicaid, I would imagine a lot of it's in the private sector as well, doesn't go to really good health care, goes to other things."

Across the political spectrum there is emerging consensus that the amount of fraud in our healthcare system is very significant and totally unacceptable. Yet efforts thus far have failed to make a major dent in the problem.

The Government Accountability Office (GAO) has produced literally hundreds of reports over the last 30 years outlining waste, fraud and abuse in Medicare and Medicaid. A simple visit to GAO.gov and use of their search engine confirms this fact.

GAO designated Medicare a "high-risk" program in 1990 and Medicaid in 2003. The two programs combined will total $1 trillion in 2010 and their "high risk" status perseveres. An April 2009 report on the "High-Risk Series" estimated that the improper payment rate in Medicaid in 2008 was 10.5 percent with home health care administration and durable medical equipment being disproportionate contributors.[1] By contrast, the improper payment rate for non-health government agencies in 2008 was 3.9 percent.[2]

Secretary Sebelius sent a letter to Senator John Cornyn last week that outlined the first ever state-by-state breakdowns of improper payment rates. There were two notable takeaways—the improper payments are indeed excessive across a sampling of over half the states, but they are heavily concentrated in fee-for-service Medicaid and not in managed care.[3]

The Office of the Inspector General at the Department of Health and Human Services is equally dire in its reports and warnings. In just one example, on August 26, 2009 they sent a letter to CMS Director of State Operations Cindy Mann essentially saying that the Medicaid's data collection is so poor they cannot even accurately measure how bad the fraud is.[4]

Thomson Reuters released a comprehensive study in October 2009 showing that between $600 and $850 billion of what we spend on healthcare each year is wasted. That is approximately one-third of our entire national health spending. The report suggested that between $125 and $175 billion of that is pure fraud, with the remainder mostly made up of administrative waste, provider errors and waste

[1] Government Accountability Office, "Progress Made but Challenges Remain in Estimating and Reducing Improper Payments," April 22, 2009. http://www.gao.gov/highlights/d09628thigh.pdf.

[2] Garret Hatch & Virginia McMurtry, "Improper Payments Information Act of 2002: Background, Implementation, and Assessment," Congressional Research Service, October 8, 2009. http://assets.opencrs.com/rpts/RL34164_20091008.pdf.

[3] Letter from Secretary Kathleen Sebelius to Senator John Cornyn, February 25, 2009.

[4] Stuart Wright, "Memorandum Report: 'MSIS Data Usefulness for Detecting Fraud, Waste, and Abuse,' OEI-04-07-00240," Office of Inspector General, Department of Health & Human Services, August 26, 2009. http://oig.hhs.gov/oei/reports/oei-04-07-00240.pdf.

largely characterized by unnecessary and duplicative diagnostic testing.[5]

The CBS news magazine show *60 Minutes* had a segment hosted by Steve Kroft on October 25, 2009 on Medicare fraud. It started with Kroft warning viewers that the following piece, "might make your blood boil." He asserted that $60 billion a year is stolen from Medicare by criminals like one they profiled.[6] Other news outlets confirm that organized crime in particular is rapidly moving into Medicare fraud because the risk is so low and the payoff so high.[7]

The American people are becoming aware of how bad the problem is. In a poll conducted last summer by Insider Advantage, the American people by a margin of 61-27 said Congress should eliminate fraud in existing public programs before creating another one.[8] A Zogby poll from around the same time asked Americans what is their preferred way to pay for modernizing our healthcare system. Eighty-eight percent said "eliminate fraud" placing well ahead of the second place finished "standardize administrative forms" at 77 percent and "reduce medical errors" at 72 percent.[9] In other words, Americans prefer going after criminals before ensuring their own personal safety from medical mistakes!

More broadly speaking, Americans believe that 50 cents of every dollar spent by the federal government is wasted according to a September 2009 Gallup poll. Democrats pegged it at 41 cents, Republicans at 54 cents and independents at 55 cents.[10] This is a startling lack of faith in the ability of the federal government to spend tax dollars efficiently.

Prior to getting into specific, workable solutions however, it is important to mention third-party payer as the root cause of excessive waste, fraud and abuse in our healthcare sector. I appreciate that this is well beyond the scope of today's hearing. But it must be acknowledged that third-party payer arrangements dominate all of Medicare and Medicaid and nearly all of what we call "private insurance." They encourage patients and healthcare providers to be less than vigilant about dollars being spent and billed. Consumers of health care services are simply more mindful of their spending when they have skin in the game as shown by the classic Rand Health Insurance Experiment[11] and more recently by the experience of Indiana state employees.[12]

Absent confronting the inherent perverse incentives of third-party payer, the next best solutions are exponentially better use of available information technology, better data sharing, metrics-based management and more transparency. Fortunately, these cost relatively little, should have few partisan boundaries and done properly would have a massively positive effect on rooting out waste, fraud and abuse.

Consider the example of the credit card industry. There are over $2 trillion in credit card transactions annually in the United States which makes it more than twice as large as Medicare and Medicaid combined. There are roughly 800 million cards in circulation, millions of vendors and countless products available for purchase. Yet, fraud in the credit card industry is less than one-tenth of one percent. It is perhaps 100 times worse in Medicare and Medicaid.

[5]Thomson Reuters, "Healthcare Reform Starts with the Facts," October 27, 2009. http://thomsonreuters.com/content/corporate/articles/healthcare_reform.

[6]*60 Minutes*, "The $60 Billion Fraud," October 25, 2009. http://www.cbsnews.com/video/watch/?id=5419844n.

[7]Kelli Kennedy, "Mafia, violent criminals turn to Medicare fraud," Newsvine.com, October 6, 2009. http://www.newsvine.com/_news/2009/10/06/3354515-mafia-violent-criminals-turn-to-medicare-fraud.

[8]Insider Advantage poll of 636 registered voters, July 15, 2009. http://www.healthtransformation.net/cs/IAPollJul09.

[9]Zogby International/University of Texas Health Science Center poll of 3,862 adults, June 2009. http://www.zogby.com/news/ReadNews.cfm?ID=1722.

[10]Gallup, "Americans: Uncle Sam Wastes 50 Cents on the Dollar," September 15, 2009. http://www.gallup.com/poll/122951/Americans-Uncle-Sam-Wastes-50-Cents-Dollar.aspx.

[11]RAND Health Insurance Experiment. http://www.rand.org/health/projects/hie

[12]Mitch Daniels, "Hoosiers and Health Savings Accounts," Wall Street Journal, March 1, 2010. http://online.wsj.com/article/SB10001424052748704231304575091600470293066.html?mod=WSJ_Opinion_LEFTTopOpinion.

Why is this true? For one, the credit card industry does a much better job at screening out bad vendors in the first place. Medicare fee-for-service consistently fails at that. The *60 Minutes* segment referenced earlier gives a flavor for that.

Second, the credit card industry uses advanced information technology that flags suspicious purchases in real time. All of us know that if we traveled to Fargo, North Dakota, tomorrow and tried to buy three plasma televisions, our credit card company would signal the store clerk to ask for us for identification in the space of seconds. Most of us have had similar experiences with seemingly more routine purchases. Medicare fee-for-service is light years behind the credit card industry in its ability to identify criminals and deny their payments.

It is worth noting that there are not thousands of federal and state law enforcement officials assigned to police rampant and ongoing credit card fraud. The problem is almost entirely nipped in the bud by proper pre-screening of vendors and advanced algorithms that spot outliers instantly.

Law enforcement plays a critical role in combating healthcare fraud but it is by definition reactive. The cost in time and money of indicting, prosecuting and imprisoning a criminal is significant and unfortunately the deterrent effect appears to be minimal as organized crime continues its march into Medicare and Medicaid fraud. Keeping up with and stopping the latest scams in a third-party payer system with poor use of information technology is like the mythical character Sisyphus trying to push the rock up to the top of the hill only to have it crash to the bottom every time he seems to be making progress.

That said, the Health Care Fraud Prevention and Enforcement Action Team (HEAT) has been a successful joint effort between the Justice Department and Health and Human Services. The level of cooperation and data sharing has been extensive and they notched up several significant successes in 2009. Aggressive, innovative United States Attorneys like Luis Perez in South Florida are making important contributions.

But the fact is, these efforts simply do not have and will never have the amount of resources and manpower to try and convict all the criminals guilty of Medicare and Medicaid fraud. James Mehmet, the former chief state investigator for Medicaid fraud in New York said in 2005, "40 percent of all claims are questionable."[13] In a Medicaid program the size of New York's that is in the neighborhood of $20 billion annually in questionable claims. To re-emphasize—that is one state's Medicaid program in one year. With all due respect to the honorable and hardworking men and women in law enforcement, a number of this magnitude makes the busting of $50 million dollar fraud rings seem like a drop in the ocean especially when factoring in all costs associated with the investigation, prosecution and eventual jail time for those convicted. One percent of annual Medicare spending is $5 billion.

Many of the attorneys and investigators I have spoken with off the record say that prosecutions focus almost exclusively on very large cases where convictions are a virtual slam dunk. The message criminals hear is that they should just not get too greedy. So long as their theft remains in the tens of thousands of dollars, they need not fear prosecution. Those smaller activities multiplied across the country thousands of times likely add up to far more dollars than the marquee indictments, prosecutions and convictions.

So because law enforcement cannot reach these smaller and vastly more numerous crimes, we must think of innovative and low cost ways to prevent and deter fraud that utilize the all-hands-on-deck approach as suggested by Secretary Sebelius.

There is no Constitutional right to become and remain a supplier to the Medicare program. This may sound obvious. But there is a mentality among too many that simply because an application is filled out properly and various token requirements are met, everyone can supply Medicare patients. This leads to

---

[13]Clifford J Levy and Michael Luo, "New York Medicaid Fraud May Reach Into Billions," *The New York Times*, July 18, 2005. http://www.nytimes.com/2005/07/18/nyregion/18medicaid.html?pagewanted=print

ridiculous situations where there are 897 licensed home health agencies in Miami-Dade County (as of April 2009) which was more than in the entire state of California.[14] There is simply not a need for that many home health providers in such a small geographic area. The Medicare fee-for-service program essentially accepts all eligible applicants regardless of patient need or demand. By contrast, commercial insurers don't have 40 suppliers in a region when five are sufficient.

Here are nine action items that would significantly reduce fraud and abuse:

1. **Add the phrase, "under penalty of perjury" to CMS form 855 and its various subforms.** These are the applications used by people wanting to become suppliers to Medicare. This very minor tweak would be a big asset to prosecutors going after bad actors because perjury is a more serious offense.

2. **Medicare and Medicaid should use private sector standards for establishing the number of suppliers for a product or service in a defined area.** California's Medicaid program has been doing this for the better part of a decade now in the durable medical equipment space. While there was some pushback from frustrated potential providers, there were no reports of access to care issues from beneficiaries.

In a related experiment last year, the South Carolina Medicaid program told its 48 Medicaid beneficiaries with the most number of prescriptions that they could select any pharmacy. That one pharmacy would be their sole provider of needed medications. After eight months those 48 individuals had 40 percent fewer prescriptions which translated into a savings of $320,000 for the Medicaid program.

3. **Reduce the administrative red tape and lengthy appeals that suppliers too often exploit.**

Currently, suppliers can drag out the process for months and usually get reinstated. In 2007 and 2008 the OIG conducted 1,581 unannounced site visits of durable medical equipment providers in South Florida and found 491 either didn't have an actual facility or were not staffed accordingly. All 491 billing privileges were revoked. 243 of them appealed and 222 (or 91 percent) of those were reinstated. Of the 222 reinstated, 111 had their billing privileges revoked again.[15]

The Florida Medicaid program requires suppliers to sign contracts that the state has the right to terminate a supplier at any time, "without cause." This has been effective in Florida without harming access to care. Any public or private purchaser of a service should retain the right to stop buying that service whenever they see fit.

4. **Authorize demonstration projects whereby the authentication of new suppliers to Medicare fee-for-service is outsourced by and to an entity *not* CMS.** Congress could identify a handful of counties with a history of Medicare fraud and designate an agency that is not CMS to conduct the bidding. Perhaps the Office of Personnel Management could run a small handful of these initial experiments as OPM has experience in this area. Entities such as credit card companies, financial institutions or health insurers among others would be free to bid.

5. **Data sharing across departmental jurisdictions and with state and local governments should be done with the same seriousness as in national security.** Prior to 9/11 the CIA and FBI rarely communicated. Now they compare intelligence frequently. There are multiple databases of Medicare and Medicaid providers and

---

[14]Craig Smith, "South Florida: Ground Zero for Healthcare Fraud," Stop Paying the Crooks, ed. James Frogue (Washington, DC: Center for Health Transformation Press) 47

[15]Ibid.

suppliers along with their disciplinary records.[16] But these databases are not as universally comprehensive or as accessible as say the National Instant Criminal Background Check System (NICS) used to keep guns out of the hands of people with criminal records. The National Crime Information Center is another law enforcement tool that allows a local officer to have instant access to a suspect criminal background across the country. These systems are not perfect, but they represent good examples of how individuals with criminal records and/or disciplinary actions in the healthcare field can at least be flagged early. This concept was part of President Obama's revised health proposal unveiled on February 22nd and based on legislation introduced by Congressman Mark Kirk so it has bipartisan support. Utilize data from the Social Security Administration and IRS as well.

6. **Open up Medicare claims data to audits conducted by contingency-fee based companies beyond the standard four recovery audit collection companies.** The status quo is not working. Higher contingency fees of perhaps 20 percent and new eyes would introduce more powerful incentives, fresh ideas and modern research techniques to the fraud hunt. The same could be done by governors with their Medicaid programs to stir up new lines of inquiry beyond what is produced by the Medicaid Fraud Control Units.

7. **Create a website where payments to Medicare providers and suppliers are posted for public access.** This would allow for better identification of outlier billing practices, particularly among providers with similar geography and patient demographics.

The South Carolina Medicaid program has three years of claims data available broken out by provider name, county, number of patients treated, number of patient visits, total payments for billed claims, and average cost per billed claim.[17] Future iterations could have increasing granularity around specific treatments per patient, outcomes and how those compare with peer providers around the state. A version for Medicare would be most useful if complete patient data were posted and not made available only in Part A, Part B and Part D silos (with Medicaid data for the very expensive "dual eligibles" in still another silo). It must be clearly emphasized that all "patient data" be devoid of any individual identifiers that could compromise patient privacy. Fortunately, Medicare has successfully shared its claims data with academic institutions for decades without breaching patient privacy.

8. **Consider the feasibility of having all Medicare suppliers and providers publicly post their requests for payment *before* they are reimbursed by taxpayers.** Again, it would have to be scrambled appropriately to guarantee patient privacy. The volume of that raw data would no doubt be massive and few people would comprehend it initially. But eventually sense would be made of the seeming chaos and patterns would emerge, some of them unflattering. This need not interfere with Medicare's existing requirement for prompt payment. President Obama spoke of the need to post legislation on the Internet for 72 hours before it is voted on by Congress. This suggestion is in that spirit of transparency.

9. **Hold hearings about the governance of CMS and its ability to be truly effective in fighting fraud and abuse.** But instead of having CMS political appointees and senior bureaucrats as witnesses as is nearly always the case, invite current and former Medicare contractors for example and others who could testify about how impactful CMS policies really are at the street level. Those witnesses would be most

---

[16]The National Supplier Clearinghouse, the Healthcare Integrity and Protection Data Bank, the OIG Exclusion List, and CMS's Medicare Exclusion Database, etc.

[17]South Carolina Department of Health and Human Services, Transparency Reporting of Medicaid. http://www.scdhhs.gov/Transparency.asp

effective if they were not in positions where they feared retribution from CMS. Some of their ideas would shock.

The fraud, waste and abuse in Medicare and Medicaid are vast but it is possible to fix the problems.

Law enforcement will always play a key role in prosecution and deterrence. But our best hope for solving the problem is far more aggressive use of technology, better management of the programs and more transparency. Taxpayers have the right to know where and how their dollars are being spent.

DISCUSSION QUESTIONS

1. What does Frogue's testimony have to do with the systems approach?

2. What do you think the difference is between "waste" and "fraud"? Should those differences mean that behaviors should be treated differently by officials in the justice system?

3. How does this testimony, and the problem of health care fraud in general, impact your life?

READING

In this article, criminologists Dean Dabney and Richard Hollinger use data from interviews conducted with 50 recovering drug dependent pharmacists to examine whether familiarity with drugs contributed to drug use by pharmacists. The authors review prior research showing a high rate of dependency among this occupational group. The interviews were conducted as part of a larger study conducted in the mid 1990s by Dabney. They found that the pharmacists had engaged in an extensive amount of drug using behaviors in the past. Types of drug abusing pharmacists included garbage heads and titraters. Because the pharmacists considered themselves drug experts, they believed they would be able to use the drugs in a safe way.

Illicit Prescription Drug Use Among Pharmacists

Evidence of a Paradox of Familiarity

Dean A. Dabney and Richard C. Hollinger

Literature on Illicit Drug Use Among Pharmacists

In 1982, the American Pharmaceutical Association (APhA, 1982) issued its first ever policy statement acknowledging that substance abuse is a problem among its membership. However, given the sensitive nature of this problem, we are left without accurate incidence or prevalence data on the problem—only rough estimates. The National Association of Retail

SOURCE: Dabney, D., & Hollinger, R. (1999). Illicit prescription drug use among pharmacists: Evidence of a paradox of familiarity. *Work and Occupations, 26,* 77–100. Copyright © SAGE, Inc.

Druggists (NARD, 1988) estimates that profession-wide, one in seven pharmacists will succumb to chemical dependency at some point in their careers. A survey conducted among the licensed pharmacists in a New England state (McAuliffe et al., 1987) found that 46% of the 312 practitioners responding had admitted to the use of some form of controlled substance at least once in their lives, 19% within the past year. Moreover, more than 20% of the respondents had engaged in illicit prescription drug use. The McAuliffe et al. (1987) data also offer estimates of the problematic effects of drug use as 2.3% of the respondents admitted drug dependency,[2] 8.9% reported experiencing adverse effects in their private or professional life due to their usage, and another 6% were identified as being at risk of drug dependency. Thus, the authors conclude that 18% of the respondents were already dependent on drugs or at risk of future drug dependency.

Another study conducted among practicing North Carolina pharmacists ($N = 1,370$) revealed that 24% of the respondents had worked with a colleague who they believed was either abusing or addicted to drugs (Normack, Eckel, Pfifferling, & Cocolas, 1985a). This study estimated that 21% of the respondents admitted to personal behaviors that placed them at risk of chemical impairment.[3]

Extrapolating from the available estimates of drug use/abuse onto the overall population of more than 190,000 U.S. practicing pharmacists nationwide (Martin, 1993), one can conservatively estimate that tens of thousands of pharmacists presently engage in some form of illicit prescription drug use. Moreover, the prevalent data suggest that a considerable segment of this sub-population of drug-using pharmacists engages in high levels of usage or experience personal or professional problems as a result.

Pharmacists are not the only people who use drugs while at work. Data from the National Household Survey on Drug Abuse (NHSDA) show that 3.1% of full-time U.S. employees older than the age of 12 have used some form of illicit prescription drug in the past year (Hoffman, Brittingham, & Larson, 1996). The larger NHSDA data set that includes a random sample of individuals older than age 12 (employed or not) shows that 10.1% had used illicit prescription drugs

within the past year (Substance Abuse and Mental Health Services Administration, 1996). Self-report studies that ask various samples of U.S. employees about their substance abuse behaviors (Decima, 1990; Lehman, Holcom, & Simpson, 1990; Schneck, Amodei, & Kernish, 1991) show that 1% to 3% report some level of illicit prescription drug use in the past year. Studies that analyze the results of employers' drug testing of job applicants (Normand, Salyards, & Mahony, 1990) or current employees (Lehman et al., 1990; Sheridan & Winkler, 1989) show that anywhere from .2% to 7% of employees test positive for prescription drug use. None of these estimates, however, approach the above prevalence estimates for the pharmacy profession (McAuliffe et al., 1987).

Growing concern over the problem of illicit drug use among pharmacists has spawned a number of other studies that inquire more deeply into the nature and dynamics of this form of employee deviance. Bissell, Haberman, and Williams (1989) asked a sample of 86 drug-recovering pharmacists to describe their substance abuse experiences in hopes of explaining drug use within this special population.[4] These researchers found that 24% of the interviewees focused their drug use on nonnarcotic prescription drugs, 22% preferred mild narcotics, and 31% chose strong narcotics. Ingestible medications such as benzodiazepines and amphetamines were among the most popular, whereas injectable drug use was rare. It was not uncommon for respondents in the Bissell et al. study to report using remarkably large amounts of prescription medications on a daily basis. Moreover, significant numbers of the abusing pharmacists reported that they engaged in complex consumption patterns and had progressed into the latter stages of the substance abuse process (i.e., exhibiting visible signs of mental, physical, and emotional problems) before they entered treatment.

Laypersons are often surprised to learn that the pharmaceutical profession is confronted with problems of drug use among its ranks. They expect that druggists, perhaps more so than any other members of society, should know better than to engage in such self-destructive behaviors. They assume that pharmacists' respect for the dangers of potentially addictive substances coupled with their professional ethics will protect them. The flaw in this logic is that it assumes that greater knowledge about the effects of medications should prevent illicit prescription drug use by pharmacists. We contend that the opposite may actually be true.

Research Methods

The data for this analysis were drawn from a larger multimethod data collection effort[5] that took place between 1993 and 1995 (Dabney, 1997). The present analysis focuses principally on personal interviews with recovering drug-abusing pharmacists. These interview data offer firsthand accounts of the attitudes and behaviors of pharmacists who use drugs; thus, they provide an important first step toward understanding this complex social problem.

The face-to-face interviews were designed to examine the personal life histories of a random sample (Berg, 1998) of 50 pharmacists who were in recovery for past prescription drug abuse. The process began with the development of a loosely structured interview guide. This interview guide was divided into 13 topical areas that allowed the interviewer to probe various aspects of the individual's pharmacy career, paying particular attention to the intertwined dynamics of his or her personal drug use.

Interview participants were recruited with the assistance of leaders in the recovering impaired pharmacists' movement. Most every American state has developed a recovery network for impaired pharmacists. Although organizational structures, funding sources, and other administrative aspects differ from state to state, each of these social assistance networks is committed to serving as a liaison between drug- and/or alcohol-using pharmacists and the governing social control and sanctioning bodies (e.g., state board of pharmacy, pharmacy employers, Drug Enforcement Administration [DEA]) that oversee pharmacy practice. Three key figures in these networks were enlisted to implement our sampling strategy.[6] Each individual was asked to contact members of his or her recovery network and make them aware of the research project and a forthcoming data collection trip to the area. The recruiters provided program participants[7] with contact information and encouraged interested parties to call the researchers for further information and/or to schedule an interview time. This process was continued until 50 pharmacists with prescription drug problems had initiated contact and the interviews were completed. None of the participant-initiated contracts resulted in a refusal to participate. All of the interviews were conducted by the senior author.

The interviews took place in 1994 during four data collection trips to pharmacy conferences and recovery network locales. They were conducted in a wide variety of physical locations (i.e., hotel rooms, dormitory rooms, public parks, restaurants, respondents' homes, respondents' places of employment, meeting rooms). Each interview involved only the interviewer and the voluntarily participating pharmacist.

The fifty interviews were completed with pharmacists from 24 different states. The tape-recording of each one was transcribed verbatim. Thematic content analysis (Berg, 1998) was used to analyze the data. First, the paper copy of each interview transcription was coded by hand. This involved identifying general thematic categories within the interview conversations. These mundane categories included but were not limited to the various topical areas contained in the above-described interview guide. Eight-symbol codes were handwritten in the margins to mark conversational excerpts that illustrated the given thematic category. Once general themes were developed and labeled within the interview transcriptions, the process was repeated using more specific thematic categories. For example, prescription drug use with medicinal motivations (i.e., self-medication) was a general theme that was identified and labeled in the original coding pass. Subsequent coding passes further delineated the self-medication issue by affixing codes that specified the type of ailment or condition that the self-medication was intended to treat (e.g., work stress, physical pain, insomnia). By sorting and resorting from general to more specific themes, we were able to search for and identify more specific themes in the data. Several phases of this sorting and coding process were conducted until we developed a comprehensive classification of all interview data. At this point, all codes were entered into the Qualpro computer program, thus allowing us to organize and retrieve data more easily. This program allowed us to visualize thematic patterns in the data, determine the prevalence of a given theme, and save the direct quotations for each theme into separate computer files.

 ## Pharmacists' Drug Use Trends and Patterns

Each of the 50 pharmacists who were interviewed spoke at length and in detail about their personal drug use histories. As expected, there were many unique aspects to each individual's past drug abuse; however, the thematic content analysis revealed several consistent trends and patterns in their drug use behaviors.

Nature and Extent of Drug Use

Each recovering pharmacist's past was marked by an extensive drug addiction history. All 50 individuals recounted daily drug use. All showed clear signs of being chemically dependent on one or more prescription drugs. The constant presence or threat of physical withdrawal was the most obvious indicator of chemical dependency. Most described a pattern of progressive drug use situations wherein even short periods of abstinence would lead to withdrawal symptoms. For example, one 39-year-old male pharmacist said,

Two years before I sobered up I was really reaching my bottom. I would chase these delivery trucks down in the morning because I didn't come to my store until midafternoon. I was in withdrawal in the morning, and I was without drugs, so I had to have it—I was just going nuts. Many mornings

I had gone to work sweating. It would be 30 degrees, it would be January, and the clerk would say, "You look sick," and I would say, "It's the flu."

Almost all of the respondents spoke about a conscious or unconscious recognition of their chemical dependency, especially the coinciding threat of physical withdrawal. To counter this threat, most of the pharmacists maintained a near perpetual state of chemical intoxication. They generally designed a tightly structured and continuous drug use pattern to avoid physical withdrawal. This trend was demonstrated in the following comment made by a 38-year-old female pharmacist: "During the last 4 years of my use, I used every single day. Day in and day out, all the time to try to stay out of withdrawal and just maintain."

Many individuals described how they had progressed to dosage intervals of an hour or less. One 45-year-old male pharmacist said,

It was just crazy. . . . I just kept taking more and more stuff because I loved it . . . Percosets [narcotic analgesic], you know. CIIs, it was unbelievable. And I would be popping these things, and 30 minutes later I'd have to pop some more. It just really snowballed fast on me until I wasn't knowing what I was doing. . . . Oh gosh, I was probably doing 20 Percoset a day at work.

Only 10 of the 50 interviewees described a drug habit that focused on a single type or class of prescription medication.[9] Three of these individuals engaged in heavy, daily use of cocaine (up to 5 grams per day). The other eight individuals claimed that their drug habit was exclusively focused on narcotic analgesics.[10]

The remaining 40 respondents can be described as poly-drug users.[11] Their daily drug use behaviors included multiple types and classes of controlled substances. Thirty-two of these 40 poly-drug users were regularly using at least one type of narcotic analgesic. However, their narcotic analgesics habit usually coincided with the use of some other class of prescription medication, such as amphetamines (e.g., Dexedrine, Ritalin), barbiturates (e.g., Seconal, Phenobarbital), or benzodiazepines (e.g., Valium, Xanax). As a 45-year-old male pharmacist explained, "I was taking amphetamines, not necessarily every day but occasionally. The opiates [narcotic analgesics] I was taking every day. And the benzodiazepines I was taking sporadically . . . daily. So, it was mainly opiates."

It also should be noted that many of the interviewees chose to mix alcohol with prescription medications. In fact, a considerable number of the respondents described daily or weekly drinking habits. Most of the alcohol consumption can be described as binge drinking behavior wherein the individual drank a high volume over a short period of time. Similarly, a number of respondents indicated that they sometimes mixed illegal street drugs with the prescription drugs. For example, five of the respondents described occasional marijuana use. In most cases, the street drug use was not daily but rather taken weekly, monthly, or on a special occasion.

Garbage Heading

Each poly-drug user was asked if he or she considered him- or herself to be a "garbage head." This is a term used within the drug treatment and support group communities to refer to an individual who is not particular and will use any type of drug to which he or she can gain access. Thirty of the 40 poly-drug users characterized themselves as garbage heads. They routinely described extensive drug use experimentation. For example, a 48-year-old male pharmacist explained that his Narcotics Anonymous sponsor once required him to write down the name of every drug type that he had used over the course of his 15-year career. He claimed that this exercise yielded a list of 144 different medications. The following interview excerpts are indicative of the types of responses that were received when asking about the breadth of garbage head practices. A 43-year-old male pharmacist said,

> I did it all. You know we were kind of garbage cans. My drug of choice was codeine. I did a

lot of acetaminophen with codeine. I started out with aspirin and codeine, like Empirin, but the Empirin hurt my stomach. So, you know, being really dumb I went to Tylenol with codeine and stayed strictly with that [all narcotic analgesics]. But I was not a downer lover, I didn't like to be zoned out like pot made me. I liked to be up and fired up and moving. Codeine did that to me. Unlike others, it didn't cause the drowsiness, it gave me a surge. But still, I had to try other things to see what worked best together.

Similarly, when asked what types of drug he preferred to use, a 42-year-old male pharmacist replied, "anything. In the beginning anything. No matter what it was. If it had that 'C'[12] with the little lines in there . . . CII, CIII, CIV . . . I had to go and do it."

Most of the respondents described how they would ingest large amounts of drugs each day. Only a small minority engaged in what would be considered approved or recommended dosage levels of the myriad of prescription medications that they were taking. Some pharmacists recounted staggering daily dosage schedules. For example, one pharmacist described how he was injecting 500 mg of morphine each day. Another individual claimed that he was injecting 500 mg of Demerol each day. Several other respondents described how they were injecting in excess of 100 mg of a narcotic per day. Intravenous users were not the only ones who displayed heavy drug use patterns. Several individuals were ingesting more than 100 Percodan or Percoset pills each day. Two separate cocaine users explained how their habits had progressed to a daily intake of an impressive 5 grams per day.

Titrating

An interesting trend emerged from the inquiry into the development of drug tolerance. Early in the interview process, pharmacists began speaking about a drug use practice called titrating. This term refers to a practice whereby individuals apply their pharmaceutical knowledge to manage their personal drug use, enhancing or neutralizing specific drug effects by ingesting counteracting drugs. In effect, they would walk a chemical tightrope that allowed them to remain high, function, and disguise the obvious physical signs of drug abuse. For example, one 44-year-old male pharmacist said,

> When I was out partying I could drink. See, I didn't drink at work. That's one of the ways that I got heavier into the benzos [benzodiazepines] and the barbs [barbiturates]. . . . You could take something like that and get the sedative effects, but it wouldn't smell on your breath. So I would not drink, but basically I had to wake up. . . . I would put about four Percosets [narcotic analgesic] and four biphetamine 20 mg or Dexedrine [amphetamine] with the Percoset. When it was time to roll out of bed, to try to get to work, I would swallow all that and wait a little bit until it would start to kick in. And then I would just compulsively swallow whatever Percoset I could get my hands on. And swallow amphetamines as needed to titrate my energy levels to being productive and not to appear impaired from the opiate.

This pharmacist used his titrating knowledge to achieve three different goals: (a) physical euphoria, (b) avoidance of negative side-effects, and (c) avoidance of detection. All three of these themes were found in varying degrees among the 28 pharmacists who recounted titrating practices.

Regardless of the origin, there is clear evidence that titrating behavior evolves from pharmaceutical training. Most pharmacists did not hesitate to state that they had learned how to titrate by applying what they had learned in class lectures or by reading books or articles on pharmacology. This is illustrated in the following exchange between the interviewer (I) and a 56-year-old male pharmacist (P).

I: It seems like you were really putting your expertise to work there?

P: Yep, all my knowledge of pharmacology so I could get perfectly titrated. And I'd go in there [to work], and 15 minutes later I could be snowed over.

Widespread presence of garbage heading and titrating offers important support for our assertion that being and becoming a pharmacist affects the individuals' drug use. Clearly, these pharmacists were exploiting their access to prescription drugs and applying their educationally acquired knowledge to enhance and inform their drug use.

Paradox of Familiarity

Without exception, every interviewed pharmacist saw his- or herself as a drug expert. They argued that pharmacists, more so than doctors, were best prepared to dispense and counsel patients about the nature and dynamics of prescription drugs. For example, a 33-year-old male pharmacist said,

> You are the guardian of their health. The doctor might not know what they're doing. It's your idea to make sure that the right meds are used. We are supposed to question the doctors in a good way. We say "Hey look, don't come off arrogant, but hey doc, why are you doing this?"

This individual emphasizes the important role that pharmacists play in the greater health care delivery system. This was a common sentiment offered by many respondents.

The naive observer might expect that a strong professional identity as well as extensive knowledge regarding the effects of prescription drugs should be the perfect deterrent against abuse. However, we found that this was not always the case. Often, addicted pharmacists described how their intimate familiarity with prescription medicines actually was a contributing factor to abuse. In particular, the interview data show that the professional socialization process exposes pharmacists to a dangerous combination of both access to drugs and detailed knowledge about them. This professional pharmacy socialization process produces what we wish to call a paradox of familiarity.

The seeds of this paradox can be traced back to the pharmacy school experience. The interview data reveal that pharmacy school offers students very limited training in the dangers of addiction. For example, when asked about his addiction education, one pharmacist offered up the following types of responses:

> I had no [drug abuse] education. I was a drug expert and knew nothing about the [addictive effects of these] substances.
>
> It was just that junkies shoot heroin.
>
> Never did we ever have a class like "addiction." Never did anyone ever come in.
>
> Absolutely not. That was not even considered. That never came up, That was the sum total of pharmacy education on substance abuse. "Keep your hands off the stuff, ha, ha, ha." That's it, that's all I ever learned.

What little drug education training these pharmacists did receive was usually quite technical and rudimentary. For each drug type, they were made aware of the addiction potential ratings that are contained in the Controlled Substance Act of 1970 (Shulgin, 1992). Pharmacy students were provided general information about the signs of abuse that accompany various controlled substances. This is not to say that pharmacists in training are not told about the dangers of drugs. On the contrary, instructors did stress that people can and do get addicted to prescription medicines. However, the message was conveyed on a very general and impersonal level. Rarely were they told that pharmacists just like them could get addicted to prescription medicines. This can be seen in the comments of a 59-year-old male pharmacist:

> In school it was cold, clinical—"Yes, this can be habit forming and addictive." But as far as the addiction process is described in detail,

you know, the mental and the physical part of it and how those interact, and all those self-esteem issues, that's totally lost in it. It's just totally clinical. . . . They did touch on it, actually, but from a legal and a clinical standpoint. "If you do this, you will get in trouble. There are the penalties, this is what they'll do to you. This class of drugs has this addiction potential."

The insufficient and abstract nature of the drug addiction awareness is also expressed in the following exchange between the interviewer (I) and a 46-year-old male pharmacist (P):

I: Do you think that they teach you everything that you need to know about substance abuse?

P: Substances of abuse? Absolutely not.

I: Did they teach you anything? I guess would be the better question?

P: Let me tell you, we went on rounds to [a hospital], which was the alcoholic ward. And we saw society's [alcohol problem], we learned how to manage it. We learned about drugs that we used for DTs [delirium tremors] and that was about it. And I think that many classes even after that received very little more than that, basic stuff such as . . . "This is addiction and how to treat it." Not even that, "These are the physical effects of alcoholism, etc. And this is the medical management of those physical effects." No treatment of the disease at all, ever.

Drug use in pharmacy school is further exacerbated by the presence of other educationally related factors. For example, we found widespread evidence that pharmacy school helped foster benign attitudes toward prescription drugs. This belief system was affected by easy access to prescription medication, relaxed attitudes toward occasional drug use, heavy social drinking and drug use in pharmacy fraternities and other social get-togethers, and exposure to drug-using pharmacy mentors (i.e., internship preceptors).

A major element of the paradox of familiarity is rooted in a pharmacist's constant exposure to prescription drugs. Throughout a pharmacist's career (both during and after college), his or her every day is filled with repeated contact to a host of prescription medicines. This continued exposure to pharmaceutical company representatives and their sample medicines effectively erodes the individual's fear of drug addiction danger. For example, a 41-year-old male pharmacist commented,

I: You say that work desensitized you further. How so?

P: Because of pharmacy school, I didn't realize the dangers of the chemicals, and I see so many prescriptions for Valium [benzodiazepine] and codeine [narcotic analgesic] . . . that over a period of years it seemed okay. I wasn't smoking marijuana, I wasn't doing anti-Baptist alcohol, so I was okay.

The combined effect of constant access to prescription drugs is also seen in the remarks of a 52-year-old female pharmacist:

Well, the accessibility helped. I mean, I used the profession because you're accessible to all these drugs. And I mean, I know. I'm a trained pharmacist. I know what can make you feel good, and what can make you feel quiet, and all the different kinds of drugs, so my drug knowledge helped me pick the best one for me.

The situation is exacerbated by the multimillion-dollar drug marketing offensive waged by the pharmaceutical companies. Pharmacists in training are constantly being told about the powerful, therapeutic effects of the prescription medicines that they dispense. This reinforcement comes from a variety of sources, such as patient consultations, coworker discussions, professional organizations, and especially personal interactions with sales representatives from the pharmaceutical industry. A few examples of this positive, pro-drug reinforcement are offered below. A 44-year-old male pharmacist stated,

P: That's the way I grew up. . . . If there's a problem—if you have a headache—you can take a pill. If there's a stomachache, you can take a pill. There was a pill for everything.

I: Like, "better living through chemistry"?

P: I think that that's right.

I: Did you buy into that?

P: I think I definitely did. If there was something wrong, regardless if it was one of my kids or whoever it was, we made something that could take away anything that you had. I mean any problem that you had. It wasn't looked at like it is now. Now it's "say no to drugs" and blah, blah, blah.

Similarly, a 34-year-old male pharmacist said,

I: A lot of people talk about that [a "better living through chemistry" mentality] as being an age when everyone was just so mesmerized by the healing potential of these drugs and not really the side effects hadn't caught up to—you know—people were just so impressed by what they can do. Is that what you're kind of talking about?

P: Yeah. Exactly, Xanax, for instance, was touted as the greatest drug ever. I remember going to an UpJohn [a drug manufacturer] lecture in probably the late '80s. The lecture was at a local pharmacy group. He said, "It's not habit forming. Basically, when you stop taking it, the symptoms of anxiety that reoccur are the original symptoms coming back of why you took the drug." This was a guy representing UpJohn doing that lecture. I mean, you laugh now, but I came home and told my dad,

"No. no." That's what I told him, I said, "It's not habit forming." He was like, "Naa." I don't know why he knew or thought he knew, but he had always said it was okay. Later on, we learned from psychiatrists and psychiatrists that Xanax was very habit forming. . . . I believed the [UpJohn] guy.

I: So coming out of pharmacy school you bought into that kind of relaxed orientation towards the medicine?

P: I would say so.

Exposure to marketing propaganda about prescription drugs was clearly one-sided in nature. The positive aspects of the drugs were never tempered by any real effort to educate the pharmacists about corresponding dangers. For example, a 46-year-old male pharmacist said,

> Yeah, what we learned back in the '70s, was "Yes, this was indeed a problem for society. Isn't it fortunate that pharmacy doesn't have it." We know too much. We know what these drugs will do, so obviously it could never happen to a pharmacist.

Respondents described how this combination of open access and positive professional reinforcement led to a feeling of familiarity and closeness toward the drugs. Pharmacists eventually let their guard down and began to adopt a benign belief system toward prescription medicines. They believed that these drugs could only improve lives; and therefore, they dismissed or minimized the dangers. Self-medication became a viable and attractive form of medicating every problem. The paradox of familiarity is clearly articulated in the following exchange that occurred between the interviewer (I) and a 40-year-old female pharmacist (P):

P: But as far as respect for the medications, yes, I had that right out of school. A lot of respect for the power of good that the medications could do.

I: What do you mean by that?

P: Well, we have a lot of people who are alive today that would not be alive without some of the pharmaceuticals that we have. And that I think is [a source] of respect.

I: What about substance abuse? Did you know anything about it at that point?

P: Zero.

I: Nothing in school or at work?

P: Right. Pretty scary, huh?

The interview data clearly demonstrate that pharmacists were able to deny the dangers and maintain an attitude of invincibility when it came to the issue of drug addiction. As professional pharmacists, they thought that they were immune to drug addiction. For example, a 33-year-old male pharmacist said.

P: I felt that I could handle it better than the average layperson. Because, after all, I'm a professional. So yeah, it was a very cavalier attitude towards drugs. Very cavalier.

I: So you bought into that "I'm a professional" thing?

P: Yeah, and I know what I'm doing. I know what the edge is, and I'm not going to go over the edge, but clearly I was well over the edge. In the end, I got very paranoid, and I got very out of control. And it's hard for me to talk about it, because it's a shameful thing. Because I do consider myself a professional, and I let myself down, and I let a lot of people down. But for me it was a very cavalier— kind of, "I can handle this"—kind of attitude. I know what I'm doing.

Similarly, a 43-year-old female pharmacist said.

I don't know that I really thought about it. I figured, well yeah, I know more about these drugs than anybody, so maybe that justified my use and perhaps I thought being an educated, intellectual type person that I would be able to detect any problems. . . . Yeah, that's about it. I know what all these things do, I can handle it. Absolutely. I knew all about the drugs and I could quit any time I wanted to. That was a real liability. Because that's where I rationalized it out. I'm a pharmacist I know about these drugs, and they're not going to bother me. I can quit any time I want.

In all, 46 of the 50 pharmacists interviewed spoke directly about this paradox of familiarity. All expressed little doubt that this dangerous combination of access and knowledge contributed to the onset of their drug use. This paradoxical mind-set did not simply affect pharmacists' decisions to start using prescription drugs. It also seemed to offer the pharmacists a convenient rationalization to continue and even increase their drug use. For example, it was not at all uncommon for interviewees to describe how they continuously broadened their definitions of acceptable use levels. This is seen in the comments of a 33-year-old male pharmacist.

I was on the hospice team and did patient consultations, evaluating their pain situations and figuring out ways to use drugs to control their pain. One of the ironic things is that I was an expert in the use of narcotics. I knew how to administer them for patients. I guess I felt that I knew so much about them that I would not get into trouble with abusing them myself. But there's a difference between knowledge and understanding. I thought that figuring out milligrams and durations and intervals that I would protect myself. None of that protects you in the long run. . . . You end up with your thought processes in one area, in another area you're impaired. Before long, you're not following the rules you set down. So you change the rules. You change them because they don't apply to you anymore. I had rules like "never two days in a row," but that

was probably the first rule that I had made that I broke. Once I didn't take an opiate two days in a row. I would be okay. You can't become an addict if you're not using all the time. I kept that rule for quite awhile. Recreational use, lower level of use for quite awhile, not doing it every day.

In many cases, pharmacists even described how they used their pharmacy knowledge to fine-tune their drug use, maximizing the drugs' pharmaceutical potential. This tendency can be seen in the comments of a 47-year-old male pharmacist.

P: Yeah, because now that I knew more. I knew how to be more careful about it. To fine-tune my taste. I knew what to stay away from and what to go towards. I knew how to keep from overloading my own system. I knew when I was starting to get toxic, and I could adjust my drug use. Because I was still at the point where I hadn't quite crossed that line yet.

I: So it didn't slow down your use, it didn't cause you to think, "Oh, this is bad." It allowed you to see more exactly how to do it and do it better.

P: Exactly right. For example, access to the pharmaceuticals. If I didn't steal Percodan [narcotic analgesic], I knew that I could take a Tylenol #3 [narcotic analgesic] and something else and enhance the high. I knew how to create that synergistic effect so that much inventory wouldn't be missing. Because it wasn't always Percodan. I would sometimes do a Tylenol #3, and those were so liberally kept, sold by the thousands for a week type of thing, it was such a big mover. So I could keep myself high and keep myself from developing the toxicity by combining other drugs and that sort of thing.

Similarly, a 41-year-old male said,

I used my training to its fullest potential. Fullest potential. . . . Do you remember John Lily?

The guy did a lot of work, experimental work with dolphins. He had a book called the *Center of the Cyclone*. In his book, he made a statement that one cannot consider oneself a true researcher unless one is willing to do the experiment on oneself. I said, "Exactly." That was one of my defining moments. So I would take that statement . . . If you didn't try it, you can't consider yourself a true researcher. That's how I viewed myself. I always believed in constant improvement.

As these pharmacists progressed into the later phases of their drug abuse period, they were forced to ponder the significance of their drug use habit. At some point, they came to the realization that they had a drug problem. However, very few individuals voluntarily sought help. Instead, they kept their problem a secret, reasoning that their knowledge would again afford them the vehicle to get themselves out of any predicament that they were in. To them, only uneducated street addicts needed professional drug treatment. This characterization can be seen in the comments of a 33-year-old female pharmacist.

Yeah, I didn't think that it would happen to me. I was pissed. I thought those [drug abusers] were people that lived under bridges. People who didn't have college educations. People who . . . I guess I was just kind of a snob.

Even when they got caught for stealing or using drugs, many pharmacists still maintained their shield of overconfidence. In the following quote, a 39-year-old female describes what happened when she was hospitalized for drug related health problems.

P: I was judgmental too. You know I [thought] those [drug abusers] were people who had no self-will. In the ER [emergency room] they did treat me like an addict and I'd get very angry, very angry.

I: Why?

P: Well, because I wasn't an addict. I would say things like, "Don't you know who I am? I am a pain specialist in this hospital; I know when I need narcotics," and they, you know, looking back on it, it must have just been humorous.

 ## Discussion

The above excerpts from personal interviews demonstrate how pharmacists' professional expertise contributes to the detriment of their health. These druggists were all aware that their drug use was wrong. They knew that their employers and the federal law made it illegal for them to remove drugs from pharmacy stock or ingest drugs while on the job. However, they were adept at developing vocabularies of adjustment (Cressey, 1953) or techniques of neutralizations (Sykes & Matza, 1957) to offset negative normative judgments. They came up with a series of excuses or justifications that served as post hoc rationalizations and a priori justifications for their behaviors. Faced with a growing drug problem, they convinced themselves that they were capable of controlling it without any outside assistance. Without exception, these behaviors and their accompanying vocabularies of adjustment were rooted in the experiences and expertise that they had gained while becoming a member of the pharmacy profession.

The above outlined interview data raises some very troubling suggestions about the ways that being and becoming a pharmacist can inadvertently produce deviant drug habits. We have been able to identify a number of aspects within the educational, occupational, and professional socialization processes that seemed to contribute to the initial onset, progression, and maintenance of these individuals' illicit prescription drug habits. The occupational and professional literature offers several possible insights into our findings.

The central argument of this article is that drug abuse among pharmacists does not solely have its origins in the problems of individual actors; but rather, it is rooted in the nature of the profession itself. Numerous scholars (Freidson, 1970; Greenwood, 1957; Pavalko, 1971) have described how the professional socialization process instills neophyte members with a sense of perceived power and authority over the knowledge and social objects that are unique to the profession. In applying his concept of "professional dominance" to the professional socialization process that affects doctors, Freidson (1975) and others (Becker et al., 1961; Bloom, 1973; Haas & Shaffir, 1987; Konner, 1987) have documented how medical professionals routinely overestimate the limits of their professional knowledge or abilities. As an example, note that members of the medical profession routinely use the term God complex to refer to a doctor who thinks he or she is capable of curing any physical ailment regardless of the circumstances. In the same way that some doctors think that they can remedy any physical ailment, it is possible that some pharmacists may reason that they are capable of self-medicating with any prescription drug without putting themselves in significant risk of drug dependency.

The potential for a pharmacist to abuse his or her professional power may be exacerbated by yet another issue. It has long been argued that pharmacy is merely an occupation or, at best, a marginal or quasi-profession. This is because it has failed to exercise strict controls over its object and the behavior of its members (Denzin & Metlin, 1968). Pharmacists have always had great difficulty in convincing others that they are really society's drug experts because it is the medical profession that controls the disbursement of medications to the general public (i.e., via an authorizing prescription). Denzin and Metlin point out that, almost like a machine, the pharmacist merely fills the prescription order that the patient's medical doctor has dictated. Although contemporary pharmacists would like us to believe otherwise, doctors still provide the "primary medical advice" to the sick and ailing patient (Denzin & Metlin, 1968, p. 379).

Notes

2. Pharmacists in the McAuliffe et al. (1987) study were asked to offer a self-assessment of drug dependency to any one of a number of psychoactive controlled substances. This list included

prescription as well as nonprescription medications. Individuals were classified as being at risk of drug abuse if they reported more than 100 total drug use episodes and experienced more than one drug-related interference with functioning (as determined by a standard checklist of items such as calling in late to work due to substance use, seeking treatment, etc.).

3. Normack, Eckel, Pfifferling, and Cocolas (1985a) used a scaled usage inventory that sampled the presence and frequency of an individual's use of a variety of substances to establish their criteria for impairment risk. Similar to the McAuliffe et al. (1987) study, they did not limit their inquiry to prescription drug use. Anyone scoring more than a 2 on the usage scale that ranged from 0 to 4 was identified as being at risk.

4. The researchers used a broad definition of drug use, stating that they were interested in "pharmacists recovering from alcohol and other drug addictions" (Bissell, Haberman, & Williams, 1989, p. 21). Similar to the above studies, they have not limited their analysis to pharmacists' use of the substances that they are responsible for dispensing.

5. Three separate data sources were used in the original inquiry to achieve a more comprehensive inquiry into pharmacists' illicit prescription drug use behaviors. These data sources included (a) in-depth interviews with pharmacists who were recovering from illicit prescription drug use behaviors; (b) incident reports detailing officially discovered cases of pharmacists' drug related wrongdoings occurring in two major retail pharmacy chains; and (c) a self-administered, anonymous survey of a random sample of practicing pharmacists.

6. These recruiters functioned as present or past coordinators of their respective state recovery network. They had access to the names of all current and past network members and were able to contact them without violating the confidentiality agreements that are a cornerstone of the recovery movement.

7. Recruiters were explicitly asked to refer only pharmacists who had a past history of prescription drug use. Several individuals who contacted us or were interviewed had no prescription drug use history (i.e., they used alcohol or street drugs only). These individuals were not included in the present analysis.

8. The membership list of the American Pharmaceutical Association was used to generate a random sample of 2,000 practicing U.S. pharmacists. Completed surveys were returned by 1,016 individuals (50.5% response rate). The data presented in Table 1 include only those 312 respondents who reported five or more lifetime episodes involving the illicit use of one of the following 10 addictive substances: cocaine, amphetamines, other stimulants, barbiturates, benzodiazepines, narcotic analgesics, nonnarcotic analgesics, inhalants, muscle relaxants, and antidepressants. Data on marijuana/hashish use and antibiotic use were available. However given the fact that these two do not fit the description of mind-altering prescription drugs, we chose to exclude them from our

analysis. We maintain that the presence of five or more lifetime use episodes is indicative of a relaxed approach to unauthorized drug use, thus suggesting that the individual has progressed past the experimental or one time occasion of drug use.

9. The term drug class refers to the groupings of drugs that have similar psychoactive effects. For example, the narcotic analgesic drug class includes all opiate-based medications. All drugs of this class are prescribed principally for pain relief. Some of the other drug classes that will be discussed in this paper include amphetamines, barbiturates, benzodiazepines, stimulants, and nonnarcotic analgesics. Each of these drug classes has its own distinguishing characteristics. The term drug types refers to the different medications contained in each drug class. Each drug type is assigned its own generic or brand name. Examples of drug types that fall into the narcotic analgesic class include Percodan, Morphine, Demerol, and Dilaudid. Note that there are often hundreds of drug types within each drug class.

10. The term narcotic analgesic is commonly used to refer to opiate-based medications. All narcotic analgesic drug types are classified as CII substances under the Controlled Substance Act of 1970 (Shulgin, 1992). Each of these substances is a highly addictive pain medication and is subject to the most strict inventory and dispensing controls. Narcotic analgesic drug types include morphine, Dilaudid, Demerol, Percodan, Percoset, Codeine, and Hydrocodone.

11. The term poly-drug user refers to an individual who routinely uses multiple types or classes of drugs and alcohol. Poly-drug use behaviors usually result in states of cross-addiction as the body develops a tolerance and dependence on multiple forms and combinations of drugs. This advanced type of drug habit is generally very difficult to reverse or control and treatment becomes a very complicated detoxification process.

12. The letter C is commonly used to abbreviate the word class. The Controlled Substance Act of 1970 (Shulgin, 1992) classifies prescription medications in five separate classes or schedules according to their medicinal purpose and addiction potential.

References

Alasuutari, P. (1992). *Desire and craving: A cultural theory of alcoholism.* Albany: State University of New York Press.

Allen, I. (1994). *Doctors and their careers: A new generation.* London: Policy Studies Institute.

American Nurses Association. (ANA). (1984). *ANA cabinet on nursing practice, statement on scope for addiction nursing practice.* Kansas City, MO: Author.

American Pharmaceutical Association. (APhA). (1982). Report of the American Pharmaceutical Association Policy Committee on Professional Affairs. *American Pharmacy, NS22,* 368-380.

Apter, T. E. (1993). *Working women don't have wives: Professional success in the 1990s.* New York: St. Martin's.

Baldwin, J. N., Light, K. E., Stock, C., Ives, T. J., Crabtree, B. L., Miederhoff, P. A., Tommasello, T., & Levine, P. J. (1991). Curricular guidelines for pharmacy education: Substance abuse and addictive disease. *American Journal of Pharmaceutical Education, 55*(4), 311-316.

Becker, H. S., Geer, B., Hughes, E. C., & Strauss, A. L. (1961). *Boys in white: Student culture in medical school.* Chicago: University of Chicago Press.

Benson, M. L. (1985). Denying the guilty mind: Accounting for involvement in a white collar crime. *Criminology, 23,* 583-607.

Berg, B. L. (1998). *Qualitative research methods for the social sciences* (3rd ed.). Needham Heights, MA: Allyn & Bacon.

Bissell, L., Haberman, P. W., & Williams, R. L. (1989). Pharmacists recovering from alcohol and other drug addictions: An interview study. *American Pharmacy, NS29*(6), 19-30.

Bissell, L., & Jones, R. W. (1981). The alcoholic nurse. *Nursing Outlook, 29*(2), 96-101.

Bloom, S. W. (1973). *Power and dissent in the medical school.* New York: Free Press.

Bogardus, D. E. (1987). *Missing drugs.* Salt Lake City, UT: Medical Management Systems.

Briles, J. (1994). *The Briles Report on women in healthcare.* San Francisco: Jossey-Bass.

Candib, L. M. (1996). How medicine tried to make a man out of me (and failed, finally). In D. Wear (Ed.), *Women in medical education* (pp. 135-144). Albany, NY: SUNY Press.

Carlson, H. B., Dilts, S. L., & Radcliff, S. (1994). Physicians with substance abuse problems and their recovery environment: A survey. *Journal of Substance Abuse Treatment, 11*(2), 113-119.

Chi, J. (1983). Impaired pharmacists: More programs move to handle the problem. *Drug Topics, 127*(47), 24-29.

Cressey, D. R. (1953). *Other people's money.* Glencoe, IL: Free Press.

Dabney, D. A. (1995a). Neutralization and deviance in the workplace: Theft of supplies and medicines by hospital nurses. *Deviant Behavior, 16,* 313-331.

Dabney, D. A. (1995b). Workplace deviance among nurses: The influence of work group norms on drug diversion and/or use. *Journal of Nursing Administration, 25*(3), 48-54.

Dabney, D. A. (1997). *A sociological examination of illicit prescription drug use among pharmacists.* Unpublished doctoral dissertation. University of Florida, Gainesville.

Dalton, M. (1959). *Men who manage.* New York: John Wiley.

Decima. (1990). *Final report of transport Canada on the results of the substance use and transportation safety study.* Toronto, Canada: Decima Research.

Denzin, N. K. (1987). *Recovering alcoholic.* Newbury Park, CA: Sage.

Denzin, N. K., & Metlin, C. J. (1968). Incomplete professionalization: The case of pharmacy. *Social Forces, 46,* 375-381.

Ditton, J. (1977). *Part-time crime: An ethnography of fiddling and pilferage.* New York: Macmillan.

Epstein, D. (1990). Theft: How safe are your pharmacies? Part I: The chains. *Drug Topics, 130*(41), 12-23.

Epstein, D. (1991). Theft: How safe are your pharmacies? Part II: The independents. *Drug Topics, 131*(1), 13-25.

Freidson, E. (1970). *Professional dominance.* Chicago: Aldine.

Freidson, E. (1975). *Doctoring together.* New York: Elsevier North-Holland.

Gallegos, K. V., Veil, F. W., Wilson, P. O., Porter, T., & Talbott, G. D. (1988). Substance abuse among health professionals. *Maryland Medical Journal, 37*(3), 191-197.

Geis, G. (1967). The heavy electrical equipment antitrust cases of 1961. In M. B. Clinard & R. Quinney (Eds.), *Criminal behavior systems: A typology* (pp. 139-151). New York: Reinhart and Winston.

Gouldner, A. (1954). *Patterns of industrial bureaucracy.* New York: Free Press.

Green, P. (1989). The chemically dependent nurse. *Nursing clinics of North America, 24*(1), 81-94.

Greenwood, E. (1957). Attributes of a profession. *Social Work, 2,* 45-55.

Haas, J., & Shaffir, W. (1987). *Becoming doctors: The adoption of a cloak of competence.* Greenwich, CT: JAI.

Hankes, L., & Bissell, L. (1992). Health professionals. In J. H. Lowinson, P. Ruiz, R. Millman, & J. G. Langrod (Eds.), *Substance abuse: A comprehensive textbook* (2nd ed., pp. 897-908). Baltimore: Williams & Wilkins.

Harris, A. M. (1995). *Broken patterns: Professional women and the quest for a new feminine identity.* Detroit, MI: Wayne State University Press.

Hoffman, J. P., Brittingham, A., & Larson, C. (1996). *Drug abuse among U.S. workers: Prevalence and trends by occupation and industry category.* Rockville, MD: U.S. Department of Health and Human Services.

Hollinger, R. C. (1991). Neutralizing in the workplace: An empirical analysis of property theft and production deviance. *Deviant Behavior, 12,* 169-202.

Hood, J. C., & Duphome, P. L. (1995). To report or not to report: Nurses' attitudes toward reporting co-workers suspected of substance abuse. *Journal of Drug Issues, 25*(2), 313-339.

Horning, D. (1970). Blue collar theft: Conceptions of property, attitudes toward pilfering, and work group norms in a modern industrial plant. In E. O. Smigel & H. L. Ross (Eds.), *Crimes against bureaucracy* (pp. 46-64). New York: Van Nostrand Reinhold.

Hughes, P. H., Conrad, S. E., Baldwin, D. C., Storr, C., & Sheehan, D. (1991). Resident physician substance use in the United States. *Journal of the American Medical Association, 265*(16), 2069-2073.

Hughes, P. H., Storr, C., Sheehan, D. V., Conn, J., & Sheehan, M. F. (1990). Studies of drug use and impairment in the medical profession. *Addiction and Recovery, 10,* 42-45.

Hutchinson, S. (1986). Chemically dependent nurses: The trajectory toward self-annihilation. *Nursing Research, 35*(4), 196-201.

Kanter, R. M. (1977). *Men and women of the corporation.* New York: Basic Books.

Konner, M. (1987). *Becoming a doctor.* New York: Penguin.

Kurzman, M. G. (1972). *Drug abuse education in pharmacy schools.* A report prepared for the Drug Enforcement Administration by the American Association of Colleges of Pharmacy, Washington, DC.

Lehman, W. E. K., Holcom, M. L., & Simpson, D. D. (1990). *Employee health and performance in the workplace: A survey of municipal employees in a large southwest city.* Fort Worth, TX: Texas Christian University, Institute of Behavioral Research.

Levers, L. L., & Hawes, A. R, (1990). Drugs and gender: A woman's recovery program. *Journal of Mental Health Counseling, 12,* 527-531.

Lorber, J. (1993). Why women physicians will never be true equals in the American medical profession. In E. Riska & K. Wegar (Eds.), *Gender, work and medicine* (pp. 62-76). London: Sage Ltd.

Mars, G. (1982). *Cheats at work: An anthropology of workplace crime.* London: George Allen & Unwin.

Martin, S. (1993). Pharmacists number more than 190,000 in United States. *American Pharmacy, NS33*(1), 22-24.

McAneny, L., & Moore, D. W. (1994). Annual honesty & ethics poll. *The Gallup Poll Monthly, 349,* 2-4.

McAuliffe, W. E., Rohman, M., Fishman, P., Friedman, R., Wechsler, H., Soboroff, S. H., & Toth, D. (1984). Psychoactive drug use by young and future physicians. *Journal of Health and Social Behavior, 25*(3), 35-54.

McAuliffe, W. E., Santangelo, S. L., Gingras, J., Rohman, M., Sobol, A., & Magnuson, E. (1987). Use and abuse of controlled substances by pharmacists and pharmacy students. *American Journal of Hospital Pharmacy, 44*(2), 311-317.

McDuff, D. R., Tommasello, A. C., Hoffman, K. J., & Johnson, J. L. (1995). Addictions training for physicians and other licensed health care professionals in Maryland. *Maryland Medical Journal, 44*(6), 453-459.

Michigan Nurses Association. (MNA). (1986). Fact sheet: Chemical dependency of nurses. East Lansing, MI: Author.

Miederhoff, P., Allen, H. D., McCreary, G. J., & Veal. A. F. (1977) A study of pharmacy students' attitudes toward drug abuse. *American Journal of Pharmaceutical Education, 42,* 129-131.

Moodley-Kunnie, T. (1988). Attitudes and perceptions of health professionals toward substance use disorders and substance dependent individuals. *The International Journal of the Addictions, 23*(5), 469-475.

National Association of Retail Druggists. (NARD). (1988). *NARD'S guide to programs for the impaired pharmacist.* Alexandria, VA: Author.

National Institute of Justice. (NIJ). (1997). *1996 Drug use forecasting: Annual report on adult and juvenile arrestees.* Washington, DC: Author.

Normack, J. W., Eckel, F. M., Pfifferling, J., & Cocolas, G. (1985a). Impairment risk in North Carolina pharmacists. *American Pharmacy, NS25*(6), 45-48.

Normack, J. W., Eckel, F. M., Pfifferling, J., & Cocolas, G. (1985b). Impairment risk in North Carolina pharmacy students. *American Pharmacy, NS25*(6), 60-62.

Normand, J., Salyards, S. D., & Mahony, J. J. (1990). An evaluation of preemployment drug testing. *Journal of Applied Psychology, 75,* 629-639.

Pavalko, R. M. (1971). *Sociology of occupations and professions.* Itasca, IL: F. E. Peacock.

Poplar, J. F., & Lyle, W. (1969). Characteristics of nurse addicts. American Journal of Nursing, 69, 117-119.

Riska, E., & Wegar, K. (1993). Women physicians: A new force in Medicine? In E. Riska & K. Wegar (Eds.), *Gender, work and medicine* (pp. 77-94). London: Sage Ltd.

Rosenthal, M. M. (1995). *The incompetent doctor: Behind closed doors.* Philadelphia: Open University Press.

Rudy, D. R. (1986). *Becoming an alcoholic: Alcoholics Anonymous and the reality of alcoholism.* Carbondale: Southern Illinois University Press.

Schneck, D., Amodei, R., & Kernish, R. (1991). *Substance abuse in the transit industry.* Washington, DC: Office of Technical Assistance and Safety.

Secundy, M. G. (1996). Life as a sheep in the cow's pasture. In D. Wear (Ed.), *Women in medical education* (pp. 119-126). Albany, NY: SUNY Press.

Shaffer, S. (1987) Attitudes and perceptions held by impaired nurses, *Nursing Management, 18*(4), 46-50.

Sheffield, J. W., O'Neill, P., & Fisher, C. (1992a). Women in recovery: From pain to progress: Part 1. *Texas Pharmacy, 8*(1), 29-36.

Sheffield, J. W., O'Neill, R., & Fisher, C. (1992b). Women in recovery: From pain to progress: Part 2. *Texas Pharmacy, 8*(2), 22-34.

Sheridan, J. R., & Winkler, H. (1989). An evaluation of drug testing in the workplace. In S. W. Gust & J. M. Walsh (Eds.), *Drugs in the workplace: Research and evaluation data* (NIDA Research Monograph 91). Rockville, MD: National Institute of Drug Abuse.

Shulgin, A. T. (1992). *Controlled substances: A chemical guide to the federal drug laws.* Berkeley, CA: Ronin.

Sich, E. W. (1987). Garment workers: Perceptions of inequity and employee theft. *British Journal of Criminology, 27,* 174-190.

Smith, H. C. (1989). Substance abuse among nurses: Types of drugs. *Dimensions of Critical Nursing, 8*(3), 159-167.

Steinberg, J. A. (1984). *Climbing the ladder of success in high heels.* Ann Arbor: University of Michigan Press.

Substance Abuse and Mental Health Services Administration. (1996). *National household survey on drug abuse: Main findings, 1994.* Rockville, MD: U.S. Department of Health and Human Services.

Sullivan, E. J. (1987). Comparison of chemically dependent and non-dependent nurses on familial, personal, and professional characteristics. *Journal of Studies on Alcohol, 48*(6), 563-568.

Sykes, G., & Matza, D. (1957). Techniques of neutralization: A theory of delinquency. *American Journal of Sociology, 22*(4), 664-670.

Tatham, R. L. (1974). Employee views of theft in retailing. *Journal of Retailing, 50,* 49-55.

Wilensky, H. L. (1964). The professionalism of everyone. *American Journal of Sociology, 70,* 137-158.

Winick, C. (1961). Physician narcotic addicts. *Social Problems, 9,* 174-186.

Wivell, M. K., & Wilson, G. L. (1994). Prescription for harm: Pharmacist liability. *Trial, 30*(5), 36-39.

DISCUSSION QUESTIONS

1. Should pharmacists who have been convicted of drug crimes be allowed to continue in their profession? Explain.

2. Do you think similar levels of drug use would be found among other health care professionals? Why or why not?

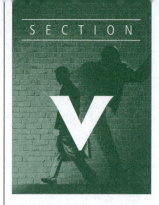

V

Crime in Systems of Social Control

White-Collar Crime in Criminal Justice, Political, and Religious Systems

- Crimes in the Criminal Justice System
- Crimes in the Political System
- Crimes by Officials in the Religious System

 Introduction

It sounds like a bad joke—a police officer, lawyer, judge, correctional officer, politician, military officer, and priest walk into a bar together. What do you think they could discuss that they have in common? Several answers come to mind. For example, they could talk about the fact that they each are public servants. Their occupations exist to serve members of the public. They could also talk about the fact that their salaries are not the highest one would find among various occupations. Or, they could talk about their colleagues who have been caught committing white-collar crimes. After all, no profession is immune from white-collar misconduct. As well, they could also talk about the main thing their professions have in common across all of their professions: they each work in systems of social control.

As examples of the crimes committed by professionals in these systems of social control, consider the following examples quoted from their original sources:

- Jorge De Castro Font, a former senator in the Commonwealth of Puerto Rico, pleaded guilty on January 21, 2009, to honest services wire fraud and conspiracy to commit extortion.... De Castro Font directly and indirectly solicited between approximately $500,000 and $525,000 in cash payments and other benefits, such as campaign contributions in excess of the legal limits, lodging, private flights, meals, and other things of value from individuals. (U.S. Department of Justice, 2010c, p. 48).
- Former United States District Court Judge Samuel B. Kent was sentenced to 33 months of imprisonment.... He previously pled guilty to obstructing an investigation of a judicial misconduct complaint (U.S. Department of Justice, 2010c, p. 6).
- Beverly Masek, former Alaska state representative, was sentenced on September 24, 2009, to 6 months of imprisonment followed by 3 years of supervised release. Masek had previously pleaded guilty to conspiring to commit bribery. Masek received multiple cash payments from Bill Allen and one of his relatives during the time she had knowledge that VECO had matters pending before the Alaska state legislature, which she knew were important to Allen's business interests. In return, Masek withdrew a piece of legislation at the request of Allen one day before she accepted a cash payment of approximately $2,000 from Allen. (U.S. Department of Justice, 2010c, p. 46)
- Ramon Bazan, a former special agent of the Bureau of Alcohol, Tobacco, Firearms and Explosives ("ATF"), was charged on December 23, 2009, in an information for allegedly making false statements in connection with a series of fraudulent visa referrals. (U.S. Department of Justice, 2010c, p. 35)
- A Roman Catholic pastor of two city parishes, including one that counted Vice President Joe Biden as a past congregant, is being accused of embezzling more than $350,000 from his parishes. (O'Sullivan, 2011)

One irony arises when considering crimes by officials in social control systems: Their occupations exist in order to reduce/govern against wrongful behaviors, but in some cases, those given the duty to stop misconduct actually engage in misconduct themselves.

Crimes in the Criminal Justice System

Entrusted to enforce the law, criminal justice officials have duties that are not given to any other occupational group. Unfortunately, as with other professions, crime occurs in the criminal justice professions. The types of white-collar crime occurring in the criminal justice system include:

- Police corruption
- Attorney misconduct
- Judicial misconduct
- Prosecutorial misconduct
- Correctional officer misconduct

Police Corruption

Police corruption occurs when police officers violate the trust they have been given and abuse their law enforcement authority (Punch, 2009). Different typologies have been presented to characterize the numerous types of police corruption known to occur. One of the clearest (and earliest) typologies was set forth by Barker and Roebucks (1973), who identified the following types of police corruption:

Corruption of authority (e.g., using the law enforcement role to gain favors such as gratuities)

Kickbacks (e.g., sending victims or offenders to certain service providers—like tow truck drivers—in exchange for a fee from the service provider)

Opportunistic theft (e.g., stealing from crime scenes when the opportunity arises)

Shakedowns (e.g., taking or soliciting bribes from offenders in exchange for not enforcing the law)

Protection of illegal activities (e.g., protecting gangs, organized crime units, or others in exchange for payment)

Fixing cases (e.g., fixing traffic tickets or changing testimony)

Direct criminal activities (e.g., engaging in crime while on the job)

Internal payoffs (e.g., engaging in schemes where other criminal justice officials are paid off for their illicit participation in the scheme)

Police sexual misconduct is another variety of police corruption. Maher (2003) offers the following definition of police sexual misconduct:

Any behavior by a police officer, whereby an officer takes advantage of his or her unique position in law enforcement to misuse his or her authority and power to commit a sexually violent act or to initiate or respond to some sexually motivated cure for the purpose of personal gratification. This behavior must include physical contact, verbal communication, or a sexual implicit or explicit gesture directed towards another person. (p. 355)

Examples of sexual misconduct exist on a continuum, ranging from situations where no contact occurs between the officer and the citizen to situations where forced contact occurs. Surveys of 40 police officers by Maher (2003) found evidence of police behaviors dictated by sexual interests. Officers reported routinely stopping motorists to "check out" those that they found attractive. A study of 501 cases of police sexual violence found that many of the offenders committed multiple acts of sexual violence (McGurrin & Kappeler, 2002). The authors suggested that the badge and gun were substitutes for physical force, particularly in situations where police officers solicited sexual favors in exchange for police decisions that would benefit the victim.

The consequences of police corruption can be far reaching. As Hunter (1999) notes, "one incident of police misbehavior in a distant locality can have adverse effects on police community relationships in police agencies across the country" (p. 156). For departments where corruption occurs, the corruption diminishes police effectiveness, creates demoralization in the department, and creates barriers between the department and the community (Hunter, 1999).

Various perspectives have been offered in an effort to explain police corruption. The phrase "bad apples" has frequently been used to suggest that corruption is limited to a few rogue officers in a department. More recently, it has been suggested that the phrase "bad orchards" would more aptly describe how the broader police culture and dynamics of policing contribute to police misconduct (Punch, 2009). Others have suggested that overreaching cultural and community factors are potential causes of police misconduct (Kane, 2002).

In an effort to identify the individual officer characteristics that contribute to police misconduct, one study compared all 1,543 police officers dismissed from the New York Police Department between 1975 and 1996 with a sample of police recruits who had never been disciplined. This study found that those who were dismissed for misconduct were more likely to have past arrests, traffic violations, and problems with previous jobs. Those who had college degrees were less likely to be dismissed (Fyfe & Kane, 2005).

Others have attributed police misconduct to a lack of policies to prevent misconduct, faulty control mechanisms, and a lack of appropriate training (Kinnaird, 2007). Suggestions for preventing police misconduct have centered on addressing these potential causal factors. One author stresses that police agencies must have policies that clearly define police misconduct so officers are aware of the rules and sanctions (Martinelli, 2007). Other strategies that have been suggested include promoting external accountability (Barker, 2002), improving police supervision strategies (Hunter, 1999; Martinelli, 2007), focusing on early warning signs (Walker & Alpert, 2002), and promoting ethics (Hunter, 1999).

Hunter (1999) surveyed 65 police officers to determine which strategies the officers most supported to deal with police misconduct. Strategies that officers supported the most included strict and fair discipline, clear policies, professional standards, promoting capable supervisors, and having administrators serve as examples or role models. The need for adequate policies to prevent and respond to police corruption is in line with the systems theme guiding the discussion in this text—systems must develop policies to address misconduct in occupations that are a part of the system, clearly define misconduct, identify ways to detect the misconduct, describe ways to respond to the misconduct, and clearly communicate the sanctions that will be imposed for misconduct.

Attorney Misconduct

It is likely that many readers, criminal justice majors in particular, have at one point considered a career as an attorney. After all, the media—in television, movies, and books—has glorified the careers of attorneys. From *Perry Mason* to *L.A. Law* to *Law and Order*, attorneys enter our homes on a regular basis through our televisions. While criminal justice majors might tend to have favorable attitudes toward attorneys, members of the public tend to view attorneys in a less favorable light. One author notes that lawyers are viewed as "simply a plague on society" (Hazard, 1991, p. 1240).

This negative view of attorneys likely contributes to formal complaints about attorney conduct (or misconduct). Over the past several decades, the number of accusations against attorneys has increased to the point that a heightened concern about being accused of misconduct has arisen (Payne & Stevens, 1999). The reason for their concern is that complaints to their respective state bar associations have the potential to result in drastic consequences to an attorney's career.

States have different expectations and definitions for what is viewed to be appropriate conduct for attorneys. In Alabama, for example, the state bar identifies the following behaviors as warranting discipline toward attorneys:

- Failing to respond to charges brought forth by the state bar
- Violating disciplinary rules

- Neglecting a legal matter
- Felony conviction
- Misdemeanor conviction
- Keeping a client's money that should have been returned
- Keeping a client's money after failing to provide services
- Keeping fraudulently obtained money
- False statements to authorities
- False statements to clients
- Misuse of the client's funds
- Failure to provide competent representation
- Disciplined for a violation in another state
- Failure to comply with an order from a disciplinary authority
- Excessive, unfair, or unclear fees
- Failure to meet legal education requirements
- Financial conflict of interest with a client
- Behavior unbecoming of a court official (Payne & Stevens, 1999).

Of the few studies that have been done on attorney misconduct, the focus tends to be on types of sanctions levied against attorneys. Morgan (1995) identified three reasons why such research is important, both for society and the field of criminal justice. First, understanding how and why attorneys are sanctioned helps to clarify "what the substantive law really is" (p. 343). Second, such research helps to formulate degrees of misconduct by understanding how severity of sanction is tied to misconduct type. Third, such research helps to dispel misguided beliefs that "professional standards are largely unenforced and unenforceable" (p. 343). In fact, research shows that offenders are routinely disciplined and this discipline may result in loss of prestige, destruction of self-worth, embarrassment, social and professional ostracism, loss of professional affiliation, and strain in personal relationships.

If attorneys violate criminal or civil laws, they can be subjected to penalties stemming from those bodies of law (e.g., incarceration, probation, fines, restitution, etc.). Research shows that allegations of misconduct against solo, inexperienced attorneys are more likely to be prosecuted, particularly during economic recessions (Arnold & Hagan, 1992). This relationship is attributed to (a) the powerlessness of solo professionals, and (b) conceptions about the legal profession that suggest that inexperienced attorneys are more likely to engage in deviance that results in more surveillance of these attorneys. As an analogy, if law enforcement targets particular neighborhoods prone to crime, they will arrest more offenders from those neighborhoods. If controlling authorities target inexperienced attorneys more, they will catch more inexperienced attorneys engaging in misconduct.

Various sanctions can be given to attorneys by their professional associations. Such sanctions usually include warning letters, private reprimands, public reprimands, suspensions, and disbarment. With the exception of the private reprimands all of the sanctions are public knowledge, and many states identify sanctioned attorneys on the state bar website. Note that simply participating in the disciplinary complaint process can be an informal sanction for attorneys accused of misconduct.

Researchers have also considered factors that contribute to sanctioning decision making. Authors have examined how attorneys are sanctioned in Alabama (Payne & Stevens, 1999) and Virginia (Payne, Time, & Raper, 2005). The Alabama study found gender patterns: Female attorneys were more likely to be publicly reprimanded and they were slightly more likely to be accused of failing to provide competent representation. One third of female attorneys were accused of this, as compared to one fifth of male attorneys.

These patterns can be at least partially understood through an application of the systems approach or patriarchal theory. Broader societal changes resulted in more females in the legal field in the 1980s. Because female attorneys, in general, have fewer years experience than male attorneys, the lack of experience may contribute to the accusation of failing to provide competent representation. Indeed, research shows that years of experience is tied to allegations of misconduct. Conversely, it could be that a male-dominated profession uses its sanctioning body to control females. Such a possibility is in line with patriarchal theory.

Figure 5.1 compares the ways attorneys are sanctioned in Alabama and Virginia. A few interesting patterns are evident in the figure. For example, suspensions were used more often in Virginia, with one third of the disciplined attorneys suspended in Virginia, as compared to one fourth of Alabama attorneys. Also, private reprimands were routinely used in Alabama, but rarely used in Virginia. In addition, license revocation occurred frequently in Virginia, but infrequently in Alabama.

On the surface, these differences point to the varied response systems between states. Also, the difference in the way misconduct is defined between states is in line with a social construction definition of white-collar misconduct, or attorney misconduct in this case. Though these differences exist, the bottom line is that all states define appropriate behavior for attorneys and all states have formal structures they use to respond to and control attorney misconduct. A similar pattern is evident when examining judicial misconduct.

Figure 5.1   Sanctions Against Attorneys in Virginia and Alabama

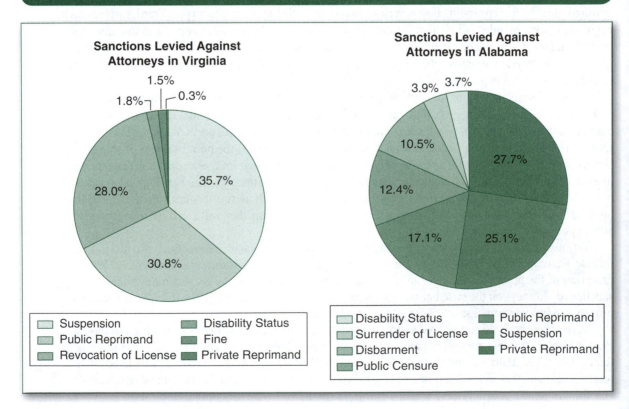

Judicial Misconduct

Just as lawyers are depicted in certain ways in television shows and movies, judges are also a regular part of the "cast of characters" portrayed in crime-related media. These portrayals often show cantankerous judges controlling their courtrooms by humiliating attorneys and other courtroom participants. Such a portrayal is not an accurate depiction of judicial conduct. In fact, in many situations if judges actually behaved the way they are portrayed on television shows and in the media, they would face disciplinary behaviors for conduct unbecoming of a judge. Consider the following description of the popular *Judge Judy* show:

> Visually, Judge Judy's courtroom looks very much like one might imagine a New York State courtroom to appear if they had never actually been inside one. . . . However, there is one very significant difference between what is seen in Judge Judy's courtroom and what occurs in a real courtroom: the behavior of the judge. Judges have several checks on how they do their job. . . . In addition to laws that prescribe how the judiciary will function, the personal reputation of judges is a major incentive to do their job in an appropriate manner. . . . Because the behavior of a syndic-court judge has Nielsen ratings as a standard, they are allowed to engage in acts that would generally not be appropriate in court. The more "straight-talking" that a judge appears, which often means being as mean as possible to unlikable litigants, the better ratings he or she receives. (Kimball, 2005, p. 150)

The Model Code of Judicial Conduct outlines various rules that prescribe appropriate behavior by judges. The rules cover judicial behavior throughout the entire justice process, which means that misconduct can occur at different phases of judicial proceedings. During jury deliberations, for example, two kinds of misconduct are known to occur: (1) pressuring the jury for a verdict and (2) communicating with jurors in private. Instances where misconduct occurs during jury deliberation may result in an appeal, but appellate courts will not automatically overturn the jury's decision. The cases of judicial error are reviewed on a case by case basis (Gershman, 1999).

Similar to the way that states define attorney misconduct differently, states also offer different typologies for judicial misconduct. Kentucky, for example, identifies three general types of judicial misconduct: (1) improper influence, (2) improper courtroom decorum, and (3) improper illegal activities on or off the bench. Within each of these general categories, specific types of misconduct are identified. In California, a more exhaustive list of types of judicial misconduct is provided by the state's judicial commission. The acts identified as misconduct in California include the following:

▲ **Photo 5.1** Judith Sheindlin ("Judge Judy"). If judges in criminal or civil courts behaved like Judge Judy, they would have numerous complaints about their conduct filed with review boards.

- Abuse of contempt/sanctions
- Administrative malfeasance, improper comments, treatment of colleagues
- Alcohol or drug related criminal conduct

- Bias/appearance of bias towards particular group
- Bias/appearance of bias not towards particular group
- Comment on pending case
- Decisional delay
- Demeanor/decorum
- Disqualification/disclosure/post-disqualification conduct
- Ex parte communications
- Failure to cooperate with regulatory authority
- Failure to ensure rights
- Gifts/loans/favors/ticket fixing
- Improper business, financial, or fiduciary activities
- Improper political activities
- Inability to perform judicial duties
- Miscellaneous off bench conduct
- Misuse of court resources
- Non-performance of judicial functions/attendance/sleeping
- Non-substance abuse criminal conviction
- Off-bench abuse of authority
- On-bench abuse of authority
- Pre-bench misconduct
- Sexual harassment/inappropriate comments
- Substance abuse

Just as allegations of attorney misconduct increased in the past few decades, allegations of judicial misconduct increased significantly in the early 1990s (Coyle, 1995). Part of this increase was likely caused by the development of formal commissions in different states that provided citizens with a mechanism they could use to file judicial complaints. In California, voters approved Proposition 190 around this same time. Proposition 190 created the Commission on Judicial Performance and authorized the commission to review judicial misconduct cases and impose sanctions, which would be reviewed by the state Supreme Court.

The way the complaint process is designed in California mirrors the complaint process followed in other states. Anyone can file a written complaint to the commission. If the complaint describes an allegation of misconduct, the judge is asked to provide information in response to the allegation. Members of the commission will interview witnesses and review court transcripts and case files. The judge will be given 20 days to respond to the complaint. After the information has been reviewed, the commission meets to review cases. On average, the commission meets every seven weeks or so (State of California Commission on Judicial Performance, 2010). In recent years, the number of judicial complaints filed has been relatively stable (see Figure 5.2).

In Focus 5.1 provides an overview of one of the cases reviewed by the California Commission on Judicial Performance. This case provides an interesting depiction of a serious form of misconduct in which the judge sexually harassed attorneys and colleagues on several occasions. Note that the judge was ultimately removed from the bench for these actions. In most cases, judges are not removed from the bench because this sanction is reserved for the most obvious and most severe types of misconduct. Advisory letters are commonly used, as are private admonishments, and public sanctions are used less frequently. Also, as others have noted, in some cases involving judicial misconduct, judges resign before they are sanctioned in order to keep their pensions intact (Lewis, 1983).

Figure 5.2 New Complaints Considered by California Commission on Judicial Performance

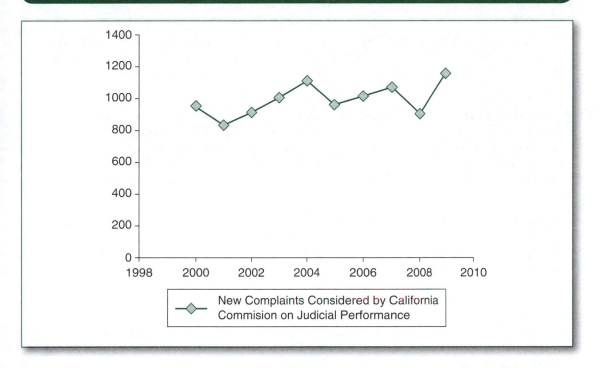

New Complaints Considered by California Commision on Judicial Performance

In Focus 5.1

Case Study: When Judges Go Bad

The following is an excerpt from a decision of misconduct rendered by the California Commission on Judicial Performance.

This is a disciplinary matter concerning Judge Arthur S. Block, a judge of the Riverside County Municipal Court from June 29, 1982 to July 28, 2000, and a judge of the Riverside County Unified Superior Court from July 29, 2000 to December 1, 2002. Formal proceedings having been instituted, this matter came before the Commission on Judicial Performance pursuant to rule 127 of the Rules of the Commission on Judicial Performance.

The commission concludes, based on Judge Block's stipulation, that Judge Block engaged in a pattern of inappropriate sexual conduct, attempted to intimidate potential witnesses during the investigation of the alleged sexual conduct, and improperly attempted to use his office to intercede in a pending matter on behalf of an acquaintance. The commission hereby publicly censures Judge Block and bars him from receiving an assignment, appointment, or reference of work from any California state court.

(Continued)

(Continued)

Count One

A. In approximately October 2000, Deputy County Counsel Tanya Galvan appeared before Judge Block in a contested juvenile dependency case. During Ms. Galvan's argument, Judge Block wrote "relax" on her hand with a pen. Ms. Galvan felt humiliated and sat down without finishing her argument.

. . .

B. In approximately February 2001, Judge Block was on the bench during a recess in a juvenile dependency calendar, while attorneys in the courtroom were attempting to resolve cases. Judge Block called Deputy County Counsel Tanya Galvan to sidebar. Judge Block did not ask any other attorney to sidebar. While discussing a legal issue with Ms. Galvan, Judge Block reached out as if to fasten a button on the front of Ms. Galvan's suit. Ms. Galvan was startled and offended. She backed away and buttoned her suit herself. . . .

C. On May 8, 2001, Judge Block presided over a contested juvenile dependency hearing. Deputy County Counsel Tanya Galvan represented the Department of Social Services. During the hearing, Judge Block declared a recess and requested that Ms. Galvan and the attorneys for the father and the mother meet with him in chambers. After discussing certain issues in the case, the attorneys began to leave chambers to return to the courtroom to resume the proceedings. Judge Block asked Ms. Galvan to remain and to close the door. Judge Block was seated behind his desk, with Ms. Galvan seated across from him. Judge Block told Ms. Galvan that he was attracted to her. Judge Block walked around his desk to Ms. Galvan and had Ms. Galvan stand. Judge Block kissed Ms. Galvan, putting his tongue in her mouth. When Judge Block released Ms. Galvan, she left chambers and returned to court. Judge Block returned to the bench and presided over further proceedings in the case without disclosing what had happened in chambers. . . .

Count Two

A. On August 2, 2000, during a conversation between Judge Block and attorneys and court staff in the courtroom, it was suggested as a joke that court interpreter Margie Stafford be held in contempt for being late. When Ms. Stafford arrived in the hallway outside the courtroom, a public area where people were present, Deputy Rosas handcuffed Ms. Stafford over her protests and resistance and took her into the courtroom. The following then took place:

THE COURT: Ms. Stafford, will you listen to the People please. What were you about to say?

THE INTERPRETER: I said this better be a joke. Take them off.

THE COURT: What were you going to say, Mr. —

MR. DAILY: I was going to say perhaps this is the appropriate time for the order to show cause re contempt.

THE COURT: All right. I understand bail is not available; is that correct?

MR. DAILY: There is no bail for that.

THE COURT: Ms. Stafford, I'm sorry but your vacation plans are somewhat awry.

Judge Block then told Ms. Stafford that it was a joke and had Deputy Rosas remove the handcuffs. Ms. Stafford felt humiliated. . . .

The case description goes on to describe additional counts against the judge.

It is estimated that 90% of complaints filed against judges are dismissed (Gray, 2004). Many of the complaints are dismissed because the allegations do not rise to levels of misconduct outlined in judicial regulations. By the very nature of their jobs, judges will, at the end of the day, make decisions that disappoint, or even anger, several of the individuals participating in the judicial process. The result is that a number of egregious allegations are made. Gray describes a case where a prison inmate filed a complaint against the judge—described as his former wife in the complaint. The inmate said that the judge was biased against him because of their prior marriage. Upon reviewing the case, it was learned that the judge and the inmate did not, in fact, have a prior marital relationship.

It is also important to note that a difference exists between "making a mistake" and committing judicial misconduct. Said Gray (2004), "It is not unethical to be imperfect, and it would be unfair to sanction a judge for not being infallible while making hundreds of decisions under pressure" (p. 124). Somewhat related, if a judge makes an error, that error will not automatically result in the judicial decision being overturned. Instead, the case would be reviewed and the relevance of the mistake would be considered in determining whether the case should be overturned. It is important to stress that judicial misconduct commissions cannot overturn judicial decisions made in courts of law. Only appellate courts have the authority to reverse judicial decisions.

An entire section of this text/reader will discuss why white-collar misconduct occurs. In terms of judicial misconduct, some have argued that a combination of three factors contributes to misdeeds by judges. These factors include: (1) office authority, (2) heavy caseloads, and (3) interactions with others in the judicial process (Coyle, 1995). Briefly, judges have a great deal of power, but they are expected to express that power under demands of large caseloads, and their interactions with others in the judicial network may provide opportunities for misconduct. One group they interact with is prosecutors—a group that also is not immune from misconduct.

Prosecutorial Misconduct

The prosecutor position has been described as "the most powerful position in the criminal justice system" (Schoenfeld, 2005). In addition to deciding whether charges should be filed against individuals, prosecutors have a strong voice in deciding what sanction should be given to defendants. While the judge ultimately assigns the sanction, it is the prosecutor who decides what types of charges to file against defendants, and these charges will help to determine the sentence given by the judge. For instance, it is the prosecutor who decides whether a defendant should be tried for capital murder—a crime that may ultimately result in the death penalty.

Criminologist Jocelyn Pollock (2004) has identified five different types of prosecutorial misconduct. First, instances where prosecutors have improper communications with defendants (e.g., without their attorney present if one was requested, personal communications, etc.) are examples of misconduct. Second, if prosecutors have ex parte communications (without the other party present) with the judge, then the prosecutor has developed an unfair advantage over the defense. Third, if prosecutors fail to disclose evidence, which they are required to do by law, then misconduct has occurred. Fourth, if a prosecutor knows that a witness has provided false testimony and fails to correct the testimony, the prosecutor has committed misconduct just as the perjurer did. Fifth, Pollock points to unnecessary and unwarranted displays of courtroom theatrics as types of misconduct.

Legal expert Alschuler (1972) discussed a different set of prosecutorial misconduct examples. Examples of misconduct he discussed include:

- Commenting on the defendant's lack of testimony
- Asserting facts that are not supported by the evidence

- Expressing personal beliefs about the defendant's guilt
- Verbal abuse of the defense attorney
- Verbal or mental abuse of the defendant

More recently, Cramm (2009) discussed additional forms of prosecutorial misconduct including (a) withholding, destroying, or changing evidence, (b) failing to preserve evidence, (c) making prejudicial comments about the defendant during opening or closing remarks, (d) coercing guilty pleas from defendants, (e) intimidating defense witnesses, and (f) obstructing defense attorney access to prosecution witnesses.

Although it is difficult to identify precisely how often prosecutorial misconduct occurs, estimates suggest that these behaviors are particularly common. One author notes that prosecutorial misconduct is "a factor in 42 percent of DNA exonerations" according to Barry Scheck and Peter Neufeld's Innocence Project (Roberts, 2007). Roberts also quotes a report from the Center for Public Integrity, which includes a group of journalists who analyzed 11,000 appellate opinions where prosecutor misconduct appeared to occur. The Center found: "Since 1970, individual judge and court panels cited prosecutorial misconduct as a factor when dismissing charges, reversing convictions, or reducing sentences in over 2000 cases" (Roberts, 2007).

A number of direct and indirect negative consequences arise from prosecutorial misconduct. Beyond limiting the defendant's right to a fair trial, influencing the jury, and creating public resentment (Alschuler, 1972), prosecutorial misconduct also has the potential to breed crime. If the most powerful representatives of the justice system break the rules, others might use the "official misbehavior" to justify their own transgressions. Also, and perhaps more significant, prosecutorial misconduct has the potential to wrongfully sentence individuals to life in prison, or even worse, death. Schoenfeld (2005) cites a *Chicago Tribune* study that found: "Since 1963, 381 people have had their convictions for homicide overturned because of prosecutorial misconduct. Sixty-seven of those defendants were sentenced to death" (p. 266).

Students should not think that they are insulated from cases of prosecutorial misconduct. Consider the case of the Duke Lacrosse players accused of raping Crystal Gail Magnum. Overzealous in his efforts to prosecute the students from the moment the allegations surfaced, former prosecutor Mike Nifong was initially praised by advocates, university faculty, and feminists because he was demonstrating a willingness to prosecute seemingly elite students accused of raping an African American woman. His zeal for the case did not dissipate, even after evidence surfaced that seemed to refute the woman's claim. Eventually, the case was dismissed.

A state bar examination of Nifong's actions in the case found that he had (a) refused to hear exculpatory evidence, (b) made false statements to the media to "[heighten] public condemnation of the accused," (c) failed to provide evidence to the defendants, (d) failed to provide the results of tests to the defendants, and (e) denied knowing about the results of a rape kit exam that potentially exonerated the defendants. Nifong was disbarred, but not before sending some rather interesting letters to the state bar. In one letter, for instance, Nifong claimed that the license he was surrendering to the state bar was damaged because his puppy had chewed on it. According to *News and*

▲ **Photo 5.2** This is the home where an alleged sexual assault by Duke University Lacrosse players is supposed to have occurred. Mike Nifong was disbarred after bringing charges against the students when the evidence suggested that they were innocent.

Observer, the falsely accused students incurred legal expenses in excess of three million dollars in their efforts to respond to Nifong's misconduct.

Few studies have empirically assessed prosecutorial misconduct, or any of the types of misconduct by upper-class criminal justice professionals for that matter. Describing the need to broaden research past conceptual divides, McBarnet (1991) writes, "We need to explore how economic elites actively use the institutions, ideologies, and methods of law to secure immunity from legal control" (p. 324). Taking this a step farther, much more research needs to focus on how power elites within the justice system misuse their legal authority to protect their own interests.

Correctional Officer Misconduct

Much more research has focused on police corruption, judicial misconduct, and attorney misconduct than corruption by correctional officers. One of the first studies done on corruption by correctional officers was a doctoral dissertation by Belinda McCarthy (1981). McCarthy's dissertation was a case study of misconduct in one state's prison system. Varieties of corruption she focused on included embezzlement (stealing from the institution), drug smuggling into the institution, coercion, and transporting contraband into the prison system. Her case study uncovered three patterns that contributed to misconduct in the prison system. First, the degree of discretion given to low level workers in an isolated work environment appeared to promote the opportunity for corruption. Second, the nature of the prison as an institution was such that inmate demand for contraband was high. Third, low morale (with workers' individual goals being different from the collective goal of the criminal justice system) was also viewed as a predictor of correctional misconduct.

As with the law enforcement profession, sexual misconduct has also been cited as a variety of misconduct occurring in the corrections profession. Varieties of sexual misconduct in the corrections field have been categorized as sexual contact offenses, sexual assault, and sexual gratification between officer and supervisee (Smith & Yarussi, 2007). Another author classifies sexual misconduct by corrections officials into the following four categories: (1) verbal harassment, (2) improper visual surveillance, (3) improper touching, and (4) consensual sex (Burton, Erdman, Hamilton, & Muse, 1999). It is believed that "consensual relations" are the most common forms of sexual misconduct between correctional officers and inmates, with rape believed to be infrequent (Layman, McCampbell, & Moss, 2000).

The notion of consensual, however, is somewhat ambiguous. Consider that sexual relations between probation/parole officers and their supervisees are prohibited by the criminal law in many states. While little research has been done in this area, experts warn against assuming that probationers and parolees (or inmates, for that matter) are able to fully consent to such relationships (Buell, Layman, McCampbell, & Smith, 2003).

A General Accounting Office study focused on sexual misconduct allegations in women's prisons in the Federal Bureau of Prisons as well as the Texas, California, and District of Columbia's Corrections departments between 1995 and 1998. The study uncovered 506 complaints of sexual misconduct by staff. Criminal prosecutions were rare, and less than one fifth of the complaints were substantiated. When complaints were substantiated, termination from employment was the most common response (Burton et al., 1999).

The consequences of sexual misconduct for sexual assault victims are likely no different from the consequences that other sexual assault victims experience. It is important to note, however, that sexual misconduct by corrections officials will lead to consequences that also impact the correctional system. Potential consequences of correctional sexual misconduct include:

- Jeopardizing staff safety if inmates react against non-offending staff members
- The risk of legal action for staff members, supervisors, and the agency

- Health risks for inmates and staff exposed to sexually transmitted diseases
- Family problems for offenders, victims, and staff responding to the allegations
- Negative perceptions of the corrections department among community members
- Reduced trust between inmates and staff (Smith & Yarussi, 2007)

Concern about an increase in sexual misconduct by community corrections officers led the National Institute of Corrections to develop a 36-hour training program to assist officials in their efforts to prevent and intervene in cases of sexual misconduct. The training focused on defining misconduct, policy development, legal issues, ethical issues, investigatory strategies, and other related topics (Buell & Mc Campbell, 2003). General strategies that have been suggested to prevent sexual misconduct include (a) developing clear policies that are enforced as needed, (b) improving the quality of workers, (c) enhancing supervisory practices, (d) implementing various social control mechanisms, and (e) providing ethics training to officers and staff (Souryal, 2009).

⊠ Crimes in the Political System

Readers are likely not surprised by the suggestion that crimes also occur in the political system. Unlike professionals working in some of the other systems, professionals in the political system routinely confront suspicion and distrust from citizens. This distrust stems at least partly from several high profile political and government scandals that have occurred over the years. Table 5.1 shows the number of public corruption convictions prosecuted by U.S. Attorneys since 1990. As shown in the table, the number of prosecuted federal public corruption cases has decreased some since 1990, but the number of local and state officials prosecuted increased slightly over this timeframe. To be sure, these cases continue to occur and they tend to receive a great deal of public scrutiny.

Indeed, it seems every decade has been marked by national political scandals. In the 1970s, Watergate served as an introduction to political corruption on the grandest scale. In June 1972, burglars connected to the Committee to Re-elect the President broke into the Democratic National Committee's offices in the Watergate Office Complex. After the investigation began, President Nixon insisted that he knew nothing about the burglary. During the course of the investigation, recordings were uncovered showing that the president participated in covering up the break in. The investigation also revealed other abuses, including warrantless wiretaps to listen in on the conversations of reporters. Watergate has been described as "the touchstone, the definitive point of reference for subsequent political scandals in the United States" (Schudson, 2004, p. 1231). Another author noted that political corruption is not new, but that efforts to control corruption through public law enforcement efforts can be traced to the 1970s in the aftermath of Watergate (Mass, 1986).

Abscam was the next major national political scandal following Watergate. In the late 1970s and early 1980s, Abscam was an FBI investigation in which undercover agents used the fictional identity of Abdul Enterprises, Ltd., to offer bribes to various officials in exchange for help making it easier for two sheiks "to emigrate to the U.S." (Gershman, 1982, p. 1572). At least a handful of congressmen immediately accepted bribes. A few offered assistance after being groomed by undercover agents. The same "scam" was repeated in Philadelphia where local officials agreed to the bribe. Once the case became public, media attention uncovered wide-ranging instances of corruption. Gershman (1982) wrote:

Seen as public theatre, Abscam cast the three branches of government in a morality play whose plot called for the portrayal of disguised heroes and hidden villains, intricate charades with racial overtones, and lavish scenery against invitations to corruption set the characters in motion. (p. 1565)

The **Iran-Contra affair** was the next major national political scandal. In the mid-1980s, political officials authorized the sale of weapons to Iran, despite the presence of an arms embargo, as part of a covert effort to trade arms for hostages. Proceeds from the weapons sales were then diverted to the Contras (anticommunist rebels) in Nicaragua despite the fact that Congress had prohibited Contra funding. More than a dozen of President Reagan's officials were indicted, and 11 were convicted. All of the convictions were later overturned or pardoned by President George H. W. Bush. While evidence suggested that Reagan was involved in the cover up, he escaped negative fallout from the scandal, prompting one reporter to call the Iran-Contra affair "the cover up that worked" (Brinkley, 1994) to distinguish the scandal from Watergate.

The 1990s and 2000s saw a series of ongoing political scandals. From the Clintons being tied up in allegations of real estate fraud in Whitewater to President Clinton's sexual contact with Monica Lewinsky to President George W. Bush's failure to uncover weapons of mass destruction in Iraq, it seemed that at any given moment in time, a political scandal was brewing over these two decades. To provide a framework for understanding these crimes in the political system, attention can be given to the following types of crimes occurring in the political system:

- Election law violations
- Campaign finance violations
- Political corruption related to extortion and bribery
- Apolitical white-collar crime
- Crimes in the military
- State-corporate crime

These varieties of crimes are discussed below.

Table 5.1   Federal Convictions: Federal, State, and Local Public Corruption Cases, 1990–2009

Year	Federal	State	Local
1990	583	79	225
1991	665	77	180
1992	532	92	211
1993	595	133	272
1994	488	97	202
1995	438	61	191
1996	459	83	190
1997	392	49	169
1998	414	58	264
1999	460	80	219
2000	422	91	183
2001	414	61	184
2002	429	132	262
2003	421	87	119
2004	381	81	252
2005	390	94	232
2006	407	116	241
2007	405	85	275
2008	458	123	246
2009	426	102	257

Election Law Violations

Election law violations are situations where political officials violate rules guiding the way that elections are supposed to be conducted. Election fraud laws exist in order to guard against crimes such as voter registration fraud, vote counting fraud, and balloting fraud (Aycock & Hutton, 2010). More specifically, election fraud involves situations where individuals try to corrupt "the process by which ballots are obtained, marked, or tabulated; the process by which election results are canvassed or certified; or the process by which voters are registered" (Donsanto & Simmons, 2007, p. 25). Schemes are characterized as either public or private, depending on who initiated the fraud. The Federal Election Commission can levy civil fines against those who violate provisions of the Federal Election Campaign Act. Criminal prosecutions would be initiated by the U.S. Department of Justice (Aycock & Hutton, 2010).

▲ **Photo 5.3**   At press time, it was not clear whether Edwards would be convicted for campaign finance violations. Some have argued that his fall from grace as a politician has been a punishment in and of itself.

Campaign Finance Violations

Campaign finance laws place restrictions on the way political campaigns are financed, with specific attention given to contributions and expenditures. Expenditures are limited only if candidates "elect to participate in a public funding program" (Aycock & Hutton, 2010, p. 358). Contributions from certain groups are prohibited (e.g., current or former government contractors, foreign nationals, contributions in the name of another). Tom Delay, former House Majority Leader, was convicted in November 2010 of violations of Texas campaign finance laws after he funneled corporate donations made to the Republican National Committee to candidates in Texas. Texas law prohibits corporate contributions to candidates. In February 2011, Delay's attorneys appealed the case on the grounds that the Texas law was unconstitutional (Epstein, 2011).

Campaign finance laws also stipulate that contributions cannot be used for personal use. At the time of the writing of this text, former vice presidential candidate and North Carolina Senator John Edwards was indicted after a grand jury investigation that focused on how his campaign used funds to pay his mistress for work she did for his campaign. In particular, she produced three videos for the campaign at a cost of $250,000. Prosecutors alleged that the funds were actually a payment to get his mistress to keep quiet about her affair with the former senator (Smith, 2011).

Political Corruption Related to Extortion and Bribery

In this context, **political extortion/bribery** refers to situations where political officials use their political power to shape outcomes of various processes, including lawmaking, awarding of contracts, policy development, and so on. Operation Bid Rig is an ongoing political corruption investigation case by the FBI. One recent sting as part of this investigation resulted in the arrests of 44 suspects, including three mayors, a city council president, two state legislators, and five rabbis. In this sting, hundreds of hours of audio and video recordings were collected. In one of the recordings, a newly elected mayor, Peter Cammarano from Hoboken, New Jersey, bragged that he would have won his election even if he had been indicted because he had votes of certain groups "locked down" (Richburg, 2009). The newly minted mayor had been mayor for less than a month when he was arrested. He allegedly took a bribe of $25,000 in exchange for his support of a lower Manhattan building project (McShane, 2009).

Research shows that political corruption is tied to historical/cultural factors, political forces, and bureaucratic forces (Meier & Holbrook, 1992). Research by Meier and Holbrook found that political corruption is lower in "a political system that has closely contested elections and higher voter turnouts" (p. 151). The underlying premise is that politicians will be on their guard more if more voters are voting and the politicians have a higher likelihood of losing an election. If no one is voting and elections are shoo-ins, the message given to the politician is that constituents really don't care about politics.

The consequences of such political corruption can be significant. In particular, individuals lose faith in their government as a result of public corruption. Criminology professor Alan Block (1996) said, "there is a loss of faith in the U.S.A. today in public institutions because of the sense that they do not work ... for they either have been corrupted or are run by nincompoops" (p. 18). As well, political scandals have made it more difficult for honest politicians to lead and govern. According to Ginsberg and Shefter (1995), "efforts to link members of the opposition party to ethical lapses have become important weapons in American political warfare" (p. 497). Government officials must spend at least part of the time that could be spent governing and leading warding off ethics attacks from their opponents.

Apolitical White-Collar Crime

Apolitical white-collar crime refers to situations where politicians get into trouble for doing things that are outside of the scope of politics but are violations of the public trust. Mark Sanford, former governor of South Carolina, came under fire after he told his staff that he was "hiking on the Appalachian trail" when, in fact, he was in Argentina with his mistress. His wife later divorced him and his ability to govern in South Carolina took a significant hit. Once a presidential hopeful, he was subsequently censured by his state government for misusing travel funds to support his "hiking."

The violations of trust in apolitical white-collar crimes often seem far out of character for the politicians caught in the scandals. In May 2010, U.S. Representative Mark Souder resigned from office "after admitting to an affair with a female staffer" ("Congressman Resigns Over Affair," 2010). One news outlet found that Souder had actually filmed a public service video with the staffer he had an affair with. The topic of the video was abstinence.

Former mayor of Washington, D.C., Marion Barry's conviction for using crack cocaine in 1990 showed a similar irony. Only a few hours before his arrest, Barry "preached an anti-drug sermon to high school students" ("Hours Before Arrest," 1990). More recently, Eliot Spitzer resigned as governor of New York after he was caught in a prostitution sting. As attorney general, Spitzer had orchestrated several prostitution busts himself.

A well-publicized case of apolitical white-collar offending involved Larry Craig, a former U.S. Republican senator. In September 2007, Craig was caught in an undercover sex sting and accused of trying to initiate sex in an airport bathroom with an undercover officer. He tapped his foot in a bathroom stall in a way that signaled his interest in "sharing some time" with the individual in the next stall. Craig pleaded guilty, though he later tried to recant his guilty plea. That he was caught in such a scandal was somewhat ironic given his history of voting for legislation restricting the rights of homosexuals. One fellow Republican senator, John Ensign from Nevada, called Craig's actions embarrassing. Less than 2 years later, Ensign admitted having an "affair with a former campaign staffer who is married to one of the lawmaker's former legislative aides" (Kane & Cillizza, 2009, p. A01).

Crimes in the Military

As a system of social control, the military system includes several branches of the military that are charged with various duties related to wartime efforts and the promotion of peace. Clifford Bryant (1979) used the phrase *khaki-collar crime* for situations where individuals in the military break rules guiding their workplace activities. According to Bryant, khaki-collar crime occurs in five contexts:

- **Intra-occupational crimes** are crimes committed against the American military system. These crimes include property crimes (e.g., theft of military property, misuse of property, and destruction of property), crimes against persons (e.g., cruelty to subordinates and assaults against superiors), and crimes against performance (e.g., mutiny, faking illness, conduct unbecoming an officer).

- **Extra-occupational crimes** are committed against the American civilian social system. These crimes include property crimes (theft, forgery, and vandalism), personal crimes (rape, robbery, assault, murder), and performance crimes (e.g., fighting and disturbing the peace).
- **Foreign friendly civilian crimes** are committed against citizens of another country. The same types of crimes found under extra-occupational crimes, but committed against foreigners, are examples.
- **Enemy civilian social system crimes** are crimes against residents of countries in which the U.S. military is fighting. Examples of crimes include property crimes (e.g., looting and pillaging), personal crimes (e.g., committing atrocities and massacres), and performance crimes (e.g., colluding with citizens to harm the U.S. military).
- **Inter-occupational crimes** are crimes committed against the enemy military system. These include property crimes (e.g., misappropriation of captured supplies), personal crimes (e.g., torture and mistreatment of prisoners of war), and performance crimes (e.g., helping the enemy).

Bryant notes that the source of law for military crimes, and the application of laws, is different than what would be found with other white-collar crimes. Depending on where the crime was committed, and which crime was committed, sources of law in khaki-collar crime cases include the U.S. Uniform Code of Military Justice, international treaties, the Law of Land Warfare, and the laws of the government of the country where the crime was committed.

It is safe to suggest that the military has more rules than other occupations guiding workplace behavior. Consider the following examples:

- If my colleagues in my department (that I chair) don't do as I ask them to do, it will make me sad. If members of the military do not do as their bosses tell them, they can be charged with insubordination.
- If I get tired of my job as department chair and quit going to work, I would be fired. If a member of the military leaves his or her military assignment, this would be called desertion.
- If my colleagues try to overthrow my department and run me off as chair, again I would be sad. If members of the military try to overtake their commanding officer, mutiny has occurred.
- If I fake being sick and try to get out of going to a meeting, this would be a minor form of occupational deviance. If members of the military feign illness to get out of their assignments, this would be called malingering and could be met with a court martial.
- If I quit my job and go work for another university, I would miss my current colleagues tremendously. If I leave the military and go work for another military, this would be called foreign enlistment.
- Up until recently, if a gay or lesbian soldier told people about his or her sexual orientation, he or she could have been disciplined by the military (see Bryant, 1979).

The list could go on and on. The simple point is that there are more rules to break in the military than there are in other occupations. One recent Navy scandal involved Captain Owen O. Honors, the former commanding officer of the USS *Enterprise*. Honors was relieved of his command in January 2011 after videos he produced while at sea were shown on the *Virginian-Pilot's* website as part of a news article the newspaper published about Honors's activities. Allegedly in an effort to promote morale among those on the ship, Honors produced videos starring himself as the emcee. In the videos, he used patriarchal types of humor—making fun of women, gays, and his superiors. In one of the videos, for example, Honors said: "Over the years, I've gotten several complaints about inappropriate material during these videos—never to me personally, but gutlessly through other channels. . . . This evening, all of you bleeding hearts—and you fag SWO [Surface Warfare Officer] boy—why don't you go ahead and hug yourself for the next 20 minutes or so, because there's a good chance you're going to be offended tonight" (Reilly, 2011). After the videos surfaced publicly (more than 3 years after he had made them), Honors was sanctioned by the military. Two of his superiors were also sanctioned by the military.

One current controversy regarding crimes in the military centers around the use of private contractors such as Xie, Dyncorp International, and Triple Canopy to provide military security functions. Regulations stipulate that private contractors should use only defensive types of violence; however, evidence points to several horrific situations where private military contractors initiated violence (Welch, 2009). The case of Blackwater (since renamed Xie), a security firm created in 1997 by a former Navy Seal, is particularly illustrative. By all accounts, Blackwater has been overrepresented in allegations of offensive force by private military contractors. Welch (2009) wrote that Blackwater has a "shooting rate" two times higher than similar private military security businesses. He added that the

> company has gained a reputation as one that flaunts a quick-draw image, thereby enticing its guards to take excessively violent actions. Some suggest that its aggressive posture in guarding diplomats reflects the wishes of its principle client, the State Department's Bureau of Diplomatic Security. (p. 356)

Another current controversy has to do with the way members of the military treat prisoners of war. The tortures occurring at Abu Ghraib made international headlines when photos surfaced showing military officials sexually degrading prisoners. Hamm (2007) noted that three explanations had been offered to explain abuses at Abu Ghraib. First, the government promoted a "bad apples explanation" suggesting that just a few bad members of the military were involved in the abusive activities. Second, some suggested that Zimbardo's "automatic brutality" theory applied (suggesting that all individuals have the capacity to torture if they are placed in a situation where it is possible). Third, historian Alfred McCoy argued that the practices had a long history in the Central Intelligence Agency. Hamm concluded that McCoy's theory made the most sense. He said that evidence suggests "that the torturing of detainees at Abu Ghraib followed directly from decisions made by top government officials, from President George W. Bush on down" (p. 259). Hamm stated that the Bush administration "took off the gloves in prisoner interrogation" (p. 259).

State-Corporate Crime

The phrase **state-corporate crime** draws attention to the fact that governmental agencies are employers (or "corporations") and these agencies and their employees sometimes commit various types of

▲ **Photo 5.4** Evidence of war crimes and torture surfaced when photos of prisoners at Abu Ghraib showing the prisoners in various shameful poses were released to the press.

misconduct—either independently or in conjunction with other corporations. The concept of state-corporate crime was first introduced by Ronald Kramer in a series of presentations he made at the Southern Sociological Association, the Edwin Sutherland Conference on White-Collar Crime, and the Society for the Study of Social Problems (Kramer, Michalowski, & Kauzlarich, 2002, p. 263). Kramer notes that the term came from a "spontaneous comment" he made at a restaurant while discussing his research with colleagues. Although Kramer developed the concept, he credits Richard Quinney's work with serving as its "intellectual origins." Quinney's early work drew attention to the need to categorize white-collar crime into corporate crime and occupational crime, and another body of his research focused on the sociology of law, with an emphasis on the way that the powerful shape the law to protect their interests. Combining Quinney's white-collar crime research with his sociology of law research lends credence to Kramer's call for a focus on "state-corporate crime." The concept of state-corporate crime is useful in (a) demonstrating how the consequences of behaviors are tied to interrelationships between social institutions and (b) highlighting the power of formal (e.g., political and economic) institutions to harm members of society (Kramer et al., 2002).

Scholars also use the phrase **state crime** to describe situations where governments, or their representatives, commit crime on behalf of the government. Again, bear in mind that a government can be seen as a corporation. International law is seen as the "foundation for defining state crime as this includes standards such as human rights, social and economic harms, as well as the judicable offenses" (Rothe, 2009, p. 51). From this perspective, state crime has been defined as

> any action that violates international public law and/or a state's own domestic law when these actions are committed by individual actors acting on behalf of, or in the name of the state, even when such acts are motivated by their own personal, economical, political, and ideological interests. (Mullins & Rothe, 2007, p. 137)

Not surprisingly, it is extremely unlikely that formal governmental institutions will self-police or impose sanctions on themselves for the commission of state crimes. As a result, efforts to control state crime often stem from the actions of advocates, including individuals and organizations, seeking to expose the wrongdoing of particular governmental officials. According to Ross and Rothe (2008), those who expose state crime offenders run the risk of experiencing the following responses from the state:

1. **Censure:** officials may withdraw support or withhold information

2. **Scapegoating:** officials may blame lower level employees for the misconduct

3. **Retaliation:** officials may target the advocates exposing the wrongdoing

4. **Defiance**/resistance: officials may block any efforts toward change

5. **Plausible deniability:** officials may conceal actions to make behavior seem appropriate

6. **Relying on self-righteousness:** officials minimize allegations

7. **Redirection/misdirection:** officials feign interest, but change the subject

8. **Fear mongering:** officials create fear to "overshadow" real issues

State crime scholars have addressed a number of different topics, including President Reagan's war on Nicaragua (Rothe, 2009), the state of Senegal's role in the sinking of a ferry, killing more than 1,800 citizens

(Rothe, Muzzatti, & Mullins, 2006), the violent deaths of more than 400,000 civilians in the Darfur region of Sudan (Mullins & Rothe, 2007), and the torture of prisoners in Abu Ghraib (Rothe & Ross, 2008).

Although research on state crime has grown significantly over the last decade, in general, criminological attention to the concept is seemingly rare (Rothe & Ross, 2008). Critical criminologists Dawn Rothe and Jeffrey Ross recently reviewed leading criminology texts to determine how much attention was given to state crime. They found that authors typically provided only a description of incidents by governmental officials when discussing crimes by state officials, thereby "failing to provide the contextual, theoretical, and historical factors associated with this subject" (p. 744). The authors attribute this lack of attention to "the perceived potential of the market" (p. 750). Despite this lack of attention, state crime experts have come a long way in advancing understanding about this phenomenon and it is entirely likely that an entire field of study will develop in the next several decades, just as the field of study focusing on white-collar crime has grown since the 1940s (see Rothe & Friedrichs, 2006).

Crimes by Officials in the Religious System

In the past, many individuals probably gave little thought to the possibility that crime occurs in the religious system. However, like other occupational settings, churches and religious institutions are not immune from misconduct. To provide a general introduction to crimes in the religious system, attention can be given to financial offenses in the religious system, deception in the religious system, and the Catholic Church sexual abuse scandal.

Financial Offenses in the Religious System

One type of white-collar crime occurring in the religious system involves financial offenses where church leaders embezzle funds from church proceeds. Such acts are relatively simple to commit because church funds are easy to target and there is often little oversight of the church's bank accounts (Smietana, 2005). One pastor, for example, who was accused of stealing more than a million dollars from his church over a 10-year time frame alleged that he had the authority to use the church funds as he saw fit because he was the "pastor and overseer" of the church ("Ex-Pastor Testifies in Embezzlement Trial," 2010).

One of the most famous instances of embezzlement by a religious leader involves the case of Rev. Jim Bakker, a former televangelist who co-hosted the TV show *The PTL Club* with his wife Tammy Faye. Bakker's television show, whose acronym stood for "Praise the Lord," brought in millions of dollars. Eventually Bakker and his wife created their own network and organization called the PTL Television Network. In 1989, Bakker was convicted of stealing $3.7 million from the PTL organization. At his sentencing hearing, prosecutor Jerry Miller focused on the vulnerable groups that had given money to Bakker's organization so Bakker could divert funds to support his lavish lifestyle. The judge, nicknamed "Maximum Bob" in reference to the long sentences he had given offenders, sentenced Bakker to 45 years in prison, with parole eligible after 10 years (Harris, 1989). An appeals court ruled that a new sentencing hearing should be held, and Bakker was subsequently sentenced to 8 years and paroled in 1994. He is now the host of the *Jim Bakker Show,* which appears on various networks.

Financial offenses by church leaders are often stumbled on only by accident. In one case, for example, it was not until a pastor left his church and "collections went up dramatically" that officials had any suspicion of wrongdoing. The subsequent investigations revealed that the pastor had stolen about one million dollars from his church over a 5-year time frame (Smietana, 2005). Other times, offenses are uncovered as a result of routine audits (O'Sullivan, 2011). Regardless of how the financial offenses are detected, their consequences can be devastating to the church that was victimized. Said one pastor about these consequences, "It's not about the money so much. It's about the trust" (Smietana, 2005).

Deception in the Religious System

Religious system deception refers to situations where church leaders lie to their **congregants** in an effort to promote an appearance of "holier than thou." Lying in and of itself is not illegal. However, the violation of trust that arises in these situations warrants that these cases be classified as white-collar crime. Consider, for instance, the case of Jimmy Swaggart, who was banned from preaching for 3 months by national leaders of the Assemblies of God Church after he confessed to liaisons with a prostitute. Ironically, Swaggart was implicated by a pastor he had exposed for adultery 2 years before (Kaufman, 1988). In a more recent case, in the fall of 2006, Rev. Ted Haggard's affair with a former male escort came to light. At the time, Haggard was the president of the National Association of Evangelicals and the founding pastor of the Colorado Springs–based New Life Church—a mega church with 14,000 members. After his adultery became public, he resigned from his presidential position and the board of his church dismissed him from pastoral duties (Banerjee & Goodstein, 2006). Haggard and his wife now travel around the United States, appearing in different churches to talk about forgiveness (Jacobson, 2009).

Catholic Church Sexual Abuse Scandal

Historically, the Catholic Church has been viewed as a safe haven where individuals can retreat for protection. Over the past 15 years, however, the image of the Church became more and more tarnished as cases of child sexual abuse by priests began to be reported in the media with increasing frequency. After a while, it was clear that the number of allegations was not indicative of a few events, but of a problem that appeared to be structurally situated within the church. To address the sexual abuse scandal, the U.S. Catholic Bishops approved the Charter for the Protection of Children and Young People. Among other things, the Charter developed a National Review Board that was charged with commissioning a study on sexual abuse in the church. All dioceses were required to participate in the study. The board hired the John Jay College of Criminal Justice of the City University of New York to conduct the study. The resulting study provided the most comprehensive picture of the issue of sexual abuse in the Catholic Church (United States Conference of Catholic Bishops, 2011).

Utilizing a variety of research methodologies, including interviews, reviews of case files, mail surveys, and so on, the John Jay study provided the following highlights:

- Four percent of active priests "between 1950 and 2002 had allegations of abuse."
- In all, 10,677 individuals accused priests of sexually abusing them as children. Approximately one sixth of them "had siblings who also were allegedly abused."
- Two thirds of allegations were made since 1993, though most incidents occurred in the 1970s and 1980s.
- It was estimated that the church had already spent $650 million in settlements and in treatment programs for priests.
- One fifth of the priests were believed to have substance abuse problems that may have been related to the misconduct.
- About half of the victims were between the ages of 11 and 17 years.

Figure 5.3 shows the priest's role in the church when the allegation occurred. As shown in the figure, the vast majority of the suspects were serving as some form of a pastor/priest, though a variety of different roles were represented among the accused. Figure 5.4 shows the location where the abuse occurred. As shown in the figure, most of the incidents occurred in the priest's home, the church, or the victim's home.

Researchers have used the John Jay data to examine similarities between sexual abuse in the Church and victimization/offending patterns among other offender groups. For example, Smith, Rengifo, and Vollman (2008) examined disclosure patterns and found that disclosure of child sexual abuse by clergy in the Catholic Church did not mimic disclosure patterns found in other child sexual abuse cases. In 2002, nearly 3,000 incidents of child sexual abuse by priests were reported. Of those, 90% had occurred more than 20 years earlier.

Alex Piquero and his colleagues (Piquero, Piquero, Terry, Youstin, & Nobles, 2008) used the John Jay data to examine the criminal careers of the clerics and compare their careers to the careers of traditional criminals. The research team found similarities and differences between the two types of offenders. In terms of similarities, both clerics and traditional career criminals exhibited relatively similar rates of

Figure 5.3   Priest's Primary Function at Time of Alleged Incident in Cases From John Jay Study

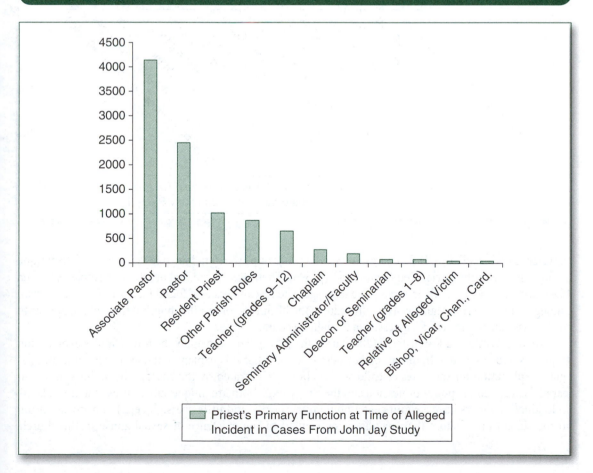

Figure 5.4   Location Where Abuse Occurred in Sexual Assault Cases Examined in John Jay Study

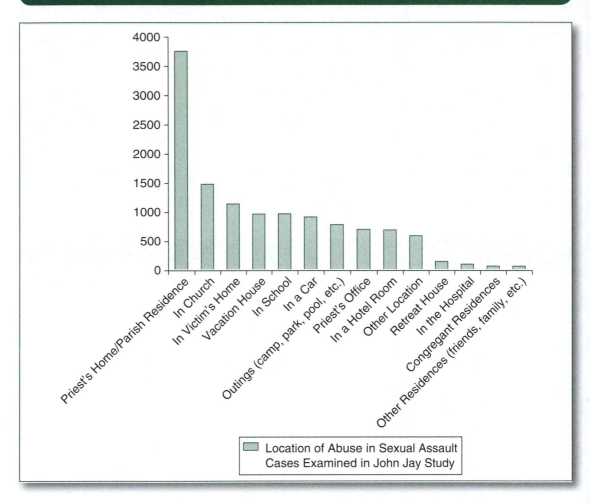

prevalence and recidivism. Differences between the two groups were attributed to "a function of the unique position in which the clerics find themselves." (p. 596). Their age of criminal onset, for example, is higher, likely because they enter their careers at a later age. The researchers also found higher rates of recidivism among married clerics. Marriage typically reduces the likelihood of re-offending, but this did not appear to be the cases among the clerics assessed in the John Jay data.

Michael White and Karen Terry (2008) used the John Jay data to apply the rotten apples explanation to the sex abuse scandal. In doing so, they demonstrated that this explanation does not provide an adequate explanation for the cases of child sexual abuse perpetrated by the clerics. The authors draw out parallels between the police profession and the clergy (e.g., both are unique subcultures that are isolated, individual members have a significant amount of authority and little oversight, etc.) to bring attention to the subcultural factors that may have contributed to the existence of sexual abuse in the church.

The authors also addressed police deviance prevention strategies that could have been used to limit the abuse. These included: (a) careful selection of personnel/training, (b) supervision and accountability, (c) guidelines, (d) internal affairs units, (e) early warning systems, (f) changing the subculture, (g) criminal cases, (h) civil liability, and (i) citizen oversight. The authors conclude that "church leaders would be well-advised to follow the lead of professional police departments who institute rigorous internal and external accountability controls" (p. 676).

Mercado, Tallon, and Terry (2008) used the John Jay data to examine those factors that increased the likelihood that priests would victimize more than one victim. Their analyses identified the following three factors as increasing the likelihood that priests would target multiple victims:

- Having victims older or younger than typical victims
- Age of cleric when abuse began (younger at onset more likely to abuse multiple victims)
- Targeting male victims

Also using the John Jay data to increase understanding about the causes of child sexual abuse, Marcotte (2008) examined the structural factors associated with Catholicism and changes in the American culture that may have contributed to the high rates of child sexual abuse in the Catholic Church. He notes that the offending priests tended to be socialized in the church in the 1950s and 1960s and this socialization process potentially explained the high number of incidents occurring in the 1960s and 1970s.

Other researchers have focused on the Catholic Church scandal, collecting original data. Many of these other studies have examined the consequences of the child sexual abuse for individuals, parishes, the Church, and society. Research shows that, like other child sexual assault victims, those assaulted by priests are more likely than those who never experienced any sexual abuse to experience social isolation and require extensive therapy (Isely, Isely, Freiburger, & McMackin, 2008). Some researchers have identified consequences that may be unique to victims of clergy. Surveys of 1,810 Catholics found that those who had been abused by priests were more distrustful of religion than those who were sexually abused by someone other than a priest. All sexual assault victims were more likely to experience various forms of "spiritual damage" (Rossetti, 1995). Other studies have found no difference between those abused by priests and victims abused by someone else (Shea, 2008). The long-term consequences are particularly salient for both groups.

Kline, McMackin, and Lezotte (2008) conducted three focus groups with Catholics whose church had been involved in one of the sex abuse scandals. The author team focused on the consequences of the scandal for the parish community. Themes they uncovered included (a) a reflection on past church wrongdoings, (b) hurt over betrayal by church leaders, (c) recognizing that one's relationship with God is separate from one's relationship to a parish, and (d) interest in children and spiritual needs.

The impact of the scandal on the Church cannot be understated. Beyond the economic toll that has come along with paying for settlements and treatment programs, raising funds was likely more difficult for Church leaders during these times. Also, the child sexual abuse scandal received widespread coverage in the press, far more coverage than other forms of child sexual abuse have received (Cheit & Davis, 2010). There are no simple answers as to what can be done to help victims, or the Church, recover. Still, lawsuits, therapy, and punishing offenders are all seen as elements that can help victims recover (Dreese, 1998).

As far as what the Church can do, experts have noted that it must take measures to prevent these actions in the future. Some experts have suggested that situational crime prevention ideals be applied to prevention strategies developed by the Church. This would entail limiting access to potential victims, increasing awareness about prevention strategies among potential victims, strengthening surveillance, and reducing risk factors (Terry & Ackerman, 2008).

Some will question whether sexual abuse by priests is actually a form of white-collar crime. After all, the offense of child sexual abuse seems more like a violent street crime than a white-collar crime. A. R. Piquero and his colleagues (2008) do an outstanding job making an argument that these offenses can be characterized as white-collar crimes. The offenses are committed: (a) by a trusted professional (b) who is respected by members of society (c) during the course of work. Also, recall Rosoff's (1989) concept of status liability: by the very nature of their status, when priests "fall from grace," the response from the public will be far more severe than other offenders might experience.

Summary

- Varieties of police misconduct include corruption of authority, kickbacks, opportunistic theft, shakedowns, protection of illegal activities, fixing cases, direct criminal activities, internal payoffs (Barker & Roebucks, 1973) and sexual misconduct.
- McCarthy (1981) identified four varieties of corruption in corrections: embezzlement (stealing from the institution), drug smuggling into the institution, coercion, and transporting contraband into the prison system.
- The public's negative view of attorneys likely contributes to formal complaints about attorney conduct (or misconduct).
- States have different expectations and definitions for what is viewed to be appropriate conduct for attorneys.
- Of the few studies that have been done on attorney misconduct, the focus tends to be on types of sanctions levied against attorneys.
- If attorneys violate the criminal or civil laws, they can be subjected to penalties stemming from those bodies of law (e.g., incarceration, probation, fines, restitution, etc.). A variety of different sanctions can be given to attorneys by their professional associations. Most commonly, these sanctions include warning letters, private reprimands, public reprimands, suspensions, and disbarment.
- Just as lawyers are depicted in certain ways on television shows and movies, judges are also a regular part of the "cast of characters" portrayed in crime-related media.
- According to the Model Code of Judicial Conduct, judges are held to "higher standards of ethical conduct than attorneys or other persons not invested with the public trust."
- Kentucky identifies three general types of judicial misconduct: (1) improper influence, (2) improper courtroom decorum, and (3) improper illegal activities on or off the bench.
- Allegations of judicial misconduct increased significantly in the early 1990s (Coyle, 1995).
- It is estimated that 90% of complaints filed against judges are dismissed (Gray, 2004).
- Some have argued that a combination of three factors contributes to misdeeds by judges. These factors include: (1) office authority, (3) heavy caseloads, and (3) interactions with others in the judicial process (Coyle, 1995).
- Criminologist Jocelyn Pollock (2004) has identified five different types of prosecutorial misconduct. Legal expert Alschuler (1972) discussed a different set of prosecutorial misconduct examples.
- While it is difficult to identify precisely how often prosecutorial misconduct occurs, estimates suggest that these behaviors are particularly common.

- A number of direct and indirect negative consequences arise from prosecutorial misconduct.
- Students should not think that they are insulated from cases of prosecutorial misconduct. Most of us likely assume that our health care providers would never even consider breaking their ethical code or the criminal law.
- Unlike professionals working in some of the other systems, professionals in the political system routinely confront suspicion and distrust from citizens.
- Types of crimes occurring in the political system include election law violations, campaign finance violations, political corruption related to extortion and bribery, apolitical white-collar crime, crimes in the military, and state-corporate crime
- Election law violations refers to situations where political officials violate rules guiding the way that elections are supposed to be conducted.
- Campaign finance laws place restrictions on the way political campaigns are financed, with specific attention given to contributions and expenditures.
- In this context, political corruption related to extortion or bribery refers to situations where political officials use their political power to shape outcomes of various processes including lawmaking, awarding of contracts, policy development, and so on.
- Apolitical white-collar crime refers to situations where politicians get into trouble for doing things that are outside of the scope of politics but are violations of the public trust.
- Clifford Bryant (1979) used the phrase *khaki-collar crime* to describe situations where individuals in the military break rules guiding their workplace activities.
- The phrase *state-corporate crime* draws attention to the fact that governmental agencies are employers (or "corporations") and these agencies and their employees sometimes commit various types of misconduct—either independently or in conjunction with other corporations.
- Historically, the Catholic Church has been viewed as a safe haven where individuals can retreat for protection.
- Utilizing a variety of research methodologies including interviews, reviews of case files, mail surveys, and so on, the John Jay study found that 4% of active priests "between 1950 and 2002 had allegations of abuse."
- Researchers have used the John Jay data to examine similarities between sexual abuse in the Church and victimization/offending patterns among other offender groups.
- Alex Piquero and his colleagues (Piquero, Piquero, et al., 2008) used the John Jay data to examine the criminal careers of the clerics and compare their careers to the careers of traditional criminals.
- Michael White and Karen Terry (2008) used the John Jay data to apply the rotten apples explanation to the sex abuse scandal.
- Other researchers have focused on the Catholic Church scandal, collecting original data. Many of these other studies have focused on the consequences of the child sexual abuse for individuals, parishes, the Church, and society.
- The impact of the scandal on the Church cannot be understated.
- As far as what the Church can do, experts have noted that the Church must take measures to prevent these actions in the future.
- Some will question whether sexual abuse by priests is actually a form of white-collar crime. A. R. Piquero and his colleagues (2008) do an outstanding job making an argument that these offenses can be characterized as white-collar crimes.

KEY TERMS

Apolitical white-collar crime

Campaign finance laws

Censure

Defiance

Election law violations

Enemy civilian social system crimes

Extra-occupational crimes

Fear mongering

Foreign friendly civilian crimes

Inter-occupational crimes

Intra-occupational crimes

Iran-Contra affair

Misdirection

Plausible deniability

Police corruption

Police sexual misconduct

Political extortion/bribery

Redirection

Religious system deception

Relying on self-righteousness

Retaliation

Scapegoating

State-corporate crime

State crime

DISCUSSION QUESTIONS

1. Discuss the similarities and differences between the types of crimes discussed in this section.

2. All white-collar crimes involve violations of trust. Review the crimes discussed in this section and rank them from the highest trust violation to the lowest trust violation.

3. Compare and contrast the terms *white-collar crime* and *khaki-collar crime.*

4. Should police officers lose their jobs if they commit workplace misconduct? Explain.

5. Why do you think judges commit white-collar crime?

6. Explain how a college education might reduce corruption in the criminal justice system.

7. Review the case study included in In Focus 5.1. What do you think should be done to this judge?

8. What is state-corporate crime? How is it different from khaki-collar crime?

WEB RESOURCES

Commission to Combat Police Corruption: http://www.nyc.gov/html/ccpc/html/home/home.shtml

Judicial and Attorney Misconduct: http://www.clr.org/ostates.html

Bishop Accountability: http://www.bishop-accountability.org/

Scambusters Church Scams: http://www.scambusters.org/churchscam.html

Political Corruption: http://www.politicalcorruption.net/

Report Public Corruption: http://www.reportpubliccorruption.org/

READING

In this article, Heather Schoenfeld describes prosecutorial misconduct as a violation of trust and uses occupational crime literature to create a foundation from which understanding about the causes of prosecutorial misconduct can be presented. Schoenfeld notes that criminological research on prosecutorial decision making has focused on issues centering around sentencing and plea bargaining and calls for broader research on prosecutorial conduct. Conceptualizing misconduct as stemming from the nature of the trust given to prosecutors, Schoenfeld examines how traditional criminological explanations such as culture of competition, neutralization theory, and opportunity contribute to prosecutorial misconduct. She also discusses the ties between opportunity structures and punishment structures. Schoenfeld concludes with a number of hypotheses and directions for future research.

Violated Trust

Conceptualizing Prosecutorial Misconduct

Heather Schoenfeld

In the past 30 years, the prosecutor has become the most powerful position in the criminal justice system (Saltzburg & Capra, 2000). Unfortunately, this power has contributed to convictions of innocent defendants. Although the full extent of prosecutorial misconduct is unknown (Meares, 1995), recent studies suggest cause for concern. Prosecutorial misconduct was a factor in 45% of recent cases overturned because of DNA evidence (Scheck, Neufeld, & Dwyer, 2000, p. 361) and 24% of recently overturned death penalty cases (Warden, 2001). The Center for Public Integrity found that since 1970, appellate courts have reviewed 11,452 criminal cases where the defendant claimed the prosecutor acted improperly. In 20% of the cases, the court dismissed, reversed, or reduced the original sentence partly because of the misconduct (Weinberg, Gordon, & Williams, 2005).

The aforementioned reports and the recent media coverage of wrongdoing by prosecutors point to the need for systematic analyses of prosecutorial misconduct and

its causes.[1] New empirical research on misconduct should be grounded in a comprehensive theory. However, existing theories of prosecutorial misconduct do not take into account the structure of the prosecutorial profession while specifying conditions under which prosecutorial misconduct is more likely. This article proposes an alternative more comprehensive theory—with the goal of generating testable hypotheses. The theory builds from the characterization of prosecutors as agents of trust and prosecutorial misconduct as violations of the norms of trust. Borrowing from theories of occupational crime to explain how the structure of the trust relationship creates motivation and opportunities for misconduct, the theory can explain why some prosecutors, despite their mandate to seek justice, use improper and unethical tactics.

Prosecutorial misconduct can occur during any part of the criminal justice process, including presentation to the grand jury, charging decisions, discovery, plea negotiations, trial, and post conviction appeals.

SOURCE: Schoenfeld, Heather. (2005). Violated trust: Conceptualizing prosecutorial misconduct. *Journal of Contemporary Criminal Justice, 21,* 250–271.

However, the following argument focuses on prosecutorial misconduct around criminal trials—either during pretrial discovery, trial, or posttrial appeals—because this type of misconduct is most implicated in wrongful conviction cases.[2] Because most convictions are obtained through a guilty plea, the scope of the argument is necessarily limited. However, because approximately one third of murder defendants' cases go to trial (Rainville & Reaves, 2003), including many high-profile cases, the potential incidence of prosecutorial misconduct presents a significant obstacle to the legitimacy and reliability of the current criminal justice system.

 # Explanations for Prosecutorial Misconduct

Knowledge of prosecutorial conduct is derived mainly from journalistic accounts and legal scholarship, none of which adequately explains why some prosecutors engage in misconduct and others do not. Alternatively, social scientists have developed theories of legal decision making; however, these theories do not specifically address misbehavior.

Legal Accounts of Misconduct

Legal analysts usually rely on either a so-called tunnel vision or a conviction psychology explanation for prosecutorial misconduct. The first contends that prosecutors ultimately seek justice, and because most defendants are guilty, prosecutors feel compelled to sidestep problems that could sacrifice a guilty verdict (Jonakait, 1987). For example, some prosecutors feel justified allowing a witness to lie about his or her background because they believe this behavior serves the interest of so-called truth (Dershowitz, 2003). Tunnel vision, or the cognitive process of applying stereotypes to cases, can also cause legal actors to discount conflicting information (Anderson, Lepper, & Ross, 1980) or neglect evidence that is contrary to their version of events (Martin, 2002; McCloskey, 1989). In this scenario, prosecutors' unwavering belief in the defendant's guilt is the prime cause of their misconduct.

Other accounts blame misconduct on prosecutors' "score-keeping mentality" or conviction psychology that compels them to win at all costs (Felkenes, 1975).[3] This mentality stems from institutional, professional, and political pressures to win convictions (Bresler, 1996; Fisher, 1988; Gershman, 2001). For example, district attorneys (DAs) feel pressure to convict because voters use convictions as a quantifiable measure of success when choosing a DA candidate (Gordon & Huber, 2002). Legal analysts argued that the desire to win convictions, coupled with limited sanctions for misconduct, can lead to misconduct (Meares, 1995).

Prosecutorial Decision Making

Sociologists and criminologists' analyses of decision making by prosecutors, defense attorneys, and judges have primarily focused on plea bargaining (Albonetti, 1986; Emmelman, 1997; Sudnow, 1965) or sentencing (Albonetti, 1991; Maynard, 1982; Steffensmeier, Ulmer, & Kramer, 1998) as these activities constitute the core activity of most courts (Ulmer, 1997).[4] They posited that to make decisions under conditions of uncertainty, legal actors use socially constructed subjective definitions of "normal crimes" or "typical defendants" that act as "shorthand reference terms for [legal actors'] knowledge of the social structure and criminal events" (Sudnow, 1965, p. 275; see also Albonetti, 1986; Farrell & Holmes, 1991). These notions develop through the interaction and interdependency of prosecutors, defense attorneys, and judges who must work together to run an efficient system with limited financial or human capital (Eisenstein, Flemming, & Nardulli, 1988; Ulmer, 1997).

Professional identities and internal organizational culture also structure legal actors' decisions. In their comprehensive research of nine court communities in the late 1970s, Hemming, Nardulli, and Eisenstein (1992) identified three DA leadership styles. Insurgent DAs work aggressively to increase the power of their office, organize their offices hierarchically, employ lax charging standards but implement strict restrictions on plea bargaining in favor of tough punishment. Reformer DAs, also interested in increasing the power of their office, tend to focus more on office efficiency—requiring tight charging standards along with plea-bargaining restrictions. Finally, conservator DAs are satisfied with the status quo and allow their assistant district attorneys (ADAs) more discretion within a decentralized organization structure.

While neither of these literatures directly focus on prosecutorial misconduct, they identify structural realities and individual-level cognitive factors that could contribute to misconduct. Legal scholarship, for example, points to the inherent contradictions within the profession and the external and internal systems of rewards and sanctions for misconduct. The decision making literature points to cases that, falling outside of understood categories of crime and criminals, are less likely to be subject to plea bargaining and more likely to be subject to the adversarial process (Sudnow, 1965). It is often in the context of these so-called exceptional cases that the opportunity for misconduct arises (Farrell & Holmes, 1991).

 ## Prosecutors as Agents of Trust

Characterizing the Trust Relationship

The Supreme Court held in 1935 that prosecutors have a unique role in the legal system as the "representatives" of the "sovereignty." The opinion states

> The United States Attorney is the representative not of an ordinary party to a controversy, but of a sovereignty whose obligation to govern impartially is as compelling as its obligation to govern at all. . . . As such, he is in a peculiar and very definite sense the servant of the law, the twofold aim of which is that guilt shall not escape or innocence suffer. He may prosecute with earnestness and vigor—indeed he should do so. But, while he may strike hard blows, he is not at liberty to strike foul ones. (*Berger v. United States,* 1935, p. 88)

Where the sovereignty derives its power from the people, prosecutors represent the public within the bounds of a trust relationship. In the sociology of trust, principals (in this case the public) transfer power and delegate resources to agents (prosecutors), so that the agents may perform specialized services or complex projects (Shapiro, 1990, p. 348). In the United State's judicial system, the public entrusts prosecutors to develop specialized skills and gain specialized knowledge through the powers bestowed on the role (such as the right to subpoena; Guerrieri, 2001). The public then trusts prosecutors to use their skills, knowledge, and power to prosecute people who break the law.

Trust relationships are inherently unbalanced for three reasons. First, agents hold monopolies of information from which their actions are based. Second, because of their status as repositories for delegated power and their rights to resources and discretion they have the power to control principals' well-being. Third, agents' role is ambivalent, creating conflict between an "acting for" role and self-interest (Shapiro, 1990, p. 348). To properly balance the trust relationship, both parties tacitly agree to the following norms of the trust: (a) both parties disclose fully and honestly, (b) agents put the interests of principals above their own, and (c) agents maintain role competence and duties of diligence and prudence (Shapiro, 1990). Agents who violate the trust relationship do so by violating the norms of trust—of disclosure, disinterestedness, and role competence.

Violations of the Norms of Trust

Prosecutors' acts of misconduct are essentially violations of the norms of trust and, therefore, stem from the nature of trust relationships. The courts have identified three categories of prosecutor misconduct during trial: personal remarks, remarks promoting bias, and improper conduct around the facts of the case. The Court's opinions about the first two types of misconduct clearly demonstrate how the trust relationship creates the violation.

> It is fair to say that the average jury, in a greater or less degree, *has confidence* [emphasis

added] that . . . [obligations to serve justice] will be faithfully observed. Consequently, improper suggestions, insinuations and, especially, assertions of personal knowledge are apt to carry much weight against the accused when they should properly carry none. (*Berger v. United States*, 1935, p. 88)

Later, in *United States v. Young* (1985), the Court wrote that the "prosecutor's opinion carries with it the imprimatur of the Government and *may induce the jury to trust the Government's judgment* [emphasis added] rather than its own view of the evidence" (p. 18).

The third category of misconduct, improper conduct, includes knowingly presenting false testimony, letting false testimony stand without correction, making material misstatements of law or fact (or evidence),[5] and not disclosing evidence favorable to defendant (Hetherington, 2002). Each jurisdiction has its own rules of disclosure.[6] However, because of constitutional requirements for a fair trial, prosecutors must also disclose evidence that is "material either to guilt or punishment" or of "sufficient probative value" to create reasonable doubt as to guilt.[7] While the criteria for materiality and probative value can be ambiguous, the Court has increasingly ruled in the spirit of *United States v. Agurs* (1976) that the "prudent prosecutor will resolve doubtful questions in favor of disclosure" (p. 108). It is these violations of disclosure that are most often implicated in wrongful convictions (Innocence Project, 2001).

Role Duality in Trust Relationships

The problem of prosecutorial misconduct is intimately linked to the role of the prosecutor in the U.S. legal system as the repository for delegated power. As agents in trust relationships, prosecutors have a dual role— they are to be impartial representatives and vigorous advocates (Fisher, 1988). Recall the Supreme Court opinion, *Berger v. United States* (1935), which obliges prosecutors to "govern impartially" and "prosecute with earnest and vigor." The American Bar Association (1993) also recognizes this duality calling the prosecutor an "administrator of justice, an advocate, and an

officer of the court" (sec. 3-1.2). Prosecutors, similar to other agents of trust, can face a conflict between their acting-for role and their self-interest as a vigorous lawyer. As an impartial judicial officer of the court, prosecutors seek truth, fairness, and the rights of the accused. As a zealous advocate, prosecutors seek convictions and penal severity (Fisher, 1988). Thus, the role of a prosecutor, as an agent of trust, necessitates constant discretion concerning when to act impartially and when to advocate.

The nature of the trust relationship with its monopoly on information, necessary discretion, and role conflict generates conditions that can lead to prosecutorial misconduct. A theory of prosecutorial misconduct should start from the premise that prosecutorial misconduct is a violation of delegated trust. In this sense, theoretical explanations for occupational crimes that violate the norms of trust are useful in generating a comprehensive theory of prosecutorial misconduct (Shapiro, 1990).[8] Although differential association theory (Akers, 1998) or social control theory (Hirschi, 1969) could be used to explain occupational crime, an integrated theory of occupational crime can better explain how structural factors interact with individual-level social-psychological variables to cause misconduct. Borrowing from integrated theories of occupational crime that focus on confluence of motivation, opportunity, and choice (Coleman, 1987; McKendall & Wagner, 1997), the following sections lay out a theory of prosecutorial misconduct that posits that misconduct occurs when prosecutors positively evaluate motives and opportunities for misconduct in a way that neutralizes symbolic constraints against misconduct.

 Toward a Theory of Prosecutorial Misconduct

Prosecutorial Motivation

In his often-cited article synthesizing the research on white-collar crime, Coleman (1987) used a symbolic interactionist approach to define motivation as the "meaning that individuals attribute to a particular situation and to social reality … [which] structures their experience and makes certain courses of action seem appropriate while others are excluded or ignored"(p. 410). Socially created meanings or symbolic constructs (Blumer, 1969; Goffman, 1959) also allow individuals to anticipate the responses of others that, in turn, help them to define the situation. Prosecutors' motivation to engage in misconduct is structured by the meanings they attach to so-called success, their perceived expectations of their role as prosecutors, and the availability of neutralizations for misbehavior.

Defining Success

Coleman (1987) argued that motivation to engage in occupational crime originates in the "culture of competition" that stresses the value of personal gain, winning, and success as measures of people's intrinsic worth. Essentially, prosecutors want, as do most professionals, to be good at their job. As one prosecutor who had four cases reversed because of misconduct said, "Nobody told us to cheat. Nobody told us to do wrong. It was to be smart, be tenacious … [be] the best prosecutors in the office" (Armstrong & Possley, 1999c, p. 1). It is how prosecutors understand the role of a so-called good prosecutor that motivates their behavior.

However, because of the intrinsic nature of the trust relationship, prosecutors are likely to have role ambivalence. If, as suggested by many legal scholars, DAs use convictions as a criteria for raises and promotions, ADAs are likely to define success through convictions (Bresler, 1996; Ferguson-Gilbert, 2001; Fisher, 1988). Political ambitions and the political impetus to be "tough on crime" (Garland, 2001) may also cause prosecutors to tend toward their advocate role (Fisher, 1988; Medwed, 2004). In addition, insurgent DAs could induce ADAs to emphasize punishment over fairness (Flemming et al., 1992). For example, one DA who was cited for misconduct in more than 20 felony trials stated, "It's my obligation as District Attorney to present the evidence in the light most favorable to the state … the people are entitled to have a D.A. who argues their position very vigorously" (Armstrong & Possley, 1999b, p. 13).

Neutralizations

The meaning that prosecutors attribute to situations not only motivates behavior, but also constrains it. For example, while prosecutors want to be good at their jobs and meet their supervisors' expectations, their actions are also constrained by their understanding that fabricating evidence is wrong. Consequently, when people behave against norms they must neutralize their symbolic constraints (Sykes & Matza, 1957). Common techniques to neutralize occupational crime include denial that the act causes harm to others, insistence that the laws violated are wrong or unfair, arguing that the position necessitated the illegal behavior, or taking the so-called everyone does it stance (for a review, see Coleman, 1987). These neutralizations allow people who behave illegally to construct their behavior as "right," thus becoming part of their motivational framework.

While there is no systematic data on prosecutors' neutralizations for their misbehavior, certain structural realities of the prosecutorial profession make various neutralizations available—increasing the likelihood that prosecutors could think they are doing the right thing despite their misconduct. First, because part of the prosecutors' role is to serve justice—an undefined concept—prosecutors can neutralize misconduct that ultimately ends in their idea of justice. Commenting on the indictment of three former prosecutors and four police officers for the framing of Rolando Cruz, who spent 12 years wrongfully incarcerated, Larry Marshall, a leading expert on wrongful convictions, stated, "There's a feeling that that is how it works, that it's legitimate to bend the truth sometimes when you are doing it with—'the greater good'—in mind" (as cited in Armstrong & Possley, 1999d, p. 1).

Second, prosecutorial behavior often walks a fine line between legitimate behavior and misconduct. For example, when selecting a jury prosecutors are not allowed to use race as a determining factor in peremptory challenges (*Batson v. Kentucky*, 1986). After the defense claimed that prosecutors deliberately eliminated African Americans from the jury in all three trials of the Ford Heights 4 in Illinois, who were later exonerated, the lead prosecutor stated "I wouldn't say it [race] was a totally irrelevant factor—but it certainly wasn't a determining factor" (Armstrong & Possley, 1999d, p. 1).

Third, because the system (including prosecutors and defense attorneys) in practice assumes defendants' guilt, prosecutors could neutralize misconduct because they believe they are prosecuting guilty defendants (Sudnow, 1965; Ulmer, 1997). As one judge stated about a prosecutor whose office has repeatedly wrongly withheld evidence:

> From [the prosecutor's] perspective, bad guys are bad guys and whatever we need to do to put them away is OK. But the problem is, every now and then, it's not a bad guy. Every now and then, you've got the wrong guy. (Armstrong & Possley, 1999e, p. 1)

Fourth, prosecutors are held to different standards than defense attorneys who have "a special prerogative to engage in truth defeating tactics" (Fisher, 1988). Consequently, some legal scholars argue that prosecutors engage in misconduct because they find it difficult to understand why defense attorneys can behave in ways that are prohibited for prosecutors (Dershowitz, 2003). Prosecutors could potentially use this discrepancy as a neutralization technique.

 Opportunity for Prosecutorial Misconduct

Motivation alone, however, does not lead to improper behavior. For improper behavior to take place, the actor must have opportunities to misbehave. Coleman (1987) defined *opportunity* as "a potential course of action, made possible by a particular set of social conditions, which has been symbolically incorporated into an actor's repertoire of behavioral possibilities" (p. 424). According to research on occupational crime, certain structural realities provide more opportunities for misbehavior (McKendall & Wagner, 1997). Similarly, routine activity theory suggests that, given the motivation, certain situations will give rise to misconduct (Clarke & Felson, 1993; Cohen & Felson, 1979). In the case of

prosecutorial misconduct, the nature of trust relationships shape opportunities through the structure of professional standards, office organization, and informal and formal social control.

Professional Standards

In a trust relationship, principals must allow agents discretion within the norms of trust because principals do not have access to all pertinent information (Shapiro, 1990). Accordingly, prosecutors have discretion within the rules laid out by court decisions and are not subject to uniform standards (B. A. Green & Zacharias, 2004, p. 843). For example, although it is clear that prosecutors must disclose evidence that points to defendants' innocence, the law does not explicate guidelines that help prosecutors make the determination between exculpatory and nonexculpatory evidence. This type of ambiguity provides a central opportunity for misconduct. In fact, the Illinois Governor's Commission on Capital Punishment (2002) cited lack of standards for disclosure as one of the factors behind wrongful convictions in Illinois. The Commission recommended that the state Supreme Court adopt a rule defining exculpatory evidence to provide clear guidance to prosecutors (Governor's Commission on Capital Punishment, 2002).

Organizational Structure

The organizational characteristics of trust relationships can also lead to opportunities for deception. Although prosecutors' offices are not all organized in the same manner (Flemming et al., 1992), organizational theory suggests that similarly situated professional organizations will tend toward uniformity for reasons of efficiency (DiMaggio & Powell, 1983). For example, Flemming et al. (1992) found that DA office size affects organizational structure: Smaller offices can maintain looser structures, while large offices have to bureaucratize, with midsize offices variable. As such, the following are opportunities that develop from potential organizational impediments to informal social control.

First, agent activities tend to be socially, organizationally, temporally, and geographically distant from their principals (Shapiro, 1990). In other words, agents' activities are not transparent to the intended beneficiaries. Likewise, the activities of prosecutors' offices are hidden from public purview, except in the case of trials. While the public holds prosecutors accountable through elections, the public does not scrutinize prosecutors' daily activities. Even when trials face heavy public scrutiny, as in the trials of the Oklahoma City bombers, prosecutors can fail to disclose evidence and present perjured testimony (Romano, 2003; Thomas, 2001).

Second, the organizational structure common to trust relationships includes hierarchy, specialization, and internal diversification—all of which mask illicit acts and block the flow of information, not only from outsiders but also from insiders as well (Shapiro, 1990). For example, ADAs in midsize to large offices are often responsible for certain types of cases or cases from certain geographical areas (Flemming et al., 1992). This segmentation could allow prosecutors to act in bad faith without internal checks (B. A. Green & Zacharias, 2004).

Third, the outputs of trust relationships provide few red flags indicating violation. In other words, an outcome (or process) that involves misconduct may look exactly like a legitimate outcome (or process; Shapiro, 1990). Consequently, misconduct can be concealed as discretionary decision making. Violations such as nondisclosure or allowing perjured testimony are very difficult to detect because the violations are based on the prosecutors' discretion and knowledge. Finally, trust services are typically carried out and recorded in documents that can be destroyed or easily falsified (Shapiro, 1990). Demonstrating prosecutorial misconduct often requires, for example, uncovering documents that prove that evidence was not turned over or documents that show that the prosecutor made a deal with a witness.

Punishment Structure

In addition to the opportunities created by the organizational structure, trust relationships also bring about formal punishment structures that make misconduct a viable option. Punishment structures are particularly important because the attractiveness of misconduct is strongly influenced by perceptions of the certainty and severity of punishment (Nagin, 1998). Perceptions, although not always in line with reality, will necessarily be based on the actual structure and imposition of available sanctions (Keppler & Nagin, 1989). Shapiro (1990) argued that accountability and punishment are difficult within trust relationships because, one, agents can easily diffuse culpability for their misdeeds to others or to the nature of their position; and two, enforcers are reluctant to destroy the organizational apparatus through individual sanctioning (see also Hagan & Parker, 1985). The trust relationship enjoyed by prosecutors similarly leads to an underused and ineffective system of sanctions including appellate review and reversal, professional or judicial sanctions, civil penalties, and criminal prosecution (Lawless, 2003; Meares, 1995).

Appellate review and reversal. The Supreme Court has held that if prosecutorial misconduct violates a defendant's due process, federal appeals courts must reverse the conviction unless the "error was harmless beyond reasonable doubt" (*Chapman v. California*, 1967). If harmless, appeals courts must ignore the error in the interest of the "prompt administration of justice" (*United States v. Hasting*, 1983). Circuit courts use a variety of factors to determine so-called harmless error such as the severity of the misconduct, the curative measures taken by the trial court, if the weight of the evidence made conviction certain absent the improper conduct, and the impact on the jury (Hetherington, 2002). In general, courts are reluctant to use reversal as a means to discipline prosecutors because of concern for finality and trial resources (Gershman, 1985).

Professional or judicial sanctions. State bar associations or disciplinary agencies can provide professional sanctions (such as censure, temporary suspension, or permanent disbarment) for prosecutors who engage in misconduct. However, bar associations, interested in upholding the credibility of the legal profession, infrequently sanction prosecutors for misconduct (Meares, 1995). The 1999 investigation by the *Chicago Tribune* found that of 381 convictions that were reversed on appeal because of misconduct, not one single prosecutor received a public sanction from the state disciplinary agency and only two were privately censured (Armstrong & Possley, 1999a, p. 1). Internal review offices are also often ineffective in sanctioning misconduct because of lack of will or resources (Abramowitz & Scher, 1998; Meares, 1995).

In addition, courts are unwilling to use judicial sanctions (such as contempt of court, fines, public reprimand, suspension and/or recommendation for a professional investigation) to punish prosecutors for misconduct. Rarely do courts identify the violating prosecutor by name, and when they do, the court writes an unpublished opinion (Ferguson-Gilbert, 2001).

Civil penalties. Prosecutors are granted wide immunity from civil suits, even if their conduct at trial is unlawful and malicious or causes direct harm to defendants. The courts hold that for prosecutors to fulfill their duties as an advocate they must be free from the threat of litigation (*Imbler v. Pachtman*, 1976). Consequently, victims of wrongful convictions can rarely sue the individual prosecutors responsible for their convictions.

Criminal prosecution. Criminal sanctions for misconduct are practically nonexistent. In one rare case, a prosecutor who was convicted of fabricating evidence, withholding evidence, and knowingly introducing misleading and perjured testimony received a US $500 fine and an official censure from the court (Hessick, 2002). The criminal prosecution of prosecutors creates a conflict of interest because the state attorney's office is usually responsible for initiating criminal proceedings against prosecutors, yet doing so is tantamount to prosecuting one of their own—thereby bringing public scrutiny to the office as a whole. In addition, the individuals charged with investigating and indicting the prosecutor may be current or former coworkers of the accused.

◼ Dynamics of Choice

The negligible likelihood of detection, punishment or official rebuke, coupled with ambiguous professional standards, creates opportunities for prosecutorial misconduct. However, despite the opportunities trust relationships provide for misconduct, many, if not most, agents adhere to the norms of trust. A rational choice framework suggests that, in general, agents make decisions to violate the norms of trust loosely based on the expectation that their choice will provide benefits with minimal risk (for a review, see Tallman & Gray, 1990). Alternatively, a framework of "bounded rationality" suggests that actors do not always maximize outcomes but choose the first alternative that is "good enough" (Simon, 1979). Either way, agents' evaluation of their options is influenced by the ethical context of the decision and moral considerations.

Ethical Environment

Theorists of occupational crime recognize that choice to engage in illegal activity on the job often depends on the ethical climate of the workplace (McKendall & Wagner, 1997). Coleman (1987) noted that members of professions such as medicine and law enforcement are expected to identify with their profession, support their colleagues, and work to advance their common interests. The more insular a work-related subculture, the easier it is for members of the subculture to "maintain a definition of certain criminal activities as acceptable or even required behavior, when they are clearly condemned by society as a whole" (Coleman, 1987, p. 423).

Prosecutors function within the subculture of law enforcement in their district and the occupational subculture of prosecutors in general. Some initial work on these subcultures suggests that law enforcement officers are isolated, insular, and defend each other to outsiders (Jackall, 1997). This behavior may be reinforced by conservator-style DA offices, where ADAs are chosen for their similar views (Flemming et al., 1992). The tendency to defend other prosecutors' actions is evidenced, in part, by a pattern among prosecutors to defend police officer testimony and resist postconviction claims of innocence in the face of new evidence highly suggestive of innocence (Liptak, 2003; Medwed, 2004; Possley & Mills, 2003). For example, in spite of the resignation of the ADA assigned to defend Rolando Cruz's conviction (because of her belief that Cruz was innocent), the Illinois Attorney General stated

> It is not for me to look at the record and make a ruling . . . a jury has found this individual guilty and given him the death penalty. It is my role to see to it that it is upheld. That's my job. (Frisbie & Garrnett, 1998, p. 224)

Prosecutors also work within their immediate organizational subculture that can vary on the value placed on punishment and/or efficiency and inform office practices such as charging or plea bargaining (Flemming et al., 1992). As one former ADA commented about prosecutors who place a high value on punishment:

> They cannot make the distinction, in my opinion, between innocence and not guilty, and there is a distinction. An innocent man never committed the crime; a not guilty one cannot be proved without a reasonable doubt. They say he's either innocent or he's guilty. There is no middle ground. There's no not guilty. (Flemming et al., 1992, p. 42)

On the other hand, an organizational culture that places equal emphasis on punishment and efficiency reinforces prosecutors' "reasonableness" and concern with fairness (Flemming et al., 1992, p. 44). Finally, the culture of the so-called court community could either encourage or constrain misconduct (Eisenstein et al., 1988).

Moral Considerations

The values, attitudes, and beliefs that individuals bring to the workplace also play a role in "determining which of the definitions they learn on the job become part of their taken-for-granted reality . . . and which are rejected out of hand" (Coleman, 1987, p. 423). Consequently, even when the workplace defines motivations and opportunities for illegality as acceptable, individual actors have the capacity to reject them because of earlier socialization on acceptable behavior (McKendall & Wagner, 1997; Paternoster & Simpson, 1993). However, some actors bring attitudes to the workplace that make it easier for them to construe misbehavior as right.

Prosecutors who engage in misconduct may exhibit orienting attitudes and beliefs that neutralize normative constraints on misconduct. For example, some prosecutors could have preconceived notions of the prototypical criminal because of media portrayals of young African-American men as criminals (Russell, 1998) and residential segregation by race (therefore limiting their exposure to people of color; Massey & Nancy, 1993). As suggested by analysts of prosecutorial decision making in routine situations (Albonetti, 1986; Farrell & Holmes, 1991; Sudnow, 1965), these preconceived notions then play out in criminal investigations (as, e.g., when police and prosecutors focus their investigations in minority communities), and decisions to prosecute (as when prosecutors feel justified in ignoring signs of innocence because the suspect fits the criminal profile; Lofquist, 2001). Conversely, those who become prosecutors without racial prejudices or with the goal of increasing social justice may be less likely to take advantage of opportunities for misconduct (see Smith, 2001, for a discussion of so-called well-intentioned prosecutors).

 ## Conclusion: Studying Prosecutorial Misconduct

The report by the Center for Public Integrity concludes that prosecutors in all 2,341 jurisdictions in the United States "have stretched, bent or broken rules to win convictions" (Weinberg et al., 2005, p. 2). The theory of prosecutorial behavior presented here explains why misconduct is potentially widespread and why some prosecutors (or DA's offices) are more likely to engage in misconduct than others. The theory develops from the intrinsic nature of the trust relationship between prosecutors and the public that requires prosecutors to act for the public and adhere to the norms of trust—disclosure, disinterestedness, and role competence. However, prosecutors' trust relationship with the public is inherently conflictual as prosecutors strive to be successful in their roles. Prosecutors' misbehavior depends on the confluence of motivation, opportunity and choice—thus emphasizing the structural realities of the occupation and the agency of prosecutors. Motivation to engage in misconduct is a result of prosecutors' definitions of success, which are influenced by the reward structure and the availability of techniques of neutralization. Opportunities for misconduct arise because of the organization of the prosecutorial role and weak informal and formal sanctions for prosecutors' behavior. Finally, prosecutors' decision to engage in misconduct, given the motivation and opportunity, depends on their evaluation of existing opportunities for rewards and risks, which is influenced by their workplace subculture and their values and beliefs.

Generating Hypotheses

Although the nature of the prosecutorial profession creates opportunities for misconduct through lack of informal and formal social control, variation in the organizational structure of prosecutors' offices allow for variation in the probability that prosecutors will decide to misbehave. Thus, it can be hypothesized that opportunities for misconduct will be more available if (a) the jurisdiction has no guidelines (or underemphasized guidelines) for prosecutorial decision making, (b) the organization of the DA's office is highly compartmentalized and provides little daily supervision of prosecutors, or (c) the DA's office lacks an effective internal (or external) review system.

Individual prosecutors will also vary in how they define success and interpret their situation. Prosecutors are more likely to positively evaluate opportunities to engage in misconduct if (d) they face a competitive reward structure or evaluations based on the number of convictions they win, (e) they feel political pressure to win convictions, or (f) they adopt available neutralizations for misbehavior. Finally, the context of prosecutors' evaluation of opportunities for misconduct will increase the likelihood of misconduct if (g) prosecutors' are firmly embedded in law enforcement culture, (h) the DA's office culture emphasizes punishment over

fairness, and (i) prosecutors' hold prejudices against minority group members.

Developing a Research Agenda

Testing these hypotheses will require multiple research projects with different foci. For example, to learn which organizational variables affect prosecutorial misconduct, researchers could survey a national sample of DA offices to gather information on hiring and promotion policies, size, internal organizational structure, existence of guidelines, office political affiliation, and presence of internal review system. Researchers could then test for correlations between these variables and the jurisdictions' number of cases appealed that include claims of misconduct during a specific time frame. Researchers could also use a comparative case study method to identify organizational factors in misconduct by selecting for variation on the dependant variable.

Ethnography or comparative ethnography of prosecutors' offices could uncover how prosecutors manage their dual role and whether they employ neutralizations if they subvert the law. Although it is difficult to generalize from a few cases, ethnographies can help refine theories of prosecutorial misbehavior, just as Sudnow's (1965) classic ethnography did 40 years ago. Only through systematic observation of the daily routine and narratives of prosecutors can researchers identify the meanings prosecutors attach to winning, succeeding, losing, and/or sanctions.

Finally, researchers could also replicate the self-report survey methods of occupational crime research to identify individual-level factors that contribute to misconduct. Survey questions could solicit information about why prosecutors chose their profession, their prejudices, values, ambitions, and their degree of embeddedness in law enforcement culture. Researchers could look for which of these factors correlate with prosecutors' own admission of various types of misbehavior. Self-report surveys could also provide a benchmark for future research.

Most studies of prosecutorial behavior were completed before the mid-1980s, yet prosecutors' circumstances have changed dramatically in the past 20 years.

With the proliferation of sentencing guidelines, mandatory minimum sentences, and truth-in-sentencing legislation, prosecutors' decisions about who and what to charge have increasing consequences for defendants, their families, and crime victims (Zimring, Hawkins, & Kamin, 2001). Although DNA technology now provides the occasional ability to detect wrongful convictions because of misconduct, most defendants have little recourse if wrongfully convicted. Thus it is vitally important that research begin anew on this topic. The alternative is the continued conviction of innocent people through prosecutorial misconduct and the eventual undermining of the legal system through the loss of the public's trust.

 Notes

1. See, for example, the following news stories. In October 2003 and April 2005, a federal district court judge in Boston released two mafia members because of federal prosecutors' "extraordinary misconduct" (Murphy, 2005). In January of 1999, the *Chicago Tribune* ran a 5-part series titled "Trial & Error: How Prosecutors Sacrifice Justice to Win." The *Tribune* investigation found that since 1963, 381 people have had their convictions for homicide overturned because of prosecutorial misconduct during trial. Sixty-seven of those defendants were sentenced to death (Armstrong & Possley, 1999e). The *Pittsburgh Post-Gazette* published a similar 10-part series in 1998 titled "Win at All Costs" that exposed systematic misconduct in the federal prosecutor's office.

2. In addition this argument focuses on wrongdoing designated by the courts as "misconduct" (such as personal remarks or remarks promoting bias, and improper conduct around the facts of the case). Even though this type of misconduct is often in contention, it differs from behavior that is deemed "unethical" by some, but not misconduct by the courts (see Smith, 2001). Thus the argument does not address practices of overcharging or undercharging (Alschuler, 1968; Brunk, 1979; Meares, 1995).

3. For a recent review of examples, see Ferguson-Gilbert, 2001, p. 291.

4. Feminist criminologists have been especially concerned with the decision making around domestic violence and sexual assault cases (Frohmann, 1991, 1997; Spears & Spohn, 1996; Spohn, Beichner, & Davis-Frenzel, 2001).

5. The Supreme Court has established that prosecutors' deliberate use of perjured testimony violates due process constitutionally guaranteed to defendants (*Mooney v. Holohan*, 1935). The Court later ruled that prosecutors' failure to correct testimony known to be false (*Alcota v. Texas*, 1957) and false testimony on witness credibility (*Napue v. Illinois*, 1959) also violates due process.

6. Rules of disclosure at a minimum require that prosecutors turn over to the defense statements made by the defendant, the defendant's prior record, documents, objects and reports to be used at trial, and expert witness testimony (see Federal Rule of Criminal Procedure, Rule 16[a]).

7. In *Brady v. Maryland* (1963) the Supreme Court held that a defendant's due process is violated when the prosecution suppresses evidence requested by the defense that is "material either to guilt or punishment" irrespective of the intentions of the prosecution (p. 87). This includes evidence that could impeach a government witness (*Giglio v. United States*, 1972). Later, the Court defined evidence as "material" if there is "reasonable probability" that the result of the proceeding would have been different if the evidence had been disclosed (*United States v. Bagley*, 1985, p. 682). When evidence is not specifically requested by the defense, prosecutors must disclose evidence of "sufficient probative value" to create reasonable doubt as to guilt (*United States v. Agurs*, 1976). In addition, prosecutors have "a duty to learn of any favorable evidence known to the others acting on the government's behalf in the case, including the police" (*Kyles v. Whitley*, 1995, p. 421). The *Brady* rule includes evidence relevant to sentencing proceedings (*Banks v. Dretke*, 2004) and evidence discovered postconviction if it "casts doubt upon the correctness of the conviction" (*Imbler v. Pachtman*, 1976, p. 427).

8. G. S. Green (1990) defined *occupational crime* as "any act punishable by law which is committed through opportunity created in the course of an occupation that is legal" (p. 12). Early conceptions of occupational crime hinged on the violation of delegated or implied trust (Sutherland, 1940).

 References

Abramowitz, E., & Scher, P. (1998, January 6). The Hyde Amendment: Congress creates a toehold for curbing wrongful prosecution. *New York Law Journal*, 3.

Akers, R. L. (1998). *Social learning and social structure: A general theory of crime and deviance.* Boston: Northeastern University Press.

Albonetti, C. A. (1986). Criminality, prosecutorial screening, and uncertainty: Toward a theory of discretionary decision making in felony case proceedings. *Criminology, 24*(4), 623-643.

Albonetti, C. A. (1991). An integration of theories to explain judicial discretion. *Social Problems, 38*(2), 247-266.

Alcota v. Texas, 355 U.S. 28 (1957).

Alschuler, A. W. (1968). The prosecutor's role in plea bargaining. *University of Chicago Law Review, 36*, 50-96.

American Bar Association. (1993). The function of a prosecutor. In *Standards for criminal justice prosecution function and defense function standard* (3rd ed., pp. 3-115). Chicago: American Bar Association.

Anderson, C. A., Lepper, M. R., & Ross, L. (1980). Perseverance of social theories: The role of explanation in the persistence of discredited information. *Journal of Personality and Social Psychology, 39,* 1037-1049.

Armstrong, K., & Possley, M. (1999a, January 14). Break rules, be promoted, series: Trial and error, how prosecutors sacrifice justice to win, five in a five part series. *Chicago Tribune,* p. 1.

Armstrong, K., & Possley, M. (1999b, January 10). 'Cowboy Bob' ropes wins—but at considerable cost, Oklahoma County prosecutor has put 53 defendants on death row but records show he's broken many rules to do so. *Chicago Tribune,* p. 13.

Armstrong, K., & Possley, M. (1999c, January 11). The flip side of a fair trial, series: Trial and error, how prosecutors sacrifice justice to win, second in a five part series. *Chicago Tribune,* p. 1.

Armstrong, K., & Possley, M. (1999d, January 12). Prosecution on trial in DuPage, series: Trial and error, how prosecutors sacrifice justice to win, third in a five part series. *Chicago Tribune,* p. 1.

Armstrong, K., & Possley, M. (1999e, January 10). The verdict: Dishonor, series: Trial and error, how prosecutors sacrifice justice to win, first in a five part series. *Chicago Tribune,* p. 1.

Banks v. Dretke, 124 S.Ct. 1256 (2004).

Batson, v. Kentucky, 476 U.S. 79 (1986).

Berger v. United States, 295 U.S. 78 (1935).

Blumer, H. (1969). *Symbolic interactionism: Perspective and method.* Englewood Cliffs, NJ: Prentice Hall.

Brady v. Maryland, 373 U.S. 83 (1963).

Bresler, K. (1996). "I never lost a trial": When prosecutors keep score of criminal convictions. *Georgetown Journal of Legal Ethics, 9,* 537-580.

Brunk, C. G. (1979). The problem of voluntariness and coercion in the negotiated plea. *Law and Society Review, 13,* 527-553.

Chapman, v. California, 386 U.S. 18 (1967).

Clarke, R. V., & Felson, M. (Eds.). (1993). *Routine activity and rational choice* (Vol. 5). New Brunswick, NJ: Transaction Publishers.

Cohen, L. E., & Felson, M. (1979). Social change and crime rate trends: A routine activity approach. *American Sociological Review, 44,* 588-608.

Coleman, J. W. (1987). Toward an integrated theory of white-collar crime. *American Journal of Sociology, 93*(2), 406-439.

Dershowitz, A. (2003). Foreword. In J. F. J. Lawless (Ed.), *Prosecutorial misconduct* (3rd ed.). San Francisco: Matthew Bender & Co.

DiMaggio, P. J., & Powell, W. W. (1983). The iron cage revisited: Institutional isomorphism and collective rationality in organizational fields. *American Sociological Review, 48,* 147-160.

Eisenstein, J., Flemming, R., & Nardulli, P. (1988). *The contours of justice: Communities and their courts.* Boston: Little, Brown.

Emmelman, D. S. (1997). Gauging the strength of evidence prior to plea bargaining: The interpretive procedures of court-appointed defense attorneys. *Law and Social Inquiry, 22*(4), 927-955.

Farrell, R. A., & Holmes, M. D. (1991). The social and cognitive structure of legal decision-making. *Sociological Quarterly, 32*(4), 529-542.

Felkenes, G. (1975). The prosecutor: A look at reality. *Southwestern University Law Review, 7,* 98.

Ferguson-Gilbert, C. (2001). It is not whether you win or lose, it is how you play the game: Is win-loss scorekeeping mentality doing justice for prosecutors? *California Western Law Review, 38,* 283-309.

Fisher, S. Z. (1988). In search of the virtuous prosecutor: A conceptual framework. *American Journal of Criminal Law, 15,* 197-254.

Flemming, R., Nardulli, P., & Eisenstein, J. (1992). *The craft of justice: Work and politics in criminal court communities.* Philadelphia: University of Philadelphia Press.

Frisbie, T., & Gannett, R. (1998). *Victims of justice: The true story of two innocent men condemned to die and a prosecution out of control.* New York: Avon Books.

Frohmann, L. (1991). Discrediting victims' allegations of sexual assault: Prosecutorial accounts of case rejection. *Social Problems, 38,* 213-226.

Frohmann, L. (1997). Convictability and discordant locales: Reproducing race, class, and gender ideologies in prosecutorial decision making. *Law and Society Review, 31*(3), 531-555.

Garland, D. (2001). *Culture of control: Crime and social order in contemporary society.* Chicago: University of Chicago Press.

Gershman, B. (1985). The Burger Court and prosecutorial misconduct. *Criminal Law Bulletin, 21*(3), 217-226.

Gershman, B. (2001). The prosecutor's duty to truth. *Georgetown Journal of Legal Ethics, 14,* 309-354.

Giglio v. United States, 405 U.S. 150 (1972).

Goffman, E. (1959). *The presentation of self in everyday life.* Garden City, NY: Doubleday.

Gordon, S. C., & Huber, G. A. (2002). Citizen oversight and the electoral incentives of criminal prosecutors. *American Journal of Political Science, 46*(2), 334-351.

Governor's Commission on Capital Punishment. (2002). *Report of the Governor's Commission on Capital Punishment.* Chicago: State of Illinois.

Green, B. A., & Zacharias, F. C. (2004). Prosecutorial neutrality. *Wisconsin Law Review,* 837-904.

Green, G. S. (1990). *Occupational crime.* Chicago: Nelson-Hall.

Guerrieri, F. (2001, Winter). Law and order: Redefining the relationship between prosecutors and police. *Southern Illinois Law Journal, 25,* 353-388.

Hagan, J., & Parker, P. (1985). White-collar crime and punishment: The class structure and legal sanctioning of security violations. *American Sociological Review, 50,* 302-316.

Hessick, C. (2002). Prosecutorial subornation of perjury: Is the fair justice agency the solution we have been looking for? *South Dakota Law Review, 47,* 255-281.

Hetherington, A. M. (2002). Thirty-first annual review of criminal procedure: III. Trial: Prosecutorial misconduct. *Georgetown Law Journal, 90,* 1679-1689.

Hirschi, T. (1969). *Causes of delinquency.* Berkeley: University of California Press.

Imbler v. Pachtman, 424 U.S. 409 (1976).

Innocence Project. (2001). *Police and prosecutor misconduct.* Available at www.innocenceproject.org/causes/policemisconduct.php

Jackall, R. (1997). *Wild cowboys: Urban marauders and the forces of order.* Cambridge, MA: Harvard University Press.

Jonakait, R. N. (1987). The ethical prosecutor's misconduct. *Criminal Law Bulletin, 23,* 550.

Keppler, S., & Nagin, D. (1989). Tax compliance and perceptions of the risks of detection and criminal prosecution. *Law and Society Review, 23,* 209-240.

Kyles v. Whitley, 514 U.S. 419 (1995).

Lawless, J. F. J. (Ed.). (2003). *Prosecutorial misconduct* (3rd ed.). San Francisco: Matthew Bender & Co.

Liptak, A. (2003, August 29). Prosecutors fight DNA use for exoneration. *New York Times,* p. 1.

Lofquist, W. S. (2001). Whodunit? An examination of the production of wrongful convictions. In J. A. Humphrey & S. D. Westervelt (Eds.), *Wrongly convicted: Perspectives of failed justice* (pp. 174-198). New Brunswick, NJ: Rutgers University Press.

Martin, D. L. (2002). Lessons about justice from the "laboratory" of wrongful convictions: Tunnel vision, the construction of guilt and informer evidence. *University of Missouri at Kansas City Law Review, 70,* 847-864.

Massey, D. S., & Nancy, D. A. (1993*). American apartheid: Segregation and the making of the underclass.* Cambridge, MA: Harvard University Press.

Maynard, D. (1982). Defendant attributes in plea-bargaining: Notes on the modeling of sentencing decisions. *Social Problems, 29,* 345-360.

McCloskey, J. (1989). Convicting the innocent. *Criminal Justice Ethics, 8,* 2-70.

McKendall, M. A., & Wagner, J. A. (1997). Motive, opportunity, choice and corporate illegality. *Organizational Science, 8*(6), 624-647.

Meares, T. L. (1995). Rewards for good behavior: Influencing prosecutorial discretion and conduct with financial incentives. *Fordham Law Review, 64,* 851-921.

Medwed, D. S. (2004). The zeal deal: Prosecutorial resistance to post-conviction claims of innocence. *Boston University Law Review, 84,* 125-183.

Mooney v. Holohan, 294 U.S. 103 (1935).

Murphy, S. (2005, April 13). Judge throws out mobster's sentence. *Boston Globe,* p. A1.

Nagin, D. (1998). Criminal deterrence research at the outset of the twenty-first century. *Crime and Justice: A Review of the Research, 25*(1), 1-42.

Napue v. Illinois, 360 U.S. 499 (1959).

Paternoster, R., & Simpson, S. (1993). A rational choice theory of corporate crime. In R. V. Clarke & M. Felson (Eds.), *Routine activities and rational choice: Advances in criminological theory* (Vol. 5). New Brunswick, NJ: Transaction Publishers.

Possley, M., & Mills, S. (2003, April 19). State backs sentence despite DNA. *Chicago Tribune,* p. 12.

Rainville, G., & Reaves, B. A. (2003). *Felony defendants in large urban counties, 2000* (No. 202021). Washington, DC: Bureau of Justice Statistics.

Romano, L. (2003, May 1). McVeigh lawyers express ire over letter. *Washington Post,* p. A10.

Russell, K. K. (1998). *The color of crime: Racial hoaxes, White fear, Black protectionism, police harassment, and other macroaggressions.* New York: New York University Press.

Saltzburg, S. A., & Capra, D. J. (2000). *American criminal procedure* (6th ed.). St. Paul, MN: West Group.

Scheck, B., Neufeld, P., & Dwyer, J. (2000). *Actual innocence: When justice goes wrong and how to make it right.* New York: Signet.

Shapiro, S. (1990). Collaring the crime, not the criminal: Reconsidering the concept of white collar crime. *American Sociological Review, 55,* 346-365.

Simon, H. (1979). Rational decision making in business organizations. *American Economics Review, 69,* 493-513.

Smith, A. (2001). Can you be a good person and a good prosecutor? *Georgetown Journal of Legal Ethics, 14,* 355-400.

Spears, J. W., & Spohn, C. C. (1996). The genuine victim and prosecutors' charging decisions in sexual assault cases. *American Journal of Criminal Justice, 20*(2), 183-205.

Spohn, C., Beichner, D., & Davis-Frenzel, E. (2001). Prosecutorial justifications for sexual assault case rejection: Guarding the "gateway to justice." *Social Problems, 48*(2), 206-235.

Steffensmeier, D., Ulmer, J., & Kramer, J. (1998). The interaction of race, gender, and age in criminal sentencing: The punishment cost of being young, Black and male. *Criminology, 36*(4), 763-798.

Sudnow, D. (1965). Normal crimes: Sociological features of the penal code in a public defender office. *Social Problems, 12,* 255-275.

Sutherland, E. H. (1940). White-collar criminality. *American Sociological Review, 5,* 1-12.

Sykes, G. K., & Matza, D. (1957). Techniques of neutralization: A theory of delinquency. *American Sociological Review, 22,* 667-670.

Tallman, I., & Gray, L. N. (1990). Choices, decisions, and problem-solving. *Annual Review of Sociology, 16,* 405-433.

Thomas, J. (2001, September 6, 2001). Oklahoma prosecutor to seek death for bombing. *New York Times,* p. 14.

Ulmer, J. (1997). *Social worlds of sentencing: Court communities under sentencing guidelines.* Albany: State University of New York Press.

United States v. Agurs, 427 U.S. 97 (1976).

United States v. Bagley, 473 U.S. 667 (1985).

United States v. Hasting, 461 U.S. 499 (1983).

United States v. Young, 470 U.S. 1 (1985).

Warden, R. (2001). *An analysis of wrongful convictions since restoration of the death penalty following Furman v. Georgia.* Chicago: Center on Wrongful Convictions.

Weinberg, S., Gordon, N., & Williams, B. (2005). *Harmful error: Investigating America's local prosecutors.* Washington, DC: Center for Public Integrity.

Zimring, F, Hawkins, D., & Kamin, S. (2001). *Punishment and democracy: Three strikes and you're out in California.* Oxford, UK: Oxford University Press.

DISCUSSION QUESTIONS

1. How does the author describe prosecutorial misconduct?

2. What does the author think the cause of prosecutorial misconduct is?

3. What do you think the cause of this behavior is?

4. How does her discussion fit in with the systems approach?

READING

In this article, Alex Piquero and his colleagues use the John Jay data to determine how well the career criminal paradigm addressed the behaviors of clerics accused of child sexual abuse as part of the Catholic Church's sex abuse scandal. The research team provides a thorough review of the paradigm and a detailed account of the sex abuse scandal. Because so many experts have questioned whether sex crimes by priests should be considered white-collar crimes, the authors make an extremely convincing case for why these behaviors should be considered as white-collar crimes. They note that their findings provide mixed support for applying the assumptions of the career criminal paradigm to sexual misconduct by clerics. The authors point to a number of possible questions for future research.

Uncollaring the Criminal

Understanding Criminal Careers of Criminal Clerics

Alex R. Piquero, Nicole Leeper Piquero, Karen J. Terry, Tasha Youstin, and Matt Nobles

A careful description of criminal activity is the cornerstone of contemporary criminological theory (Blumstein, Cohen, Roth, & Visher, 1986; A. R. Piquero, Farrington, & Blumstein, 2003; Wolfgang, Figlio, & Sellin, 1972). Such a characterization of the nature and pattern of offending during the life course also serves to generate important facts of crime (Farrington, 2003), which though often debated, are critical to the development and advance of any strong theory of crime (Braithwaite, 1989).

The more general criminal careers literature has been largely based on the offending patterns of individuals followed in (typically) official police contact, arrest, and conviction records in the first two to three decades of life (Blumstein et al., 1986; Farrington, 2003; A. R. Piquero et al., 2003; Wolfgang et al., 1972). Within that research, several key findings have emerged, including the following seven key pieces

that are used to form the foundation for the present article.

First, the age of onset of offending is between ages 8 and 14, whereas the age of desistance from offending is between 20 and 29. Few offenders continue past age 30. Second, the prevalence of offending peaks in late adolescence (between ages 15 and 19). Third, an early age of onset foreshadows a lengthy criminal career and the commission of more offenses. Fourth, there is marked continuity in offending and antisocial behavior across different phases of the life course; there is relative stability of the ordering of people on some measure of antisocial behavior over time, and people who commit relatively many offenses during one age range are likely to also commit many offenses during another age range. Fifth, a small number of offenders commit a large percentage of all crimes; these chronic offenders exhibit an early onset, a high individual offending frequency, and a lengthy

SOURCE: Piquero, A., Piquero, N. L., Terry, K. J., Youstin, T., & Nobles, M. (2008). Uncollaring the criminal: Understanding the criminal careers of criminal clerics. *Criminal Justice and Behavior, 35,* 583–599. Published by SAGE, Inc., on behalf of the International Association for Correctional and Forensic Psychologists.

criminal career. Sixth, offending is more versatile than specialized, but although diversification increases up to age 20, afterward diversification decreases and specialization increases. Seventh, offenders tend to be involved in a wide range of acts that are elements of a larger syndrome of antisocial behavior that includes reckless driving, heavy drinking, and promiscuous sex.

Other longitudinal-based criminal careers research using self-report records of offending has generated some similar and some unique results. For example, the age of onset tends to be earlier in self-report compared to official records; the prevalence and frequency of offending is higher in self-reports; and persistence in crimes with a low probability of detection is a common feature in self-reported estimates of offending.

Although the totality of these summary conclusions have provided important information with respect to the longitudinal patterning of criminal activity, they remain limited because they rely on limited samples, focusing almost exclusively on juveniles followed into early adulthood and focusing on more traditional street offenses. N. L. Piquero and Benson (2004) noted that, by failing to recognize and account for other crime and offender types, such as acts committed by white-collar offenders, criminal career criminology is falling prey to the same mistake pointed out by Sutherland (1940) many years ago: acting as though common street crime is the only crime type that exists. As such, conclusions drawn from the criminal career body of research, such as those listed above, will "inevitably lead to a biased and incomplete understanding of trajectories in crime" (N. L. Piquero & Benson, 2004, p. 149). Unfortunately, little information is known about the criminal careers of white-collar offenders (but see Benson & Kerley, 2000; Weisburd & Waring, 2001) or of other types of offenders who occupy positions of trust and power, such as the sample that forms the basis for the current study, clerics who sexually abused minors.

As a result of the recent media attention garnered by the sexual abuse scandal in the Catholic Church, researchers were able to collect basic descriptive offending information on priest abusers, which did not exist for this group of offenders prior to this time. It is

this sample for whom we examine basic criminal career parameters and dimensions.

Church Abuse Scandals

A series of church abuse scandals has resulted in a large public outcry that shocked Catholic parishioners with tales of long-term abuse. This has generated a number of negative consequences not only for the victims of the abuse cases but also for the respective churches more generally. For example, from January 2002 through April 2004, the *Boston Globe* alone printed 1,454 articles relating to the sexual abuse perpetrated by members of the Catholic Church clergy (see "The *Boston Globe* Spotlight Investigation," 2004). The overwhelming press and shocking revelations of a massive church cover-up led to an increase in the public outcry regarding sex offenders. Although the state of popular and legislative discourse regarding sex offenders was already leaning toward increased punitiveness (Terry, 2006; Zimring, 2004), as seen through highly celebrated policies such as Megan's Law in 1994, the Catholic Church sex abuse scandal had several negative effects that did not necessarily serve the cause of child protection (Finkelhor, 2003).

In many ways, these church sex scandals became a sensationalized flashpoint for what has been a persistent and elusive social problem. First, it focused the public attention solely on child sexual abuse, placing nonsexual child abuse in the background, despite the fact that sexual maltreatment makes up only 10% of reported child abuse cases (U.S. Department of Health and Human Services, Administration on Children Youth and Families, 2002). The scandals also reinforced many stereotypes about sexual offenders, making it difficult for professionals to reestablish public awareness of the full spectrum of offenders. This led to a zero-tolerance policy for a priest who sexually abused a child at any point in his career, and subsequently, public perceptions of sex offenders leaned toward the view of untreatable offenders who offend throughout their lifetimes (Finkelhor, 2003). This viewpoint is contrary to extant research suggesting that cognitive-behavioral treatment programs can reduce recidivism by as much as 40% (Hanson et al., 2002) and that sex offenders are not necessarily the recidivistic, specialized, dangerous offenders that some believe (see Sample & Bray, 2003; Zimring, Piquero, & Jennings, 2007). And although the extent to which the church sex abuse scandals have increased public fear of child sexual abuse is unclear, the public has continually pressed for more severe and enduring penalties for sex offenders, including public notification, electronic monitoring, and proposed legislative policies that would incorporate mandatory minimum sentences up to life in prison for repeat offenders.

Initially, the Catholic Church addressed the scandal (and its underlying etiology) indirectly. After critics demanded a full and thorough accounting of sexual abuse at the hands of priests, the bishops created the Charter for the Protection of Children and Young People. The Charter called for creation of two oversight offices (the Office of Child and Youth Protection and the National Review Board) and two studies on the abuse crisis. Despite these steps taken to address the issue, survivors' groups and other critics perceived Church officials to be secretive and inaccessible. Maier (2005) noted that applying principles of openness, attentiveness, and responsiveness to public opinion would have aided the Church in negotiating the crisis, instead of simply obscuring it behind internal politics. However, the perception that the Church simply adopted a position emphasizing damage control for the organization and isolation for known abusers is comparable to the perception that corporations shield themselves from liability when their employees engage in white-collar crime (Gross, 1980).

This linkage—between clergy abuse and white-collar crime—is one that can provide a useful backdrop and analogy within which to understand this abuse crisis. On this score, Dunne (2004) suggested that the Catholic Church operates in a "client-independent" organizational framework built around controlling essential public services, as would a municipality, rather than a "client-dependent" system that relies on commerce and customer service. The Church's delayed response to the abuse scandal can be attributed to the fact that it does not rely on a free market system for its longevity and can be interpreted by critics as nothing more than a fundamental desire to protect its own image. Unaccountable to stockholders and government regulation in the corporate sense, and apparently unconcerned with consumers'

willingness to "brand switch" to an alternative denomination, the Church has few incentives to face true accountability. To the degree that the abuse scandal can be interpreted as white-collar crime, the Church represents a corporate entity characterized by malfeasance in knowingly concealing a history of sexual abuse on the part of its "employees." Furthermore, Kochansky and Herrmann (2004) suggested that the scandal and response evolved from a phenomenon that they call "institutional narcissism," which they define as "a focus on self-protection that threatens to overshadow the dedication and service of the vast majority of the clergy and to compromise the work of the Church itself" (p. 301).

Cleric Abuse as a Form of White-Collar Crime

Some scholars might argue that the cleric sex abuse scandals fall outside the purview of white-collar crime and therefore should be studied separately (Friedrichs, 2007, p. 104). However, we believe that the complete separation of the two would be premature, because the study of white-collar crime can inform and provide useful insights into the understudied phenomena of cleric abuse from an organizational perspective. The issue of what exactly constitutes white-collar crime has a long debated history that begins with Sutherland's (1940, p. 9) introductory definition of white-collar crime as "a crime committed by a person of respectability and high social status in the course of his occupation." In this definition, he purposely highlighted the use of offender characteristics (e.g., respectability and high social status) as defining elements of white-collar crime. This was a significant contribution at the time, insofar as he pushed scholars to look beyond existing causal factors (e.g., poverty and social disorganization) that were dominating causal explanations of crime and encouraged them to recognize that crimes were not exclusive to individuals who composed the lower classes.

Sutherland's offender-based definition soon proved to be limiting in two respects. First, the requirement of high or respectable social status restricted the array of offenses that could be examined. Second, by including social status in the definition, it could not be used as an explanatory variable (see Coleman, 2006, for detailed discussion). These limitations led to the development of an offense-based definition by Edelhertz (1970, p. 3), who defined white-collar crime as "an illegal act or series of illegal acts committed by nonphysical means and by concealment or guile to obtain money or property, to avoid the payment or loss of money or property, or to obtain business or personal advantage." This definition proved useful when dealing with official statistics because it followed the legal codes, but it was criticized as being too broad and losing sight of the very population that Sutherland wished to emphasize.

The definition of white-collar crime continues to evolve, with scholars arguing that the central factor in the definition should be the violation or abuse of trust (Friedrichs, 2007; Shapiro, 1990). This approach deals with the earlier criticisms of the offender-based definition by excluding social status as part of the definition but allowing the definition to stay truer to Sutherland's (1940) original conception as he characterized white-collar crime as a "violation of delegated or implied trust." Shapiro (1990) argued that this latest amendment to the concept of white-collar crime is important to "integrate the 'white-collar' offender into mainstream scholarship by looking beyond the perpetrators' wardrobe and social characteristics and exploring the modus operandi of their misdeeds and the ways in which they establish and exploit trust" (p. 363).

Therefore, we believe that the abusive behavior of clerics broadly constitutes a type of white-collar crime when it is defined as a violation of trust, because there is no question that clerics hold prestigious, if not revered, positions within society. As religious leaders are commonly regarded as the source of moral guidance and inspiration, they violate a sacred form of trust (Friedrichs, 2007). Because they have gained their positions of trust through their occupational role, this violation of trust can be construed as a type of professional or occupational crime.

Current Study

This article reports on our effort to provide the first descriptive account of the criminal careers of sexually abusing clerics. To undertake this task, we surveyed all dioceses and religious communities about sexual abuse allegations against clerics from 1950 to 2002 and obtained data on offending from church personnel files. A comprehensive portrait of the criminal careers of these clerics represents an important step in describing key criminal career parameters so as to provide a comparison against the criminal career parameters evinced by other samples that have served traditional criminology research in general and criminological theory in particular. More generally, our research helps to fill one of the gaps with respect to the absence of research on how the offending careers of white-collar criminals are similar to or different from those of street criminals. In addition to this portrait, we also investigate how several key predictors employed in the more general criminal career literature relate to the number of police investigations accumulated by the clerics.

Data

The data for this article are derived from the Nature and Scope Study of Child Sexual Abuse in the Catholic Church (John Jay College, 2004). The John Jay College Research Team compiled three survey instruments and sent them to the presiding bishops in all Catholic dioceses, eparchies, and religious communities in the United States. A diocesan survey sought information about the diocese, such as size and population; a cleric survey sought information about all priests with allegations of abuse; and a victim survey sought information about individuals who made allegations of sexual abuse against priests as well as the circumstances of the abuse.

The data in the Nature and Scope study are based on diocesan personnel records. The researchers did not collect the information personally; rather, diocesan employees who had access to personnel files were selected to complete the surveys. All information collected was anonymous, and the researchers had no access to information that could identify the dioceses, priests, or victims. To ensure the greatest level of uniformity possible in filing in the surveys, the researchers provided each diocese with written instructions, a video explaining how to complete the surveys, a research participation statement that reviewed the confidentiality protocols of the study and provided information about counseling, a Web site with a regularly updated list of frequently asked questions, and access to a 1-800 number for these employees to call with questions about the survey instruments. Once the dioceses completed the surveys, they sent them in a double-envelope to an independent auditor at a national accounting firm. The independent auditor identified the diocese, matched it to a list of randomized numbers, coded the inner envelope with that number, and discarded the outer envelope (which had the postmark). He mailed the envelope with only the code and no other identifying information to the researchers. For a more detailed account of the methodology, see Terry (2008).

Offending Records

Both the cleric and victim surveys asked for information pertaining to criminal actions taken against priests with allegations of abuse. For the purposes of completing the survey, the information was derived from personnel files, which contained information about the priests' criminal records. This information provided by the dioceses was consistent with what was publicly known at the time regarding criminal charges, investigations, convictions, and sentencing of priests with allegations of sexual abuse.

There are limitations to relying on criminal history data for analysis. Most important, sexual offenses are significantly underreported, and when reported, it is often after a long delay. As such, the statute of limitations prohibits the states from filing criminal charges against many of those with allegations of child sexual abuse. However, most studies that analyze criminal career data do use official records, and the criminal history data of priest abusers can serve as a useful, initial evidentiary backdrop for us to study some of the basic criminal career dimensions of clerics.

Plan of Analysis

There are a wide variety of criminal career dimensions that can be explored, including prevalence, frequency, specialization, recidivism, escalation, career duration, and desistance. A full undertaking of these dimensions is beyond the scope and size of this article;

instead, we provide some basic information with respect to participation/frequency, onset age, recidivism, and career duration—all of which have been studied in great detail using other samples of street offenders and which would provide a nice complement and base of comparison to these extant findings. Furthermore, we also examine the extent to which several key variables found to relate to criminal activity in extant criminal career studies (prior abuse, marriage, problem behaviors, substance abuse history, and age at first offense) also relate to cleric abuse as measured through the number of police investigations accumulated by the clerics.

 Results

Participation/Frequency/Chronicity

The prevalence of offending (measured via police investigations) is 22.6%, suggesting that more than three quarters of the sample were not investigated by the police. Compared with extant criminal career studies of more traditional samples (see review in A. R. Piquero et al., 2003), this is an underestimate even with the use of official offending records. The 959 offending clerics accumulated a total of 2,066 police investigations in the study period, for an average of 0.48 per cleric. Table 5.2 presents the information necessary for identifying chronic offenders using the Wolfgang et al. (1972) designation of chronic offending as those individuals with five or more offenses.

Here, it can be seen that chronic offenders represent 1.76% of the full sample, or 7.82% of all offenders, but were responsible for 36.3% of all police investigations. Like those obtained by Wolfgang et al. (1972), these findings suggest that a small percentage of the cohort is responsible for a large share of the convictions. Figure 5.5 displays the relationship between police investigation number and the percentage of the full and offender samples.

Offense Skewness

Fox and Tracy (1988) outlined a measure of offense skewness, termed alpha (α), which provides researchers with a mechanism to make comparisons about

Table 5.2 Chronicity Analysis

Full Sample (N = 4,244)								Offender Sample (N= 959, k ≥ 1)					
k	N_k	Pn_k	O_k	Po_k	cPn_k	cPo_k	Area	K	N_k	Pn_k	cPn_k	Area	Cumlarea
0	3,285	0.77403	0	0	1	1	0.77403						
1	604	0.14232	604	0.29235	0.22597	1	0.12152	1	604	0.62982	1	0.53776	0.53776
2	169	0.03982	338	0.16360	0.08365	0.70765	0.02492	2	169	0.17623	0.37018	0.11029	0.64805
3	72	0.01697	216	0.10455	0.04383	0.54405	0.00834	3	72	0.07508	0.19395	0.03692	0.68497
4	39	0.00919	156	0.07551	0.02686	0.43950	0.00369	4	39	0.04067	0.11887	0.01634	0.70131
5	25	0.00589	125	0.06050	0.01767	0.36399	0.00197	5	25	0.02607	0.07821	0.00870	0.71001
6	12	0.00283	72	0.03485	0.01178	0.30349	0.00081	6	12	0.01251	0.05214	0.00358	0.71359
7	7	0.00165	49	0.02372	0.00895	0.26864	0.00042	7	7	0.00730	0.03963	0.00187	0.71546
8	4	0.00094	32	0.01549	0.00730	0.24492	0.00022	8	4	0.00417	0.03233	0.00099	0.71645
9	8	0.00189	72	0.03485	0.00636	0.22943	0.00040	9	8	0.00834	0.02815	0.00177	0.71822
10	1	0.00024	10	0.00484	0.00448	0.19458	4.53E-05	10	1	0.00104	0.01981	0.00020	0.71842
11	6	0.00141	66	0.03195	0.00424	0.18974	0.00025	11	6	0.00626	0.01877	0.00109	0.71951
12	2	0.00047	24	0.01162	0.00283	0.15779	7.16E-05	12	2	0.00209	0.01251	0.00032	0.71982
13	2	0.00047	26	0.01259	0.00236	0.14618	6.59E-05	13	2	0.00209	0.01043	0.00029	0.72012
14	1	0.00024	14	0.00678	0.00189	0.13359	3.07E-05	14	1	0.00104	0.00834	0.00014	0.72025
15	2	0.00047	30	0.01452	0.00165	0.12682	5.63E-05	15	2	0.00209	0.00730	0.00025	0.72050
23	2	0.00047	46	0.02227	0.00118	0.11229	4.77E-05	23	2	0.00209	0.00521	0.00021	0.72071
26	1	0.00024	26	0.01259	0.00071	0.09003	1.97E-05	26	1	0.00104	0.00313	8.73E-05	0.72080
29	1	0.00024	29	0.01404	0.00047	0.07744	1.66E-05	29	1	0.00104	0.00209	7.34E-05	0.72087
131	1	0.00024	131	0.06341	0.00024	0.06341	7.47E-06	131	1	0.00104	0.00104	3.31 E-05	0.72091
Total	4,244		2,066	1			0.93693		959	1		0.72091	

NOTE: k = police investigation number; N_k = number of individuals investigated by police k times; Pn_k = fraction of the cohort with exactly k police investigations; O_k = number of offenses multiplied by the number of offenders, or $k \times N_k$; Po_k = fraction of the offenses committed by member with exactly k offenses; cPn_k = fraction of sample members with k or more offenses; cPo_k = fraction of the offenses committed by cohort members with at least $k+1$ offenses; Cumlarea = cumulative area.

chronicity within and across data sources. This coefficient of offense skewness is the area between the curve and the diagonal line of the even distribution (i.e., one in which all cohort members commit the same number of offenses). Alpha measures the extent of departure of the cumulative offense curve from the diagonal. The curve is piecewise linear (Fox & Tracy, 1988, p. 263), so one must first calculate the area by:

$$\text{Area} = \Sigma Pn_k(Po_k/2 + cPo_{(k+1)}) - 0.5$$

Figure 5.5 Threshold of Chronic Offender

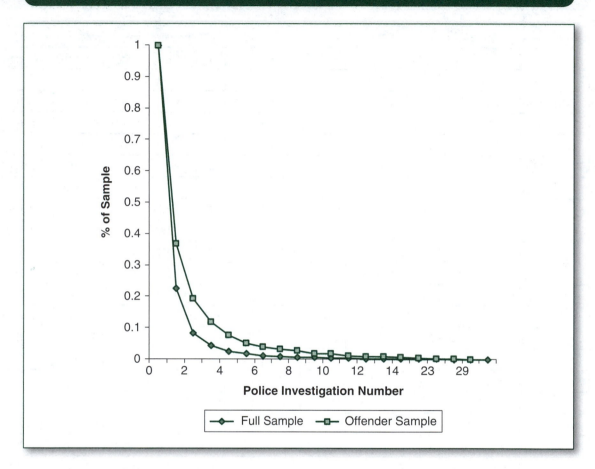

where Pn_k is the fraction of the cohort with exactly k offenses, Po_k is the fraction of the offenses committed by members with exactly k offenses, and $cPo_{(k+1)}$ is the fraction of the offenses committed by cohort members with at least $k + 1$ offenses. The area achieves a value of 0 if every cohort member had the same number of offenses, and the area approaches a limit of one half if the same person committed all offenses (Fox & Tracy, 1988, p. 264). To obtain the measure of skewness, alpha (α), the area between the observed curve and the diagonal is doubled:

$$\alpha = 2\Sigma Pn_k(Po_k/2 = cPo_{(k+1)}) - 1$$

Alpha ranges from 0 for complete equality in offense share to 1 for complete unevenness in offense share. Although alpha is influenced by both the distribution of offenses among offenders and the prevalence of offending itself, by calculating alpha for the offenders only in addition to calculating alpha for the full cohort, one can obtain a measure of the skewness in offense share distribution without the effect of prevalence.[1] And although there is no standard criterion for deciding when skewness is or is not substantial, alpha can be compared against other measures of alpha calculated for other cohort studies.

Two cautions with respect to alpha should be noted. First, cumulative offense plots should always be inspected when interpreting alpha. Second, because alpha assumes that the offenses held by a group are evenly distributed among its members, it assumes that there is no remaining skewness beyond the truncation point (Fox & Tracy, 1988, pp. 271-272). Thus, care must be taken with respect to truncation points in the offense distribution.

Data for assessing offense skewness may be found in Table 5.2. As stated earlier, alpha is calculated by subtracting 1 from twice the sum of the area. Among the full sample, alpha is equal to .87, and among the offenders, alpha is equal to .44. In comparing the estimates from the cleric database to those from both general population and offender-based studies, it is important to note that the cleric offense skewness estimates are quite comparable to existing skewness estimates (see A. R. Piquero, Farrington, & Blumstein, 2007).

Onset Age

Figure 5.6 displays a histogram depicting the age at the first reported abuse incurred by the clerics, a key variable referred to in the criminal career literature as onset age. What is striking about this figure is how much it does *not* resemble the standard onset age depictions found in the extant literature, which we believe is because of the nature of the sample and the nature of the offending. The average onset age among the clerics was 38.91 (median = 36.00, standard deviation = 11.19), well greater than the averages appearing in the more general population and offender-based studies (ranging from 12 to 17, depending on the use of self-report [earlier] or official [later] records). This onset age also appears to resemble other types of samples, white-collar offenders in particular, who tend to evince later ages of onset as well. For example, Weisburd and Waring (2001) reported an average age of onset for their white-collar offender sample of 35 years. In short, the criminal career parameter of onset age among the clerics depicts a much later onset age than most extant criminal career data, largely because of the nature of the offense (clerics are typically older when they are ordained, so that the opportunity to

Figure 5.6   Onset Age of First Cleric Abuse

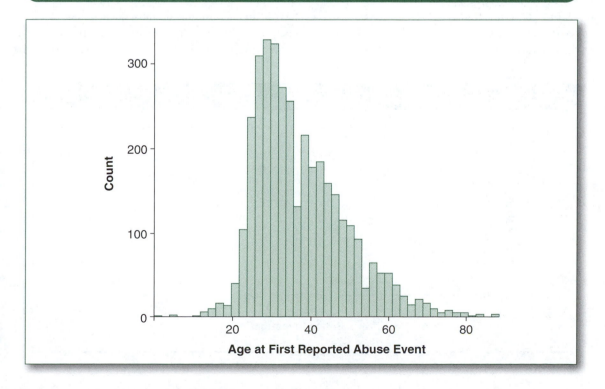

offend is contingent on their securing a position, which often does not occur until adulthood).

Recidivism

Blumstein, Farrington, and Moitra (1985) argued that the arbitrary calculation used by Wolfgang et al. (1972) that identifies chronic offenders as 6% of the Philadelphia 1945 Birth Cohort overdramatizes the chronic offender effect because many cohort members will not incur an official criminal justice contact. Instead, they urge that the ever-arrested subjects be the base used to calculate the chronic offender effect. These researchers also noted that the proportion of chronic offenders observed by Wolfgang et al. could have resulted from a homogenous population of persisters. Although those with five or more arrests accounted for the majority of arrests among the persisters, this finding could have occurred even if all subjects with three or more arrests had identical recidivism probabilities (Blumstein et al., 1985, p. 189). Thus, the chronic offenders who were identified retrospectively as those with five or more arrests could not have been distinguished prospectively from offenders with three or four arrests.

Recidivism probabilities through the first 10 police investigations are graphed in Figure 5.7. As can be seen, the recidivism probabilities begin at .22 (the prevalence of offending in the data), and jump quickly (because of the large proportion of one-time offenders who do not recidivate) to .37 for Offense 2, as expected. Between Offenses 2 and 3, the recidivism probability increases to .52, and then increases to .61 and .65 at Offenses 4 and 5, respectively. After Offense 5, and beginning with Offense 6, the recidivism probability increases to .66 and follows a steady incline until it reaches a high point at Offense 9, where the recidivism probability is .87.

Because the recidivism probabilities are very close and based on a small number of individuals, we conclude that beginning at Offense 7, the recidivism probabilities are quite stable and can be seen to reflect a homogenous group of persisters. The recidivism probabilities, especially the flattening and stability of recidivism beginning after Offense 6, are quite clear and confirm the benefit from partitioning the persister population.

The observed difference between a recidivism probability of .61 (at Offense 4) and .81 (at Offense 8) may appear small, but it can make an appreciable difference in the amount of subsequent offending. This effect is highlighted by a focus on the probability of *non*recidivism, which is reduced from .38 to .18. For the

Figure 5.7   Recidivism Probability

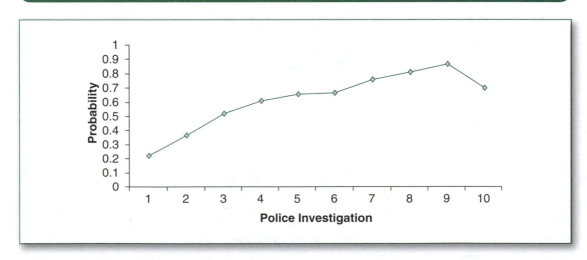

geometric distribution, the expected number of future police investigations after any given conviction from the third conviction onward is $q / (1 - q)$, so that if $q = .61$, then each persister can expect to experience an additional 1.57 police investigations; if the recidivism probability is .81, however, the expected number of future police investigations is 4.40, which is 180% ([4.40 – 1.57] / 1.57) larger.

In short, this brief analysis of the recidivism probabilities indicates that there is a rapidly increasing probability of recidivism through the first few (three to four) involvements with the law and a higher but stable recidivism rate for subsequent involvement—more than 66% at and after the sixth police investigation. This estimate is comparable to those obtained by Blumstein et al. (1985, p. 192) for the Philadelphia 1945 Birth Cohort Study, where they found that the recidivism rate increased to about 80% between the sixth and seventh arrest, and to the 1942 Racine, Wisconsin Birth Cohort, where Blumstein and colleagues (1985, p. 194) found that the recidivism rate increased to about 88% between the fifth and sixth arrest. The rise in the observed aggregate recidivism probability in the cleric database reflects the changing composition of the offenders at each stage of involvement; the desisters stop relatively early and so leave a residue composed increasingly of the high-recidivism persisters (Blumstein et al., 1985, p. 216). From a policy perspective, these results suggest the possibility of early discrimination between the more and the less frequently offending clerics and also

> endorses the appropriateness of representing the typical observation of growth in recidivism probability with successive involvements with the criminal justice system as a process involving a changing mix of a high- and low-recidivism group that is increasingly composed of the high-recidivism group. (Blumstein et al., 1985, p. 217)

Career Duration

The last criminal career dimension examined in this study is career duration, or the time between the first and final recorded abuse event. The issue of career duration, though infrequently studied in the criminal career literature because of the lack of long-term data on criminal activity, is important especially for policy matters insofar as knowledge on career length speaks directly to the need (or lack thereof) for lengthy incarceration sentences. To the extent that careers are short, then lengthy sentences will waste scarce resources, but if careers are long, then this may provide support for lengthier sentences. Estimates of career duration in the more general criminal career literature are varied (ranging from 5 to 11 years), ranging widely depending on the data source, type of sample, and length of follow-up period (see A. R. Piquero et al., 2003). Within a sample of white-collar offenders, Weisburd and Waring (2001) found a mean duration of criminal career length of about 14 years.

Figure 5.8 shows career duration in the cleric database, and as can be seen, career length is left-censored; that is, most criminal careers are short in magnitude, with an average career length of 5.29 years (median of 2 years). It also is the case that more than 30% of careers are less than 1 year in length, whereas only 10% of careers are more than 15 years in length. This 5-year average is not that far removed from other career length estimates of 5 to 7 years in the Rand Inmate Survey (Spelman, 1994).

Predicting Number of Police Investigations

In this final analysis, we examine the predictors of the number of police investigations. Because of the count-oriented nature of the outcome variable, we turn to the family of count models, poisson and negative binomial regression. The latter model, which allows for overdispersion (present in the number of police investigations variable), provided a better fit to the data, and we present those estimates. Five variables are used to predict the number of police investigations: whether the cleric was married (no/yes, 1.19%), whether the cleric had any sort of substance abuse history including alcohol or drugs (no/yes, 18.63%), whether the cleric was previously abused (no/yes, 6.83%), the age at the first

Figure 5.8 Career Duration

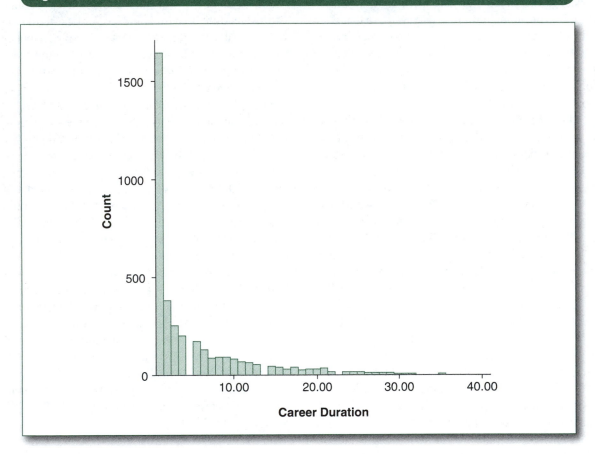

reported abuse by the cleric (mean = 38.90 years), and a count of the number of different problematic behaviors in the cleric's personnel files (mean 0.43).[2] The results may be found in Table 5.3.

The negative binomial regression results indicate that three variables significantly relate to the number of police investigations. Married clerics are significantly more likely to accumulate many police investigations, as are clerics with a history of previously being abused. Furthermore, clerics who exhibited an earlier age at first abuse were significantly more likely to accumulate many police investigations. The latter two coefficient effects are similar to those reported in the extant criminological literature (i.e., prior abuse → more crime and early onset → more crime); however, the marriage effect observed indicated an opposite sign compared to the extant criminal career literature: whereas marriage serves to inhibit crime among general population and offender samples, it serves to increase the number of police investigations among clerics. In short, married clerics evince a higher number of police investigations than nonmarried clerics.

 Discussion

The purpose of this article was to examine the extent to which previous findings regarding basic criminal career parameters that have emerged from more general population and offender-based samples replicate when using a heretofore unstudied population: priests

Table 5.3 Negative Binomial Regression Results Predicting the Number of Police Investigations

Independent Variable	Coefficient	SE	Z Value
Married	.763	.385	1.98*
Substance history	.131	.109	1.20
Problem count	−.024	.053	−0.46
Prior abuse history	.573	.156	3.67*
Age at first abuse	−.033	.003	−8.85*
Constant	.543	.152	3.56*
/lnalpha	1.432	.058	1.317
Alpha	4.190	.247	3.733*
Log likelihood = −2932.400			

*$p < .05$.

who sexually abused children. In this article, we employed data on more than 4,000 clerics and examined basic criminal career dimensions (prevalence, frequency, chronicity, onset age, recidivism, career duration) as well as how several key risk factors (marriage, substance abuse history, previous abuse, behavior problems, and onset age) related to offending as measured via the number of police investigations accumulated by the clerics. A number of key findings emerged from our effort, some of which replicated previous criminal career studies and others that yielded discrepant findings.

With respect to prevalence and frequency, we found that 23% of the sample had a non-zero rate of offending (as measured through police investigations). The 959 offenders accumulated 2,066 police investigations, yet the number of police investigations was not equally distributed throughout the sample. For example, 1.76% of the full sample of clerics (or 7.82% of the offender clerics) accounted for 36.3% of all offenses in the data. This finding indicates a somewhat lower prevalence than other longitudinal studies of the general population

(about a third in the Philadelphia Birth Cohort Study; Wolfgang et al., 1972). The prevalence and frequency estimates from the cleric data are difficult to compare with more traditional white-collar criminal databases because those studies are traditionally based on an already-identified (selected) sample of offenders. At the same time, the cleric data reveal a comparable chronic offender effect, indicating a small percentage of individuals are responsible for a large percentage of offenses. An investigation of the probability of recidivism further indicated that recidivism became constant after the accumulation of about four to five police investigations, and especially after six police investigations. This implies that there exists variation within the persister population, especially at the low end, but a more homogenous group of offenders at the high end. From a policy perspective, criminal justice policy makers should be careful about making lengthy incarceration decisions among the low-persister group but at the same time take great care in identifying those who may go on to become high-rate recidivists.

Turning to an analysis of onset age, the significant finding emerging from the cleric data indicates that the average age of first abuse was appreciably higher among the clerics, averaging almost 39 years of age, compared to the early adolescence figures observed among general population and offender-based samples but more similar to the average age of 35 found for white-collar offenders. Our analysis of the key analog to onset age, career duration, generated findings indicating that most careers are left-censored; that is, they are relatively short. In fact, 30% of all careers among this sample of clerics were less than 1 year, and only 10% were more than 15 years. The average career duration, recognizing that we did not observe the full career (offenders always have some sort of non-zero probability of offending), was 5.29 years.

Last, our regression analyses predicting the total number of police investigations indicated that three variables were important predictors: prior abuse of the cleric, marriage, and onset age. Interestingly, although we observed effects consistent with previous criminal careers research with respect to previous abuse and early onset (both increase the total number of police investigations), the effect of marriage on the number of police investigations was positive, indicating that married clerics were more likely to accumulate many more police investigations than nonmarried clerics. This finding runs counter to the more general observation in criminology that marriage serves to inhibit criminal activity, a finding that emerges among general population and offender samples (Laub & Sampson, 2003; A. R. Piquero, Brame, Mazerolle, & Haapanen, 2002; Sampson & Laub, 1993; Weisburd & Waring, 2001). Although we wish to take care in speculating about the meaning of this finding, it may be that married clerics looked outside of their marriage to explore alternative sexual interests that their current marriage will not allow.

In total, these findings simultaneously provide confirmatory and contradictory findings with respect to extant criminal career findings. Similarities exist with the cleric data with regard to both the more general criminal career findings and with the study of white-collar criminal careers. For example, the cleric data appears to be somewhat similar to the general criminal career research with regard to prevalence (though at the low end) and recidivism, yet differences also arise as a function of the unique position in which the clerics find themselves. Not only are they likely to be older when they enter their occupation, they also occupy positions of authority and power and encounter specific sorts of opportunities to engage in specific sorts of offenses. This difference is remarkably similar to the white-collar crime data of Weisburd and Waring (2001). In both the cleric and white-collar crime samples, the average age of onset occurs in the mid-to-late 30s. However, the cleric data exhibits differences from what was found with the sample of white-collar offenders in that the average length of the criminal career was noticeably shorter for the clerics, approximately 5 years, whereas the length for the white-collar offenders was much longer, approximately 14 years.[3] Therefore, this sample of offenders appears to be both similar to and different from both common street offenders and white-collar offenders.

To be sure, our data are limited in some respects. For example, our key outcome variable is based on official police records; thus, some unknown level of bias is likely integrated into our principal outcome measure. Also found in many other criminal career studies, this sort of bias may lead to an underestimate of the true offense level of the clerics. Second, our limited data miss the priests who did not come to the attention of authorities and/or who were not part of the larger data collection effort. Third, we were limited by the range and extent of key theoretical predictors that could explain the phenomenon of cleric abuse. All of these limit our ability to generalize from the data, but in any area of research for which basic descriptive data do not exist, we think that some basic portrait is a useful starting point.

Going forward, perhaps the next set of steps in this area of research should be an application of extant criminological theories to account for cleric abuse. For example, given the findings here with respect to previous abuse, perhaps Agnew's (1992) general strain theory would offer insight into how negative experiences relate to crime indirectly, as they operate through the production of negative emotions. Also, it would be interesting to examine the extent to which Gottfredson and Hirschi's (1990) general theory of crime would explain cleric abuse. These authors claim that low self-control accounts for all patterns of crime and deviance among all offenders; yet, by the very nature of their profession and what it entails, it would appear that clerics likely evince some semblance of self-control, but perhaps this self-control varies according to the situation (see A. R. Piquero & Bouffard, 2007). This is particularly interesting in light of the fact that this theory has not fared so well in explaining white-collar and corporate crime (Benson & Moore, 1992; Simpson & N. L. Piquero, 2002), especially given some of the similarities between the cleric sample and that of the criminal careers of white-collar criminals. If, in fact, the cleric sample is more similar to samples of white-collar offenders, other individual difference explanations will need to be examined (see N. L. Piquero, Exum, & Simpson, 2005). Last, it may be useful to examine how developmental or life-course theories of crime account for cleric abuse. Do the cleric abusers, who offend predominantly in adulthood, fit the stereotype of Moffitt's (1993) life-course-persistent offender or a failed adolescent-limited offender? Or are they unaccounted for, as suggested by N. L. Piquero and Benson (2004)? Could it be that this group of offenders constitutes those who can be classified as "punctuated situationally dependent"? That is, as a group, they follow similar trajectories, as described by the criminal career research, in that they have a brief flirtation with delinquency during adolescence that ends in their mid-20s; but, after a period of conformity, these individuals begin to offend again (N. L. Piquero & Benson, 2004).

The descriptive findings emerging from the cleric data generate a large array of research questions, ones that we hope the field will pursue. One approach to begin assessing these questions is with an anonymous self-report survey to currently employed clerics. Though we recognize the sensitivity and likely difficulty associated with such an endeavor, the collection of self-report data, with its inclusion of a rich array of predictor variables, would help begin to fill an important set of voids in this particular strand of criminal careers research.

 Notes

1. A larger prevalence implies that offensivity is more widely spread; thus, the distribution is less skewed (Fox & Tracy, 1988, p. 269).

2. This variable is a count of the number of different problem behaviors (out of 17): (a) social inhibition, (b) boundary problems, (c) narcissism, (d) sex with adult women, (e) sex with adult men, (f) coercive sex with adult men, (g) coercive sex with adult women, (h) other sexual behaviors, (i) hostility, (j) financial problems and/or gambling, (k) medical problems, (l) depression, (m) bipolar symptoms, (n) anger/stress, (o) other Axis I disorder, (p) alcohol/substance abuse, and (q) civil or criminal actions (John Jay College, 2004).

3. We recognize, of course, that there are key differences in the sample compositions and length of observation periods that could account for these discrepancies.

 References

Agnew, R. (1992). Foundation for a general strain theory of crime and delinquency. *Criminology, 30,* 47-87.

Benson, M. L., & Kerley, K. R. (2000). Life course theory and white-collar crime. In H. N. Pontell & D. Shichor (Eds.), *Contemporary issues in crime and criminal justice: Essays in honor of Gilbert Geis* (pp. 121-136). Upper Saddle River, NJ: Prentice Hall.

Benson, M. L., & Moore, E. (1992). Are white-collar and common offenders the same? An empirical and theoretical critique of a recently proposed general theory of crime. *Journal of Research in Crime and Delinquency, 29,* 251-272.

Blumstein, A., Cohen, J., Roth, J., & Visher, C. A. (1986). *Criminal careers and "career criminals."* Washington, DC: National Academy Press.

Blumstein, A., Farrington, D. P., & Moitra, S. (1985). Delinquency careers: Innocents, desisters, and persisters. In M. Tonry & N. Morris (Eds.), *Crime and justice: An annual review of research, Vol. 6.* (pp. 187-219). Chicago: University of Chicago Press.

The *Boston Globe* Spotlight Investigation: Abuse in the Catholic Church. (2004). *Boston Globe.* Retrieved from http://www .boston.com/globe/spotlight/abuse/

Braithwaite, J. (1989). *Crime, shame, and reintegration.* New York: Cambridge University Press.

Coleman, J. W. (2006). *The criminal elite: Understanding white-collar crime* (6th ed.). New York: Worth Publishers.

Dunne, E. A. (2004). Clerical child sex abuse: The response of the Roman Catholic Church. *Journal of Community & Applied Social Psychology, 14,* 490-494.

Edelhertz, H. (1970). *The nature, impact, and prosecution of white collar crime.* Washington, DC: Government Printing Office.

Farrington, D. P. (2003). Developmental and life-course criminology: Key theoretical and empirical issues—the 2002 Sutherland award address. *Criminology, 41,* 221-256.

Finkelhor, D. (2003). The legacy of the clergy abuse scandal. *Child Abuse and Neglect, 27,* 1225-1229.

Fox, J. A., & Tracy, P. E. (1988). A measure of skewness in offense distributions. *Journal of Quantitative Criminology, 4,* 259-273.

Friedrichs, D. O. (2007). *Trusted criminals: White collar crime in contemporary society* (3rd ed.). Belmont, CA: Thomas-Wadsworth.

Gottfredson, M. E., & Hirschi, T. (1990). *A general theory of crime.* Palo Alto, CA: Stanford University Press.

Gross, E. (1980). Organizational structure and organizational crime. In G. Geis & E. Stotland (Eds.), *White-collar crime: Theory and research* (pp. 52-76). Beverly Hills, CA: Sage.

Hanson, R. K., Gordon, A., Hams, A. J. R., Marques, J. K., Murphy, W., Quinsey, V. L., et al. (2002). First report of the Collaborative Outcome Data Project on the effectiveness of psychological treatment for sexual offenders. *Sexual Abuse: A Journal of Research and Treatment, 14,* 169-194.

John Jay College (Principal Investigator and Author). (2004). *The nature and scope of sexual abuse of minors by Catholic priests and deacons in the United States, 1950-2002.* Washington, DC: United States Conference of Catholic Bishops.

Kochansky, G. E., & Herrmann, F. (2004). Shame and scandal: Clinical and Canon Law perspectives on the crisis in the priesthood. *International Journal of Law and Psychiatry, 27,* 299-319.

Laub, J. H., & Sampson, R. J. (2003). *Shared beginnings, divergent lives.* Cambridge, MA: Harvard University Press.

Maier, C. T. (2005). Weathering the storm: Hauser's vernacular voices, public relations and the Roman Catholic Church's sexual abuse scandal. *Public Relations Review, 31,* 219-227.

Moffitt, T. E. (1993). "Life-course-persistent" and "adolescence-limited" antisocial behavior: A developmental taxonomy. *Psychological Review, 100,* 674-701.

Piquero, A. R., & Bouffard, J. A. (2007). Something old, something new: A preliminary investigation of Hirschi's redefined self-control. *Justice Quarterly, 24,* 1-27.

Piquero, A. R., Brame, R., Mazerolle, P., & Haapanen, R. (2002). Crime in emerging adulthood. *Criminology, 40,* 137-169.

Piquero, A. R., Farrington, D. P., & Blumstein, A. (2003). The criminal career paradigm. In M. Tonry (Ed.), *Crime and justice: A review of research* (Vol. 30, pp. 359-506). Chicago: University of Chicago Press.

Piquero, A. R., Farrington, D. P., & Blumstein, A. (2007). *Key issues in criminal careers research: New analyses from the Cambridge Study in Delinquent Development.* New York: Cambridge University Press.

Piquero, N. L., & Benson, M. L. (2004). White-collar crime and criminal careers: Specifying a trajectory of punctuated situational offending. *Journal of Contemporary Criminal Justice, 20,* 148-165.

Piquero, N. L., Exum, M. L, & Simpson, S. S. (2005). Integrating the desire for control and rational choice in a corporate crime context. *Justice Quarterly, 22,* 252-280.

Sample, L. L., & Bray, T. M. (2003). Are sex offenders dangerous? *Criminology and Public Policy, 3,* 59-82.

Sampson, R. J., & Laub, J. H. (1993). *Crime in the making.* Cambridge, MA: Harvard University Press.

Shapiro, S. P. (1990). Collaring the crime, not the criminal: Reconsidering the concept of white-collar crime. *American Sociological Review, 55,* 346-365.

Simpson, S. S., & Piquero, N. L. (2002). Low self-control, organizational theory, and corporate crime. *Law and Society Review, 36,* 509-547.

Spelman, W. (1994). *Criminal incapacitation.* New York: Plenum.

Sutherland, E. H. (1940). White collar criminality. *American Sociological Review, 5,* 1-12.

Terry, K. (2006). *Sexual offenses and offenders: Theory, practice, and policy.* Belmont, CA: Wadsworth.

Terry, K. (2008). Stained glass: The nature and scope of child sexual abuse in the Catholic church. *Criminal Justice and Behavior, 35,* 549-569.

U.S. Department of Health and Human Services, Administration on Children Youth and Families. (2002). *Child Maltreatment 2000: Reports from the states to the National Child Abuse & Neglect Data System.* Washington, DC: Government Printing Office.

Weisburd, D., & Waring, E. (2001). *White-collar crime and criminal careers.* Cambridge, UK: Cambridge University Press.

Wolfgang, M. E., Figlio, R. M., & Sellin, T. (1972). *Delinquency in a birth cohort.* Chicago: University of Chicago Press.

Zimring, F. E. (2004). *An American travesty: Legal responses to adolescent sexual offending.* Chicago: University of Chicago Press.

Zimring, F. E., Piquero, A. R., & Jennings, W. G. (2007). Sexual delinquency in Racine: Does early sex offending predict later sex offending in youth and young adulthood? *Criminology & Public Policy.*

DISCUSSION QUESTIONS

1. How are abusive priests similar to and different from other criminals?

2. How can these findings be used to prevent child sexual abuse in the religious system?

3. Why do you think the priests committed sexual abuse?

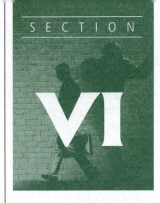
Crimes in the Educational System

 Introduction

About a decade ago, College of William and Mary adjunct English professor Sam Kashner penned an article titled "The Professor of Desire" in *GQ* magazine. In the article, he wrote firsthand about sexual relationships he had with his students at the small liberal arts college located in Williamsburg, Virginia. The article made local, state, and national headlines. One story repeated over and over in the news focused on how Kashner described a sexual relationship with a married student. According to the professor, the affair led to the husband's suicide. It was not long after the *GQ* article that William and Mary passed a policy restricting student/professor sexual relationships.

The case was particularly problematic because of the honesty underlying Kashner's open confession. The stories read almost as if they should have been shared in a locker room, if they should have been shared at all. College professors are supposed to educate students about topics that will help them in their future careers; they are not supposed to have sex with their students—and then promote their career by writing about it. College professors are supposed to help students learn to think and write critically about their world, so that they can better understand the worlds in which they live.

▲ **Photo 6.1**   It was like something out of Carrie Bradshaw's *Sex and the City*, except it could have been named "Sex and the University." Sam Kashner, adjunct professor of English at the College of William and Mary (shown in picture), wrote openly about his sexual escapades with students in a 2000 article of *GQ*.

To be sure, a variety of different types of misconduct occur in the educational system. Consider the following examples as they were described verbatim from their original sources:

- Jane Gallop, an English professor at the University of Wisconsin . . . wrote about her affairs, first with her professors at Cornell while she was doing her dissertation and later with her students, saying that they led her to new levels of intellectual and creative energy. Professor Gallop once joked at a conference on gay and lesbian studies that "my sexual preference is graduate students," and then French-kissed in public the graduate student she was advising. The student later accused the professor of sexual harassment and of declining to write a recommendation because she had refused to sleep with her. (Schemo, 2001)

- A recent graduate from Edinboro University contends a professor sexually harassed him with repeated references to the movie *Brokeback Mountain* and retaliated after he refused to date the professor. The defendant, *****, referred to *******, who graduated in August, and a classmate as "Brokeback buddies," asking, "Why don't you have a Brokeback moment with your hunting buddy?", according to the lawsuit . . . suing the school, some administrators, and *****. ("Edinboro University Graduate," 2009)

- An economics and finance professor at Kean University has resigned after being accused of copying large parts of her doctoral dissertation from a dissertation written six years earlier at Louisiana Tech University, according to today's *New York Times*. *****, who had tenure at the New Jersey institution, received her doctorate from Nova Southeastern University, in Florida. Both Kean and Nova Southeastern are investigating the matter. ("Accused of Plagiarizing Dissertation," 2007)

- ORI made fifteen findings of misconduct in science based on evidence that ***** knowingly and intentionally fabricated and falsified data reported in nine PHS grant applications and progress reports and several published papers, manuscripts, and PowerPoint presentations. The findings [include]: 1. Respondent knowingly and intentionally falsified a figure that was presented in manuscripts submitted to the *Journal of Experimental Medicine* and the *Journal of Virology* and in several PowerPoint presentations that purported to represent rectal mucosal leukocytes in some instances and lymph nodes in other instances. 2. Respondent knowingly and intentionally falsified portions of a three-paneled figure included in several manuscript submissions, PowerPoint presentations, and grant applications. 3. Respondent knowingly and intentionally falsified a figure included as Figure 1N in *American Journal of Pathology* 54:1453–1464, 1999, three NIH grant applications, and several PowerPoint presentations. (Office of Research Integrity, 2010a)

In this section, attention is given to crimes committed in the educational system. The majority of the discussion will focus on crimes by professors and researchers working in the educational system. After discussing how professionals have committed misconduct in this system, attention will be given to the way that students have committed workplace crimes in the educational system.

◪ Crimes by Professionals in the Educational System

It's probably not something we go around bragging about, but as professors we work in an occupation that is not immune from white-collar crime. Not only do we study white-collar crime, we also are a part of an occupational subculture that experiences various forms of white-collar crime. Four types of misconduct that appear to be among the more common types of academic misconduct include:

- Research misconduct
- Ghostwriting
- Pecuniary-oriented offenses
- Sexual harassment

After discussing these varieties of crimes in higher education, attention will be given to crimes by students as types of occupational crimes.

Research Misconduct by Professors

Research misconduct refers to a range of behaviors that center around researchers (many of whom are faculty members) engaging in various forms of wrongdoing during the course of their research. These forms of wrongdoing include, but are not limited to, fabricating data, masking findings, plagiarism, and treating research subjects unethically. Over the past two decades or so increased efforts have been directed toward identifying research misconduct. Such activities have always been known to occur, but they are now perceived and responded to differently. Describing this shift in philosophy, one author writes:

> Sadly, history includes many egregious examples of fraudulent scientists, but they were, until recently, regarded as isolated oddballs who did little to damage science, a self-correcting enterprise. But, in the past twenty years, country after country has recognized increasing examples of fraud and has come to think that it cannot be ignored, but needs to be recognized and managed. (R. Smith, 2006, p. 232)

In the United States, efforts to recognize and manage research misconduct are typically led by the funding agencies providing financial support for the research. The Office of Research Integrity (ORI), part of the Office of Public Health and Sciences within the U.S. Department of Health and Human Services, oversees research supported by the Public Health Services (PHS). The mission of ORI focuses on:

> (1) oversight of institutional handling of research misconduct allegations involving research, research training, or related research activities support by the PHS; (2) education in the responsible conduct of research; (3) prevention of research misconduct; and (4) compliance with the PHS Policies on Research Misconduct. (Office of Research Integrity, 2010b)

The increased federal oversight and efforts to respond to research misconduct have not gone unnoticed. Some researchers have tried to explain why the federal government has become so intense in its efforts to weed out research misconduct. Hackett (1993) identified several factors that contributed to the increased oversight. First, the federal government has been investing more and more money in scientific endeavors and science has become more visible to members of society as a result of this increased funding. Second, science is viewed as a "resource for power" and those who control science would potentially become more powerful through that control. Third, to some, science is like a religion and enforcement efforts toward misconduct are defined as ways to protect the "religion" of science. Fourth, Hackett noted that opposition to the "intellectual elite" may have contributed to political officials' decisions to increase efforts toward controlling research misconduct. Finally, science has become increasingly important to universities, businesses, and the government. The growing importance of science potentially increased the need of the government to expand its ability to control science.

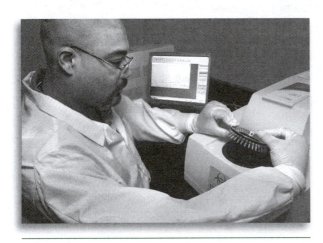

▲ **Photo 6.2** White-collar crimes even occur in laboratories when scientists fabricate data or violate rules guiding their profession. This scientist, like most scientists, did not break any workplace rules. The few who do, however, create enormous problems for the field of science.

Like other forms of white-collar crime, it is difficult to estimate how often research misconduct occurs. It may, however, be even more difficult to estimate for the simple reason that few researchers have actually empirically assessed research misconduct. Experts have noted that research misconduct is "real and persistent" (Herman, Sunshine, Fisher, Zwolenik, & Herz, et al., 1994). Anecdotally, the former editor of the *British Medical Journal* indicated that he "dealt with about 20 cases [of research misconduct] a year" (R. Smith, 2006).

One of the more infamous cases of research misconduct involved Ward Churchill, a professor of ethnic studies at the University of Colorado at Boulder. Prior to the allegations of misconduct, Churchill had come under fire for making disparaging comments about the victims of the 9/11 attacks. His notoriety grew and greater attention was given to his work, and at least five different scholars indicated that Churchill had misrepresented either their work or their colleague's work. In 2005, an investigation followed and the university's investigative committee found that Churchill engaged in "serious research misconduct." Another university committee recommended suspension without pay with a 3–2 vote (University of Colorado Investigative Committee Report, 2007). The two dissenting voters wanted him fired. In July 2007, the university's regents fired Churchill. He appealed the decision and though a jury found in his favor—awarding him one dollar—the judge overturned the verdict and upheld the university's actions.

One of the charges against Churchill was that he plagiarized some of his writings. Interestingly, researchers have suggested that plagiarism by professors is more likely to occur in the humanities and social sciences than in the hard sciences due to the nature of the disciplines. In particular, the level of creativity required in the humanities and social sciences is higher, and the need for creativity may create situations where professors are more apt so borrow someone else's creativity (Fox, 1994). In the hard sciences, where several authors typically appear on published manuscripts, loose authorship—where some authors are included on the manuscript who should not be—is believed to be more problematic.

Today, plagiarism is often uncovered when computer-based text searching tools are used to search for it (Huckabee, 2009). Plagiarism is discovered in at least four other ways:

- Researchers accidentally stumble upon it.
- Reviewers identify it during the peer review process.
- A disgruntled colleague or subordinate searches for it and finds it.
- The plagiarized author finds it.

In what would seem to be a plagiarism case, but technically is not, one professor recently published parts of one of his student's dissertation in an article he wrote. Jeannette Colman was a graduate student working on her dissertation under the supervision of Rimco Polman. After she successfully completed her dissertation, Professor Polman used parts of Colman's dissertation in a work he published in the *Journal of Sports Sciences* in 2007. Polman listed Colman as third author of the article. Because she was listed as a coauthor, he didn't technically plagiarize her work, even though she never gave him permission to use her work. The university panel reviewing the case found that Colman (the student) "did not own copyright to her dissertation" (Newman, 2010). As a result, the professor was found not guilty of research misconduct.

Research misconduct has severe consequences on several different levels. These include: (1) consequences for the individual faculty member, (2) financial consequences for the college or university, (3) morale consequences for the college or university, (4) image consequences for science, (5) consequences for members of society, and (6) consequences for various cultures. In terms of individual consequences, when research misconduct is exposed, the status of the offender takes a significant hit. While some may be able to overcome allegations—the president of the Southern Illinois University system was accused of plagiarizing both his Master's thesis and 1984 dissertation in 2007, but he remains as president in 2011 after he told the Board of Trustees that his faculty committees never told him he had to use quotation marks—others are not able to overcome allegations. For example, the former president of University of Texas–Pan American resigned after it was alleged that she had plagiarized parts of her dissertation 35 years ago (Montell, 2009).

Colleges and universities will also suffer financial consequences from research misconduct. On one level, federal funding agencies may withhold funding if it is determined that the college or university was complacent in its efforts to limit research misconduct. Such a loss could amount to millions of dollars for the higher education institution. On another level, donors may be less likely to give to institutions if they believe that research misconduct has occurred. As with the losses in federal support, such economic losses can prove to be significant.

Higher education institutions will also experience morale consequences from the negative exposure that comes along with the allegations of research misconduct. Instances where professors are caught engaging in research misconduct are sure to make the news. Consider the following headlines from several different news sources:

- University of Colorado will investigate allegations of misconduct against controversial professor (Smallwood, 2005b)
- Former scientist at University of Vermont to plead guilty to vast research fraud (Smallwood, 2005a)
- List of research fraud grows as MIT star is fired for faking data (Shepherd, 2005)
- MIT dismisses biology professor for faking data (Jacobson, 2005)
- Fraud, greed in the academy: Once-respected researcher heads to jail in landmark fraud case (Interlandi, 2006)

- Study data at UCLA falsified: In 2005, a researcher faked interviews and took participants' funds, a federal notice says (Chong, 2007)
- Professor whose article was retracted resigns from Harvard Medical School (Huckabee, 2009)
- UAB animal transplant studies by two researchers found falsified (Parks, 2009)
- Two CMU math faculty members violate integrity policy; university returns $619,489 in grant money (Bolitho, 2009)
- Reports allege misconduct at UConn (Schmidt, 2003)
- Research-fraud investigation leads to departures from Northern Kentucky University (Wilson, 2003)

Two interesting patterns appear in these headlines. First, note that none of the headlines identify the professor's name. Second, and on the other hand, note that all but one of the headlines lists the name of the college or university where the misconduct occurred. In many ways, research misconduct may damage the higher education institution's image as much as it damages the actual professor who engaged in the misconduct.

Colleges and universities will also experience significant time losses in responding to cases of research misconduct. Investigations can take a great deal of time and resources. For example, a University of Washington investigation took 7 years to conclude that an assistant professor should be fired. The investigation concluded that the researcher "had falsified seven figures and tables in two research papers" (Doughman, 2010). Time that administrators and faculty could have spent in productive activities had to be directed toward addressing misconduct by the assistant professor.

Research misconduct also has consequences for the image of science. In particular, these sorts of activities ultimately paint the scientific enterprise in a negative light. Consider the case of one anesthesiologist who fabricated his findings in 21 studies. Consequently, "the reliability of dozens more articles he wrote is uncertain, and the common practice supported by his studies—of giving patients aspirin-like drugs and neuropathic pain medicines after surgery instead of narcotics is now questioned" (Harris, 2009).

In a similar way, research misconduct has ramifications for members of society who are exposed to new practices and policies as a result of research. While a goal of research is to provide information that can be used to improve the human condition, if new practices and policies are based on data obtained through flawed research, then individuals exposed to those new practices and policies are put at risk. Giving patients aspirin instead of narcotics after surgery, for example, may have been a risk for patients. Also, the results of another fabricated research study (described below) led doctors to prescribe hormones to treat menopause for years. In effect, treatments were being determined by "fake" research. Once the research was exposed as fabricated, one couldn't help but wonder whether prescribing hormones was actually helpful or harmful.

Research misconduct can also have negative consequences for an entire culture. In China, Jiangton University professor Chen Jin was heralded as a top scholar until it was revealed that his prize invention—a mobile phone chip—was simply a Motorola phone chip that had been sanded down with sandpaper. The "revelation . . . shocked China, where the 'home-grown' invention had become a source of national pride" (Burns, 2006). Just as Olympic athletes who cheat embarrass their countries when they are caught, internationally recognized researchers caught cheating have a similar effect.

Two patterns are common in research misconduct cases—one that is common in other white-collar crime cases and one that is not. First, as in other white-collar crime cases, many of those who commit research misconduct commit various forms of misconduct on multiple occasions. If researchers engage in one type of misconduct, like fudging data—it is likely that they have engaged in others, like fudging accounting data on funded research (see Schmidt, 2003). Consider the case of James David Lieber, a former staff research associate for UCLA's Semel Institute for Neuroscience and Human Behavior. Working on a study focusing on the long-term experience of female opiate addicts who visited methadone clinics three decades ago, Lieber "knowingly and intentionally falsified and fabricated interviews, urine samples, and urine sample records" (Chong, 2007). The investigation showed that Lieber had not interviewed the subjects he was supposed to interview, and had altered their urine samples. It was also revealed that he stole travel funds. Hence, he committed multiple types of violations.

A second pattern in these cases—and one that distinguishes it from many other white-collar crimes—is that in most cases the offenders acted alone. This is part of the process of committing research misconduct. Whereas certain types of health care fraud, for example, might require multiple participants to carry out the fraud, for research misconduct, a rogue professor aiming to achieve a certain end is able to accomplish this task without the help of others. Working alone insulates the professor from detection and allows the academic to continue to use his or her research to gain power and prestige.

Some have pointed to the pressure to publish and get grants as being the source of research misconduct. Fox (1994) notes that economic incentives may play more of a role and points out that "the economic stakes of science have heightened" (p. 307). Top professors—with strong research portfolios—can earn hundreds of thousands of dollars in their annual salary from their college or university, and some will earn far more providing consulting services. While most of these scientists conduct their research legitimately, it is plausible that those who commit misconduct are doing so, at least partly, for economic reasons.

Another possible reason that faculty engage in these activities is that their mentors did not supervise them appropriately (Brainard, 2008). Brainard cites a study that found that in three fourths of misconduct cases, the supervisors did not give the supervisee appropriate training in reviewing lab results. Recall the university president who indicated that his allegations of plagiarism could be explained by the fact that his faculty committees never told him he was supposed to put quotation marks around quotes.

Because of the potential role that mentors have in contributing to misconduct, some have argued that mentors should play an active role in training their students how to conduct research appropriately. One author team suggests that mentors should train students how to (a) review source data, (b) understand research standards, and (c) deal with stressful work situations (Wright, Titus, & Cornelison, 2008). In a similar way, mentors should also teach their students how to protect the rights of their research subjects, the consequences of research misconduct, and the importance of research integrity.

Typically, accusations of misconduct begin with information from someone involved in the research on at least some level. Rarely are local or state criminal investigations undertaken against researchers, and federal investigations are conducted only when direct evidence of wrongdoing exists. In a rather controversial move, Virginia Attorney General Ken Cuccinnelli launched an investigation into the work of meteorology researcher Michael Manns (McNeill, 2010; Walker, 2010). The case is controversial for at least four reasons:

- The attorney general issued a subpoena for data from the University of Virginia, where Mann *used to* work.
- It is alleged by some that the attorney general was using the case to gain "cool points" from the political Right for "going after" a researcher whose findings showed support for the evidence of global warming.
- State agencies don't typically address these types of issues.
- The professor had already been cleared of misconduct by a Penn State University review panel. (McNeill, 2010; Walker, 2010)

The investigation was ongoing when this book was written. The outcome remains to be seen.

Ghostwriting

Ghostwriting refers to situations where professors or researchers have their work written by someone else, but the professor's name appears on the work. Typically, "papers are produced by companies or other parties whose names do not appear as authors" (Lederman, 2009). Situations where university professors allow their names to be put on papers written by ghost authors hired by pharmaceutical companies have been described as "distressingly common in top medical journals" (Basken, 2009). In some cases, the real author's name appears on the article along with a top scientist who did not actually contribute to the article. In these cases, the top scientists can be labeled "honorary" authors, though in print it appears that they were actually contributing authors.

A recent study of ghostwriting and honorary authorship published in the *Journal of the American Medical Association* found the following rates of ghost authorship and use of honorary authors among six top medical journals in articles published in 2008: 26% of the articles had honorary authors, 8% had ghostwriters, and 2% had both honorary and ghostwriters (Wislar, Flanagin, Fontanarosa, & Dangelis, 2010). This means that more than one third of the articles published in the top medical journals listed authors who actually should not be listed! Figure 6.1 provides a visual portrayal of the degree of ghostwriting/honorary authorship in these journals.

Research shows that ghostwriting occurs more in research articles than in reviews and editorials (Wislar et al., 2010). In an effort to limit the extent of ghostwriting, many journals now ask authors to sign a form indicating that they are the only authors of the manuscript and that all of the authors listed did, in fact, contribute to the manuscript. For the record, the author of this book is no ghost, and he certainly isn't an honorary author.

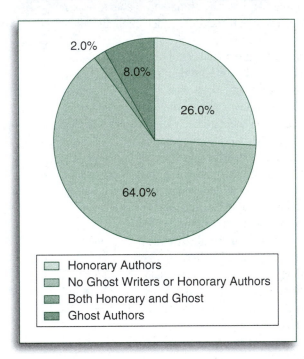

Figure 6.1 Percentage of Articles With Ghostwriters and Honorary Authors in Six Medical Journals, 2009

Legend:
- Honorary Authors
- No Ghost Writers or Honorary Authors
- Both Honorary and Ghost
- Ghost Authors

2.0%
8.0%
26.0%
64.0%

Pecuniary-Oriented Offenses

In this context, **pecuniary-based offenses** include misbehaviors that are ultimately done by professors for the economic gain that comes along with the commission of the offenses. Four varieties of pecuniary-oriented offenses exist. These include:

- Embezzlement
- Textbook fraud
- Double billing
- Engaging in unapproved outside work

Embezzlement

Embezzlement occurs when faculty members or college/university staff steal funds from an account to which they have access. Consider the case of Robert Felner, a former dean of the School of Education at the University of Louisville who was convicted of misappropriating $2.3 million from contracts with three schools and a federal grant he was supervising. Felner was sentenced to more than five years in federal prison (Glen, 2010).

Not all cases of **faculty embezzlement** are necessarily million-dollar scams. Ansley Hamid, former professor of anthropology at John Jay College, was accused of stealing $5,000 in grant funds to fund personal trips, purchase heroin, and buy ABBA CDs, an allegation that one author called "the most heinous accusation—a crime against humanity" (Morris, 1999). Incidentally, the charges against Hamid were eventually dropped, but not before he lost his job.

Textbook Fraud

Textbook fraud, in this context, refers to instances where faculty sell the complimentary textbooks they receive from publishers to book dealers who resell the books. Some faculty may see nothing wrong with these activities. As a new faculty member, I recall my then-dean's take on this issue. He explained that our college at the time viewed it as unethical and inappropriate to sell textbooks that we had requested from publishers; however, it was legitimate in his view to resell textbooks that we did not actually request from the publisher but received as part of an unsolicited marketing campaign. Not surprisingly, research shows that faculty members view it as more ethical to sell unsolicited books than it is to sell solicited books (Robie, Kidwell, & King, 2003).

Many colleges and universities have express, written policies forbidding the selling of complimentary textbooks under any circumstances. Some of these policies even state that book dealers are not permitted on campus. Here is how my university, Georgia State University, spells out its policy on selling textbooks:

313.05 Ethical Behavior with Regard to Complimentary Textbooks

The University Senate passed the following resolution on February 2, 1989:

The distribution of complimentary textbooks is an important part of the process whereby professors review the full range of instructional materials available for their courses. However, the integrity of this process must be respected.

Selling complimentary copies of textbooks adversely affects the entire academic community.

Professor-authors are deprived of economic return in royalties, and incentives to write textbooks are diminished.

Students generally do not benefit from the sale of complimentary copies, as these books are sold at or only slightly below the new book price.

Selling complimentary textbooks inflates the cost of all textbooks, as publishers must compensate for revenue lost from the sale of new books.

Selling complimentary copies violates the tradition of respect by professors for the intellectual work of their colleagues and for the textbook publishers.

The future of availability of complimentary textbooks may be seriously jeopardized by the reluctance of publishers to risk further financial loss.

Faculty members receive complimentary textbooks as a result of their position at the University. These textbooks should not be viewed as a source of faculty income. We recommend the following:

1. Complimentary textbooks are not to be resold for faculty profit. The books may be maintained for faculty reference or contributed to a library for student reference.

2. Solicitors for complimentary copies are forbidden from campus.

3. The campus bookstore may not sell copies which are identifiable as complimentary copies whatever their source may be. (*Georgia State University Faculty Handbook,* 2010)

More than 20 years ago, it was estimated that publishers lost $60 million a year to these activities (Sipes, 1988). The practice appears to remain widespread, and likely costs publishers far more today. A survey of 236 faculty from 13 community colleges and universities found that 30% of the sample had resold complimentary books in the prior year, and they made $80 per sale on average (Robie et al., 2003).

To address this, some publishers stamp the word "complimentary" or "not for resale" on many of the textbooks' pages, others put the professor's name on the book, and some even tell professors that if they do not plan on using the book, they can return it to the publisher who will make a donation to charity for each returned complimentary book received (Hamermesh, 2009).

For the record, if faculty try to sell their complimentary copies of this book to book dealers, an invisible ink will explode all over both the faculty member and the book dealer.

Double Billing

Faculty double billing occurs when professors bill more than one source for the same effort of work or reimbursement. Examples of double billing include (a) instances where professors bill two sources for the same travel reimbursements and (b) instances where faculty bill multiple universities for the same instructional effort. In one case involving double billing for travel reimbursements, Florence Lopez-de-Silanes resigned after being placed on unpaid leave after being caught double billing travel expenses for $150,000. What makes his case particularly interesting is that he was—at the time—the head of Yale's International Institute for Corporate Governance (Sherman, 2005). Sherman quotes the *Wall Street Journal* as describing the professor as "a strong advocate of prompt disclosure of financial misdeeds."

In an a case showing how multiple universities can be double billed, a married couple from Georgia Tech made headlines in newspapers in Georgia and Minnesota when it was reported that the couple—Francois Sainfort (an associate dean at the time) and Julie Jacko (a biomedical engineering professor) were paid by both Georgia Tech and the University of Minnesota in the 2008 spring semester (Jones, 2008). In August 2007, the two Georgia Tech employees were offered positions at the University of Minnesota—Sainfort was offered $285,000 to be the head of the Division of Health Policy and Management and Jacko was offered $216,000 to serve as the Director of the School of Health Informatics. Their contracts, which they signed in October, stipulated a start date of January 1, 2008. The couple left Atlanta but never officially resigned from their Georgia Tech positions. They continued to collect salaries and allegedly even sought travel reimbursement expenses from Georgia Tech after they were hired at Minnesota (Jones, 2008). When his boss noticed the problem, he e-mailed Sainfort to ask about it. Sainfort e-mailed his boss back on February 11, stating: "As a matter of fact, Julie and I have not even signed an employee contract yet with Minnesota . . . we have only agreed to unofficially start this semester with full residence starting in May"

(Shelman, 2008a). In September 2008, citing too much pressure from the media scrutiny, Sainfort stepped down from his leadership position but kept his position as a professor (Shelman, 2008b).

Engaging in Unapproved Outside Work

Faculty working full-time for a college or university also commit workplace offenses by engaging in outside work that is not approved by the institutions. Three overlapping types of conflicts arise with unapproved outside work: (1) research-based conflicts of interest, (2) teaching/service-based conflicts of interest, and (3) time-based conflicts of interest. With regard to research-based conflicts of interest, colleges and universities have policies restricting outside work to ensure that the institution's research agenda does not seem to be influenced by specific companies. For example, medical schools would not want their research to appear to be partial to certain pharmaceutical companies. As a result, these schools limit the amount of consulting and outside work that professors can do with such companies.

The case of Charles Nemeroff, former chair of the Emory University's Department of Psychiatry, is illustrative. His bosses suspected that Nemeroff was doing too much consulting for GlaxoSmithKline so they ordered him to limit his outside income from the drug company to less than $10,000 a year. The very same day that he signed this agreement, he was paid $3,000 in consulting fees from the company. The following year, he received $170,000 from the company. In all, Nemeroff received $500,000 in payments he never reported to his university (Goldstein, 2008). Nemeroff's misdeeds came to light when U.S. Senator Charles Grassley "released documents indicating that Nemeroff earned millions of dollars in fees from drug companies, but reported little of that money to Emory" (White & Schneider, 2008). The subsequent investigation revealed that the professor made more than $2.8 million between 2000 and 2007 from consulting with drug companies (Harris, 2008). As a result of his actions, the National Institutes of Health suspended a $9.3 million grant that had been awarded to the university, and Emory's entire federal funding portfolio was in jeopardy.

In terms of teaching/service-based conflicts of interest that arise from unapproved outside work, when full-time faculty are hired by colleges and universities, the institution in effect "owns" that person's efforts for the duration of the contract. Institutions gain notoriety when certain professors are on their payrolls. Also, having the best professors at a college or university allows institutions to promote their educational mission by suggesting that students will be exposed to some of the greatest minds in higher education. By forbidding outside work, administrators are able to maintain their competitive edge and keep professors from working for their competitors.

In terms of time conflict and unapproved outside work, the expectation is that full-time faculty will work 40 hours a week in performing teaching, research, and service activities. The reality is that most faculty likely work in excess of 55 hours a week on these activities. A handful, however, may actually work fewer hours in teaching, conducting research, and engaging in service activities.

Those who have unapproved outside jobs, for example, might be unable to meet the hourly obligations of a full-time job in higher education. Rarely would these behaviors be treated as illegal criminally, but professors could face formal or informal repercussions from their supervisors or university administrators for these behaviors. If your white-collar crime professor, for instance, routinely canceled class because of outside work (or other unapproved reasons, for that matter), your professor could be subjected to a range of potential disciplinary actions. In some instances, canceling even one class could be problematic, and I suspect that readers are grossly disappointed when their professor cancels a class. Typically, colleges and universities will permit occasional cancellations as long as students are given an assignment that corresponds to the topic that students would have covered in class and the topic at hand.

The advent of online classes poses different issues in that classes would never be canceled. Most faculty who teach online actually spend more time engaging with their students than faculty spend in traditional courses. For full-time faculty, issues arise when faculty fail to correspond with students and instruct them in ways that are necessary in order to teach students adequately about the topic (in this case, white-collar crime). Again, faculty won't be criminally prosecuted for failing to meet the time demands of the class. Imagine if they were, and if they were actually sent to jail for abusing class time. The following conversation would occur in jail:

Street offender to professor: Why are you in the pokey?

Professor to street offender: I canceled a few too many of my classes.

Street offender to professor: You know you're going to get beat up in here, right?

 ## Sexual Harassment

Sexual harassment refers to a range of behaviors where employees perform sexually inappropriate actions against their colleagues or students. Legal definitions of sexual harassment suggest that sexual harassment is "any unwelcome or unwanted sexual attention [that affects] an individual's job, raise, or promotion" (Andsager, Bailey, & Nagy, 1997, p. 33). Fitzgerald (1990) identified four categories of sexual harassment:

- **Gender harassment:** sexist remarks and behavior
- **Seductive behavior:** inappropriate sexual advances
- **Sexual bribery:** offering rewards for sex
- **Sexual coercion:** threatening punishment to get sex

For purposes of this book, sexual harassment offenses committed by college professors include (a) sexualized comments, (b) sexualized behaviors, (c) academic incest, (d) sexual relationships with students taking their classes, (e) grades for sex, and (f) rape.

With regard to **sexualized comments,** harassment occurs when professors make comments to students that are of a sexual nature. One criminal justice professor, for example, told a researcher that one of her former professors would "make comments about my breasts" (Stanko, 1992, p. 334). Note that simply using foul language is not in and of itself sexual harassment. Typically, the language would need to be of a sexual nature to be considered harassment. I recall one of my sociology professors who began the semester asking the class if anyone minded if he used the "f-word." He didn't use the phrase "f-word" when he asked—he actually said the word. And this really was the very first thing he said to our class that semester. Then he even wrote the four letters making up the word in huge letters on the chalk board (this was back when professors used the chalk board to communicate course notes). The professor explained that by itself, the word is just a word. Depending on the context in which the word is used, the word will have different meanings, consequences, and ramifications. We knew that we would not be taking notes that day—other than writing one word in our notebook.

Sexualized behaviors go beyond comments and include actual activities of a sexual nature committed by the offending party. This could include staring, touching, groping, hugging, and a range of other behaviors. In some cases, such behavior may be unintentional. As an example, at my prior university all professors were required to attend a sexual harassment seminar mandated by our administration. During the seminar, the presenter shared a story about one of our colleagues who taught biology. When teaching about the male reproductive system, he used a picture of a male penis from a medical book. When teaching about female reproductive system, he used a picture from *Playboy*. It did not occur to the professor that at least half of the class would find this offensive until he was reported to the equal opportunity office.

Academic incest refers to consensual "student faculty relationships in which both participants are from the same department but not necessarily in a student-teacher relationship" (Skinner et al., 1995, p. 139). Surveys of 583 university students and 229 community college students by Skinner and her research team found that students tend to define such relationships as ethically inappropriate. Surveys of 986 students uncovered gender patterns regarding stereotypes about sexual harassment (Hippensteele, Adams, & Chesney, 1992). Perhaps not surprisingly, males were found to have more stereotypical attitudes. They were more likely than females to agree with statements such as, "It is only natural for a man to make sexual advances to a woman he finds attractive."

Sexual contact with students refers to instances where the professor has some form of direct contact of a sexual nature with students in his or her classes or under his or her supervision. Questions are sure to rise about whether sexual relationships are consensual or not between students and faculty. The types of policies that

▲ **Photo 6.3** President Barack Obama met his future wife, Michelle Robinson, when she was assigned as his mentor in the Sidley Austin law firm. Obama, a first-year law student at Harvard, was serving as a summer associate there. Because of their professional relationship, she turned him down when he asked her out and tried to fix him up with her friends, putting him off because she felt "self-conscious" being his mentor (Mundy, 2008). Eventually, she agreed to go out with him.

colleges have to address student/faculty relationships exist on a continuum. On one end of the continuum, some colleges and universities have either no policy or permissive policies that allow such relationships so long as they are consensual. At the other end of the continuum, other colleges and universities have more restrictive policies, with some even forbidding consensual relationships altogether. Not only do the policies exist on a continuum, perceptions of harassment exist on a continuum. Consider the following comments from a university dean:

> A couple of weeks ago, a troubled member of staff came to see me for a confidential meeting. He had started a relationship with an undergraduate and thought he'd better confess. "She's a third year," he blurted, hoping this might mitigate the offense. "Oh, well, that certainly helps," I mused . . . wondering where I filed the number of the university attorney.
>
> "Is she in your course?" [I asked]. She wasn't. *She wasn't even in his department. I breathed a sigh of relief. At least he wasn't teaching her.* (Feldman, 2009, p. 29, emphasis added)

Another type of sexual harassment in college settings involves professors awarding **grades for sex.** Euphemistically called "an A for a lay" (Fearn, 2008, p. 30), these situations use the power of grading in order to solicit sexual favors from students. Some experts contend that exchanging grades for sex "is accepted without question or noticeable comment by most members of the university community" (Reilly et al., 1986, p. 341).

Rape is sometimes classified with sexual harassment, although it is actually a violent, felonious assault. It is the most rarely reported type of sexual assault or harassment. In one recent case, a 62-year-old criminal justice professor was indicted in January 2010 on grounds that he sexually assaulted a 21-year-old student ("Troy Criminal Justice Professor Indicted on Rape Charge," 2010). According to court records, the sexual assault allegedly occurred in the Fall 2009 semester at a polygraph business that the professor ran. Incidentally, the same professor was charged with misdemeanor harassment on the grounds that he had inappropriately touched a woman 4 years earlier. He was found not guilty on the earlier charge (Elofson, 2010). Although cases of rape are clearly violations of the criminal law, many instances of sexual harassment are not generally treated as crime violations, but are treated as either civil wrongs or administrative violations.

Recall from the introduction that different cultures define workplace misconduct in varying ways. Cross-cultural definitions of sexual harassment demonstrate this pattern. As an illustration of the cultural variations in defining sexual harassment, note that other countries—like Britain—are more accepting of faculty/student romantic relationships (Fearn, 2008). Part of their openness to these relationships is based on the differences in the way that colleges function in Britain, as compared to the United States. In Britain, students tend to be slightly older and faculty begin teaching at a younger age—making the age difference between faculty member and student less pronounced. Also, in the United States, the system of grading creates more power than what is found in grading systems used in Britain (Fearn, 2008). To put this in perspective, Fearn cites a British study that found that one fifth of "academics reported having sexual relations with a student."

Fearn is quick to note that an increasing trend in Britain is to be less tolerant of these sorts of relationships. Describing this trend firsthand, one British professor commented about her experiences as a student:

> I have been chased around offices, leapt on in a lift, groped under . . . tables and been the recipient of unpleasantly explicit anonymous notes, and I do not think I am any different from any other woman of my generation. . . . I welcome the fact that today young women are sufficiently empowered to know that they have a right to complain about it. (Bassnett, 2006, p. 54)

It is difficult to know how often sexual assaults occur as students, though they are empowered to report them, often decide not to report their harassment experiences to authorities or to researchers studying the topic. One author team cites estimates that suggest that one fourth to one half of female university students are sexually harassed as students, with 5% to 10% of them experiencing serious forms of harassment (Skinner et al., 1995). A survey of 597 students found that 15.2% of the respondents reported being "hit on" by one their professors (Anderson, Bailey, & Nagy, 1997). Fourteen of the students said they had sexual relationships with a professor. Another study focused on the sexual harassment experiences of female college students ($n = 319$) and employees ($n = 446$) (Kelly & Parsons, 2000). This study found that 42% of the sample had experienced at least one incident of sexual harassment, and that different patterns of harassment exist between students and employees. For example, undergraduate students were sometimes harassed by graduate teaching assistants, graduate students were harassed by male faculty, and employees were more likely to experience gender harassment than students were.

Sexual harassment occurs in all academic disciplines, including criminal justice. A survey of 65 criminologists found that 59% of them experienced some form of sexual harassment during graduate school (Stanko, 1992). One third of the respondents said they were harassed in their field research by criminal justice professionals or the subjects they were studying. The criminal justice professors described a range of harassment experiences, including the following:

- An ongoing problem occurred when I was a graduate assistant and actually ended up with the professor trying to kiss me. Most of the time, though, he simply managed to direct the conversation ... to sex.
- My research professor would make comments about my physical attractiveness and invite me to dinner. I declined.
- Faculty told me as a graduate student that my demeanor was not feminine enough.
- At the interview for the RA position which led to my main fellowship in grad school, he grabbed me out of the blue and started kissing me. I did not know what to do, so I pulled away and continued as if nothing happened. He kissed me several more times, my response was the same. . . . On several occasions, he pulled up my shirt and fondled my breast. I started wearing fondle-proof clothes. (Stanko, 1992, p. 334)

The consequences of sexual harassment can be quite devastating for students—both in the short term and the long term. In the short term, being exposed to harassing experiences will make it more difficult for students to learn, which will affect their grades, mental health, and attachment to school. Students might change majors, transfer, or even drop out of college. Each of these decisions will have long-term consequences for victims of sexual harassment. As well, the experience of sexual harassment may impact the victim's own personal relationships with loved ones.

Describing her experience of being sexually harassed by her counseling professor, one former student wrote the following:

My anxiety was of such concern that I began seeing a therapist. She helped me understand that I had certain personality traits that had made me a likely target for Professor X. I had always idealized teachers and had done so particularly with him. I had trusted him implicitly during a busy, stressful time. . . . My experience of being sexually harassed by my counseling professor has changed my life forever. I know that although the trauma has lessened considerably, it will never disappear. (Anonymous, 1991, p. 506)

As noted above, students who are harassed by their professors tend not to report their victimization to anyone. In fact, as compared to university employees, students are more likely to ignore the behavior whereas employees are more likely to tell their supervisor or file a complaint (Kelly & Parsons, 2000). One study identified the following as reasons why students, in this case medical students, chose not to report their harassment experience: (a) loyalty to the "team," (b) seen as not serious enough, (c) reporting defined as a weakness, (d) reporting defined as futile, and (e) concern about repercussions on future evaluations (Wear, Aultman, & Borges, 2007).

Of course, colleges are not the only workplace where sexual harassment occurs. The topic was discussed in the context of colleges and universities for two reasons. First, as students, readers will likely better understand the topic by seeing it through the lens of students. Second, colleges and universities "are institutions that reflect reality in the greater society" (McCormack, 1985, p. 23). What is going on in colleges and universities simply reflects activities that occur in other institutions. Unfortunately, what this means is that you won't escape the risk of sexual harassment when you graduate from college. Instead, when you enter your careers, you will be confronted with the potential for different types of sexual harassment.

⬙ Disciplining "Bad" Professors

Some professors actually ended up in prison for their wrongdoing, but these cases are typically ones where quite serious wrongdoing occurred. Even more rarely are criminal sanctions applied to researchers who fabricate research findings. Eric Poehlman, a former tenured professor at the University of Vermont, became the first scientist jailed for research misconduct in the United States after he "pleaded guilty to lying on a federal grant application and admitted to fabricating more than a decade's worth of scientific data on obesity, menopause, and aging" (Interlandi, 2006).

Incidentally, the fraud came to light when Walter DeNino, one of his former students who had become a lab worker for Poehlman, noticed some discrepancies in the lab reports. DeNino viewed his professor as a mentor but still notified university administrators about his concerns—which eventually panned out after an investigation. His former student was in the courtroom when Poehlman pled guilty. The disgraced professor apologized to his former student (Interlandi, 2006). Poehlman was sentenced to 366 days in federal prison. His case has been described as the "most extensive case of scientific misconduct in the history of the National Institutes of Health" (Kintisch, 2006). One can only imagine what DeNino went through as he mulled over the decision to report his former professor to administrators. Think about it—would you report your professor for misconduct? See In Focus 6.1, When Professors Go Bad, to read the press release issued by the U.S. Department of Justice describing the case and its outcome.

In Focus 6.1

When Professors Go Bad: A Case of Research Misconduct

Press Release—Dr. Eric T. Poehlman

U.S. Department of Justice

United States Attorney
District of Vermont

United States Courthouse and Federal Building
Post Office Box 570
Burlington, Vermont 05402-0570

(802) 951-6725
Fax: (802) 951-6540

Burlington, Vermont—March 17, 2005

The United States Attorney's Office for the District of Vermont, the U.S. Department of Health and Human Services (HHS) Office of Inspector General (OIG) and Office of Research Integrity (ORI) announced today that Dr. Eric T. Poehlman, 49, a former tenured research professor at the University of Vermont (UVM) College of Medicine in Burlington, Vermont, has agreed to a comprehensive criminal, civil, and administrative settlement related to his scientific misconduct in falsifying and fabricating research data in numerous federal grant applications and in academic articles from 1992 to 2002.

According to court documents filed today, Dr. Poehlman has agreed to plead guilty to making material false statements in a research grant application in April 1999, upon which the National Institutes of Health (NIH) paid $542,000 for Dr. Poehlman's research activities. In addition, Dr. Poehlman has agreed to pay $180,000 to settle a civil complaint related to numerous false grant applications he filed while at UVM. In addition, Dr. Poehlman will pay $16,000 in attorney's fees to counsel for Walter F. DeNino, a research assistant whose complaint of scientific misconduct spurred an investigation by UVM. Also, Dr. Poehlman has agreed to be barred for life from seeking or receiving funding from any federal agency in the future, including all components of the Public Health Service, and to submit numerous letters of retraction and correction to scientific journals related to his scientific misconduct. Dr. Poehlman also agreed to be permanently excluded from participation in all Federal health care programs. In these agreements, Dr. Poehlman has admitted that he acted alone in falsifying and fabricating research data and filing false grant applications.

"Preserving the integrity of the grant process administered by the Public Health Service is a priority for the Department of Justice," said United States Attorney David V. Kirby. "This prosecution demonstrates that academic researchers will be held fully accountable for fraud and scientific misconduct. Dr. Poehlman fraudulently diverted millions of dollars from the Public Health Service to support his research projects. This in turn siphoned millions of dollars from the pool of resources available for valid scientific research proposals. As this prosecution proves, such conduct will not be tolerated."

Acting Assistant Secretary for Health, Cristina V. Beato, M.D., acknowledges the "invaluable assistance of the Department of Justice in bringing this case to a conclusion and upholding the high standards for research integrity in research supported by the Public Health Service." HHS actions against Dr. Poehlman include a life time debarment from receiving Public Health Service research funds and an agreement to retract or correct ten scientific articles due to research misconduct. Dr. Beato added that "while criminal charges against research scientists are rare, the egregiousness of Dr. Poehlman's conduct in this case fully supports the actions of the U.S. Attorney's Office and the administrative actions taken by HHS." Through ORI, HHS is authorized to investigate and oversee institutional investigations of allegations of research misconduct in order to protect the integrity of Public Health Service funded research.

Dr. Poehlman will appear for arraignment and to plead guilty to the criminal charge filed today at a date to be determined by the Court. Dr. Poehlman faces up to five years imprisonment on the criminal charge, but the United States has agreed to take no position on a request by Dr. Poehlman to receive a more lenient sentence based upon his cooperation with authorities and his acceptance of responsibility. The civil settlement agreement will become effective after approval by the Court. The administrative settlement will be effective immediately.

From 1987 to 2001, Dr. Poehlman held various research positions as an assistant, associate, and full professor of medicine at the UVM College of Medicine in Burlington, Vermont (1987–1993; 1996–2001), and the University of Maryland in Baltimore, Maryland (1993–1996). In these academic positions, Dr. Poehlman conducted research on human subjects related to exercise physiology and other topics that was funded primarily by grants from federal public health agencies and departments, including the NIH, the U.S. Department of Agriculture ("USDA"), and the Department of Defense.

(Continued)

(Continued)

From in or about 1992 to 2000, Dr. Poehlman submitted seventeen (17) research grant applications to federal agencies or departments that included false and fabricated research data. In these grant applications, Dr. Poehlman requested approximately $11.6 million in federal research funding. In most cases, Dr. Poehlman falsified and fabricated research data in the "preliminary studies" sections of grant applications in order to support the scientific basis for and his expertise in conducting the proposed research. Reviewers of these grant applications relied on the accuracy of the "preliminary studies" to determine if a grant should be recommended for award. While many of the grant applications were not awarded, NIH and USDA expended approximately $2.9 million in research funding based on grant applications with false and fabricated research data.

Dr. Poehlman falsified and fabricated research data in grant applications and research papers related to several topics including his study of the impact of the menopause transition on women's metabolism ("the Longitudinal Menopause Study"), his study of the impact of aging in older men and women on a wide range of physical and metabolic measures ("the Longitudinal Study of Aging"), and his proposal to study the impact of hormone replacement therapy ("HRT") on obesity in post-menopausal women ("the Prospective HRT Study"). Dr. Poehlman also presented falsified and fabricated data in grant applications and academic papers related to his study of metabolism in Alzheimer's patients and the effect of endurance training on metabolism.

Very few professors end up prosecuted in the criminal justice system for their misdeeds; more often administrative sanctions are applied by the university. Common types of discipline against professors include: (a) oral reprimands, (b) written reprimands, (c) recorded reprimands, (d) loss of benefits for a period of time, such as forgoing a raise, (5) restitution, (6) fines, (7) salary reductions, (8) suspensions with or without leave, (9) dismissals, (10) tenure revocations, and (11) departmental reassignments (Euben & Lee, 2005). A number of court cases have focused on the appropriateness of these sanctions after professors sued for being disciplined. Table 6.1 provides an overview of some of these cases. One thing that stands out in these cases is that the courts have tended to uphold the sanctions unless it was clear that the professor's rights were violated. For example, the courts have said that professors cannot be placed on unpaid leave until after a hearing has occurred (Euben & Lee, 2005).

Also, note that the types of discipline will vary according to the type of misconduct. Faculty who "blow off" class a little too often would be subjected to one form of discipline, whereas those who fabricate data would be subjected to another form of discipline. Also, even within specific types of misconduct, different forms of discipline are necessary. For example, "no single punishment is appropriate for all sexual harassment cases, but it is the faculty member's misconduct, not his ideas, that should be punished" (Knight, 1995, as cited in Euben & Lee, 2005). The key is that behaviors are disciplined, not beliefs or ideas.

Crimes in the Educational System by Students

Some may question whether crimes by students are actually white-collar crimes. In this context, it is argued that a broad conceptualization of white-collar crime that views white-collar crime as offenses committed in various occupational systems allows one to consider student offenses as white-collar misconduct. Three types of behavior by students, in particular, can be seen as white-collar crimes: (1) offenses students commit on their jobs, (2) academic dishonesty, and (3) Internet/digital piracy by college and university students.

Table 6.1 Legal Decisions Regarding Faculty Discipline

Case	Sanction	Action	Judicial Decision
Hall v. Board of Trustees of State Institutions of Higher Learning	Warning/ reprimand	Faculty member touched a student's breasts after she asked a question about mammograms	Sanction did not violate the faculty member's rights
Newman v. Burgin	Public censure	Plagiarism	Sanction was upheld
Wirsing v. Board of Regents of Univ. of Colorado	One-time denial of salary increase	Professor refused to use departmental evaluation forms	Sanction upheld
Williams v. Texas Tech University Health Sciences Center	Permanent salary reduction	University told him to bring in more grants, but he didn't	The university could do this, particularly because the faculty member was given 6 months to do so.
Edwards v. California Univ. of Pennsylvania	Paid suspension	Bad language in classroom	No violation of the professor's rights
Bonnell v. Lorenzo	Unpaid suspension	Suspended without pay pending hearing on sexual harassment charges	University must pay salary before hearings
Klinge v. Ithaca College	Demotion in rank	Professor plagiarized and was demoted from professor to associate professor	No violation of rights
McClellan v. Board of Regents of the State Univ.	Modified teaching assignments	Made sexual comments to students, was told he couldn't teach specific class for years	No violation of rights
Bauer v. Sampson	Mandatory counseling	Alleged to have anger management issues because of temperament	Violated free expression rights

With regard to offenses committed on their jobs, note that many of the occupational offenses discussed in earlier sections of the book might actually entail crimes committed by students employed in those professions. Restaurants and other service industries, for instance, routinely hire students as employers. In addition to students as occupational offenders in jobs outside of the college/university setting, students also have opportunities to commit white-collar crimes in their positions as student workers or students affiliated with university workers. Consider the following cases as examples:

- A student worker at one university "was caught changing 75 Fs to As for 8 students" (Dyer, 2004).
- A university student in California was arrested after being charged with stealing two professors' identities and using those stolen IDs to change her grades and several other student's grades (La, 2005).

- Students in Louisiana collaborated in a scheme with an assistant registrar to have their grades changed. The worker also "manufactured entire academic transcripts for people who never enrolled on . . . the campus." It was estimated that grades were changed for 541 students in the scheme, at prices ranging from $200 to $500 (Dyer, 2004).

Academic dishonesty can also be seen as a variety of white-collar crime. On one level, students are "pre-professionals" seeking an education that will hopefully prepare them for their future professional careers. On another level, students assume the role of a "worker" in their efforts to pursue an education. They perform "work-like" activities as part of their coursework. Just as some workers in legitimate occupations break occupational rules and criminal laws while performing their jobs, some students break college and university rules (and various laws) while performing as students.

In this context, academic dishonesty can be defined as "intellectual theft" (Petress, 2003). One author cites estimates suggesting that between 63% and 75% of students self-report cheating (Iyer & Eastman, 2006). Interviews with 31 undergraduates found that the "students did not seem to have any deep moral dilemmas about plagiarism" (Power, 2009, p. 643). Over recent years, plagiarism using information copied from the Internet has been described as a "monumental problem" (Strom & Strom, 2007, p. 108), noting that of the 30,000 papers reviewed in one popular plagiarism detection tool each day, "more than 30% of [the] documents include plagiarism" (Strom & Strom, 2007, p. 122).

Research on academic dishonesty has focused on the characteristics of dishonest students, the connections between academic dishonesty and white-collar crime, the causes of academic dishonesty, the role of instructors in academic dishonesty, and appropriate response strategies and policies to limit academic dishonesty. To gain insight into the characteristics of students who engage in academic dishonesty, Iyer and Eastman (2006) compared 124 business students with 177 non-business students and found that business students were more honest than non-business students. They also found that males, undergraduates, and members of fraternities and sororities were more likely be dishonest than females, graduate students, and students who are not members of fraternities and sororities. Focusing specifically on types of business students, one research team surveyed 1,255 business students and found that accounting majors were more honest than management majors (Rakovski & Levy, 2007). This study also found that males, and students with lower grade point averages, were less honest than females and students with higher grade point averages.

Examining the connection between academic dishonesty and crime at work, Sims (1993) surveyed 60 MBA students, asking about various forms of academic dishonesty and workplace misconduct. Sims found that respondents "who engaged in behaviors considered severely dishonest in college also engaged in behaviors considered severely dishonest at work" (p. 207).

Researchers have identified a number of potential predictors of academic dishonesty. Reviewing prior studies on academic dishonesty, one author team cited the following causes: (1) low self-control, (2) alienation, (3) situational factors, and (4) perceptions that cheating is justified (Aluede, Omoregie, & Osa-Edoh, 2006). A survey of 345 students found that the more television they watched, the more likely they would engage in academic dishonesty (Pino & Smith, 2003). Some have argued that academic dishonesty is part of a developmental process "in which students learn to behave professionally and morally by making choices, abiding by consequences, and (paradoxically) behave immorally" (Austin, Simpson, & Reynen, 2005, p. 143).

In a rather interesting study that may raise some critical-thinking questions among readers, one professor focused on the ties between opportunity and self-control (Smith, 2004). The professor had his students complete a self-control survey at the beginning of the semester. Later in the semester, the professor returned exams to the students and told them that he did not have time to grade the exams. Students were told they would have to grade their own exams and were given a copy of an answer key to complete this task. In reality, the professor had made copies of all students' exams before returning them ungraded to the students. This allowed the professor to grade the students' exams and compare their "earned" grade with the grades the students gave themselves. Of the 64 students in the class, 30 scored their exams higher than they should have. The author found that opportunity seemed to play a role in fostering the academic misconduct and that low self-control was related to academic dishonesty. Incidentally, the students received the "earned" grade on their exams and the professor waited until the end of the semester to tell them about his experiment.

Some researchers have focused on the college professor's role in promoting (and preventing) academic dishonesty. Surveys of 583 students found that an instructor's perceived credibility influenced academic dishonesty (Anderman, Cupp, & Lane, 2010). If students perceived a professor as credible, they were less likely to commit academic dishonesty in that professor's course. Somewhat referring to this possibility, one author commented, "the value of individual and collective honesty has to be taught, role modeled, and rewarded in schools; to neglect or refuse to do so is malfeasance" (Petress, 2003). Also highlighting the professor's role in preventing academic dishonesty, Lee (2009) advises professors to:

- Demonstrate to students why academic dishonesty is wrong
- Develop assignments and class activities that make it virtually impossible for students to engage in academic dishonesty
- Promote and foster values of respect and honesty between students and faculty

Some authors have also noted that professors can prevent (or at least detect) these offenses by implementing aggressive academic dishonesty policies and using available tools to identify cases of academic dishonesty. For example, computer software is available that detects cheating on multiple choice exams that use scantrons to score the exams. The software detects similar wrong answer patterns and alerts professors to possible academic dishonesty (Nath & Lovaglia, 2008). A popular company, Turnitin, provides software that reviews papers submitted in classes and identifies plagiarized papers. Turnitin has been hailed as a "potent weapon against academic dishonesty" (Minkel, 2002, p. 25). Recently, students filed a lawsuit against Turnitin, arguing that the collection tool violated students' copyright ownership rights over the papers they wrote because the tool stored their papers in order to compare them with past and future submissions to Turnitin, and the company made money off of the students' papers. In 2008, a federal judge ruled that the software program does not violate copyright laws (Young, 2008).

Internet and digital piracy is another type of white-collar crime believed to be particularly popular on college campuses across the United States. This topic will be addressed in detail in the section focusing on computer crime. At this point, it is prudent to warn you that that the authorities take digital piracy by college students seriously. Not long ago, Michel Crippen, a student at California State University, Fullerton, was arrested by Homeland Security officers after he modified "Xbox video game consoles to play copied games" (Sci Tech Blog, 2009). So, if you are sitting in your dorm room or at home near your computer, make sure that you haven't illegally downloaded materials from the Internet or stored illegally copied software on your computer. The next knock on your door could be Homeland Security officers coming to take you away. The irony is that the Homeland Security officers were once college students themselves. One can't help but wonder if they broke any rules when they were college students.

✉ Summary

- In this section, attention was given to crimes committed by professionals and students in the educational system.
- Four types of misconduct that appear to be among the more common types of academic misconduct include: research misconduct, ghostwriting, pecuniary-oriented offenses, and sexual harassment.
- Research misconduct refers to a range of behaviors that center around researchers (many of whom are faculty members) engaging in various forms of wrongdoing during the course of their research. These forms of wrongdoing include, but are not limited to, fabricating data, masking findings, plagiarism, and treating research subjects unethically. Experts have noted that research misconduct is "real and persistent" (Herman et al., 1994).
- Researchers have suggested that plagiarism by professors is more likely to occur in the humanities and social sciences than in the hard sciences due to the nature of the disciplines.
- Research misconduct has severe consequences on several different levels. These consequences include: (1) consequences for the individual faculty member, (2) financial consequences for the college or university, (3) morale consequences for the college or university, (4) image consequences for science, (5) consequences for members of society, and (6) consequences for various cultures.
- Because of the potential role that mentors have in contributing to misconduct, some have argued that mentors should play an active role in training their students how to conduct research appropriately.
- Ghostwriting refers to situations where professors or researchers have their work written by someone else, but the professor's name appears on the work.
- Pecuniary-based offenses include misbehaviors that are ultimately done by professors for the economic gain that comes along with the commission of the offenses. Four varieties of pecuniary-oriented offenses include: embezzlement, textbook fraud, double billing, and engaging in unapproved outside work.
- Embezzlement occurs when faculty members or university staff steal funds from an account to which they have access.
- Textbook fraud refers to instances where faculty sell complimentary textbooks that they receive from publishers to book dealers who resell the books.
- Double billing occurs when professors bill more than one source for the same effort of work or reimbursement.
- Faculty working full-time for a college or university also commit workplace offenses by engaging in outside work that is not approved by the institutions. Three overlapping types of conflicts arise with unapproved outside work: (1) research-based conflicts of interest, (2) teaching/service-based conflicts of interest, and (3) time-based conflicts of interest.
- Sexual harassment refers to a range of behaviors where employees perform sexually inappropriate actions against their colleagues or students.
- Sexual harassment offenses committed by college professors include (1) sexualized comments, (2) sexualized behaviors, (3) academic incest, (4) sexual relationships with students in class, and (5) grades for sex.
- Eric Poehlman, a former tenured professor at the University of Vermont, became the first scientist jailed for research misconduct in the United States after he "pleaded guilty to lying on a federal grant application and admitted to fabricating more than a decade's worth of scientific data on obesity, menopause, and aging" (Interlandi, 2006).

- Common types of discipline against professors include: (1) oral reprimands, (2) written reprimands, (3) recorded reprimands, (4) loss of benefits for a period of time, e.g., no raise, (5) restitution, (6) fines, (7) salary reductions, (8) suspensions with or without leave, (9) dismissals, (10) tenure revocations, and (11) departmental reassignments.
- Three types of behavior by college students can be seen as white-collar crimes: (1) offenses students commit on their jobs, (2) academic dishonesty, and (3) Internet piracy by college and university students.

KEY TERMS

Academic dishonesty	Grades for sex	Sexual contact with students
Academic incest	Pecuniary-based offenses	Sexual harassment
Faculty double billing	Research misconduct	Sexualized behavior
Faculty embezzlement	Seductive behavior	Sexualized comments
Gender harassment	Sexual bribery	Textbook fraud
Ghostwriting	Sexual coercion	

DISCUSSION QUESTIONS

1. Which is worse—sexual assault by a fellow student or sexual assault by a professor? Explain.

2. What are some similarities and differences between crime in the educational system and crime in the health care system?

3. Should professors be fired for plagiarism? Explain.

4. If professors have their names listed on articles they didn't actually write, would this violate the honor code established for students? Explain.

5. Who is responsible for preventing research misconduct?

6. If you found out that one of your professors committed research misconduct, would it change the way you evaluated them on the teaching evaluations? Explain.

7. What are appropriate penalties for academic dishonesty by students?

8. How can academic dishonesty be categorized as white-collar crime? Explain.

WEB RESOURCES

Office of Research Integrity: http://ori.dhhs.gov/

Sexual Harassment at School: http://www.equalrights.org/publications/kyr/shschool.asp

Online Plagiarism Checker: http://plagiarisma.net/

READING

In this reading, Elizabeth Stanko describes the results of a survey of members of the American Society of Criminology's (ASC) Division on Women and Crime. ASC is a professional association including professors, researchers, and other scholars who conduct research and teach about issues related to crime and criminal justice. Chances are that some of your professors are either current or past members of ASC. Stanko's survey found that most of the female respondents experienced some forms of sexual harassment when they were in graduate school. She provides some specific examples the respondents experienced, and some of those experiences are, to put it bluntly, horrific. Stanko suggests that training of female graduate students in criminology and criminal justice should include sexual safety training. She notes that by recognizing that these behaviors occur, measures can follow to address the behaviors.

Intimidating Education

Sexual Harassment in Criminology

Elizabeth A. Stanko

The Anita Hill/Clarence Thomas sexual harassment case was rated the third most important event in the United States in 1991. The public airing of one woman's story, an accomplished academic woman at that, hit many raw nerves of women throughout the United States and elsewhere. Earlier that summer, I was asked to conduct a survey about sexual harassment among the members of the Women and Crime Division of the American Society of Criminology. This paper presents the findings of that survey and highlights the implications for the way women are educated and trained as criminal justice professionals. These findings raise fundamental questions about women's treatment as graduate students, colleagues, and researchers within the field of criminal justice.

Sexual Harassment and Sexual Safety

I had no knowledge that any form of sexual harassment was inappropriate. We had no word for it, except graduate school.

Sexual harassment, one form of intimidating behavior by men, takes many forms. A general definition includes unwanted sexual attention, such as leering; sexual teasing; jokes, comments, or questions aimed at one's sexuality; unwanted pressure for sexual favors or dates; unwanted touching or pinching; and unwanted pressure for sex with implied threats of retaliation for noncooperation. Some women also report sexual assault and rape as sexual harassment (Stanko 1985; see also Erez and Tontodonato 1992).

Sexual harassment and its commonness in American academic settings is itself well documented (for a review, see Reilly, Lott, and Gallogly 1986). The early work of Benson and Thompson (1982) suggested that one female student in five met some form of sexual intimidation at the hands of professors and instructors. A growing body of research is confirming that substantial numbers of women are at risk of sexual assault on U.S. campuses (Berger et al. 1986; Ehrhart and Sandler 1985; Koss, Gidycz, and Wisniewski 1987; Lott, Reilly, and Howard 1982; Warshaw 1988).

Women's safety in the criminal justice system must be explored within the context of women's safety

SOURCE: Stanko, Elizabeth. (1992). Intimidating education: Sexual harassment in criminology. *Journal of Criminal Justice Education, 3*, 331–340.

apart from their experiences as college students. All crime surveys, for example, note that women are much more concerned about crime than are men (Gordon and Riger 1988; Stanko 1990). At the heart of women's concern about personal safety is their awareness of lack of sexual safety. Potential danger, moreover, is typically at the hands of men, often men known to the women they endanger. As research consistently shows, many women have experienced men's threatening, intimidating, or violent behavior (Kelly 1988; Russell 1982; Stanko 1985; Warshaw 1988), and their assailants are usually familiar and familial.

There is little doubt that female criminal justice professionals encounter widespread sexism and situations of sexual harassment. Female police officers, corrections officers, lawyers, victims, and defendants, to name a few, have all reported many instances of sexually intimidating conduct (Hunt 1984; Martin 1980; Schafran 1987; Zimmer 1986). Women in academe are not immune. Ramazanoglu suggests that women in higher education confront "male dominated hierarchies, [which] leads to widespread defense of male privilege and to institutionalized forms of violence" (1987:61). Closely tied to issues of gender, power, and control, sexual harassment surfaces as the metaphor for gender relations and sexuality in the wider society. Locating this metaphor within our own understanding as female professionals will necessarily raise questions about how we educate, train and support women to work in an often hostile atmosphere.

The Survey

The impetus for the survey arose from a growing concern of a number of members of the Women and Crime Division of the American Society of Criminology about the problem of sexual harassment on their campuses. The author, herself a survivor of a sexual harassment lawsuit and a researcher of violence against women, agreed to poll ASC Division members on their own experiences. The survey was distributed in late August/September 1991, just around the time of the Supreme Court hearings.

Of the 220 questionnaires, 65 were returned, a completion rate of approximately 27 percent. Six (6)

men and 58 women took part. Respondents ranged in age from the mid-twenties to the early sixties; half of the respondents were aged between 40 and 49. The sample was overwhelmingly Caucasian, and most of those surveyed were employed as full-time university professors.

Respondents were asked to reflect on their experiences in three areas: professional and graduate school training; research and fieldwork; and current working context. The questionnaire focused explicitly upon unwanted sexual attention and sexual harassment. Many respondents, though, took the opportunity to include comments about working climates that may not have been sexually harassing but were demeaning and degrading of women and women's research (see also Ramazanoglu 1987).

Graduate Training

Nearly three out of five respondents (59%) reported that they had received some unwelcome comments about their sexuality during their graduate training. These remarks occasionally were colored by racist and homophobic references.

There continues to be controversy about the effect or importance of "mere" remarks. Examples reported on the survey included the following irritating, worrying, or frightening comments:

> Outside my office in the hall [I heard] "If she fucks niggers, she'll fuck anything."

> [Comment from a faculty member] You know, you have great legs. I'm a leg man.

> An ongoing problem occurred when I was a graduate assistant and actually ended up with the professor trying to kiss me. Most of the time, though, he simply managed to direct the conversation, regardless of what it was about, to sex.

> My research professor would make comments about my physical attractiveness and invite me to dinner. I declined.

> Comments about my breasts. [I was] discouraged from taking "male" skills classes. Groping. Sex-for-grades "bargain" offers.

The body of evidence about sexual harassment suggests that women respond in a variety of ways to such "face-to-face discriminatory behavior" (McClelland and Hunter 1992). Some women confronted the sexist remarks; some remained silent; others found ways of deflecting any possible harm. Many women developed techniques to protect themselves from harassment, such as avoiding the individual or the situation where harassment could arise. Comments from professors, fellow graduate students, or research supervisors must be considered according to how women negotiate safety with men in a variety of locations. One woman cited the following experience in graduate school:

> Male doctoral students [were] circulating memos about female doctoral student members of a women's caucus needing to be fucked and raped.

Feelings of humiliation, degradation, and embarrassment were common: women reported feeling angry, frustrated, saddened, confused, hurt, and frightened. One woman was told she could never quite fit in:

> Faculty told me as a graduate student that my demeanor was not feminine enough (too serious, not smiling enough), or that my attitudes were too feminine (lack of ambition in career plans, insufficiently competitive behavior).

Whereas "putting up" with comments seemed to be part of being a woman in graduate school, 11 women (17% of the respondents) felt sexually intimidated by someone in authority during graduate school. Sexual intimidation was defined as a threat or bribe by a person in a position of authority to coerce sexual contact with another person. Threats involved withholding recommendations, giving poor grades in courses, and withdrawing supervision. Bribes included promises of grants, promotions, recommendations, and/or research assistance. Respondents reported offers of financial and academic support in exchange for sex, refusals to process data for a dissertation because the woman refused sexual advances, threats or promises regarding grades and recommendations, and being given pornography as part of "professional" reading materials.

The intimidation had wide-ranging effects. Respondents changed courses of study, changed supervisors, or dropped out of programs for a while. All reported feeling angry, horrified, confused, or self-doubting; many feared they would fail to receive their PhDs. Some "real horror stories" were reported, such as the following:

> At the interview for the RA position which led to my main fellowship in grad school, he grabbed me out of the blue and started kissing me. I didn't know what to do, so I pulled away and continued as if nothing happened. He kissed me several more times, my response was the same. I took the job on the condition that there would be a professional relationship between us. I was explicit. Looking back, I don't think he said anything. Then he started getting physical. On several occasions, he pulled up my shirt and fondled my breast. I started wearing fondle-proof clothes. Then it came time for job recommendations. He showed me the letter he was going to send to some college. It read like a probation report, citing deficiencies and whether he thought I could ever make them up. I took it out of the out-going basket before it was mailed and told him not to write. He threatened to terminate my grant, laughed and told me I had no power. He could do what he wanted. As it turned out, he was unable to cancel my grant and I asked him to resign from my dissertation committee.

Such situations can overshadow an entire graduate school education.

It is important to note at this point that the persons who reported these events are now successful academics. By "successful" I mean that they now hold university jobs, and are actively teaching and researching aspects of women's lives in the field of criminology. All the respondents completed or are about to complete PhDs, although they were treated by faculty members and fellow students in a demeaning and at times frightening way. Some of the respondents are prominent women in the field. Yet their memories of graduate school, and of their initial experiences of fieldwork and research, were peppered with reminders from mentors, faculty members, and fellow students that they were, after all, "only women." Until now, most of these women had chosen to remain silent about how they were treated during graduate school. Then, as now, women (as all the evidence suggests) occupied and continue to occupy marginalized, sexualized, and subordinate positions in society (see, for instance, Faludi 1992 and French 1992).

Research and Fieldwork

To become a professional in the field of criminology, one must master the art and skill of doing fieldwork in some aspect of the criminal justice system. Collecting information on the working of the courts, the prisons, the police service, or probation means entering yet another domain occupied largely by men.

Approximately one respondent out of three (31%) reported encountering sexual comments and/or intimidation during their fieldwork and research. No doubt this experience is testimony to the cult of masculinity underpinning so much of the criminal justice system. For some individuals, such comments and intimidation meant that they felt unable to continue in their research site, either because they refused to be humiliated or were frightened of the intimidation. Women told of the following experiences:

> Working in a correctional setting, we were "expected" to flirt with guards/supervisors. It was normative and a way to get access to data.

> [The] language and touching from police officers when [I was] collecting data. [I] needed to do follow-up work, but opted not to.

> Constant harassment from police officers, humiliation in prison visits; sexist comments

from court officers. Somehow [I] got used to it. Don't work [now] in male prisons at all.

> A male colleague where I was conducting my research talked incessantly of women's bodies and his conquests. I stopped using him as a resource, as I was not comfortable in his presence. Even though he was very knowledgeable in the area and could have been a great help.

Some women encountered situations that put their own safety at risk:

> [While I was doing a police ride-along] a sergeant drove to a dark, deserted alley and turned off the engine. [It was] about one a.m. He said he wanted to show me something. It was just a come on. He proceeded to give me a "tour" of homeless shacks.

> Certainly the most memorable (but not the only one) was when a man (an executive in a factory) whom I was interviewing at his home attempted to rape me. But if I did not know judo he would probably have raped me. Finally he let me go when I screamed and threatened to bring charges of rape against him.

> The judge I was interviewing asked me to turn off the tape recorder and came over to the desk attempting to touch me. I turned on the tape recorder and said "Oh your Honor!" He stopped.

After many such experiences, the respondents reported a variety of ways of coping and managing harassment. One woman stated:

> Doing work in prisons and law enforcement has led to a variety of comments over the years, from cj professionals and offenders/inmates alike. It has sometimes led to minor problems with cj professionals until they learned that I knew what I was talking about. I learned to handle it.

Another reflected:

Respondents have made passes but most have backed down when firmly told it was inappropriate. I interview drug users/abusers. I am more cautious and frankly more nervous when interviewing men. No, dealing with unwanted male advances is something every women has to deal with.

As in graduate school, women learn that becoming a professional means negotiating their sexuality with men who are their supervisors, their access points to research sites, their interview subjects, and their colleagues. Again, it is important to note that these comments come from women who, by their professional achievements, have managed their "femaleness" in a male field. What have we learned from this exploratory study? These are the lessons about coping with and negotiating sexuality, and it is essential to share them with female graduate students who are currently training to enter the criminological profession.

Sexuality, Sexual Harassment, and Professionalism

The emphasis on sexual harassment thus far, as opposed to a wider discussion of sexuality, is purposeful. It sets a context within which to view a range of sexual encounters that adults have in their professional and private lives. Alongside coercive sexual intrusions, say some researchers (Kelly 1988; Russell 1982; Stanko 1985), are those sexual liaisons which are not coercive. The attack on women alleging sexual harassment is that the allegation is the complaint of a woman scorned. In other words, all sexual advances are assumed to be harmless; rejected by humorless or sexless women; rejected by lesbians (thus all women who reject men are lesbians); about sex and not about power.

I asked respondents to reflect on their voluntary sexual involvement as students. Participants thus were asked whether they had engaged *voluntarily* in sexual relations with their professors during their undergraduate or graduate academic careers. Eleven (17%) replied that they had sexual relationships with their professors. These liaisons ranged from one-night encounters to lifelong commitments. Some respondents offered the following reflections:

OK, they were affairs, exciting and interesting at the time. Although I had fantasies of fame and fortune at the side of these august figures, they never panned out. I've no regrets.

Looking back, I realize that I was flattered by his attention and too naive to know how to deal with it. I actually learned a lot, including how painful it was when his wife found out (I liked her a lot) and that I never wanted to be in a situation like that again. I never have.

In retrospect, I define it as harassment. Indeed, it was institutionalized sexual harassment since most women grad students there had at least one affair with a faculty member. Many of the faculty were continually having affairs with graduate students. One, then another, then another and on through the years. How can it not be coercive, given the power differential [between student and faculty member]?

The guy was a jerk, but being young and stupid at the time, I found him charming. I regret the relationship now, but it was not in any way coercive on his part.

Some married their professors and established enduring partnerships; others married and discovered later that the subordinate relationship was the attraction to the professor, and that a partnership could not be sustained. One woman painfully revealed:

I made the choice [to marry my professor] but had no idea of the long term negative effects it would have on my career. He *should* have known [10 years older than me, and a full professor at the time]. He had no concern for my professional life but wanted a pretty young grad student. This was the *worst* choice of my life I'll always pay for. We must make young women aware of the dangers of these liaisons. The appeal of romance with a professor is the linkage of sexual and intellectual union/ acceptance with the symbol of power, the male professor.

Sexual intimidation and sexual attraction stand along the same continuum. Forms of serialization occur in unspoken, yet recognized, situations. Although some experiences are implicit and others are explicit, sexual bargaining is very much a part of professional life for many women. Sorting out the wanted from the unwanted sexual encounter is very confusing at times (Stanko 1990). At other times, however, the fact and the experience of coercion and threat are clearly recognized.

The work of Catharine MacKinnon (see especially 1987) helps clarify this confusion between sex and coercive sex. In her short essay titled "Sex and Violence: A Perspective," MacKinnon argues that *from women's point of view* "what women experience does not so clearly distinguish the normal, everyday things from those abuses from which they have been defined by distinction" (1987:86). Sexuality and power are inextricably linked; subordination is eroticized. Female graduate students and junior faculty members are structurally less powerful than others in the setting, so the *potential* for abuse is ever-present. Women's lives, as I have argued elsewhere (Stanko 1990), exist along a continuum of unsafety.

Any threat or irritating/harassing comment reported in this survey occurred during the intellectual and professional training for respondents' careers. If women are to be accepted as competent members of the criminal justice profession, we must debate and discuss the impact of sexual harassment/sexual discrimination/sexuality for women as professionals in the field. Women who feel that they are untouched by discrimination must understand that a significant group of women feel so aggrieved. Not only are they aggrieved by intermittent (and, for some, constant) encounters with sexual harassment and intrusions; they also feel devalued as women who have chosen to

concentrate their intellectual pursuits on matters important to women, as either victims, offenders, or fellow professionals in the field. Those of us who teach women and train the next generation of researchers and academics must be prepared to include discussions about coping with sexism, often combined with homophobia and racism, in our courses. Men who value their female colleagues and feel that women contribute to the field must be prepared to confront other men about their behavior.

The purpose of this paper is to articulate what has been endured in silence by many women in the criminal justice system: sexual harassment and demeaning treatment. In raising the dilemmas and the contradictions of women's lives, then *at least* we can cope better with knowing that we are choosing a career where we will be a minority for a long time. We need support and recognition of the abuse that many women already have experienced in order to confront behavior that is professionally unacceptable.

References

Benson, D. and G. Thompson (1982) "Sexual Harassment on a University Campus: The Confluence of Authority Relations, Sexual Interest and Gender Stratification." *Social Problems* 29(3):236-51.

Berger, R. J., P. Searles, R. G. Salem, and B. A. Pierce (1986) "Sexual Assault in a College Community." *Sociological Focus* 19(1):1-26.

Ehrhart, J. K. and B. R. Sandler (1985) *Campus Gang Rape: Party Games?* Washington, DC: Project on the Status and Education of Women, Association of American Colleagues.

Erez, E. and P. Tontodonato (1992) "Sexual Harassment in the Criminal Justice System." In I. Moyer (ed.), *The Changing Roles of Women in the Criminal Justice System*, pp. 227-52. Prospect Heights, IL: Waveland.

Faludi, M. (1992) *Backlash*. London: Chatto and Windus.

French, M. (1992) *The War against Women*. London: Hamish Hamilton.

Gordon, M. and S. Riger (1988) *The Female Fear*. New York: Free Press.

Hunt, J. (1984) "The Development of Rapport through the Negotiation of Gender in Fieldwork among the Police." *Human Organization* 43:283-96.

Kelly, L. (1988) *Surviving Sexual Violence*. Oxford: Polity.

Koss, M., C. A. Gidyez, and N. Wisniewiki (1987) "The Scope of Rape Incidence and Prevalence of Sexual Aggression and Victimization in a National Sample of Higher Education Students." *Journal of Consulting and Clinical Psychology* 55:162-70.

Lott, B., M. E. Reilly, and D. Howard (1982) "Sexual Assault and Harassment: A Campus Community Case Study." *Signs* 8:296-319.

MacKinnon, C. (1987) "Sex and Violence: A Perspective." In C. MacKinnon (ed.), *Feminism Unmodified*, pp. 85-92. London: Harvard University Press.

Martin, S. (1980) *Breaking and Entering*. Berkeley: University of California Press.

McClelland K. and C. Hunter (1992) "The Perceived Seriousness of Racial Harassment." *Social Problems* 39(1):92-107.

Ramazanoglu, C. (1987) "Sex and Violence in Academic Life or You Can Keep a Good Woman Down." In J. Hanmer and M. Maynard (eds.), *Women, Violence and Social Control,* pp. 61-74. Atlantic Highlands, NJ: Humanities Press International.

Reilly, M. E., B. Lott, and S. M. Gallogly (1986) "Sexual Harassment of University Students." *Sex Roles* 15(7/8):333-58.

Russell, D. E. H. (1982) *Rape in Marriage.* New York: Macmillan.

Schafran, L. H. (1987) "Practicing Law in a Sexist Society." In L. Crites and W. Hepperle (eds.), *Women, The Courts and Equality.* Newbury Park, CA: Sage.

Stanko, E. A. (1985) Intimate Intrusions: Women's Experience of Male Violence. London:

____. (1990) *Everyday Violence: How Women and Men Experience Physical and Sexual Danger.* London: Pandora.

Warshaw, R. (1988) *I Never Called It Rape.* New York: Free Press.

Zimmer, L. (1986) *Women Guarding Men.* Chicago: University of Chicago Press.

DISCUSSION QUESTIONS

1. What do you think causes sexual harassment?

2. Did these findings surprise you?

3. What can be done to stop sexual harassment in higher education?

4. Do you think the results would be any different if the study was replicated today? Explain.

READING

In this study, Sandra Reynolds examined the types of misconduct addressed by ORI and the National Institutes of Health between 1992 and 2002. She paid particular attention to the characteristics of offenders, types of studies, and sanctions given to offenders. Reynolds focused primarily on misconduct in clinical trials. She found that all of the clinical trial misconduct cases involved falsification or fabrication of data. Plans of supervision were the most common type of sanction given to offenders.

ORI Findings of Scientific Misconduct in Clinical Trials and Publicly Funded Research, 1992–2002

Sandra M. Reynolds

Introduction

Research is a collaborative enterprise in which trust is essential. This trust is violated when scientists report results based on fabricated or falsified data or claim plagiarized work as their own. Misconduct in research funded by government agencies is a misuse of public funds, a point brought home by the hearings conducted by the Oversight and Investigations Subcommittee of the House Energy and Commerce Committee in the late 1980s and 1990s [1]. Several of the cases investigated by the Committee stemmed from allegations of data

SOURCE: Reynolds, S. M. (2004). ORI findings of scientific misconduct in clinical trials and publicly funded research, 1992-2002. *Clinical Trials, 1*, 509-516.

fabrication or falsification in clinical trials, most notably the National Surgical Adjuvant Breast and Bowel Project (NSABP) [2-4]. In the multicenter NSABP, study results and treatment recommendations had already been published when the coordinating center reported that some data from a single clinical center had been falsified. Public reaction to this disclosure showed the extent to which misconduct can shake confidence in trial results. Women whose treatment decisions had been guided by the NSABP's published results feared that their survival had been compromised, and testified to their sense of betrayal in Congressional hearing [5]. The perception of unreliability can weaken public confidence in the validity of evidence based medicine, affect support for future funding, and increase pressure to eliminate scientific misconduct. Since 1992, The Office of Research Integrity has reviewed investigations of scientific misconduct in research funded by the Public Health Service.

History of ORI

The Office of Research Integrity developed through legislation beginning with the 1985 amendment to the Public Health Act which directed the Secretary of Health and Human Services to establish regulations requiring entities which apply for Public Health Service (PHS) funds to report findings of scientific misconduct to the Secretary. The amendment also required the Secretary to set up a process for reviewing these reports of scientific misconduct. These regulations were codified in 42 CFR subpart A which defined scientific misconduct, described the required reporting process, and established the Office of Scientific Integrity (OSI) and the Office of Scientific Integrity Review (OSIR).

In June 1992, OSI and OSIR were consolidated in the Office of Research Integrity (ORI) in the Office of the Assistant Secretary for Health. In addition to being responsible for education and prevention programs in the area of scientific misconduct, ORI was directed to review and monitor investigations of scientific misconduct, conduct inquiries and investigations when necessary, and propose findings of scientific misconduct and suggested sanctions [6]. The NIH Revitalization Act of 1993 established ORI as an independent entity within

the US Department of Health and Human Services [7]. An appeals procedure was introduced in November 1992 and revised in 1994. In 1999, the responsibility for conducting investigations shifted from ORI to the Office of the Inspector General, Department of Health and Human Services, which has subpoena power [8]. ORI continues to review the results of investigations and submit findings and proposed administrative actions to the Assistant Secretary.

Definition of Scientific Misconduct

The evolution of the definition of scientific misconduct has had a long and contentious history [9-12], a full discussion of which is beyond the scope of this paper. Since 1999, ORI has been moving toward the adoption of the Office of Science and Technology Policy definition [10,13: p 1-2]. Proposed changes to Public Health Service policies on scientific misconduct, including the new definition, were recently published for public comment [14]. Throughout the period surveyed, ORI was governed by the definition of scientific misconduct in 42 CFR §50.102:

> Misconduct or Misconduct in Science means fabrication, falsification, plagiarism, or other practices that seriously deviate from those that are commonly accepted within the scientific community for proposing, conducting, or reporting research. It does not include honest error or honest differences in interpretations or judgments of data.

ORI's Procedure

Institutions receiving PHS funds are required to notify ORI at the start of each investigation of scientific misconduct and to give a final report of their conclusion [15]. If on review ORI finds the investigation adequate to support a conclusion of scientific misconduct, this finding and appropriate administrative action are recommended to the Assistant Secretary for Health. Respondents may appeal to the Departmental Appeals Board (DAB) [16].

ORI also receives inquiries from both individuals and institutions [17: p 8]. When an allegation is received, ORI must determine that the alleged misconduct falls within its jurisdiction. That is, it must have occurred in a situation supported by the PHS or in an application for PHS support, and it must satisfy the definition of scientific misconduct cited in 42 CFR § 50.102 above. If the matter falls within its jurisdiction, ORI then determines whether there is sufficient evidence to open a case. ORI may request additional information or may ask the respondent's institution to conduct an investigation. Before the revision of procedure in 1999, ORI could conduct its own investigations. After that time, ORI could recommend that the Office of the Inspector General, HHS conduct an investigation [8, 18: p 1-2].

Although institutions are discouraged from making a finding of scientific misconduct at the inquiry stage without carrying out a full investigation [19], ORI sometimes reported inquiries closed with findings of no scientific misconduct. Cases opened by ORI may be closed administratively when further review establishes that the matter does not involve PHS funding, the evidence proves to be insufficient, or the matter does not fit the definition of scientific misconduct [19]. Institutions must report promptly any indication of criminal activity to ORI which will notify the Office of the Inspector General [15].

Administrative Actions

Many cases of scientific misconduct are concluded by an agreement in which respondents voluntarily exclude themselves from US Government grants and contracts or from participation in certain PHS funded activities for a given time period. In the absence of such an agreement, ORI recommends administrative actions to exclude or limit the respondents' participation. Similar sanctions are imposed in either case. Respondents may be debarred or voluntarily excluded from government grants and contracts or from serving in an advisory capacity to the PHS. They may be subject to supervision, or required to have certification of the accuracy of their work. ORI also compels retraction or correction of publications affected by scientific misconduct.

Debarment is defined in 45 CFR § 76 as "An action taken . . . to exclude a person from participating in covered transactions". Debarred individuals may not receive or benefit from federal funds. They may not receive US Government grants or contracts, and they may not use materials or facilities paid for with these funds. Debarred individuals are placed on the List of Parties Excluded from Federal Procurement and Nonprocurement Programs which is maintained by the General Services Administration [20]. The list is available in print and through the internet [21]. Exception to the debarment may be granted for specific activities [22], but an institution which continues to support the debarred individual with US Government funds without such an exception could face loss of funding [23]. Lesser penalties would allow the respondent to benefit from government funds provided that the specific requirements of the action are met. An individual subject to supervision could receive funds only if the grant application included a plan for the individual's supervision. A respondent who had plagiarized work in the past might be required to present certification that others' contributions are adequately credited in each future submission.

Methods

Summaries of ORI's findings of scientific misconduct are published in the Federal Register, ORI newsletters, and the NIH Guide for Grants and Contracts [24]. ORI annual reports reprint these summaries and also give brief accounts of investigations concluded with findings of no scientific misconduct [13, 17, 18, 25-32]. Each report from the establishment of ORI in May 1992 through the end of 2002 was read to identify cases in which a clinical trial was the setting of the purported misconduct.

Exceptions to debarment were drawn from the annual reports [26: p 21, 27: p 13-15, 17-18, 28: p 41-42, 45-48, 31: p 29]. For five of the six cases reported in 1996, details of the exceptions were published in the NIH Guide for Grants and Contracts [33-36]. Reports of cases closed during this time period with a finding of no scientific misconduct sometimes note that the alleged misconduct occurred in the context of a "clinical trial".

These instances were tabulated, but it is possible that clinical trials were involved in more cases closed with findings of no scientific misconduct in which the words "clinical trial" did not appear. Where no scientific misconduct was found, identifying information was removed from the report unless the respondent had asked to be identified. This prevented identification of clinical trials in which scientific misconduct had been alleged but not found. In some years, ORI reported both inquiries and investigations closed with findings of no scientific misconduct. For consistency, only investigations are considered here. Decisions of the DAB are published in full on the worldwide web [37] and summarized in the annual reports.

 Results

From 1993 to 2002, ORI reported 249 closed cases in annual reports (Table 6.2). Six more cases of scientific misconduct were published in the NIH Guide for Grants and Contracts in 1993, but were not included in the annual report for that year. Altogether, scientific misconduct was found in 136 cases. Investigations were closed with no finding of scientific misconduct in 108 cases and 11 cases were closed administratively. ORI annual reports from 1993 to 2002 summarize three DAB decisions affirming ORI's findings and three concluding that ORI failed to prove its case by the preponderance of the evidence. Two cases were not decided

Table 6.2   Disposition of Closed Investigations

Year	Misconduct	No Misconduct	Administrative Closure	Total Closed Investigations
1993	10	6	0	16
1994	11	14	1	26
1995	24	14	3	41
1996	17	19	2	38
1997	14	14	1	29
1998	9	12	0	21
1999	12[a]	10	1	23
2000	7	6	1	14
2001	14	4	1	19
2002	12[b]	9	1	22
Total from Annual Reports	130	108	11	249
From 1993 NIH Guide for Grants and Contracts	6			
Findings of scientific misconduct	136			

a. Two cases summarized for one individual are tabulated only once.
b. One case summarized in the annual report was a duplicate from the previous year.

because the appeal was withdrawn or the respondent agreed to a voluntary exclusion.

Of the 136 cases of scientific misconduct reported, 17 (13%) occurred in clinical trials, 19 (14%) in other clinical research, 78 (57%) in basic research and five (4%) in other research. In 17 (13%) cases, the type of research could not be determined from the summary (Table 6.3). Debarment was applied in 85 (63%) cases. In 129 (95%) cases, respondents were excluded from serving in an advisory capacity to the PHS. Requirements for supervision of work or certification of accuracy were imposed in 65 (48%) cases. Sanctions could occur in any combination. Exceptions to debarment were granted in 13 cases. One report did not indicate the excepted activity. The remaining 12 allowed support for nonresearch activities including training or practice in clinical medicine (10 cases), nursing (one case) and clinical laboratory (one case). One exception allowed "Federal funds used for purposes of teaching or training medical students, residents, or fellows, in clinical matters" [31: p 29]. Another excepted student loans and educational grants for nonresearch training [33], Of the 52 cases where debarment was not imposed, 49 respondents were subject to supervision or certification of future work (Table 6.3). One respondent received no sanction from ORI because the institution's administrative action was deemed sufficient [26: p 19], and another respondent was excluded only from serving in an advisory capacity to the PHS. The most frequent offence was fabrication or falsification of data which occurred in 119 (88%) cases. Falsification of credentials was cited in 11 (8%) cases and plagiarism in 14 (10%).

All of the 17 cases of misconduct in clinical trials involved fabrication or falsification of data (Table 6.4). Only six (35%) respondents were debarred from US Government funding (Table 6.5). The remaining 11 (65%) were permitted to continue to work in positions funded by the PHS provided that the funded institution submitted a plan for supervision of their work. In contrast, debarment was applied in 79 (66%) of the 119 cases of scientific misconduct in other types of research. Only three (18%) respondents in clinical trials held doctorates compared with 81 (60%) in all other types of research combined.

In clinical trials, debarment was imposed upon the two respondents in faculty positions, two clinic coordinators, one medical student and one employee. Two of the three respondents with doctorates were

Table 6.3   Sanction by Type of Research

Type of Research	Debarment From Funding[a]		Funding Subject to Supervision or Certification[b]		Neither		Total	
	n	(%)	n	(%)	n	(%)	n	(%)
Basic	59	(76)	18	(23)	1	(1)	78	(57)
Clinical trial	6	(35)	11	(65)			17	(13)
Other clinical	9	(47)	10	(53)			19	(14)
Other	3	(60)	1	(20)	1	(20)	5	(4)
Not specified	8	(47)	9	(53)			17	(13)
Total	85	(63)	49	(36)	2	(1)	136	

a. May include other sanctions.
b. Not debarred.

debarred. One of these was a principal investigator and the second, who was cited for falsifying data in a grant application, may have been the principal investigator as well.

However senior investigators were not always held accountable for misconduct which occurred under their supervision. Clinical trials were noted in 12 (11%) of the 108 brief reports of investigations closed with

Table 6.4   Scientific Misconduct in Clinical Trials by Position of Respondent

Acts Cited	Faculty	Clinic Coordinator	Data Coordinator/ Manager	Employee/ Staff	Research Assistant	Medical Student	Interviewer/ Counselor	Total
Switched randomization assignment for four pairs of patients							1	1
Fabricated or falsified preenrollment test data	1		2					3
Falsified entry criteria and follow-up data. Forged signature on consent form			1					1
Fabricated or falsified follow-up data			1					1
Fabricated or falsified lab results, test dates. Falsely reported prerandomization evaluation. Falsely reported that procedures were performed by certified personnel		1						1
Falsified monthly logs and Human Investigation Committee research approval forms				1				1
Falsely reported that measurements were done according to study protocol				1				1
Altered nuclear magnetic resonance data in grant application	1							1
Fabricated data for three environmental intervention forms for visits not made and two phone calls not made							1	1
Fabrication or falsification not further specified		1		3	1	1		4
Total	2	2	4	5	1	1	2	17

Table 6.5   Administrative Actions Imposed in Cases of Scientific Misconduct in Clinical Trials by Position of Respondent

Position of Respondent	Years Debarred From Funding				Years Excluded From PHS Boards			Years Supervision			Total
	0	2	3	8	0	3	8	0	1	3	
Faculty			1	1		1	1	2			2
Clinic coordinator			2		1	1		2			2
Data coordinator/manager	4					4				4	4
Employee/staff	4	1				5			1[a]	4	5
Research assistant	1					1				1	1
Medical student			1			1		1			1
Interviewer/counselor	2					2				2	2
Total	11	1	4	1	1	15	1	5	1	11	17

a. Year of supervision follows 2-year debarment.

finding of no scientific misconduct. Four of these reports point to mismanagement or lack of supervision as a cause of the erroneous data [13: p 34, 28: p 56, 30: p 24-25]. In two of those cases, the respondent was a principal investigator or senior clinical trial investigator. One report noted that the senior clinical trial investigator had not provided adequate training for the nurse coordinator, but "the respondent was not the individual responsible for apparently altered data submitted to the coordinating center" [30: p 25]. In the other case, the report stated that, "The institution concluded that the respondent had neglected some of his responsibility as PI by not responding to and correcting recurring problems regarding data that had been submitted to the coordinating center" [30: p 24], but was not responsible for submitting seven falsified monthly logs to the coordinating center and altering several research approval forms. The absence of identifying information makes it difficult to link these gentle rebukes of senior investigators with corresponding reports of scientific misconduct. Nevertheless, the latter case is very likely the same as a subsequent one in which a former clinical trial employee was subject to three years of supervision for the very acts of scientific misconduct for which her PI had been absolved of responsibility [13, p 28-29]. It is worth noting that at the conclusion of the case this individual was no longer employed on the trial which freed the principal investigator from devising a plan for her supervision. He was not required to submit a plan for "responding to and correcting recurring problems in his center's data".

 Discussion

Scientific misconduct in clinical trials accounted for 17(13%) of the cases reported by ORI from May 1992 to 2002. Whether this is proportional to the number of clinical trials funded by the PHS is difficult to determine. Most recently, Nathan and Wilson reported the number of awards and amount of funds allocated for clinical research, including grants for research projects, training grants, career awards and contracts, in each of the years 1996–2001 [38]. The number of awards ranged from 2767 to 3874 or 24-27% of all awards. This accords well with the combined percent of clinical trials (13%) and other clinical research (14%) in the cases decided by ORI. Nathan and Wilson did not report the proportion of awards to clinical trials, but they remarked that clinical trials accounted for about a third of funding for clinical research. Funding for clinical research ranged from 32 to 38% of all funding [38], implying clinical trial funding of ~11-13%.

Rather than debarment, a plan of supervision was required in 65% of 17 cases of scientific misconduct in clinical trials, suggesting that the respondent was a subordinate whose work could be overseen effectively. This sanction does not address problems in trial design or supervision which may have contributed to misconduct in the first place. If the employee had left the trial, the principal investigator had no obligation to draw up a plan for improved supervision.

During the period of this survey, ORI's oversight of scientific misconduct investigations was limited by the definition of scientific misconduct in 42 CFR § 50:102. This definition has been criticized as both too broad and too narrow. It includes the vague and potentially troublesome "other practices that seriously deviate" clause which could stifle innovation [39]. On the other hand it excludes "honest error". The DAB clarified that negligence in research does not constitute misconduct, and charged ORI with the burden of proving that the alleged misconduct was not simple error [9, 40]. Nevertheless, incompetence and negligence constitute poor stewardship of research funds. Steneck has suggested that, "It could be the case that more public funds are wasted and more error creeps into research through carelessness and sloppiness than through intentional misconduct" [41]. The proposed policy changes would shift the burden of proof to the respondent. "Once the institution or HHS makes a prima facie showing of research misconduct, the respondent has the burden of proving any affirmative defenses raised, including any honest error or difference of opinion. . ." [14]. The proposed definition also drops

"other practices which seriously deviate", but a finding of research misconduct would require a "significant departure from accepted practices of the relevant research community" [14].

The causes of scientific misconduct can be complex [11]. ORI proceedings sanction a limited, specifically defined set of offenses. Suggestions for a more substantive approach to the problem include broadening the definition of scientific misconduct, promoting education in good research practice, decreasing pressures to publish and adopting wider use of data audits. Resnik suggests that the purpose of a definition can be multifold, encompassing promoting education and setting moral and political goals, as well as establishing clear and enforceable rules. A narrow, legalistic definition encourages compliance with a minimum standard rather than aspiration toward exemplary behavior. He proposes a definition which takes account of a continuum of ethical lapses with punishable misconduct at one end [11]. Goldner suggests that legal concepts clarify some of the issues in prosecution of scientific misconduct [9]. He cites Dresser's proposal that "culpable mental state concepts" from the Model Penal Code be applied in the development of graded sanctions. Misconduct committed purposely, knowingly or recklessly would be severely punished, but negligence would be handled by the institution at which it occurred "through education, close supervision, and other remedial activities" [42]. Rennie and Gunsalus argued against including culpable mental state concepts in the definition of misconduct, observing that consideration of culpability interfered with a clear-headed determination of fact [43]. They proposed ". . . defining precisely what constitutes good scientific practices and desirable behavior in specific areas. These should include data recording and retention, authorship practices, and student mentoring" [43].

Establishment of training programs in responsible conduct of research has been a requirement of NIH training grants since at 1990. ORI proposed a policy change to extend the requirement to all institutions which apply for PHS funds. After being submitted for comment, the final policy was published in December 2000 and suspended in February 2001 after a Congressional request for review [44]. In 2002,

ORI noted that this review had been completed [32]. The policy had not been reenacted as of this writing. In a review of research on the effectiveness of these programs of education in the responsible conduct of research, Steneck found the evidence to be inconclusive [45]. He claimed stronger evidence for the effectiveness of data audits, observing, "If results matter, then one of the most effective ways to educate researchers about their responsibilities may be to check more carefully the work they produce" [45].

Good scientific practice, education and monitoring are especially important in multicenter trials with their distribution of responsibility for observing study protocol in patient recruitment, treatment administration and data integrity. Knatterud and colleagues note that quality assurance should be incorporated into the study design from the start [46]. The plan should encompass clear communication of study procedure, training of investigators, monitoring and data quality assurance procedures, as well as plans for detecting fraud and dealing with misconduct. A clearly written protocol and manual of procedures, carefully developed data collection forms, and training of investigators can help prevent errors [46]. Study design must include adequate training to certify (and periodically recertify) study personnel as competent to carry out their responsibilities [47]. Ongoing oversight is necessary. Planned site visits not only deter misconduct, but also allow for early detection and correction of deviations from protocol [46]. Central review of data by alert personnel and routine reports that call attention to unusual center performance can facilitate the detection of fraud [46,48].

In a long-running trial, all personnel should be reminded periodically of the importance of protocol adherence and accurate and timely data reporting. However, regular reminders and discussion have become more difficult as funds for meetings of all study personnel have been constrained so that meetings are held less frequently and the participating personnel have been restricted to senior investigators. Finally, study leaders should establish the standard of conduct expected of all participating investigators and personnel early in the clinical trial and be prepared to take preventive or corrective actions whenever and wherever required.

References

1. Dingell JD. Shattuck lecture —misconduct in medical research. *N Engl J Med* 1993; 328: 1610-15.
2. What is truth? (editorial). *Lancet* 1994; 343: 1443-44.
3. Sawyer K. NIH chiefs rebuked over fraud. *Washington Post* April 14, 1994: Al.
4. Seachrist L. NIH tightens clinical trials Monitoring. *Science* 1994; 264: 499.
5. Altaian LK. Officials apologize for delay in uncovering falsified data in cancer study. *New York Times* April 14, 1994: A17.
6. 57 Fed. Reg. 24262 (1992).
7. 42 USC § 289b.
8. Office of Research Integrity, about ORI, historical background, http://ori.dhhs.gov/html/about/historical.asp updated April 26, 2002 (last accessed 03/23/04).
9. Goldner JA. The unending saga of legal controls over scientific misconduct: a clash of cultures needing resolution. Am J Law Med 1998; 24: 293-343.
10. 65 Fed. Reg. 76260 (2000).
11. Resnik DB. From Baltimore to Bell Labs: reflections on two decades of debate about scientific misconduct. *Account Research* 2003; 10: 123-35.
12. Shamoo AE, Resnik DB. *Responsible conduct of research.* New York: Oxford University Press 2003, 99-103.
13. US Department of Health and Human Services, Office of the Secretary, Office of Public Health and Science. ORI Annual Report 1999.
14. 69 ed. Reg. 20777-20803 (2004).
15. 42 CFR §50.103-104
16. Office of Research Integrity, about ORI, function, http://ori.dhhs.gov/html/about/function.asp updated March 17, 2004 (last accessed 03/23/04).
17. Department of Health and Human Services, Office of the Assistant Secretary for Health. ORI Annual Report 1993. September 1994.
18. Department of Health and Human Services, Office of the Secretary Office of Public Health and Science. ORI Annual Report 2001, July 2002.
19. Office of Research Integrity. Handling misconduct; ORI addresses issues in inquiries and investigations, http://ori.dhhs.gov/html/misconduct/inquiry_issue-s.asp August 14, 2003 (last accessed 11/26/03).
20. 48 CFR § 9.404.
21. Excluded Parties Listing System, http://epls.arnet.gov (last accessed 7/14/04).
22. 45 CFR §76.120.
23. 45 CFR § 76.225.
24. National Institutes of Health, Office of Extramural Research, NIH guide: notices, http://grantsl.nih.gov/ grants/guide/notice-files (last accessed April 6, 2004).
25. Office of Research Integrity. ORI annual reports. http://ori.dhhs.gov/html/publications/annual-report-s.asp updated Nov 29, 2003 (last accessed 03/23/04).

26. Department of Health and Human Services, Office of the Assistant Secretary for Health. ORI Annual Report 1994. April 1995.

27. Department of Health and Human Services, Office of the Secretary, Office of Public Health and Science. ORI Annual Report 1995. July, 1996.

28. Department of Health and Human Services, Office of the Secretary, Office of Public Health and Science. ORI Annual Report 1996.

29. Department of Health and Human Services, Office of the Secretary, Office of Public Health and Science. ORI Annual Report 1997.

30. Department of Health and Human Services, Office of the Secretary, Office of Public Health and Science. ORI Annual Report 1998.

31. Department of Health and Human Services, Office of the Secretary, Office of Public Health and Science. ORI Annual Report 2000.

32. Department of Health and Human Services, Office of the Secretary, Office of Public Health and Science. ORI Annual Report 2002. November 2003.

33. US Department of Health and Human Services. NIH Publication not96-080. Bethesda, Maryland: US Department of Health and Human Services, 1996. also available on the internet at http://grantsl.nih.gov/grants/guide/notice-files (last accessed April 6, 2004).

34. US Department of Health and Human Services. NIH Publication not96-114. Bethesda, Maryland: US Department of Health and Human Services, 1996. also available on the internet at http://grantsl.nih.gov/grants/guide/notice-files.

35. US Department of Health and Human Services. NIH Publication not96-l77. Bethesda, Maryland: US Department of Health and Human Services, 1996. also available on the internet at http://grantsl.nih.gov/grants/guide/notice-files.

36. US Department of Health and Human Services. NIH Publication not96-125. Bethesda, Maryland: US Department of Health and Human Services, 1996. also available on the internet at http://grantsl.nih.gov/grants/guide/notice-files.

37. Office of Research Integrity, Departmental Appeals Board decisions and rulings, http://ori.dhhs.gov/html/ programs/dabrulings.asp (last accessed April 6, 2004).

38. Nathan DG, Wilson JD. Clinical research and the NIH -a report card. *N Engl J Med* 2003; 349: 1860-65.

39. Silverstein SC. Statement of Samuel C. Silverstein, MD to the Commission on Research Integrity. FASEB Newsletter 1994; 27: 6-7.

40. US Department of Health and Human Services, Office of Research Integrity, Departmental Appeals Board. Dr Rameshwar K. Sharma, DAB No. 1431 at 13 (1993). Available at Office of Research Integrity, Departmental Appeals Board decisions and rulings, http: //ori.dhhs .gov/html/programs/dabrulings.asp.

41. Steneck NH. Tensions of the times: science and scientists. *J NIH Research* 1996; 8: 26-29.

42. Dresser R. Defining scientific misconduct; the relevance of mental state. *JAMA* 1993; 269: 895-97.

43. Rennie D, Gunsalus CK. Scientific misconduct, new definition, procedures, and office—perhaps a new leaf. *JAMA* 1993;269:915-17.

44. Office of Research Integrity responsible conduct of research (RCR) education, http://ori.dhhs.gov/html/ programs/congressionalconcern sresponse.asp (last accessed 08/12/04).

45. Steneck NH. Assessing the integrity of publicly funded research, in Office of Research Integrity, Investigating research integrity: proceeding of the first ORI research conference on research integrity, 2000.

46. Knatterud GL, Rockhold FW, George SL et al. Guidelines for quality assurance in multicenter trials: a position paper. *Control Clin Trials* 1998; 19: 477-93.

47. DeMets DL. Distinctions between fraud, bias, errors, misunderstanding, and incompetence. *Control Clin Trials* 1997; 18: 637-50.

48. DeMets DL, Meinert CL. Data integrity. *Control Clin Trials* 1991; 12: 727-30.

DISCUSSION QUESTIONS

1. What patterns appear in terms of the types of individuals cited for misconduct?

2. What do you think about the sanctions given to the offenders?

3. Do you think misconduct happens more or less often in criminal justice research? Explain.

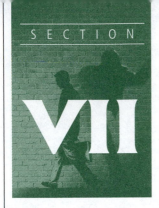

VII

Crime in the Economic and Technological Systems

 Introduction

Many readers likely have Facebook pages. When visiting your friends' pages, tagging their photos, making cute comments on their posts, and posting information yourself, you likely have given very little thought to how Facebook relates to white-collar crime. Believe it or not, the social networking site relates to white-collar crime in four ways. First, some people (when they are supposed to be working) spend time lurking through their friends' Facebook pages. Second, some workers have actually lost their jobs for information they posted on Facebook pages. Third, the computer technology that makes Facebook possible is the same technology that provides the opportunity for computer crimes by white-collar offenders. Fourth, Mark Zuckerberg—the founder of Facebook—has been accused of various white-collar crimes related to his creation of the website and the administration of it.

As an undergraduate student at Harvard, Zuckerberg worked for Divya Narenda and Cameron and Tyler Winklevoss on a social network called ConnectU. After his experiences at ConnectU, Zuckerberg created Facebook, but was sued by his former bosses on the grounds that he stole ConnectU's source code to create Facebook. So, his first accusation of white-collar crime was for copyright infringement (or theft of computer

▲ **Photo 7.1** From student to creator of Facebook, Mark Zuckerberg has faced his share of accusations of white-collar misconduct.

codes). Eventually, the parties reached an out-of-court settlement where ConnectU was sold to Facebook and the owners were given $65 million, with much of the payment being in the form of shares in Facebook. Later, however, it was learned that the stocks included in the settlement agreement were actually worth much less than what the ConnectU creators were led to believe.

It was eventually determined that the settlement was paid in cheaper shares (known as preferred shares) rather than the more expensive shares (known as common shares). The result—the original owners appealed the out-of-court settlement and accused Zuckerberg of securities fraud (Thomas, 2010). So, his second accusation of white-collar crime arose. The court subsequently found in favor of Zuckerberg. Interestingly, while these allegations were being reviewed, some unwelcome information about Zuckerberg surfaced. While a 19-year-old Harvard student, Zuckerberg instant messaged a college friend the following comments about the information social networkers sent in to be posted on ConnectU: "People just submitted it. I don't know why. They 'trust' me. Dumb fu**s" (Carlson, 2010). The instant message he sent years ago came to light while Facebook users were criticizing the site for its lax privacy policies. Thus, a third possible allegation of white-collar crime has surfaced—misuse of computer information.

Incidentally, Divya Narenda—the one who sued Zuckerberg after he created Facebook—joined Facebook in 2008 (Carlson, 2009). Perhaps with too much time on my hands, I checked to see if Narenda had "friended" Zuckerberg. At the time of the writing of this book, he had not.

The accusations against Zuckerberg are examples of the kinds of white-collar crimes occurring in the economic and technological systems. Zuckerberg is not alone in being accused of misconduct occurring in these systems. Consider the following examples quoted verbatim from their original sources:

- A contract security guard at the North Central Medical Plaza on North Central Expressway in Dallas, pleaded guilty . . . to felony offenses related to his compromising and damaging the hospital's computer system . . . [the defendant], a/k/a "Ghost Exodus," 25, of Arlington, Texas pleaded guilty to an indictment charging two counts of transmitting a malicious code. . . . [The defendant] gained physical access to more than 14 computers located in the North Central Medical Plaza, including a nurses' station computer on the fifth floor and a heating, ventilation and air conditioning (HVAC) computer located in a locked room. The nurses' station computer was used to track a patient's progress through the Carrell Memorial Clinic and medical staff also used it to reference patients' personal identifiers, billing records and medical history. . . . [The defendant] installed, or transmitted, a program to the computers that he accessed that allowed him, or anyone with his account name and password, to remotely access the computers. He also impaired the integrity of some of the computer systems by removing security features, e.g., uninstalling anti-virus programs, which made the computer systems and related network more vulnerable to attack. (U.S. Department of Justice, 2010a, May 14)

- ***** appeared before U.S. Magistrate Judge Nancy A. Vecchiarelli and pleaded guilty to a two-count Information filed on May 14, 2010, which charged ***** with causing damage to a protected computer system and possessing 15 or more unauthorized access devices. According to court documents, ***** admitted that between August 2006, and March 2007, while enrolled as a student at the University of Akron, he used the University's computer network to access IRC channels on the Internet to control other computers and computer networks via computers intentionally infected and taken over, known as "BotNet" zombies, which were located throughout the United States and in other countries. (U.S. Department of Justice, 2010b)

- The Securities and Exchange Commission today charged a former Citigroup investment banker for repeatedly tipping his brother about upcoming merger deals in an insider trading scheme that involved friends and family throughout Northern California and the Midwest and reaped more than $6 million in illicit profits. The SEC alleges that *****, a former director in Citigroup Global Markets' investment banking division in New York, repeatedly told his brother Michael Kara of Walnut Creek, Calif., about upcoming deals involving Citigroup's health care industry clients. The SEC further alleges that *****, in addition to buying stock and options in target companies that were the subject of the Citigroup deals, leaked the information to a network of friends and family who also traded in advance of the deals. The SEC has charged the ***** brothers and six others in the case. (Securities and Exchange Commission [SEC], 2009b)

These examples demonstrate the breadth of offenses that are committed in the economic and technological systems. These two systems share several similarities. These similarities include:

- Both systems cross international boundaries.
- The two systems are more interdependent than independent—the economic system relies on technology to survive and the technological system requires economic advances to grow.
- Workers in these systems typically possess specialized knowledge about the careers operating in the systems.
- White-collar crimes occur in both systems.

With the term *white-collar offender*, it is often images of offenders from the economic or technological systems that come to mind. Prominent white-collar offenders who committed crimes against at least one of these systems include Bernie Madoff, Ken Lay, Martha Stewart, Michael Milken, and others. While many people recognize these names, the actual behaviors that got them into trouble are less understood. In this section, attention is given to white-collar crimes committed in the economic and technological systems.

Crime in the Economic System

The economic system includes banks, investment companies, stock markets across the world, commodities markets, and other exchanges/markets where individuals are able to make investments, purchase raw materials, and secure goods. Generally speaking, crimes in the economic system can be classified as investment frauds. In describing these behaviors, real examples are discussed in order to better illustrate each offense type.

 ## Investment Fraud

Investment fraud occurs when investments made by consumers are managed or influenced fraudulently by stockbrokers or other officials in the economic system. **Securities and commodities fraud** is a broad concept capturing a range of behaviors designed to rip off investors. At the broadest level, securities fraud refers to fraudulent activities related to stocks, bonds, and mutual funds. Consider a case where Andrew McKevley, the former head of the employment recruitment firm Monster Nationwide Inc., was charged with fraud and conspiracy after he backdated several employees' stock options. In doing so, the value of their stock options was fraudulently changed. In another case, four executives were convicted after backdating contracts and filing false SEC documents, lying in press releases, and being dishonest with the company's own auditors (Taub, 2006). Again, these actions were done to increase the value of the company's stocks. In Focus 7.1 provides an overview of how one investment advisor "went bad."

In Focus 7.1

When Investment Advisors Go Bad

The sole owner and president of Magnolia Capital Advisors, a registered investment adviser [was convicted of securities fraud].

This Decision bars Don Warner Reinhard (Reinhard) from association with any broker or dealer or investment adviser. He was previously enjoined from violating the antifraud provisions of the federal securities laws, based on his wrongdoing while associated with a registered investment adviser and a registered broker-dealer in trading collateralized mortgage obligations. Additionally, he was convicted of several federal crimes involving dishonest conduct. . . .

His May 13, 2009, Plea Agreement includes a Factual Basis for Plea that describes Reinhard's conduct that violated each of the above provisions. Reinhard was sentenced to fifty-one months of imprisonment and ordered to pay restitution of $667,890.28 and a special assessment of $700.

As set forth in the Factual Basis for Plea, Reinhard committed numerous dishonest acts. For example, in order to obtain a $223,245 boat loan in 2003 to fund a $265,394 purchase of a boat, Reinhard submitted financial documents to a bank that included a copy of his purported income tax return that grossly inflated his income as compared with the income stated on the return that he

(Continued)

(Continued)

actually filed. In 2006, he filed a voluntary petition for bankruptcy and failed to disclose numerous significant assets, such as the boat, other objects, and investment accounts. Additionally, Reinhard falsely represented that he had made no gifts of $200 or more during the preceding year, when in fact he had paid $20,240 for plastic surgery for his girlfriend, paid off $7,554 of her car loan, and paid $11,200 into her bank account during that timeframe. While the bankruptcy proceeding was pending, he transferred unreported assets, and deposited most of the approximately $40,000 in proceeds in his girlfriend's bank account. Additionally, he filed materially false tax returns for 2001, 2002, and 2005, that included false representations including overstating expenses and understating income. The amount of intended loss involved in the bank, bankruptcy, and tax fraud was approximately $995,874. . . .

Reinhard will be barred from association with a broker-dealer or an investment adviser. His criminal conduct was egregious, involved a high degree of scienter, and was recurrent, extending over a period of three years. His occupation, if he were allowed to continue it, would present opportunities for future violations of the securities laws. The degree of harm to investors and the marketplace from the conduct underlying Reinhard's antifraud injunction is quantified in his ill-gotten gains of $5,857,241.09 plus prejudgment interest of $2,258,940.58 that the court ordered disgorged. . . . Even disregarding the injunction entered by default or assuming *arguendo* that Reinhard was the victim, not the perpetrator, of conduct referenced in the injunctive complaint, as he has suggested in this proceeding, his criminal conduct shows a lack of honesty and indicates that he is unsuited to function in the securities industry. The degree of harm to the public from the conduct underlying his criminal conviction was approximately $995,874. Bars are also necessary for the purpose of deterrence.

Commodities fraud is defined as the "fraudulent sale of commodities investments" (FBI, 2009b). **Commodities** are raw materials like natural gas, oil, gold, agricultural products, and other tangible products that are sold in bulk form. Consider a case where one offender was convicted after he convinced 1,000 victims to invest in commodities such as oil, gold, and silver. The problem was that the commodities did not exist ("Kingpin of Commodities Fraud," 2006).

Commodities fraud is believed to be particularly prevalent in Florida. In 2006, one-fourth of advisories of enforcement activities by the Commodity Futures Trading Commission were tied to companies in Florida. It is believed that the weather, proximity to other countries, and established telemarketing firms contributed to the high rate of commodities fraud in that state (Katz, 2007).

While "securities and commodities" fraud is a general label given to fraud in the economic system, several specific varieties of these frauds exist. These include:

- Market manipulation
- Broker embezzlement
- Hedge fund fraud
- Insider trading
- Futures trading fraud

- Foreign exchange fraud, high yield investment schemes, and advanced fee fraud
- Ponzi and pyramid schemes

Each of these is discussed below. Because most white-collar crime students have likely had little exposure to the workings of the stock market and other financial institutions, where appropriate, analogies to the experiences of college students are made in an effort to better demonstrate the context surrounding the offenses. After discussing these fraud types, attention will be given to Bernie Madoff's historic scheme and patterns surrounding these offenses, with a specific focus on the consequences of these frauds for individuals, community members, and society at large.

Market Manipulation

Market manipulation refers to situations where executives or other officials do things to artificially inflate trading volume and subsequently affect the price of the commodity or security. This is sometimes called "pump and dump" because participants will "pump" up the price of the stocks by sharing false information in chat rooms, e-mails, or other forums before "dumping" (or selling) the stocks that have been artificially inflated (FBI, 2009b).

A scene from the classic Rodney Dangerfield film *Back to School* comes to mind. Thornton Melon (the likable nouveau riche character Dangerfield was playing) was standing in a long line with his son and two of his son's friends, waiting to register for classes, when he thought of a way to make the line shorter. He had his chauffeur stand in front of his limousine with a sign that read "Bruce Springsteen" on it. Eventually word spread through the registration area that "The Boss" was in the limo and all of the students stampeded out of the registration hall to get to the limo. Melon and the other three were immediately at the front of the line and able to register for their courses. In effect, Melon's lie had manipulated others to behave differently. In terms of market manipulation, officials share false information to get others to invest differently, and by dumping their own stocks after prices increase, they profit from their lies.

Market manipulation is believed to be pervasive in the natural energy industry, particularly in the gas and electricity markets. In fact, according to some, market manipulation is partly to blame for the unprecedented energy crisis in California in the early 2000s, a crisis that threatened to make the state go bankrupt (Oppel, 2003). Not surprisingly, market manipulation has been described as a "contentious topic" in energy markets (Pirrong, 2010). Energy industry leaders make a distinction between "market power" manipulation and "fraud-based" manipulation. Market power manipulation strategies manipulate the market through aggressive buying and selling strategies. Fraud-based manipulation strategies manipulate the market by distorting information (Pirrong, 2010).

The Enron scandal included fraud-based market manipulations. Among other things, the energy giant's operatives "used names such as 'Fat Boy,' 'Death Star,' 'Get Shorty,' and 'Ricochet' for programs to transfer energy out of California to evade price caps and to create phony transmission congestion" (Bredemeier, 2002, p. A04). The strategies allowed the company to charge a higher price for the energy it was supplying than what the energy was worth. Enron executives unjustly profited more than $1.1 billion from these efforts.

Three federal statutes exist to "prohibit manipulation of various energy commodities and empower federal agencies to impose penalties" (Pirrong, 2010). These laws include the Commodity Exchange Act, the Energy Policy Act of 2005, and the Energy Independence and Security Act of 2007. This latter act, in particular, calls upon the Federal Trade Commission to treat market manipulations by petroleum and oil company insiders as false and deceptive business practices that could be subjected to fines of up to one million dollars.

Broker Fraud and Embezzlement

Broker fraud occurs when stockbrokers fail to meet their legal obligations to investors. It is believed that "one of the most common frauds is brokers omitting important types of information that investors need to make intelligent decisions about where to put their money" (Knox, 1997, p. 56). Imagine if your professor failed to tell you about the due date for a paper and then held you accountable for not turning the paper in on time? Omitting useful information can create negative consequences for investors.

Broker embezzlement occurs when brokers take money that is supposed to be in an investment account and use it for their own personal use (Ackerman, 2001). Trust is an important element of these offenses. Investor-broker relationships are built on trust. It is not uncommon to hear of situations where fraudulent brokers developed that trust through forming relationships at various institutions that have historically been seen as trustful. Consider the case of Gregory Loles, a broker accused of stealing more than two million dollars from three parishioners of St. Barbara's Greek Orthodox Church in Easton, Connecticut. Loles "allegedly used the funds to support his private businesses" (McCready & Tinley, 2009).

Hedge Fund Fraud

Somewhat similar to broker embezzlement, **hedge fund fraud** refers to fraudulent acts perpetrated in **hedge fund systems.** A hedge fund is a "private investment partnership . . . [with] high net worth clients" (FBI, 2009b). Problems that arise include situations where the hedge fund managers overstate the assets in a fund in an effort to lie to the investors about their investments. In one case, a hedge fund manager mailed investors false statements making it appear as if the investors' accounts were doing well, when in fact the accounts had lost money. While hedge fund managers have many motives for lying, in this particular case the manager did it so he could continue to receive the 2% fee for managing the account. One client was led to believe he had $6.3 million, when all he had was $173,000. Think about the 2% commission—2% of $6.3 million is $126,000. By continuing to make the investor think he had more than six million dollars, the hedge fund manager was able to collect $126,000 in commission—just on this client alone!

As an analogy, consider a situation where a college or university fraternity has a tight-knit group of members who all contribute their membership fees to the treasurer. The treasurer is supposed to transfer the fees to the national membership, but steals the funds instead. While not exactly hedge fund fraud, such a situation would be similar in that the deception integrates the dynamics of (a) a privatized/elite partnership and (b) deceit by the trusted manager of the funds.

Various strategies have been suggested for curbing hedge fund fraud. These include hiring external agencies to do internal compliance, developing a hedge fund information depository, and conducting routine assessments of compliance officers with the aim of evaluating their effectiveness (U.S. Government Accountability Office, 2005). Insider trading is a type of fraud that occurs regularly in hedge funds.

▲ **Photo 7.2**   Accused of insider trading, but convicted of perjury.

Insider Trading

Insider trading occurs when individuals share or steal information that "is material in nature" for future investments. The notion of "material in nature" means that the information "must be significant enough to have affected the company's stock price had the information been available to the public" (Leap, 2007, p. 67). Media mogul Martha Stewart was accused of insider trading after it was learned that she sold some ImClone stocks upon hearing that one of the company's drugs was not going to be approved. Ultimately, Stewart was convicted of perjury and not insider trading.

In testimony before the U.S. Senate Judiciary Committee, Linda Chatman Thomsen (2006), who at the time was the Director of the Division of Enforcement for the U.S. Securities and Exchange Commission, provided this historical overview of insider trading:

- In the mid-1980s, information that was illegally traded focused on information about pending takeovers and mergers.
- In the late 1980s and early 1990s, due to the recession, illegally traded information tended to be "bad news" information about upcoming company closings or downsizings.
- In the mid-2000s, illegally traded information tended to involve illegally obtained or distributed information about technology, globalization, mergers, and hedge funds.

Somewhat reflecting Thomsen's assertions, in 2007, *Wall Street Journal* reporter Kara Scannell (2007) penned an article titled, "Insider Trading: It's Back With a Vengeance." Not coincidentally, Thomsen described insider trading as "an enforcement priority" at the time.

To put into perspective why insider trading is so unfair, imagine if the student sitting next to you in your white-collar crime class is dating a student worker from the criminal justice department, and your classmate accesses copies of the exam ahead of time. In the end, the student would have an unfair advantage over the rest of the students in your class. In a similar way, those who receive material information about stocks and other investments have an unfair advantage over the rest of us. Of course, simply receiving the information is not in and of itself criminal; the action becomes illegal when the investor acts on the inside information.

By their very nature, these cases typically involve more than one offender, and in some cases, insider trading schemes may involve several offenders. In November 2009, Preet Bharara, a Manhattan U.S. Attorney, charged nine defendants for their intricate scheme of receiving, selling, and buying inside information. As evidence of the breadth of this case, here is how the SEC summarized this scheme:

The Securities and Exchange Commission today announced insider trading charges against nine defendants in a case involving serial insider trading by a ring of Wall Street traders and hedge funds who made over $20 million trading ahead of corporate acquisition announcements using inside information tipped by an attorney at the international law firm of Ropes & Gray LLP, in exchange for kickbacks. The SEC alleges that Arthur J. Cutillo, an attorney in the New York office of Ropes & Gray, misappropriated from his law firm material, nonpublic information concerning at least four corporate acquisitions or bids involving Ropes & Gray clients. . . . The complaint alleges that Cutillo, through his friend and fellow attorney Jason Goldfarb, tipped inside information concerning these acquisitions to Zvi Goffer, a proprietary trader at the broker-dealer Schottenfeld Group, LLC ("Schottenfeld"). The complaint further alleges that Zvi traded on this information for

▲ **Photo 7.3** Insider trading occurs even at Disneyland. We must protect the magic in more ways than one.

Schottenfeld, and had numerous downstream tippees who also traded on the information, including other professional traders and portfolio managers at two hedge fund advisers. (SEC, 2009c)

In another recent case demonstrating the "group" nature of insider trading, Yonni Sebbag was arrested along with his girlfriend, Disney employee Bonnie Hoxie, in May 2010. Hoxie, an administrative assistant at the resort, acquired insider information on Disney's quarterly earnings and shared that information with her boyfriend. He called 33 different investment companies offering to sell the insider information. Several of the investment companies he called notified the authorities about Sebbag's offers (Johnson, 2010).

Insider trading is attributed to a number of factors, including an increase in the number of mergers, lightly regulated hedge funds, and more complex funding strategies (Scannell, 2007). Scannell also notes that the "rapid trading style" of hedge funds makes it "harder to pin trades on non-public information."

Futures Trading Fraud

Futures trading fraud refers to fraud occurring in the trading of futures contracts and options on the futures trading market. **Futures contracts** are "agreement[s] to buy or sell a given unit of a commodity at some future date" (Schlegel, 1993, p. 60). Brokers "in the pits" buy and sell commodities based on a contract between the investor and the broker. The sale could be contingent on a specific date or a specific value of the commodity.

Schlegel (1993) describes several types of futures trading fraud including prearranged trading, front running, and bucketing. Here is how he describes these schemes:

- **Prearranged trading:** "brokers, or brokers and local brokers, first agree on a price and then act out the trade as a piece of fiction in the pit, thereby excluding other potential bidders from the offering. The prearranged deal ensures a given profit for the colluding traders while denying their customers the best possible price." (p. 63)
- **Front running:** "broker takes advantage of the special knowledge about a pending custom order and trades on his or her own account before executing that order." (p. 63)
- Bucketing: "a floor trader will take a position opposite that of a customer's position, either directly or by using another floor trader, again in collusion." (p. 63)

In each of these actions, the broker unjustly profits from the fraudulent actions. To limit the extent of fraud in the futures markets, in 1974 the Commodity Futures Trading Commission (CFTC) was created.

Sometimes the actions of the fraudulent futures market brokers aren't terribly sophisticated. In a recent case, the CFTC charged a broker for stealing $14 million from 44 different investors. The broker simply stole their funds and bought himself "a $2.4 million house, luxury vehicles, jewelry, and gold bullion instead of trading commodity futures and options contracts" (Danner, 2009).

Foreign Exchange Fraud, High-Yield Investment Schemes, and Advanced Fee Fraud

Other types of securities and commodities fraud include foreign exchange fraud, high yield investment schemes, and advanced fee fraud. **Foreign exchange fraud** occurs when brokers or other officials induce "victims to invest in the foreign currency exchange market" through illegitimate and fraudulent practices (FBI, 2009b). Typically, the frauds involve situations where offenders either don't provide the investor what was promised or they simply take the funds and fail to perform the promised financial transaction.

High yield investment schemes promise investors low-risk or even no-risk investment strategies, when in fact the funds are not actually invested (FBI, 2009b). Sometimes offenders claim to the investor that the investment schemes are backed by the Federal Reserve or the World Bank, when they have no backing whatsoever (Behrmann, 2005). Investors are also told that they are being given access to a "prime" bank, thereby making investors falsely believe that they are a part of an exclusive group of investors in a "private club" (Welch, 2008). The offender fakes the investment and moves it through several international bank accounts, making "the chase futile for the original investors" (Behrmann, 2005).

Advanced fee fraud occurs when investors are promised certain actions in exchange for an upfront fee. Investors are pressured to invest, they pay the broker, and they never receive any services. This is the top online scam reported to the SEC (Welch, 2008). Imagine if your professor charged an advanced fee for a study session, and then the professor doesn't show up for the event. Not only would you be ripped off, you'd probably be a bit angry at the professor.

Ponzi and Pyramid Schemes

Ponzi and pyramid schemes scam investors by paying them from future investors' payments into the offender's scheme. Table 7.1 shows the differences between Ponzi and pyramid schemes. Pyramid schemes recruit individuals by promising them profits from getting others to invest, whereas Ponzi schemes do not require participants to recruit investors. In pyramid schemes, the participants' interactions are generally limited to interactions with the investor who got them to join the scheme; in Ponzi schemes, interactions are often with the individual who created the scheme. The source of payments in both schemes is from new participants—those in pyramid schemes know this, but those in Ponzi schemes do not. Pyramids collapse quickly, but Ponzi schemes may not (SEC, 2009a).

To illustrate how these schemes are developed, consider the basic definitions of the schemes. Here is how the SEC defines **Ponzi schemes:**

A Ponzi scheme is an investment fraud that involves the payment of purported returns to existing investors from funds contributed by new investors. Ponzi scheme organizers often solicit new investors by promising to invest funds in opportunities claimed to generate high returns with little or no risk. In many Ponzi schemes, the fraudsters focus on attracting new money to make promised payments to earlier-stage investors and to use for personal expenses, instead of engaging in any legitimate investment activity.

Table 7.1   Differences Between Pyramid and Ponzi Schemes

	Pyramid Scheme	Ponzi Scheme
Typical "hook"	Earn high profits by making one payment and finding a set number of others to become distributors of a product. The scheme typically does not involve a genuine product. The purported product may not exist or it may only be "sold" within the pyramid scheme.	Earn high investment returns with little or no risk by simply handing over your money; the investment typically does not exist.
Payments/profits	Must recruit new distributors to receive payments.	No recruiting necessary to receive payments.
Interaction with original promoter	Sometimes none. New participants may enter scheme at a different level.	Promoter generally acts directly with all participants.
Source of payments	From new participants—always disclosed.	From new participants—never disclosed.
Collapse	Fast. An exponential increase in the number of participants is required at each level.	May be relatively slow if existing participants reinvest money.

Ponzi schemes have received a great deal of scrutiny in recent times. To understand the increase in these schemes in the United States, it is helpful to understand the history of the schemes. Charles Ponzi was the mastermind behind the first Ponzi scheme (and because the schemes are named after him, this is one of the few white-collar crimes that begins with a capital letter). Promising investors returns of 200%, he developed a scheme in 1919 where he convinced investors to invest in an international postage stamp program. He paid off early investors with funds contributed by new investors. His scheme was uncovered when *The Post* asked Clarence Barrons, who published the *Barron's Financial Report* at the time, to review Ponzi's company. Barron learned that Ponzi's investors were making significant profits without Ponzi actually investing any money. A federal investigation followed and Ponzi eventually pleaded guilty and served 3.5 years in federal prison. He was later convicted in state courts as well (Zuckoff, 2005).

Today, Ponzi schemes seem to be so common in the United States that some have referred to the country as "a Ponzi nation" (2009). One author labeled 2009 as the "Year of the Ponzi" (C. Anderson, 2010). In 2009, 150 Ponzi schemes collapsed, as compared to 40 in 2008. Also, in 2009, one fifth of the SEC's workload was directed toward responding to Ponzi schemes. By comparison, in 2005, just one tenth of their workload was for Ponzi schemes. C. Anderson notes that the financial crisis brought the scams to light more quickly. Investors, in need of funds to respond to the economic downturn, tried to withdraw from their investments only to learn that their investor was actually operating a Ponzi scheme. The most famous of these Ponzi schemes was orchestrated by Bernie Madoff.

Bernie Madoff's Ponzi Scheme: From Armani Suits to a Bulletproof Vest

Bernie Madoff was the mastermind behind what has come to be called the largest Ponzi scheme in the history of the United States. Madoff's scheme was simple. Figure 7.1 shows a time line highlighting Madoff's scheme. Starting in the early 1990s, he marketed his scheme as an exclusive investment opportunity with clients waiting

Figure 7.1 Madoff Time Line

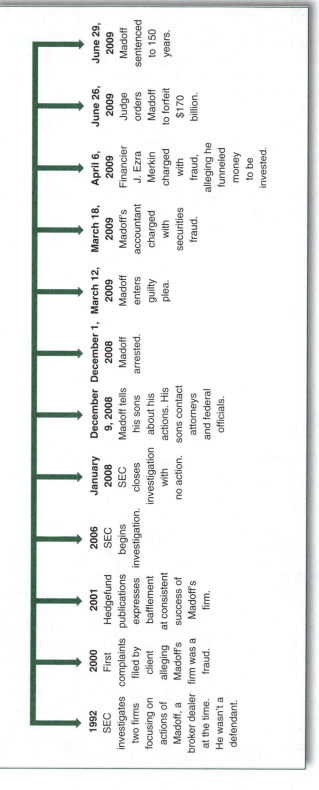

1992
SEC investigates two firms focusing on actions of Madoff, a broker dealer at the time. He wasn't a defendant.

2000
First complaints filed by client alleging Madoff's firm was a fraud.

2001
Hedgefund publications expresses bafflement at consistent success of Madoff's firm.

2006
SEC begins investigation.

January 2008
SEC closes investigation with no action.

December 9, 2008
Madoff tells his sons about his actions. His sons contact attorneys and federal officials.

December 1, 2008
Madoff arrested.

March 12, 2009
Madoff enters guilty plea.

March 18, 2009
Madoff's accountant charged with securities fraud.

April 6, 2009
Financier J. Ezra Merkin charged with fraud, alleging he funneled money to be invested.

June 26, 2009
Judge orders Madoff to forfeit $170 billion.

June 29, 2009
Madoff sentenced to 150 years.

SOURCE: Adapted from McCoy, 2009

a year to be given the opportunity to invest with him (Healy & Syre, 2008). It was a privilege to have Madoff investing on an investor's behalf. Investors sent him millions, but instead of investing the money, he deposited it in a bank account at Chase Manhattan (Healy & Mandell, 2009). Eventually, thousands of investors had invested $65 billion in Madoff's accounts (Glovin, 2009a). Madoff had a few complaints about his activities, which opened up SEC investigations, but the investigations never substantiated wrongdoing.

Madoff's scheme continued for more than 17 years. Two elements of his scheme allowed it to continue for so long: (1) investors were receiving positive returns on their investments and (2) Madoff was extremely secretive in sharing information about investors' accounts. In terms of positive returns, a hedge fund managed by Madoff averaged a 10.5% annual return over 17 years (at least it appeared to average those returns; Appelbaum, Hilzenrath, & Paley, 2008). With returns like that, investors were likely extremely satisfied with their interactions with Madoff.

Regarding his secretiveness, Madoff provided very little information about his "investments" to his investors. When he was asked questions by his investors about how his investment strategy paid so well, he told investors, "secrecy as to information is a key issue for everyone" (Glovin, 2009b, p. C4). Madoff was so extreme in his secrecy that he did not allow clients electronic "access to their accounts" (Appelbaum et al., 2008). This practice was described by the head of a consulting firm as "extremely secretive, even for the non-transparent world of hedge funds" (Appelbaum et al., 2008).

One day in the fall of 2008, clients asked Madoff to withdraw seven billion dollars. His account, however, did not hold the funds. He called a meeting with his sons and told them about his scheme. The next day, his sons turned their father in to the FBI (Healy & Syre, 2008). Incidentally, his wife "withdrew ten million dollars from a brokerage account the same day her sons turned him in" (Healy, 2009a). On March 12, 2009, Madoff pled guilty to the largest Ponzi scheme to date. At his court hearing he very directly admitted, "I operated a Ponzi scheme through the investment advocacy side of my business" (Glovin, 2009b).

Madoff's victims were stunned by the revelations. Both individual and organizational investors lost huge amounts of funds. Victims included nonprofits and charities that had trusted Madoff to manage their foundation's finances. Several philanthropic organizations lost hundreds of millions and charities experienced large losses. Madoff managed "nearly 45% of Carl and Ruth Shapiro's Family Foundation," which lost 145 million dollars (Healy & Syre, 2008). Jewish charities, in particular, were hit quite hard. The Women's Zionist Organization of America lost 90 million dollars, Yeshiva University lost 14.5 million dollars, and the Eli Weisel Foundation for Humanity lost the 15.2 million it had invested with Madoff. Mark Charendoff, the Jewish Funders Network president, lamented, "It's an atomic bomb in the world of Jewish philanthropy" (Campbell, 2009, p. 70). Madoff's individual victims included well-known clientele such as Sandy Koufax (baseball Hall of Fame pitcher), Fred Wilpon (owner of the New York Mets), Larry King (CNN anchor), Jeffrey Katzenberg (Hollywood mogul), Kevin Bacon (actor), Zsa Zsa Gabor (actress), and John Malkovich (actor) ("Madoff's Victims," 2009). Thousands of others also lost money to Madoff's scheme.

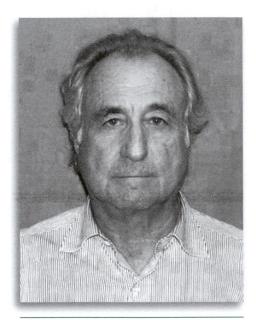

▲ **Photo 7.4** Bernie Madoff operated an enormous Ponzi scheme through the investment advocacy side of his business. When he was sentenced for it, few individuals spoke out on his behalf.

One task that has proven to be particularly difficult has been to accurately estimate the losses. Initially, Yeshiva University was believed to have lost $110 million to the scheme. However, when examining actual losses, they actually lost $14.5 million. Why the discrepancy? Because the university officials (and Madoff's investors) were basing their losses on amounts that Madoff told them they had in their accounts—fictitious amounts for his victims. Yeshiva never actually had $110 million. So, their loss was calculated as the actual amount it invested. Beyond the economic losses, foundations and charities also experienced negative consequences from having their names attached to Madoff.

As an analogy, imagine if unbeknownst to you someone broke into your white-collar crime professor's grade book online and changed all of the student's grades to make it look like everyone had an A+. You would not know the other students' grades, but you would "know" (or assume) that you had a perfect score in the class. You would likely be feeling pretty good about the class. Then, if the professor became aware of the scheme and changed everyone's grades back to their actual grade, how would you feel? Would you think that you "lost" points? Many of you probably have legitimate A+ grades, but for those who would have the grade changed to something lower, understanding your actual grade in the class would be somewhat confusing. For Madoff's victims, understanding the precise extent of their losses was confusing—both on an economic level and an emotional level.

Not surprisingly, Madoff was not well liked by Americans. As an indicator of the hatred that Americans had for him, it is significant to note that Madoff wore a bulletproof vest when going to and from court. Somewhat telling of his betrayal to his friends and family, the judge in Madoff's case, Manhattan federal judge Denny Chin, "noted he had not gotten a single letter from friends or family testifying to Madoff's good deeds" during his sentencing hearing (Zambito, Martinez, & Siemaszko, 2009). In statements to the court, his victims called him "a psychopathic lying egomaniac," "ruthless and unscrupulous," and "a devil" (Dey, 2009).

It is not entirely clear where all of the money went. Madoff lent millions to his family members and paid their corporate credit card bills, even for those family members who worked for a different corporation. He also paid bills for the captain of his boat (Efrati, 2009). But even these expenses would account for only a miniscule amount of the funds. Douglas Kass, a hedge fund manager himself, told a reporter, "It appears that at least $15 billion of wealth, much of which was concentrated in southern Florida and New York City, has gone to 'money heaven'" (Stempel & Plumb, 2008).

The fallout from Madoff's fraud continues. Civil charges were filed against his broker, Robert Jaffe, for "knowingly and recklessly participating in Madoff's Ponzi scheme" (Healy, 2009b, p. 1). Stanley Chais, a California investment advisor, was charged with fraud for funneling his clients' funds to Madoff. Frank Dipascali Jr., Madoff's top aide, pleaded guilty in August 2009 for his role in helping to deceive investors in the scheme. The U.S. Marshall's service recently auctioned off Dipascali's belongings in an effort to help make up for losses. During an auction preview, one woman attending the auction commented, "For someone who stole millions, this stuff isn't all that nice" (Debusmann, 2010).

The SEC has faced enormous criticism for not stopping the scheme sooner. After all, on six separate occasions, they had received complaints about Madoff's activities. A recent report by the SEC's Office of Investigations titled *Investigation of the Failure of the SEC to Uncover Bernard Madoff's Ponzi Scheme* noted that

> the SEC received more than ample information in the form of detailed and substantive complaints over the years to warrant a thorough and comprehensive examination and/or investigation of Bernard Madoff . . . for operating a Ponzi scheme, and that despite three examinations and two investigations being conducted, a thorough and competent investigation or examination was never performed. (SEC, 2010)

The 499-page report provides a scathing review of the SEC's failure, but offers suggestions on how to avoid such a failure in the future.

Strategies to improve the investigation of these offenses will be discussed in a later section. At this point, one benefit that has come out of Madoff's actions is that increased attention is being given to the warning signs or "red flags" of Ponzi schemes. These red flags include:

- Complicated trading strategies
- Irregular investment payments
- Unique customer statements
- Delays in withdrawals/transfers
- Promises of high investment returns with little or no risk
- Overly consistent returns
- Unregistered investments
- Unlicensed sellers
- Secretive strategies
- Issues with paperwork
- Difficulty receiving payments (SEC, 2009a)

Wells (2010) suggests that "the flag that flies the highest is a rate of return for an investment that greatly exceeds the norm" (p. 6). Madoff's scheme flew this red flag as high as it could be flown. Recognizing patterns surrounding fraud in the securities and commodities industry should help to prevent and respond to these offenses in the future.

Patterns Surrounding Investment Fraud

Several patterns characterize various dynamics surrounding investment fraud. Some of these patterns are similar to other forms of white-collar crime, while others seem more specific to cases of investment fraud. These patterns include:

- Significant press attention
- Attributions of greed
- Increasing punitiveness
- "White-collar gangs"
- Multiple offenses
- Negative consequences

Addressing these patterns will provide a full understanding of investment fraud.

First, several cases of investment fraud, or related offenses, receiving significant press attention were prominently highlighted in the national media over the past few decades. Table 7.2 shows 12 offenders that I would characterize as "infamous," the offenses they were accused of committing, the specific behaviors they performed, and the outcomes of these behaviors. Each of these individuals received a great deal of press attention for his or her misdeeds. In fact, so much press coverage focused on these scandals that some researchers have focused on how the press reported specific cases of investment fraud. One author team, for example, reviewed media reports about Enron and noted that the reports demonstrated four consistent themes about

Table 7.2 Top Twelve Infamous Offenders Committing White-Collar Crimes Against the Economic System

Name	Former Job Title	Offense Title	Offense Description
Ivan Boesky	Chairman of The Beverly Hills Hotel Corp.	• Insider trading	Boesky made several large stock purchases in the days before corporate takeovers and he would sell the newly purchased stocks soon after the takeovers were complete and the value of the stock increased. The breadth of his purchases alerted investigators to possible wrongdoing.
Bernard Ebbers	WorldCom CEO	• Conspiracy • Securities fraud • False regulatory filings	Ebbers exaggerated WorldCom's earnings and hid company losses for 2 years. WorldCom went bankrupt and the investigation uncovered $11 billion in false accounting entries. More than 17,000 employees lost their jobs and the incident harmed investor confidence.
Andrew Fastow	Enron CFO	• Wire fraud • Securities fraud	Fastow helped to hide Enron's debt and exaggerated the company's profits. He conspired with Skilling to lie to investors. Some see him as a scapegoat in the Enron fiasco. Fastow plead guilty and agreed to testify against Lay and Skilling.
Walter Forbes	Cendant chairman	• False statements • Conspiracy to commit securities fraud	Forbes was involved in a scheme in which company's stock was inflated by $500 million. Upon hearing of the fraud, public confidence dropped and the company's market value decreased $14 billion in a 24-hour period.
Dennis Kozlowski	Tyco CEO	• Grand larceny • Conspiracy • Falsifying records	Kozlowski took $120 million in bonuses without the approval of the board of directors. He also lied about the value of his company to increase stock prices.
Kenneth Lay	Enron chairman and CEO	• Fraud • Conspiracy • Lying to banks	With other Enron executives, Lay lied about Enron's finances. Enron, a Houston-based company that was once the top energy trading company in the U.S., eventually collapsed and 20,000 employees lost their jobs and retirement packages. Lay was convicted but died of heart disease before his sentencing. The judge, following traditional policies in death of offenders presentence, vacated the conviction.
Bernie Madoff	• Founder of Bernard L. Madoff Investment Securities • Chairman of the NASDAQ Stock Market	• Securities fraud • Ponzi scheme	Madoff stole several million dollars from thousands of investors through a Ponzi scheme he developed. The scheme took place over years as he did not rapidly increase the amount of positive returns to investors, but he increased the amounts slowly over time. Victims describe him as an angry man. *Newsweek* (2010) quotes Madoff telling a fellow inmate who was badgering him about his victims: "F--k my victims," Madoff reportedly said. "I carried them for 20 years, and now I'm doing 150 years."

(Continued)

Table 7.2 (Continued)

Name	Former Job Title	Offense Title	Offense Description
Michael Milken	Wall Street financier	• Securities fraud	Milken was involved in the crackdown on Wall Street misconduct in the late 1980s, early 1990s. He pleaded guilty to securities fraud after Boesky indicated he would testify against Milken. Some blame Milken for the Savings and Loan collapse 30 years ago, a charge he vehemently denies. Milken is now a philanthropist, consultant, and sought-after speaker. Some credit him with making several important changes to the medical field. He has raised hundreds of millions of dollars for medical research, particularly for cancer research. His net worth is 2.5 billion, which is just 200 million below Oprah.
Charles Ponzi	Founder of Old Colony Foreign Exchange Company	• Ponzi scheme	Ponzi convinced thousands of individuals to invest in a postage stamp program that would provide, according to Ponzi, a 50% return in less than 3 months. Ponzi used international mail coupons to begin his scheme, and then used incoming investments from new investors to maintain the scheme and pay former investors.
John Rigas	Adelphia CEO	• Securities fraud • Lying to investors • Conspiracy	Rigas hid $2.3 billion of his company's debt. He allegedly "helped himself" to so much of the company's funds that his son limited the elder Rigas's withdrawals to $1,000,000 a month.
Jeffrey Skilling	President and chief operating officer of Enron	• Fraud • Conspiracy • Lying to auditors • Insider trading	Skilling was second in command to Lay at Enron. Part of their scheme included reporting the value of their company based on future estimates rather than current estimates.
Martha Stewart	Martha Stewart Living CEO	• False statements • Obstruction of justice	Stewart sold $228,000 worth of her ImClone stock the day before the Food and Drug Administration (FDA) announced they were not going to approve one of ImClone's cancer drugs. The investigation revealed that she had the same stockbroker as the CEO of ImClone. She later was convicted of lying to investigators (perjury) and obstruction of justice. Ironically, at the time of her sentencing, the stocks she sold had increased in value to $315,000.
Samuel Waksal	ImClone CEO	• Insider trading	Waksal unloaded 79,000 shares of ImClone stock upon hearing that the company's cancer drug, Erbitux, was not being approved by the FDA in 2001. Later the drug was approved and was instrumental in the sale of ImClone to Eli Lilly for $6.5 billion. Waksal served 5 years in prison, but because he still owned stock options in ImClone, he profited from the sale.

"Not so" critical thinking question: Which of the following do the above offenders have in common?

a. All but one are male

b. They are all white

c. All but two have beards

d. All of the above

the scandal: risk, gratification, pride, and fantasy imagery (Knottnerus, Ulsperger, Cummins, & Osteen, 2006). Perhaps partly because of the press coverage given to the Enron fiasco, Friedrichs (2004) notes that Enron became a metaphor for a series of corporate scandals in the past decade. Cases involving executives from WorldCom, Adelphia, Tyco, Rite Aid, and other recognizable companies received significant press attention.

A second pattern has to do with attributions of greed that are used to explain cases of investment fraud. Reporters seemed either directly or indirectly to focus on greed explanations in explaining investment fraud. The high salary of executives has been a particular source of contention, both in the media and in private discussions. By focusing on their salaries when discussing the offenses by executives, it is as if the reporters are suggesting that the crimes are somehow tied to salary, when—in fact—the root causes of investment fraud are much more complex.

Still, the notion that greed causes investment fraud persists. The movie *Wall Street*, starring Michael Douglas and Charlie Sheen, is illustrative. Douglas stars as Gordon Gekko—a white-collar criminal engaging in a variety of investment frauds, and Sheen plays Bud Fox—a character new to Wall Street and aiming to learn from Gekko. In one scene, Gekko tells a group of share holders:

> The point is, ladies and gentleman, that greed—for lack of a better word—is good.
> Greed is right.
> Greed works.
> Greed clarifies, cuts through, and captures the essence of the evolutionary spirit.
> Greed, in all of its forms—greed for life, for money, for love, knowledge—has marked the upward surge of mankind.
> And greed—you mark my words—will not only save Teldar Paper, but that other malfunctioning corporation called the USA.

I won't spoil the end of the movie for those who have not yet seen it, but it is important to note that Gekko's speech has been linked to the following comments Ivan Boesky once told a group of University of California, Berkley students: "Greed is all right, by the way. I want you to know that. I think greed is healthy. You can be greedy and still feel good about yourself."

A third pattern consistent in these recent investment frauds is that the criminal justice system has demonstrated increasing punitiveness toward these offenders (Payne, 2003b). It is a myth that white-collar offenders are always sentenced more leniently than conventional offenders, and this will be discussed in more detail later in the section focusing on corrections. For now, it can simply be stated that judges and prosecutors seem intent on penalizing investment fraud offenders severely, particularly those investment fraud offenders who receive a great deal of attention from the media (Payne, 2003b). Some have attributed the increased punitiveness to the fact that the schemes often bilk elderly persons out of their life savings, as well as the fact that concern about white-collar crime in general has heightened (Hansard, 2007). The stiff "public sentence" allows judges to "send a message" that the (justice) system is not tolerant of these behaviors. In fact, judges and prosecutors often use the phrase "send a message" or some variation when describing the sentence given to investment fraud offenders. Here are a few examples of this practice:

- "The *message must be sent* that Mr. Madoff's crimes were extraordinarily evil," Judge Denny Chin said when he sentenced Madoff. (McCoy, 2009)
- A prosecutor urged a judge "to '*send a message*' to Wall Street that insider trading won't be tolerated, especially when the offender ran a 'billion-dollar hedge fund' and was 'at the pinnacle' of his profession." (Glovin & Hurtado, 2010)

- "Judge Nottingham just imposed the maximum fine of $19 million, calling Nacchio's offenses 'crimes of overarching greed.' The judge said he wants to *send a message* that crime does not pay. 'Not only does it not pay, it costs,' he said. 'It costs far and above and beyond.'" (Lewis, 2007)
- "The judge said she wanted to *send a message* that those who commit white-collar crimes will be punished severely. . . . The judge said Caplan, who worked at Brean Murray, Carret & Co. LLC, stole from at least seven investors." ("He Made His Own Bed," 2006)
- "Imposing the 121-month sentence, Judge Walter noted the recent 'staggering increase' in investor-advisor frauds and said that he wanted to '*send a message* that these crimes will result in significant prison sentences.'" (FBI, 2010a)

Another pattern surrounding these offenses can be called **white-collar gangs.** One criminologist defines a gang as

> a self-formed association of peers, bound together by mutual interests, with identifiable leadership, well-developed lines of authority, and other organizational features, who act in concert to achieve a specific purpose or purposes which generally include the conduct of illegal activity and control over a particular territory, facility, or type of enterprise. (Miller, 1975, p. 121)

The very nature of most investment frauds requires that offenders work together with other offenders "in concert to achieve a specific purpose" and their behaviors "include the conduct of illegal activity." Highlighting the themes surrounding the investment scandals of the early 2000s, Friedrichs (2004) drew attention to the "cooperative involvement of a broad network of other parties" that was found in the scandals. While the behaviors of "street gangs" and "white-collar gangs" are substantively different, the point is that investment offenders almost always work with other conspirators in committing their crimes.

A related pattern has to do with the fact that investment offenders tend to commit multiple offenses. It is rare that these offenders engage in their illicit behaviors only once or twice, and rarely do they commit just one type of misconduct. As an example, one offender: (a) lied to investors about funds, (b) falsely solicited payments from investors, (c) did not tell investors information they needed to know about their accounts, and (d) did not pay his taxes for 4 years (Mclaughlin, 2010). That investment offenders commit crimes in groups and commit these offenses on multiple occasions is useful information for investigators—if they find evidence of one offender committing one offense, by broadening the scope of their investigation, they can identify additional offenses and offenders.

A final pattern surrounding investment frauds involves the negative consequences that stem from these offenses. Beyond the direct economic toll for society in general, the offenses negatively impact investors' confidence in their immediate aftermath, and this reduction in confidence may result in fewer investments and lower stock values (Friedrichs, 2004). For specific victims of the investment frauds, different consequences may surface, and these consequences may linger, at least for some victims.

To address the long-term consequences of investment frauds, Shover and his research team (Shover, Fox, & Mills, 1994) interviewed 47 victims of fraud a decade after their victimization. The sample included victims of the Southland Industrial Banking Commission collapse, which was a result of fraudulent and criminal activities committed by the commission's executives. The researchers found that the long-term effects were minimal for many victims, but some described significant effects. Elderly victims, in particular, seemed to experience more negative consequences from the victimization. One victim told an interviewer:

> It's destroying us. It's destroying us. She was trained to look up to and obey an authority figure. I don't necessarily agree with that. Sometimes the authority figures are wrong. So as a result, she's a walking bag of nerves, very short-tempered. (Shover et al., 1994, p. 87)

The results of the Shover research team's study showed that delegitimation effects dissipated over time, suggesting that investor confidence can be restored. They also found, though, that when these effects lingered, they tended to be a result of the actions of state officials responding to the misconduct more than the actual misconduct itself.

Others have also commented on the way that investors "get over" investment scandals. A few years after the series of corporate scandals in the early 2000s, one author team wrote in the High Yield Report: "It was the same story in the U.S. secondary market last week. Everyone was buying everything and anything" (Appin & O'Connor, 2003). The article was appropriately titled "Market Rises as Spectre of Corporate Fraud Fades."

These patterns demonstrate the pervasiveness of investment frauds. As a type of crime in the economic system, investment fraud cases typically involve large profits for offenders and large dollar losses for scammed investors. A similar pattern is found in crimes in the technological system.

Crimes in the Technological System

Our technological system has made massive strides during our lifetime. Cell phones, lcd televisions, laptops, and handheld technological devices are relatively recent creations. These items are all relatively recent creations that came about as the result of technological advancements. While technological advancements have resulted in new products, the same advancements have also resulted in new types of crimes. In particular, computer crime (or cyber crime) has also become an international concern.

The term **computer crime** refers to a range of computer-related behaviors that are criminally illegal or otherwise harmful. In cases of computer crime, the computer is either a target of the offense (e.g., sabotage), a tool for the crime (e.g., cyber fraud, piracy), or is incidental to the crime (e.g., containing evidence about a crime; Hale, 2002; Sinrod & Reilly, 2000). While not all "computer crimes" are necessarily illegal—consider times when workers spend the day surfing the Internet rather than working—legal changes beginning in 1978 have provided criminal definitions that prohibit computer crime. In 1978, Florida and Arizona became the first two states to pass laws related to computer crime. Florida's Computer Crime Act "defined all unauthorized access as a third degree felony regardless of the specific purpose" (Hollinger & Lanza-Kuduce, 1988, p. 114). Within 10 years, the majority of states and the federal government had followed suit.

Hollinger and Lanza-Kuduce note that the public was somewhat apathetic with regard to the creation of these new laws. They also note that, unlike other legal developments, the media's reporting was "indispensable to the criminalization process" (p. 113). They also wrote that unlike other legal developments that are promoted by advocacy groups, efforts to reform the criminal law so it responded more directly to computer crimes was led by "computer crime experts and legislators rather than moral entrepreneurs" (p. 101). More than three decades after these laws were first developed, computer crime laws have expanded and are routinely enforced by state and federal authorities.

Since 1995, the Computer Security Institute (CSI) has conducted an annual survey titled the Computer Crime and Security Survey. The 2008 survey sampled 522 computer security professionals working in a variety of businesses (Richardson, 2008). Among other things, the most recent survey found that financial

Table 7.3   Types of Computer Crimes Reported in Computer Security Survey

Table	2007	2008
Denial of services	25%	21%
Laptop theft	50%	42%
Telecom fraud	5%	5%
Unauthorized access	25%	29%
Virus	52%	50%
Financial fraud	12%	12%
Insider abuse	59%	44%
System penetration	13%	13%
Sabotage	4%	2%
Theft/loss of property info	8%	9%
From mobile devices		4%
From all other sources		5%
Abuse of wireless network	17%	14%
Web site defacement	10%	6%
Misuse of web application	9%	11%
Bots	21%	20%
DNS attacks	6%	8%
Instant messaging abuse	25%	21%
Password sniffing	10%	9%
Theft/loss of costumer data	17%	17%
From mobile devices		8%
From all other sources		8%

SOURCE: Adapted from Richardson (2009).

computer crimes cost an average of nearly a half million dollars per incident. The survey also found that 44% of virus incidents were done by someone inside the organization. Table 7.3 shows the types of incidents respondents said their business had experienced.

It is important to bear in mind that not all computer crimes are white-collar crimes. Instances where individuals look at child pornography in the privacy of their own home would not be considered white-collar crime. If, however, they had child pornography on their work computer, as one professor at the University of Georgia did, this could be considered a white-collar crime. To provide a full understanding of crimes committed in the technological system, in the following paragraphs attention is given to the following:

- Types of computer crimes
- Explaining computer crimes
- Problems responding to computer crimes
- Preventing computer crime
- Students and computer crime

The dynamic and changing nature of computer crimes will be demonstrated through this discussion, and the way that the systems approach relates to this form of white-collar crime will be particularly evident.

Types of Computer Crimes

Experts have identified a laundry list of different types of computer crimes. These include hacking, cracking, phishing, extortion, child pornography, software piracy, money laundering, fraud, corporate espionage, cyber-terrorism, surveillance, identity theft, online stalking, and hate speech (Sinrod & Reilly, 2000; Yar, 2006). Figure 7.2 shows some of the common computer crimes committed by employees. For our purposes, the simplest way to understand computer crimes as white-collar crimes is to focus on general categories of computer crimes that target, or occur in, businesses. The following overlapping types of computer crimes warrant discussion: theft, unauthorized access, virus introduction, software crimes, and Internet crimes.

Theft as a Computer Crime

Theft as a type of computer crime refers to a variety of computer-related activities that result in the offender stealing something from the business. Items stolen include funds, information, and

Figure 7.2   Common Types of Computer Crimes by Employees

intellectual property (Carter & Katz, 1996). In terms of theft of funds, computer crimes include computer fraud and computer embezzlement. In computer fraud cases, offenders gain access to an account they are not supposed to enter and steal from the account. In computer embezzlement cases, the offender already has authorized access to the account by virtue of his or her position in the business.

Theft of information occurs when offenders steal information including (a) information that can be used to trade securities and stocks and (b) intellectual property (Carter & Katz, 1996). One type of information theft, the theft of intellectual property, occurs when offenders steal information that is protected by copyright. Estimates suggest that 62% of computer theft of proprietary information is done by current employees or employees of other businesses (Sinrod & Reilly, 2000). In Focus 7.2, When Computer Geeks Go Bad, describes a case of an offender using a computer to steal information from his former company.

In Focus 7.2

When Computer Geeks Go Bad

United States Attorney David C. Weiss
District of Delaware

For Immediate Release

Contact: Robert F. Kravetz
Tuesday, June 8, 2010

Former Dupont Chemist Pleads Guilty

*Dr. Hong Meng Admits Theft of DuPont Trade
Secrets Relating to Organic Light Emitting Diodes (OLEDs)*

WILMINGTON, DE—David C. Weiss, United States Attorney for the District of Delaware and Richard A. McFeely, Special Agent in Charge of the Baltimore Federal Bureau of Investigation (FBI) Field Office announced today that HONG MENG, age 43, a former research chemist for E.I. du Pont de Nemours and Company ("DuPont"), waived indictment and pleaded guilty to one count of theft of trade secrets, in violation of 18 U.S.C. § 1832. The offense carries a maximum prison sentence of 10 years, a fine of up to $250,000.00, and restitution. United States District Judge Sue L. Robinson scheduled a sentencing hearing for September 14, 2010 at 8:30 a.m.

According to facts admitted to by MENG in a plea agreement, MENG was involved in research in the field of Organic Light Emitting Diodes ("OLED") during his tenure at DuPont. OLED technology represents the next generation of display and lighting applications, and DuPont has expended significant resources on OLED research and development. In early 2009, DuPont's OLED research efforts resulted in the development of a breakthrough chemical process that increased the performance and longevity of OLED displays. The chemical process was considered to be a "trade secret" by DuPont, which took commensurate measures to protect it. MENG was aware of these security measures and knew that the chemical process was a DuPont trade secret. In Spring 2009, while still employed by DuPont and without company permission, MENG accepted a position as a faculty member at Peking University (PKU) College of Engineering, Department of Nanotechnology, in Beijing, China. After MENG accepted employment with PKU, he hired an assistant and graduate student; received office space, lab space, and an email address; was listed as a faculty member on the PKU website; and gave a presentation to officials of a regional Chinese government, soliciting funding to commercialize his OLED research at PKU. MENG failed to inform DuPont about his actions.

On July 30, 2009, MENG emailed a Microsoft Word document to his PKU email account which contained, embedded on the second page, the protected chemical process. In August 2009, MENG downloaded the same Word document from his DuPont work computer to a thumb drive, which he subsequently uploaded to his personal computer. MENG admitted that he knew to a practical certainty that his conduct in misappropriating the chemical process would injure DuPont. . . .

United States Attorney David C. Weiss said of the case: "The conviction of Dr. Hong Meng demonstrates our office's commitment to prosecuting offenses involving the unauthorized accessing of trade secret information. We will continue to vigilantly enforce intellectual property offenses, particularly when such offenses involve the possible transmittal of sensitive trade secret information outside the United States."

"Ensuring the protection of sensitive technologies created by our trusted partners in the private sector has, and will remain, a critical goal of the FBI's Wilmington office," said Richard McFeely, Special Agent in Charge. "We remain committed to investigating and prosecuting individuals who exploit U.S. technologies for their own gain."

Unauthorized Access as a Computer Crime

Unauthorized access occurs when individuals break into various computer databases to which they do not have legitimate access. *Hacker* is a term used to describe those who have the skills to access various secure computer databases and programs, but do so only out of a desire to experiment to see if they are able to access these programs. **Crackers** crack into computer systems "with [the intent] to sabotage and cause chaos to [the] corporation" (Wiggins, 2002, p. 20). Health care providers and utility companies are believed to be especially vulnerable to these incidents (Rogers, 2002).

Two types of crackers exist—those outside the targeted business and those inside the business. Crackers outside the business engage in their activities to "cause disruption to the networks for personal or political motives" (Sinrod & Reilly, 2005, p. 5). Hactivism is the concept of politically motivated cracking and hacking. When insiders are the crackers, a different set of concerns arise. According to Sinrod and Reilly, "disgruntled employees are the greatest threat to a computer's security" (p. 7).

Virus Introduction as a Computer Crime

Virus introduction is another type of computer crime. Viruses are introduced for various reasons. Crackers typically introduce viruses for recreational reasons, pride, profit, protection, or cyber-terrorism reasons. Recreationally, just as some unsupervised youth might vandalize public property, crackers find pleasure in "vandalizing" computer programs. In terms of pride, successfully sabotaging computer programs that are difficult to break into provides crackers a sense of accomplishment. In terms of profit, crackers can profit either from stealing funds themselves or by being paid by a coconspirator who is unable to carry out the crime alone. Also, viruses are introduced as a form of protection by employees to cover up evidence of their thefts and protect them from being identified (Carter & Katz, 1996).

With regard to cyber-terrorists, crackers aim to use viruses to threaten public security. Note that the types of activities of cyberterrorists are much different than the virus introducing activities of traditional crackers. Consider the following two examples described by Barry C. Collin (2001) of the Institute for Security and Intelligence at the 11th Annual Symposium of Criminal Justice Issues:

- A CyberTerrorist will remotely access the processing control systems of a cereal manufacturer, change the levels of iron supplement, and sicken and kill the children of a nation enjoying their food. That CyberTerrorist will then perform similar remote alterations at a processor of infant formula. The key: the CyberTerrorist does not have to be at the factory to execute these acts.
- A CyberTerrorist will attack the next generation of air traffic control systems, and collide two large civilian aircraft. This is a realistic scenario, since the CyberTerrorist will also crack the aircraft's in-cockpit sensors. Much of the same can be done to the rail lines.

Some will question whether cyber-terrorism is a form of white-collar crime. To be sure, not all cases would necessarily fit within the types of behaviors typically characterized as white-collar crimes. However, note that some companies might commit cyber-terroristic activities against others, and when businesses are targeted, it can be suggested that they have experienced a form of white-collar victimization. The enormous threats that cyber-terrorists pose for businesses and governments has led state and federal officials to develop cyber-terrorism law enforcement units.

Software Crime as Computer Crime

Software crimes refer to situations when computer software is central to the offense. Four overlapping types of software crimes exist: (1) theft of software, (2) counterfeiting software, (3) copyright violations of computer software, and (4) piracy (Wiggins, 2002). **Theft of software** refers to instances when workers steal computer software that their company owns and use it for their personal use. Imagine a situation where a worker has a copy of a photo editing program, for example. The computer software is supposed to be loaded only on the worker's office computer. If the worker takes the software home and loads it on his or her home computer so family members can use the software for personal reasons, then misconduct has occurred.

Counterfeiting software crimes occur when individuals make counterfeit copies of particular software programs. Microsoft (2010) describes these crimes as resulting from "unauthorized copying, reproduction, or manufacture of software products." Once the counterfeit software is produced, it is sold to consumers (a) by fraudulent business owners, (b) through e-mail scams, (c) in online auction sites like eBay, (d) on websites like Amazon.com, and (e) by street vendors (Microsoft, 2010). In what was called the "most significant crackdown on software piracy," the FBI and Chinese authorities recently arrested more than two dozen individuals as part of an offense involving "more than $500 million worth of counterfeit Microsoft and Symantec software that was being made in China and distributed worldwide" (Barboza & Lohr, 2007).

Copyright violations of computer software occur when users use software for purposes beyond what was intended under the copyright agreement described on the software. This could include illegally reproducing, altering, selling, or misrepresenting software programs. Piracy is also seen as a type of copyright violation.

Electronic and software piracy refers to theft of copyright protected electronic information including software, electronic programs, and electronic files such as movies and music. The Digital Millennium Copyright Act of 1998 was passed in an effort to limit piracy and copyright violations. The law stipulates that it is illegal to possess, sell, or distribute code cracking devices and calls for stiff penalties for offenders (Higgins, 2006). Much more will be written about piracy (see below) when considering students and computer crime. At this point, it is significant to note that the government has been building its efforts to respond to piracy. These efforts are captured in a recent statement Vice President Joe Biden made to reporters: "Piracy is theft. Clean and simple. It's smash and grab. It ain't no different than smashing a window at Tiffany's and grabbing [merchandise]."

Internet Crimes

Internet crimes are a range of offenses committed by offenders through the use of the Internet. A decade ago, it was estimated that Internet crime losses totaled one trillion dollars across the world (Rataj, 2001). Examples of Internet crimes reported to the FBI (2010b) include:

- Fake e-mails from the FBI: scammers send potential victims e-mails requesting funds as part of an FBI investigation.
- Non-delivered merchandise: not receiving merchandise purchased on an Internet website
- Non-payment for items sold on the Internet: not being paid for items sold through auction sites or other Internet websites
- Advanced fee fraud: requesting fees for goods or services that will never be provided
- Identity theft: stealing and falsely using someone's personal identity information
- Overpayment fraud: sending a counterfeit check for a purchase and asking for the difference to be returned

Table 7.4 shows the number of complaints the FBI's Internet Complaint Center received and the losses attached to those complaints between 2004 and 2009. As shown in the table, the number of complaints increased more than 20% between 2008 and 2009. Note that the financial losses more than doubled between these 2 years—from $265 million in 2008 to nearly $560 million in 2009. New e-mail scams identified by the FBI include (a) a hit man scheme where individuals receive e-mails from an assassin offering not to kill them in exchange for money, (b) pop-ups promising free astrological readings that turn out not to be free, (c) economic stimulus scams where recipients are told how to receive funds from the stimulus package, but only after entering their personal information, and (d) fake pop-up ads that download viruses (FBI, 2010b).

Table 7.4 Internet Crime Complaints to the FBI, 2004–2009

Year	Complaints	Loss (in millions)
2009	336,655	$559.7
2008	275,284	$265
2007	206,884	$239
2006	207,492	$198
2005	231,493	$183
2004	207,449	$68

Explaining Computer Crime

Although it is impossible to know for certain why computer crimes occur, a handful of explanations that are routinely cited will likely help to understand the source of many of these offenses. In particular, computer crimes are commonly attributed to opportunity, structural changes, and peer associations. Each of these explanations will be briefly reviewed here and discussed in more detail when causes of all forms of white-collar crime are considered later in this text.

Opportunity explanations center on the ease by which these offenses are committed, particularly for those who have a high degree of knowledge about computers. Offenders can target a high number of victims with great ease and relatively quickly—sometimes with a few key strokes on the computer keyboard. From this perspective, the steady availability of and access to computers provides offenders opportunities to commit all sorts of crimes. Many criminal justice sanctions for convicted computer criminals are based on the belief that opportunity contributes to the crime. As a condition of probation, many offenders are not allowed to own computers or live in a home where computers are present. The assumption is that restricting the opportunity for computer crime will prevent computer crimes from occurring.

Some experts attribute computer crimes to *structural changes*, an explanation that fits well within the ideals of the systems perspective. When I was born in the early 1980s (okay, I'm fibbing about the date), there was virtually no concern about computer crime. Technology was extremely limited. I have fond memories of playing Pong with my brother on our 26-inch black and white Zenith television. The television didn't have a remote control—unless you consider my brother and me as my father's remote control. In any event, changes in the technological, educational, social, and political systems resulted in technological advancements that have changed our society. One technological change entailed an increase in the use of computers to the point that virtually all businesses and most individuals in the United States now are computer literate. The increased presence of computers, then, provides new criminogenic opportunities. Consider that the advent of the Internet has resulted in different types of computer crimes (Yar, 2006). It is important to note that the crimes committed with computers are not all necessarily new crimes, but that the technologies for committing the crimes are new (Montano, 2001). As shown above, crimes such as theft, trespassing, and vandalism are committed with computers. These are not new crimes per se, though new laws are used to respond to instances where these crimes are committed with the use of computers.

Computer crimes have also been explained by *peer association* explanations, which suggest that the crimes occur as the result of individuals being associated with peers who might be more prone to commit these offenses. Studies of college students have supported these explanations. One study found the seriousness of computer crimes committed by college students was tied to negative peer associations—the more negative peer associations students had, the more serious types of computer misconduct they committed (Morris & Blackburn, 2009). In another study, a survey of 581 college students found that factors contributing to piracy and illegal access included differential associations, imitation, and differential reinforcement (Skinner & Fream, 1997).

Of course, there is no definitive explanation for why computer crimes occur. Explanations vary across offenders and offense types. For example, factors that lead males to commit computer crimes might be different from the factors that contribute to females' decisions to commit these offenses. As well, the causes of virus introductions might be different from the causes of computer fraud or computer embezzlement. Unfortunately, few studies have focused on the motivations for computer crime. Being unable to accurately pinpoint the causes of these behaviors has made it more difficult for authorities to respond to computer crimes.

Problems Responding to Computer Crimes

In addition to the fact that the causes of computer crime are not clear, other factors have made it more difficult to respond to computer crimes. These problems stem from the dynamics of the offense, offender characteristics, criminal justice dynamics, victim characteristics and decisions, and general crime prevention issues. With regard to the dynamics of the office, four issues arise. First, computer crime is an offense that occurs very quickly (Carter & Katz, 1996). Some have referred to them as "hit and run" offenses because of how quickly the offenses occur (McMullan & Perrier, 2007). Second, the offenses, by their very nature, are international in scope, making it difficult to even know where the crime actually occurred (Speer, 2000). Third, the technological nature of the crimes allows the offenses to occur without victims even realizing that they have been victimized until hours, days, weeks, or even months after the offense occurred. Fourth, the nature of computer offenses is constantly changing, making it more difficult to watch for signs of the crimes.

In terms of offender characteristics, computer offenders tend to be highly educated people who are able to go to great lengths to conceal their crime and their identity. When a conventional offender robs a bank, witnesses see the offender and cameras may even provide pictures of the suspect. When a computer criminal robs a bank, no one sees the criminal and pictures are certainly not available. Offenders' technical knowledge is the equivalent of the stereotypical ski mask that conventional offenders wear in old cops-and-robbers movies.

Criminal justice dynamics also contribute to problems in responding to computer crimes. Often, criminal justice professionals are not adequately trained how to respond to computer crimes (Carter & Katz, 1996). Also, solving these offenses requires collaboration between criminal justice agencies, and such collaboration may be difficult to carry out at times (Montano, 2001). In some cases, international collaboration may be necessary (Speer, 2000). Criminal justice officials also must grapple with resource deployment issues in deciding the amount of fiscal resources and workload to devote to responding to computer crimes (McMullan & Perrier, 2007).

Victim characteristics and behaviors also inhibit the response to computer crimes. On one level, it is difficult in some cases to identify victims of computer crimes, especially when businesses and individuals do not even know they have been victimized (Speer, 2000). On another level, even when businesses are victimized by a computer crime, many will decide not to report the offense to the authorities. If the offense is not reported, authorities cannot respond to the offense. Table 7.5 shows common reasons that security officials listed for not reporting computer victimizations to the authorities. As shown in the table, the strongest reasons for not reporting include perceptions that the incident was too small, beliefs that law enforcement couldn't help, and concern over negative publicity.

General crime prevention issues may also make it more difficult to respond to computer crimes. For the most part, law enforcement prevention programs focus on preventing traditional crimes (Rataj, 2001). Businesses are told to identify/mark property, install cameras, hire security guards, keep shrubs away from windows, put bars on their windows, and so on. Prevention strategies rarely focus on what can be done to prevent computer crime, or other forms of white-collar crime for that matter. In order to better prevent computer crime, an expanded focus must be given to prevention measures. It is important to note that some colleges and universities have developed prevention measures to address computer crimes by college and university students.

Table 7.5 Reasons for Not Reporting Computer Crime Victimizations

Reasons for Not Reporting	Average Response (on a 1 to 7 scale)[a]
Incident too small to bother reporting	4.33
Believed law enforcement couldn't help	4.07
Negative publicity	3.71
Other	3.21
Competitors would use to advantage	3.14
Civil remedy pursued	2.78
Unaware of law enforcement interest	2.66

a. 1 = of no importance; 7 = of great importance.

Students and Computer Crimes

In Section VI it was briefly noted that a current concern on college and university campuses is digital and Internet piracy by students. Most colleges have specific policies that prohibit piracy by students. By developing these policies, colleges and universities are able to insulate themselves from blame when students are caught misusing college/university computers. In effect, officials can say that the student was violating an institutional policy, showing that the officials do not support the student's actions.

Internet piracy is "the illegal duplication and distribution of copyrighted materials from the Internet" (Hohn, Muftic, & Wolf, 2006), and digital piracy is the illegal duplication of copyright protected software. These forms of piracy are believed to cost society between $25 and $30 billion a year

(Hohn et al., 2006). The music and movie industries have been particularly vigilant in their efforts to suppress Internet piracy.

Lars Ulrich, drummer from the heavy metal band Metallica, was among the most vocal critics of file-sharing programs that allowed computer users to illegally download and share music. After learning that his band's unreleased music was being distributed on Napster, the band sued Napster for copyright infringement and racketeering. Testifying before the Senate Judiciary Committee on Downloading Music on the Internet on July 11, 2000, Ulrich said,

> We were startled to hear reports that five or six versions of our work-in-progress were already being played on some U.S. radio stations. We traced the source of this leak to a corporation called Napster. Additionally, we learned that all of our previously recorded copyright songs were, via Napster, available for anyone around the world to download from the Internet in a digital format known as MP3. In fact, in a 48-hour period, where we monitored Napster, over 300,000 users made 1.4 million free downloads of Metallica's music. Napster hijacked our music without asking. They never sought our permission. Our catalog of music simply became available for free downloads on the Napster system. I do not have a problem with any artists voluntarily distributing his or her songs through any means that artist so chooses. But just like a carpenter who crafts a table gets to decide whether he wants to keep it, sell or give it away, shouldn't we have the same options? We should decide what happens to our music, not a company with no rights to our recordings, which has never invested a penny in our music or had anything to do with its creation. The choice has been taken away from us. (Ulrich, 2000)

▲ **Photo 7.5**   Metallica became embroiled in efforts to control computer crime when drummer Lars Ulrich led efforts of the music industry to stop individuals from illegally downloading music.

Metallica and Napster settled out of court.

Over the past few years, high-profile cases of college students being convicted for various forms of digital piracy have made the news headlines. In 2009, Joel Tenenbaum, a Boston University graduate student, was fined $675,000 after the court had found that he had illegally downloaded 30 songs from four record labels ("Joel Tenenbaum Fined," 2009).

Research shows that college students routinely engage in various forms of digital and Internet piracy. A study of 114 students found that 79.8% said they had illegally downloaded music and more than a third said they had pirated software (Hohn et al., 2006). A 2007 survey by SurveyU found that two thirds of the 500 students surveyed were not concerned about illegally downloading music or repercussions from doing so. The survey also found that "only 57% of the students' total libraries had been purchased" (Yoskowitz, 2007).

Researchers have tested various theories in an effort to explain software piracy by students. One author team surveyed 342 students and found support for the idea that low self-control contributes to software piracy (Higgins, Fell, & Wilson, 2006). In another study, of 507 college students, a researcher found that broadband connections combined with prior experience using CD-ROMs increased the risk of Internet piracy (Hinduja, 2001).

 ## Preventing Computer Crime

Three different types of strategies are used to prevent computer crimes by white-collar offenders. These include employer-based strategies, criminal justice system-based strategies, and employee-based strategies. In terms of *employer-based strategies*, employers use a range of tactics to protect their businesses from computer crimes. Most commonly these tactics include encryption, firewalls, employee training, routine audits, and physical surveillance (Carter & Katz, 1996). Many large private businesses have security personnel whose sole efforts are directed toward preventing and/or identifying cases of computer crime.

With regard to *criminal justice system-based strategies,* law enforcement agencies have become more vigilant in their efforts to prevent and respond to computer crimes. Computer crime units have been developed in the FBI, Secret Service, Air Force Office of Special Investigations, and other local, state, and federal law enforcement agencies (Carter & Katz, 1996). Some have called for using community policing ideals to respond to computer crimes (Jones, 2007). Applying community policing ideals to these offenses would provide employees and businesses the power to prevent computer crimes. Others have also highlighted the need to have governmental agencies and companies work together to respond to computer crime (Wiggins, 2002). Such cooperation is believed to help to educate law enforcement officials about the technical and complex dynamics of computer offenses.

Employee-based strategies call upon employees to make active efforts to prevent computer crimes. Such strategies include rewards for reporting computer crimes, updating virus protection programs, employee-initiated audits of computer use, taking additional precautions to protect one's work computer from victimization, and formal agreements whereby employees agree to use computers only for work-related activities (Carter & Katz, 1996). Including employees in prevention strategies ensures that well-rounded prevention programs are in place.

Do As I Say, Not As I Do

In what can be filed under the category of "Do as I say, not as I do," an interesting anecdote about my own experience with computer victimization comes to mind. While working on this section, I decided that I would search the Internet for additional information about computer viruses. I found a few useful websites and took some notes on the material I read. About 2 hours later, I realized that my computer had become infected by a computer virus called the "control center virus." Somehow, during my search, I had clicked on a website that downloaded this virus to my laptop. I had to stop work immediately, save my work to that point, and shut down the computer. The next day I delivered my computer to one of the computer tech employees in my college. He confirmed that my computer had become infected and that he would need to take a few days to get rid of the virus and restore the computer to its appropriate state. Fortunately, I didn't lose any files or data—I just lost some time.

So, if you are writing a paper about computer viruses for your white-collar crime class, do not search the Internet for information—make sure you search your library database and rely on scholarly journal articles published by top publishing companies such as Sage. This little bit of advice will take you a long way in your academic career.

⊠   Summary

- A wide range of offenses is committed in the economic and technological systems, two systems that share several similarities.

- When the term white-collar offender comes to mind, it is often images of offenders from the economic or technological systems that come to mind.

- The economic system includes banks, investment companies, stock markets across the world, commodities markets, and other exchanges/markets where individuals are able to make investments, purchase raw materials, and secure goods.

- The phrase "securities and commodities fraud" covers a broad concept, capturing a range of behaviors designed to rip off investors.

- Several specific varieties of these frauds exist, including market manipulation, broker embezzlement, hedge fund fraud, insider trading, futures trading fraud, foreign exchange fraud, high yield investment schemes, advanced fee fraud, and Ponzi and pyramid schemes.

- Market manipulation refers to situations where executives or other officials do things to artificially inflate trading volume and subsequently affect the price of the commodity or security.

- Three federal statutes exist to restrict market manipulation by energy companies: the Commodity Exchange Act, the Energy Policy Act of 2005, and the Energy Independence and Security Act of 2007.

- Broker fraud occurs when stockbrokers fail to meet their legal obligations to investors. Broker embezzlement occurs when brokers take money that is supposed to be in an investment account and use it for their own personal use.

- Hedge fund fraud refers to fraudulent acts perpetrated in hedge fund systems.

- Insider trading occurs when individuals share or steal information that "is material in nature" for future investments.

- Futures trading fraud refers to fraud occurring in the trading of futures contracts and options on the futures trading market.

- Ponzi and pyramid schemes scam investors by paying them from future investors' payments into the offender's scheme.

- Bernie Madoff was the mastermind behind what has come to be called the largest Ponzi scheme in the history of the United States.

- One benefit that has come out of Madoff's actions is that increased attention is being given to the warning signs or "red flags" of Ponzi schemes.

- Several patterns characterize various dynamics surrounding investment fraud, including significant press attention, attributions of greed, increasing punitiveness, "white-collar gangs," multiple offenses, and negative consequences.

- To address the long-term consequences of investment frauds, Shover and his research team interviewed 47 victims of fraud a decade after their victimization. The results of the Shover research team's study showed that *delegitimation effects dissipated over time, suggesting that investor confidence can be restored.*

- The phrase "computer crime" refers to a range of computer-related behaviors that are criminally illegal or otherwise harmful.

- In 1978, Florida and Arizona became the first two states to pass laws related to computer crime.

- Not all computer crimes are white-collar crimes.

- The following overlapping types of computer crimes are often cases of white-collar crime: theft, unauthorized access, virus introduction, software crimes, and Internet crimes.

- Theft as a type of computer crime refers to a variety of computer-related activities that result in the offender stealing something from the business. Items stolen include funds, information, and intellectual property.
- Theft of information occurs when offenders steal information including (a) information that can be used to trade securities and stocks and (b) intellectual property.
- Unauthorized access occurs when individuals break into various computer databases to which they do not have legitimate access.
- Crackers typically introduce viruses for recreational reasons, pride, profit, protection, or cyber-terrorism reasons.
- Four overlapping types of software crimes exist: (1) theft of software, (2) counterfeiting software, (3) copyright violations of computer software, and (4) piracy.
- The phrase "Internet crimes" refers to a range of offenses committed by offenders through the use of the Internet.
- Computer crimes are commonly attributed to opportunity, structural changes, and peer associations.
- Problems in responding to computer crime stem from the dynamics of the offense, offender characteristics, criminal justice dynamics, victim characteristics and decisions, and general crime prevention issues.
- Most colleges have specific policies that prohibit piracy by students. One author team surveyed 342 students and found support for the idea that low self-control contributes to software piracy (Higgins et al., 2006).
- Three different types of strategies are used to prevent computer crimes by white-collar offenders: employer-based strategies, criminal justice system-based strategies, and employee-based strategies.

KEY TERMS

Advanced fee fraud	Foreign exchange fraud	Investment fraud
Broker embezzlement	Front running	Market manipulation
Broker fraud	Futures contracts	Ponzi schemes
Commodities	Futures trading fraud	Prearranged trading
Commodities fraud	Hedge fund fraud	Software crimes
Computer crime	Hedge fund systems	Theft of software
Counterfeiting software crimes	High yield investment schemes	Unauthorized access
Crackers	Insider trading	White-collar gangs
Electronic and software piracy	Internet crimes	

DISCUSSION QUESTIONS

1. Which crimes do you think do more harm—crimes against the economic system or street crimes? Explain.

2. How are crimes in the economic system similar to crimes in the technological system? What are some differences in the two categories of crime?

3. Do you think Martha Stewart's penalty was accurate? Why or why not?

4. What are some patterns surrounding investment fraud?

5. How does investment fraud impact your life as a student?

6. How serious are computer crimes on your campus?

7. Why do you think hackers engage in computer crime behaviors?

8. How do you think investment crimes and computer crimes will change in the next decade?

WEB RESOURCES

SEC Law and Insider Trading: http://www.mystockoptions.com/articles/index.cfm/secID/D851C4F4-43AD-450C-A3EEB399AEFDED48

Investor Tip: http://www.investortrip.com/how-to-recognize-stock-market-manipulation-vs-normal-stock-market-movement/

Identity Theft: http://www.ftc.gov/bcp/edu/microsites/idtheft/

IT Crime Prevention: http://www.interpol.int/public/technologycrime/crimeprev/itsecurity.asp

Internet Crime Complaint Center: http://www.ic3.gov/default.aspx

READING

In this article, Elizabeth Szockyj describes a case study in which she examined the processing of an insider trading offense in the criminal and civil justice systems. She focuses specifically on the case of Carl Karcher, the founder of a fast-food chain with more than 400 restaurants, and Alvin Deshano, Karcher's head accountant. She provides a detailed account of the charges levied against both offenders, noting that insider trading was a priority for the SEC in the early to mid-1980s. The author also highlights the interplay between political system maneuverings and justice system outcomes. Karcher's defense—that he had a legal right to avoid economic losses—is detailed. The importance of legal definitions is made clear, particularly in the author's discussion of how the prosecutor had to demonstrate that the information was "material in nature." The case study demonstrates the complexity of insider trading.

Insider Trading

The SEC Meets Carl Karcher

Elizabeth Szockyj

Corporate officers and major shareholders are restricted as to when and on what grounds they may trade company stock, but insider trading is not illegal in the United States. On the contrary, allowing officers and directors of corporations to own and to deal in stock in their company is supported in order to reward past performance and to supply an incentive for future profitability. What is illegal is when an insider trades on information that is confidential or not available to the general public, such as advance knowledge regarding a new product or unanticipated profits or losses. Trading on nonpublic information, or tipping other people who then trade, is said to undermine "the fair and honest operation of our securities markets."[1]

In 1988, the California office of the Securities and Exchange Commission (SEC) filed a civil insider trading action against Donald Karcher, the president, and Carl Karcher, the founder of Carl Karcher Enterprises (CKE), a fast-food chain, and against 13 members of the Karcher family. Before the case was over, the head of the CKE accounting department, Alvin DeShano, was prosecuted criminally by the Department of Justice for alleged illegal insider trades. After much publicity, negotiation, and expense, the Karcher family members settled with the SEC. DeShano was acquitted of criminal charges by a jury whose members felt uncomfortable convicting him on the basis of entirely circumstantial evidence.

Both the civil and criminal nature of insider trading are illustrated in this case. The civil suit reveals the motivations, on the part of all parties, for pursuing a settlement, the most frequent method of disposal of insider trading cases. By not forcing the defendants to admit to committing the offense, that is, by allowing them to settle without admitting or denying guilt, the SEC is able to assess penalties that the court might deny, while the defendants may be better off financially and emotionally by avoiding possible higher fines, additional legal fees,

SOURCE: Szockyj, Elizabeth. (1993). Insider trading: The SEC meets Karl Karcher. *The Annals of the American Academy of Political and Social Science, 525,* 46–58.

disruption to the corporate functioning, psychological stress, and potential adverse publicity.

The criminal trial in this case depicts the subtleties of a jury trial for a white-collar offense. The jury's shift from an initial stance favoring guilt to an acquittal of the defendant reveals the dynamics of the jury deliberation process, particularly when a respectable defendant is being tried. The uncertainty of proving criminal intent based on circumstantial evidence has haunted attempts to prosecute insider traders. Set in a time when insider trading had become a household word and when penalties from the newly passed Insider Trading Sanctions Act of 1984 (ITSA) could be applied, the Karcher case takes the reader from the circumstances surrounding suspect securities trades to the discovery of possible illegality and then to a final resolution.

Discovery of Suspicious Trades

Aroused by unusual trading activity, the computer in the Washington offices of the National Association of Securities Dealers (NASD) red-flagged shares trading in Carl Karcher Enterprises, Inc. Heavy selling of stock on 22 October 1984 resulted in a fourfold increase in volume from the previous day, with a jump from 21,250 to 107,620 shares. On 23 October the volume rose to 182,000 shares after CKE released its startling profit expectations, under the wire service headline "Carl Karcher Said Third Quarter Net Could Be Off by 50%." NASD, now alerted, surveyed the brokers involved in the trades to determine the individuals who had bought and sold CKE stock. By January 1985, NASD, whose suspicions of illegal insider trading appeared confirmed, turned its findings over to the SEC for further investigation and possible official action.[2]

The stock under scrutiny was fairly new to the over-the-counter market. The company, CKE, had gone public in 1982 after decades of nurturing by its founder, Carl Karcher. From his humble beginnings in Los Angeles in 1941, with a small hot dog stand purchased for $326, Carl Karcher had watched his investment grow into a chain of 449 restaurants spanning four states.[3]

Precursors to the 1984 News Release

As the three-and-a-half-year SEC investigation progressed, the events of the days prior to the news release regarding the drop in CKE earnings were revealed. Due to some poor business ventures, primarily an ill-fated national expansion attempt, as well as a slump in the Los Angeles fast-food industry following the 1984 summer Olympics, the CKE earnings for the fiscal period ending 5 October 1984 were approximately 83 percent lower than for the same period the previous year, as stated in the SEC charges; the Department of Justice estimated the decline at 65 percent. These reduced period-nine earnings had a strong impact on CKE earnings for the third quarter ending 2 November 1984.

DeShano, the director of general accounting for the corporation, received the preliminary report for period nine on Friday, 12 October. Between that Friday and Tuesday, 16 October, DeShano, the controller, and staff members adjusted and corrected the information in the report. On 16 and 17 October the final report was distributed to the CKE executives. Donald Karcher, the president of the corporation, was notified in Europe of the period-nine results. Not only were the results devastating news for the company, but Donald was scheduled to speak at a conference on 23 October and there were certain to be questions regarding the economic status of CKE. At a meeting of company executives on Saturday, 20 October, it was decided that in lieu of releasing the customary report of earnings in November, a special press notice would be issued just prior to Donald Karcher's speaking engagement. CKE had never before made a midquarter announcement. The release was transmitted Tuesday morning, 23 October, over the Dow Jones newswire. That day the CKE stock opened at 21½, declined to a low of 16 1/2, and closed at 17 1/4.

In a flurry of activity before the time of the press release, stocks and debentures were sold by several of Carl Karcher's children, relatives of Donald Karcher, and Alvin DeShano. Sales by the Karcher family members accounted for 27.5 percent of the total trading volume of CKE common stock for 22 October 1984.[4]

It was these trades, which occurred after the preliminary report but before the press release, that were of concern to the SEC; it was during this time that non-public information that would affect the price of the stock was in the hands of Donald and Carl Karcher.

The SEC Indictment

Insider trading was at this time a well-known priority for the SEC. With increased sanctions for insider trading legislated just months before by the ITSA, the SEC was moving full-steam ahead. On the East Coast, the agency made media headlines in 1984 and 1985 with insider trading charges against Paul Thayer, the Deputy Secretary of Defense to President Reagan, and against *Wall Street Journal* reporter R. Foster Winans.

In 1984, when Irving Einhorn arrived in Los Angeles to head the regional SEC office, he found the branch "in an embarrassing state of disarray."[5] What the office needed was the successful prosecution of a major securities-fraud case. With the Karcher case, the office was guaranteed national exposure. Because of the sheer number of possible defendants—16 in all—this was the largest insider trading case the Los Angeles SEC had encountered.

After countless interviews with CKE officials, traders, and family members, and after tracing telephone conversations and stock reports, the SEC announced, on 14 April 1988, three and a half years after the relevant events, its charges against a number of Karcher family members and the CKE accountant. According to the SEC, Carl Karcher and his wife, Margaret,[6] had conveyed information regarding the impending decline in profits to three daughters, a son, and two sons-in-law. Karcher had assumed the role of advising his children in their financial affairs; and all the children charged were heavily in debt from stock margin accounts.[7] Donald Karcher and his wife, Dorothy, were also charged with relaying confidential information to four relatives.

The complaint claimed that the 10 relatives avoided a total of $310,000 in losses by trading on the confidential information before the public announcement of 23 October. Neither Donald nor Carl Karcher was accused of selling CKE stock themselves, only of tipping the others.

Finally, both the accountant, Alvin DeShano, and Carl Karcher's son and vice president of manufacturing and distribution, Carl Leo Karcher, were said to have been aware of the drastic decline in earnings because of their position. DeShano was accused of selling all of his 1725 shares of CKE stock, thereby avoiding losses of $9367—the Department of Justice estimated this sum at $7107—while it was alleged that Carl Leo Karcher avoided approximately an $8000 loss through his sale of stock.

In the complaint, the SEC sought, for all defendants, a permanent injunction from engaging in insider trading violations. For those guilty of trading illegally, disgorgement of the avoided loss, to be paid to the stockholders defrauded, and fines up to triple the amount disgorged—in accordance with the ITSA—were requested. The individuals charged with passing the information would be responsible for damages up to triple the amount of the losses avoided by those they allegedly tipped. Under these stipulations, Carl Karcher would be required to pay close to $1 million in fines.

A Determination of Guilt

Carl Leo Karcher, a vice president of the company at the time in question, was aware of the period-nine report by virtue of his position. At the monthly meeting of company officers, he was startled to see the drastic period-nine drop in earnings and the dismal third-quarter profit expectations. Two days later, Carl Leo instructed his broker to sell 75 debentures. He hoped to reduce his $836,000 debt to his brokerage firm, thereby avoiding a margin call.

In testimony before the SEC, Carl Leo stated that after he had made the phone call to his broker, the chief financial officer for CKE warned him not to sell the debentures until after the public announcement on the third-quarter earnings. Upon receiving this information, Carl Leo canceled his order, but 50 debentures already had been sold. He did not attempt to reacquire these debentures. Within an hour after the earnings news release, he sold another 50 debentures.

The SEC charged Carl Leo with trading on inside information to avoid potential losses estimated at $8000. During testimony before the SEC, Carl Leo admitted to receiving and acting on the confidential earnings information, stating that at the time he believed that as long as he was selling at a loss, this act would not be considered insider trading. Carl Leo explained, "I had a legal right to sell the debentures because the sale would result in a loss to me."[8]

With this evidence in hand, the SEC asked that Carl Leo be found guilty and fined without a trial. Carl Leo proved to be the only defendant to admit to using the inside information to trade. In the summary proceedings that took place on 12 September 1988, the defense argued that Karcher had not intended to defraud, deceive, or manipulate but had simply made a mistake. Los Angeles Federal Court Judge Edward Rafeedie found that there was enough evidence without a trial to convict the former vice president of insider trading. Carl Leo's personal knowledge of the law was not relevant to his guilt.[9]

Armed with the ITSA, which allows civil penalties of up to three times the amount gained or avoided, the SEC requested that Carl Leo pay $10,500, including interest, for the losses that he avoided, plus up to $34,500 in civil penalties. The judge granted the $10,500 disgorgement and enjoined Carl Leo from committing future securities violations, but he refused to impose the treble penalty. Judge Rafeedie felt that the provision should be used for "a more egregious case." He continued, "This involved a single trade [and] is not the type of case that has been in the headlines involving . . . secret transactions [referring to the Levine-Boesky-Siegel insider trading cases]."[10]

The Carl Leo Karcher case, one of the first that attempted to use the triple-damages provision in the ITSA, dealt a blow to SEC enforcement ambitions.[11] Ironically, the standard SEC settlement incorporates a civil penalty equal to the profit obtained or loss avoided, which is more stringent than the civil court sentence handed down in the Carl Leo case. This is contrary to the normal plea-bargaining assumption that one will receive a more lenient sentence by waiving the trial alternative. As discussed later in this article, the remainder of the Karchers settled with the SEC by agreeing to pay a penalty equal to the amount disgorged.

The DeShano Trial

The only criminal charge in the Karcher episode was laid in March of 1989 against the head accountant, Alvin DeShano. This was a case where the link between the confidential period-nine report and the sale of CKE stock was direct. Since neither Carl nor Donald Karcher sold his own stock, the government would have to show that the brothers first had access to the nonpublic report and then relayed the information to their families and that thereafter the relatives charged sold the stock based on that knowledge. In the accountant's case, the government did not have the difficult task of proving the middle step.

A long-time employee of CKE, DeShano, who turned 55 during the course of the trial, was depicted as an unsophisticated investor, an honest man whose major fault was that he procrastinated. The defense claimed that DeShano had intended to sell the stock long before the preliminary ninth-period report was compiled but never quite got around to doing so.

Held in Los Angeles federal court from 23 May to the final jury verdict on 5 June 1989, the DeShano criminal trial demonstrated the difficulty of litigating insider trading cases. For the defense, there was the presupposition of guilt in the jurors' minds to be overcome. For the prosecution, a case based on circumstantial evidence is always risky.

The judge's instruction to the jury had explicated the elements that constitute insider trading. Essentially, the jurors were required to find, beyond a reasonable doubt, that the defendant (1) was a corporate insider, (2) was in possession of nonpublic material information, (3) used and relied on that information, and (4) intended to defraud. It was primarily the third and fourth elements that led the jurors to reach a verdict of not guilty.

When DeShano took the stand, he denied that he sold his stock because of the unfavorable preliminary report; instead, he claimed that he had intended to sell weeks before but had procrastinated. It was argued by the defense that DeShano was a numbers cruncher; he was not in a position to step back and view the entire picture, nor was he able to forecast the drastic decline in the stock price from the limited information he possessed. One of the jurors countered this position with his own analysis of the situation:

> My argument against that was ... that he could have almost done it in his head. You can look at your checkbook and you don't have to run it all the way through to know that you've got a lot less money than you had a month ago at this time, not right to the dollar amount, but you know.[12]

In his summation to the jury, the defense attorney, David Wiechert, explained that the case is "as complicated as the human mind. You have to determine what he [DeShano] was thinking when he sold his stock."[13] The jury took this advice to heart.

One of the jurors, who originally had voted for guilt, reflected:

> I relented only because one of the elements that the judge had instructed us on, as a prerequisite for a guilty finding, was something that couldn't possibly be reached. It was asking us for a smoking gun and there was no such thing possible. . . . In the instructions to the jury, Judge Tashima pointed out that we would have to conclude he [DeShano] had used it [the preliminary report] in his decision to sell. And, of course, that's an impossibility. I mean how can we presuppose what went on in his mind?[14]

The same juror later added, "The last element, of course, was that he did in fact use it in determining whether to sell his stock. And that was the one that stopped everybody, because, like I say, you can't delve into the man's mind."[15]

The consensus appeared to be that the circumstantial evidence presented was not sufficient to judge that DeShano had a guilty mind. Another juror stated, "Nobody saw him [DeShano]. Nobody knew what he was thinking. That's what broke the jurors down."[16] The acquittal, my interviews indicated, was the result of the jury's inability to determine positively that DeShano was aware of the drastic fiscal implications of the preliminary report and that he used this information in his decision to sell.

This ambivalence on the part of the jury is significant particularly in light of a statement made by the judge in *Herman and MacLean v. Huddleston:*

> The proof ... required in fraud cases is often a matter of inference from circumstantial evidence. If anything, the difficulty of proving the defendant's state of mind supports a lower standard of proof [lower than a preponderance of the evidence]. In any event, we have noted elsewhere that circumstantial evidence can be more than sufficient.[17]

This and other court decisions allow intent to be liberally inferred from the circumstantial evidence presented,[18] but the jury in the DeShano case chose not to do so.

Often, nonlegal characteristics of the offender, such as socioeconomic status, moral character, and severity of the possible sentence, may induce juror sympathy and leniency. The finding on whether socioeconomic status has an effect on juror judgment is inconclusive;[19] however, juror responses indicate that DeShano's class was noted. One juror described the defendant's appearance in court as follows: "[DeShano] was well presented, [a] calm, serene individual. . . . He was likable. Both he and his wife presented themselves as a very nice mid-aged couple. I think that impressed everybody."[20]

The moral character of the defendant also was raised by the jurors in the interviews. Studies have found that a defendant's emotional demeanor is influential in a judgment of conviction; those who suffer or appear remorseful may be treated more leniently.[21] An example of this sentiment was expressed by a juror who stated, "I think justice being done in this world, if it ever is, I think it was done in this case because I really think that Al DeShano is the kind of person that suffered . . . over this thing."[22] Moreover, at least one juror may have had sympathy for the defendant because he could picture himself in a similar situation. One of the jurors, commenting on the attitude of another juror, explained, "He made it look like it was okay for [DeShano] to do that because he was a white-collar worker and he might do it, too. He might have done it."[23]

Finally, the five-year maximum prison term that DeShano possibly faced may have swayed some individuals. Krupa has shown that jurors are less likely to convict where the prosecutoral evidence was weak, the prescribed punishment severe, and the final sentence outside of their control.[24] A juror commented:

> We talked about that in the jury room . . . what would they do to him in a case like this. We couldn't possibly see a prison sentence, for instance. I think perhaps that may have been uppermost in the minds of some of those who were [for] not guilty in the beginning, who just couldn't see [giving him] a strong life-changing kind of punishment [that would cause a] loss of a job and all the rest of it. I think they were thinking more along the lines of the punishment situation.[25]

The jury was able to justify its decision to acquit based on the evidence presented. They did not feel the prosecutor established beyond a reasonable doubt that DeShano used the information in the preliminary report in his decision to sell the stock. Yet, factored into the conversion toward an acquittal were several extralegal variables: the socioeconomic status of the defendant, his demeanor at the trial, and the length of the potential prison sentence.

 ## Motivations for Prosecuting DeShano

There are several factors the SEC considers before it decides to pursue a case. In her analysis of SEC docket investigations, Shapiro lists the following elements, among others: (1) recurrence of the offense, (2) recency, (3) nature of the offense, (4) amount of money involved, (5) culpability, and (6) strength of evidence. Shapiro found that the prior record of investigated offenders was unrelated to the likelihood of SEC prosecution.[26] The Karcher case exemplifies these findings; the extent of the illegal activity, the total of 16 persons charged, and the sum of money involved, $314,000, amounted to sufficient reason for the SEC to devote three years of resource-intensive labor to the case. An added incentive was the publicity that the Karcher name guaranteed.

The SEC generally refers cases to the Department of Justice for consideration of criminal charges. Such was the situation with DeShano. He was the only individual in the case not connected to the Karcher family by blood or marriage. There was no denial that DeShano had access to the confidential preliminary report and that he had read it. Einhorn, the regional administrator of the SEC, stated that DeShano "had the books in front of him and he acted on that information. The rest who traded are either tippees or tippers, and they aren't company employees."[27] DeShano himself perceived the strength of the case against him, stating, "They [the SEC] thought that it would be a good lead case because it was different. They thought because I actually sold they had more [of an] ability to prove that I was guilty."[28] But he also added that both he and the Karchers felt "all along that I was being used as a scapegoat to get to them [the Karchers]. . . . No one knows me, but they sure know his [Carl Karcher's] name."[29] The defense counsel, a former assistant U.S. attorney, reflecting on why the Department of Justice brought the criminal case against DeShano, stated, "They wanted to bring an insider trading case. It's a high priority. There haven't been many in the office."[30]

When taken on its own merit, out of the context of the Karcher family trades, the DeShano case appeared petty and inconsequential. Here was a man who was depicted by witnesses as honest and loyal, who, by all appearances, had never traded on inside information before, and whose loss avoided amounted to only $7107. Small cases such as this may be advantageous from a deterrence standpoint, conveying the message to the community that the district attorney will prosecute small-time offenders. But, as one of DeShano's defense attorneys remarked,

> if you want to use that as a goal of the prosecution, the deterrence aspect, then you've got to pick a case that's a strong case because if you lose it then you may have the opposite effect. The word may go out that you can't even win the little one.[31]

The jurors did not view this case as particularly strong; there was no eyewitness testimony as to DeShano's intent. They could only infer it from the circumstantial evidence presented in court. A juror remarked:

> It was a case that I wondered why the government brought in the first place. . . . I think everybody should be prosecuted . . . [when there is] sufficient evidence to bring a case. But I don't think that, in this case for instance, they were wisely using the taxpayers' money to bring this case unless they had something more to go on than they did.[32]

The Department of Justice believed it had a strong case. Circumstantial evidence, such as that presented in this case, had been sufficient in the past to return a guilty finding. DeShano was an insider who sold stock after he received the preliminary report. But, when there is only circumstantial evidence, the jury must infer the thought process of the defendant based solely on the timing of the stock trade and the information he had available. Although arguably the strongest case, taken by itself, out of the context of the Karcher family trades, the DeShano trade appeared insignificant. In light of the blatant abuse of inside information by individuals such as Boesky, the case against DeShano made the jury question the prudence of the government's decision to prosecute.

Settlements With the SEC

The Karcher family civil trial was set for May of 1989. Numerous defense motions had been filed, including one to have the case dismissed and another to try each Karcher separately. The motions served to tie up SEC resources and undoubtedly enriched the Karcher attorneys. As the trial date approached, two of the three lawyers of the SEC's litigation department were devoting their full attention to the case. But there was no trial.

Donald Karcher and those he allegedly tipped settled the civil charges with the SEC in February of 1989. The six defendants agreed to pay a total of $187,560 to settle their portion of the case. This included disgorgement of the loss avoided by those trading, with fines of the same amount, and a fine of $62,520 for Donald and his wife. All the defendants consented to an injunction from future securities violations.

The cases against the other Karchers were based primarily on circumstantial evidence: Carl had talked with his children during this time frame and they all sold their securities around the same time. An SEC lawyer later stated, after an unsuccessful defense motion to dismiss charges against the family, "They've never been able to explain what it was that triggered those sales. It's a little too much to believe that they coincidentally all decided to dump their stock on the same weekend."[33] The Karcher children claimed that they had personal financial reasons for selling more than $1 million worth of stock in the days before the announcement.

On 2 May 1989, the day the Karcher trial was to begin and more than a year after the complaint had been first filed by the SEC, headway was being made toward a settlement. Wes Howell, Carl Karcher's attorney, explained:

> "The money we're talking about is not going to make an enormous amount of difference [to Karcher]. [But] he was seeing his whole family being swept up. . . . He was seeing his company, with all of the principal executives, being subpoenaed. . . . And I couldn't promise him that he'd win."[34]

Before the SEC settlement could be completed, however, Karcher wanted assurance that the Department of Justice would not later file criminal charges. In July, the final settlement was reached, and it was formalized in August 1989. Karcher and the remaining family members neither admitted nor denied guilt. The stipulations in the consent agreement included an injunction from violating the insider trading regulations, disgorgement from the tippees of a total of $332,122 in profit, in addition to fines totaling the same amount, and $332,122 in fines for Carl Karcher. An SEC attorney pointed out that this settlement was fairly standard for insider trading cases.[35]

A *Los Angeles Times* interview with Karcher's attorney, Thomas Holliday, revealed that, "by settling the case, Karcher chose to avoid both the emotional and financial costs of a trial. . . . 'We had a winnable case,' Holliday said, 'but the monetary cost, in terms of lawyers and personal impact on the family, far outweighed the desire to win' at trial."[36]

Alvin DeShano formally settled the SEC civil charges against him in August of 1989. While neither admitting nor denying guilt, he agreed to an injunction against future insider trading infractions and consented to a disgorgement of $12,386, the amount he saved, plus interest, by selling the stock, in addition to a fine for the same amount.

Conclusion

The Karcher case study sheds light on the difficulties encountered when prosecuting either a civil or criminal white-collar crime. It was through the computer surveillance program at NASD that the Karcher trades were initially discovered. The case was then turned over to the SEC, which decided to investigate and file a complaint against those involved. Proactive market surveillance is one of the most frequently used insider trading detection techniques, but, at the same time, it has the greatest inaccuracy rate.[37] Approximately 0.6 percent of the initial inquiries made by self-regulatory organizations, such as the New York Stock Exchange or NASD, into anomalies detected by their surveillance strategies were referred to the SEC for the fiscal years 1985 and 1986. Of these 468 insider trading referrals, only 45, approximately 10 percent, resulted in SEC enforcement actions.[38] The Karcher case was one of the few that made it to the final stage of the process.

As affluent, prominent members of the community, the Karchers were able to engage the SEC in numerous pretrial motions. In the end, Carl Karcher was not prosecuted criminally, and, like most white-collar defendants, agreed to the sentence without admitting or denying guilt. By settling the case, both the SEC and the defendants avoided the time-consuming, resource-draining alternative of a trial. Yet, because of the reluctance of the trial judge in the Carl Leo Karcher case to use the treble penalties available under the ITSA, the defendants who settled with the SEC were financially penalized to a greater extent than the only defendant sentenced by the court.

The criminal prosecution of DeShano, in which his stock sale was examined by itself and not in the context of the other Karcher trades, appears trivial and insignificant when compared to more heinous criminal offenses. Ordinarily, though, a theft of approximately $7000 by a street criminal would be considered egregious. The average loss from robbery in 1987, for instance, was $447, with only 6 percent of the completed robberies involving property valued at more than $1000.[39]

Unlike a bank robbery, however, where the offense is not debated, the prosecutor in insider trading cases must prove that an offense was indeed committed. The complexities of the definition of the offense and the reliance on circumstantial evidence are common problems that prosecutors of white-collar crime must overcome. What looked like the strongest case for the government resulted in a not-guilty finding, leaving jurors questioning the wisdom of allocating resources to the prosecution of this offense.

Notes

1. U.S., Congress, House, Committee on Energy and Commerce, Insider Trading and Securities Fraud Enforcement Act of 1988, Report no. 100-910, 100th Cong., 2d sess., 1988, p. 8.

2. Eric Shine, "A Little Bell Set Carl Karcher Probe in Motion," *Los Angeles Times,* 15 Apr. 1985.

3. Mary Ann Galante, "Karcher: Cloudy Chapter in Horatio Alger Success Story," *Los Angeles Times,* 15 Apr. 1988.

4. Gary G. Lynch et al., "Recent SEC Enforcement Developments," in *Insider Trading, Fraud, and Fiduciary Duty under the Federal Securities Laws* (Washington, DC: American Law Institute, American Bar Association, 1989), 1:508.

5. David A. Vise and Steve Coll, *Eagle on the Street* (New York: Charles Scribner's Sons, 1991), p. 260.

6. Charges against Margaret Karcher were dropped in March 1989.

7. A margin account allows investors to buy securities on credit as long as they maintain a minimum amount of equity in their account. If the securities in the account drop in value, the brokerage firm may request that the investor provide more equity; this is known as a margin call.

8. Declaration of Carl Leo Karcher to the Securities and Exchange Commission, filed 9 Aug. 1988, para. 5.

9. Mary Ann Galante, "Judge Rules Karcher Son Violated Stock Sale Laws," *Los Angeles Times,* 13 Sept. 1988.

10. Ibid.

11. Theodore A. Levine, Arthur F. Mathews, and W. Hardy Callcott, "Current Legal Developments Affecting Insider Trading Enforcement Actions and Litigation, 1988–1989," in *Insider Trading, Fraud, and Fiduciary Duty,* 1:5.

12. Personal interview.

13. Personal interview.

14. Personal interview.

15. Personal interview.

16. Personal interview.

17. 459 U.S. 375, 384 (1983).

18. See John W. Bagby, "The Evolving Controversy over Insider Trading," *American Business Law Journal,* 24:571, 606-7 (1986).

19. Francis C. Dane and Lawrence S. Wrightsman, "Effects of Defendants' and Victims' Characteristics on Jurors' Verdicts," in *The Psychology of the Courtroom,* ed. N. L. Kerr and R. M. Bray (New York: Academic Press, 1982).

20. Personal interview.

21. Dane and Wrightsman, "Effects of Defendants' and Victims' Characteristics."

22. Personal interview

23. Personal interview.

24. Cited in Martin F. Kaplan, "Cognitive Processes in the Individual Juror," in *Psychology of the Courtroom,* ed. Kerr and Bray.

25. Personal interview.

26. Susan P. Shapiro, *Wayward Capitalists: Target of the Securities and Exchange Commission* (New Haven, CT: Yale University Press, 1984).

27. Mary Ann Galante, "Carl's Jr. Chief Accountant Charged with Stock Fraud," *Los Angeles Times,* 17 Feb. 1989.

28. Personal interview.

29. Personal interview.

30. Personal interview.

31. Personal interview.

32. Personal interview.

33. David Greenwald, "Karcher Denies Telling His Children to Sell Their Stock," *Orange County Register,* 21 Mar. 1989.

34. Mary Ann Galante, "Tentative Settlement in Suit against Karchers," *Los Angeles Times,* 21 Mar. 1989.

35. Personal interview.

36. Mary Ann Galante, "Karchers Settle Insider-Training Case with Fine," *Los Angeles Times,* 25 July 1989.

37. Shapiro, *Wayward Capitalists.*

38. U.S., General Accounting Office, *Securities Regulation: Efforts to Detect, Investigate and Deter Insider Trading* (Washington, DC: General Accounting Office, 1988).

39. U.S., Department of Justice, Bureau of Justice Statistics, *Special Report: Robbery Victims* (Washington, DC: Department of Justice, Apr. 1987).

DISCUSSION QUESTIONS

1. Do you agree with the penalties in this case? Explain.

2. How does character influence jurors' perceptions of white-collar offenders?

3. What does this case study have to do with the systems approach?

READING

In this reading, BJS statistician Ramona Rantala describes the results of a survey of 7,818 businesses. The survey found that two thirds of the businesses experienced at least one form of computer crime. Businesses with the highest rates of computer crime victimization included telecommunications businesses, computer systems design companies, and durable goods manufacturers. Computer virus infections were the most common type of cyber crime reported by the businesses. One in 10 of the businesses reported experiencing cyber theft. Employees accounted for approximately three fourths of the cyber thefts.

SOURCE: Rantala, R. (2008). Cybercrime against businesses, 2005. Bureau of Justice Statistics.

Cybercrime Against Businesses, 2005

Ramona R. Rantala

Among 7,618 businesses that responded to the National Computer Security Survey, 67% detected at least one cybercrime in 2005. Nearly 60% detected one or more types of cyber attack, 11% detected cyber theft, and 24% of the businesses detected other computer security incidents. Respondents, representing 36 economic industries, said they detected more than 22 million incidents of cybercrime in 2005. The vast majority of cybercrimes (20 million incidents) were other computer security incidents, primarily spyware, adware, phishing, and spoofing. There were nearly 1.5 million computer virus infections and 126,000 cyber fraud incidents.

The effects of these crimes were measured in terms of monetary loss and system downtime. Ninety-one percent of the businesses providing information sustained one or both types of loss. The monetary loss for these businesses totaled $867 million in 2005. Cyber theft accounted for more than half of the loss ($450 million). Cyber attacks cost businesses $314 million. System downtime caused by cyber attacks and other computer security incidents totaled 323,900 hours. Computer viruses accounted for 193,000 hours and other computer security incidents resulted in more than 100,000 hours of system downtime.

Of the businesses responding to the survey, telecommunications businesses (82% of these businesses), computer system design businesses (79%), and manufacturers of durable goods (75%) had the highest prevalence of cybercrime in 2005. Utilities, computer system design businesses, manufacturers of durable goods, and internet service providers detected the highest number of incidents, with a total of more than 10.5 million incidents. Administrative support, finance, and food service businesses incurred

the highest monetary loss with a combined total of $325 million, more than a third of the total for all businesses.

Forestry, fishing, and hunting (44% of businesses) and agriculture (51%) had the lowest prevalence of cybercrime in 2005. Agriculture, rental services, and business and technical schools incurred the least monetary loss (S3 million).

Insiders (i.e., employees, contractors, or vendors working for the business) were responsible for the cyber thefts against nearly 75% of businesses victimized by cyber theft. Conversely, more than 70% of businesses victimized by cyber attacks or other computer security incidents said the suspected offenders were outsiders (i.e., hackers, competitors, and other non-employees).

Overall, few businesses that detected an incident (15%) reported cybercrimes to official law enforcement agencies. More than 50% of victimized businesses reported cyber thefts to police, while cyber attacks and other computer security incidents were reported to authorities by 6% and 12% of victimized businesses, respectively.

The National Computer Security Survey Provides the Nation's First Large-Scale Measure of Cybercrime

The President's National Strategy to Secure Cyberspace directs the Department of Justice to develop better data about the nature and prevalence of cybercrime and electronic intrusions.[1] Other data collections address cybercrime, but no large-scale (or nationally representative) survey collects sufficient information to accurately measure cybercrime and its consequences or to develop risk factors.

---

[1]The National Strategy to Secure Cyberspace, February 2003; Recommendation A/R 2-1.

The National Computer Security Survey (NCSS) was developed by the U.S. Department of Justice (DOJ), Office of Justice Programs, Bureau of Justice Statistics in partnership with the U.S. Department of Homeland Security, National Cyber Security Division. The DOJ Computer Crime and Intellectual Property Section, the Computer Intrusion Section of the Federal Bureau of investigation Cyber Division, and the U.S. Secret Service also collaborated on the project. The survey was also supported by a wide variety of trade associations and industry groups. (A complete list is available online at http://www.ojp.usdoj.gov/bjs/survey/ncss/ncss.htm.)

The NCSS documents the nature, prevalence, and impact of cyber intrusions against businesses in the United States. This report examines three general types of cybercrime:

- Cyber attacks are crimes in which the computer system is the target. Cyber attacks consist of computer viruses (including worms and Trojan horses), denial of service attacks, and electronic vandalism or sabotage.
- Cyber theft comprises crimes in which a computer is used to steal money or other things of value. Cyber theft includes embezzlement, fraud, theft of intellectual property, and theft of personal or financial data.
- Other computer security incidents encompass spyware, adware, hacking, phishing, spoofing, pinging, port scanning, and theft of other information, regardless of whether the breach was successful or damage or losses were sustained as a result.

More Than 8,000 Businesses Participated in the Survey

The National Computer Security Survey sample was a stratified, random sample of businesses designed to produce national and industry-level estimates. The sample was stratified by industry, risk level, and size of business. Thirty-six industries, as defined by the North American Industrial Classification System (NAICS), were within the scope of the survey.

To produce national and industry-level estimates a sample of nearly 36,000 businesses was selected. Responses were received from more than 8,000 businesses, giving an overall response rate of 23%. Response rates varied by business size, with larger businesses responding at a higher rate. Response rates also varied by industry. Response rates were highest for utility businesses (37%). Telecommunications (16%) had one of the lowest response rates. Though response rates were not sufficient to support national or industry-level estimates, they were the highest of any survey of this kind.

Computer Virus Infections Were the Most Prevalent Cybercrime Among Businesses in 2005

Of the 8,000 respondent businesses representing 36 economic industries, more than 7,800 used some type of computer system. Two-thirds of the businesses that used computers detected at least one computer security incident (5,081 businesses) in 2005. Nearly three-fifths detected one or more types of cyber attack. A tenth detected a cyber theft. A quarter of the businesses detected other computer security incidents, such as spy-ware or phishing.

Computer virus infection was the most prevalent type of cyber attack, detected by 52% of responding businesses. Nearly 90% of respondents reported that they were able to stop a virus before it caused an infection. Of those businesses able to intercept viruses, 40% said they were successful in preventing all virus infections.

Cyber fraud was the most common type of cyber theft, having been detected by 5% of the businesses responding to the survey.

Of the businesses detecting theft of intellectual property, 70% indicated at least one incident involving the theft of trade secrets. For victims of theft of personal or financial data, names and dates of birth were taken from 60% of businesses. More than 75% of the businesses detecting other computer security incidents indicated that some type of malware (primarily adware) was installed, and 58% of victims discovered spyware or keystroke logging applications. Slightly more than 50% of the businesses detecting other computer security incidents were victims of corporate identity theft in the form of phishing or spoofing.

Prevalence of cybercrime varied by industry and risk level, in 2005, telecommunications businesses (82% of these businesses), computer system design businesses (79%), and manufacturers of durable goods (75%) had the highest prevalence of cybercrime. These three industries also showed the highest prevalence of cyber attacks. Finance (33% of businesses) and Internet service providers (21%) had the highest proportion of businesses detecting cyber theft. About a third of responding telecommunications businesses, manufacturers of durable goods, and architecture and engineering businesses detected other computer security incidents.

Forestry, fishing, and hunting (44% of businesses) and agriculture (51%) had the lowest prevalence of cybercrime in 2005. Forestry, fishing, and hunting also had the lowest proportion of businesses detecting cyber theft (3%), followed by warehousing (4%) and social services (5%).

86% of Victimized Businesses Detected Multiple Incidents

The majority of victimized businesses (86%) detected multiple incidents, with half of these (43%) detecting 10 or more incidents during the year. However, the percentage of businesses detecting multiple incidents varied by type of incident. For victims of computer viruses, denial of service attacks, fraud, and other computer security incidents, the majority of victims detected multiple incidents. Conversely, fewer than half of the victims of vandalism or sabotage, embezzlement, theft of intellectual property, or theft of personal or financial data detected multiple incidents.

91% of Businesses Detecting Cybercrime Incurred Losses

The effects of cybercrime were measured in terms of monetary loss and system downtime. During testing of the survey instrument, many businesses indicated that they had no reliable way to estimate the costs associated with system downtime. The businesses cited various reasons for difficulty in estimating the cost: employees were able to work offline, customers could return after systems were restored, and there was no method for measuring lost sales. For these reasons, the NCSS asked only for duration of downtime rather than a dollar loss equivalent.

Ninety-one percent of the businesses that detected incidents and answered questions on loss sustained one or both types of loss. Forty-one percent of businesses sustained both monetary loss and system downtime.

Type of loss	Percent of business*
No loss	9
Any loss	91
Monetary loss only	38
Downtime only	12
Both	41

*Based on 4,083 businesses answering at least one question on monetary loss or downtime.

Of the 3,591 businesses that detected incidents and responded to monetary loss questions, 3,247 (90%) incurred monetary loss from the computer security incidents. The amount of monetary loss depended on the type of incident. Approximately 68% of the victims of cyber theft sustained monetary loss of $10,000 or more. By comparison, 34% of the businesses detecting cyber attacks and 31% of businesses detecting other computer security incidents lost more than $10,000. The other computer security incidents category had the highest proportion of businesses experiencing some form of cybercrime but incurring no monetary loss (20%).

There was no downtime for a tenth of the businesses detecting cyber attacks or other computer security incidents. System downtime lasted between 1 and 24 hours for half of the businesses and more than 24 hours for a third of businesses detecting these types of incidents.

The duration of system downtime varied by type of incident. Denial of service attacks noticeably affected the computer systems of 92% of victims. By comparison, incidents of vandalism or sabotage shut systems down for 73% of businesses, and other computer security incidents caused system downtime for 68% of victimized businesses.

Cybercrime Resulted in Monetary Loss of $867 Million Among Businesses Responding to the Survey

Nearly 4,500 businesses provided information on 22 million cybercrime incidents in 2005. The 3,247 businesses that incurred monetary loss from cybercrime lost a total of $867 million. About 2,000 businesses said their business networks, PCs, or web sites (or combinations of the three) were down for a total of 324,000 hours.

Cyber attacks accounted for nearly 1.6 million incidents, more than $300 million in loss, and 220,000 hours of system downtime. Computer viruses accounted for about 90% each of: cyber attack incidents (1.5 million incidents), monetary loss ($281 million), and system downtime (193,000 hours).

Cyber theft accounted for less than 1% of all incidents but more than 50% of the total monetary loss ($450 million). Theft of intellectual property had the fewest number of incidents (607), and the greatest amount of monetary loss of all types of cyber theft (nearly $160 million). Embezzlement also cost businesses nearly $160 million. System downtime data were not collected for cyber theft.

Although 24% of businesses detected other computer security incidents, these other incidents accounted for 92% of the total number of incidents, or 20 million incidents. Other computer security incidents accounted for 12% of all monetary loss ($103 million) and 32% of system downtime (104,000 hours).

Two-Thirds of Computer Security Incidents Were Targeted Against Critical Infrastructure Businesses

The number of incidents varied by risk level and industry. Ninety-five percent of victimized scientific research and development businesses detected multiple incidents. By comparison, fewer than 80% of victimized

businesses operating in management of companies; forestry, fishing, and hunting; or other services detected more than one incident.

Critical infrastructure businesses detected 13 million incidents (nearly two-thirds of the total). High risk industries detected more than 4 million incidents (a fifth of the total).

Risk Level	Number of Incidents
All businesses	22,138,250
Critical infrastructure	13,039,900
High risk	4,133,800
Moderate risk	1,979,400
Low risk	2,985,100

Utilities, computer system design businesses, durable goods manufacturers, and internet service providers detected the most incidents. Businesses in these four industries detected more than 10.5 million incidents in 2005. Forestry, fishing, and hunting; food service; and rental service businesses detected the lowest number of incidents. Combined, these 3 industries detected fewer than 10,000 incidents.

Computer system design businesses (98%) incurred monetary loss more frequently than any other industry. In 2005 computer security incidents resulted in losses of $10,000 or greater for more than half of the finance businesses, manufacturers of durable goods, insurance businesses, and mining businesses.

Critical infrastructure ($288 million) and low-risk businesses ($298 million) sustained the greatest monetary loss from cybercrime in 2005.

Risk level	Monetary loss (in thousands)
All businesses	866,600
Critical infrastructure	287,600
High risk	205,100
Moderate risk	76,100
Low risk	297,800

Specifically, administrative support, finance, and food service businesses incurred the greatest monetary loss with a combined total of $325 million, more than a third of the total for all businesses. Agriculture businesses, rental services, and business and technical schools incurred the least monetary loss with a combined loss of $3 million.

More than half of the manufacturers of durable goods (56%) sustained system downtime of 25 hours or longer. By comparison, more than a third of legal services and accounting businesses had a total of 1 to 4 hours of system downtime. Critical infrastructure industries suffered 152,200 hours of system downtime (nearly half of the total). Health care businesses reported the greatest duration of system downtime (34,800 hours). Accounting; forestry, fishing, and hunting; and warehousing had the least downtime—a total of 2,500 hours, with fewer than 1,000 hours each.

Insiders Were Involved in Cyber Theft for 74% of Businesses in 2005

A third of the victimized businesses indicated that they were unable to determine what affiliation any computer security offenders had with the business. The type of incident for which businesses had the least information about the offender was denial of service (50% of businesses). Conversely, some offender information was known by the majority of victims of theft of intellectual property (94% of businesses) and embezzlement (93%).

In 2005 someone from outside the business, such as a hacker or competitor, was responsible for at least one computer security incident against 71% of the businesses that were able to make a determination about the suspected offender. For cyber attacks and other computer security incidents, nearly 75% of businesses said the suspected offender was an outsider. By comparison, the majority of businesses detecting cyber theft reported that the suspected offender was an insider (employee, contractor, or vendor working for the business). For embezzlement, more than 90% of businesses said the suspected offender was an insider, which is to be expected due to the nature of the crime.

For thefts of intellectual property, nearly 85% of businesses said an insider was involved.

Motion picture and sound recording businesses (87% of victimized businesses) had the highest percentage of outside offenders. By comparison, arts and entertainment businesses had the lowest (55%). Retail (54%), finance (50%), and utility businesses (50%) showed the highest percentage of inside offenders. Petroleum businesses (24%), architecture and engineering businesses (25), and business and technical schools (26%) had the lowest. Computer system design businesses had the second highest prevalence of outside offenders (84% of victimized businesses) and one of the lowest prevalence rates of inside offenders (29%).

Most Businesses Did Not Report Cyber Attacks to Law Enforcement Authorities

When a computer security incident was detected, businesses responded in a variety of ways. The majority of businesses (87%) reported the incident to some person or organization. Eighty percent of responding businesses reported incidents to someone within their business. Fifteen percent of respondents reported incidents to another organization, such as their computer security contractor or internet service provider. Fifteen percent of victimized businesses reported incidents to law enforcement. Law enforcement includes federal, state and local law enforcement agencies, and official organizations affiliated with law enforcement such as InfraGard (an organization that works with the Federal Bureau of Investigation), the United States Secret Service (USSS) sponsored Electronic Crimes Task Forces, USSS Cyber Investigative Section (CIS), and CERT CC (an organization that works with the Department of Homeland Security).

Reporting of incidents to law enforcement authorities varied by the type of incident. The majority of businesses reported embezzlement (72%), fraud (63%), and theft of personal or financial data (60%). Few businesses reported theft of intellectual property (27%), any type of cyber attack (6%), or other computer security incidents (12%) to law enforcement officials.

Among businesses not reporting incidents to law enforcement authorities, the majority (86%) indicated that incidents were reported elsewhere (within the business or to an organization such as their security contractor) rather than to law enforcement. Half of the businesses responded that they thought there was nothing to be gained by reporting an incident to law enforcement. Other businesses said they did not think to report the incident (22%), did not know who to contact (11%), or thought the incident was outside the jurisdiction of law enforcement authorities (7%).

Few businesses (3%) indicated that their decision not to report an incident to law enforcement was based on the possibility of negative publicity or decreased confidence in the business.

Three-Fifths of the Businesses Detecting Cyber Attacks Reported That the Internet Was Involved

One critical aspect of computer security is determining which networks were accessed in an incident. (Accessed networks include networks that were breached, used to get into another part of the computer system, or affected by the incident—for instance, networks vandalized or on which malware was surreptitiously installed.) NCSS data identify which systems tended to be targeted. Nearly 1,600 businesses that detected incidents also provided information on the systems the business used and which ones were accessed during an incident.

A majority of the businesses detected at least one incident involving the Internet and/or a local area network (LAN). The Internet was the most prevalent vehicle or target of cyber attacks (64% of businesses), while cyber thieves tended to access a business's LAN (57% of businesses). For victims of other computer security incidents, half of the businesses reported the Internet, half reported their LAN, and more than a quarter said their wide area network (WAN) was accessed.

Other networks were accessed to a lesser extent. Intranet or Extranet connections were accessed during computer breaches for 17% of respondents, stand-alone workstations (15%), other networks such as

virtual private networks (12%) and wireless connections (8%) were also accessed.

Another critical aspect of computer security is determining whether laptops not owned by the business posed more of a security threat than business-owned laptops. Nearly a third of the businesses said a business-owned laptop was involved in at least one computer security incident. Business-owned laptops were cited less frequently as having been used in cyber attacks (10% of businesses) or cyber thefts (20%) than in other computer security incidents (38%). In comparison, 8% of the businesses reported non-business laptops were used in a cyber attack, 7% in a cyber theft, and 16% in another computer security incident.

Of the 4,000 businesses detecting a virus infection, 51% provided information on how viruses were introduced into their computer systems. E-mail attachments were the most commonly cited vehicle (77% of businesses) for introducing computer virus infections.

Small businesses (83%) were somewhat more vulnerable to virus-laden e-mails than large businesses (72%). Conversely, large businesses (37%) were more vulnerable to portable media such as CDs or thumb drives as a source of virus infections, compared to small businesses (14%). This difference might be explained by a greater tendency of larger businesses to use portable media.

Internet downloads were the second most prevalent source of computer virus infections. Sixty-one percent of businesses detected virus infections from Internet downloads. This percent did not vary by business size.

Insufficient Anti-Virus Software Was the Most Prevalent Vulnerability

Overall, 62% of the businesses using anti-virus software said the software was inadequate in preventing incidents. Nearly half of the businesses using anti-spyware or anti-adware said the software did not prevent an incident. Internal controls (31% of businesses), e-mail logs and filters (27%), and firewalls (26%) were also commonly cited as insufficient.

Security insufficiencies differed depending on the type of incident. The most prevalent security deficiencies were anti-virus software for cyber attacks (66% of businesses), misuse of authorized access for cyber theft (46%), and anti-spyware and anti-adware for other computer security incidents (62%).

Other security measures appeared to be more successful in preventing incidents. Biometrics (5% of businesses), digital certificates (5%), password generators (6%), and encryption (7%) were least frequently cited as the mechanisms that were inadequate to prevent incidents.

Businesses That Outsourced All or Part of Their Computer Security Had a Greater Prevalence of Incidents

Businesses that outsourced all or part of their computer security had a higher prevalence of cybercrime compared to businesses that performed all security in-house.

Sixty-four percent of businesses that outsourced at least one security measure detected one or more cyber attacks in 2005. By comparison, 55% of businesses that kept all security functions in-house detected a cyber attack that same year.

The security measure that showed the greatest difference in prevalence of attacks between outsourcing and in-house was physical security. Businesses that outsourced physical security had the highest prevalence of cyber attacks (73%), compared to businesses that managed their own physical security (60%). Several security measures showed little or no difference between the businesses that outsourced computer security and those that kept it in-house. These include business continuity plans and formal audit standards. Two security measures showed a slightly lower prevalence of cyber attacks when outsourced: network watch centers and configuration management.

DISCUSSION QUESTIONS

1. What can be done to prevent computer crimes against businesses?

2. Why do you think these offenses occur?

3. Why are certain businesses over represented as victims of computer crime?

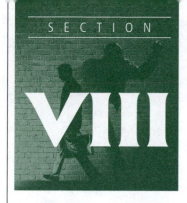

Crimes in the Housing System

- Mortgage Fraud
- Types of Mortgage Fraud
- Consequences of Mortgage Fraud
- Patterns Surrounding Mortgage Fraud
- Slumlords as White-Collar Criminals
- Consequences of Slumlord Behaviors
- Responding to Slumlords

 Introduction

"College students are irresponsible. Their negative reviews and the 'slumlord' reference makes me laugh because it's skewed and spoken from an already jaded point of view," wrote Mary McMaster ("My Dad Is Not a Slumlord," 2010) in a letter to the editor published in Columbia, South Carolina's *Free Times: Columbia's Free Weekly.* She was responding to a news article the weekly publication published the week before titled "Henry McMaster: Slumlord Millionaire?" (Hutchins, 2010). The article painted a picture of her father— then South Carolina's attorney general and a candidate for the soon-to-be-vacated governor's seat—as a ruthless and unresponsive slumlord. McMaster rented properties near the University of South Carolina to several different renters, including college students. Hutchins summarized the following complaints from two dozen tenants:

> Bad plumbing, broken windows, awkward confrontations with Henry, windows painted shut, bats, insects, mice . . . potentially dangerous gas leaks, rude text messages from [Henry's wife] . . . water pouring from light fixtures . . . being forced out of apartments . . . discrimination, severe water damage, mold, breach of contract, and withholding of security deposits.

University of South Carolina student Emrys McMahon told Hutchins: "He's a slumlord. . . . He has a bunch of shitty places he doesn't care about. He's a slumlord."

Local interest in the article soared and many readers made comments on a blog linked to the article. Many of the comments came from former tenants. Here are a few examples:

- After enduring the torture for what seemed like ages, my roommates and I finally broke free of the McMaster B.S. Winters of no heat except for a hole in the floor from the heater downstairs . . . roof leaks, delay in move-in, gas leaks.

▲ **Photo 8.1**   Is it a crime for landlords not to maintain their apartments?

- After reading this article and the comments that followed, it is refreshing to know that I was not alone in my disputes with the McMasters.
- As a former tenant of the McMaster's at a house on Greene Street, I can honestly say that South Carolina is in serious trouble if he treats its residents anything like he does his renters. They refused to fix a broken window. . . . Henry told me "Darlin', you're in the big city now. You have to get used to that."

Some readers may have lived in shoddy conditions themselves at some point during their college years, but did you think of your landlord as a white-collar criminal? Most likely, if we encountered them, we did not define slumlords as criminal. However, their actions fall within the domain of white-collar crime. They are not alone in committing crimes in the housing system. In fact, an increase in mortgage fraud has made crimes by slumlords seem rare by comparison. Consider the following examples, quoted verbatim from their original sources, as additional illustrations of crimes by slumlords, officials in the mortgage industry, and other professionals:

- [The defendant] . . . acted as a settlement agent in closing four home loans totaling about $978,500 in 2006. ***** secretly used his own money to pay closing costs on behalf of straw buyers and subsequently was reimbursed by a third party. ("NC Man Sentenced," 2010)
- [The defendant] was sentenced to 27 months in prison for his role in a real estate development fraud scheme that took place in 2006 and 2007. According to information presented in court, ***** assisted his father, Gary, in fraudulently obtaining financing for a number of high-end homes in

Ladue and Town & Country that they intended to rehab. In all, the [defendants] submitted fraudulent loan applications—including phony tax returns and profit/loss statements—for five different loans at five different area financial institutions. (Internal Revenue Service, 2010)

- [The defendant] was sentenced to twelve months and one day in federal prison on charges of bank fraud and money laundering. ***** was also ordered to pay restitution of $288,171. *****, a former Certified Public Accountant whose license has been suspended by the Oregon Board of Accountancy, previously admitted guilt in a scheme to defraud Countrywide Financial Corporation ("Countrywide") and Silver Falls Bank. According court documents, ***** used his financial expertise as an accountant to defraud Countrywide and Silver Falls Bank of funds by fabricating and submitting fraudulent individual income tax returns, between the years of 2003 and 2007, to his mortgage broker in support of applications to the financial institutions. The Silver Falls Bank has since been closed by the Federal Deposit Insurance Corporation. (Internal Revenue Service, 2010)

- [The defendant] was sentenced to twelve months and one day in prison on his conviction of wire fraud conspiracy and willful failure to file income tax returns. According to information presented to the court, ***** participated in a mortgage fraud scheme involving closing loans where ***** and his co-conspirator were supposed to pay off other mortgages, but instead used that money for their own purposes. As a result, there ended up being two mortgages on properties when there was only supposed to be one. Thus, when it came time to foreclose on the properties, the second lending institutions were not in the first lien position and they suffered over $670,000 in losses. (Internal Revenue Service, 2010)

- The violations have led to injuries for several tenants, according to their suit. Faustino Velasquez's 7-year-old daughter was bitten by so many bedbugs she needed to be treated at the hospital. A cockroach crawled into Jose Bonilla's ear, sending him to the hospital. Broken windows have fallen on several tenants, resulting in head or back injuries. A girl suffered smoke inhalation after an explosion in the basement. (B. Smith, 2006)

In this section, attention is given to crimes committed in the housing system. As will be shown, a number of different types of white-collar crimes occur in this system. Generally speaking, these crimes can be classified as (a) mortgage fraud and (b) renting unsafe properties (e.g., being a slumlord).

✉ Mortgage Fraud

Mortgage fraud involves cases of "intentional misrepresentation to a lender for the purpose of obtaining a loan that would otherwise not be advanced by the lender" (Financial Crimes Enforcement Network [FinCEN], 2009). Mortgage fraud has always been a problem in the United States, but it has increased in recent years. In a 2005 press release describing a mortgage fraud operation called Quick Flip, the FBI (2005) described mortgage fraud as "one of the fastest growing white-collar crimes in the United States." For the first time ever, losses to mortgage fraud exceeded one billion dollars in 2005 (FDIC, 2007). Not long after that, it was estimated that mortgage fraud costs banks and lenders more than four billion dollars a year (Creswell, 2007).

Experts have tied increases in mortgage fraud to the cooling real estate market. According to Vickers (2007), "as business dries up, there's increasing pressure on lenders, brokers, title companies, and appraisers to be profitable." Federal responses demonstrated an increase in mortgage fraud. In fact, the number of mortgage fraud investigations by the FBI doubled from 2008 to June 2010 (Pelofsky, 2010). As evidence of the breadth of these cases, consider that in June 2010, federal officials "charged 1,215 people in hundreds of mortgage fraud cases that resulted in losses of 2.3 billion dollars" (Pelofsky, 2010).

Reports from banking institutions also demonstrate a significant increase in mortgage fraud cases. Suspected cases of mortgage fraud are reported by banking officials "through Suspicious Activity Reports (SARs) required under the Bank Secrecy Act" (FinCEN, 2009). SARs have been described as "one of the most important sources of lead information for law enforcement in fighting financial crimes" (FinCEN, 2010d). To put in perspective the increase in mortgage fraud cases, at least suspected mortgage fraud cases, consider that in fiscal year 2004 banks across the United States filed 17,127 SARs about mortgage fraud. In fiscal year 2009, bank officials filed 67,190 SARs about mortgage fraud. This means that the number of suspected mortgage fraud cases quadrupled within a 5-year timeframe! As of March 2010, the FBI had 2,989 active investigations related to mortgage fraud. More than two thirds of the cases involved losses exceeding a million dollars.

It is important to stress that not all cases of mortgage fraud are necessarily white-collar crimes committed by employers. Indeed, some cases entail situations where consumers scam banks by committing fraud in order to benefit from deceiving the lender. Many cases of mortgage fraud, particularly those that are the most pervasive, can be classified as white-collar crimes. Between June 1, 2009, and June 30, 2009, the Financial Crimes Enforcement Network (2010d) reported that 32,926 SARs describing mortgage fraud cases were filed by banks. While many of the reports focused on allegations against consumers, about half clearly implicated white-collar offenders. Figure 8.1 shows the types of employers accused of mortgage fraud during this timeframe. As shown in the figure, real estate professionals, brokers, and appraisers were listed in more than half of all the reports. In fact, broker-facilitated mortgage fraud has been hailed as "the most prevalent segment of mortgage fraud nationwide" (FDIC, 2007).

Figure 8.1   Mortgage Fraud Suspect's Employee Role in Suspicious Activity Reports filed to FinCEN, January 1, 2009–June 30, 2009

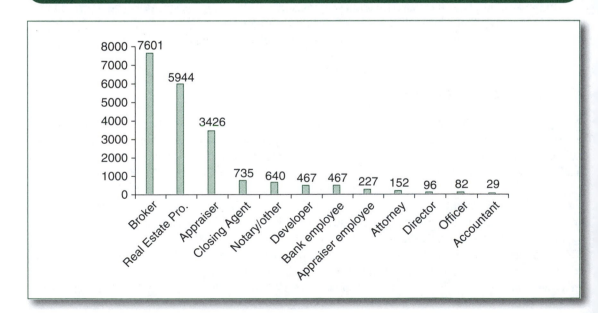

Beyond focusing on type of offender in these cases, attention can also be given to the types of mortgage fraud committed by professionals working in the housing system. In doing so, a fuller understanding of the nature of mortgage fraud will be possible. After discussing these types of mortgage fraud, attention will be given to the patterns surrounding these cases and the consequences of these behaviors.

Types of Mortgage Fraud

At the most general level, experts distinguish between "mortgage fraud-for-profit" and "mortgage fraud-for-housing." **Fraud-for-housing** cases occur when borrowers lie about their financial information in order to secure the mortgage so they can purchase a home (Glink & Tamkin, 2008). In contrast, **fraud-for-profit** occurs when offenders commit the fraud in order to reap a monetary benefit from the mortgage transaction. Mortgage fraud-for-profit is also known as "industry insider fraud" because the vast majority of cases involve schemes with employers inside the business transaction playing a prominent role (FBI, 2009b). In these situations, offenders could be real estate professionals, employees of property management companies, appraisers, financial advisors, loan officers, processors, underwriters, closing attorneys, or bank employees. The underlying thread across fraud-for-profit cases is that they involve multiple participants who commit an assortment of schemes over time (Fannie Mae, 2007).

Several different types of mortgage fraud exist. In terms of types of "for-profit-fraud," the following warrant discussion: (a) straw buyer fraud, (b) short sale fraud, (c) appraisal fraud, (d) equity skimming, (e) reverse mortgage fraud, (f) fraud during closing/settlement, (g) foreclosure rescue scams, (h) builder initiated fraud, (i) flipping, (j) qualifications fraud, and (k) real estate agent/investor fraud. Each of these is discussed below.

Straw Buyer Frauds

Straw buyer fraud occurs when individuals who do not plan on living in or even owning a house purchase the house and then deed it over to the person who will live there. In many cases, the straw buyers do this for a fee (Fannie Mae, 2007). In other cases, the straw buyers do this with the intent of unloading the mortgage on an unsuspecting homeowner who is unaware of the true costs of the home and, in most cases, probably unable to pay the actual mortgage amount. Based on these dynamics, Curry (2007) identified two types of straw buyers: (1) conspirator straw buyers who are in on the scheme and (2) the victim straw buyers who are not in on the scheme but who believe they will either legitimately own the home or be able to rent it. In the latter cases, the victim is often an "unsophisticated buyer, without cash or good credit" (Martin, 2004).

A few examples will help to distinguish between these different strategies used in straw buying fraud. In terms of coconspirator straw buyers, consider a case where a loan officer worked with a coconspirator to "take out more than $38 million in bank loans by recruiting strangers to fill out applications" (J. C. Anderson, 2010). All individuals involved in the scheme were aware of the straw buying fraud. On one side of the transaction, straw buyers purchase homes. The funds provided by the bank are given to the conspirator in the scheme. The straw buyer who owns the home either sells the home to another straw buyer or simply defaults on the loan. In these situations, the straw buyers are often offenders who have been convicted of other offenses. This dynamic somewhat blurs the line between street offenders and white-collar offenders. Browning (2010) describes a case where a man who had been imprisoned for selling cigarettes without paying taxes was caught in a straw buyer scheme one year after being released from prison.

The case of Lessie Towns provides an example of unsuspecting victims getting involved in a straw buying scheme. The 75-year-old Chicago homeowner learned that her house was being foreclosed on even though she "never missed a payment." In 2005, Towns "signed what she thought was a refinancing agreement with Oak Based Trust One Mortgage" (Meincke, 2009). What had actually occurred was she had transferred her home to another owner without knowing it. In fact, her home was sold twice without her knowledge through straw buyers. "I'm not angry," she told a reporter. "I'm disgusted. Just tired of fraud, tired of people using people" (Meincke, 2009). This victimization almost resulted in Towns losing her home. She had to enlist the services of a real estate attorney and spend a significant amount of time recovering ownership of her home. She was able to stop the foreclosure process on her home on the stipulation that she prove that she did not mean to sell her home when she signed the paperwork 4 years earlier. Incidentally, an Illinois law was passed in August 2009 in an effort to crack down on mortgage fraud and strengthen homeowners' rights. The governor signed the bill in Lessie Towns's backyard (Kass, 2009). He referred to the law as the "Lessie Towns Act" to honor the older woman's efforts to save her home. Towns lamented that she knew the governor was coming to her home only 20 minutes before he arrived.

Short Sale Fraud

The phrase "short sale" refers to instances where lending institutions allow homes to be sold for amounts that are lower than what the homeowner owed on the home's mortgage. These sales typically occur for houses that have been foreclosed on or those that are nearing foreclosure. To put this in perspective, a homeowner might have a $400,000 mortgage. Unable to sell the home for that amount, the bank may allow the homeowner to sell it for less, even waiving any additional future costs to the homeowner in some cases. Short sales in and of themselves are entirely legal and offer homeowners a way to get out from a mortgage and home they are no longer able to afford. These sales allow lending institutions to avoid lengthy and costly foreclosure processes. Still, the lending institution loses money on a short sale. Consider the following example:

1. Susan buys a home from Chandra and gets a $300,000 mortgage.

2. The bank gave $300,000 to Chandra as part of the transaction.

3. Susan is unable to pay her mortgage and asks for a short sale.

4. The home is sold for $270,000 to Randy.

5. The bank lost $30,000

Short sale fraud occurs when parties involved in the short sale manipulate the process in order to convince the lending institution to permit the short sale to occur. One variety of short sale fraud is "premeditated short sale fraud." This occurs when the offender "uses straw buyers to purchase and ultimately default on a home loan, creating a short sale situation so that the perpetrator himself can take advantage and purchase the home at a steep discount" (FBI, 2009b). Consider the example above. If Susan is a straw buyer and Randy asked her to buy the home and default on the loan so he could buy the home at a lower price, premeditated short sale fraud has occurred.

Another variety of short sale fraud can be coined "secondary short sale fraud." Secondary short sale fraud involves situations where the home has a second mortgage or equity loan attached to it. If a short sale occurs on a home with a second mortgage or an equity loan, by law, the entire proceeds from the short sale go to the primary mortgage holder. Secondary short sale fraud occurs when the owner of the secondary mortgage contacts settlement agents and asks for a cut that will not be shown on the settlement statement (Olick, 2010). One executive who arranges short sales told Olick that he had been contacted by 200 settlement agents who had been asked by bank employees to do this. The victim in these cases would be the primary lending institution, which would get even less from the short sale.

Appraisal Fraud

Appraisal fraud occurs when appraisers misrepresent the actual value of a home (Curry, 2010). Appraisers are called upon to determine a home's value so the lending institution can determine if the home is worth the amount of money that the lending institution would need to lend the buyer for the purchase. Four types of appraisal fraud occur. First, **inflated appraisals** overestimate the value of a home in order to allow it to be sold at an inflated price. This is also known as value fraud (Rudra, 2010). Second, **deflated appraisals** underestimate the value of the home in order to force the seller to lower the home price. Third, **windshield appraisal fraud** occurs when appraisers fail to do a thorough appraisal of a home (and may not even go into the home to determine its value—hence they determine its value by looking through the windshield of their automobile) (FDIC, 2007). Fourth, **conspiracy appraisal frauds** occur when appraisers work with other offenders as part of broader mortgage schemes. For example, for straw buying or flipping schemes to be successful, appraisers must provide inflated appraisals of targeted homes on a regular basis for their coconspirators. In Focus 8.1, When Real Estate Appraisers Go Bad, is a press release from the Department of Justice describing the conviction of an appraiser involved in a complex conspiracy that was designed to artificially inflate property values in order to defraud lenders.

In Focus 8.1

When Real Estate Appraisers Go Bad

Department of Justice Press Release

For Immediate Release

January 29, 2010
United States Attorney's Office
Central District of California
Contact: (213) 894-2434

Real Estate Appraiser Sentenced to Three Years in
Prison in Mortgage Fraud Scheme That Led to $46 Million in Losses

LOS ANGELES—A former state-licensed real estate appraiser was sentenced today to three years in federal prison and ordered to pay more than $46 million in restitution for her role in a massive mortgage fraud scheme that caused tens of millions of dollars in losses to federally insured banks.

Lila Rizk, 43, of Rancho Santa Margarita, received the three-year prison term after her conviction last summer on conspiracy, bank fraud and numerous loan fraud charges.

Rizk was sentenced by United States District Judge Dean D. Pregerson, who warned that other professional real estate appraisers should know that if they inflate appraisals and lie about the value of homes, "there is an overwhelming likelihood that they will be caught and go to prison."

(Continued)

(Continued)

The evidence presented at Rizk's trial last summer showed that she was part of a wide-ranging and sophisticated scheme that obtained inflated mortgage loans on homes in some of California's most expensive neighborhoods, including Beverly Hills, Bel Air, Holmby Hills, Malibu, Carmel, Mill Valley, Pebble Beach, and La Jolla. Members of the conspiracy sent false documentation, including bogus purchase contracts and appraisals, to the victim banks to deceive them into unwittingly funding mortgage loans that were hundreds of thousands of dollars more than the homes actually cost. Lehman Brothers Bank alone was deceived into funding more than 80 such inflated loans from 2000 into 2003, resulting in tens of millions of dollars in losses.

The evidence presented at trial showed that Rizk profited by collecting hundreds of thousands of dollars in fees for providing inflated appraisals in the scheme. Her appraisals typically valued the homes three times higher than what the homes really cost. In order to supposedly justify these inflated values, Rizk used "comps," or comparable homes, that were far bigger, more luxurious, and in better neighborhoods than the homes she appraised. Once she had inflated a few dozen homes, she then used those homes as "comps" to supposedly justify inflated prices for homes later in the scheme.

Ten other real estate professionals have been convicted of federal charges related to the scheme.

This case is the result of an investigation by the Federal Bureau of Investigation and IRS–Criminal Investigation.

Equity Skimming/Equity Fraud

Equity skimming occurs when investors convince financially distressed homeowners to use their home equity to "hire" the investor to buy the home, or part of the home, from the homeowner and rent it back to the homeowner. The investor receives funds from the equity loan, collects fees for rent, and then defaults on the mortgage (Donahue, 2004). Figure 8.2 shows the stages of equity skimming. Here is the foundation of the equity skimming process:

Homeowners facing foreclosure sell their homes to a third-party investor, typically located by a foreclosure consultant, but continue living in them for one year. The original homeowners use that time to build their credit or otherwise improve their financial position. Fees for the investor and the foreclosure consultant are paid from equity in the property, and at the end of the year the property is sold back to the original owner if that person can obtain a new mortgage. (Londoño, 2007)

If the process unfolds as described, then fraud has not necessarily occurred. Fraud occurs when the investor decides not to pay the equity loan or the mortgage, resulting in the homeowner losing his or her home to foreclosure.

Another related variety of **equity fraud** occurs when offenders steal the equity of a home by forging a homeowner's signature on equity loan forms and then directs the funds from the equity loan to the offenders' bank account. Sometimes the funds are maneuvered through several different bank accounts, including offshore and international accounts, making it virtually impossible to track the funds. As an analogy, think of a home that has a $30,000 theater system installed. The theater system has significant monetary value. If an offender breaks in and steals the theater system, the homeowner has been victimized by theft. Now, think of a home that has $30,000 in equity (meaning that the home is worth $30,000 more than the amount of money the

Figure 8.2 Stages of Equity Skimming

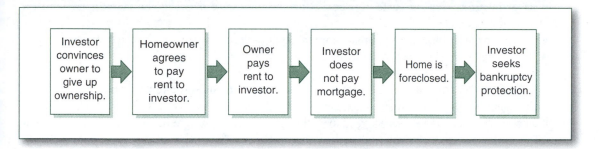

homeowner owes the lending institution). Just as burglars could break in and steal a theater system, offenders can steal a homeowner's equity by committing fraud against a lending institution using the homeowner's property information. Homeowners know they have been burglarized when they enter an empty home, but they may not learn of their equity theft victimization until they "receive an eviction notice" (Fannie Mae, 2007).

Reverse Mortgage Fraud

A reverse mortgage is a transaction where homeowners over the age of 62 sell their homes back to the lending institution and are able to live in their homes until they move or pass away. The homeowner can receive either a lump sum or monthly payments from the bank. The use of reverse mortgages has increased over the past decade, partly because of the higher number of older persons seeking strategies to increase their income. As a result, reverse mortgage frauds tend to target the elderly (FBI, 2010b). In general, **reverse mortgage fraud** refers to situations where fraudulent activities occur as part of the reverse mortgage transaction. One financial expert cites the following types of reverse mortgage fraud: charging for free information, misrepresenting pre-loan counseling, forgery of homeowner's signature, posing as government officials hired to help seniors get reverse mortgages, and bundling unnecessary services with reverse mortgage transactions (Paul, 2006). Another scheme occurs when closing agents fail to pay off the homeowner's original mortgage and pocket funds from the reverse mortgage transaction, instead of sending those funds to the lending institution (Tergesen, 2009).

Some offenders have been known to actively engage in the real estate process with the aim of committing reverse mortgage fraud. In these situations, the offenders target a foreclosed or distressed home, purchase the home with a straw buyer who lives in the home for a short while, and then get a reverse mortgage where the bank gives the schemers a lump some of money for the equity in the home. Then the conspirators disappear and stop making payments on the original mortgage (Glink, 2009).

Fraud During Closing/Settlement

Real estate closings or settlements refer to the end of the real estate transaction, when buyers and sellers sign the paperwork transferring ownership and agreeing to the terms of the sale and mortgage. Types of fraud that are possible during this phase of the real estate transaction include:

- Closing fee kickback fraud where settlement agents give kickbacks to real estate professionals who convinced the parties to use the settlement agent

- Failure to reveal settlement costs that one of the parties will have to pay the lending institution, real estate professionals, or the other party
- Overstating settlement costs and pocketing the difference between the stated costs and the actual costs
- Increasing fees above those promised for real estate services provided to the buyer or seller
- Providing kickbacks to lenders (Castillo, 2007).

A related type of fraud during closing is called **dual settlement statements fraud.** In these cases, settlement agents send one settlement statement to the bank and a different copy to the seller. The one given to the seller has the actual sales price agreed to by the seller. The one given to the bank has a higher selling price. The bank gives the higher amount to the settlement agent. The settlement agent gives the seller the amount he or she expected. The agent, and conspirators if there are any, keep the difference. In some cases, the buyer and seller are aware of the scheme (IRS, 2010).

Foreclosure Rescue Scams

Foreclosure rescue scams include various illicit activities designed to use impending foreclosures or a homeowner's financial distress as an element of the offense. These scams include arson, unauthorized bankruptcy filings, advanced fee frauds, and stimulus frauds. Arson as a type of foreclosure rescue scam occurs when investors, flippers, or homeowners destroy their property by fire in order to have the insurance company pay off the debt that has accumulated with the mortgage (Glink, 2009). If homeowners do this on their own, the action would not necessarily be a white-collar crime. If investors or business owners destroy their business or investment properties, these behaviors could be classified as white-collar crimes.

Unauthorized bankruptcy filings occur after a homeowner has hired a financial consultant who is paid to help the homeowner overcome his or her financial distress. The financial consultant promises to get the lending institution to stop bothering the homeowner to make mortgage payments. Without the homeowner's knowledge, the consultant files for bankruptcy on behalf of the homeowner. The homeowner stops receiving calls from the lending institution and assumes that the consultant has fixed the situation. When the homeowner fails to show up for the bankruptcy hearing (which he or she does not know about), the foreclosure process begins (FBI, 2009b).

Advanced fee fraud occurs when financial consultants or other individuals charge fees in advance to help homeowners address their financial problems. In many cases, the fraud occurs when offenders charge homeowners up front for help refinancing their mortgage. Federal officials have noted that these schemes have become increasingly popular over the past few years (FinCEN, 2010c). The popularity of advanced fee schemes led some states to pass laws to address the offenses. In California, for instance, a law was passed that stated:

It is illegal for . . . any person including lawyers, real estate brokers, real estate professionals, corporations, companies, partnerships, or any other licensed or unlicensed person or party to demand, charge, or collect any advance, up-front, or retainer fees, or any other type of pre-payment compensation, for loan modification work or services, or any other form of mortgage loan forbearance. (California Department of Real Estate, 2009)

Stimulus frauds occur when offenders use government stimulus programs as a tool for foreclosure rescue frauds (FinCEN, 2010b). Offenders hide behind the guise of government support and recruit potential victims through well-organized "clinics" they hold at luxury hotels or other posh settings. One approach that is used is the "redemptionist" approach where distressed homeowners are promised that their debt will go away if they participate in a redemption program (FinCEN, 2010b). Those in financial distress, a vulnerable state, trust the "financial consultants" and end up passing along private information that the offenders use to steal from the homeowner. Foreclosure schemes "are particularly evil because they prey on people with big enough financial problems that they're in danger of losing their home" (Curry, 2007).

Builder-Initiated Fraud

Builder-initiated mortgage frauds occur when builders or developers engage in behaviors that are designed to defraud the lender or the buyer. Such behaviors include (a) pump-and-pay schemes, (b) builder bailout schemes, and (c) faulty credit enhancements. With regard to **pump-and-pay schemes,** some builders work with others in the housing system to fraudulently increase their property's value. The builder has the property refinanced and collects the fraudulently obtained equity (Glink, 2009). The builder might actually repay the equity loan, but the fact remains the equity was fraudulently created.

In **builder bailout schemes,** builders offer buyers "excessive incentives" but hide those offers from the mortgage company to make it appear that the property is worth more than it is actually worth (FBI, 2010b). It has become increasingly common, for example, for builders to give homeowners a new car to get them to purchase a new home. As long as the builder reports this incentive to the lender, such practices are legitimate. When builders hide these incentives, they are able to increase the amount of profit they actually get from the lender.

Faulty credit enhancements by builders occur when builders engage in measures that make it appear as if buyers have better credit than they actually have. They do this to ensure that buyers are able to secure a mortgage. For instance, builders might put money in a buyer's account to make it appear that the buyer has a strong credit rating and the funds needed for the down payment (Glink, 2009). The problem is that the buyer actually does not have good credit and his or her risk of not being able to repay the mortgage is higher than the lending institution realizes. The builder sells the home, gets the money, and then the lending institution may in the not-so-distant future end up having to begin the foreclosure process on the home.

Flipping

Flipping occurs when scammers buy and resell properties with inflated prices. Sometimes the same home will be sold over and over at escalating prices as part of these schemes. This should not be confused with legitimate flipping businesses where investors purchase homes, fix them up, and then sell the homes for a profit (Curry, 2007). In the illegal flip, the home is bought, sold, resold, resold, and so on, with no changes made to the property. Fraudulent appraisals are used to resell the property at inflated prices (FBI, 2009b).

Reselling the same property creates numerous problems for neighborhoods. Typically, these homes are not well maintained, and the presence of dilapidated structures potentially breeds additional problems. Also, by reselling the home at higher prices, those who legitimately own their homes will have their property values artificially inflated. This is problematic for at least two reasons. First, the homeowners' property taxes will increase as the result of the artificially inflated prices. Second, if homeowners purchase neighboring homes based on appraisals including the flipped home's artificially inflated price, they will be purchasing their home at an inflated price. At some point, the home will potentially be worth less than the amount of money the homeowner owes on mortgage. This is known as the mortgage being "under water." In Focus 8.2, Flip This, provides a detailed description of the way that the flipping process is carried out.

In Focus 8.2

Flip This

Here is a case description of property flipping excerpted from an FDIC (2007) publication:

During a routine examination of a $1 billion financial institution, examiners became suspicious when they noticed that one loan officer worked apart from other loan originators and had processing personnel dedicated to his loan originations. Bank management indicated the loan officer was the bank's highest producer and that "even a bad month was a good month" for that loan officer. The loan officer maintained a high number of loan originations, even though he took no referrals from the phone queue. On further investigation, the FDIC discovered that the loan officer had an undisclosed relationship with a local mortgage broker. Examiners' review of the officer's lending activity revealed several loans that had been originated, sold, and then quickly fell into foreclosure. Properties were also refinanced rapidly, with an affiliate of the broker placing second mortgages on the property that would immediately be paid from the next refinance. A sample of the officer's loan documentation discovered altered or falsified account statements, purchase and sale agreements, income figures, credit reports, and verification of deposit forms. The loan officer has since resigned from the institution and is the subject of an ongoing criminal investigation. Total loss exposure to the bank is still being determined; however, the bank has already had to repurchase several loans as a result of this officer's actions.

Qualifications Fraud

Qualifications fraud refers to situations where professionals lie about a buyer's qualifications in order to secure a mortgage that allows the buyer to purchase the home. Industry professionals will lie about or exaggerate any of the following: income, assets, collateral, length of employment, employment status, and property value (FBI, 2005). Those items most commonly misrepresented are "employment, income, and occupancy intentions" (FDIC, 2007). In some cases, professionals might help buyers appear to be qualified when they are not (IRS, 2010). For instance, real estate developers or agents might tell buyers to have their names added to a family member's or friend's bank account so they look like they have more funds available for the home purchase than they do (FBI, 2009b).

Real Estate Agent/Investor Fraud

Real estate agent/investor fraud refers to a variety of scams committed by agents and investors. For example, **home improvement scams** include instances when agents or investors conceal problems with homes that should be disclosed to potential buyers. **Fraudulent loan origination** scams occur when professionals help buyers qualify for loans even though the buyers are not actually qualified. **Chunking** occurs when investors buy several properties without telling banks about properties other than the one the bank is financing. **Liar loans** refer to situations where investors lie about loans they have or are trying to get. **Churning** refers to "excessive selling [of the same property] for the purpose of generating fees and commissions" (Fannie Mae, 2007). Many of these scams occur as part of a broader scheme involving several coconspirators. As an illustration, churning may occur as part of a flipping scheme where homes are sold and resold. The agent's role in these schemes is to broker the deal and collect commissions. As well, in many appraisal fraud cases, "unscrupulous real estate agents . . . conspire with appraisers to fraudulently declare artificially high market values for homes" (Bennett, 2007).

Another variety of real estate agent fraud—which involves the help of fraudulent appraisers—are "inflate and crash" schemes (Bennett, 2007). In these situations, homes are sold at inflated prices (thousands of dollars above the listing price) and when the bank gives the seller the funds from the transaction, the seller gives the amount of funds that was over the listing price back to the coconspirators. Here are the steps in this fraud:

1. Randy lists his house for sale for $400,000.

2. Susan offers Randy $600,000 for his house on the condition that he gives $180,000 back to her at closing. This would mean that Randy is selling the house for $420,000.

3. Real estate agents negotiate the deal and approve it because it increases their commissions.

4. The appraiser appraises the house value at an inflated value of $600,000.

5. After closing the sale, Randy gives Susan the $180,000 and she divides the proceeds with the real estate agents and the appraiser.

6. Susan lives in the home for a short period, but then stops paying the mortgage and is evicted. The lending institution is unable to recover its losses as the home is not worth more than $400,000.

One mortgage fraud investigator alone said he had encountered 400 cases of "inflate and crash" fraud (Bennett, 2007).

Consequences of Mortgage Fraud

The consequences of mortgage fraud are widespread. To fully understand these consequences, it is necessary to focus on the consequences for (a) individual victims of mortgage fraud, (b) business victims of mortgage fraud, (c) communities and neighborhoods where the frauds occur, and (d) the real estate market. In terms of individual victims of mortgage fraud, homeowners victimized by mortgage fraud experience tragic consequences as a result of these crimes. Consumers who have lost their homes due to these offenses offer "stories of financial ruin" (J. C. Anderson, 2010). James Frois, director of the federal government's Financial Crime Enforcement Network, lamented that the most "troubling aspect" of some types of mortgage fraud is that the fraudulent actions "take advantage of senior citizens who have worked hard over their entire lives to own their homes" (FinCEN, 2010a).

When businesses are victimized by mortgage fraud, similar stories of financial ruin may surface. Beyond the dollar losses that lending institutions experience from fraud, many businesses face problems with morale and potential business failures as a result of fraud. After Lee Farkas, chairman of the bankrupted mortgage lender Taylor, Bean, and Whitaker Mortgage Corporation, perpetrated a mortgage scheme that resulted in millions in overdrafts to the bank, the fraud "contributed to the downfall of Colonial Bank" ("Ex U.S. Mortgage Executive Charged," 2010). Many employees lost their jobs and the bank ceased to exist because of the illicit actions of Farkas.

Communities will also experience negative consequences from mortgage fraud. Abandoned homes used in various mortgage frauds become targets of vandals (Fannie Mae, 2007) and the vandalism results in neighboring homes having lower property values (Creswell, 2007). The abandoned homes also increase levels of disorganization in the neighborhood, which may serve to breed conventional crime. Alternatively, as noted above, some types of mortgage fraud, like variations of appraisal fraud, may artificially increase property values and subsequently raise homeowners' property taxes (Fannie Mae, 2007).

The real estate market also experiences consequences from mortgage fraud. At the simplest level, increased mortgage rates/fees and difficulties determining actual home values have been linked to fraud (Fannie Mae, 2007). Federal officials suggested that "a direct correlation between fraud and distressed real estate markets [exists]" (FBI, 2009b). Others have suggested that the inflated home prices found during the real estate boom of the early to mid-2000s could be attributed to mortgage fraud (J. C. Anderson, 2010). In somewhat of a cyclical pattern, then, the current housing crisis can be seen as stemming at least partly from potentially fraudulent activities. Many homeowners now have mortgages that are higher than the value of their homes. The high rate of foreclosures has dropped home values even further. Ironically, the lack of business for mortgage industry insiders is now being seen as a motivating factor for current fraudulent activities.

Patterns Surrounding Mortgage Fraud

Because mortgage fraud is a recent social and crime problem, virtually no criminological studies have examined the offense type. Still, from news reports and governmental studies, three patterns seem to characterize these offenses. First, somewhat similar to other white-collar crimes, the offenses generally involve large dollar losses. Second, and also similar to other white-collar crimes, mortgage fraud cases often occur over long periods of time. Third, governmental studies show that mortgage fraud is distributed differently across the country. Table 8.1 shows the top 10 regions where suspicious activity reports for mortgage fraud occurred between January 1, 2009 and June 10, 2010. As shown in the table, the top three areas where suspicious reports come from include regions of Miami, Los Angeles, and New York City.

Table 8.1 Top Ten Regions With SARs for Mortgage Fraud

Location	Subjects	Rank
Miami-Fort Lauderdale-Pompano Beach, FL	5,029	1
Los Angeles-Long Beach-Santa Ana, CA	4,839	2
New York-Northern New Jersey-Long Island, NY-NJ-PA	3,447	3
Chicago-Naperville-Joliet, IL-IN-WI	2,973	4
Washington-Arlington-Alexandria, DC-VA-MD-WV	1,848	5
Riverside-San Bernardino-Ontario, CA	1,791	6
Phoenix-Mesa-Scottsdale, AZ	1,674	7
Atlanta-Sandy Springs-Marietta, GA	1,667	8
San Francisco-Oakland-Fremont, CA	1,364	9
Orlando-Kissimmee, FL	1,326	10

NOTE: The table shows the top ten metropolitan regions ranked by the concentration of local subjects of all mortgage loan fraud SARs reported between January 1, 2009 and June 10, 2010.

States that are believed to have significant mortgage problems include: (1) Florida, (2) New York, (3) California, (4) Arizona, (5) Michigan, (6) Maryland, (7) New Jersey, (8) Georgia, (9) Illinois, and (10) Virginia (Mortgage Asset Research Institute, 2010). State laws have been somewhat successful in curbing mortgage fraud. Georgia, for example, dropped from being the state with the highest ranking for mortgage fraud to eighth after the state passed laws addressing mortgage fraud and increased its efforts to become more vigilant in responding to these crimes (Glink & Tamkin, 2008).

Based on the patterns surrounding mortgage fraud, warning signs for these offenses have been identified. These warning signs include:

- Inflated appraisals
- Increased commissions for brokers and appraisers
- Exclusive use of one appraiser
- Requests to sign blank forms
- Higher than customary fees (FBI, 2009c).

The Mortgage Bankers Association (MBA, 2007) has called for a number of changes to increase efforts to prevent and more easily identify cases of mortgage fraud. In particular, the MBA supports:

- Mandatory reporting requirements to law enforcement about certain types of transactions
- Better communication between the mortgage industry and law enforcement
- A database of censored or debarred mortgage officials
- Increased funding for preventing and prosecuting these offenses
- Assigning law enforcement responsibility to one specific U.S. Department of Justice Office
- Enhancing intergovernmental collaborations in prosecuting mortgage fraud cases

The relative newness of the mortgage fraud crisis has forced criminal justice officials to respond using strategies and tools built for other types of crimes. These agencies have adapted, and continue to change in an effort to improve the response to these cases. As an example, in March 2010, the Financial Fraud Enforcement Task Force (created by President Barack Obama in Fall 2009) held a summit in Phoenix, Arizona, to address mortgage fraud. At that summit, U.S. Attorney General Eric Holder announced that an additional 8 million dollars would be provided to agencies to step up their efforts to address mortgage fraud. Similar summits have been held in other cities with high rates of mortgage fraud. The summits brought together criminal justice officials, community leaders, officials from lending institutions, and other real estate professionals to promote the coordinated response needed to address mortgage fraud effectively.

▲ **Photo 8.2** Attorney General Eric Holder, at the podium, has called for a collaborative response among various agencies involved in the response to mortgage fraud. Summits have been held across the United States with the aim of bringing stakeholders together to discuss effective ways to respond to mortgage fraud.

Slumlords as White-Collar Criminals

Another pervasive crime in the housing system is the failure of landlords to provide adequate housing. The concept **slumlord** is used to describe landlords who profit from renting run-down apartments that are not maintained by the property owner. While some may think that these behaviors are not criminal, the **Uniform Residential Landlord and Tenant Act (URLTA)** is a federal law stipulating that homes must be inhabitable, up to code, safe, and capable of providing the necessary utilities (Richter, 2010). States and localities have similar laws and codes. One issue that arises, though, is that local officials must decide which is worse: (1) forcing impoverished tenants to move out of their homes and perhaps end up homeless or (2) doing nothing and allowing the slumlord's activities to continue (Thomas, 2005).

In some instances, local officials are excluded from decision making processes designed to respond to slumlords. Lawsuits against slumlords are a perfect example. Adam Murray, executive director of the Inner City Law Center in California, described a case where one landlord was sued by 56 tenants after the landlord had been cited for 2,700 code violations. Here are some of the problems uncovered as described in the out-of-court settlement:

- Dilapidated plumbing that caused a ceiling to collapse onto a tenant
- Cockroach infestations so overwhelming that roaches lodged themselves in the ears of sleeping tenants and mothers had to stand watch over their sleeping babies
- An elevator that was out of service for three years, requiring mothers of small children to carry their baby's strollers up as many as four flights of stairs
- Sewage pipes that had leaked into an apartment, soaking the tenant's living room rug with raw sewage (Murray, 2009b).

The case was settled out of court with the slumlord agreeing to pay the tenants 3.3 million dollars.

Imagine the horror of the parents who found a cockroach lodged in their child's ear. The consequences of such filth are enormous. In the following paragraphs, attention is given to the numerous types of negative consequences that slumlords' activities have on individuals, communities, and society.

Consequences of Slumlord Behavior

Few criminological studies have focused on the consequences of slumlords' behaviors. However, using sociological, public policy, and public health literature, one can identify a host of different consequences that are likely to arise when landlords fail to maintain their property. These consequences include the following:

- Health consequences
- Financial consequences
- Dehumanization
- Emotional consequences
- Decreased property values
- Social disorganization
- Crime
- Legislative consequences
- Grassroots efforts

Each of these consequences is addressed below.

With regard to *health consequences*, public health scholars have long noted that individuals' health outcomes are tied to the types of environments in which the individuals live. Those who live in run-down apartments that are not well maintained are more likely to experience negative health outcomes. As one expert notes, "ill health and living in slums are intrinsically interwoven" (Sheuya, 2008, p. 298). According to one estimate, in Los Angeles, 48,000 people "get sick each year from living in slum conditions" (Murray, 2009a).

To be sure, landlords are not to blame for all of the problems that arise in slums, but if they actively choose not to maintain their property, then one can suggest that they have at least some blame in the negative health outcomes that are tied to slum conditions.

Financial consequences also arise from the behaviors of slumlords. On one level, it must be stressed that the health conditions are tied to financial consequences for those exposed to slum conditions. Individuals who get sick from living in slums will have health care bills to pay. They also will miss work as a result of the health conditions. Health care bills and missing work result in very real financial consequences for those living in slums. On another level, it is important to note that living in slums can actually cost residents and members of society significant financial costs. As a simple example, for residents, utility bills for utilities connected to broken appliances can be exorbitant. A leaky faucet or broken toilet not fixed by the landlord can drastically raise the tenant's water bill. Or, an outdated furnace or air conditioner can add precious dollars to the tenant's heating and cooling bill. While tenants will "pay more" to live in a slumlord's property, residents and city officials will also pay more as a result of the slumlord's behavior. Four decades ago, the National Commission on Urban Problems (1972) noted that "slums are expensive to city administrations" (p. 5). The same comment remains true today.

Dehumanization is another consequence of the slumlord's behaviors. Residents of slums are in positions of powerlessness while the property manager and landlords have significant power over the tenants. The degree of control given to property owners is such that the lives of tenants are truly in the landlord's hands. For those who don't maintain their properties, it can be suggested that the landlords are, in effect, treating human beings in dehumanizing ways. Arguing for the need for laws to protect residents, Colorado Representative Michael Merrifield commented that the living conditions of pets and animals are better protected than humans' living conditions are. He pleaded before the state legislature: "It's time—it's past time for Colorado's human animals to have the same rights as Colorado's dogs and cats" (Gathright, 2008).

Tenants will also experience *emotional consequences* from living in a slumlord's property. Perhaps the simplest way to explain how slum residents experience emotional consequences is to apply Maslow's hierarchy of needs to tenants. Maslow argued that all individuals have certain needs, and these needs could be categorized as a hierarchy including lower level needs and higher level needs (see Figure 8.3). According to Maslow, we direct our behaviors toward meeting our lower level needs, and once those needs are fulfilled, we then direct our behaviors toward fulfilling the higher level needs. The most basic needs individuals have are physiological needs—the need for food, clean air, water, usable toilets, and so on. The next level of needs are security needs—the need to feel safe. If we have our physiological and security needs met, then we are able to focus on meeting higher level needs—including belonging, self-esteem, and self-actualization. It is very likely that those who live in slums will face problems with food, air, water, and other physiological needs. As well, many will feel threatened by crime. As a result, most of their efforts will be spent on behaviors targeting physiological and security needs, meaning they won't be able to address their emotional needs.

A simple example might clarify how slumlords' behaviors contribute to these processes. In one case in which a landlord was convicted for not making repairs ordered by code officials, one of the residents described how his "girlfriend's seven-year-old missed school because of a lack of water to bathe in" (Yaniv & Moore, 2008, p. 18). In effect, the child could not go to school and work toward meeting his higher level needs because he was not able to have his lower level needs fulfilled.

Figure 8.3   Maslow's Hierarchy of Needs

Self-Actualization

Esteem Needs

Social Needs

Safety Needs

Physiological Needs

Another consequence of slumlords' behaviors are *decreased property values*. As noted above, property values in a particular neighborhood are tied to the value of nearby properties. If landlords fail to maintain their property, the value of the property will plummet, and the value of the neighboring properties will go down as well.

Slumlords' behaviors also contribute to *social and physical disorder*. Social disorder refers to social activities of residents that lack order and cohesion. Activities such as open-market drug dealing, unsupervised youth, public drunkenness, and so on are examples. Physical disorder refers to changes in properties or other physical structures. Graffiti, burglar bars, vandalism, litter, and other physical changes to the environment are examples. In this context, it is reasonable to suggest that when landlords fail to maintain their properties, the likelihood for social and physical disorder increases. Said one representative to a reporter, "these slumlords destroy a block, and that destroys a neighborhood" (Singer, 1999). Describing this phenomenon, Justice William O'Douglas once said in a court opinion, "The misery of housing may despoil a community as an open sewer may ruin a river" (cited in Murray, 2009a).

Slumlords' behaviors may also contribute to *crime* in a particular neighborhood. This notion is related to broken windows theory. Broken windows theory suggests that disorder leads to crime because disorder sends a "signal that no one cares" (Wilson & Kelling, 1982, p. 31) to potential offenders. As an example, when I was in the second grade, my family lived in a home near the railroad tracks and across the street from an abandoned milk factory. I was with some kids playing ball in the street when a baseball went through one of the windows in the abandoned building. Like many young (unsupervised) youth might do, we all ran home. A few months later a group of kids (again unsupervised) was hanging out and looking at the broken window on the old factory. The kids assumed that "no one cares" about the building and, out of boredom, proceeded to throw rocks at the windows and break virtually every window in the building. In effect, one broken window, left unfixed, led to dozens of broken windows.

With regard to slumlords, when landlords fail to maintain their property, it is possible that the degraded property sends messages to potential offenders "that no one cares." Some problem-oriented policing practices have integrated landlords into efforts to restore neighborhoods, and in some places landlords are held criminally liable for contributing to neighborhood decay. Interestingly, while it is possible that slumlords' behaviors (white-collar crimes) lead to street crimes, no criminological studies have assessed how this form of white-collar misconduct potentially breeds additional crimes. This is a fruitful area of study. Perhaps readers looking for capstone, thesis, or future dissertation topics will find this area of research interesting enough to address. The potential implications—for theory, policy, and future research—from such a study are laudable.

Legislative consequences have also resulted from the pervasiveness of slumlords' behaviors. States have passed a number of different laws in an effort to control slumlords. In Washington state, legislators passed a tenant relocation assistance bill that stipulated that landlords had to pay tenants three times their monthly rent (up to $2,000) if the tenants were displaced because housing code violations forced the residence to be condemned. If landlords do not pay the tenants, the law stipulates that local governments may pay and then collect funds plus interest from landlords. The new law also requires landlords to return deposits in these situations (Thomas, 2005).

In Colorado, HB 1356, passed in 2008, stipulated, "In every rental agreement, the landlord is deemed to warrant that the premises are fit for human habitation" (Kopel, 2008). Arizona's Residential Landlord and Tenant Act offered a little more direction in defining expectations of landlords. This law requires landlords of rental properties to:

- Meet building and health codes
- Make repairs to make the home inhabitable
- Keep common areas clean and safe
- Keep appliances supplied by the landlord working and safe
- Provide for trash removal
- Supply water, heating, and cooling (Volunteer Lawyers Program Community Legal Services, 2009)

Failure to meet these expectations can result in civil penalties for landlords.

Grassroots responses are a final type of consequence resulting from slumlords' behaviors. In some cases, tenants and community members may come together in an effort to address specific slumlords. In other cases, advocacy groups have been formed to help residents exposed to slumlords. One rather interesting grassroots effort is the use of the Internet to share information about bad landlords. A website called Landlord Ratings was created to allow renters to rate their landlords. Renters are given the opportunity to rate landlords on various measures. Go to http://landlordratings.org/ to see if your landlord has been rated. If you still live with your parents, you may want to think twice about rating them.

Responding to Slumlords

Tenants who encounter slumlords are advised to follow a formal and written process in addressing their concerns. One expert recommends the following steps to register complaints about landlords:

1. Notify landlord of concerns in writing

2. Report the complaints to the local housing authority. The U.S. Housing and Urban Development website includes contact information for all housing authorities

3. Arbitration

4. File a lawsuit

Ideally, the tenant's concerns can be addressed before they reach the point of a lawsuit, but this is not always the case.

In reporting complaints to the local housing authority, tenants will find tremendous variation in the way that localities respond to misconduct by landlords. Many major cities now have housing courts where these disputes are heard. Typically, the sanctions administered in these courts are fines and directives to fix up the property. The fines are collected by the city (and are not necessarily given to the victims). Ideally, such funds can be used to address slumlord behavior on a community scale. In Brooklyn, New York, the Housing Preservation and Development court collected 4.52 million in fines in 2007 ("Landlord Jailed," 2008).

Criminal penalties are applied less often to slumlords, but they are occasionally used. Not long ago, Hamid Khan was sentenced to 9 days in jail and ordered to pay $156,000 in fines after a 94-unit Bronx apartment building he owned racked up more than 2,000 code violations (Brown, 2008). Note that his sanction was not for the violations, but for the failure to fix the violations after he was ordered to do so.

In what *Newsweek* called "the prescription to fit the crime," some judges have sentenced slumlords to live in the slums they owned. Milton Avol's tenants "repeatedly complained of horrors: rats roaming through bedrooms, frayed electrical wiring, foul water seeping through cracked plaster." Avol earned the nickname "ratlord" ("R[X] for the 'Ratlord,'" 1987, p. 54). Other landlords have faced similar sanctions. In Boston, a judge ordered a slumlord to live in his rental property until the property was repaired *and* the judge said the family living in the rental property could live in the slumlord's own home (Zeman & Howard, 1992). In Washington, D.C., a landlord who pleaded guilty to 70 building code violations was sentenced to live for 2 months "where his tenants lived without heat, hot water, and basic sanitation (Leonning, 2001, p. B1). Later, officials recommended that the landlord be placed on electronic monitoring to ensure that he actually lived on the decayed property (Kovaleski, 2002).

Clearly, the behavior of slumlords presents numerous problems for residents, community members, city administrators, and the rest of society. Efforts to control slumlords have been largely unsuccessful. Still, the continuing local, state, and federal activities is warranted. Without some form of intervention, slums could be in even more dire straits than they currently are.

Summary

- In this section, attention was given to crimes committed in the housing system.
- The most commonly committed crimes in the housing system include mortgage fraud and renting unsafe properties (e.g., being a slumlord).
- Mortgage fraud involves cases of "intentional misrepresentation to a lender for the purpose of obtaining a loan that would otherwise not be advanced by the lender" (FinCEN, 2009).
- It is important to stress that not all cases of mortgage fraud are necessarily white-collar crimes committed by employers.
- At the most general level, experts distinguish between "mortgage fraud-for-profit" and "mortgage fraud-for-housing."
- In terms of types of "for-profit-fraud," the following types of mortgage fraud were discussed: (1) straw buyer fraud, (2) short sale fraud, (3) appraisal fraud, (4) equity skimming, (5) reverse mortgage fraud, (6) fraud during closing/settlement, (7) foreclosure rescue scams, (8) builder initiated fraud, (9) flipping, (10) qualifications fraud, and (11) real estate agent/investor fraud.

- Curry (2007) identified two types of straw buyers: (1) the conspirator straw buyers who are in on the scheme and (2) the victim straw buyers who are not in on the scheme but who believe they will either legitimately own the home or be able to rent it.
- The phrase "short sale" refers to instances where lending institutions allow homes to be sold for amounts that are lower than what the homeowner owed on the home's mortgage.
- Appraisal fraud occurs when appraisers misrepresent the actual value of a home.
- One variety of equity fraud occurs when offenders steal the equity of a home by forging a homeowner's signature on equity loan forms and then directs the funds from the equity loan to the offender's bank account.
- Reverse mortgage fraud refers to situations where fraudulent activities occur as part of the reverse mortgage transaction.
- Foreclosure rescue scams include various illicit activities designed to use impending foreclosures or a homeowner's financial distress as an element of the offense.
- Builder-initiated mortgage frauds occur when builders or developers engage in behaviors that are designed to defraud the lender or the buyer including (1) pump-and-pay schemes, (2) builder bailout schemes, and (3) faulty credit enhancements.
- Flipping occurs when scammers buy and resell properties with inflated prices. Sometimes the same home will be sold over and over at escalating prices as part of these schemes.
- Qualifications fraud refers to situations where professionals lie about a buyer's qualifications in order to secure a mortgage and allow the buyer to purchase the home.
- Real estate agent/investor fraud refers to a variety of scams committed by agents and investors.
- To fully understand these consequences, attention was given to (1) individual victims of mortgage fraud, (2) business victims of mortgage fraud, (3) communities and neighborhoods where the frauds occur, and (4) the real estate market.
- Because mortgage fraud is a recent social and crime problem, virtually no criminological studies have examined the offense type.
- The concept "slumlord" is used to describe landlords who profit from renting run-down apartments that are not maintained by the property owner.
- The consequences of failing to maintain rental properties include health consequences, financial consequences, dehumanization, emotional consequences, decreased property values, social disorganization, crime, legislative consequences, and grassroots efforts.
- Tenants who encounter slumlords are advised to follow a formal and written process in addressing their concerns.

KEY TERMS

Advanced fee fraud	Churning	Equity skimming
Appraisal fraud	Conspiracy appraisal frauds	Flipping
Builder bailout schemes	Deflated appraisals	Foreclosure rescue scams
Builder-initiated mortgage frauds	Dual settlement statements fraud	Fraud-for-housing
Chunking	Equity fraud	Fraud-for-profit

Fraudulent loan origination

Home improvement scams

Inflated appraisals

Liar loans

Mortgage fraud

Qualifications fraud

Real estate agent/investor fraud

Reverse mortgage fraud

Short sale fraud

Slumlord

Straw buyer fraud

Uniform Residential Landlord and Tenant Act (URLTA)

Windshield appraisal fraud

DISCUSSION QUESTIONS

1. Which type of mortgage fraud do you think is the most serious type?

2. What are three similarities between mortgage fraud and the behaviors of slumlords? What are three differences between the two types of crimes?

3. You are elected mayor of a large city that has several properties that appear to be run by slumlords. If you close the slums down, your homeless population will increase. If you allow the slumlords to continue their practices, other negative consequences will surface. What will you do?

4. Describe how mortgage fraud and slumlord activity might actually cause street crime.

5. List four concepts that come to mind when you think of the word "slumlord." What do these concepts have to do with white-collar crime?

6. What does the systems approach have to do with mortgage fraud and slumlord activities?

7. If you could choose a career responding to either mortgage fraud, slumlord behavior, or other types of white-collar crime, which career would you choose? Why?

WEB RESOURCES

Guide to Mortgage Fraud: http://www.realtor.org/library/library/fg330

Slumlord Laws: http://definitions.uslegal.com/s/slumlord/

Mortgage Assistance Relief Scams: http://www.ftc.gov/bcp/edu/pubs/consumer/credit/cre42.shtm

Flipping Frenzy: http://www.flippingfrenzy.com/

READING

In this article, Donald Palmer and Michael Maher, two Management and Accounting scholars, examine whether the mortgage crisis can be attributed to what their disciplines call a "normal accident." The authors' discussion demonstrates how white-collar misconduct crosses many academic disciplines, and the various disciplines will use different perspectives to understand and explain the misconduct. Notions of the systems approach are tightly wound into the discussion, particularly in their discussion of the way that complicated interactions result in "unexpected relationships." They draw attention to the way that complex relationships between various systems—including the financial system, social system, and housing system—influence the development of laws to regulate and control misconduct. The authors provide an insightful discussion about applying natural law and socially constructed law (though they don't call it that) to the way the mortgage system is regulated. They also argue that definitions of law change as social control agents expand their efforts to address concerns related to the systems the agencies control.

The Mortgage Meltdown as Normal Accidental Wrongdoing

Donald Palmer and Michael W. Maher

 Introduction

In this essay, we analyze the mortgage meltdown as a 'normal accident' (Perrow, 1984). We begin by briefly outlining normal accident theory—both Perrow's original version and Mezias's (1994) subsequent extension. We then use normal accident theory to analyze the mortgage meltdown and draw a few insights from our account. Following that, we consider the relationship between normal accidents and wrongdoing, a vexing question for both normal accident theory and observers of the meltdown. We conclude by briefly contemplating the policy implications of our analysis.

Our normal accident account of the mortgage meltdown diverges in important ways from the dominant discourse on the meltdown. This discourse attributes the meltdown to the unbridled greed and fraudulent behavior of mortgage industry participants. Our analysis suggests that the mortgage industry's complex and tightly coupled technology made it vulnerable to failure and that the greed and fraudulent behavior of mortgage industry participants, however reprehensible, played a minor role in the meltdown. The dominant discourse on the mortgage meltdown also attributes the meltdown to insufficient regulatory control. Our normal accident analysis also suggests that insufficient regulatory oversight contributed to the debacle. But our analysis implies that simply increasing the amount of regulation over the mortgage industry is unlikely to reduce its susceptibility to failure in the future. Indeed, if additional regulation increases the system's complexity and coupling, it could increase the system's susceptibility to failure.

SOURCE: Palmer, Donald, and Maher, Michael. (2010). The mortgage meltdown as normal accidental wrongdoing. *Strategic Organization, 8,* 83–91.

Normal Accident Theory

Perrow developed normal accident theory to explain the failure of technological systems in industrial contexts (e.g., petrochemical facilities and nuclear power plants). He contends that technological systems composed of many complex and tightly coupled interactions are prone to failure. He defines complex interactions as unexpected relationships: relationships that are either not designed into a system or are designed into a system but occur infrequently. Complex interactions are hard to manage because system operators do not anticipate them and have little experience dealing with them. Perrow defines tightly coupled interactions as rapid and unmediated relationships: relationships that unfold quickly and unconditionally. Tightly coupled interactions are hard to manage because system operators do not have the time or the means to respond to them.

Mezias used Perrow's normal accident theory to analyze the savings and loan crisis in the late 1970s and 1980s, which caused many S&L institutions to go bankrupt and many investors and depositors to lose vast sums of money. Mezias contends that the S&L crisis was the product of increasing complexity and tight coupling in the industry. Over the decades leading up to the crisis, financial markets became global, trading became continuous (round the clock), new technologies were instituted, the pace of transactions accelerated, new sophisticated financial instruments were created and a plethora of government regulations were promulgated, all of which increased the number of unexpected and unmanageable interactions.

 ## The Mortgage Meltdown as Normal Accident

The Argument

Davis (2010, this issue) argues convincingly that over the last few decades a bewildering array of assets have been securitized, leading to changes in the structure of the banking system and alterations in the way households think and behave. We focus narrowly on that part of the larger financial system whose failure constituted the mortgage meltdown. And we argue that this part of the larger financial system was complex and tightly coupled on at least four levels (each of which can be thought of as a different subsystem): the field, firm, fund and transaction levels.

We do not have the space here to elaborate our argument in detail at any, let alone all four levels. Instead, we provide illustrations of complexity and coupling at the firm, fund and field levels. And we present a crude analysis of complexity and coupling at the transaction level. Our illustrations of complexity and coupling at the firm, fund and field levels are quotes from persons directly involved in the events surrounding the demise of Bear Stearns, an investment bank heavily committed to mortgage-backed securities. These quotes, taken from a comprehensive journalistic account of the firm's downfall (Cohan, 2009), provide insight into how actors on the ground perceived the events in question. Our analysis of complexity and coupling at the transaction level comes from our reading of newspaper and magazine articles too numerous to cite here.

Illustrations of complexity and coupling at the firm, fund and field levels. Complexity at the firm level is well illustrated by an email message written by Paul Friedman, COO of Bear Stearns' Fixed Income Division (presented in Exhibit A), which describes recent developments in the firm's effort to merge into J. P. Morgan Chase. In a two- to three-day period in March 2008, Bear Stearns moved from being highly profitable to being almost bankrupt, a fate it sought to avoid by merging into J. P. Morgan. The key element of Friedman's message from the standpoint of normal accident theory is the succession of unexpected turns of events (in bold), ending with Friedman's summary assessment, 'you could not make this stuff up'. They indicate that even a person with intimate knowledge of the situation could not have foreseen the developments.

EXHIBIT A

An Illustration of Complexity at the Firm Level

As of this moment, **the world has shifted again. It had suddenly dawned on JPM** [J. P. Morgan Chase] that if the [Bear] stockholders vote down the deal—and they will—that they will have to leave their guarantee in place for a year without having control. **In addition, the Fed,** which had previously agreed to buy $30 billion of our stuff, now says that what they really meant was that they'd buy it after the deal closed. **As a result, JP[M] has informed us** that unless we grant them sufficient stock to guarantee that the deal is approved, **they're telling the world** on Monday that they're pulling the guarantee. **They will also** stop lending to us (currently around $10 billion) and demand repayment. Whether they can do that legally is another question, but they're doing it anyway, damn the consequences. **Meanwhile, our board** has said that we can't give away something that the shareholders currently have without getting something in exchange. **So we're deadlocked** and we're back to thinking about going b/k [bankrupt]. **You can't make this stuff up.**

(Paul Friedman, COO of Bear Stearns' Fixed Income Division, as quoted in Cohan, 2009: 138)

Tight coupling at the fund level is well illustrated by an account (presented in Exhibit B) given by an anonymous Bear Stearns executive of the developments that precipitated the rapid demise of the firm's Enhanced Leverage Fund in May 2007. One of the fund's counterparties, Goldman Sachs, issued an unexpectedly low valuation of some of the fund's mortgage-backed assets at the end of April. And this low valuation led to other low valuations, which caused the fund's overall value to plummet. The key part of the executive's account from the standpoint of normal accident theory is the repeated use of the phrases 'got to' and 'have to', culminating in the sentence fragments 'we got nothing we can do' and finally 'and that's game fucking over'. They indicate that there was little the fund's managers could do to alter the direction of the chain of events.

EXHIBIT B

An Illustration of Tight Coupling at the Fund Level

They give us these 50 and 60 prices. What we got from the other counterparties is 98. The SEC rules say that when you do this, you **either have to** average them—they're meant to be averaging 97s and 98s, not 50s and 98s—or you can go ask if those are the correct marks. But you can't ask the low mark. **You've got to** go back and ask the high mark. Everybody knows the procedure. So **we got to** go ask the high mark. We ask the 98 guy—another major Wall Street firm—and you know what he says? Remember, he knows he's high now. He goes, 'You're right. We were wrong. It's 95.' In other words, he gave himself a margin of error, and he said, 'I'm going to drop it severely.' He looked at it with great intensity and said 95. **Now we got nothing we can do** but take the 50 and 95 and average them. **We have to** repost our NAV. And now we go from minus 6 to minus 19—minus 18.97 to be exact—and **that is game fucking over**. By the way, the firm that sent us the 50 made a shit pot full of money in 2007 shorting the fucking market.

(Anonymous Bear Stearns Enhanced Leverage Fund executive, as quoted in Cohan, 2009: 337)

Complexity and tight coupling at the field level are illustrated by explanations offered by Ben Bernanke, chairman of the Federal Reserve Board of Governors, and Tim Geithner, New York Federal Reserve Bank president (presented in Exhibit C), to justify their role in orchestrating the acquisition of Bear Stearns by J. P. Morgan Chase. One key element of these justifications is the perceived dense web of interconnections linking Bear Stearns to other actors in the mortgage field (including trading counterparties and other investment banks) as well as actors in related fields of economic activity—a sign of complexity. Another key element is the predicted uncontrollable and rapid unwinding of those relationships if the government failed to stem Bear Stearns' bankruptcy and broker its combination with J. P. Morgan—an indication of tight coupling.

EXHIBIT C

An Illustration of Complexity and Tight Coupling at the Field Level

Our financial system is extremely complex and interconnected, and Bear Stearns participated extensively in a range of critical markets. The sudden failure of Bear Stearns likely would have led to a chaotic unwinding of positions in those markets and could have severely shaken confidence. The company's failure could also have cast doubt on the financial positions of some of Bear Stearns's counterparties and perhaps companies with similar businesses. Given the exceptional pressure on the global economy and financial system, the damage caused by a default by Bear Stearns could have been severe and extremely difficult to contain. Moreover, and very importantly, the adverse impact of a default would not have been confined to the financial system but would have been felt broadly in the real economy through its effects on asset values and credit availability.

(Ben Bernanke, chairman of the Federal Reserve Board of Governors, as quoted in Cohan, 2009: 100)

Bear Stearns occupies—occupied—a central position in the very complex and intricate relationships that characterize our financial system. And, as important, it reached the brink of insolvency at an exceptionally fragile time in global financial markets. In our judgments, an abrupt and disorderly unwinding of Bear Stearns would have posed systemic risks to the financial system and magnified the downside risk of economic growth in the United States. A failure to act would have added to the risk that Americans would face lower incomes, lower home values, higher buying costs for housing, education, other living expenses, lower retirement savings, and rising unemployment.

(Tim Geithner, New York Federal Reserve Bank president, as quoted in Cohan, 2009: 99-100)

An analysis of complexity and coupling at the transaction level. The financial system whose failure constituted the mortgage meltdown became increasingly complex at the transaction level over the three decades preceding the meltdown. Before 1970, the transaction system was very simple. Home buyers entered the market, lenders (mostly S&L institutions) wrote mortgages to facilitate their home purchases, and lenders typically held the mortgages as investments. Beginning in 1970, financial innovators (such as Louis Ranieri), aided by technological advances (such as the development of the mathematical formula known as the Copula), extended the transaction stream. Mortgage holders (either the lenders that wrote the mortgages or diversified financial institutions that purchased them from the lenders) began bundling the mortgages into multi-tiered bonds called collateralized debt obligations (CDOs) that were then sold to investors, many of which were diversified financial institutions. Often the diversified financial institutions that purchased the CDOs recombined their component tiers into second order bonds (CDO2s), which they then sold to still other investors. In addition, interconnected with this stream of transactions was a parallel stream of transactions that involved insurance policies on these mortgage-backed assets called credit default swaps (CDSs). Importantly, coupling in the system remained tight throughout the post-1970 period. The central players in the new system lobbied successfully to deregulate the system, by supporting passage of the Commodity Futures Modernization Act and the repeal of the Glass-Steagall Act. This meant that there were relatively few ways for government officials to intervene to alter the speed and direction of market interactions.

Several developments served to increase the through-put of this transaction system. The flow of mortgages into the system was increased by US Department of Housing and Urban Development (HUD) policies, which loosened lending criteria and provided lenders with incentives to write mortgages for low income home buyers. Further, as Davis (2009) points out, households began thinking of homes as investments, spurring them to purchase new and additional homes. This increased the supply of potential home buyers, which drove up home prices, which increased the viability of adjustable rate mortgages (ARMs), which further increased the supply of potential home buyers, which further boosted home prices. But other developments served to reverse the trend in home prices. Perhaps most importantly, construction firms responded to the rise in home prices by building more units. And this caused prices to level off, which caused some holders of ARMs to default, which caused the housing supply to increase, which caused home prices to drop, and more home owners to default.

The system might have reached equilibrium at this point. But the financial institutions that held the sophisticated mortgage-backed assets (the CDOs, CDO2s, CDSs, etc.), as well as their counterparties, lenders and investors, found it difficult to estimate the effects of the defaults on the value of the assets. Some institutions sensibly but somewhat arbitrarily reduced valuation of their assets. And others holding similar assets, bound by mark to market accounting requirements, were forced to do the same. This led to a spiral of asset devaluations, which caused the financial institutions' counterparties, lenders and investors to withdraw from the market, precipitating the credit crunch. Seen in this way, the mortgage meltdown was the result of close interconnections built into the financial system that did not frequently come into play during periods of normal operation (when default rates were low), and thus were poorly understood by and not subject to the control of the operators of the system when they were triggered by changes in the state of the system (when default rates increased).

Theoretical Insights

On the basis of our preliminary normal accident analysis of the mortgage meltdown, we have come to conclude that financial systems in capitalist economies are even more complex than technological systems in industrial contexts. This is true for at least two reasons.

First, technological systems in industrial contexts are typically designed by a relatively small number of individuals according to primarily technical criteria. As a result, they are designed so as to achieve a relatively limited number of compatible goals with system-wide viability in mind. Financial systems, by contrast, are typically designed by a multitude of quasi-independent actors, with different and in some cases incompatible interests, and with little concern for system-wide integrity. Imagine a petrochemical plant designed by multiple engineering teams, each of which operates in semi-independence, constructs its part of the plant with the goal of obtaining outputs that it alone values, and that communicates only rarely with the other teams regarding matters of plant-wide concern. This is an apt analogy for the mortgage field circa 2007.

Second, most technological systems are composed of interactions that are largely regulated by natural laws. For example, when a petrochemical plant holding tank's cooling apparatus fails, its liquid contents warm. And when the liquid warms, its vaporization rate increases. These interactions unfold in this way regardless of how human beings who might or might not be aware of the interactions interpret them, as long as human beings do not intervene in the interactions. Certainly system interactions in industrial contexts are also governed by formal rules and norms, such as those designed to insure system safety. But these governance mechanisms play a relatively small role in the system's overall functioning.

Financial systems are composed of interactions that are regulated by a larger variety of mechanisms. Some of these mechanisms resemble natural laws. For example, the 'law of supply and demand' appears to have regulated the interactions among the number of home buyers, the number of homes available for purchase and the price of those homes. But some mechanisms that appear to resemble laws are influenced by human agency. For example, demand for mortgage-backed securities and credit default swaps hinged partly on analysts' perceptions of the integrity of the mortgages that backed those securities and swaps. And analysts' perceptions of the integrity of these underlying assets hinged partly on analysts' faith in rating agencies' assessments of those assets.

Further, some interactions in financial systems are regulated by a plethora of other mechanisms that do not resemble natural laws, even laws that are mediated by human agency. Some interactions are regulated by formal policies, established by the government, industry governing bodies and professional associations. Other interactions are regulated by informal understandings, such as norms. Some interactions are regulated by trust, status and resource dependence-based power relationships. We think that the operation of these mechanisms, when compared to the operation of natural laws, is influenced by a greater number of variables, that are less well understood, and that perhaps relate to one another in stochastic rather than deterministic ways.

Our preliminary analysis of the mortgage meltdown as a normal accident has also led us to suspect that the current US financial system is more complex and tightly coupled than many other capitalist financial systems. The complexity of the current US financial system is likely underpinned partly by self-interest on the part of its designers. The complex financial instruments at the center of the mortgage meltdown were difficult for investors and government officials

to comprehend. The harder it was for investors to comprehend the financial instruments, the more dependent they were on the designers of those instruments, and thus the more the designers could charge for their services. The harder it was for government officials to understand the financial instruments, the less able they were to monitor and control them, and thus the more financial executives were free to act as they chose.

Tight coupling in the current US financial system is likely underpinned partly by the dominance of a cognitive frame that Abolofia (2010) calls 'market fundamentalism'. This frame assumes that the free market is an efficient, even flawless, regulator of economic relations and led the creators of the financial instruments at the center of the mortgage meltdown to develop a principled objection to government regulation of the system. Indeed, we suspect that market fundamentalism led market participants to develop a principled disinterest in understanding the mechanisms regulating the system. If one believes that self-conscious design and management of the financial system leads to suboptimal outcomes, then there is no point in developing an understanding of the system other than to satisfy idle curiosity.

The Mortgage Meltdown as Wrongdoing

There has been much public finger-pointing and a substantial amount of law enforcement activity in the wake of the mortgage meltdown. An orthodox normal accident explanation of the mortgage meltdown does not sit comfortably with this public outcry and legal action. Perrow and Mezias consider normal accidents and wrongdoing to be mutually exclusive, presumably because they implicitly adopt a legal point of view, defining wrongdoing as intentional behavior and accidents as unintentional. Thus Perrow developed a special label, 'executive failure', to denote events that appear to be normal accidents but are in fact incidents of wrongdoing. And Mezias contrasted his normal accident explanation of the S&L crisis with a wrongdoing account, contending that the evidence fit the normal accident explanation better than the wrongdoing one. From the standpoint of received normal accident theory, if the mortgage meltdown is a prototypical normal accident, the public outcry and law enforcement activity in response to the meltdown is by definition misplaced. And if the public outcry and law enforcement activity is on target, the mortgage meltdown is by definition not a prototypical normal accident.

We think the orthodox normal accident theory treatment of wrongdoing has merit. But we also think it has drawbacks. Most importantly, we believe it limits the empirical examination of the relationship between accidents and wrongdoing. Accidents and wrongdoing need not be considered mutually exclusive if one adopts a 'labeling theory' approach, which defines wrongful behavior as any behavior that social control agents designate as wrongful, regardless of whether or not the perpetrators of the behavior acted intentionally or unintentionally (Becker, 1963). Such an approach finds support in evidence that the location of the line separating right from wrong changes from time to time, as demonstrated by Hirsch and Morris (2010) in their essay on the meltdown in this issue of *SO!*. If one takes a labeling theory approach, then one is freed to theorize and examine the relationship between normal accidents and wrongdoing. And taking this approach, we have drawn the following tentative conclusions.

First, wrongdoing can contribute to normal accidents. A number of mortgage brokers and lenders falsified documentation attesting to home buyers' eligibility for loans at the height of the housing bubble (Temple-Raston, 2008). This fraudulent behavior injected more low income home buyers into the system, supplementing the impact of HUD's policies and the ARM loan boom. As devastating as this behavior was to unsuspecting home buyers, though, it likely played a minor role in precipitating the crisis. The number of fraudulent loans injected into the system was infinitesimal compared with the number of marginal loans entering the system via other completely legal means.

Second, normal accidents can increase the likelihood that largely unrelated wrongdoing is detected. Bernard Madoff and Allen Stanford orchestrated elaborate Ponzi schemes that stole hundreds of millions of dollars from investors in the years leading up to the mortgage meltdown. This theft, while catastrophic from the standpoint of the defrauded investors, contributed little to the mortgage meltdown. But as the meltdown unfolded, investors sought to liquidate their Madoff and Stanford fund holdings so as to place them in safer investment havens. And when they did, the investors found that Madoff and Stanford could not meet their liquidation requests, because the fund managers had spent their money rather than invested it.

Third, normal accidents can lead actors involved in a failing system to engage in wrongdoing. Countrywide Financial, the nation's largest single home lender during the housing boom, suffered huge losses in the course of the meltdown and was eventually acquired by Bank of America. The SEC has charged Countrywide's CEO Angelo Mozilo for selling a large portion of his Countrywide stock holdings while remaining publically upbeat about the firm's prospects during a period when he knew the firm was in trouble. Mozilo's actions are presumed to have been motivated by a desire to protect Countrywide Financial from mass stockholder defection and his personal wealth from serious deterioration.

Finally, normal accidents can lead social control agents to more vigorously police the line between right and wrong and even label previously acceptable behavior as wrongful. Social control agents, which include organizations and the persons who inhabit them, have interests and capacities that shape their behavior. And social control agents can use normal accidents as opportunities to pursue their interests. For example, the FBI, which had over 600 mortgage fraud cases underway at the onset of the mortgage meltdown, used the meltdown as an opportunity to organize its cases into a high profile program that it dubbed 'Operation Malicious Mortgage'. And this program drew considerable attention and funds to the agency, funds that it had lost to counterterrorism efforts in the wake of the 9/11 attacks. And at this writing, lawmakers are considering a variety of new regulations designed to reduce the likelihood of mortgage meltdowns in the future.

Conclusion

We have briefly summarized normal accident theory, presented a preliminary normal accident analysis of the mortgage meltdown, enumerated some insights that we have gleaned from this analysis and considered the relationship between normal accidents and wrongdoing. While we are not policy experts, we hope that our planned fully developed normal accident analysis of the meltdown will provide some insight into the sort of policies that might reduce the chances of a similar crisis in the future. At the moment, though, we can only speak in very general terms. Perrow has demonstrated how safety mechanisms can add complexity and coupling to a system, thus increasing its propensity to fail. We think that government regulation can have a similar effect. Thus, if regulatory changes are to be contemplated, changes that decrease complexity and coupling should be at the top of the list.

 References

Abolofia, M. Y. (2010) 'Can Speculative Bubbles be Managed? An Institutional Approach', *Strategic Organization* 8(1): 93-100.

Becker, H. (1963) *Outsiders: Studies in the Sociology of Deviance*. New York: The Free Press.

Cohan, W. D. (2009) *House of Cards*. New York: Doubleday.

Davis, G. F. (2009) *Managed by the Market: How Finance Re-shaped America*. Oxford: Oxford University Press.

Davis, G. F. (2010) 'Not Just a Mortgage Crisis: How Finance Maimed Society', *Strategic Organization* 8(1): 75-82.

Hirsch, P. and Morris, M.-H. (2010) 'Immoral but not Illegal: Monies vs mores amid the Mortgage Meltdown,' *Strategic Organization* 8(1): 69-74.

Mezias, S. J. (1994) 'Financial Meltdown as Normal Accident: The Case of the American Savings and Loan Industry', *Accounting, Organizations and Society* 19: 181-92.

Perrow, C. E. (1984) *Normal Accidents: Living with High-Risk Technologies*. New York: Basic Books.

Temple-Raston, D. (2008) 'FBI Sweep Reveals New Twists to Mortgage Fraud', *NPR report*, 3 December.

DISCUSSION QUESTIONS

1. Which of the principles of science (discussed in the introduction) are related to the author's discussion?

2. In what ways is mortgage fraud a "normal accident"?

3. Which other white-collar crimes could be seen as "normal accidents"? Explain.

READING

This report provided by the Federal Bureau of Investigation describes the problem of mortgage fraud, with a particular focus given to the patterns of mortgage fraud seen in 2009. Because the crime is a relatively recent phenomenon, few criminological studies have focused on this topic. This report demonstrates the ties between the government system and the educational system in that, as researchers and scholars, we must often rely on government data and reports to form a foundation from which empirical understanding about certain types of white-collar crime can evolve. The report begins by highlighting an increase in mortgage fraud cases and describes governmental efforts to address this white-collar crime. The report suggests that some types of mortgage fraud—like foreclosure rescue scams—may increase as a result of the crisis in the economic system. Fraud-for-profit is described as particularly problematic. The regional variation in mortgage fraud is also considered.

SOURCE: Federal Bureau of Investigation. (2010). 2009 Mortgage Fraud Report "Year in Review." Washington, DC. Retrieved June 21, 2011, from http://www.fbi.gov/stats-services/publications/mortgage-fraud-2009

2009 Mortgage Fraud Report "Year in Review"

Federal Bureau of Investigation

 ## Introduction

Mortgage fraud continued to increase in 2009[a] despite modest improvements in various economic sectors. While recent economic indicators report improvements in various sectors, overall indicators associated with mortgage fraud, such as foreclosures, housing prices, contracting financial markets, and tighter lending practices by financial institutions, indicate that the housing market is still in distress. In addition, the discovery of mortgage fraud via mortgage industry loan review processes, quality control measures, regulatory and industry referrals, and consumer complaints lag behind these indicators, often up to two years or more.

Mortgage Fraud Defined

Mortgage fraud is a material misstatement, misrepresentation, or omission relied upon by an underwriter or lender to fund, purchase, or insure a loan. Mortgage loan fraud is divided into two categories: fraud for property and fraud for profit. Fraud for property/housing entails misrepresentations by the applicant for the purpose of purchasing a property for a primary residence. This scheme usually involves a single loan. Although applicants may embellish income and conceal debt, their intent is to repay the loan. Fraud for profit, however, often involves multiple loans and elaborate schemes perpetrated to gain illicit proceeds from property sales. Gross misrepresentations concerning appraisals and loan documents are common in fraud for profit schemes, and participants are frequently paid for their participation. Although there is no centralized reporting mechanism for mortgage fraud complaints or investigations, numerous regulatory, industry, and law enforcement agencies collaborate to share information used to assess the current fraud climate.

SOURCE: FBI Financial Crimes Section, Financial Institution Fraud Unit, *Mortgage Fraud: A Guide for Investigators*, 2003.

U.S. housing inventory increased from 127 million units to 130 million units from 2007 to 2009,[1] U.S. properties in foreclosure increased more than 120 percent,[2] and U.S. home prices declined each consecutive year since 2007.[3] Meanwhile unemployment increased from 7.7 percent in January 2009 to 10 percent in December 2009.[4] The ongoing discovery of the lack of due diligence in historical subprime loans, loan modification re-defaults,[5] increasing prime fixed-rate loan delinquencies,[6] and the expected increases over the next three years[7] in the interest rates on Alternative A-paper (Alt-A)[b] and Option Adjustable Rate Mortgage (ARM)[c] loans raise the chance for future mortgage defaults. During the next two years, a total of $80 billion of prime and Alt-A loans and a total of $50 billion subprime loans are due to recast.[8] These

---

[a]There is no 2008 loss data from which to compare as 2009 was the first year any entity had attempted to quantify a fraud loss.

[b]Designed for prime-quality borrowers often requiring no documentation.

[c]Designed for slightly better than subprime borrowers.

factors combine to fuel a mortgage fraud climate rife with opportunity. Consequently, mortgage fraud perpetrators are continuing to take advantage of the opportunities provided in a distressed housing market.

Mortgage fraud continued through 2009 despite increased government-mandated scrutiny of mortgage loan applications and institutions and recent government stimulus interventions. From 2008 through 2009, the U.S. Congress passed various stimulus packages[d] aimed at stabilizing the current economic climate and releasing enormous funds into the economy, but each has potential fraud vulnerabilities. Additionally, the FBI, HUD, Federal Trade Commission, Federal National Mortgage Association (Fannie Mae), Federal Home Loan Mortgage Corporation (Freddie Mac), and other entities have taken steps to increase mortgage fraud awareness and prevention measures, including posting mortgage fraud warnings and alerts on their websites and offering training and educational opportunities to consumers, law enforcement, regulatory, and industry partners.

Federal programs and initiatives resulting from the American Recovery and Reinvestment Act (ARRA)—including the Hope for Homeowners Program, the Home Affordable Modification Program, and the Home Price Decline Protection Program—will likely assist a majority of vulnerable homeowners with refinancing and loan modifications needed to remain in their homes. This should help to reduce the pool of potential scam victims and minimize the number of homeowners entering into foreclosure.

Additionally, other programs implemented by Congress as a result of the Emergency Economic Stabilization Act (EESA) and the Housing and Economic Recovery Act (HERA) (Congress authorized $25 million to be allocated each year from FY 2009 through 2013 to provide FHA with improved technology and processes and to help reduce mortgage fraud)[9] that were designed to stimulate the economy have the potential to provide new targets for mortgage fraud activity as perpetrators vie for billions of dollars provided by these programs.[10]

Vulnerabilities associated with these and similar programs include the lack of transparency, accountability, oversight, and enforcement that predisposes them to fraud and abuse. These vulnerabilities could potentially lead or contribute to an increase in government, mortgage, and corporate frauds, as well as public corruption.

Several mortgage fraud schemes, especially foreclosure rescue schemes, have the potential to spread if the current distressed economic trends and associated implications continue through and beyond 2010, as expected. Increases in defaults and foreclosures, declining housing prices, and decreased housing demand place pressure on lenders, builders, and home sellers to maintain the productivity and profitability they enjoyed during the boom years. These and other market participants are perpetuating and modifying old schemes, including property flipping, builder bailouts, short sales, debt eliminations, and foreclosure rescues. Additionally, they are facilitating new schemes, including credit enhancements, property thefts, and loan modifications in response to tighter lending practices. Consequently, mortgage fraud perpetrators are continuing to take advantage of the opportunities provided in a distressed housing market. When the market is down and lending is tight, perpetrators gravitate to loan origination schemes involving fraudulent/manufactured documents. When the market is up they gravitate to inflating appraisals and equity skimming schemes. According to MARI reporting, "Collusion among insiders, employees, and consumers is highly effective in times of recession because everyone has something to gain in times of desperation."[11]

Victims of mortgage fraud activity may include borrowers, mortgage industry entities, and those living in neighborhoods affected by mortgage fraud. As properties affected by mortgage fraud are sold at artificially inflated prices, properties in surrounding neighborhoods also become artificially inflated. When this occurs, property taxes also artificially increase. As unqualified homeowners begin to default on their

[d]The stimulus packages include the $300 billion Housing and Economic Recovery Act (HERA) of 2008, the $4 billion Community Block Grant, the $700 billion Emergency Economic Stabilization Act (EESA), the $787 billion American Recovery and Reinvestment Act (ARRA), and the Neighborhood Stabilization Program.

inflated mortgages, properties go into foreclosure and neighborhoods begin to deteriorate, and surrounding properties and neighborhoods witness their home values depreciating. As this happens, legitimate homeowners find it difficult to sell their homes.

Additionally, the decline in U.S. home values has a direct correlation to state and local governments' ability to provide resources for schools, public safety, and other necessary public services that are funded in large part from property tax revenue.[12] According to the National League of Cities (NLC), the municipal sector likely faces a combined estimated shortfall of $56 to $83 billion from 2010 to 2012. The NLC expects that revenue from residential and, more recently, commercial property tax collections will see a significant decline from 2010 to 2012. City managers are responding with layoffs, furloughs, payroll deductions, delays and cancellations of capital infrastructure projects, and cuts in city services.[13] According to the National Association of Realtors, local tax formulas and assessment cycles do not reflect rapid home price declines. This results in high property taxes for homeowners as median home prices continue to decline 22.3 percent from 2006 to 2009.[14]

The schemes most directly associated with the escalating mortgage fraud problem continue to be those defined as fraud for profit. Prominent schemes include loan origination, foreclosure rescue, builder bailout, short sale, credit enhancement, loan modification, illegal property flipping, seller assistance, bust-out, debt elimination, mortgage backed securities, real estate investment, multiple loan, assignment fee, air loan, asset rental, backwards application, reverse mortgage fraud, and equity skimming. Many of these schemes employ various techniques such as the use of straw buyers, identity theft, silent seconds, quit claims, land trusts, shell companies, fraudulent loan documents (including forged applications, settlement statements, and verification of employment, rental, occupancy, income, and deposit), double sold loans to secondary investors, leasebacks, and inflated appraisals.

Mortgage Fraud Perpetrators

Mortgage fraud perpetrators are industry insiders, including mortgage brokers, lenders, appraisers, underwriters, accountants, real estate agents, settlement attorneys, land developers, investors, builders, and bank and trust account representatives. Perpetrators are also known to recruit ethnic community members as victims and co-conspirators. FBI reporting indicates numerous ethnic groups are involved in mortgage fraud either as perpetrators or victims. This type of mortgage fraud is known as affinity fraud. Ethnic groups involved in mortgage loan origination fraud include North Korean, Russian, Bulgarian, Romanian, Lithuanian, Mexican, Polish, Middle Eastern, Chinese, and those from the former Republic of Yugoslavian States. Street gangs such as the Conservative Vice Lords, Black P. Stone Nation, New Breeds, Four Corner Hustlers, Bloods, and Outlaw Motorcycle Gang are also involved in various forms of mortgage loan origination fraud as a means to launder money from illicit drug proceeds. Additionally, African, Asian, Balkan, and Eurasian organized crime groups have also been linked to various mortgage fraud schemes.

 ## Mortgage Fraud in a Sluggish Economy and a Distressed Housing Market

Economic Growth

The U.S. economy has experienced some growth in the fourth quarter of 2009 and into the first quarter of 2010; the Mortgage Bankers Association predicts that this growth will flatten or decline for the remainder of 2010 and into 2011 while rebounding in 2012.[15] The housing market is expected to remain volatile for the next couple of years.

According to the Comptroller of the Currency and the Office of Thrift Supervision, the performance of mortgage loans serviced by the largest national banks and federally regulated thrifts declined for the seventh consecutive quarter in December 2009 though home foreclosures slowed and new home retention actions continued strong.[16]

According to MortgageDaily.com, bank failures doubled from 2008 to 2009. Coupled with the nearly double increase in regulatory actions against U.S. financial institutions during the same period, it is unlikely that the acceleration of bank failures will abate.[17] According to the Federal Deposit Insurance Corporation (FDIC), 140 banks failed in 2009, costing the nation's Deposit Insurance Fund $37.4 billion. As of May 31, 2010, 78 banks had failed in 2010, with the year-end total expected to exceed the 2009 rate. Although the FDIC does not make official projections, the cost is expected to be even greater in 2010 but is expected to begin to diminish in 2011.[18]

Unemployment

Unemployment, mortgage loan recasts, and federal loan modification efforts are factors that will influence the number of foreclosures in the next few years.[19] The impact of unemployment may be difficult to capture as unemployment data are aggregated and do not capture the effects of job losses on individual households. According to the U.S. Government Accountability Office (GAO), a large number of payment-option ARMs are scheduled to recast beginning in 2010 which may result in an increase in foreclosures as these Alt-A borrowers may not be able to afford the higher payments. There is conflicting information on the true impact that unemployment is having on default and foreclosure rates. Fifty-eight percent of homeowners receiving foreclosure counseling by the National Foreclosure Mitigation Counseling (NFMC) program established by Congress listed unemployment as the main reason for default. However, the Center for Responsible Lending asserts that while unemployment compounds the current economic crisis, it is not responsible for the current increasing foreclosure rate as during previous periods of high unemployment when foreclosures remained flat.[20]

Negative Equity/Underwater Mortgages

At the end of fourth quarter 2009, more than 11.3 million, or 24 percent, of all residential properties with mortgages were in negative equity, meaning their mortgage balance exceeded their home's current market value. This accounted for $801 billion with another 2.3 million properties approaching negative equity.[21] Nevada, Arizona, Florida, Michigan, and California were the top five states reporting negative equity.

California and Florida accounted for 41 percent of all negative equity loans. Negative equity can occur because of a decline in value, an increase in mortgage debt, or a combination of both. Negative equity makes borrowers more vulnerable to foreclosure and foreclosure rescue schemes, which can contribute to homeowners eventually defaulting on their mortgages.[22]

Foreclosures

National bank and federally regulated thrift servicers expect new foreclosure actions to increase in 2010 as alternatives to prevent foreclosures are exhausted and a larger number of seriously delinquent mortgages go into foreclosure.[23]

Home Prices

According to the Federal Reserve, while a few districts indicated a modest improvement in their housing markets in 2009 resulting from homebuyer tax credits, low mortgage rates, and more affordable prices, overall the U.S. housing market remained depressed. This trend will continue until results of the efforts initiated by the authority of HERA and other market factors begin to stabilize the economy. U.S. residential property values fell from $21.5 trillion in 2007 to $19.1 trillion in 2008, an 11 percent decrease.[24] In early 2009, U.S. home prices were at their lowest levels since May 2004 due to accelerated depreciation in 75 percent of all metropolitan markets, and housing inventory remained very high.[25] According to Standard and Poors (S&P)/Case-Shiller Home Price Indices and U.S. Census estimates of total housing inventory, home prices have declined and inventory remains high in 2010.[26] S&P/Case-Shiller data indicate that the Las Vegas MSA had the greatest decline in home price from 2008 to 2009 (see Table 8.2). S&P/Case-Shiller, Federal Housing Finance Agency (FHFA), IHS Global Insight, and Freddie Mac forecasters indicate that house-price changes will play a key role in future mortgage performance and project declines in 2010.[27] Rapid contraction in the economy in addition to deteriorating labor markets, large inventories of unsold homes, and increasing foreclosures and defaults have contributed to the continued decline in home prices in 2010.

Table 8.2   S&P/Case-Shiller Home Price Index and FiServe Data Through December 2009

Location	Percent Change 2008–2009
U.S. National Index	−2.5
Metropolitan area	
Las Vegas	−20.6
Tampa	−11
Detroit	−10.3
Miami	−9.9
Phoenix	−9.2
Seattle	−7.9
Chicago	−7.2
New York	−6.3
Portland	−5.4
Atlanta	−4

According to First American CoreLogic, during the first 13 months of the federal housing stimulus programs, home sales and home prices stabilized. It is likely that the collective set of federal programs, including the home buyer tax credit, Federal Reserve mortgage-backed security purchases, and federal foreclosure prevention programs (Home Affordable Modification Program [HAMP], Home Affordable Refinance Program [HARP], Home Affordable Foreclosure Alternatives [HAFA]), contributed to the housing market stabilization.[28] Under a simulation scenario of extended federal support, home prices are expected to increase year-over-year by more than 4 percent in February 2011. However, if the federal support ends, home prices are expected to decline by more than 4 percent year-over-year in February 2011.

Mortgage Industry

Industry participants are taking steps to increase due diligence efforts by looking more broadly and deeply at loan originations. This includes re-underwriting, fraud screening, review of closing packages, and executing a series of tolerance tests from a state and federal regulatory standpoint.[29]

However, regarding loan origination schemes, industry insiders allege that while credit quality is up, there is still evidence of significant error rates in the loan closures. There is also concern that new Real Estate Settlement Procedures Act (RESPA) requirements are confusing the very people who must adhere to them.

The Mortgage Bankers Association

According to the MBA's National Delinquency Survey (NDS), 10.44 percent of all residential mortgage loans in 2009 were past due. Five percent of the loans serviced were 90 days or more past due, and 9.7 percent were seriously delinquent (more than 90 days past due).[30] The MBA estimates that mortgage loan originations will decrease 37 percent through 2010 (see Figure 8.4).[31] The MBA NDS examines 85 percent of the outstanding first-lien mortgages in the market. The NDS reported 44.4 million first-lien

Figure 8.4   Mortgage Origination Forecast, MBA as of 15 March 2010

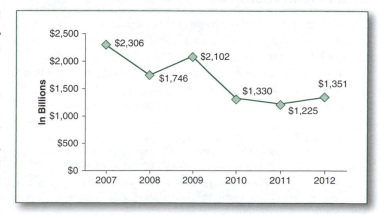

mortgages on one- to four-unit residential properties in 2009 compared with 45.4 million in 2008. Conversely, the NDS reported a fourth-quarter increase in foreclosure rates for the same period.[32] FHA's market share increased dramatically since FY 2007 as subprime lending decreased, lending tightened, and borrowers and lenders were looking for federally insured loans (see Figure 8.5).[33]

The MBA reports an increase in foreclosure rates for all loan types (prime, subprime, FHA, and VA) from 2008 to 2009, and serious delinquencies increased 327

Figure 8.5   FHA Share of Home Purchase Activity, FY 2007 to FY 2010 (through 1 April 2010)

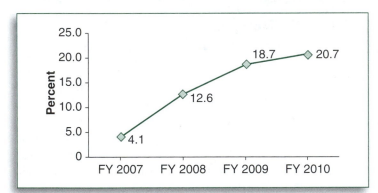

basis points for prime loans, 745 basis points for subprime loans, 244 basis points for FHA loans, and 130 basis points for VA loans.[34]

Loan Modifications

Historic increases in loss mitigation efforts, delinquencies, and foreclosures are overwhelming an already burdened mortgage servicing system.[35] Loan modification fraud flourishes because of increasing demand for these loans by public and political officials, unreasonable time constraints to complete modifications, and

borrowers submitting financial packages that cannot always be independently confirmed.[36] Loan modification implications that may impede a lender from modifying a delinquent mortgage include specific investor guidelines, the impact on mortgage insurance, lien position, other interest parties in the property, and borrower qualifications.[37] These implications also may impede borrowers from seeking or securing a loan modification and add to their frustration in dealing with lenders, which makes them more vulnerable to fraud perpetrators.[38]

According to the HAMP, of the more than 3 million eligible homeowners, only 230,000 have been granted permanent modifications, while 1.1 million are in trial modifications as of April 30, 2010.[39] More than half of all loan modifications are redefaulting, falling 60 or more days past due nine months after modification.[40]

 ## Financial Institution Reporting of Mortgage Fraud Increases

SARs from financial institutions indicate an increase in mortgage fraud reporting.[e] There were 67,190 mortgage fraud-related SARs filed with FinCEN in FY 2009, a 5.1 percent increase from FY 2008 and a 44 percent increase from FY 2007 filings. SAR filings in the first six months of 2010 exceed the same period in FY 2009 by more than 4,400 (or 13 percent) (see Figure 8.6).[f]

SARs reported in FY 2009 revealed $2.8 billion in losses, an 86 percent increase from FY 2008 and a 250 percent increase from FY 2007 (see Figure 8.7). Additionally, SAR losses reported in the first six months of FY 2010 exceeded the same period in FY 2009 by more than $788 million (or 67 percent). While total

---

[e]Mortgage loan fraud (MLF) SAR time lag versus fraud reporting for calendar year 2009: SAR filers reported suspicious activities that were more than a year old in 77 percent of MLF SARs; fourth quarter mortgage loan fraud SAR filings indicated that 65 percent of reported activities occurred more than two years prior to the filing compared with 43 percent in the fourth quarter of 2008. Source: FinCEN, April 2010.

[f]The dates of the SAR filings are not always indicative of the dates of the underlying suspicious activities. Many SARs reflect activity dates that preceded the filing of the SARs by a number of years. Therefore, an increase in the filings during this period is not necessarily indicative of an increase in mortgage loan fraud activity during the same period.

Figure 8.6   Mortgage Fraud–Related SARs, FY 2005 to 31 March 2010

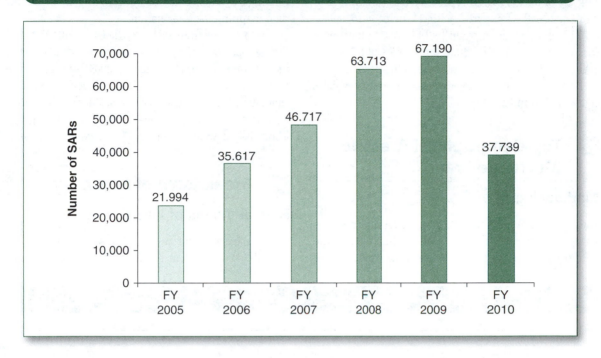

Figure 8.7   Mortgage Fraud SAR Losses, FY 2005 to 31 March 2010

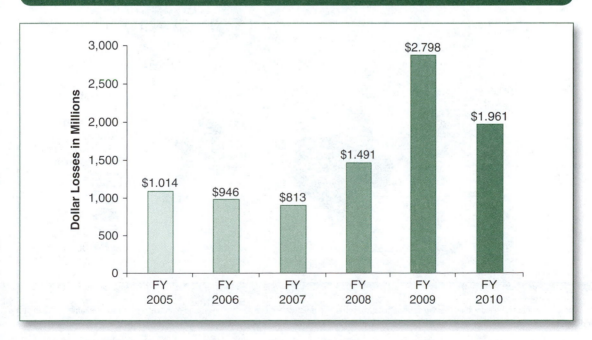

SAR losses in FY 2009 were $2.8 billion, only 22 percent (14,737 of 67,190 SARs) reported a loss (an average of $189,862/SAR) compared with 11 percent (6,789 of 63,713 mortgage loan fraud [MLF] SARs) reporting a loss ($1.5 billion) in FY 2008 (an average of $219,619/SAR). While there was an increase in the percentage of SARs filing a loss, the average loss amount per SAR decreased from FY 2008 to FY 2009.

 ## Top Geographical Areas for Mortgage Fraud

Methodology

Data from law enforcement and industry sources were compared and mapped to determine which areas of the country were most affected by mortgage fraud during 2009. This was accomplished by compiling the state rankings by each data source, collating by state, and then mapping the information.

Information from the FBI, HUD-OIG, FinCEN, MARI, Fannie Mae, RealtyTrac, Inc., and Interthinx indicate that the top mortgage fraud states for 2009 were California, Florida, Illinois, Michigan, Arizona, Georgia, New York, Ohio, Texas, the District of Columbia, Maryland, Colorado, New Jersey, Nevada, Minnesota, Oregon, Pennsylvania, Rhode Island, Utah, and Virginia (see Figure 8.8).[g]

 ## Breakdown of Sources

Federal Bureau of Investigation

FBI mortgage fraud investigations totaled 2,794 in FY 2009, a 71 percent increase from FY 2008 and a

Figure 8.8 Top Mortgage Fraud States by Multiple Indicators, 2009

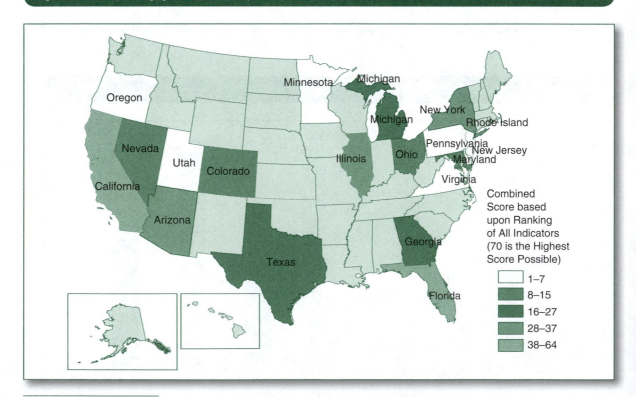

[g]A score of 70 would represent a state that was ranked first across all seven indictors, while a score of one would represent a state that was ranked 10th in only one indictor. The highest score observed was a 64 (California) while two states received a score of 1 (Pennsylvania and Utah).

131 percent increase from FY 2007 (see Figure 8.9). As of April 2010, there were 3,029 pending cases. According to FBI data, 66 percent (1,842) of all pending FBI mortgage fraud investigations opened during FY 2009 (2,794) involved dollar losses totaling more than $1 million. As of April 2010, 68 percent (2,060) of all pending FBI mortgage fraud investigations involve dollar losses totaling more than $1 million.

Based on regional analysis of FBI pending mortgage fraud-related investigations as of FY 2009, the West region ranked first in mortgage fraud investigations, followed by the Southeast, North Central, Northeast, and South Central regions, respectively (see Figure 8.10).

FBI field divisions that ranked in the top 10 for pending investigations during FY 2009 were Tampa, Los Angeles, New York, Detroit, Portland, Washington Field, Miami, Chicago, Salt Lake City, and Dallas, respectively (see Figure 8.11).

FBI field divisions that ranked in the top 10 for an increase in pending investigations from FY 2008 to FY 2009 were Portland, with a 465 percent increase,

followed by Tampa (363 percent), New Haven (327 percent), Jacksonville (247 percent), Omaha (230 percent), Washington Field (221 percent), Phoenix (217 percent), San Juan (200 percent),[h] Seattle (181 percent), and Minneapolis (155 percent), respectively (see Figure 8.12).

FBI information indicates that the states of Arizona, California, Florida, Ohio, and Tennessee were consistently on the top 10 lists for property flips occurring on the same day, within 30 days, and within 60 days in 2009. Traditionally, any exchange of property that occurs on the day of sale is considered suspect for illegal property flipping. Figures 8.13, 8.14, and 8.15 indicate (where data was available) the number of property transactions recorded at the county clerk's office that occurred on the same day, within 30 days, and within 60 days from the date of sale.

Financial Crimes Enforcement Network

According to SAR reporting, the Los Angeles, Miami, Tampa, San Francisco, Chicago, Sacramento, New York,

Figure 8.9   Increase in FBI Mortgage Fraud Pending Investigations, FY 2005 Through 14 April 2010

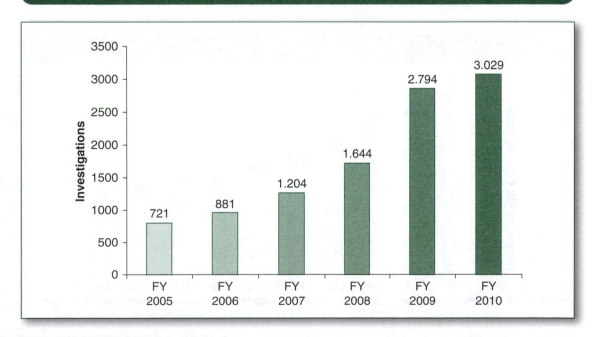

---

[h]FBI San Juan investigations increased from two cases in FY 2008 to six cases in FY 2009.

Figure 8.10   FY 2009 Percent of FBI Pending Mortgage Fraud Investigations by Region

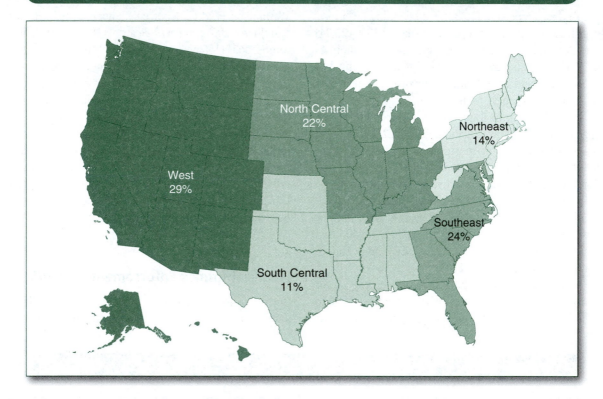

Figure 8.11   Top 10 Field Offices by Pending Cases, FY 2009

Figure 8.12 Top Field Offices by Increase in Pending Cases, FY 2008 to FY 2009

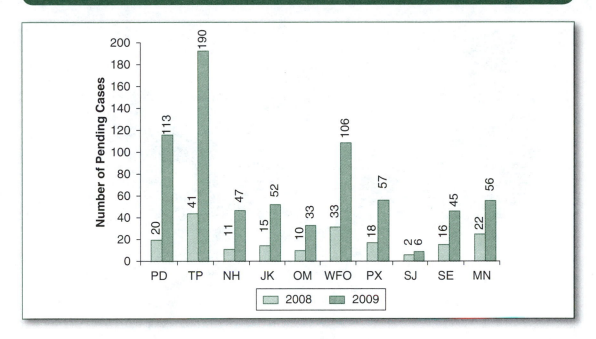

Atlanta, Phoenix, and Memphis Divisions, respectively, were the top 10 FBI field offices impacted by mortgage fraud during FY 2009 (see Figure 8.14).

U.S. Department of Housing and Urban Development—Office of Inspector General

In FY 2009, HUD-OIG had 591 pending single family (SF) residential loan investigations, a 31 percent increase from the 451 pending during FY 2008.[41] This also represented a 27 percent increase from the 466 pending during FY 2007. HUD-OIG's top 10 mortgage fraud states based on pending investigations in FY 2009 were Illinois, California, Florida, Texas, New York, Maryland, Georgia, Colorado, Ohio, Virginia, and Pennsylvania (see Figure 8.15).

HUD-OIG data indicates that there was a 700 percent increase in the number of investigations opened in

Nevada[i] in FY 2009, followed by New Hampshire, Florida, and Tennessee (see Figure 8.16).

LexisNexis Mortgage Asset Research Institute

During 2009, Florida, New York, California, Arizona, Michigan, Maryland, New Jersey, Georgia, Illinois, and Virginia were MARI's top 10 states for reports of mortgage fraud across all originations (see Figure 8.17).[42]

Florida continues to rank first in fraud reporting since 2006, and its fraud rate was almost three times the expected amount of reported mortgage fraud in 2009 for its origination volume. Virginia, Arizona, and New Jersey replaced Rhode Island, Missouri, and Colorado from 2008 reporting.

MARI indicates the top five MSAs reporting fraud in 2009 were New York City-Northern New Jersey-Long

---

[i]HUD-OIG reported that Nevada had one investigation opened in FY 2008 compared with eight in FY 2009, which caused the data to reflect such a drastic change.

Figure 8.13 Same-Day Property Flip Transactions, 2009

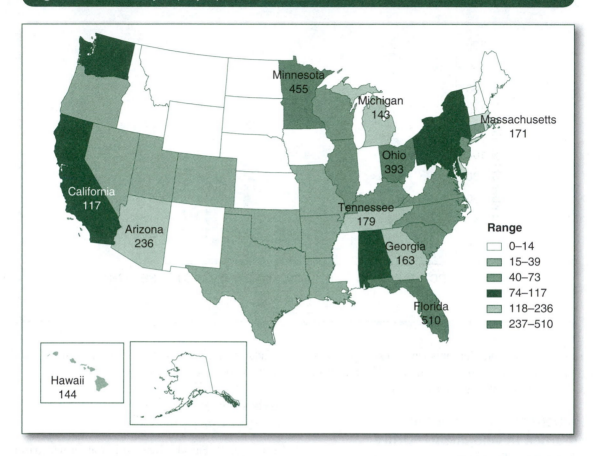

Figure 8.14 Top Ten FBI Field Divisions for FY 2009 Mortgage Fraud SARs

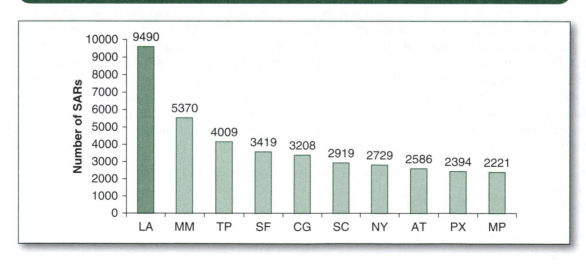

Figure 8.15   Top 11 States by HUD-OIG Pending Cases, FY 2009

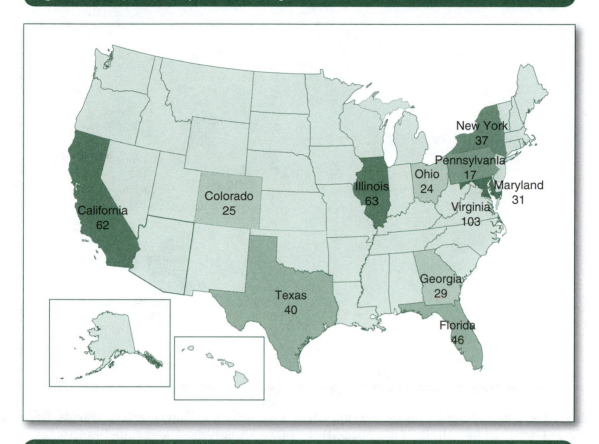

Figure 8.16   Top Ten States by Percent Change in Cases Opened, FY 2008 to FY 2009, HUD-OIG

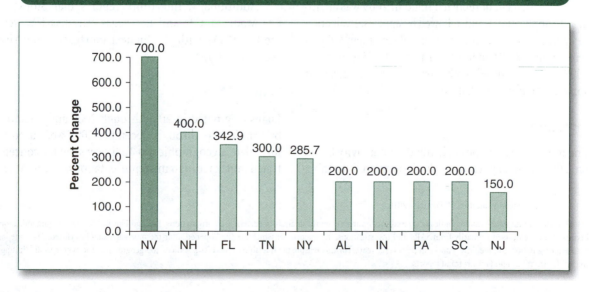

Figure 8.17 Top 10 States by MARI, 2009

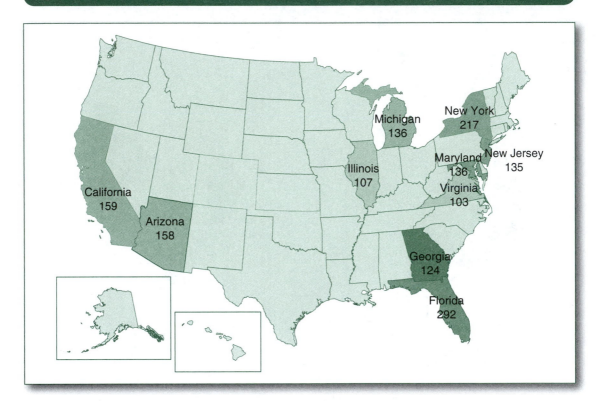

Island; Los Angeles-Riverside-Orange County, CA; Chicago-Gary-Kenosha, IL-IN-WI; Miami-Fort Lauderdale, FL; and Washington-Baltimore, DC-MD-VA. Fifty-nine percent of reported fraud in 2009 was attributed to application fraud, followed by appraisal/valuation (33 percent), and tax return/financial statement (26 percent) fraud. MARI indicates that overall, 75 percent of 2009 loans reported with appraisal fraud included some form of value inflation.[43]

Interthinx®

The top 10 states for possible fraudulent activity based on 2009 loan application submissions to Interthinx

were Nevada, California, Arizona, Florida, Colorado, Ohio, Rhode Island, Michigan, the District of Columbia, and Maryland, respectively (see Figure 8.18).[j]

Additionally, Interthinx reports that Stockton, CA; Modesto, CA; and Las Vegas-Paradise NV, were the top MSAs with the highest mortgage fraud risk (see Table 8.3).[k]

Fannie Mae

Loans originated in 2008 through 2009 and reviewed by Fannie Mae through December 2009 were used to formulate a geographic top 10 list by state for concentrated mortgage loan misrepresentations. Fannie Mae's

[j]Information provided by Interthinx®, February 2010.

[k]The Interthinx indices are leading indicators based predominantly on the analysis of current loan originations. FBI and FinCEN data are lagging indicators because they are derived primarily from SARs and investigations, the majority of which are filed/opened after the mortgage loan has closed. The time lag between origination and the SAR report can be several years. For this reason, the Interthinx Fraud Risk Indices' top geographies and type-specific findings may differ from FBI and FinCEN fraud reports.

Figure 8.18   Top 10 States by Interthinx, 2009

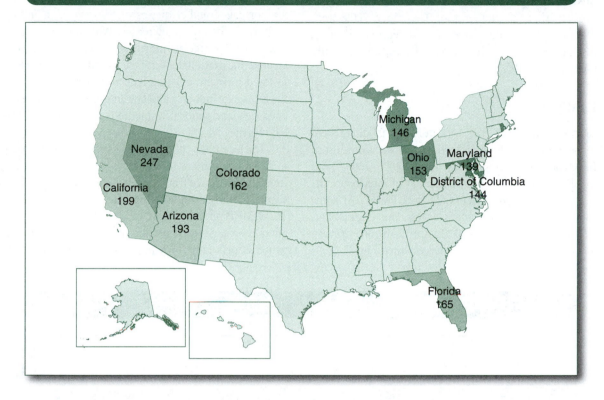

Table 8.3   Top 10 MSAs With Mortgage Fraud Risk per Interthinx, 2009

Rank by Mortgage Fraud Risk Index	MSA	Percent Change in Index From 2008 to 2009
1	Stockton, CA	61
2	Modesto, CA	66.4
3	Las Vegas-Paradise, NV	41
4	Riverside-San Bernardino-Ontario, CA	62.6
5	Merced, CA	52.1
6	Reno-Sparks, NV	44.1
7	Vallejo-Fairfield, CA	54.2
8	Bakersfield, CA	40.2
9	Cape Coral-Fort Myers, FL	44.7
10	Fresno, CA	37.9

top 10 mortgage fraud states based on significant misrepresentations discovered by the loan review process through the end of December 2009 were Florida, California, New York, Georgia, Illinois, Michigan, Arizona, Texas, New Jersey, and Virginia (see Figure 8.19).[44]

RealtyTrac

According to RealtyTrac, Inc., during 2009, there were more than 2.8 million U.S. properties with foreclosure filings, a 120 percent increase from 2007 to 2009.[45] The top 10 states ranked by the number of foreclosure filings per housing unit were California, Florida, Arizona, Illinois, Michigan, Nevada, Georgia, Ohio, Texas, and New Jersey (see Figure 8.20). In April 2010, one in every 386 housing units received a foreclosure filing.[46]

 ## FBI Response

As mortgage fraud crimes escalate, the burden on federal law enforcement increases. With the anticipated continued upsurge in mortgage fraud cases, the FBI created the National Mortgage Fraud Team (NMFT), fostered new and existing liaison partnerships within the mortgage industry and law enforcement, and developed new and innovative methods to detect and combat mortgage fraud.

In December 2008, the FBI established the NMFT to assist field offices in addressing the financial crisis, from the mortgage fraud problem and loan origination scams to the secondary markets and securitization. The NMFT provides tools to identify the most egregious mortgage fraud perpetrators, prioritizes investigative efforts, and provides information to evaluate

Figure 8.19   Top 10 States by Fannie Mae, 2009

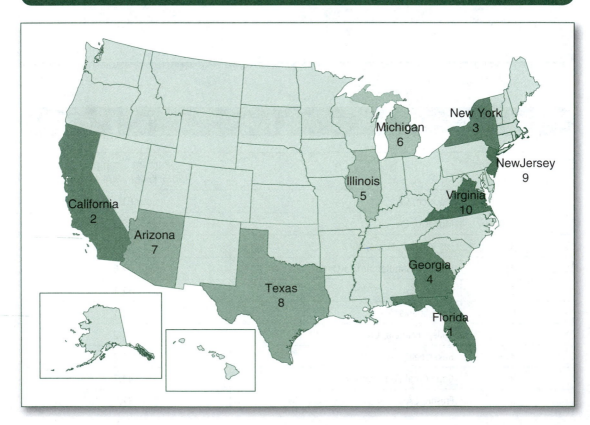

Figure 8.20 Top 10 States by RealtyTrac, 2009

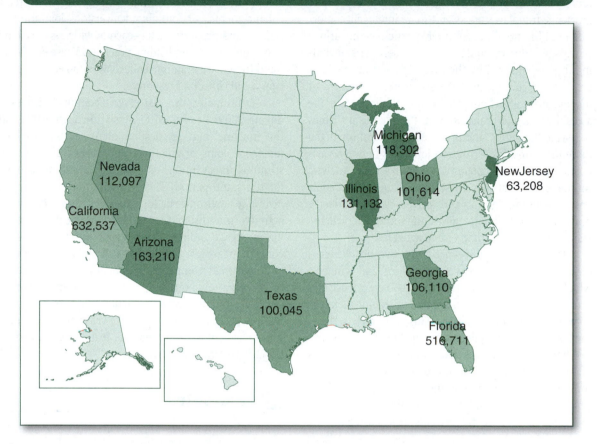

resource needs. For example, the FBI began implementing the DOJ's Strike Force Approach to mortgage fraud wherein DOJ trial attorneys were detailed to the FBI Las Vegas Field Office to collaborate with assistant United States attorneys and FBI investigative personnel in a coordinated effort to prosecute a large number of egregious mortgage fraud offenders in a short time period.

The FBI continues to support 23 mortgage fraud task forces and 67 working groups. The FBI also participates in the DOJ National Mortgage Fraud and National Bank Fraud Working Groups and the Financial Fraud Enforcement Task Force (FFETF) formed by Attorney General Eric Holder. The FFETF's mission is to enhance the government's effectiveness in sharing information to help prevent and combat financial fraud. The FBI actively participates in the FFETF's Mortgage Fraud Working Group. Other task forces and working groups include, but are not limited to, representatives of the HUD-OIG, the U.S. Postal Inspection Service, the U.S. Securities and Exchange Commission, the Commodities Futures Trading Commission, the IRS, FinCEN, the FDIC, and other federal, state, and local law enforcement officers across the country. Representatives of the Office of Comptroller of the Currency, the Office of Thrift Supervision, the Executive Office of U.S. Trustees, the Federal Trade Commission, and others participate in national and ad-hoc working groups. Additionally, the Financial Intelligence Center was initiated as part of the NMFT to provided tactical analysis of intelligence data to identify offenders and emerging mortgage fraud threats.

The FBI continues to foster relationships with representatives of the mortgage industry to promote mortgage fraud awareness and share intelligence information. FBI personnel routinely participate in various mortgage industry conferences and seminars, including those sponsored by the MBA. Collaborative efforts are ongoing to educate and raise public awareness of mortgage fraud schemes with the publication of the annual Mortgage Fraud Report, the Financial Crimes Report to the Public, and press releases and through the dissemination of information jointly or between various industry and consumer organizations. Analytic products are routinely disseminated to a wide audience, including public and private sector industry partners, the intelligence community, and other federal, state, and local law enforcement agencies.

The FBI employs sophisticated investigative techniques, such as undercover operations and wiretaps, which result in the collection of valuable evidence and provide an opportunity to apprehend criminals in the commission of their crimes. This ultimately reduces the losses to individuals and financial institutions. The FBI has also established several intelligence initiatives to support mortgage fraud investigations and has improved law enforcement and industry relationships. The FBI has established methodology to proactively identify potential mortgage fraud targets using tactical analysis coupled with advanced statistical correlations and computer technologies.

Outlook

The current housing market, while showing modest signs of improving, continues to suffer from high inventories, sluggish sales, and a high foreclosure rate. It remains an attractive environment for mortgage fraud perpetrators who discover methods to circumvent loopholes and gaps in the mortgage lending market whether the market is up or down. Market participants are employing and modifying old schemes, such as loan origination, short sales, property flipping, builder bailouts, seller assistance, debt elimination, reverse mortgages, foreclosure rescues, and identity theft. Additionally,

they are adopting new schemes, including fraud associated with economic stimulus disbursements, credit enhancements, condominium conversions, loan modifications, and property theft—each of which is surfacing in response to tighter lending practices. These emerging fraud trends are draining lender, law enforcement, regulatory, and consumer resources.

Additionally, the distressed economy witnessed during 2009 is expected to persist through 2011, and the housing market, despite increased scrutiny of mortgage loan originations and recent government stimulus interventions, is expected to remain volatile for the same period. This will continue to provide a favorable environment for expanded mortgage fraud activity. In addition, the discovery of mortgage fraud via mortgage industry loan review processes, quality control measures, regulatory and industry referrals, and consumer complaints lags behind indicators such as foreclosures, housing prices, contracting financial markets, and the establishment of tighter mortgage lending practices, often up to two years or more, which means law enforcement may not realize a downturn in fraud reporting until 2013.

 Endnotes

1. Internet site; U.S. Census; http://www.census.gov/hhes/www/housing/hvs/historic/files/his_tab7a_v2008_web.xls; December 31, 2009; Source information is data pertaining to the total housing inventory for the United States.

2. RealtyTrac, National Real Estate Trends, March 2010; URL: http://www.realtytrac.com/trendcenter; accessed on April 23, 2010.

3. Online Report; S&P/Case-Shiller Home Price Indices; Real Estate Indices; December 2009; URL: http://www.standardandpoors.com/indices/sp-case-shiller-home-price-indices/en/us/?indexId=spusa-cashpidff--p-us----; accessed on March 8, 2010.

4. U.S. Bureau of Labor Statistics, Labor Force Statistics from the Current Population Survey, May 31, 2010, URL: http://data.bls.gov/PDQ/servlet/SurveyOutputServlet?data_tool=latest_numbers&series_id=LNS14000000, accessed on May 31, 2010.

5. Online Article; Office of the Comptroller of the Currency and the Office of Thrift Supervision, OCC and OTS Release Mortgage Metrics Report for Fourth Quarter of 2009, March 25,

2010, URL: www.occ.gov/ftp/release/printview/2010-36.htm, accessed on May 7, 2010.

6. Online Article; Mortgage Bankers Association, National Delinquency Survey, December 31, 2009.

7. Online Article: Zach Fox, SNL Financial, Credit Suisse: $1 trillion worth of ARMs still face resets, February 25, 2010, URL: http://www.snl.com/interactivex/article.aspx?CDID=A-10770380-12086, accessed on June 7, 2010.

8. Online Article; UPI, Recasting Mortgages Worth $47 Billion Will Increase Defaults, January 11, 2010, URL: http://www.upi.com/Real-Estate/2010/01/11/Recasting-Mortgages-Worth-47-Billion-Will-Increase-Defaults/9721263236699/, accessed on June 6, 2010.

9. Testimony of John A. Courson, President and Chief Executive Officer, Mortgage Bankers Association, Before the House Financial Services Subcommittee on Housing and Community Opportunity Hearing on The FHA Reform Act of 2010, March 11, 2010.

10. Government Accountability Office; GAO-09-161; available at www.gao.gov/new.items/d09161.pdf; Troubled Asset Relief Program: Additional Actions Needed to Better Ensure Integrity, Accountability, and Transparency; December 2008

11. Lexis Nexis Mortgage Asset Research Institute, Twelfth Periodic Mortgage Fraud Case Report, p. 4, April 26, 2010.

12. U.S. Conference of Mayors, U.S. Metro Economies, June 2008, URL: www.usmayors.org, accessed on March 3, 2010.

13. National League of Cities, Research Brief: City Budget Shortfalls and Responses: Projections for 2010, December 2009, URL: http://www.nlc.org/ASSETS/0149CE492F8C49D09516019530 6B6E08/BuddgetShortFalls_FINAL.pdf, accessed on March 28, 2010.

14. The Wall Street Journal, Homeowners Hold Ground Against Rising Property Taxes, March 6, 2010, URL: http://online .wsj.com/article/SB1000142405274870454130457509943085723873 8.html, accessed on March 10, 2010.

15. Mike Fratantoni, Vice President of Research and Economics, Mortgage Bankers Association, The Current State of the Industry, Speech given at the April 27, 2010 MBA National Fraud Issues Conference.

16. Office of the Comptroller of the Currency and the Office of Thrift Supervision, OCC and OTS Release Mortgage Metrics Report for Fourth Quarter of 2009, March 25, 2010, URL: www.occ .gov/ftp/release/printview/2010-36.htm, accessed on May 7, 2010.

17. MortgageDaily.com, Bank Failures Double, April 12, 2010, URL: www.mortgagedaily.com/PressRelease041210.asp, accessed on April 20, 2010.

18. Online news article; Maurice Tamman and David Enrich; The Wall Street Journal; Local Banks Face Big Losses: Journal Study of 940 Lenders Shows Potential for Deep Hit on Commercial Property; May 19, 2009; http://online.wsj.com/article/SB124269114847832587 .html; July 7, 2009.

19. U.S. Government Accountability Office, Loan Performance and Negative Home Equity in the Nonprime Mortgage Market, December 16, 2009, URL: www.gao.gov/products/GAO-10-146R, accessed on March 18, 2010.

20. Testimony of Julia Gordon, Center for Responsible Lending Before the U.S. House of Representatives Committee on Financial Services, The Private Sector and Government Response to the Mortgage Foreclosure Crisis, December 8, 2009, URL: http://www.responsiblelending.org/mortgage-lending/policy-legislation/congress/Gordon-Loan-Modification-Testimony-12-8-09-final.pdf

21. First American CoreLogic, Underwater Mortgages on the Rise According to First American CoreLogic Q4 2009 Negative Equity Data, February 23, 2010.

22. U.S. Government Accountability Office, Loan Performance and Negative Home Equity in the Nonprime Mortgage Market, December 16, 2009, URL: www.gao.gov/products/GAO-10-146R, accessed on March 18, 2010.

23. Office of the Comptroller of the Currency and the Office of Thrift Supervision, OCC and OTS Release Mortgage Metrics Report for Fourth Quarter of 2009, March 25, 2010, URL: www.occ .gov/ftp/release/printview/2010-36.htm, accessed on May 7, 2010.

24. First American CoreLogic LoanPerformance HPI, Residential Property Values Fell $2.4 Trillion During 2008 Based on First American CoreLogic and LoanPerformance Home Price Index Analytics, Media Alert, February 18, 2009, URL: www.loanper formance.com.

25. Ibid.

26. First American CoreLogic LoanPerformance HPI, Residential Property Values Fell $2.4 Trillion During 2008 Based on First American CoreLogic and LoanPerformance Home Price Index Analytics, Media Alert, February 18, 2009, URL: www.loan performance.com.; Internet site; U.S. Census; http://www.census .gov/hhes/www/housing/hvs/historic/files/his_tab7a_v2008_web .xls; December 31, 2009; Source information is data pertaining to the total housing inventory for the United States. Online Report; S&P/ Case-Shiller Home Price Indices; Real Estate Indices; December 2009; URL: http://www.standardandpoors.com/indices/index-announcements/en/us/?index=sp-case-shiller-home-price-indices &type=All&category=Real+Estate accessed on March 8, 2010.

27. U.S. Government Accountability Office, Loan Performance and Negative Home Equity in the Nonprime Mortgage Market, December 16, 2009, URL: www.gao.gov/products/GAO-10-146R, accessed on March 18, 2010.

28. First American CoreLogic, Research Brief, A Simulation: Measuring the effect of Housing Stimulus Programs on Future House Prices, April 2010 URL: http://www.corelogic.com/ uploadedFiles/Pages/About Us/News/Tax_Credit_White_Paper_ final_0410.pdf, accessed on May 28, 2010.

29. Digital Risk, Solid Diligence an Emphasis at Fraud Conference, April 23, 2010.

30. Mortgage Bankers Association, National Delinquency Survey, December 31, 2009.

31. Mortgage Bankers Association, MBA Mortgage Finance Forecast: Mortgage Originations, March 15, 2010, URL: http://www.mortgagebankers.org/files/Bulletin/InternalResource/72219_.pdf Estimates; accessed on May 28, 2010.

32. Mortgage Bankers Association, National Delinquency Survey, December 31, 2009

33. U.S. Department of Housing and Urban Development, FHA Share of Home Purchase Activity, URL: http://www.hud.gov/utilities/intercept.cfm?/offices/hsg/comp/rpts/fhamktsh/fhamkt1209.pdf; accessed on May 28, 2010.

34. Mortgage Bankers Association, National Delinquency Survey, December 31, 2009.

35. Elizabeth DeSilva and Robert Maddox, Fraud in Loss Mitigation and Loan Modification, April 27, 2010, Mortgage Bankers Association's National Fraud Issues Conference, Chicago, Illinois.

36. Elizabeth DeSilva and Robert Maddox, Fraud in Loss Mitigation and Loan Modification, April 27, 2010, Mortgage Bankers Association's National Fraud Issues Conference, Chicago, Illinois.

37. Loan modification scam presentation, MBA National Fraud Issues Conference April 26, 2010, Chicago, Illinois.

38. Online Article; ABC News, Brian Ross and Avni Patel, On Hold: Even Congresswoman Gets the Runaround on Bank Help Lines: Rep. Maxine Waters Dials and Redials Attempting to Get Help for Constituents, January 22, 2009, URL: http://abcnews.go.com/Blotter/story?id=6702731&page=1, accessed on May 20, 2010.

39. Making Home Affordable, Servicer Performance Report Through March 2010, April 14, 2010, URL: www.makinghomeaffordable.gov/pr_04142010b.html, accessed on April 19, 2010.

40. Office of the Comptroller of the Currency and the Office of Thrift Supervision, OCC and OTS Release Mortgage Metrics Report for Fourth Quarter of 2009, March 25, 2010, URL: www.occ.gov/ftp/release/printview/2010-36.htm, accessed on May 7, 2010.

41. Data; U.S. Department of Housing and Urban Development, provided on March 3, 2010.

42. Lexis Nexis Mortgage Asset Research Institute, Twelfth Periodic Mortgage Fraud Case Report, p. 4, April 26, 2010.

43. Lexis Nexis Mortgage Asset Research Institute, Twelfth Periodic Mortgage Fraud Case Report, p. 11, April 26, 2010.

44. Fannie Mae, Fraud Finding Statistics, January 2009, URL: https://www.efanniemae.com/utility/legal/pdf/fraudstats/fraudupdate0110.pdf, accessed on April 6, 2010.

45. RealtyTrac, RealtyTrac Year-end Report Shows Record 2.8 Million U.S. Properties with Foreclosure Filings in 2009, January 14, 2010, URL: http://www.realtytrac.com/contentmanagement/pressrelease.aspx?channelid=9&itemid=8333, accessed on April 29, 2010.

46. RealtyTrac, National Real Estate Trends, April 2010, URL: www.realtytrac.com/trendcenter, accessed on May 25, 2010.

DISCUSSION QUESTIONS

1. What is mortgage fraud?

2. How does mortgage fraud impact your life as a student?

3. Which systems are involved in contributing to, and responding to, mortgage fraud?

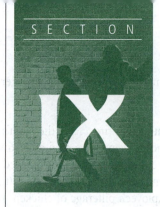

Crimes by the Corporate System

Section Highlights

- Conceptualizing Corporate Crime
- Types of Corporate Crime
- Dynamics of Corporate Offending
- Public Concern About Crimes by the Corporate System

 ## Introduction

A student interested in learning more about a specific for-profit college completed a website registration form indicating interest in the college. Minutes later, the individual received a phone call from a marketing specialist from the college. The student told that marketer that he was interested in criminal justice. The marketer told the student that he should consider a medical assistant certificate instead because he would potentially earn $70,000 a year after just 9 months of coursework. In reality, 9 out of 10 employees in the medical assisting field make under $40,000 a year. And the marketer knew this. What the marketer did not know, however, was that the "student" was actually an undercover employee working on an investigation focusing on the marketing practices of for-profit colleges for the U.S. Government Accountability Office (USGAO, 2010).

In this case, the marketer's illicit actions were conducted to benefit the company for which he worked. This distinguishes the misconduct from those discussed earlier in this work. Indeed, all of the offenses discussed in the prior sections were conducted by the employee and for the employee's benefit.

Other white-collar offenses either benefit, or are committed by, an employer or business. Consider the following examples:

- "On September 3, 1991, the [Imperial Food Products, Inc.] plant caught fire.... Of the plant's 230 workers, 90 were in the plant at the time the fire started. Of those, twenty-five died and 56 were injured.... Immediately, survivors reported that exit doors had either been locked or blocked and their escape from the plant had been severely hampered. Apparently, the firm's owner, Emmett Roe, had authorized the doors to be padlocked due to suspected employee's pilferage of chicken parts. The locked doors, however, were only part of the problem. The building ... did not have a plantwide sprinkler system" (Wright, Cullen, & Blankenship, 1995, p. 21)
- "On September 26, 2002, at approximately 11:00 p.m., the Senegalese ferry Le Joola capsized off the Gambian coast.... Over 1,800 passengers perished, making this the second worse maritime disaster of the modern era. In the wake of the sinking, it became clear that the state of Senegal held liability for the ferry's failure" (Rothe, Muzzatti, & Mullins, 2006, p. 159)
- On April 30, 2010, Johnson & Johnson subsidiary McNeil Consumer Healthcare "recalled more than 40 types of widely used children's medicine" (Erickson, 2010, p. 22)
- "Sarah Price had just laid her daughter down for a nap when she heard the sharp crack of breaking wood. The seam of the baby's bed had split open. Her [four-month-old] daughter fell through a gaping hole" (Sorkin, 2008)
- "The drug thalidomide caused some 8,000 babies in nearly 50 countries to be born severely deformed" (Punch, 2000, p. 244)
- "In U.S. v. Nelson, the Division successfully prosecuted ... three corporations involved in illegally harvesting from the Chesapeake Bay and selling millions of dollars worth of striped bass. The investigation ... was a long-term undercover operation that conducted purchases and sales of the fish. To date, the defendants have pleaded guilty to charges including Carey Act, conspiracy, and false labeling violations" (U.S. Department of Justice, 2010, Environment and Natural Resources Division, p. 28)

In this context, the phrase "crimes by the corporate system" is used to characterize the body of offenses that are committed to benefit the corporation for which the employee (or employees) works. To fully understand this body of offenses, in this section attention is given to conceptualizing corporate crime, types of corporate crime, dynamics of corporate offending, and public concern about crimes by the corporate system. By addressing these areas, readers will see how corporations also commit, and benefit from, various types of misconduct.

⬚ Conceptualizing Corporate Crime

As noted in Section I, the term *corporate crime* was initially discussed by Clinard and Quinney who, in *Criminal Behavior Systems*, showed how white-collar crime can be classified into "corporate crime" and "occupational crime." From this perspective, the crimes discussed in the prior sections can be seen as "occupational crimes." To understand what is meant by corporate crime, it is useful to first define *corporation*.

The concept of corporation can be seen four different ways (see Figure 9.1). First, one can suggest that a corporation is a *business*. Second, one can also point to the *physical or structural location* where a business

Figure 9.1 What Is a Corporation?

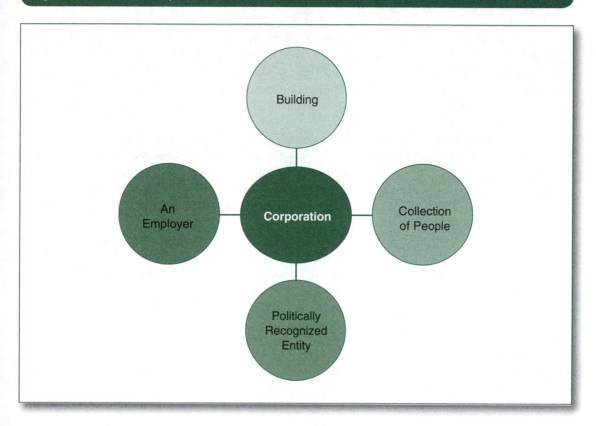

exists as a corporation (or an organization). Third, if businesses become incorporated, that *legally recognized status* can be seen as indicating the presence of a corporation that is separate from the presence of a specific person or persons owning or running an organization. Fourth, a corporation can be seen as a *collection of employees* who work for an employer.

The employment arrangement in a corporation is hierarchal in nature. At the bottom of the corporate hierarchy are workers with no supervisory responsibilities. Direct supervisors are at the next level of the corporation. Managers and administrators are above the supervisors. Many corporations also have a specific corporate board. A chief executive officer or president of the board is ultimately the highest ranking individual in a corporation. In theory, the corporation exists to meet its goals—which typically include profit, growth, and success.

Understanding these levels helps to shed light on the concept of corporate crime and the persistence of misconduct in businesses. As Ermann and Lundman (2002) note, corporations are not technically "collections of people," but are collections of "replaceable people." What this means is that individuals can lose their jobs if they are not performing in a way that helps the corporation to meet its goals. Consequently, individuals—through direct or indirect pressures—might break rules or violate the law in order to promote corporate growth. In some cases, criminal decision making might be clearly intentional in nature.

In other cases, harm arising from corporate misdeeds might be the result of organizational processes that do not actually intend for the harmful behavior to occur.

The abstract nature of corporate offending has resulted in an assortment of terms and definitions to describe these behaviors. One author has suggested that corporate crime "includes the vast majority of regulatory offenses subsumed under regulatory law" (Snyder, 1990, p. 374). Frank and Lynch (1992) describe corporate crime as including behaviors that are "socially injurious and blameworthy acts, legal or illegal that cause financial, physical, or environmental harm, committed by corporations and businesses against their workers, the general public, the environment, other corporations or businesses, the government, or other countries" (p. 17).

Some scholars have used phrases such as organizational crime (Schrager & Short, 1978), organizational deviance (Ermann & Lundman, 1978), and organizational misconduct (Vaughan, 2001) to describe similar behaviors. Organizational misconduct, for example, refers to "violations of laws, rules, or administrative regulations by an individual or group of individuals in an organization who, in their organizational role, act or fail to act in ways that further the attainment of organizational goals" (Vaughan, 2001, p. 46).

These behaviors can be distinguished from the other forms of white-collar crime (discussed earlier in this text) in at least four different ways. First, the offenses are committed either *for the organization* or *by the organization*. Many of the crimes discussed earlier are committed *against the organization* and *by an individual*. Second, many corporate crimes are committed in groups, as part of an organizational decision-making process. Third, while the consequences of all forms of white-collar crime are serious, the consequences of corporate misdeeds can be particularly devastating. Fourth, the misdeeds of corporations are more rarely defined as criminally illegal.

Because corporate crime is different from the other forms of white-collar crime, it is best seen as a distinct form of white-collar crime. As a distinct form of white-collar crime, one can point to several specific types of corporate crime.

Types of Corporate Crime

In a classic corporate crime study, Clinard and Yeager (1980) reviewed 1,553 corporate offenses and uncovered the following varieties: (1) administrative violations, (2) environmental violations, (3) financial violations, (4) labor violations, (5) manufacturing violations, and (6) unfair trade practices. Their research was useful in showing that the concept of corporate crime could be subdivided into types of corporate misdeeds. Depending on the level of analysis, it would be possible to list hundreds of different types of corporate misconduct. To keep the discussion manageable, it is useful to focus on general types of corporate wrongdoing. Therefore, the following seven types of corporate crimes warrant attention:

- Antitrust offenses
- False advertising
- Deceptive sales
- Unfair labor practices
- Unsafe work environments
- Harmful consumer products
- Harmful treatment of consumers

Antitrust Offenses

Our economy is based on principles of open market competition. The price of goods and services is tied to supply and demand. Businesses compete with one another by selling goods and services at prices that can be determined by a freely competitive marketplace. This helps to keep prices low and stimulates new businesses that form to enter the competitive marketplace (U.S. Department of Justice [USDOJ], n.d., p. 2). Such a process, in theory, ensures that consumers pay fair prices for goods and services. Some corporations, however, commit crimes known as antitrust offenses to control competition. Put simply, antitrust offenses are those that restrict competition. **Antitrust laws** are designed to promote and protect competition. In the United States, antitrust laws cover business activities in the areas of (1) pricing distribution, (2) mergers, (3) joint ventures, and (4) intellectual property use (Jacobsen, Seat, Shugarman, & Gildea, 1991).

   The most prominent laws to control antitrust offenses are the Sherman Antitrust Act, the Clayton Act, and the Federal Trade Commission Act (FTC) (see Table 9.1). The **Sherman Antitrust Act,** often called the

Table 9.1   Major Antitrust Laws

Law	Descriptions
Sherman Antitrust Act	The Sherman Act outlaws all contracts, combinations, and conspiracies that unreasonably restrain interstate and foreign trade. This includes agreements among competitors to fix prices, rig bids, and allocate customers. The Sherman Act also makes it a crime to monopolize any part of interstate commerce. An unlawful monopoly exists when only one firm controls the market for a product or service, and it has obtained that market power, not because its product or service is superior to others, but by suppressing competition with anticompetitive conduct. This Act is not violated simply when one firm's vigorous competition and lower prices take sales from its less efficient competitors—that is competition working properly. Sherman Act violations involving agreements between competitors usually are punished as criminal felonies.
Clayton Act	The Clayton Act is a civil statute (carrying no criminal penalties) that was passed in 1914 and significantly amended in 1950. The Clayton Act prohibits mergers or acquisitions that are likely to lessen competition. Under the Act, the government challenges those mergers that a careful economic analysis shows are likely to increase prices to consumers. All persons considering a merger or acquisition above a certain size must notify both the Antitrust Division and Federal Trade Commission. The Act also prohibits other business practices that under certain circumstances may harm competition.
Federal Trade Commission Act	The Federal Trade Commission Act prohibits unfair methods of competition in interstate commerce, but carries no criminal penalties. It also created the Federal Trade Commission to police violations of the Act.
Other Laws	The Department of Justice also often uses other laws to fight illegal activities, including laws that prohibit false statements to federal agencies, perjury, obstruction of justice, conspiracies to defraud the United States and mail and wire fraud. Each of these crimes carries its own fines and imprisonment terms which may be added to the fines and imprisonment terms for antitrust law violations.

Sherman Act, passed in 1890, is the broadest antitrust law. This act makes it illegal for competitors to engage in activities that restrict competition. The Antitrust Division of the U.S. Department of Justice has the responsibility for prosecuting these crimes. Common types of antitrust offenses include:

- Price fixing
- Bid rigging
- Price discrimination
- Price gouging
- Market allocation
- Group boycotts

As will be shown below, it is extremely difficult to determine whether these crimes occur or whether behaviors in the corporate system simply reflect fluctuations in the economy.

Price Fixing

Price fixing offenses occur when competitors agree on a price at which goods or services should be sold. The competitors do not need to agree on the same price; they simply need to agree to set prices. Other examples of price fixing include instances where competitors agree to: (1) establish price discounts, (2) hold prices firm, (3) eliminate discounts, (4) adopt a standard formula for a competing price, (5) maintain certain price differentials between different types, sizes, and quantities of products, (6) fix credit terms, (7) not advertise prices, (8) agree on financing rates, (9) set shipping fees, and (10) fix warranties (U.S. Department of Justice, n.d.; Federal Trade Commission, n.d.).

A distinction can be made between horizontal and vertical price fixing. **Horizontal price fixing** occurs when competitors agree to set prices at a certain level. **Vertical price fixing** refers to situations where parties from different levels of the production and distribution chain agree to set prices at a certain level. Traditionally, vertical price fixing has been regarded as illegal. A manufacturer, for example, is not allowed to tell retailers and distributors how much to charge for products produced by the manufacturer. In a recent U.S. Supreme Court case, *Leegin Creative Leather Products, Inc. v. PSKS, Inc.*, this premise was changed and the Court ruled that the "rule of reason" should be used to determine whether agreements between various levels of the production distribution chain are illegal. The rule of reason refers to the premise that "courts must weigh all of the circumstances of the restraint, and the restraint's history, nature and effect in the market involved, in order to ascertain whether anti-competitive effects outweigh any pro-competitive benefits" (Martin, 2007, p. 1). The Court cited "a growing consensus in economic theory that vertical pricing agreements, while sometimes anti-competitive, can often have pro-competitive effects" (as cited in Martin, 2007).

Bid Rigging

Bid rigging (or collusion) occurs when competitors conspire to set specific bids for goods or services they would supply in response to a request for bids. At least four types of bid rigging exist. First, **bid suppression** refers to instances where competitors agree not to submit a bid for a particular job on the understanding that a specific competitor will likely be selected for that job. Second, **complementary bidding** (also known as "cover" and "courtesy" bidding) occurs when competitors submit bids with artificially high estimates or specific demands that cannot be met so that a specific competitor with a lower price or without the demands is selected. Third, **bid rotation** occurs when competitors take turns submitting the lowest bid on a series of bids. Fourth, **subcontracting** occurs when competitors hire one another on subcontracts after the winning bid has been selected (USDOJ, n.d., p. 4).

It is believed that bid rigging is more likely to occur if: (1) there are fewer competitors, (2) the products or services are standardized, (3) competitors know one another, and (4) bidders or businesses submit their bids in the same physical location at the same time (USDOJ, n.d., p. 4). This last item refers to the possibility that competitors will meet one another in the building when submitting their bids and this "chance meeting" will give them the opportunity to "compare notes" or otherwise discuss their bids. Imagine if a professor told students to turn their take-home exams in at a specific time and in a specific location. The possibility that students might run into one another and engage in wrongdoing potentially increases by creating a situation where it is likely they will see one another.

Price Discrimination

On the surface, one might assume that the term *price discrimination* means that businesses cannot charge individuals two different prices based on protected classes like gender, race, religion, and so on. While civil rights laws do prohibit charging for goods based on the characteristics of the consumer, price discrimination actually refers to practices where different prices are charged simply to restrict competition between competitors (Knopp, 1966). It is problematic, however, to determine whether different prices are being offered to limit competition, or if the price differences are just a natural part of business. Indeed, there are many instances where consumers can legally be charged two different prices. Rawkowski (2004) uses the example of charging business travelers more for airfare. One can point to several other examples where consumers are charged different prices:

- Two consumers buy the same car on the same day, with one paying more than the other.
- Two consumers stay in a hotel on the same day, with one paying more than the other.
- Two concertgoers pay two different prices to see Justin Beiber in concert.
- Two students in the same class are charged two different prices for the class (one student is a graduate student and the other is an undergraduate student).
- A grocery store charges two consumers two different prices for the same goods because one of the consumers has a "grocer card" that allows discounts.
- On "Ladies'" night, women are admitted free into a bar but men have to pay a cover charge.

What it comes down to is the fact that price discriminations "are generally lawful, particularly if they reflect the different costs of dealing with different buyers or are the result of a seller's attempts to meet a competitor's offering" (FTC, 2010b). Made illegal under the **Robinson-Patman Act,** price discrimination is illegal if it is done to lessen competition.

Price Gouging

Price gouging refers to situations where businesses conspire to set artificially high prices on goods and services. Check cashing businesses have been implicated in price gouging. These businesses, which exist primarily in minority neighborhoods, charge consumers relatively high fees to cash their paychecks. Some states have passed laws capping the amount that these businesses can charge for cashing checks. Such laws have been found to reduce the number of minority households that do not have bank accounts (Washington, 2006).

Price gouging claims often surface after disasters because of seemingly inflated prices for goods and services such as gas, hotel rooms, food, and so on. After Hurricane Katrina, politicians were quick to blame the oil industry and local gas stations for the high gas prices consumers were forced to pay in the hurricane's aftermath. State attorneys general charged gas stations with gouging although "it was later found by the FTC that gas prices were being set in competitive markets" (Carden, 2008).

Some states have passed laws making it illegal for businesses to raise prices if a state of emergency has been declared. Critics of such laws suggest that selling commodities at prices below market value will actually create more problems and cause shortages on a quicker basis. The higher price, it is believed, helps to prevent shortages. Indeed, after Hurricane Katrina, a call for federal anti-gouging laws was opposed by FTC Chairwoman Deborah Platt Majoras because such a law "could hurt consumers by causing fuel shortages" (McNamara, 2006). Other experts have also warned against federally mandated price controls, suggesting that such practices harm consumers by increasing the amount of time it would take goods to reach consumers (Montgomery, Baron, & Weisskopf, 2007). Montgomery and his colleagues note that price controls on gasoline after Hurricanes Katrina and Rita would have increased economic damage by $1.5 to 2.9 billion.

Other critics of federal price controls suggest that such laws and policies would keep many businesses from "providing goods and services after natural disasters" (Carden, 2008, p. 531). If there is no economic incentive to deliver goods to a disaster area where it may take more resources to deliver the goods, businesses may choose to deliver their goods elsewhere. Critics also suggest that the policies assume that the government better knows how to "allocate resources more efficiently than the market" (Culpepper & Block, 2008, p. 512). To these critics, price controls place artificial constraints on demand and supply, which makes it difficult to promote a free market economy. Culpepper and Block further suggest that "government regulation is nothing short of a disaster as far as satisfying customers is concerned" (p. 512).

Of course, some scholars support the use of price controls in responding to disasters. The assumption is that while natural laws of supply and demand exist during routine days:

In times of disaster, this assumption is often void. A gouger has a local monopoly on the scarce commodity and exploits this monopoly. Gougers violate social norms that dictate that one should help out in times of disaster, not seek profit from them. (Angel & McCabe, 2009, p. 283)

Based on the premise that gougers violate social norms, some have also suggested that gougers are immoral. Drawing on principles of supply and demand, one economist, however, argues that (1) anti-gouging laws are not morally justified, (2) price gouging is not necessarily morally reprehensible, and (3) gouging "offenders" are not necessarily immoral (Zwolinski, 2008). The ambiguity surrounding the utility of these laws reflects the general difficulties that arise when defining white-collar crime (discussed earlier in this text).

Market Allocation

Market allocation occurs when competitors agree to divide markets according to territories, products, goods, or some other service (USDOJ, n.d., p. 4). Perhaps an analogy can be made to drug dealing. It is well known that drug dealers have specific territories where they sell their drugs. Efforts to deal drugs in a rival drug dealer's neighborhood would likely be met with a violent response from the rival dealer. In effect, the drug dealers have engaged in market allocation. In terms of legitimate goods and services, market allocation is illegal because it restricts competition and potentially allows one business to have a monopoly over the jurisdiction or territory it serves or the product/services it provides.

Group Boycotts

Group boycotts are situations where competitors agree not to do business with specific customers or clients. Consider a case in which a group of competing attorneys in the District of Columbia agree not to provide services to indigent defendants unless the District paid the attorneys more for their services. The FTC investigated the case and found the attorneys in violation of antitrust laws, group boycotting in particular. The attorneys appealed the decision and the case eventually made its way to the Supreme Court. The Supreme Court upheld the FTC's decision (FTC, 2010b).

Dynamics Surrounding Antitrust Offenses

Several varieties of antitrust offenses exist, and four patterns are consistent across these offenses. These patterns include (1) the way that "agreement" is conceptualized, (2) the seriousness of harm arising from the offenses, (3) globalization, and (4) difficulties proving (and punishing) offenses.

First, in terms of the way "agreement" to limit competition is conceptualized, some might assume that agreements occur only through verbal or written agreements. This is not the case. In each of the antitrust offenses discussed above, agreements can be in writing, verbally agreed, or *inferred from the conduct of businesses*. As a result, to prove an antitrust offense, officials may rely on either direct evidence—like testimony of participants or witnesses—or circumstantial evidence such as expense reports, telephone records, fluctuations, or bidding histories (USDOJ, n.d., p. 4) . Note also that if the behaviors of competitors result in an antitrust offense, like price fixing, competitors can be found in violation of the laws. Consider the following example provided by the FTC (2010b):

> A group of competing optometrists agreed not to participate in a vision care network unless the network raised reimbursement rates for patients covered by its plan. The optometrists refused to treat patients covered by the network plan, and eventually the company raised reimbursement rates. The FTC said that the optometrists' agreement was illegal price fixing, and that its leaders had organized an effort to make sure other optometrists knew about and complied with the agreement.

Second, it is important to draw attention to the serious harm that arises from antitrust offenses. Estimates suggest that antitrust offenses "can raise the price of a product by ten percent . . . and that American consumers and taxpayers pour billions of dollars each year into the pockets of [those participating in these schemes]" (USDOJ, n.d., p. 4). As evidence of this harm, consider that 6 of the top 10 corporate offenders from the 1990s, as defined by the *Corporate Crime Reporter,* were convicted of antitrust offenses (see Table 9.2).

One of the most prominent recent antitrust offenses involved vitamin producers in the late 1990s. Firms across the world conspired to set caps on how many vitamins each firm would produce, how much they should charge, and who they would sell the vitamins to. The scheme was so large that the U.S. Department of Justice suggested that "In the end, for nearly a decade, every American consumer—anyone who took a vitamin, drank a glass of milk, or had a bowl of cereal—ended up paying more so that the conspirators could reap hundreds of millions of dollars in additional revenue" (USDOJ, n.d., p. 4). Those involved in the conspiracy included executives from F. Hoffman-LaRoche, Ltd., and BASF AG.

A third pattern surrounding antitrust offenses centers around the globalization of our economy. As the world has become more global in nature, the types of antitrust offenses have become more globally

Table 9.2 Top Ten Corporate Offenders, 1990s

Corporation	Type of Crime Committed	Criminal Fine	Where to Read More
F. Hoffman-LaRoche	Antitrust	$500 million	12 Corporate Crime Reporter 21(1), March 24, 1999
Daiwa Bank Ltd.	Financial	$340 million	10 Corporate Crime Reporter 9(3), March 4,1996
BASF Aktiengesellschaft	Antitrust	$225 million	12 Corporate Crime Reporter 21(1), March 24,1999
SGL Carbon Aktiengesellschaft (SLG AG)	Antitrust	$135 million	12 Corporate Crime Reporter 19(4), May 10, 1999
Exxon Corporation and Exxon Shipping	Environmental	$125 million	5 Corporate Crime Reporter 11(3), March 18, 1991
UCAR International, Inc	Antitrust	$110 million	12 Corporate Crime Reporter 15(6), April 13, 1993
Archer Daniels Midland	Antitrust	$100 million	10 Corporate Crime Reporter 40(1), October 21,1996
(tie) Banker's Trust	Financial	$60 million	12 Corporate Crime Repoter 11(1), March 15, 1999
(tie) Sears Bankruptcy Recovery Management Services	Fraud	$60 million	13 Corporate Crime Reporter 7(1), February 15, 1999
Haarman & Reimer Corp.	Antitrust	$50 million	11 Corporate Crime Reporter 5(4), February 3, 1997

oriented. The federal response to antitrust offenses has shifted to adjust to the types of issues arising in a global economy. For example, historically the United States would apply only civil actions against businesses from other countries that engaged in violations of U.S. antitrust laws. In the 1990s, however, U.S. officials began to apply criminal sanctions to businesses in other countries. The criminalization of foreign antitrust cases through an application of the Sherman Act was upheld in *U.S. v. Nippon Paper Industries* (Lee, 1998).

The fourth pattern surrounding antitrust cases centers on the difficulties officials have establishing that crimes occurred and subsequently applying appropriate punishments. Interestingly, difficulties convicting antitrust offenders have been traced to efforts to "get tougher" against this group of offenders. In particular, some scholars have argued that it became harder to convict antitrust offenders in the 1980s after a 1970s law made offenses such as price fixing a felony rather than a misdemeanor (Snyder, 1989, 1990). The rationale for this argument is that offenders put up less of a defense when they were charged with misdemeanors. Facing a felony conviction, alternatively, potentially raises the bar for the kinds of penalties convicted offenders would receive, and as a result, may cause defendants to seek more remedies to avoid a conviction.

False Advertising

False advertising occurs when businesses make inaccurate statements about their products or services in order to facilitate the sale of those items or services. Put more simply, false advertising laws prohibit "untrue or misleading information given to you to get you to buy something, or to come to visit their store" (LA County Division of Consumer Affairs, 2010). False advertising is illegal through the Federal Trade Commission Act, which stipulates:

- Advertising must be truthful and non-deceptive
- Advertisers must have evidence to back up their claims
- Advertisements cannot be unfair (FTC, 2001)

The concept of "deceptive" suggests that businesses cannot mislead or provide irrelevant information in their efforts to promote products. The concept "unfair" means that businesses cannot use advertisements to injure or harm consumers. Types of false advertising include:

- **Bait and switch practices** where customers are lured into the store with the promise of a sale item that does not exist, or is not available in an appropriate amount
- **Resale fraud** where used items are sold as new
- **Misuse of "on sale" phrases** where regular prices are presented as if they are sale prices
- **Misrepresenting the product's capabilities** where consumers are told that the product can do things that it cannot
- **Misrepresenting items as made in the USA** when parts of the product were made elsewhere (LA County Division of Consumer Affairs, 2010)

The FTC regularly addresses cases of false advertising. In 2004, Kentucky Fried Chicken settled charges with the FTC that the company "made false claims in a national television advertising campaign about the relative nutritional value and healthiness of its fried chicken" (FTC, 2004). The company was also charged with comparing the nutritional value of its chicken to "certain popular weight loss programs." KFC promoted their chicken breasts as having less fat than a Burger King Whopper, which, while true, hides the facts that because of the way they way they were cooked, the chicken breasts in fact did "have more than three times the trans fat and cholesterol, more than twice the sodium, and more calories" (FTC, 2004).

In a more recent false advertising case, Eli Lilly and Company pleaded guilty to false advertising after they promoted their drug Zyprexa as a treatment for Alzheimer's disease despite the fact that the FDA had not approved the drug as a treatment for the disease. As part of the plea, the company received a $515 million criminal fine and forfeited $100 million in assets. As part of the civil settlement, the company agreed to pay up to $800 million to federal and state governments (U.S. Department of Justice, 2009).

According to the FTC, the types of advertisements that will receive the most scrutiny from the federal government are those that (1) make claims regarding the consumer's health or safety or (2) include statements that consumers could not realistically be able to evaluate on their own (FTC, 2001). Consider the following false advertising cases as examples:

- Bayer was successfully sued for advertising that one of its vitamins reduced the risk of prostate cancer. As a result of the court's decision, the company had to re-develop its advertising program (Cooper, 2009).
- After being charged with false advertising by the Federal Trade Commission, Nestle agreed to stop advertising that its products "would prevent kids from getting sick or missing school." The settlement did not carry a monetary award, but the company agreed it would not advertise the product as promoting health unless the FDA found such a relationship ("Nestle Subsidiary," 2010).
- Kellogg's settled with the FTC after the agency found that the company falsely advertised Rice Krispies by stating on the cereal box that the product "now helps support your child's immunity," [with] "25 percent Daily Value of Antioxidants and Nutrients—Vitamins A, B, C, and E" on one part of the box, and "Kellogg's Rice Krispies has been improved to include antioxidants and nutrients that your family needs to help them stay healthy" on another part of the box. (FTC, 2010a)

Two common trends in advertising include going-out-of-business sales and the use of celebrities to promote goods. Laws exist to govern these advertising practices. For example, a business cannot advertise that it is going out of business unless it is actually going out of business. With regard to celebrity ads, the advertisement must accurately reflect the celebrity's view of the product. If a celebrity states that he or she uses a product in an ad, he or she must actually use that product. If the celebrity decides at a later date not to support the product any longer, the advertiser can no longer promote the product as if it were endorsed by the celebrity (FTC, 2001). For example, if P. Diddy endorsed this book upon its release, the book could be promoted with his endorsement. If P. Diddy later writes his own white-collar crime book and decides not to support this one, later promotions would not be able to use the music mogul's endorsement.

Some have suggested that the recession starting in 2008 contributed to an increase in false advertising by businesses trying virtually anything to offset the negative consequences of the downturn in the economy (Cooper, 2009). While such a suggestion is speculative, it is in line with the assumptions of the systems perspective suggesting that changes in the one system (e.g., the economic system) will have ramifications for other systems (e.g., marketing practices in the corporate system).

Deceptive Sales

Deceptive sales are illicit sales practices that are driven by corporate policies and directives. Certainly, corporate policies and pressures can promote deceptive sales practices by employees. Consider a 1991 undercover investigation by California's Department of Consumer Affairs that found that the commission structure used in Sears Auto Centers promoted fraud by sales staff. The undercover visitors posed as customers seeking automobile services 38 different times. Of those 38 visits, sales staff recommended unnecessary services 34 times, with one of the visits resulting in needless repairs costing nearly $600 (Fisher, 1992). Interviews with the workers found that under the commission structure, which was instituted in 1990, employees were expected to sell a certain amount of services and products over an 8-hour shift. Failure to sell the expected amounts would result in punitive responses from employers, including having their hours cut or being moved to another department. After the fraud charges by the Department of Consumer Affairs surfaced, the company changed its policy and now pays its auto center salespersons hourly wages (Halverson, 1992).

Despite the change in corporate policy, charges against the company were not dropped, and similar charges against Sears were filed in 41 other states. Eventually Sears settled the charges, paying out $23 million, with California receiving $8 million to pay for "reimbursement costs, new employee training, and coupons for discounts at the service center" (Jennings, 2008, p. 507). Sears' net loss that year was $3.9 billion, the worst year for the company in 60 years. Since then, the amount of sales in auto centers has been below the pre-1992 levels (Jennings, 2008). In the interest of full disclosure, I should note that I worked for Sears from 1989 through 1992, not in the auto centers, but in hardware, sporting goods, and lawn and garden. The fall in auto center sales probably had more to do with the fraud investigation than with my departure.

In a more recent case involving deceptive sales practices, and one many students might be able to relate to, a large for-profit college came under fire in 2004 after a federal investigation by the Department of Education (DOE) revealed that the college recruiters systematically lied to students about how courses would transfer, the amount of financial aid available, and class size (Coutts, 2009). The DOE report said that the college "based its recruiters' pay on the number of students they brought in, and punished underperforming recruiters by isolating them in glass-walled rooms and threatening to fire them if they failed to meet management goals" (Brown, 2004). Here's how a recruiter from the college described the process:

> One thing we would be told to do is call up a student who was on the fence and say, "all right, I've only got one seat left. I need to know right now if you need me to save this for you, because this class is about to get full." Well, that wasn't true. We were told to lie.... One of the things we were to do was ... say we are regionally accredited, which means that [credits] are transferred anywhere. (Coutts, 2009, n.p.)

Those of you who have transferred know that transfer decisions are made by the college or university to which the student is transferring, and not by an accreditation standard. Such deceptive practices were done to benefit the college, not the employee.

The DOE ruled that the recruiting strategies violated Title II of the Higher Education Act. A subsequent audit found that other violations related to the use of financial aid funds were also committed by the college. The parent company of the for-profit college eventually paid the Department of Education $9.8 million. Later it was ordered to pay shareholders $280 million because investors were fraudulently misled about the school's recruiting practices ("University of Phoenix Parent," 2008).

Problems with deceptive practices to recruit students were not limited to this one for-profit college. In a recent U.S. Government Accountability Office (USGAO, 2010) investigation, four undercover employees registered on the websites of 15 different for-profit colleges. After registering on the websites, they began receiving phone calls from recruiters. Some calls were made within 5 minutes after the employee registered on the website. One received an average of six calls a day for an entire month.

The active recruiting by the for-profit recruiters was not problematic in and of itself. After all, they were hired to recruit students to their colleges. Instead, the problems arose when recruiters made deceptive statements about (1) accreditation, (2) graduation rates, (3) employment possibilities, (4) expected salaries, (5) program duration, and (6) cost. Four of the colleges encouraged the undercover applicant to lie about their income and savings in order to gain federal support for their education. All 15 of the colleges "made some type of deceptive or otherwise questionable statement to undercover applicants" (USGAO, 2010, p. 7). Table 9.3 summarizes the deceptive practices.

Table 9.3   Fraudulent Actions Encouraged by For-Profit Colleges

Location	Certification/ Course of Study	Type of College	Fraudulent Behavior Encouraged
California	Certificate–computer-aided drafting	Less than 2-year, privately owned	• Undercover applicant was encouraged by a financial aid representative to change the FAFSA [Free Application for Federal Student Aid] to falsely increase the number of dependents in the household in order to qualify for Pell Grants. • The representative told the undercover applicant that by the time the college would be required by Education to verify any information about the applicant, the applicant would have already graduated from the 7-month program. • This undercover applicant indicated to the financial aid representative that he had $250,000 in the bank, and was therefore capable of paying the program's $15,000 cost. The fraud would have made the applicant eligible for grants and subsidized loans.
Florida	Associate's degree–radiologic technology	2-year, privately owned	• Financial aid representative suggested to the undercover applicant that he not report $250,000 in savings on the FAFSA. The representative told the applicant to come back once the fraudulent financial information changes had been processed. • This change would not have made the applicant eligible for grants because his income would have been too high, but it would have made him eligible for loans subsidized by the government. However, this undercover applicant indicated that he had $250,000 in savings—more than enough to pay for the program's $39,000 costs.
Pennsylvania	Certificate–web page design	Less than 2-year, privately owned	• Financial aid representative told the undercover applicant that he should have answered "zero" when asked about the money he had in savings—the applicant had reported a $250,000 inheritance. • The financial aid representative told the undercover applicant that she would "correct" his FAFSA form by reducing the reported assets to zero. She later confirmed by e-mail and voicemail that she had made the change. • This change would not have made the applicant eligible for grants, but it would have made him eligible for loans subsidized by the government. However, this applicant indicated that he had about $250,000 in savings—more than enough to pay for the program's $21,000 costs.
Texas	Bachelor's degree–construction management	4-year, privately owned	• Admissions representative encouraged applicant to change the FAFSA to falsely add dependents in order to qualify for Pell Grants. • Admissions representative assured the undercover applicant that he did not have to identify anything about the dependents, such as their Social Security numbers, nor did he have to prove to the college with a tax return that he had previously claimed them as dependents. • Financial aid representative told the undercover applicant that he should not report the $250,000 cash he had in savings.

The types of deceptive statements made by recruiters might resonate some with readers who, as students, have their own set of expectations about the value of their education. Consider the following examples quoted from the GAO report:

- A college owned by a publicly traded company told our applicant that, after completing an associate's degree in criminal justice, he could try to go work for the Federal Bureau of Investigation or the Central Intelligence Agency. While other careers within those agencies may be possible, a position as an FBI special agent or CIA Clandestine Officer require a bachelor's degree at a minimum.
- A small beauty college told our applicant that barbers can earn $150,000 to $200,000 a year. While this may be true in exceptional circumstances, the Bureau of Labor Statistics (BLS) reports that 90% of barbers make less than $43,000 a year.
- A representative at a college in Florida owned by a publicly traded company told an undercover applicant that the college was accredited by the same organization that accredits Harvard and the University of Florida when in fact it was not. The representative told the undercover applicant: "It's the top accrediting agency—Harvard, University of Florida—they all use that accrediting agency.... All schools are the same; you never read the papers from the schools." (USGAO, 2010, p. 91)

The undercover investigation revealed that deceptive sales practices by college recruiters seemed to occur far too regularly. To date, no charges have been filed against the colleges, but charges remain possible. To view a video of the undercover applicants talking with recruiters, go to www.gao.gov/products/gao-10-948t.

Unfair Labor Practices

Unfair labor practices refer to corporate violations where workers are subjected to unethical treatment by their bosses and corporate leaders. In this context, two general types of unfair labor practices can be identified: (1) exploitation and (2) systemic discrimination.

Exploitation

Exploitation refers to situations where businesses take advantage of their workers. Pay exploitation is an example. An assignment I give my white-collar crime students asks them to write about types of white-collar crimes they have experienced. Each semester, at least a handful of students write about jobs where they work parts of their shifts for free. From my students' reports, this seems to be particularly popular in the restaurant industry—where waiters and waitresses stick around after their shifts to help clean the restaurants, being paid the standard waiter/waitress wage of $2.13 an hour if they are paid at all.

Sweatshops are examples of unfair labor practices. Such businesses "regularly violate both wage and child labor laws and safety or health regulations" (Foo, 1994, p. 2179). In many sweatshops, undocumented workers are hired and paid reduced wages. Such practices are criticized because they cheat the government out of tax dollars and deprive workers of necessary benefits (Foo, 1994). These activities are not simply a modern phenomenon. In 1892, Florence Kelley identified three types of sweatshops in the garment industry:

- *Inside shops* are those created by manufacturers inside a factory.
- *Outside shops* include contractors hired to produce goods or materials to be used by the manufacturer.
- *Home shops* (aka family groups) are run out of the exploited worker's home.

Even then, she drew attention to the problems of infection and disease that stemmed from such practices.

Some may point to greed and profit as the primary motivators for the creation and persistence of sweatshops. However, the reasons for the development of sweatshops are more complex than this. Foo (1994) cites a GAO report that attributed the existence of sweatshops to:

- The presence of a vulnerable population
- The presence of an exploitable population
- Labor intensive industries
- Low profit margin industries
- Lack of inspection staff
- Weak penalties
- Inadequate cooperation among enforcement agencies

Barnes and Kozar (2008) examined the types of exploitation targeted at pregnant workers in the textile industry in China, Mexico, Nicaragua, and the Philippines. Their research identified an assortment of types of exploitation including forced abortions, unpaid overtime, forced job requirements harmful to the fetus, and lack of appropriate benefits. The authors note that U.S. firms are linked to these practices in that "governments of developing nations continue to lure [U.S. firms] in with promises of tax breaks, no duties, longer work weeks, and low minimum wage requirements" (p. 291).

Discrimination

Discrimination is another type of unfair labor practice committed in the corporate system. Some may question whether these offenses are actually corporate crimes. It is significant to note that Clinard and Yeager (1980) cited discrimination under the category of labor violations in their discussion of corporate crime. What this suggests is that discrimination has been considered a type of corporate misconduct ever since scholars first began to discuss these misdeeds.

Four federal statutes prohibit employment discrimination: Title VII, the Americans with Disabilities Act, the Age Discrimination Act, and the Equal Pay Act of 1963 (Goldman, Gutek, Stein, & Lewis, 2006). These laws prohibit the unfair treatment of employees based on their membership in a protected class including race, sex, religion, national origin, and disability status (Chien & Kleiner, 1999). Table 9.4 shows the number of discrimination complaints individuals filed with the Equal Employment Opportunity Commission (EEOC) between 1996 and 2009. One trend stands out: the number of complaints was higher in 2008 and 2009 than any other time. When releasing the 2009 data, officials from the EEOC attributed the differences to several possible factors, including "greater accessibility of the EEOC to the public, economic conditions, increased diversity and demographic shifts in the labor force, [and] employees' greater awareness of their rights under law" (Equal Employment Opportunity Commission, 2010).

Women are more likely than men to experience discrimination because of stereotypes, perceptions of a lack of fit in the workforce, and the inability of recruiters to identify with women (Chien & Kleiner, 1999). Chien and Kleiner argue that these factors "inhibit women's career development and advancement and subsequently undermine women's contributions to the labor market" (p. 34).

Basing employment decisions on stereotypes has been regarded as a form of discrimination. In *Price Waterhouse v. Hopkins* (1989), a woman was denied a promotion in an accounting firm because she was

Table 9.4 Complaints Filed With EEOC, 1997–2009

	FY 1997	FY 1998	FY 1999	FY 2000	FY 2001	FY 2002	FY 2003	FY 2004	FY 2005	FY 2006	FY 2007	FY 2008	FY 2009
Total charges	80,680	79,591	77,444	79,896	80,840	84,442	81,293	79,432	75,428	75,768	82,792	95,402	93,277
Race	29,199	28,820	28,819	28,945	28,912	29,910	28,526	27,696	26,740	27,238	30,510	33,937	33,579
	36.2%	36.2%	37.3%	36.2%	35.8%	35.4%	35.1%	34.9%	35.5%	35.9%	37.0%	35.6%	36.0%
Sex	24,728	24,454	23,907	25,194	25,140	25,536	24,362	24,249	23,094	23,247	24,826	28,372	28,028
	30.7%	30.7%	30.9%	31.5%	31.1%	30.2%	30.0%	30.5%	30.6%	30.7%	30.1%	29.7%	30.0%
National origin	6,712	6,778	7,108	7,792	8,025	9,046	8,450	8,361	8,035	8,327	9,396	10,601	11,134
	8.3%	8.5%	9.2%	9.8%	9.9%	10.7%	10.4%	10.5%	10.7%	11.0%	11.4%	11.1%	11.9%
Religion	1,709	1,786	1,811	1,939	2,127	2,572	2,532	2,466	2,340	2,541	2,880	3,273	3,386
	2.1%	2.2%	2.3%	2.4%	2.6%	3.0%	3.1%	3.1%	3.1%	3.4%	3.5%	3.4%	3.6%
Retaliation—all statutes	18,198	19,114	19,694	21,613	22,257	22,768	22,690	22,740	22,278	22,555	26,663	32,690	33,613
	22.6%	24.0%	25.4%	27.1%	27.5%	27.0%	27.9%	28.6%	29.5%	29.8%	32.3%	34.3%	36.0%
Retaliation—Title VII only	16,394	17,246	17,883	19,753	20,407	20,814	20,615	20,240	19,429	19,560	23,371	28,698	28,948
	20.3%	21.7%	23.1%	24.7%	25.2%	24.6%	25.4%	25.5%	25.8%	25.8%	28.3%	30.1%	31.0%
Age	15,785	15,191	14,141	16,008	17,405	19,921	19,124	17,837	16,585	16,548	19,103	24,582	22,778
	19.6%	19.1%	18.3%	20.0%	21.5%	23.6%	23.5%	22.5%	22.0%	21.8%	23.2%	25.8%	24.4%
Disability	18,108	17,806	17,007	15,864	16,470	15,964	15,377	15,376	14,893	15,575	17,734	19,453	21,451
	22.4%	22.4%	22.0%	19.9%	20.4%	18.9%	18.9%	19.4%	19.7%	20.6%	21.4%	20.4%	23.0%
Equal Pay Act	1,134	1,071	1,044	1,270	1,251	1,256	1,167	1,011	970	861	818	954	942
	1.4%	1.3%	1.3%	1.6%	1.5%	1.5%	1.4%	1.3%	1.3%	1.1%	1.0%	1.0%	1.0%

seen as "too macho" (Malos, 2007, p. 97). Managing partners of the company said she needed to act more feminine and wear more makeup. The Supreme Court ruled that businesses could not base promotion decisions on gender stereotypes. Courts have also held that employers can be held liable for discrimination if they make employment decisions based on a woman's status as a mother. If employers assume, for instance, that a job would be too difficult because the employee is a new mother, the employer could be held liable for discrimination.

Discrimination does not just stem from employment decisions; instead, hostile or harassing behaviors of employees against other employees can be seen as discriminatory. Consider the following illustration:

> An African American employee at an East Coast Company took the day off to celebrate Martin Luther King Jr. Day. Upon returning from work, he discovered a note that had been scribbled on his desk calendar. It read: "Kill four more, get four more days off." (Solomon, 1992, p. 7)

In many cases, such attitudes stem from the top of the corporation and reflect corporate culture. Indeed, one court has recognized that "top level officials are 'in a position to shape the attitudes, policies, and decisions of corporate managers'" (Sorenson, 2009, p. 194, citing *Ercegovich v. Goodyear Tire and Rubber Co.,* 1998). It is through this perspective that corporations can be held accountable for discriminatory practices of its employees. Consider, as an illustration, a recent survey of nearly 700 business leaders focusing on hiring disabled workers that found that "86% agreed that employers would pick a non-disabled candidate, while 92% said there was still discrimination against disabled people in employment and recruitment" (Faragher, 2007, p. 22).

In a recent case highlighting how corporate leaders are involved in discrimination, an investigation by the Office of Inspector General (USOIG) and the Office of Professional Responsibility found that U.S. Deputy Assistant Attorney General Bradley S. Schlozman "considered political and ideological affiliations in hiring career attorneys and in other personnel actions affecting career attorneys in the Civil Rights Division" (USOIG, 2008). As part of the evidence to substantiate the investigation, investigators found e-mails with comments such as "I have an interview with some lefty who we'll never hire but I'm extending a courtesy interview as a favor," "[I] just spoke with [the attorney] to verify his political leanings and it clear he is a member of the team," and in response to a request to hire an attorney, Schlozman e-mailed, "Conservative?" Ironically, while the Civil Rights Division exists to protect against civil rights violations, in this case a top-ranking official from the division committed multiple civil rights violations.

Discrimination has negative consequences for individuals, groups, and organizations. At the individual level, discrimination can negatively impact one's health, self-esteem, and job performance. At the group level, groups receive unfair pay differences and are assigned to different jobs based on group identities. At the organizational level, the corporation suffers from a negative reputation, law suits, and fines from the EEOC (Goldman et al., 2006). In fact, in 2009, the EEOC "recovered more than $376 million in monetary relief for thousands of discrimination victims."

Unsafe Work Environments

Crime also occurs in the corporate system when employers place employees at risk of harm in *unsafe work environments*. Labeled corporate violence by Frank and Lynch (1992), unsafe work environments can result in death, illnesses, and injuries. In terms of death, one author describes corporate murder as including deaths from industrial "accidents" and "occupationally related diseases, the majority of which are caused by the knowing and willful violation of occupational health and safety laws by corporations" (Kramer, 1984, p. 7). One scholar has suggested that "managers and corporations commit far more violence than any serial killer or criminal organization" (Punch, 2000, p. 243). According to the Occupational Safety and Health Administration (OSHA, 2010a), 14 employees are killed on the job every day in the United States. OSHA (2006) estimates that 50,000 employees die each year from work-related illnesses. Depending on how one defines "work-related illnesses," this number may be far higher.

Consider stress-induced illnesses, for example. Did the stress come from the workplace or some other aspect of the individual's life? One author points to three issues that make it difficult to link illness to the workplace. First, determining the precise cause of illnesses, and linking the illness to the workplace, is difficult. Second, disease is seen as a normal part of the aging process. If individuals develop a workplace illness after years of work, the assumption is that the illness came from "getting old" rather than working. Third, and somewhat related, diseases are "considered normal" and accepted as a part of our lives (Frank, 1993, p. 110).

Workplace injuries can be either acute or chronic. Acute injuries are immediate injuries that one might experience on the job. Chronic injuries refer to those that occur over time. The nature of some types of jobs can lead to long-term injuries. Standing on a cement floor and packing boxes in a 100° Fahrenheit factory for 40 hours a week over 30 years (a job my dad had) can lead to knee and shoulder problems. Bending over and serving school children lunch for 22 years (a job my mom had) can lead to back problems. Typing on a computer over several years (a job I have) can result in carpel tunnel syndrome, a disease that makes it difficult to move one's hands (see Frank, 1993).

In terms of acute injuries, in 2009, 117 out of 10,000 full-time workers missed at least one day of work as the result of an occupational injury or illness (Bureau of Labor Statistics [BLS], 2010). This was a 5% decrease from the prior year. Figure 9.2 shows the number of injuries/illnesses between 2003 and 2009. As shown in the figure, 2009 was the only year that there were fewer than a million workplace injuries. Somewhat in line with the systems perspective and the assumption that changes in one system will lead to changes in other systems, experts attribute this decrease to the downturn in the economic system. In particular, they note that because of problems in the economic system, there were fewer hours worked in construction and manufacturing—two industries that typically have more injuries (BLS, 2010). Because fewer workers were in these industries, the number of possible injuries would also decrease. Changes in the economic system, in this case, reduced the number of workplace injuries in the corporate system.

Despite this reduction, certain industries seem to be more at risk for workplace injuries than others. Table 9.5 shows the number of injuries in various industries. One clear pattern, and one that is not entirely surprising, is that "blue-collar" industries have more workplace injuries/illnesses than "white-collar" industries. The most frequent types of OSHA violations in 2010 reflect this dynamic. In particular, the top 10 most

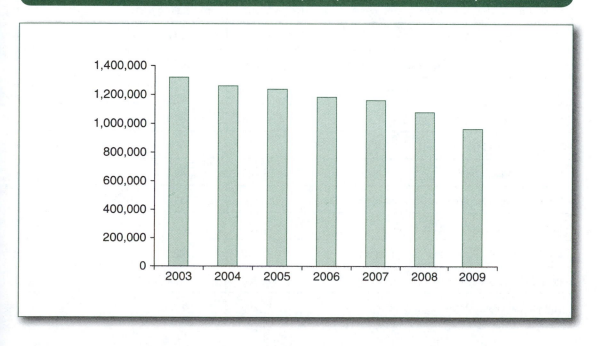

Figure 9.2 Number of Injuries and Illnesses With Days Away From Work, Private Industry, 2003–2009

Table 9.5 Number, Incidence Rate, and Median Days Away From Work for Nonfatal Occupational Injuries and Illnesses, 2009

Occupation	Number	Incidence Rate (per 10,000)	Median Days Away From Work
Total	1,238,490	117	8
Management Occupations	24,020	39.0	4
Business and Financial Operations Occupations	7,760	15.6	5
Computer and Mathematical Occupations	2,940	10.0	7
Architecture and Engineering Occupations	5,330	24.8	7
Life, Physical, and Social Science Occupations	3,360	31.5	5
Community and Social Services Occupations	15,510	101.1	6
Legal Occupations	1,549	17.3	2
Education, Training, and Library Occupations	33,260	51.5	4
Arts, Design, Entertainment, Sports, and Media Jobs	7,150	53.2	7
Health Care Practitioners and Technical Occupations	64,800	111.6	7
Health Care Support Occupations	79,660	266.3	6
Protective Service Occupations	92,610	342.6	10
Food Preparation and Serving Related Occupations	77,220	105.4	6
Building/Grounds Cleaning/Maintenances Jobs	98,250	303.7	7
Personal Care and Service Occupations	31,330	134.5	7
Sales and Related Occupations	69,130	65.0	8
Office and Administrative Support Occupations	83,260	49.0	7
Farming, Fishing, and Forestry Occupations	12,160	134.1	7
Construction and Extraction Occupations	106,330	212.3	12
Installation, Maintenance, and Repair Occupations	95,210	208.3	10
Production Occupations	112,800	143.6	9
Transportation and Material Moving Occupations	211,290	282.0	12

frequently cited OSHA standards in fiscal year 2010 included: (1) scaffolding, (2) fall protection, (3) hazard communication, (4) respiratory protection, (5) ladders, (6) lockout/tagout, (7) electrical/wiring methods, (8) powered industrial trucks, (9) electrical, general requirements, and (10) machine guarding (OSHA, 2010a). Where these problems exist, the possibility of workplace injuries increases. Note that I made an intentional decision not to refer to injuries as "accidents." As will be shown below, injuries occurring in the corporate system are often far from accidental.

Beyond the physical costs, the costs of workplace injuries and illnesses are significant. These costs include: (1) settlement costs to victims and family members, (2) negative publicity, (3) increases in insurance premiums, (4) higher worker compensation rates, and (5) increased attention from governmental agencies (Yakovlev & Sobel, 2010). In terms of economic costs, it is estimated that "the cost of occupational injuries and illnesses totals more than $156 billion" (OSHA, 2006, p. 5).

Some authors have suggested that corporations are more concerned with profit than worker health and safety. One author even suggests that such a statement "seems incontrovertible" (Tombs, 2008, p. 26). However, economists have found that companies actually maximize profit if they provide safer working environments for their employees. In some cases, this means replacing workers with technological devices that are safer and "reduce worker exposure to danger and lead to lower injury rates over time" (Yakovlev & Sobel, 2010, p. 435). This may mean fewer jobs in "dangerous" jobs but more jobs in technologically oriented occupations that develop the technologies to make workplaces safer.

A summer job I had in college comes to mind. For 4 years I spent my summers working in the bottle factory where my dad worked. College students had various summer jobs in the factory, including painting, packing bottles in boxes, driving forklifts, cleaning, and so on. One job was called "snapping." In this job, workers waited on the basement floor of the factory to stack packed bottles of boxes on a pallet. The packed boxes were carried on a conveyor belt, with as many as 30 boxes a minute coming before the "snapper." The snapper would grab several boxes at once, "snap" the lids of the boxes strategically, and flip them over while turning around to place them in a predetermined pattern on a pallet. The job was actually somewhat exciting to those of us who rarely did it. Trying to stack all of the boxes without creating a mess made the task more like a game than a job. If we fell behind, a full-time worker was there to help us out (while making fun of us for being unable to keep up). Each summer, someone got hurt from either dropping boxes (filled with bottles—which would become broken bottles) or from trying to lift too many boxes at once.

Years later I learned that the "snapper" job no longer existed. A machine was created that would simultaneously pack the bottles in boxes and then stack the packed boxes on a pallet. A worker had to watch the machine to make sure it was working properly. Sitting and watching a machine stack boxes is much safer than stacking the boxes yourself!

The Occupational Safety and Health Administration, situated in the Department of Labor, is the federal agency charged with addressing health and safety issues in businesses. OSHA exists to "ensure safe and healthful working conditions for working men and women by setting and enforcing standards and by providing training, outreach, education, and assistance" (OSHA, 2010a). About 2,400 inspectors work for OSHA and related state agencies. In 2005, OSHA conducted "close to 39,000 inspections and issued just over 85,000 citations for violations" (OSHA, 2006). The types of violations OSHA issues citations for are outlined in Table 9.6.

OSHA was created in 1970 as part of the Occupational Safety and Health Act. This act covers all employees working in the private sector. State and local government workers are covered under specific state occupational acts, which by law must be similar to the federal law. The act does not cover (1) self-employed

Table 9.6 Types of OSHA Violations

Violation	Definition
Willful	The employer knew that a hazardous condition existed but made no reasonable effort to eliminate it and in which the hazardous condition violated a standard, regulation, or the OSH Act.
Serious	The workplace hazard could cause injury or illness that would most likely result in death or serious physical harm, unless the employer did not know or could not have known of the violation.
Other-than-serious	A situation in which the most serious injury or illness that would be likely to result from a hazardous condition cannot reasonably be predicted to cause death or serious physical harm to exposed employees but does have a direct and immediate relationship to their safety and health.
De minimis	Violations that have no direct or immediate relationship to safety or health.
Other	Violations that have a direct relationship to job safety and health, but are not serious in nature.
Failure to abate	The employer has not corrected a violation for which OSHA has issued a citation and that abatement date has passed.
Repeated	Employer may be cited for a repeated violation if that employer has been cited previously for a substantially similar condition.

workers, (2) immediate family members of self-employed farmers, and (3) workers covered by another federal agency (OSHA, 2010a). The act stipulates that workers have the following rights (see OSHA, 2010a):

1. Receive information and training about hazards, methods to prevent harm, and the OSHA standards that apply to their workplace.

2. Observe testing that is done to find hazards in the workplace and get the testing results.

3. Review records of work-related injuries and illnesses.

4. Get copies of their medical records.

5. Request OSHA to inspect their workplace.

6. Use their rights under the law to be free from retaliation and discrimination.

Under this last provision, employees cannot be punished by employers for exercising their rights. If employers engage in any form of adverse action, the corporation/business could face additional penalties from OSHA. Types of adverse actions that would warrant a response from OSHA include any of the following actions directed toward the employee who reported a concern to OSHA: firing/laying off, making threats, blacklisting, reassigning, reducing pay or hours, demoting, denying overtime, disciplining, denying benefits, failure to rehire, and intimidation (OSHA, 2010b).

Workplace injuries and illnesses are rarely treated as crimes. A study of Finnish police officers found a systematic lack of interest in responding to workplace safety offenses (Alvesalo & Whyte, 2007). In this study, one officer told an interviewer that such cases were "worthless shit" that should not receive police intervention.

Typically, workplace injuries and illnesses are handled within the regulatory environment. This presents problems in that victims' needs may not be fully addressed through an administrative response system. To address this problem, one expert called for broader workers compensation policies, civil lawsuits, and criminal prosecutions of companies responsible for harming their employees (Frank, 1993).

With regard to workers compensation, the specific features of the policies are not "worker friendly" policies. Under worker compensation systems, it is up to workers to prove that their ailment was caused by the occupational setting. If workers agree to the compensation, they typically give up their right to sue their company for negligence (Frank, 1993). The pursuit of criminal remedies is complicated by perceptions of workplace injuries as accidents rather than avoidable injuries inflicted by the corporate system employing the injured employee.

Some have criticized the use of the word *accidents* to describe workplace injuries (Alvesalo & Whyte, 2007). The basis for the criticism is fourfold. First, many of the injuries are foreseeable and can be attributed to decisions made by managers and supervisors to place workers at risk. Second, the term accident also implies that the injured party is to blame. Keep in mind that injured parties more often work in blue-collar occupations. Third, by construing injuries as accidents, the managers increase their power over the workers, who get blamed for getting hurt on the job. Finally, by defining injuries as accidents, workers are less likely to pursue civil and criminal remedies to address their injuries. As an example of how defining workplace injuries as accidents helps to keep the cases out of the justice system, consider the following comments from one police officer: "It's not the responsibility of the employer if some idiot blunders by oneself, does something stupid. There cannot be someone looking over every Tom, Dick, and Harry" (Alvesalo & Whyte, 2007, p. 69).

Reflecting the connections between constructions of definitions of deviance, workplace injury, and the system's response, author Maurice Punch (2000) observed the following:

> Corporations can create an environment that leads to risk-taking, even recklessness, resulting in high casualties and severe harm. Companies then get away with "murder" because the courts are not geared to organizational deviance and corporate violence. (p. 243)

Discussing these ideas in the abstract may make it difficult for some students to fully appreciate the dynamics of workplace injuries and illnesses. However, many students are likely already employed in either full- or part-time jobs. Students must recognize that in their role as "worker" they too have certain rights that their employer is expected to recognize. In Focus Box 9.1 includes information about these rights from an OSHA publication titled "Young Workers."

In Focus 9.1

Young Worker's Rights: What Every College Student Needs to Know

You Have a Right to a Safe and Healthy Workplace and a Responsibility to Be Safe

You may work to earn spending money, buy a car, save for college or gain work experience. Whatever the reason, plans for your job and for your future don't include getting hurt.

(Continued)

(Continued)

Each year, 60–70 teens die from work-related injuries and about 200,000 young workers seek emergency medical treatment.

It doesn't have to be this way. You have the right to be safe and healthy at work and you have a responsibility to be safe. And there are simple, practical steps that you and your employer can take to help make sure that your job helps you build a better future.

Employer Responsibilities:

Provide a workplace that protects workers from injuries, illnesses and fatalities.

Know the law about working limits for teens, including the number of hours they can work and the kinds of jobs that can be performed.

Emphasize the importance of safety.

Make sure that young workers are trained properly.

Teach workers to recognize hazards and use safe work practices.

Teen Worker Responsibilities:

Trust your instincts about dangerous situations.

Follow all safety rules.

Wear proper safety equipment.

Ask questions about potentially dangerous situations or equipment.

Tell your supervisor or parent if you suspect unsafe conditions.

Be aware of your work environment.

Work safely.

Stay sober and drug-free.

Know your workplace rights.

What Is OSHA?

OSHA is the Occupational Safety and Health Administration. Its role is to assure the safety and health of America's workers by setting and enforcing standards; providing training, outreach, and education; establishing partnerships; and encouraging continual improvement in workplace safety and health.

Finding Answers:

Employers are responsible for providing a safe and healthy workplace for their employees. If you are worried about a specific workplace hazard or interested in learning more about keeping yourself and others safe and healthy at work, visit the OSHA Teen Workers website at www.osha.gov/teens. Or call OSHA toll-free at 1-800-321-OSHA to report a problem, ask questions or request information.

To protect yourself:

Know your workplace rights.

Talk to your employer.

Stay alert and work safely.

Get safety and health training.

Visit the OSHA Teen Workers website at www.osha.gov/teens.

Common workplace hazards and injuries:

Slips, trips and falls

Strains and sprains

Chemical exposure

Burns and cuts

Eye injuries

Hearing loss

Motor vehicle crashes

Electrocution

Machinery malfunctions

Harmful Consumer Products

Crimes also occur in the corporate system when corporations create **harmful consumer products**. Companies produce all sorts of goods for our use. In most cases, these goods are safe. Occasionally, however, goods enter the marketplace that create significant harm to consumers. Consider that in 2010, the United States Consumer Product Safety Commission issued 427 recalls for millions of goods "that either violated mandatory standards or were defective and presented a substantial risk of injury to the public" (USCPS, 2010a).

While virtually any product can be unsafe if used inappropriately, goods that have been linked to serious harm include:

- Harmful toys
- Certain automobiles
- Types of food
- Specific types of construction material
- Recalled goods from China

These goods are discussed below.

Table 9.7	Number of Toy-Related Injuries Requiring Emergency Room Intervention, 2005–2009		

Year	All Ages	Under 15	Under 5
2005	202,300	152,400	72,800
2006	220,500	165,100	78,400
2007	232,900	170,100	80,200
2008	235,300	172,700	82,300
2009	250,100	169,200	80,900

Harmful Toys

Children's products are those that are often found to be the least safe. One advocacy group, Kids in Danger, lamented that children are "used as guinea pigs for unsafe products" because government "safety tests aren't required for children's products" (Sorkin, 2008). Interestingly, the number of toy-related injuries has grown since 2005. Table 9.7 shows the number of toy injuries requiring emergency room treatment between 2005 and 2009. During this time, the number of toy injuries increased from 202,300 to 250,100, which represented a statistically significant increase. Incidentally, approximately 130,000 toy injuries requiring emergency room treatment occurred in 1996. This means that the number of injuries nearly doubled from 1996 to 2009. Approximately 75% of those injured by toys were under 15 years of age. In 2009, twelve kids died from toy injuries (USCPS, 2010d).

Certain Automobiles

On August 28th, 2009, a 911 operator received a call from Mark Saylor, an off-duty California highway patrol officer. He told the operator, "We're in a Lexus . . . and were going north on 125 and our accelerator is stuck . . . we're in trouble . . . there's no brakes . . . we're approaching the intersection . . . hold on . . . hold on and pray . . . pray" (Frean & Lea, 2010). He and three family members were killed in what was later attributed to a problem with the accelerator sticking to the floor mat.

Initially, National Highway and Traffic Safety Administration (NHTSA) investigators found that the mat in Saylor's vehicle was longer than it should have been and it was believed that this potentially contributed to the crash. Until Toyota found a fix, owners of certain models were advised to remove the mats from the driver's side ("Fatal Crash Spurs Review," 2009). Another review of the incident found that the design of the gas pedal could have forced it to get lodged with the mat (Bensinger & Vartabedian, 2009). A subsequent investigation revealed that similar problems in other cars made by Toyota "led to thousands of accidents and nineteen deaths" (Frean & Lea, 2010).

In response to these concerns, in 2009 Toyota recalled 4.26 million automobiles. The recall resulted in Toyota's shares dropping 0.9% (Keane & Kitamura, 2009). It is estimated that the recall cost Toyota $900 million (Glor, 2010) and U.S. sales of Toyota vehicles dropped to under 100,000 vehicles for the first time since the late 1990s ("There's No Brakes," 2010). Obviously, this drop in sales was the result of a reduction in consumer confidence. In Focus 9.2 includes the testimony Toyota's chief executive gave before the U.S. House Committee on Oversight and Reform on February 24, 2010.

▲ **Photo 9.1** The number of kids who required emergency room treatment for injuries they experienced from playing with toys in the United States doubled between 1996 and 2009.

In Focus 9.2

Toyota Chief Executive Akio Toyoda's
Remarks to the House Committee on Oversight and Reform

I am Akio Toyoda of Toyota Motor Corporation. I would first like to state that I love cars as much as anyone, and I love Toyota as much as anyone. I take the utmost pleasure in offering vehicles that our customers love, and I know that Toyota's 200,000 team members, dealers, and suppliers across America feel the same way. However, in the past few months, our customers have started to feel uncertain about the safety of Toyota's vehicles, and I take full responsibility for that. Today, I would like to explain to the American people, as well as our customers in the U.S. and around the world, how seriously Toyota takes the quality and safety of its vehicles. I would like to express my appreciation to Chairman Towns and Ranking Member Issa, as well as the members of the House Oversight and Government Reform Committee, for giving me this opportunity to express my thoughts today.

I would like to focus my comments on three topics—Toyota's basic philosophy regarding quality control, the cause of the recalls, and how we will manage quality control going forward. First, I want to discuss the philosophy of Toyota's quality control. I myself, as well as Toyota, am not perfect. At times, we do find defects. But in such situations, we always stop, strive to understand the problem, and make changes to improve further. In the name of the company, its long-standing tradition and pride, we never run away from our problems or pretend we don't notice them. By making continuous improvements, we aim to continue offering even better products for society. That is the core value we have kept closest to our hearts since the founding days of the company.

At Toyota, we believe the key to making quality products is to develop quality people. Each employee thinks about what he or she should do, continuously making improvements, and by doing so, makes even better cars. We have been actively engaged in developing people who share and can execute on this core value. It has been over 50 years since we began selling in this great country, and over 25 years since we started production here. And in the process, we have been able to share this core value with the 200,000 people at Toyota operations, dealers, and suppliers in this country. That is what I am most proud of.

Second, I would like to discuss what caused the recall issues we are facing now. Toyota has, for the past few years, been expanding its business rapidly. Quite frankly, I fear the pace at which we have grown may have been too quick. I would like to point out here that Toyota's priority has traditionally been the following: First; Safety, Second; Quality, and Third; Volume. These priorities became confused, and we were not able to stop, think, and make improvements as much as we were able to before, and our basic stance to listen to customers' voices to make better products has weakened somewhat. We pursued growth over the speed at which we were able to develop our people and our organization, and we should sincerely be mindful of that. I regret that this has resulted in the safety issues described in the recalls we face today, and I am deeply sorry for any accidents that Toyota drivers have experienced.

(Continued)

(Continued)

Especially, I would like to extend my condolences to the members of the Saylor family, for the accident in San Diego. I would like to send my prayers again, and I will do everything in my power to ensure that such a tragedy never happens again.

Since last June, when I first took office, I have personally placed the highest priority on improving quality over quantity, and I have shared that direction with our stakeholders. As you well know, I am the grandson of the founder, and all the Toyota vehicles bear my name. For me, when the cars are damaged, it is as though I am as well. I, more than anyone, wish for Toyota's cars to be safe, and for our customers to feel safe when they use our vehicles. Under my leadership, I would like to reaffirm our values of placing safety and quality the highest on our list of priorities, which we have held to firmly from the time we were founded. I will also strive to devise a system in which we can surely execute what we value.

Third, I would like to discuss how we plan to manage quality control as we go forward. Up to now, any decisions on conducting recalls have been made by the Customer Quality Engineering Division at Toyota Motor Corporation in Japan. This division confirms whether there are technical problems and makes a decision on the necessity of a recall. However, reflecting on the issues today, what we lacked was the customers' perspective. To make improvements on this, we will make the following changes to the recall decision making process. When recall decisions are made, a step will be added in the process to ensure that management will make a responsible decision from the perspective of "customer safety first." To do that, we will devise a system in which customers' voices around the world will reach our management in a timely manner, and also a system in which each region will be able to make decisions as necessary. Further, we will form a quality advisory group composed of respected outside experts from North America and around the world to ensure that we do not make a misguided decision. Finally, we will invest heavily in quality in the U.S., through the establishment of an Automotive Center of Quality Excellence, the introduction of a new position—Product Safety Executive, and the sharing of more information and responsibility within the company for product quality decisions, including defects and recalls.

Even more importantly, I will ensure that members of the management team actually drive the cars, and that they check for themselves where the problem lies as well as its severity. I myself am a trained test driver. As a professional, I am able to check on problems in a car, and can understand how severe the safety concern is in a car. I drove the vehicles in the accelerator pedal recall as well as the Prius, comparing the vehicles before and after the remedy in various environmental settings. I believe that only by examining the problems on-site, can one make decisions from the customer perspective. One cannot rely on reports or data in a meeting room. Through the measures I have just discussed, and with whatever results we obtain from the investigations we are conducting in cooperation with NHTSA, I intend to further improve on the quality of Toyota vehicles and fulfill our principle of putting the customer first.

My name is on every car. You have my personal commitment that Toyota will work vigorously and unceasingly to restore the trust of our customers.

Toyota was not the first automobile company to face concerns about safety. In the early 2000s, the Ford Explorer faced public scrutiny after it was found that tread separation problems on the Explorer's Firestone tires resulted in the deaths of 134 individuals in the United States. The investigation found that separately the tires and the vehicles were safe. However, when combined, they were a "toxic cocktail," according to Rep. Edward Markey (D. Mass.) (White, Power, & Aeppel, 2001). Ford and Firestone recalled more than 27 million tires in a 10-month time frame, and in 2001, Ford cut its 100-year supply relationship with Firestone (Ackman, 2001).

Of course, this was not the first time that the safety of a Ford vehicle was called into question. Recall the discussion of the Ford Pinto case earlier in this text. The Pinto was linked to a series of deaths "because of gas-tank explosions in rear-end collisions" (Glazer, 1983, p. 37). Ford was sued in 50 different lawsuits between 1971 and 1978 as a result of these collisions. One employee, Frank Camps, a design engineer, "questioned the design and testing procedure and later charged publicly that his superiors who knew of this danger were so anxious to produce a lightweight and cheap car . . . that they were determined to overlook serious design problems" (Glazer, 1983, p. 36).

Types of Food

Certain types of food can also be seen as unsafe consumer products. Walters (2007) notes that genetically modified food has the potential to harm consumers. He also draws attention to the "sale of contaminated meat" and "the illegal use of chemicals" on food items. Whereas the Consumer Product Safety Commission has the authority to recall many products, consumable products such as food are under the authority of the Food and Drug Administration.

In September 2008 concern surfaced over potentially contaminated peanut butter. An investigation revealed that Peanut Butter Corporation of America, a peanut butter producer in Georgia, had distributed peanut butter contaminated with salmonella. Initially, the FDA found that the company actually knew about the tainted peanut butter but engaged in "lab shopping" to find another lab that would approve the peanut butter before distribution. A subsequent report by the FDA found that the company had actually distributed the peanut butter before even receiving approval from the second laboratory. Congress held a hearing, inviting food safety experts and subpoenaing representatives from Peanut Butter Corporation. Officials from the corporation did not testify, invoking their Fifth Amendment right against self-incrimination ("FDA: Georgia Plant Knowingly Sold," 2009). By April 2009, at least nine individuals had died from eating the peanut butter and more than 700 had become seriously ill (Centers for Disease Control [CDC], 2009). The company filed for bankruptcy and the entire peanut butter industry experienced economic losses as consumers cut back on their peanut butter consumption. The Georgia Bureau of Investigation indicated it would not criminally prosecute the company because the state criminal laws did not allow for serious penalties in the case. A federal criminal investigation is ongoing, as are several lawsuits against the corporation.

Many cases of food poisoning from harmful food products likely go unnoticed. Research by CDC scientists estimates that 48 million (or one in six Americans) individuals get sick from food poisoning each year (Scallan et al., 2011). Also, it is estimated that approximately 228,000 individuals are hospitalized in the United States from food poisoning each year, and approximately 3,000 die from tainted food.

Specific Types of Construction Material

Certain types of construction materials have also been shown to be unsafe products. Asbestos is perhaps the most well known construction material deemed to be unsafe. Asbestos is a mineral used in the past in various construction processes and products, including insulation, siding, roofing materials, shipyard construction materials, and so on. Initial concern about asbestos can be traced to the 1920s when one physician wrote about the potential for harm from exposure to this product. It was not until the mid-1970s, however, that widespread concern about the product surfaced. Workers in various industries exhibited different illnesses that were traced to exposure to asbestos. It is now known that asbestos exposure can lead to asbestosis (an illness making it difficult to breath), lung cancer, and mesothelioma—a rare type of cancer that "attacks the lining of the lungs, heart, and abdomen" ("Maryland Contractor Fined," 2010). Between the early 1970s and 2002, 730,000 individuals filed asbestos claims at a cost of $70 billion. Estimates suggest that by 2029, a half million Americans will have died from asbestos related diseases (Morris, 2010).

Asbestos is rarely used in building products today, though materials containing it are still found in older buildings and homes. Left alone in the construction material, the asbestos poses little harm. However, when cut, damaged, or moved, the asbestos fibers can become airborne and cause health problems.

Chinese drywall is another type of unsafe building material. In 2008, the U.S. Consumer Product Safety Commission began receiving complaints about problems homeowners were having with drywall installed in their homes. The drywall was imported from manufacturers in China between 2003 and 2007 when the U.S. levels of drywall were low because of the building boom and the need for drywall to repair homes after Hurricanes Katrina and Rita. Residents with the drywall in their homes reported (1) rotten egg smells or odors that smelled like fireworks, (2) corroded or black metals, (3) corroded electrical wiring, and (4) an assortment of health problems. The health problems they described included "irritated and itchy eyes, difficulty breathing, persistent coughing, bloody noses, runny noses, headaches, sinus infections, fatigue, asthma attacks, loss of appetite, poor memory, and irritability; testing of the homes with the drywall found that the Chinese drywall emitted 100 times the amount of hydrogen sulfide that non–Chinese drywall emitted (U.S. Consumer Product Safety Commission [CPSC], 2010b; Hernandez, 2010).

It is estimated that seven million sheets of the tainted drywall were installed in tens of thousands of homes in the United States, and that property damage from the defective drywall will rise to $3 billion. By March 2010, approximately 2,100 homeowners filed lawsuits over the drywall against builders, insurers, manufacturers, realtors, suppliers, developers, and others. Around the same time, the CPSC recommended that homeowners remove the drywall from their homes, an expense that would need to be covered by the homeowners. Estimates suggested that such a process would cost an average of $100,000 per home (Hernandez, 2010).

In the fall of 2010, a judge held that insurers could not be held liable because of traditional exclusions found in insurance policies ("Insurer's Recent Success," 2010). In October 2010, Knauf Plasterboard Tianjin Co., the company responsible for some of the tainted drywall, agreed to fix the homes that had its drywall installed in them (Burdeau, 2010). By January 2011, the CPSC had received 3,770 complaints from consumers in 41 states saying that the defective drywall caused problems in their homes. At present, the agency is still conducting an investigation; it is described as "the largest compliance investigation in agency history" (CPCS, 2010c).

Recalled Goods From China

The drywall was not the first imported goods from China that were deemed to be unsafe. The year 2007, deemed "Year of the Recall," saw a particularly high number of Chinese goods recalled by the Consumer Product Safety Commission. To put this in perspective, in 2007, the CPSC issued 473 recalls. Of those 473,

82% were for imported goods, most of which included toys and jewelry from China (CPSC, 2010a). Many of the recalls centered on what was deemed to be an unsafe level of lead paint in the goods. In September 2007, the CPSC signed an agreement with China's equivalent agency stipulating that China would no longer export toys containing lead paint to the United States ("Chinese Goods Scare Prods Regulators," 2007). The CPSC's Office of International Programs and International Affairs enhanced its efforts to work with China and other foreign manufacturers to focus on product safety. Part of their efforts entailed the coordination of U.S.–China Consumer Product Safety Summits. The agency also staffed an employee in China for the first time beginning in December 2009 (CPSC, 2010a).

To be sure, globalization has had ramifications for the way that corporations create and distribute unsafe products. On the one hand, it is hard to hold manufacturers in other countries accountable "because attorneys can't establish jurisdiction" (PR Newswire, 2007). On the other hand, the way that goods are now created, a specific product may include parts that were created in several different countries. It becomes particularly difficult to determine where the faulty part of an unsafe product was made (Wahl, 2009).

Harmful Treatment of Consumers

Harmful treatment of consumers refers to situations where businesses either intentionally or unintentionally put consumers who are using their services at risk of harm. Institutional neglect in nursing homes is one example. Offenses that have been known to occur in nursing homes include instances where nursing homes fail to:

1. Check and update each resident's assessments every 3 months.

2. Have a program to keep infection from spreading.

3. Give proper treatment to residents with feeding tubes to prevent problems.

4. Make sure that each resident gets a nutritional and well-balanced diet.

5. Try to resolve each resident's complaints quickly.

6. Make sure each resident is being watched, and has assistant devices when needed, to prevent accidents.

7. Make sure that residents are well nourished.

8. Keep residents free from physical restraints, unless needed for medical treatment.

9. Keep the rate of medication errors (wrong drug, wrong dose, wrong time) to less than 5% (Payne, 2011).

Note that these offenses in and of themselves may not produce harm. However, they raise the likelihood that consumers might experience harm.

Businesses have a duty to ensure that consumers are as safe possible. A landmark case demonstrating this involved pop singer Connie Francis. In 1974, she was raped at a Howard Johnson's hotel in New York. After her victimization, she sued the hotel for failing to provide her adequate security after learning that the lock on the door of the room where her rape occurred had not been fixed a year after she was raped. She was awarded more than three million dollars, which is believed to be one of the largest amounts of civil damages awarded at the time (Barrows & Powers, 2009).

A more recent case demonstrating how businesses and corporations can commit misconduct by failing to keep consumers safe involves the band Great White. The 1980s band is best known for its hit, "Once Bitten, Twice Shy." Like many eighties bands, Great White was still entertaining audiences two decades later by playing in nightclubs and local establishments across the country. On February 20, 2003, they were playing at The Station, a popular nightclub in West Warwick, Rhode Island. To start the show, the band's tour manager, Dan Biechele—with the approval of the owners of the establishment—set off a fireworks display that shot flames 15 feet in the air and into soundproofing foam installed in the ceiling (Kreps, 2010).

The establishment erupted in fire. Concertgoers could not even see the exit signs at the doors because of the smoke. Some of them had problems getting past a local television camera person who was there, ironically, to film a story about nightclub safety. Within 3 to 5 minutes, The Station was engulfed in flame. By the time the fire was over, 100 people were killed and at least 230 suffered physical injuries (Kreps, 2010).

Band manager Biechele later pleaded guilty to 100 counts of manslaughter. In May 2006, he was sentenced to 15 years in prison with 11 years suspended. He was paroled in March 2008. The owners of the club—brothers Michael and Jeffery Derderian—pleaded guilty after Biechele, while still claiming that they did not know that the soundproofing was flammable. Several entities involved in the concert were sued, including the band, the installer of the soundproofing foam, the promoters, alcohol suppliers, the owners, their insurance companies, and the television station doing the story on nightclub safety. In 2010, the case was settled for $176 million ("Great White Band Manager," 2006; Kreps, 2010). That so many defendants were listed in the lawsuit demonstrates the complexity of these cases. The Great White case also shows that the failure to keep consumers safe is defined as a criminal wrong for those directly involved in the event, and a civil wrong for those indirectly involved.

Dynamics of Corporate Offending

It is clear that several varieties of corporate crime exist. At least four patterns run through these varieties of crime. These patterns include:

- The benefits of corporate crime
- The complexity of intent
- The breadth of victimization
- Problems responding to corporate crime

With regard to the *benefits of corporate crime*, it is clear that corporations benefit from wrongdoing, assuming they don't get caught. Even when they get caught, many believe that the low penalties given to offenders result in corporations still benefiting from the misconduct. It is important to stress that some individuals also benefit from corporate offending. The discussion has tended to suggest that it is the corporation that benefits from these misdeeds (Glasberg & Skidmore, 1998a). However, employees may also benefit, particularly if the misdeeds results in promotions, favorable job evaluations, and bonuses.

The *complexity of intent* is another dynamic of corporate crimes. Punch (2000) categorized three levels of knowledge to describe managerial involvement in corporate violence: (1) fully conscious conspiratorial behavior over time, (2) incompetent and negligent, and (3) unaware of criminal risks, perceived legitimate behavior. This third level may be particularly difficult to group. In effect, it is entirely reasonable that no one did anything wrong, but a corporate harm nonetheless occurred. As Vaughan (2001) notes, "traditionally, when things go wrong in organizations, individuals are blamed." Vaughan goes on to say that organizations "have their dark side" and that organizational processes can produce "harmful outcomes, even when personnel are well-trained, well-intentioned, have adequate resources, and do all the correct things" (p. 57). Ermann and Lundman (2002) offer a similar perspective: "Well-intentioned individuals in organizational settings may produce deviant actions, even though none of them have deviant knowledge, much less deviant motivations. Indeed, individuals may do their jobs well and nevertheless produce deviance" (p. 9).

Consider the Ford Pinto case, the first time a prosecutor tried to criminally prosecute an automobile company for corporate misconduct tied to the gas tank explosions of the Pinto. While many may want to place blame on the Ford executives and attribute the misdeeds to profit seeking motivations, Lee and Ermann (1999), after a thorough review of the case, "argue[d] that institutionalized norms and conventional modes of communication at the organizational and network level better explain available data" (p. 33). They also note that "routine processes can generate unintended tragedy" (p. 43) and concluded that the accidents were the result of "unreflective action" writing: "The Pinto design emerged from social forces both internal and external to Ford. There was no 'decision' to market an unsafe product, and there was no decision to market a safe one" (p. 45).

As another example, recall the Great White tragedy. The tour manager and bar owners were simply doing their jobs—trying to entertain the concertgoers. They did not intend to create the harm that arose that winter night. But, their actions did nonetheless result in harm.

One can also point to the **breadth of victimization** as another corporate crime dynamic. One single corporate offense could harm thousands, if not millions, of individuals. One author has classified corporate crime victims into primary, secondary, and tertiary victims (Shichor, 1989). Primary victims are those directly harmed by the corporate offense (i.e., the individual who used the unsafe product). Secondary victims are impersonal victims, typically not individuals (e.g., businesses that are harmed by the misdeeds of a corporation). Tertiary victims include members of the community harmed by victimization. Another author has noted that victims of corporate crime include workers, consumers, investors, taxpayers, and other corporations (Barnett, 1981). In addition, scholars have noted that corporations can victimize themselves through what is called collective embezzlement, defined as "crimes by the corporation against the corporation" (Calavita & Pontell, 1991). Instances where top executives allow a corporation to fail, knowing that they will profit from the failure, are examples of collective embezzlement.

Another dynamic surrounding corporate crime has to do with *problems responding to corporate crime.* Corporations "possess an economic and political power that is great relative to that generally possessed by victims of corporate crime" (Barnett, 1981, p. 4). With this power, corporations are believed to be able to influence criminal justice decision making and use their resources to "manipulate politicians and the media" (Garoupa, 2005, p. 37). As an example, one expert has shown how some types of corporate misconduct are not defined as crime, but as "risky business" by various parties (Pontell, 2005).

⬛ Public Concern About Crimes by the Corporate System

Corporate crimes do not typically receive the same level of public scrutiny that other crimes do. One author attributed this to the belief that these offenses "are usually less sensational, better concealed, and harder to prove" (Minkes, 1990, p. 128). Members of the public often do not know they have been victims of corporate offenses, nor are they aware of the harm from these offenses or of possible strategies to recover the costs of the harm (Tombs, 2008).

Some have attributed the lack of understanding about corporate crime to media coverage of these offenses. Research by Burns and Orrick (2002) suggested that (1) corporate crime coverage is less frequent than traditional crime coverage, (2) when corporate crime is covered in the media, the coverage will influence policy makers, (3) the public receives a distorted image of corporate crime, and (4) reporters do not define corporate misconduct as deviant or criminal. The authors also suggested that when corporate crime is addressed in the media, the focus is on the harm and the incident, but not on the criminal or the factors contributing to the crime.

News reporters are not the only ones to ignore corporate crime. Criminologists also pay relatively little attention to the topic. Figure 9.3 shows the subjects of articles in criminal justice journals from a study by Lynch, McGurrin, and Fenwick (2004). As Lynch's study shows, compared to articles and studies on other forms of crime, few studies focused on corporate crime. In fact, articles on antitrust offenses were the least frequent type of article.

Figure 9.3   Topics Addressed in Criminal Justice Journals

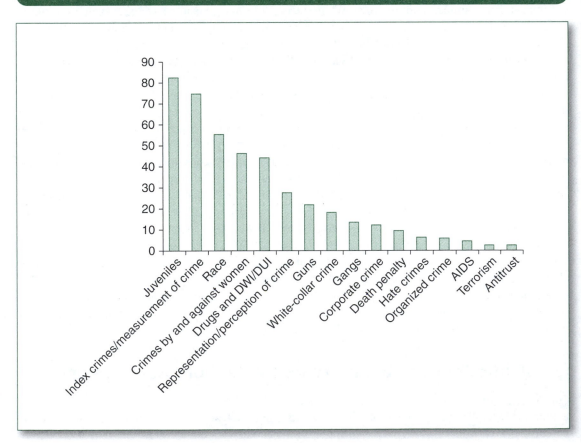

⊠ Summary

- The phrase "crimes by the corporate system" is used to characterize the body of offenses that are committed to benefit the corporation for which the employee (or employees) works.
- The concept of corporation can be seen four different ways—as a business, a location, a legally recognized status, and a collection of employees.
- Frank and Lynch (1992) describe corporate crime as including behaviors that are "socially injurious and blameworthy acts, legal or illegal, that cause financial, physical, or environmental harm, committed by corporations and businesses against their workers, the general public, the environment, other corporations or businesses, the government, or other countries" (p. 17).
- Antitrust offenses are offenses that restrict competition. Antitrust laws are designed to promote and protect competition.
- Price fixing offenses occur when competitors agree on a price at which goods or services should be sold.
- Bid rigging (or collusion) occurs when competitors conspire to set specific bids for goods or services they would supply in response to a request for bids.
- Made illegal under the Robinson-Patman Act, price discrimination is illegal if it is done to lessen competition.
- Price gouging refers to situations where businesses conspire to set artificially high prices on goods and services.
- Market allocation occurs when competitors agree to divide markets according to territories, products, goods, or some other service (U.S. Department of Justice, n.d., p. 4).
- Group boycotts refer to situations where competitors agree not to do business with specific customers or clients.
- Four patterns are consistent across these antitrust offenses—(1) the way that "agreement" is conceptualized, (2) the seriousness of harm arising from the offenses, (3) globalization, and (4) difficulties proving (and punishing) offenses.
- False advertising occurs when businesses make inaccurate statements about their products or services in order to facilitate the sale of those items/services.
- Two common trends in advertising include going-out-of-business sales and the use of celebrities to promote goods.
- Deceptive sales refers to illicit sales practices that are driven by corporate policies and directives.
- Unfair labor practices refer to corporate violations where workers are subjected to unethical treatment by their bosses and corporate leaders. Two general types of unfair labor practices can be identified: (1) exploitation and (2) systemic discrimination.
- Discrimination has negative consequences for individuals, groups, and organizations.
- Labeled corporate violence by Frank and Lynch (1992), unsafe work environments can result in death, illnesses, and injuries.
- Crimes also occur in the corporate system when corporations create *harmful consumer products*. In 2010, the United States Consumer Product Safety Commission issued 427 recalls for millions of goods "that either violated mandatory standards or were defective and presented a substantial risk of injury to the public" (USCPS, 2010a).
- The year 2007, deemed "Year of the Recall," saw a particularly high number of Chinese goods recalled by the Consumer Product Safety Commission.

- Globalization has ramifications for the way that corporations create and distribute unsafe products.
- *Harmful treatment of consumers* refers to situations where businesses either intentionally or unintentionally put consumers who are using their services at risk of harm.
- At least four patterns run across these varieties of crime—the benefits of corporate crime, the complexity of intent, the breadth of victimization, and problems responding to corporate crime
- Corporate crimes do not typically receive the same level of public scrutiny that other crimes receive.

KEY TERMS

Antitrust laws	False advertising	Price gouging
Bait and switch practices	Group boycotts	Resale fraud
Bid rigging	Harmful consumer products	Robinson-Patman Act
Bid rotation	Harmful treatment of consumers	Sherman Antitrust Act
Bid suppression	Horizontal price fixing	Subcontracting
Breadth of victimization	Market allocation	Unfair labor practices
Complementary bidding	Organization misconduct	Vertical price fixing
Deceptive sales	Price discrimination	
Exploitation	Price fixing	

DISCUSSION QUESTIONS

1. Watch the GAO video showing college recruiters lying to undercover applicants available online at www.gao.gov/products/gao-10-948t. Do you think any crimes were committed? How can the recruiters' behaviors be characterized as corporate crime?

2. Write two personal ads for yourself: one that is accurate and one that is a "false advertisement." What is it that makes the advertisement false?

3. Visit the Federal Trade Commission's website and find an example of an antitrust offense. Search the web to find how often the specific offense was discussed on various websites. How does the attention given to the antitrust offense compare to the attention given to other offenses?

4. What do you think should be done to companies that produce unsafe products? Explain.

5. How can companies save money by providing a safer work environment? What factors would influence a business leader to provide an unsafe environment?

6. Is food poisoning a crime? Explain.

7. Review the types of corporate crime discussed in this section. Rank the offenses from least serious to most serious.

8. Describe a way that you have been a victim of a corporate crime.

9. Review the testimony provided by Toyota Chief Executive Akio Toyoda in In Focus 9.2. Do you think his statements reflect suggestions by Ermann and Lundman that corporate harm sometimes comes from unreflective action and organizational processes? Explain.

WEB RESOURCES

FTC Guide to Antitrust Laws: http://www.ftc.gov/bc/antitrust/index.shtm

World Vision Child Labor: http://www.worldvision.org/content.nsf/learn/globalissues-childprotection-childlabor

U.S. Consumer Product Safety Commission: http://www.cpsc.gov/cpscpub/prerel/prerel.html

Food and Drug Administration: http://www.fda.gov/

Reporting Corporate Crimes: http://www.quackwatch.com/02ConsumerProtection/complaint.html

Citizen Works: http://www.citizenworks.org/admin/press/corpreforms.php

READING

In this reading, criminologist Ronald Kramer considers the seriousness of corporate crime. Kramer provided one of the first, and most useful, frameworks for viewing the seriousness of corporate crime. He examines the economic, physical, and moral costs of corporate crime and draws comparisons between corporate and conventional crimes. Some of the estimates provided by Kramer are staggering. Kramer also discusses public concern about corporate crime and includes a number of recommendations to address corporate misconduct.

Is Corporate Crime Serious Crime?

Criminal Justice and Corporate Crime Control

Ronald C. Kramer

One frequent objection to both the criminological study and greater legal control of corporate crime is the argument that these crimes are not as serious (i.e., harmful) as other forms of crime, particularly "street crime." Business spokesmen and some criminologists contend that corporate crime has only diffuse economic effects and is, therefore, unimportant. Even if the great economic costs of corporate crime are recognized, it is argued that these crimes are not serious or not violent is then used to justify their exclusion from criminological study and greater legal control (Wilson, 1975; Nettler, 1978; Brown, 1978).

The purpose of this paper[1] is to counter that argument. Drawing on evidence from a wide variety of sources, we shall demonstrate that corporate crime is indeed "serious" crime, with economic, physical, and moral costs far greater than those associated with conventional "street crime."[2] Thus, we argue that the criminal justice system must become more concerned with the issue of controlling corporate crime in the future.

 Economic Costs

Although it is difficult to measure the economic costs of corporate crime precisely, even the most conservative estimates show that the total loss to the public from these crimes is extremely high. As Geis (1973:185) points out, "Corporate crime . . . imposes an enormous financial burden on society." Furthermore, the economic costs associated with corporate crimes such as consumer fraud, anti-trust and restraint of trade violations, commercial bribery, tax violations, and others, simply dwarf the financial costs of conventional property crimes like robbery, burglary, and larceny.

There are varying estimates of the actual costs of corporate crimes. A Department of Justice estimate put the total annual loss to taxpapers from reported and unreported violations of federal regulations by corporations at $10 to $20 billion (Clinard and Yeager, 1980:8). The Chamber of Commerce of the United States (1974), a conservative pro-business organization, has estimated that various white-collar crimes costs the public some $40 billion a year. One of the most thorough attempts to

SOURCE: Kramer, R. (1984). Is corporate crime serious crime? Criminal justice and corporate crime control. *Journal of Contemporary Criminal Justice, 2,* 7–10. Copyright © SAGE, Inc.

calculate the financial loss to the country from corporate crimes was that of the Subcommittee on Antitrust and Monopoly of the U.S. Senate Judiciary Committee headed by the late Senator Philip Hart. This subcommittee put the cost of corporate crime at between $174 and $231 billion a year. Compared to even the least of these estimates, the $3 to $4 billion annual loss to street crime represents nothing more than a drop in the bucket. In light of these figures, it is difficult not to agree with Conklin (1977:2) that "The costs of business crime are pervasive and exorbitant."

Physical Costs

Discussions of corporate crime traditionally have focused only on the economic costs of these types of offenses. But the impact of corporate crime is not limited to these costs. There are serious "physical costs" associated with the criminal acts of corporations as well. As Geis (1973:183) notes, "Corporate crime kills and maims." Each year corporations are responsible for causing thousands of deaths and injuries around the world (Braithwaite and Condon, 1978; Clinard and Yeager, 1980; Geis, 1973, 1975; Goff and Reasons, 1978; Reiman, 1979). As with the economic costs of corporate offenses, these physical costs far exceed those caused by the more conventional street crimes of the poor and the powerless. As Liazos (1972:11) points out, "the corporate economy kills and maims more, is more violent, than any violence committed by the poor."

The extent of this "corporate violence" in our society is staggering. For example, over 100,000 deaths a year are attributed to occupational related diseases, the majority of which are caused by the knowing and willful violation of occupational health and safety laws by corporations (Ashford, 1976; Berman, 1978; Lens, 1979; Page and O'Brien, 1972; Reasons, Peterson, and Ross, 1981; Scott, 1974; Swartz, 1975; Tataryn, 1979). Additionally, 14,200 workers are killed in industrial "accidents", with two million more receiving disabling injuries (National Safety Council, 1971). Again, the majority of these deaths and injuries can be attributed to dangerous work conditions maintained by corporations in violation of federal law (Reiman, 1979).

Workers are not the only victims of corporate crime, however. The general public is often victimized simply by being in an environment made unsafe by corporate acts. As Schrager and Short (1978:415) have noted, the "potential impact ranges from acute environmental catastrophes such as the collapse of a dam to the chronic effects of diseases resulting from industrial pollution." One study recently estimated that 140,000 deaths a year (9% of all U.S. deaths) may be attributed to air pollution (Mendelsohn and Orcutt, 1979). The victimization of the public by corporate violation of environmental pollution laws is probably best exemplified by the pain and anguish suffered by the residents of New York's "Love Canal" who were needlessly exposed to toxic chemical wastes dumped by the Hooker Chemical Company (Brown, 1979).

Consumers are a segment of the general public who are victimized by corporate criminal acts. It has been estimated by the Consumer Product Safety Commission that approximately 20 million serious injuries are annually associated with unsafe and defective consumer products (unsafe food and drugs, defective autos, tires, appliances, contraceptive devices, and others). One hundred and ten thousand of these injuries result in permanent disability and 30,000 result in death (Schrager and Short, 1978). In addition to this "domestic" corporate violence, a number of U.S. corporations have been involved in the dumping of defective medical devices, lethal drugs, known carcinogens, toxic pesticides, and contaminated foods on Third World nations after these products were banned in the United States (Dowie, 1979).

These data show that corporate crimes do have enormous physical costs. After comparing these physical costs to the average 20,000 murders and nonnegligent manslaughters reported to police agencies each year, it must be concluded that, "'Far more persons are killed' through corporate criminal activities than by individual criminal homicides" (Clinard and Yeager, 1980:9).

Social and Moral Costs

Finally, it must be pointed out that corporate crimes have social and moral costs as well. As Conklin (1977:7) notes, "Even more significant than the financial and physical costs of white-collar crime may be the destructive impact of such behavior on public confidence in the economy and commercial world." Corporate criminal acts violate trust and undermine social institutions as Sutherland (1949:13) pointed out long ago:

> The financial loss from white collar crime, great as it is, is less important than the damage to social relations. White collar crimes violate trust and, therefore, create distrust; this lowers social morale and produces social disorganization. Many of the white collar crimes attack the fundamental principles of the American institutions.

Even more so than street crime, corporate crime is thought to erode the moral base of society. The President's Commission on Law Enforcement and Administration of Justice (1967:5) argued that these crimes "are the most threatening of all . . . because of their corrosive effect on the moral standards by which American business is conducted." Most importantly, however, the existence of corporate crime may set an example of lawlessness for the general public and serve to justify street crimes. As Conklin (1977:8) points out, "Crimes by the upperclass, especially if they do not lead to conviction and imprisonment, serve as rationalization for the lower classes to justify their own criminal behavior."

◪ Increasing Public Concern

Even if the social harm of corporate crime is recognized, it is asserted that the public is not concerned with these offenses and tolerant of corporate offenders. Given the low level of concern and the lack of moral condemnation on the part of the public, it is argued that criminologists should slight the topic of corporate crime and redirect their efforts toward the study and control of the kind of crime that the public is concerned about— common street crimes (Wilson, 1975; Brown, 1978).

The notion that the public is unconcerned with corporate crime is a taken for granted assumption that runs through much of the literature in this area. As early as 1907, E. A. Ross noted that white-collar criminals ("criminaloids" was his term) were not under the "effective ban of public opinion" (pp. 69-70). In a comment on Hartung's study of white-collar offenses in the wholesale meat industry in Detroit, Burgess (1950:24) argued that these men were not criminals because they were not regarded as such by society. The highly respected criminologist George Void (1958:249) argued that laws defining white-collar crime "have never been regarded generally by the community as of the same kind, to be handled in the same way, as those involving the historic common law crimes." Even Sutherland (1949:49) himself noted the "relatively unorganized resentment of the public toward white-collar crime."

The conventional wisdom in this case is simply not true. A large number of studies show that the public has always been somewhat concerned with corporate crime,[3] and this concern has increased dramatically in recent years (Clinard and Yeager, 1980; Schrager and Short, 1980; Cullen, Link, and Polanzi, 1982; Meier and Short, 1982). What accounts for this increasing public concern over corporate crime? Clinard and Yeager (1980) have identified some of the "specific social forces that have contributed to the rise in interest in and concern with corporate crime," such as: highly publicized corporate violations, increased recognition of corporate irresponsibility, the growth of the consumer movement, increased concern for the environment, over-concentration on lower-class crime, the protests and demonstrations of blacks in the late 1960s and early 1970s, the prison reform movement of the 1970s and the influence of conflict analysis and Marxist theory on criminology (pp. 14-16).

All of these factors have undoubtedly contributed to the increasing public concern with the issue of corporate crime. However, it appears that Clinard and Yeager have passed over an important point. The public could not become very concerned about corporate crime until it became convinced that these offenses were just as serious, if not more serious, than ordinary street crimes. And, they would not become convinced of that until they recognized that corporate crimes have *serious physical impact*. The recent increase in public concern over corporate crime can be attributed to the increasing recognition of the *physical harm* caused by these offenses. As columnist Jack Anderson (1979:8A) has noted:

> the American people—and Congress—are becoming increasingly aware that criminal misconduct by Big Business executives can be deadlier than the mass murders of a Richard Speck or a Charles Manson. And there is a growing demand that corporate fatcats, whose profit-motivated decisions cause death or injury to thousands of Americans, be punished at least as severely as a ghetto kid who holds up a neighborhood liquor store.

A recent study by Schrager and Short (1980) supports this conclusion. They found a high degree of public concern for illegal corporate acts with "serious adverse physical impact." Their study supports the importance of physical impact in the public's evaluation of the seriousness of corporate crime. As Schrager and Short (1980:26) point out:

> Individuals not only consider organizational (corporate) crimes with physical impact to be far more serious than those with economic impact, but they also rate physical organizational crimes as equal in seriousness to a range of common crimes which theorists such as Nettler and Wilson consider central to the "crime problem." People appear to evaluate both common and organizational offenses in terms of impact. They respond to the physical dimension of both common and organizational crimes in a similar manner, and the same was found for the economic dimension.

The evidence is clear that the public evaluates corporate crimes with physical impact to be just as serious, if not more serious, than ordinary street crimes; and they are just as concerned about controlling corporate crime as they are about street crime.[4] Still, the erroneous belief that the public is less concerned about

and more tolerant of these crimes is prevalent among politicians and law enforcement officials (and some criminologists). The consequences of such a belief may be tragic. As Conklin (1977:17) notes, "Failure to seek a conviction because of a belief in public tolerance of business crime may reduce the deterrent effect of the law and increase the amount of such crime."

 ## The Criminal Justice Response: A Challenge for the Future

Given the grave social harm caused by corporate crime and the increasing public concern with these criminal acts, there is an obvious need to develop more effective legal controls over corporate behavior. In recent years, there have been numerous calls for the greater use of criminal sanctions against corporate offenders (Elkins, 1976; Anderson, 1979; Conyers, 1980). Two criminologists have, in fact, recently argued that corporate crime is more preventable by criminal justice intervention than traditional crime (Braithwaite and Geis, 1982). Before the criminal justice system can become more active and more effective in controlling corporate crime, however, two things must happen: 1) major reforms will have to be implemented in the existing system and 2) more resources will have to be devoted to criminal justice in general and corporate crime control in particular.

Most of those who call for the greater use of the criminal justice system to combat corporate crime recognize that as it is currently structured, that system is inadequate for the task. Thus, numerous proposals have been made to reform the criminal justice system with the objective of increasing corporate crime control (Stone, 1975; *Yale Law Journal,* 1979; Coinard and Yeager, 1980; Coffee, 1980, 1981; Fisse, 1981; Braithwaite, 1982; Braithwaite and Geis, 1982; Ermann and Lundman, 1982; Skoler, 1980). These proposals include:

1. The creation of new criminal laws that deal specifically with harmful actions engaged in by corporate (organizational) entities.

2. The adoption of a proactive enforcement stance with regard to corporate crime.

3. The creation of special corporate crime units within enforcement agencies with "special focus" training of the police personnel who will start these units.

4. Changing the law to make it easier to convict corporations in a criminal court. For example, including strict liability provisions for corporate organizations (because juries are incapable of understanding the complex issues involved in many corporate offenses).

5. Increasing the level of fines for corporations.

6. The creation of new sanctions which penetrate the corporate structure, that is, reach inside and attempt to restructure its management structure and decision making process.

With or without these reforms, the criminal justice system will never be able to control harmful corporate behavior without a dramatic increase in financial resources and personnel. As it stands now, the system cannot adequately control traditional crime with its existing resources. More money and manpower must be allocated to the system in general and a higher priority for these resources needs to be placed on corporate crime control.

Both the task of reforming the criminal justice system and providing it more resources to effectively combat corporate crime are political issues. Absent sustained political activity, they will not occur and the economic, physical, and social costs of corporate crime will continue to mount. In my view, criminologists must take the lead in presenting the political case for stemming the tide of corporate crime. That is our most important challenge for the future.

Notes

1. There are no official statistics, of course, on corporate crime.

2. Street crime is, of course, a serious problem. The intent here is to demonstrate that corporate crime is equally serious, if not more serious.

3. For a review of these studies, see Meier and Short (1982).

4. Further evidence for this is provided by a 1969 Louis Harris Poll (*Time*, June 6, 1969:26), by a study carried out by Cullen, Link, and Polanzi, (1982) and by a study carried out by Sinden, (1980).

References

Anderson, Jack 1979 "Deadly decisions by profit-seekers." The Detroit Free Press (October 10).

Ashford, Nicholas A. 1976 Crisis in the Workplace: Occupational Disease and Injury. Cambridge, MA: MIT Press.

Berman, Daniel M. 1978 Death on the Job. New York: Monthly Review Press.

Braithwaite, John 1982 "Enforced self-regulation: A new strategy for corporate crime control." Michigan Law Review 80 (June): 1466-1507

Braithwaite, John and Barry Condon 1978 "On the class basis of criminal violence." Pp. 232-251 in Paul R. Wilson and John Braithwaite (eds.) Two Faces of Deviance. St. Lucia, Queensland: University of Queensland Press.

Braithwaite, John and Gilbert Geis 1982 "On theory and action for corporate crime control." Crime and Delinquency 28 (January): 292-314.

Brown, Michael H. 1979 Laying Waste: The Poisoning of America by Toxic Chemicals. New York: Pantheon Books.

Brown, Robert 1978 "The new criminology" in E. Kamenka, R. Brown, and A. Erh-Soon Tay (eds.), Law and Society. New York: St Martin's Press.

Burgess, Ernest W. 1950 "Concluding comment." American Journal of Sociology 56 (July): 34.

Chamber of Commerce of the United States 1974 A Handbook on White Collar Crime. Washington, DC: Chamber of Commerce of the United States.

Clinard, Marshall B. and Peter C. Yeager 1980 Corporate Crime. New York: The Free Press.

Coffee, John C, Jr. 1980 "Making the punishment fit the corporation: The problem of finding an optimal corporation criminal sanction." Northern Illinois University Law Review: 3-36.

Coffee, John C, Jr. 1981 "No soul to damn—No body to kick: An unscandalized inquiry into the problem of corporate punishment." Michigan Law Review 79 (January): 386-459.

Conklin, John E. 1977 Illegal But Not Criminal: Business Crime in America. Englewood Cliffs, NJ: Prentice-Hall.

Conyers, John, Jr., 1980 "Corporate and white-collar crime: A view by the chairman of the house subcommittee on crime." American Criminal Law Review 17 (Winter): 287-300.

Cullen, Francis T., Bruce G. Link, and Craig W. Polanzi 1982 "The seriousness of crime revisited: Have attitudes toward white collar crime changed?" Criminology 20 (May): 83-102.

Dowie, Mark 1979 "The corporate crime of the century." Mother Jones (November): 23-25.

Elkins, James 1976 "Corporations and the criminal law: An uneasy alliance." Kentucky Law Journal 65: 73-129.

Ermann, M. David and Richard J. Lundman 1982 Corporate Deviance. New York: Holt, Rinehart, and Winston.

Fisse, Brent 1981 "Community service as a sanction against corporations." Wisconsin Law Review (September).

Geis, Gilbert 1973 "Deterring corporate crime." Pp. 182-197 in Ralph Nader and Mark J. Green (eds.), Corporate Power in America. New York: Grossman.

Goff, Colin H. and Charles E. Reasons 1978 Corporate Crime in Canada: A Critical Analysis of Anti-Combines Legislation. Scarborough, Ontario: Prentice-Hall of Canada, Ltd.

Lens, Sidney 1979 "Dead on the job." The Progressive (November): 50-52.

Liazos, Alexander 1972 "The poverty of the sociology of deviance: Nuts, sluts, and 'preverts.'" Social Problems 20 (Summer): 103-120.

Meir, Robert F. and James F. Short, Jr. 1982 "The consequences of white-collar crime." Pp. 23–49 in Herbert Edelhertz and Thomas D. Overcast (eds.), White-Collar Crime: An Agenda for Research. Lexington, MA: Lexington Books.

Mendelsohn, Robert and Guy Orcutt 1979 "An empirical analysis of air pollution dose response curves." Journal of Environmental Economics and Management 6 (June): 85-106.

National Safety Council 1971 Accident Facts. Washington, DC: National Safety Council.

Nettler, Gwynn 1978 Explaining Crime (Second Edition), New York: McGraw-Hill.

Page, Joseph A. and Mary-Win O'Brien 1972 Bitter Wages, New York: Grossman

The President's Commission on Law Enforcement and Administration of Justice 1967 Task Force Report: Crime and Its Impact—An Assessment Washington DC: U.S. Government Printing Office.

Reasons, C. L., C. Paterson, and L. Ross 1981 Assault on the Worker. Toronto: Butterworth.

Reiman, Jeffrey 1979 The Rich Get Richer and The Poor Get Prison. New York: John Wiley & Sons.

Ross, Edward Alsworth 1907 "The criminaloid." The Atlantic Monthly 99 (January): 44-50.

Schrager, Laura Shill, and James F. Short, Jr. 1978 "Toward a sociology of organizational crime." Social Problems 25 (June): 407-419.

Schrager, Laura Shill and James F. Short, Jr. 1980 "How serous a crime" Perceptions of organizational and common crimes." Pp. 14-31 in Gilbert Geis and Ezra Stotland (eds.), White-Collar Crime: Theory and Research. Beverly Hills, CA: Sage Publications.

Scott, Rachel 1974 Muscle and Blood. New York: E. P. Dutton.

Sinden, Peter G. 1980 "Perceptions of crime to capitalist America: The question of consciousness manipulation." Sociological Focus 13 (January): 75-83.

Skoler, Daniel L. 1980 "White-collar crime and the criminal justice system: Problems and challenges." Pp. 57-75 in Herbert Edelhertz and Charles Rogovin (eds.), A National Strategy for Containing White-Collar Crime. Lexington, MA: Lexington Books.

Stone, Christopher D. 1975 Where the Law Ends: The Social Control of Corporate Behavior. New York: Harper and Row.

Sutherland, Edwin H. 1949 White Collar Crime. New York: Dryden. Re-issued by Holt, Rinehart, and Winston. New York, 1961.

Swartz, Joel 1975 "Silent killers at work." Crime and Social Justice 3 (Summer): 15-20.

Tataryn, L. 1979 Dying for a Living. Toronto: Deneau and Greenberg.

Time Magazine 1969 "Changing morality: The two Americas." Time 93 (June 6): 26.

Vold, George 1958 Theoretical Criminology. New York: Oxford University Press.

Wilson, James Q. 1975 Thinking About Crime. New York: Basic Books.

Yale Law Journal 1979 "Structural crime and institutional rehabilitation: A new approach to corporate sentencing." Yale Law Journal 89: 353-375.

DISCUSSION QUESTIONS

1. Which costs of corporate crime do you think are the most serious? Explain.

2. How might Kramer frame the costs of corporate crime today?

3. Review the recommendations made by Kramer. Do you think the justice system has completed any of these recommendations? Explain.

READING

In this reading, Michael Lynch and his colleagues describe the reporting practices of the Food and Drug Administration by analyzing how the organization reports its practices in the FDA Enforcement Report and the FDA Consumer. The authors discuss the structure and history of the FDA as well as the way the organization is perceived by outsiders. Lynch and his coauthors suggest that the FDA attempts to portray certain images in an effort to control the perceptions that outside entities have of the agency. To assess this possibility, the authors reviewed more than 8,500 articles published by the FDA in the two publications. The authors found that the image of the FDA is portrayed differently in the two reports.

SOURCE: Lynch, M. J., Ronald G. Burns, and Jefferson E. Holcomb. (2005). Food for Thought: An Investigation of Food and Drug Administration Reporting Practices, 1995–1999. *Criminal Justice Review, 30*, 293–311. Published by SAGE, Inc., on behalf of the Georgia State University Research Foundation.

Food for Thought

An Investigation of Food and Drug Administration Reporting Practices, 1995–1999

Michael J. Lynch, Ronald G. Burns, and Jefferson E. Holcomb

The majority of research performed in the fields of criminology and criminal justice focuses on laws that are primarily applied to people of lower socioeconomic status. Despite periodic calls for greater attention to the crimes of the powerful and the laws, regulations, and forms of justice that apply to these behaviors, little empirical research on these issues is found in criminological and criminal justice literature. There has been a particular lack of attention to research regarding regulatory responses to violations of law (for a review, see Friedrichs, 2004, pp. 247-259). There is even less emphasis on the behavior of specific regulatory agencies assigned the duty of policing corporate crime within the literature on regulatory agencies produced by criminologists (e.g., see Jamieson, 1994, on the Federal Trade Commission; Burns & Lynch, 2004; Szasz, 1986, on the Environmental Protection Agency [EPA]). This neglect is telling and speaks to the criminological penchant for focusing on the behavior and control of the powerless as opposed to the powerful (Reiman, 2004). This tendency remains strong in criminology despite (a) widely accepted evidence that corporate criminality is more costly and more violent than ordinary crime (e.g., Frank & Lynch, 1992; Hills, 1987; Reiman, 2004; Simon, 1995; Sutherland, 1949) and (b) criticism pointing toward the continued neglect of corporate criminality and its processing (Burns & Lynch, 2002; Jamieson, 1994; Reiman, 2004; Simon, 1995; Sutherland, 1949).

As with other regulatory agencies of social control that deal with powerful actors, there has been little analysis of the Food and Drug Administration (FDA) by criminologists (see Braithwaite, 1984; Clinard & Yeager, 1980). Furthermore, when the FDA is discussed in the corporate crime literature, it is usually scrutinized only in relation to its drug approval procedures or the issue of deregulation (Quirk, 1980) and not as an agency of social control that plays an important role in defining and controlling behaviors that could be considered crimes. However, a considerable body of literature has developed exploring how various social issues become identified as social problems. The present study contributes to the growing body of constructionist research literature by examining the FDA's reporting practices about its regulatory activities. Given the tenuous position of regulatory agencies such as the FDA, exploring how such agencies report their behavior to various audiences may provide insight into how they respond to the challenges of regulation.

The FDA

Originally recognized as the "Division of Chemistry" and the "Food, Drug, and Insecticide Administration" the FDA added regulatory functions to its scientific mission in 1906 with passage of the Federal Food and Drugs Act. The agency was originally housed under the Department of Agriculture, although it is currently located in the Department of Health and Human Services (Swann, 1998). The FDA employs about 9,000 workers who are spread throughout approximately 170 sites maintained by the FDA. The agency is relatively small and lacks resources compared to other federal regulatory agencies. Its annual budget of roughly $1.3 billion requires FDA administrators to creatively identify a means to use such relatively few resources to address an increasingly wide array of responsibilities (Hilts, 2003). According to Hilts (2003), despite a wide scope of responsibilities, limited resources, and recent calls to dismantle the agency, the FDA has ... proved itself an essential part of modern society. Its history demonstrates that regulatory agencies can not only establish effective protections but make high scientific standards the starting point for industry and the basis of modern government policy as well. (p. xvi)

Hilts (2003) highlights the extensive nature and broad scope of the FDA in noting that "[i]t is required to keep tabs on the products of about 95,000 businesses, amounting to about $1 trillion worth of goods a year, about a quarter of the American economy" (p. xvi). The FDA annually catalogs over "200,000 reports of harmful effects from prescription drugs and medical devices each year" (p. xvi) and fields an immense number of consumer questions and information requests. Thus, the FDA is a complex agency responsible for a wide array of tasks and issues. For instance, the FDA is responsible for ensuring safety and effectiveness with regard to food products, veterinary and human drugs, biological products, medical devices, cosmetics, and electronic products that emit radiation. Hilts (2003) adds that the FDA, the most scrutinized regulatory agency, has retained extremely high standards as the first agency in the world to attempt to scientifically evaluate drugs and food. In addition to regulating food and drugs, the FDA created the "scientific base for industry—defining what is safe and what works or does not" (Hilts, 2003, p. xiv).

The complexity and wide-ranging scope of the FDA result in the agency constantly facing pressure from, and trying to maintain positive relations with, various interest groups. Hawthorne (2005) asserts that even though the FDA staffs "a corps of dedicated, careful scientists," the agency "is, and always has been, buffeted by the conflicting demands of scientific accuracy and public pressure, of industry and consumers, and by the contradictions between two types of public need" (p. 27). With reference to the latter, the FDA faces often contradictory forms of consumer activism: Those citizens who feel the FDA impedes progress and should more quickly allow potentially helpful products become publicly available and those who believe the FDA too easily permits potentially harmful products to become

available (Hawthorne, 2005). In other words, some consumers wish to have access to as many treatments as possible, whereas others remain concerned about harmful products reaching the general public. The former group is often identified as representing the voice of industry, whereas the latter is frequently supported by consumer advocate groups and public health organizations (Hawthorne, 2005).

Hawthorne (2005) describes the pressures faced by the FDA from various industries such as pharmaceutical companies that frequently characterize the FDA as

the all-powerful, arbitrary, nitpicky naysayer that keeps their desperately needed medicines off the market until they run a zillion unnecessary tests to prove things they already proved. The agency is unreliable, one week saying it wants to help manufacturers get their products out to patients quickly, then the next week panicking after too many reports of dangerous side effects. It is mysterious; there is no way of knowing just what a company must do to move its product past the regulatory box-checkers. At best, the FDA is a bunch of bureaucrats who mean well but are scared to be the first to approve something new. Most of all, the agency must be obeyed. It is almost impossible to get through a 10-minute interview with a pharmaceutical executive without hearing at least one complaint or fear about the FDA. (p. x)

An example of the conflict faced by the FDA in regulating industry without seeming overbearing is found in a 2002 appearance by FDA Deputy Commissioner Lester Crawford on Capitol Hill. Crawford faced questions from politicians who wished to know why the agency referred to regulated drug companies as "clients" and "customers" and why the FDA was "bragging" about how it had helped the U.S. drug industry's global market share (Dickinson, 2002, p. 16). Crawford responded that the FDA "treads a tightwire of remaining correct but aloof in terms of its enforcement in its consideration of industry. Referring to the industry as a 'client' or 'customer' is sort of the new emphasis on stakeholder investment"

(Dickinson, 2002, p. 18). Among other things, the agency's ties and responsiveness to government pressures are affected by the pharmaceutical industry's close ties to government (the industry is the "most powerful lobbying force in Washington, DC," and is always among the most prominent donors to political campaigns [Hawthorne, 2005]) and the notable influence of those in the food industry.

That the head of the FDA was facing questions from politicians is not surprising given the relationship between the agency and government officials. Hawthorne (2005) noted that

> it would be bad enough if the only political pressures that the FDA had to withstand were from powerful drug and food companies with multi-million-dollar lobbying budgets, consumer groups that pounce every time a drug shows serious side effects, and consumer groups that want drugs for their disease approved now. But there is more. As a federal agency, run by a commissioner who must be confirmed by the Senate, who must go to Congress every year for money, and who must report to another political appointee (the secretary of Health and Human Services), the FDA also has to live in the hardcore world of Democrats and Republicans, Congress and the White House—the world of pure politics. (p. 209)

The FDA is a government agency whose budget is set by government officials. The president appoints the FDA commissioner, and agency decisions are vetted by the Department of Health and Human Resources (Hawthorne, 2005). Although it is hoped that the agency's decisions are based purely on science, industry, political, and consumer pressures likely result in FDA actions being affected by a range of variables and not just science.

Despite constantly facing pressures from many directions, the FDA, first and foremost, is a regulatory agency charged with responding to and protecting the public. The agency serves the general public primarily through regulating food and drug products, although information dissemination is also an important part of

the FDA's charge. The FDA keeps the public (and others) informed through information-based publications such as FDA Consumer, providing a wealth of information about the agency on its Web site, maintaining a staff of public affairs specialists (who have been deemed "walking encyclopedias" [Adams & Henkel, 1995, p. 22]) and other means.

Of particular significance to the present work, the FDA is charged with ensuring that information pertaining to products in these areas is accurately, honestly, and informatively presented to various groups. The FDA accomplishes its information dissemination mission through the publication of two different reporting mechanisms: FDA Enforcement Report (hereafter Report) and FDA Consumer (hereafter Consumer). These outlets, which are described more completely in the Data and Method section, contain information that reflects actions taken by the FDA. The data and descriptions found in each outlet, however, are filtered or constructed by discretionary actions on behalf of FDA officials charged with determining how a case is classified and by the reporting format itself. In other words, the data and descriptions found in these reporting mediums may reflect organizational efforts to construct a particular image of FDA practices. To examine this possibility, we compared the information reported in each FDA information outlet within the theoretical context of social constructionism.

 ## Data and Method

Generally, the FDA regulates industry behavior through one of four mechanisms: recalls, injunctions, seizures, or criminal action (which includes prosecution, indictment, information, and disposition). The definitions and responsibilities associated with these actions are provided in Table 9.8.

We collected two different sets of data concerning the FDA's regulatory behavior to examine the FDA's reporting behavior and image management. The data were drawn from Report and Consumer. Report is a weekly publication of the FDA that, in theory, includes information on all cases that come to the attention of the FDA. Report can be considered official data, containing

Table 9.8   FDA Classification and Definitions of Violations as Recorded in FDA Enforcement Report

	Definition	Responsibility
1. Recalls and field corrections	An action taken by a firm to remove a product from the market or to conduct a field correction	FDA request, FDA order, or firm initiative
2. Injunction	A civil action taken against an individual or firm, which seeks to stop continued production or distribution of a violative product	FDA
3. Seizure	Action taken to remove a product from commerce because it is in violation of law	FDA; the FDA initiates a seizure by filing a complaint with the U.S. District Court; the U.S. Marshall is then directed by the court to seize the product until the matter is resolved
4. Criminal action	A criminal action taken against a company or individual	FDA

NOTE: FDA = Food and Drug Administration.

information on charges, prosecutions, violations, convictions, and recalls. Specifically, as stated in each edition of the Report, "the FDA Enforcement Report is published weekly by the FDA, U.S. Public Health Service, Department of Health and Human Services. It contains information on actions taken in connection with agency regulatory activities." The FDA is mandated to report its actions in this way by the regulations that define FDA responsibilities. Analyzing the content found in Report involved limited subjectivity because of the direct presentation of information provided. For each edition of Report, we coded the frequency of each type of regulatory action (i.e., "recalls and field corrections," "injunctions" "seizures," and "criminal actions") reported and the seriousness class (i.e., Class I, II, or III) assigned to that action.

In addition, we extend our analysis of the FDA's behavior by examining the stories the FDA publishes about its own activities in its official magazine, Consumer. The stories concern the FDA's involvement in specific incidents that the FDA chooses to highlight in this popular magazine format. Consumer is best viewed as a general information magazine sponsored by the FDA; it does not contain information on all cases brought to the attention of the FDA. Rather, Consumer contains materials on only those cases the FDA chooses

to highlight or publicize in this specific format. The majority of Consumer's featured articles are designed to make consumers (more) aware of defective products and/or various safety tips.

After reviewing several dozen editions, it was decided that two sections or "departments" of each Consumer publication would be used for the analyses: the "Investigators' Reports" and "Summary of Court Actions." As noted in each edition of Consumer, the "Investigators' Reports" contains "selected cases illustrating regulatory and administrative actions—such as inspections, recalls, seizures, and court proceedings— by FDA's regional and district offices across the country." Summary accounts (in each edition of Consumer) describe "cases involving seizure proceedings, criminal proceedings, and injunction proceedings. Seizure proceedings are civil actions taken against goods alleged to be in violation, and criminal and injunction proceedings are against firms or individuals charged to be responsible for violations." Because of their focus on FDA enforcement actions, the information found in these departments of Consumer were selected as representative of how the FDA presents itself to consumers and thus deemed worthy of comparison to the information found in Report.

Perhaps the most subjective aspect of the study, latent content analysis was used to assess the essence of each article found in these reports. The process involved reading each article and determining its main focus as related to the four categories of FDA regulation (recalls, seizures, injunctions, and criminal actions). In general, determining the main focus of each article was quite simple. Given the fact that the articles are written for the general public, the authors are typically straightforward in presenting the details. Some articles ($n = 15$; 11.3%) found in the "Investigators' Reports," however, did not specifically relate to an enforcement action and thus were categorized as "other."

All editions of both Report and Consumer published during the years 1995 to 1999 were analyzed to assess the reported enforcement behaviors of the FDA. Two hundred sixty editions of Report were used in the present study and were accessed through the FDA Web site (www.fda.gov). Thirty-nine editions of Consumer were included in the analyses and were found in publicly available print format. The 39 Consumer editions constitute all that were published during the 1995-1999 time period. Specifically, 10 editions of Consumer were published annually during 1995 and 1996 (two editions were bimonthly). In 1997, the publication became bimonthly, with a total of seven editions published during that year. Six editions were published during both 1998 and 1999.

 Findings

Presentation of the findings is divided into three areas: (a) Consumer (including results from "Investigators' Reports" and "Summary of Court Actions" departments), (b) Report, and (c) the FDA's recall practices.

Consumer

There were 133 articles found in the 5 years of "Investigators' Reports" examined. There was an average of 3.4 articles per edition, the majority of which involved criminal actions. A sampling of titles from selected editions of Consumer suggests that the FDA used this outlet to demonstrate its punitive approach to regulating private industry. For example, headlines such as "Drug

Firm President and Other Officials Sentenced" (Consumer, March 1995) and "Illegal Use of Vet Drug Results in Fines, Probation" (Consumer, April 1996) suggest that the FDA strongly punishes industry misbehavior. The "Investigators' Reports" section had lead stories related to criminal actions in 31 of the 39 editions (79.5%) of Consumer. Analysis of the content of Report provided below lends support to the notion that the agency appears to employ Consumer as a public forum for image construction. The next most frequent article category in Consumer involved injunctions and seizures. These articles typically addressed the FDA practice of restricting certain "troubling" business behaviors (e.g., "Drug Manufacturer Enjoined," Consumer, April 1995) or the FDA's power to physically seize and destroy illegal goods (e.g., "Unapproved Drugs End Up at Hazardous Waste Site," Consumer, September-October 1997). Finally, we discovered that only a small percentage of articles in Consumer had recalls as the main focus. This finding, which is inconsistent with the results from our analyses of Report, is discussed more fully at a later point in this work.

Report

According to the FDA, "the FDA Enforcement Report ... contains information on actions taken in connection with agency regulatory activities" (FDA Web site). That stated, much of what appears in these reports concerns recalls, with few mentions of criminal actions or injunctions. In addition to information on recalls, criminal actions, and injunctions, Report also includes data on "Alerts." Specifically, alerts are

> any communication issued by a manufacturer, distributor, or other responsible party or FDA to inform health professionals or other appropriate persons or firms of a risk of substantial harm from a medical device in commercial use. Notifications are issued at the request of FDA. Safety Alerts are voluntarily issued. (FDA web site)

Most FDA activity listed in the *Report* involved "recalls and field corrections." Of the total number of

7,999 FDA "agency regulatory activities" that were recorded during the time period under study, only a small portion (1%) involve anything besides recalls and field corrections. Seizures and alerts appear infrequently in this publication, suggesting that the agency primarily uses recalls to regulate industry. Comparing the results from Report and Consumer, a discrepancy in the number of serious cases reported seems evident. Specifically, in the "Investigators' Reports" section of Consumer, more than 100 articles examining criminal cases, injunctions, and seizure were noted. In Report, fewer than 40 such cases are evident. The reason this occurs is that several articles may be written about the same case in Consumer, and in fact, specific cases may be followed over time and appear on numerous occasions. For example, an individual case may be discussed as a seizure and later as a criminal case both at the stage of charging and initial investigation and still later, after the penalty in the case has been determined. Thus, the discrepancy between the two sources is not a recording error but one that reflects the additional emphasis placed on depictions of criminal cases in Consumer.

FDA Recall Practices

Clearly, the vast majority of FDA actions (99%) involve recall and field correction activity. To further investigate the agency's use of recalls, the first step was to analyze the seriousness of all recalls found in Report. To do so, we used the FDA's own seriousness rating system (Class I, Class II, and Class III). Each edition of Report defines the seriousness of various recalls as follows:

> A Class I recall is a situation in which there is a reasonable probability that the use of or exposure to a violative product will cause serious adverse health consequences or death.

> A Class II recall is a situation in which use of or exposure to a violative product may cause temporary or medically reversible adverse health consequences or where the probability of serious adverse health consequences is remote.

A Class III recall is a situation in which use of or exposure to a violative product is not likely to cause adverse health consequences.

These definitions are reasonably clear; the seriousness of an offense is to be judged by the outcomes associated with the use of the product in question.

Of the 7,924 total FDA recalls, only 6.1% were judged to be very serious (Class I) or as conditions in which a "reasonable probability" of adverse health consequences exists. Roughly 60% (59.4%) of cases were recorded as Class II recalls or involved products that could result in temporary or medically reversible adverse health consequence. The final 34.5% of the cases were Class III recalls or represented conditions that are not likely to lead to adverse health consequences. In general, it appears that the majority of FDA recalls are "less serious" in nature, involving Class II and III recalls. These findings are addressed below.

Discussion

Our findings indicate that when Consumer was employed to determine the nature of the regulatory work performed by the FDA, it appeared that more than 81% of cases were serious in nature and involved criminal charges or outcomes, seizures, and injunctions. Furthermore, recalls appeared to be insignificant and to compose a very small fraction of the work of the FDA. In contrast, when Report was employed to assess the type of regulatory activity in which the FDA engages, a completely different picture emerges in which recalls and field corrections compose 99% of FDA activity. Why would the image of the FDA that emerges from these two data sources be so different?

From a constructionist framework, such actions appear to be a logical response given the demands and constraints placed on a large bureaucracy operating within a complex social and political environment. The FDA's precarious position between the public and the business world seemingly require that it manipulate its image in an effort to appeal to different constituencies. With respect to the public, the FDA desires to appear to be a strong advocate of public health as an agency that fulfills its mission by taking a strong stance against offenders who threaten public health. Meanwhile, the FDA cannot afford to present such an image to all audiences because doing so would generate energetic responses from the business community. Such actions might include enhanced efforts to undermine the FDA's credibility, expanded lobbying, and an expansion of the argument that the FDA stifles free market incentives and operations. In other words, given its mission and the need to present very different images to potentially conflicting audiences, it would not be unusual to discover that an agency such as the FDA might engage in image management. Indeed, this is what the data we have reviewed suggest. Although such a practice is not uncommon in popular culture (e.g., Playboy and Sports Illustrated target males; Play girl and Redbook target females), a problem occurs when we remove ourselves from popular culture and focus on a regulatory agency responsible for protecting and reporting about human safety. Targeting information to particular groups does not necessarily infer that the FDA is neglecting its responsibilities. Constructing an image through presenting select information, however, does present problems. If the FDA alters its reporting practices as part of its image-making efforts, where does this leave the consumer? More personally, where does this leave researchers?

In general, information reported in Consumer portrays the image that the FDA takes a punitive approach toward industry misbehavior. The titles of Consumer magazine sections (e.g., "Summary of Court Actions"), the omission of reports on recalls (an activity that constitutes the majority of FDA actions), and its focus on a small number of criminal actions in the "Investigators' Reports" all provide evidence of how the FDA attempts to manage its public image. The image portrayed in Consumer is in stark contrast to the information reported in Report, which indicated that the majority of the FDA efforts are classified by the agency itself as being of a less serious nature.

 Conclusion

Originally at issue was a question of how the FDA processed cases that come to its attention. We quickly discovered that the FDA maintained two publications that recorded its official behavior. We wondered why there might be two such publications and decided to examine these publications to determine if each presented a different image of FDA activity and, if so, what these differences were. Our analysis reveals that these publications present dramatically different images of what the FDA actually does. Report is constructed to be circulated to industries, government policy analysts, and watchdog groups, whereas the stories and records contained in Consumer report on a small sample of all FDA activities to a public audience. Although it is unclear the direct role that FDA administrators have in the selection and preparation of materials published in Consumer, the agency is clearly accountable to a variety of conflicting interest groups. Such pressures certainly dictate that public relations efforts and information dissemination receive careful consideration, and the present findings demonstrate that the information provided in FDA outlets is not randomly selected.

Furthermore, our findings suggest that the public is presented with an image of the FDA as an energetic and vocal advocate for public health justice. However, it appears that the dramatic activities reported in the public magazine are not representative of the typical, regulatory behavior as reported in its publication for government and industry. The situation we have uncovered is of a contextually embedded agency that is charged with serving as an advocate of public health, a watchdog over an industry, and a mediator of public-industry conflicts.[1] As noted, this may occur because the FDA needs industry's cooperation to carry out its assigned task of protecting public health. Beyond this, however, the situational context must also be understood in relation to broader political and economic constraints that define and limit the relationship between the actors involved in the construction of the FDA's image and the FDA's ability to provide an environment in which public health justice can flourish. Most certainly, the FDA's image as a fetter on the free market (industry and some government view) and as an ineffective mechanism for protecting public health (public and some government view) is something the FDA would like to alter.

We believe that research into the nature and organization of agencies charged with regulating corporations and policing corporate crime must become more central to criminology. The public howls at the ineffectiveness of the criminal justice system in detecting, catching, prosecuting, and punishing crime and criminals. The situation that currently exists relative to the social control of deviant corporations and businesses, however, makes the criminal justice system appear very efficient in comparison. Many of those most concerned with street crime, such as the middle class, are much more likely to be harmed by crimes of the powerful compared to crimes of the powerless. The image of crime as the work of the powerless, without proper recognition of the crimes of the powerful, is often reinforced in traditional criminology and criminal justice textbooks (Lynch, McGurrin, & Fenwick, 2004).

Finally, if, as we are told in a contemporary advertisement, "image is everything," then the construction of multiple images is certainly useful for an agency operating in an environment as challenging and conflicted as the FDA. Although the existence of the FDA may deter some from marketing unsafe and harmful products—and most assuredly, the FDA has kept harmful products from reaching the market—the effect of such a deterrent is limited by an image of FDA incompetence and ineffectiveness. However, the FDA needs to be concerned with more than just its image of ineffectiveness and how the data it keeps affect that image; it needs to be concerned with its actual behavior. The problems the FDA has encountered are not entirely of its own making, nor are they confined to image management. Extremely limited budgets, lingering cutbacks from the Reagan-Bush years, and continual corporate challenges make the FDA tasks of protecting the public much more difficult. Greater criminological interest in the political and economic climate surrounding the FDA, as well as the activities, tasks, and enforcement practices of the agency, may help produce enhanced understanding not only of this agency but also of the federal regulatory process more generally

and stimulate criminological interest in the laws and practices governing agencies that police corporate and other powerful offenders.

 Note

1. As further evidence of the controversial nature of FDA rulings and procedures, see the literature on the health impacts of the diet drug Fen-Phen (Abenhaim et al., 1996; Brenot et al., 1993; Cannistra, Davis, & Bauman, 1997; Connolly et al., 1997; Curfman, 1997; Graham & Green, 1997; Mark, Patalas, Chang, Evans, & Kessler, 1997).

 References

Abenhaim, L., Moride, Y., Brenot, F., Rich, S., Benichou, J., Kurz, X., et al. (1996). Appetite-suppressant drugs and the risk of primary pulmonary hypertension. The New England Journal of Medicine, 335, 609-616.

Adams, B., & Henkel, J. (1995). Public affairs specialists: FDA's walking encyclopedias. FDA Consumer, 29, 22-26.

Barak, G. (Ed.). (1994). Media, process, and the social construction of crime. New York: Garland.

Berger, P., & Luckman, T. (1966). The social construction of reality. Garden City, NJ: Doubleday.

Best, J. (1989). Images of issues: Typifying contemporary social problems. New York: Aldine de Gruyter.

Best, J. (1991). 'Road warriors' on 'hair trigger highways': Cultural resources and the media's construction of the 1987 freeway shootings problem. Sociological Inquiry, 61, 327-345.

Best, J. (Ed.). (1995). Images of issues: Typifying contemporary social problems (2nd ed.). New York: Aldine de Gruyter.

Braithwaite, J. (1984). Corporate crime in the pharmaceutical industry. London: Routledge and Kegan Paul.

Brenot, F., Herve, P., Petipretz, P., Parent, F., Duroux, P., & Simmonneau, G. (1993). Primary pulmonary hypertension and fenfluramine use. British Heart Journal, 70, 537-541.

Burkholz, H. (1994). The FDA follies: An alarming look at our food and drugs in the 1980s. New York: Basic Books.

Burns, R., & Crawford, C. (1999). School shootings, the media, and public fear: Ingredients for a moral panic. Crime, Law and Social Change, 32(2), 147-168.

Burns, R., & Lynch, M. (2002). Another fine mess . . . A preliminary examination of the use of fines by the National Highway Traffic Safety Administration. Criminal Justice Review, 27, 1 -25.

Burns, R., & Lynch, M. (2004). Environmental crime: A sourcebook. New York: LFB Scholarly Publishing.

Cannistra, L., Davis, S., & Bauman, A. (1997). Valvular heart disease associated with dexfenfluramine. The New England Journal of Medicine, 337, 636.

Chermak, S, (1994). Crime in the news media: A refined understanding of how crimes become news. In G. Barak (Ed.), Media, process, and the social construction of crime (pp. 95-129). New York: Garland.

Claybrook, J. (1984). Retreat from health and safety: Reagan's attack on America's health. New York: Pantheon.

Clinard, M., & Yeager, P. (1980). Corporate crime. New York: Free Press.

Cohen, S. (1972). Folk devils and moral panics: The creation of mods and rockers. London: MacGibbon and Kee.

Connolly, H., Crary, J., McGoon, M., Hensrud, D., Edwards, B., Edwards, W., et al. (1997). Valvular heart disease associated with Fenfluramine-Phentermine. The New England Journal of Medicine, 337, 581-588.

Cullen, F., Maakkestad, W., & Cavender, G. (1987). Corporate crime under attack: The Ford Pinto case and beyond. Cincinnati, OH: Anderson.

Curfman, G. (1997). Editorial: Diet pill redux. The New England Journal of Medicine, 337, 9.

Dickinson, J. (2002). The Bush FDA: A friend of industry? Medical Marketing & Media, 37(4), 16,18,20,

Frank, N. (1985). Crime against health and safety. Albany, NY: Harrow and Heston.

Frank, N. (1993). Maiming and killing: Occupational health crimes. The Annals of Political and Social Science, 525,107-118.

Frank, N., & Lynch, M. (1992). Corporate crime, corporate violence. Albany, NY: Harrow and Heston.

Friedrichs, D. (2004). Trusted criminals (2nd ed.). Belmont, CA: Wadsworth.

Gale, F. (1994). Political literacy: Rhetoric, ideology, and the possibility of justice. Albany: State University of New York Press.

Graham, D., & Green, L. (1997). Further cases of valvular heart disease associated with Fenfluramine-Phentermine. The New England Journal of Medicine, 337, 635.

Hall, S. (1985). Signification, representation, ideology: Althusser and the post-structuralist debates. Critical Studies in Mass Communication, 2, 91-114.

Hawthorne, F. (2005). Inside the FDA: The business and politics behind the drugs we take and the food we eat. Hoboken, NJ: John Wiley.

Hills, S. (1987). Corporate violence. Totowa, NJ; Rowman and Littlefield.

Hilts, P. J. (2003). Protecting America's health: The FDA, business and one hundred years of regulation. New York: Knopf.

Holcomb, J. E. (1997), Social constructionism and social problems research: Images of issues. Social Pathology, 3, 165-176.

Jamieson, K. (1994). The organization of corporate crime: The dynamics of antitrust violation. Thousand Oaks, CA: Sage.

Jenkins, P. (1992). Intimate enemies: Moral panics in contemporary Great Britain. New York: Aldine de Gruyter.

Katovich, M., & Reese, W. A., II. (1993). Postmodern thought in symbolic interaction. The Sociological Quarterly, 34, 391-411.

Lynch, M. (1990). The greening of criminology: A perspective for the 1990s. The Critical Criminologist, 2-3, 3-4, 11-12.

Lynch, M., McGurrin, D., & Fenwick, M. (2004). Disappearing act: The representation of corporate crime research in criminological literature. Journal of Criminal Justice, 32(5), 389-398,

Lynch, M., Nalla, M., & Miller, K. (1989). Cross-cultural perceptions of deviance: The case of Bhopal. Journal of Research in Crime and Delinquency, 26, 7-35.

Lynch, M., & Stretesky, P. (2003). The meaning of green: Contrasting criminological perspectives. Theoretical Criminology, 7, 217-238.

Mark, E., Patalas, E., Chang, H., Evans, R., &Kessler, S. (1997). Brief report: Fatal pulmonary hypertension associated with short-term use of Fenfluramine and Phentermine. The New England Journal of Medicine, 337, 602-606.

Meier, K. (1985). Regulation. New York: St. Martin's.

Musolf, G. (1992). Structure, institutions, power, and ideology. New directions within symbolic interactionism. The Sociological Quarterly, 33, 171-190.

Quirk, P. (1980). Food and Drug Administration. In J. Q. Wilson (Ed.), The politics of regulation (pp. 226-232). New York: Basic Books.

Reiman, J. (2004). The rich get richer and the poor get prison (7th ed.). Boston: Allyn and Bacon.

Reynolds, L. (1987). Interactionism: Exposition and critique. Dix Hills, NY: General Hall.

Schneider, J. (1985). Social problems theory: The constructionist view. American Sociological Review, 11, 209-219.

Schneider, J., & Kituse, J. (Eds.). (1984). Studies in the sociology of social problems. Norwood, NJ: Ablex.

Sholle, D. (1988). Critical studies: From the theory of ideology to power/knowledge. Critical Studies in Mass Communications, 5, 16-41,

Simon, D. (1995). Elite deviance. Boston: Allyn and Bacon.

Spector, M., & Kituse, J. (1977). Constructing social problems. Menlo Park, CA: Cummings.

Surette, R. (1994). Predator criminals as media icons. In G. Barak (Ed.), Media, process, and the social construction of crime (pp. 131-158). New York: Garland.

Sutherland, E. (1949). White-collar crime. New York: Holt, Rinehart & Winston.

Swann, J. (1998). Food and Drug Administration. In G. T. Kurian (Ed.), A historical guide to the U.S. government (pp. 248-254), New York: Oxford University Press.

Szasz, A. (1986). Corporations, organized crime and hazardous waste disposal: Making a criminogenic regulatory structure. Criminology, 24, 1-27.

Wright, J., Cullen, F., & Blankenship, M. (1995). The social construction of corporate violence: Media coverage of the Imperial Food Products fire. Crime & Delinquency, 41, 20-36.

DISCUSSION QUESTIONS

1. Why do you think the image presented by the FDA varies across the two types of publications?

2. Should the FDA be doing anything different in the way it presents its image?

3. How could this study be replicated with other agencies?

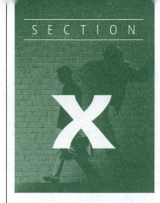

Environmental Crime

Introduction

On April 20, 2010, an explosion on BP's Deepwater Horizon rig occurred in the Gulf of Mexico. Eleven rig workers were killed and oil began to spill out of the Macondo well into the Gulf of Mexico. The oil poured into the Gulf for 3 months, with some estimates suggesting that a million gallons of oil flowed into the Gulf every day. By most measures, this seemed to be the "world's worst oil spill" (Randall, 2010). Referring to the harm from the spill, one reporter called the Gulf an "unsolved crime scene" (Sutter, 2010).

It is still too early to know all the consequences of the spill. As of August 2010, the National Science Foundation provided $7 million in research funding to study the long-term effects of the disaster. BP pledged to spend $500 million to address the consequences of the disaster, though it may be some time until we fully understand the effects of the unprecedented spill. After all, the consequences of the *Exxon Valdez* disaster are still being identified two decades after that oil spill occurred (Sutter, 2010).

Some consequences are obvious. Eleven men died. Fishermen in the Gulf were forced to give up their livelihoods. Birds, fish, and oysters died from the exposure to oil. Some have argued that the disaster will impact ecosystems across the world (Adams, 2010). Said the editor of naturalnews.com, "We may have just done to ourselves, . . . what a great meteorite did to the dinosaurs" (Adams, 2010). The cleanup effort cost an

▲ **Photo 10.1**   Crime Scene or Accident Scene. . . . Emergency responders work to put the fire out that was caused by the explosion on BP's Deepwater Horizon rig.

▲ **Photo 10.2**   A massive effort was put in place to clean up the oil spill in the Gulf.

estimated $6 million a day, and a long-term focused financial analysis estimated that cleanup costs alone will amount to $7 billion (Condon, 2010).

BP received criticism on a daily basis. The criticism targeted BP for misrepresenting various aspects of the response, underestimating the extent of the problem, paying out claims too slowly to affected workers, and having a flawed response plan (Searcey, 2010; Webb & Pilkington, 2010). The response plan received the brunt of the criticism. One rather disturbing criticism was that the response plan listed "a wildlife expert who died in 2005" (Webb & Pilkington, 2010, n.p.). Also, the response plan listed marine animals (walruses, seals, etc.) as "sensitive biological resources," despite the fact that these mammals do not "[live] anywhere near the Gulf" (Mohr, Pritchard, & Lush, 2010, n.p.). Mohr and his coauthors (2010) referred to BP's response as "on-the-fly planning." It did not help when the world saw BP chief executive Tony Hayward vacationing on his 52-foot yacht just weeks after the explosion. Hayward explained that he just "wanted to get [his] life back." He was removed as chief executive not long after making these comments.

One news headline that comes to mind read "Officials dismayed with BPs response." A colleague of mine cut this headline from the paper and hung it on my door, referring to my own initials (and maybe my own response to departmental issues). Suddenly my initials weren't as cool as they used to be.

BP established a $20 billion fund that was to be used to respond to claims that individuals brought against the company (Searcey, 2010). The confusing nature of the claims process made it difficult to process the claims. Ironically, those involved with administering the fund on behalf of BP noted that they "had to sift through fraudulent claims" against the company (Searcey, 2010).

Some have argued that the blame for the disaster cannot be placed solely on BP. One author noted that it was "American firms that owned the rig AND the safety equipment that failed" (Pendlebury, 2010). This same author noted that the United States uses more oil than any other country and that the United States leased drilling rights in coastal waters to BP to generate revenue. It is safe to suggest that several companies were involved in the disaster.

On December 15, 2010, the U.S. Department of Justice filed a lawsuit against BP and eight other companies for their role in the rig explosion. Filed under the Oil Pollution Act and the Clean Water Act, the lawsuit alleged the following:

- Failure to take necessary precautions to secure the Macondo well prior to the April 20th explosion
- Failure to use the safest drilling technology to monitor the well conditions
- Failure to maintain continuous surveillance of the well
- Failure to utilize and maintain equipment and materials that were available and necessary to ensure the safety and protection of personnel, property, and the environment ("Attorney General Holder Announces," 2010).

The lawsuit sought costs for governmental removal efforts, the damage to the environment, and the impact on the economy.

BP and these other companies are not the only businesses to harm the environment. Consider the following, quoted verbatim from the press release or media description of the environmental crime cases:

- The investigation documented 331 occasions in which both hazardous and non-hazardous waste did not arrive at the given destination. The investigation documented 273 occasions in which disposal facility signatures were forged to show receipt of the waste at a designated disposal facility. The criminal complaint alleges 18 counts of fraud and 6 counts of forgery. The complaint alleges that hazardous waste was illegally disposed of, including hazardous from a plating operation. (California Environmental Protection Agency, 2005)
- The U.S. Environmental Protection Agency is citing Gardnerville, Nevada, businessman ***** with violating federal law governing the safe handling and disposal of solid and hazardous waste. ***** operates an auto dismantling business and an un-permitted illegal waste disposal site that has resulted in open dumping and illegal disposal of hazardous waste over an 80-acre site. The facility is located in Indian Country located near Gardnerville, Nevada, in Douglas County. . . . Wastes included abandoned automobiles, trailers, tires, car batteries, construction waste, used oil, used appliances, televisions and computer monitors, waste paint, and aerosol cans. (Peck, 2010)
- A man already charged with five felonies and five gross misdemeanors for allegedly turning two Kent properties into hazardous-waste sites was in court again yesterday, a day after he was arrested on suspicion he committed environmental crimes at an illegal wrecking yard in Seattle. (Green, 2005)
- ***** chief executive officer and president of Eco Finishing Company, a Fridley, Minnesota, metal finishing business, was sentenced to 15 months in prison and paid $250,000 in restitution for violating the Clean Water Act and the U.S. Criminal Code. ***** conspired to discharge chromium, zinc and cyanide in the company's industrial wastewater at well above permitted levels. The investigation also revealed that the company on several occasions altered its production and wastewater treatment practices when regulators were conducting on-site compliance testing. The alterations were designed to deceive the government by limiting the discharge of pollutants when the company was being monitored. (U.S. Environmental Protection Agency [EPA], 2008)

In each of these cases, businesses or employees harmed the environment as part of their work efforts. To fully understand environmental crime within the context of white-collar crime, it is necessary to consider the following topics: the conceptualization of environmental crime, types of environmental crime, consequences of environmental crime, the EPA and environmental crime, and problems addressing environmental crime. A full understanding of these topics will help students understand how environmental crime fits within the broader concept of white-collar crime.

Conceptualizing Environmental Crime

Pollution is a problem that affects all of us. Several different types of pollution exist, including water pollution, air pollution, noise pollution, soil pollution, waste disposal, and so on. Concern about environmental pollution escalated in the United States in the 1970s, a decade labeled the "environment decade in reference to the increase in environmental legislation and political support for laws regulating pollution" (Barnett, 1993, p. 120). Elsewhere, Barnett (1999) refers to this time period as "a decade long surge of environmental concern" (p. 173). As a result of this public and political concern, hundreds of environmental protection laws were passed by state and federal governments. At the federal level, the best known environmental protection laws include:

- Atomic Energy Act
- Chemical Safety Information, Site Security, and Fuels Regulatory Relief Act
- Clean Air Act
- Clean Water Act
- Comprehensive Environmental Response, Compensation, and Liability Act
- Emergency Planning and Community Right to Know Act
- Endangered Species Act
- Energy Independence and Security Act
- Energy Policy Act
- Federal Food, Drug, and Cosmetic Act
- National Environmental Policy Act
- Noise Control Act
- Occupational Safety and Health Act
- Ocean Dumping Act
- Oil Pollution Act
- Pollution Prevention Act
- Safe Drinking Water Act
- Resource Conservation and Recovery Act
- Shore Protection Act
- Toxic Substance Act (EPA, 2010c)

These acts provide a foundation from which one can consider criminal and civil definitions of environmental crime. In particular, violations of these acts are environmental crimes. Some environmental crime scholars have called for broader, more philosophical conceptualizations of environmental crime. Barnett (1999) used Aldo Leopold's land ethic to conceptualize environmental crime: "A thing is right when it tends to preserve the integrity, stability, and beauty of the biotic community. It is wrong when it tends otherwise" (p. 161). Such an approach highlights the fact that many behaviors that harm the environment are often not codified in law. As a result, some authors have argued that a need exists to distinguish between those behaviors labeled as environmental crime and those that are "serious instances of ecological destruction" (Halsey, 1997, p. 121).

Two fundamental statements about environmental crime need to be made to adequately discuss this concept within the context of white-collar crime. First, pollution in and of itself is not an environmental crime. Many individuals and businesses routinely pollute the environment without actually committing environmental crimes. When we drive our automobiles to get to class, we pollute the environment. If we are running late for our white-collar crime class and speed to make up for lost time, we pollute the environment even more, but we have not committed an environmental crime. Indeed, routine activities we engage in on a daily basis produce different levels of pollution or destruction. Here is how one author described the seemingly routine nature of environmental harm:

> Not only is it profitable to be environmentally destructive (in the sense of mining, manufacturing cars, clearfelling forests), it feels good too (in the sense of purchasing a gold necklace, driving on the open road, looking at a table, chair, or house constructed from redwood, mahogany, mountain ash, or the like). (Halsey, 2004, p. 844)

Second, it is important to understand that not all environmental crimes are white-collar crimes. If an individual throws their old washer and dryer away along the side of a rural road, they have committed an environmental crime, but they have not committed a white-collar crime because the offense was not committed as part of their work efforts. As another example, if an individual buys new tires for his or her automobile, asks to keep the old tires, and then dumps the old tires in an empty field, the individual has committed an environmental crime, but not a white-collar crime.

White-collar environmental crimes, then, involve situations where individuals or businesses illegally pollute or destroy the environment as part of an occupational activity. Here are a few examples quoted from the U.S. Environmental Protection Agency (2010d) that demonstrate what is meant by white-collar environmental crimes:

- A plant manager at a metal finishing company directs employees to bypass the facility's wastewater treatment unit in order to avoid having to purchase the chemicals that are needed to run the wastewater treatment unit. In so doing, the company sends untreated wastewater directly to the sewer system in violation of the permit issued by the municipal sewer authority. The plant manager is guilty of a criminal violation of the Clean Water Act.
- In order to avoid the cost of paying for proper treatment of its hazardous waste, the owner of a manufacturer of cleaning solvents places several dozen 5-gallon buckets of highly-flammable and caustic waste into its dumpster for disposal at a local, municipal landfill that is not authorized to receive hazardous waste. The owner of the company is guilty of a criminal violation of the Resource Conservation and Recovery Act.
- The owner of an apartment complex solicits bids to remove 14,000 square feet of old ceiling tiles from the building. Three bidders inspect the building, determine that the tiles contain dangerous asbestos fibers, and bid with the understanding that, in doing the removal, they would be required to follow the work practice standards that apply to asbestos removal. The fourth bidder proposes to save the owner money by removing the tiles without following the work practice standards. The owner hires the fourth bidder on this basis and, so, the work is done without following the work practice standards. The owner is guilty of a criminal violation of the Clean Air Act (no pagination, available online).

In each of these cases, the offender committed the offense as part of an occupational routine. Note that although each of these cases could be handled as violations of criminal law, in many cases white-collar environmental offenses are handled as civil wrongs or regulatory violations.

Varieties of Environmental White-Collar Crime

Recognizing the distinction between environmental crime and environmental white-collar crime helps to identify the roles of workplace and class status in the commission of these offenses. The distinction also helps to recognize that several varieties of environmental white-collar crimes exist. These varieties include:

- Illegal emissions
- Illegal disposal of hazardous wastes
- Illegal dumping
- Harmful destruction of property/wildlife
- Environmental threats
- Environmental state crime
- International environmental crimes

It is important to note that these varieties are not mutually exclusive because there is overlap between them.

Illegal Emissions

Illegal emissions, as a variety of environmental white-collar crime, refer to situations where companies or businesses illegally allow pollutants to enter the environment. Water pollution and air pollution are examples of illegal emissions. Sometimes water and air pollution occur as a result of the production process. The smoke billowing out of factory towers contains pollutants that are the result of the production process. Companies are permitted to allow a certain amount of pollutants into the environment. They pay what is called a "sin tax" to cover the perceived costs of polluting the environment. If they exceed the "permissible" amount of pollution, then civil and criminal laws can be applied.

Other times, the pollution might be the result of unintended processes or neglectful behavior by employees. Consider the *Exxon Valdez* incident in March 1989, when the ship ran aground on Bligh Reef off the Alaskan shore. The crash spilled more than 11 million gallons of oil into Prince William Sound. It has been reported that the ship was on autopilot while the ship's captain was sleeping off a drunken stupor below deck and the third mate ran the ship on less than 5 hours sleep. Exxon did not technically intend for the disaster to occur, but because the company overworked ship employees (not giving them enough rest) and allowed someone with an alcohol problem to serve as the captain of the ship, the company eventually settled both criminal and civil charges resulting from the incident.

Under the **Federal Water Pollution Control Act,** companies are required to self-disclose to the EPA instances when they have discharged potentially harmful substances into navigable waters. After disclosing the incident, they can still be assessed civil penalties, like fines. Criminal justice students might quickly ask if this is a violation of the Fifth Amendment right against self-incrimination. In an early test of the self-disclosure rule, the owner of an oil refinery in Arkansas, who had self-disclosed that oil from his property had leaked into a nearby tributary, appealed a $500 fine on the grounds that his Fifth Amendment right had been violated (*U.S. v. Ward*). The U.S. Supreme Court upheld the fine on the grounds that the self-disclosure resulted in a civil penalty and not a criminal penalty (Beck, 1981; Melenyzer, 1999).

Illegal Disposal of Hazardous Wastes

Illegal disposal of hazardous wastes involves situations where employees or businesses dispose of wastes in ways that are potentially harmful to individuals and the environment. These offenses are actually quite easy to commit. For example, it is easy to mix hazardous substances with nonhazardous substances, but difficult to detect (Dorn, Van Daele, & Vander Beken, 2007). Often, the cases are detected through witnesses who anonymously report the misconduct. In one case, for instance, an anonymous caller contacted the Maryland Department of Environment to tell them "that asbestos debris was being dumped [by contractors] through a trash chute into an open dumpster on the street below, potentially exposing both workers and the community to toxic asbestos fibers" ("Maryland Contractor Fined," 2010). Officials recovered 7,000 bags full of asbestos debris. The contractor was fined $1.2 million. In another case, a company was fined $819,000 after its workers threw asbestos into public trash receptacles, including one located at a high school (Hay, 2010).

In the past, illegal hazardous waste disposal was attributed to private truckers or waste management contractors who were hired to get rid of waste and dumped it illegally, and there were no repercussions for the businesses that created the waste. The Resource Conservation and Recovery Act, passed in 1976, provided greater controls over the way that hazardous waste was created, monitored, and discarded. Of particular relevance is the "Cradle to Grave" provision of the act, which requires a "manifest system" to keep track of the waste from the time it is created through its disposal. The manifest system refers to the record keeping process used to monitor the waste. The creator of the waste must monitor the waste when it is created and keep track of the waste all the way through its disposal. The law states that those who create the waste are accountable for all aspects of the disposal of the waste. The business can be held liable if it doesn't complete the manifest forms, if it hires an unlicensed contractor to get rid of the waste, or if the waste is eventually dumped illegally by the contractor hired to dispose of it (Stenzel, 2011).

One of the most well-known environmental crimes involving hazardous wastes is the Love Canal tragedy. Located in Niagara Falls, New York, the Love Canal was initially designed to be a canal, but it ended up being a waste disposal site for Hooker Chemical. After Hooker filled the canal with waste, and covered the waste in ways the company thought were safe, they sold the property to the Niagara Falls school board for one dollar in the mid-1950s. The company never hid the fact that the property was on top of a waste site (Beck, 1979).

The school board developed a school and several homes were built on and around Love Canal. In the late 1970s, chemicals from the abandoned site leaked into the homes and residents began to experience a number of different health problems (Baldston, 1979). An EPA report cited "a disturbingly high rate of miscarriages" among pregnant women in the neighborhood (Beck, 1979). One EPA administrator wrote:

> I visited the canal area. Corroding waste disposal drums could be seen breaking up through the grounds of backyards. Trees and gardens were turning black and dying . . . puddles of noxious substances were pointed out to me by the residents. . . . Everywhere the air had a faint, choking smell. Children returned from play with burns on their hands and faces. (Beck, 1979)

Eventually, the federal government and the state of New York declared an emergency and provided a temporary relocation of 700 families (In Focus 10.1 includes a press release from the White House describing the declaration of emergency).

In Focus 10.1

EPA, New York State Announce
Temporary Relocation of Love Canal Residents

[EPA press release—May 21, 1980]

President Carter today declared an emergency to permit the Federal government and the State of New York to undertake the temporary relocation of approximately 700 families in the Love Canal area of Niagara Falls, New York, who have been exposed to toxic wastes deposited there by Hooker Chemical Company.

Barbara Blum, Deputy Administrator of the U.S. Environmental Protection Agency, in announcing the President's action—taken at the request of Governor Carey of New York—said that the Federal government and the State will jointly fund the relocation effort.

"This action is being taken," said Blum, "in recognition of the cumulative evidence of exposure by the Love Canal residents to toxic wastes from Hooker Chemical Company and mounting evidence of resulting health effects.

"Health effects studies performed by others so far are preliminary. Taken together, they suggest significant health risks. Ordinarily, we would not subject the public and affected families to the disruption of temporary relocation unless conclusions on adverse health have been fully documented and confirmed after independent review," she said.

"But this is not an ordinary situation. This case presents special circumstances warranting this extraordinary action. The studies completed to date are sufficiently suggestive of a threat to public health that prudence dictates the residents be relocated while further definitive studies are being completed," Blum declared.

The families eligible for temporary relocation assistance live in the area from 103rd Street on the east to both sides of 93rd Street on the west, Black Creek on the north to Frontier Avenue on the south.

The temporary relocation will last until long-range studies of the environmental exposures and resulting health effects suffered by the affected families are completed. These studies, which will be conducted by EPA, will be completed within the next few months.

Governor Carey's request to declare an emergency will make funds available on a matching basis with the State of New York to fund the temporary relocation under the Federal Disaster Relief Act.

The temporary relocation will be assisted by the Federal Emergency Management Agency and the New York Department of Transportation. Personnel from these two agencies are currently at the Love Canal site to begin assisting families.

Under existing Federal law, this temporary housing may be provided rent free for a period of up to one year. Pending the location of such temporary housing, residents may seek shelter with family members or in hotels, motels or other transient accommodations and will be reimbursed by the Federal government.

"The Hooker Chemical Company's dumping of toxic wastes at Love Canal," said Blum, "and the resulting health and environmental damages are a stark symbol of the problems created by the improper disposal of hazardous wastes by our society. The implementation of the regulatory program by EPA and the States under the Resource Conservation and Recovery Act should prevent new Love Canals. But Americans will not be free of the effects of our toxic waste heritage without the passage of Superfund legislation to give EPA the authority and funds to clean up hazardous waste sites before they damage public health."

The complaint in the Governor's suit against Hooker Chemical Company will be amended to seek reimbursement for costs expended in this effort. The Justice Department has requested that Hooker pay the costs of temporary relocation, but the company has refused.

EPA believes this action is required at Love Canal even though it may not be necessary at other hazardous waste sites. A review by EPA's Hazardous Waste Enforcement Task Force indicates that a larger number of people in Love Canal are directly exposed to a broader range of toxic chemicals at high levels than now known at other abandoned hazardous waste sites around the country. In addition, President Carter has previously declared an emergency at Love Canal, the only hazardous waste site to be identified as such. Finally, the Government's lawsuit against Hooker Chemical Company requests relocation of the affected families, the only case involving a hazardous waste site where such relief has been requested.

In 1979, the EPA and DOJ (U.S. Department of Justice) filed four suits against Hooker Chemical alleging violations of the Resource Conservation and Recovery Act, the Clean Water Act, the Safe Drinking Water Act, and the Refuse Act. The basis for the suits was that Hooker had illegally disposed of its waste, which included 21,000 tons of chemical waste. The State of New York filed a similar lawsuit against the company. By the mid-1990s, the company had settled for $20 million and its parent company agreed to pay $129 million to the federal government and $98 million to the state of New York to support cleanup efforts (Moyer, 2010).

Illegal Dumping

Illegal dumping, in this context, is different from illegal disposal of hazardous waste. Also known as "fly dumping" "wildcat dumping," and "midnight dumping," **illegal dumping** refers to situations where employees or businesses dump products they no longer need in sites that are not recognized as legal dump sites (U.S. Environmental Protection Agency, 1998). Common products that are illegally dumped include automobile tires, construction waste (like drywall, roofing materials, plumbing waste), landscaping waste, and automobile parts.

These materials present different types of risk than might be found with the illegal disposal of hazardous wastes. For example, many of the products are not biodegradable and will destroy the usefulness of the land where they are dumped. Also, the site where offenders dump these products will become an eyesore and attract future illegal dumpers. In addition, some of the products, like tires, will trap rainwater and attract mosquitoes, thus becoming a breeding ground for disease (EPA, 2010c). In one recent case the owner of a used tire shop in Ohio was sentenced to 6 years in prison after he was caught illegally dumping tires on five separate occasions (Futty, 2010).

Illegal dumping is primarily done for economic reasons. Business owners wanting to avoid the costs of waste disposal dump their goods in the unregulated open dump areas. The offenses also present significant economic costs, particularly in terms of cleanup costs. In Columbus, Ohio, for example, city crews "cleaned up 621 tons of illegally dumped tires in 2009" (Futty, 2010, n.p.). Assuming that the average city worker makes $30,000 a year, this suggests that three full-time employees were hired solely to clean up illegally dumped tires in Columbus. And this estimate accounts for only one type of illegal dumping.

Harmful Destruction of Property/Wildlife

Harmful destruction of property and wildlife by companies or workers during the course of their jobs can also be seen as environmental white-collar crimes. Before businesses can clear land for development, thus destroying habitat, they must gain approval from the local government. Failing to gain such approval would be a regulatory violation. Also, instances where workers destroy wetlands are examples of environmental crimes. Additional examples of harmful destruction of property include using unsafe chemical pesticides, using chemical fertilizers, and logging on public land (Barnett, 1999).

Harmful treatment of animals can also be seen as an environmental white-collar crime. This could include illegal trading of wildlife or illegal fishing by companies or sailors (Hayman & Brack, 2002) and overharvesting sea life (Barnett, 1999). Illegal fishing also includes unregulated and unreported fishing. These activities include "fishing in an area without authorization; failing to record or declare catches, or making false reports; using prohibited fishing gear; re-supplying or re-fueling illegal, unregulated, or unreported vessels" (National Oceanic and Atmospheric Administration, 2010). In October 2010, a new federal rule was passed stipulating that the United States would deny foreign vessels suspected of illegal fishing entry into U.S. ports.

Harmful treatment of animals, as an environmental white-collar crime, also includes instances where those whose work centers on animals do things to harm the animals. Two examples include harmful treatment of animals in zoos and crimes by big game operators. In one case of the former, a zoo owner was fined $10,000 and ordered to shut down his zoo for 30 days after the U.S. Department of Agriculture found the owner in violation of the Animal Welfare Act for failing to build appropriate fences around the animals, failing to keep the food safe from contamination, and failure to provide the animals proper housing (Conley, 2007). Just 3 years before, the same owner was fined after two Asiatic bears that escaped from the zoo had to be shot and killed (Chittum, 2003).

Crimes by big game operators include situations where they or their clients kill endangered species or hunt on protected land. In one case, a big-game operator and his sons pleaded guilty "for illegally guiding clients on Brown bear hunts on federal property" (USDOJ, Environment and Natural Resources Division, p. 28)." The owner was fined $71,000 and his sons were sentenced to 3 months of house arrest. Those getting paid to help individuals in these hunts commit a white-collar crime when they intentionally perform activities that harm animals. For the hunters (e.g., clients involved in a

▲ **Photo 10.3**   Zoo owners can be found criminally or civilly liable for mistreating or neglecting animals housed at their zoo.

big-game hunt), a crime is also committed, but it would not be characterized as a white-collar crime because the activities were not committed during work. Note that the crime is not when the hunters actually harm the animals, but it is the act of intending to harm the protected animals that is illegal (U.S. DOJ, Environment and Natural Resources Division, 2010, p. 28).

Environmental Threats

A number of environmental threats exist that have the potential to harm the environment. The federal government has identified five "significant threats" to the environment. First, *knowing endangerment* refers to situations where individuals or businesses intentionally mishandle hazardous wastes or pollutants that pose risks to their workers or community members. Second, *repeat offenders* are a threat inasmuch as the government recognizes that some businesses repeatedly violate environmental laws on the assumption that it is cheaper to pay the fine and harm the environment, rather than fix the problem. Third, the federal government closely monitors *misuse of federal facilities/public lands* to protect properties from further environmental harm. Fourth, the government has called attention to the need to be prepared for catastrophic events. Finally, *organized crime entities* like the Mafia are believed to be intricately involved in the waste disposal industry (U.S. Department of Justice, 1994).

Scholars have drawn attention to the way organized crime groups are involved in illegal waste offenses. In fact, some have used the phrase "environmental organized crime" to describe the Mob's involvement in these crimes (Carter, 1999). The organized nature of the illegal waste disposal enterprise has allowed authorities to use RICO statutes to prosecute environmental offenders.

In New York City, the Mafia had such a strong hold on the waste disposal industry that other businesses rarely tried to enter the waste disposal marketplace. In the early 1990s, Browning Ferris Industries (BFI) began its efforts to become one of the businesses responsible for collecting waste in the city. Carter (1999) quotes a *Fortune* magazine writer who described the Mob's reaction shortly after learning of BFI's intentions:

> The freshly severed head of a large German Shepherd [was] laid like a wreath on the suburban lawn of the one of the company's top local executives. A piece of string tied to the dog's mouth around a note . . . read, "Welcome to New York." (p. 19)

Fans of the former HBO hit *The Sopranos* might recall the following exchange between Tony Soprano and his daughter Meadow in an episode where the crime boss and his daughter were visiting colleges during Meadow's senior year in high school:

Meadow Soprano:	Are you in the Mafia?
Tony Soprano:	Am I in the what?
Meadow Soprano:	Whatever you want to call it. Organized crime.
Tony Soprano:	That's total crap, who told you that?
Meadow Soprano:	Dad, I've lived in the house all my life. I've seen the police come with warrants. I've seen you going out at three in the morning.

Tony Soprano:	So you never seen Doc Cusamano going out at three in the morning on a call?
Meadow Soprano:	Did the Cusamano kids ever find $50,000 in Krugerrands and a .45 automatic while they were hunting for Easter eggs?
Tony Soprano:	I'm in the waste management business. Everybody immediately assumes you're mobbed up. It's a stereotype. And it's offensive. And you're the last person I would want to perpetuate it. . . . There is no Mafia.

A braver white-collar crime text author might follow up this exchange with a joke about the Mafia and the waste management industry. This author does not want to find the head of a German Shepherd in his front yard, so he will pass on the opportunity for a joke.

Environmental State Crime

In Section V, the way that governments are involved in corporate offending was discussed. One type of crime that governments can commit can be called **environmental state crime.** In this context, environmental state crime refers to criminal or deviant behaviors by a governmental representative (or representatives) that result in individuals and/or the environment being harmed by pollutants and chemicals. Examples include situations where government officials illegally dispose of waste or use harmful chemicals in unjustified ways.

As an illustration, White (2008) describes how depleted uranium was used in the Gulf Wars. The product was used in armor and as weapons, and has been linked to various illnesses in Iraqis and Gulf War veterans. Governmental officials have denied that the use of the product was criminal, which is not surprising given that, as White notes, "one of the features of state crime is in fact denial on the part of the state that an act or omission is a crime" (p. 32). White quotes the former director of the Pentagon's Depleted Uranium Project, Dough Rokke, to highlight the criminal nature of the use of depleted uranium. Rokke remarked:

> This war was about Iraq possessing illegal weapons of mass destruction, yet we are using weapons of mass destruction ourselves. Such double standards are repellent. . . . A nation's military personnel cannot willfully contaminate another nation, cause harm to persons and the environment, and then ignore the consequences of their actions. To do so is a crime against humanity. (p. 42)

White points out that Rokke has, himself, suffered negative health effects from exposure to depleted uranium.

International Environmental Crimes

International environmental crimes include environmental offenses that cross borders of at least two different countries or occur in internationally protected areas. Instances where companies ship their waste from an industrialized country to a developing nation are an example (Dorn et al., 2007). In some cases, companies might bribe "Third World government officials to establish toxic waste dumps in their countries" (Simon, 2000, p. 632).

Other examples of international environmental crimes include illegally trading wildlife, illegally trading substances harmful to the ozone, illegal fishing, and illegal timber trading/logging (Hayman & Brack, 2002). International environmental crimes are potentially more difficult for regulatory agencies to address because of issues surrounding jurisdiction, economic competition, and language barriers. Still, it is clear that environmental crime has become an international issue that has evolved as the process of globalization has unfolded in our society. As evidence of the globalization of environmental crime, consider that more than 100 countries have passed laws stipulating that environmental assessments must be conducted before a business will receive approval to begin a construction project (McAllister, 2008). Indeed, world leaders have recognized that environmental crime has serious consequences.

Consequences of Environmental Crime

It is overly simplistic to say that the consequences of environmental crime are devastating. But, it must be stated that these crimes threaten the existence of human life (Comte, 2006). Not surprisingly, environmental crime has more victims than others crimes, but these victims are often not aware of their victimization (Hayman & Brack, 2002). O'Hear (2004) provides a useful taxonomy that outlines the following types of harm potentially arising from environmental crime: (1) immediate physical injury from exposure to harmful products that may burn or kill individuals, (2) future physical injuries, (3) emotional distress from fear of future injuries, (4) disruption in social and economic activities, (5) remediation costs, (6) property damage, and (7) ecological damage. In general, the types of consequences can be classified as *physical costs*, *economic costs*, and *community costs*.

With regard to *physical costs*, there are absolutely no studies that show that pollution is good for one's health. It is impossible to accurately determine the precise extent of physical injuries from environmental crimes, but estimates are somewhat startling:

- It is estimated that 20,000 to 60,000 individuals die from pollution causes annually in the United States (Hopey & Templeton, 2010).
- Estimates suggest that 24,000 people die prematurely each year from fine particle pollution from U.S. power plants, dying an average of 14 years prematurely (Schneider, 2004)
- Across the world, it is estimated that two million individuals die prematurely from air pollution (World Health Organization, 2008)
- Unsafe water and poor sanitation are believed to kill 1.6 million a year (World Health Organization, 2005)
- Estimates from one study that considered all forms of pollution suggest that as many as 60 million deaths can be attributed to pollution, suggesting that 40% of all deaths are pollution related (Pimentel et al., 2007)

Of course, it is not just deaths that increase with pollution; physical illnesses are also tied to the problem. One estimate suggests that 38,000 people have heart attacks each year that were caused by pollution from U.S. power plants (Schneider, 2004). Schneider also suggests that pollution causes hundreds of thousands of individuals to have respiratory problems. As well, research shows that lead exposure causes "intellectual and behavioral deficits in children and hypertension and kidney disease in adults" (Schwemberger et al., 2005, p. 518). Rather than listing ill effects from all pollutants, it can be stated that for virtually any pollutant, one can point to potentially harmful health effects.

As with other forms of white-collar crime, environmental crime has enormous *economic costs*. A study by a research team at California State University, Fullerton, found that the state of California loses $28 billion a year to the consequences of pollution (Hall & Brajer, 2008). Costs stem from a variety of sources including missed work, missed school days, visits to the doctor, and visits to the emergency room. One can also note that taxpayers pay for enforcement and cleanup costs associated with white-collar environmental crime. In addition, employees end up "paying for" the violations of corporations and businesses when—after a company is caught engaging in environmental offending—they lose their jobs, become unemployed, and must find other ways to make a living (Barnett, 1981).

Environmental crime also presents different *costs to the community*. In communities where these crimes occur, quality of life is reduced. These offenses create public eyesores and reduce property values around the areas exposed to environmental pollution. Also, consistent with other corporate crimes, environmental crimes have the potential to "erode the moral base" of the community (Kramer, 1984, p. 8). While not specifically tested, it is plausible that environmental crime is correlated with traditional crimes. Criminologists have noted that socially disorganized communities have higher crime rates than other communities. Environmental pollution has the potential to produce social disorganization, and therefore potentially contributes to conventional crimes.

Environmental crimes also harm the community by posing a number of risks to those around the "environmental crime scene." For example, illegal waste disposals create the following risks for the immediate area surrounding the site where the illegal disposal occurred:

- Fire and explosion
- Inhaling toxic gases
- Injury to children playing around the site
- Soil or water contamination
- Plant or wildlife damage (Illinois Environmental Protection Agency, 2010)

A large body of research has shown that minorities and minority communities are more at risk for experiencing the ill effects of environmental crime. The term **environmental racism** is used to describe this heightened risk of victimization for minorities. Consider, for example, that research shows that minority children are significantly more likely than non-minority children to have higher levels of lead in their blood (Schwemberger et al., 2005).

Various efforts have been promoted to address environmental racism. For example, the Southern Center on Environmentally-Driven Disparities in Birth Outcomes was created at Duke University to study the links between environmental, social, and individual factors and how those factors contribute to health disparities in birth outcomes. The Center's ongoing projects include "Mapping Disparities in Birth Outcomes," "Peri-natal Environmental Exposure," and "Healthy Pregnancy, Healthy Baby." The Center is funded by the U.S. Environmental Protection Agency (EPA) (Duke University, 2010).

The EPA has also addressed concerns about environmental racism by developing an Office of Environmental Justice in the early 1990s and giving the office the responsibility of promoting environmental justice activities in the agency. According to the EPA (2010c), environmental justice is "the fair treatment and meaningful involvement of all people regardless of race, color, national origin, or income with respect to the development, implementation, and enforcement of environmental laws, regulations, and policies." The two assumptions of the federal Environmental Justice Initiative are fair treatment and meaningful involvement. Fair treatment refers to the notion that no group should be disproportionately impacted by pollution. Meaningful involvement refers to the following assumptions:

- People have an opportunity to participate in decisions about activities that may affect their environment and/or health;
- The public's contribution can influence the regulatory agency's decision;
- Their concerns will be considered in the decision making process; and
- The decision makers seek out and facilitate the involvement of those potentially affected. (EPA, 2010c)

On December 15, 2010, the first ever White House Forum on Environmental Justice was convened, with six cabinet secretaries and several other senior agency officials participating in the discussion. Much of the discussion focused on the way that poor and minority communities experience more pollution than other communities, a fact that led to the development of the Office of Environmental Justice in the first place nearly two decades earlier. Indeed, not all environmental activists in attendance viewed the forum favorably. Suzie Canales, who helped create the Texas-based advocacy group Citizens for Environmental Justice after her sister died from what Canales believed was environmentally induced breast cancer, told the director of the EPA, "We need to stop being studied to death. . . . What I'm saying to you is that with all these powerful agencies . . . instead of giving us more documents that have no value to us, you need to roll up your sleeves." She gave the EPA a report in which she wrote of the forum, "There's no cause for celebration. . . . All the executive order has really done to date is spawn more bureaucracies that give false hope to communities with promises and words" (Mcardle & Nelson, 2010).

To be sure, the consequences of environmental crime are serious and warrant a response from formal control agencies. Local police are not trained or equipped to respond to these offenses, which are complex and potentially harmful to those responding to environmental crimes involving hazardous materials (Dorn et al., 2007). Some have noted that criminal penalties are rarely applied and that while enforcement is done by local, state, and federal regulatory agencies, the law enforcement response is not as aggressive as compared to other crimes (Shover & Routhe, 2005). At the federal level, the U.S. Environmental Protection Agency (EPA) is the largest agency, with 17,000 employees, responsible for addressing environmental crimes.

The U.S. Environmental Protection Agency

The **Environmental Protection Agency** was created in 1970 when President Richard Nixon reorganized several federal agencies to create one federal agency responsible for addressing environmental pollution. In developing his message to Congress about the EPA, President Nixon indicated that the agency's roles and functions would include the following:

- The establishment and enforcement of environmental protection standards consistent with national environmental goals
- The conduct of research on the adverse effects of pollution and on methods and equipment for controlling it, the gathering of information on pollution, and the use of this information in strengthening environmental protection programs and recommending policy changes

- Assisting others, through grants, technical assistance and other means in arresting pollution of the environment
- Assisting the Council on Environmental Quality in developing and recommending to the President new policies for the protection of the environment

Four decades later, the roles and functions have not changed a great deal, though the authority of the agency has expanded significantly. Today, the actions of the EPA can be characterized in four overlapping ways: (1) as an enforcer of criminal and civil laws, (2) as an agency trying to protect public health, (3) as an agency aiming to deter future misconduct, and (4) as a facilitator of fund generation and cost savings. As you read about these areas, consider whether you would want to work in environmental protection careers (see In Focus 10.2. Students and the EPA). Each of these areas is addressed below.

In Focus 10.2

Help Wanted: College Students and the EPA

Several opportunities are available at the EPA for college students.

Student Career Experience Program (SCEP). The Student Career Experience Program in EPA's Office of Enforcement and Compliance Assurance (OECA) and in the Office of Prevention, Pesticides and Toxic Substances offers career-related employment that will enrich your academic experience through valuable work experience. To qualify, you must be at least 16 years old and enrolled as a degree-seeking student. More specifically, you must be taking at least a half-time academic or vocational and technical course load at one of the following:

- accredited high school,
- technical or vocational school, or
- a two- or four-year accredited college or university at the undergraduate, graduate, or professional school level.

U.S. citizenship is required to be considered for a possible conversion to permanent employment.

National Network for Environmental Management Studies (NNEMS). A comprehensive fellowship program designed to provide undergraduate and graduate students with practical research opportunities and experiences. The projects are narrow in scope to allow students to complete the research by working full-time during the summer and/or part-time during the school year. Research fellowships are available in:

- Environmental Policy, Regulation, and Law;
- Environmental Management and Administration;
- Environmental Science; and
- Public Relations and Communications.

NNEMS fellows receive a stipend at a level determined by the student's level of education and the duration and location of the research project. Fellowships are offered to undergraduate and graduate students. Students must meet certain eligibility criteria. The application deadline for the NNEMS Program is in the winter of each year with all projects beginning the following summer. Complete application information and materials can be obtained:

- in the Career Service Center (or equivalent) of colleges and universities;
- on the NNEMS Web site; or
- by writing to Ginger Potter, NNEMS Program, US EPA (1704A), 1200 Pennsylvania Avenue, NW, Washington, D.C. 20460.

Student Services Contracting Authority. EPA's Office of Research and Development offers a unique and exciting career opportunity for students seeking scientific or administrative services experience in support of our mission. This opportunity is open to individuals at least 18 years old who are currently enrolled in a degree program at a recognized educational institution or are recent graduates (within one year of graduation for BS and MS degrees and two years of graduation for post docs). By means of flexible Personal Services Contracts, students are hired as Student Services Contractors to work with our various laboratories, research centers and offices located across the country. Student contractors partake in an intensive hands-on employment experience over a 12-month period (with an option for an additional 12 months) working side-by-side with EPA mentors and/or scientists, who will provide day-to-day direction and oversight.

Greater Research Opportunities (GRO) Undergraduate Fellowships. The GRO fellowship program helps build capacity in universities with limited funding for research by awarding undergraduate fellowships to students in environmental fields. The purpose of the fellowship program is to encourage promising students to obtain advanced degrees and pursue careers in environmental fields.

Eligible students will receive support for their junior and senior years of undergraduate study and for an internship at an EPA facility during the summer between their junior and senior years. For more information contact Georgette Boddie, USEPA Office of Research and Development, National Center for Environmental Research or visit epa.gov/ncer/fellow.

Student Career Experience Program (SCEP). The Student Career Experience Program in EPA's Office of Enforcement and Compliance Assurance (OECA) offers career-related employment that will enrich your academic experience through valuable work experience. To qualify, you must be at least 16 years old and enrolled as a degree-seeking student. More specifically, you must be taking at least a half-time academic or vocational and technical course load at one of the following:

- accredited high school,
- technical or vocational school, or
- a two- or four-year accredited college or university at the undergraduate, graduate, or professional school level.

EPA as an Enforcer of Criminal and Civil Laws

The EPA works with other federal and state agencies to enforce environmental crime laws. The EPA's Office of Criminal Enforcement responds to: (1) Clean Water Act and Clean Air Act violations, (2) Resource Conservation and Recovery Act (RCRA) violations, (3) illegal disposal of waste, (4) exporting hazardous waste, (5) illegal discharge of pollutants, (6) illegal disposal of asbestos, (7) illegal importation of chemicals, (8) tampering with drinking water supplies, (9) mail fraud, (10) wire fraud, and (11) money laundering (EPA, 2010e).

Figure 10.1 shows the number of criminal cases opened by the EPA between 1999 and 2010. As shown in the table, the agency opened 472 criminal investigations in 1999 and dropped to 305 investigations in 2006, but increased to opening 346 criminal investigations in 2010. These changes can be attributed to changing priorities, changes in workload, and shifts in administrative structures.

The EPA takes an active stance toward detecting environmental criminals. In 2008, they borrowed from the traditional fugitive posters that other federal agencies used and began to publish fugitive posters of "wanted" environmental offenders. Figure 10.2 shows the wanted poster of environmental crime suspect Raul Chavez-Beltran, whose company was accused of illegally transporting soil that was contaminated with mercury. You can check out the other wanted environmental crime fugitives online at http://www.epa.gov/compliance/criminal/fugitives/index.html.

It is important to note that the EPA works with other agencies in its efforts to enforce criminal and civil laws. The cases will be adjudicated by the Department of Justice. The process for criminally prosecuting these types of crimes will be discussed later in the text.

Figure 10.1 Number of EPA Cases in Which Criminal Charges Were Initiated, 1999–2009

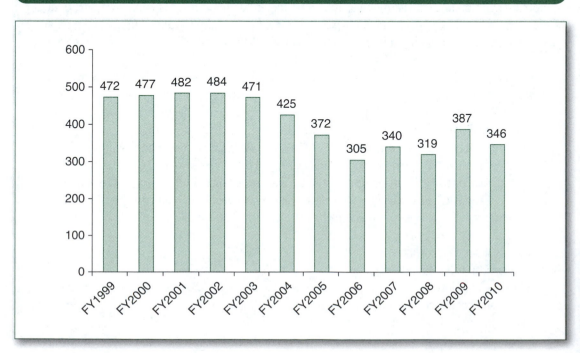

Figure 10.2 Environmental Protection Agency Wanted Poster

WANTED

by the
U.S. Environmental Protection Agency
CRIMINAL INVESTIGATION DIVISION

Name:	Chavez-Beltran, Raul
Alias:	
Sex:	Male
Race:	White
Date of Birth:	07/20/1961
Place of Birth:	Saltillo, Coahuila, Mexico
Height:	5'08"
Weight:	180 lbs
Eyes:	Brown
Hair:	Black
Scars/Tattoos:	
FBI #:	
NIC #:	W724108332

Last Known Address: Mexico

Case Summary:
- Chavez-Beltran was charged in the Western District of Texas - El Paso Division.
- Chavez-Beltran's alleged violations include:
  - Resource Conservation and Recovery Act (RCRA)
  - Conspiracy
  - Mail Fraud
- Chavez-Beltran's company is called En-Con Environmental Services, Inc. illegally transported mercury contaminated soil.
- Chavez-Beltran has been a fugitive living and working in Mexico.

Anyone with information regarding this fugitive should contact the U.S. Environmental Protection Agency, Criminal Investigation Division – Dallas Texas Office at: 1-214-665-6600 or complete the form located at: http://www.epa.gov/compliance/criminal/fugitives/report-location-form.html

U.S. EPA/CID Wanted Poster November 1, 2008   **www.epa.gov/fugitives**

EPA as a Protector of Public Health

The adverse health effects of pollution were discussed above. Activities of the EPA can be seen as protecting public health in three ways. First, a significant proportion of the agency's efforts are directed toward educating members of the public about environmental issues. The agency's website (http://www.epa.gov) includes a wealth of information about the environment, causes of pollution, the consequences of pollution, and effective remedies. Various types of search tools are available, allowing website visitors to gather information about an assortment of environmental topics. As well, one search tool allows visitors to determine how much air pollution exists in their neighborhood. Many of you have likely heard of sex offender registries, and may have even searched them. A similar tool, called AirData, exists for air pollution. As noted on the EPA's website, the tool provides information about air pollution from two EPA databases: (1) Air Quality System database, which provides air monitoring data primarily in cities and towns, and (2) National Emission Inventory database, which provides estimates of annual emissions of hazardous air pollutants. It is available online at http://www.epa.gov/air/data/.

A second way that the agency protects public health is through research programs that investigate how various chemicals and pollutants harm individuals and the environment. The EPA's Office of Research and Development (ORD) conducts and oversees various scientific studies on different aspects of pollution. ORD oversees several research centers, laboratories, and research programs, including the National Center for Environmental Research, the National Center for Computational Toxicology, the National Center for Environmental Assessment, the National Health and Environmental Effects Research Laboratory, and the National Homeland Security Research Center. Research by ORD is focused on assessing environmental risks, characterizing harm from the pollutants, and developing management practices to deal with risk (EPA, 2010e).

Environmental risk assessment research encompasses three domains. Hazard identification refers to efforts to identify the negative health consequences of various pollutants. Exposure assessment refers to efforts to identify specific locations where the pollutants exist, how much of the pollutants exist, and how long they have existed. Dose-response assessment refers to efforts to determine how much of specific pollutants produce specific effects (EPA, 2010e). Using this risk assessment process as a foundation, researchers can then assess how to characterize environmental risks and how best to manage them.

A third way that EPA protects public health is through its enforcement efforts. When cases are resolved, agency representatives include a discussion on the way various chemicals/pollutants involved in that particular settlement/case harmed individuals and the environment. For example, in December 2010, North America's largest lead producer, Doe Run Resources Corporation of St. Louis, Missouri, settled charges that it violated several federal laws including the Clean Air Act, the Clean Water Act, the Resource Conservation and Recovery Act, the Emergency Planning and Community Right-to-know Act, and the Comprehensive Environmental Response, Compensation, and Liability Act. The settlement required Doe Run Resources to implement measures to reduce the amount of the following pollutants in the environment: lead, sulfur dioxide, nitrogen oxides, volatile organic compounds, carbon monoxide, carbon dioxide, particulate matter, arsenic, cadmium, copper, and zinc. Table 10.1 shows the adverse

Table 10.1   Types of Harm From Pollutants in the Doe Run Resources Corporation Case

Pollutant	Harm
Lead	At high levels can cause convulsions, coma, and even death. Lower levels of lead can cause adverse health effects on the central nervous system, kidney, and blood cells. Fetuses, infants, and children are more vulnerable to lead exposure than adults since lead is more easily absorbed into growing bodies, causing delays in physical and mental development, lower IQ levels, shortened attention spans, and increased behavioral problems.
Sulfur dioxide	High concentrations affect breathing and may aggravate existing respiratory and cardiovascular disease. Sensitive populations include asthmatics, individuals with bronchitis or emphysema, children, and the elderly. Sulfur dioxide is also a primary contributor to acid rain.

Pollutant	Harm
Nitrogen oxides	Can cause ground-level ozone, acid rain, particulate matter, global warming, water quality deterioration, and visual impairment. Nitrogen oxides play a major role, with volatile organic chemicals, in the atmospheric reactions that produce ozone. Children, people with lung diseases such as asthma, and people who work or exercise outside are susceptible to adverse effects such as damage to lung tissue and reduction in lung function
Volatile organic compounds	Play a major role in the atmospheric reactions that produce ozone, which is the primary constituent of smog. People with lung disease, children, older adults, and people who are active can be affected when ozone levels are unhealthy. Ground-level ozone exposure is linked to a variety of short-term health problems, including lung irritation and difficulty breathing, as well as long-term problems, such as permanent lung damage from repeated exposure, aggravated asthma, reduced lung capacity, and increased susceptibility to respiratory illnesses such as pneumonia and bronchitis.
Carbon monoxide	Colorless, odorless gas that is formed when carbon in fuel is not burned completely. It is a component of motor vehicle exhaust, which contributes about 56 percent of all Carbon Monoxide emissions nationwide. Carbon monoxide can cause harmful health effects by reducing oxygen delivery to the body's organs (like the heart and brain) and tissues.
Particulate matter	Short term exposure to PM can aggravate lung disease, cause asthma attacks and acute bronchitis, may increase susceptibility to respiratory infections and has been linked to heart attacks.
Arsenic	A carcinogen, and chronic exposure can result in fatigue, gastrointestinal distress, anemia, neuropathy, and skin lesions that can develop into skin cancer in mammals.
Cadmium	A probable carcinogen, and can cause pulmonary irritation and kidney disease.
Copper	Drinking water containing large concentrations of copper can cause gastrointestinal distress and liver or kidney damage. High concentrations of copper can become toxic to aquatic life.
Zinc	Can cause stomach cramps, nausea, vomiting, and anemia.

effects of these pollutants. The amount of pollution reduced in this case was significant. In fact, estimates suggest that the settlement actions will reduce the amount of lead pollution by the company by 822 tons annually (EPA, 2010, Doe Run Resources Corporation Settlement).

In its annual reports, the EPA estimates how their actions have impacted the health of citizens. In fiscal year (FY) 2010, it was estimated that the agency's largest resolved Clean Air Act cases reduced emissions of harmful pollutants to the degree that the following reductions occurred:

- Between 680 and 1,700 fewer premature deaths
- 1,100 fewer emergency room visits or hospital admissions
- 450 avoided cases of chronic bronchitis
- 1,100 avoided nonfatal heart attacks
- 12,000 avoided cases of aggravated asthma
- 650 avoided cases of acute bronchitis
- 22,000 avoided cases of upper and lower respiratory symptoms
- 87,000 avoided days when people would miss work or school
- 520,000 avoided days when people must restrict their activities

EPA as a Deterrent

Settlements are designed not just to punish environmental offenders, but to ensure that the offenders develop measures to stop future offending. Consider the case of Beazer Homes, USA, Inc., one of the top 10 builders in the United States. On December 2, 2010, the company settled a civil suit with the EPA and DOJ after the company was charged with violating the Clean Water Act in 21 states. The charges centered on the company's discharging of pollutants into storm water without a permit and failure to use best management practices to deal with pollutants at 362 separate construction sites across 21 states (EPA, 2010a).

The company agreed to pay a $975,000 fine as a result of their plea. But, perhaps more importantly, they also agreed to change their practices to reduce future offending. In particular, the lawsuit settlement stipulated that Beazer Homes would develop a compliance program in line with federal laws. Beazer's compliance program was required to include:

- Designation of a company storm water compliance manager who will oversee the compliance program nationwide
- Designation of trained and qualified site-level and division-level storm water compliance managers for each site who will be responsible for compliance at that site
- Specific requirements for site-specific storm water Pollution Prevention Plans
- A requirement to conduct and document a preconstruction inspection and review at every site prior to commencing construction activity
- Requirements for routine site inspections including the use of standardized forms approved by EPA that require Beazer to document completion of all responsive actions taken to achieve or maintain compliance at a site
- A requirement that the division-level storm water compliance manager conduct an oversight compliance inspection and review at every site within his or her division once every calendar quarter
- Implementation of a storm water training program for Beazer employees that includes annual refresher training for storm water compliance managers
- Implementation of a storm water orientation program for contractors
- A requirement to submit national compliance summary reports to EPA; the national compliance summary reports are based on each division's summary of its quarterly oversight inspections and reviews

In theory, the compliance program would reduce the likelihood of the home builder engaging in future offending (EPA, 2010a).

EPA as a Fund Generator and Cost Savings Entity

The EPA can be seen as a resource generator and a cost savings entity. The agency generates resources through the fines that are imposed in cases they investigated. Table 10.2 shows amount of fines in EPA cases between 1974 and 2009. Since 1996, the EPA cases have recovered more than $150 million every year, and the amount was even more than $250 million a few years. In 2009, the EPA cases recovered just over $186 million in fines.

The EPA is also instrumental in collecting fines to help in cleanup costs of environmental pollution sites in the United States. The **Comprehensive Environmental Response Compensation and Liability Act,** also known as the Superfund Act, was passed in 1980 "to clean up past environmental sins" (Barnett, 1993, p. 120). This law placed the economic onus of fixing environmental harm on corporations and provided a legislative remedy that assisted in determining how funds should be collected and distributed. Funds come from taxes

Table 10.2	EPA, FY 1974–FY 2009 Penalties Assessed			
Fiscal Year	**Civil Judicial**	**Administrative**	**Criminal**	**Total**
74	$5,000	NA	NA	$5,000
75	$75,250	NA	NA	$75,250
76	$314,500	NA	NA	$314,500
77	$4,423,960	NA	NA	$4,423,960
78	$1,313,873	$25,000	NA	$1,338,873
79	$4,028,469	$56,800	NA	$4,085,269
80	$10,570,040	$159,110	NA	$10,729,150
81	$5,634,325	$742,910	NA	$6,377,235
82	$3,445,950	$949,430	NA	$4,395,380
83	$5,461,583	$2,419,898	$369,500	$8,250,981
84	$3,497,579	$3,385,344	$198,000	$7,080,923
85	$13,071,530	$9,707,480	$1,526,000	$24,305,010
86	$13,178,414	$7,449,993	$1,936,150	$22,564,557
87	$17,507,499	$6,818,374	$2,475,051	$26,800,924
88	$25,001,221	$11,908,300	$8,660,275	$45,569,796
89	$21,473,087	$13,778,859	$11,601,241	$46,853,187
90	$38,542,015	$22,747,652	$5,513,318	$66,802,985
91	$41,235,721	$31,868,407	$14,120,387	$87,224,515
92	$50,705,071	$28,028,260	$62,895,400	$141,628,731
93	$85,913,518	$29,219,896	$29,700,000	$144,833,414
94	$65,635,930	$48,020,941	$36,812,000	$150,468,871
95	$34,925,472	$35,933,856	$23,221,100	$94,080,428
96	$66,254,451	$29,996,478	$76,660,900	$172,911,829
97	$45,966,607	$49,178,494	$169,282,896	$264,427,997
98	$63,531,731	$28,041,562	$92,800,711	$184,374,004
99	$141,211,699	$25,509,879	$61,552,874	$228,274,452
00	$54,851,765	$29,258,502	$121,974,488	$206,084,755
01	$101,683,157	$23,782,264	$94,726,283	$220,191,704
02	$63,816,074	$25,859,501	$62,252,318	$151,927,893
03	$72,259,713	$24,374,718	$71,000,000	$167,634,431

(Continued)

Table 10.2 (Continued)

Fiscal Year	Civil Judicial	Administrative	Criminal	Total
04	$121,213,230	$27,637,174	$47,000,000	$195,850,404
05	$127,205,897	$26,731,150	$100,000,000	$253,937,047
06	$81,807,757	$42,007,029	$43,000,000	$166,814,786
07	$39,771,169	$30,696,323	$63,000,000	$133,467,492
08	$88,356,149	$38,197,194	$63,454,493	$190,007,837
09	$58,496,536	$31,608,710	$96,000,000	$186,105,246

and enforcement-initiated penalties on corporations and companies (Barnett, 1993). In 2010, the EPA received commitments of $1.4 billion to support the investigation and cleanup of environmental crime sites. Sites selected to use Superfund dollars are referred to as Superfund sites.

The EPA also helps to save future costs through its compliance efforts. By ensuring that companies are in compliance with environmental laws, in theory the agency is reducing future costs of pollution. Though it is difficult to gauge the degree to which these savings occur, it nonetheless seems safe to suggest that fewer environmental crimes in the future means reduced costs of environmental crimes (controlling for business growth and inflation).

It is important to reiterate that state and local environmental protection agencies also respond to environmental crimes, particularly those that are more manageable given the resources of those agencies. These local and state agencies can be seen as fulfilling functions similar to those of the federal agency. More will be written about how these agencies identify and respond to these crimes in a later section.

Criticisms of EPA

In discussing the functions of the EPA, it also important to draw attention to the criticisms that individuals and groups have made about the agency. In particular, the EPA has been criticized for the following:

- An ineffective response to the September 11, 2001, terror attacks
- Overregulating rural areas
- Overstepping its boundaries regarding state issues
- Politicizing the science process

In terms of an ineffective response to September 11, the EPA was criticized for not providing enough information about the harmful effects of the air around New York City's "Ground Zero" after the September 11 terror attacks. The agency was also criticized for not providing enough assistance in cleanup efforts. Rep. Jerrold Nadler (D-NY) commented that "New York was at the center of one of the most calamitous events in American history and the EPA has essentially walked away" (Lyman, 2003b). The EPA's Office of Inspector General conducted its own investigation into the EPA's response to September 11. The report claimed that "the White House reviewed and even changed EPA statements about public health risks to make them sound less alarming" and that the EPA understated the potential health effects of the attack (Lyman, 2003a).

The EPA has more recently been accused of over-regulating in rural areas and making it difficult for farmers to make a living by producing goods they have been producing for centuries. With changes in rules, including one proposed rule that would have supposedly allowed the EPA to regulate dust, farmers and their advocates were in an uproar about the EPA's actions. Tamara Thies, the National Cattlemen's Beef Association chief environmental council, accused the EPA of "waging an unprecedented war to end modern production of animal agriculture" (K. Anderson, 2010). In September 2010, Senate Agriculture Committee Chairman Blanche Lincoln (D-Ark) held a committee hearing to "examine the impact of the U.S. Environmental Protection Agency regulation on agriculture" (Clayton, 2010). At the hearing, Lincoln was critical of the EPA, stating, "Farmers

▲ **Photo 10.4** The EPA was heavily criticized for what was perceived to be a lax response to 9/11 and the environmental dangers that arose when the World Trade Center collapsed.

need certainty and stability, not additional burdensome and costly regulation" [and said that many of EPA's initiatives reflected] "dubious rationales and . . . they will be of questionable benefit" (Kopperud, 2010).

Critics have also claimed that the EPA oversteps its boundaries into states' issues all too often. Texas Governor Rick Perry has been especially critical of the EPA. In a statement released on May 26, 2010, Perry made the following comments:

> An increasingly activist EPA is ignoring the 22 percent reduction in ozone and 46 percent decrease in NOX emissions that Texas has achieved since 2000. On behalf of those Texans whose jobs are threatened by this latest overreach, and in defense of not only our clean air program but also our rights under the 10th Amendment, I am calling upon President Obama to rein in the EPA and instruct them to study our successful approach for recommended use elsewhere. (Office of the Governor Rick Perry, 2010)

In Fall 2010, federal regulations changed in terms of how greenhouse gas permits should be issued to businesses, a task that had been done by state agencies previously. A spokesman from Perry's office told reporters, "The existing permits in Texas have helped our state achieve dramatic improvements in air quality and we believe they will ultimately be upheld in the courts. In their latest crusade, the EPA has created massive job-crushing uncertainty for Texas companies" (Plushnick-Masti, 2010). In December 2010, Perry vowed to "defend Texas' freedom to continue our successful environmental strategies free from federal overreach" (Powell, 2010). The battle reached the point where six Texas legislators developed a proposal to establish autonomy from the federal government.

The EPA has also faced criticisms of politicizing the science process. A 2008 survey of 1,586 EPA scientists administered by the by Iowa State University's Center for Survey Statistics and Methodology on behalf of the Union of Concerned Scientists found that 889 of the scientists (60%) "reported personally experiencing what they viewed as political interference in their work over the last five years." ("Meddling at EPA?" 2008). Additional findings from the survey showed that that about one fourth of the scientists witnessed EPA officials misrepresenting findings, 284 witnessed situations where officials selectively used data, and 224 scientists said they had been told to engage in such activities. One EPA scientist made the following comments in the study: "Do not trust the Environmental Protection Agency to protect your environment.

Ask questions. Be aware of political and economic motives. Become politically active. Elect officials with motives to protect the environment and hold them accountable" (Union of Concerned Scientists, 2008, p. 6). Francesca Grifo, Senior Scientist with the Union of Concerned Scientists, presented a summary of the findings in a hearing titled *Oversight Health on Science and Environmental Regulatory Decisions* before the U.S. Senate Committee on Environment and Public Works Subcommittee on Public Sector Solutions to Global Warming, Oversight, and Children's Health Protection. In her testimony, Grifo said,

> Science is not the only element of effective policy making. However, because science enjoys widespread respect, appointed officials will always be tempted to manipulate or suppress scientific findings to support predetermined policies. Such manipulation is not only dishonest; it undermines the EPA's credibility and affects the health and safety of Americans.

Problems Addressing Environmental Crimes

▲ **Photo 10.5** Political leaders are expected to protect the environment and are held accountable in the media when they appear to respond too lightly to environmental disasters. Former President Bush took a lot of flack in the media for this picture, taken of him flying over New Orleans in the aftermath of Hurricane Katrina. President Obama received similar criticism from members of the media for his response to the BP oil spill.

Like other white-collar crimes, environmental white-collar offenses are complex, with a number of barriers making it difficult for control agencies to respond to the problem. In general, the three barriers are (1) media portrayals of environmental crime, (2) evidentiary issues, and (3) an empirical void.

Media Portrayals of Environmental Crime

With regard to the *media portrayals of environmental crime,* it is safe to suggest that the media provide little information about environmental crimes, and the information provided may give the public and policy makers a distorted image of environmental crime. One author team examined how often chemical spills were reported in the *Tampa Tribune*—the largest newspaper in Hillsborough County, Florida—between 1987 and 1997 (Lynch, Stretesky, & Hammond, 2000). The study found that 878 chemical spills were reported to the EPA in the county over the decade. Of those 878, 9 were reported in the newspaper. The authors note that newspapers fail to focus on environmental crimes because they do "not fit the public's image of crime" (p. 123). Another study, this one of 162 EPA cases between 2001 and 2002, also found that the cases received little scrutiny from the press. The cases that did receive press attention were deemed as more serious, which was determined by the penalty given to the offender (Jarrell, 2007).

Another problem related to the media and environmental crime is that environmental disasters tend to be politicized by commentators in the media. After the BP disaster, President Barak Obama was criticized for not doing enough to respond to the environmental situation in the Gulf. Fox News showed a daily description of Obama's

White House schedule and compared the president's schedule with the daily activities in the Gulf in the aftermath of the oil spill ("Disaster in the Gulf," 2010). In a similar way, President George W. Bush was vilified by commentators for what was perceived to be a lackadaisical response to Hurricane Katrina. One photo that created controversy showed President Bush looking out of the window of Air Force One as it flew over New Orleans. Five years later, in his memoir, the former president said he regretted having that photo taken.

Evidentiary Issues and Environmental Crime

Evidentiary issues also make it difficult to address environmental crimes. Environmental crime pioneer Gerhard Mueller (1996) identified 10 such problems that hindered the criminal justice response to environmental crime (see Table 10.3). These problems include

- Identifying the harm from environmental crimes
- Determining the amount of "permissible" pollution
- Identifying liability
- Issues around vicarious liability (e.g., holding an employer responsible for an employee's actions)
- Determining ways to hold corporations liable
- Establishing proof
- Lack of enforcement
- Power abuses
- Changing priorities
- Decriminalization/determining the appropriate penalty

Of course, the criminal justice system cannot respond to environmental crime by itself. Some have argued that better controls in the form of self-regulation, improved marketing of safe products, and improved communication about environmental risk will help to address environmental crime (Grabosky & Gant, 2000).

Empirical Issues and Environmental Crime

Empirical issues have also made it difficult to address environmental crime. On a general level, one can point to a dearth of research on the topic, which is surprising given the wealth of compliance and violations data available from the EPA that could be used to study various types of white-collar crime (Burns & Lynch, 2004). Indeed, the data available are virtual gold mines for future researchers. Perhaps those of you doing theses or dissertations in the near future could "mine" some of the EPA data to help generate empirical understanding about environmental crime.

On another level, the existing environmental crime research has given limited attention to "the place of the upper class in environmental research" (Simon, 2000, p. 633). What this means is that the research has failed to adequately address environmental crime *as a white-collar crime*. In doing so, opportunities for contextualizing, characterizing, and explaining "environmental white-collar crime" have been missed.

Simon (2000) also draws attention to the lack of research on global aspects of environmental offending. In a similar way, one can point to a lack of research on the way that environmental crime is influenced by various societal systems. Certainly, the environmental system can be seen as a system that interacts with other societal systems on various levels. As noted earlier in this text, the interrelated nature of systems is central to the systems perspective. Put another way, changes in one system will lead to changes in other

Table 10.3   Problems Responding to Environmental Crime

Problem	Why It's a Problem	Can This Problem Be Addressed?
Problem of qualification	Harm is not always immediately visible, causing some criminal justice officials and policy makers to misunderstand the problem.	Through education and awareness, improved response systems have evolved.
Problem of quantification	It is difficult to determine how "much" pollution is permissible, and how much harm is appropriate, with decisions somewhat arbitrary.	Laws have placed a "sin tax" on companies exceeding permissible pollution, but this may not help.
Problem of strict liability	Laws too narrowly defined on intent make it difficult to prove intent.	Laws became more flexible in the U.S., focusing on mens rea, but not in other countries.
Problem of vicarious liability	Can be counterproductive to deterrence if offenders are held accountable for things they did not intend.	Responsible corporate officers can be held accountable for environmental offending.
Corporate criminal liability	Identifying specific corporate officers with the decision making power that was abused is difficult, with "blame passed downwards."	Through complex investigations and plea bargains, officers can be identified.
Problem of proof	Hard to prove damage, effects, guilt, mens rea, and connection between the crime and the consequences.	With time and resources, cases can be proven, but it is complex. Also, corporations can't plead the fifth (must provide information)
Problem of abuse of power	Powerful businesses might control policy makers and regulators.	Must be addressed on a case by case basis.
Problem of inadequate enforcement	In the 1970s, only 130 cases were referred by EPA to DOJ for criminal prosecution.	The EPA has been opening more criminal investigations this decade.
Problem of changing priorities	Industrialization is seen as progress and consequences are virtually ignored.	Advocates must continue efforts to generate awareness about environmental issues.
Problem of decriminalization	Cases were routinely kept out of the justice system in the past.	The criminal justice system has increased its efforts responding to environmental crime cases.
Problem of penalization	Mixed evidence on the deterrent potential of punitive policies.	Need more research to determine appropriate sentences.

systems. Some have argued that as our industrial system developed the environmental system "has been cast in the role of a commodity for use in the production and consumption" (Barnett, 1999, p. 167). Then, as our technological system grew, new forms of chemical wastes were created and new areas of concern for the environmental system arose. The task at hand is to recognize how our changing societal systems have changed the nature of environmental white-collar crimes occurring in communities across the world.

⊠ Summary

- On April 20th, 2010, an explosion on BP's Deepwater Horizon rig occurred in the Gulf of Mexico. Eleven rig workers were killed and oil began to spill out of the Macondo well into the Gulf of Mexico.
- On December 15, 2010, the U.S. Department of Justice filed a lawsuit against BP and eight other companies for their role in the rig explosion.
- Concern about environmental pollution escalated in the U.S. in the 1970s, a decade labeled the "environment decade in reference to the increase in environmental legislation and political support for laws regulating pollution" (Barnett, 1993, p. 220).
- It is important to understand that not all environmental crimes are white-collar crimes.
- White-collar environmental crimes involve situations where individuals or businesses illegally pollute or destroy the environment in the course of occupational activity.
- The varieties of environmental white-collar crime include illegal emissions, illegal disposal of hazardous wastes, illegal dumping, harmful destruction of property/wildlife, environmental threats, environmental state crime, and international environmental crimes.
- Illegal emissions, as a variety of environmental white-collar crime, refers to situations where companies or businesses illegally allow pollutants to enter the environment.
- Illegal disposal of hazardous wastes involves situations where employees or businesses dispose of harmful wastes in ways that are potentially harmful to individuals and the environment.
- One of the most well known environmental crimes involving hazardous wastes is the Love Canal tragedy.
- Also known as "fly dumping," "wildcat dumping," and "midnight dumping," illegal dumping refers to situations where employees or businesses dump products they no longer need in sites that are not recognized as legal dump sites (EPA, 1998).
- Harmful destruction of property and wildlife by companies or workers during the course of their jobs can also be seen as environmental white-collar crimes.
- The federal government has identified five "significant threats" to the environment: knowing endangerment, repeat offenders, misuse of federal facilities, catastrophic events, and organized crime.
- Environmental state crime refers to criminal or deviant behaviors by a governmental representative (or representatives) involving the intentional use of pollutants and chemicals to harm individuals and the environment.
- International environmental crimes include those environmental offenses that cross borders of at least two different countries or occur in internationally protected areas.
- Environmental crime has more victims than others crimes, but victims are often not aware of their victimization (Hayman & Brack, 2002). In general, the types of consequences can be classified as *physical costs*, *economic costs*, and *community costs*.
- The Environmental Protection Agency has also addressed concerns about environmental racism by developing an Office of Environmental Justice in the early 1990s and giving the office the responsibility of promoting environmental justice activities in the agency.
- The EPA was created in 1970 when President Richard Nixon reorganized several federal agencies to create a single federal agency responsible for addressing environmental pollution.
- The actions of the EPA can be characterized in four overlapping ways: (1) as an enforcer of criminal and civil laws, (2) as an agency trying to protect public health, (3) as an agency aiming to deter future misconduct, and (4) as a facilitator of fund generation and cost savings.

- The EPA has been criticized for the following: an ineffective response to the aftermath of September 11, over-regulating rural areas, overstepping its boundaries regarding state issues, and politicizing the science process.
- Three barriers to addressing environmental crime include (1) media portrayals of environmental crime, (2) evidentiary issues, and (3) an empirical void.

KEY TERMS

Comprehensive Environmental Response Compensation and Liability Act

Environmental Protection Agency (EPA)

Environmental racism

Environmental state crimes

Federal Water Pollution Control Act

Illegal dumping

Illegal emissions

International environmental crimes

Knowing endangerment

White-collar environmental crimes

DISCUSSION QUESTIONS

1. Check out the EPA fugitives at http://www.epa.gov/compliance/criminal/fugitives/index.html. Categorize them based on (a) whether they are white-collar offenders, (b) the type of offense they committed, and (c) the harm from their offenses. What patterns do you see regarding gender, race, age, and geography? Explain.

2. Go to http://www.epa.gov/air/data/. Check to see how much air pollution exists in your hometown as well as your college town (if it is different from your hometown). Compare and contrast the amount of pollution in the two places.

3. Watch Doug Rokke's presentation about depleted uranium on Youtube: http://www.youtube.com/watch?v=e-VkpR-wka8. How can use of depleted uranium be characterized as white-collar crime? Is its use an environmental crime?

4. What is it that makes big-game hunting illegal in some situations? Do you think these crimes are serious? Explain.

5. Rank the various types of environmental crime from least serious to most serious. Explain your rankings.

6. Would you be interested in working for the Environmental Protection Agency? Explain.

7. How can scientists commit environmental crime? Explain.

8. Imagine the world 20 years from now. What do you think environmental crime will be like then?

WEB RESOURCES

Earth Liberation Front: http://earth-liberation-front.org/

Interpol Environmental Crime: http://www.interpol.int/public/environmentalcrime/default.asp

Department of Environmental Protection: http://www.ct.gov/dep/site/default.asp

Zero Waste America: http://www.zerowasteamerica.org/RefuseNewsIllegalDumping.htm

United Nations Environment Program: http://www.mea-ren.org/ecmu.php

READING

In this reading, white-collar crime expert David Simon draws attention to the lack of environmental crime research on the role of class status and global issues as the topics relate to crimes against the environment. Simon notes that explanations of environmental crime failed to consider how large, global corporations used their economic and class power to perpetrate offenses that have an international reach. He provides a detailed description of the way that large companies in the United States are actively involved in the commission of these offenses and highlights the way that government officials allow organized crime syndicates control over the waste management industry. Simon concludes with some important recommendations for future research.

Corporate Environmental Crimes and Social Inequality

New Directions for Environmental Justice Research

David R. Simon

zasz and Meuser (1997) note that environmental justice research may have "excluded" certain questions of import (p. 114). Among the topics they list as thus far neglected are (a) the place of the upper class in environmental research and (b) the lack of both a global and a historical perspective. This article represents a furtherance of suggestions concerning their proposed research agenda. First, however, it is necessary to establish a theoretical context in which such research can take place.

Specifically, the place of many upper-class behaviors in environmental concerns involves the commission of environmental and other deviant offenses. As noted below, environmental corporate crimes are but a portion of an entire genre of corporate crime. Ever since Sutherland (1949), numerous criminologists have pointed out a form of differential association among these corporate executives and firms, making certain deviant and illegal practices routine (Simon, 1995, p. 35

and following; Simon, 1999, pp. 50-90; Simon & Hagan, 1999, pp. 20-23, 40-43). As noted below, a number of illegal and deviant acts have become institutionalized practices among certain industries that pollute, dump toxic waste, and make environmental crime victims of various global minorities.

Thus, it is members of the upper class who are the CEOs and leading stockholders of the nation's largest industrial corporations, those very firms most frequently charged with various corporate violations including environmental harms. Moreover, numerous studies demonstrate that globally (Ridgeway & St. Clair, 1998; Simon, 1999, pp. 183-188), nationally (Blumberg & Gottleib, 1989; Gedicks, 1993), and locally (Gedicks, 1993; Hurley, 1995; Pulido, 1996), upper-class business owners have consistently opposed certain environmental regulations, approved of those that benefited them economically, and used others as a form of social control of the lower and working classes (Taylor, 1997, 1998).

SOURCE: Simon, D. (2000). Corporate Environmental Crimes and Social Inequality: New Directions for Environmental Justice Research. *American Behavioral Scientist, 43*(4), 633–645.

Moreover, as demonstrated below, environmental crime is part of an entire pattern of criminal behavior in which many of these industrial giants engage with alarming frequency. The patterns of corporate wrongdoing and their relationship to environmental deviance are in need of further research. Thus far, environmental crime anthologies (Clifford, 1998; Edwards, Edwards, & Fields, 1996) have largely overlooked the social power context in which environmental deviance occurs.

Second, concerning the global context of environmental inequalities, most large American environmental polluters are transnational in scope. Not only do these firms commit environmental offenses within the United States, but many exhibit a disturbing pattern of international environmental wrongdoing. Moreover, anecdotal evidence indicates that these same international corporations commit a wide variety of criminal offenses. Likewise, extant research on environmental inequalities has focused on those offenses against environmental law that affect oppressed minorities within the United States. Such offenses, I will contend, represent a small portion of a much more widespread pattern of global victimization of the poor and peoples of color. Further knowledge of a more inclusive context of corporate criminality holds the promise of providing a much richer picture concerning global corporate criminal activity and its relationship to environmental offenses. Much evidence indicates that environmental law violations are what sociologists term "socially patterned" (Simon, 1995, p. 6). That is, these crimes are not merely random or accidental. They are examples of institutionalized behaviors that take place among a number of organizations in the same industry or agencies of government. As is explored below, these patterned "green crimes" are, in turn, related to other patterns of corporate criminal violations.

Finally, any further environmental inequality research must include the role of government, both nationally and globally. As will be argued, government is frequently a major environmental polluter and, at times, engages in acts of environmental deviance in consort with major industrial corporations. This state-corporate crime (Simon, 1999, pp. 303-328) is frequently well

hidden and largely unresearched. Suggestions for further inquiry are made below. I begin with an agenda for domestic corporate crime research.

 ## Criminogenic Corporate Patterns, Environmental Crime, and the Missing Upper Class

Corporate crime rates are not evenly spread across all industries. Some industrial groups are much more corrupt and criminogenic than others. Thus, Clinard (1979) found that 60% of all corporate offenses prosecuted by the Department of Justice between 1974 and 1976 occurred in just three industries: petrochemicals, pharmaceuticals, and automobile manufacturing. All three of these industries contain long-established patterns of criminal activity.

Patterns of deviant behavior in these industrial sectors fit C. Wright Mills's (1956, pp. 343-361; Simon, 1999, pp. 50-90) description of "the higher immorality," an institutionalized insensitivity to right and wrong. If this depiction is correct, firms in the above-mentioned industries not only engage in the frequent violation of environmental laws; they also (with alarming frequency) regularly violate other white-collar crime laws as well.

General Electric (GE) represents perhaps the quintessential case study of these criminogenic patterns. Currently, GE is named by the Environmental Protection Agency (EPA) as a primarily responsible party (PRP) in more than 80 hazardous waste sites in need of cleanup in the United States (*Congressional Quarterly*, 1998, p. 549). More than this, GE has a longstanding criminal record in many other areas dating back decades (Simon, 1995, p. 35 and following).

Although the exact extent of petrochemical hazardous waste is difficult to determine, there are suggestive statistics. There are some 1,200 chemical firms operating some 11,500 production facilities. The 50 largest industrial organic chemical firms account for nearly 90% of all shipments, and the 50 largest agricultural chemical firms account for slightly more than 90% of all shipments. The 50 largest inorganic chemical firms account for roughly three fourths of all shipments. One study by Booz Allen concluded "that these three industrial segments are the major source of petrochemical industry hazardous waste" (Barnett, 1994, p. 19).

Three electronics firms, including GE and Westinghouse, were also identified in the EPA's Clean Water Project as PRPs at Superfund sites (hazardous waste sites in need of cleanup). Westinghouse is identified as a PRP at 90 EPA Superfund sites. Ford and General Motors, two automotive firms, are identified as PRPs at 19 and 21 Superfund sites, respectively (Barnett, 1994, p. 21). Consistent with the higher immorality, there is evidence that major chemical corporations, including DuPont, Union Carbide, and others, have hired organized criminal syndicates to illegally dispose of hazardous waste in New York, New Jersey, and other locations (*ABC News,* 1988; Rebovich, 1992, pp. 64-76). In a number of states, mob-connected garbage haulers obtained permits and set themselves up as solid-waste disposers. Landfill owners were then bribed to sign for shipments that were never received, while the actual shipments were dumped illegally in sewers, in waterways, or into the ocean (Albanese & Pursley, 1993, pp. 325-326).

The hiring of organized criminal syndicates to perform various services for corporations and the federal government, especially the CIA, has a long and sordid history. The Mafia was hired by naval intelligence during World War II to secure the New York docks from potential threats from Nazi submarines, to plan the invasion of Sicily and Italy, and to run the military government in Italy after the Allied victory. Moreover,

- The CIA has been linked to the furtherance of drug trafficking for the past 50 years, including the French connection heroin route (1950), the Golden Triangle opium production (1950-1970s), and Afghan heroin production and Latin American cocaine traffic (1980s). There is some evidence that the CIA played a role in spreading crack cocaine sales in African American and other minority communities in the 1980s.

- The CIA hired organized crime figures in the 1950s and 1960s to assassinate Fidel Castro.

- Organized crime money and/or electioneering favors were used by the Kennedy campaign in 1960, Nixon in 1968, and Reagan in 1980 to win election to office.

- Organized crime has provided finance capital to major corporations in various business ventures, especially building casinos, prevented unions from forming or helped unions win recognition, and provided arson services to slumlords and banks. Likewise, organized crime syndicates and numerous large banks, investment houses, jewelry exchanges, and check-cashing services have conspired together to launder drug money (Simon, 1999, pp. 2-3, 77-80, 292-296).

In short, organized criminal syndicates have proved useful to corporate, labor, and political elites for the past 50 years, sometimes for anti-environmental purposes in the pursuit of profit.

Consistent with Clinard's (1979) findings, the majority of environmental violations by U.S. corporations are found in only a few industries: petrochemicals, petroleum, automobiles, and electrical products. These corporations are members of oligopolistic industries that are heavily concentrated, wherein four or fewer firms control 50% or more of a market. The corporations in these industries have some important common characteristics.

1. Their boards of directors contain upper-class executives from the largest banks and insurance companies. Many of the directors sit on more than one corporate board. They are thus interlocked (Simon, 1999, pp. 16-24).

2. They are among the 500 largest industrial firms that sponsor 90% of the nation's network television programs.

3. They are among those corporations that spend the most money (hundreds of millions per election cycle) to lobby Congress and back political candidates.

4. Some are annually among the 100 largest defense contracting firms. A number of them have been involved in waste-disposal scandals at federally owned facilities, sometimes aided and abetted by the federal government.

5. They are among the largest 500 industrial corporations that make 80% of all after-tax profits in manufacturing. Many of the firms involved in environmentally polluting industries also own other firms in other industries. Philip Morris, for example, which owns Marlboro cigarettes, also owns Kraft Foods, Tang, Oscar Meyer, Jell-O, Miller Beer, Post cereals, and Maxwell House coffee. Monsanto, which makes herbicides, insecticides, and fertilizers, also makes pharmaceuticals, NutraSweet, and soap (Ridgeway & St. Clair, 1998, pp. 82, 130).

6. They are among the largest 500 corporations that make 90% of all profits involved in U.S. foreign trade (Simon, 1999, p. 20 and following).

7. A number of large chemical firms have been guilty of hiring organized criminal syndicates to dispose of toxic waste.

8. The victims of illegal hazardous waste disposal tend to be the most poor and powerless populations in both the United States and around the world.

One reason why corporate crimes of all types flourish within certain industries is that the mainstream press underreports both individual incidents of crime and the seriousness of such violations. In 1994 alone, 6 of the top 10 *Project Censored* stories were ecologically related (Curran, 1995), and this pattern has been consistent since Carl Jensen (1993) began the project. Consider just a few of *Project Censored's* 1997 summary of its top 200 stories for the past 20 years:

- In 1976, a story related that 500,000 people annually in the world's poorest nations were poisoned by pesticides. By 1995, the United States had exported 58 million pounds of banned pesticides and prescription drugs to the world's poorer nations.

- Another censored story related that Mobil Oil had for years done business with Zimbabwe, a major human rights violator embargoed and condemned by most of the world's nations. In 1996, Mobil continued to do business with Zimbabwe, and Texaco had illegally done business with Haiti, a major global drug-trafficking and rights-violating nation.

- In the 1970s, baby formulas made by Nestle and Bristol Meyers were advertised by giving free samples to mothers in poor nations and with promises of modernization and increased social status. These formulas caused the deaths of 35,000 Third World infants and numerous cases of brain damage, in part because of a lack of facilities to boil the water that was mixed with the formulas. By 1995, despite international boycotts, formula manufactures still advertised their products, which by then had contributed to more than 1 million infant deaths per year in poor nations (Jensen, 1997, pp. 37-39, 52-53).

Thus, because companies like GE and Westinghouse also own major media outlets, news stories of GE's criminal violations are consistently given short shrift by mainstream media. The lack of stories is also accompanied by vigorous public relations efforts that function to cover up environmental harms (Ridgeway & St. Clair, 1998, pp. 135-152; Stauber & Rampton, 1995; see below).

What all this means is that corporate violators of ecological criminal laws are part of an entire political economy, a macro environment over which they exert considerable control. Part of this environment concerns the global political economy in which such transnational corporations operate. Often, corporate violations are international in scope and involve not just violations of hazardous waste laws but corruption statutes as well.

The problem of environmental destruction thus represents one of the most dangerous contradictions of giving priority to the value of accumulating wealth without regard to the means of doing so. Environmental problems also represent the outgrowth of an international system of nations in which corporations have been allowed to set priorities without regard to the welfare of individuals, especially the poorest and most powerless individuals in Third World nations, Third World workers, and poor men, women, and children around the globe.

 ## Global Patterns of Environmental Victimization

The victimization of non-elites by environmental harms is a global pattern, one that especially strikes people of color. *Environmental racism* is the term used to describe the victimization of people of color by corporate polluters. Various studies have established that minorities in the United States are at considerable risk from such victimization (Billiard, 1994, p. 6 and following; Parenti, 1995, p. 112; Rosen, 1994, p. 225).

Likewise, there are a large number of toxic-waste problems that are exported to foreign countries, many of which have involved the illegal bribery of officials of foreign governments. The advanced nations of the world generate about 400 million tons of toxic waste annually; 60% comes from the United States. A shipment of toxic waste leaves the United States every 5 minutes every day of the year. The vast majority of America's internationally exported toxic waste, 80%, is sent to Canada and Britain (Cass, 1994, p. 2). The EPA requires U.S. companies to provide onsite disposal facilities for toxic waste, which cost upward of $30 million and take years to build. However, such waste can be dumped in Third World nations for a fraction of the cost, sometimes for as little as $20 a ton (Cass, 1994, p. 7). In 1991, an internal memo written by one of the World Bank's chief economists advocated that the World Bank encourage "more migration of dirty industries to the Less Developed Countries" (Rosen, 1994, p. 226), thus giving credence to those who believe that environmental racism is an intentional policy. European nations also export toxic waste to the world's poorer nations.

At times, multinational corporations have provided handsome financial rewards to the recipient nations. For example, Guinea-Bissau, which has a gross national product of $150 million, will make $150 million to $600 million over a 5-year period in a deal to accept toxic waste from three European nations.

Typically, bribes are paid to Third World government officials to establish toxic waste dumps in their countries. Third World participation in the waste dumping of advanced nations has generated a host of scandals.

- In April 1988, five top government officials in the Congo were indicted after they concluded a deal to import 1 million tons of chemical waste and pesticide residue, receiving $4 million in "commissions" from a firm specializing in hazardous waste disposal. The total contract was worth $84 million.

- After dumping toxic waste in Nigeria and Lebanon, in 1988, Italy agreed to take back some 6,400 tons. What's more, Nigeria recalled its Italian ambassador and arrested 25 people when it discovered some of the waste was radioactive. To complicate matters, Italian dock workers in 10 port cities have refused to handle the waste. Italy has pledged to ban further toxic exports to the developing world and plans to spend $7 billion a year to clean up its own toxic dumps at home. The Italian government has also sued 22 waste-producing firms to force them to turn over $75 million to pay for transporting and treating incoming waste.

- In 1987, Weber Ltd., a West German waste transporter, found a Turkish cement plant willing to accept 1,500 tons of toxic-waste-laden sawdust for about $70 a ton. Instead of being burned, the sawdust waste sat in the open air for nearly 16 months, slowly leaking poison into the ground. A newspaper reported the sawdust contained lethal PCBs, and a scandal ensued. Under pressure form the governments of Turkey and West Germany, Weber finally agreed to transport the waste back to West Germany. Normally, Weber charges its customers $450 to $510 a ton to dispose of waste in Germany. With Third World costs of $110 per ton or less, the amount of profit involved is substantial.

- In late 1991, three South Carolina metal smelting firms contracted with a waste-disposal firm to send waste containing life-threatening levels of cadmium and lead to Bangladesh. Once in that country, the waste was used to make fertilizer used by Bangladeshi farmers (Brooks, 1988; Cass, 1994; Leonard, 1994, p. 9; *Newsweek,* 1988).

Closer to home, there are currently about 1,800 maquiladora plants owned by multinational firms along the U.S.-Mexican border. Of 600 plants owned by America's *Fortune* 500 firms, only 91 have thus far complied with Mexican law requiring that waste generated by American corporations be transported to the United States for disposal (Kelly, 1993).

On both sides of the U.S.-Mexican border, there have been reports of deformed fish, increased cancer rates, and a doubling of typhoid and infectious hepatitis and other problems, including birth defects (Kelly, 1993, pp. 13, 16-17; Wolkomir, 1994, pp. 27, 30).

Finally, in 1995, it was learned that Shell Oil's parent firm paid the Nigerian military to use force against environmental protestors and that Shell offered bribes to witnesses at the trials of murdered protestors to testify against environmental activists (Ridgeway & St. Clair, 1998, pp. 22-23; Simon, 1999, p. 191). Taken collectively, all of this indicates that the global "waste industry is one of the most corrupt industries in the world" (Jensen, 1993, p. 57). Most of its victims include the least powerful people on the face of the earth, poverty-stricken people of color, most of whom are powerless to resist the environmental deviance of multinational firms (Bullard, 1994, p. 6 and following). Moreover, many times the federal government has covered up and at other times been a coconspirator in the violation of environmental and other laws.

The Government as Polluter

According to Helen Caldicott (1992), "The U.S. government is the nation's chief polluter" (p. 7). Thanks to large campaign contributions and other forms of political influence, the federal government has all but become an ally of major polluters and their upper-class stockholders. Federal facilities discharge almost 2.5 million tons of toxic and radioactive waste annually without reporting it. The Government Accounting Office estimates that 95% of U.S. government toxic pollution is exempt from the government's own reporting procedures. At Department of Defense weapons plants alone, there are 14,401 potentially contaminated dumpsites.

Various agencies of the U.S. government are named as PRPs at 8% of the Superfund sites, but this estimate is considered very conservative because the federal government is exempt from EPA regulations in more than 90% of cases. It is estimated that 60 million Americans live within 50 miles of one of the military-related nuclear waste storage sites. Almost every U.S. domestic military facility

> works with hazardous materials and generates toxic waste through such activities as the production, cleaning, and use of weapons, explosives and rocket fuels, vehicles, aircraft, and electronic equipment. Substances like PCBs, dioxin, heavy metals, and cyanides are emitted directly into the air, soil, and ground water. (Ridgeway & St. Clair, 1998, p. 108)

Likewise, more than half of the 10.5 billion pounds of toxic chemicals released into the air, soil, and water are not covered by EPA regulations (Caldicott, 1992, p. 7).

Aside from the government's own abysmal record of polluting the environment, the EPA itself has demonstrated an alarming degree of corruption, misfeasance, and malfeasance. A 1992 Environmental Research Foundation report concludes that the EPA often opposes congressional attempts to pass environmental laws and spends more time trying to figure out how to exempt corporations from its regulations than it does regulating them (Jensen, 1993, p. 56).

Conclusion: Research Agenda for Ecological Crime

The above discussion allows for some important conclusions concerning patterns of environmental crime and the place of those patterns within the structure of the

American political economy (Simon, 1995, p. 42-54). Further research in this area needs to focus on the interrelationships between environmental/hazardous waste violations and other forms of corporate and political crime. Specifically,

1. What additional violations of corporate crime laws are exhibited by the various chemical and other firms that have been convicted of multiple violations of hazardous waste and other environmental laws?

2. What are the specific relationships between the firms convicted of numerous violations of various environmental laws and the EPA?

3. What influence do powerful petrochemical and other firms frequently convicted of environmental criminal violations have on Congress and on the executive branch of the federal government?

4. What patterns of criminality exist in which government agencies and corporations violate environmental laws in a conspiratorial fashion?

5. Reportage by the media of environmental racism and other green crimes has been slanted in favor of corporate polluters and governmental agencies (Rosen, 1994, p. 224), and frequently these crimes have been dramatically underreported (Curran, 1995; Jensen, 1993; Rosen, 1994, pp. 228-229). Studies are needed to ascertain when and if victims of ecological crimes are viewed in an objective light by the press. In addition, at what point does the mainstream media become concerned enough about environmental crimes to give them major and/or sustained attention?

6. Finally, in the structural sense, what corporate interlocks exist between firms in environmentally related fields and other sectors of American capitalism, especially finance capital sectors (multinational banks and insurance firms)?

Such research would aid in answering key questions concerning the distribution of power within the American political economy, the emerging nature of the higher immorality (including its international patterns), and the degrees of harm caused by various forms of environmental crime.

This article has described a set of institutionalized deviant behaviors among some corporate fields that are environmentally related. It has argued that such firms use a variety of political and media influences to persuade the public that they are actually environmentally concerned. Frequently, the government itself acts as a coconspirator in environmental crimes. In addition, these firms are interlocked with other segments of corporate America in understudied ways. These realities alone indicate that a new research agenda for environmental deviance is needed.

Finally, it is important for criminologists to study patterns of ecological crime as a way of empirically testing major criminological theories. Two dominant theoretical notions regarding organizational offenses are differential association and neo-Mertonian anomie theory (Messner & Rosenfeld, 1994). Differential association holds that criminal activity and the methods of committing it are learned as socially approved behaviors. How and why such behaviors are learned within the petrochemical and related industries are important in assessing the role of organizational culture and the organizational environment in causing ecological crime.

Neo-Mertonian anomie theory focuses on the overall macro cultural and institutional structure in which environmental violations take place. Messner and Rosenfeld (1994) have correctly argued that America's social structure involves institutional dominance by business institutions and cultural values that emphasize individualism, achievement, competition, and the fetishism of money. This overarching social structure creates a climate in which ends (especially profit and power) are emphasized over means (lawful business practices). Thus, the values associated with the American Dream result in pressures on both individuals and organizations to achieve material success while neglecting the means of doing so (i.e., engaging in criminal activity). Ecological crime provides something of a laboratory for testing and refining these two theories of organizational criminal behavior. Likewise, the study of the context in which environmental crime takes places promises to enrich the environmental justice movement as well.

References

ABC News. (1988). Sons of Scarface: The new mafia [documentary].

Albanese, J., & Pursley, R. D. (1993). *Crime in America: Some existing and emerging issues.* Englewood Cliffs, NJ: Prentice Hall.

Barnett, H. (1994). *Toxic debts and the Superfund dilemma.* Chapel Hill: University of North Carolina Press.

Blumberg, L., & Gottlieb, R. (1989). *War on waste: Can America win its battle with the garbage.* Covelo, CO: Island Press.

Brooks, J. (1988, July 17). Waste dumpers turning to West Africa. *New York Times*, p. 1.

Bullard, R. D. (Ed.). (1994). *Unequal protection: Environmental justice and communities of color.* San Francisco: Sierra Club Books.

Caldicott, H. (1992). *If you love this planet: A plan to heal the Earth.* New York: Norton.

Cass, V. (1994, November). *The international toxic waste trade: Who gets left holding the toxic trash bag?* Paper presented at the 1994 meeting of the American Society of Criminology.

Clifford, M. (Ed.). (1998). *Environmental crime.* Baltimore, MD: Aspen.

Clinard, M. B. (1979). *Corporate crime.* Washington, DC: Government Printing Office.

Congressional Quarterly. (1998, 19 June), p. 549.

Curran, R. (1995, March 29-April 4). Too hot to handle. *San Francisco Bay Guardian*, pp. 15-17.

DiMaggio, P., & Powell, W. (1983). The iron cage revisited: Institutional isomorphism and collective rationality in organizational fields. *American Sociological Review, 48,* 147-160.

Edwards, S., Edwards, T., & Fields, C. (Eds.). (1996). *Environmental crime and criminality.* New York: Garland.

Freeman, A. (1994, July/August). Bad chemistry at EPA. *Multinational Monitor*, p. 5.

Gedicks, A. (1993). *The new resource wars: Native environmental struggles against multinational corporations.* Boston: South End.

Hurley, A. (1995). *Environmental inequalities: Class, race, and industrial pollution in Gary, Indiana, 1845-1980.* Chapel Hill: University of North Carolina Press.

Jensen, C. (1993). *Censored: The news that didn't make it—and why.* Chapel Hill, NC: Shelburne.

Jensen, C. (and the Project Censored Staff). (1997). *Twenty years of* Project Censored. New York: Seven Stories.

Kelly, M. (1993, October). Free trade and the politics of toxic waste. *Multinational Monitor*, pp. 13-20.

Leonard, A. (1994, September). Dumping Pepsi's toxic waste. *Multinational Monitor*, pp. 7-10.

Lewis, C. (1998). *The buying of Congress.* New York: Avon.

Messner, S., & Rosenfeld, R. (1994). *Crime and the American dream.* Monterey, CA: Brooks/Cole.

Mills, C. W. (1956). *The power elite.* New York: Oxford University Press.

Newsweek. (1988, November 7), p. 68.

Parenti, M. (1995). *Democracy for the few* (6th ed.). New York: St. Martin's.

Pulido, L. (1996). *Environmentalism and economic justice: Two Chicano struggles in the Southwest.* Tucson: University of Arizona Press.

Rebovich, D. J. (1992). *Dangerous ground: The world of hazardous waste crime.* New Brunswick, NJ: Transaction.

Ridgeway, J., & St. Clair, J. (1998). *A pocket guide to environmental bad guys.* New York: Thunder's Mouth.

Rosen, R. (1994, Spring). Who gets polluted: The movement for environmental justice. *Dissent*, pp. 223-230.

Simon, D. R. (1995). *Social problems and the sociological imagination.* New York: McGraw-Hill.

Simon, D. R. (1999). *Elite deviance* (6th ed.). Needham Heights, MA: Allyn & Bacon.

Simon, D. R., & Hagan, F. (1999). *White-collar deviance.* Needham Heights, MA: Allyn & Bacon.

Stauber, J. C, & Rampton, S. (1995). *Toxic sludge is good for you.* Monroe, ME: Common Courage.

Sutherland, E. H. (1949). *White-collar crime.* New York: Holt, Rinehart & Winston.

Szasz, A. (1986). The process and significance of political scandals: A comparison of Watergate and the "sewergate" episode at the Environmental Protection Agency. *Social Problems, 33,* 200-217.

Szasz, A., & Meuser, M. (1997). Environmental inequalities: Literature review and proposals for new direction in research and theory. *Current Sociology, 45,* 99-120.

Taylor, D. E. (1997). American environmentalism: The role of race, class and gender in shaping activism, 1820-1995. *Race, Gender and Class, 5*(1), 16-62.

Taylor, D. E. (1998). The urban environment: The intersection of White middle class and White working class environmentalism, 1820-1950s. *Advances in Human Ecology, 7,* 207-292.

Wolkomir, R. (1994, May). Hot on the trial of toxic dumpers and other eco-outlaws, Texas style. *Smithsonian*, pp. 26-37.

DISCUSSION QUESTIONS

1. Are all environmental crimes white-collar crimes? Explain.

2. Review Simon's recommendations for future research. Which research strategies might be used to address these research questions?

3. How can the government be characterized as a polluter?

READING

In this reading, Harold Barnett addresses how the Superfund initiative has been used to address environmental crimes. The initiative requires corporations to pay for the costs of cleaning up environmental offenses. He traces the history of Superfund and places the policy within the context of shifts in environmental attitudes in the 1970s and 1980s. Barnett discusses how different EPA administrators promoted varying approaches to enforcing Superfund. He also shows how public concern about the environment outweighed corporate opposition to policies regulating companies and businesses. In addition, he draws attention to the power of corporations to shape legislative responses to environmental offending.

Crimes Against the Environment

Superfund Enforcement at Last

Harold C. Barnett

In his pioneering study of corporate crime, Edwin Sutherland emphasized the ability of corporations to shield themselves from stigma and liability for socially harmful actions. He lamented the absence of organized public resentment, a potential counterbalance to corporate political power.[1] Writing in 1949, Sutherland made no substantive reference to crimes against the environment. Since his time, however, we have come to recognize the dangerous legacy of the industrial and chemical revolutions and have witnessed the growth of a broad-based environmental movement that has provided political support for the environmental legislation of the 1970s. The history of this legislation and its implementation reveal continuous tension between economic necessity and environmental quality.[2]

Legislation during the "environmental decade" was primarily prospective. Law was fashioned to limit and control future emissions and disposal of pollutants and contaminants into air and water and onto land. By the end of the 1970s, however, attention shifted from control of future pollution to the correction of harms already imposed upon the environment. In 1980, Congress enacted the Comprehensive Environmental Response Compensation and Liability Act, commonly referred to as the Superfund Act. Its purpose is to provide a means to clean up past environmental sins. A reading of the legislative history makes clear that major corporations in the petrochemicals, metals, electrical, and transportation industries were perceived by Congress as the perpetrators of the severe environmental damage to be addressed by Superfund. A primary intent of the act was to place the cost of correction on corporations to the extent that they were responsible for environmental problems. Superfund in this regard

SOURCE: Barnett, H. (1993). Crimes Against the Environment: Superfund Enforcement at Last. *Annals of the American Academy of Political and Social Science,* 525, 119–133.

[1] Edwin H. Sutherland, *White Collar Crime* (New Haven, CT: Yale University Press, 1983), pp. 53–62.

[2] For recent discussion of the politics of environmental protection, see P. C. Yeager, *The Limits of Law* (New York: Cambridge University Press, 1991).

represents a major social initiative to sanction[3] powerful corporations for their decades of environmental neglect.[4] The history of Superfund provides insight into the impact of organized public resentment on regulatory enforcement and the strategies adopted by industry to blunt that impact.

Superfund Strategy

The Superfund Act of 1980, amended in 1986, was intended to clean up some of the nation's worst uncontrolled hazardous waste sites. Documented health hazards at New York's Love Canal alerted the public to the dangers posed by these toxic time bombs and to the absence of any meaningful government response. To date, the Environmental Protection Agency (EPA), the federal agency charged with implementation, has included some 1200 sites on its list of Superfund cleanup priorities. Each site has its own story of risk, loss, and fear. At Times Beach, Missouri, the residents of a scenic town on the Ozark River were evacuated to protect them from dioxin-contaminated soil. The residents of Woburn, Massachusetts, were exposed to chlorinated organic solvents in two municipal wells and to groundwater contaminated with organic pollutants and heavy metals. Excess rates of leukemia, lung/respiratory, and kidney/urinary disorders in children; perinatal mortality; and birth defects were observed among those with greater access to the contaminated water. The Stringfellow Acid Pits in Glen Avon, California, was used as a surface impoundment; over 30 million gallons of a large variety of liquid hazardous wastes were disposed there. Surface and groundwater contamination threatens a major source of drinking water for some 500,000 people in the area. The Sylvester site in Nashua, New Hampshire, a former sand and gravel pit, received at least 240,000 pounds of hazardous waste, and a wide variety of hazardous substances were found in groundwater, surface waters, and air. The plume of contamination threatens drinking water for several Massachusetts towns.

Cleanup of the hazardous areas is financed by a combination of revenues raised primarily through a tax on petrochemical industry corporations and enforcement-induced cleanup expenditures from many of these same corporations. This strategy's enforcement component has several underlying premises. First, those responsible for conditions at Superfund sites are held liable whether or not they were negligent in their disposal practices; that is, liability is strict. Second, strong enforcement and liability provisions can facilitate privately funded cleanup at the 40 to 50 percent of sites where responsible parties are identified. In particular, where contribution to the need for cleanup is not divisible, each responsible party can be held liable for the total cost of cleanup regardless of proportionate contribution; that is, liability is joint and several. If a responsible party refuses to conduct a cleanup after the EPA issues a unilateral order, the agency can pay for cleanup and then bring suit to recover costs and to impose penalties for three times these costs.[5] The penalties are paid into the cleanup fund. Sites also can be cleaned up with Superfund monies when responsible parties cannot be identified or are insolvent. The logic of the Superfund Act suggests that an aggressive application of enforcement powers is essential if the program is to achieve a level of funding commensurate with cleanup goals.

Superfund has been mired in continuous conflict over who will bear the substantial costs of cleanup, which are expected to exceed $100 billion. Superfund strategy in general, and enforcement policy in particular, have been shaped by this conflict. Over $10 billion has been spent to date. Advocates of an aggressive policy, including environmental interest groups, see the Superfund Act as a primary mechanism to impose

---

[3]Conceptualizing private sector contributions to hazardous waste site cleanup as a sanction is consistent with much of the corporate crime literature. See, for example, Marshall B. Clinard and Peter C. Yeager, *Corporate Crime* (New York: Free Press, 1980).

[4]The following analysis draws heavily on my research for a book on the Superfund program, *Toxic Debts: The Superfund Dilemma*, forthcoming from the University of North Carolina Press.

[5]The cleanup fund provides a unique opportunity for the EPA to leverage settlements on recalcitrant responsible parties. Most other regulatory programs do not allow an agency the resources to take corrective actions.

the cost of cleanup directly on those responsible for the environmental damage. Enforcement, they argue, is necessary since the funds raised through taxation are inadequate to the magnitude of the cleanup task. On the other hand, many potential defendant corporations oppose aggressive enforcement and the act's underlying liability standards. They argue that society as a whole, having benefited from the chemical revolution, should bear responsibility for correcting its environmental consequences. They contend that a socialization of cleanup costs through general revenues or a broad-based tax on American industry is more equitable. This proposed strategy is similar to that currently being utilized to bail out savings and loan institutions. All taxpayers, not just those who looted the thrifts, have to pay the bill. Opponents of strong enforcement efforts further argue that conflicts between the government and defendants as well as between the defendants and their insurers impose substantial transaction costs on society in the form of litigation expenses and cleanup delays. They favor a shift in emphasis from enforcement to a more broadly based no-fault system, which they believe will reduce the total cost of achieving cleanup and make the program more efficient and more equitable.

Conflict over Superfund implementation has produced three distinct EPA enforcement strategies. The first, a strategy of nonconfrontational voluntary compliance, developed under EPA Administrator Ann Burford, made sparing use of Superfund and of the agency's enforcement powers. The second, a fund-first approach promulgated under EPA Administrators William Ruckelshaus and Lee Thomas, emphasized use of the fund to leverage enforcement. The third, an enforcement-first strategy recently advanced under EPA Administrator William Reilly, elevates the role of enforcement. Thus an aggressive enforcement component has emerged only at the end of the first decade of Superfund implementation, though, given the strong opposition by major polluting corporations, it is striking that an aggressive enforcement strategy has emerged at all.

Can Enforcement First Last?

A review of the first decade of Superfund implementation highlights factors that constrained aggressive enforcement, including White House opposition to active regulatory action and related White House and congressional decisions to limit the EPA's enforcement budget. Limitations imposed on the Superfund program as a whole and on its enforcement component can be attributed to the political influence of powerful corporations and to official concern with negative economic consequences of environmental protection. The impact of these constraints has been lessened by societal concern for environmental and public health threats and by active oversight and involvement on the part of environmental advocates, the latter buttressed by continuing public support for environmental programs. Later, an enforcement-first strategy was backed or, at least, minimally opposed by the Bush White House.

Bush administration endorsement for enforcement-first can be traced in part to the federal government's fiscal crisis: a mounting federal budget deficit, a recessionary economy, and strong antitax sentiments have reduced the government's capacity to absorb the economic burden of environmental problems. Cleanup, strongly favored by the public, is expensive, and costs that are not imposed on responsible parties through enforcement programs have to be borne by taxpayers. In addition, the federal government has its own hazardous waste sites on Department of Energy and Department of Defense properties to clean up.

White House support also reflects the desire of the Bush administration to present itself as pro-environment. The appointment of Reilly and subsequent White House lobbying for the Clean Air Act are clearly consistent with this desire. While the administration gave minimal support to the reauthorization of Superfund taxing authority during debate on the 1991 budget package, it did not actively stand in opposition.[6] This reflects recognition that Superfund is among the most visible of environmental programs and that efforts to hurt it

---

[6]Major corporations and their insurers had hoped that a full debate over reauthorization would afford them the opportunity to present their case against Superfund liability standards and their case for a greater socialization of cleanup costs.

would be unacceptable to the public. The White House learned from the Sewergate scandal that overt efforts to undermine the program are politically damaging. However, decisions to add to already rising regulatory costs may be due more to inadvertence than to conscious White House design. Domestic policy has not been a high priority for the administration. The pre-election 90-day moratorium on new regulations was to advertise that the White House was concerned with regulatory costs and to allow President Bush to unfurl a deregulatory banner prior to the elections.[7]

Major corporations are not pleased with the EPA's new strategy.[8] They claim that the agency has failed to negotiate settlements. They urge the EPA to offer to pay for the share of a cleanup for which there is no identifiable responsible party as an inducement to corporations to settle. The EPA, they charge, fails to force small contributors to hazardous site contamination to bear their share of cleanup costs. Major targets of EPA enforcement see themselves as being liable for far more than their proportionate share of cleanup costs, and they believe that their primary viable option is compliance with unilateral EPA orders followed by efforts to recover costs from the fund if they can prove that part of the cleanup was not necessary—or through third-party contribution suits.

Industry's effort to illuminate the cost and inequity of enforcement includes increased use of third-party suits. Municipalities are a prime target.[9] Du Pont, Rohm & Haas, and others have brought suit against 50 municipalities for cleanup costs at a New Jersey landfill. B. F. Goodrich and Uniroyal Chemical Co. have targeted 24 Connecticut communities for litigation, while General Electric and Polaroid are suing 12 Massachusetts municipalities. Occidental Petroleum, Lockheed, Proctor &

Gamble, and 61 other companies are demanding that 29 Los Angeles suburbs pay 90 percent of a cleanup expected to cost from $650 to $800 million. In bringing suit against municipalities, major corporations are forcing government officials to deal firsthand with perceived inequities in the law as well as with high transaction costs. The underlying message is that if municipalities consider this situation unfair, they should join industrial plaintiffs in pressuring Congress to change the law.

Corporations have begun actively to investigate site records to identify responsible parties that have fallen through the EPA's underfunded investigative net. Monsanto, for example, was able to reduce its liability for a $40 million cleanup by 40 percent after identifying 20 additional responsible parties.[10] Potentially liable minor contributors, faced with the threat of third-party suits, have found settlement to be less expensive than litigation.

Providers of environmental damage insurance have long protested the inequity and high cost of Superfund liability standards. They feel most the extra expense involved with litigation since, in many cases, they must pay the cleanup costs imposed on their industrial clients. Four insurers said that in 1985 they paid out an average of $15,600 on 176 claims. In 1989, they paid out an average of $64,400 on 786 closed claims. Insurers also reported spending about $158 million on lawsuits involving pollution coverage issues. At the close of the 1980s, they were engaged in 1962 lawsuits with insured parties over coverage involving about 6000 hazardous waste sites, and these numbers are expected to increase.[11]

Corporate targets of EPA enforcement have attempted to recruit financial institutions against the enforcement-first strategy, since commercial lenders

---

[7]See Bob Davis, "January Surprise: Bush Plans to Unveil a 90-Day Moratorium on New Regulation," *Wall Street Journal*, 20 Jan. 1992.

[8]The following is based in part on interviews with Lloyd Guerci, former Director of the EPA Superfund enforcement division, 9 Aug. 1991; Dell Perelman, Assistant General Counsel, Chemical Manufacturers Association, 9 Aug. 1991; Arthur Weissman, Chief, Super-fund enforcement guidance and evaluation branch, 8 Aug. 1991.

[9]See Robert Tomsho, "Pollution Ploy: Big Corporations Hit by Superfund Cases Find Way to Share Bill," *Wall Street Journal*, 2 Apr. 1991; idem, "Gumshoes Help Companies Cut Dump Cleanup Bills," ibid., 5 Nov. 1991.

[10]As reported in Tomsho, "Gumshoes."

[11]See U.S. General Accounting Office, *Pollution Claims Experience of Property/Casualty Insurers* (Washington, DC: Government Printing Office, Feb. 1991).

can be exposed to Superfund liability when they acquire contaminated property through foreclosure. Such liability became a source of concern in the late 1980s with an increase in business failures and loan defaults on commercial property and resultant savings and loan failures. The Chemical Manufacturers Association, for instance, has argued that if lenders face cleanup problems, it is because of Superfund's severe liability standard.[12]

Industry and its insurers continue to advocate a socialization of Superfund cleanup costs via taxation. Ultimately, major industrial contributors to Superfund cleanup problems wish to establish that an explicit socialization of cost is more equitable, less expensive, and less painful than enforcing sanctions against the powerful. As the primary target of enforcement, industry has acted to allocate the financial burden via third-party suits while imposing transaction costs involved with litigation. They anticipate that municipalities, lending institutions, and other third parties drawn into the Superfund liability net will demand a rationalization of Superfund strategy. Industry arguments that transaction costs are excessive find considerable support in academic studies of environmental enforcement. The latter view Superfund's liability provisions as little more than an extremely costly funding mechanism.[13] A soon-to-be-released RAND Corporation study predicts that legal fees and other transaction costs will rise as a proportion of the total bill.[14]

 ## Conclusion

The development of an aggressive Superfund enforcement policy supports Sutherland's prediction that organized public resentment can counter the political influence of industry. The response of industry to this policy, however, highlights inherent limitations on the ability of an environmentally conscious public both to demand cleanup and to impose its costs on industrial polluters. Congressional and executive-branch sensitivity to industrial interests and the need to promote capital accumulation stands in direct opposition to many environmental initiatives. To resolve such conflict, Congress often has chosen to socialize corrective costs. In this way, government is legitimized while corporate profits are protected. The current Superfund tax is in part passed forward to consumers and, as a deduction in calculating the corporate profit tax, is passed backward to taxpayers. Thus a portion of cleanup costs is already socialized and the actual burden on industry is generally overstated.

Industry argues that a further broadening of the tax base in combination with a greatly restricted enforcement program is the appropriate way to resolve an ongoing conflict over the financing of Superfund. Holding industry liable is inequitable, they argue, since past disposal practices conformed to existing law, and society as a whole benefited from the production that gave rise to hazardous wastes.

For environmentalists and those in Congress who reject the argument that industry should be held blameless for its past deeds, the case for socialization rests on the assertion that the gain in equity from preservation of a polluter-pays principle is not justified by the related loss in efficiency. This assertion sanitizes enforcement and casts it merely as an alternative and high-transaction-cost funding option; it rests on the premise that there is no ethical dimension to corporate decisions that caused damage to human health and the environment. The implication is that enforcement in this area should not be compared, for example, to that against drug dealing, where perceived social damage justifies even inefficient efforts to sanction perpetrators. Further, emphasis on the high cost of litigation is often another way of saying that it is too expensive to make powerful violators pay.

[12]See testimony of the Chemical Manufacturers Association on lender liability under Superfund before U.S., Congress, Senate, Committee on Environment and Public Works, Subcommittee on Superfund, Ocean, and Water Protection, 10 Apr. 1991, pp. 5, 17.

[13]See, for example, Jan P. Acton, *Understanding Superfund: A Progress Report* (Santa Monica, CA: RAND, 1989) and, more recently, Peter S. Menell, "The Limitations of Legal Institutions for Addressing Environmental Risks," *Journal of Economic Perspectives,* 5:93–113 (Summer 1991).

[14]See "Toxic Waste: Paying for the Past," *Economist,* 29 Feb. 1992, p. 80.

If industry's equity or equity-efficiency trade-off arguments prevail, those responsible for environmental damage will avoid both stigma and substantial liability for past actions and may feel free to pursue environmentally unsound practices in the future. Organized public resentment will have promoted cleanup but will not have toppled barriers to sanctioning the powerful. The Superfund program will come to more closely resemble the bailout of the savings and loan insurance fund. As we approach the next Superfund reauthorization, Congress is faced with a decision either to accept the high social cost of imposing sanctions on polluting corporations or to simply pay for cleanup and hope that history will not repeat itself.

DISCUSSION QUESTIONS

1. Who should pay for the costs of environmental offenses? Explain.

2. How have companies avoided paying the costs of environmental crimes?

3. What can members of the public do to address barriers created by organizational opposition to regulatory policies?

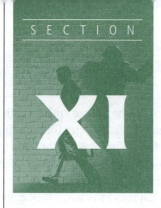

XI

Explaining White-Collar Crime

Section Highlights

- Culture and White-Collar Crime
- Deterrence Theory/Rational Choice Theory and White-Collar Crime
- Strain Theory and White-Collar Crime
- Learning Theory and White-Collar Crime
- Neutralizing and Justifying White-Collar Crime
- Control Theory and White-Collar Crime
- Self-Control and White-Collar Crime
- Routine Activities and White-Collar Crime
- Conflict Theory and White-Collar Crime
- Explaining White-Collar Crime
- Theories Ignored in the White-Collar Crime Literature
- Integrated Efforts to Explain White-Collar Crime
- Systems Theory

Introduction

In the movie *Office Space,* the workplace experiences of a group of coworkers who are not entirely enthused with their employer are chronicled in a rather humorous manner. The lead character Peter Gibbons, played by Ron Livingston, decides to put in as little effort as possible at his job and is rewarded for this effort with a significant promotion. Later in the movie he and his disgruntled coworkers, who learn they are going to be fired, concoct a scheme to embezzle a small amount of money that should go unnoticed from the company on a regular basis until they have collected millions over time. The plan goes awry when they embezzle a large amount of funds that would be noticed by company officials. Fearing the repercussions that they will experience once they are caught, they write a letter confessing their workplace misconduct and telling where the embezzled funds are located. After they slide their confession under their boss's door, Milton Waddams, another disgruntled coworker, played by movie director Mike Judge, decides to burn the business to the ground because he is fed up with the emotional abuses perpetrated by his bosses. Subsequent scenes show Milton enjoying the spoils of the embezzlement scheme and the offending team moving on in their respective careers.

A close look at the movie shows how various criminological theories can be used to explain the behaviors of workers in the movie. According to Sutherland (1941), "many white-collar crimes are made possible because a businessman holds two or more incompatible and conflicting positions of trust, and is analogous to a football coach who umpires a game in which his own team is playing" (p. 112). In the *Office Space* example, the workers used the trust placed in them by their employers to steal money from company accounts. In reviewing the movie, readers can likely identify how several other theories are relevant to the story line.

Criminological theory is central to the study of white-collar crime. Five comments about using criminological theory to understand and explain white-collar crime will help create a foundation from which readers can gain an appreciation of white-collar crime explanations. First, it is important to stress that theories are potential explanations of behaviors or phenomena. Recall the principle of skepticism discussed in Section I: There are no truths when it comes to social science theories. Or, maybe there is one truth: We do not know for certain what causes white-collar crime. Still, theories are useful because they help us research white-collar crime and determine appropriate responses to the problem.

Second, for white-collar crime explanations to have practical utility, the theories or explanations must point to changes that would reduce (rather than increase) white-collar misconduct. For example, based on his review of the multidimensional causes of white-collar crime, Passas (2001) identified the need to: (1) watch for fraud among high-level managers—especially when competition and corporate pressures are high, (2) develop strong internal control mechanisms to strengthen companies, (3) institutionalize internal and external strategies that can limit the ability of offenders to make excuses for or rationalize their misconduct, (4) improve publicity surrounding incidents of white-collar crime victimization, and (5) increase the amount of accountability given to external auditors. In essence, his explanations for white-collar crime led to specific policy implications.

Third, it is important to realize that multiple factors likely contribute to white-collar crime. We cannot say that one variable or one event automatically leads to white-collar misconduct. Although theories are discussed separately below, the most accurate explanations combine various theoretical assumptions and explanations to address human behavior.

Fourth, a great deal of theory building centers on explaining individual motivations for white-collar crime. Attempts to explain white-collar crime often center on identifying individual motivations for white-collar offending. Consider how two offenders explained their crimes in the following two examples:

- I committed the offenses because I was in financial difficulties. I ended up in debt and due to the personal circumstances with my family and my wife, it meant that I couldn't deal with the debt. I was unable to control our expenditure . . . both the children were at a private school. . . . And I was pressured to pay up to meet the family commitments. . . . I had borrowed lots of money and owed lots of money to friends. My wife was terrified by the idea of debt so I could not share this with her; it would have devastated her so I tried to solve it all by myself. (Gill, 2005, p. 18)
- I was living the high life. I had become a high net worth individual and I was keeping up the lifestyle, cars, spending a lot of money on other people—especially my kids. The greed drove the demand for keeping up a lifestyle and the pride part was that I did not want my family and peers to see me on the rack. . . . I knew I was digging a hole but I felt that something would turn up. I looked at it as a cash flow problem, I knew it was theft. . . . I was fiddling the books to make it look good. I was taking the money from the company . . . the three words that sum it up are lies, pride, and greed. (Gill, 2005, pp. 18–19)

Fifth, while explanatory attempts often focus on individual behavior, it is important to realize that structural variables and macro-level features are also useful in explaining and understanding white-collar crime. Consider, for example, that structural factors of the medical profession have been used to explain health care fraud (Wilson, Lincoln, Chappell, & Fraser, 1986). As well, structural features of other occupations might promote or inhibit white-collar offending in those occupations. Put another way, reasons that one occupational group engages in wrongdoing might be different from the reasons that other occupational groups engage in wrongdoing. Of course, some criminologists would dispute this statement vehemently and suggest that the same phenomena that cause any specific type of crime are that same phenomena that cause all types of crime (Hirschi & Gottfredson, 1987). The key to keep in mind is that micro-level theories will address individual-level motivations for white-collar offending while macro-level theories will address societal factors that contribute to rates of white-collar offending.

Criminologists have devoted a great deal of effort to trying to identify the causes of white-collar crime. In this section, the following topics are addressed to provide readers with a basic understanding about the potential causes of white-collar crime: culture, deterrence theory and rational choice theory, strain theory, learning theory, neutralizing and justifying white-collar crime, control theory, self-control, routine activities theory, conflict theory, explaining corporate crime, theories ignored in the white-collar crime literature, integrated efforts to explain white-collar crime, and systems theory. This should give readers a general understanding of the efforts to explain white-collar misconduct.

Culture and White-Collar Crime

Some criminologists attribute white-collar crime to cultural influences that seemingly promote wrongdoing by workers and corporations. James Coleman (1987), for example, argued that industrial capitalism promotes a "culture of competition." Within the social structure that has developed in our industrialized capitalist society, upper-class workers are presented with various types of opportunities for white-collar crime. Based on this, Coleman suggested that white-collar crime "results from a coincidence of motivation and opportunity." The culture of competition is not just about competing to succeed, it is also reflective of a fear of failing that rests on apparent insecurities individuals have about their careers and their roles in their respective organizations. In effect, workers might bend, or even break, workplace rules in an effort to compete in the workplace.

As evidence of the presence of this culture of competition, consider a study in which Jenkins and Braithwaite (1993) reviewed violations in 410 nursing homes in Australia. They found that for-profit nursing homes had more violations than non-profit nursing homes, and that non-profit homes, when they do commit violations, often do so in response to the broader goals of the nursing home (e.g., their violations result from competing toward the organization's goals).

Greed is an often cited explanation for white-collar misconduct that fits within this notion of a culture of competition. Both practitioners (Miller, 1993) and researchers (Braithwaite, 1991; Robinson & Murphy, 2009) have attributed corporate wrongdoing to greed that stems from cultural influences. Braithwaite (1991) wrote that "greed motivates crime even after a need has been satisfied" (p. 42). Miller (1993), a former federal probation officer who worked extensively with white-collar probationers, wrote the following reflections upon his retirement after a career that spanned 30 years:

> I am often asked what the offenders I supervised had in common. A large portion were professionals—doctors, pharmacists, lawyers, accountants, stockbrokers, and even a few former judges and high-level politicians. And the one common thread I noted, year after year, was greed. . . . This common denominator has changed society's priorities and damaged the nation's value system. One goal now dominates—to achieve material things at any cost. (p. 22)

Tied into this competitive culture is ego-seeking by workers. As Wheeler, Weisburd, Waring, and Bode (1987–1988) wrote, the corporate "ladder is shaped like a pyramid" and competition for advancement becomes stiffer as employees move up the workplace ladder (p. 356). When the competition becomes extremely tight, some individuals might "slip over the boundary of legality" (p. 356). Also reflective of the ties between a competitive culture and greed, a study of 91 companies over a 3-year period found that executive compensation was a factor in manager-controlled firms. In particular, more compensation for executives meant more crime in these firms (Bilimoria, 1995).

Poverty can also be seen as a cultural influence that potentially promotes white-collar crime. Criminologists have long suggested that a culture of poverty is correlated with street crime. Historically, though, it has been assumed that poverty explanations were not relevant in terms of white-collar crime. Indeed, when Sutherland first discussed white-collar crime he rejected poverty explanations as causes of the behavior because poverty, on the surface, does not seem to cause white-collar offending. After all, white-collar offenders are not impoverished. In an effort to broaden our understanding of poverty and crime, criminologist John Braithwaite (1991) has argued that poverty explanations may actually be useful to explain how power is used to perpetrate white-collar crime if one considers the ties between poverty and inequality. He explained:

> When needs are satisfied, further power and wealth enable crime motivated by greed. New types of criminal opportunities and new paths to immunity from accountability are constituted by concentrations of wealth and power. Inequality thus worsens both crimes of poverty motivated by need for goods for use and crimes of wealth motivated by greed enabled by goods for exchange. (p. 43)

In other words, poverty is correlated with both street crime and white-collar crime. For poor individuals, crimes are motivated by a need for goods that arises out of poverty. For white-collar offenders, crimes are motivated by greed, and poverty provides them power to commit offenses. The more powerful that wealthy individuals become, the more pathways they have to white-collar crime, particularly in the face of limited responses to crimes committed by those with power.

Hirschi and Gottfredson (1987) have been extremely critical of cultural theories. On the most basic level, they argue that white-collar crime is far rarer than would be expected if culture actually caused white-collar crime. From their perspective, if a culture of competition or culture of poverty led to white-collar crime, then more professionals should be involved in workplace offending. Most doctors do not commit crime. Most accountants are honest. Most textbook authors do not plagiarize. Most lawyers are ethical. Most investors are law abiding. They also implied that if white-collar crime were caused by cultural values, then coworkers and citizens should be more accepting of the offenders and the offenders would not feel the need to hide their crimes or their criminal identities. To Hirschi and Gottfredson, if white-collar crime emanated from values central to our society, then we would not expect the offenders to experience shame, embarrassment, or stigma when their crimes are exposed.

Deterrence Theory/Rational Choice Theory and White-Collar Crime

Deterrence theory can be traced to Cesare Beccaria's *On Crimes and Punishments*, a work that many have defined as the foundation of the classical school of criminological thought. In this brief work, Beccaria outlined his theory of punishment, which was based on the assumption that punishment can stop individuals from offending. In order for punishment to be effective, however, he argued that it must meet three criteria: (1) punishment must be swift so that the offender links the behavior of crime with the response of punishment in his or her mind, (2) punishment must be certain so that offenders know if a crime is committed then a negative consequence will occur, and (3) punishment must be proportional to the crime so that the punishment outweighs the positive benefits individuals experience from committing crime.

The underlying assumption of deterrence theory is that individuals are rational beings. This assumption has direct bearing for the theory's applicability to white-collar crime. John Braithwaite (1982) wrote: "White-collar criminals are more deterrable than common criminals because their crimes are more rational and calculating and because they have more of all of the things that can be lost through criminal justice sanctions" (Braithwaite, 1982, p. 760). Somewhat in line with this assumed rationality, interviews with judges found that the judges tended to view punishment as necessary in order to deter white-collar misconduct (Pollack & Smith, 1983).

Research by Sally Simpson and various colleagues (Simpson & Koper, 1992; Elis & Simpson, 1995; Piquero, Exum, & Simpson, 2005) has been instrumental in demonstrating how deterrence ideals can be used to explain various forms of workplace misconduct. One of her studies found some evidence that stiffer sanctions might deter corporations from future wrongdoing, though the likelihood of repeat offending in corporate crime cases was found to be more influenced by industry type than sanction severity (Simpson & Koper, 1992). In particular, automobile and oil industry firms were found to be more likely to reoffend than firms in the aircraft industry.

In another study, surveys of 96 business school graduates and executives conducted by Elis and Simpson (1995) examined the importance of punishment threat and morality in preventing corporate misconduct. Their findings showed that risk of informal detection and costs from informal sanctions did not deter corporate misconduct; however, the research team did find four factors that appeared to prevent intentions to commit corporate misconduct: (1) certainty of informal sanctions, (2) beliefs about immorality, (3) corporate climate, and (4) pressures from the boss.

Rational choice theory, the modern variation of deterrence theory, considers the limits of human rationality while still considering humans as rational and suggests that offenders will consider the benefits of offending and weigh those benefits against possible negative consequences that arise from misconduct (Clarke & Cornish, 1985). Piquero, Exum, and Simpson (2005) integrated rational choice theory with the idea of "desire for control" to explain how such a desire influences decision making that may lead to corporate offending. To test this premise, Piquero and her research team surveyed 13 business executives and 33 MBA students. They found that desire for control was related to support for white-collar misconduct. From this finding, they suggested that corporate crime is committed in order to "gain control over environments that are uncertain or irrational" (p. 272). They also found a vicarious effect of internal reprimands. If coworkers were reprimanded, individuals were less likely to indicate intentions to engage in white-collar crime. In addition, they found that informal sanctions deterred intentions to offend, but formal sanction threats did not.

Some authors have used deterrence ideals to speculate why white-collar crime persists. Albrecht and Searcy (2001) attributed white-collar misconduct to a failure to identify the crimes in the workplace, the absence of formal efforts to respond to fraud, and inadequate control mechanisms. Each of these elements has to do with the certainty of punishment: If offenders are not identified, and they know there is little likelihood of getting caught, they will be more likely to engage in workplace misconduct. Other authors have suggested that lenient sanctions promote wrongdoing. For example, one author noted that it is cheaper for some businesses to break the law than it is to abide by the law (Millspaugh, 2001). From this perspective, fines are seen as providing very little deterrent power. Still other authors have suggested that deterrence strategies alone are not enough to prevent white-collar misconduct and that deterrence strategies and theories must consider values of individuals, businesses, and communities (Payne & Gainey, 2004).

✖ Strain Theory and White-Collar Crime

In general, **strain theory** focuses on the way stresses and strains contribute to offending. The source of strain varies across types of strain theories. Some theories point to the social and economic structures as the source of strain, others point to the individual, and others point to the organization. In terms of white-collar offending, three types of strain theories warrant discussion: classical strain theory, institutional anomie theory, and general strain theory.

Classical Strain Theory

Classical strain theory traces the source of strain to interactions between the social and economic structures. As a macro-level theory, classical strain theory addresses how macro-level variables influence individual behavior. Robert Merton (1938) developed his version of strain theory in "Social Structure and Anomie," a brief article published in *American Sociological Review.* Merton based this theory on four assumptions:

- Capitalism promotes financial success as a goal
- Individuals are socialized to follow legitimate means such as working hard and getting an education to meet financial goals
- Some individuals face barriers or strain in their efforts to attain financial success
- When individuals experience strain, they change either the goals or the means to address the strain

Merton's theory was developed to explain why poor individuals engage in crime, and this has led some to question whether the theory can be used to explain crimes by white-collar workers. The assumption of Merton's theory is that being unable to achieve economic success makes some individuals engage in illegitimate activities. White-collar workers have already achieved economic success. As Langton and Piquero (2007) wrote, "the basic focus on the stresses associated with being poor was incompatible with studies of white-collar crime" (Langton & Piquero, 2007, p. 1). Despite this focus of Merton's theory, Langton and Piquero demonstrate how the theory can explain white-collar offending.

According to Merton, five modes of adaptation characterize how individuals adapt to the way goals and means are prescribed (see In Focus 11.1). **Conformists** accept the goals prescribed by society and follow legitimate means to attain the goals. Most white-collar professionals can be characterized as conformists. I am a conformist. I want material success and I am awfully concerned about doing things the right way to attain material success.

In Focus 11.1

Merton's Modes of Adaptation

Mode	Goals	Means
Conformist	Accept	Accept
Innovator	Accept	Reject
Ritualist	Reject	Accept
Retreatist	Reject	Reject
Rebel	Reject/Replace	Reject/Replace

Innovators accept the goal of financial success but replace legitimate means with illegitimate means. Consider how embezzlers steal funds after experiencing strain caused by financial problems (Cressey, 1953; Green, 1990). Or, consider how computer criminals find ways to get around the rules to attain material success. They maintain the goal of financial success, but use illegitimate means to attain their goals.

Ritualists are white-collar workers who do not accept the goals of society but go through the motions of engaging in the means prescribed by society. Companies that violate the law repeatedly and pay fines because the fines are seen as costs of doing business have been described as ritualists (Braithwaite, 1993). These companies go through the motions with regulators in a ritualistic way to make it seem like they are playing by the rules, but in reality they have no intention to actually follow the rules.

Retreatists are white-collar workers who accept neither the goals of society nor the means to attain those goals. Merton noted that this is the least common adaptation. He wrote that retreatists are "*in* the society, but not *of* it" (p. 677). To Merton, ritualists included those with drug and alcohol addictions. One could also suggest that workers who allow their drug and alcohol problems to influence their workplace activities are retreatists. Also, one could point to workers who show up for work but do not do any work as retreatists. They are "*in* the workplace," but they are not a part "*of* the workplace."

Rebels are workers who reject the goals and means of society and replace the societal-prescribed goals and means with their own goals and means. Recall the notion of collective embezzlement developed by Kitty Calavita and her coauthors (Calavita, Pontell, & Tillman, 1997). They described **collective embezzlement** as crime committed by the organization against the organization. Rather than focusing on success as the goal, workers developed failure as the goal so that the governmental insurance programs would bail out the failed business. As I have noted elsewhere, "those participating in collective embezzlement reject the standard goal of success, replace it with the goal of failure, and reject the legitimate ways to attain success" (Payne, 2003b).

Merton's strain theory can be used to understand deviance by Olympic athletes, which, with a bit of a stretch, can be conceptualized as occupational deviance (Payne & Berg, 1999). Most Olympic athletes can be described as conformists—they want success and they work hard in legitimate ways to attain success. Those who use performance enhancing strategies like blood doping and the consumption of illegal substances can be seen as innovators. Ritualists would be those athletes who have little interest in winning or succeeding. Retreatists include former athletes who "drop out of organized sports to become 'beer-belly' softball players" (p. 103) or develop substance abuse problems. Rebels include athletes who defy the rules of the sport and replace the sport's rules with their own. Consider examples of "podium politics" where athletes make symbolic gestures while they are receiving their Olympic medals. Such gestures, prohibited by Olympic rules, are committed with the aim of meeting the athlete's own political or social goals (rather than the Olympic Games' apolitical and pro-social goals). In 1968, for example, gold medalist Tommie Smith and bronze medalist John Carlos were suspended from the U.S. Olympic team after they raised their fists on the Olympic podium to protest against racism.

▲ **Photo 11.1**   Tommie Smith and John Carlos were reprimanded and treated as rebels after they protested racism while receiving their gold and bronze medals in the 1968 Olympic Games.

Institutional Anomie Theory

Another variety of strain theory, **institutional anomie** theory, is a more modern macro-level approach to explaining how societal institutions promote crime (Messner & Rosenfeld, 2007). In *Crime and the American Dream,* Steve Messner and Richard Rosenfeld describe how society promotes values related to financial success but fails to promote values consistent with using legitimate means to attain financial success. Culture, as it is described by the authors, affects societal institutions. Messner and Rosenfeld note that four values central to the American culture are a breeding ground for crime (see Table 11.1). First, the focus on achievement encourages Americans to always want more. Once we achieve a goal, new goals are developed. Second, universalism suggests that everyone should want material success, despite the fact that such a goal is unrealistic. Third, individualism suggests that we should be able to attain our financial goals on our own, which is also unrealistic. Fourth, materialism refers to the way that our society encourages us to be enamored with material goods and the acquisition of the best new products.

Table 11.1 Values That Are Central to the American Dream

Value	What It Means	How It Relates to White-Collar Crime
Achievement	Individuals are socialized to work hard and direct their efforts toward achieving financial goals. Once certain goals are achieved, new goals are developed.	Individuals keep working toward getting more and more. Eventually a fear of failure may cause some individuals to engage in wrongdoing in the workplace.
Universalism	All individuals are encouraged to strive for monetary success regardless of whether that is realistic.	As individuals move up the workplace ladder, advancement becomes more competitive. It is unrealistic to assume that everyone can be promoted. Individuals might engage in wrongdoing to increase their likelihood of advancement.
Individualism	Individuals are socialized to believe that they can succeed on their own.	Efforts to build careers on one's own can be stressful and counterproductive. Individuals might resort to wrongdoing to address the shortfalls of working alone.
Materialism	Individuals are socialized to want material goods.	The desire for better and new goods in order to "keep up with the neighbors" might cause individuals to engage in wrongdoing to have the finances needed to acquire the goods and services, and it may cause corporations to use shortcuts and provide products desired by the public but that are unsafe.

The underlying assumption of institutional anomie theory is that individuals are socialized to succeed at any cost, but not all individuals are (1) given the opportunities to succeed or (2) socialized in how to succeed in legitimate ways. Hence, anomie (e.g., normlessness) exists at the institutional level between the prescription of societal goals and legitimate means. The result of this anomie is unbridled aspirations to "get rich." According to one white-collar crime scholar, "Regardless of their social background and social capital available to them, people are encouraged to desire more than they presently have" (Passas, 2001, p. 122). Describing these aspirations, one author team wrote:

> Monetary success has no limit. There are always possibilities to acquire more. When money has inherent value as it does in America, and a person's "success" is measured in financial terms, there is also no limit to a person's status. American culture perpetuates these assumptions because to do so is productive to its advancement as a corporate nation. If American citizens become satiated with wealth at a certain level, American industry can move no further than this limit. (Trahan, Marquart, & Mullings, 2005, p. 606)

Messner and Rosenfeld's early editions of their work made little mention of white-collar crime, though they began their book with a description of Michael Milken's experiences as a white-collar offender. Schoepfer and Piquero (2006) point out that because institutional anomie theory "assumes that criminal activity relates to the pursuit of monetary success ..., white-collar crimes should not only be able to be explained under this theoretical framework, but also should expand the generalizability of the theory" (p. 228). In later editions,

Messner and Rosenfeld (2007) added a significant amount of discussion about the way white-collar crime was tied to the American dream, and they began their book with a discussion of how the Enron scandal created a foundation for understanding institutional anomie theory. They also noted that "the same social forces that lead to higher levels of serious crime also produce the contrasting social responses to street crime and suite crime" (p. 32).

Schoepfer and Piquero (2006) tested institutional anomie theory through a consideration of embezzlement cases included in the FBI's Uniform Crime Reports in 1991. They used 1990 census data to determine how well structural variables related to institutional anomie predicted embezzlement cases in 1991. The researchers found some support for institutional anomie: more high school dropouts (a sign of increased anomie) meant more embezzlement, and more voters (a sign of decreased anomie) meant less embezzlement.

Institutional anomie theory has also been used to understand victim behavior in white-collar crime cases. Adam Trahan and his research team (2005) used data from a survey of 434 victims of a Ponzi scheme and information from investor files contained in prosecutors' case files to determine how the "American dream" influenced victim behavior. The survey revealed that a desire for money influenced decisions to invest in the scheme for 86% of the victims. Victims found it difficult to believe that they were victimized by a crime, or that the offender had actually done anything criminal. After all, their efforts to invest were simply part of their American dream. The authors concluded:

> The victims of the Ponzi scheme examined here clearly sought financial success with no apparent stopping point. Prior to their involvement in the scheme, they were relatively successful. . . . Some would argue that they had already achieved the American dream. However, the American dream is entirely unattainable because it is always possible to acquire more money, status, and so forth. (p. 616)

General Strain Theory

Developing what is known as **general strain theory,** Robert Agnew (1985, 1992) used a social psychological approach to explain how crime is an adaptation to stress and frustration. Agnew highlighted three sources of strain that could lead to crime:

1. The failure to achieve positively valued goals

2. The removal or expected removal of positively valued stimuli

3. Confronting or expecting to confront negative stimuli

Agnew argued that stress leads to crime if the stress leads to negative affective states, such as anger.

First, the *failure to achieve positively valued goals* could lead to strain. In terms of white-collar crime, not being promoted, given raises, or paid fairly could result in offending. White-collar workers direct a great deal of effort toward meeting the organization's goals. If the organization meets its goals but the worker is not rewarded for his or her efforts in working toward those goals, strain occurs and this strain could result in offending.

Second, *the removal or expected removal of positively valued stimuli* results in strain because individuals must confront losing something they find valuable. With regard to white-collar crime, individuals, who have invested so much in their careers and moved up the organizational ladder, might face stress maintaining their status. Donald Cressey's (1953) classic study on embezzling found that the embezzlers engaged in offending because they developed an "unshareable financial problem." In other words, they lost the amount of "positively valued stimuli" they needed to address their financial needs. Wheeler and his coauthors (Wheeler, Weisburd, & Bode, 1988) noted that the "fear of failing"—the fear of "losing what they have worked so hard to gain" (p. 356)—might lead these offenders to engage in misconduct. They also suggested that these types of offenders feel remorse (or "social pain") when they are caught.

Third, *confronting or expecting to confront negative stimuli* refers to instances where individuals confront negative events in their lives. Those who experience unpleasant work settings, for example, would be more prone to commit misconduct from this perspective (Van Wyk, Benson, & Harris, 2000). Surveys of 1,116 nursing home employees found that employees who reported being abused by patients were more likely to steal from patients and physically abuse them (Van Wyk et al., 2000). The authors found that motivations (confronting negative stimuli) were more important than opportunities because offenders would find or create the opportunities to commit the misconduct if they wanted to.

Langton and Piquero (2007) used data from the "Nature and Sanctions of White-Collar Criminals Study" (see Wheeler, Weisburd, & Bode, 2000) to assess the ties between strain and white-collar offending. They found that the presence of strain was related to financial motivations to offend. In addition, they found that types of strain experienced by white-collar offenders possibly vary across white-collar offenders by status. Lower status white-collar offenders might respond more to one type of strain while higher status white-collar offenders might respond more to other types of strain. For lower status offenders, financial motives seemed to be more likely types of strain. For white-collar offenders, like security violators, strain appeared to be linked more often to the fear of losing one's status. The authors compared this suggestion to Wheeler et al.'s conclusion that a "fear of failing in their professional careers" might lead some upper status workers to engage in wrongdoing.

Learning Theory and White-Collar Crime

Some criminologists have focused on the way that white-collar crime can be understood as learned behavior. The most prominent of these **learning theories** is **differential association theory,** which was developed by Edwin Sutherland. Differential association theory includes a series of nine propositions (see In Focus 11.2) that describe how individuals learn criminal behavior. The general thrust of the theory is that individuals learn from their peers through a process in which they learn how to commit crimes, why to commit those crimes, and why laws restricting those crimes are inappropriate. An often cited example of the way that Sutherland (1949) viewed his differential association theory as explaining crime in the workplace is the comment of a shoe salesman who said that his manager conveyed the following message to him when he was hired:

> My job is to move out shoes, and I hired you to assist in this. I am perfectly glad to fit a person with a pair of shoes if we have his size, but I am willing to misfit him if it is necessary in order to sell him a pair of shoes. I expect you to do the same. If you do not like this, someone else can have your job. While you are working for me, I expect you to have no scruples about how you sell shoes. (p. 238)

In Focus 11.2

Sutherland's Differential Association Theory

1. Criminal behavior is learned.

2. Criminal behavior is learned in interaction with other persons in a process of communication.

3. The principle part of the learning of criminal behavior occurs within intimate personal groups.

4. Learning criminal behavior includes learning the techniques of committing the crime, which are sometimes very complicated and sometimes very simple, and learning the specific direction of motives, drives, rationalizations, and attitudes.

5. The specific direction of motives and drives is learned from perceptions of various aspects of the legal code as being favorable or unfavorable.

6. A person becomes criminal when he or she perceives more favorable than unfavorable consequences to violating the law.

7. Differential associations may vary in frequency, duration, priority, and intensity.

8. The process of learning criminal behavior by association with criminal and anticriminal patterns involves all of the mechanisms involved in any other learning.

9. While criminal behavior is an expression of general needs and values, it is not excused by those general needs and values since noncriminal behavior is also an expression of the same needs and values.

Although Sutherland created both the concept of white-collar crime and the differential association theory, few studies have tested the theory's ability to explain white-collar crime. In one of the few studies, Nicole Piquero and her colleagues (Piquero, Tibbetts, & Blankenship, 2005) used data from a survey of 133 MBA students to see whether the theory would explain students' decisions to market and produce a hypothetical drug that was about to be recalled (and respondents knew this about the drug). They found support for differential association. Decisions to market the drug even though it was going to be recalled were tied more to corporate climate and coworkers' attitudes, and were not tied to connections with peers and friends outside of the workplace. Put simply, if I am Bernie Madoff's coworker, I would be more likely to offend than if I were his friend or family member.

Learning theory is relevant in terms of the skills needed to commit white-collar offenses and the motives for offending. In terms of skills, many white-collar crimes involve "highly complex and technically skilled acts" (Robin, 1974, p. 259). Computer crimes, for example, often require a level of technological skills that many do not possess. Cases of embezzlement involving computers might require a similar level of skills. Physicians need certain skills to commit unnecessary surgery. Researchers need skills to fudge data. In essence, one needs the skill set required to do a job in order to commit crime on that job.

Learning theorists have suggested that in addition to learning the skills to commit white-collar crimes, white-collar offenders learn motives or reasons for committing crime on the job. Some researchers have examined how academic training influences attitudes supportive of white-collar offending. As an illustration, one author team surveyed 350 medical students to examine how the students perceived public health insurance programs and found that "the students viewed Medicare and Medicaid in the same unflattering light as physicians" (Keenan, Brown, Pontell, & Geis, 1985, p. 171). One third of the students attributed health care fraud to structural aspects of health care programs, and many students called for structural changes of the programs to improve the ability of doctors to deliver health care to impoverished groups. What this suggests is that the students had already learned to attribute fraud to an external source even before they became practicing health care professionals. In another study, a survey of 537 students compared MBA students to nonbusiness students and found that the business students "were more likely to be tolerant of business practices with ethical issues "(Yu & Zhang, 2006, p. 185). Business students tended to follow "a law-driven approach to business ethics," which suggests that "if it is legal, it is ethical" (p. 185). Somewhat ironically, the authors suggest that teaching business law classes may result in students becoming more accepting of unethical practices (e.g., if they learn that certain behaviors are technically legal, they would be more supportive of those behaviors regardless of whether the behaviors are ethical).

Learning theory has been criticized on a number of grounds. Some have questioned the source of learning: who did the first "white-collar criminal" learn the skills and motives from (see Martin, Mutchnick, & Austin, 1990)? Randy Martin and his colleagues (1990) also note that learning theory, differential association in particular, is difficult to test empirically. Researchers have also found that the actual relevance of learning from coworkers is overstated. Research by Spahr and Alison (2004) on 481 fraud offenders found that most offenders worked alone, and when there were collaborators, the co-offenders tended to come from outside of the white-collar offenders' workplace.

Neutralizing and Justifying White-Collar Crime

Neutralization theory was developed by Gresham Sykes and David Matza (see Matza, 1964; Sykes & Matza, 1957) in an effort to explain how juvenile delinquents drift in and out of delinquent behavior. They argued that juveniles understand right from wrong and that before they commit delinquent acts they neutralize or rationalize their behavior as appropriate. Researchers have highlighted the difference between neutralization and accounts. Neutralizations occur before the criminal act and provide offenders with the mental strength they need to commit the crime. Accounts are offered after the act and allow the offender to minimize the criminal label (Benson, 1985a). After showing how neutralizations are used to commit white-collar misconduct, attention will be given to the types of accounts offered by white-collar offenders to describe their behaviors and the purposes served by these accounts.

Neutralizations and White-Collar Offending

Sykes and Matza (1957) described five techniques of neutralization they believed juveniles used to rationalize their misconduct. Given that white-collar workers are rational beings, it is plausible that white-collar offenders use similar types of neutralizations. First, **denial of injury** refers to situations where offenders justify their actions on the grounds that no one was harmed or injured as a result of their misconduct. One study found that individuals neutralized the marketing of unsafe products by suggesting that the government overstates the degree of harm to consumers (Piquero, Tibbetts, & Blankenship, 2005).

Denial of victim refers to situations where the offenders convince themselves that victims deserve the harm they experience. As an illustration, Bernie Madoff told a fellow inmate about his misdeeds: "F*ck my victims. I carried them for 20 years and now I'm doing 150 years" (Ruiz, 2010, n.p.). In embezzlement cases, this denial arises when offenders convince themselves that "the victim mistreated the offender and deserved to be victimized, the money belonged to the offender anyway" (Green, 1993, p. 102).

Appeal to higher loyalties neutralizations occur when offenders justify their wrongdoing by suggesting that the misbehavior was done for the good of a larger group. Instances where white-collar offenders attribute their misdeeds to efforts to help their company make a profit are indicative of an appeal to a higher loyalty (Piquero, Tibbetts, & Blankenship, 2005). As another example, situations where prosecutors allow witnesses to lie on the grounds that the lie will help achieve justice can be seen as appeals to higher loyalties. In these cases, prosecutors possibly "neutralize misconduct because they believe they are prosecuting guilty defendants" (Schoenfeld, 2005, p. 258).

Denial of responsibility refers to situations where offenders neutralize their behaviors by suggesting that they are not responsible for their misconduct. An auto repair shop owner, for example, told a colleague: "You can't be honest in this business and make a decent living" (Seibel, 2009, n.p.). In another example, an offender involved in a complex fraud told investigators, "My mandate was to keep the bank running until a final solution to the financial problems is found. That was the mandate given to me by the president ... when the security is involved ... you do not always go by the rule of the book" (Passas, 2001, p. 130).

Condemnation of condemners is a neutralization where offenders blame the criminal justice and social control systems for their misdeeds. They argue that those who are persecuting them for their misdeeds also engage in wrongdoing. This rationalization is closely aligned with "claims that everyone does it" rationalizations. In addition, from their perspective, lenience would be a natural response from a system that is perceived to be run by individuals who engage in misconduct themselves. One offender convicted after defrauding victims in a $14 million commodities fraud scheme said that "he deserved mercy for helping fellow alcoholics like himself" ("Kingpin of Commodities Fraud," 2006).

Several studies have considered how different types of white-collar offenders justify their misdeeds with neutralizations. Research shows that older individuals are more likely to neutralize their misconduct than younger workers are (Piquero, Tibbetts, & Blankenship, 2005). Research also shows that workers learn the types of rationalizations to use on the job from their coworkers (Dabney, 1995).

One team of researchers conducted an ethnographic study using participant observation, in-depth interviews, and survey methodologies to examine how speech therapists, occupational therapists, and physical therapists neutralized Medicaid fraud (Evans & Porche, 2005). Findings showed that "claims everyone else does it" were the most common neutralizations offered. Denials of responsibility and injury were the second and third most commonly used types of neutralization. Table 11.2 shows how these different neutralizations were offered by health care providers in situations when the providers billed for more time than was actually provided to the care recipient (e.g., they would bill for an hour after spending only 45 minutes with the patient) or submitted individual bills after providing group services.

An ethnographic study of three private veterinary practices over a 5-year time span focused on "ethical lapses" made by workers in this industry and the role of various neutralizations in promoting these misdeeds (Gauthier, 2001). The study found evidence of rationalizations paralleling those offered by Sykes and Matza (1957). For example, similar to a denial of responsibility, the defense of necessity was found to be "the primary justification invoked for professional lapses" (Gauthier, 2001, p. 475). This defense was frequently used to justify dishonest billing procedures. For instance, in one case a veterinarian billed a client for euthanizing a dog when the dog had in fact died on its own. The vet wanted the dog owner to feel like the owner had made the decision to put the dog down.

Gauthier also found claims of "everyone else is doing it," particularly with regard to price fixing. The vets also engaged in denial of injury, denial of victim, claims of entitlement, condemnation of condemners, and appeal to higher loyalties. In the latter case, Gauthier provides the example of billing for euthanizing a healthy animal when in fact the vet had put the pet up for adoption. Gauthier suggested this happened on

Table 11.2 Neutralizations Offered by Speech, Occupational, and Physical Therapists

Neutralization	Verbatim Comments Quoted by Evans and Porche (2005)
Everyone does it	• I feel it is very accepted around here. You see it all the time. • I think it is very acceptable. It may not be right, but we all do it. (p. 260)
Denial of responsibility	• Sometimes the patient just won't work with you, especially if their family is visiting. Patients' families really interfere also. • Sometimes my patients are sick and coughing all over so I cut the session short. Other times they are just uncooperative. (p. 262)
Denial of injury	• It's not like the patients care when I end their session 5 or 10 minutes early. Most of them are eager to leave and get back to their family or the activities the nursing home has going on. • Besides, we do actually give each patient individual attention. The patients are still getting their therapy. (p. 265)

at least a few occasions. In these cases, vets did not believe it was appropriate to put down a healthy animal and their loyalty to animals led them to not euthanize the animal, even though they billed for it.

Criminologist Dean Dabney (1995) interviewed 25 nurses with an aim to identifying how differential association, social learning, and neutralization theories work together to explain deviance by nurses. His interviews showed a significant amount of deviance (23 reported engaging in theft and all 25 said they saw their coworkers steal). Items stolen included supplies, over-the-counter medicines, and narcotics. Comments from the nurses suggested that neutralizations are learned from the workgroup "through an informal socialization process" (p. 328), and nurses used the neutralizations before committing a deviant act. They also used the neutralizations to condone misconduct by their peers.

Accounts and White-Collar Crime

While offenders use neutralizations to give them the mental fortitude to engage in wrongdoing, accounts are offered after the fact to describe their behaviors. An account is "a statement made by a social actor to explain unanticipated or untoward behavior" (Scott & Lyman, 1968, p. 46). Three types of accounts exist: denials, justifications, and excuses. Denials involve situations where offenders deny a specific aspect of the crime: They deny that they committed the crime or they deny knowing anything about the crime. Types of denials attributed to white-collar offenders include the following:

- Denial of crime: offenders say they did not commit the crime they are accused of
- Denial of fact: offenders deny specific aspects of the crime
- Denial of awareness: offenders indicate that they did not understand that their actions were violations of workplace rules
- Denial of guilt: offenders admit doing something but deny that the action was criminal (Payne, 2003b)

The denial of guilt may be particularly common among white-collar offenders. For example, former governor of Illinois Rod Blagojevich was convicted of using his position as governor of Illinois to "sell off" Barack Obama's Senate seat, which he was charged with filling after Obama was elected president. Blagojevich never denied having conversations about filling the seat. He argued that his actions were "business as usual" in the political arena and that he was being persecuted. As another example, John Rigas, the former chairman of Adelphia Communications, was sentenced to 15 years in prison for fraudulent accounting practices. After his conviction, he maintained that his case was not "about fraud" (Cauley, 2007). He told a reporter, "because you know, there was no fraud.... It was a case of being in the wrong place at the wrong time. If this had happened a year before, there wouldn't have been any headlines" (Cauley, 2007).

Interviews with 30 white-collar offenders by Benson (1985a) focused on the types of denials offered by white-collar offenders for their misconduct. Within the context of "denying the guilty mind," Benson showed how different types of white-collar offenders used different denials that, on the surface, seemed to be tied to the nature of each occupation where the misdeeds occurred. Antitrust offenders, for example, told Benson about the "everyday character and historical continuity of their offenses" (p. 591). They described their actions as "blameless," and condemned prosecutors, while showing how their alleged crimes were not like street crime. Tax offenders, on the other hand, commonly made claims that everyone engages in the offenses. Those who committed financial trust violations were more likely to accept responsibility for their behavior. Fraud and false statement offenders denied "committing any crime at all," and suggested that prosecutors were politically motivated and inept. Because of the nature of fraud, Benson suggested that "defrauders are most prone to denying any crime at all" (p. 597). The nature of fraud is such that offenders lie to commit the crime. They continue to lie after the crime in an attempt to conceal their offending.

In contrast to denials where offenders reject responsibility for the act, justifications are "accounts in which one accepts responsibility for the act in question but denies the pejorative quality associated with it" (Scott & Lyman, 1968, p. 47). Types of justifications offered by white-collar offenders include:

- Denial of law: professionals describe the law as unfair (Coleman, 1994)
- Defense of entitlement: workers indicate that they are underpaid, overworked, and entitled to the funds
- Borrowing: workers say that they planned to return the money (Coleman, 1987)
- Metaphor of the ledger: workers suggest that occasional wrongdoings are okay (Minor, 1981)
- Denial of wrongfulness: offenders suggest that there was nothing wrong with their behavior (Payne, 2003b)

Excuses are different from justifications and denials. Scott and Lyman (1968) defined excuses as "socially approved vocabularies for mitigating or relieving responsibility" (p. 47). Examples of excuses Scott and Lyman described that are relevant to white-collar crime include appeal to accidents, appeal to defeasibility, and scapegoating. Appeal to accidents refers to excuses where offenders describe the outcome as an accident. The portrayal of the BP oil spill by BP executives and the way that OSHA violations are constructed as accidents are examples of the "appeal to accidents" excuse type.

Appeal to defeasibility includes situations where offenders deny intent, deny knowledge, or minimize the harm surrounding the offense. Consider a case where a white-collar offender said, "I would never have done this business if I wasn't told by my lawyers that it was legal. I didn't believe in my heart of hearts that I did anything wrong" ("Kingpin of Commodities Fraud," 2006). At his sentencing, Madoff tried to minimize his intent. He told the court: "When I began the Ponzi scheme, I believed it would end shortly and I would be able to extricate myself and my clients. But, that ended up being impossible" (Healy, 2009b).

Scapegoating refers to excuses where white-collar offenders blame others for their wrongdoing. In some cases, for example, white-collar offenders blame their billing directors and administrative staff for wrongdoing. Also, cases where corporate executives blame lower level workers or "disgruntled" workers for corporate harm can be seen as examples of scapegoating.

Gibson (2000) discussed four types of excuses that workers make for workplace misconduct. These excuses include:

- "I was told to do it" (let's call this the authority excuse)
- "Everybody is doing it" (we can call this the institutional excuse)
- "My actions won't make a difference" (this can be called the minimization excuse)
- "It's not my problem" (the ostrich excuse)

Those who use the authority excuse might actually believe that their misconduct was the result of their being ordered by their boss to engage in the wrongful behavior. Gibson (2002) cites the power of authority as demonstrated in Stanly Milgram's *Obedience to Authority* study as an example of this power.

With regard to institutional excuses, Gibson notes that offenders know their actions are wrong, so they look around the workplace to find others who are engaging in similar acts. The minimization excuse parallels Sykes and Matza's (1957) denial of injury neutralization. Finally, the "ostrich" excuse refers to situations where workers ignore their coworkers' misdeeds because they believe that is not their responsibility to stop misconduct.

Purposes of Rationalizations and Accounts

Rationalizations and accounts serve four purposes for white-collar offenders (Payne, 2003b). First, given that white-collar offenders know right from wrong, rationalizing behavior allows then to engage in behavioral drifting: they can drift in and out of acceptable and unacceptable behavioral patterns (see Matza, 1964). Second, rationalizations and accounts promote intrinsic identity management, which simply means that they allow offenders to "maintain a positive self image" (Payne, 2003b). Third, rationalizations and accounts also promote extrinsic identity management, meaning that offenders are able to control that others see them in a positive way. Fourth, accounts allow offenders to try to minimize the types of sanctions given to them. In effect, by making excuses or using justifications, offenders can avoid punishment, reduce the sanction, and delay the sanction altogether (Payne, 2003b).

Control Theory and White-Collar Crime

Control theory approaches the question of crime causation somewhat differently than other criminological theories. Rather than asking "why do people commit crime," the question from a control theory perspective is "why don't people commit crime" (Hirschi, 1969). Travis Hirschi (1969) answered this question in *Causes of Delinquency* by suggesting that individuals' bonds to society keep them from engaging in criminal behavior. According to Hirschi, four elements make up an individual's bond to society: attachment, belief, involvement, and commitment. Attachment refers to the degree of attachment that individuals have to their parents, schools, and other pro-social institutions. Belief refers to whether individuals believe in social rules and laws. Involvement refers to whether individuals are involved in pro-social activities, because those who are would have less time to commit criminal or delinquent acts. Commitment refers to whether individuals are committed to the values and goals prescribed by society. According to Hirschi, society is largely organized around conventional behavior, with supports and rewards given to promote conventional behavior. The theory is quite simple—the stronger an individual's societal bond is, the less likely the person will engage in criminal behavior; the weaker the bond, the more likely criminal behavior will follow. Hirschi's research confirmed his theory with the exception of his focus on involvement. He found that involvement in pro-social activities does not reduce likelihood of offending, possibly because it does not take that much time to commit a crime.

Finding that involvement in pro-social activities does not reduce criminal activities has direct implications for applying his theory to crime in the workplace. In particular, having a job is a pro-social activity, yet the fact that one has a job does not reduce the likelihood that one will commit a white-collar crime. In fact, the very definition of white-collar crime requires that individuals have jobs at which to commit crimes. Also, one does not have to be involved in a number of outside activities in order to keep from engaging in white-collar crime (Makkai & Braithwaite, 1991).

Lasley (1988) conducted surveys of 435 executives employed by a large multinational auto manufacturing company to consider how well Hirschi's control theory explained white-collar crime. He used Hirschi's theory to develop four "theorems of white-collar offending." These theorems included:

- Executives with stronger attachments to their company and coworkers will have lower workplace offending rates.
- Executives with stronger commitments to "lines of action" will have lower workplace offending rates.
- Executives with stronger involvement in corporate activities will be less likely to engage in white-collar crime.
- Executives who believe in workplace rules will be less likely to violate those rules.

The results of Lasley's (1988) study showed support for Hirschi's control theory. Executives with stronger (1) attachments to their corporation, (2) commitment to "corporate lines of action," (3) stronger involvement in corporate activities, and (4) stronger belief in organizational rules were less likely to commit white-collar crime. Lasley emphasized the importance of attachment to one's organization (or the lack of attachment) as being problematic for organizations. He wrote,

> It cannot be denied, in most cases, that unpleasant attitudes held by an executive toward his or her employing organization will result in some denial of legitimacy of the controlling organization's rules and policies. For some, white-collar criminality may even be a means for relieving organizational pressures brought about by unpleasant working conditions. (p. 359)

Not all studies have found support for an application of control theory to explain white-collar crime. One study found that white-collar offenders have stronger social bonds to society as is evidenced through participation in religious activities and membership in community organizations (Benson & Kerley, 2001). To some, bonds to a company might actually promote lawbreaking rather than inhibit it. This would be particularly likely in cases where individuals commit crime on behalf of their business. Some regard loyalty as central to corporate decision making. According to Robinson and Murphy (2009), "the reason loyalty is so important . . . is simple: loyalty means moving up in the corporate organization; disloyalty means failing" (p. 63).

Self-Control Theory and White-Collar Crime

Self-control theory was created by Michael Gottfredson and Travis Hirschi (1990), who argued in *A General Theory of Crime* that all types of crime were caused by the presence of low self-control. Self-control was described by the theorists as "the individual characteristic relevant to the commission of criminal acts" (p. 88). They characterized individuals with low self-control as "impulsive, insensitive, physical (as opposed to mental), risk-taking, short-sighted, and non-verbal" (p. 90). According to Gottfredson and Hirschi, self-control levels are tied to parenting, with bad parenting resulting in low self-control, and levels of self-control are stable throughout one's life after early childhood.

The authors put a great deal of effort into arguing that their theory explains white-collar crime and street crime, and they critiqued white-collar crime theories for being narrow in scope (see Hirschi & Gottfredson, 1987). In their first effort to describe how their general theory of crime explained white-collar crime, the authors used the concept of "criminality" to describe what is now known as self-control. They wrote that

> criminality is the tendency of individuals to pursue short-term gratification with little consideration for the long-term consequences of their act. . . . People high on this tendency are relatively unable or unwilling to delay gratification; they are relatively indifferent to punishment and to the interests of others. (p. 960)

As evidence of the ties between criminality and white-collar crime, and their suggestion that white-collar crime and street crime are caused by criminality, Hirschi and Gottfredson compared arrest data for fraud and embezzlement with murder arrests. They suggested that similar age distributions for offenders across offense types showed evidence for a general theory, with their premise being that "a major correlate of ordinary crime is similarly correlated with white-collar crime" (p. 966). They also compared gender and race data for the three offense types and found that arrest rates were similar across the offenses.

Hirschi and Gottfredson (1987) were extremely critical of white-collar crime theories that explained the behavior by focusing on the nature of the occupation rather than the characteristics of the individual offender. They argued that focusing on motives and opportunities limited to the workplace "confuse[s] social location with social causation" (p. 971). In their view, the cause of white-collar crime lies within the individual: Those with low self-control should be more prone to engage in white-collar misconduct. They also suggested that when low self-control interacts with opportunity, misconduct results (Gottfredson & Hirschi, 1990).

Several different studies have examined the utility of self-control theory in explaining various forms of occupational misconduct. Some of these studies offer support for self-control theory's applicability to white-collar crime. For example, one study found that low self-control of corporate managers was tied to corporate crime (Mon, 2002). As well, a study of 522 "fraud" and "force" offenders examined the self-control levels of the offenders and found that lower levels of self-control were more likely among those who committed more offenses (Longshore & Turner, 1998). The authors of this study found an important distinction between the two offense types: self-control was tied to fraud by the presence of criminal opportunity, but opportunity was not a factor in force crimes. In another study, surveys of 342 undergraduates revealed that the tie between low self-control and digital piracy was mediated by learning theory (Higgins, Fell, & Wilson, 2006). The authors suggested that those with low self-control must learn how to commit white-collar crimes, and they must also be presented with opportunities to offend.

Alternatively, research by Grasmick, Tittle, Bursik, and Arneklev (1993) found that self-control predicted fraud, but the presence of opportunity had independent effects on fraud. They noted that opportunity is tied to social structure and that their findings "direct attention back toward features of the social environment that influence the number and distribution of criminal opportunities" (p. 24). The authors suggested that researchers look more closely at motivations and caution not to assume that motivations are the same for all low self-control offenders.

In addition to being linked to offending, low self-control has been described as "a powerful predictor of victimization" (Holtfreter, Reisig, & Pratt, 2008, p. 208). In terms of white-collar crime victimization, a study of 922 Florida residents by Holtfreter and her colleagues found that low self-control increases consumers' risks of fraud victimization. The authors explained that "individuals who lack self-control tend to make impulsive decisions that are associated with negative life outcomes" (p. 207).

Some studies offer mixed support for using self-control theory to explain white-collar crime. Benson and Moore (1992) analyzed presentence reports to compare 2,462 convicted white-collar offenders to 1,986 convicted conventional offenders, all of whom were convicted in federal court between 1973 and 1978. Addressing Gottfredson and Hirschi's assumption that white-collar offenders and conventional offenders share similar characteristics, Benson and Moore uncovered several differences between the two types of offenders. For instance, white-collar offenders exhibited fewer past problems in school and less excessive drinking. However, they found that white-collar offenders with more extensive criminal histories were, in fact, similar to conventional offenders.

Based on their findings, Benson and Moore suggested that self-control operates differently based on circumstances and situational factors. First, some occupational offenders with low self-control levels engage in misconduct just as conventional offenders do. These offenders commit criminal and delinquent acts somewhat frequently in the workplace. Second, high self-control offenders commit white-collar crime in order to meet organizational/economic goals that arise from our culture of competition. Third, opportunistic self-control offenders engage in misconduct as a result of personal situations (like unshareable financial problems) and do so only when opportunities are presented. Benson and Moore (1992) described this group of offenders in the following way: "If their positions in life are somehow threatened, a formerly adequate level of self-control may become inadequate and criminal opportunities that once were resisted are now accepted" (p. 257).

At least a handful of studies have found virtually no support for using self-control theory to explain various types of white-collar crime. For example, research shows that the theory does not explain corporate offending (Simpson & Piquero, 2002). Also, surveys of 1,116 nursing home workers found that self-control was not related to occupational offending in cases of theft or patient abuse (Van Wyk et al., 2000). In a more recent study, N. L. Piquero and her coauthors (Piquero, Schoepfer, & Langton, 2010) surveyed 87 working adults enrolled in business courses using a vignette survey to determine how well self-control and desire for control explained "intentions to destroy damaging workplace documents" (p. 640). While they found that desire for control predicted intentions to offend, they also found that self-control level was not a significant predictor of offending intentions. They suggested that "self-control offers little by way of helping criminologists better understand corporate offending" (p. 642).

Several criticisms have been cited regarding the theory's application to white-collar crime. In general, these criticisms can be classified as conceptualization issues, empirical concerns, and problems with logical consistency. With regard to conceptualization issues, scholars have noted that Gottfredson and Hirschi conceptualize crime as an irrational act, though white-collar crime is generally rational behavior (Simpson

& Piquero, 2002). Also, Gottfredson and Hirschi have been critiqued for oversimplifying the complex nature of white-collar crime in their efforts to conceptualize the relationship between self-control and workplace offending (Geis, 2000; Simpson & Piquero, 2002). Criminologist Gilbert Geis (2000) noted the complexities of explaining white-collar crime and highlighted the fact that many workplace decisions are driven by complex organizational processes and structural factors. He said, "to say an absence of self-control prods the decisions of top-level business officers who violate the law is to trivialize the roots of their actions" (p. 44).

Empirical criticisms of Gottfredson and Hirschi's efforts to explain white-collar crime as based on self-control centered on the way that the authors operationalized white-collar offending (Geis, 2000; Reed & Yeager, 1996). In particular, their reliance on arrest data, and their focus on the offenses of fraud and embezzlement, was seen as both narrowly and ambiguously defining white-collar crime. Their empirical effort was regarded as narrow because it focused only on arrests (excluding acts that did not result in arrests) for two specific types of offenses. Their effort was also seen as ambiguous because many offenders arrested for these crimes were likely not actually white-collar offenders.

Self-control theory's application to white-collar crime has also been criticized on the grounds of logical consistency. In effect, it is illogical to some to suggest that white-collar crime can be caused by low self-control because most white-collar workers would not achieve their levels of status unless they possess high self-control (Piquero, Exum, & Simpson, 2005; Spahr & Alison, 2004). Employees higher up in the workplace theoretically should have higher levels of self-control and more job stability, and they tend to be older than conventional offenders described by Gottfredson and Hirschi (Spahr & Alison, 2004). In other words, white-collar offenders are different from conventional offenders.

Gottfredson and Hirschi (1990) addressed the issue of whether executives have high levels of self-control by critiquing white-collar crime studies. They noted that their theory would not predict a great deal of offending by white-collar employees because they recognized that most white-collar employees need a high level of self-control in order to ascend up the workplace ladder. They suggested that some white-collar crime authors misinterpret statistics and exaggerate the extent of the problem to make white-collar crime seem more prevalent than it actually is. They also follow a strictly "legal" approach in defining white-collar crime.

Routine Activities Theory and White-Collar Crime

Routine activities theory was developed by Cohen and Felson (1979) as a structural theory to explain how different societal changes work together to impact crime rates. In particular, the theorists contended that crime occurs when the following three elements exist at the same time and place: (1) the presence of motivated offenders, (2) the absence of capable guardians, and (3) the availability of suitable targets. As an example of their theory, they described how changes in the 1960s involving more televisions in homes (as a result of technological influences) and fewer individuals at home during the day (as a result of more women entering careers) resulted in an increase in burglaries by motivated offenders.

Various features of different types of white-collar crime discussed earlier in this text can be understood through an application of routine activities theory. Consider, for example, the following:

- A decrease in the number of workers in retail settings means that more workers are working alone in retail jobs. This means that there will not be as many capable guardians available to keep the workers from engaging in misconduct.

- The number of individuals injured in the workplace decreased significantly between 2007 and 2010. This decrease is potentially attributed to fewer individuals in manufacturing jobs. This means that there are fewer vulnerable targets for workplace injuries.
- With a downturn in the economy, businesses have been forced to become more competitive. This may mean that some businesses are more motivated to engage in wrongdoing such as false advertising or price fixing.

The theory is particularly useful for analyzing specific occupational situations to determine the likelihood of workplace crime. For example, experts have noted that the "presence of other employees close by is assumed to act as a form of guardianship" (Van Wyk et al., 2000, p. 35). In addition, research has shown that higher rates of unemployment are tied to lower rates of embezzlement (suggesting there a fewer motivated offenders available to embezzle when fewer individuals are employed) (Schoepfer & Piquero, 2006). Also, researchers have noted that consumers who engage in certain types of risky behaviors (like remote buying on the phone or Internet) are more at risk for fraud victimization (Holtfreter, Reisig, & Pratt, 2008). As well, scholars have used the theory as a guide to determine how vulnerable different groups are for white-collar victimization and which strategies to use to reduce vulnerability (either by developing capable guardians or limiting the presence of motivated offenders).

▲ **Photo 11.2** Security cameras may be useful for stopping some types of offenses, but their utility in stopping many types of crimes by executives is limited.

Several researchers have suggested that elderly persons are more likely to be vulnerable targets or "attractive targets for consumer fraud" (Braithwaite, 1989b, citing research by Fattah & Sacco, 1989). A study of **medical fraud** found that the vast majority of the fraudulent acts were "directed at elderly persons, regardless of whether they were receiving therapy in nursing homes, hospitals, or through home health agencies" (Evans & Porche, 2005, p. 266). Evans and Porche went on to state, "This population seemed to be viewed as the ideal population to defraud," primarily because they are seen as unlikely to report fraud.

Because of these age-related vulnerabilities, it should not be surprising that the theory has been used to address crimes in nursing homes (see Payne & Burke-Fletcher, 2005). Randy Gainey and I (see Payne & Gainey, 2006) used routine activities theory as a guide to understanding the nature of crime and victimization in a sample of 801 cases of patient abuse perpetrated by different types of occupational offenders against nursing home residents. Our research found that the image of a stressed worker as a "motivated offender" mischaracterized the apparent dynamics underlying these offenses. We identified three types of motivated offenders:

- The *serial abuser* committed multiple offenses. Serial abusers were identified in 47.9% of the cases where motivation could be assessed.
- The *pathological tormentor* committed offenses to torment or control the victim. This involved 27.5% of the cases.
- The *stressed out caregiver* appeared to commit abuse as a reaction to something the patient did to the worker. Just under one fourth of the offenders were characterized this way.

While stress played a role in less than a fourth of the cases as a motivation for offending, in three fourths of the cases, offenders were motivated by other factors, including histories of employee misconduct and the desire to torment patients. Here are two case descriptions of motivated offenders that we categorized as pathological tormentors:

- An aide "taped a resident's buttocks together with masking tape" (*Medicaid Fraud Reports,* March, 1996, p. 10).
- "A certified nursing assistant found the . . . resident with a washcloth stuffed inside her tracheotomy mask, which effectively cut off her oxygen supply. . . . Interviews with employees placed defendant in the resident's room approximately ten minutes prior to the discovery of the washcloth. [The aide] was not assigned to this resident and was under orders she was not to care for the resident because of past incidents. . . . Interviews with facility employees stated the parents of the victim would leave a note on a chalk board in the victim's room saying, "Terri, we love you." When the family would leave, [the aide] would go into the victim's room and erase the message. Employees have seen her turn the television set away from the resident so she could not see the screen and turn family photographs face-down so the resident could not see the photographs" (*Medicaid Fraud Reports,* September, 1998, p. 13).

From our analysis, we characterized vulnerable targets based on their age (older patients had increased vulnerability) and presence of cognitive impairments (which also increased vulnerability). We focused on the presence of mandatory reporting laws, which require officials to report suspected cases of elder abuse, and on penalty enhancement laws, which provide for stiffer penalties for those who abuse the elderly. Our analysis suggested that mandatory reporting laws did not affect victimization rates, and states with penalty enhancement statutes actually gave shorter prison/jail sentences than those states without the statutes. This finding calls into question whether certain types of policies can be seen as capable guardians.

Conflict Theory and White-Collar Crime

Conflict theorists explain white-collar crime from a more critical perspective, focusing on the way that those with power exert influence in order to use the law as an instrument of power. Several different types of conflict theory exist, including but not limited to Marxist conflict theory, conservative conflict theory, radical conflict theory, anarchist criminology, left realist theory, feminist criminology, critical criminological theory, and peacemaking criminology (Bohm & Vogel, 2011; Williams & McShane, 2009). These theories tend to be macro-level theories, focusing on the way institutional forces (controlled by those with power) shape wrongdoing. While various themes are presented with these different types of conflict theories, one common theme is an assumption that power differences between classes (upper vs. lower) result in differential treatment of those without power.

Richard Quinney's (1974) *The Social Reality of Crime* is a classic work that accurately shows how class differences potentially result in differential applications of the law. In this work, Quinney outlines six propositions that demonstrate how the powerful classes exert their power to define behaviors as criminal. These propositions include:

Proposition 1: Definition of crime: Crime is a definition of human conduct that is created by authorized agents in a politically organized society.

Proposition 2: Formulation of criminal definitions: Criminal definitions describe behaviors that conflict with the interests of the segments of society that have the power to shape public policy.

Proposition 3: Application of criminal definitions: Criminal definitions are applied by the segments of society that have the power to shape the enforcement and administration of criminal law.

Proposition 4: Development of behavior patterns in relation to criminal definitions: Behavior patterns are structured in segmentally organized society in relation to criminal definitions, and with this context persons engage in actions that have relative probabilities of being defined as criminal.

Proposition 5: Construction of criminal conceptions: Conceptions of crime are constructed and diffused in the segments of society by various means of communication.

Proposition 6: The social reality of crime: The social reality of crime is constructed by the formulation and application of criminal definitions, the development of behavior patterns related to criminal definitions, and the construction of criminal conceptions (Quinney, 1974, pp. 15–23, as cited in Martin et al., 1990, pp. 389–390)

Quinney's thesis is that powerful classes use the law to exert influence over less powerful classes. In particular, the way law is developed, enforced, and applied is seen as a tool for increasing the amount of power that controlling groups have over minority groups. This assumption parallels many aspects of white-collar crime. Consider that many types of white-collar offending are not typically defined as criminally illegal. Doctors, for example, do not go to jail for making medical errors. Corporate executives are not sent to prison for creating unsafe products. Environmental pollution is defined as a cost of doing business and those exposed to the pollutants are defined as unfortunate, but are not defined as crime victims. As criminologist Ronald Kramer and his colleagues (Kramer, Michalowski, & Kauzlarich, 2002) note, "the social process of naming crime is significantly shaped by those who enjoy the economic and political power to ensure that the naming of crime . . . will reflect . . . their worldview and interests" (p. 266).

Conflict theorists are concerned not only with how crime is defined, they are also concerned with how crime is perceived and addressed by criminal justice officials. With regard to perceptions about crime, conflict theorists would draw attention to the misguided perception that white-collar offenders are less serious offenders than conventional offenders. For example, some criminal justice officials have justified shorter prison sentences for white-collar offenders in the following two ways: (1) "prison is much harder" on white-collar offenders than it is on conventional offenders, and (2) "it is not class bias to consider prison a greater hardship for the middle class because the loss of reputation is very serious" (Pollack & Smith, 1983, p. 178). To conflict theorists, such perceptions are inaccurate, unfair, and reflective of the influence that powerful classes have over those that are less powerful.

In a similar way, conflict theorists are critical of the criminal justice system's response to white-collar offending. Some criticize the system for punishing white-collar offenders too leniently; though it will be shown in a later section that convicted white-collar offenders may not be receiving as lenient sentences as believed. Others point out that most white-collar offenders commit a "prison escape" by preventing their cases being brought into the criminal justice system in the first place (Gerber, 1994). Conflict theorists also point out that the overemphasis on street crimes (like the war on drugs) and lack of emphasis on white-collar crimes are indicative of unfair treatment of less powerful groups.

More than a quarter of a century ago, Kramer (1984) pointed to six proposals to control corporate crime that had been identified in studies conducted between 1975 and 1982. Quoted verbatim from Kramer, these proposals included:

- New criminal laws that deal specifically with harmful actions engaged in by corporate (organizational) entities;

- The adoption of a proactive enforcement stance with regard to corporate crime;
- The creation of special corporate crime units within enforcement agencies;
- Changing the law to make it easier to convict corporations in a criminal court;
- Increasing the level of fines for corporations;
- The creation of new sanctions which penetrate the corporate structure, that is, reach inside and attempt to restructure its management structure and decision making process. (p. 9)

Those approaching white-collar crime from a conflict theory orientation would note that only one of these six proposals has been fulfilled over the past three decades: the size of fines has increased. Interestingly, these fines can be used by the criminal justice system to increase the power that it has over less powerful groups. Indeed, one could envision a study concluding this year with these same implications. In effect, conflict theorists draw attention to the apparent lack of interest that some officials have in treating behaviors "close to home" as criminal behavior.

Explaining Corporate Crime

Thus far, the discussion of theories has focused primarily on explaining individual behavior in white-collar crimes. Recall from the discussion in the corporate crime section that in some cases the crime is committed either by the organization or for the good of the organization. The nature of corporate crime is such that individual-level variables may not sufficiently explain the misconduct. As a result, several theorists have devoted specific attention to explaining corporate crime. One thing is clear from these efforts— while it is difficult to explain individual behavior, it may be even more difficult to explain corporate behavior (Albanese, 1984). Describing the conceptual roadblocks that arise when trying to explain corporate crime, Tillman and Pontell (1995) said that organizations "have a dual nature." They explained about organizations: "They both structure and constrain action by providing a context in which decisions are made, while at the same time existing as resources to be used by individual actors or groups to further their interests" (p. 1459).

Punch (2008) suggested that the "corporate setting provides MOM—motive, opportunity, and means." He described motives as including power, growth, profit, and so on. He said that the opportunity for offending occurs in boardrooms and executive offices that are not policed. The means for offending refers to the strategies employers use to carry out corporate offending. While Punch provides a simple framework for explaining corporate crime, the nature of the offending is so complex that identifying precise predictors of the behavior is not a simple task. In general, explanations of corporate crime have focused on (1) the structure of the organization, (2) organizational processes, and (3) dynamic organizational explanations.

Organizational Structure and Corporate Crime

Some theorists have noted how variables related to an organization's structure are also related to corporate crime. For example, Tillman and Pontell (1995) suggested that corporate crime is more often found in: larger organizations, organizations growing quickly, and organizations with complex ownership structures. Other authors have also suggested that size and complexity influence corporate crime (Punch, 2008). One author suggested that corporate crime is more likely in larger organizations because larger businesses (1) see penalties as a cost of doing business and (2) are more resistant to any stigma that arises from misconduct (Yeager, 1986).

Organizational Processes and Corporate Crime

Theorists have also described the way that organizational processes influence wrongdoing. From this orientation, one can consider the definition of corporation offered by Ermann and Lundman, (2002): "Organizations are collections of positions that powerfully influence the work-related thoughts and actions of the replaceable people who occupy positions in them" (p. 6). The notion of "replaceable people" is particularly important. Coleman (1982) described the "irrelevance of persons," writing that "persons have become, in a sense, that [which] was never before true, incidental to a large fraction of the productive activity in society" (p. 26).

Corporations have goals, and rules are assigned that prescribe behaviors corporate actors are expected to follow in their efforts to attain corporate goals. Although goals and rules are prescribed, there is evidence that pressure from the top of an organization may encourage wrongdoing by employees. Describing this top-down pressure, it has been suggested that "organizations, like fish, rot from the head down" (Jenkins & Braithwaite, 1993, p. 220). Another way to suggest it is that those with power influence "replaceable people" to engage in misconduct so that they, the "replaceable people," do not become "*replaced.*" Simpson and Piquero (2002) note that "when employees are ordered to do something by a supervisor, most will do what is expected of them because they are only partial moral agents, limited in their responsibility and liability" (p. 537).

Figure 11.1 shows the cycle of corporate crime following a process-oriented explanation of corporate crime. Employees learn rules of what is expected in their corporation. In some cases, organizational rules may come into conflict with societal laws. The employees' behaviors, because the employees are "replaceable," may break societal laws to further the organization's goals. Employees are rewarded for helping the organization move toward its goals. If they are caught breaking the rules, they may be fired. In such cases, new employees are hired into the position (after all, employees are "replaceable people"), and the cycle begins anew.

Dynamic Organizational Explanations and Corporate Crime

Dynamic organizational theories explore the links among societal factors, organizational processes, and individual motivation. These approaches recognize the limited nature of other organizational theories in explaining corporate crime. Simpson and Piquero (2002) called for an integration of organizational theories in order to develop stronger explanations of corporate misconduct. They theorized that less successful firms might engage in misconduct in order to become more successful; however, individuals in those firms must accept and conduct wrongdoing in order for misconduct to occur. Based on this, they call for the integration of macro- and micro-level theories and develop their own organizational contingency theory to "explain the circumstances and conditions under which corporate crime is likely" (p. 515). In line with this thinking, Simpson and Koper (1997) demonstrated how both external (political changes, market pressures, competition levels, legal changes) and internal dynamics (changes in organizational management) potentially influence corporate wrongdoing.

Simpson and Piquero (2002) conducted a factorial survey with 96 students to examine the impact of organizational factors and self-control on attitudes about offending. They found that self-control and organizational factors (e.g., corporate offending propensity) were not tied together; however, they also found that "variables consistent with an integrated materialistic and cultural organizational theory predicted managers' offending intentions" (p. 309). They found additional support for integrating macro- and

Figure 11.1 The Cycle of Corporate Crime

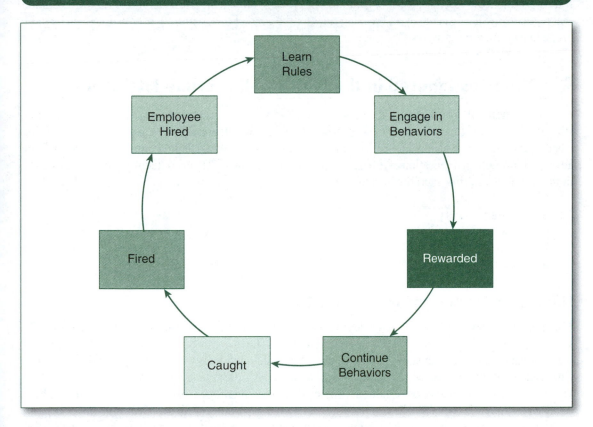

micro-level explanations. Managers were more likely "to offend if they perceived career benefits," and concerns about job security kept some from offending. They summarized their findings:

> Offending is more likely when companies are not doing well economically and when illegality is apt to garner significant financial gains for the firm . . . managers who believed their illegal act would negatively affect the firm's reputation were significantly less willing to offend. (p. 536)

Diane Vaughan (1992) has also noted the importance of bringing together the micro- and macro-levels to explain corporate offending. According to Vaughan, "the link between individual choice and the structural determinants of those choices is paramount to understanding misconduct both in and by organizations" (p. 134). Vaughan's theory of organizational offending uses Merton's theory as a framework to link together individual and institutional motivations. According to Vaughan, three features of the interactions between individuals and the organizations where they work promote crime in the organization:

- A competitive environment generating pressures for organizational law violations
- Organizational characteristics including processes that provide opportunities for offending
- A relationship with regulators that minimizes the likelihood of detection and prosecution

When these elements are present in an organization, the likelihood of corporate misconduct increases. If a corporation, for example, places a great deal of pressure on its employees and there is little likelihood that regulators will catch employees breaking rules for the good of the organization, employees will be more prone to commit wrongful acts.

Theories Ignored in the White-Collar Crime Literature

At least a handful of criminological theories have received very little, if any, attention in white-collar crime studies. This is unfortunate because the strength of these "ignored" theories can be assessed by determining whether the theories explain white-collar crime, and our understanding about white-collar crime could be advanced through an application of different theories to the behavior. Theories that warrant more attention in the white-collar crime literature include:

- Life course theory
- Social disorganization theory
- Gender theories
- Labeling theory

Life Course Theories and White-Collar Crime

Life course theory uses a social psychological orientation to identify how events early in one's life course shape experiences later in one's life (Payne & Gainey, 2009). The theory is regularly used to explain violence, with a great deal of research showing that many, but not all, individuals who have violent childhoods also have violent adulthoods. As Michael Benson and Kent Kerley (2001) note, white-collar crime researchers have not used life course theory to address white-collar crime, and life course theorists have not used white-collar crime to test the theory. The authors note that such a gap between the two areas of research is problematic because of recent research showing relatively lengthy criminal histories among many white-collar offenders and evidence that white-collar offenders do not fit "the stereotypical image of the white-collar offender as a person who comes from the privileged sectors of society" (p. 12). In other words, a need exists to consider the past lives of white-collar offenders in order to understand how past experiences influenced decision making in offending.

To address this obvious gap in the white-collar crime literature, Benson and Kerley (2001) compared the life histories of a sample of convicted conventional offenders with a sample of convicted white-collar offenders. The authors culled data from the presentence investigation reports of offenders convicted in eight federal districts between 1973 and 1978. Their analysis showed that the life histories of white-collar and conventional offenders were different. White-collar offenders were much more likely to come from intact families and less likely to have problems in school. They were more likely to be involved in pro-social activities, had fewer prior arrests, and were older when their criminal careers began.

Benson and Kerley (2001) point to the need to consider how turning points later in life contribute to white-collar offending. Possible turning points they identify include dire family consequences, stressors related to occupational dynamics, and changes in business revenues. In addition to calling for more attention being directed toward the causes and consequences of white-collar crime for individual offenders, the authors suggest that white-collar crime be examined "as a social event in the life course" (p. 134).

Piquero and Benson (2004) described the need to expand the use of life course theory to address white-collar crime. They highlighted the differences between white-collar and conventional offenders, and also the similarities, to provide a framework that future researchers could use to address white-collar crime from a life-course perspective. As Piquero and Benson (2004) pointed out, "we simply need more information about the life histories of white-collar offenders" (p. 160).

Social Disorganization Theory and White-Collar Crime

Social disorganization theory suggests that a neighborhood's crime rate is shaped by the ability of its members to agree upon and work toward a common goal, such as crime control. The ability of a neighborhood to be organized is predicted to be determined by neighborhood structural characteristics, in particular the mobility of its population, racial/ethnic heterogeneity, and poverty. Thus, neighborhoods that are less able to agree to work together toward controlling criminal behavior tend to have the following in common: a large percentage of the residents do not stay very long (a mobile population), residents are a diverse mix from different racial and ethnic origins, and many of the residents are poor. Many studies have found strong support for the idea that social disorganization breeds street crime.

At least one study used social disorganization theory to assess the factors that business owners take into account when deciding which types of crime prevention tools to use (Casten & Payne, 2008). Not surprisingly, business owners consider neighborhood factors in deciding how to develop loss prevention strategies.

What is not clear is whether social disorganization contributes to white-collar crime. Such a question could be addressed several different ways. For example, it would be useful to identify whether retail settings in disadvantaged areas have more employee theft than retail settings in more advantaged areas. In addition, it would be interesting to determine whether corporations located in disadvantaged areas have different rates of regulatory violations than corporations located in non-disadvantaged areas. As well, more research needs to be done on the way white-collar crime promotes social disorganization in disadvantaged communities. It seems as though the application of social disorganization theory to white-collar crime is an area ripe for empirical efforts.

Gender Theories and White-Collar Crime

Gender theories are also under-represented in the white-collar crime literature. These theories call attention to the need to consider crime from the perspective of women (Danner, 1998). In "Three Strikes and It's Women Who are Out: The Hidden Consequences for Women of Criminal Justice Policy Reforms," Mona Danner outlines the way that laws such as three strikes policies negatively impact women. Similar questions arise with regard to white-collar crime theories and policies: (1) how do white-collar crime policies impact women? (2) do patriarchal values contribute to white-collar crime? (3) are women disproportionately victims of certain types of white-collar crime? and (4) how can the feminist perspective promote understanding about white-collar crime?

Research by Kathleen Daly (1989) shows that theories used to explain women's involvement in white-collar crime may need to be different from those traditionally used to explain men's involvement in workplace offending. Reviewing data from Wheeler et al.'s data set of white-collar offenders, Daly found significant differences between male and female white-collar criminals. She found that many of the women did not fit the image of the typical upper-class white-collar offender. A third of the women were unemployed, and many who worked were in clerical positions, while many of the men worked in managerial positions.

In addition, the women were less likely to have college degrees and more likely to be non-White. Daly also found that that their crimes were better described as "occupational marginality" as opposed to mobility (the women worked on the fringes of the organization rather than in its upper echelons). She also found that women were more likely to work alone in their offending, and financial need was more commonly a motive for them. Daly notes that individuals do not need a white-collar job to commit the crimes of embezzlement, fraud, and forgery. Citing research by Howe (1977), she notes that a "'pink-collar world' suffices, as does having no ties to the labor market" (p. 179). In addition, Daly argues that white-collar crimes by women should be addressed with theories—not with a focus on how the crimes "deviate" from men's white-collar crimes, but instead, "women's illegalities should be explained on their own terms" (p. 790).

Labeling Theory and White-Collar Crime

Labeling theory focuses on the way that individuals develop criminal labels. Some labeling theorists have suggested that the process of labeling individuals certain ways results in behaviors consistent with those labels. The notion of "self-fulfilling prophecy" comes to mind. It is widely accepted, for example, that if children are treated as intelligent, they will be more likely to show signs of intelligence. If children are labeled as bad, they will be more likely to misbehave. Criminologist Ruth Triplett (1993) has noted that it is not simply the process of being labeled that results in deviant outcomes; instead, negative labels increase the number of delinquent peers one has, which can increase support for subsequent misconduct. In other words, some individuals are able to reject negative labels, while others might respond to the labels by joining forces with others who have the same delinquent or criminal label.

The way labeling relates to white-collar crime has been only tangentially addressed in the literature. Research by Benson (1980) shows how white-collar offenders reject the criminal label as a coping strategy to deal with the consequences of their sanction. Elsewhere, Benson (1990) wrote the following:

> Few events produce stronger emotions than being publicly accused of a crime. Especially for the individual who has a stake in maintaining a legitimate persona, the prospect of being exposed as a criminal engenders "deep emotions" (Denzin, 1983): shame, humiliation, guilt, depression, and anger.

Consistent with Triplett's hypothesis, if convicted white-collar offenders avoid contacts with other offenders and reject the criminal label, they should be less prone to re-offend. Alternatively, the labeling of white-collar offenders as criminals may serve to increase their offending if the strength of the labeling is such that white-collar offenders are not able to reject the label. Such a label could create additional opportunities for offending. David Weisburd and his colleagues (Weisburd, Waring, & Chayet, 1995) described this process in the following way:

> Once prestige and status are lost, they may be perceived as difficult to regain. Once the cost of illicit behavior has been minimized, recidivism may be more likely. In some sense, the model of a spiraling process of deviance set into play by a labeling experience (Wilkins, 1965) may be more appropriate for white-collar criminals than for the common criminals for whom the concept was initially developed. (p. 590)

It is plausible that labels attach differently based on offender type. Labeling a young male in a disadvantaged community as a gang member or criminal may serve to increase his social status in his community and the rewards that come along with being labeled a criminal could perpetuate wrongdoing (Triplett, 1993). Labeling an older male in an affluent community a white-collar criminal would not increase his social status in his neighborhood. The negative consequences of the "white-collar criminal" label, as opposed to the rewards that others might get from the criminal label, might actually serve to promote future wrongdoing. Such an assumption has not yet been addressed in the white-collar crime literature. Indeed, research on how labels affect white-collar criminality is needed.

▲ **Photo 11.3** Sometimes being labeled a criminal creates rewards in terms of increased status for conventional offenders. For white-collar offenders, the label of "criminal" is unlikely to result in status-related rewards.

Integrated Efforts to Explain White-Collar Crime

Thus far, the various theoretical perspectives addressing white-collar crime have been discussed separately. Many scholars, however, have suggested that the best way to explain white-collar crime is to use an integrated approach that brings together multiple perspectives (Gerber, Jensen, & Fritsch, 1996). Even among specific types of occupations, misconduct by employees is likely not "a unidimensional phenomenon" (Hollinger et al., 1992, p. 155).

The call for integrated theories gained popularity in criminology in the mid- to late-1980s, so the importance of bringing together multiple perspectives is not a new idea. The value of theoretical integration is demonstrated in the way that Donald Cressey (1953) explained the causes of embezzlement in *Other People's Money*. Later, summarizing Cressey's research, Green (1993) highlighted four steps that Cressey saw as leading to embezzlement:

- An unshareable financial problem
- Embezzlement defined as a means to fix the financial problem
- The offender has the skills to commit the crime
- Neutralization occurs to give the offender the mental strength to commit the crime

In these steps, one can point to the linking together of four different theoretical perspectives: (1) the unshareable financial problem relates to strain theory, (2) the values suggesting that it is OK to steal can be linked to cultural theory, (3) the skills needed to steal can be linked to learning theory, and (4) the neutralization can be linked to neutralization theory.

Other researchers have noted the need to use integrated models to explain different forms of white-collar misconduct. Makkai and Braithwaite (1991) conducted a multi-method study involving interviews with regulatory officials, surveys of nursing home directors, and reviews of compliance data to determine how well four theories addressed violations by nursing homes: control theory, opportunity theory, subcultural theory, and differential association theory. They found that none of the theories on their own predicated compliance rates and called for theory integration to explain regulatory violations by nursing homes. As well, describing how strain (or greed) leads to white-collar crime, one author team showed how various factors such as individual personality characters, social controls, personal controls, reward and punishment, loyalty, executive ideology, and opportunity work together to foster misconduct in the workplace (Robinson & Murphy, 2009).

Systems Theory

As noted throughout this book, **systems theory** offers a foundation from which white-collar crime can be addressed. The theory does not explain why white-collar crime occurs on an individual level; instead it provides insight into the interconnections among various societal systems and the way that various systems influence white-collar wrongdoing.

As an illustration, activities in the political system have a direct influence on white-collar misconduct. For example, changes in the political system routinely lead to changes in the health care system. These systemic changes are tied to changes in the social, educational, and technological systems. Together, these changes influence the types of crimes committed in the health care system. Consider the nature of crimes committed in the home health care field:

> In the late 1980s and early 1990s, changes in health care payment plans encouraged hospitals to shorten hospital stays, technological advancements allowed hospital equipment to be mobile, and a graying population led to an explosion in the use of home health care services. . . . In the state-operated Medicaid system, which serves the impoverished population, home health care spending quadrupled between 1985 and 1992. (Payne & Gray, 2001, p. 210)

During this same time frame, the amount of fraud occurring in the home health care industry increased dramatically as well.

Also showing how the political system influences white-collar crime, some have attributed white-collar crime to types of economic policies developed in legislation (Mon, 2002). From this perspective, researchers have blamed the rampant fraud found in the savings and loan industry in the late 1980s on federal policies promoting deregulation (Glasberg & Skidmore, 1998a;). Under deregulation policies, rules governing thrifts and savings and loan companies were changed "so that the behaviors that previously fell within the definition of corporate or executive crime were no longer violations but, rather, were enabled by the structure of the legislation" (Glasberg & Skidmore, 1998b, p. 124). Among other things, deregulation policies relaxed federal control over interest rates, provided federal insurance on deposits up to $100,000 for thrift institutions, and removed "restrictions on the intermingling of commercial banking, real estate, and securities investing," thereby encouraging the institutions to engage in risky behaviors (Glasberg & Skidmore, 1998a, p. 432). Pontell (2005) suggested that financial policies were too lax and wrote: "public policies that 'whitewash' white-collar crime and that do not explicitly recognize the potential devastation of control fraud, will not only be ineffective, but will serve as virtual blueprints for financial disasters" (p. 319). Indeed, scholars argued that the deregulation policies resulted in the collapse of the thrift industry, with billions lost to fraud perpetrated by those employed in the industry (Calavita et al., 1997).

Glasberg and Skidmore (1998a) attributed the failure of deregulation and the fraud that resulted to "unintended consequences of the dialectics of state projects" (p. 424). They pointed to the need to look at how external factors came together to foster misbehavior by organizations in the thrift industry and called attention to the need to address how policies are implemented and the consequences of those policies (Glasberg & Skidmore, 1998b). In other words, in line with systems theory, they recognized that policy making in the political arena will impact other societal systems.

The activities of other systems and behaviors of individuals in those systems also demonstrate how white-collar crime can be understood from a systems perspective. Consider the following:

- It has been argued that the criminal justice system's crackdown on different types of white-collar crime in the 1980s occurred because the government viewed white-collar crime as "undermin[ing] the legitimacy of the political and financial systems" (Newbold & Ivory, 1993, p. 245).
- With changes in the economic system, it is possible that "downsizing will promote more corporate crime because corporate personnel will be especially pressured to take risks to maximize profits as an alternative to the public trauma associated with downsizing" (Friedrichs, 1997, p. 360). Friedrichs also noted that economic changes could inhibit wrongdoing because people are more afraid of losing their jobs in times of downsizing. Whether corporate downsizing leads to, or prevents, white-collar crime, it seems safe to suggest that such changes at the broader economic and corporate system levels have direct bearing on white-collar offending.
- Technological changes in the technological system influence the commission of white-collar crime and the way the justice system responds to the crimes (Croall, 1989). One author team noted that the "criminal law cannot keep up with a technologically advanced, constantly changing business environment" (Simpson & Koper, 1992, p. 367). In a similar way, highlighting how changes in the technological system influence the criminal justice system, Albanese (1984) wrote, "increasing sophistication of law enforcement techniques may produce only more sophisticated forms of organized crime" (p. 18).

Again, the main premise of systems theory is that all systems are interrelated. Changes in one system will lead to changes in other systems. Such changes have direct implications for the commission of white-collar crime and appropriate response strategies.

✉ Summary

- Criminological theory is central to the study of white-collar crime. It is important to stress that theories are potential explanations of behaviors or phenomena, and for white-collar crime explanations to have practical utility, the theories or explanations must point to changes that would reduce (rather than increase) white-collar misconduct.
- Some criminologists attribute white-collar crime to cultural influences that seemingly promote wrongdoing by workers and corporations. James Coleman (1987), for example, argued that industrial capitalism promotes a "culture of competition."
- Deterrence theory can be traced to Cesare Beccaria's *On Crimes and Punishments*, a work that many have defined as the foundation of the classical school of criminological thought. Research by Sally Simpson and various colleagues has been instrumental in demonstrating how deterrence ideals can be used to explain various forms of workplace misconduct.
- Three types of strain theories were discussed: classical strain theory, institutional anomie theory, and general strain theory.
- Classical strain theory traces the source of strain to interactions between the social and economic structures.

- In *Crime and the American Dream,* Steve Messner and Richard Rosenfeld (2007) describe how society promotes values related to financial success but fails to promote values consistent with using legitimate means to attain financial success.
- Developing what is known as general strain theory, Robert Agnew (1985, 1992) used a social psychological approach to explain how crime is an adaptation to stress and frustration.
- Some criminologists have focused on the way that white-collar crime can be understood as learned behavior. The most prominent learning theory is differential association theory, which was developed by Edwin Sutherland.
- Sykes and Matza (1957) described five techniques of neutralization they believed juveniles used to rationalize their misconduct. Given that white-collar workers are rational beings, it is plausible that white-collar offenders use similar types of neutralizations.
- While offenders use neutralizations to give them the mental fortitude to engage in wrongdoing, accounts are offered after the fact to describe their behaviors.
- Rather than asking "why do people commit crime," the question from a control theory perspective is "why don't people commit crime" (Hirschi, 1969). Some have regarded loyalty as central to corporate decision making.
- Self-control theory was created by Michael Gottfredson and Travis Hirschi (1990), who argued in *A General Theory of Crime* that all types of crime are caused by the presence of low self-control. Hirschi and Gottfredson (1987) were extremely critical of white-collar crime theories that explained the behavior by focusing on the nature of the occupation rather than the characteristics of the individual offender.
- Routine activities theory suggests that crime occurs when the following three elements exist at the same time and place: (1) the presence of motivated offenders, (2) the absence of capable guardians, and (3) the availability of suitable targets.
- Conflict theorists explain white-collar crime from a more critical perspective, focusing on the way those with power exert influence in order to use the law as an instrument of power.
- The nature of corporate crime is such that individual-level variables may not sufficiently explain the misconduct. In general, explanations of corporate crime have focused on (1) the structure of the organization, (2) organizational processes, and (3) dynamic organizational explanations.
- Theories that warrant more attention in the white-collar crime literature include life course theory, social disorganization theory, gender theories, and labeling theory.
- Many scholars have suggested that the best way to explain white-collar crime is to use an integrated approach that brings together multiple perspectives.
- As noted throughout this book, systems theory offers a foundation from which white-collar crime can be addressed. The theory does not explain why white-collar crime occurs on an individual level; instead it provides insight into the interconnections among various societal systems and the way that various systems influence white-collar wrongdoing.

KEY TERMS

Appeal to higher loyalties	Conflict theorists	Denial of victim
Collective embezzlement	Control theory	Deterrence theory
Condemnation of condemners	Denial of responsibility	Differential association theory

General strain theory	Medical fraud	Routine activities theory
Innovators	Neutralization theory	Scapegoating
Institutional anomie	Rational choice theory	Self-control theory
Labeling theory	Rebels	Social disorganization theory
Learning theories	Retreatists	Strain theory
Life course theory	Ritualists	Systems theory

DISCUSSION QUESTIONS

1. Which theory do you think most accurately explains white-collar crime? Which one is least effective? Why?

2. Watch the movie *Office Space* and apply four different theories to the movie.

3. How can theory influence the criminal justice system's response to white-collar crime? Explain.

4. Select two theories and explain how white-collar crime prevention strategies might be developed using those theories.

5. Are white-collar offenders born to be bad? Explain.

6. Find two examples of white-collar crimes in recent news articles. Apply two theories of white-collar crime to the articles.

7. Which types of rationalizations do you think are most commonly used by white-collar offenders? Are there any rationalizations that you think justify white-collar misconduct?

8. Do you think corporations cause people to commit crime? Explain.

WEB RESOURCES

Criminological Theory on the Web: http://www.umsl.edu/~keelr/200/Diane_Demelo/diane.pdf

Crimetheory.com: http://www.crimetheory.com/

READING

To test Hirschi and Gottfredson's self-control theory, Michael Benson and Elizabeth Moore used data from the presentence reports of 2,462 white-collar offenders and 1,986 conventional offenders convicted in eight federal districts between 1973 and 1978. The researchers focused specifically on the criminal versatility of white-collar offenders and whether they exhibited similar levels of deviance. The authors found that, in general, white-collar offenders did not have the same level of criminal histories that conventional offenders had, and they were less involved in deviant activities. Some chronic white-collar offenders were more comparable to conventional offenders. The authors advise that self-control theory needs to focus on motives for offending and, based on this recommendation, they suggest that white-collar offenders follow three different paths to white-collar offending.

Are White-Collar and Common Offenders the Same?

An Empirical and Theoretical Critique of a Recently Proposed General Theory of Crime

Michael L. Benson and Elizabeth Moore

Gottfredson and Hirschi (1990) recently proposed a general theory of crime. The theorists contend that all crime, including white-collar crime, can be explained by the same causal principles. Their theory is one of a number of recent efforts to promote a more interdisciplinary approach to crime. The central thesis of this movement is that theories of crime that are solely sociological ignore individual traits that account for a significant, if not the major, proportion of variation in individual criminal activities (Andrews and Wormith 1989; Wilson and Herrnstein 1985). For the theory of crime by Gottfredson and Hirschi, the causally important individual trait is self-control. Because white-collar offenders often are cited as counter-examples to trait theories, it is important to determine how well such theories apply to them. If propositions derived from the theory do not hold for those who commit white-collar offenses, its claim to generality must be qualified and its underlying causal structure reevaluated.

The theory proposed by Gottfredson and Hirschi combines elements of opportunity and control theories (1990, p. 23). From opportunity theory, the proposition is taken that environmental conditions influence criminal opportunities. For example, the availability of suitably attractive and unguarded targets influences whether particular crimes are likely to occur. From control theory, the proposition is borrowed that people differ in their propensity to take advantage of criminal opportunities. According to the theory, persons with low self-control are more likely to steal the unattended pocketbook or vandalize the unpoliced subway train than those with high self-control. In this view, then, the two major causal factors that explain crime are self-control and opportunity.

SOURCE: Benson, M., and Moore, E. (1992). Are white-collar and common offenders the same? An empirical and theoretical critique of a recently proposed general theory of crime. *Journal of Research in Crime and Delinquency, 29,* 251–272.

The idea that the causes of white-collar crime, or any other crime for that matter, involve "unique, specific cultural motives" is rejected, as are the traditional sociological processes thought to generate such motives (Hirschi and Gottfredson 1987b, p. 971). According to this theory, the only motive involved in crime is something akin to greed, that is, a desire to pursue one's short-term pleasure, gratification, or gain; this motive derives from an internal characteristic of the individual—low self-control.

This article addresses two propositions on white-collar crime derived from the general theory of crime proposed by Gottfredson and Hirschi (1990; see also Hirschi and Gottfredson 1986, 1987a, 1987b, 1989). This theory predicts that those who commit white-collar crimes are (a) as criminally versatile and (b) as prone to deviance as those who commit common street crimes. To assess the validity of these propositions, we investigate the criminal records of a large sample of individuals convicted of white-collar and ordinary street offenses and their respective levels of participation in deviant activities.

Contrary to the claims of Gottfredson and Hirschi, we find that those who commit even run-of-the-mill, garden-variety white-collar offenses can, as a group, be clearly distinguished from those who commit ordinary street offenses. We contend that the Gottfredson and Hirschi theory is inadequate in explaining white-collar crime; its rejection of motives as important causal forces is misguided. Because motives are generated by macro social and organizational processes, a fully developed theory of white-collar crime must take these processes into account.

Implications From the General Theory of Crime

The theory proposed by Gottfredson and Hirschi conceives of the criminal as a person with low self-control who engages in a variety of criminal and deviant acts (1990, pp. 85-120). Self-control is a behavioral propensity that varies over individuals but remains stable for any given person (Gottfredson and Hirschi 1990, p. 137). Individuals with low self-control tend to pursue "short-term

gratification in the most direct way with little consideration for the long-term consequences of their acts" (Hirschi and Gottfredson 1987b, p. 959).[1]

Low self-control is not always manifested by criminal behavior. Depending on the situation, it may come out in other risky, disreputable, or deviant behaviors, such as reckless driving, alcohol and drug abuse, promiscuous sex, and job quitting (Hirschi and Gottfredson 1987a, p. 14; 1987b, p. 960). Criminal and other such "equivalent" behaviors express an underlying general propensity for deviance (Hirschi and Gottfredson 1987a, p. 15). How this propensity is manifested depends on the situations and opportunities confronting potential offenders as they go through life.

According to Gottfredson and Hirschi, this conceptualization also fits those who commit what are typically thought of as white-collar crimes. Indeed, for purposes of causal explanation, labels such as "white-collar offender" and "common street offender" are said to be misleading because similar types of persons commit both types of offenses.

> There is no reason to think that the offenders committing these crimes are causally distinct from other offenders.... The assumption that white-collar criminals differ from other criminals is simply the assumption, in another guise, that offenders specialize in particular crimes, an assumption for which there is no good evidence.... The central elements of our theory of criminality are ... easily identifiable among white-collar criminals. They too are people of low self-control, people inclined to follow momentary impulse without consideration of the long-term costs of such behavior. (Gottfredson and Hirschi 1990, pp. 190-91)

If this view of criminality and white-collar offenders is correct, two related empirical implications follow. The first is that so-called white-collar offenders do not specialize in white-collar offenses. Rather, they commit a variety of crimes in the spontaneous, impulsive manner of street criminals. We call this the criminal versatility proposition. Empirically, it implies that if known offenders are divided into two groups (white-collar and common) on the basis of a conviction or an arrest, both groups will display similar levels of versatility in their criminal careers; those labeled white-collar offenders will exhibit criminal careers similar to those labeled common offenders. Examination of the criminal careers of the white-collar offenders should reveal lack of specialization in white-collar offenses and general similarity between their careers and those of street offenders.

The second implication involves levels of participation in deviance. According to this theory, criminals are attracted to a wide variety of "disreputable" behaviors, such as "drug, alcohol and cigarette use, promiscuous sex, divorce, job quitting, and fast cars" (Hirschi and Gottfredson 1987b, p. 960). If this deviance proposition is true of criminals in general, it must also be true of so-called white-collar criminals. Like the criminal versatility proposition, the deviance proposition implies that if offenders are divided into two groups (white-collar and common), both will be similar in regard to these specified kinds of behavior. Thus the theory predicts that white-collar offenders engage in non criminal but nevertheless unconventional or disreputable acts to the same extent as common offenders.

In effect, the criminal versatility and deviance propositions make the same prediction: those who violate white-collar criminal statutes are like those who violate other criminal statutes in certain regards. This prediction follows from the premise that there is only one type of offender. Hence, for causal explanation it is said to be a mistake to distinguish between offenders on an offense-specific basis. In the words of Gottfredson and Hirschi (1990), "The distinction between crime in the street and crime in the suites is an *offense* rather than an *offender* distinction . . . offenders in both cases are likely to share similar characteristics" (p. 200, emphasis in original).

Related Research

Wheeler, Weisburd, Bode, and Waring (1988) compared a large sample of persons convicted of white-collar and common crimes on a variety of social and demographic indicators. They found that those convicted of white-collar crimes tend to have higher educational attainment than those convicted of common crimes and the general public. They also are more likely to have histories of steady employment than common criminals. In their sample, the typical white-collar criminal was a White male aged 40. The typical common criminal was a Black male aged 30. Contrary to the Gottfredson and Hirschi theory, Wheeler, Weisburd, Bode, and Waring conclude that as a group white-collar criminals can be clearly distinguished from common criminals (1988, p. 347).

Weisburd, Chayet, and Waring (1990) used the Wheeler, Weisburd, Bode, and Waring (1988) data to investigate the criminal careers of white-collar offenders. Contrary to Gottfredson and Hirschi they found significant differences between the criminal careers of white-collar and common offenders. The former "begin later and evidence a lower frequency of offending" than the latter (Weisburd et al. 1990, p. 352). But other results appear to lend some support to the position of Gottfredson and Hirschi. A nontrivial proportion of white-collar offenders were found to be repeat offenders and some had "serious and lengthy criminal records" (Weisburd et al. 1990, p. 343). The data did not permit Weisburd et al. to track the form of white-collar offending careers. Hence, they could not investigate the criminal versatility of white-collar offenders in detail. Nevertheless, they found suggestive evidence that white-collar offenders do not specialize in white-collar crime (Weisburd et al. 1990, pp. 349-52).

In evaluating the Gottfredson and Hirschi theory, results based on the Wheeler, Weisburd, Bode, and Waring (1988) data must be interpreted cautiously. The data were collected from jurisdictions that may not be representative of federal districts generally (Benson and Walker 1988), and the sampled offenders may not represent convicted white-collar criminals generally. The same may be said of the sample and data we subsequently describe, but to the extent that our findings overlap with theirs, the external validity of both studies is enhanced.

More important, the analyses conducted so far do not address propositions derived directly from the general theory. Wheeler, Weisburd, Bode, and Waring (1988) examined indicators of conventionality rather than criminality and deviance. Although Weisburd et al. (1990)

appear to provide some support for the general theory, they did not directly address either the versatility or deviance propositions.[2]

Research Design

Defining White-Collar Crime

The definition of white-collar crime continues to provoke significant controversy. Disagreement centers largely on whether it should be defined according to offense- or offender-based criteria (Shapiro 1980, 1990; Coleman 1989; Steffensmeier 1989; Edelhertz 1970). We employ an offense-based definition. That is, we designate offenders as white-collar by the offenses they committed rather than their social or occupational status. This approach was used in a number of recent studies on white-collar crime (Weisburd et al. 1990; Benson and Walker 1988; Wheeler, Weisburd, and Bode 1982; Hagan, Nagel-Bernstein, and Albonetti 1980). The offenses that we designate as white-collar are bank embezzlement, bribery, income tax violations, false claims and statements, and mail fraud. This set of offenses is similar to the offenses analyzed by Wheeler, Weisburd, Bode, and Waring (1988) and Hagan et al. (1980). Although we do not claim that it is representative of the total body of white-collar crime, we do believe that all of the offenses fit at least one definition of white-collar crime and provide a broad and heterogeneous view of what most scholars and laypersons would regard as white-collar criminal activity (cf. Wheeler, Weisburd, Bode, and Waring 1988).

This approach toward white-collar crime has been widely used in recent research, but it is not universally accepted. Some would not regard all of the offenders studied here as "real" white-collar criminals (Steffensmeier 1989). We chose to approach white-collar crime in this way primarily because the offenses that we designate as white-collar appear to fit Gottfredson's and Hirschi's conception of white-collar crime, in that they all involve the use of fraud in pursuit of self-interest. Because our objective is to test their theory, we use a definition that fits their use of the concept.

There is another reason for taking this approach. As Hirschi and Gottfredson (1987b) have noted, a weakness of the white-collar crime literature is its over-reliance on egregious, highly publicized, and largely atypical cases. Previous researchers generally ignored the more common run-of-the-mill, garden-variety white-collar offenders and offenses (but see Wheeler, Weisburd, Bode, and Waring 1988 and especially Weisburd, Wheeler, Waring, and Bode 1991 for important exceptions). Although these "middle class offenders" as Weisburd et al. (1991) call them may not make for dramatic headlines, they nevertheless account for the major proportion of officially recorded white-collar crimes. Any theory of white-collar crime must, therefore, explain these middle-class crimes as well as the crimes of more highly publicized and egregious offenders.

Sample and Data

In this study, we reanalyze data from a project designed to provide information on sentencing patterns in federal district courts.[3] The sampling frame for the original study consisted of defendants sentenced in eight federal district courts between 1973 and 1978. The eight districts were selected to represent variation in regional location and size.[4] The time frame is about the same as in the Wheeler, Weisburd, Bode, and Waring (1988) study, but the districts included in the present analysis differ from the ones used in that study.

The cases involve 2,462 individuals sentenced for the white-collar crimes noted earlier (bank embezzlement, bribery, income tax violations, false claims, and mail fraud) and three common crimes ($N = 1,986$). The common crimes include narcotics offenses, postal forgery, and bank robbery.[5] These offenses cover a broad range of violent and nonviolent, economic and noneconomic activities, but they are not representative of the total body of common crime. For the comparative and theory-testing purposes at issue here, however, they are well-suited. It is reasonable to expect that common offenders processed in federal courts are more like white-collar offenders than common offenders processed in state or local courts. Hence these data provide for a conservative test of our position and a liberal test of the Gottfredson and Hirschi argument.

Data were gathered primarily from presentence investigation (PSI) reports. The most recent 120 PSI reports per offense from each of the five largest districts and the most recent 40 PSI reports per offense from the three smaller districts were selected for the sample.[6]

Our investigation involves data on prior arrests, drug and alcohol use, and academic performance and social adjustment in high school. We treat prior arrests as measures of criminal activity. Substance abuse and poor academic performance and social adjustment in high school are considered indicators of deviance.

Another potentially more serious objection to these data concerns what criminal records mean in the case of white-collar crime. Some argue that because white-collar offenses are so difficult to detect, an offender may commit a whole series of crimes before one is discovered and officially entered into the records. Further, unlike typical common crimes, white-collar crimes may not take place at any one particular time or place, but may consist of a pattern of activities that is geographically and temporally scattered. The basic argument is that criminal records do not capture the full extent of illegal activity by white-collar offenders. In its general form, this contention is difficult to counter; to what extent do bureaucratic records of *any* sort ever capture the full lived reality of human activity? Whether this problem is any more severe in the case of white-collar as opposed to common crime, however, is open to debate.

Consider the matter of detection. True, a bank teller may engage in a series of small embezzlements before being caught. In this case, the teller's single arrest would underestimate both the extent of her criminal activity and her specialization in embezzlement. But exactly the same logic can be applied to many, if not most, common crimes. Is the probability of being arrested for any *single* burglary or illegal narcotics transaction really significantly higher than the probability of being arrested for any *single* episode of embezzlement? Because of auditing controls, tellers who embezzle may actually face a higher risk of detection for any single offense than those who commit common street offenses. So may those who violate other white-collar statutes. Entire investigative agencies are devoted to detecting particular white-collar offenses—securities fraud, tax violations, postal and wire frauds, and lending and credit fraud. These agencies may not have high success rates, but it is not clear

that they are any less successful than the police at identifying and apprehending individuals engaged in criminal activities. As indicators of criminality, official records may be no less valid for white-collar offenders than they are for other types of offenders.

Results

Criminal Versatility

As a group, the white-collar offense sample appears much less involved in crime than common criminals. Less than half as many white-collar criminals (39.0%) as common criminals (81.1%) have a prior arrest. The mean number of arrests for white-collar criminals (1.79) is also much smaller than that of common criminals (5.63). Nevertheless, like Weisburd et al. (1990), we find that a nontrivial proportion of white-collar offenders have prior records.

The aggregate figures hide variation within both groups of offenders. For example, mail fraud offenders are more than three times as likely to have a prior arrest (65.9%) as bank embezzlers (18.4%). There is also considerable variation among the white-collar offense groups in average number of prior arrests. Among the common offense groups, forgers and bank robbers have significantly more involvement in criminal behavior than narcotics offenders.

Note that one of the white-collar offense groups, mail fraud offenders, has a higher average number of prior arrests than narcotics offenders, and sizable proportions of those convicted of income tax and false claims offenses have prior arrests. These findings coincide remarkably well with those of Weisburd et al. (1990) and support their claim that the commonplace assumption that those who violate white-collar statutes are not recidivists is mistaken.

We now turn to the issue of specialization and the transition matrix analysis. To ensure equal sample sizes for all the transition matrices, the sample was restricted to offenders with at least five prior arrests. This permitted us to average FSCs [forward specialization coefficients] over multiple transitions (four, in this case), as is the common practice in research on specialization (Farrington et al. 1988; Kempf 1987). Unfortunately, this restriction reduced the N to 890 for common offenders and 302 for white-collar offenders, 44% and 12%, respectively, of the original samples.

The transition probabilities for all offenses for both common and white-collar offenders remained stable through all four transitions. This stability indicates that the underlying pattern of transition is the same in all matrices. The ASR [adjusted standardized residual] in diagonal cells was significant in all cases.

Like others, we find limited evidence for specialization among offenders. For the criminal versatility proposition, the results are mixed. Contrary to the proposition, white-collar offenders appear to specialize most in white-collar offending.

The results suggest that white-collar offenders may be somewhat less criminally versatile than common offenders, but they must be treated with caution. Only 12% of the white-collar sample was included in the analysis; information on prior arrests for almost 90% of this sample was excluded. The transition matrix analysis, therefore, may present a misleading picture of white-collar criminal versatility.

To investigate this possibility, we compared the distribution of prior arrests for the white-collar and common offender samples as a whole. This procedure permits us to take into account all of the available information on arrests for the two offense groups. As expected, the white-collar offender sample has many fewer prior arrests than the common offender sample (4,306 to 11,196, respectively). The distribution of arrests among both samples is remarkably similar. In both groups 43% of the prior arrests were for minor offenses. The major substantively notable difference involves prior arrests for white-collar offenses. The white-collar offenders had proportionately four times as many prior arrests for white-collar offenses as the common offenders (15% versus 4%, respectively). The common offenders had proportionately more prior arrests for violent and property crimes.

Taken together, our analyses of white-collar arrest histories suggest that, as a group, those who commit white-collar offenses have far fewer prior arrests than those who commit street offenses. Among the different types of white-collar offenders, however, there is considerable variation in the extent of their criminal activities. Those convicted of mail fraud have notably more prior

arrests than those who violate other white-collar crime statutes. Two different methods of analysis show that those who commit white-collar offenses are somewhat more likely to specialize in white-collar crimes than common offenders, but also display versatility in their offending. In short, there is a relatively big difference between the white-collar and common offense samples in their frequency of offending and a smaller, but still notable, difference in the nature of their offending.

Deviance

Gottfredson and Hirschi (1990, p. 200) contend that white-collar offenders and ordinary offenders are "likely to share similar characteristics." According to their theory, both groups are composed of individuals with a propensity for disreputable behavior and living outside of the mainstream.

Neither white-collar nor common offenders are likely to have drinking problems. Although common offenders are twice as likely as their white-collar counterparts to drink excessively, the percentage of problem drinkers in both groups is small and the absolute differences are negligible.

The results on performance in high school are less favorable to the deviance proposition. On average, those convicted of white-collar offenses appear much less likely to receive below-average high school grades or be below average in social adjustment than those convicted of common crimes. There are some exceptions to this general pattern. Offenders convicted of mail fraud and false claims are as likely to have trouble in school as narcotics offenders. Overall, 21.5% of the white-collar offense sample had poor social adjustment in school and 24.6% received poor grades. Roughly twice these percentages in the common offense sample had poor adjustment and poor grades.

With respect to deviant activities, white-collar and common criminals differ principally in illegal drug use. Only 6% of white-collar criminals are reported to have used illegal drugs, compared to almost half of the common criminals.

Our analysis of prior arrests revealed that some white-collar offenders have extensive criminal careers. Because the theory predicts a positive correlation between crime and deviance (Gottfredson and Hirschi 1990, p. 118), we compared the high-rate white-collar offenders to their less criminal counterparts on deviance. Recidivist white-collar offenders (defined as those with at least four prior arrests) are notably more deviant than their nonrecidivist counterparts. The former's problems with alcohol abuse and poor school performance resemble that observed among common offenders. Overall, a comparison suggests that this select group of white-collar offenders, which constitutes about 16% of the white-collar sample, is much like common criminals in its involvement in deviant activities.

Taken together, the results do not support the deviance proposition. The white-collar offense sample clearly differs from the common offense sample on three out of four measures of deviance. White-collar offenders with extensive prior records are very similar to common offenders on these measures.

Reconsideration of the Theory

Overall, do the results support this theory of crime? In one sense, the consistency of the differences between the two samples provides some support for the position of Gottfredson and Hirschi. Their theory predicts a positive correlation between crime and deviance (Gottfredson and Hirschi 1990, p. 118). In effect, this is what was found: White-collar offenders with low levels of involvement in crime had similarly low levels of involvement in deviance; those with high levels of criminal activity (about 16% of the white-collar sample) also had high levels of participation in deviance. Further, although the white-collar offenders displayed greater specialization than the common offenders, they also evidenced considerable versatility in offending. The theory receives partial support.

But in another and perhaps more important sense, the results clearly do not support the theory. As a group, the overwhelming majority of offenders labeled white-collar are much less involved in crime and deviance than those labeled common. The former are less likely to have prior arrests, drinking problems, used illegal drugs, or performed poorly in high school than the latter. Contrary to the theory, those convicted of white-collar offenses have criminal careers that differ from those convicted of common offenses, especially with respect to frequency of offending. Insofar as the theory predicts that distinguishing between offenders on the basis of conviction offenses is meaningless because all offenders share similar characteristics, these findings, as well as those of Wheeler, Weisburd, Bode, and Waring (1988) and Weisburd et al. (1990), contradict it.

But how should these findings be interpreted? Must we reject Gottfredson's and Hirschi's commendable goal of pursuing a general theory of crime and retreat to special theories of white-collar crime? We think not, at least not entirely. Rather, we suggest that self-control and opportunity are related more complexly than is envisioned in this theory as currently formulated and that motives cannot be ignored as important causal forces.

It is easy to agree with Gottfredson and Hirschi that persons with little or no self-control probably are prone to engaging in a wide variety of criminal and deviant acts. However, as our research and that of others show, the majority of those who commit white-collar offenses do not display this kind of generalized deviance. This suggests that these offenders have at least moderate, if not considerable, self-control. Yet at some point in their lives they commit white-collar offenses. This finding is particularly troubling for a theory based on stable behavioral propensities, because as Weisburd et al. (1990) show, these offenders typically start much later in life than common offenders. In this case, the theoretical problem becomes under what conditions is self-control turned off, overcome, or redirected such that normally law-abiding individuals come to commit white-collar crimes.

According to Gottfredson and Hirschi, it is an absence or low level of self-control that leads to crime. This assumes that whenever self-control is present it always acts so as to prevent illegal behavior. But there is no logical reason why someone, sufficiently motivated, may not pursue illegal or deviant ends in a disciplined and self-controlled manner (Tittle, 1991). From Sutherland (1949) on, a wealth of case studies of corporate and other white-collar crimes clearly document cases in which people who have enough self-control to obtain positions of power and influence commit serious crimes.[7] If, as Gottfredson and Hirschi contend, self-control is a stable behavioral propensity, then it cannot suddenly disappear in these people and its absence cannot explain their crimes. Some people with a good deal of self-control, therefore, commit crimes, though the prevalence of criminal behavior among such people may be, as Gottfredson and Hirschi contend, relatively low.

If absence of self-control does not cause some white-collar crimes, what does? The answer, we believe, involves both opportunities and motives generated by macro social, economic, and organizational processes, which create other paths or routes to white-collar crime.

Working in the sociological tradition of Bonger (1969), Coleman (1987) traces one path to white-collar crime. He argues that white-collar crime is in part a function of certain cultural traits of capitalism. According to Coleman (1987), capitalism is based on a "culture of competition," which promotes and justifies the pursuit of material self-interest and individual achievement, often at the expense of others and in violation of the law. The culture of competition creates a context in which aggressive, talented high achievers are rewarded for pursuing their own interests in a calculated and unprincipled manner. These individuals fit public and media stereotypes of the high-powered corporate white-collar offender. They are the offenders that traditional white-collar crime theory holds rarely appear in official records of white-collar offending. Their offenses often are complex, long-lasting and costly, typically affecting large numbers of victims. Their crimes are a function of well-known motives (greed, lust for power, and ego gratification) combined with opportunities created by their occupational and organizational positions (Wheeler and Rothman 1982).

Recent research by Wheeler, Weisburd, Bode, and Waring (1988) and Weisburd et al. (1991) shows this description does not fit the bulk of those who appear in federal court for white-collar crimes. These individuals typically are not high-status corporate or political elites. Rather, they are more aptly described as middle-class people, neither social elites nor social outcasts. They are not heavily involved in crime or deviance, and they do not commit highly complex and costly offenses

(Wheeler, Weisburd, Bode, and Waring 1988; Weisburd et al. 1991). They commit garden-variety white-collar offenses. On the continuum of self-control, they fall somewhere between Gottfredson's and Hirschi's impulsive, uncontrolled, generalized deviant and the aggressive, cold-blooded, calculating white-collar offender popularized by Sutherland (1949) and others.

Following Wheeler, Weisburd, Bode, and Waring (1988) and Cressey (1953), we speculate that these offenders may follow a different route to white-collar crime. This route derives from a different feature of the culture of competition: the ever present possibility of failure. The motive is the desire to avoid failure and to protect one's relative position in life. It may explain why those convicted of white-collar offenses as a group appear to be so different from those convicted of common offenses.

Middle-class individuals who violate white-collar statutes may have sufficient self-control to hold back from crime and deviance most of the time. Their self-control enables them to obtain more or less secure positions in legitimate society. But then something happens to threaten the security of their positions. In Cressey's theory of embezzlement, they suffer a financial problem. For example, an economic downturn may threaten a small businessperson with bankruptcy and loss of a lifetime of effort spent building a business. This problem may appear to be solvable through recourse to a white-collar crime, such as, for example, making false statements on a business loan application. Similarly, a mid-level sales manager in a large corporation may, in response to organizational pressures for greater profits, resort to commercial bribery to improve sales and thus keep her position secure. Under such conditions, the person has a strong motive to commit a white-collar crime and a formerly adequate level of self-control becomes inadequate. The individual resorts to fraud to avoid failure and to protect his or her position. Self-reports from white-collar offenders suggest that they often are motivated not so much by greed as by a desire merely to hang on to what they already had (Benson 1985; Rothman and Gandossy 1982; Denzin 1977; Cressey 1953).

These offenders have motives that are specifically related to their class positions in the larger social structure. Unlike the vast majority of common offenders, they have attained a degree of material success and at least middle- if not upper-class positions in life. Hence, unlike common offenders, they can be threatened by the prospect of losing their positions and associated material well-being. The fear of failure or of a downturn in one's standard of living, then, may be unique class-based causes of white-collar crime. To understand and explain white-collar crime, we must take these motives and the larger economic and organizational forces that activate them into account in our theories.

In summary, we suggest there are three paths or routes to white-collar crime along which motives, opportunities, and self-control operate differently. The first route is followed by offenders with low self-control who impulsively pursue their own self-interest through fraud whenever opportunities arise. Gottfredson and Hirschi probably are correct that it makes no sense to distinguish between these offenders and common offenders on the basis of the offenses they happen to be convicted of at any particular point in their careers. The second path involves offenders with high self-control, who employ it to pursue ego gratification in an aggressive and calculating manner. In a culture based heavily on materialism and competition, such personalities are bound to appear frequently and to often be able to obtain positions of power and influence. Between the two extremes, on a middle path, are offenders who may take advantage of criminal opportunities depending on other aspects of their personal situations. If their positions in life are somehow threatened, a formerly adequate level of self-control may become inadequate and criminal opportunities that once were resisted are now accepted.

Appendix B: Offenses Constituting Crime Categories

Violent: criminal homicide, forcible rape, robbery, assault, other crimes against persons.

Property: burglary, larceny, motor vehicle theft, forgery and counterfeiting, stolen property, loan sharking, other organized crime, arson, vandalism, other crimes against property.

White-collar: fraud, embezzlement, corporate crime, other white-collar offenses.

Public order and minor offenses: weapons, prostitution and vice, sex offenses, narcotics, gambling, offenses against the family, driving under the influence, liquor laws, drunkenness, disorderly conduct, vagrancy, contempt, other nuisance offenses.

⬡ Notes

1. In their 1986, 1987a, and 1987b articles, Hirschi and Gottfredson use the term "criminality." More recently, they have substituted the generic term "low self-control" for "criminality" (Gottfredson and Hirschi 1990).

2. In a recently published monograph Weisburd, Wheeler, Waring, and Bode (1991) do consider some of the deviance issues addressed in this article.

3. The data used in this study were made available by the Inter-University Consortium for Political and Social Research. The data for SENTENCING IN EIGHT UNITED STATES DISTRICT COURTS, 1973-1978 were originally collected by Brian Forst and William Rhodes. Neither the collector of the original data nor the Consortium bear any responsibility for the analyses or interpretations presented here.

4. The jurisdictions were New Jersey, Eastern New York, Connecticut, Northern Ohio, Middle Florida, Western Oklahoma, Northern New Mexico, and Northern California.

5. Following Wheeler, Weisburd, Bode, and Waring (1988), we designated postal forgery as a common crime offense primarily because it is a nonviolent, financially oriented property crime that is unlikely to be committed by offenders of white-collar social status. In the federal judiciary, most cases of postal forgery involve individuals who have stolen government issued checks for welfare or social security benefits from mail boxes. Whether the defendant is charged with the crime of postal theft or postal forgery depends mainly on whether he or she is caught at the time of the theft or while trying to cash the check by forging the recipient's endorsement.

6. Due to the relative scarcity of PSI reports for false claims, bribery, and mail fraud, about 500 cases were selected nationwide for each category. We deleted cases where the defendant was a corporation.

7. Readers familiar with the white-collar crime literature will need no documentation of this point, but others may wish to consult the following works for examples of the types of cases to which we refer: Geis (1977); Reiman (1979); Braithwaite (1984); Hochstedler (1984); Cullen, Maakestad, and Cavender (1987); Levi (1987); Hills (1987); Coleman (1989); Simon and Eitzen (1990).

References

Andrews, D. A. and J. Stephen Wormith. 1989. "Personality and Crime: Knowledge Destruction and Construction in Criminology." *Justice Quarterly* 6:289-310.

Benson, Michael L. 1985. "Denying the Guilty Mind: Accounting for Involvement in a White-Collar Crime." *Criminology* 23:583-608.

Benson, Michael L. and Esteban Walker. 1988. "Sentencing the While-Collar Offender." *American Sociological Review* 53:294-302.

Bonger, Willem. 1969. *Criminality and Economic Conditions*. Bloomington: Indiana University Press.

Braithwaite, John. 1984. *Corporate Crime in the Pharmaceutical Industry*. London: Routledge & Kegan Paul.

Bursik, Robert J. 1980. "The Dynamics of Specialization in Juvenile Offenses." *Social Forces* 58:851-64.

Coleman, James E. 1987. "Toward an Integrated Theory of White-Collar Crime." *American Journal of Sociology* 93:406-39.

———. 1989. *The Criminal Elite*. 2nd ed. New York: St. Martin's.

Cressey, Donald R. 1953. *Other People's Money*. New York: Free Press.

Cullen, Francis T., William J. Maakestad, and Gray Cavender. 1987. *Corporate Crime Under Attack*. Cincinnati, OH: Anderson.

Denzin, Norman K. 1977. "Notes on the Criminogenic Hypothesis: A Case Study of the American Liquor Industry." *American Sociological Review* 42:905-20.

Edelhertz, Herbert. 1970. *The Nature, Impact and Prosecution of White-Collar Crime*. Washington, DC: U.S. Government Printing Office.

Farrington, David P., Howard N. Snyder, and Terrence A. Finnegan. 1988. "Specialization in Juvenile Court Careers." *Criminology* 26:461-85.

Geis, Gilbert 1977. "The Heavy Electrical Equipment Antitrust Cases of 1961." Pp. 102-16 in *White-Collar Crime*, edited by Gilbert Geis and Robert F. Meier. New York: Free Press.

Goodman, Leo. 1962. "Statistical Methods for Analyzing Processes of Change." *American Journal of Sociology* 68:57-78.

Gottfredson, Michael R. and Travis Hirschi. 1990. *A General Theory of Crime*. Stanford, CA: Stanford University Press.

Hagan, John, Ilene Nagel-Bernstein, and Celesta Albonetti. 1980. "The Differential Sentencing of White-Collar Offenders in Ten Federal District Courts." *American Sociological Review* 45:802-20.

Hills, Stuart L., ed. 1987. *Corporate Violence*. Totowa, NJ: Rowman & Littlefield.

Hirschi, Travis and Michael Gottfredson. 1986. "The Distinction Between Crime and Criminality." Pp. 55-69 in *Critique and Explanation: Essays in Honor of Gwynn Nettler*, edited by Timothy F. Hartnagel and Robert Silverman. New Brunswick, NJ: Transaction.

———. 1987a. "Toward a General Theory of Crime." Pp. 8-26 in *Explaining Crime: Interdisciplinary Approaches*, edited by Wouter Buikhuisen and Sarnoff Mednick. Leiden: Brill.

———. 1987b. "Causes of White-Collar Crime." *Criminology* 25:949-74.

———. 1989. "The Significance of White-Collar Crime for a General Theory of Crime." *Criminology* 27:359-71.

Hochstedler, Ellen., ed. 1984. *Corporations as Criminals*. Beverly Hills, CA: Sage.

Kempf, Kimberly L. 1987. "Specialization and the Criminal Career." *Criminology* 25:399-420.

Levi, Michael. 1987. *Regulating Fraud*. London: Tavistock.

Reiman, Jeffrey H. 1979. *The Rich Get Richer and the Poor Get Prison*. New York: Wiley.

Rothman, Martin and Robert F. Gandossy. 1982. "Sad Tales: The Accounts of White-Collar Offenders and the Decision to Sanction." *Pacific Sociological Review* 4:449-73.

Shapiro, Susan. 1980. *Thinking About White-Collar Crime: Matters of Conceptualization and Research*. Washington, DC: U.S. Government Printing Office.

———. 1990. "Collaring the Crime, Not the Criminal: Reconsidering 'White-Collar Crime.'" *American Sociological Review* 55:346-65.

Simon, David R. and D. Stanley Eitzen, eds. 1990. *Elite Deviance*. 3rd ed. Boston: Allyn & Bacon.

Simpson, Sally. 1987. "Cycles of Illegality: Antitrust Violations in Corporate America." *Social Forces* 65:943-63.

Steffensmeier, Darrell. 1989. "On the Causes of 'White-Collar' Crime: An Assessment of Hirschi and Gottfredson's Claims." *Criminology* 27:345-58.

Sutherland, Edwin. 1949. *White-Collar Crime*. New York: Drysden.

Tittle, Charles A. 1991. "Review of *A General Theory of Crime*." *American Journal of Sociology* 96:1609-11.

Weisburd, David, Ellen F. Chayet, and Elin J. Waring. 1990. "White-Collar Crime and Criminal Careers: Some Preliminary Findings." *Crime & Delinquency* 36:342-55.

Weisburd, David, Stanton Wheeler, Elin Waring, and Nancy Bode. 1991. *Crimes of the Middle Classes*. New Haven, CT: Yale University Press.

Wheeler, Stanton, Kenneth Mann, and Austin Sarat. 1988. *Sitting in Judgement*. New Haven, CT: Yale University Press.

Wheeler, Stanton and Mitchell Rothman. 1982. "The Organization as Weapon." *Michigan Law Review* 80:1403-26.

Wheeler, Stanton, David Weisburd, and Nancy Bode. 1982. "Sentencing the White-Collar Offender: Rhetoric and Reality." *American Sociological Review* 47:641-59.

Wheeler, Stanton, David Weisburd, Nancy Bode, and Elin Waring. 1988. "White-Collar Crime and Criminals." *American Criminal Law Review* 25:331-57.

Wilson, James Q. and Richard J. Hermstein. 1985. *Crime and Human Nature*. New York: Simon & Schuster.

Wolfgang, Marvin E., Robert M. Figlio, and Thorsten Sellin. 1972. *Delinquency in a Birth Cohort*. Chicago: University of Chicago Press.

DISCUSSION QUESTIONS

1. Do you think white-collar offenders have low self-control? Explain.

2. What do you think accounts for differences between white-collar and conventional offenders?

READING

In this article, Nicole Piquero and her coauthors consider whether self-control or desire for control is related to corporate offending. The authors conceptualize desire for control as involving the "wish" to be in control of daily activities. While self-control and desire for control are both psychologically oriented, the authors distinguish between the two phenomena. They conducted a survey with business students to determine how the two explanations were related to support of corporate offending (as described in a vignette). The researchers found that self-control did not explain corporate offending, but desire for control did.

Completely Out of Control or the Desire to Be in Complete Control?

How Low Self-Control and the Desire for Control Relate to Corporate Offending

Nicole Leeper Piquero, Andrea Schoepfer, and Lynn Langton

Over the past two decades, Gottfredson and Hirschi's general theory of crime (1990) has occupied a central role in criminological theory in terms of sparking criminological thought, research, and debate. At its core, the theory contends that individuals who lack self-control are more likely to engage in problematic behavior (i.e., criminal and analogous behavior) over their life course because of its time-stable nature. In addition, Gottfredson and Hirschi contend that low self-control is "*the* individual level cause of crime" (p. 232; emphasis in original). In other words, once individual propensity, or self-control, is taken into account, all other variables should be rendered insignificant in predicting crime and other high-risk behaviors. Evidence from Pratt and Cullen's meta-analysis (2000) provides good empirical support for the effect of self-control on criminal and analogous behaviors. Moreover, this finding has even held with controls for rival theoretical variables, and it has emerged regardless of whether the measurement of self-control is behavioral or attitudinal (Tittle, Ward, & Grasmick, 2003).

At the same time that the general theory has been witnessing such empirical support, it has rarely been applied to the study of white-collar or corporate crime. The few attempts have revealed mixed success (see Benson & Moore, 1992; Simpson & Piquero, 2002). This becomes problematic for the generality component of the theory because if it is indeed a general theory of crime, then it should be able to explain all forms of crime, including white-collar and corporate crimes. Gottfredson and Hirschi (1990; also see Hirschi & Gottfredson, 1987, 1989) do content that their theory is applicable to the study of white-collar crime because crime, in all its varieties, is a unitary phenomenon capable of explanation by a single theoretical explanation. However, many scholars have countered and critiqued their conceptualization of white-collar crime (for the debate, see Geis, 2000; Reed & Yeager, 1996; Steffensmeier, 1989).

SOURCE: Piquero, N., Schoepfer, A., & Langton, L. (2010). Completely Out of Control or the Desire to Be in Complete Control? How Low Self-Control and the Desire for Control Relate to Corporate Offending. *Crime and Delinquency, 56,* 627–647.

The unsuccessful attempts of self-control to explain corporate criminality prompted N. L. Piquero, Exum, and Simpson (2005) to search for another possible individual-level explanation of corporate wrongdoing. Specifically, the authors examined the ability of desire for control—an understudied personality trait referring to the general need to be in control of everyday life events—to account for corporate offending. Based on data from a sample of MBA students, their analysis indicated that individuals high in desire for control were more likely to report that they would engage in corporate crimes. The analysis, however, could not speak to whether desire for control was a better predictor of corporate offending when compared to low self-control because, unfortunately, the researchers did not have a measure of self-control in their data. Therefore, caution must be drawn from their results owing to the possibility of a misspecified model.

This article builds off prior research and joins these two individual difference explanations in an effort to adjudicate which personal characteristic—desire for control or low self-control—relates best to corporate offending decisions. If Gottfredson and Hirschi (1990) are correct, then low self-control should not only significantly relate to corporate offending but also render insignificant any other personal characteristic, including desire for control. On this point, Gottfredson and Hirschi could not be clearer, claiming that the search for personal characteristics has produced nothing "contrary to the use of low self-control as the primary individual characteristic causing criminal behavior" (p. 111).

 Desire for Control

Desire for control is the general wish to be in control over everyday life events (Burger & Cooper, 1979), and it is believed to exhibit specific measurable behavioral manifestations. It is an important concept in the psychological literature, given that researchers have long viewed the need to have control over outcomes as one of the strongest human motivations (see, e.g., Bandura, 1977). Central to this research on desire for control is Burger and Cooper's 20-point Desirability of Control

Scale, which has been cited in more than 130 articles (Gebhardt & Brosschot, 2002).

According to Burger and Cooper (1979), those high in desire for control tend to be assertive, decisive, and active; they generally seek to influence others when influence is advantageous; and they tend to avoid unpleasant situations (i.e., failure) through the manipulation of events. Psychologists have developed self-report questionnaires, with the foremost being the Desirability of Control Scale, that measure these underlying behavioral traits while remaining sensitive to the fact that levels of desire for control may vary across individuals (Burger & Cooper, 1979).

Although desire for control is an important concept in psychological literature, it has received sparse attention in the criminological literature. The underlying concept of desire for control, however, may actually be beneficial for the study of white-collar and corporate crime. N. L. Piquero et al. (2005) conducted the first criminological study of desire for control by incorporating it into a study of corporate crime. Using scenario-based data, the study examined the effects of desire for control as it related to rational choice considerations and corporate criminal decision making. The researchers predicted that individual corporate offenders with high desire for control would be more likely to engage in corporate offending because of their susceptibility to an illusion of control, or an exaggerated sense of personal success over everyday life events, including those governed by chance (Langer, 1975; see also N. L. Piquero et al., 2005). In addition, individuals with high desire for control were believed to be more attuned to sanction threats and less so to the personal benefits of the act.

N. L. Piquero and colleagues (2005) found that desire for control was positively and significantly related to intentions to offend in a corporate context, suggesting that individuals of high desire for control engage in corporate crime as a means to gain control over uncertain or irrational environments. Findings were mixed regarding the relationship between desire for control and the rational choice framework. As predicted, high desire for control was positively related to individually perceived sanction threats, but contrary to expectations, desire for control was negatively related to individually perceived benefits. The researchers concluded that corporate crime decision making was influenced by situational, individual, and personality characteristics—mainly, the desire for control.

Furthermore, desire for control is arguably similar to low self-control in terms of behavioral manifestations and influence on the decision-making process. Although N. L. Piquero et al. (2005) were unable to directly compare the two theories with their data, they did suggest that desire for control appears to be better equipped for explaining corporate criminality, whereas low self-control appears to be better equipped for explaining more traditional offending (e.g., street offenses). These scholars maintained that the most important distinction between desire for control and low self-control is in how the future is viewed: Individuals with high desire for control like to be in control and should therefore be more responsive to how their actions will affect their world—both in the here and now and in the future. Yet, individuals of low self-control also have a here-and-now orientation, allowing them to react to situations without regard to future consequences. Although individuals of high desire for control and low self-control view the future differently, the two concepts do not necessarily identify opposite propensities in individuals. In other words, the presence of one trait does not necessarily require the absence of the other, because individuals can be impulsive and yet still be in control (whether real or perceived) of their everyday lives (N. L. Piquero et al., 2005).

In fact, N. L. Piquero and her colleagues (2005) are not alone in their idea that possessing self-control and exerting self-control are two overlapping but separate concepts. Tittle and colleagues (2004) have made similar reference to the fact that Gottfredson and Hirschi's formulation (1990) of low self-control fails to acknowledge an important distinction between ability to exert self-control and the desire to exert self-control. Their Desire to Exert Self-Control Scale is quite different from the more common measures of low self-control, such as the attitudinal scale developed by Grasmick and colleagues (1993; i.e., the Low Self-Control Scale), which tends to focus on the ability to regulate impulses and

not the desire or will to control them. Their conclusion that self-control may not be the only personality-related cause of crime and deviance is in line with the reasoning of N. L. Piquero and colleagues (2005) and the research endeavor at hand.

Current Study

This article seeks to empirically differentiate two individual difference explanations—low self-control and the desire for control—in explaining corporate crime. Following Braithwaite (1984), the current research defines *corporate crime* as "the conduct of a corporation, or of employees acting on behalf of a company, which is proscribed and punishable by law" (p. 6).

Although white-collar crimes and corporate crimes are not generally considered synonymously, corporate crime tends to be a more narrow or specific form of white-collar crime. Whereas low self-control has been successful in predicting more traditional forms of crime (e.g., street offending), it has not fared as well in explaining white-collar or corporate offending; because of this, researchers have looked toward other explanations to account for corporate crime and toward the desire for control. To date, both concepts have been independently used to predict corporate offending, but research has yet to examine how (if at all) the two personal characteristics operate together. The current research seeks to fill that void.

Based on the findings reviewed above, Hypothesis 1 posits that low self-control and the desire for control will be distinct but related concepts (N. L. Piquero et al., 2005). Given that Gottfredson and Hirschi's self-control explanation (1990) has received substantial support in predicting deviant and criminal behavior, additional research hypotheses are derived from that perspective. If Gottfredson and Hirschi are correct, then low self-control should be positively related to corporate offending (Hypothesis 2), and it should render insignificant any other personal characteristic (including the desire for control) in explaining criminal offending (Hypothesis 3). Finally, following N. L. Piquero et al. (2005), the desire for control should be a positive and significant predictor of corporate offending (Hypothesis 4).

Data

The data used to empirically investigate the relationship between low self-control and desire for control are derived from a vignette survey, an approach common in criminology in general (Nagin & Paternoster, 1993; A. Piquero & Tibbetts, 1996) and in the study of white-collar and corporate offending in particular (N. L. Piquero et al., 2005; Simpson, Paternoster, & Piquero, 1998; Simpson & Piquero, 2002). Data were collected from 87 working adults who were returning to higher education and were enrolled in several business courses. Before the distribution of the survey, all respondents were informed that they were part of a study, and all participants gave voluntary consent. Each individual was given a questionnaire containing a scenario in which a manager is told to "take care" of documents relevant to a specific account and so instructs his or her employees to destroy (i.e., shred) the problematic documents. Respondents were asked to indicate the likelihood that they would act as the manager depicted in the scenario and to respond to a variety of questions following the scenario that namely included demographic information and personal behaviors, as well as the Desire for Control Scale (Burger & Cooper, 1979), the Grasmick et al. Low Self-Control Scale (1993), and a behavioral self-control measure.

Dependent Variable

After reading the scenario, respondents were asked, "What is the chance that you would act as the manager did under these circumstances?" The dependent variable represents the respondent's self-reported intentions to engage in corporate offending. Response options ranged on a Likert-type scale from *no chance* to *100% chance* but were recoded into a dichotomous variable (called *commit*) because approximately half the sample (49%) indicated a nonzero chance of offending.

Independent Variables

Self-control. Two indicators of self-control were utilized: attitudinal and behavioral. First, respondents were presented with the Grasmick et al. attitudinal scale (1993; the Low Self-Control Scale), comprising 24 questions. Response options ranged from 1 (*strongly agree*) to 4 (*strongly disagree*). Higher scores on the scale represent lower self-control, whereas lower values indicate higher self-control. The scale was tested for reliability and found to have strong internal consistency ($\alpha = .79$). Because Gottfredson and Hirschi (1990) strongly argue in favor of behavioral indicators of low self-control, a seven-item count index (referred to as *analogous*) of behavioral indicators of self-control was also created. The items forming this index include cigarette smoking, drinking alcohol, using marijuana, speeding, car accidents, motor vehicle violations, and being suspended or let go from a job. Response options (0 = *no*, 1 = *yes*) accompanied each item in the survey. As such, the behavioral self-control index could range from 0 to 7, but no respondent admitted to all seven items, so the scale range is 0 to 5. Higher values represent lower self-control.

Desire for control. Respondents were asked to complete Burger and Cooper's Desire for Control Scale (1979). After reading each of the 20 statements, respondents were asked to indicate how well it described them (1 = *does not apply to me at all*, 7 = *always applies to me*). A total scale score is computed as the sum of the items (after the appropriate reverse-scoring of selected items), with higher scores indicative of greater desire for control. The Desire for Control Scale evinced good internal consistency ($\alpha = .72$).

Control variables. Three variables were used to control for respondents' demographic characteristics. Age of the respondent was a continuous variable that ranged from 21 to 54, with a mean of 32 years. Sex was coded as 0 (female) or 1 (male), with 45% of the sample consisting of men. Race was coded as 0 (non-White) or 1 (White), with 51% of the sample being White. Finally, to ensure that the gender of the individual depicted in the scenario did not have an influence on the outcome, a dichotomous variable (entitled *scenario*) was included that coded the gender of the supervisor depicted in the scenario (0 = Mary, 1 = Tom). Approximately half the sample (49%) randomly received the male scenario.

Analytic Plan

The analysis was conducted in a series of steps. First, the bivariate correlations of all variables were examined. This was done to allow for a better understanding of the relationship between the variables, to examine the relationship between low self-control and desire for control, and to check for multicollinearity. Next, a series of logistic regression analyses were estimated where each personal characteristic—low self-control (attitudinal and behavioral) and desire for control—was independently examined and then added in a stepwise fashion. The final logistic regression model presents the full model containing all three personal characteristics, as well as the control variables.

 Results

To understand the relationship between self-control and desire for control (Hypothesis 1), the correlations were examined among the two indicators self-control, the desire for control, and the other variables in the model. As expected, desire for control and self-control are related but distinct concepts. Both indicators of self-control, the attitudinal scale as well as the behavioral indicator, exhibit positive but nonsignificant associations with desire for control. Also, as Gottfredson and Hirschi (1990) would predict, there is a positive and significant association between the two measures of self- control ($r = .34$). Only one variable, race ($r = .24$), exhibits a significant (and positive) association with the dependent variable, whereas another (desire for control; $r = .22$) is approaching significance. Finally, none of the correlations between the independent variables exceeded .60; so, multicollinearity does not appear to be a problem. Other indicators of multicollinearity (e.g., variance inflation factor scores) were examined, and all tests indicated that there were no such problems.

Next, a multivariate analysis was estimated that examines the effects of the various independent variables on corporate offending intentions. Following Gottfredson and Hirschi (1990), a positive and significant relationship was expected between self-control and intentions to offend (Hypothesis 2). The attitudinal predictor of self-control is in the expected positive

direction but does not attain significance. Meanwhile, the behavioral indicator of self-control was neither significant nor in the expected direction. Consistent with Hypothesis 4, desire for control exerts a positive and approaching significant effect on intentions to offend. Race also exerts an approaching significant and positive effect across all models, indicating that Whites are more likely to report intentions to offend.

 Conclusion

Extant research has not been particularly supportive of the ability of low self-control to account for white-collar or corporate offending, despite Gottfredson and Hirschi's claims (1990) to the contrary. However, N. L. Piquero and colleagues (2005) have found a divergent personal characteristic, desire for control, to be positively related to intentions to engage in corporate crimes. Recognizing a need for a better understanding of the individual-level characteristics of white-collar and corporate offenders, this research was designed to compare the ability of desire for control versus low self-control for predicting intentions to destroy damaging workplace documents. Several key findings emerged from the analyses.

Most important, desire for control was a significant predictor of intentions to engage in corporate offending. Even after controlling for behavioral and attitudinal measures of low self-control—both independently and together in the same model—desire for control retained significance, whereas neither measure of low self-control attained significance, directly contrary to Gottfredson and Hirschi's expectation (1990). Based on what is known about the educational, social, and monetary attainments of many white-collar offenders (Benson & Moore, 1992), combined with the complexity and foresight involved in so many of these offenses (Calavita & Pontell, 1990; Sonnenfeld & Lawrence, 1978), this finding is not surprising to those who study white-collar crime and, especially, corporate crime. The impulsivity, self-interest, and present-day orientation of the individual with low self-control are inconsistent with the concepts of company loyalty and acting for the good of the company rather than personal benefit. However, desire for control is typified by high aspirations, personal expectancies of success, leadership positions, and a future-focused orientation, most of which provide a much better fit for the profile of the average corporate offender.

In addition, the current study utilized both an attitudinal and a behavioral measure of low self-control to maximize the effects of self-control. Because the different measures of low self-control are equally prevalent in the extant literature, the decision was made to operationalize low self-control in both ways to see if the effects would vary across the measurement of the construct. Neither measure emerged as a significant indicator of intentions to engage in corporate crime. This is consistent with prior research that found a nonsignificant relationship between behavioral measures of low self-control and corporate crime (Simpson & Piquero, 2002). Although Hirschi and Gottfredson (1987, 1990) anticipate that behavioral measures in particular will be able to predict criminal offenses, empirical evidence does not suggest this to be the case, at least with corporate offenses.

There is much to be learned about the desire for control and its ability to account for not only corporate offending but criminal offending in general. These preliminary findings suggest that it is a personal characteristic warranting further examination. Future research should strive to answer some of the many questions that remain regarding the desire for control. For instance, research should further examine the relationship between low self-control and desire for control to determine whether these concepts are mutually exclusive or whether they can be found to varying degrees within the same individual. In this regard, future research should examine the interactive effects between the two concepts. Scholars should also consider the ways in which desire for control can be integrated into other theoretical frameworks. For example, an integration of desire for control into organizational theories could examine whether company leaders high in desire for control are more likely to foster a criminogenic workplace with their expectations of success and illusion of control. Finally, desire for control should be applied to more typical criminal (i.e., street crimes) and analogous behaviors to understand how the concept operates across different crime types.

In closing and in concert with at least two other research findings (Benson & Moore, 1992; Simpson & Piquero, 2002), the results of this study suggest that self-control offers little by way of helping criminologists better understand corporate offending. In addition to examining the work of others (Geis, 2000; Simpson & Piquero, 2002), scholars should revisit Gottfredson and Hirschi's claim of generality (1990) and especially reconsider their strong position regarding self-control as "the" cause of crime. As of right now, it appears as though the general theory of crime may not be so general after all, at least when it comes to understanding corporate offending—especially when considering that corporate crimes appear to fall better under the purview of more traditional rational-choice theories (Paternoster & Simpson, 1996), organizational accounts (Simpson et al., 1998; Vaughan, 1996), and even other personal characteristic theories (N. L. Piquero et al., 2005). In the end and in contrast to Gottfredson and Hirschi's claims, self-control simply may not be the sole personal characteristic implicated in criminal offending.

 Note

1. At the request of a reviewer, supplemental analysis was performed in which management level was included as a control variable (1 = upper management, 0 = lower and middle). This variable did not exert any effect on any of the outcome variables, nor did its inclusion substantively alter any of the coefficient effects—namely, that of low self-control and desire for control.

 References

Arneklev, B. J., Grasmick, H. G., Tittle, C. R., & Bursik, R. J., Jr. (1993). Low self-control and imprudent behavior. *Journal of Quantitative Criminology, 9,* 225-247.

Bandura, A. (1977). *Social learning theory.* Englewood Cliffs, NJ: Prentice Hall.

Benson, M. L., & Moore, E. (1992). Are white-collar and common offenders the same? An empirical and theoretical critique of a recently proposed general theory of crime. *Journal of Research in Crime and Delinquency, 29,* 251-272.

Braithwaite, J. (1984). *Corporate crime in the pharmaceutical industry.* London: Routledge & Kegan Paul.

Burger, J. M. (1992). *Desire for control: Personality, social, and clinical perspectives.* New York: Plenum Press.

Burger, J. M., & Cooper, H. M. (1979). The desirability of control. *Motivation and Emotion, 3,* 381-393.

Calavita, K., & Pontell, H. N. (1990). "Heads I win, tails you lose": Deregulation, crime, and crisis in the savings and loan industry. *Crime and Delinquency, 36,* 309-341.

Gebhardt, W. A., & Brosschot, J. F. (2002). Desirability of control: Psychometric properties and relationships with locus of control, personality, coping, and mental and somatic complaints in three Dutch samples. *European Journal of Personality, 16,* 423-438.

Geis, G. (2000). On the absence of self-control as the basis for a general theory of crime. *Theoretical Criminology, 4,* 35-53.

Gibbs, J. J., Giever, D. M., & Martin, J. (1998). Parental management and self-control: An empirical test of Gottfredson and Hirschi's general theory. *Journal of Research in Crime and Delinquency, 35,* 42-72.

Gottfredson, M. R., & Hirschi, T. (1990). *A general theory of crime.* Stanford, CA: Stanford University Press.

Grasmick, H. G., Tittle, C. R., Bursik, R. J., Jr., & Arneklev, B. J. (1993). Testing the core empirical implications of Gottfredson and Hirschi's general theory of crime. *Journal of Research in Crime and Delinquency, 30,* 5-29.

Green, D. (1989). Measures of illegal behavior in individual-level deterrence research. *Journal of Research in Crime and Delinquency, 26,* 253-275.

Higgins, G. K (2005). Can low self-control help with the understanding of the software piracy problem? *Deviant Behavior, 26,* 1-24.

Hirschi, T., & Gottfredson, M. R. (1987). Causes of white-collar crime. *Criminology, 25,* 949-974.

Hirschi, T., & Gottfredson, M. R. (1989). The significance of white-collar crime for a general theory of crime. *Criminology, 27,* 359-371.

Hirschi, T., & Gottfredson, M. R. (2000). In defense of self-control. *Theoretical Criminology, 4,* 55-69.

Keane, C., Maxim, P. S., & Teevan, J. J. (1993). Drinking and driving, self-control, and gender: Testing a general theory of crime. *Journal of Research in Crime and Delinquency, 30,* 30-46.

Kim, M., & Hunter, J. (1993). Relationships among attitudes, behavioral intentions, and behavior: A meta-analysis of past research. *Communications Research, 20,* 331-364.

LaGrange, T. C., & Silverman, R. A. (1999). Low self-control and opportunity: Testing the general theory of crime as an explanation for gender differences in delinquency. *Criminology, 37,* 41-72.

Langer, J. R. (1975). The illusion of control. *Journal of Personality and Social Psychology, 32,* 311-328.

Mustaine, E. E., & Tewksbury, R. (2002). Workplace theft: An analysis of student-employee offenders and job attributes. *American Journal of Criminal Justice, 27,* 111-127.

Nagin, D. S., & Paternoster, R. (1993). Enduring individual differences and rational choice theories of crime. *Law and Society Review, 27,* 467-496.

Paternoster, R., & Simpson, S. (1996). Sanction threats and appeals to morality: Testing a rational choice model of corporate crime. *Law and Society Review, 30,* 549-583.

Piquero, A., & Tibbetts, S. G. (1996). Specifying the direct and indirect effects of low self-control and situational factors in offender decision-making: Toward a more complete model of rational offending. *Justice Quarterly, 13,* 481 -510.

Piquero, N. L., Exum, M. L., & Simpson, S. S. (2005). Integrating the desire for control and rational choice in a corporate crime context. *Justice Quarterly, 22,* 252-280.

Pogarsky, G. (2004). Projected offending and contemporaneous rule-violation: Implications for heterotypic continuity. *Criminology, 42,* 111-135,

Pratt, T. C., & Cullen, F. T. (2000). The empirical status of Gottfredson and Hirschi's general theory of crime: A meta-analysis. *Criminology, 38,* 931-964.

Reed, G. E., & Yeager, P. C. (1996). Organizational offending and neoclassical criminology: Challenging the reach of a general theory of crime. *Criminology, 34,* 357-382.

Sellers, C. (1999). Self-control and intimate violence: An examination of the scope and specification of the general theory of crime. *Criminology, 37,* 375-404.

Simpson, S. S. (2002). *Corporate crime, law, and social control.* New York: Cambridge University Press.

Simpson, S. S., Paternoster, R., & Piquero, N. L. (1998). Exploring the micro-macro link in corporate crime research. In P. A. Bamberger & W. J. Sonnenstuhl (Eds.), *Research in the sociology of organizations: Deviance in and of organizations* (Vol. 15, pp. 35-68). Stamford, CT: JAI Press.

Simpson, S. S., & Piquero, N. L. (2002). Low self-control, organizational theory, and corporate crime. *Law and Society Review, 36,* 509-548.

Sommerfeld, J., & Lawrence, P. R. (1978). Why do companies succumb to price fixing? *Harvard Business Review, 56,* 145-157.

Steffensmeier, D. (1989). On the causes of "white-collar" crime: An assessment of Hirschi and Gottfredson's claims. *Criminology, 27,* 345-358.

Stylianou, S. (2002). The relationship between elements and manifestations of low self-control in a general theory of crime: Two comments and a test. *Deviant Behavior, 23,* 531-557.

Tittle, C. R., Ward, D. A., & Grasmick, H. G. (2003). Self-control and crime/deviance: Cognitive vs. behavioral measures. *Journal of Quantitative Criminology, 19,* 333-365.

Tittle, C. R, Ward, D. A., & Grasmick, H. G. (2004). Capacity for self-control and individuals' interest in exercising self-control. *Journal of Quantitative Criminology, 20,* 143-172.

Vaughan, D. (1996). *The Challenger launch decision.* Chicago: University of Chicago Press.

Winfree, L. T., & Bemet, F. B. (1998). Social learning, self-control, and substance abuse by eighth grade students: A tale of two cities. *Journal of Drug Issues, 28,* 539-558.

DISCUSSION QUESTIONS

1. What are the similarities and differences between self-control and desire for control?

2. Where does one's "desire for control" come from? Explain.

Life course criminology has grown significantly over the past two decades. Despite this growth in the life course perspective, the application of the life course theory to white-collar offending is relatively rare. To fill this gap in the literature, Nicole Piquero and Michael Benson show how life course criminology can be applied to white-collar crime. The authors note that white-collar offenders come from different social backgrounds than conventional offenders and discuss the age at which white-collar criminals begin their criminal careers. They also discuss desistance from offending, referring to the factors that cause offenders to end criminal careers. Particularly interesting is the fact that white-collar crime careers tend to last longer than the criminal careers of conventional offenders. Piquero and Benson also note several research implications for using the life course perspective to examine white-collar crime.

White-Collar Crime and Criminal Careers

Specifying a Trajectory of Punctuated Situational Offending

Nicole Leeper Piquero and Michael L. Benson

The rise of the life course approach has been a breath of fresh air for criminology. Even though it is a relatively recent development, it has already produced a number of significant results (for many examples, see the articles in Thornberry & Krohn, 2003). More important, it has provided a new way of looking at offenders, a more realistic view that recognizes that behavior— especially the behavior of young people—results from complex, multifaceted, and interacting developmental processes. Despite its accomplishments and its promise, however, life course criminology runs the risk of making an old mistake, a mistake pointed out long ago by Sutherland (1940). The mistake is acting as though common street crime is the only type of crime there is. Sutherland criticized the criminologists of his day for relying on samples limited to street offenders, for having an overly narrow conception of offending and offenders, and for ignoring illegalities that did not conform to the common stereotypical image of street crime. Exactly the same charges could be leveled today at life course criminology. With very few exceptions, it too has relied on limited samples; it too implicitly conveys the impression that juvenile delinquency and street crime are the only forms of crime there are; and it too neglects the crimes of the powerful and well-to-do.[1] If continued, these practices will, we argue, inevitably lead to a biased and incomplete understanding of trajectories in crime.

The developmental explanations that have been put forth to explain offending patterns over the life course assume that offending almost always begins early in life; that is, sometime during the first or second decade of life. The primary issues that researchers have investigated are age at which offending starts,

SOURCE: Piquero, N., and Benson, M. (2004). White-Collar Crime and Criminal Careers: Specifying a Trajectory of Punctuated Situational Offending. *Journal of Contemporary Criminal Justice, 20*, 148–165.

how long it lasts, and how the age of onset relates to the length of career. One important theory posits that there are only two general patterns: those who show signs of antisocial behavior very early in life and persist in antisocial and criminal behavior throughout adulthood versus those who show no signs of antisocial behavior early but who undergo a brief period of criminality during adolescence (Moffitt, 1993; also see Patterson, DeBaryshe, & Ramsey, 1989). That such patterns are followed by many individuals is undoubtedly true, but there is another pattern that has been left out of the picture. It includes those who seem to begin or, as we argue, resume offending in adulthood, presumably after most other offenders have "aged out" of crime. Existing theoretical models have yet to acknowledge, let alone account for, this group of offenders.

White-Collar Crime and Criminal Careers: What Do We Know?

A statistically valid picture of white-collar offenders is hard to come by because of the virtual lack of quantitative data on these offenders. Until the late 1980s, most of what was known about white-collar offenders was based on qualitative accounts of highly publicized and egregious offenders and offenses (Benson, 2002). Following Sutherland's lead, investigators conducted detailed case studies of the offenses of powerful upper-class business executives from the privileged sectors of society (e.g., Braithwaite, 1984; Calavita & Pontell, 1990; Geis, 1977; Simpson & Piquero, 2000).[2] The case study approach has done much to keep white-collar crime on the criminological map, and it has confirmed many of Sutherland's original conjectures concerning the high social status of the offenders, the seriousness of their offenses, and the leniency of their treatment in the justice system.

In the 1980s, two data collection efforts were undertaken that for the first time permitted statistical analyses of the characteristics of white-collar offenders,

offenses, and offending careers. The first dataset was constructed under the guidance of Stanton Wheeler (Wheeler, Weisburd, Waring, & Bode, 1988). The other dataset was collected by Brian Forst and William Rhodes. Both studies were based on samples of individuals who had been convicted in selected U.S. federal courts of presumptively white-collar crimes in the mid-1970s. In the Wheeler dataset, the white-collar offenses included antitrust offenses, securities fraud, mail fraud, false claims, bribery, income tax fraud, lending and credit fraud, and bank embezzlement with a sample size of 1,342. In the Forst and Rhodes data, the white-collar offenses included embezzlement, bribery, income tax fraud, false claims, and mail fraud with a sample size of 2,462. Data were collected from presentence investigation (PSI) reports, which are prepared by federal probation officers after an offender is convicted for the sentencing judge (for more complete information on the sampling designs and data collection methods, see Forst & Rhodes, n.d.; Weisburd, Wheeler, Waring, & Bode, 1991). The PSI report provides detailed information on the current offense, criminal history, and background characteristics of offenders (e.g., education, employment, family, etc.). Although both studies were originally designed to investigate how white-collar offenders were treated in the federal judicial system, the quality and depth of information available from the PSIs permitted investigators to examine the social characteristics of the offenders and various aspects of their offending careers (Benson & Kerley, 2000; Benson & Moore, 1992; Weisburd & Waring, 2001; Weisburd et al., 1991; Wheeler et al., 1988). It is important that both studies also sampled a comparison group of individuals convicted of non-white-collar offenses, enabling comparisons between individuals who commit different types of offenses.

A great deal has been learned from these data collection efforts that challenges existing assumptions in the study of white-collar crime and criminal careers. For example, two notable findings emerged that call into question the stereotype of the white-collar offender as a person of wealth, power, and high social status, who has led an upstanding and otherwise impeccable life. First, most of the individuals convicted of white-collar crimes in the federal system are not wealthy high-powered corporate executives. Rather, they tend to look more like members of the middle classes with moderate incomes and ordinary jobs—small-time entrepreneurs and midlevel office workers (Benson & Kerley, 2000; Weisburd et al., 1991). Second, a substantial proportion of persons convicted of white-collar offenses are repeat offenders, that is, they have had at least two official contacts with the criminal justice system (Benson & Moore, 1992; Weisburd et al., 1991). In both studies, approximately 40% of the white-collar offenders had at least one other arrest in addition to the white-collar type offense that made them eligible for inclusion in the study.

Even though in these studies white-collar offenders turn out to be not as elite or law abiding as the standard stereotype would envision them, there are still substantial differences between white-collar and common offenders. After carefully comparing the persons convicted of ordinary street crimes with those convicted of white-collar crimes on a host of social background and status characteristics, Weisburd and his colleagues (1991) concluded that

> whatever else may be true of the distinction between white-collar and common criminals, the two are definitely drawn from distinctively different sectors of the American population. (p. 73)

Similar analyses of the Forst and Rhodes data came to the same conclusion (Benson & Kerley, 2000; Benson & Moore, 1992). The people who commit white-collar crimes do not come from the same social backgrounds nor occupy the same social space as the people who commit ordinary street crimes. To the extent that criminal careers are seen as arising out of one's social background, these offenders offer a challenge to existing developmental theories of criminal offending.

In an important follow-up study based on the Wheeler data, Weisburd and Waring (2001) gathered additional data on the subsequent criminal records of the original Wheeler sample. Using FBI rap sheets, the investigators were able to construct longitudinal criminal record data on the offenders that ran from the time of their original white-collar crime convictions in the mid-1970s up to 10 years later. They found that almost one third of the white-collar offenders were rearrested after their original convictions (p. 28).

An important issue for life course criminology and for the criminal career paradigm is the age of onset. As noted above, research based on ordinary street offenders and juvenile delinquents finds that most of these offenders have official contacts with the justice system sometime in their teenage years. However, for white-collar criminals, the average age of onset is found to be substantially later. In the Wheeler data, the average age of onset, defined as an arrest, for all white-collar offenders was 35. Of course, many of the white-collar offenders were first-time offenders, but even when the sample is restricted to offenders with at least two arrests, the average age of first arrest for white-collar offenders is 33.5. For first-time offenders, the average age is 40.9 (Weisburd & Waring, 2001, pp. 33-34). Benson and Kerley (2000, p. 132) found exactly the same average age of onset (40) for first-time white-collar offenders as in the Forst and Rhodes data. For white-collar offenders with prior records, the average age of onset was 24 compared to 19 for common offenders.

When and how offenders end their criminal careers also are important questions for the criminal career perspective. Weisburd and Waring (2001) examined the issue of desistance for white-collar offenders. They found notable differences between white-collar and common offenders with regard to desistance. The average age of last arrest for repeat white-collar offenders in their study was 43, considerably older than the late 20s and early 30s, which is the time period during which most common offenders are assumed to age out of crime. It is surprising that a substantial number of the repeat offenders in their sample were arrested in their 50s, and a small number of offenders continued to be active into their 70s (Weisburd & Waring, 2001, p. 37).

Weisburd and Waring (2001) also found other differences between the careers of their white-collar offenders and the careers of street offenders. For instance, the repeat offenders in their sample had on average considerably longer periods of career activity than is typically found in samples of street offenders. Research on street offenders typically finds that criminal careers last not much longer than 5 years (Farrington, 1992). Among the white-collar offenders studied by Weisburd and Waring, however, the average duration between first and last arrest was 14 years. In addition, even though these white-collar offenders were criminally active for relatively long periods of time, they tended to commit, or at least to be arrested for, relatively few offenses during the duration of their careers. As Weisburd and Waring (2001) note, in light of their relatively low levels of criminal activity, it may not even make sense to apply the concept of criminal career to white-collar offenders (p. 43).

One area in which those who commit white-collar offenses do appear to be similar to those who commit ordinary street offenses is in their lack of specialization in offending. Although a large proportion of white-collar offenders are repeat offenders, in the sense of having other arrests, their other offenses tend not to be other white-collar crimes (Benson & Moore, 1992; Weisburd & Waring, 2001). Rather, they are arrested for a variety of other types of crimes. At least as indicated by arrests, white-collar offenders do not specialize in white-collar crimes to any notable degree. Of course, it is entirely possible that successful white-collar offenders specialize in one type of offense but are simply never caught.

On such limited evidence, it would, of course, be unwise to draw many firm conclusions about the criminal careers or absence of criminal careers of white-collar offenders. We simply need more data. The two most useful datasets available are now more than 20 years old, and no effort has been made to gather data on contemporary white-collar offenders. Nevertheless, we can make two observations that we think are likely to stand the test of time and new data. First, the people who commit white-collar crimes come from more privileged or less troubled social and personal backgrounds than the people who commit ordinary street crimes. Second, white-collar offending starts and ends later in the life course than street crime. Although these observations may appear blazingly obvious to some, their significance for life course and developmental approaches to crime should not be overlooked. To the extent that these approaches emphasize biological and early family background factors in the etiology of crime, it would seem that they are going to have difficulty accounting for patterns in white-collar offending.

 ## Theoretical Expansions to Account for White-Collar Offenders

To date, our understanding or picture of trajectories in crime assumes that offending starts early in life, stops after a short while for most people, but continues on longer for a small subset of offenders. We suspect that this view misses another potential pattern, a pattern that is followed by those who become involved in white-collar crime. We call this pattern *punctuated situationally dependent offending*.[3] This pattern assumes that white-collar offenders follow the same developmental trajectories in crime and delinquency that most people do. That is, they have a brief flirtation with delinquency during adolescence that ends in the late teens or early 20s. However, after a period of conformity during their 20s and 30s, they begin to offend again later in life by committing white-collar crimes. Their offending is situational in the sense that it is triggered by or dependent on factors external to the offender. This situational dependence can come about in two ways. First, white-collar offending may be situationally dependent in the sense that the opportunity to offend may not become available to the individual until after he or she has obtained a certain occupational position. Second, it may be situationally dependent in the sense that the individual experiences some crisis in his or her personal or occupational life that motivates the commission of a white-collar crime. The key point about this pattern, however, is that it is not a continuation of the offending that took place during adolescence. Rather, the offender's criminal trajectory is punctuated by a period or periods of conformity, and when offending resumes, it is of a different character from the indiscretions of youth.

Existing developmental explanations do not account for this punctuated period of conformity, nor do they address the resumption of criminal activity. In fact, two common themes running throughout existing life course explanations are that offending begins early in life and that once offenders have become socially integrated into conventional society, criminal activities will be forever deterred. It would appear then that white-collar offenders, who begin offending in adulthood and who are already educated, employed, and married, offer a unique challenge to life course explanations of criminal behavior, particularly with regard to onset and desistance of offending. We offer below some suggestions for orienting future investigations and a challenge to white-collar crime and life course scholars to begin to address this seemingly unique pattern of behavior.

Unlike street crime opportunities, which are often assumed to be ubiquitous and available to all, opportunities to engage in white-collar crime are not likely to be so prevalent or so democratically distributed. Rather, they arise out of certain occupational positions (Weisburd & Waring, 2001). Access to white-collar crime opportunities, therefore, is shaped by the same structural factors that determine how occupations are distributed to individuals. Structurally shaped opportunities play a much bigger role in white-collar as opposed to street crime. Criminological theories typically assume the presence of opportunities and do little to articulate how offenders and opportunities come together in time and space (however, see Cohen & Felson, 1979). For example, Gottfredson and Hirschi (1990) have garnered much attention with respect to both street offending as well as white-collar crime with their general theory of crime. The basic premise of their theory is that variation in an internal trait explains variation in offending; that is, individuals with low self-control will engage in more crime than individuals with greater self-control. Very little attention is paid to explaining or conceptualizing opportunities to offend. It is simply assumed that opportunities for offending

are more or less a constant for everyone. White-collar and corporate crime scholars, on the other hand, are acutely aware of how opportunities for white-collar crime are situated within occupations and organizations and their corresponding commercial, economic, and legal environments (Simpson & Piquero, 2002).

As middle- and upper-class individuals grow older, they are exposed to different kinds and perhaps more white-collar criminal opportunities as they move into more trusted occupational positions. Because potential white-collar criminals have worked their way up to positions of trust and authority, they have unique opportunities to engage in crime that are not available to others. Because so many jobs are now located in large organizations, it is important to consider how organizations influence individual behavior. The structure and culture of an organization may influence how individuals perceive and take advantage of criminal opportunities. An organization may not only expose individuals to various criminal opportunities but may also encourage them in different ways. For example, the hierarchical division of labor and diffuse decision making found in many organizations permits individuals to hide behind the company "web" to avoid being held responsible (Coleman, 1998, p. 133). In addition, the organization may encourage employees through awards and promotional incentives to find innovative solutions to meet company needs (Reed & Yeager, 1996). Obviously, the study of organizational behavior is a large and complex topic, one that is beyond the scope of this article. We merely wish to note that organizations create both opportunities for white-collar crime and pressure to take advantage of those opportunities. Hence, organizations are an important situational element in white-collar offending, an element that comes into play at a different stage in the life course from the usual causal factors associated with crime.

Another important consideration is that unlike many ordinary street crime offenders, white-collar offenders often have acquired some level of material, occupational, and social success. In other words, they have something to lose. We usually think of these trappings of success and achievement as factors that promote conformity. In theory, middle-class people conform in part because they have a stake in conformity and the collateral consequences of being caught doing something untoward are more severe for them than they are for someone who has not achieved middle-class levels of success and who has less to lose. However, situations may arise in which these very same factors can motivate crime rather than conformity. If, for example, the individual experiences some sort of personal or occupational crisis that threatens their middle-class standing, white-collar crime may appear as a way out of the crisis (Benson & Moore, 1992; Cressey, 1953; Weisburd & Waring, 2001; Wheeler, 1992). Evidence suggests that some white-collar offenders, particularly women, are likely to respond to family emergencies and poor family economic conditions by engaging in crime (Daly, 1989; Zietz, 1981). Weisburd and Waring (2001) found that a substantial proportion of the white-collar offenders they studied appeared to fit this pattern. That is, they were people who had gotten into a troublesome situation and who thought that white-collar crime was the only way out. Stanton Wheeler (1992) describes this factor as the fear of falling. He argues that the reasons for engaging in criminal activities may not lie with greed or financial gain but rather with the fear of losing what one has already attained. Individuals in the middle or upper classes have invested much time and effort into conventional society and when things start to go astray, they will grasp onto what they have already worked so hard to attain. Therefore, it is not necessarily the fear of failing but rather the fear of falling that explains some white-collar offending (Wheeler, 1992).

Theoretical expansions always make evident the need for more research. Although we do not claim to have provided a major theoretical expansion here, we do think that our approach recommends several fruitful avenues for research. First, at the most basic level, we simply need more information about the life histories of individual white-collar offenders. Do they really conform to the punctuated pattern that we have hypothesized? That is, is it really true, as we theorized, that most white-collar offenders engage in minor delinquencies during adolescence, then stop, and then start

again much later with white-collar offenses? Or, is there some other pattern? Second, if the pattern of punctuated offending is observed, then we need more information on the situational factors that trigger offending later in life. The groundbreaking work by Weisburd and Waring (2001) is very helpful, but it is limited in that it is based on a sample of convicted offenders. By definition, these are people who have responded to situational pressures with offending, but the question we really need to answer is this: Of those who experience situational pressures, how many respond to the pressure with offending? And further, what separates those who respond with offending from those who do not? Third, we speculate that a lot of the pressure arises from organizational and job-related influences. So, it is important to document that and better understand just how organizations exert pressures on individuals. A potentially useful line of investigation would be to compare employees or managers in law-abiding companies to their counterparts in companies that are known to have been involved in white-collar offenses. If our theory is correct, then we should expect to observe differences between these individuals in the pressures they feel from the company's leaders. Fourth, future research needs to further explore the role of individual motivations. It very well could be that the motivations for white-collar offending are similar to the motivations for street offending, or it could be that researchers have yet to tap into the full array of individual factors. For example, white-collar crime may simply be a means to alleviate stressful experiences as suggested by traditional strain theories or yet unexplored individual characteristics, such as fear of falling, could better account for such criminal events. These are among the many research avenues to be explored by the intersection between the criminal career paradigm and the existing white-collar crime research.

Summary and Conclusion

In a number of ways, white-collar crime is different from ordinary street crime. Involvement in it occurs at a different point in the life course. It has a dramatically different opportunity structure. Those who participate in it are drawn from a different sector of the American social structure. Finally, it may have significantly different motivations from those who engage in street crime.

We are not the first to draw attention to the differences between white-collar crimes and street crimes nor are we the first to note that most criminological theories fail to account for white-collar offending behaviors (Sutherland, 1949). Although existing developmental theories may eventually be able to account for developmental patterns in juvenile offending, they appear to have little to offer with regard to crimes that occur later in life, such as white-collar crimes. Most of the theorizing about crime over the life course simply ignores white-collar crime and white-collar crime research. We think this is a mistake. A full understanding of crime over the life course will require criminologists to take a closer look at all forms of offending, including those that begin, persist, and end during adulthood. In our view, white-collar offending cannot be explained by the theoretical perspectives currently popular in life course criminology. Rather, a new perspective is needed, one that focuses on adults and on the intersection of occupations, organizations, and white-collar criminal opportunities. Toward that end, we have offered a way of conceptualizing white-collar criminal careers that takes note of the punctuated situationally dependent nature of white-collar offending.

 Notes

1. Crimes of the elite can include both white-collar crimes, those crimes committed for the benefit of the individual, or corporate crimes, those crimes committed for the benefit of the corporation or organization (Clinard & Quinney, 1973). Although it is recognized that organizations are held accountable and responsible for the actions of their employees and therefore possible to study the criminal careers of organizations (see Simpson & Koper, 1992), this is beyond the scope of this article. Our focus will remain on individual actors engaging in criminal behaviors, even though they may on occasion be acting in the interests of an organization.

2. There are exceptions, of course; studies by Cressey (1953) and Zietz (1981) portrayed the lives of white-collar offenders who often came from middle- or even lower class backgrounds. See also Croall (1989).

3. Those familiar with the work of Steven Jay Gould (2002) undoubtedly will not miss that our term echoes the evolutionary theory of punctuated equilibrium that he and Niles Eldredge proposed in 1972. The echo is intentional, in that we speculate that for many white-collar offenders their offenses are episodic events that occur within a background of conformity, just as for Gould major evolutionary changes occur suddenly and episodically within a long time frame of stasis and lack of change.

 References

Benson, M. L. (2002). *Crime and the life course.* Los Angeles: Roxbury Publishing Co.

Benson, M. L., & Kerley, K. R. (2000). Life course theory and white-collar crime. In H. N. Pontell & D. Shichor (Eds.), *Contemporary issues in crime and criminal justice: Essays in honor of Gilbert Geis* (pp. 121-136). Upper Saddle River, NJ: Prentice Hall.

Benson, M. L., & Moore, E. (1992). Are white-collar and common offenders the same?: An empirical and theoretical critique of a recently proposed general theory of crime. *Journal of Research in Crime and Delinquency, 29,* 251-272.

Blumstein, A., Cohen, J., Roth, J. A., & Visher, C. A. (1986). *Criminal careers and "career criminals."* Washington, DC: National Research Council.

Braithwaite, J. (1984). *Corporate crime in the pharmaceutical industry.* London: Routledge & Kegan Paul.

Calavita, K., & Pontell, H. N. (1990). "Heads I win, tails you lose": Deregulation, crime, and crisis in the savings and loan industry. *Crime & Delinquency, 36,* 309-341.

Clinard, M. B., & Quinney, R. (1973). *Criminal behavior systems: A typology.* New York: Holt, Rinehart & Winston.

Cohen, L. E., & Felson, M. (1979). Social change and crime rate trends: A routine activities approach. *American Sociological Review, 44,* 588-608.

Coleman, J. W. (1998). *The criminal elite: Understanding white-collar crime.* New York: St. Martin's Press.

Cressey, D. (1953). *Other people's money.* New York: Free Press.

Croall, H. (1989). Who is the white-collar criminal? *British Journal of Criminology, 29,* 157-174.

Daly, K. (1989). Gender and varieties of white-collar crime. *Criminology, 27,* 769-794.

Elder, G. H., Jr. (1994). Time, human agency and social change. *Social Psychology Quarterly, 57,* 4-15.

Elliot, D. S. (1994), Serious violent offenders: Onset, developmental course and termination. *Criminology, 32,* 1-22.

Farrington, D. (1992). Criminal career research in the United Kingdom. *British Journal of Criminology, 32,* 521-536.

Forst, B., & Rhodes, W. (n.d.). *Sentencing in eight United States District Courts, 1973-1978.* Codebook (Interuniversity Consortium for Political and Social Research Study No. 8622). Ann Arbor: University of Michigan.

Geis, G. (1977). The heavy electrical equipment antitrust cases of 1961. In G. Geis & R. Meier (Eds.), *White-collar crime* (Rev. ed. pp. 117-132). New York: MacMillan.

Gottfredson, M. R., & Hirschi, T. (1990). *General theory of crime.* Stanford: Stanford University Press.

Gould, S. J. (2002). *The structure of evolutionary theory.* Cambridge, MA: Harvard University Press.

Hagan, J. (1997). Defiance and despair: Subcultural and structural linkages between delinquency and despair in the life course. *Social Forces, 76,* 119-134.

Hagan, J., & Palloni, A. (1998). Crimes as social events in the life course: Reconceiving a criminological controversy. *Criminology, 26,* 87-100.

LeBlanc, M., & Loeber, R. (1998). Developmental criminology updated. In M. Tonry (Ed.), *Crime and justice: A review of research* (pp. 115-198). Chicago: University of Chicago Press.

Moffitt, T. E. (1993). Adolescence-limited and life-course-persistent antisocial behavior: A developmental taxonomy. *Psychological Review, 100,* 674-701.

Moffitt, T. E. (1997). Adolescence-limited and life-course persistent offending: A complementary pair of developmental theories. In T. P. Thornberry (Ed.), *Developmental theories of crime and delinquency* (pp. 11-54). New Brunswick, NJ: Transaction Publishers.

Moffitt, T. E., Caspi, A., Rutter, M., & Silva, P. A. (2001). *Sex differences in antisocial behaviour: Conduct disorder, delinquency, and violence in the Dunedin longitudinal study.* Cambridge: Cambridge University Press.

Nagin, D. S., & Land, K. C. (1993). Age, criminal careers, and population heterogeneity: Specification and estimation of a nonparametric, mixed Poisson model. *Criminology, 31,* 327-362.

Patterson, G. R., DeBaryshe, B., & Ramsey, E. (1989). A developmental perspective on antisocial behavior. *American Psychologist, 44,* 329-335.

Piquero, A. R., Farrington, D. P., & Blumstein, A. (2003). The criminal career paradigm. In M. Tonry (Ed.), *Crime and justice: A review of research* (pp. 359-506). Chicago: University of Chicago Press.

Reed, G. E., & Yeager, P. C. (1996). Organizational offending and neoclassical criminology: Challenging the reach of a general theory of crime. *Criminology, 34,* 357-382.

Sampson, R. J., & Laub, J. H. (1993). *Crime in the making.* Cambridge: Harvard University Press.

Simpson, S. S., & Koper, C. S. (1992). Deterring corporate crime. *Criminology, 30,* 347-375.

Simpson, S. S., & Piquero, N. L. (2000). The Archer Daniels Midland antitrust case of 1996: A case study. In H. N. Pontell & D. Shichor (Eds.), *Contemporary issues in crime and criminal justice: Essays in honor of Gilbert Geis* (pp. 175-194). Upper Saddle River, NJ: Prentice Hall.

Simpson, S. S., & Piquero, N. L. (2002). Low self-control, organizational theory, and corporate crime. *Law and Society Review, 36,* 509-548.

Sutherland, E. H. (1940). White collar criminality. *American Sociological Review, 5,* 1-12.

Sutherland, E. H. (1949). *White-collar crime.* New York: Holt, Rinehart & Winston.

Thornberry, T. P. (1987). Toward an interactional theory of delinquency. *Criminology, 25,* 863-892.

Thornberry, T. P., & Krohn, M. D. (2003). *Taking stock of delinquency: An overview of findings from contemporary longitudinal studies.* New York: Kluwer Academic/Plenum Publishers.

Void, G. B., Bernard, T. J., & Snipes, J. B. (1998). *Theoretical criminology.* New York: Oxford University Press.

Weisburd, D., & Waring, E. (2001). *White-collar crime and criminal careers.* New York: Cambridge University Press.

Weisburd, D., Wheeler, S., Waring, E., & Bode, N. (1991). *Crimes of the middle classes: White-collar offenders in the federal courts.* New Haven, CT: Yale University Press.

West, D. J., & Farrington, D. P. (1977). *The delinquent way of life.* London: Hienemann.

Wheeler, S. (1992). The problem of white-collar crime motivation. In K. Schlegel & D. Weisburd (Eds.), *White-collar crime reconsidered* (pp. 108-123). Boston: Northeastern University Press.

Wheeler, S., Weisburd, D., Waring, E., & Bode, N. (1988). White collar crime and criminals. *American Criminal Law Review, 25,* 331-357.

Zeitz, D. (1981). *Women who embezzle or defraud: A study of convicted felons.* New York: Praeger.

DISCUSSION QUESTIONS

1. How might events early in one's life course impact white-collar offending?

2. What are some similarities and differences between the "criminal careers" of white-collar offenders and conventional offenders?

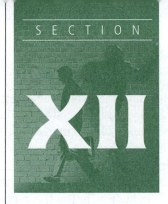
Policing White-Collar Crime

✖ Introduction

In his senior year of college, criminology student Garrett Speaks was approached by his professor and told about an opportunity that ultimately shaped his career. In particular, Speaks was told that the attorney general's office was searching for a possible undercover agent to send into nursing homes in an effort to detect misconduct by nursing homes. After meeting with the investigator overseeing the investigation, Speaks was selected to participate in the undercover investigation. He had to change his identity from criminology student to nurse's aide. He went through a nurse's aide training program to receive the necessary certification. A fictional employment history was created for him. Eventually, he was hired as a nurse's aide in a nursing home. Working in the nursing home for a short period, he did not see any evidence of wrongdoing. So, he sought employment at another nursing home. In the second home, where he was paid just $3.75 an hour, he uncovered several horrific examples of misconduct. Eventually, his undercover investigation resulted in the criminal prosecution of the nursing home (Speaks, 1997).

It was no coincidence that the attorney general sought out the services of a graduating senior rather than a seasoned officer. First, it would likely have been very difficult to convince more experienced police officers to give up their careers to work in a nursing home. Second, the excitement of undercover activities is likely higher among those new to the career. Third, in a case such as this, it is easier for a younger individual to become an undercover operative than it would be for an older agent (alternatively, a new graduate would not be able to pull off an undercover investigation in many other white-collar settings where one's level in the corporation is based on experience and age). Finally, most new college graduates have a clean slate when it comes to law enforcement practices. If they are new to law enforcement, they are not yet cynical and they are possibly easier to train than those who already have experience and a set of expectations that may not match the reality of the undercover assignment.

As an example, a police trainer once told me that he would rather train someone who has never shot a gun how to shoot a gun, as opposed to training someone who was raised as a hunter. The trainer's rationale: Many people learn the wrong way to shoot guns and it is harder to teach them the right way than it is to teach someone who has never even touched a gun. In a very real sense, Speaks was like the "new gun owner" who had never touched a gun. Training him how to go into a corporation and serve as an undercover agent was likely much simpler because of this.

While Speaks's experience as a lone undercover investigator is illustrative of a successful way to police white-collar crime, several different types of policing efforts and strategies are used to uncover white-collar crime. Consider the following cases:

- In July 2010, 24 suspects were arrested after an undercover mortgage fraud FBI investigation called "Operation Madhouse . . . in which law enforcement agents posed as home buyers seeking assistance in financing and closing fraudulent mortgages" ("24 Arrested," 2010).
- In November 2010, a bookkeeper at an elementary school was arrested after "the results of a routine audit at Freedom Park Elementary school . . . [found $24,000] missing from the school's student activity account" (Terry, 2010, n.p.).
- In December 2010, a doctor was arrested for violating whistleblower retaliation laws after he retaliated against two nurses who told authorities about substandard care the doctor was providing, including "suturing a rubber scissor tip to a patient's finger, using an unapproved olive oil solution on a patient with a highly resistant bacterial infection, failing to diagnose a case of appendicitis and conducting a skin graft without surgical privileges" (Sack, 2010, n.p.).
- In May 2010, three ranch workers were arrested after an undercover investigation, which entailed the installation of hidden cameras and the hiring of an undercover ranch hand, was initiated by the Chicago-based advocacy group Mercy for Animals. The video showed the defendants "jabbing cows with pitchforks, stomping on their heads, beating them with crowbars and breaking their tails" (Zachariah & Johnson, 2010, n.p.).
- In October 2010, former *CHiPs* actor Larry Wilcox was sued by the SEC after an undercover investigation showed that Wilcox was involved in several stock-related kickback schemes (Kell, 2010).

These examples highlight four important themes regarding the policing of white-collar crimes. First, white-collar crimes come to the attention of the police through several different avenues. Second, a number of different agencies are involved in the police response to white-collar crime. Third, the notion of "police response" describes different forms of policing, including criminal policing, private policing, and regulatory policing. Fourth, the specific police techniques used to address white-collar crimes are tied to the types of white-collar crime under investigation. An official responding to pollution, for example, performs one set of activities, while an officer responding to stock fraud would perform another set of activities.

⬚ Agencies Involved in Responding to White-Collar Crime

Generally speaking, three types of agencies are involved in responding to white-collar crime. These include private agencies (or self-policing by corporations or businesses), formal criminal police agencies, and governmental regulatory agencies. Private agencies are involved in policing misconduct inasmuch as a specific business guards against employee misconduct through the development of security and prevention measures. Formal criminal policing agencies at all levels of government respond to white-collar crime, though local police more rarely respond to these cases. State police agencies may become more involved, while federal law enforcement is engaged in even more policing of white-collar misconduct (see Figure 12.1). With regard to regulatory responses, at the local level, different governmental agencies have responsibility for ensuring that businesses are not in violation of local ordinances. At the state level, regulatory agencies enforce state health-, safety-, and sales-related laws. The federal government has several regulatory agencies whose purpose is to make sure that businesses and their workers are abiding by federal laws and regulations.

It is important to note that many white-collar crime cases are addressed through joint policing efforts by agencies from each level of government (local, state, and federal) and each type of policing agency (criminal policing, regulatory policing, and self-policing). Table 12.1 shows some of the federal agencies involved in responding to white-collar crime. Note that this list is not exhaustive. Dozens of other federal agencies are involved in responding to different forms of white-collar crime. Perhaps one way to think of it is to recognize that for each profession/industry, a different type of policing/regulatory agency exists to guard against occupational misconduct in that occupation. A discussion of the FBI's response to white-collar crime helps to frame an understanding of the way that law enforcement agencies address these offenses.

Figure 12.1   Police Agencies Involved in White-Collar Crime Cases

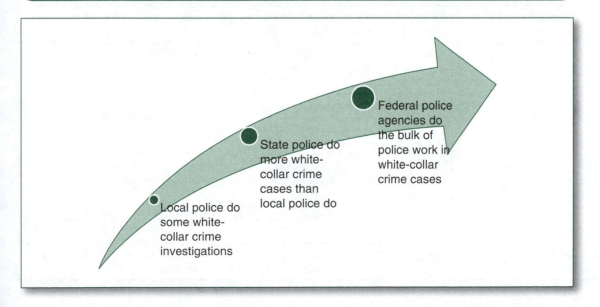

Table 12.1 Some Federal Agencies Involved in Policing/Regulating White-Collar Crime

Agency	What the Agency Does That Is Related to White-Collar Crime[a]	Where to Learn More
Consumer Product Safety Commission	Regulatory agency responsible for protecting the public from unreasonable risk of injury from thousands of products.	www.cpsc.gov
Commodities Futures Trading Commission	Regulatory agency responsible for regulating U.S. commodities and futures markets and preventing fraud and abuse in the markets	www.cftc.gov
Environmental Protection Agency	Government agency responsible for protecting the environment through compliance efforts and criminal and civil law enforcement practices	www.epa.gov
Equal Employment Opportunity Commission	Federal agency responsible for enforcing federal employment discrimination laws; has authority to file lawsuits if necessary	www.eeoc.gov
Federal Bureau of Investigation	Federal law enforcement agency that addresses white-collar crime through its Financial Crimes Section	www.fbi.gov
Federal Deposit Insurance Corporation	Independent agency that insures bank deposits, supervises financial institutions and examines their activities, and manages failed banks	www.fdic.gov
Federal Trade Commission	Addresses antitrust laws, anticompetitive practices, and false advertising practices by businesses.	www.ftc.gov
Financial Crimes Enforcement Network	Has regulatory duty to administer the Bank Secrecy Act. Assists law enforcement through analysis of information gathered as part of the Bank Secrecy Act.	www.fincen.gov
Financial Industry Regulatory Authority	Independent regulatory agency regulating more than 4,500 securities firms operating in the United States (largest of its kind)	www.finra.org
Food and Drug Administration	Ensures safety and effectiveness of certain food and drug products, investigates potential manufacturing violations	www.fda.gov
HHS Center for Medicare and Medicaid Services (CMS)	Administers nursing home inspections by contracting with states who hire inspection teams and provide inspection data to CMS.	www.cms.gov
HHS Office of Research Integrity	Has regulatory authority to promote the responsible conduct of research and monitors college and university reviews of research misconduct cases	ori.hhs.gov
Internal Revenue Service	Federal agency enforcing tax laws; becomes involved in white-collar crime cases when businesses/corporations break tax laws.	www.irs.gov
National Highway Traffic Safety Association	Federal agency that develops and enforces motor vehicle performance standards including gas mileage standards, and investigates motor vehicle safety, and detects odometer fraud	www.nhtsa.gov
National Labor Relations Board	Independent agency administering the National Labor Relations Act, addressing unfair labor practices	www.nlrb.gov
Occupational Safety and Health Administration	Federal agency that sets and enforces safety and health standards for work settings, and maintains data on workplace injuries and illnesses	www.osha.gov

Agency	What the Agency Does That Is Related to White-Collar Crime[a]	Where to Learn More
Office of the Comptroller of the Currency	Independent agency responsible for chartering and regulating national banks, and ensuring fairness and equal access to the banks	www.occ.treas.gov
Office of Thrift Supervision	Independent agency that regulates savings associations and their holding companies	www.ots.treas.gov
Public Company Accounting Oversight Board	Ensures that publicly registered accounting firms are in compliance with various federal laws	pcaobus.org
Securities and Exchange Commission	Regulates the U.S. securities market, using civil enforcement actions and administrative proceedings	www.sec.gov
U.S. Army Corps of Engineers	Has responsibility of protecting nation's water from harmful and illegal discharge of dredged and fill material	www.usace.army.mil
U.S. Department of Agriculture	Inspects and monitors poultry, eggs, and meat products sold in the United States	www.usda.gov
U.S. Department of Education, Office of Inspector General	Conducts independent investigations, audits, and inspections of DOE personnel, activities, and programs receiving DOE funding	www2.ed.gov/about/offices/list/oig/programs.html
U.S. Department of Health and Human Services, Office of Inspector General	Conducts independent audits, investigations, and inspections to guard against fraud and abuse in Health and Human Services programs and to protect program beneficiaries	oig.hhs.gov
U.S. Department of the Interior, Office of Inspector General	Provides oversight of programs, employees, and operations occurring in the Department of Interior	www.doioig.gov
U.S. Department of Justice, Office of Inspector General	Conducts independent investigations of DOJ personnel and programs to determine whether fraud, abuse, or waste is occurring	www.justice.gov/oig
U.S. Fish and Wildlife Service	Administers Endangered Species Act and responds to white-collar crimes when businesses/corporations harm endangered species	www.fws.gov
U.S. Postal Inspection Service	Federal law enforcement agency addressing fraud conducted through the mail	Postalinspectors.uspis.gov
Wage and Hour Division of Department of Labor	Enforces federal labor laws, including minimum wage laws, overtime laws, and family and medical leave laws	www.dol.gov/whd

a. Information in this column adapted from each agency's website. All agencies do activities other than those listed here.

The FBI and White-Collar Crime

In the FBI, the **Financial Crimes Section (FCS),** located in the agency's Criminal Investigations Division, investigates cases of white-collar crime. The FCS is composed of the Economic Crime Unit (ECU), Health Care Fraud Unit (HCFU), Forensic Accountants Unit, National Mortgage Fraud Unit, and Asset Forfeiture/ Money Laundering Unit. The ECU addresses fraudulent behavior (excluding health care fraud). The HCFU investigates various forms of health care fraud committed against insurance companies and individuals.

▲ **Photo 12.1** FBI Badge and Gun. The FBI plays a central role in many white-collar crime investigations.

The National Mortgage Fraud Team investigates mortgage frauds perpetrated against banks. The Asset Forfeiture/Money Laundering Unit assists agents in using asset forfeiture laws to support their investigations of white-collar crimes. The Forensic Accountants Unit, created in 2009, assists in white-collar crime investigations that require the services of a financial accountant or financial analyst (FBI, 2010b).

Recent initiatives by the FBI include the agency's Health Care Fraud Initiative and the Forensic Accounting Program. The former initiative included expanded efforts to address frauds involving (a) durable medical equipment (beginning in December 2006), (b) infusion therapy (beginning in April 2008), and (c) home health care (beginning in January 2010). The Forensic Accounting Program (FAP) is an initiative that started in March 2009 with the purpose of attracting and retaining **forensic accountants** in the battle against white-collar crime (FBI, 2010b). Initiatives of the FAP are outlined in Table 12.2.

Figure 12.2 shows the number of FBI white-collar crime cases between 2005 and 2009 for four types of white-collar crime. As shown in the figure, while some types of cases have increased, others have decreased. Note that these fluctuations are potentially a reflection of law enforcement behavior rather than changes in the prevalence of white-collar crimes.

Table 12.2 Initiatives of the FBI's Forensic Accounting Program	
Initiative	**Description**
Forensic accountant core training session training course	In FY 2009, the FAU [Forensic Accounting Unit] initiated development of a rigorous training curriculum titled the Forensic Accountant Core Training Session ("FACTS"). FACTS is a comprehensive introductory program of instruction designed to increase a FoA's [forensic auditor] proficiency in the critical areas necessary to conduct a financial investigation. This extensive course will develop the FoA's aptitude and knowledge in handling a financial investigation according to pertinent rules and regulations across a wide variety of subject matters. The FAU developed the FACTS training curriculum and will be responsible for administering the training. The material covered will focus primarily on providing an overview of FBI programs and systems, financial investigative topics and techniques, resources available to develop an investigation, legal training, and expert witness-testifying techniques.
BankScan initiative	BankScan is an in-house-created software application which translates physical bank and credit card statements into an electronic medium, thus dramatically decreasing the time-consuming data-entry process. In FY 2009, FAU deployed the BankScan training initiative "Train the Trainer" with the goal of full field office deployment by the end of FY 2010. The Train the Trainer Initiative was completed, and each field office "Trainer" received the requisite training and was supplied with the necessary software and equipment to implement the BankScan Project. Since its implementation, the FBI has benefited through an exponential increase in financial investigative efficiency and productivity.

Initiative	Description
Electronic subpoena production	The Electronic Subpoena Production initiative represents a joint undertaking of the FBI's CID, DOJ's Criminal Division Fraud Section, and the IRS. Electronic Subpoena Production requires financial institutions to digitally produce account data stored electronically by relying on existing Rule 17 of the Federal Rules of Criminal Procedure. When used in conjunction with BankScan, the introduction of this new process will substantially increase the efficiency and effectiveness of FBI forensic financial investigations.
Financial analyst conversion	In FY 2009, the FAU developed a selective conversion process to transition qualified FAs [forensic accountants] to the FoAP [Forensic Accounting Program] to provide the FBI's investigative programs with the highest caliber of financial investigative work-product and support. This effort will ensure only those individuals who meet the FoA requirements are selectively converted to the FoAP.

Figure 12.2 FBI Investigations of Different White-Collar Crimes, 2005–2009

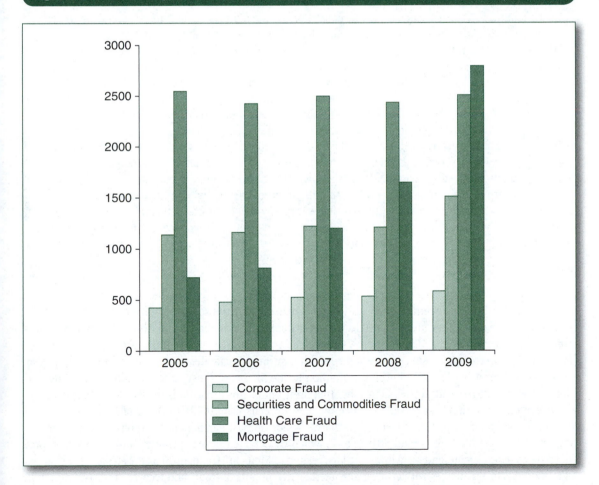

"Long standing partnerships" are hailed by the FBI as "one of the best tools in its arsenal" for addressing various types of white-collar crime (FBI, 2010b) as well as various local and state agencies. In Focus 12.1 provides an overview of the National Mortgage Fraud Team (NMFT) as an example of such a partnership. In some cases, the FBI is the leading partner in the effort, while in others the agents are members of a supporting cast.

In Focus 12.1

The FBI National Mortgage Fraud Team

In December 2008, the FBI established the NMFT to assist field offices in addressing the financial crisis, from the mortgage fraud problem and loan origination scams to the secondary markets and securitization. The NMFT provides tools to identify the most egregious mortgage fraud perpetrators, prioritizes investigative efforts, and provides information to evaluate resource needs.

The FBI continues to support 18 mortgage fraud task forces and 53 working groups; and participates in the National Mortgage Fraud and National Bank Fraud Working Groups, the National Securities and Commodities Fraud Working Group, and the President's Corporate Fraud Task Force to maximize intelligence sharing between stakeholder agencies and coordinate multi-agency, multi-jurisdictional mortgage fraud initiatives. Task forces and working groups include, but are not limited to, representatives of the HUD-OIG, the US Postal Inspection Service, the US Securities and Exchange Commission, the Commodities Futures Trading Commission, the IRS, FinCEN, the Federal Deposit Insurance Corporation, and other federal, state, and local law enforcement officers across the country. Additionally, representatives of the Office of Comptroller of the Currency, the Office of Thrift Supervision, the Executive Office of U.S. Trustees, the Federal Trade Commission, and others participate in national and ad-hoc working groups.

The FBI continues to foster relationships with representatives of the mortgage industry to promote mortgage fraud awareness and share intelligence information. FBI personnel routinely speak at and participate in various mortgage industry conferences and seminars, including those sponsored by the MBA [Mortgage Bankers Association]. Collaborative efforts are ongoing to educate and raise public awareness of mortgage fraud crimes with the publication of the annual Mortgage Fraud Report; the Financial Crimes Report to the Public; press releases; and through the dissemination of information with and between various industry and consumer organizations. Analytical products are routinely disseminated to a wide audience to include public and private sector industry partners, the intelligence community, and other federal, state, and local law enforcement.

Other federal law enforcement agencies also recognize the benefits of partnerships in addressing white-collar crimes for which they are responsible. Consider the Health Care Fraud and Abuse Program, which is jointly administered by the U.S. Attorney General and U.S. Department of Health and Human Services (HHS). The program was created as part of the Health Insurance Portability and Accountability Act of 1996. Since its creation it has "returned over $15.6 billion to the Medicare Trust Fund" (Health Care Fraud and Abuse Program, 2010). One active partnership that grew out of this program is the Health Care Prevention and Enforcement Action Team (HEAT), which includes officials from the HHS Office of Inspector General and U.S. Department of Justice (DOJ). This initiative builds on past partnerships and has developed initiatives including the Medicare Fraud Strike Force, which was created in the spring of 2007. The strike force coordinates federal, state, and local investigations related to Medicare fraud. In 2010, the strike force charged 88 individuals or businesses with crimes, convicted 89 defendants of fraud, and recovered "$71.3 million in investigative resources" (U.S. Department of Health and Human Services [HHS], 2010).

A few points about the agencies involved in responding to white-collar crime need to be stressed. First, a plethora of different agencies are involved in controlling and responding to white-collar crimes, and these agencies go by different names depending on the state or locality where they exist. It can be somewhat confusing to keep track of jurisdictional issues and determine who is responsible for preventing and policing specific types of white-collar crime. Here is how one author described this issue:

> There is no reason to believe that decisions as to which agency responds to a white-collar crime challenge are in any way related to resources or other capabilities of that agency. Rather, who becomes involved is likely to reflect which agency moved first, or which has greater clout or resources. Agencies have overlapping jurisdiction and there is little to prevent dysfunctional duplication of effort or significant matters falling through the gaps. (Edelhertz, 1983, p. 128)

A second issue has to do with the way that agencies have historically defined "white-collar crime." In the 1970s, the Department of Justice declared white-collar crime "an investigative priority." Poveda (1992) argued that in their declaration of "priority," agencies reconceptualized what scholars meant by white-collar crime in a way that resulted in the importance of class status, in defining white-collar crime, being cast aside. He wrote: "We need to consider whether the justice department's institutionalization of a white-collar crime represents a 'real' effort at combating the crimes of the elite or simply a 'symbolic' gesture" (p. 24). Simon and Swart (1984) offered a similar observation, stating that the DOJ's definition of white-collar crime was "so non-specific that it could include everything from welfare cheating by the poor to antitrust violations by upper-class businessmen" (p. 109).

Recognizing the conceptual and jurisdictional issues that surface with regard to law enforcement efforts to address white-collar crime should help us to appreciate the complexities surrounding the police and regulatory response to occupational misconduct. These complexities are particularly evident when considering the use of traditional policing strategies to address white-collar crime.

 # Law Enforcement Strategies and White-Collar Crime

A major portion of the police response to white-collar crime involves law enforcement strategies carried out by officials in the justice system. The law enforcement response to white-collar crime is similar to how the police respond to traditional crimes in several ways. For example, police use both reactive and proactive strategies in both types of cases. **Reactive strategies** entail situations where the police respond to reports of criminal incidents, and **proactive strategies** entail situations where the police develop criminal cases in an active way. Also, an enormous amount of power is afforded police officers responding to both types of cases. In addition, law enforcement officers have an enormous amount of discretion in deciding how to proceed in both types of cases.

Despite these similarities, as will be shown below a number of specific features of white-collar crime investigations make them substantively different from responses to traditional forms of crime. To provide insight into the law enforcement response to white-collar crimes, attention is given to the following:

- Stages of the white-collar crime investigation
- Evidence gathering strategies
- Problems addressing white-collar crime through a law enforcement response
- Suggestions for improving the law enforcement response to white-collar crime

Stages of the White-Collar Crime Investigation

White-collar crime investigations can be discussed as part of the broader criminal justice process. In discussing investigations from this perspective, one can point to the fact that white-collar crime investigations begin one of two ways. First, some white-collar crime investigations begin when cases are referred to law enforcement agencies that are responsible for addressing specific forms of white-collar crime. Such referrals come from consumers who are victims of white-collar crime, coworkers of the individual or individuals committing white-collar crime, competitors of the white-collar or corporate offender, the suspect's employer, and local, state, and federal agencies that uncover evidence of wrongdoing (Payne, 2003a). With regard to local agencies in particular, in some cases individuals might contact the local police to report white-collar offenses. In these situations, it is entirely likely that the local police do not have the resources or jurisdiction over the misconduct. In these cases, the local police will refer the report to the appropriate agency charged with addressing that specific form of misconduct, which could be a state or federal agency.

A second way that white-collar crime investigations begin is as the result of evidence uncovered as part of routine reviews of financial records by agencies proactively searching evidence of wrongdoing. For example, auditors in Medicaid Fraud Control Units routinely review insurance claims submitted by health care providers in an effort to identify signs of misconduct. If the auditor finds signs of fraud, the investigation officially begins.

Once a white-collar crime investigation begins, a series of stages are followed. One expert suggested that white-collar crime investigations be conducted in the following stages:

- Identify target, including conspirators
- Locate documents
- Review and confirm false statements on the records
- Interview participants (Bradley, 2008, p. 4)

Bradley draws attention to the need to gather information through records reviews before interviewing participants. This is somewhat different from traditional investigations, perhaps because of the how the crimes are reported.

Compare a domestic violence incident to a white-collar crime, for example. In the domestic violence incident, the police are called, they arrive on the scene, and they immediately question participants about the incident. Records (like threatening notes the offender wrote, phone records, etc.), if needed, might be gathered at a later date. If a banking employee is suspected of embezzling money from the bank, however, the investigators will wait until they have reviewed the records before interviewing participants.

In many white-collar crime cases, multiple suspects might be involved. For example, mortgage fraud cases might involve appraisers, real estate agents, mortgage brokers, developers, home builders, and other conspirators. In these situations, Bradley (2004) suggests that investigators "begin with the least culpable and work . . . toward the primary suspects" (p. 4). There are a number of possible reasons to start with the "least culpable" participant. For example, the person who has done the "least amount of harm" is not going to want to take the blame for the harm committed by conspirators. Somewhat related, the "least culpable" suspect will be in a better position to receive plea bargain offers later in the criminal justice process.

As an illustration of the "least culpable" recommendation, consider an incident of academic dishonesty that occurred in my class not long ago. Two students had written exactly the same wrong answers on their quizzes. Their wrong answers were so preposterously incorrect that it was clear to me that academic dishonesty had occurred. It was also clear that student B had copied from student A (because student A was an "A" student and student B . . . well, let's just say it was obvious). I asked student A to come by my office and asked her about the situation. In my view, student A was the least culpable because this student was not the "copier," but was the "supplier" who had the answers correct on her own. After I asked her about the incorrect answers, student A immediately confessed that student B had copied her answers. I asked student B to come by my office. Initially, he insisted that he did not copy, but that he and student A had simply studied together. I asked if he really wanted to stick with that story. Shortly later, he confessed to the academic dishonesty. Had I started my "investigation" with student B, it is entirely likely that the process would not have flowed as smoothly.

Evidence Gathering Strategies

White-collar crime investigations also differ from traditional crime investigations in the way that evidence is gathered. Common strategies to gather evidence in white-collar crime cases include (1) audits, (2) record reviews, (3) undercover strategies, (4) the use of whistleblowers, and (5) the use of technological devices. Each of these strategies is discussed below.

Audits

As noted above, some agencies routinely conduct **audits** in search of evidence of white-collar misconduct. Sometimes audits are done through data-mining techniques, which involve searching data sets for patterns that might indicate fraud (Rejusus, Little, & Lovell, 2004). Whether conducted in a proactive or reactive manner, audits are typically conducted by financial fraud accountants with specific skills designed to enhance their abilities to identify fraud.

Recall the principle of skepticism discussed in Section I. This principle encourages individuals to have an open mind and to question and re-question everything, to never assume that anything is true. Financial fraud investigators are skeptical by nature and review cases from the perspective that the records are not accurate (Wells, 2003b). Such a perspective is believed to help find evidence of wrongdoing. Describing this skeptical approach to conducting audits, one investigator said, "Audits are like an onion. You keep peeling away the different levels until you get to that level where you know what happened" (Payne, 2003a, p. 121).

Audits can be complex and time consuming, but the payoff is significant. In most cases, however, an audit by itself is not necessarily enough to establish that a white-collar crime was committed, or to identify who the white-collar offender is. Instead, as one investigator said, audits are "an indicator of the problem . . . they do not indicate automatically that a crime occurred" (Payne, 2003a, p. 121). While not always sufficient by themselves, when combined with other forms of evidence-gathering strategies, audits can provide the evidence needed to substantiate wrongdoing.

Record Reviews

White-collar crime investigators will also conduct **record reviews** in building their case. The amount of records law enforcement investigators will need to review in these cases can be enormous. Investigators will review all sorts of records, including financial records, banking records, sales records, e-mail correspondence, phone records, property deeds, loan applications, and any other records that are relevant to the case under investigation.

As part of the search for records, white-collar crime investigators will examine whether suspects tried to destroy records, which would be a separate offense, as well as evidence supporting the belief that they engaged in the offense under investigation. In one recent case, a state legislator was indicted for bribery and extortion after he led a proposal to develop an academic center and asked the university to hire him in the center if it was approved by the legislature. After the center was approved by the legislature, the university did, in fact, hire the legislator. A news reporter began to investigate the matter and asked for copies of e-mails between the legislator and university employees. The legislator asked university employees not to release the records. The evidence that he tried to hide the evidence was used to indict him in December 2010 (Sizemore, 2011).

In another case, nine employees were convicted of neglecting an at-risk child who was in their care. An autopsy revealed that the child had starved to death. In the course of the investigation, officials from the HHS Office of Inspector General found that the employees "attempted to conceal the incident by destroying old records and creating new false records" (HHS, 2010, p. v). Again, the fact that they destroyed records was used to show that they knew that they had done something wrong. Had the records been left alone, it would have been more difficult to establish intent.

E-mails are a relatively recent type of record that can be used in white-collar crime investigations. Two misconceptions about e-mails exist. First, some assume that once an e-mail is deleted that it is gone forever. However, e-mail servers save deleted e-mails for set periods of time and investigators have been able to access deleted e-mails to use as evidence in white-collar crime cases. Second, many people assume that their e-mails are private; however, most businesses have e-mail use policies that allow employers to access workers' e-mails without their consent. Also, for government workers who work in states with liberal open records laws, any of the workers' e-mails can be made public through freedom of information requests.

Undercover Investigations

Undercover investigations are also used in white-collar crime cases. On the surface, these investigations are no different from undercover criminal investigations in conventional criminal cases. However, as will be shown below, important differences exist between white-collar and conventional undercover investigations.

One basic difference is that **white-collar undercover investigations** are not typically begun unless there is already evidence of wrongdoing by the suspect or the corporation. Whereas many undercover drug investigations involve "reverse sting" activities where undercover officers pose as drug dealers and arrest whoever happens to try to purchase drugs, white-collar crime investigations are rarely conducted without already knowing who the specific target of the investigation is. In other words, typically, "there are no random spot checks" of white-collar employees (Payne & Berg, 1997, p. 226).

As an illustration of how undercover investigations are "built into" the broader criminal investigation in white-collar crime cases, consider the following stages of a recent white-collar crime investigation:

1. A senior official at PepsiCo receives an envelope offering to sell him confidential, private information about Coca-Cola.

2. The Pepsi executive contacts Coca-Cola.

3. Coca-Cola executives call the FBI and tell them about the case.

4. The FBI opens the investigation and interviews witnesses.

5. Undercover agents offer to buy the secret information from the suspect, a Coca-Cola employee.

6. Agents give the employee $30,000 stuffed in a Girl Scout cookie box.

7. A Coca-Cola employee provides information to the undercover agents.

8. A review of Coca-Cola video surveillance found proof of the employee stealing documents and product samples.

9. The employee and two coconspirators were arrested (McKay, 2006).

All of this happened in a 3-month time span. Note that the undercover investigation was just one component of the case, albeit a significant component.

Criminologist Gary Marx (1982) has discussed several criticisms of undercover policing. While he focused on all types of undercover policing (e.g., undercover prostitution stings, drug stings, etc.), Marx used several examples of undercover white-collar crime investigations to frame his discussion. One criticism he levied against these investigations is that they deceive individuals and may coerce individuals into offending. He also noted the significant amount of stress police officers experience from undercover policing and he argued that the independence given to law enforcement officers in these cases may be a breeding ground for corruption. In addition, over-relying on informers may give informers too much power and become problematic if informers take advantage of the undercover investigation. Marx also suggested that undercover work may promote poor police/community relationships.

One can envision how these criticisms have merit in undercover investigations involving street crimes and organized crime. The criticisms may not be as relevant when considering undercover investigations of white-collar crimes. Table 12.3 shows the similarities and differences between the two types of investigations. First, in terms of danger, there is very little risk for undercover agents in white-collar crime cases. Consider a case where an undercover officer goes to a pharmacist suspected of committing prescription fraud. There is virtually no danger in that assignment. Alternatively, for undercover investigations of street crimes, the investigations occur in dangerous areas and often target dangerous offenders.

Another difference between the two types of undercover assignments has to do with the time element given to the undercover investigation. For many undercover investigations of street crimes or organized crime, undercover agents infiltrate the criminal subculture and spend significant amounts of time in the dangerous settings. For white-collar crime investigations, it is rare that an undercover agent would join the occupational subculture under investigation for an extended period of time.

Somewhat related, one can also distinguish the two types of investigation based on the role that the undercover work has in the broader investigation. For investigations of drug crimes or organized crime, the undercover work is central to the investigation. The centrality of the undercover work to the investigation is what justifies spending the extended amount of time on the case. For white-collar crime cases, the undercover investigation is typically a "supplemental component" to the investigation. This is not to diminish the importance of undercover work in these cases, as the cases may not be solved without the undercover work.

Table 12.3   Distinguishing Undercover Investigations of White-Collar Crime and Conventional Crime Cases

	White-Collar Undercover Investigation	Conventional Undercover Investigation
Potential for danger	Minimal	High
Time to complete undercover investigation	Short period of time	Lengthy period of time
Centrality to the case	Supplemental evidence	Evidence central to case
Role playing	Some (as consumer)	Identity change (as criminal)
Stress potential	Unlikely	Likely

Another difference between the two types of investigation has to do with the nature of the role playing in white-collar and conventional undercover investigations. In undercover investigations of conventional crimes, the undercover agent must often act as if he or she is a criminal—a drug dealer, prostitute, thief, mobster, gang member, or some other identity relevant to the investigation. In white-collar crime investigations, the agent often does not have to take on the role of the criminal, but may take on the role of a consumer. Consider a case in which a broker is suspected of stealing clients' funds. If an undercover investigation is initiated, the agent simply poses as someone interested in investing. Or, if a doctor is being investigated for submitting fraudulent bills to insurance companies, the investigator just has to act sick. Who among us has not acted sick at some point in our lives? Maybe some of us have acted sick to get out of work. For undercover investigations in health care fraud cases, undercover investigators act sick as part of their work.

▲ **Photo 12.2**   It is safe to suggest that traditional policing is much more dangerous than white-collar crime policing.

Based on the dynamics noted above, one can assume that level of stress in the two types of cases varies. Undercover investigations of conventional crimes are dangerous, time consuming, and involve situations where individuals have to pretend to be criminals. Certainly, one can accept Marx's premise that such activities would potentially stress undercover police officers. As well, these dynamics could potentially contribute to police corruption. For white-collar crime investigations, the fact that the investigations are short, in safe settings, and do not involve a great deal of role-playing should reduce the amount of stress arising from these cases.

Whistleblower Evidence

White-collar crime investigations often involve the collection of whistleblower evidence. **Whistleblowers** are individuals who notify authorities about wrongdoing in their organization. Two types of whistleblowers exist: internal whistleblowers and external whistleblowers (Vinten, 1994). **Internal whistleblowers** share information with officials within the organization where they work, often reporting the misconduct to the company's security program. **External whistleblowers** share the information with outside organizations like law enforcement agencies or the media. Table 12.4 shows some whistleblowers whose stories eventually made it to Hollywood.

Working with whistleblowers can strengthen white-collar crime investigations significantly. One author team argued that such evidence "may be the best evidence for proving a case" (Botsko & Wells, 1994, p. 21). The same author team suggested that investigators must make sure that the emotional impact of participating in the investigation is minimized. One strategy they suggested for minimizing the emotional impact on whistleblowers is to not ask for too much information until the worker is at a place where he or she is comfortable providing the information. They wrote:

Effective management of witnesses represents one of the most challenging responsibilities for white-collar crime investigators. To overcome such barriers as anger and fear and to collect and preserve the most accurate testimony possible from . . . whistleblowers, investigators should focus on the informer's emotional agenda. (p. 21)

| Table 12.4 | You're Going to Hollywood: Whistleblowers Who Made It to Hollywood |

Whistleblower	Description	Name of Movie or Show	Actor Who Played Whistleblower
W. Mark Felt	Felt was "Deep Throat," the individual who fed information about the Watergate scandal to reporters Bob Woodward and Carl Bernstein. He announced his role in Watergate three decades after the scandal.	*All the President's Men*	Hal Holbrook
Frank Serpico	Serpico told the *New York Times* about NYPD corruption and was subsequently suspiciously shot in the face during a drug bust. He also provided testimony in the Knapp Commission's investigation of corruption.	*Serpico*	Al Pacino
Karen Silkwood	Silkwood, a nuclear plant worker, was providing information about her factory's safety violations to a reporter. One night when she was delivering evidence to a coworker, she was suspiciously killed in a car accident. The evidence documents were not found in the wrecked car.	*Silkwood*	Meryl Streep
Linda Tripp	Tripp tape-recorded conversations she had with Monica Lewinsky about Lewinsky's sexual relations with President Clinton and provided the tapes to Independent Counsel Kenneth Starr.	*Saturday Night Live*	John Goodman
Sherron Watkins	Watkins sent a letter to Enron's CEO, Ken Lay, detailing Enron's misdeeds. She was named "2002 Person of the Year" by *Time* magazine, along with two other whistleblowers.	*Enron: The Smartest Guys in the Room*	Self (documentary)
Mark Whitacre	Whitacre was the FBI's highest level executive whistleblower in the early 1990s when he provided evidence about price fixing at Archer Daniels Midland (ADM). ADM settled the case for $100 million and alleged wrongdoing by Whitacre. An FBI investigation revealed that Whitacre had stolen $9 million himself. He served 8 years in prison for his fraud.	*The Informant*	Matt Damon

Research shows that whistleblowers decide to report their coworker's or organization's misconduct for several reasons (Latimer, 2002). Some workers report white-collar misconduct out of a sense of obligation or duty. Other workers report misconduct because they want to see the offender punished for the misconduct. Still other employees report misconduct so they will not get into trouble themselves. In many cases, whistleblowers are able to collect monetary awards, and these awards can be sizeable. Some whistleblowers report misconduct because of the positive attention they get from participating in the investigation. These whistleblowers "have aspirations to become a hero" (Latimer, 2002, p. 23).

A study of whistleblowers found that workers were more likely to blow the whistle on evidence they saw, as opposed to evidence they heard about (Near & Miceli, 2008). This same study found that workers who perceived their company as retaliatory in nature were more likely to report misconduct than those who did not see their company in this light. In addition, compared to non-whistleblowers, whistleblowers were (a) more likely to be supportive of cash rewards, (b) paid more, and (c) more educated.

Technological Devices and White-Collar Crime Evidence

Various types of technological devices are used to search for evidence in white-collar crime cases. Several types of software, for example, are used to search for evidence of computer crimes against corporations. As well, cameras and tape recorders are sometimes used to substantiate wrongdoing. As an illustration, in one recent case a senior financial analyst for WellCare—Sean Hellein—alerted authorities that his coworkers had defrauded Medicaid of approximately a half billion dollars. After alerting authorities about the misconduct, he was asked to wear "hidden microphones and miniature cameras disguised as buttons" (Hundley, 2010). He collected 1,000 hours of evidence that led the authorities to raid the company's headquarters.

In another case, a physician, two nurses, and six aides were arrested after a camera was hidden in a nursing home resident's room for 5 weeks. The video from the hidden camera revealed the following:

- To prevent contractures, this patient's physician ordered that the patient receive 30 minutes of range of motion therapy twice a day. The camera revealed that the patient consistently did not receive this therapy.
- To prevent the development of dangerous pressure sores or promote their healing, the patient was required to be turned and repositioned every 2 hours and to receive incontinence care every 2 hours as well, but the camera revealed that the patient often went without this care.
- To ensure proper nutrition and hydration, the patient was supposed to receive total assistance while eating. The camera further revealed that the patient often failed to receive assistance in eating and often went without eating or drinking at all.
- To avoid seizures, combat pressure sores, prevent depression, reduce pain, and to maintain proper nutrition, the patient was required to receive a series of medications, including Tegretol, an anti-seizure medication; Celexa and Remeron, anti-depressants; Baclofen, a muscle relaxant and pain reducer; and a liquid protein nutritional supplement. The camera revealed that the nurses charged to do so often failed to administer these medications as prescribed. (*Medicaid Fraud Reports*, 2006, November, p. 1)

In these cases, the presence of audio and video recordings provides valuable evidence that will increase the likelihood of a conviction.

Problems Addressing White-Collar Crime Through a Law Enforcement Response

Few criminal cases are actually simple to detect and investigate. White-collar crime cases are no exception. Problems that surface in criminal white-collar crime investigations include the following:

- Resource problems
- Relationship dynamics
- Time
- Complexity
- Proof
- Perceptions of white-collar crime police work

Resource Problems

Resources are a problem inasmuch as white-collar crime police units are grossly under-resourced in comparison to police units focusing on conventional crimes. To be sure, police departments are underfunded in general, and many recent budget cuts have forced departments to eliminate various programs and services. It is likely much easier to reduce services addressing crimes like white-collar crime, which is often viewed as less serious than conventional crime. State and federal agencies have also experienced funding problems when it comes to responding to various types of white-collar crimes (Payne, 2006).

Resource problems are a little different for white-collar crime investigations than they are for conventional crime investigations. In particular, whereas most conventional offenders have limited resources that they can use to build their defense against the charges, white-collar offenders typically have significant resources that can be devoted to defending against the allegations. During investigations, corporations will often "lawyer up" as soon as the investigation begins (Williams, 2008, p. 322). Said one investigator, "This is one of the biggest things I've noticed in every interview we do. There's lawyers, upon lawyers, upon lawyers" (Williams, 2008, p. 322).

To be sure, many interviews with conventional offenders are conducted without defense attorneys present. This is less common in white-collar crime investigations. Williams (2008) highlights a process called *litigotiation,* where corporate lawyers engage with police in a way that makes it seem like they are cooperating through "interaction rituals." But they are simply protecting their client through "legal gamesmanship" (p. 322). Examples of litigotiation would include participating in interviews but stalling the case by making unnecessary requests of the police—requests that are not typically made in investigations of conventional criminal cases.

Varying amounts of resources will need to be assigned to different types of cases. Agencies must make decisions about the amount of resources they will devote to different cases. The SEC, the federal agency responsible for addressing securities fraud through civil actions, provides its enforcement division guidance in the Division of Enforcement's enforcement manual. In particular, home office Associate Directors and Regional Directors are asked to prioritize their top three cases and list their top 10 cases based on three criteria: "programmatic importance of enforcement action," "magnitude of potential violations," and "resources required to investigate potential violations" (Securities and Exchange Commission, Division of Enforcement, 2010, p. 9). Table 12.5 shows what is meant by each of these items.

Relationship Dynamics

Relationship dynamics also present problems in white-collar crime investigations. Three types of relationships are relevant: (1) the victim/offender relationship, (2) the offender/witness relationship, and (3) the officer/offender relationship. First, in terms of the victim/offender relationship, recall that in many cases white-collar crime victims are not aware of their victimization, perhaps partly because of the trust the victim (consumer, client, coworker, etc.) places in the offender (Bucy, 1988). As a result, they are unable to report the victimization to the police and subsequently unable to participate as a witness in the investigation.

With regard to the offender/witness relationship, many of the witnesses that investigators want to interview will be in trusting relationships with the offender. These relationships might be work relationships or personal relationships. Either way, the relationship makes it more difficult for investigators to get accurate information from witnesses. For example, if the witness is a coworker or subordinate of the suspect, the witness has a level of trust in the suspect but may not trust the white-collar crime investigator (Payne, 2003a).

Table 12.5   Criteria Used to Decide Resource Allocation in Securities Fraud Investigations

Programmatic Importance Indicators	Indicators of Magnitude Potential	Indicators of Resources Required
• whether the subject matter is an SEC priority • whether the subject matter is a Division priority • whether an action would fulfill a programmatic goal of the SEC or the Division • whether an action would address a problematic industry practice • whether the conduct undermines the fairness or liquidity of the U.S. securities markets • whether an action would provide an opportunity for the SEC to address violative conduct targeted to a specific population or community that might not otherwise be familiar with the SEC or the protections afforded by the securities laws • whether an action would present a good opportunity to work together with other civil and criminal agencies • whether the conduct can be addressed by any other state or federal regulators • whether an action would alert the investing public of a new type of securities fraud	• the egregiousness of the conduct • the length of time the conduct continued, or whether it is ongoing • the number of violations • whether recidivists were involved • whether violations were repeated • the amount of harm or potential harm to victims • the amount of ill-gotten gains to the violators • whether victims were specifically targeted based on personal or affinity group characteristics • for issuers or regulated entities, whether the conduct involved officers, directors, or senior management • whether gatekeepers (such as accountants or attorneys) or securities industry professionals are involved	• the complexity of the potential violations • the approximate staff hours required over the course of the investigation • the number of staff assigned • the amount of travel required • the duration of the relevant conduct • the number of potential violators • the number and locations of potential witnesses • the number and location of relevant documents to be reviewed

As well, in certain professions, the occupational subculture is perceived as protecting members of that subculture in law enforcement investigations (Wilson, Lincoln, Chappell, & Fraser, 1986). When witnesses are interviewed, they often tell investigators that the suspects are "pillars of the community," making white-collar offenders, in the words of one investigator, "sympathetic defendants who do not look like criminals" (Payne, 2003a, p. 145). In other cases, witnesses might actually be colluding or conspiring with the suspect, thereby making it less likely that they will be cooperative witnesses (Payne, 2006).

The police officer/offender relationship may also present barriers in white-collar crime investigations. The relationship dynamics between officers and offenders are different in white-collar crime and conventional crime cases (see Table 12.6). First, one can note that class status differences between officers and white-collar offenders make these white-collar crime cases different from conventional crime cases. In white-collar crime cases, offenders typically come from a higher social class than most officers do. Alternatively, officers are in a higher social class than conventional offenders are in. This is potentially problematic when white-collar suspects try to use their class status to gain power over officers.

Table 12.6   Relationship Dynamics Between Police Officers and White-Collar and Conventional Offenders

	White-Collar Offenders	Conventional Offenders
Class status	Have a higher class status than police officers	Have a lower class status than police officers
Education	Have either more or a different type of education than police officers	Tend to be less educated than police officers
Economic power	Have more economic power than police officers	Have less economic power than police officers
Political power	Have more political clout and political contacts than police officers	Have less political power than police officers
Familiarity with criminal justice	Very little prior contacts with police	Have longer criminal histories and more contacts with the police

Educational differences might also exist between officers and white-collar offenders. While more and more police officers are required to have college degrees, especially at the federal level, the vast majority of white-collar offenders will have higher educational levels than conventional offenders, and their educational expertise will be different than police officers' expertise. This can be problematic in that officers will need to be acquainted with the offender's occupational specialization in order to understand the nature and dynamics of the occupational misconduct. While those of us trained in Criminology and Criminal Justice are well versed in our own fields, understanding the intricacies of careers in other fields is a difficult task.

White-collar offenders will also have more political and economic power than police officers, while police officers have more economic and political power than conventional offenders. This becomes problematic when offenders use their expertise to try and call in favors from politicians, business leaders, and community leaders. In a case involving a 16-year-old kid from an inner-city neighborhood, few outsiders might try to intervene on behalf of the kid. In a case involving a powerful white-collar offender, officers will sometimes need to take more precautions to ensure that the offender is not able to exert political power over the investigation. As an example, they might wait longer to proceed with a white-collar case in order to have the strongest case possible.

One can also point to the familiarity that police officers have with conventional offenders (as opposed to white-collar offenders) as another relationship barrier in these cases. Conventional offenders are typically more "familiar" with the criminal justice system, having longer arrest records and more contacts with law enforcement officers. Scholars have long talked about a courtroom workgroup to describe familiarity between actors in the courts. For offenders arrested many times, police officers and offenders have—in a very real sense—an informal relationship, albeit one that is based on formal control mechanisms. No such relationship exists between police officers and white-collar offenders, most of whom have had few prior contacts with the police. In the end, police officers lack familiarity with white-collar offenders. Ironically, the familiarity element might actually result in officers "liking" conventional offenders more than white-collar offenders. Said one white-collar crime investigator, "You cannot trust these white-collar criminals. They are not 'honest criminals' like traditional ones" (Alvesalo, 2003, p. 129).

Time

Time is another problem in white-collar crime investigations. Time becomes problematic in three ways. First, because white-collar crime victims often do not know they were victimized, a long period of time may pass between the time the crime was committed and the time the investigation begins. The longer the amount of time that elapses between the commission of the offense (whether it is a white-collar crime or conventional crime) and the time police become aware of the offense, the less likely that an arrest will occur in the case.

Second, time is problematic in that it can take an inordinate amount of time to collect all of the necessary records in white-collar crime cases (Payne, 2003a). While the collection of electronic evidence has made record collection more efficient, it still takes time to identify which records are needed and then to review all of the records. As well, writing up the results of the record review can be quite time consuming.

Third, some have argued that it takes longer to prepare for a white-collar crime interrogation than it takes to prepare for an interrogation of a conventional offender (Alvesalo, 2003). Alvesalo notes that interrogations of conventional offenders are usually not prepared ahead of time. Investigators, perhaps because they routinely complete such interrogations, are able to conduct the interrogations "by free narration" (p. 127). Describing the interrogation of white-collar offenders, he quotes one investigator who said:

> In the uniformed police, . . . you never had to prepare for the . . . interrogation at all. You just went in there and asked, "What is going on?" and took the statements. In cases of economic crime, you might write questions for a week and you have to do background work for a month and when you start to interrogate, you check the questions, and prepare yourself with all kinds of documents that you have to show the suspects . . . a totally different world. (p. 127)

As an analogy, think of a class you could attend, never study, and then ace the exams. This would be like interrogating conventional offenders. Alternatively, think of a class you have to work hard in, like most of your criminal justice classes. This would be like interrogating white-collar offenders.

Complexity

Complexity is another problem in white-collar crime investigations. Three issues that make the cases particularly complex include (1) complex record searches, (2) extensive collaborations with partners, and (3) the lack of a systematic approach. In terms of complex record searches, the amount of records collected in white-collar crime cases can be overwhelming to the investigations. It is estimated that the "average fraud case can entail fifty boxes of evidence" and 150,000 to 250,000 pages of information (Taylor, 2001, p. 22). Sifting through all of those records is not only time consuming, but a complex endeavor arises in efforts to take that information and narrow it down to evidence indicating that a crime has been committed.

The extensive collaborations with partners in white-collar crime cases can also make the investigations more complex than might be found in investigations of conventional crimes. In home health care fraud cases, for example, investigators will work with the following agencies to pursue the white-collar crime investigation:

- Adult protective services
- Auditor of state
- Crime Victim's Coordinator
- Department of Family Services
- Department of Health

- Division on Aging
- Division on Medical Assistance
- Federal Bureau of Investigation
- Internal Revenue Service
- Local law enforcement
- Local county and prosecuting attorneys
- State Medicaid agency
- State police
- State professional licensing boards (e.g., Board of Nursing, Pharmacy)
- U.S. Attorney's Office
- U.S. Postal Inspection Service
- U.S. Department of Health and Human Services, Office of Inspector General (Payne, 2003a)

Collaboration is necessary in many white-collar crime investigations and can result in adding complexities to the investigation (Middlemiss & Gupta, 2007). For example, it may be difficult to determine which agencies should be involved in the investigation. As well, statutes may keep agencies partnering with one another from sharing relevant information (Payne, 2011). In addition, turf wars may erupt during the course of the investigation. Also, participants in the partnership might have different goals—some might be obsessed with crime statistics, while others might be involved in the effort because they want a part of the funds recovered through the investigation. Also, bureaucratic inertia, which refers to situations where a large group of individuals is unable to move forward, may keep the partnership from attaining its goal (Middlemiss & Gupta, 2007). In effect, having to partner with other agencies can make white-collar crime investigations more complex.

The lack of systematic approaches has also contributed to complexity in some white-collar crime investigations. For example, some authors have contended that environmental crime investigations do not always follow systemic approaches (Van den Berg and Eshuis, 1996). Without a systematic approach, the investigatory process becomes more difficult than it needs to be. Remember the principle of parsimony discussed earlier in the text. This principle suggests that theorists must keep their explanations of white-collar crime as simple as possible. In a similar way, investigators must try to simplify the complexities of white-collar crime investigations. To do so, it has been argued that white-collar crime investigations need to be better planned, prioritized, and sensitive to group dynamics (Van den Berg & Eshuis, 1996).

Keep in mind that the police processing of white-collar crime cases varies across offense types. Some white-collar crime cases will be less complex, and subsequently easier to investigate, than other white-collar crime cases. FBI agent Daniel Bradley (2008) has suggested that records in real estate fraud cases are easier to review than those found in other white-collar crimes. According to Bradley, "these false statements are clear and simple, provable through documentation and witness testimony, and therefore easily conveyed. For example, it is easy to compare a home value estimate from an appraisal form to the estimate actually listed on a mortgage document" (no pagination).

Establishing Proof

It is also difficult for investigators to gather evidence that prosecutors will be able to use to prove various aspects of the misconduct. In some white-collar crime cases, it is so difficult to establish intent that investigators might end up having to "devote their endeavors to less serious charges" (Wilson et al., 1986, p. 139). Consider Martha Stewart's case. She was accused of insider trading, but ultimately convicted of perjury.

In a similar way, it is difficult to prove that specific suspects are responsible for the misconduct. This is particularly the case in corporate crimes where it is difficult to determine which employees participated in

▲ **Photo 12.3**   Traditional police work is seen as exciting. White-collar crime investigations are not held in the same regard. Rarely do you see kids playing "white-collar crime cops and robbers."

the offense. In investigations of conventional crimes, "the police ask 'Who did it?' In [white-collar] crime cases, they ask 'which one of the known suspects is responsible?'" (Alvesalo, 2003, p. 124). One criminal justice official commented, "as in any white-collar crime . . . , defendants usually assert that they did not understand the complicated regulations, were bad record keepers, etc., but had no criminal intent. Absent a confession, that defense is difficult to overcome" (Payne, 2003a, p. 137).

Perceptions of White-Collar Crime Police Work

Another barrier in the response to white-collar crime is that police work in these cases is often perceived pejoratively, as if the activity is not real police work. On the one hand, such perceptions become problematic when funding for these activities is withheld or reduced based on perceptions such as that police work is not "real" police work. On the other hand, given that some police officers even view white-collar crime police work as "not real police work" (see Alvesalo & Whyte, 2007), it may be difficult to recruit and retain seasoned criminal justice professionals into policing careers targeting white-collar offenders.

 ## Suggestions for Improving the Law Enforcement Response to White-Collar Crime

A number of different suggestions have been made to improve the law enforcement response to white-collar crime. For example, just as the media show celebrated white-collar offenders doing the "perp walk" to the police car, police department, or courthouse, some researchers have suggested that efforts should be undertaken to make sure that arrests are "publicized" to those in the workplace by arresting suspects when a lot of people are at work, like during shift changes (Payne & Gray, 2001). This same author team warns officers against assuming that labels given to white-collar crime are accurate descriptors of the behavior. For instance, some believe that "financial crimes" are not harmful, and this would, in turn, diminish the value that officers give to the work. Recognizing the seriousness of the offenses potentially increases the value that officers would place on law enforcement activities targeting white-collar crimes.

The search for a **"smoking gun"** has also been suggested as a strategy to improve investigations in white-collar crime cases (Payne & Gray, 2001). In this context, the phrase "smoking gun" refers to indisputable evidence that substantiates that a crime has been committed. One contracted employee, for example, billed an employer for 800 consecutive days of work. Think about that. That's 27 straight months with no day off from work. Incidentally, this employee held a separate full-time job and took three vacations to New York, Aruba, and Mexico during the 27-month scam (Payne, 2003a). Figure 12.3 shows some additional smoking gun cases.

Figure 12.3 The Smoking Gun and White-Collar Crime

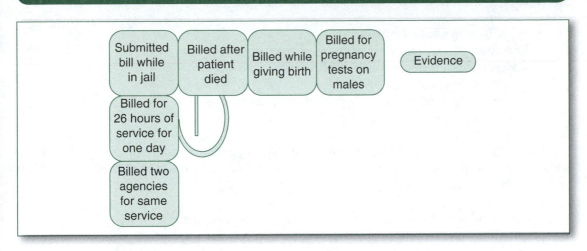

Another recommendation for improving the police response to white-collar crime is related to the popular movie *Jerry McGuire*. Even if you have not seen the movie, you have probably heard the quote by Rod Tidwell, played by Cuba Gooding Jr., who said to Jerry, "Show me the money." The quote is among the most recognized movie lines. There's another quote that financial investigators recognize: "Follow the money" (Wells, 2003a, p. 84). Certainly, in many white-collar crime cases, money is the target. If investigators can find the money, they find evidence that substantiates the crime. As Wells (2003b) wrote, "Money from any source—lawful or not—can be dispersed only four ways: It can be spent, saved, used to acquire assets, or to pay debts." Thus, investigators will review the suspects' assets (e.g., their possessions), liabilities, sources of funds, and expenditures.

Improved educational programs have also been hailed as strategies to help law enforcement officers respond to white-collar crime. Over the past decade, efforts have expanded to involve colleges and universities in preparing current and future investigators to address white-collar crime. One example is the Internal Revenue Service Criminal Investigation's (IRS CI) Adrian Project. In this project, the IRS CI partners with a college and assigns a coach to work with students on an applied learning exercise. The students are given crime scene scenarios, including white-collar crime scenarios, and asked to investigate the offenses. The program has been found to improve students' detection skills, abilities to gather and organize data, abilities to use multiple investigative tools, and interviewing and communication skills (Brickner, Mahoney, & Moore, 2010).

At the University of West Virginia, the College of Business and Economics developed a Fraud Accounting and Fraud Investigator program to improve the skills of future fraud fighters. This is a certificate program that includes four courses: "Fraud Investigation, Fraud Data Analysis, Criminology and Legal Issues, and Advanced Fraud Investigation" (Richardson, 2010, p. 10). Assignments include hands-on crime scene investigation.

At Gonzaga University, the Justice for Fraud Victims project was created as a joint effort between forensic accountants, faculty, the police, and local prosecutors. Accounting students assigned to teams work on real fraud cases involving small businesses and nonprofit organizations. The students help gather evidence, recover money for businesses, and prosecute offenders (Sowa, 2010). The number of college-level fraud courses has grown significantly between the 1990s and 2003 (from 19 to 150) (Wells, 2003b). These courses aim to teach students the following skills that are needed among fraud investigators:

- Expertise with financial matters
- Understanding motivations for white-collar crime
- Understanding the laws surrounding white-collar crime
- Insight into legal and ethical issues
- Communication and writing skills, particularly report writing
- Critical thinking skills (Peterson, 2004)

Following this same line of thinking, some have called for a more proactive educational response to white-collar crime that addresses the changing nature of societal systems. Said one official employed in a statistical financial analysis unit:

The authorities find themselves in this position of running after the problems and their perpetrators—the robbers always keeping the advantage over the cops. With the advantage and with the ever increasing innovations in technology that can be used for illicit ends, the risk grows that the criminal act cannot be [stopped]. (Nardo, 2004, 139)

Increasing technological awareness about white-collar crime should help to improve the police response to white-collar crime.

Self-Policing and White-Collar Crime

Self-policing refers to efforts by companies and businesses to develop their own policing responses to white-collar crime. Businesses develop self-policing strategies for practical and economic reasons. Practically speaking, it is impossible for law enforcement agencies to police businesses on a daily basis, so businesses develop their own private policing systems. Economically, self-policing strategies help businesses to protect their bottom lines by minimizing the economic costs of employee misconduct. Types of self-policing efforts used by business to detect or prevent white-collar crime include: loss prevention strategies, compliance programs, audits, and forensic accounting.

Loss Prevention Strategies

Loss prevention strategies are efforts that businesses use to keep employees from stealing from the business. Traub (1996) cites three types of loss prevention strategies. Category I strategies refer to efforts where businesses emphasize security. Security officials perform a number of different activities including "surveillance, plain-clothes detective work, and undercover operations directed at criminal activity and other forms of misconduct" (p. 248). Some businesses have increased their reliance on security strategies to detect and prevent workplace crimes. Consider that the number of investigators hired in some accounting firms doubled in the wake of the Enron and WorldCom scandals in the early 2000s (Wells, 2003b).

Category II loss prevention strategies emphasize screening and education (Traub, 1996). During recruiting stages, workers are screened intensively in an effort to weed out those who have a likelihood of engaging in criminal acts on the job. Background checks and reference checks have long been used to screen out applicants that employers think might steal from the workplace. With the advent of technology, some employers now also conduct media and Internet searches to learn more about prospective employees. These searches can be quite enlightening. In one media search, the following information was uncovered:

> A candidate said he had been working in the family business for a few years, when in fact he has been in prison. A Kroll media search found out that the candidate had been in prison because he had shared a cell with mass murderer Fred West at some point and on being released, sold his story to a newspaper. (Huber, 2010, p. 145)

Facebook and similar social network sites have also been searched to determine the employability of job candidates. Criminal justice students should take note of this particular statement. In a recent conference presentation titled "What Were You Thinking? Criminal Justice Students and Their Social Networking Sites," a criminal justice professor and his graduate student discussed a research project where they reviewed public Facebook pages of criminal justice students at their university (Lee, 2010). The research team showed some of the pictures they found on students' Facebook pages. Many of the criminal justice majors included pictures of drunken celebrations and marijuana use. One that stood out showed two students in a bathroom, with one of them bent over the toilet. Even if the pictures were not of the students themselves, simply having these pictures on one's Facebook page might be enough to raise concern in future employers. (Note to readers—after you read this chapter, review your Facebook page to make sure it won't keep you unemployed in the future. Make sure you finish this chapter first, though.)

Category III strategies emphasize getting employees to share information about their coworkers' misconduct through efforts such as whistleblowing and anonymous hotlines (Traub, 1996). Anonymous hotlines have been found to be particularly effective "if accompanied by positive support from management" (Holtfreter, 2004, p. 89). What this means is that the leaders of the business must promote a culture that advances and supports ethical decision making in the workplace.

In conducting workplace investigations, it is imperative that information is secured and not shared with coworkers of suspects until necessary. Most workplace settings have tight-knit relationships among coworkers. Coworkers will share information—whether it is accurate or not—with one another. If information about an ongoing investigation becomes public, the internal investigation could be derailed.

The internal investigation process will follow stages similar to those followed in law enforcement investigations of white-collar crime (discussed above). Some differences are worth noting. For example, if a business catches an employee engaging in misconduct, it may simply fire the employee and not refer the case to the authorities. This is often done to avoid negative publicity or simply to minimize the amount of time that would be spent in the criminal justice process.

Another difference has to do with the way interviews are conducted in self-policing and in law enforcement investigations. Public law enforcement officers are held to a higher standard with regard to the rights of the individual they are interrogating. If, for example, a suspect "pleads the Fifth" and says that he or she will not answer specific questions in a criminal investigation, this cannot be held against the suspect at trial. If a suspect refuses to cooperate in an internal investigation, the person's employer can make decisions about the outcome of the investigation by inferring from the employee's refusal to answer questions (Schiff & Kramer, 2004).

Some also make a distinction between a "custodial interrogation" of arrested offenders and a **workplace interview** conducted in internal investigations. One expert advised:

> The interview is not a forum for cross-examination, but for information gathering. If cross examination techniques are used, then often little is achieved. However, it is important for the investigator to use assistance language, "can you help me?," "can you be of assistance to me?," or "I do not understand some issues." (Coburn, 2006, p. 348)

The key distinction centers on a more inquisitorial approach found in internal investigations, as opposed to the adversarial approach used in criminal investigations.

Also similar to criminal investigations, internal investigations might entail a significant number of records that need to be collected, analyzed, and secured. Coburn (2006) recommended that organizations develop policies for collecting and securing records. In particular, Coburn suggested the following:

- "Have a written procedure for the collection of evidence;
- Document the collection of evidence, detailing, time, place of origin, and circumstances of collection;
- Identify documents;
- Obtain relevant primary documents, i.e., contracts, invoices, share certificates, financial transaction documents, etc.;
- Obtain relevant secondary documents, e.g., entry documentation to buildings, telephone, facsimile and computer information;
- Verify primary and secondary documents;
- Secure documents inside the organization." (Coburn, 2006, p. 348)

Whereas a criminal investigation secures records in the law enforcement agency, self-policing efforts keep their records in-house. Whether those records become public depends on the seriousness of the offending and whether the business decides to report the case to the authorities.

Compliance Strategies

Compliance strategies are another form of self-policing. A **compliance program** is an "organizational system aimed at comprehensively detecting and preventing corporate criminality" (Goldsmith & King, 1997, p. 9). Such programs provide a mechanism for identifying and reporting misdeeds with an aim toward keeping the misconduct from occurring in the first place. Strategies used in compliance programs include "audits, employee training, reporting mechanisms, and sanctions for illegal actions" (Goldsmith & King, 1997, p. 10).

Under the 1991 U.S. Sentencing Guidelines, corporations with strong compliance programs are eligible to receive lighter sanctions for misconduct. The sentencing guidelines offer guidance to organizations to indicate what is expected in compliance programs in order to be eligible for reduced sanctions. The guidelines state:

1. The organization must have established compliance standards and procedures to be followed by its employees and other agents that are reasonably capable of reducing the prospect of criminal conduct.

2. Specific individual(s) within high-level personnel of the organization must have been assigned overall responsibility to oversee compliance with such standards and procedures.

3. The organization must have used due care not to delegate substantial discretionary authority to individuals whom the organization knew, or should have known through the exercise of due diligence, had a propensity to engage in illegal activities.

4. The organization must have taken steps to communicate effectively its standards and procedures to all employees and other agents, e.g., by requiring participation in training programs or by disseminating publications that explain in a practical manner what is required.

5. The organization must have taken reasonable steps to achieve compliance with its standards, e.g., by utilizing monitoring and auditing systems reasonably designed to detect criminal conduct by its employees and other agents and by having in place and publicizing a reporting system whereby employees and other agents could report criminal conduct by others within the organization without fear of retribution.

6. The standards must have been consistently enforced through appropriate disciplinary mechanisms, including, as appropriate, discipline of individuals responsible for the failure to detect an offense. Adequate discipline of individuals responsible for an offense is a necessary component of enforcement; however, the form of discipline that will be appropriate will be case specific.

7. After an offense has been detected, the organization must have taken all reasonable steps to respond appropriately to the offense and to prevent further similar offenses—including any necessary modifications to its program to prevent and detect violations of law. (U.S. Federal Sentencing Guidelines)

Beyond allowing a lighter sanction if a corporation is found liable for corporate misconduct, compliance programs are valuable because they can potentially deter workplace transgressions. Scholars have offered suggestions for how to ensure that compliance programs effectively police workplace misconduct. Nestor (2004) argued that executives should "drive compliance from the top" (p. 348). He called for the development of a corporate code of ethics and mandated reporting by officials. If executives show they are serious about preventing corporate misconduct, Nestor suggested, the compliance program will serve as an effective self-policing strategy.

Audits

Audits are included as a part of many organizations' compliance programs and can be seen as an effective self-policing strategy. In this context, audits are different from those discussed above. Criminal investigation audits are conducted by law enforcement representatives for the purpose of searching for wrongdoing. **Self-policing audits** are done by the organization, and as a result, the organization has more control over the direction and timing of the audit.

Audits have been described as "a widely used organizational defense against fraud" (Holtfreter, 2004, p. 89). Audits are done either as part of routine procedures or they may be initiated out of a concern that fraud is occurring in the organization. Organizations will conduct either internal or external audits. **Internal audits** are conducted by the organization's accounting department, while **external audits** are conducted by consultants hired by the corporation (Holtfreter, 2004). Some red flags that surface from audits include the following:

- A lack of documentation for new projects
- Significant payments to new vendors
- Larger payments than usual
- Signs of managers systematically overriding internal controls (Heslop, 2004)

When fraud is discovered during a routine audit, it is believed that the detection is typically "by chance" (Hemraj, 2002, p. 85). **Fraud audits,** or audits conducted for the purpose of exposing fraud, are more likely to reveal fraud. The objectives of a fraud audit include: (1) identifying control mechanisms in a business, (2) identifying weaknesses in a business that place the business at risk for fraud, and (3) identifying those with access who have taken advantage of the weaknesses (Buckhoff, Higgins, & Sinclair, 2010). Some estimates suggest that nearly half of frauds against businesses are uncovered through audits (Peterson, 2004).

Audits are also useful in helping companies to identify parts of the company that are not profitable as well as potential areas of concern. In addition, audits help companies determine whether they are at risk of criminal and civil liability, and if conducted as part of a strong compliance program, audits allow companies more control over the direction of any subsequent criminal or civil investigation (Goldsmith & King, 1997).

In July 2002, the Sarbanes Oxley Act was passed in reaction to the scandals that were occurring at the time, including Enron's and WorldCom's crimes. Among other things, the act, known as SOX, developed standards for auditor independence in publicly traded companies and public accounting firms. The act states that an external auditor:

- Cannot have been an employee of the company being audited in the prior year
- Must be approved by the company's audit committee
- Cannot offer additional services (like bookkeeping) without the approval of the audit committee
- Cannot perform audits more than 5 years in a row for the same company
- Must communicate policies and changes to the audit committee
- Must publicly disclose fees (Nestor, 2004)

The SOX act included a number of other provisions relevant to the criminal and civil processing of corporate crimes. These other provisions will be discussed later in the text.

Forensic Accounting

Students are likely familiar with television shows like *CSI: Crime Scene Investigation,* where forensic scientists review crime scene evidence and solve the crime by the end of the show. Just as forensic scientists are able to piece together evidence to identify suspects, forensic accountants are able to review financial records and determine whether evidence indicates that a crime has been committed. As such, forensic accounting is another self-policing strategy some businesses will use to detect fraud.

When using forensic accountants, businesses will typically hire external consultants to perform the investigation. Just as a large private investigator business exists in the United States, an industry called "Forensic Accounting and Corporate Investigation" also exists (Williams, 2005). This industry has been described as "a diverse and loosely coupled network of private firms and professional groups providing investigative, advisory, and adjudicative service to clients embroiled in cases of economic and financial wrongdoing, whether as 'victims' or 'offenders'" (Williams, 2005, p. 188). Williams described three tiers in this industry: (1) specialized forensic accounting units housed in large accounting firms, (2) large forensic accounting firms devoted solely to corporate investigations, and (3) small private investigation agencies. When hired, forensic accountants can do investigative accounting searching for evidence of fraud, economic loss calculations determining how much a company has lost to fraud or other events, and appraisals of the business to determine whether the company made or lost money as a result of misconduct (Rasmussen & Leauanae, 2004). For corporate offenders, forensic accounting firms also offer services as expert witnesses, consulting about federal policies and laws, witness preparation, and a number of other services.

It is important to note that forensic accountants will also collect and scrutinize evidence other than financial records. They will review work schedules, read e-mails, interview workers and bosses, gather and review other available evidence, and develop a report detailing their conclusions about the presence of fraud in the business: (1) whether it is occurring in the business, (2) why it is occurring, and (3) who is possibly committing the fraud. A survey of 252 academics and forensic accountants found that the most necessary skills for forensic accountants included deductive reasoning, critical thinking, and the ability to serve as an expert witness (DiGabriele, 2008). The author of this study notes that an accounting education often focuses on a structured way to do accounting, but forensic accounting is different because the practitioners need to be able to improvise.

⊠ Regulatory Policing and White-Collar Crime

Regulatory agencies are governmental agencies responsible for making sure that regulations are followed in industries and businesses across the United States. In this context, regulations are rules that guide workplace activities. Note that the violation of a "rule" may not necessarily be treated as a violation of the criminal law, but these violations can be seen as white-collar crimes. To provide a framework for understanding regulatory policing, the following areas will be addressed:

- Conceptualizing Regulatory Policing
- Regulatory Officials as Police Officers
- Regulatory Policing Styles
- Criticisms of Regulatory Policing

Conceptualizing Regulatory Policing

Different types of businesses are regulated by different regulatory agencies depending on the different types of products/services the business provides. In reality, most businesses are regulated by multiple regulatory agencies. For example, restaurant/bars are regulated by (1) local and state agencies responsible for ensuring that food safety laws are not violated, (2) state alcohol control agencies to make sure that liquor laws are not violated, (3) occupational safety and health agencies to make sure businesses are not violating workers' rights or making them unsafe, and (4) local, state, and federal agencies charged with ensuring waste is disposed of correctly.

Regulatory agencies engage in policing activities in different ways that are tied to the specific agency's mission statement. Regulatory enforcement has been defined as "the consistent application of formal rules and sanctions to secure compliance with the enabling legislation and promulgated regulations" (Snider, 1990, p. 374). As Hazel Croall (1979) points out, regulatory officers "proceed very much like police" (p. 166). Others have added that regulators "are required to set in motion a process to identify . . . and punish those who have been irresponsible" (Jayasuriya & Sharp, 2006, p. 51).

▲ **Photo 12.4** In September 2009, inspectors from the Consumer Product and Safety Commission—the regulatory agency responsible for reviewing the safety of various products—closed 200 pools across the United States because the pools did not have the right drains installed.

Some have said that the financial crisis of the early 2000s actually served to "awaken the world to the role of the regulator in the fight against financial crimes" (Pusey, 2007, p. 300). Pusey draws attention to the changing nature of the regulator's role. Recently, the Obama administration increased regulatory efforts. Describing crackdowns on unsafe products and unsafe workplace settings, one reporter commented, "The new regulators display a passion for rules and a belief that government must protect the public from dangers lurking at home and on the job—one more way the new White House is reworking the relationship between government and business" (Layton, 2009).

Regulatory Officials as Police Officers

In general, agencies receive information about violations through referrals, site inspections, news reports, and record reviews. In terms of referrals, regulatory agencies receive information about potential rule breaking from investors, consumers, anonymous tips, competitors, and other governmental agencies that uncover potential wrongdoing (Rutledge, 2006). Regulatory officials will review the referral by using traditional investigatory techniques, including interviewing witnesses, visiting the site of the alleged violation, reviewing records, and so on.

In addition to visiting business sites to follow up on complaints, regulatory officers will also carry out routine site visits to conduct periodic reviews of businesses. Inspectors from local or state health departments, for example, will visit restaurants to ensure that the businesses are in compliance with food safety and health regulations. The inspectors assign the restaurant a score based on the inspection. In some places, the inspection reports are posted online. Inspectors can force a business to shut down until the violations are addressed. Consider a recent case in which an inspector temporarily closed a restaurant in south Florida for 17 violations uncovered as part of the inspection. Among other things, the inspection found "raw sewage in the back yard of the restaurant; more than 100 fresh rodent droppings in the kitchen; a live roach in the kitchen; ready-to-eat, potentially hazardous food prepared on site and held more than 24 hours and not properly date-marked" (Trischitta, 2011, n.p.). In another case, a restaurant was shut down by inspectors who found employees butchering a deer in the kitchen when they visited the establishment to follow up on an anonymous tip ("Restaurant Closed Briefly," 2008).

As another example of site visits as part of regulatory policing of white-collar crime, the Center for Medicare and Medicaid Services contracts with states to have state inspectors visit nursing homes receiving Medicare or Medicaid at least once a year and conduct health and safety inspections. The inspectors conduct a thorough investigation assessing the degree to which the business is adhering to more than 150 different rules. Based on their findings, the team can fine the nursing homes, deny payments, and suspended the nursing home from participation in Medicare and Medicaid if they fail to address violations found by inspectors (Medicare.Gov, 2008). See In Focus 12.2 for a description of the thoroughness of the site visits.

In Focus 12.2

The Nursing Home Inspection Process

The inspection team observes resident care processes, staff/resident interaction, and environment. Using an established protocol, the team interviews a sample of residents and family members about their life within the nursing home, and interviews caregivers and administrative staff. The team reviews clinical records.

The inspection team consists of trained inspectors, including at least one registered nurse. This team evaluates whether the nursing home meets individual resident needs. In addition, fire safety specialists evaluate whether a nursing home meets standards for safe construction. When an inspection team finds that a home does not meet a specific regulation, it issues a deficiency citation.

The regulations cover a wide range of aspects of resident life, from specifying standards for the safe storage and preparation of food to protecting residents from physical or mental abuse or inadequate care practices. (Medicare.gov, 2008)

Regulatory investigations sometimes stem from news reports demonstrating how a particular agency or industry is violating regulations. In July 2010, for example, the Department of Housing and Urban Development initiated an investigation after a *New York Times* article titled "Need a Mortgage? Don't Get Pregnant," by reporter Tara Bernard (2010), showed that pregnant women and new moms were being denied loans because of their new babies. After the article appeared in print, HUD released a statement to the press that included the following comments:

A published report in the New York Times indicated that some mortgage lenders may be denying credit to borrowers because of a pregnancy or maternity leave. As a result, HUD's Office of Fair Housing Equal Opportunity is opening multiple investigations into the practices of lending institutions to determine if they are violating the Fair Housing Act.

"This report is profoundly disturbing and requires immediate action," said John Trasviña, HUD's Assistant Secretary for Fair Housing and Equal Opportunity, the office that will be directing these investigations. "Lenders must not carry out due diligence responsibilities in ways that have the practical effect of discriminating against recent or expectant mothers."

Regulatory agencies also learn about violations through record reviews. For businesses that receive payments from the government, regulatory officials review the bills submitted by the business to ensure the business is in compliance and to determine whether regulatory rules were violated. If officials detect errors in the claims, additional examination is conducted to determine if the error was intentional or accidental. For accidental errors, the funds are recovered from business. For intentionally submitted false bills, the case is referred to another office for criminal and civil investigations. In securities fraud investigations, federal and "state regulators have authority to issue subpoenas for documents" (Rutledge, 2006).

▲ **Photo 12.5** New babies are supposed to be an exciting part of individuals' lives. A *New York Times* article reported that mortgage lenders were denying loans to pregnant women or new mothers in a discriminatory way. Based on the news article, the Department of Housing and Urban Development initiated an investigation. "Denying a mortgage to people just because they're having a baby is flat wrong," Vice President Joseph R. Biden Jr. said in a press release from HUD.

Regulatory Policing Styles

Generally speaking, two types of regulatory strategies exist—persuasion/cooperation strategies and retributive/punishment strategies (Frank, 1984; Snider, 1990). Persuasion strategies promote "education, negotiation, and cooperation" to get businesses and corporations to comply with regulations (Frank, 1984, p. 237). Retributive strategies emphasize finding violations and punishing offenders. An analogy to traffic enforcement helps to distinguish between the two strategies. If your campus police develop strategies to educate and persuade students to obey traffic laws, this would be a persuasion strategy. If your campus police focus solely on catching traffic violators and giving them stiff fines, this would be a retributive strategy. Among regulatory agencies, some are more persuasion oriented, while others are more punishment oriented.

A question that often arises is whether regulatory officers are police officers. Using James Q. Wilson's typology of police officers, criminologist Nancy Frank (1984) shows how regulatory policing styles are similar to traditional law enforcement styles. First, some regulatory agencies follow a "service style" where the agencies serve the community through the provision of various services. According to Frank, administrators in these agencies see themselves as serving the government and not the public.

Second, some agencies follow a "watchman" style in their efforts to regulate corporate behavior—using discretion and staying out of the way, with officers who are described by Frank as possessing "only marginal competence" (Frank, 1984, p. 242). Consider the movie *Larry the Cable Guy: Health Inspector*, which one or two readers may have seen. In the movie, Larry the Cable Guy is portrayed as a health inspector letting businesses get away with all sorts of atrocities and enforcing laws only as a last resort. I won't give away the plot because it truly is worth watching to learn more about regulatory policing.

Third, "legalistic" agencies address regulatory violations more aggressively. Officers are more competent and more professional in such agencies and the agencies likely "have formal guidelines instructing enforcement officers when to bring actions" (Frank, 1984, p. 245). These officers likely see their occupations as being oriented toward law enforcement and play by the book in their efforts to regulate businesses and corporations.

Fourth, the "free agent" style is similar to the legalistic style, but regulatory officers are given more leeway in deciding how to proceed with the case. Imagine Clint Eastwood's Dirty Harry character as a regulatory officer. Instead of a .44 magnum he would be armed with a clipboard, rule book, and BlackBerry, but his efforts to root out corporate rule breaking would be similar to the way the fictional officer sought out criminals in the five movies about the detective's crime fighting.

As long as we are using a Dirty Harry an analogy, in the 1983 Dirty Harry movie *Sudden Impact*, Detective Harry Callahan was pointing his gun at his nemesis when he said, "Go ahead, make my day"—a quote that has become part of our lexicon. Callahan was, in effect, communicating a very clear message to the offender—he wanted to shoot the suspect in the head. In a no-nonsense way, regulatory officers are expected to communicate messages to the businesses and organizations they regulate.

Researchers have suggested that how compliance messages are communicated to managers in the business or corporation may have an impact on how they respond to the regulatory activity (Makkai & Braithwaite, 1994). If the regulator's behaviors/messages are perceived as overly punitive, the business might continue to engage in rule breaking. Makkai and Braithwaite call for a reintegrative shaming model to notify businesses about misconduct. They suggest that regulators do the following:

(a) communicate noncompliance in a way that is perceived as procedurally fair, (b) communicate noncompliance in a way that does not communicate distrust, (c) communicate noncompliance in a way that shows respect for professionalism, (d) give praise to low self-efficacy actors when they fix one of the problems, and (e) encourage disengagers to become reengaged. (p. 365)

In other words, the "Dirty Harry style of communicating" may not be the best way for regulators to communicate with corporations.

Criticisms of Regulatory Policing

A number of different criticisms have been levied against regulatory policing, with most of these criticisms suggesting that the regulatory efforts do little to stop misconduct. In fact, some say that rather than stopping misconduct, such efforts may actually breed rule breaking. For example, one author team suggested that "much regulation . . . represents a facilitation, rather than diminishment, of environmental harm" (Halsey & White, 1998, p. 347). Others have blamed regulatory agencies for recent economic woes on the grounds that "light-handed" regulation allowed corporate misconduct to escalate to the point that markets collapsed and criminal prosecutions were inevitable (Tomasic, 2011).

Scholars have also argued that corporate power weakens the regulatory system. Snider (1990) suggested that "the entire agenda of regulation is the result of a struggle between the corporate sector opposing regulation and the much weaker forces supporting it" (p. 284). Another criticism that has been levied is that regulatory efforts are too lenient and corporate misconduct should be handled as violations of the criminal law with more severe sanctions given to offenders.

While some have said the corporations, businesses, and offenders should be criminally punished rather than regulated, criminologist Susan Shapiro (1985) has argued that a clear sign that regulatory agencies have failed is the use of the criminal law to respond to corporate misconduct. From this perspective, if regulatory agencies were working, companies would be abiding by corporate regulations and there would be no need for the criminal law in these cases.

The Global Police and White-Collar Crime

As noted throughout this book, white-collar offending occurs internationally. Consequently, police agencies from across the world have been called upon to use law enforcement strategies to detect, respond to, and prevent white-collar crime. A number of different issues arise in efforts to address international white-collar crimes. Such barriers include the following:

- Countries vary in the types of records they maintain
- Linguistic barriers make it difficult for officers to communicate with one another
- Cultural barriers create situations where misconduct and offenders might be perceived differently
- Gaining cooperation between agencies from different countries is difficult
- Variation in international laws results in misconduct being defined differently across the world
- Determining whether international enforcement policies are effective is an arduous task (Passas, 2004)

These barriers can be overcome, or at least minimized. For example, cooperation can be enhanced if officers are aware of cultural differences between countries (Larsson, 2006). Also, resource commitments by specific agencies involved in international partnerships would help to demonstrate that countries are committed to responding to white-collar crime (Berkman et al., 2008). Larsson (2006) suggested that international cooperation can be improved if officials do the following: (1) create networks where police officers can develop a "common language" (p. 463), (2) provide appropriate education and training to those involved in the international response to white-collar crime, (3) ensure that police agencies have the information they need to prevent crime, and (4) identify communication channels.

⬚ Summary

- White-collar crimes come to the attention of the police through several different avenues, and a number of different agencies are involved in the police response to white-collar crime.
- The notion of "police response" to white-collar crime describes different forms of policing, including criminal policing, private policing, and regulatory policing.
- Three types of agencies are involved in responding to white-collar crime. These include private agencies (or self-policing by corporations or businesses), formal criminal police agencies, and governmental regulatory agencies.
- In the FBI, the Financial Crimes Section (FCS), located in the agency's Criminal Investigations Division, investigates cases of white-collar crime.
- A major portion of the police response to white-collar crime involves law enforcement strategies carried out by officials in the criminal justice system.
- White-collar crime investigations begin one of two ways—from referrals or as a part of a proactive policing initiative.
- Common strategies to gather evidence in white-collar crime cases include (1) audits, (2) record reviews, (3) undercover strategies, (4) the use of whistleblowers, and (5) the use of technological devices.
- While not always sufficient by themselves, when combined with other forms of evidence-gathering strategies, audits can provide the evidence needed to substantiate wrongdoing.
- White-collar crime investigators will also review an assortment of records in building their case. The amount of records law enforcement investigators will need to review in these cases can be enormous.
- On the surface, undercover white-collar crime investigations are no different from undercover criminal investigations. However, important differences exist between white-collar and conventional undercover investigations.
- Compared to conventional undercover investigations, white-collar crime undercover investigations are less dangerous, less time consuming, involve lower degrees of role playing by officers, and are not as central to the case as undercover investigations in criminal cases.
- Whistleblowers are individuals who notify authorities about wrongdoing in their organization. Two types of whistleblowers exist: internal whistleblowers and external whistleblowers (Vinten, 1994).
- Various types of technological devices are used to search for evidence in white-collar crime cases.
- Problems that surface in criminal white-collar crime investigations include the following resource problems: relationship dynamics, time, complexity, proof, and perceptions of white-collar crime police work.
- Resources are a problem inasmuch as white-collar crime police units are grossly under-resourced in comparison to police units focusing on conventional crimes.
- Three types of relationships present obstacles in white-collar crime investigations: (1) the victim/offender relationship, (2) the offender/witness relationship, and (3) the officer/offender relationship.
- Three issues that make white-collar crimes particularly complex are (1) complex record searches, (2) extensive collaborations with partners, and (3) the lack of a systematic approach.
- It is difficult for investigators to gather evidence that prosecutors will be able to use to prove various aspects of the misconduct.

- Police work in these cases is often perceived pejoratively, as if the activity is not real police work.
- A number of different suggestions have been made to improve the law enforcement response to white-collar crime, including searching for the "smoking gun," "following the money," and educating officials.
- Self-policing refers to efforts by companies and businesses to develop their own policing responses to white-collar crime.
- Types of self-policing efforts used by business to detect or prevent white-collar crime include: loss prevention strategies, compliance programs, audits, and the use of forensic accountants.
- Loss prevention strategies are efforts that businesses use to keep employees from stealing from the business.
- A compliance program is an "organizational system aimed at comprehensively detecting and preventing corporate criminality" (Goldsmith & King, 1997, p. 9).
- Criminal investigation audits are conducted by law enforcement representatives for the purpose of searching for wrongdoing. Self-policing audits are done by the organization.
- Forensic accountants are able to review financial records to determine whether there is evidence indicating that a crime has been committed. As such, forensic accounting is another self-policing strategy some businesses use to detect fraud.
- Regulatory agencies are governmental agencies responsible for making sure that regulations are followed in industries and businesses across the United States.
- Different types of businesses are regulated by different regulatory agencies depending on the different types of products/services the business provides.
- In general, agencies receive information about violations through referrals, site inspections, news reports, and record reviews.
- Two types of regulatory strategies exist: persuasion/cooperation strategies and retributive/punishment strategies (Frank, 1984; Snider, 1990).
- A number of different criticisms have been levied against regulatory policing, with most of these criticisms suggesting that the regulatory efforts do little to stop misconduct.
- Police agencies across the world have been called upon to use law enforcement strategies to detect, respond to, and prevent white-collar crime.
- Larsson (2006) suggested that international cooperation can be improved if officials do the following: (1) develop networks where police officers can create a "common language" (p. 463), (2) provide appropriate education and training, (3) ensure that police agencies have the information they need to prevent crime, and (4) identify communication channels.

KEY TERMS

Audits	Internal audits	Self-policing
Compliance program	Internal whistleblower	Self-policing audits
External audit	Loss prevention strategies	Smoking gun
External whistleblower	Proactive strategies	Whistleblower
Financial Crimes Section (FCS)	Reactive strategies	White-collar undercover investigations
Forensic accountant	Record reviews	Workplace interview
Fraud audits	Regulatory agencies	

DISCUSSION QUESTIONS

1. How are white-collar crime investigations different from investigations of conventional crimes?

2. Review the police/regulatory agencies that respond to white-collar crimes. Which of those agencies would you want to work for? Explain.

3. Compare and contrast law enforcement strategies and regulatory strategies to control white-collar crime.

4. What would you like most about being a white-collar crime investigator? What would you like the least?

5. Should businesses be required to report their employees to the police if they catch them stealing from the business? Explain.

6. Compare and contrast self-policing efforts with traditional policing efforts.

7. Which types of evidence gathering strategies do you think are the most effective for building white-collar crime cases?

8. Why is white-collar crime so difficult to address with law enforcement and regulatory efforts?

9. You are elected President. A representative from the banking industry, which helped get you elected, asks you to sign an executive order calling for deregulation. What do you do?

10. How would you feel if you found out that one of your coworkers is an undercover investigator posing as an employee in your work setting? Explain.

WEB RESOURCES

Whistleblower Laws: http://www.whistleblowerlaws.com/whistleblower-protections-act/

Cisco Loss Prevention: http://www.cisco.com/web/strategy/docs/retail/Video_Surveillance_BR.pdf

COPS Website: http://www.cops.usdoj.gov/

READING

In this reading, Garrett Speaks, a special agent from the Bureau of Criminal Investigation (Pennsylvania Office of Attorney General), writes about his experience of being hired as an undercover investigator to investigate crimes in nursing homes after he graduated from college. Speaks describes how a cover story was created and how traditional white-collar crime strategies guided the development of the investigation. After working in one nursing home where no crimes were seen, he was hired in a second home where he saw various forms of criminal behavior committed. Speaks provides a detailed account of the types of crimes he witnessed. His undercover work led to a conviction 2 years later.

Documenting Inadequate Care in the Nursing Home

The Story of an Undercover Agent

Garrett E. Speaks

While completing my undergraduate degree in Criminology, I received a call from a professor who told me that the Pennsylvania Office of Attorney General (OAG) was seeking to hire a young undercover agent. I went to Harrisburg for an interview and met with a Deputy Attorney General, who said that the Office was interested in securing an undercover agent to go inside nursing homes and other settings to investigate possible patient abuse. If I were hired, I would be working as a nurse's aide. Even after learning about the arduous and unpleasant duties that a nurse's aide performs, the work still interested me.

A second interview followed with the Deputy Attorney General and others in the Office. To judge my reaction to sick and injured persons, I was shown photographs of patients who had been wounded or killed in health care settings. An OAG agent drove me to Philadelphia where I was directed to fill out an application for employment at a Philadelphia nursing home. I was immediately brought back to Harrisburg where I was asked to describe, in detail, everything I observed

on my trip. It was not until later did I realize why this exercise was important. As an undercover agent, it was my job to record and report everything I saw and heard. I was not to pass judgment or form opinions based on my observations. After the second extended interview process, I was advised that I might be contacted again.

The next contact came after I graduated from college. I had just been hired as an insurance salesman and was in the process of studying to take the life insurance test for my new sales job. I immediately accepted the position of working undercover as a nurse's aide because it seemed to be more satisfying to me than the prospect of selling insurance. I was told to pack for an extended stay since it was unclear when I would return home.

I crammed my Volkswagen Diesel Rabbit with clothes and books, quit my part-time waiter job, dropped off the insurance manuals that I was studying, and left the next morning for the State Capitol in Harrisburg, Pennsylvania. I immediately enrolled in a two-week nurse's aide training course at a local nursing

SOURCE: Speaks, G. (1997). Documenting Inadequate Care in the Nursing Home: The Story of an Undercover Agent. *Journal of Elder Abuse & Neglect, 8*(3), 37–45.

home, along with two other Office of Attorney General agents. All Pennsylvania nurse's aides are required to complete training and pass a test to become certified as a nurse's aide. Nursing homes may hire uncertified aides, but the aide must become certified no later than 120 days after employment. At the completion of the two week course, I took the state's nurse's aide test which consisted of a written component and a clinical section performed in front of a nurse. In general, I gained an understanding of basic human care for nursing home residents from the course. I passed the exam and was certified as a nurse's aide.

Once certified, I moved to Philadelphia and secured employment in a reputable nursing home known to deliver adequate care in order to gain hands-on experience with patient care. The nursing home that hired me was located in a suburban middle-class area of Philadelphia. This home paid me $7.00 per hour. I found it well staffed with a large amount of family participation. While there, I felt that the residents were well cared for; I saw only one decubitus ulcer. After approximately two months, it was decided that I should attempt to gain employment in the target nursing home. This particular home, located in West Philadelphia, was selected because of the numerous complaints of patient abuse that had been received about it.

First, a cover story had to be developed for me; that is, a complete employment and education history, including legitimate appearing references. I told the nursing home staff that I had recently moved to Philadelphia to live with my brother. I needed to work in Philadelphia because I would be attending school at a local computer training center. I used my last real job as a reference and also a fictitious nursing home. If the target home chose to contact the fictitious home, the phone call would be received at the Attorney General's Office in Harrisburg on a telephone maintained for undercover operations. The telephone line is not traceable to the Office.

Two weeks after applying to the nursing home, I received a call and was scheduled for an interview. The home was located in a low income and minority neighborhood. During the interview I was asked why I wanted to work in this field. I informed them of my plans to go to computer school and because of my class schedule needed to work the 3:00 PM to 11:00 PM shift. This shift was chosen because it would give me a better opportunity to observe patient care while administrators and most supervisors were not apt to be present in the facility.

I was hired at the rate of $3.85 an hour with no benefits until completing six months of employment. A five-day training course was required, held in the basement of the facility. My class consisted of 14 other newly hired aides, most of whom had no prior nursing home experience, and none were state certified. After only three days of classroom instruction, the course participants were asked to sign a paper stating that training had been completed in all areas of patient care. In actuality, the training had been cut short because the facility did not have enough staff, and we were needed right away in the units.

On July 2, 1991, I was assigned the 3:00 PM to 11:00 PM shift on a non-skilled floor unit. On that unit I observed that the floors were always covered with food particles. Most of the call bells did not work, with some even having exposed wiring. Some of the residents' urine smelled of ammonia and their stools were very dark. My state's nurses' aide training program taught me that these conditions indicated possible dehydration, so I attempted to increase my residents' water intake.

In some of the rooms, the air conditioners were not working so I brought in a thermometer to record the temperatures. One room which housed three male residents consistently had readings over 90 degrees. At the beginning of my shift, I frequently discovered these men restrained in bed sweating profusely. I gave them water, got them out of bed, and took them to the air-conditioned lounge. Not long after coming to that unit, an LPN told me one of these men had been taken to the hospital with pneumonia and that the heat had definitely had an impact on him.

I noticed that one of the residents had a small decubitus ulcer on his buttocks, and at times the treatment had not been done. When I reported it, the LPN said that it was not her problem; treatments were to be done on the day shift.

I soon realized that if I was to find more severe patient abuse at the facility, I needed to move off the non-skilled floors and work with residents who depended on staff to provide them with care. I made a request to the Director of Nursing to work with the skilled care patients explaining that I hoped some day to become an LPN. I also requested a change to the 7:00 AM to 3:00 PM shift.

On the skilled unit, I was frequently assigned 10 to 12 total care residents at a time, which meant working feverishly just to get these residents out of bed and cleaned each day. Despite the fact that I was an undercover agent, my first responsibility was to take care of the residents. However, I did carry a small notebook which I took into the staff bathroom each day to record my observations. I wrote down the information about the residents I cared for, what I observed, and what I heard from co-workers about the resident care. Later, a decision was made that I should photograph the residents' conditions. A camera was given to me which I eventually used to photograph decubitus ulcers on eleven residents who were living in the skilled care unit where I worked.

Treatments of decubiti in this facility were done once a day during the 7:00 AM to 3:00 PM shift. As a nurse's aide, I was required to remove the day-old bandages and leave the residents in bed with the wounds exposed until the treatment nurse could come and treat them. This procedure made it very easy to photograph the wounds. I hid the camera in my pocket, went into the room of my residents, closed the door, and placed a wheelchair or some obstruction near the door so if anyone came into the room, I could hear the door bang and could hide the camera. My task was simply to photograph the exposed and uncovered wounds. On the days that I brought the camera in and out of the facility, I was very nervous. Because of a large amount of theft inside the facility, management had the right to randomly search any worker coming and going. Fortunately, I was able to use the camera without incident.

In the skilled care unit, I found a large number of residents with severe decubitus ulcers. One of the nurses, to my surprise, told me that the other skilled care unit had residents with more serious decubiti. The first resident I worked with on the skilled care unit had five ulcers; the one on her back was four inches in circumference and one-half inch deep. One morning I was called to the resident's room to assist the nurse in changing wound dressings. My notes of that date read: "A.B.'s decubitus: one on left buttock, one-half inch in circumference and a quarter inch deep; one on lower back, approximately four inches in circumference, black in color; and one on her left heel, bleeding, and appears that her whole heel is gone. Agent observed heel bone sticking out of the back of her foot."

An RN said that the reason the facility had so many patients with decubiti was that the staff did not have enough time to properly care for the residents. She also stated that this particular resident came to the facility approximately seven months prior with only blisters on her feet. The RN also stated that A.B. was dying because her blood was "poisoned due to sores on her heel." Another RN said that the family would not allow A.B.'s leg to be amputated.

Soon after I photographed one of the residents, I heard that she had died. The records indicated that she had sepsis; a nurse stated that the bed sores had killed her. Around the same time, a nursing home administrator called all the staff on our floor to a meeting and said that she expected the state Department of Health to come soon for an inspection of the facility. Meanwhile, she stated the corporation's quality assurance people would be in the facility to inspect and find the problems before the state did. Also, five new LPN's had been hired.

Following this meeting, four nurse's aides with name tags that indicated they were from the corporation's quality assurance program were on our unit cleaning rooms, bathing and shaving patients, trimming fingernails, and putting name tags on laundry and residents' doorways. For the first time, soft music began to play over the public address system. I noticed extra paperwork being done at the nurse's station and a social worker filling out dietary meal observation cards in the lounge. When I asked him what he was doing there, he said that he filled the forms out every day, even though I had never seen him there before. Prior to our state inspection, my floor averaged six nurse's aides. This number was increased to eight or nine during the inspection, which occurred not long after our meeting with the administrator.

The inspection lasted approximately one week; for the first time I felt we had enough staff to get all our work done. A nurse's aide said she wished the state was there all the time. When the inspection was over, the quality assurance workers disappeared, the extra nurse's aides left, and the music was turned off. We were called to a meeting and informed that we had passed inspection. I was surprised because I knew most of the facility's nurse's aides were not state certified as the law requires. When I asked the personnel director how we had passed, she said that during the state inspection, the state only checks the aides who were hired during the previous 120 days when certification is not required. She said, "that is lucky for us." One of the supervisors stated that, "everyone is so uptight when the state comes. If we did things the right way, the way it's supposed to be done all the time, we'd have nothing to worry about."

During my employment inside the nursing home, I continually reported what I saw and heard. Typically, I would observe a problem in the home and then ask an RN, an LPN, or a nurse's aide about it. I had been in the facility for approximately three months when I realized that I rarely observed physicians in the facility. I once recalled seeing a doctor stand outside a resident's room with a dictaphone and describe the condition of the resident. I would often receive complaints from my residents about never seeing their doctors. One of the LPNs stated that the physicians at the facility never actually looked at the residents; they only looked at the medical records and walked around the facility for awhile.

While working on the skilled care unit, I befriended an LPN. I found her to be a very conscientious nurse who demonstrated genuine concern for the condition of the facility's residents. Her complaints to me were typical of others I heard while at the facility. She complained about the doctors' lack of care, the lack of proper staff, and the lack of training. She blamed the staff on the non-skilled care floors of the facility for the development of resident decubiti. Her belief was that residents' skin would break down on the non-skilled care floors, where staffing levels were the lowest. When the sores were finally discovered by the staff, often when they were more numerous and serious, the residents would

be sent to her. She blamed the sores on nurses and nurses's aides whom she felt had not properly cared for the residents. She said she would come back to work after her days off and find wound dressings she had put on residents still in place and unchanged.

When the residents woke up, the aides removed the bandages. They remained on their beds with the wounds exposed until the nurse had a chance to get to treat them. It was not unusual for a resident to lie in bed possibly all morning with sores exposed waiting for treatment.

The facility had only one treatment nurse who worked on the two skilled care floors of the facility. She pushed a small cart stacked high with wound kits from room to room once a day treating the decubitus ulcers. She dressed the wounds from the moment she began her shift at approximately 8:00 AM, finishing the treatments around 1:00 PM and working steadily without breaks to get all the sores covered.

I discovered that the company which managed the nursing home owned most of the subsidiaries that dealt with the facility including the ambulance company, the durable medical goods and staffing company, the pharmacy company, the rehabilitation company and, of course, the check-cashing van. Each pay day, the check cashing van arrived and charged the employees a fee to cash their checks. It seems the company was even making money off the money it was paying its employees.

One of the biggest problems I experienced while at the facility was the number of temporary nurse's aides that were assigned to work there by the corporation's staffing company. This company routinely provided nurse's aides to the facility when it was short-handed. The problem was that the facility was always short-handed and the staffing company never seemed to send enough staff. The residents' full-time aides were already underpaid, undertrained and overworked.

The replacement nurse's aides caused a lot of resentment among the full-time staff because they were paid almost as much an hour as the regular staff. Unfortunately, the presence of the staffing company aides did not guarantee better nursing care because these temporary workers knew that they were not going to be at the facility long. They felt that they did not have to listen to anyone's instructions. Lacking familiarity with the residents' needs, they also caused a breakdown in the continuity of care and contributed to the deterioration in the residents' care.

This type of abuse is not what could be called a "one time event," such as hitting or pushing a resident. What I observed was long-term neglect of residents through continuing deterioration of care that eventually resulted in the breakdown of the resident's health and led to decubitus ulcers and contractures. During my employment in the facility, I observed at least 100 decubitus ulcers. Some residents had one wound, while others had as many as 16. I was taught in the state certification training program that decubitus ulcers were preventable, except in cases where underlying disease, such as vascular compromise in the extremities or cancer brought on these wounds.

As part of my nurse's aide training, I learned that residents had to be turned every two hours and range of motion exercises were needed to prevent contractures. Throughout the time I was undercover, I continually reported that residents were not turned at the facility. This practice was neither recommended nor enforced by the administration or the nursing supervisory personnel. The facility had no turning schedule posted nor did they announce over the public address system to turn patients. I also never saw range of motion exercises done on a resident in the six months I was at the facility.

Ideally, nurse's aides should know to do these procedures on their own. However, if an aide is overworked and underpaid, as well as undertrained, it is reasonable to believe that proper resident care will not be performed and that skin integrity and other care issues will suffer. The numbers and severity of decubitus ulcers that I observed confirmed these assumptions.

As a nurse's aide, I realized that 95% of the care a nursing home resident receives comes from the aides. If care fails at the aide level, it is almost irrelevant how good the care might be at any other level. It always bothered me during my time in the nursing home that while 95% of the care was provided to residents by nurse's aides, the aides received the lowest pay. In my case at this facility, I was paid less than I could have earned as a worker in a fast food restaurant.

Receiving $3.85 an hour did not add to my sense of worth as a person or as an aide. I was further aggravated by being forced to pay monthly dues to a union which claimed to represent the aides at the facility. This union was actually the waitress and bartender union of Philadelphia. In my experience, it accomplished little for the staff at the facility.

Toward the end of the investigation, I met a resident (M.W.) for the first time when I went to her room to assist her nurse's aide in bathing her. At her door the odor was so bad I could barely go any further. Inside the room, I found a severely contracted black female who was moaning in terrible pain. She was lying in a milky white substance which I later learned was the contents of her colon draining out of a decubitus ulcer on her right hip. She had at least eight decubitus ulcers that I observed. The medical records reported that she had Alzheimer's disease, contractures, and multiple "horrible decubiti (a total of eight), all stages three and four." M.W.'s sister told me during a brief conversation that when M.W. arrived at the facility three years earlier, she was walking and talking and had no wounds. When I inquired of the treatment nurse why M.W. had so many wounds, I was informed that it was because of lack of nourishment and not having been turned properly. She stated that M.W.'s decubiti were "rotting."

Another nurse told me that M.W. "is rotting to death from poor nursing care." Only Tylenol had been ordered for her, when she should have been given morphine due to the severity of her pain. The nurse then looked at me and asked me if I could imagine my own pelvis rotting? I recall that on November 27, 1991, while photographing her, she lay in bed and moaned because of constant pain. She died two days later on November 29, 1991. I attended the autopsy of M.W. at the Philadelphia Medical Examiner's Office, and the medical examiner confirmed what the nurse had previously told me. I saw her pelvic bone on the side where her deepest wound was and where the contents of her colon had been draining. The medical examiner was able to pass a probe from the outside of her hip through the sore and into her colon and out of her left lower back.

Shortly after the death of M.W., I ended my employment at the facility, and the investigation moved into the next stage which involved securing the medical records of those residents the Attorney General's Office felt might have received inadequate care at the facility.

Based on what I reported, a search warrant was obtained and the facility was searched and medical records were seized. The evidence gathered was presented to the Statewide Investigating Grand Jury in Harrisburg which would decide on the merits on the case. My part as an undercover agent was over.

This investigation continued for two more years before ending in a conviction. The most important observation I made during the undercover operation was that residents whose family or friends participate in day-to-day care receive substantially higher quality of care from nursing home staff. Unfortunately in today's society, our elderly are too often "hidden away" and forgotten. We must make the care and protection of our elderly a top priority. It is both an issue of morality and self preservation.

DISCUSSION QUESTIONS

1. Would you want a similar job after you graduate from college? Explain.

2. Describe how this undercover investigation might differ from an undercover investigation of a street gang?

3. Do you think undercover investigations are ethical? Explain.

READING

In this reading, authors Carleen Botsko and Robert Wells examine how whistleblowers are used in white-collar crime investigations. The authors consider the emotional impacts of whistleblowing and point to strategies investigators can use to make sure that emotional issues do not derail white-collar crime investigations. They describe how white-collar crime whistleblowers are technically victims of white-collar crime. The authors note that issues related to victimization must be addressed to gain the most effective information from whistleblowers.

Government Whistleblowers

Crime's Hidden Victims

Carleen A. Botsko and Robert C. Wells

For the past 8 years, Tom has worked for the same Federal agency. He earns a good salary as a senior research analyst and owns a home in a quiet suburb. He and his wife have two children and a third is on the way. Although Tom is, by all accounts, a model employee, he is about to make a decision that will place his career, and eventually other aspects of his life, in jeopardy.

SOURCE: Botsko, C., and Wells, R. (1994, July). Government whistleblowers: Crime's hidden victims. *FBI Law Enforcement Bulletin*, pp. 17–21.

During the past several months, Tom has observed his supervisor taking routine lunches with a local contractor who does business with Tom's section. He also has learned from several knowledgeable sources that this same contractor paid for many of the frills included in his supervisor's recent Hawaiian vacation. While irritated by the apparent lack of judgment demonstrated by his supervisor. Tom did not wish to make waves in an otherwise ideal work situation.

Now, as his supervisor rummages through bids submitted by contractors for an upcoming project, Tom observes him dial the phone and ask for the contractor with whom he lunches regularly. In partial disbelief, Tom overhears his supervisor read off the bid totals.

Tom knows that this information must be reported to the appropriate authorities. While he has no interest in becoming involved in a lengthy federal investigation, he does what he has been encouraged to do during numerous agency security awareness briefings—he dials his agency's hotline number.

Reluctantly, Tom has joined the ranks of an often-misunderstood circle referred to as government whistleblowers. Unfortunately, these potentially invaluable witnesses to serious criminal acts and breaches of public trust routinely must endure what Tom fears most—protracted and tedious inquiries carried out by investigators who appear insensitive as they methodically pursue "the facts."

This need not be the case. White-collar crime investigators can take steps to alleviate the fear and anxiety often experienced by whistleblowers. In doing so, they can successfully sustain these witnesses through the long and often-bewildering investigative/judicial process.

 # The Emotional Impact of Crime

In white-collar crime investigations, the testimony provided by government whistleblowers may be the best evidence for proving a case. Investigators need to preserve the testimony of these important eye witnesses just as they would protect corporate financial records.

An integral component of this effort includes understanding the emotional impact witnesses experience. Investigators must ensure that these emotional factors do not become barriers to the quality and quantity of information disclosed by these informers.

The Whistleblower as Victim

Traditionally, in many white-collar crime cases, the government is labeled as the victim. But what about individuals like Tom? In the months, or even years, ahead, his role will be that of a witness for the government. *Still, his emotional response—including nervous distress caused by the retaliatory actions of his supervisor—closely parallels those of violent crime victims.* In order to deal effectively with such witnesses, investigators must understand how the impact of crime affects an investigation.

A psychologist and former New York City police officer, Morton Bard, provided the first glimpse of the emotional impact of crime from the perspective of the victim. In a behavioral profile of victims and witnesses,[1] he identified three separate stages in the process of resolving the crisis brought on by their involvement in a crime. These three stages are impact, recoil, and reorganization.

Stage 1: Impact

The impact stage is characterized by disbelief, disorientation, disorganization/confusion, feelings of vulnerability, suggestibility, and difficulty in recalling details. In the case of whistleblowers, *the impact stage begins when they report the crime and can last up to 72 hours.*

Stage 2: Recoil

In the recoil stage, whistleblowers commonly exhibit intense anger, resentment, extreme fear, shame, or guilt, as well as phobic reactions to details of the crime, particular places, times of day, and kinds of people. This is the stage during which most white-collar crime investigators deal with witnesses. *For whistleblowers, this stage begins several days after reporting the crime and continues until the investigation ends.*

The recoil stage represents a particularly difficult period for most victims and witnesses. During this period, their thinking often focuses on understanding why the crime occurred or why they chose to get involved. Most will wake early each morning, as Tom did, thinking about the crime and mentally replaying the events in an attempt to understand it fully. During this period, some will take an emotional roller coaster ride. Moods will fluctuate between feelings of apathy and anger, resignation and rage, serenity and anxiety. Victims/witnesses may be obsessed with the crime one minute and deny such feelings the next.

In Tom's case, he became haunted by fears of reprisal at the hands of his supervisor. Because he experienced all of the emotional reactions common to the recoil stage, his family, friends, and coworkers noticed changes in his behavior. Once well-liked and well-respected, Tom no longer felt a part of the organization. He increasingly isolated himself from coworkers. Ultimately, his supervisor was able to exploit these changes in his behavior as justification for a series of negative job actions against him.

Stage 3: Reorganization

During the reorganization stage, feelings of fear and rage slowly diminish as the victim thinks and talks less about the crime. Like Tom, most victims, witnesses, or whistleblowers will be unable to achieve this stage of resolution while the case is pending.

White-Collar Crime Investigations

White-collar crime investigators should realize that criminal investigations may escalate the crisis experienced by whistleblowers. While Tom struggles with a disorienting assortment of emotional reactions, the justice system may add elements to his ordeal.

In addition to the emotional reactions experienced in the impact, recoil, and reorganization stages, whistleblowers also face challenges brought on by the investigative process itself. Investigators should realize that these elements, often unique to white-collar crime cases, may affect an informer's ability to sustain the rigors of the investigative and judicial processes.

Perhaps the most profound of these factors is the time required to investigate and to prosecute a white-collar crime case successfully. Most citizens get their information concerning the workings of the criminal justice system from television. Of course, on television, cases move quickly—in sharp contrast to the slow, methodical process of investigating and prosecuting a case of fraud against the government. Whistleblowers should be informed from the outset that white-collar crime investigations may last 1 to 5 years.

The types of guilt experienced by whistleblowers may seriously affect their ability to provide information. Many whistleblowers will experience not one but two layers of guilt. As a whistleblower, the individual may initially feel guilty about "turning in" an employer, particularly one who has provided the employee with a "real" job or an opportunity to excel. Once the whistleblower resolves this layer of guilt, another often develops—guilt over not reporting the illegal activities when they first took place. Whistleblowers may believe that investigators view them as irresponsible for not reporting the incidents sooner. Investigators should reassure whistleblowers who place such undue pressure on themselves.

In addition, whistleblowers may fear losing their positions while the case is investigated. This fear results from the pressure of continuing to work within an environment that is under investigation. Whistleblowers often question whether their identity as the complainant has been disclosed. To allay these fears, investigators should assure whistleblowers that every effort will be taken to protect their identity.

 ## Dealing With Whistleblowers

To gather the most accurate information, investigators should first focus on the needs and concerns of whistleblowers. When whistleblowers sense a genuine interest in their welfare, they focus more energy on the needs of an investigation. Accordingly, investigators should learn more about the emotional reactions common to whistleblowers.[2]

Additionally, investigators should ask questions to find out whether informers are experiencing any emotional reactions. Are they getting along with coworkers, supervisors, spouses, children? Are they having trouble keeping focused either at home or at the office? Are they experiencing anger or guilt? Are they having difficulty sleeping?

If whistleblowers admit to a problem, investigators should discuss it with them. Most important, investigators should make sure that whistleblowers fully understand the process in which they are involved. Investigators may need to review whistleblowers' roles continually during the judicial process, depending on their emotional state and ability to deal with the situation.

It is important to give a whistleblower the opportunity to vent feelings of anger or fear before initiating any questioning. Investigators should ask how things are going and watch to see whether the whistleblower's body language and other nonverbal reactions match verbal responses. If the verbal response is positive while a frown forms on the subject's face, then investigators should understand that the whistleblower may not be emotionally prepared to cooperate fully.

Investigators should prompt whistleblowers to break down their resistance by eliciting questions from them before the inquiry begins. For example, they might consider saying, "We are going to be asking you a lot of questions, but before we do, do you have anything that you would like to ask?" A common response might be, "Yes. I have a question. How long is it going to take for the government to get this case to trial?" Such a question allows investigators to respond sympathetically, thus building trust and breaking down emotional barriers. A proper response would be, "You are right. We know this has not been easy for you. We would like to tell you where we are with the investigation."

Investigators should also acknowledge whistleblowers' agendas in order to help disarm the hidden anger that may develop toward the government. By letting whistleblowers know what to expect, investigators

remove another barrier, allowing whistleblowers to devote more energy to recalling information, thus enhancing the investigation.

As part of this effort, investigators should also keep whistleblowers informed of the status of the investigation. Generally, it is best to keep them advised as major events unfold, such as possible indictment, arrest, or trial dates.

Finally, investigators should advise whistleblowers of their rights. Because these rights differ from State to State and among agencies, investigators must be fully aware of the laws, regulations, and court decisions that fall under their jurisdiction.

Getting Past Emotions

Whistleblowers do not arrive for interviews bearing clear indicators of their emotional state or agenda. However, imagine if a whistleblower did arrive for an interview wearing a nametag complete with an emotional reading: Bob—angry. Investigators would first acknowledge, then help to diffuse, the anger. Likewise, investigators' reactions should be the same, even though they may have to prompt whistleblowers to reveal their true emotional state.

Consider the following example. For the past 6 months, an employee's marriage has been deteriorating. Because she fears her marital problems may interfere with her work performance, she decides to speak to her supervisor. As she haltingly begins to relate her problems, her supervisor interrupts—telling her that a report he had wanted at the end of the week will have to be on his desk by this afternoon.

Chances are that the supervisor will get the report. But how good will it be? The fact that the supervisor failed to address the employee's emotional concerns will directly affect the quality of the report.

For white-collar crime investigators, the same thing can occur if they ask for information before dealing with the emotional agendas of whistleblowers. Consider how much of their attention and energy remains focused on such concerns as job loss rather than on the questions being asked of them by investigators.

Conclusion

Effective management of witnesses represents one of the most challenging responsibilities for white-collar crime investigators. To overcome such barriers as anger and fear and to collect and preserve the most accurate testimony possible from government whistleblowers, investigators should focus on informers' emotional agendas.

Investigators must also remember that good information is best preserved by keeping the source of that information informed. In the final analysis, a whistleblower who knows what to expect from the investigative and judicial process is more likely to be an effective and credible witness when called upon to recall facts or to testify.

 ## Endnotes

1. Morton Bard and Dawn Sangrey, *The Crime Victim's Book,* 2d ed. (New York: Brunner/Mazel Publishers), 1986.

2. To assist investigators, the Behavioral Science Division at the Federal Law Enforcement Training Center (FLETC) in Glynco, Georgia, developed a course to address these specific issues.

DISCUSSION QUESTIONS

1. What factors would influence your decision to report misconduct in the workplace?

2. Are whistleblowers victims? Explain.

3. Other than emotional issues, what other types of issues might arise with whistleblowers?

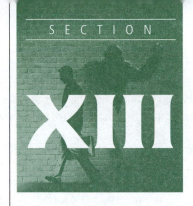

XIII

Judicial Proceedings and White-Collar Crime

Introduction

Bernie Madoff stood before Judge Denny Chin, having pled guilty to defrauding investors out of billions of dollars. Several individuals were in the court with him. His defense attorney, Ira Sorkin, stood by his side. At the table to his right were U.S. Attorneys, including Marc O. Litt, one of the lead prosecutors of the case. Behind him were victims of his schemes, members of the press, family members, and other members of the public wanting to see how justice would be served. Some victims were given the opportunity to address the court and describe the devastating impact of Madoff's crimes. Discussing the sentence he was giving to Madoff, Judge Chin remarked, "Here the message must be sent that Mr. Madoff's crimes were extraordinarily evil and that this kind of manipulation is not just a bloodless crime that takes place on paper, but one instead that takes a staggering toll" (Zambito, Martinez, & Siemaszko, 2009). The judge sentenced Madoff

▲ **Photo 13.1**   Judge Denny Chin sentenced Bernie Madoff to 150 years in prison, describing Madoff's actions as "extraordinarily evil" and hoping to send a message to others that such behavior would not be tolerated.

to 150 years in prison. Several viewers in the court cheered and applauded when the sentence was announced. The next day, Sorkin was on television news shows arguing that the sentence was "absurd" (McCoy, 2009).

This one court hearing was scrutinized across the world. In some ways, it may have seemed as if this hearing was the most important part of the judicial process. However, the bulk of the criminal justice system's judicial process in Madoff's case, and every other criminal case for that matter, occurs before the actual sentencing. In other ways, it may have seemed as if this hearing marked the end of the judicial process. But, as is the case with many white-collar crime convictions, a series of civil proceedings followed in an effort to determine how to recover as much money as possible for victims.

The scrutiny the court hearing received demonstrated several important facets regarding the judicial response to white-collar crime. In particular, the Madoff case showed how white-collar crimes (1) are processed through several different judicial proceedings, (2) involve the efforts of many different actors in the judicial process, and (3) present numerous complexities to those involved in adjudicating the cases. To shed some light on the way the judicial system responds to white-collar crimes, in this section attention is given to the following: types of judicial proceedings; the roles of judges, prosecutors, and defense attorneys; other actors involved in white-collar crime judicial proceedings; civil lawsuits; and issues in white-collar judicial proceedings. Addressing these areas will help students to appreciate the complexities surrounding the judicial response to white-collar crime.

 ## Types of Judicial Proceedings Responding to White-Collar Misconduct

White-collar misconduct cases are adjudicated in at least five different types of judicial or quasi-judicial proceedings: (1) criminal proceedings, (2) civil proceedings, (3) administrative proceedings, (4) professional-disciplinary proceedings, and (5) workplace-disciplinary proceedings (see Figure 13.1). In **criminal proceedings,** criminal charges are filed against the defendant and sanctions could include imprisonment, fines, probation, community service, and restitution. Because an individual's liberty is at stake (through incarceration) criminal proceedings offer offenders more protections than other proceedings, and the standard of proof is higher. The bulk of this chapter addresses criminal judicial proceedings as they relate to white-collar offenders.

In **civil proceedings,** an individual or government representative, referred to as a plaintiff, files civil charges against an individual or business. The charges focus on violations, allegedly committed by the defendant, that brought some sort of harm to the plaintiff. In some white-collar crime cases, the government will file motions in civil court that seek injunctive remedies. For instance, officials routinely ask civil courts to issue "cease and desist" orders, which tell a business or corporation to refrain from the activities under judicial review until the proceeding is completed. In civil proceedings, the standard of proof is less (e.g., plaintiffs must prove by a preponderance of evidence) and defendants are not afforded the same level of protections (e.g., while they may refuse to testify, the judge and jury are permitted to make inferences about such a refusal). Also, sanctions are primarily monetary in nature. More on civil proceedings will be provided below.

Administrative proceedings are different from criminal justice and civil proceedings. Technically, these proceedings are not designed to punish but are designed "to restrict . . . certain future actions" (Cohen, 1992, p. 1059). These proceedings are used more commonly for white-collar offenses than for conventional offenses. Many regulatory agencies use administrative proceedings to adjudicate cases brought to their attention. Depending on the laws that govern the regulatory agency, the types of decisions made in administrative proceedings could include the following:

Figure 13.1 Types of Judicial Proceedings in White-Collar Misconduct Cases

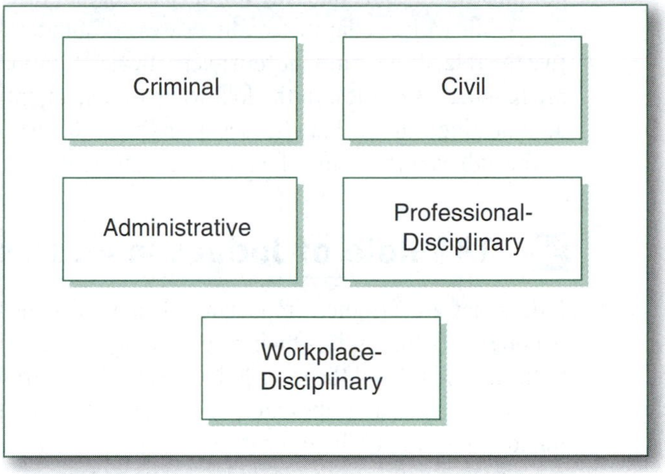

- Criminal
- Civil
- Administrative
- Professional-Disciplinary
- Workplace-Disciplinary

- Issue civil fines
- Issue cease and desist orders to protect the health and safety of workers, consumers, citizens, and others
- Prevent specific individuals/groups from participating in corporate activities
- Prohibit the corporation from participating in specific types of government programs (Van Cleef, Silets, & Motz, 2004)

As an illustration, the Securities and Exchange Commission (SEC) will hold administrative proceedings before the Commission or an administrative law judge. The SEC has the authority to impose administrative sanctions including cease and desist orders and monetary penalties. One issue that arises in the judicial processing of white-collar crime cases is that the boundaries between criminal, civil, and administrative proceedings "are often very fuzzy" (Cohen, 1992, p. 1060).

Professional-disciplinary proceedings are also used to address different types of white-collar misconduct. Recall the discussion of the ways bar associations discipline lawyers in Section V. These proceedings are administered through the state bar association, with the professional disciplinary association processing the case and deciding whether and how to sanction the attorney. Other professions have similar proceedings. For instance, medical professionals accused of misconduct could have their cases adjudicated by state medical boards, which are responsible for licensing different types of medical professionals. Other occupations that have professional boards reviewing their allegations of wrongdoing include but are not limited to social workers, counselors, barbers, teachers, and clergy.

Workplace-disciplinary proceedings are similar to the professional-disciplinary proceedings, except they are conducted entirely within the workplace where the misconduct was alleged. Cases heard in the workplace (quasi-judicial hearings) often include labor violations and discrimination. The cases are typically handled through a company's equal opportunity office or human resources department. These cases may not necessarily be resolved in the workplace because the offended party might file a claim in civil or administrative court once the workplace proceedings are completed.

While white-collar misconduct cases are adjudicated in different ways, from a criminological perspective the role of the criminal court is particularly important in understanding how white-collar crime cases are handled as crimes. In the following section, attention is given to various actors involved in criminally adjudicating white-collar offenses. This will be followed by a discussion of civil lawsuits and issues that arise in the judicial processing of white-collar offenders.

⧗ The Role of Judges in Addressing White-Collar Crime

Judges play an extremely important role in processing white-collar crime cases through the justice system. Among other things, it is their responsibility to ensure that the justice process unfolds in a way that is fair to the defendant and the state. Judges oversee cases from the time they are filed until they are resolved. They approve plea negotiations and oversee trials. They also sentence convicted offenders and even make recommendations about where incarcerated offenders will serve their sentences. Clearly, judges are afforded a great deal of power in the criminal justice system.

Unfortunately, few recent studies have examined the judicial role in white-collar crime cases, though a few classic studies create a foundation from which understanding about judges and white-collar crime can evolve. These earlier studies focused on how judges perceive white-collar offenders, offenses, and sanctions. With regard to studies on perceptions about offenders, one early study found that judges perceive public officials (e.g., politicians) as deserving of more severe sanctions than other offenders (Pollack & Smith, 1983).

Stanton Wheeler, Kenneth Mann, and Austin Sarat (1985) authored the seminal work, *Sitting in Judgment: The Sentencing of White-Collar Criminals,* which was based on interviews with 51 federal judges who had significant involvement with hearing white-collar crime cases. Among other things, their research showed that judges varied in how they received information and used the information available to them. Their research also showed that the three most salient factors influencing judicial decision making in white-collar crime cases included (1) harm from the offense, (2) blameworthiness, and (3) consequences of the punishment.

In terms of harm, the more harm caused, the less favorably judges perceived white-collar offenders. In the words of the authors, for some judges, "if an offense is more serious, its perpetrator is therefore more culpable" (p. 54). Judges determined harm by considering how much was lost, the duration of the offending, whether there were identifiable victims and the types of victims, and whether trust violations occurred. In assessing blame, judges considered prior records, offender motive, the offender's life history, and evidence presented at the trial.

In terms of sentencing, the author team noted elsewhere that the judges perceived white-collar offenders as having a special sensitivity to imprisonment (Mann et al., 1980). They viewed this special sensitivity as providing a powerful general deterrent that would keep white-collar employees from engaging in future misconduct. As a result, the judges viewed publicity as an important ingredient in increasing the deterrent potential of jail. One judge indicated that "he had tried to make sure" that certain types of cases would receive publicity (p. 137). Others have also suggested that judicial sanctions such as jail have the ability to deter white-collar misconduct (Pollack & Smith, 1983).

More will be written about sentencing of offenders in the next section. At this point, attention can be given to factors contributing to judges' sentencing behaviors and judges' perceptions of criminal sanctions.

With regard to the former, a study of U.S. federal anti-trust sentences from the mid-1950s through the early 1980s found that sentences appeared to be tied to judges' goals. For example, those seeking promotion to higher courts sentenced differently than those who did not aspire to a higher court (Cohen, 1992).

A number of researchers have drawn attention to the short sentences that white-collar offenders receive (Payne, 2003b). According to Mann and his colleagues (1980), judges justified these shorter sentences on three grounds. First, the judges did not want to do additional harm to the offender's family. Second, a shorter sentence was seen as providing offenders the opportunity to contribute back to the community. Third, with shorter sentences, offenders would be in better positions to pay victims back and make reparations for their misdeeds. The judges did not see fines as being useful for white-collar offenders.

Early legal scholars highlighted the difficulties that judges faced in sentencing corporate offenders. Orland

▲ **Photo 13.2**   The judge oversees the trial and ensures that the rights of both sides are protected. In white-collar crime cases, judges will assess blame and harm differently than they might in other cases. In one recent case, a judge lamented that he "lost a lot of sleep over the right thing to do in this case," referring to his concern about how to appropriately sentence a white-collar offender (Collins, 2010).

(1980), for example, wrote, "Often judges find it difficult to condemn the acts of corporate executives which are undertaken not only to advance personal career goals, but also to maximize the profits of the corporation" (p. 511). He continued, "Many judges find it less difficult to punish criminal conduct undertaken at the expense of the corporation than conduct in which the corporation and its stakeholders are the ultimate beneficiaries of the criminal act" (p. 511). As will be shown below, corporations make better "victims" than "offenders."

Federal and state sentencing guidelines now give judges less discretion in deciding how to punish white-collar offenders. Under these guidelines, judges refer to the guidelines to determine the sentence recommended for a specific offense. The sentence (time to be served) is typically offered as a range (e.g., 6 months to 1 year). Judges can depart from the recommended range, either increasing or decreasing the actual sentence given to the offender. In white-collar crime cases, upward departures usually result from significant monetary harm, emotional harm, offenses targeting vulnerable groups, and abuses of trust (Barnard, 2001).

Departures have been found to be related to white-collar crime type. For example, a review by the U.S. Sentencing Commission (1996) found that computer criminals were more likely than other white-collar offenders to receive downward departures from the guidelines range, and no computer criminal had received an upward departure. The Commission suggested that computer criminals were more educated than other white-collar criminals and all federal defendants in general.

The Role of Prosecutors in Addressing White-Collar Crime

Prosecutors have a central role in processing white-collar crime cases through the justice system. At the federal level, U.S. Attorneys are the prosecutors responsible for prosecuting federal offenses. At the state and local level, prosecutors go by different names including district attorney, commonwealth's attorney, solicitor, attorney general, and so on. In some jurisdictions, specific units devoted to white-collar crimes exist, while other jurisdictions rely on prosecutors who seem to have more expertise with white-collar crimes. Regardless of what they are called and their levels of expertise, these officials are responsible for making several important decisions about white-collar crime cases. Decisions prosecutors make include:

- Deciding whether to prosecute a white-collar crime case
- Deciding what to charge offenders with
- Deciding whether to accept plea bargains
- Deciding whether to charge corporations
- Deciding whether to defer prosecution

Each of these areas is addressed below.

Deciding Whether to Prosecute a White-Collar Crime Case

The prosecution of white-collar criminals is seen as necessary in order to demonstrate "moral outrage" for white-collar misconduct (Cohen, 1992). Obviously, not all white-collar crimes are prosecuted in the justice system (see Figure 13.2). Some crimes never come to the attention of authorities, others are detected but not investigated, and others are investigated but not prosecuted. The question that arises is how prosecutors

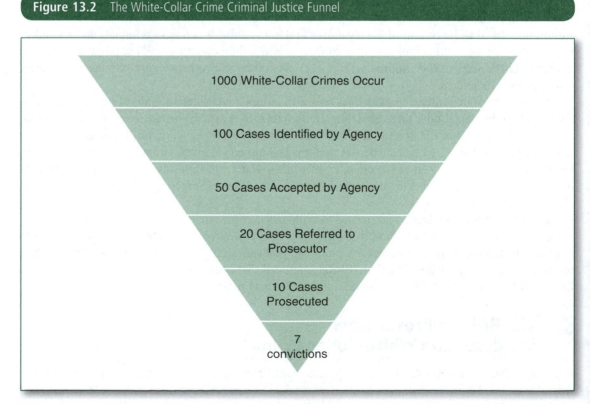

Figure 13.2 The White-Collar Crime Criminal Justice Funnel

1000 White-Collar Crimes Occur

100 Cases Identified by Agency

50 Cases Accepted by Agency

20 Cases Referred to Prosecutor

10 Cases Prosecuted

7 convictions

NOTE: Numbers are hypothetical and meant to illustrate how few cases are prosecuted compared to the amount of white-collar crime.

decide which cases to prosecute. Kitty Calavita and Henry Pontell (1994) noted that "major cases" are determined based on dollar amount. Major cases would be those selected for prosecution.

In a 1994 memo, Earl Delaney, director of the EPA's Office of Criminal Enforcement, offered environmental law enforcement agents guidance in determining which cases should be treated as criminal as opposed to civil or administrative wrongs. He suggested that the decision to handle cases criminally be guided by two factors: **significant environmental harm** and **culpable conduct.** He specified that harm includes (1) actual harm, (2) threat of harm, (3) failure to report potentially harmful activities, and (4) the possibility that the behavior will escalate if it is not handled criminally. Delaney did not define culpable conduct as intent per se, but as including (1) a history of misconduct, (2) deliberate misconduct, (3) concealing misconduct, (4) tampering with monitoring equipment, and (5) practicing business without a license.

While Delaney's memo focused solely on environmental crime, other researchers have cited similar factors that are believed to guide prosecutorial decision making. For example, Cohen (1992) argued that prosecutors will consider the following factors when deciding whether to prosecute white-collar offenders: the defendant's knowledge and intent, harm from the offense, whether misconduct continued after the regulatory agency initiated its investigation, amount of evidence, and how much the defendant benefited from the wrongdoing. A survey of state attorneys general found that seriousness of the offense was the most important factor prosecutors considered when deciding whether to prosecute white-collar crimes (Ayers & Frank, 1987). Incidentally, this same study found that political factors were among "the least important factors."

Some have noted that decisions to prosecute may be tied to the way the referral is made to the prosecutor. According to one group of white-collar crime experts, referral agencies must "sell a case to a prosecutor" (Pontell, Jesilow, & Geis, 1984, p. 413). Pontell and his colleagues quote one fraud investigator who said of U.S. Attorneys:

> Their priorities are bank robberies, drugs, immigration, and terrorists. . . . Somebody goes and blows up nine airplanes and then you come in the next day with a doctor who is [stealing] from Medicare or Medicaid. Where are their priorities? They will be more concerned with violent crimes. (p. 413)

Federal statistics support the suggestion that white-collar crime cases are declined for prosecution by U.S. Attorneys more often than other types of crimes. In 2004, 148,229 cases were referred to U.S. Attorneys for review and to be considered for prosecution. Of those cases, 22% were declined for prosecution. Consider the declination rates based on the agency referring the case to the U.S. Attorneys:

- Small Business Administration—69% of cases declined for prosecution
- Land Management Bureau—68% of cases declined for prosecution
- U.S. Environmental Protection Agency—54% of cases declined for prosecution
- U.S. Army—5% of cases declined for prosecution
- Citizen and Immigration—2% of cases declined for prosecution

Also, supporting this suggestion that white-collar crime cases are declined more often, here are the declination rates for offenses:

- Food and drug cases: 50.3% of cases declined for prosecution
- Regulatory offenses: 62.2% of cases declined for prosecution

- Embezzlement offenses: 32% of cases declined for prosecution
- Fraud: 39.7% of cases declined for prosecution
- Drug offenses: 15.3% of cases declined for prosecution
- Immigration offenses: 1.5% of cases declined for prosecution (Bureau of Justice Statistics, 2006)

It should not automatically be assumed that cases are declined out of some sort of intentional bias on the part of prosecutors toward lower-class offenders. Three traditional explanations addressing why prosecutors choose not to prosecute include the organizational advantage argument, the alternative sentencing argument, and the system capacity argument (Tillman, Calavita, & Pontell, 1997). The **organizational advantage argument** suggests that "organizational structure may serve as a buffer between the white-collar offender and social control mechanisms" (p. 55). The **alternative sanctions argument** points to the use of less costly civil and administrative procedures to respond to misconduct. The **system capacity argument** points to the difficulties officials face in responding to these crimes (Tillman et al., 1997).

Tillman and his research team (1997) examined how the criminal justice system responded to the savings and loan crisis to see which argument might best address the system's response to the fiasco. The researchers found limited support for the first two arguments, and moderate support for the third argument—at least in some jurisdictions. They added a fourth possible explanation, which they coined a **damage control argument.** This orientation emphasizes the importance of "symbolic, high-visibility prosecutions in restoring public confidence" (p. 72).

Prosecutors face a number of other issues that may influence their decision-making process in white-collar crime cases. Issues include: (1) trials may be harder to win in white-collar crime cases, (2) the time to complete the cases is significant, (3) resource issues, (4) establishing intent, and (5) practical issues. With regard to trials, several features of the white-collar criminal trial mean that the cases may be harder for the prosecutor to win. The cases use complex evidence, the trials last a long time, and the defense attorneys are often among the most talented attorneys prosecutors will face. Brickey's (2006) review of the white-collar crime trials of the executives involved in the scandals that occurred in the early 2000s found that 18 defendants were convicted, 11 were acquitted, and 15 had their cases result in mistrials. By comparison, in conventional cases, trials almost always result in a victory for prosecutors.

The time to complete white-collar crime cases is also significant. These cases take far longer to complete than prosecutions of conventional crimes take. An investigation by the Government Accounting Office (USGAO, 2003) found that more than half of the Medicaid fraud cases prosecuted by fraud control units took more than 2 years to process from identification through adjudication. A review by the Bureau of Justice Statistics (2006) focusing on the amount of time it took U.S. Attorneys to file charges (or decline the case) from the time they received notification about the case from the referral agency found the following:

- The median amount of time for fraud cases was 14.6 months
- The median amount of time for regulatory offenses was 15.9 months
- The median amount of time for drug offenses was 6.6 months
- The median amount of time for immigration offenses was 1.1 month
- The median amount of time for violent offenses was 6.5 months

In other words, it took more than twice as long to decide how to proceed with white-collar crimes as it took to decide how to proceed with drug crimes and violent offenses.

Resource issues also potentially influence prosecutors' decisions about white-collar crime cases. In this context, "resources" refer to time, funds, staff, and materials needed to process the case through the justice system. Particularly at the local level, prosecutors lack the resources they need to address white-collar crimes. As a result, when prosecuted, the cases are more often handled by federal prosecutors (Benson 1990). As illustrated above, even at the federal level many cases are not prosecuted.

Problems establishing intent may also influence prosecutors' decisions to prosecute white-collar crime cases. As one author noted, "it is quite difficult to judge the motivation and behavior" of many white-collar offenders (Punch, 2000, p. 251). In fact, surveys from fraud prosecutors revealed that "the burden of the commonwealth/government to prove the mental state . . . beyond a reasonable doubt (knowledge and intent) . . . is the most difficult element of [white-collar] crime to establish" (Payne & Berg, 1997, p. 228).

Practical issues refer to an assortment of issues that commonly arise in the prosecution of most white-collar crime cases. For example, the cases typically require much more expertise to prosecute than conventional crimes might require (Jesilow, Geis, & O'Brien, 1985). Also, prosecutors will often need technical assistance in these cases and many have not been trained adequately in how to prosecute white-collar crimes (Payne, 2011). One topic for which prosecutors need specific training is deciding which charges to file against white-collar offenders.

Deciding Charges

Prosecutors must also decide what charges to file against white-collar criminals. At the federal level, prosecutors have hundreds of possible statutes to choose from. In some instances, white-collar offenders are charged with violations of the **Racketeer Influenced and Corrupt Organizations (RICO) Act.** Because it is Title IX of the Organized Crime Control Act, many have assumed that RICO is limited to prosecutions of mobsters and other participants in organized crime ventures. However, as Beare (2002) notes, Robert Blakely, who drafted the law, supported the use of controlling white-collar crime with the RICO act. In Blakely's words,

> There is nothing in RICO that says that if you act like a racketeer you will not be treated like a racketeer. Whatever the color of your shirt or your collar . . . people who run groups by extortion or violence or fraud ought to be called racketeers. (p. 184)

When considering the text of the RICO act, one can see how the act can be used in white-collar crime prosecutions. As one author notes:

> Section 1962 of RICO prohibits "any person" from (i) using income derived from a pattern of racketeering activity, or from the collection of an unlawful debt, to acquire an interest in an enterprise affecting interstate commerce; (ii) acquiring or maintaining through a pattern of racketeering activity, or through collection of an unlawful debt, an interest in an enterprise affecting interstate commerce; (iii) conducting, or participating in the conduct of, the affairs of an enterprise affecting interstate commerce through a pattern of racketeering activity or through collection of an unlawful debt; or (iv) conspiring to participate in any of these activities. (Argust, Litvack, & Martin, 2010)

Clearly the breadth of this statute is such that many white-collar crime cases fall within the realm of RICO violations.

Other common charges against white-collar offenders at the federal level include violations of mail fraud statutes, the False Statements Act, the False Claims Act, and specific acts targeting specific forms of white-collar misconduct (Alshuler et al., 2008). **Mail fraud statutes** prohibit the use of the U.S. mail service to commit crimes. The **False Statements Act and False Claims Act** govern against the submission of fraudulent claims or bills for services. The False Claims Act was passed during the Civil War to guard against situations where individuals tried to defraud the government. It has gone through several changes since then, but covers situations where individuals or businesses bill for goods that were not delivered or services that were not provided. In Focus 13.1 shows some specific laws targeting specific forms of white-collar misconduct. As shown in these statutes, the laws stipulate minimum and maximum sentences. Thus, the type of charge prosecutors file will have ramifications for the sentence convicted offenders receive. Charge type also influences decisions about plea bargaining.

In Focus 13.1

U.S. Laws Governing Against White-Collar Crimes

§ 1344. Bank fraud—Whoever knowingly executes, or attempts to execute, a scheme or artifice—(1) to defraud a financial institution; or (2) to obtain any of the moneys, funds, credits, assets, securities, or other property owned by, or under the custody or control of, a financial institution, by means of false or fraudulent pretenses, representations, or promises; shall be fined not more than $1,000,000 or imprisoned not more than 30 years, or both.

§ 1347. Health care fraud—Whoever knowingly and willfully executes, or attempts to execute, a scheme or artifice—(1) to defraud any health care benefit program; or (2) to obtain, by means of false or fraudulent pretenses, representations, or promises, any of the money or property owned by, or under the custody or control of, any health care benefit program, in connection with the delivery of or payment for health care benefits, items, or services, shall be fined under this title or imprisoned not more than 10 years, or both. If the violation results in serious bodily injury (as defined in section 1365 of this title), such person shall be fined under this title or imprisoned not more than 20 years, or both; and if the violation results in death, such person shall be fined under this title, or imprisoned for any term of years or for life, or both.

§ 1348. Securities and commodities fraud—Whoever knowingly executes, or attempts to execute, a scheme or artifice—(1) to defraud any person in connection with any commodity for future delivery, or any option on a commodity for future delivery, or any security of an issuer with a class of securities registered under section 12 of the Securities Exchange Act of 1934 (15 U.S.C. 78l) or that is required to file reports under section 15(d) of the Securities Exchange Act of 1934 (15 U.S.C. 78o (d)); or (2) to obtain, by means of false or fraudulent pretenses, representations, or promises, any money or property in connection with the purchase or sale of any commodity for future delivery, or any option on a commodity for future delivery, or any security of an issuer with a class of securities registered under section 12 of the Securities Exchange Act of 1934 (15 U.S.C. 78l) or that is required to file reports under section 15(d) of the Securities Exchange Act of 1934 (15 U.S.C. 78o (d)); shall be fined under this title, or imprisoned not more than 25 years, or both.

Deciding About Plea Bargains

Prosecutors will also make decisions about **plea bargains** in deciding whether to allow a defendant to plead guilty in exchange for a reduce sentence or some other incentive. A common estimate is that 90% of offenders (white-collar and conventional) plead guilty (O'Hear, 2004). Consider that 90% of those involved in the corporate scandals of the early 2000s (Adelphia, WorldCom, HeathSouth, Enron, etc.) entered guilty pleas (Brickey, 2006). After pleading, nearly all of them became cooperating witnesses "who assisted the government in developing the case against their peers" (Brickey, 2006, p. 403).

While similar proportions of white-collar and conventional offenders plead guilty, their reasons for pleading guilty might vary. For conventional offenders, a common reason is to avoid the costs of a trial that come along with paying the defense attorney higher fees for trial services. For white-collar offenders, many likely plead guilty in order to avoid the stigma and shame that would come along with a public trial. For both groups of offenders, a lighter sentence also drives the decision to accept a plea bargain offered by prosecutors.

Deciding Whether to Charge Corporations

Dating back as far as Sutherland (1941), some criminologists have claimed that prosecutors are reluctant to prosecute corporations or businesses. A common explanation for this refusal is that prosecutors are "persuaded by the argument that punishing a corporation in effect punishes innocent shareholders" (Plimton & Walsh, 2010, p. 331) and workers.

In the face of this resistance to prosecuting corporations, one can point to three reasons justifying the prosecution of corporations. First, the harm from many corporate crimes is more severe than the harm from other crimes. Second, it is believed that corporate criminals are "just as morally culpable as traditional criminals" (Page, Savage, Stitt, & Umhoffer, 1999, p. 520). Third, corporate prosecutions send a message to other corporations that misconduct will not be tolerated.

Another reason corporations were not prosecuted was that it was not always clear when such a prosecution would be appropriate. To offer guidance to U.S. Attorneys in determining when to prosecute corporations, the Deputy Attorney General sent a memo in November 2006 offering federal prosecutors guidance in making this determination. The factors McNulty (n.d.) addressed included offense characteristics, organizational characteristics, and the consequences of different types of reactions by the justice system. In terms of offense characteristics, the memo drew attention to the seriousness of the offense, the consequences of the offense, as well as the risk of harm from the offense. Attention was also given to whether the nature of the offense fit in with national priorities. Table 13.1 shows the types of questions prosecutors might now ask in determining whether to prosecute corporations.

In terms of organizational characteristics, McNulty (n.d.) urged prosecutors to consider the pervasiveness of wrongdoing in the corporation, with specific attention given to past misconduct by the business. Also, whether the corporation disclosed the misconduct in a timely manner was noted as a factor to consider along with whether the corporation had a strong compliance program. In addition, prosecutors were encouraged to consider the remedial actions taken by company officials to address the wrongdoing (e.g., replacing corporate leaders, disciplining workers, revising compliance policies, etc.).

In addition to addressing offense and corporate characteristics, attention was also drawn to the consequences of the system's intervention. For example, if a prosecution would have a disproportionate adverse effect on those not responsible for the misconduct, prosecutors were encouraged by McNulty (n.d.) to take

| Table 13.1 | Factors U.S. Attorneys Are Urged to Consider in Deciding to Prosecute Corporations |

Factor		
Is the offense serious with a high risk of harm?	Yes	No
Was misconduct pervasive in the organization?	Yes	No
Has the corporation been involved in past allegations of misconduct, whether criminal, civil, or regulatory violations?	Yes	No
Did the corporation voluntarily disclose wrongdoing in a timely way?	Yes	No
Does the corporation have an adequate compliance program that was in place before the misconduct occurred?	Yes	No
Did the corporation address this misconduct through appropriate remedial actions?	Yes	No
Are there collateral consequences for groups that were not responsible for the misconduct?	Yes	No
Would prosecuting individuals responsible for the misconduct be adequate?	Yes	No
Would civil or regulatory actions be adequate?	Yes	No

that into consideration. He also encouraged prosecutors to consider the adequacy of prosecution as well as "the adequacy of remedies such as civil or regulatory enforcement actions" (p. 4).

Despite these guidelines, or maybe because of them, corporations are still rarely prosecuted in the criminal justice system. According to one author, structural features of the criminal justice system assigning responsibility for handling these cases to regulatory agencies results in infrequent use of criminal laws to address corporate offenses (Slapper, 1993). This same author notes that corporate offenses are often framed as accidents, thereby allowing companies to hide behind this conceptual frame. Consider the BP oil disaster in the Gulf of Mexico in July 2010. The disaster was routinely portrayed as an "accident," implying that corporate wrongdoing did not occur.

Local and state prosecutors also have authority to prosecute corporate crimes. Michael Benson and Frank Cullen (1998) described the most detailed study on how local prosecutors responded to corporate crime in *Combating Corporate Crime: Local Prosecutors at Work*. Among other things, they examined the impact of resources, the presence of alternative remedies, legal and technical difficulties, and political factors on local prosecutors' decisions to prosecute corporate crime. In terms of resources, attention was given to the lack of staff, funds, and time to prosecute corporate crime. With regard to alternative remedies, attention was given to deferring the cases to federal officials, relying on regulatory agencies, and filing civil suits against corporate criminals. Legal and technical difficulties considered included investigatory problems, proving intent, inappropriateness of criminal sanctions, and lack of expertise. Political factors included the state of the local economy, the corporation's level of resources, and the prosecutor's career goals.

Part of their research efforts included a survey of district attorneys in California to determine how local prosecutors perceived corporate crime, how often they prosecuted these cases, and how community factors might contribute to decision making (see Benson, Cullen, & Maakestad, 1988). Their research found that "a significant majority of the district attorneys had prosecuted a variety of corporate crimes" (p. 505). The main barriers prosecutors confronted had to do with the limited resources available to respond to corporate misdeeds. They also found that rural prosecutors were more sensitive to prosecuting businesses that the community relied on, presumably because the rural prosecutors did not want to lose a business and harm the entire community. Elsewhere, Benson and his colleagues (1990) reported that half of the urban district attorneys said that corporate crime was "not serious" and only 11% of rural prosecutors said that the misconduct was serious or somewhat serious. Prosecutors described harm and blameworthiness as influencing their decisions to prosecute along with other factors such as multiple offenses, victim preference, and regulatory inaction at the federal level.

Scholars have noted other problems that arise when prosecuting corporations. For example, it is extremely difficult to identify the decision-making processes that led to the corporate misconduct (Punch, 2000). Take BP's case, for example. What decisions were made by executives that contributed to the explosion in the Gulf of Mexico? Who made those decisions? Were those decisions made in good faith? Identifying this decision-making process is complex and sometimes impossible. In addition, laws are written and interpreted as applying to individuals, and not organizations, resulting in atypical offenders in corporate crime prosecutions (Punch, 2000).

Although these obstacles exist, some corporate offenses are prosecuted in the criminal justice system. Geis and Dimento (1995) point to five principles of **corporate crime liability** that support the need to prosecute corporations criminally. These principles include:

- A corporation is the sum of the actors in the organization.
- It is ineffective to punish individuals for corporate misconduct.
- It is more shameful for a corporation to be prosecuted than it is for an individual.
- Corporations can change more than individuals.
- It is easier to prove intent in corporations than it is with individuals.
- The corporation has resources to pay fines.

Geis and Dimento (1995) stress that the principles are not empirically grounded and are potentially misguided and harmful (e.g., if executives continue their misconduct). They concluded:

> Punishing the corporation alone might well induce it to clean up its act, but such punishment, almost always a fine, could be regarded as not much more than an unfortunate consequence.... Punishing perpetrator and corporation together appears to offer the best deterrence, although it remains to be demonstrated that such punishment produces the kinds of results claimed for it. (p. 84)

When corporations are prosecuted, different legal standards apply to the prosecution. For example, business entities do not have the right to "plead the Fifth" (e.g., the Fifth Amendment of the U.S. Constitution offers protection against self-incrimination). This is an individual right, not an organizational right (Nakayama, n.d.). Also, intent is determined somewhat differently in corporate crimes. For example, in corporate crime cases intent is: (1) demonstrated through uncovering evidence of conspiracies, (2) inferred to a new corporation after two corporations merge, (3) applied if corporate officials actively try to conceal a felony, and (4) present if corporate officials actively ignore criminal activity (Plimton & Walsh, 2010).

Common defenses that corporations use are "rogue employee" defenses and due diligence defenses (Plimton & Walsh, 2010). The **rogue employee defense** argues that the corporate misconduct was the result of an individual employee and not the result of any corporate activities. To counter this defense, prosecutors must show that the employee was acting within the scope of employment, that the employee's actions were done to benefit the corporation, and that "the act and intent can be imputed to the organization" (Plimton & Walsh, 2010, p. 332).

Under the **due diligence defense,** the corporation contends that it did everything it could do, in good faith, to abide by the law. In determining whether the organization acted with due diligence, the court will consider seven factors. In particular, the organization must have:

- An established compliance program
- Assigned the responsibility for supervising the compliance program to a high ranking employee
- Demonstrated that it did not give significant responsibility to an employee prone to misconduct
- Communicated compliance messages to employees
- Made a reasonable effort to meet compliance
- Enforced compliance standards when wrongdoing occurred
- Responded to wrongdoing and initiated measures to keep that misconduct from re-occurring (Goldsmith and King, 1997, p. 20)

Some have argued that prosecutors have become "unjustifiably heavy-handed" in corporate crime cases, "compelling corporations to cooperate in criminal investigations" (Bharara, 2007, p. 54). Strategies that have come under fire include situations where prosecutors (1) force companies to waive attorney-client privilege, (2) require corporations to fire employees, and (3) make unrealistic requests in exchange for leniency (Bharara, 2007). Bharara quotes several other legal scholars who used the following concepts to describe the notion of holding corporations criminally liable: "unprincipled, pointless, counterproductive, indiscriminate, incoherent, illogical, puzzling, and extreme" (p. 67).

Deciding Whether to Defer Prosecution

Another decision prosecutors will make is whether to enter into deferred prosecution agreements or non-prosecution agreements with corporations/businesses. Prosecutors have used pretrial diversion programs routinely over the last several decades for individual offenders. Their use for corporate offenders has been somewhat sparing until recently.

In a **deferred prosecution agreement (DPA),** the prosecutor agrees not to prosecute the corporation if the corporation agrees to certain conditions to be completed over a probationary period. In a **non-prosecution agreement (NPA),** the prosecutor indicates that the prosecution will not occur based on the corporation's agreement to certain conditions. A DPA is filed with the court, while an NPA is not (USGAO, 2009). Conditions that are imposed on corporations include the development of improved compliance programs, removal of certain personnel, fines, and a waiver of privileges (Spivack & Raman, 2008).

The number of DPAs and NPAs doubled between 2002 and 2005, as compared to the number of agreements the entire decade before. The agreements have become so frequent that some have suggested they have "become the standard means for concluding corporate crime prosecutions" (Spivack & Raman, 2008, p. 159). Deferrals are seen as advantageous because they save prosecutorial resources and protect "innocent" employees from experiencing collateral consequences that stem from corporate crime prosecutions (Spivack & Raman, 2008). They have been critiqued because it is not always clear that the agreements are used consistently (USGAO, 2009).

Table 13.2 shows the number of corporate crime prosecutions, DPAs, and NPAs by U.S. Attorneys and the Department of Justice's Criminal Division between 2003 and 2009. There was an increase in their use

Table 13.2   Number of Corporate Prosecutions Compared to Each Deferred Prosecution Agreement or Non-prosecution Agreement Entered Into by U.S. Attorneys Offices and the Criminal Division, FY 2004–2009

Year	U.S. Attorney's Office	Criminal Division
Fiscal Year 2004		
Prosecutions	297	5
DPAs and NPAs	4	1
Prosecutions per DPA or NPA	74.3	5.0
Fiscal Year 2005		
Prosecutions	350	3
DPAs and NPAs	11	9
Prosecutions per DPA or NPA	31.8	0.3
Fiscal Year 2006		
Prosecutions	304	5
DPAs and NPAs	19	5
Prosecutions per DPA or NPA	16.0	1.0
Fiscal Year 2007		
Prosecutions	257	11
DPAs and NPAs	31	10
Prosecutions per DPA or NPA	8.3	1.1
Fiscal Year 2008		
Prosecutions	257	6
DPAs and NPAs	12	13
Prosecutions per DPA or NPA	21.4	0.5
Fiscal Year 2009		
Prosecutions	194	8
DPAs and NPAs	17	6
Prosecutions per DPA or NPA	11.4	1.3
Total FY 2004 through FY 2009		
Prosecutions	1659	38
DPAs and NPAs	94	44
Prosecutions per DPA or NPA	17.6	0.9

between 2003 and 2007. Among U.S. Attorneys, for every 17.4 corporate crime prosecutions, one NPA or DPA was issued. In the Criminal Division, for every .9 corporate crime prosecutions, one NPA or DPA was issued. A recent investigation by the U.S. Government Accountability Office (2009) concluded that while the DOJ has improved its ability to monitor the number of DPAs/NPAs, the next step is to determine the actual effectiveness of the agreements in controlling corporate misconduct.

 ## The Role of Defense Attorneys in White-Collar Crime Cases

The defense attorney is responsible for defending the accused offender against the criminal charges. One legal scholar indicated that defense attorneys have four goals in defending white-collar defendants, depending on where the case is in the judicial process. These goals include: (1) keep the defendant from being indicted, (2) if indicted, keep the defendant from being convicted, (3) if convicted, keep the defendant from being imprisoned, and (4) if imprisoned, keep the sentence shorter (Lawless, 1988).

Kenneth Mann (1985), author of *Defending White-Collar Criminals: A Portrait of Attorneys at Work,* has provided the most descriptive overview of the defense attorney's role in white-collar crime cases. Conducting interviews with 44 defense attorneys experienced with defending white-collar offenders, Mann's work demonstrated how some attorneys have made a career out of white-collar crime defense work. Mann's research showed how attorneys worked to control the flow of information and showed white-collar offenders how to act in the criminal justice process.

Several features of the white-collar criminal case make these cases different from traditional criminal cases for defense attorneys. Just as the complex record search creates problems for prosecutors and investigators, the sheer number of records can be difficult for defense attorneys to review (Leto, Pogrebin, & Stretesky, 2007). Also, the cases typically involve more witnesses than might be found in conventional crimes (Leto et al., 2007). In addition, defense attorneys will need to direct efforts toward dealing with the media more than they might in other cases (Preiser & Swisher, 1988). Somewhat related, defense attorneys will spend more time preparing the white-collar defendant for the emotional impact of the trial and for the attention the case will get from the media (Lawless, 1988). Note also that prosecutors will select only white-collar crime cases that are very strongly in their favor (Lawless, 1988).

Stereotypes about white-collar offenders can also make the cases a little more challenging for defense attorneys. For instance, one author team noted that the cases are harder for defense attorneys because juries are predisposed to assume that white-collar defendants are guilty (Preiser & Swisher, 1988). Also, some defense attorneys perceive white-collar offenders as "defendants who are manipulative and [who] attempt to influence their defense team" (Leto et al., 2007, p. 106). In short, white-collar defense attorneys may have quite a task in front of them when they agree to defend white-collar defendants.

In-depth interviews of five federal public defenders by Jessica Leto and her colleagues (2007) found that defense attorneys used three strategies to manage their cases and their clients. First, the **process-oriented defense** strategy is guided primarily by a process that flows from one step to the next step (e.g., 1. read the indictment, 2. contact the defendant, 3. contact the prosecutor, 4. construct the defense, etc.). The attorneys "process" these cases the same way regardless of case or offender characteristics.

Second, the **discovery-oriented defense** is a more flexible defense strategy that is dictated by the characteristics of the charges, with no set formula used to respond to the cases. Attorneys using this strategy rely more on records and may not view the defendant (or the case) in a favorable light. The authors quote one attorney who—when asked what was the first thing he did when assigned a white-collar crime case—responded, "Go tell [the chief] to kiss my ass for giving it to me. Then, I don't know beyond that" (Leto et al., 2007, p. 97).

Third, the **client-oriented defense** strategy involves situations where the client "direct[s] the way the attorney defends the case" (Leto et al., 2007, p. 100). In these situations, the client is given a little involvement in the beginning stages of the judicial proceedings, and then more and more as the case progresses. The underlying assumption is that white-collar defendants have a great deal to offer in building and orchestrating their own defense strategies.

Leto and her research team (2007) note that strategies may change as the case proceeds. For example, sometimes a defense case may begin using process- or discovery-oriented strategies and then shift to a client-oriented defense case. They note that the attorneys in Mann's (1985) seminal research project tended to use "mistake of fact" defenses, but none of the attorneys in their study used this defense. The strategy they used if the case made it to trial was to "find flaws in the government's case in order to cast doubt upon their client's guilt" (Leto et al., 2007, p. 104).

Mann (1985) suggested that defense attorneys will "portray the [white-collar] defendant as an innocent victim of circumstance" (p. 40). Benson (1989) argued that defense attorneys will paint a picture of the defendant as an upstanding member of the community who, through the publicity surrounding the case, has already been punished enough. To be sure, white-collar crime defense attorneys will use a variety of defenses that are tailored to the specific type of white-collar crime the defendant is charged with. Some of the common types of defenses used to defend white-collar defendants include:

1. The **good faith defense** is based on the argument that defendants lack knowledge and intent. They did not know the crime was being committed; therefore, they could not have formed the intent to commit the crime. The "ostrich instruction" means that this defense does not apply if defendants actively avoided finding out about the crime by simply ignoring behaviors they should have been monitoring (Fischer & Sheppard, 2008).

2. The **meeting competition defense** is raised in price discrimination cases to show that a business's price discriminations were done "in good faith to counter actions of a competitor" (Hill & Lozell, 2010, p. 257).

3. The **isolated occurrence defense** argues that the misconduct was a rare event done by a single employee and not part of any systematic criminal activity. This defense is "one of the most frequently litigated defenses in OSH Act citations" (Trumka, 2008, p. 348). The business must show that measures were implemented to stop similar incidents from occurring in the future.

4. The **lack of fraudulent intent defense** argues that the defendant did not intend to commit a criminal act (Heenan, Klarfeld, Roussis, & Walsh, 2010).

5. The **withdrawal from conspiracy defense** is used in antitrust offenses to argue that the defendant withdrew his or her involvement from the misconduct before the illegal actions occurred. The defendant must demonstrate active efforts to stop the conspiracy. Reporting the crime to authorities is seen as one strategy for demonstrating withdrawal from a conspiracy (Hill & Lozell, 2010).

6. The **reliance on the advice of counsel defense** is raised when defendants argue that their actions were carried out simply because they were following the advice of their attorneys. This is technically

not a defense that would mitigate guilt, but this information may sway a jury to side with the defendant (Heenan et al., 2010).

7. The **ignorance defense** is raised to show that the defendant did not know that the criminal acts were occurring (Alshuler et al., 2008).

8. The **multiplicity of indictment defense** argues that the offender is being charged for one single offense on several different counts in the indictment. This defense suggests that the defendant is being tried twice and the defendant's double jeopardy rights are violated (Fischer & Sheppard, 2008).

Denial of criminal intent is among the most common denials offered by white-collar defendants (Benson, 1985). In fact, one group of legal scholars wrote that "a typical defense ... begins with a denial that the defendant carried out any violations with a criminal or fraudulent purpose" (Heenan et al., 2010, p. 1027). In addition to serving as a legal defense, such a denial allows white-collar offenders to shield themselves from the social stigma of a criminal label.

In cases where a corporation, business, or organization is the defendant, the company may rely on its internal general legal counsel for assistance and advice. In these situations, defendants sometimes raise the attorney-client privilege in an effort to keep information out of court (Yohay & Dodge, 1987). **Attorney-client privilege** has been described as "the oldest and most widely applied doctrine protecting confidential information" (Goldsmith & King, 1997, p. 24). There are restrictions regarding what type of information is protected under this privilege. Judges will occasionally use the "subject matter" test to see if the privilege applies. Under this test, five elements are necessary for the privilege to apply:

1. The communication must be made for the purpose of securing legal advice

2. The employee making the communication must do so at the direction of a supervisor

3. The direction must be given by the supervisor to obtain legal advice for the corporation

4. The subject matter of the communication must be within the scope of the employee's corporate duties

5. The communication may not be disseminated beyond those persons who need to know information (Goldsmith & King, 1997, p. 27)

Corporate attorneys often direct their efforts toward delaying the investigation and prosecution by filing motions and using an assortment of tactics to give them more time to build their own cases. One expert suggested that legal counsel should not see settling as a rational decision if a corporate executive is facing both criminal and civil charges (Zane, 2003).

Other Actors Involved in White-Collar Crime Judicial Proceedings

When watching an episode of *Law and Order* or another television show depicting the trial process, viewers will always see other "actors" involved in the courts. These other actors include (1) jurors, (2) witnesses, (3) defendants, and (4) victims. While these actors are involved in all types of court proceedings, certain dynamics of white-collar crime cases mean that the roles of these participants is substantively different in white-collar versus traditional cases.

Jurors

In cases where trials are held before juries, jurors will determine guilt or innocence of accused offenders. In some places, juries may play a role in sentencing and they also may make recommendations about the amount of damages to be awarded in civil trials. Some have argued that juries are harsher than judges—in determining guilt and in meting out penalties (Levine, 1983).

Some researchers have hypothesized that offenders who do not have specific characteristics of what would be expected for different types of crimes will be judged by external or situational factors, meaning that jurors might be assessing offenders based on whether they look like the "typical offender" in a certain type of crimes (Gordon, Michels, & Nelson, 1996). Gordon and his coauthors' mock juror study found that respondents sentenced White embezzlers to longer sentences than Black embezzlers, but Black burglars were given longer sentences than White burglars. The authors suggest that mock jurors "viewed a white defendant committing the white-collar crime as a more typical event than the black defendant committing the white-collar crime" (p. 195).

Such a finding is relevant to other forms of white-collar crime as well. In effect, jurors might be reluctant to see certain types of white-collar defendants as capable of engaging in wrongdoing (Jesilow, Geis, & O'Brien, 1986). It may be difficult, for example, for jurors to accept that that a trusted physician actually engaged in fraud. Fraud by some types of professionals is not a "typical event" among those professionals. Hence, jurors' perceptions are influenced by cognitive processes that define and assess defendants by preconceived notions.

Juries will occasionally "make mistakes" in white-collar crime cases—either failing to come to a unanimous agreement or engaging in behavior that allows defendants to appeal a conviction. In the Tyco case, for example, a mistrial was declared after a juror gave a thumbs-up sign to the defense table. In the first Enron trial, which lasted 3 months, a mistrial was declared after the jury was unable to come to an agreement on nearly 180 of the 202 charges filed against the executives (Brickey, 2006). The jury deliberated for only 4 days.

The complexity of white-collar crime cases sets them apart from many traditional criminal cases decided by jurors. Consider a robbery as opposed to a securities fraud case. In the robbery, the jury hears one type of evidence, and the evidence is typically easy to follow. In securities fraud cases, the jury will hear different types of evidence, which may not always be easy to follow. On the one hand, prosecutors will make efforts to simplify proceedings so all can understand the evidence. On the other hand, defense attorneys may use the complexity of the cases to help demonstrate why the defendant should not be convicted. Brickey (2006) quotes a securities lawyer who said, "If you look at Bernie Ebbers, Adelphia, and Martha Stewart, the government has done an exceptional job when they keep it simple so juries understand" (p. 417).

The amount of time that jurors must devote to white-collar crime cases is also different from other types of cases. The time estimates for different types of white-collar crimes have been provided elsewhere. At this point it is important to suggest that "time" can influence juror decision making in that some jurors might vote certain ways out of a desire to end their involvement in the case.

Witnesses

Witnesses are also involved in white-collar crime trials. Generally speaking, types of witnesses include government witnesses, lay witnesses, cooperating witnesses, character witnesses, and expert witnesses.

Government witnesses are police officers, investigators, auditors, and other officials who developed the case as part of the investigation process. These witnesses are trained in how to share information so that the evidence best reflects the government's interests. In terms of white-collar crimes, much of the testimony of government witnesses will be directed toward the records reviewed as part of the investigation.

Lay witnesses are individuals who have some relevant information to share about the white-collar crime case based on something they saw or experienced. Two issues arise in white-collar crime cases that limit the use of lay witnesses. First, white-collar crimes are not committed openly; few witnesses are available to describe the offense. Second, white-collar crime victims were often not aware of the victimization when it occurred and may, as a result, have little to offer at a trial.

Cooperating witnesses are witnesses who are cooperating with the prosecution as a result of some involvement they had in the case. In terms of white-collar crime cases, cooperating witnesses often include coworkers, subordinates of the defendant, supervisors, or informants who participated in the criminal investigation. Cooperating witnesses are sometimes offered a reduced sentence in exchange for their testimony.

Character witnesses are individuals who share information about the defendant that demonstrates, in theory, that it is not in the defendant's "character" to engage in wrongdoing. For white-collar crime trials, character witnesses are called upon to demonstrate that the defendant's work ethic, long history of contributions to the community, and good citizenship are not consistent with evidence that suggests wrongdoing. White-collar offenders, in particular, may have access to well-known and powerful character witnesses like celebrities and politicians. There is debate surrounding the utility of such witnesses. After former Los Angeles Mayor Richard Riordan testified in the criminal case of an executive accused of fraud, one former prosecutor turned white-collar criminal defense attorney told a reporter, "High-profile character witnesses never concerned me. . . . While they are interesting to watch testify, they by definition don't know the facts of the case being prosecuted, and therefore the impact of their testimony is usually quite limited" (Pfiefer, 2010).

Expert witnesses are witnesses who share their professional insight and interpretation of the evidence used in the case. Typically hired for a fee, these witnesses are actually involved throughout the justice process (see Figure 13.3). At the pretrial phase, expert witnesses review evidence and provide advice about how the evidence can be used at trial. During the trial, the expert will testify and educate the jury about the evidence under review. After the trial, the expert will assist in filing, helping to identify the grounds for appeal. Also, experts will be called upon to help white-collar offenders prepare for their punishment experience.

Perhaps the more important part of experts witnesses role involves their testimony in court. They will discuss the strength of evidence for the side that hired them and will also address the limitations of the other side's evidence. In white-collar crime cases, they will communicate complex financial information or other industry-specific information in a way that jurors can understand.

Expert witnesses must exhibit a level of scientific expertise that is consistent with what would be expected in the expert's scientific area of study (Summerford, 2002). The judge determines whether someone is able to serve as an expert witness. In selecting experts for white-collar crime cases, one author team suggests that those hiring the expert consider the following: (1) the expert's academic training, (2) whether the expert is accredited by an accreditation body, (3) the expert's match to the specific type of case, (4) the expert's level of expertise, and (5) what the expert looks like (Rasmussen & Leauanae, 2004). This fifth factor might surprise readers. The authors use the phrase "beauty contest" in suggesting that "better looking" experts who have "charisma" will be better received by jurors.

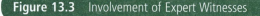

Figure 13.3   Involvement of Expert Witnesses

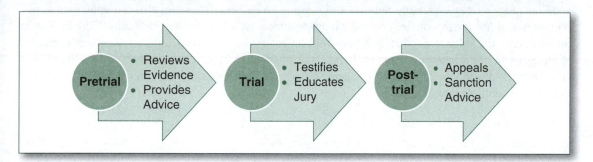

The Role of White-Collar Defendants

White-collar defendants also play a role in judicial proceedings. Many scholars have pointed to the way that white-collar offenders will deflect blame from themselves and onto others in an effort to portray themselves as honest professionals (Croall, 1993). This blame deflection is particularly evident during the judicial process when defendants will blame the wrongdoing on administrative errors, coworker errors, unclear policies, or unfair regulations (Jesilow et al., 1986). Some white-collar defendants will describe their misdeeds as if they are analogous to what can be called a "Robin Hood defense" (e.g., their crimes help the poor). Here is how Paul Jesilow and his colleagues (1985) described efforts to shape perceptions about physicians accused of fraud: "Physicians are many times able to cast shady actions in a positive light. For example, providers who knowingly bill for unnecessary services can argue that the procedures were necessary for the health of the patient" (p. 14).

In most trials, white-collar defendants will not take the stand. The messages of denial and blame deflection are communicated through their attorneys. If white-collar defendants take the stand, their efforts to lie and minimize would be frowned upon by the judge (Mann, 1985). Consider Judge Marian Cedarbaum's comments to Martha Stewart at her sentencing hearing: "Lying to government agencies during the course of an investigation is a very serious matter, regardless of the outcome of the investigation" ("Martha Stewart Reads a Statement," 2004, July 17). Jurors also look unfavorably on white-collar defendants when they lie or blame others for their transgressions (Brickey, 2006).

For white-collar defendants, the trial experience will be different from the trial experience of many traditional offenders in four ways. First, in some cases, the corporation or business is on trial, not an individual offender. Second, many white-collar trials will have multiple defendants; one study showed that two thirds of the celebrated corporate fraud cases of the mid-2000s had more than one defendant (Brickey, 2006). Third, recall that many white-collar offenders have no criminal record, meaning that they have never been on trial before. Presumably, this could make the trial more stressful. Fourth, the longer length of white-collar crime trials can be particularly problematic for white-collar defendants (Wright, 2006). Depression, anxiety, and mental health problems have anecdotally been found among white-collar defendants. These problems can be attributed to: (1) their lack of prior exposure to the trial process creates added stress, (2) they are used to being in control as leaders and executives but are not in control in court, (3) they have a great deal to lose if they are found guilty, and (4) a significant amount of shame or stigma is part of the trial process.

While they typically will not take the stand, if convicted, white-collar offenders will go to great lengths to convince the judge why they should be punished leniently. For example, many white-collar offenders will send the judge a letter expressing remorse and begging for lenience. They will also call upon their family members and friends to write letters to the judge to appeal for a light sentence (Mann, 1985). In Martha Stewart's case, the judge received 1,500 letters from supporters who urged the judge to issue a light sentence to Stewart. One of the letters was from Stewart herself. In Focus 13.2 includes an excerpt of the letter Stewart sent. Note the direct appeal to the judge where Stewart said, "My hopes that my life will not be completely destroyed lie entirely in your hands."

In Focus 13.2

It's a Good Thing: Excerpt of Martha Stewart's Letter to Her Judge

Dear Judge Cedarbaum:

We have never had the opportunity to speak one on one, you and I, despite the fact that I sat before you for five weeks. I am sorry that the legal system is such that even when a person's life is at stake—and for me that means my professional and personal life, not my physical being—the constraints prohibit conversation, communication, true understanding and complete disclosure of every aspect of the situation. I am not a lawyer, I am not skilled in legal processes, I am not even knowledgeable about many legal terms and legal procedures. I am still, after two and a half years of legal maneuverings and countless hours of preparation and trial time, abysmally confused and ill prepared for what is described to me as the next step in this process.

I am a 62 year old woman, a graduate of the excellent Nutley, New Jersey public school system and Barnard College. I have had an amazing professional life and several exciting careers, and I am grateful for that. I have a lovely family and a beautiful, upright, intelligent daughter (also a graduate of Barnard College), and I feel blessed and proud.

For more than a decade I have been building a wonderful company around a core of essential beliefs that are centered on home, family values and traditions, holidays, celebrations, weddings, children, gardening, collecting, home-making, teaching and learning. I have spent most of my professional life creating, writing, researching, and thinking on the highest possible level about quality of life, about giving, about providing, so that millions of people, from all economic strata, can enjoy beauty, good quality, well made products, and impeccably researched information about many hundreds of subjects which can lead to a better life and more rewarding family lifestyle.

I ask that in judging me you consider all the good that I have done, all the contributions I have made and the intense suffering that has accompanied every single moment of the past two and a half years. I seek the opportunity to continue serving my community in a positive manner, to attempt to repair the damage that has been done and to get on with what I have always considered was a good, worthwhile and exemplary life.

My heart goes out to you; my prayers are with you, and my hopes that my life will not be completely destroyed lie entirely in your hands.

Respectfully and most sincerely,
Martha Stewart

The Role of Victims in White-Collar Judicial Proceedings

Victims also have a role in white-collar judicial proceedings, though their role is limited. Criminologist Gilbert Geis (1976) has observed that the victim's role in the criminal justice process can be compared to the role that an expectant father has in the delivery room during the birth of his child. The father had a major role in the beginning of the pregnancy, but when the baby is being born, the father is tangential to the process. According to Geis, the victim has a similar role in the criminal justice process.

In white-collar crime proceedings at the federal level, historically victims were not permitted to participate in the allocution process. **Allocution** refers to the part of the trial process where individuals are permitted to address the court prior to sentencing. Federal law reserved allocution for victims to those who had been victimized by violent crimes. This changed in 2004 with the passage of the **Crime Victims Rights Act,** which permitted victims of all types of federal offenses to participate in the allocution process.

The importance of victim allocution cannot be understated. A sampling of the comments victims made in Bernard Madoff's sentencing hearing include:

- "Last year, my mother died. Now I don't have my mother or my money."
- "Your sons despise you.... [You] are an evil lowlife."
- "For the first time in my life, I'm very, very frightened about my future."
- "I calculate again and again how long it is I can hold out." (Barnard, 2009)

Hearing victims' voices and seeing them in court reinforces that white-collar crimes are not victimless crimes.

It is certainly plausible that the voices could actually provide support for increasing offenders' sentences. Beyond the sentencing enhancement, participating in the process can be empowering and rehabilitative to victims (Barnard, 2002). Drawbacks include time and resources, identifying which victims should participate, how to deal with emotional outbursts, revictimization in the justice process, inarticulate victims, and emotional letdowns for victims (Barnard, 2002).

In some cases, the victim may be a business or corporation. A question that has come up is the degree to which the business/corporation can contribute to the prosecutorial efforts in terms of financial support. In one case involving insurance fraud, an insurance company paid for some of the prosecutorial costs (see *People v. Eubanks*). The defendant appealed the case and the California Supreme Court ruled that such activity has the potential to result in unfair treatment of the defendant, and that the activity could lead to a conflict of interest. Courts do allow victims to provide assistance to the prosecution in some cases (e.g., they may hire a private investigator), though financial contributions are generally not permitted (Nahra, 1999).

Civil Lawsuits and White-Collar Crime

As noted above, white-collar crime cases can also be adjudicated in civil court through the use of lawsuits. Types of lawsuits can be categorized by the plaintiff/defendant relationship. The following types of lawsuits are relevant to white-collar crime:

- Individuals suing businesses
- Businesses suing businesses
- Government agencies suing individuals

- Government agencies suing businesses
- *Qui tam* suits
- Class action suits

Within these types of lawsuits, different varieties of lawsuits exist. Two that are particularly relevant for white-collar crimes include tort lawsuits and contract lawsuits. A **tort lawsuit** involves "one party alleging injury, damage, or loss stemming from the negligent or intentional acts of another party" (Cohen, 2009, p. 1). **Contract lawsuits** "involve fraud, employment discrimination, tortiuous interference, or allegations of unfulfilled agreements between buyers and sellers [and] lenders and borrowers" (Farole, 2009, p. 1). These lawsuits can be filed in either state or federal court.

The Civil Justice Survey of State Courts collects information on types of tort and contract trials held in state general jurisdiction courts. The survey was conducted in 1991, 1996, and 2005. In 2005, 7.4 million claims were filed in all types of state courts. Just under 27,000 cases were heard in courts of general jurisdiction, which are the trial courts that hear more serious cases (Langton & Cohen, 2008). Table 13.3 shows the types of defendants (individual, government, or business) in state court tort and contract trials in 2005 by misconduct type. Businesses were defendants more often for each case type, except for medical malpractice cases (which had hospitals as defendants most often).

Table 13.4 shows the types of defendants in contract and tort cases for the same year and whether the case was decided by a judge or a jury. Lawsuits for failing to provide services were more likely to be heard through a bench trial (with 80% of the cases heard in this manner), while lawsuits for medical practice were

Table 13.3   Types of Defendants in State Court Tort and Contract Trials, 2005

	Individual	Government	Business	Hospital
Tort trials				
Fraud	34.9	0.8	64.2	0.1
Failure to provide services	19.3	0.0	80.6	0.0
Employment discrimination	0.6	35.4	59.9	4.1
Other employment disputes	23.0	8.1	58.3	10.6
Interfering with contractual relationship	32.0	4.6	61.4	0.0
Contract trials[a]				
Medical malpractice	38.5	0.4	5.2	55.6
Professional malpractice	36.0	0.0	37.3	2.7
Asbestos	6.0	2.4	88.0	0.0
Other product liability	1.1	0.0	89.9	0.0

a. Includes only cases where an individual is the plaintiff. The percentage refers to percentage of all cases.

Table 13.4 Types of Defendants' Trials in State Court Tort and Contract Trials, 2005

	Number	Percentage of Total[a]	Jury (%)	Bench (%)
Tort trials				
Fraud	1,113	12.5	50.1	49.9
Failure to provide services	2,591	29.1	16.6	83.4
Employment discrimination	319	3.6	91.2	8.8
Other employment disputes	558	6.3	62.9	37.1
Interfering with contractual relationship	15.2	1.7	61.8	38.2
Contract trials				
Medical malpractice	2,449	14.9	98.7	1.3
Professional malpractice	150	0.9	60.0	40.0
Asbestos	87	0.5	95.4	4.6
Other product liability	268	16.3	92.5	7.5

a. Refers to percentage of total trials.

more likely to be decided by jury trials (nearly 99% of medical malpractice cases were jury trials). Additional findings from the 2005 Civil Justice Survey of State Courts include the following:

- 80% of torts were individuals suing businesses or other individuals.
- Jury trials lasted, on average, 2 days longer than bench trials in both tort and contract cases.
- Plaintiffs won two thirds of contract trials.
- Half of all plaintiffs in tort trials received $24,000 or less in damages.
- Half of the tort cases were completed within 2 years after the complaint was filed. (Cohen, 2009; Farole, 2009)

At the federal level, 512,000 civil cases were completed in district courts in 2002–2003, the most recent year for which data were available. About one fifth of the cases were tort claims where the plaintiffs sued alleging that they were injured or damaged by the defendant's negligent actions (Cohen, 2005). Additional characteristics of federal lawsuits over this timeframe include:

- 90% of tort cases were personal injury cases
- 71% of cases were decided by juries
- 48% of cases were won by the plaintiff
- 84% of the plaintiffs who won received monetary awards, with the median award being $201,000 (Cohen, 2005)

Government agencies, particularly regulatory agencies, might also file civil lawsuits against individuals and businesses in an effort to stop white-collar offending, punish the individual/offender for the wrongdoing, and recover the economic costs arising from the misconduct. Recall the discussion in an earlier section of the billions of dollars that the EPA has recovered from environmental criminals. Most of these funds were recovered through civil enforcement actions.

In other cases, known as **qui tam lawsuits,** an individual can actually sue a corporation or company on behalf of the government. These lawsuits give private citizens the authority to take on the role of the government and sue corporations that have defrauded the government. Citizens who bring the charges can receive 25%–30% of the damages received from the lawsuit. These are also known as whistleblower lawsuits in reference to the economic incentive given to whistleblowers to bring charges against a company (Payne, 2003a). Citizens must show that the information they are using to file their suit did not come from public disclosures made by other parties. In other words, the citizen must be the "original source of the information" (Pacini, Qiu, & Sinason, 2007, p. 68).

As long as the lawsuits are filed in good faith, employees cannot be punished by their companies for filing the lawsuits. Employers, of course, do not see qui tam policies favorably. Beyond getting employees to report misconduct, the lawsuits "supplement the strained resources of government attorneys and investigators" (Pacini et al., 2007, p. 65). In one recent case, John Kopchinski and five others were awarded $51.5 million after they filed a lawsuit against Pfizer Inc. for defrauding Medicaid through its marketing practices for various drugs. Pfizer settled the case without admitting wrongdoing (Neil, 2009).

Class action lawsuits are also used to address corporate wrongdoing. In these situations, a group of victims sues a business or corporation jointly for the harm caused by the corporation. Victims agree to be a part of the lawsuits with the understanding that any damages received would be split in a predetermined way. These lawsuits can be quite lucrative for attorneys and plaintiffs. A website even exists that publishes current class action suits—http://classactionworld.com/.

⊠ Issues in White-Collar Judicial Proceedings

A number of different issues arise concerning the judicial processing of white-collar offenders through the justice system. Some of these issues exist throughout the entire criminal justice system's processing of white-collar offenders, while others are unique to the judicial processing of white-collar offenders. These issues include:

- The need for networking
- Class bias
- The use of parallel proceedings
- Conceptual ambiguity surrounding corporate crime prosecutions

Each of these issues is discussed below.

Networking and the Judicial Process

As with the police response to white-collar crime, prosecutors must work with a number of different agencies in their efforts to battle white-collar misconduct. Unfortunately, interagency conflict and a lack of information sharing prohibits collaboration in some instances (Hammett & Epstein, 1993). Benson and his colleagues (1990) commented that the "continued rarity of intergovernmental cooperation is troubling" (p. 371).

In effect, some prosecutors would likely pass on white-collar crime prosecutions simply to avoid the headache of collaboration. As an analogy, think of group projects in courses. Many students despise such projects and may even drop courses simply to avoid group projects. Prosecutors do the same thing in white-collar crime cases.

Class Bias

Class bias is also implicit throughout the judicial processing of white-collar crime cases. Such bias is evident in four ways: (1) the hiring of high-powered defense attorneys, (2) complacency of criminal justice officials adjudicating the cases, (3) the disparate treatment of corporations, and (4) inadequate laws. In terms of *hiring high-powered defense attorneys,* some white-collar defendants are able to assemble powerful defense teams that are paid hundreds of thousands, if not millions of dollars, to defend the white-collar defendant. These defense teams are able to use resources that far outweigh the types of resources prosecutors have available. Traditional defendants, by comparison, have few, if any, resources available to support their defense.

Class bias is also evident regarding the *complacency* that some officials show toward the judicial processing of white-collar crimes. Some authors have noted that white-collar crimes are not a priority for prosecutors (Hammett & Epstein, 1993), while others have suggested that the failure to take action potentially contributes to future misconduct (Van den Berg & Eshuis, 1996). Consider the war on drugs. Prosecutors devote tremendous resources to battling drug crimes. These prosecutions tend to focus more on poor and minority suspects. So, white-collar crimes are ignored while drug crimes are "attacked" in a war-like fashion. In terms of a lack of enforcement contributing to future misconduct, one can point to the way that drivers speed on certain highways because police officers never stop speeders on those highways. In Atlanta, Georgia, where I live, you have to go 20 miles an hour over the speed limit on some roads just to keep from being run over. The lack of traffic enforcement results in drivers speeding. The lack of white-collar crime prosecutions may contribute to future white-collar misconduct.

One can also recognize bias when considering the *disparate treatment of corporations.* Criminologist John Hagan drew attention to the dual role that corporations can have in the criminal justice system: (1) they can be victims of white-collar crime or (2) they can be perpetrators of crime. Hagan (1982) wrote, "Corporate entities not only have successfully avoided large-scale prosecutions, they also have proven themselves effective in using criminal prosecutions to penalize those who offend them" (p. 994). Hagan suggested that prosecutors spend significant resources protecting corporations, but by comparison, fewer resources are devoted to prosecute corporate entities. Hagan concluded that the criminal justice system "better serves corporate than individual interests" (p. 1016). Another scholar noted that businesses have a significant amount of "power" to get out of trouble (Punch, 2000, p. 273). Or, as suggested above, they make great victims but lousy offenders.

Inadequate laws are another indicator of class bias in the judicial response to white-collar crimes. Conflict theorists have argued that laws are developed in a way that protects the powerful and weakens the poor and minority groups. This assumption will be discussed later. At this point, it is sufficient to point out that the consequences of inadequate laws are borne out in the judicial process. To be fair, it is important to note that efforts have been made to improve the laws to better address white-collar offending. For example, states have expanded their laws to make them apply to different types of white-collar crime. In New York, for example, a "scheme to defraud" statute was passed because it was recognized that the "false pretense larceny" statute was not sufficient for many white-collar crime cases (Clarey, 1978).

Still, problems remain that make traditional laws weak when processing white-collar crime cases. In one case, for example, a prosecutor charged contractors who tried to defraud an older woman with burglary.

His rationale—the contractors committed the elements of "breaking" and "entering" into a home with "the intent to commit a crime." Incidentally, this prosecution was successful. More often than not, other prosecutors would have forgone charging the offenders because of the very real perception that the laws do not always cover the behavior of the white-collar offender.

The Use of Parallel Proceedings

Another issue that arises is the use of **parallel proceedings** in adjudicating a white-collar crime case. What this means is that a specific white-collar crime can be heard in more than one court simultaneously. There are different ways that proceedings might occur simultaneously. A criminal case could be processed with a civil or administrative proceeding, or a civil proceeding could be processed along with an administrative proceeding. Parallel proceedings are warranted under two circumstances: (1) criminal proceedings may need to parallel civil or administrative hearings that address immediate needs to protect health and safety, and (2) simultaneous proceedings may be necessary to respond to cases that are especially serious (Nakayama, n.d.).

Table 13.5 shows the advantages and disadvantages of using parallel proceedings in white-collar crime cases. Reasons criminal proceedings might be completed on their own include the following: (1) the ability to use evidence from the criminal proceeding in the civil case, (2) ensuring the civil case does not negatively impact the criminal case, (3) gaining an evidentiary advantage by not disclosing evidence too early, and (4) avoiding the surfacing of unnecessary issues. Reasons proceedings might occur simultaneously include: (1) the need to address an immediate threat, (2) the threat of losing assets or bankruptcy, (3) the civil case was already under way when the criminal case began, and (4) the civil case fits within a national priority (Nakayama, n.d.).

The use of parallel proceedings has been questioned on various grounds such as concerns about double jeopardy, excessive fines, and due process violations (McDade & O'Donnell, 1992). Despite these questions, the use of parallel proceedings remains a popular alternative. Note that the proceedings are expected to remain separate. For example, it is deemed unethical for authorities to "use the threat of a criminal enforcement to resolve a civil matter" (Nakayama, n.d., p. 8).

Table 13.5   Pros and Cons of Parallel Proceedings Instead of Completing Criminal Proceedings First

Pros of Parallel Proceedings	Cons (Reasons Criminal Prosecution Should Be First)
• Immediate threats to health and safety can be dealt with through injunction • Defendant's assets could "disappear" • Pending statute of limitations • Pending deadline for bankruptcy • Civil case is farther along in justice process when criminal proceeding begins • Civil case directly relates to a national priority and failing to address the case would jeopardize the national priority	• Criminal sanctions have potential to deter and punish offenders • Civil sanction could undermine criminal case and lessen penalty given to offender • Civil proceedings could expose ongoing investigation • Defendant could gain prosecutor's evidence prematurely • Officials from one proceeding may need to address unnecessary issues arising from other proceeding • Witnesses would be interviewed too frequently within short period of time

Conceptual Ambiguity Surrounding Corporate Crime Prosecutions

Another issue surrounding corporate crime prosecutions centers on our lack of understanding about the number of corporate crime prosecutions, how to define them, measure them, and study them. Legal scholar Leonard Orland (1980) expressed great disgust over the way that criminologists discussed corporate crime adjudications. He argued that criminologists considered some adjudications as corporate crimes when, he believed, those acts were not truly corporate crimes. For example, criminologists often include civil and administrative judicial proceedings that result in violations, warnings, and injunctions as indicators of corporate crime. Orland contended that by wasting its time studying these sorts of behaviors, the criminal justice system is given the freedom to ignore serious acts of wrongdoing that should be handled criminally. Describing these beliefs, Orland (1980) wrote:

> Ultimately, the investigative power of the government, and not the musings of criminologists, should be used to quantify the actual amount of reported corporate crime. These data will permit criminologists to estimate the prevalence of underreported corporate crime and it is likely they will discover that the amount of "hidden" corporate crime is vast, and that true corporate crime is substantially underreported. (p. 518)

Summary

- White-collar misconduct cases are adjudicated in at least five different types of judicial or quasi-judicial proceedings: (1) criminal proceedings, (2) civil proceedings, (3) administrative proceedings, (4) professional-disciplinary proceedings, and (5) workplace-disciplinary proceedings
- Judges play an extremely important role in processing white-collar crime cases through the justice system.
- The three most salient factors influencing judicial decision making in white-collar crime cases include (1) harm from the offense, (2) blameworthiness, and (3) consequences of the punishment.
- At the federal level, U.S. Attorneys are the prosecutors responsible for prosecuting federal offenses.
- The prosecution of white-collar criminals is seen as necessary in order to demonstrate "moral outrage" for white-collar misconduct (Cohen, 1992).
- Cohen (1992) argued that prosecutors will consider the following factors when deciding whether to prosecute white-collar offenders: the defendant's knowledge and intent, harm from the offense, whether misconduct continued after the regulatory agency initiated its investigation, amount of evidence, and how much the defendant benefited from the wrongdoing.
- Prosecutors face a number of other issues that may influence their decision-making process in white-collar crime cases, including: (1) trials may be harder to win in white-collar crime cases, (2) the time to complete the cases is significant, (3) resource issues, (4) establishing intent, and (5) practical issues.
- Dating back as far as Sutherland (1941), some criminologists have claimed that prosecutors are reluctant to prosecute corporations or businesses.
- The factors prosecutors are encouraged to address in deciding whether to prosecute corporations include offense characteristics, organizational characteristics, and the consequences of different types of reactions by the justice system.
- Common defenses that corporations use are "rogue employee" defenses and due diligence defenses (Plimton & Walsh, 2010).

- Another decision prosecutors will make is whether to enter into deferred prosecution agreements or non-prosecution agreements with corporations/businesses.
- The defense attorney is responsible for defending the accused offender against the criminal charges.
- Kenneth Mann (1985), author of *Defending White-Collar Criminals: A Portrait of Attorneys at Work,* has provided the most descriptive overview of the defense attorney's role in white-collar crime cases.
- In-depth interviews of five federal public defenders by Jessica Leto and her colleagues (2007) found that defense attorneys used three strategies to manage their cases and their clients: *process-oriented, discovery-oriented,* and *client-oriented strategies.*
- Denial of criminal intent is among the most common denials offered by white-collar defendants (Benson, 1994).
- Other actors in the court include (1) jurors, (2) witnesses, (3) defendants, and (4) victims.
- Jurors might be reluctant to see certain types of white-collar defendants as capable of engaging in wrong-doing (Jesilow et al., 1986).
- Types of witnesses include government witnesses, lay witnesses, cooperating witnesses, character witnesses, and expert witnesses.
- Many scholars have pointed to the way that white-collar offenders will deflect blame from themselves and onto others in an effort to portray themselves as honest professionals (Croall, 1993).
- The 2004 Crime Victims Rights Act permitted victims of all types of federal offenses to participate in the allocution process.
- Two types of lawsuits that are particularly relevant for white-collar crimes include tort lawsuits and contract lawsuits.
- In *qui tam lawsuits*, an individual can actually sue a corporation or company on behalf of the government.
- Issues arising in the adjudication of white-collar crime cases include the need for networking, class bias, the use of parallel proceedings, and conceptual ambiguity surrounding corporate crime prosecutions.

KEY TERMS

Administrative proceedings

Allocution

Alternative sanctions argument

Attorney-client privilege

Character witnesses

Civil proceedings

Class action lawsuits

Class bias

Client-oriented defense

Contract lawsuits

Cooperating witnesses

Corporate crime liability

Crime Victims Rights Act

Criminal proceedings

Culpable conduct

Damage control argument

Deferred prosecution agreement (DPA)

Discovery-oriented defense

Due diligence defense

Expert witnesses

False Statements Act and False Claims Act

Good faith defense

Government witnesses

Ignorance defense

Isolated occurrence defense

Lack of fraudulent intent defense

Lay witnesses

Mail fraud statutes

Meeting competition defense

Multiplicity of indictment defense

Non-prosecution agreement (NPA)

Organizational advantage argument

Parallel proceedings

Plea bargains

Process-oriented defense

Professional-disciplinary proceedings

Qui tam lawsuits

Racketeer Influenced and Corrupt Organizations (RICO) Act

Reliance on the advice of counsel defense

Rogue employee defense

Significant environmental harm

System capacity argument

Tort lawsuit

Withdrawal from conspiracy defense

Workplace-disciplinary proceedings

DISCUSSION QUESTIONS

1. Describe the roles of various actors involved in the judicial response to white-collar crimes.

2. Do you think class bias exists in prosecuting white-collar crimes? Explain.

3. What are the advantages and disadvantages of prosecuting corporations?

4. How are civil proceedings different from criminal justice proceedings? How are different types of judicial proceedings punitive?

5. Would you want to defend white-collar offenders as a defense attorney? Why or why not?

6. Go to classactionworld.com. Review five cases. How are those cases like white-collar crimes? How are they different?

7. If you were called for jury duty, would it matter to you whether the type of case was a white-collar crime case or a conventional case? Explain.

8. How is prosecuting white-collar offenders similar to group projects your professors give you in your college courses?

9. What factors influence prosecutorial decision making?

10. What types of defenses are most commonly used by defense attorneys in white-collar crime trials?

WEB RESOURCES

Legal Information Institute White Collar Crime: http://topics.law.cornell.edu/wex/White-collar_crime

White Collar Crime: Who Does Time? http://www.businessweek.com/magazine/content/06_06/b3970083.htm

Lawyers.com—White Collar Crime: http://white-collar-crime.lawyers.com/

READING

In this reading, Michael Benson, Francis Cullen, and William Maakestad address the way that local prosecutors perceive and respond to corporate crime. The researchers found that although the prosecutors did not see corporate crime as extremely serious, they were nonetheless willing to prosecute corporate crime if corporations caused harm or other agencies did not intervene in the cases. The authors uncovered community differences, with urban prosecutors being more likely to view corporate crime as serious. Nearly 70% of urban prosecutors prosecuted a corporate crime in the prior year, as compared to about a third of rural prosecutors. Benson and his coauthors discuss a number of implications for better controlling corporate crime.

Local Prosecutors and Corporate Crime

Michael L. Benson, Francis T. Cullen, and William J. Maakestad

Traditionally, the criminal law has been used primarily against conventional violent and property crimes. Corporate illegalities have been handled by special procedures designed to eliminate the stigma of crime, if not ignored altogether (Sutherland [1949] 1983, pp. 54-55). Recently, however, growing interest in white-collar and corporate crime by legislators, law enforcement officials, and environmental and consumer groups has led some observers to proclaim that a "social movement" against white-collar crime is under way (Cullen, Maakestad, and Cavender 1987; Katz 1980). A potentially important dimension of this movement is an apparent increase in local prosecutions of corporate offenders (Cullen et al. 1987; Magnuson and Leviton 1987; Maakestad 1986).

Although this development may strike some as long overdue (Coleman 1989; Geis 1972), how best to control corporate misconduct in a free market economy is a matter of substantial controversy, and the wisdom of using criminal sanctions against corporate offenders has been vigorously debated.

The bulk of funds spent on law enforcement come from local governments. A widespread increase in corporate prosecutions at this level would represent remarkable shifts in local law enforcement priorities and societal reactions to corporate misconduct. Such potentially significant public policy developments deserve careful consideration. Surprisingly, then, systematic evidence on what local prosecutors think and do about corporate crime is hard to find. Indeed, putting aside a few studies of isolated and sensational cases, we know little about local prosecutors and corporate crime (Cullen et al. 1987; Magnuson and Leviton 1987).

This article begins by noting some evidence suggesting that corporate crime is an emerging priority for local prosecutors. From an ongoing study of local prosecutors, we next present data on prosecutors' attitudes toward corporate crime, the prevalence of corporate prosecutions, and the use of control networks against corporate crime. We conclude by addressing the implications of these findings for corporate crime control in the United States.

SOURCE: Benson, M., Cullen, F. T., & Maakestad, W. (1990). Local Prosecutors and Corporate Crime. *Crime and Delinquency, 36*(3), 356–372.

Local Prosecution of White-Collar and Corporate Crime

White-collar crimes committed by corporations pose special problems for law enforcement agencies. Hidden behind ordinary business routines, they often leave victims unaware of their victimization. They are difficult to uncover, and once detected, troublesome to investigate and prosecute. Business offenders hire skilled defense attorneys who take full advantage of the procedural safeguards afforded criminal defendants by the law (Mann 1985). Because evidence in corporate cases often involves arcane technical or financial data, investigations and prosecutions tend to be long and costly affairs. The federal government historically has had the dominant role in controlling white-collar and corporate crime. Many local prosecutors lack the resources and expertise to pursue corporate crime prosecutions.

In the 1970s local prosecutors began to reevaluate their stance toward these crimes. In 1973, at the instigation of a group of innovative local prosecutors, the National District Attorneys Association (NDAA) established an Economic Crime Committee. The Committee's charge was to promote local white-collar enforcement, enhance the capabilities of local prosecutors to deal with white-collar crime, and increase their professional commitment to do so (Edelhertz and Rogovin 1980a, pp. ix-xi). By 1978, over 60 district attorneys' offices were participating in the Economic Crime Project (Edelhertz and Rogovin 1980b, p. 11).

The Economic Crime Project promoted specialization and networking as strategies for containing economic and corporate crime. To overcome the lack of expertise, local prosecutors established special economic crime units. In theory, by concentrating on economic crimes, unit staff would develop necessary technical and legal skills. The special units then joined with other law enforcement and regulatory agencies to form control networks. Members of the control networks exchange information, share expertise and resources, and develop coordinated responses to local economic crimes. Evaluations of exemplary units in the

Project indicated that the control network approach could work well at the local level (Finn and Hoffman 1976; Whitcomb, Frisina, and Spangenberg 1979). Throughout the 1970s it was widely advocated by U.S. Justice Department and NDAA officials (Abrams 1980; see also the articles in Edelhertz and Rogovin 1980a). Some saw evidence that local prosecutors were responding:

> [By 1978] a clear recognition had developed, on the part of prosecutors in every part of the United States, that enforcement of laws against white-collar crime was the business of the local prosecutor as well as of federal prosecutors. Local prosecutors were more ready than ever before to commit resources of staff and dollar to this effort, even in the face of competing demands for resources to deal with violent crime and property crime. Cadres of local assistant district attorneys had been trained and battle hardened and were moving beyond simple cases to take on more sophisticated fraud schemes including state anti-trust offenses. Communication networks had developed among the assistant district attorneys staffing those economic crime units and some were coordinating actions across jurisdictional lines (sometimes across the continent). (Edelhertz and Rogovin 1980b, p. 11)

Since this assessment, the political and prosecutorial environment has changed considerably. Whereas district attorneys once concentrated almost exclusively on economic crimes such as consumer fraud, they now prosecute a broader variety of cases. Concerned with occupational safety violations and illegal dumping of toxic wastes, prosecutors in some states have sought criminal indictments against corporations for noneconomic offenses (Cullen et al. 1987, pp. 312-19). This shift reflects changing law and changing federal-state relationships. Courts have broadened traditional notions of corporate criminal liability (Brickey 1984) and new regulatory initiatives have expanded the statutory tools available for prosecutors to use against harmful corporate behavior. The federal government shifted responsibility for many programs to state and local officials. In this new environment, local officials must push the initiative against corporate crime.

We know little about how local officials have handled this new responsibility. Empirical studies of local reactions to corporate crime are rare; we know of only three completed in the past decade (Ayers and Frank 1987; Benson, Maakestad, Cullen, and Geis 1988; Gurney 1985).

It is important, then, to assess the current state of local reactions to corporate crime. We need to know whether local prosecutors regard corporate crime as a serious problem. Do they believe that strong criminal penalties improve corporate compliance with the law? Under what circumstances are they willing to conduct corporate criminal prosecutions? How many and what types of corporate offenses do they prosecute? Are they using the control network approach against corporate crime?

The Study

Data for this analysis are drawn from an ongoing study of local prosecutors and corporate crime in the United States. Part one of the study, a national survey of district attorneys, was conducted during the spring of 1989. The second part of the study is an ethnographic analysis of corporate crime control in four jurisdictions selected because of their relatively high levels of activity in this area. During the fall of 1989, we interviewed prosecutors and investigators who specialize in white-collar and corporate crime. We also interviewed representatives from the respective state attorney general's office, local police, and various state and federal regulatory agencies.

The purpose of the larger study is to investigate the relationship between community context and constraints on prosecutorial decision making in corporate cases. For the present report, we rely primarily on the survey data. Our analysis of the interviews is not yet complete, hence we draw on them only to provide tentative illustrations and interpretations of certain points.

Sample

Variations in state criminal justice systems complicate national studies of local prosecution. In most states, a locally elected official representing a county or county-equivalent geographic area conducts criminal prosecutions. But there are numerous exceptions to this pattern. For example, in some states, felony and misdemeanor prosecutions are handled by different officials. In drawing the sample of local prosecutors, we used state statutes to identify officials responsible for prosecuting locally committed felonies.

Using a mailing list provided by the National District Attorneys Association (NDAA), we sent questionnaires to 1,042 district attorneys. Every district attorney whose jurisdiction is located in a metropolitan statistical area (MSA) received a questionnaire ($N = 632$), and a 25% random sample of the remaining rural prosecutors ($N = 410$) was included in the sample. This represents approximately one third of the NDAA membership. After follow-up postcards, and two other mailings, the final response rate was 66% ($N = 686$).

Given our sampling approach, the final sample is disproportionately composed of respondents located in urban districts. For this reason and because rural districts, by definition, have little corporate or business activity and hence little business-related crime, we present the results for urban and rural districts separately.

Questionnaire

The mail survey focused on prosecutors' experiences with and attitudes toward corporate crime. Directions on the survey defined corporate crime as "a violation of a criminal statute either by a corporate entity or by its executives, employees, or agents acting on behalf of and for the benefit of the corporation, partnership, or other form of business entity." We noted explicitly that this "definition excludes crime committed by an employee against an employer for the purpose of personal gain, such as embezzlement or theft."

 Results

Critics have claimed that corporate crime is not regarded as a serious problem by the United States law enforcement establishment (Coleman 1989; Reiman 1979). In the new environment of the 1980s, is this true of local prosecutors?

What Prosecutors Say About Corporate Crime

As expected, more urban prosecutors regarded corporate crime as a serious problem than did their rural counterparts, but only 3.6% of urban prosecutors rated corporate crime as a "very serious" problem. About one third (30.1%) saw it as "somewhat serious" and about half regarded it as "not at all serious." Almost no rural prosecutors (0.4%) regarded corporate crime as a very serious problem and few (10.6%) saw it as somewhat serious. When asked about future trends in corporate criminal prosecutions, a majority of urban prosecutors (54.7%) said they anticipated doing about the same number. Just over 1 in 4 (28.8%) anticipated prosecuting more cases; very few (.5%) planned on doing less. A similar distribution was found for trends in the past. Of the urban respondents, 6 out of 10 reported that during their tenure as prosecuting attorneys the number of corporate crimes prosecuted annually had remained about the same. Just over one quarter reported an increase and less than 1% reported a decrease. Rural prosecutors were considerably less likely to have observed or to anticipate an increase in corporate prosecutions.

On the theory that local prosecutors attend only to street crime, some may regard the findings on perceived seriousness as singularly unsurprising. The interviews suggested, however, that another reason may be partially to blame for low levels of concern about corporate crime. In every jurisdiction we visited, the interviewees noted that the enormous effort against drugs has sapped resources and enforcement. It has overloaded the system, making it difficult to respond adequately to other types of crime. As one interviewee stated:

> This was my point this morning when we were talking about the system is finished. It's kaput. It's over, the game, the war. There is no war. It's over. We have filled them [jails and prisons] to max on these drug things. We have allocated all of our resources for drug things. The judges can't review the courtcalls of four or five hundred drug cases. You bring in a white-collar executive to the bar of justice, and the judge looking at all of this, goes "What, what is this?"

Later, the same prosecutor said:

> Basically we're not going to get a dime from anybody from any other area except drugs. For 8 years or so all our State's Attorney shouted was "gangs and drugs, gangs and drugs." So after 8 years of that approach the problem is 10 times worse, and it has hurt every other area of prosecution.

With varying degrees of emphasis, most of the prosecutors and investigators we interviewed offered the same analysis: The war on drugs weakens efforts against other crimes, including corporate crimes.

Considering that most district attorneys do not regard corporate crime as a serious problem, one might assume they would have little enthusiasm for criminalization as a means of control. Paradoxically, this does not appear to be the case. Nearly three fifths of the prosecutors from rural as well as urban districts felt that "weak criminal penalties" are somewhat or very important causes of corporate crime. Furthermore, when asked about "methods of improving corporate compliance with the law in your state," 7 out of 10 reported that "tougher criminal penalties" would be somewhat or very useful in achieving this goal.

Prosecutors apparently believe that criminal sanctions, especially incarceration, make a difference. The interviews shed light on the reasoning behind this belief. Commenting on the impact of imprisonment, a prosecutor noted:

> It's one thing that can't be passed on. You can fine a company a million dollars, and if they're a viable company the shareholders suffer, the consumer suffers in higher prices, and what have you. But the culprits are not the people that are paying the price. So you give them 20 years in jail, and you try to pass that on to the consumer. It really stops at that point and people start waking up. I mean, as I talk around the country to these corporate people, there's no doubt in my mind that they are prepared to pay the cost of fines at the expense of life and limb at their workplace. But, boy when Film Recovery [A case in which corporate executives received prison sentences for causing a worker's death] came down and people are like going to jail, a businessman says, "How do I pass that on?" and a criminal defense lawyer says, "You don't. You do the time." That's why people are paying attention now.

Though corporate prosecutions are costly and time consuming, prosecutors believe their general deterrent effect makes them well worth the expense. As one prosecutor pointed out:

> There's only one advantage to these prosecutions. One of these prosecutions is worth 500 as far as a deterrent value is concerned. I've prosecuted maybe 50 murderers, and I've never deterred the street murderer once. I've probably prosecuted one industrial murderer and I think we've deterred a whole lot of people, at least woke them up and some people are trying to do the right thing. So even with a lack of resources, one [of these] prosecutions is much more valuable than one streetwise, or what they call traditional, street crime prosecution.

Prosecutors believe that criminal penalties are effective, but under what conditions are they willing to use them? The survey data and the interviews suggest that prosecutors' reactions to corporate harms are largely shaped by factors deeply rooted in American legal culture: harm and blameworthiness (Wheeler, Mann, and Sarat 1988).

When asked what would increase their "willingness to prosecute a corporate criminal offense," a large majority of prosecutors focused on the substantive effects of the offense. For example, urban prosecutors said they would "probably or definitely" be more willing in cases involving "physical harm to victim or victims" (94.6%); "substantial economic harm" (92.7%); or, "a large number of victims" (92.7%). Nearly identical proportions of rural prosecutors also reported increased willingness to prosecute under these conditions.

Prosecutors' reactions to corporate crime parallel their treatment of street crime; they attend closely to what was done and who did it. Regardless of whether the perpetrator is an individual or a business, when victims lose money or are physically hurt, prosecutors believe they have a duty to investigate. The greater the number of victims involved, the greater the reason to investigate. If the loss or hurt is caused by someone acting deliberately or with disregard for the safety of others, then prosecutors define the event as criminal and are inclined to prosecute. Consider this exchange with a veteran prosecutor:

Interviewer:	Do you measure harm on a variety of different dimensions? How many people....
Prosecutor (interrupting):	You know it's not so much or how many, like it would be OK if it was one person and not OK if it was two. When there are people involved, and we can immediately say it's people, our position is when you kill somebody and if you can't demonstrate to us that this was a freak thing, you took every possible precaution, you know, we're going to look real seriously at criminal charges.

Evidence of the offender's criminality is as important as the substance of the offense. Prosecutors distinguished between the incidental and habitual corporate criminal. One interviewee posed this example:

> Let's take AT&T. Suppose AT&T does X and CM&W (a pseudonym) does X, and AT&T can demonstrate that for the last 40 years they have appropriately done everything with regard to environmental issues. We know CM&W, because we've been on CM&W's case for years. We're going to be much more inclined to go for the throat of CM&W than we are for AT&T.

Survey data corroborate this point. Over 90% of prosecutors say that "evidence of multiple offenses rather than a single offense" would "probably or definitely increase" their willingness to prosecute.

As with many street crimes, victim preferences also shaped enforcement decisions. For over 70% of the respondents "victim preference for prosecution" would increase their willingness to prosecute. Conversely, over three fourths of the district attorneys stated that "lack of cooperation from victim(s)" would limit their willingness to prosecute corporations.

The visibility of corporate conduct also appears to influence the decision to file criminal charges. Over three fourths of the sample said that "public concern over the corporate criminal offense" would increase their willingness to prosecute; just under half of the respondents admitted that "media attention on the case" would do the same thing.

There are, however, factors that limit prosecutors' willingness to conduct criminal prosecutions of corporate offenders. Some evidence suggests that local prosecutions are used only when corporate criminality has escaped appropriate penalty. Thus approximately three fourths of the district attorneys sampled indicated that their willingness to prosecute was limited by an "actual or pending action" by either a federal or a state regulatory agency. In contrast, over half the sample stated that they would be more likely to file criminal charges if "regulatory agencies failed to act."

Undoubtedly, prosecuting offenses committed in organizational settings is time-consuming and expensive. Hence the potential drain on resources, difficulty of proving intent, and availability of alternate remedies always figure into the decision-making calculus in corporate cases. Nevertheless, the survey and interviews suggest that underneath these tactical considerations lie traditional moral concerns: The corporate status of the offender, notwithstanding, prosecutors wanted to stop the victimization of innocents and punish those who callously put their own desires above the safety and well-being of others. That urban and rural prosecutors identified the same factors as increasing their willingness to prosecute evidences a consensus on the proper use of criminal sanctions. Local prosecutors appeared much like the federal judges studied by Wheeler et al. (1988). For both groups, a common culture rooted in concepts of harm and blameworthiness appears to guide reactions to white-collar and corporate crime.

Actions speak louder than words, however. It is appropriate now to turn from what prosecutors said about corporate crime to what they were doing about it.

What Prosecutors Are Doing About Corporate Crime

Of the urban districts, 69.1% and 35.1% of the rural districts prosecuted at least one corporate offense in 1988. As Table 13.6 shows, prosecutors located in urban districts were more likely to have prosecuted any given offense than were their counterparts in rural districts.

To see whether 1988 was an unusual year, we asked prosecutors how many corporate crimes they handled in a "typical year." In the urban districts the percentage who *never* prosecute corporate crimes is just under 14%. Approximately 85% of urban district attorneys prosecute corporate offenses, albeit not very frequently.

Table 13.7 shows the rates at which prosecutors located in urban districts handled specific offenses. Most prosecuted less than one case per year of the selected offenses. A small minority prosecuted more than three cases per year. No matter what the crime, a majority of local prosecutors handled less than one case per year.

Table 13.6   Percentage Prosecuting Selected Corporate Crimes in Urban and Rural Jurisdictions, 1988

	Jurisdiction	
Corporate Crime	**Rural**	**Urban**
Consumer fraud	15.3	41.1
Securities fraud	4.6	22.6
Insurance fraud	9.3	31.1
Tax fraud	4.7	15.9
False claims	10.9	31.2
Workplace offenses	2.3	10.9
Environmental offenses	12.8	30.8
Illegal payments	1.2	15.7
Unfair trade practices	1.2	7.7

NOTE: Rural jurisdictions, $N = 261$; Urban jurisdictions, $N = 424$.

The control network approach has been much touted as a corporate crime control strategy (Vaughan 1983). It calls for local prosecutors to establish in-house units specializing in white-collar and corporate crime cases. The units coordinate their activities with other agencies to form an interorganizational control network. This approach permits local prosecutors to take on more complex cases. But is it widely used and associated with higher prosecution rates?

Districts with economic and white-collar crime are located almost exclusively in urban areas. Because only three rural districts participated in a control network, we confined our analysis to the urban districts.

Just under 23% of the respondents from urban districts indicated that their office had a special "in-house unit for investigating and prosecuting economic or white-collar crimes" ($N = 97$). About 8% ($N = 32$) reported being involved in an "inter-agency task force or strike group which focuses on economic or white-collar crimes." There was considerable overlap between the two groups, as three quarters of those involved in an interagency task force also had a special unit. A total of 103 (24.4%) of the respondents appeared to use the

Table 13.7   Frequency of Prosecutions in a Typical Year (in percentages)

Corporate Crime	Never	Frequency		
		Fewer Than 1 Case per Year	**About 1-3 Cases per Year**	**More Than 3 Cases per Year**
Consumer fraud	31.6	32.6	20.8	15.0
Securities fraud	56.5	28.0	12.2	3.4
Insurance fraud	36.9	39.6	14.6	9.0
Tax fraud	61.6	25.3	7.5	5.6
False claims	40.3	33.5	14.9	11.3
Workplace offenses	67.9	25.7	5.2	1.2
Environmental offenses	45.4	33.3	13.1	8.3
Illegal payments	50.6	37.5	9.6	2.2
Unfair trade practices	75.1	17.5	3.0	4.4

NOTE: Table based on urban jurisdictions only; $N = 424$.

control network strategy. Hereafter, we refer to these as control network districts.

Participation in a control network increased prosecutions of corporate crime (see Table 13.8). The frequency of prosecutions for securities frauds, environmental offenses, illegal payments, and unfair trade practices in control network districts was particularly notable.

The significance of these findings, though, is not clear. Do prosecutors in control network districts prosecute more corporate crimes because of greater ability to do so or because corporate crimes occur more often in their jurisdictions? If we assume that population size correlates roughly with business activity and hence corporate crime, we can use it as a proxy control for corporate crime. Accordingly, we divided the sample into three groups based on population: small (under 200,000), medium (200,000 to 500,000), and large (over 500,000). We then examined prosecution rates in each group (see Table 3.9).

Controlling for population size reduces but does not eliminate the association between control networks

Table 13.8 Percentage of Network and Nonnetwork Jurisdictions That Prosecute One or More Selected Corporate Crimes per Year

Corporate Crime	Nonnetwork	Network
Consumer fraud	24.0	71.2
Securities fraud	5.5	45.6
Insurance fraud	14.5	51.5
Tax fraud	9.4	24.5
False claims	18.0	51.5
Workplace offenses	4.6	12.0
Environmental offenses	15.1	40.2
Illegal payments	5.9	30.3
Unfair trade practices	4.3	22.8

NOTE: Table based on urban jurisdictions only; nonnetwork districts, $N = 321$; network districts, $N = 103$.

and prosecution rates. Medium-sized control network districts prosecuted six offenses more often than large districts without such arrangements. For example, 78% of the medium-sized control network districts prosecuted one or more consumer frauds per year, but only 46% of the large nonnetwork districts did so. The control network strategy appears to increase prosecutorial activity independent of the amount of corporate crime.

The attitudes of prosecutors located in control network districts may account for the higher levels of prosecutorial activity found there. Compared to their counterparts, significantly higher percentages of prosecutors in offices with special units rated corporate crime as a "somewhat" (65.1 versus 18.1%) or "very serious" (10.6 versus 1.3%) problem. The specialists we interviewed manifested firm, often passionate, resolve against business crime. They argued that more could and should be done in this area. Generalizing from the interviews, we believe that specialists appreciate the seriousness of corporate crime and advocate for resources to use against it.

As its name implies, networking is an integral part of the control network strategy. To find out how extensively local prosecutors work with other agencies, we asked our respondents how often they cooperated with selected agencies on corporate crime investigations. Table 13.10 shows the results for urban districts.

There appears to be little cooperation between local prosecutors and federal law enforcement agencies. Over 70% of the respondents indicated that they never cooperate in joint investigations with federal regulatory agencies; two thirds never cooperate with the U.S. Attorney in their district, and 60% never cooperate with the FBI.

There was somewhat greater, though still not overwhelming, cooperation between local prosecutors and state agencies. Approximately 1 in 5 district attorneys cooperated more than once per year with the state police or the state attorney general's office. Just under 30% of the districts cooperated at that level with state regulatory agencies. Local prosecutors were most likely to work with the local police on corporate cases. The relatively high levels of cooperation with local police suggest that many prosecutors deal with corporate crime as they do with traditional street crime. That is, they wait for the police to bring them cases. It also may

Table 13.9   Percentage of Network and Nonnetwork Districts That Prosecute One or More Selected Corporate Crimes per Year in Different Sized Jurisdictions

Corporate Crime	Population Size					
	Large		Medium		Small	
	Network					
	No	Yes	No	Yes	No	Yes
Consumer fraud	46.2	70.2	35.6	78.1	20.1	61.5
Securities fraud	28.6	43.1	12.1	25.0	2.5	30.8
Insurance fraud	35.7	58.9	26.8	56.3	9.7	7.7
Tax fraud	8.3	29.3	13.6	25.8	8.4	0.0
False claims	30.8	53.6	22.4	45.2	16.3	58.3
Workplace offenses	16.7	8.8	5.2	10.0	3.8	30.8
Environmental offenses	33.3	47.4	22.0	34.4	12.6	23.1
Illegal payments	38.5	35.7	8.5	30.0	3.4	7.7
Unfair trade practices	16.7	23.2	5.1	28.1	0.1	7.7
Base *n*	14	58	62	32	244	13

NOTE: Table based on urban jurisdictions only; $N = 424$.

mean that the crimes involved are rather routine, garden-variety consumer frauds, as these are the offenses police are most likely to hear about (Stotland 1982).

We also investigated whether membership in a control network influences the frequency of joint investigations and found cooperation was more prevalent among control network districts. Extensive cooperation with federal agencies was still relatively uncommon. Less than 1 in 4 of these districts cooperated at least once a year with the FBI, U.S. Attorney, or federal regulatory agencies. In contrast, 3 out of 4 districts cooperated at least once a year with the local police on a corporate case and 40% cooperated with the police more than three times a year.

Overall, integration between local prosecutors and other levels of government, especially federal agencies, was not widespread. More prosecutors worked with the local police than with any other agency on corporate cases. Edelhertz and Rogovin (1980c, p. 108) observed this same pattern over a decade ago. It would appear, therefore, that calls for greater local and federal cooperation have met with only partial success.

 ## Implications for Corporate Crime Control

In the last two decades corporate harms have risen in American consciousness of the crime problem. Against this backdrop, our research investigates what local prosecutors are thinking and doing in this area, thereby providing a firmer empirical base for policy debates.

The data show that prosecutors generally do not regard corporate crime as a serious problem and most

Table 13.10   Frequency of Joint Investigations With Selected Law Enforcement and Regulatory Agencies (in percentages)

Agency	Frequency of Joint Investigations			
	Never	Less Than 1/Year	1-3 Times per Year	More Than 3 Times
Local police	28.6	33.3	22.2	15.8
State police	44.2	33.0	16.0	6.5
State Attorney General	38.6	39.6	16.4	5.4
State regulatory agency	35.4	35.9	16.5	12.2
Federal regulatory agency	70.7	22.4	5.9	1.0
U.S. Attorney	66.8	25.6	5.8	1.5
FBI	60.9	29.3	7.3	2.5
Other prosecutor	43.9	35.4	18.0	2.7

NOTE: Table based on urban jurisdictions only; $N = 424$.

do not anticipate doing more prosecutions in the future. In part, this may be because of the current push against illegal drug use. This does not mean that local district attorneys are inconsequential in the social movement against corporate crime. A substantial majority of district attorneys prosecute corporate cases, albeit infrequently. They believe these prosecutions have significant general deterrent effects on the business community, and there are theoretical reasons for agreeing with them.

The number of potential corporate offenders is much smaller than the number of potential individual offenders. In theory, when a target population is small, even a small number of prosecutions may substantially raise a potential offender's perceived risk of being sanctioned and hence may have dramatic deterrent effects. In addition to the regular media, businesspersons have other means (industry associations and trade publications) of learning about corporate prosecutions. Hence they may be more likely than ordinary individuals to learn of peers who have been caught and punished. In short, communicating the threat of punishment, a prerequisite for deterrence, may be more feasible with business as opposed to street criminals.

A decade ago, Edelhertz and Rogovin (1980b, p. 11) argued that local prosecutors were beginning to see white-collar law enforcement as part of their job. No longer willing to cede the federal government exclusive jurisdiction over corporate crimes, local prosecutors were beginning to pursue these cases. Unfortunately, without baseline data, we cannot determine how strongly this trend has continued. But there is evidence that it has continued.

As of 1978, district attorneys in 66 jurisdictions were participating in the NDAA's Economic Crime Project (Edelhertz and Rogovin 1980b, p. 11). The survey—which does not include information from the 200 or so nonresponding urban districts—indicates that there are now over 100 jurisdictions with such arrangements, representing nearly one quarter of urban districts. The growing number of special units may mean that corporate and other white-collar crimes have permanently emerged from their pre-1970 levels of obscurity in local law enforcement.

For prosecutors, interest in corporate crime control does not arise in a political or organizational vacuum. It develops out of locally generated concerns.

An egregious, highly publicized case may provide the stimulus. Alternatively, a perceptive district attorney may note nascent public concern over corporate misconduct and take a more active role against it.

Environmental crimes are a case in point. Corporate environmental violations have high salience for local prosecutors. As one said, "the danger [from] this environmental stuff is much greater than [what] we have to worry about [from] drugs." Prosecutors recognize the public's concern over environmental problems. As one prosecutor observed:

> I find that a day really does not go by without me hearing about some type of environmental issues just on television or in the newspapers. The problems are immense.

Recall from Table 13.7 that environmental crimes rank in the top four in frequency of prosecution, despite the relative newness of state statutes criminalizing environmental violations.

Local corporate crime specialists have become more common partially because of a general rise in American consciousness of the seriousness of corporate misconduct. District attorneys have responded to this trend by creating special units.

Organizational consequences follow the creation of new units. The allocation of organizational resources opens new career opportunities for assistant prosecutors, and specialization permits them to conduct high-visibility prosecutions. Favorable results in a few widely publicized cases may bring instant recognition both within the office and in the larger community. Once established, these opportunities inevitably draw some takers in each new cohort of public prosecutors.[1] For this group, corporate crime is both a serious social problem and a career opportunity.

Recognition of the seriousness of corporate crime does not, however, automatically translate into effective action against it, and the continued rarity of inter-govermental cooperation is troubling. The prosecutors and investigators we interviewed routinely remarked on the virtual necessity of interagency cooperation but also noted that it is difficult to initiate and maintain. Because we chose the field study

sites in part as a result of their high levels of inter-agency interaction, it is probably safe to assume that networking problems are even more pronounced in other jurisdictions.

Working with other people in agencies takes a lot of time, energy, and patience. It requires sharing credit and control over investigations and prosecutions. For ambitious and busy people, these are important disincentives to networking. Sometimes the benefits of cracking a big case are worth the trouble of coordinating with others and sharing credit. But much of the time the motivation to put up with the difficulties of networking comes only from the individual prosecutor's sense of professional duty.

In conclusion, for those who hold that local law enforcement should do more against business crime, our findings present reasons for both optimism and pessimism. On the positive side, prosecutors have no philosophical or conceptual objections to using the criminal law against corporate offenders. They think tougher criminal penalties would improve corporate compliance with the law and largely agree on when they should be imposed. Enthusiasm for criminalization appears strongest among prosecutors specializing in this area. There is a constituency, perhaps a growing one, within the system advocating for greater criminal control of corporate wrongdoers.

On the negative side, this constituency faces a difficult job getting resources for its work. Competing demands for funds and staff for drug crimes often take priority and networking has not really taken hold at the local level. Coordination across levels of government appears uncommon. Environmental crimes may provide a stimulus for change. To the extent they become linked with specific physical harms to individuals, we expect more local prosecutions of corporations violating environmental laws.

Note

1. The attractions of corporate criminal prosecutions for assistant prosecutors should not be overemphasized. High-visibility murder, drug, and organized crime cases are still the crimes of choice. But there are not many of these. Hence big corporate cases provide additional opportunities to make a name for oneself.

References

Abrams, Norman. 1980. "Assessing the Federal Government's War on White Collar Crime." *Temple Law Review* 53:984-1008.

Ayers, Kenneth and James Frank. 1987. "Deciding to Prosecute White-Collar Crime: A National Survey of State Attorneys General." *Justice Quarterly* 4:425-439.

Benson, Michael, William Maakestad, Francis Cullen, and Gilbert Geis. "District Attorneys and Corporate Crime: Surveying the Prosecutorial Gatekeepers." *Criminology* 26:505-518.

Brickey, Kathleen. 1984. *Corporate Criminal Liability*. Wilmette, IL: Callaghan.

Coleman, James. 1989. *The Criminal Elite*. New York: St. Martin.

Cullen, Francis, William Maakestad, and Gray Cavender. 1987. *Corporate Crime Under Attack: The Ford Pinto Case and Beyond*. Cincinnati: Anderson.

Edelhertz, Herbert and Charles Rogovin. 1980a. "Preface and Acknowledgements." Pp. ix-xii in *A National Strategy for Containing White-Collar Crime*, edited by H. Edelhertz and C. Rogovin. Lexington, MA: Lexington Books.

———— 1980b. "Symposium Background." Pp. 11-17 in *A National Strategy for Containing White-Collar Crime*, edited by H. Edelhertz and C. Rogovin. Lexington, MA: Lexington Books.

———— 1980c. "Implementing a National Strategy." Pp. 103-112 in *A National Strategy for Containing White-Collar Crime*, edited by H. Edelhertz and C. Rogovin. Lexington, MA: Lexington Books.

Finn, Peter and Alan Hoffman. 1976. *Exemplary Projects: Prosecution of Economic Crime*. Washington, DC: National Institute of Law Enforcement and Criminal Justice.

Geis, Gilbert. 1972. "Criminal Penalties for Corporate Criminals." *Criminal Law Bulletin* 8:377-92.

Gumey, Joan. 1985. "Factors Influencing the Decision to Prosecute Economic Cases." *Criminology* 23:609-628.

Katz, Jack. 1980. "The Social Movement Against White-Collar Crime." *Criminology Review Yearbook* 2:161-84.

Maakestad, William. 1986. "States' Attorneys Stalk Corporate Murderers." *Business and Society Review* 56:21-25.

Magnuson, Jay and Gareth Leviton. 1987. "Policy Considerations in Corporate Criminal Prosecutions after People v. Film Recovery Systems, Inc." *Notre Dame Law Review* 62:913-939.

Mann, Kenneth. 1985. *Defending White-Collar Crime*. New Haven: Yale University Press.

Reiman, Jeffrey. 1979. *The Rich Get Richer and the Poor Get Prison*. New York: Wiley.

Stotland, Ezra. 1982. "The Role of Law Enforcement in the Fight against White-Collar Crime." Pp. 69-98 in *White-Collar Crime: An Agenda for Research*, edited by H. Edelhertz and T. Overcast. Lexington, MA: Lexington Books.

Sutherland, Edwin. [1949] 1983. *White-Collar Crime: The Uncut Version*. New Haven: Yale University Press.

Vaughan, Diane. 1983. *Controlling Unlawful Organizational Behavior*. Chicago: University of Chicago Press.

Wheeler, Stanton, Kenneth Mann, and Austin Sarat. 1988. *Sitting in Judgment: The Sentencing of White-Collar Criminals*. New Haven: Yale University Press.

Whitcomb, Debra, Louis Frisina, and Robert Spangenberg. 1979. *An Exemplary Project: Connecticut Economic Crime Unit*. Washington, DC: National Institute of Law Enforcement and Criminal Justice.

DISCUSSION QUESTIONS

1. What factors influence prosecutors' decisions to prosecute corporate crime?

2. What community level differences exist in terms of decisions to prosecute corporate crime?

3. How do you think your local prosecutor perceives corporate crime?

READING

In this article, Barbara Belbot describes the dilemma that corporate attorneys face when they learn that their employer is committing white-collar crime. She draws attention to the important role that corporate attorneys have in corporations and illustrates how the attorney-client privilege guides attorneys' decisions about how to respond to situations where they encounter white-collar crime by their employers. Belbot also shows how government agencies have developed policies promoting whistleblowing by attorneys. She also considers the consequences of adhering strictly to attorney-client privilege in the face of potential harm to consumers, investors, and others.

SOURCE: Belbot, Barbara (1991). Whistleblowing and Lawyers. *Journal of Contemporary Criminal Justice, 7*(3), 154–166.

Whistleblowing and Lawyers

Barbara A. Belbot

 Introduction

Before the 1960s, American society and the law supported wide corporate autonomy. People assumed that corporations needed little regulation and generally functioned in the best interests of the public. The economics of the marketplace was relied upon to solve whatever problems arose (Westin 1981).

Beginning in the 1960s and 1970s, however, these traditional assumptions began to erode. The consumer protection movement focused on dangerous and substandard products. The equal rights movement challenged racial, sex and age discriminatory employment practices. The occupational health and safety movement investigated harmful and unsafe conditions in the workplace. The environmental protection movement examined the purity of our water, air and land. The Watergate scandal raised questions concerning the honesty and values of our nation's leaders and politicians (Westin 1981).

It was this social and political atmosphere that produced the whistleblower, loosely defined as a current or former employee who makes public allegations of his or her employer's wrongdoing. Unlike the muckrakers who exposed corporate and industrial wrongdoing earlier in this century, the whistleblower is new in the history of American reform because he or she exposes the wrongdoing of his or her own organization. Whistleblowers are caught between loyalty to the organizations that employ them and an ethical obligation to disclose and correct unconscionable or illegal practices (Peters and Branch 1972).

Professional employees are in an especially difficult situation because, in addition to the loyalty they owe to their employers, they owe loyalty to the profession itself and to the public. They generally have a formal ethical code that guides their performance. They also may be licensed by the state and subject to disciplinary action for violating their profession's code of ethics (Halpert 1985).

This article examines the difficulties faced by a corporate attorney who discovers that a client has committed a fraudulent act. The attorney's ethical and moral dilemma is especially troublesome because he or she is under a professional obligation to keep information confidential that has been imparted in the course of the business relationship with the client.

 The Corporate Attorney

Whether he or she is hired in-house as an employee of the corporation or is a member of a private law firm retained by the corporation, the corporate lawyer performs a role that is vastly different than the lawyer-advocate. Corporate lawyers are legal advisors, and although they are not entirely divorced from the adversarial system, they function primarily in a non litigation context. Their responsibilities are to guide and advise the client through the maze of government regulations and court decisions that address products liability, food and drugs, occupational safety, the environment, consumer protection, collective bargaining, antitrust, tax, equal employment and securities (Burke 1981). They may even sit as officers or directors of the corporation. Although they are hired to advise the corporate entity, their advice affects employees, shareholders, investors, creditors, competitors, consumers and the general public. They are privy to a large amount of information concerning the corporation's business transactions and future plans. Because of their unique position, the question arises as to the corporate lawyer's responsibilities to the public interest. How should corporate lawyers balance their obligations to clients, as those obligations are developed by the doctrines of attorney-client privilege and confidentiality, and their obligations to the public interest? (Lome, 1978). As Maureen Burke (1981) has observed,

Corporate lawyers can be a powerful source of promoting ethical corporate conduct. They have an impact on society out of proportion to their numbers due to the power and influence of their clients. Therefore, the ethical conflict of corporate attorneys over the duty of confidentiality towards clients and the duty to pursue the public welfare has far-reaching social, economic, and political implications (p. 240).

Like all professions, lawyers are guided in this area by a code of ethics. In addition, they are guided by a body of common law that has developed over the past several hundred years.

The Attorney-Client Privilege and Client Confidentiality

The attorney-client privilege prohibits the introduction at trial of any information revealed by a client in confidence to his or her attorney. The privilege originally belonged to the attorney and was designed to protect him from having to reveal a confidence and, thereby, compromise his honor as a gentleman (Luban 1988). By the 1700s, however, the privilege was understood to belong to the client, with the rationale that for a lawyer to carry out the duty to represent a client, he must know all the facts concerning the situation; full disclosure of the facts by a client is best assured if the client knows that his or her confidences will not be divulged by the lawyer (Burke 1981). The privilege encourages the client to fully disclose all the facts, knowing that those confidences will not be divulged by the lawyer (Burke 1981). The attorney-client privilege does not protect advice that an attorney has given to a client to assist the client in the commission of a crime; however, communications about past crimes are protected by the privilege (McCormick 1972).

Jeremy Bentham attacked the attorney-client privilege by arguing that if the defendant is guilty, the attorney should be made to testify against him or her and help bring a guilty person to justice. If the defendant is innocent, there is nothing for the attorney to betray; an innocent person has no reason not to disclose all the facts to a lawyer (Luban 1988).

Bentham's critics maintain that it is incorrect to assume that an innocent defendant will have no reason to withhold vital information from an attorney (Freedman 1975). It is conceivable that an innocent client may withhold information because he or she does not realize that they are innocent of wrongdoing. This is an especially compelling argument with respect to certain complex white-collar regulatory offenses that may be treated as violations of either the civil or criminal law. Forcing a lawyer to testify against a client would discourage some clients from revealing exculpatory facts.

The more compelling argument in favor of the privilege is that a criminal defendant is entitled to zealous representation under the Sixth Amendment. An advocate acts as the defendant's spokesperson. Under Bentham's scheme, a defendant who exercises his or her Sixth Amendment right to counsel and divulges all the facts to counsel is at risk of incriminating himself or herself through his or her spokesperson. In effect, Bentham's position robs a defendant of the Fifth Amendment guarantee of the right against self-incrimination.

The attorney-client privilege is limited to communications that can be introduced into evidence during a trial. It does not prohibit an attorney from revealing client confidences in other settings. The more general ethical duty of client confidentiality is a lawyer's obligation to protect any embarrassing or detrimental information about a client regardless as to how the information became known to the lawyer. The rationale for the duty of client confidentiality is the same as the rationale for the attorney-client evidentiary privilege—to encourage clients to confide in their lawyer. The duty extends, however, to protecting client secrets that are discovered by an attorney from a source other than the client. The reason for the enhanced obligation is to encourage the attorney to fully investigate a case without fear that he or she may find information that they would rather not know (Luban 1988).

The Model Rules of Professional Conduct

During the years following Watergate, the Code of Professional Responsibility came under escalating attack for its failure to make clear a lawyer's ethical obligations and because it failed to provide adequate guidance for the other roles that lawyers play—as advisors, negotiators and mediators (Hazard 1990; Burke 1981).

The American Bar Association created the Kutak Commission in 1977 to revise the Code. In 1980, the Commission released the first public draft of its work, called the Model Rules of Professional Conduct (Burke 1981). Immediately, controversy developed concerning the draft's new standards for when a lawyer can reveal a client's confidential information. Opponents of the proposals argued that lawyers would be forced to blow the whistle on their corporate clients (Hazard and Koniak 1990). David Luban (1988) described the ensuing debate as "the most celebrated donnybrook in legal ethics since the involvement of lawyers in the Watergate scandal" (p. 181).

The furor centered on proposed Rule 1.6(b) which gave a lawyer the discretion to reveal confidential information to the extent the lawyer reasonably believes disclosure is necessary:

(2) To prevent the client from committing a prospective crime or fraudulent act the lawyer believes likely to cause death or substantial bodily harm, or substantial harm to the financial interests or property of another;

(3) To rectify the consequences of a client's past criminal or fraudulent act in the commission of which the lawyer's services had been used . . .

The Kutak Commission did not limit disclosure of prospective client fraud to only criminal acts. A lawyer could reveal an act that could likely cause substantial harm to financial or property interests as well as death or bodily harm. A lawyer could also reveal past criminal or fraudulent acts in which his or her services had been

used in order to help rectify the wrongs that had been done. Critics argued that proposed rule 1.6(b) was a radical departure from the requirements of DR 7-102 (B)(1) and that it greatly broadened the scope of permissible disclosure (Hazard 1990).

In 1983, the ABA House of Delegates rejected the Kutak Commission's proposed Rule 1.6(b) and adopted a very different version. According to the officially adopted version, a lawyer has the discretionary right to reveal information he or she reasonably believes necessary:

(1) To prevent the client from committing a criminal act that the lawyer believes is likely to result in imminent death or substantial bodily harm.

Unlike the proposed rule, the adopted rule does not allow an attorney to reveal a client's confidence unless it is necessary to prevent a future criminal act, and only if the act is likely to result in imminent death or substantial bodily harm. A lawyer has no discretion to reveal information concerning a fraudulent act that occurred in the past (Nahstoll 1984).

The only recourse for an attorney who finds himself or herself in a situation that is not addressed by the adopted rule is to withdraw representation. The ABA House of Delegates argued that withdrawal from a case is an effective solution because it allows an attorney to protect himself or herself, and it puts the third-party victim of the fraud on notice that things are amiss. Unfortunately, withdrawing representation is too late if the fraud involved past conduct, and it fails as a solution if the innocent victim does not comprehend the significance of withdrawal. As Geoffrey Hazard commented, "What the ABA has done is loudly to proclaim that a lawyer may not blow the whistle, but quietly to affirm that he may wave a flag" (1984, p.797).

Model Rule 1.13 deals specifically with disclosing the confidences of the corporate client. As finally adopted by the House of Delegates, the Rule provides that if a lawyer for an organization knows that an officer, employee, or other person associated with the organization is engaged in or is intending to engage in an illegal act that may be imputed to the organization, the lawyer is obligated to do what is necessary for the organization's best interests. Rule 1.13 further provides that such efforts include referring the matter to the highest authority that can act on behalf of the organization.

As originally drafted by the Kutak Commission, Rule 1.13 also provided that when a corporation's highest authority fails to act on a matter that has been referred by corporate counsel, and counsel reasonably fears that the organization is threatened by substantial injury, counsel could take further remedial action in the organization's best interests, including revealing a confidence to directors, shareholders or other persons outside of the organization. As adopted by the House of Delegates, however, the corporate attorney has no right to take any remedial measures other than contacting the organization's highest authorities. If the attorney's efforts are unsuccessful, his or her only option is to resign.

 ## The Debate and the Conflict Continue

Many legal commentators have expressed disenchantment with the Model Rules as adopted by the ABA's House of Delegates. According to David Luban, the successful opponents of the Kutak Commission had the individual, defenseless criminal defendant in mind when they advocated the importance of client confidentiality. Their reasoning is inappropriate when considering the powerful corporation engaged in shady business practices of questionable legality. He draws from the Ford Pinto case. Defective design of the fuel tank resulted in a number of deaths and, eventually, a criminal indictment against Ford Motor Corporation for reckless homicide. Luban asks whether Ford's general legal counsel had the obligation to disclose the danger posed by the faulty design and engineering. He points out that the adopted Model Rules, as adopted by the ABA, would not have permitted legal counsel to take action. Rule 1.6 permits disclosure of only criminal acts. Until Ford was actually indicted, there was no legal

precedent to warn its attorneys that the corporation's actions might be considered criminal (Luban 1988).

Harry Jones (1978) distinguishes the lawyer as advocate from the lawyer as counsellor. As a counsellor, an attorney functions without opposing counsel present to represent the interests of many of the people who may be affected by the counsellor's advice. A judge is not present to monitor the fairness of the arrangements. He suggests that the lawyer as counsellor must be aware of both the social worth and the legality of the results he or she helps a client accomplish. Writing before the adoption of the Model Rules, Jones criticizes their predecessors, the Canons and the Code of Professional Responsibility, for failing to recognize the unique position of the nonadvocate.

R. W. Nahstoll (1984) also is concerned that the Model Rules as adopted by the House of Delegates suffer from excessive concern with the ethics of courtroom advocacy. He believes that the ABA Rules make it possible for clients to use and exploit their attorneys because the rules do not permit attorneys to act to protect third persons from injury and because they prohibit an attorney from acting according to his or her personal standards of morality.

Criticism of the ABA's Model Rules has extended beyond the academy. The ABA's Model Rules of Professional Conduct do not govern the ethical conduct of lawyers. The law of ethical conduct is actually found in rules adopted by the highest courts of each of the fifty states and the District of Columbia. There are 51 separate codes of conduct (Hazard and Hodes 1987). Many states substantially changed the provisions of Model Rule 1.6 as they pertain to an attorney's responsibilities to reveal client fraud. Like the Kutak Commission's proposal, but unlike the rule adopted by the House of Delegates, six states either permit or require lawyers to report not only future criminal acts but future fraudulent acts as well. Although the ABA rule does not allow for the rectification of past criminal or fraudulent conduct, eleven states have rules that do. Ten states also allow or require lawyers to prevent future crime that could cause financial or property damage in addition to death or bodily harm (Hazard and Koniak 1990).

One of the most powerful critiques of the Model Rules was expressed by the court-appointed Bankruptcy Trustee for O.P.M Leasing Services, Inc. O.P.M. filed a bankruptcy petition in 1981. It soon surfaced that the company had been involved in a massive fraud scheme that included creating phony leases and altering the terms of genuine leases in order to procure millions of dollars in financing from major lending institutions. For several years, O.P.M.'s law firm unknowingly assisted the fraudulent activities. At some point, the firm gained knowledge in the course of its professional relationship with O.P.M. The firm sought legal counsel concerning its ethical obligations—whether to reveal the fraud and disclose client confidences or withdraw from representation. The firm kept the fraud secret for several months after being assured by the officers of O.P.M. that the fraud had ended. Upon discovering that the fraud had not ended, the law firm resigned its representation. Upon advice of counsel, the firm refrained from disclosing the fraud to its victims or to the law firm that look over the legal representation of O.P.M. (Hazard and Koniak 1990).

In his report to the court, the Bankruptcy Trustee wrote that in his opinion O.P.M.'s law firm could have followed other courses of action consistent with their ethical obligations. In addition, he took the opportunity to comment on the ABA House of Delegate's rejection of the Kutak Commission proposals:

> The Trustee considers the ABA's action outrageous and irresponsible. The Trustee hopes that the ABA will reconsider the issue and that the state bar authorities will reject the rule in favor of one that goes at least as far as the proposed rule in permitting lawyers to prevent their clients from committing future frauds and using lawyers as instruments in fraudulent schemes (Rotunda 1988, p. 95).

⊠ Alternative Mechanisms

In addition to the formal ethical obligations that govern a lawyer's responsibilities, other measures have been instituted to augment attorneys' attempts to regulate themselves. The Securities and Exchange Commission uses its regulatory powers to encourage lawyers to report illegal activities directly to the agency. In addition to ongoing reporting requirements, securities law requires corporations to disclose certain information when issuing stock. Until recently, only attorneys who had actively participated in securities fraud with their clients were held liable by the SEC for aiding and abetting fraud. In *SEC v. National Student Marketing Corporation* (1972), however, the SEC filed a complaint against eighteen defendants, including four attorneys and two law firms. The agency charged that the law firms had violated securities laws when they allowed their clients to consummate a stockholder-approved merger on the basis of a proxy statement containing materially misleading financial information. The complaint stated that the lawyers should have insisted that the proxy statement be revised. If the corporation refused a revision, the SEC maintained that the lawyers should have withdrawn and reported the violations to the agency. A great deal of controversy surrounded the complaint because the lawyers were not directly involved in the scheme and did not benefit from it (Burke 1981). The case was eventually settled with the law firm agreeing to pay a large fine and to institute internal procedures to reduce the risk of the matter reoccurring (Lorne 1978).

Corporations themselves have developed policies to clarify the role and independence of in-house legal counsel. Connecticut General Insurance Company and Mead Corporation instruct their general legal counsel to report serious disagreements about legal matters to the chair of the board or to the full board of directors. General legal counsel for The General Motors Corporation is appointed by the board of directors so that the lines of ultimate responsibility are clear (Burke 1981).

Perhaps the least desirable attempt to force an attorney to blow the whistle on client fraud is a civil lawsuit filed against the attorney by the innocent third party victim to the fraud. Until recently, a lawyer's only liability was to his or her own client for malpractice. Privately retained lawyers are becoming increasingly more vulnerable to complaints by innocent victims even though the lawyers did not knowingly and intentionally participate in the illegal or fraudulent act (Gillers 1989).

The dilemma hits when the lawyer must disclose confidential information in order to avoid civil liability, but is unable to invoke an exception to the ethical rule imposing confidentiality in the jurisdiction in which he or she is practicing law.

For those attorneys who are employed by corporations and who elect to blow the whistle on their employers, the problems can be even more devastating than they are for a lawyer in private practice. In most states, individuals who work for private employers can be discharged at-will if they do not have a contract with the employer or a collective bargaining agreement. Certain exceptions have been created by statute, such as prohibitions against firing someone based on their race, sex, religion or national origin. Several states have also recognized an exception to discharging an employee who has disclosed employer misconduct or refused to participate in that misconduct (Howard 1988).

The legal rights of an attorney-employee should arguably stand in the same shoes as any other employee who has blown the whistle on the boss. Two recent court decisions, however, suggest that may not necessarily be the case. In *Herbster v. North American Co. for Life and Health Ins.* (1986), the court rejected the claim of a lawyer who alleged that he had been discharged from a corporation in retaliation for refusing to destroy memoranda that implicated his employer in fraud. In *Willy v. Coastal Corp.* (1986), the court rejected the claim of a lawyer who alleged that he had been discharged in retaliation for refusing to alter the findings of a report he had authored concerning his employer's noncompliance with environmental protection laws and for agreeing with state officials to correct several of the company's environmental problems.

In both cases the courts ruled that the special nature of the attorney-client relationship required a different solution than if the two plaintiffs had been ordinary employees. The courts concluded that the attorneys' professional obligations included the duty to keep client confidences. If they believed that they had

been asked to perform illegal acts, their recourse was to terminate their employment. Based on an attorney's standard of professional conduct, the courts refused to rule that the employers were liable for wrongful discharge (Gillers 1988).

 Conclusion

Corporate attorneys face major ethical and professional dilemmas. Depending on the jurisdiction in which they practice, their own rules of ethical conduct may make it impossible for them to blow the whistle on illegal activities performed by their client. Yet, the corporation's attorney, whether he or she is hired as an employee or retained from a private law firm, frequently is in the best possible position to identify illegal and fraudulent practices, take steps to prevent them or to limit the damage already done to innocent victims. As the facts surface surrounding the savings and loan and banking crises, the role played and the benefits reaped by many corporate attorneys will surely raise new concerns about the moral and ethical responsibilities of lawyers to blow the whistle.

If confidentiality is upheld as an all-important value in the nonadvocacy practice, there will be circumstances in which crimes and frauds continue; money and lives will be lost because a lawyer was prevented from disclosing wrongdoing, or was so befuddled by the state of the law that he or she did not know in which direction to turn. To date, it is a trade-off that we have been willing to make in order to encourage clients to confide in their counsel and for counsel to zealously represent their clients. It is, however, a trade-off that has proved to be too expensive, both for the public's interest and for the lawyers who have to compromise their personal morality.

 References

Burke, M. (1981). The duty of confidentiality and disclosing corporate misconduct. *The Business Lawyer, 36,* 239–295.

Freedman, M. (1975). Judge Frankel's search for truth. *University of Pennsylvania Law Review, 123,* 1060–1089.

Gillers, S. (1988). Protecting lawyers who just say no. *Georgia State University Law Review, 5,* 1–26.

Gillers, S., (1987). Ethics that bite: Lawyers' liability to third parties. *Litigation* (2), 13.8–M.

Halpert, T. A. (1985). Protecting the professional whistleblower. *Nova Law Review, 10,* 1–27.

Hazard, G., & Koniak, S. (1990). *The law and the ethics of lawyering.* Westbury, New York: The Foundation Press, Inc.

Hazard, G., & Hodes, W. (1987). *The law of lawyering: A handbook on the model rules of professional conduct.* New York: West.

Hazard, G. (1984). Rectification of client fraud: Death and revival of a professional norm. *Emory Law Journal, 33,* 78–39.

Howard, J. L. (1988). Current developments in whistleblower protection. *Labor Law Journal* (2), *39,* 67–80.

Jones, H. (1978). Lawyers and justice: The uneasy partisanship. *Villanova Law Review, 23,* 957–978.

Lorne, S. M. (1978). The corporate and securities advisor, the public interest and professional ethics. *Michigan Law Review, 76,* 425–469.

Luban, D. (1988). *Lawyers and justice: An ethical study.* Princeton, NJ: Princeton University Press.

McCormick (1972). *Evidence,* Section 87.

Nahstoll, R. W. (1984). The lawyer's allegiance: Priorities regarding confidentiality. *Washington and Lee Law Review, 41,* 421–452.

Peters, C., & Branch, T. (1972). *Blowing the whistle: Dissent in the public interest.* New York: Praeger Publishers.

Rotunda, R. (1988). Client fraud: Blowing the whistle, other options. *Trial,* November 1988, 92–97.

Westin, A. (1981). *Whistle-blowing: loyalty and dissent in the corporation.* New York: McGraw-Hill:

Cases

Herbster v. North American Co. for Life and Health Ins., 501 N.E. 2d 343(1986).

SEC v. National Student Marketing Corporation, [1977-1978 Transfer Binder] FED. SEC. L. REP. (CCH) para. 96,027 at 91,600 (D.D.C. 1977).

Willy v. Coastal Corp., 647 F.Supp. 116 (S.D. Tex. 1986).

DISCUSSION QUESTIONS

1. Do you think corporate attorneys should notify the authorities if they uncover wrongdoing?

2. In this section, you read about whistleblowers who received millions of dollars for filing qui tam suits. Should corporate attorneys be able to file these suits against their own companies? Explain.

3. Should attorneys ever be punished for exposing illegal activity by their employers? Explain.

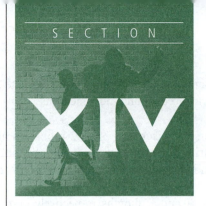
The Corrections Subsystem and White-Collar Crime

 ## Introduction

On January 10, 2011, Tom Delay, former Majority Leader of the U.S. House of Representatives, stood before Texas State District Judge Pat Priest, waiting to be sentenced after being found guilty of money laundering by a jury a few months earlier. Prosecutors urged the judge to impose the maximum 10-year sentence while Delay's defense attorneys argued that Delay had been punished enough as a result of his participation in the justice process. The judge sentenced Delay to 3 years in prison. Later Delay told a Fox News correspondent that his conviction was politically motivated by those opposed to his views. He said, "I have an ego and I have arrogance that I fight every day. But arrogance is not a crime that you put someone in jail for. This is a political trial" (Sullivan, 2011, n.p.).

Delay was not the only white-collar offender sentenced that week. Consider the following sentences handed down to less popular white-collar offenders who were sentenced around the same time:

- A pastor in Tampa, Florida was sentenced to 2.5 years in prison and 3 years probation after pleading guilty to embezzling more than $800,000. During sentencing, the judge used a Biblical quote to justify the pastor's sentence: "To whom much is given, much is expected" (Moorhead, 2011, n.p.).
- In Maryland, two men were sentenced in federal court to 30 and 37 months, respectively, in prison after pleading guilty in a kickback scheme they used to steal $1.5 million as part of one of the offender's business. The judge ordered the offenders to pay restitution and "entered an order formally forfeiting the defendant's interests in their homes to the government" (U.S. Attorneys Office Middle District of Pennsylvania, 2011).
- A developer was sentenced to 3 years probation after he pleaded guilty to "harboring stolen antiques" he removed from clients' homes. The developer was also sentenced to 500 hours of community service (Sayre, 2011).
- A Florida day care operator was ordered to pay $79,000 in restitution to the government after she pleaded guilty to defrauding the government for meals provided in her center. Because of the conviction, the woman "may not hold any professional licenses in the state and is banned from entering into any contracts with the state" (Voyles, 2011).
- Guidant LLC, a medical device manufacturing company, was sentenced to 3 years probation and ordered to pay $286 million in criminal fines and forfeiture after being convicted of "withholding information from the FDA regarding catastrophic failures in some of its lifesaving devices" (U.S. Department of Justice, 2011).

The same week that Delay was sentenced, another former politician—Edwin Edwards, the former governor of Louisiana—was released from prison after serving 9.5 years of his 10-year sentence for racketeering. The last 6 months of his sentence was to be spent on home incarceration. On house arrest, the 83-year-old was given specific rules and guidelines describing the types of behaviors he could engage in until his 10-year sentence was complete.

Other than being sentenced around the same time, or released from a sentence at the same time, these examples demonstrate several patterns relevant to the sentencing of white-collar offenders. First, white-collar offenders are subject to a wide range of sentencing alternatives. Second, as Delay's case showed, it is common for white-collar offenders to deny their criminal involvement even after being sentenced. Third, some white-collar offenders are indeed sentenced to prison. Fourth, organizations—as well as individuals—can be sanctioned in white-collar crime cases. Fifth, fines can be quite substantial in these cases.

While these patterns are evident in the punishment of white-collar offenders, to fully address how punishment is meted out against this group of offenders, in this section attention is given to sentencing dynamics, prison, probation and parole, fines, alternative sanctions, the punishing of corporations, and reasons for punishing white-collar offenders. By addressing these areas, readers will gain insight into the dynamics guiding the sanctioning of white-collar offenders and an appreciation of the underlying factors that contribute to the punishment experience for white-collar offenders.

✉ Sentencing Dynamics and White-Collar Offenders

To some, the sentencing of offenders is the most important part of the justice process in that it is through sanctioning offenders that goals of the justice system can be addressed and equal treatment of offenders can be promoted. Indeed, the ideals of justice are borne out through the application of just and fair punishments that are tied to the nature of the offense rather than to the class or status of the offender. The ability of the justice system to actually achieve "blind justice" can be assessed through an examination of the sentencing dynamics surrounding white-collar offenses. These dynamics can be understood through a consideration of sentencing practices, sentencing policies, and sentencing patterns.

Sentencing Practices and White-Collar Offenders

Research on the sentencing of white-collar offenders has provided mixed messages about issues related to the dispositions given to this group of offenders. The conventional assumption has been that white-collar offenders are sentenced more leniently than other offenders. Some studies on specific types of white-collar offenders have uncovered evidence of leniency. For example, a study of offenders convicted of Medicaid fraud in California found that this type of white-collar offenders received more lenient sentences than comparable conventional offenders (Tillman & Pontell, 1992). Tillman and Pontell (1992) cite three factors that contribute to the leniency afforded white-collar offenders. First, white-collar offenders have a "status shield" as a result of their occupational prestige, and this prestige is seen as protecting them from the stiff sentences given to street offenders. Second, white-collar offenders are able to hire better attorneys than conventional offenders. Third, the complexity of white-collar crime cases potentially creates enough doubt that more lenient sanctions are justified by criminal justice officials. Incidentally, the authors' own research found that when civil and administrative sanctions were added to the "total sentence," sanctions were more equitable.

Wheeler and his colleagues' (1982) interviews with judges found that the judges considered how the white-collar offender experienced the criminal justice process and some viewed participation in the process as a punishment in and of itself for white-collar offenders. The judges also reported considering the sanctions imposed on white-collar offenders by civil, administrative, and professional proceedings. In addition, the age of the offender, his or her health, and the impact that the sentence might have on family members were also considered by judges.

Interestingly, while the judges reported considering extra-legal variables in sentencing white-collar offenders, some studies have found that white-collar offenders actually receive longer sentences than comparable conventional offenders—they are sentenced more severely than people think. One study, for example, found that after Watergate white-collar offenders "were more likely to be sentenced to prison, but for shorter periods of time than less-educated persons convicted of common crimes" (Hagan & Palloni, 1986, p. 603). Examining presentence investigation of 1,094 crimes occurring in seven federal districts between 1976 and 1978, Wheeler, Weisburd, and Bode (1982) found that white-collar offenders were more likely to go to prison and to be sentenced for longer periods of time than comparable conventional offenders were.

Another study found that the type of sanction given to offenders was not tied to their status, but it was tied to the occupation in which the white-collar defendant worked (Hagan & Parker, 1985). Based on this perspective, Hagan and Parker suggested "that the substitution of class for status measures is crucial" (p. 312). In essence, the structure of certain occupations (which are related to the class of occupations) provides different opportunities for offenders, as well as different types of remedies from the criminal justice system.

Examining the influence of class position, Benson (1989) reviewed the sanctions given to 174 white-collar offenders sentenced in the 1970s. He found that informal social control sanctions were influenced by class position, but class position did not influence formal social control responses. Focusing on how loss of a job impacted sentence, he found that losing one's job did not influence the sentence given in the justice process. Managers and employers (as white-collar offenders) were less likely to lose their jobs than nonmanagers and employees. He also found that public officials and professionals were "more vulnerable to informal sanctioning than employers and managers," leading Benson to conclude, "the advantage of certain class positions seems to be more pronounced outside rather than inside the legal system" (p. 475).

Using the same data that they used in their 1982 study but adding a social class variable, Weisburd, Waring, and Wheeler (1990) found that class and occupational status were "complementary not competing indicators" (p. 237). They found that offenders "with high class positions receive the most severe prison sanction" (p. 237). In a subsequent study, Weisburd Wheeler, Waring, and Bode (1991) found that most offenders convicted of offenses labeled white-collar offenses are not actually upper-class offenders, but middle-class white-collar offenders.

Researchers have identified factors other than class and status that seemed to influence the sentencing of white-collar offenders. One study showed that the judicial district where the white-collar case was tried influenced sentencing outcomes at the federal level (Hagan, Negal, & Albonetti, 1980). Another study found that the combination of sanctions available to punish different types of white-collar offenders influenced the type of sentence given to them (Waldfogel, 1995). Research by Albonetti found that the sanctioning of white-collar offenders was tied to the complexity of the cases and to pleading guilty (Albonetti, 1999). In terms of guilty pleas, she noted that "pleas vary in their worth to prosecuting attorneys" (p. 321). In other words, for some guilty pleas, prosecuting attorneys are willing to offer a more greatly reduced sentence in exchange for a guilty plea. For example, a complex case that could be difficult to prove might receive a greater sentence reduction in exchange for a plea as opposed to a "smoking gun" case where the case should be easy to prove.

Sentencing Policies and White-Collar Offenders

The Sentencing Reform Act was passed in 1984 as part of the Comprehensive Crime Control Act. One aim of the act was "to remedy individualized disparity in federal criminal sentences and to equalize sentences for 'street criminals' and 'white-collar offenders'" (Ryan-Boyle, Simon, & Yebler, 1991, p. 739). The **U.S. Sentencing Commission** was created as part of the act; it has the responsibility of developing strategies to promote fairer sentencing at the federal level through the development of sentencing guidelines. As initially envisioned, judges were expected to sentence offenders within a certain range based on the recommendation found in the guidelines. Judges could decrease or increase sanctions through departures if circumstances warranted. For white-collar offenders, the guidelines promoted imprisonment because incarceration was seen "as the most effective deterrent for white-collar offenders" (Ryan-Boyle et al., 1991, p. 756). As a result, the guidelines "increased both the probability of imprisonment and the length of the sentence for most white-collar offenses" (Cohen, 1992, p. 1100).

When first created, the federal guidelines were seen as mandatory in nature, with judges required to provide a justification for departing from the guidelines. After the U.S. Supreme Court reviewed the guidelines in *Booker v. Washington,* the guidelines were revised to be advisory in nature, thus theoretically giving judges back the discretion that was taken away when the guidelines were first created.

For some white-collar crimes, sentences at the federal level became even stiffer with the passage of the Sarbanes-Oxley Act in 2002. Passed in reaction to the corporate scandals that had just occurred, the act called for a number of restrictive strategies to prevent white-collar crime. In terms of penalties, the act doubled prison sentences from up to 10 years to up to 20 years for managers who falsified financial statements. In addition to stricter penalties, the act called for improved ethics training, improved corporate governance strategies, and better understanding of internal control efforts (Canada, Kuhn, & Sutton, 2008). The act has been described as "the most comprehensive economic regulation since the New Deal" (Vakkur, McAfee, & Kipperman, 2010, p. 18). Another author recently noted that "the implications of [the act] are still an open issue" (Dey, 2010, p. 53).

Surveys of 43 corporate executives and 130 graduate students in accounting found that the threat of jail time that is prescribed in the Sarbanes-Oxley Act has limited effectiveness in deterring financial statement fraud (Ugrin & Odom, 2010). The authors found that changing from one to 10 years' incarceration had a deterrent effect, but changing from 10 to 20 years did not. Respondents indicated they would be no more deterred by a 20-year sentence than they would be a 10-year prison sentence. While research shows that the sanctions would not deter criminal behavior, research also shows that corporate risk taking declined after the act was passed; however, the decrease is possibly attributed to other types of regulations including internal controls and increased board oversight (Dey, 2010).

Sentencing Patterns

Figure 14.1 shows the types of penalties given for different types of offenses at the federal level between October 1, 2003 and September 20, 2004 (Bureau of Justice Statistics, 2006). As shown in the figure, variation exists among white-collar offenders and between white-collar offenders and conventional offenders. Overall, three fourths of all offenders were sentenced to prison. Among specific types of white-collar offenders, the following patterns are shown:

- About 60% of fraud offenders were sentenced to prison and roughly 30% were given probation.
- Roughly 45% of embezzlers were sent to prison and 40% were given probation.
- Less than a fourth of anti-trust offenders were sent to prison and just over half were given probation.
- About a third of food and drug offenders were sent to prison and about two thirds were given probation.

In reviewing the figure, it becomes obvious that a higher percentage of burglaries get prison sentences than any of the white-collar offense types. On the surface this may seem to suggest that white-collar offenders are less likely to be sentenced to prison than conventional offenders. However, these estimates do not control for past criminal histories or other factors that might influence sentencing decisions.

Table 14.1 shows the types of federal sentences and mean and median lengths of sentences for various offense types during the same time frame. A few points are worth highlighting. First, roughly 6,000 offenders were incarcerated for offenses that could be characterized as white-collar offenses (though they may not all actually be white-collar offenders). Second, white-collar offenders tend to receive shorter prison

Figure 14.1 Sentence Types for Offenders Sentenced in Criminal Cases Terminated, by Offense, October 1, 2003–September 30, 2004

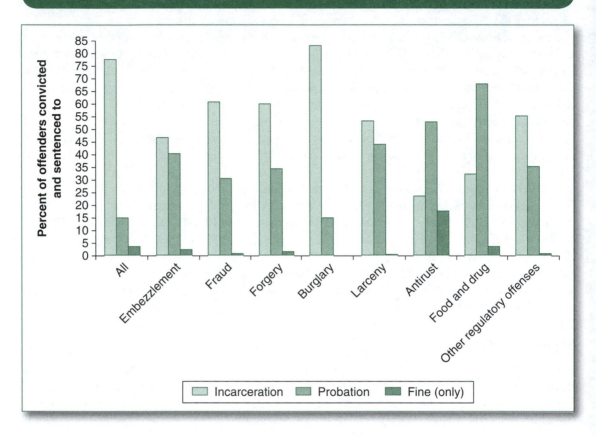

sentences than other offenders. Third, the average probation sentence for white-collar offenders tended to be higher than the average probation sentence given to other offenders.

Some have argued that the sentencing of white-collar offenders has gotten a little out of control, with some sentences seemingly far too severe. Noting that the sentences are the result of the development of sentencing guidelines, Podgor (2007) writes:

> In an attempt to achieve a neutral sentencing methodology, one that is class-blind, a system has evolved in the U.S. that fails to recognize unique qualities of white-collar offenders, fails to balance consideration of both the acts and the actors, and subjects offenders to draconian sentences that for some cases exceed their life expectancy. (p. 734)

Jonathan Simon, a law professor at the University of California, Berkley, compared the severe prison sentences given to white-collar offenders to the types of sentences given to drug offenders, stating that "both represent increasingly irrational levels of punishment" (Moyer, 2009a, n.p.).

Table 14.1 Type and Length of Sentences Imposed for Sentenced Offenders, by Offense, October 1, 2003–September 30, 2004

Offense	Offenders Convicted and Sentenced in Criminal Cases That Terminated During 2004							
	Number				Sentence Length in Months			
					Incarceration		Probation	
	Total	Incarceration	Probation	Fine (only)	Mean	Median	Mean	Median
All offenses	74,782	58,106	11,067	2,639	59.70	37.0	32.2	36.0
Embezzlement	646	302	261	14	16.00	12.0	40.1	36.0
Fraud	8,677	5,278	2,661	69	26.60	18.0	38.9	36.0
Forgery	73	44	8	1	20.00	18.0	42.2	36.0
Burglary	53	44	8	0	28.40	24.0	—	—
Larceny	1,307	695	573	6	31.30	18.0	40.3	36.0
Antitrust	17	4	9	3	—	—	—	—
Food/drug	28	9	19	1	—	—	29.4	30.0
Other regulatory offenses	791	439	281	6	28.10	18.0	33.1	36.0

Prison sentences for some first-time white-collar offenders "can exceed the sentences seen for violent street crimes, such as murder and rape" (Podgor, 2007, p. 733). Podgor contrasts white-collar sentencing with so-called three strikes laws. In the three strikes policies, the primary emphasis is on the actor. If the actor commits three offenses, a strict penalty results. In white-collar sentencing practices, attention is on the action of committing a white-collar offense. If an offender commits one white-collar offense, a stricter penalty results.

Some have suggested that the apparent disparate sentencing resulting in long sentences for white-collar offenders might simply reflect the fact that the vast majority of white-collar offenders are kept out of the justice system in the first place. Gerber (1994) commented, "The apparent harshness of sentencing of white-collar offenders proves to be the result of a diversion of less serious offenders from the criminal court" (p. 164). For those white-collar crime cases that make their way into the justice system, by the time the offenders get to the judge, the government often has substantial evidence showing that the white-collar offenders have done something remarkably harmful (Wheeler et al., 1982). In other words, white-collar offenders do not go to court unless they have done something "really really bad."

The white-collar offender with the longest prison sentence on record is Shalmon Weiss. Weiss, whose misdeeds resulted in the collapse of National Heritage Life Insurance, was sentenced in 2000 by a Florida judge to 845 years in prison. According to the Bureau of Prisons, Weiss is scheduled to be released on November 23, 2754 (Moyer, 2009b). Chances are he will not live until his release date.

⊠   The Prison Experience for White-Collar Offenders

While a handful of studies have considered sentencing issues related to white-collar offenders, very few studies have focused on the experience of white-collar offenders in prison. Part of this lack of research has to do with the relatively few white-collar inmates in prison at any given time in the United States. It is extremely difficult to gain access to these inmates and even if access is granted to a prison, it is even more unlikely that white-collar inmates would agree to participate in a study while incarcerated. Some researchers have done an excellent job locating and interviewing white-collar inmates after they have been released (Benson & Cullen, 1988). Others have relied on anecdotal accounts and media reports to generate understanding about how white-collar offenders experience prison (Payne, 2003b). From these efforts, one can point to five dynamics of the white-collar prison experience: (1) depression, (2) danger, (3) deprivations, (4) deviance, and (5) doldrums (see Payne, 2003b, for a thorough discussion of each of these dynamics). It is important to stress that the experience of incarceration for conventional offenders might be described through a discussion of similar dynamics. However, the source of these characteristics and their consequences likely vary between the two types of offenders. After discussing these dynamics, attention will be given to the way that white-collar offenders adjust to prison.

Depression and the White-Collar Offender

For some white-collar offenders, it is likely that various degrees of depression will be experienced, particularly in the initial stages of incarceration. While all inmates likely experience different forms of depression, the sources of depression for white-collar offenders manifest themselves differently. Their sources of depression include (1) stressful changes coming from one's first exposure to prison life, (2) loss of job, (3) loss of status, (4) isolation, and (5) sentencing dynamics (Payne, 2003b).

With regard to *stressful changes* as a source of depression, white-collar offenders who have never been to prison experience an enormous amount of anxiety both before their incarceration and in the early stages of the incarceration. As Michael Benson and Frank Cullen (1988) point out, "For the first-time offender, the stress created by the prospect of going to prison probably exceeds any other that the person may have experienced" (p. 209). Another expert told a reporter that for white-collar offenders, "prison is equivalent to shock therapy, suddenly exposing [white-collar] offenders to people and circumstances they never would have imagined" ("Is Martha Stewart Truly a Changed Woman?" 2005). Prison administrators have been encouraged to watch for signs of depression in an effort to prevent possible suicide attempts among white-collar offenders. For those who experience stress in their initial stages of incarceration, as time passes they will better adjust to the incarceration experience (Benson & Cullen, 1988).

Another source of depression for white-collar offenders is the *loss of their jobs.* While their crimes were often committed against their employers, and as part of their jobs, individuals define themselves by their careers. For convicted white-collar inmates, their loss of a career identity can be particularly problematic. They go from having a respectable job title to having an inmate number. Former California Republican Congressman Randy "Duke" Cunningham went from being a member of the U.S. House of Representatives to inmate 94405-198 after being sentenced to prison for accepting bribes from military contractors. Some inmates will have prison jobs to replace their former white-collar jobs. Not surprisingly, the pay is not so good in prison. White-collar inmates will go from making hundreds of thousands, if not millions of dollars, to making 12 cents an hour "for scrubbing floors and toilets" (Green, 2007). In the end, these changes in career identities can potentially be a source of depression, at least initially in the incarceration experience.

Somewhat related, *loss of status* can be another potential source of depression for white-collar inmates. These are individuals who go from being in charge in their occupations and businesses to individuals who are ordered around by prison officials and intimidated by fellow inmates. In other words, they go from being at the top of the social and occupational hierarchy outside of prison to the bottom of the social hierarchy inside of prison. Benson's (1990) interviews with white-collar offenders found that inmates experience what he referred to as status degradation as a result of their conviction. He notes that white-collar inmates even lose "control over the presentation of self" (p. 522).

Isolation is another potential source of depression for white-collar inmates. Because so few white-collar offenders are in prison at any given time, it may be difficult for them to find peers with whom they can interact in prison. Much of their time may be spent alone until they find ways to communicate with fellow inmates. For example, Bernie Madoff reportedly doled out financial advice to fellow inmates who sought it and spent his time with a fellow white-collar inmate and an organized crime boss (Searcey & Efrati, 2011).

Interestingly, *sentencing dynamics* can also be a source of depression in white-collar inmates. Recall from above that white-collar inmates receive shorter sentences than conventional inmates. What makes this particularly ironic is that depression and adjustment problems are more prone to occur in the first 6 months or so of incarceration (Payne, 2003b). After that initial introduction to incarceration, inmates are able to adjust to the incarceration experience (Benson & Cullen, 1988). By the time white-collar inmates are released from prison, many have, in effect, likely become accustomed to the incarceration experience.

▲ **Photo 14.1** Former U.S. Congressman Randy "Duke" Cunningham (R-CA) lost his identity as a career politician and was given a prison number as his new identity.

▲ **Photo 14.2** White-collar inmates have little in common with other incarcerated offenders. They are older, have different life histories, have had little exposure to violence, and have not led the traditional criminal lifestyle.

Danger and the White-Collar Offender

Another dynamic surrounding the incarceration experience of white-collar offenders centers around their concerns about being injured. Four themes arise regarding danger and white-collar offenders: (1) celebrity bashing, (2) prison placement, (3) prison culture/socialization, and (4) exaggerated concerns. With regard to **celebrity bashing,** some celebrity offenders are attacked by inmates seeking fame and notoriety. John Geoghan, a Catholic priest well known for sexually abusing more than 130 children over his career, was beaten and strangled to death by inmate Joseph Druce in August 2003. Bernie Madoff was allegedly beaten up in prison and treated for broken ribs and multiple bruises in the first year of his incarceration. While receiving widespread media attention, the story was never confirmed by prison officials or Madoff, which is not surprising given that reporting victimization would potentially place Madoff at risk for subsequent victimization.

In terms of *prison placement,* some prisons and jails are more dangerous than others for white-collar offenders. Between sentencing and admissions, offenders are often held in a detention center that may include all types of offenders. White-collar offenders, particularly those who might be targeted for an attack, might be placed in solitary confinement for their protection (Moyer, 2009b). Also, while many white-collar offenders are sentenced to minimum security prisons, where the risk of violence is much lower, with the growing trend of longer prison sentences for white-collar offenders, some are being sent to higher security level prisons, which are more dangerous (O'Donnell, 2004).

Prison culture/socialization is relevant to the danger faced by white-collar inmates in that this offender group is not typically aware of the prison culture, nor have these offenders been socialized how to behave in prison. The prison subculture includes offenders who have been exposed to, and have histories of, a great deal of violence in their lives. This is most likely not the case for white-collar offenders. One reporter quoted a prison consultant to white-collar offenders who said, "These guys have never been in a fight in their lives—they don't know what violence is, and now they're entering a world where anything can happen" (Shapiro, 2009, n.p.). Describing the importance of prison socialization, another prison consultant advised that white-collar offenders do not know prison rules, like "changing the television channel can start a fight" (O'Donnell & Willing, 2003).

Though danger exists, from a scientific perspective, one can note that the concerns about danger are somewhat over exaggerated. Violence is relatively infrequent in minimum security prisons, where most white-collar offenders are housed. As well, the rate of prison assaults against inmates is much lower today than in the past (Bureau of Justice Statistics, 2011). In some ways, the fear of harm is likely more inhibiting and significant than the actual experience of harm for white-collar offenders. With time, they adjust to the prison environment and anxiety decreases (Benson & Cullen, 1988). Here is how one incarcerated white-collar offender described this process to an interviewer: "The inmates see me as someone they can talk to because . . . I've worked with the general public. . . . I expected to be ridiculed because I've been to school. And I expected to be bullied, but I haven't been" (Dhami, 2007, p. 68).

Deprivations and the White-Collar Offender

Prison deprives inmates of liberties, rights, freedom, and lifestyles to which they were previously accustomed. For white-collar inmates accustomed to certain lifestyles, the experience of deprivations might be particularly problematic. Something as basic as food consumption will be very different for white-collar inmates. One reporter team said that the food at one low-security prison was so bad that inmates "prefer microwaved groundhogs captured in the prison yard" (O'Donnell & Willing, 2003). A law professor told a reporter the following about a white-collar offender who was preparing for a prison stint: "His meal choices will not be what he's used to. . . . His diet will be prison food, which probably makes military or college dorm food look good" (Green, 2007, n.p.). As the son of a cafeteria worker, I won't disparage cafeteria food. But the point is worth reiterating—those not accustomed to this environment will experience it differently from those who have been in similar situations in the past.

Of course, it is not just bad food that is a deprivation for white-collar offenders. The enormous status deprivation (or degradation as Benson, 1990, calls it) is particularly salient for white-collar offenders.

This degradation can be experienced as a punishment in and of itself. Trying to use this perspective as an argument for a more lenient sentence, Tom Delay's attorney pointed out in Delay's sentencing hearing that Delay "has fallen from the third most powerful position in this country to a man who is unemployed and unemployable" (Meyer, 2011).

For some offenders, the deprivations may be more significant than the danger they are concerned about in prison. Consider the following comments from former New York Chief Judge Sol Wachtler about his 13-month stay in prison as told to an interviewer:

> Believe it or not, the worst moment was not when I was stabbed and put in solitary confinement—although if you put splints under my fingernails and told me to tell you what happened in solitary, I couldn't, because the human mind locks these unpleasant thoughts out. No, the worst moment was when I was flown from one prison to another, with my wrists shackled together and a waist chain on, and I had to walk across the airport tarmac with everyone staring at me. And then the two sets of guards from the different prisons argued as to whom the chains belonged to. ("Judge Not," 1997, p. 30)

The judge was used to being above (and in control of) correctional officers. Upon his imprisonment, they were in control of him.

Prison Deviance and the White-Collar Offender

As many sociologists have noted, any time you have a group of individuals together, someone in that group will engage in some form of deviance. With a group of convicted offenders together, it seems safe to suggest that some will engage in deviant acts while incarcerated. Many offenders have long histories of rule breaking. They are not going to decide to "behave" simply because they are behind bars. Three types of violations are relevant with regard to white-collar inmates: rule violations, deviant use of the justice process, and jailstripe crimes (Payne, 2003b). In this context, the phrase rule violations simply refers to situations where inmates break prison rules. Sometimes the rule violations seem relatively minor. Martha Stewart, for example, supposedly made more ceramic figures per month than prison rules allowed. She made 12 figures in 5 months, but should have made only one per month (Waller, 2007). Other times, the rule violations might be more significant. For example, Washington, D.C., Mayor Marion Berry allegedly received oral sex from a prostitute in a crowded visiting room while he was incarcerated ("Ex-Mayor in 'Jail-Sex' Row," 1992).

Deviant misuse of the justice process refers to situations where offenders misuse the justice process in a way that gains them some sort of advantage. Filing unnecessary or unwarranted appeals, misuse of furloughs, and unnecessary participation in treatment programs are examples. Unnecessary participation in treatment programs is believed to be particularly problematic with white-collar offenders. While some believe that it is easier for white-collar offenders to be paroled than conventional offenders (e.g., one prosecutor said "they present much better than a guy with scars and tattoos and a nickname like 'Snake'"; "White-Collar Crime Rising," 2003), others have said that the nature of programming at the federal level makes it more difficult for white-collar offenders to have time taken off their sentences.

In particular, offenders receive time off of their sentences if they participate in a certain number of hours of treatment programs. The problem that arises is that white-collar inmates are often not in need of the types of treatment programs that are available. To take advantage of the opportunity to have their sanctions reduced, some white-collar offenders have allegedly "faked" their way into treatment programs. In his presentence report, for example, Sam Waksal (the former ImClone Systems Inc. CEO caught up in Martha Stewart's scandal) told the probation officer that he was a social drinker and that he consumed about five glasses of wine a week. By the time his sentencing hearing came around—about 3 months later—Waksal's attorney told the judge that Waksal had "recently developed a dependence on alcohol and would benefit from treatment for his newly acquired addiction" (Falkenberg, 2008, n.p.). Waksal is not alone in this category. Prison consultants report telling white-collar offenders how to get into the best treatment programs in order to be released earlier (Falkenberg, 2008). Of course, like Waksal, perhaps some of these offenders developed their drug abuse problems between their guilty conviction and the time they were sent to prison.

The phrase **jailstripe crimes** refers to criminal acts that offenders commit while incarcerated. In one case, for example, an offender who had been convicted of fraud and was serving his sentence in a minimum security prison orchestrated an identity theft scheme from inside prison that netted him $250,000 ("Inmate Ran Identity Theft Ring," 2011). An investigation by the Department of Justice's Office of Inspector General found that inmates routinely used prison telephones to commit criminal acts. Their investigation found that U.S. Attorneys had prosecuted 117 cases where offenders used prison phones to commit crime (U.S. Office of Inspector General, 1999). Of those 117, 25 were financial fraud cases. In one case uncovered in the investigation, an inmate used a prison telephone to run a "fraudulent employment match service" (p. 3). Consumers who contracted with the employment service would have been paying the inmate for services that he never provided. In another case, an inmate stole more than $100,000 from a trucking company (U.S. Office of Inspector General, 1999).

Doldrums

Another aspect of the white-collar inmates' experiences in prison can be characterized as "the doldrums." After becoming acquainted with the incarceration experience, white-collar inmates report being very bored with the incarceration experience. One former white-collar inmate told Benson and Cullen (1988): "It was kind of an unexperience. It was not nearly as frightening as I thought it would be" (p. 209). Perhaps that is because white-collar offenders expected the experience to be much worse than it actually was, and it turned out not to be as bad as feared, that boredom and monotony "have been cited as the worst part of the white-collar inmate's incarceration experiences" (Payne, 2003b, p. 105).

▲ **Photo 14.3** Does this look like a club to you? Would you want to be stuck here for 6 months with 1,000 offenders and 200 staff members who have control over your every move?

Adjusting to Prison Life

The above discussion is not meant to make it seem as if prison is too punitive for white-collar offenders or that white-collar offenders should be treated differently than conventional offenders. Instead, the intent was to call attention to the fact that the "incarceration experience" varies between conventional and white-collar offenders. One area where the experience is also different has to do with the tendency among members of the public to assume that white-collar offenders are not being "punished enough" during their prison stay. The moniker "Club Fed" is used to describe the supposed "club-like" atmosphere surrounding the prisons where white-collar inmates are often incarcerated. There are no bars, no fences, and no prison cells. Often, no structural barriers separate these prisons from the rest of society. Hence, it must not be that bad to be sentenced to "Club Fed."

"Club Fed" is a myth. Being incarcerated can be a difficult process for any offender. Offenders have limited rights, they have no autonomy, they are away from their family members, there is nothing to do, and they have concerns about their safety. Describing the punitive nature of prisons for white-collar offenders, one author commented,

> But the grim reality of prison life for today's white-collar criminal—the utter absence of privacy, the body-cavity strip searches, standing in line 90 minutes, much of it outdoors in any weather, to get unspeakable food—is definitely worse than they or the public expect. (Colvin, 2004, n.p.)

For white-collar offenders, the most significant part of the prison experience is their initial adjustment period. With this in mind, recall that judges justified shorter prison sentences (or no prison sentence) for white-collar offenders based on their "special sensitivity to incarceration" (Mann, Wheeler, & Sarat, 1980). Though it may be the case that the initial stages of incarceration are particularly difficult for white-collar offenders, some scholars have argued that white-collar offenders have the personalities, skills, and resources to adjust effectively to the stresses of prison life. Benson and Cullen (1988) interviewed 13 white-collar offenders incarcerated in four different correctional institutions. Their research showed that while offenders initially found incarceration to be quite stressful (probably the most stressful event they had ever faced), offenders were able to "eventually adjust to prison life" (p. 209). The authors note how some offenders found the experience "interesting in a sociological sense" (p. 209). They also found that many of the offenders denied their criminal status as a coping strategy. In addition, Benson and Cullen noted that white-collar inmates searched for ways to increase their social status (compared to fellow inmates) while incarcerated. In doing so, they "reject the prison subculture" (p. 213).

Because of an increase in the number of white-collar offenders being sentenced to prison, and convicted offenders' fears about their future incarceration experience, a new industry has evolved that can be coined the "white-collar prison consultant industry." In this field, experts (some of whom are former white-collar inmates themselves) provide future white-collar inmates advice on how to get used to prison. The consultants are hired to tell the future inmates "how to negotiate the perils of the U.S. penal system" (Kelly, 2009, p. 1). Said Kelly, "they teach you how to behave, they teach unwritten rules, most important, they teach how to survive" (p. 1). As noted above, they also teach white-collar inmates how to get into the "best" treatment programs to earn early release.

Steven Oberfest, CEO of Prison Coach, charges $200 an hour to prepare offenders for prison. He uses his past experience as an inmate as the source of his information (Shapiro, 2009). Oberfest, who calls himself an "inmate adaptation specialist," told another interviewer, "I can prepare you to go into hell" (Johnson, 2009, p. 1A). To capture this white-collar market (pun intended), one consultant even "changed his company name from American Prison Consultants to Wall Street Prison Consultants" (Johnson, 2009, p. 1A).

The Probation and Parole Experience for White-Collar Offenders

As shown above, many white-collar offenders are sentenced to probation and some are placed on parole after their incarceration in states where parole still exists. These are **community-based sanctions.** Community-based alternatives are popular for all types of offenders—conventional and white-collar alike.

There is a misperception that these sanctions are not punitive, when, in fact, offenders tend to define certain types of probation as especially punitive. While all types of offenders are subject to these sentencing alternatives, the way the sanctions are experienced varies between types of offenders.

One of the first studies on the probation experience of white-collar offenders was done by Michael Benson (1985b). He interviewed 22 federal probation officers and 30 white-collar probationers and found that for white-collar offenders the probation experience could be characterized as "going through the motions" (p. 429). He also found that the types of interactions between probation officers and white-collar offenders often allowed the offenders to continue to deny their criminal status. The officers interviewed did not believe that white-collar probationers would get in trouble while on probation and one agency viewed control as "unnecessary in the case of white-collar offenders" (p. 431). Said one probation officer, "They don't need supervision. Some of it is just chit chat" (p. 431). Other probation officers highlighted the need to help offenders get accustomed to the fact that they had been convicted and "to adjust psychologically to the stigmatization effects of conviction" (p. 432).

Focusing on their status, Benson (1985b) highlights one flaw that community supervision has for white-collar probationers. In particular, he notes that probation officers spend most of their time supervising offenders from a lower class than the officer's social class. In fact, one can argue that officers are trained both formally and informally how to supervise lower-class offenders. Conversely, officers are not always adequately prepared "to supervise their social equals or betters" (p. 435).

In a more recent study, Karen Mason (2007) interviewed 35 white-collar probationers to examine how shifts in penology have impacted their probation experiences. Her results highlighted the differences between white-collar offenders' probation experiences as compared to the experiences of other offenders. Among other things, she noted that the "workaday world of these offenders does not easily accommodate the demands of supervision, monitoring, and surveillance that are central to probation" (p. 28). The offenders described what they perceived as a bureaucratic model of probation that failed to offer offenders any sort of services or guidance. Referring to the loss of occupational status common among white-collar offenders, Mason noted that assisting white-collar offenders with reintegrative efforts "is no longer a priority in community supervision under the new penology" (p. 29).

Similar to Benson's research, Mason (2007) uncovered dynamics showing that white-collar offenders used aspects of the sanction to reject a criminal identity. In particular, she found that the probationers experienced the bureaucratic nature of probation (e.g., filling out forms and turning in records) in a way that allowed them to continue to deny their criminal status. They played by the rules in an effort to maintain "their own feelings of superiority and self-worth" (p. 30). Though maintaining a noncriminal identity, the white-collar probationers experienced a loss of autonomy, stigma, stress from the loss of autonomy, anxiety, shame for what they did to their families, and status degradation.

The notion of status degradation is particularly relevant with white-collar probationers. A power inversion occurs whereby probation officers gain a higher level of control over white-collar offenders (who are in an equal if not higher social status than probation officers). These aspects can be somewhat difficult to adjust to for white-collar offenders. Said one defense attorney about his client's probation sentence: "For someone who's not used to that, it's a real humiliation" (Sayre, 2011, n.p.). Some have warned that community corrections officers might exert extra power over white-collar offenders in order to make up for the difference in social statuses between white-collar probationers and officers. Minkes (1990) wrote:

> There is a temptation to gloat at the discomfiture of the rich and leave them to their fate. After all, poor people are sent to prison every day for property offenses of far less value; how much more should the rich be punished. However, this argument must not be turned on its head . . . probation

officers should be considering recommendations for probation, community service, compensation orders, and fines ... and using formal and informal contacts with sentencers to press home the comparisons of seriousness. (p. 130)

In other words, probation officers have an important role in ensuring that white-collar offenders are punished fairly.

⊠ Monetary Fines and White-Collar Offenders

White-collar offenders are also punished through the use of different types of monetary penalties. **Monetary penalties** include criminal fines, restitution, civil settlements, and compensatory and punitive damages awarded in civil trials. **Criminal fines** are monetary penalties awarded by the judge after an offender has been convicted of a crime. The fine is collected by the state (or federal) government and funds are allocated accordingly in the jurisdiction where the case was heard. Fines are not designed to go directly back to victims.

Some legal scholars have advocated that fines should be the primary sanction given to white-collar offenders and that imprisonment is an inappropriate, ineffective, and costly alternative. Richard Posner (1980) called for large fines to deter wrongdoing. He argued that a large fine would have deterrent power equal to imprisonment. He wrote,

> In a social cost benefit analysis of the choice between fining and imprisoning white-collar crimi-nals, the cost side of the analysis favors fining because ... the cost of collecting a fine from one who can pay it ... is lower than the cost of imprisonment. (p. 410)

From his perspective, such a practice was not unfair or biased toward the poor because he viewed a large fine as just as punitive as incarceration.

Research shows that judges do not see fines as having a significant impact on offending (Mann et al., 1980). In the judges' views, by the time offenders were convicted, many were either already bankrupt or too affluent to actually feel the effects of fines. Providing judges with guidance on when to issue fines, the federal guidelines state "that a court must impose a fine in all cases, except where the defendant establishes that he is unable to pay and is not likely to become able to pay any fine" (Schanzenbach & Yaeger, 2006, p. 764). The amount of the fine is tied to the nature of the offense and the recommendations in the guidelines. In fraud cases, consideration is given to the economic harm experienced by the victim and the gain experienced by the offender, while in antitrust cases—where it may be virtually impossible to identify economic costs and offender gains—consideration is given to the impact that the offending had on the economy (Ryan-Boyle et al., 1991).

A theoretical perspective known as optimal penalty theory predicts that fines will be used "to the maximum extent possible before they are supplemented with imprisonment" (Waldfogel, 1995, p. 107). The basis for the assumption is that fines are "costless" and prison is costly. A study by Waldfogel (an economist) examined penalties given to 7,502 fraud offenders convicted at the federal level in 1984. He found that prison sentences were tied to harm from offenses and fines were tied to the offender's ability to pay the penalty. In line with optimal penalty theory, his research found that those who were given higher fines were sentenced to prison for shorter periods of time. A study of 22,508 federal white-collar offenders sentenced under the sentencing guidelines between 1991 and 2001 found similar results: pay-ing fines reduced the amount of prison time for white-collar offenders (Schanzenbach & Yaeger, 2006). Such a finding is potentially problematic because it means that lower-class individuals are being awarded longer prison sentences because of their inability to pay a fine.

Restitution is a monetary penalty that orders an offender to pay victims back for their suffering. In terms of white-collar crime, victims could be those individuals directly harmed by the white-collar misconduct, the employer victimized by the offense, or a governmental agency that was either victimized or had to devote a great deal of resources to address the wrongdoing. The aim of restitution is to make victims "whole" through payments (Ryan-Boyle et al., 1991).

Civil courts can order defendants found liable to pay several different types of monetary penalties. Monetary penalties awarded in civil court are called "damages." Compensatory damages and punitive damages are particularly relevant to white-collar crime cases. **Compensatory damages** are awards made to plaintiffs (victims) that the defendants are ordered to pay in order to compensate victims for their victimization experience. **Punitive damages** are "awarded when the defendant's conduct is determined to have been so 'willful, malicious, or fraudulent' that it exceeds the legal criteria for mere or gross negligence" (Cohen, 2005, p. 1). Awarded by juries, in theory punitive damages are designed to punish and deter (Cohen, 2005; Stevens & Payne, 1999).

Figure 14.2 shows the median amount of compensatory and punitive damages awarded to plaintiffs in different types of citizen-initiated civil trials held in state courts in 2005. Note that the amount of damages tends to be higher in white-collar crime cases (asbestos, medical malpractice, and employment discrimination) than in other types of cases (automobile accidents, seller plaintiff—which refers to credit collections, and mortgage foreclosures).

Table 14.2 shows how the amount of damages awarded as a result of civil jury trials in specific types of white-collar crime cases changed between 1992 and 2005 in 75 of the most populated counties in the United States (Langton & Cohen, 2008). Note that between 1992 and 2005, and controlling for inflation, the amount of awards for all types of cases decreased by 40.3%, but the amount of awards given in medical malpractice and product liability cases increased by 143.6% and 386.9%, respectively. Damage awards in fraud trials increased by 6.2%.

Figure 14.2   Median Compensatory and Punitive Final Awards for Plaintiff Winners in Select Trial Cases

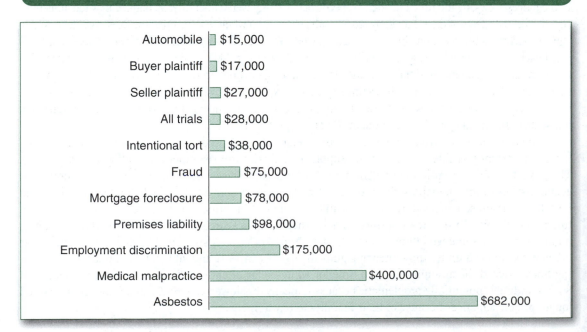

Table 14.2 Jury Trials Awards in State Courts in the Nation's 75 Most Populous Counties, by Selected Case Types, 1992, 1996, 2001, and 2005

Case Type	Median Jury Award Amounts Adjusted for Inflation				Percent Change in Median Award Amounts	
	1992	1996	2001	2005	1992–2005	2001–2005
All cases	$72,000	$44,000	$41,000	$43,000	−40.3%	4.9%
Product liability	154,000	409,000	597,000	749,000	386.9	25.5
Medical malpractice	280,000	315,000	474,000	682,000	143.6	43.9
Fraud	98,000	98,000	90,000	92,000	6.2	10.4
Buyer plaintiff	61,000	61,000	69,000	61,000	0.0	−11.6
Employment	196,000	256,000	140,000	114,000	−41.8	−18.6

Punitive damages are only rarely sought and applied in citizen-initiated civil cases. Langton and Cohen's (2008) reviews of civil jury trials in 2005 found that punitive damages were awarded to plaintiffs in about one out of 20 general civil jury trials. The same year, 8% of contract trials heard in state courts of general jurisdiction resulted in punitive damages (Farole, 2009), and just over nine percent of tort trials involved punitive damages (Cohen, 2009).

Farole's (2009) review of state court civil trials found that the amount of punitive damages awarded exceeded compensatory damages nearly two thirds of the time when damages were awarded. Tables 14.3 and 14.4 show additional patterns surrounding punitive damages in white-collar crime cases adjudicated in civil proceedings in state courts. As shown in Table 14.3, the size of punitive damages can be quite large. Table 14.4 shows the amount of compensatory and punitive damages awarded in 2001 in large U.S. counties. Again, the

Table 14.3 Plaintiff Winners Who Sought and Were Awarded Punitive Damages in Civil Trials, by Selected Case Types, 2005

Tort Trials	Number of Plaintiffs Who Sought Punitive Damages	# Awarded Punitive Damages	Median Amount	# of Cases With Punitive Damages Over $250,000	# of Cases With Punitive Damages Over $1,000,000
Fraud	259	151	100,000	67	7
Failure to provide services	372	138	53,000	20	3
Employment discrimination	84	10	115,000	1	1
Other employment disputes	93	86	10,000	12	10
Interfering with contractual relationship	42	18	6,888,000	12	11
Medical malpractice	56	6	2,835,000	5	5

Table 14.4 Comparing Compensatory to Punitive Damage Awards in Civil Trials Related to White-Collar Crimes With Plaintiff Winners in State Courts in the Nation's 75 Largest Counties, 2001

Case Types	Number of Trials With Punitive Damages	Median Damage Award Amounts		Amount of Punitive Damages Awarded: Maximum Amount	Number of Trials With Punitive Damages		Number of Punitive Damage Trials With Punitive Awards	
		Compensatory	Punitive		$1 Million or More	$10 Million or More	Greater Than Compensatory Damage Awards	More Than Four Times the Compensatory Damage Awards
All civil trials	356	$80,000	$50,000	$364,500,000	41	9	138	50
Product liability	3	16,562,000	433,000	500,000	—	—	—	—
Asbestos	2	20,000,000	500,000	500,000	—	—	—	—
Other	1	2,000,000	150,000	150,000	—	—	—	—
Medical malpractice	15	757,000	187,000	75,000,000	2	2	4	1
Professional malpractice	7	40,000	1,000	40,000	—	—	—	—
Fraud	60	119,000	63,000	275,000,000	5	2	16	2
Failure to provide services	16	160,000	275,000	5,000,000	3	—	13	3
Employment discrimination	13	493,000	606,000	3,500,000	5	—	6	—
Other employment dispute	16	150,000	151,000	1,500,000	1	—	10	—
Tortious interference	9	889,000	83,000	364,500,000	1	1	3	3

size of some of the awards is striking, and for some types of white-collar crimes (e.g., failure to provide services and employment discrimination), the median amount of punitive awards exceeded compensatory awards.

Note that these estimates do not include monetary penalties arising out of civil settlements between the offender and the government or in civil trials initiated by a government or corporation. Recall from the discussion about the U.S. Environmental Protection Agency (EPA) that such settlements can be enormous and provide a method for recovering costs and using settlement monies to help fund regulatory and criminal justice efforts.

A number of issues arise regarding the use of punitive damages. For example, large punitive damage awards against a company may inadvertently punish innocent workers who lose their jobs or consumers who pay higher prices as the punished business continues to seek profits. Also, the question of whether large damages can be seen as cruel and unusual punishment has surfaced, with the U.S. Supreme Court deciding that such damages are not violations of the Eighth Amendment. However, it is expected that the damages "bear a reasonable relationship to the actual harm they are intended to punish" (Stevens & Payne, 1998, p. 198).

One can also question the practice of justifying punitive damages on deterrent ideals. The sanction of punitive damages does not meet the tenets of classical deterrence theory, which suggests that sanctions must be swift, certain, and severe enough to outweigh offender gain without being too severe. The penalties are not applied quickly, especially given the lengthy judicial process and the fact that many defendants will tie the case up in a drawn-out appeals process. The size of the damages is random and uncertain, with little evidence that any sort of constant factors contribute to jury awards. Also, the size of some punitive damages often far exceed what might be called for from a classical deterrence theory perspective (Stevens & Payne, 1999). Note that judges have the authority to reduce punitive damage penalties and many judges exercise this right in cases involving large punitive damages.

Alternative Sanctions and White-Collar Offenders

Several types of alternative sanctions, both formal and informal, are used to punish offenders. The way these sanctions are used for white-collar offenders is at least partly distinct from how the sanctions are used for conventional offenders. In this context, alternative sanctions include (1) house arrest, (2) community service, (3) shaming, and (4) loss of a job.

House Arrest and White-Collar Offenders

Under **house arrest,** offenders are told that they must be at home either all of the time or when they are not at work, the doctor's office, or a religious service. Probation and parole officers use various strategies to make sure that offenders are at home. House arrest is used as (1) a pre-trial strategy to keep offenders out of jail before trial, (2) a sanction imposed as part of the offender's probation experience, or (3) as a condition of release after an offender has been incarcerated in jail or prison.

With regard to white-collar crime, a perception exists that suggests it is better to be on house arrest in a white-collar offender's home than it is to be on house arrest in a conventional offender's home. Before Madoff was sentenced, he was placed on house arrest. Comments such as "Madoff has been under house arrest in his $7 million Manhattan penthouse" demonstrate the frustration that people seem to have with putting affluent individuals on house arrest (Neumeister & Hays, 2009, n.p.). It is important to bear in mind that Madoff, at that point, had not yet been sentenced, and punishment is a relative experience (Payne &

Gainey, 1998). What one offender "feels" as punitive will be different from what another offender might "feel" as punitive. Where the punishment (or controlling actions of the justice system) occurs may actually have very little to do with the punitiveness of house arrest. Having said that, I'll go ahead and contradict myself—if I were to be placed on house arrest, I'd prefer to be in a penthouse than one of my old college apartments. Either way, though, the experience of house arrest would be controlling and punitive for me.

House arrest has been lauded as an appropriate sanction for some types of white-collar offenders for four reasons (Rackmill, 1992). First, it is a cost-effective sanction in that there are no incarceration costs. Second, the sanction allows offenders to find (or maintain) employment, which will help the offender pay the victim back. Third, given that most white-collar offenders are nonviolent, there is little risk that they would physically harm anyone while they are on house arrest. Fourth, the house arrest sanction minimizes the trauma that the family might endure from the criminal justice process. To be sure, a number of different types of offenders—conventional and white-collar alike—are good candidates for house arrest sanctions.

House arrest with electronic monitoring is a variation of the house arrest alternative. In these situations, offenders wear an ankle monitor and the probation or parole officer monitors the offender's whereabouts through the use of satellite technology. Many will recall how Martha Stewart was placed on house arrest with electronic monitoring after her brief stay in prison. As with house arrest in general, some assume that even the addition of electronic monitoring results in the sanction being lenient as compared to other sanctions. It is interesting to note, however, that studies show that certain types of individuals with exposure to the justice process actually prefer prison to electronic monitoring (Payne & Gainey, 1998; May & Wood, 2005). Offenders cite the degree of control that community corrections officers have over their lives as being particularly problematic for them. In other words, house arrest with electronic monitoring is a punitive experience (again, whether one lives in a penthouse or the trailer where I once lived).

Randy Gainey and I, in 1998, interviewed offenders on house arrest with electronic monitoring to shed some light on this punitive experience. We were able to identify how the sanction might apply similarly and differently to white-collar and conventional offenders. In particular, using Gresham Sykes (1958) pains of imprisonment as a guide, we highlighted how offenders on electronic monitoring experienced the types of "pains" that offenders in prison experienced, and how they also experienced additional pains that are unique to the electronic monitoring experience (see Table 14.5).

Table 14.5 The Pains of Electronic Monitoring for White-Collar Offenders

Pain	What It Means	White-Collar Offender Experience
Deprivation of autonomy	Electronically monitored offenders lose their freedom and have very little control over decisions about movement.	White-collar offenders would be permitted to leave home only for work, medical reasons, probation officer visits, and so on.
Deprivation of goods/services	Electronically monitored offenders are not permitted to do activities outside of the home that others take for granted.	White-collar offenders would lose their social activity and would not be permitted to shop, eat out, or do other things without approval.
Deprivation of liberty	Electronically monitored offenders lose many of their rights, with some losing their right to vote.	White-collar offenders would experience these same losses.

Pain	What It Means	White-Collar Offender Experience
Deprivation of heterosexual relations	Electronically monitored offenders do not lose their ability to have relations with others, but these relations are certainly influenced by the sanction.	Because of the loss of status experienced by the offender, partners may also lose status, thereby potentially influencing the relationship.
Monetary costs	Electronically monitored offenders usually have to pay to be on the sanction.	White-collar offenders would experience the same losses as conventional offenders here, though relatively speaking this may be more of a cost for conventional offenders.
Family effects	The family members of electronically monitored offenders must change their actions when someone in their home is monitored.	The loss of status would be experienced by the entire family, and some may actually lose their home as well as other taken for granted comforts.
Watching other effects	Electronically monitored offenders see others engaging in activities that they would like to be doing.	White-collar offenders would experience the same losses.
Bracelet effects	Electronically monitored offenders often complain about having to wear the bracelet.	Offenders who are working would find the most discomfort with the bracelet, especially if it was noticeable.

As an illustration of how the electronic monitoring experience can be punitive for white-collar offenders, consider the following deprivations experienced by incarcerated and electronically monitored offenders:

- *Deprivation of autonomy:* just as inmates lose control over their lives, white-collar offenders on house arrest with electronic monitoring are forced to give up their freedom and abide by controls and restrictions that are placed on them by the court and reviewed by probation officers. White-collar offenders are virtually always used to being in control of their lives and the lives of others. Having someone else control them, especially someone from a lower social status, could be difficult for some offenders.
- *Deprivation of goods and services:* just as inmates have reduced access to goods and services, white-collar offenders on house arrest with electronic monitoring will have limited access to the kinds of goods and services they are accustomed to. This could represent a major shift in an offender's life-style, which would be experienced as punitive.
- *Deprivation of liberty:* convicted felons lose many rights (e.g., in various states—the right to own a gun, to vote, etc.). For white-collar offenders involved in the political process, losing the right to participate in the political process can be especially difficult.
- *Deprivation of heterosexual relations:* whereas inmates do not have the same kinds of heterosexual relationships while they were incarcerated, monitored offenders also have their intimate relationships disrupted while on house arrest with electronic monitoring. In a very real sense, the non-monitored family members have more social power than monitored offenders because they are able to maintain a social lifestyle. For white-collar offenders accustomed to an active social life, the fact

that their social lives are put on hold while family members continue engaging in social activities can be problematic.

- *Monetary costs:* these affect all offenders because they are required to pay for the costs of the monitoring experience. For white-collar offenders, however, paying for the electronic monitoring sanction may be less difficult.
- *Family effects:* families of white-collar offenders can face a reduced quality of life, a lower social status, and a reduction in the types of materials and goods they are used to. On electronic monitoring, the stigma of wearing the ankle bracelet may also affect the family. In addition, these effects are experienced by white-collar offenders when the family loses its lifestyle, status, or other material goods as a result of the conviction. Also, the monitored offender will rarely have time alone in his or her own residence.
- *Watching-others effects:* monitored offenders have to watch others do things they are unable to participate in because of the restrictive probation conditions.
- *Bracelet effects:* refers to instances when the monitor is felt as an invasive or stigmatizing tool attached to the body as a reminder of one's misdeeds. This can be particularly difficult for women in the workplace if they are unable to conceal the monitor (Payne, 2003b).

It is important to note that the "pains of electronic monitoring" typology was developed by focusing on all types of offenders, most of which are conventional offenders. Additional research on the experience of white-collar offenders on house arrest with electronic monitoring is needed.

Community Service

Community service involves situations where offenders are told to perform a certain number of hours or days of community service. In some cases, judges will order white-collar offenders to complete a specific type of community service, while in others the offender might be ordered simply to perform some general service activities. Given the skills that white-collar offenders have, many are in positions to offer their specific skills for the good of the community. Consider the following:

- A judge ordered a pain management doctor, who pleaded guilty to knowing that her patients diverted controlled substances on four occasions, to perform 100 hours of community service, with half of the hours performed in a community clinic and half in her own office (Hoffman, 2008).
- A dentist was ordered to perform 1000 hours of community service at a local clinic after being convicted of Medicaid fraud (Lehr, 2010).
- Convicted of tax fraud and sentenced to prison, three accountants were ordered "to meet with tax professionals after they complete their prison sentences to explain to them the dangers of misleading the IRS" ("Ex-Ernst & Young Partners Get Jail Sentence," 2010).
- After a fraudulent scheme led by two men in a software start-up company resulted in more than 200 people losing their jobs, the men were ordered "to perform 80 hours of community service in a soup line or homeless shelter to give them a better perspective on the repercussions of their fraudulent actions" ("Former Entellium CEO," 2009).

Community service has numerous advantages. The sanction holds offenders accountable for their misdeeds, helps to reintegrate offenders back into the community, and the community benefits from the offenders' contributions. Despite these advantages, the sanction appears to be rarely applied. A study of home health care providers convicted of white-collar offending, for example, found that less than a third were sentenced to community service (Payne & Gray, 2001).

Shaming

Shaming is another alternative sanction strategy used to punish white-collar offenders. Shaming strategies are used for all types of offenders, but they may be particularly effective for white-collar offenders given the higher amount of stigma and shame that accompanies the conviction of white-collar offenders (Benson, 1990). As examples of shaming strategies used against white-collar offenders, consider the following sanctions:

- A Cincinnati judge made a white-collar offender send community members apologies and purchase newspaper ad space to advertise his company's environmental offenses (Ivancevich, Konopaske, & Gilbert, 2008).
- A Maryland judge made an insurance agent "clean out the stalls of the city's mounted police unit" after the agent was convicted of defrauding Maryland horse trainers (Ivancevich et al., 2008, p. 403).
- A former senior vice president of Bristol Meyers-Squibb was ordered to write a book about his conviction for lying to the Federal Trade Commission about a pharmaceutical deal that had gotten out of control (McCarthy, 2011).
- A physician was ordered to write a letter to a medical journal describing her after-the-fact involvement in a drug diversion scheme and how physicians can experience negative consequences as a result of misconduct (Hoffman, 2008).

The idea of shaming white-collar offenders as a sanction has been gaining popularity over the years. Said one legal scholar, "Some of legal academia's brightest stars have jumped on the shame train, arguing that modern versions of the dunce cap, rather than shackles, best fit the 'white collar' criminal" (Owens, 2000, p. 1047). Shaming by itself can be counterproductive. Scholars have called for what is called **reintegrative shaming,** a process characterized by a shaming sanction followed by efforts to re-engage offenders in the community.

John Braithwaite (1989a) and Michael Benson (1990) have been the leading criminologists calling for the use of reintegrative shaming for white-collar offenders. Braithwaite notes that overly punitive and stigmatizing responses to white-collar misconduct can be counterproductive and result in offenders becoming disengaged from the community. Building on Braithwaite's ideas, Benson notes that **disintegrative shaming** embarrasses offenders, causes anger, and potentially leads to additional harm. Alternatively, reintegrative shaming focuses on the bad act and communicates messages of disapproval, which are followed by efforts to reintegrate the offender back into the community.

One author team identified several reasons why reintegrative shaming strategies should be effective for white-collar offenders. These reasons included:

- White-collar offenders want to minimize the harm done to their family members, and reintegrative shaming strategies provide an opportunity to do this.
- Others possibly steer clear of white-collar misconduct because they do not want to be embarrassed.
- Those who have a higher attachment to their jobs, families, and society should be less likely to want to be shamed.
- Reintegration affirms individuals while disintegration breaks them down (Ivancevich et al., 2008).

For white-collar offenders, reintegrative shaming is effective inasmuch as offenders take responsibility for their actions. In other words, reintegrative shaming will be more powerful if offenders "respect the shamer" (Ivancevich et al., 2008). What this means is that if the offender has no respect for those doing the shaming, there is little likelihood that the shaming will have deterrent qualities.

Loss of Job

Loss of their job is another sanction that can be imposed on white-collar offenders. For many individuals, this potential loss is likely enough to keep workers from engaging in misconduct. Once caught, not only do offenders lose their current jobs, they are also often ordered out of their careers for various amounts of time. Martha Stewart, for example, was not able to serve as a CEO of a publicly traded company (including her own) from the time of her conviction until 2011. When Ivan Boesky was convicted of his securities crimes, he was barred from working in the securities industry for the remainder of his life (Adams, 2009). Boesky was not alone. A study of 2,206 individuals charged with financial misrepresentation in enforcement actions by the SEC and Department of Justice (DOJ) found that 93% of the individuals had lost their jobs by the time the enforcement action was completed (Karpoff, Lee, & Martin, 2008). When other professionals such as lawyers, doctors, educators, and so on are caught committing crime on the job, they too face the likelihood of losing their jobs.

At some point, white-collar offenders who lost their jobs and have completed their criminal justice sanction will seek new employment. A study by Kent Kerley and Heith Copes (2004) found that, for the most part, white-collar offenders "are better able to rebound following contact with the criminal justice system" (p. 65). In particular, they found that white-collar offenders were better able to find new jobs than conventional offenders were. The caveat they uncovered in their research was that white-collar offenders with more arrests and a later onset of offending found it just as difficult as conventional offenders to find a stable job.

☒ Punishing Corporations for White-Collar Crime

Corporations can also be punished both formally and informally for misconduct. If convicted (in criminal court), found liable (in civil court), or determined responsible (in administrative or regulatory proceedings), various types of sentencing alternatives arise. Criminal penalties include fines, restitution, probation, and debarment, and civil penalties including compensatory and punitive damages can be applied. In administrative proceedings, a corporate offender can be given civil fines and required to pay restitution. Corporations can also experience "marketplace sanctions," such as loss of investor confidence (Cohen, 1992). It is also important to note that when corporations are sanctioned, individuals leading the corporation are also sanctioned as individual offenders.

With regard to criminal sanctions, the *U.S. Sentencing Guidelines* includes an Organizational Guidelines section that provides judges guidance in determining how to sentence corporations. The guidelines specify three sanctions: probation, fines, and restitution. The Organizational Guidelines were implemented in November 1991 and included recommended sanctions that were stricter than the types of sanctions applied earlier. For example, fine amounts recommended in the Organizational Guidelines were 5 to 10 times higher in the guidelines than the fines that had traditionally been applied in corporate misconduct cases (Cohen, 1992). The guidelines have been critiqued for appearing to arbitrarily stipulate sanctions relative to organizational characteristics (e.g., size of the company, number of employees, etc.; Rackmill, 1992). It is an interesting philosophical question: If two companies commit the exact same offense, should one of them be punished more severely because it is larger and wealthier. (A similar question can be asked about individual white-collar offenders).

Fining Corporate Offenders

The use of fines to punish corporations is a hotly debated issue among criminologists and economists. As suggested above, some economists apply concepts of cost-benefit analysis in determining the relevance of fines to control corporate misconduct. Some criminologists, on the other hand, view fines as less than useful, to put it nicely. Snider (1990) suggested that "fines for large organizations typically represent a fraction of the profits made in one hour of operation" (p. 380). Another scholar noted that fines are simply a "cost of doing business" and that ultimately fines hurt stockholders and corporations (Orland, 1980).

Cohen (1989) has considered how corporate fines compare to the harm committed by the corporation. Focusing on 288 non-anti-trust corporate offenders prosecuted between 1984 and 1987, he found that monetary sanctions "seldom exceed—and often are much less than—total harm" (Cohen, 1989, p. 618). To quantify the difference, he suggested that "a firm convicted of causing $1.00 in harm might pay a criminal fine of $.76 in addition to any other sanctions such as criminal restitution or civil penalties" (p. 658).

While Cohen's study was done before the Organizational Guidelines were in effect, criminological studies since then also question the effectiveness of fines for corporations. A review of 405 cases where organizations were sentenced through 1996 found that organizational offenders were able to avoid paying fines "by convincing a U.S. District Court that they have no money" (Green & Bodapati, 1999, p. 556). The authors noted a particularly interesting irony: Organizations might commit crimes because of a lack of money. Then, they can argue that the "lack of money motive" can be used to avoid sanctioning the organization. They also call for organizational sales (where the business is sold) or forced dissolution (which is an organizational death penalty) in these cases. Judges are unwilling to make these decisions out of concern for workers, investors, and consumers (Orland, 1980).

More recently, Nicole Piquero and Jason Davis (2004) reviewed sanctions imposed on organizations after the guidelines were developed to see whether certain factors impacted the penalty given to corporations. They found that although legal factors consistent with the guidelines impacted sentencing to a degree, two extra-legal variables influenced organizational sentencing: (1) economic solvency and (2) closely held organizations. These two factors influenced the amount of the fine, "but did not significantly impact the placement of the fine within the guideline range" (p. 652).

Probation and Corporate Offenders

Corporations can also be sentenced to a term of probation. The first use of **organizational probation** occurred in 1971 in *U.S. v. Atlantic Richfield, Co.,* when Judge James B. Parsons, Jr., sentenced ARCO (the Atlantic Richfield Company) to probation and "ordered it to develop an oil response plan" (Lofquist, 1993, p. 160). Lofquist notes that by the eighties, one fifth of all corporate offenders convicted at the federal level were given a probation sentence. The use of organizational probation was not formalized until the development of the Organizational Guidelines in 1991. The federal sentencing guidelines specify that corporations cannot be sentenced to more than 5 years probations.

Corporations can be required to meet certain conditions while on probation. Probation conditions must be tied to the characteristic of the organization and the offense (Plimton & Walsh, 2010). Probation conditions are, as a result, tied to type of industry. For instance, judges have ordered bakeries convicted of wrongdoing to provide food for the underprivileged (Levin, 1984). One condition sometimes used is that companies are told to apologize publicly, in various media sources, for their misconduct(Cohen, 1992). Table 14.6 shows the factors that drive organizational probation decisions and the types of conditions that organizations can be ordered to abide by as part of their probation.

Issues Surrounding Corporate Sanctions

Two issues surface when considering how to sanction organizations. These include (1) determining appropriate sanctions to reduce recidivism and (2) avoiding harm to innocent parties. With regard to recidivism, one basis for punishing companies is to keep them from committing future acts of misconduct. Research shows that recidivism by corporations is tied more to the nature of the industry as opposed to the type of intervention (e.g., criminal justice, civil, or administrative) (Simpson & Koper, 1992). However, the authors found that for those corporations with past guilty verdicts, stiffer penalties (measured by changing from a misdemeanor to a felony) reduced subsequent recidivism. In terms of punishing innocent parties, some

Table 14.6 Dynamics Surrounding Corporate Probation

The court shall order a term of probation:	Mandatory conditions of the probation are:	Discretionary conditions are:
• If necessary to ensure satisfaction of other sanctions; • If an organization of fifty or more employees lacks an effective program to prevent and detect law violations; • If the organization or high-level personnel participating in the offense have been convicted of a similar offense in the past five years; • If necessary to ensure that changes are made within the organization to reduce the likelihood of future criminal conduct; • If the sentence does not include a fine; or • If necessary to accomplish one of the four purposes of sentencing.	• Commission of no further crimes; • Payment of a fine or restitution, or performance of community service; and • Any other conditions reasonably related to the instant offense and imposing no unnecessary deprivations of liberty or property.	• Publicity paid for by the defendant in media specified by the court detailing the crime, conviction, sentence, and remedial steps taken; • Development by the defendant, with court approval, of an effective program to prevent and detect future law violations; • Notification of employees and shareholders of the offense and of the details of the compliance program; • Periodic reports to the court regarding progress in implementing the compliance program, occurrence of new offenses, or investigations involving the defendant; and • Periodic examinations of facilities and records, and interviews of employees by the court or a special probation officer to monitor compliance.

sentences (corporate manslaughter and penalties for violations of safety laws) are potentially too strict and harmful to innocent employees or shareholders (Payne & Stevens, 1999). As noted above, a desire to avoid harming individuals leads some judges to give relatively lenient sentences in some corporate misconduct cases.

Reasons for Punishing White-Collar Offenders

Criminologists have described several reasons why society punishes criminals. These reasons include (1) retribution, (2) specific deterrence, (3) general deterrence, (4) rehabilitation, (5) just deserts, and (6) incapacitation, which refers to removing dangerous offenders from the street to protect society from harm. With the exception of the sixth reason, all of the reasons easily demonstrate reasons why white-collar criminals are punished.

Retribution and White-Collar Offenders

As a philosophy of punishment, **retribution** means that offenders should be punished to meet societal demands. Philosophers have long noted that formal punishment satisfies public demands. Another way to say it is that punishment of wrongdoers makes some people "happy." This may be especially the case for victims of white-collar crimes. When Bernie Madoff was being led away in handcuffs after being sentenced, one of his victims was heard saying, "What a sweet sight. What a sweet sight" (Healy & Mandell, 2009). Some members of the media could not help but gloat over Madoff's plight. Said one team of reporters about Madoff the day after he was sentenced in way that hinted at pleasure:

> The swanky East 64th Street duplex where Madoff spent the previous night must have felt like a distant memory as he looked around his Spartan cell. Instead of having his loving wife, Ruth, for company, Madoff is sharing a roof with . . . rapists, murderers, even thieves like him. (Zambito, Martinez, & Siemaszko, 2009)

Madoff is not the only white-collar offender members of society want punished. A survey of 1,512 respondents from across the United States found that more than three fourths of the respondents supported longer prison sentences for white-collar offenders (Unnever, Benson, & Cullen, 2008, p. 177). Podgor (2007) wrote that "Wealth, education, and prestige are often cited as reasons for giving white-collar offenders a harsher punishment" (p. 770). As an illustration, one U.S. Attorney commented that white-collar criminals "should be treated more harshly because you're talking about people who have gotten every opportunity that you can give them . . . the drug dealers have had no opportunities" (O'Donnell & Willing, 2003). It seems that some members of the public may be less forgiving of white-collar offenders.

Specific Deterrence and White-Collar Offenders

Specific deterrence ideals suggest that punishment should occur in order to stop the punished offender (in this context, either a white-collar offender or a corporation) from engaging in future wrongdoing. Deterrence theory has been addressed elsewhere in this text. At this point, it is sufficient to suggest that some believe that sanctions proportional to the harm committed by the offender will keep individuals and corporations from engaging in future misconduct (Spurgeon & Fagan, 1981). Note that some research has called into question the deterrent ability of imprisonment for individual offenders (Weisburd, Waring, & Chayet, 1995), while others have found that sanctions might deter corporations from future misconduct (Simpson & Koper, 1992).

General Deterrence and White-Collar Offenders

General deterrence ideals suggest that offenders should be punished in order to keep other potential offenders from engaging in misconduct. As noted earlier, judges often justify their stern responses to white-collar offenders on general deterrence ideals (Mann et al., 1980). There is a perception that fines and probation do not have general deterrent power for white-collar offenders. One government official with the Environmental Crime Division of the Department of Justice has been quoted saying, "Incarceration is the cost of business that you can't pass on to the consumer" (Stuart, 1995, p. 255). The underlying assumption is that fines are passed on to consumers, and as a result will not keep offenders from engaging in white-collar misconduct.

In line with general deterrence ideals, educators have used incarcerated white-collar offenders to teach future white-collar professionals how to avoid white-collar offending. Castleberry (2007), a marketing professor, takes his students on prison field trips as part of his efforts to teach business ethics and to make sure that students understand the laws governing workplace behaviors. He argues that the visits show students that laws apply to them, that there are consequences for bad workplace decisions, and that criminal workplace decisions sometimes results from "seemingly insignificant acts." He also argues that visits will help students understand what prison life is like for white-collar offenders and that from this it is assumed that students would be less prone to engage in workplace misconduct.

Rehabilitation and White-Collar Offenders

Rehabilitation, as a philosophy of punishment, suggests that offenders are brought into the justice process so that the government can play a role in treating whatever issues offenders have that may have contributed to their wrongdoing. White-collar offenders might receive individual-level counseling from probation and parole officers to help them deal with their status degradation and to regain employment (Payne, 2003b). In general, though, treatment programs tend to be designed more for drug and violent offenders. If individuals with a white-collar status find themselves in a treatment program, it is more apt to be the result of a commission of a drug offense.

Just Deserts and White-Collar Offenders

Just deserts as a punishment orientation suggests that offenders should be punished for one primary reason: because they deserve it. Braithwaite (1982) highlights the difficulties that arise in applying this philosophy to white-collar offenders:

- How do you indentify who is responsible?
- Do you punish the individual or the organization?
- If punishing both, how much punishment is appropriate and how would it be divided?
- How do you keep individuals (consumers and workers) from being punished? (p. 755)

Braithwaite suggests that the negative consequences arising from overly strict responses to white-collar offending supports the selective enforcement of white-collar crimes. He quotes the justice theorem: "Where desert is greatest, punishment will be the least" (p. 755).

Braithwaite draws attention to the debate about whether white-collar offenders should be punished more severely so that they are punished the same as conventional offenders. In doing so, he calls for a utilitarian approach to balance the scales of justice. His perspective is quite simple: Rather than punishing white-collar offenders more severely, why not punish conventional offenders less and white-collar offenders only slightly more so that both groups are punished similarly?

Experts recognize that effective punishments balance ideals of retribution, just deserts, deterrence, and rehabilitation. Benson (1985b) calls for short sentences of white-collar offenders that are split between a short prison sentence and a short probation sentence. Such an approach would have deterrent, retributive, and rehabilitative qualities. As well, it would be more cost effective than other remedies.

⧄ Summary

- White-collar offenders are subject to a wide range of sentencing alternatives including prison, probation, restitution, fine, and various alternative sanctions. Organizations—as well as individuals—can be sanctioned in white-collar crime cases.
- Research on the sentencing of white-collar offenders has provided mixed messages about issues related to the disposition of white-collar offenders.
- Wheeler and his colleagues' (1982) interviews with judges found that the judges considered how the white-collar offender experienced the criminal justice process; some judges viewed participation in the process as a punishment in and of itself for white-collar offenders.
- The Sentencing Reform Act was passed in 1984 as part of the Comprehensive Crime Control Act. One aim of the act was "to remedy individualized disparity in federal criminal sentences and to equalize sentences for 'street criminals' and 'white-collar offenders'" (Ryan-Boyle et al., 1991, p. 739).
- Some have argued that the sentencing of white-collar offenders has gotten a little out of control, with some sentences seeming far too severe.
- Some have suggested that the apparently disparate sentencing resulting in long sentences for white-collar offenders might simply reflect the fact that the vast majority of white-collar offenders are kept out of the justice system in the first place.
- Very few studies have focused on the experience of white-collar offenders in prison. One can point to five dynamics of the white-collar prison experience: (1) depression, (2) danger, (3) deprivations, (4) deviance, (5) doldrums.
- For white-collar offenders, the sources of depression include (1) stressful changes coming from one's first exposure to prison life, (2) loss of job, (3) loss of status, (4) isolation, and (5) sentencing dynamics (Payne, 2003b).
- Four themes arise regarding danger and white-collar offenders: (1) celebrity bashing, (2) prison placement, (3) prison culture/socialization, and (4) exaggerated concerns.
- For white-collar inmates accustomed to certain lifestyles, the experience of deprivations might be particularly problematic.
- Three types of inmate violations are relevant with regard to white-collar inmates: rule violations, deviant use of the justice process, and jailstripe crimes (Payne, 2003b).
- After becoming acquainted with the incarceration experience, white-collar inmates report being very bored with the prison.
- Benson (1985b) found that for white-collar offenders the probation experience could be characterized as "going through the motions" (p. 429).

- Monetary penalties include criminal fines, restitution, civil settlements, and the compensatory and punitive damages awarded in civil trials.
- Alternative sanctions given to white-collar offenders include (1) house arrest, (2) community service, (3) shaming, and (4) loss of a job.
- With regard to white-collar crime, a perception exists that suggests that it is better to be on house arrest in a white-collar offender's home than it is to be on house arrest in a conventional offender's home.
- Community service holds offenders accountable for their misdeeds, helps to reintegrate offenders back into the community, and the community benefits from the offenders' contributions.
- Shaming strategies are used for all types of offenders, but they may be particularly effective for white-collar offenders given the higher amount of stigma and shame that accompanies the conviction of white-collar offenders (Benson, 1990).
- A study of 2,206 individuals charged with financial misrepresentation in enforcement actions by the SEC and DOJ found that 93% of the individuals had lost their jobs by the time the enforcement action was completed (Karpoff et al., 2008).
- Corporations can be punished both formally and informally for misconduct. Depending on whether convicted (in criminal court), found liable (in civil court), or determined responsible (in administrative or regulatory proceedings), various types of sentencing alternatives are available.
- Two issues surface when considering how to sanction organizations. These include (1) determining appropriate sanctions to reduce recidivism and (2) avoiding harm to innocent parties.
- Reasons for punishing white-collar offenders include (1) retribution, (2) specific deterrence, (3) general deterrence, (4) rehabilitation, and (5) just deserts.

KEY TERMS

Celebrity bashing	General deterrence	Rehabilitation
Community service	House arrest	Reintegrative shaming
Community-based sanctions	Jailstripe crimes	Restitution
Compensatory damages	Just deserts	Retribution
Criminal fines	Monetary penalties	Shaming
Deviant misuse of the justice process	Organizational probation	Specific deterrence
Disintegrative shaming	Punitive damages	U.S. Sentencing Commission

DISCUSSION QUESTIONS

1. A blue-collar and white-collar offender commit the exact same crime. The blue-collar offender is sentenced to prison for one year. Should the white-collar offender be given the same sentence?

2. A blue-collar and white-collar offender both steal from their job. Each of them stole the same amount. The blue-collar offender is fined $500.00. Should the white-collar offender receive the same fine? Would it be unfair to punish the white-collar offender more because of the offender's higher income? Should the offender be given a lower prison sentence in exchange for the higher fine? Explain.

3. How is incarceration different for white-collar offenders as compared to conventional offenders?

4. What do you think of research that shows that white-collar offenders are more likely than conventional offenders to be sentenced to prison? What are some possible reasons for this finding?

5. Is probation an effective sanction for white-collar offenders? Explain.

6. How are fines appropriately and inappropriately used in white-collar crime cases?

7. Describe the different ways that organizations are punished. Do you think businesses should ever be forced to close as a result of misconduct? Explain.

8. Which types of alternative sanctions might be most appropriate for white-collar offenders? Explain.

9. Why do we punish white-collar offenders?

WEB RESOURCES

White-Collar Prisoners: How not to get stuck in jail: http://www.economist.com/node/13528224

Prison Activist Resource Center: http://www.prisonactivist.org/

Correctional Alternatives, Inc.: http://www.correctionalalternatives.org/

Redemption and the white collar criminal: http://business.blogs.cnn.com/2009/10/02/redemption-and-the-white-collar-criminal/

READING

Past research shows that judges sometimes conditioned their sentences given to white-collar offenders on the assumption that white-collar inmates are more sensitive to the incarceration experience. In order to examine whether white-collar offenders are more sensitive to prison, Michael Benson and Frank Cullen interviewed a sample of white-collar inmates that had been released from prison. The researchers found that white-collar inmates experienced some sensitivity to incarceration upon their admission to prison, but the offenders were able to overcome those issues and adjust to prison. The authors also found that white-collar inmates reject the inmate subculture.

The Special Sensitivity of White-Collar Offenders to Prison

A Critique and Research Agenda

Michael L. Benson and Francis T. Cullen

Judges see general deterrence and the need to provide the appearance of justice as the primary reasons for punishing white-collar criminals (Mann, Wheeler, and Sarat, 1980; Pollack and Smith, 1983; Renfrew, 1977). Although these rationales would appear to support frequent use of incarceration, judges apparently feel that mitigating circumstances can undermine the need for imprisonment (Mann et al. 1980; Pollack and Smith, 1983; Conklin, 1977). One prominent mitigating factor is the white-collar offender's "special sensitivity" to imprisonment (Mann et al., 1980).

According to the special sensitivity view, white-collar offenders' middle or upper class background and lack of experience with the criminal justice system makes imprisonment more painful for them than for offenders from lower social classes (Mann et al., 1980; Pollack and Smith, 1983; Renfrew, 1977). Bearing the material deprivations of prison life is ostensibly more difficult for high status offenders, since they are accustomed to comfortable life-styles. In addition, these offenders are thought to be embarrassed, humiliated, or to have "suffered enough" by dint of the stigma of conviction. The process serves as the punishment for upper status lawbreakers, rendering additional sanctions, such as incarceration, unnecessary.

Although this perspective is widely accepted, imprisoned white-collar offenders have never been closely studied by criminologists, sociologists, or psychologists (Geis, 1982:161-62). Research on prison life, prisonization, and the effects of incarceration on subsequent social adjustment has focused almost exclusively on juvenile delinquents in reformatories and average inmates in state prisons (Clemmer, 1958; Toch, 1977; Sykes, 1958). Thus, due to lack of research, the prevailing understanding of how white-collar offenders adjust to incarceration remains based on preconceptions of prison life and white-collar sensibilities rather than theory or research.

This article developed from a research project on white-collar offenders. As part of that research, thirty

SOURCE: Benson, M. L., & Cullen, F. (1985). The special sensitivity of white-collar offenders to prison: A critique and research agenda. *Journal of Criminal Justice, 16,* 207–215.

white-collar offenders were interviewed, fourteen of whom had been incarcerated. Although the interviews were conducted for other reasons, the offenders often mentioned their experiences while incarcerated. As the interviews progressed, certain patterns emerged that prompted reconsideration of the special sensitivity view of white-collar offenders.

This article presents a theoretical critique of the special sensitivity hypothesis. Examples are drawn from the interviews to illustrate the major points. These examples must be viewed with appropriate caution, since they are based on the experience of a limited sample. Even so, the present authors believe that the offenders' comments serve a sensitizing function, grounding the discussion in "lived reality" and suggesting hypotheses for future research.

The article begins by providing some background on the study that generated the authors' initial interest in this issue. Following the description of offenders' initial apprehensions over incarceration, is a review of research that challenges several key assumptions of the special sensitivity hypothesis. Then coping strategies employed by white-collar offenders are discussed. In conclusion, a research agenda for examining incarcerated white-collar offenders is outlined.

Background

Under the auspices of the Probation and Parole Office for the U.S. District Court for the Northern District of Illinois, letters were sent to a sample of white-collar offenders who were chosen on the basis of their crimes and occupations. The letter informed them that a study investigating the effects of conviction on white-collar offenders was under way. They were asked for interviews.

All of the offenders were white males. They ranged in age from thirty-two to seventy-three, with a mean of fifty. They pursued a variety of white-collar occupations—law, banking, and civil service among others. Their crimes were presumptively white-collar offenses and included mail fraud, false statements, embezzlement, and income tax violations (Wheeler, Weisburd, and Bode, 1982; Hagan and Palloni, 1986). Examination of pre-sentence investigation reports

and interviews with probation officers indicated that the offenders enjoyed incomes, educational attainments, and lifestyles appropriate for persons of middle to upper middle class social status.

Eight offenders served their time in the work release program at the Metropolitan Correctional Center (MCC) in Chicago. Another offender served time in MCC but not in the work release program. The remaining five were incarcerated in federal correctional institutions located in Kentucky (Lexington), Minnesota (Sandstone), and Illinois (Marion).

Initial Fear and Anxiety

For the first-time offender, the stress created by the prospect of going to prison probably exceeds any other that the person may have experienced. Even the street offender "finds his career disrupted, his relationships suspended, his aspirations and dreams gone sour" (Johnson, 1976:1). Yet, despite their initial fear and anxiety, the majority of offenders eventually adapt to prison life (Toch, 1981:3).

Among middle and upper class offenders, perceptions of prison life based on dramatizations and sensationalized news reports certainly heighten the sense of anxiety. It is easy for persons from these social strata to assume the worst and to conjure up images of solitary suffering and emotional devastation. Yet, contrary to the special sensitivity view, the white-collar offenders interviewed in this study seemed remarkably free of emotional difficulties (see also Spencer, 1965). They reported no physical or verbal abuse from other inmates. Like ordinary offenders, they appeared to undergo a process of adjustment and reconciliation once the shock of confinement passed. Consider, for example, the following statements by an offender sentenced to be confined on weekends in MCC.

> When I first went into the program, I was, you know, concerned. I didn't know what kind of place I was going to obviously, and I was very concerned about that. I was also concerned about what was going to happen to me, because you hear all these crazy

things of what happens in prisons. It upset me to no end. I really was, because I didn't know what to expect, until I really saw the layout and everything, not knowing who are all these other guys. What are they doing here? Are they mass murderers? I was a zombie standing around for about two hours and then I went to sleep.

When asked what it was like after he had been to MCC a few more times, the same offender responded in this manner:

Not bad. For the most part people that are in that program seem to be relatively, well, I don't know if the word is decent or not, but they're okay guys. There's just a few of them that are crazies. . . . You're not afraid of or mind talking to and sitting around shooting the breeze with them.

In contrast to the experience that the offenders imagined they would have, they routinely reported their actual treatment was far more benign. After a period of disorientation, they learned the institution's rules and discovered that their fellow inmates were not "crazies." Indeed, a few of the younger, college educated offenders found the experience interesting in a "sociological" sense. Two more examples are given below— first, an individual sentenced to work release at MCC, and second, an individual who did time in a federal correctional institution (FCI).

It was kind of an unexperience. It was not nearly as frightening as I thought it would be. I found out that as long as you did your chores, as long as you followed the rules, which were minimal, I had no problem whatsoever. None. Most of the people that I lived with were minorities. I had no problem with that. There were no incidents of violence or threats or anything of that nature. . . . So I didn't find it a terribly difficult experience. (MCC)

Once you're past the first initial period, it's really not so bad. I mean sitting in prison, I got all the food, three square meals a day. I really have no problems, no worries. Yeah, I'm worried about my family, but there's nothing I can do about it. I might be worried about the guy next to me cutting my throat, but I'm really not. All I got to do is just get up in the morning. Somebody gives me food. I get candy. I get movies. I get books. I can do whatever the . . . I want to do. Yeah, it's punishment, but its effect as punishment is gone after the first few days. I mean you're afraid of going to prison till you get to prison, and once you're in prison, you really don't want to go back to prison, but once you're there for a couple of months, you just kind of get into it. You live. You're there. You survive. And if it really gets down to it again, you can go back again, and you can survive. (FCI)

The experiences and attitudes related by the offenders quoted above and similar sentiments expressed in other interviews prompted an attempt to develop a framework to understand these unexpected results. It was recognized at the outset that prison life is stressful and that it forces inmates to make both behavioral and psychological adjustments. Factors influencing how individuals adjust to and cope with stress were examined, following a review of research on inmate adjustments to prison life.

 ## Adjusting to Prison: Personal and Social Resources

Research on inmate adjustments to prison life has focused almost exclusively on juvenile delinquents in reformatories and average adult offenders in state prisons. This research has shown that inmates do not respond uniformly to prison stress. Rather, the inmate's personal traits and social resources interact with the prison environment to produce a variety of adaptive responses to incarceration. For example, although prison life can lead to alienation and embitterment, the types of relationships offenders have on the outside influence the degree to which they are detrimentally affected by imprisonment (Clemmer, 1958:298-301). Inmates who have strong supportive relationships with persons outside of prison are less affected by the prisonization process (Thomas, 1975). Similarly, inmates with well-established identities and a strong commitment to traditional values tend to resist adopting the dogmas and codes of the prison world (Irwin, 1970). Finally, Porporino and Zamble (1984:413) reported an inverse relationship between education and depression in prison. In their study inmates with more education were less depressed and less anxious after six months in prison than those with little or no education. In sum, research to date has suggested that personal and social resources—education, family ties, and noncriminal identities—enhance the offender's ability to cope with the incarceration experience.

It is necessary to consider typical white-collar offenders in light of the research described above. Compared to most prison inmates, they are older, have more education, and are more likely to come from a stable family. White-collar offenders also have strong noncriminal self-conceptions (Coleman, 1985; Benson, 1985). Thus, due to their class backgrounds, many white-collar offenders are likely to possess the personal traits and social ties that research has suggested reduce the impact of incarceration on the psychological well-being of offenders. If these factors correlate with successful adjustments among low status offenders, presumably they operate in a similar manner among high status offenders.

The special sensitivity view rests on the assumption that high social class makes a person less able to deal with the stress of incarceration. Yet research on social class, stress, and personality has suggested precisely the opposite. For example, research on the general public consistently has found that higher social class reduces vulnerability to stress (Link and Dohrenwend, 1980). Studies examining social class and personality similarly have found that self-direction

and concern with internal psychological processes are more valued among persons in higher social classes than among those in lower social classes (House, 1981:549). These class-linked personality traits suggest that white-collar offenders are likely to believe in and exhibit self-efficacy. Self-efficacy means the perception that one's rewards in life are contingent upon one's own actions (Goodstein et al. 1984). Among ordinary offenders, self-efficacy is associated with lower levels of stress and a greater sense of well-being (MacKenzie and Goodstein, 1983). Upper status offenders may score highly on self-efficacy and hence experience lower levels of stress. Persons who score highly on self-efficacy find ways to assert control even when the opportunity to do so is severely limited (Bandura, 1977; Rotter, 1966), and the ability to assert control over one's personal fate characterizes mature coping in prison (Toch, 1982; Johnson, 1987). One of the offenders interviewed touched on this theme in this manner:

> I went with the attitude that I got to make the most of a bad thing. I'd gone through the Marine Corps. I'd gone to Paris Island. I figured if I can make it through there, I can make it through this.

It also seems that white-collar offenders may have greater emotional resources than ordinary offenders. Recent research in the sociology of emotions has suggested that there are class-linked variations in the ability to handle emotions. Feelings are complex social constructions (Denzin, 1983; Hochshild, 1979). They are not simply caused by factors external to individuals. Emotions can be, and are, worked on and shaped by individuals. Hochshild (1979) has called this activity "emotion work" or "emotion management." These terms refer to the strategies employed by individuals to engender, modify, or reject feelings. Individuals vary in their ability to manage their emotions, and in prison the ability to manage emotions is a useful mechanism for coping with stress. Hochshild (1979) suggested that middle and upper class occupations call upon individuals to develop skill in managing their feelings. Success in the professional and business worlds requires that one adopt a goal-oriented approach to life. Although the capacity for emotion work is not limited to upper status offenders, due to their occupational experiences they may be more adept at performing it than lower status offenders, and thus more adept at coping with the psychological stress of prison life.

Similarly, the white-collar offenders' well-known tendency to resist criminal labeling suggests that they do not passively accept feelings of shame and guilt. Highly resistant to negative interpretations of their actions, they rationalize their crimes even after conviction and display a remarkable inability to accept the moral implications of their convictions (Coleman, 1985; Benson, 1985). In rejecting negative labeling, they also reject or manage the accompanying emotions. Shame and guilt depend on the individual's acceptance of the definition of the situation imputed by a specific or generalized other (Shott, 1979). But accepting the definitions constructed by others is precisely what white-collar offenders do not do. They reject characterizations of their actions as criminally motivated. Just as they work to rationalize their behavior in moral terms, it can be expected they will also work to neutralize feelings of shame and stigma.

Another salient consideration is that white-collar offenders are likely to have had prior, and often extensive, organizational experience. Correctional facilities are complex organizations and use standard bureaucratic techniques to accomplish their goals—rules, standardized procedures, and a hierarchy of authority. White-collar offenders understand and are familiar with these procedures; submitting to autocratic rules and regulations are not completely novel experiences for them. Accordingly, this background provides them with a frame of reference for orienting themselves to the new experience of imprisonment, thus helping them to interpret and manage prison life.

Finally, in regards to ordinary prison inmates, Toch (1982) and Johnson (1987:68-69) have argued that learning to cope maturely with the stresses of prison life increases ability to cope with the stresses of life in general. Although they made their arguments in the context of the debate over prison reform,

the present authors suggest that the converse of their reasoning is applicable. That is, those who cope maturely with the stresses of life in general also may be able to cope with the stresses of prison life. If the white-collar offender's class status and financial success in life indicates coping ability, it follows that this ability can be employed in the prison environment just as it has been in everyday life.

Elitism and Conformity as Coping Strategies

The theory and research reviewed above indicates that the social backgrounds and personal traits associated with upper class status may enhance favorable adjustments to the stresses of prison life. This section presents some of the specific coping strategies that the interviews suggested are employed by incarcerated white-collar offenders. In the interviews almost every offender expressed a sense of personal superiority over fellow inmates and prison personnel. They seemed to divide fellow inmates into two broad categories—"those criminals" and "people like me." They saw themselves as the elite of the prison. One of our subjects expressed it thus:

> You'll find two distinct classifications in people at the MCC center. You'll find five percent who are professionals and the other ninety-five percent are people of very low caliber of intelligence, a very, very high percentage of uneducated Blacks, Mexicans, and Puerto Ricans, very low caliber whites. People who have had a history through childhood and everywhere else of disruptive behavior, and yet they all seem to get along nicely at MCC. You associate and pick your friends like you would elsewhere, but out of one hundred twenty there are seven or eight or ten professionals, and they stand out like sore thumbs, and they seem to gravitate and associate together. The funny part is there doesn't seem to be any middle ground.

Remarks such as the one quoted above seem to indicate two things about incarcerated white-collar offenders: They have a high sense of self-esteem and they look for ways to enhance their self-esteem while in prison.

It is suggested here that as these offenders "gravitate and associate together," they reinforce differences between themselves and ordinary offenders. Associating with fellow inmates of similar social status facilitates offenders' subjective rehabilitation, reducing feelings of stigmatization and isolation. High status fellow inmates form a set of "sympathetic others" (Goffman, 1963), sharing stigma and willing to adopt a common standpoint toward the world. These associations reduce the initial sense of isolation these offenders feel, help them put their predicaments into perspective, and, most importantly, allow them to distance themselves from the other inmates. A probation officer interviewed for the project made the following point:

> It's kind of like when you're convicted you think you're alone, and then you go over to MCC in the work release program and there are ten white-collar offenders in the same program, who have families and good jobs, and you say, "Gee, people really do this and I'm not the only one." It diminishes their own guilt and their tendency to blow things out of proportion.

Many offenders reported an almost sycophantic submission to official authority and compulsive observance of institutional rules. Unlike the often covertly hostile or openly rebellious orientation of ordinary offenders (Johnson, 1987:64), white-collar offenders go out of their way to observe the rules and make a good impression on prison authorities. Offenders often mentioned how well they had done at MCC, how they had not broken the rules, performed their duties as required, and in a few cases assisted the prison administration with their special skills. Thus, rather than identifying with the inmate culture and adopting an intransigent line with respect to institutional regulations, white-collar offenders submit to official authority. Consider the following two examples:

> I got a marvelous letter from the warden [director of MCC] saying that I was outstanding. I was never late once. One hundred and eight days and I was never late once to come back. Most guys are late. I did all the duties. I did everything that was expected of me. I cooperated every way I possibly could, and I got a very marvelous letter from the warden saying that I was an outstanding person. Just the opposite of the guys who bucked the system. I learned early in the army, you don't buck the system. When you're in a situation, do your job, and do it well, and everybody will respect you, and that's what I did.

> I get along with people perfect. I made sure, whatever they wanted, whatever they did. They gave me details to do and I did everything perfect. I was a model. When I left there (MCC), they couldn't say one bad word about me, believe me.

By conforming to institutional rules white-collar offenders accomplish two subjectively important ends. They distance themselves from other inmates, and they validate pre-offense identities. The term identities is used here in the sense developed by symbolic interactionists as an internalized sense of self and a sense of where one stands as a social object with respect to others (Stryker, 1980; McCall and Simmons, 1983). For example, one can have an identity as a good father to the extent that one thinks of oneself in this way and perceives that others also place one in the same position. The identities that white-collar offenders wish to reaffirm are based on their conceptions of themselves as people who fit in with conventional society. By conforming to institutional rules offenders reaffirm their commitment to this social world and the legitimacy of their claim to be part of it.

Unlike ordinary offenders, who may experience conflict between the demands of the inmate culture and those of prison authorities, white-collar offenders reject the inmate culture (Johnson, 1987). As members of the dominant social classes, white-collar offenders accept the basic assumptions and operating principles of their society, which the prison is designed to protect and reinforce. Thus, they are psychologically in tune with the purposes of prisons and with the reasons for having prisons. To use the argot of the prison, they are "square Johns." By rejecting the inmate culture and viewing themselves as superior to it, they reject the moral implications of prison in defining themselves and publicly demonstrate their commitments to identities as law-abiding persons. Thus, for white-collar offenders elitism and conformity are means of coping with prison and reaffirming a sense of self.

DISCUSSION QUESTIONS

1. What are the implications of the finding that white-collar inmates are able to adjust to the incarceration experience?

2. Why do you think white-collar inmates reject the inmate subculture?

READING

In this study, Jurg Gerber surveyed embezzlers incarcerated in Japan, conducted interviews with white-collar inmates, and talked with prison workers to learn more about the incarceration experiences of white-collar offenders in another country. Gerber draws attention to the appearance of lenient treatment that white-collar offenders in the United States receive. He notes that only the most serious white-collar crime cases are brought into the system in the United States and even then white-collar offenders sentenced to prison appear to serve their sentences in "Club Fed"–like institutions. His research on Japanese embezzlers suggests that their experiences are not similar to a Club Fed experience. Gerber discusses his findings within the framework of reintegrative shaming.

"Club Fed" in Japan?

Incarceration Experiences of Japanese Embezzlers

Jurg Gerber

 ## Introduction

There has been a longstanding debate in criminology over the severity of punishment meted out to street criminals and white-collar offenders. Some scholars have argued that white-collar offenders are treated more leniently than comparable street criminals (Clinard & Yeager, 1980; Ross, 1907; Sutherland, 1949; Tillman & Pontell, 1992). Others have maintained that white-collar criminals do not receive less severe

SOURCE: Gerber, Jurg. (1994). "Club Fed" in Japan? Incarceration Experiences of Japanese Embezzlers. *International Journal of Offender Therapy, 37,* 163–174.

sanctions (Benson & Walker, 1988), while yet others have found that high-status defendants at times receive harsher sentences than other defendants (Wheeler, Weisburd, & Bode, 1982). Such inconsistent findings can be reconciled at least partly by the work of Shapiro (1985, 1990), who pointed out that white-collar offenders are more likely to be subjected to civil and administrative sanctions than street offenders. Consequently, only the most serious white-collar offenses are prosecuted in the criminal courts. The apparent harshness of sentencing of white-collar offenders proves to be the result of a diversion of the less serious offenders from the criminal courts.

Regardless of the severity of sanction, it is well known that few white-collar criminals serve any time in prison. Those who do find that their sentences are short and often served in one of several minimum security federal correctional facilities sometimes referred to as "Club Fed." While these institutions have no bars or walls, their distinctiveness derives as much from the unusual inmates they sometimes house as from the surroundings they provide. From the Reverend Sun Myung Moon to the former Senator Williams, these institutions have held a surprising number of white-collar offenders (Hagan & Palloni, 1986, p. 603).

Dating back to the work of Sutherland, critics have maintained that such preferential treatment of white-collar offenders reinforces the perception that their offenses are not serious; in turn, this may make it more difficult to control such behaviors. Sentencing white-collar offenders to longer terms and forcing them to serve them in conventional prisons might enhance control efforts. Presumably, increasing the severity and certainty of incarceration would deter many potential white-collar offenders because their acts are rational and because these individuals have the most to lose if caught (Braithwaite, 1985; Geis, 1984).

One way to learn if differences in treatment produce different outcomes is by focusing on incarceration practices in other societies. Unfortunately, there is little cross-cultural research on incarceration of white-collar criminals. The current project is a pilot study of incarceration experiences of one type of white-collar criminals, embezzlers, in one society, Japan.

Japan as a Research Setting

Japan is an ideal society in which to do research aimed at testing hypotheses developed in the United States. Like the latter, it is highly industrialized, but it has low crime rates. Given its levels of industrialization and urbanization it should have high crime rates, but does not. Explanations for this fact have been many. Braithwaite (1989) uses Japan as an example of a society that relies on *reintegrative shaming* to keep crime rates low: the society labels and shames criminals, but then reintegrates them. Bayley (1976) has focused on the relative economic stability enjoyed by Japanese workers that, inter alia, leads to less employee theft than in the United States. Close police/community relations are also believed to have reduced the crime rates. Police officers in Japan know the people on their beats and are thus able to monitor them and their neighborhoods more effectively (Bayley, 1976; Clifford, 1976). Kerbo and Inoue (1990) point out that Japan's cultural homogeneity has led to pressure on people not to engage in antisocial behavior because such actions would always harm the in-group (unlike the U.S. where the victims sometimes belong to an out-group). Schneider (1992) argues that criminality is low in Japan because the Japanese see group loyalty as more important than individualism, because shame is important, and because crime control is a community issue (therefore, informal sanctions can be used more effectively in Japan, whereas in the U.S. or in the Federal Republic of Germany formal, state-administered sanctions must be used). In sum, Braithwaite (1989, p. 62), reviewing the findings of Bayley (1976), Clifford (1976), Adler (1983) and Fenwick (1985), concludes that Japan's low crime rates are caused by "high interdependency in Japanese society" and "highly developed communitarianism."

Rates of white-collar crime are difficult to estimate in Japan. Braithwaite (1989) points out that the communitarianism that makes possible low crime rates in general, also allows for the concealment of white-collar criminal subcultures. It is known, though, that Japanese pharmaceutical companies have a long history of engaging in corporate crime (Braithwaite, 1984), and that political corruption is commonplace. For instance, in the Lockheed scandal during the 1970s, Japanese Prime Minister Tanaka was convicted of accepting a bribe from the Lockheed corporation (Coleman, 1989; Simon & Eitzen, 1990), while the Recruit Cosmos Scandal of 1984 led to the resignation of 53 officials and the indictment of 19 individuals, and contributed to the defeat of the ruling party in the upper house during the 1989 elections (Kerbo & Inoue, 1990).

The question remains as to how Japan treats its white-collar criminals and whether this treatment affects crime rates in general and recidivism rates in particular. The current research represents a first step in finding answers to this question.

Methods

The data collection for this research occurred in early 1992. A fellow researcher and I were invited by the Correction Bureau of the Japanese Ministry of Justice to travel to Japan to intensify contacts between Japanese officials and American educators, and to learn about Japanese corrections. As part of this stay we were given the opportunity to implement a research project; the present article reports on one aspect of this larger project.

I was given the opportunity to administer a questionnaire to 75 inmates in one prison, Prison X, that housed "Class A" adult male inmates. In Japanese prisons, inmates are separated on the basis of age (juveniles, adults under 26 years of age, adults over 26), gender, and *degree of criminal tendency:* Class A offenders are "those who do not have an advanced criminal tendency," while Class B offenders "have an advanced criminal tendency" (Correction Bureau, 1990, p. 30). In theory, the distinction between Classes A and B is based on psychological differences, but in practice it is based on recidivism: the more convictions an inmate has, the more likely it is he will be sent to a prison for B prisoners.[1]

While we visited several prisons, the only prison in which I could conduct research with male inmates was in Prison X. In the prison we toured that held Class B inmates, Prison Y, we were not allowed to interact with inmates at all. The present findings are thus biased in an important way: only information from inmates who serve their time in the relatively relaxed atmosphere of Prison X are included.[2] Officials at the Correction Bureau told me that they selected Prison X for interviews as it was the prison in the vicinity of Tokyo that housed white-collar offenders.

Following the administration of the questionnaire to the 75 inmates, who had been selected by officials at Prison X, and so cannot be considered a random sample, I was able to interview 14 prisoners face-to-face. I was given some background information on the 75 inmates and was able to select the 14 myself. I chose them primarily on the basis of the offense for which they were convicted, picking all inmates who could be classified as having committed a white-collar offense, primarily embezzlement and fraud. Interviews with these inmates averaged about 30 minutes in length. While several guards were always present during the administration of the questionnaire to three groups of 25 inmates each, only the interpreter, the inmate, and I were in the room during the face-to-face interviews. My impression was that, cultural differences notwithstanding, inmates felt relatively free to talk to me as evidenced by some of the critical remarks they expressed.

Data were also gathered from other sources. I was able to interview eight officers and administrators of Prison X about their perceptions of inmates and prison life. Towards the end of the stay I was able to submit questions I had about the prison to the liaison officer who passed them on to appropriate prison officials. I was also able to observe inmates within the prison, which provided for at least some participant observation data. Finally, I was given an opportunity to interview a prosecutor in Tokyo who specializes in white-collar offenses.

Findings

In order to judge the severity of sanctions levied against certain kinds of offenders, information is needed on the percentage of offenders sentenced to prison terms. It is widely recognized that better statistics are kept in the United States on the adjudication of street criminals than on white-collar criminals. Indeed, it is extremely difficult to find any reliable statistics on white-collar criminals in general, and embezzlers, the focus of this study, in particular. While the Federal Bureau of Investigation reported 12,055 arrests for embezzlement during 1990 (U.S. Department of Justice, Federal Bureau of Investigation, 1991), the adjudication of these cases is unclear. Approximately 1,800 individuals were convicted of embezzlement in U.S. District Courts in 1990; about one quarter of these individuals were sentenced to some form of incarceration; the average sentence length was 17.7 months; and the average time served was 11.6 months (U.S. Department of Justice, Bureau of Justice Statistics, 1991).[3]

Japan and the United States are therefore similar in that they rarely incarcerate white-collar offenders. The question is now whether or not those who are sent to correctional institutions receive any special treatment. One important qualification notwithstanding, the "Club Fed" phenomenon that is observed in the United States is not present in Japan. One of the distinctions between Class A and Class B prisoners is the existence of previous convictions. It would follow that inmates who are classified as Class A, those without advanced criminal tendencies, would be first-time offenders. Of the 377 inmates serving time at Prison X during 1990, the most recent year for which figures are available, 84.6% were incarcerated for the first time. The same figures also imply, however, that about one sixth of the prison's population are repeat offenders who have served time previously. In this context it is important to remember that I was stationed in Prison X because, according to the liaison officer of the Correction Bureau, white-collar criminals would not likely be assigned to a Class B prison. Therefore, white-collar criminals appear to be routed to the relatively more attractive Class A prisons, which is consistent with the Club Fed phenomenon.

Though they are not sent to Class B prisons, the few white-collar offenders who end up in Class A prisons do not find a country club atmosphere as the term Club Fed implies. Indeed, they are confronted with prison conditions that are identical to those of other Class A inmates, and are of a harshness not imaginable to American street offenders, much less American white-collar offenders. The overarching goal of Japanese corrections, as is the case at least in theory in many correctional systems in the world, is resocialization and reintegration into society. As Japan is a society that values conformity and uniformity, inmates, regardless of the offenses they committed, are prepared to reenter society by learning an uncritical acceptance of rules and regulations. Officers in charge of inmates, convicted of white-collar and street offenses, expressed this idea as follows:

I try to teach the importance of group life, rules, and cooperation. (Officer E)

Prisons are places for people who have violated rules . . . I teach them to follow rules in prison, then they learn to follow them on the outside. (Officer F)

Prisons are places where sentences should be carried out . . . in Japan this means forced labor, eight hours a day . . . through the process of engaging in prison industries the importance of rules and cooperation is taught which leads to resocialization. (Officer B)

People who come to prisons are rule violators—society and prisons are both groups that depend on rules. . . . prison should teach about the importance of rules. (Officer A)

In order to achieve the goal of successful reintegration of offenders into society, the individuals must learn to control themselves. As most of them are seen as incapable of doing so, they must be forced.

The people who come to prison led lazy and disorganized lives in society; they need to be taught how to lead their lives organized. This would involve teaching manners such as sitting up straight; not doing the little things well is an indication of a mindset. (Officer G)

As the correctional officers see it, teaching such skills is complicated by the need to protect inmates from each other. The rules that regulate inmate behavior are, from a Western perspective, incredibly detailed and repressive. Among many other things, inmates who eat their meals in their cells are not allowed to share food, they are not allowed to lie down except during certain hours, while in their cells they are not allowed to lean against a wall, and they are not allowed to stand up except for the purpose of going to the bathroom. Such rules are said to ensure the protection of inmates, although guards believe that inmates often do not understand this.

> The exchange of food is prohibited. While this is okay in society, in prison strong inmates can take food from weak inmates. The way to protect weak inmates is to prohibit all food exchange. . . .
> Standing up without reason is prohibited. [If inmates are allowed to stand up without reason] they can easily commit suicide—also, if an inmate wants to conceal an activity from guards, another inmate could stand at the window and check for the guard, who would then never find out what is going on. Inmates can also be better protected from each other this way. (Officer B)

Inmates do have problems seeing the usefulness of such detailed rules. Several expressed concern about the rigidity of the regulations when they were asked about what they liked least about prison.

> Feeling of lack of freedom. . . . there are too many constraints. . . . even during free time and during exercise time officers still give a lot of orders that are not necessary; for instance, standing up in cell without reason leads to them giving orders, wrong posture when watching TV does the same. (Inmate #14, serving time for fraud and embezzlement)

> No freedom . . . I must stay in my cell on weekends. . . . if I have a legitimate request to

send a letter I have to go through official channels which are slow. (Inmate #9, serving time for theft and embezzlement)

> I would like them to stop using the military style—if prison could be more open and democratic it could be better. The language for instance is unnecessarily militaristic. (Inmate #11, serving time for embezzlement)

A second concern expressed by some inmates is related to the extent of control officers have over inmates. The amount of discretion on the part of officers was seen as problematic. Not only could the officers dictate the behavior of inmates, but they were able to do so in an arbitrary manner.

> Relationships with staff can be problematic because some officers cannot understand me and my problems because they can be rigid in their thinking. I cannot approach them with my concerns. A good officer is a fair officer, a bad officer is one who is not. (Inmate #10, serving time for embezzlement)

> One area Japanese prisons should improve is the fairness with which officers treat inmates. There are tremendous differences between officers. For instance, "talking back to an officer" is treated and defined very differently; there is great arbitrariness. (Inmate #14)

Along similar lines, there was a discrepancy according to inmates between the rhetoric of resocialization and actual treatment of inmates by correctional officers. Whereas resocialization is the overarching goal of Japanese corrections, its officers are believed by inmates to lose sight of this goal at times and to stereotype inmates. Prisoners are then seen as wholly untrustworthy and likely to fail.

> Here in prison officers look down on me. If I were the warden I would provide for more humane treatment of inmates who are already sorry for what they did. The officers act like we

are all criminals who will never change. (Inmate #5, serving time for insurance fraud and arson)

Each inmate has good and bad sides but prison officials have a tendency to look only at the bad. Please look at the good sides too. (Inmate #9)

When asked about what aspect of prison life they liked best, or disliked the least, a few inmates interestingly stated that rules and discipline appealed to them.

Learning to abide by rules is positive. (Inmate #7, serving time for breach of trust)

When I read a book about American prisons I read that they are less restrictive. I prefer Japanese prisons because prisons should be a place where inmates should be punished. Adversity in prison teaches inmates to deal with problems on the outside. (Inmate #13, serving time for violating corporate tax law)

However, it was a clear minority of inmates who saw learning about rules and regulations as beneficial or desirable. More commonly, inmates listed recreational activities, the opportunity to read, the opportunity for self-reflection and learning vocational skills as aspects of prison life they considered enjoyable. Several also listed physical education such as softball, exercise, and Tenny-Pong (a hybrid between tennis and ping-pong).

Why do inmates like, or not dislike, certain aspects of prison life in Japan? In some instances, it might be speculated that inmates gave answers they assumed were the "appropriate" answers. Inmate #13, for instance, had been admitted to Prison X less than one month prior to the administration of the interview. It is possible that he was cautious in providing only answers that he considered acceptable by the prison administration. Conversely, consistent with Braithwaite's (1989) argument concerning reintegrative shaming, it is possible that inmates, having undergone a process of resocialization, have changed their value systems so that they can be reintegrated into society. Inmate #7 had completed about 17 months of a three-year sentence at the time of the interview; he might have been successfully resocialized.

It came as a surprise to me how many of the inmates liked physical education and recreation classes, especially in light of the fact that several of the inmates were older and did not seem to be overly athletic. Guards and the liaison officer indicated that they believed that inmates like sports because it is the one activity that is regulated less than most other aspects of prison life. Softball gives inmates an opportunity to escape the harsh reality of prison life with its rules and regulations.

Discussion and Conclusions

My goal was to learn about the incarceration experiences of Japanese white-collar offenders and compare them to the experiences of their American counterparts. It is clear that incarceration in Japan is very different from the United States for white-collar offenders. While the American prison experience conjures up images of "Club Fed," Japanese white-collar criminals, if they are unfortunate enough to be incarcerated, are more likely to be treated in a fashion similar to other Class A inmates. Although Class B inmates endure much more elaborate rules and regulations, Class A inmates still must deal with a prison environment that is vastly more restrictive than what is common in the United States. Japanese prison inmates convicted of embezzlement can only dream of the relatively relaxed atmosphere of a maximum security prison in the United States. The nature of minimum security prisons in this country is probably beyond the imagination of most Japanese, inmates and ordinary citizens alike.

The question remains whether such harsh treatment is beneficial to the inmates and society. On one hand, it is unlikely that this is the case. In many ways, the correctional system in Japan today is reminiscent of the *separate* and the *silent* systems of years past (Allen & Simonsen, 1989): total control over the movement of inmates, and near-complete control over conversations has not been a feature of U.S. prisons for several decades. These systems have been abandoned because they led to abuse and violence against the inmates. It seems at least possible that Japanese prison inmates would suffer similarly from abuse.

On the other hand, it is conceivable that a repressive correctional system *may* work better in Japan than it did in the U.S. While correctional treatment of inmates in Japan is extremely control-oriented, its underlying philosophy is far more complicated than a simplistic "lock-'em-up-and-throw-away-the-key." In fact, consistent with Braithwaite's (1989) argument concerning *reintegrative shaming,* there is a strong element of rehabilitation. The emphasis on rehabilitation manifests itself in everything guards and inmates told me, although they did not always agree on the relative effectiveness of the program and methods used.

Shame was a common theme in the answers provided by inmates. They indicated repeatedly that they regretted having engaged in the criminal behavior, they wished they could undo the action, and that while they did not take into consideration the feelings of the victims at first, they learned to do so later.

> Before and during the embezzlement I felt that I was entitled to the money, in fact, the amount was appropriate. Now I am sorry and want to pay back the owner [of the business he victimized], . . . I learned about the reasons for laws from the meaning of prison rules. (Inmate #1, serving time for embezzlement)

> I just took the money that I needed. I was entitled to some money because I had to do extra work at night and because the dormitory [where he lived] was bad. . . . I no longer think that I was right in just taking it—I should have asked if I needed anything. (Inmate #2, serving time for embezzlement)

Once shame and guilt can be induced, resocialization becomes possible according to correctional officials. Prison discipline is needed to achieve this goal, but it is also needed to protect the feelings of the victim.

> Resocialization is the goal of the prison—everything works towards this goal—both punishment and education are necessary. (Officer F)

> It wouldn't be fair to [victims] if the inmates were having a good time in prison. Their behavior should be regulated. (Officer B)

It is noteworthy that this process works from the perspective of the inmates. While they bitterly complained in some instances about the rigidity and comprehensiveness of prison rules, they expected to be reintegrated fully upon release from the prison. They expected to be accepted by their family and friends, and they anticipated no significant problems in finding work upon release, although some indicated that they would lie about their backgrounds if necessary.

In sum, while few white-collar criminals serve time in prisons in Japan, as is the case in the United States, they tend to have incarceration experiences that are much more similar to those of street criminals than is the case in the United States. Although some elements of the "Club Fed" phenomenon can be observed in Japan, it is much less pronounced there than in the United States.

Notes

1. The use of the male pronoun "he" is deliberate in this context as this distinction applies to males only. Regardless of their criminal tendencies, women are sent to the same institution in each prefecture. This is similar to the situation in the U.S. and produces the same consequences:

> Since the proportion of women in each jurisdiction who are incarcerated is small, often prisoners with a variety of needs—from community custody to strictest maximum security—are held in the same prison. As a result, all the women held are subjected to enhanced security (Weisheit & Mahan, 1988, p. 71).

2. Inmates in Prison Y were not allowed to look at us as we walked by; they were forced to turn around when we were near.

3. Figures for state courts are very incomplete, but what is available suggests outcomes comparable to the findings at the federal level. In a study of six states (California, Minnesota, New York, Pennsylvania, Nebraska, and Virginia) that voluntarily participated from 1983 to 1988, 11,331 individuals were arrested for embezzlement. Of these, 70.9% were convicted of something, but only 4,833 were convicted of embezzlement. Of the latter, 80.9% were sentenced to some form of incarceration (U.S. Department of Justice, Bureau of Justice Statistics, 1992).

References

Adler, F. (1983). *Nations not obsessed with crime*. Littleton, CO: F.B. Rothman.

Allen, H., & Simonsen, C. (1989). *Correction in America* (5th ed.). New York: Macmillan.

Bayley, D. H. (1976). *Forces of order: Police behavior in Japan and the United States*. Berkeley, CA: University of California Press.

Benson, M., & Walker, E. (1988). Sentencing the white-collar offender, *American Sociological Review, 50,* 294-302.

Braithwaite, J. (1984). *Corporate crime in the pharmaceutical industry*. London: Routledge & Kegan Paul.

Braithwaite, J. (1985). White collar crime. *Annual Review of Sociology, 11,* 1-15.

Braithwaite, J. (1989*). Crime, shame and reintegration*. Cambridge, MA: Cambridge University Press.

Clifford, W. (1976). *Crime control in Japan*. Lexington, MA: D.C. Heath.

Clinard, M., & Yeager, P. (1980). *Corporate crime*. New York: Free Press.

Coleman, J. W. (1989). *The criminal elite* (2nd ed.). New York: St. Martin's Press.

Fenwick, C. R. (1985). Culture, philosophy and crime: The Japanese experience. *International Journal of Comparative and Applied Criminal Justice, 9,* 67-81.

Geis, G. (1984). White-collar and corporate crime. In R. F. Meier (Ed.), *Major forms of crime* (pp. 139-150). Beverly Hills, CA: Sage.

Gerber, J., & Weeks, S. L. (1992). Some reflections on doing crosscultural research: Interviewing Japanese prison inmates. *The Criminologist, 17*(6), 1, 7-12.

Hagan, J., & Palloni, A. (1986). 'Club Fed' and the sentencing of white-collar offenders before and after Watergate. *Criminology, 24,* 603-621.

Kerbo, H. R., & Inoue, M. (1990). Japanese social structure and white collar crime: Recruit cosmos and beyond. *Deviant Behavior, 11,* 139-150.

Ross, E. A. (1907). *Sin and society*. Boston: Houghton Mifflin.

Schneider, H. J. (1992). Crime and its control in Japan and in the Federal Republic of Germany. *International Journal of Offender Therapy and Comparative Criminology, 36,* 307-321.

Shapiro, S. (1985). The road not taken: The elusive path to criminal prosecution for white collar offenders. *Law and Society Review, 19,* 179-217.

Shapiro, S. (1990). Collaring the crime, not the criminal: Reconsidering the concept of white-collar crime. *American Sociological Review, 55,* 346-365.

Simon, D. R., & Eitzen, D. S. (1990). *Elite deviance* (3rd ed.). Boston: Allyn & Bacon.

Sutherland, E. (1949). *White collar crime*. New York: Holt, Rinehart & Winston.

Tillman, R., & Ponteil, H. N. (1992). Is justice 'collar-blind?' Punishing Medicaid provider fraud. *Criminology, 30,* 547-573.

U.S. Department of Justice, Bureau of Justice Statistics. (1991). *Federal crime case processing, 1980-89, with preliminary data for 1990*. NCJ-130526. Washington, DC: U.S. Government Printing Office.

U.S. Department of Justice, Bureau of Justice Statistics. (1992). *Forgery and fraud-related offenses in 6 states, 1983-88*. Special Report NCJ 132445. Washington, DC: Author.

U.S. Department of Justice, Federal Bureau of Investigation. (1991). *Crime in the United States, 1990*. Washington, DC: U.S. Government Printing Office.

Weisheit, R., & Mahan, S. (1988). *Women, crime and criminal justice*. Cincinnati, OH: Anderson Publishing Company.

Wheeler, S., Weisburd, D., & Bode, N. (1982). Sentencing the white-collar offender: Rhetoric and reality. *American Sociological Review, 50,* 641-649.

DISCUSSION QUESTIONS

1. How would it be different to be a white-collar inmate in Japan as compared to the U.S.?

2. What contributes to these differences?

READING

In this study, David Weisburd and his coauthors examine the question of whether convicted white-collar offenders are similar to convicted conventional offenders. The authors note that criminal justice officials and researchers assume that the two groups are different. Using data from seven federal judicial districts for offenders convicted between fiscal years 1976 and 1978, the authors found that both groups of offenders tended to have

SOURCE: Weisburd, David, Chayet, Ellen, & Waring, Elin. (1990). White-collar crime and criminal careers: Some preliminary findings. *Crime and Delinquency, 36,* 342–355.

prior criminal histories. They also found that white-collar offenders were older than conventional offenders and the offenders did not specialize in specific types of criminal careers. The authors raise the question of whether specific types of crime sentencing policies are needed to deal with chronic offenders. They also point out that many "white-collar" offenders are actually "middle-class" offenders.

White-Collar Crime and Criminal Careers

Some Preliminary Findings

David Weisburd, Ellen F. Chayet, and Elin J. Waring

The criminal career paradigm has begun to play a central role in the ways in which scholars and policymakers understand criminality. The paradigm directs attention to the factors that lead to participation in crime, the nature and extent of criminal activities of active offenders, and the duration of their involvement (e.g., see Blumstein and Cohen with Hseih 1982; Blumstein, Cohen, Roth, and Visher 1986). Scholars have increasingly focused upon the careers of "common criminals," but they have largely neglected the careers of white-collar offenders. Behind this neglect lies a common assumption about the nature of white-collar criminality. Although street criminals are assumed highly likely to recidivate, white-collar criminals are thought to be "one-shot" offenders unlikely to be processed in the justice system after their initial brush with the law. This assumption has little empirical support. But nonetheless, it is commonly stated by both researchers (see Edelhertz and Overcast 1982) and criminal justice practitioners (e.g., see Benson 1985; Wheeler, Mann, and Sarat 1988).

This article examines the extent to which this image of white-collar criminals is reflected in the criminal records of defendants convicted under white-collar crime statutes in the federal court system. We find that a substantial proportion of such criminals are repeat offenders, and that a number have serious and lengthy criminal records. Following this, we explore parameters of criminality identified in the study of criminal careers in the context of this white-collar crime sample. We conclude with a discussion of the implications of these findings for white-collar crime research and policy.

The Sample

The sample was drawn from an earlier study of convicted white-collar criminals conducted by Wheeler, Weisburd, and Bode (1988; see also Wheeler, Weisburd, and Bode 1982; Wheeler, Weisburd, Waring, and Bode 1988; Weisburd, Wheeler, Waring and Bode forthcoming). They defined white-collar crime as "economic offenses committed through the use of some combination of fraud, deception, or collusion" (Wheeler, Weisburd, and Bode 1982, p. 642; see also Shapiro 1980). Following this they examined eight such crimes in the federal system: antitrust offenses, securities and exchange fraud, postal and wire fraud, false claims and statements, credit and lending institution fraud, bank embezzlement, IRS fraud, and bribery. Wheeler and colleagues argued that their sample included those offenses "that would most frequently be identified by persons as 'presumptively' white-collar" (1982, p. 643) and that most of the crimes identified in their sample fit one or another definition of white-collar crime (Wheeler, Weisburd, Waring, and Bode 1988, p. 334). But they acknowledge that they cast a larger net for white-collar criminals than most other studies (see Weisburd et al. forthcoming).

The sample was drawn from seven federal judicial districts during fiscal years 1976-1978 with specific information about offenders coded from presentence investigation reports. The districts were chosen in part to provide geographic spread, in part because they were being examined in other studies, and in part because some of them were known to have a substantial amount of white-collar prosecution (see Wheeler, Weisburd, Waring, and Bode 1988). The districts (and their central cities) are: Central California (Los Angeles), Northern Georgia (Atlanta), Northern Illinois (Chicago), Maryland (Baltimore), Southern New York (Manhattan and the Bronx), Northern Texas (Dallas), and Western Washington (Seattle).

To allow a detailed reading of each presentence investigation, as well as to avoid having one or two offenses dominate, Wheeler, Weisburd, and Bode (1988; hereafter referred to as Wheeler et al.) chose to examine a random sample of 30 convicted defendants from each offense category in each of the seven districts.[1] The resulting sample therefore contained more antitrust and securities fraud offenders, and fewer postal fraud, IRS fraud and bank embezzlement offenders than a nonstratified random sample would. But it offered a broad and heterogeneous sample of those convicted under white-collar crime statutes in the federal courts.

A brief review of background characteristics of the sample selected by Wheeler et al. illustrates the extent to which it reflects a white-collar population of criminal defendants. For example, only 8% of the sample as a whole were unemployed at the time they committed their crimes—a stark contrast to street criminals, most of whom are not employed in legitimate occupations (Sviridoff and McElroy 1985). In the Wheeler et al. sample, most of those employed had "white-collar" jobs as defined by the federal government, and many were owners or officers of businesses. The sample also included a larger number of White offenders and a substantially older population of criminals than would be found in a sample of street criminals. Indeed, whereas bank embezzlers were on average 31 years old at the time of their conviction, the average tax offender was 47 years old, and the average securities offender was 44 years old.

Prior Criminality of the Sample

Of the eight white-collar crimes examined, only in the antitrust category did offenders fit traditional stereotypes of white-collar criminals. For every other offense, a substantial number of those examined had prior criminal records. Even in the case of embezzlement in

banks where there are generally barriers to bank employment for those with criminal records, almost one-third of the offenders had prior arrests.

Many white-collar criminals evidenced multiple prior arrests. In the case of credit fraud, false claims and mail fraud violators, about 4 in 10 offenders had two or more prior arrests, and about 3 in 10 had four or more prior arrests. Although the extent of repeat offending was much lower in other crime categories, more than a quarter of tax offenders had two or more prior arrests, and more than 1 in 10 of bank embezzlers and bribery offenders had multiple prior arrests.

A substantial proportion of offenders in every crime category (with the exception of antitrust) also had prior convictions. The proportion ranged from a low of 19% for bribery offenders to a high of 46% for those convicted of a credit fraud.

The seriousness of the criminal records of these offenders may be gauged from the number with either prior felony convictions or previous incarcerations. More than 1 in 7 securities fraud violators in the sample had prior felony convictions, and this was the case for more than a quarter of those convicted of credit fraud, false claims, and mail fraud. Whereas only 1 in 25 securities violators had spent any time in jail or prison,[2] this was true for a fifth of credit fraud, false claims, and mail fraud offenders. And many of those in this latter group had served substantial periods of time behind bars.

Certainly, many of the white-collar criminals identified in the Wheeler et al. study were repeat offenders who evidenced criminality even before the felony convictions that brought them into the sample. Yet, the fact that antitrust offenders did not evidence substantial prior criminality raises an important question about the general validity of these findings. Is a high rate of recidivism common only among low-status criminals in the sample? Perhaps, more important, do those offenders who would fit the most restrictive definitions of white-collar crime also recidivate?

To address this question we restricted our criminal history analysis to a selected group of offenders who held elite positions or owned significant assets, and committed their crimes in the course of a legitimate occupation. Thus we selected (following Katz 1979) only those sample members who worked within a bourgeois profession (such as doctors, lawyers or accountants), or who had positions as officers or managers, or who were owners of substantial capital (greater than $250,000)— and who used their occupation to commit their crimes. This procedure eliminated approximately two-thirds of the sample.[3] But even restricting the sample in this way we found that over a quarter had criminal records (see Table 14.7). Of this sample, 10% reported prior felony convictions, and 6% had prior records of incarceration. Accordingly, evidence of criminal careers can be found even within a highly restricted population of elite white-collar offenders.

Table 14.7 Prior Criminal Records of a Sample Restricted to High Status White-Collar Offenders From the Wheeler et al. Sample[a]

	Percentage of Restricted Sample	N
Percentage with any prior arrests	28	319
Percentage with any prior convictions	22	316
Percentage with 2 or more prior arrests	13	317
Percentage with prior felony convictions	10	319
Percentage previously incarcerated	6	319

a. See endnote 3 for details about the definition of this sample.

White-Collar Criminals and Criminal Careers

Having established that many white-collar criminals do recidivate, we were led to ask how their criminal "careers"[4] are similar or different from those of street criminals. The Wheeler et al. data allowed us to focus upon three dimensions of offending identified in criminal career research (see Blumstein et al. 1986): frequency, or the intensity of offending; onset, or the age of the entrance of offenders into criminality; and specialization, or the extent to which criminals repeat crimes of a similar type. We were not able to speculate on other related dimensions of criminal careers, such as duration or desistance, because the sample was drawn at time of conviction and the study included no criminal history information subsequent to that conviction.

The Wheeler et al. data showed that there is a much higher frequency of offending for white-collar criminals than has commonly been thought. But the frequency of their offending is still much lower than that of other types of criminals. In a comparison sample of common crime offenders convicted under federal forgery and postal theft statutes, for example, Weisburd et al. (forthcoming) found that 80% had prior arrests, and 74% had more than two prior arrests.[5] Similarly, studies of convicted street crime offenders have reported much higher rates of prior offending than found in this white-collar crime sample.[6]

These comparisons are, of course, complicated by the fact that the meaning of arrest for a white-collar crime is often different than that for a street crime. Prosecutors, not the police, are usually the primary investigators of white-collar crime (Katz 1979). And white-collar offenders are often "arrested" much later in the investigative process than are street criminals, because their crimes are usually difficult to unravel and seldom have the advantage of identifiable victims (Braithwaite and Geis 1982). Such offenders may not be arrested at all if prosecutors decide to use civil actions instead of a criminal prosecution (Mann 1989). Accordingly, at least in regard to white-collar crimes,[7] we might expect official records to underestimate the frequency of offending for those in a white-collar crime sample.

This underreporting bias is exacerbated by the fact that white-collar crimes generally are of longer duration than are street crimes (see Wheeler, Weisburd, Waring, and Bode 1988). A land scheme that continues over several years may, for example, produce only one arrest. But it is certainly not comparable to a single theft or mugging. Even accounting for the fact that white-collar crimes prosecuted in the federal courts seldom approximate the spectacular offenses reported in the popular press, they generally represent more complicated and longer-lived crimes than the average street offense (Wheeler, Weisburd, Waring, and Bode 1988). In this sense, we might speculate that large gaps between officially reported crimes in a white-collar criminal "career" do not necessarily mean that such offenders are inactive in those periods.

The onset of offending in the Wheeler et al. sample also points to important differences between these offenders and street criminals. Whereas street offenders are usually arrested for the first time while teenagers, in every crime category we examined, white-collar offenders were, on average, adults before they committed their first offense. Indeed, for bribery, tax, and securities offenders the mean age of first arrest was over 40.

Of course it is problematic to speak of onset in a criminal career if there is no evidence that an offender will continue criminality after a first offense. And in fact, when we examined only "chronic" offenders— those with three or more arrests (see Tillman 1987)[8]— we gained a substantially different portrait of the onset of offending in a white-collar crime sample. Although older, on average, than street criminals when they committed their first crimes, among chronic white-collar offenders the mean age of first arrest for each of the offense categories was between 20 and 30.

This discussion of white-collar criminal careers has so far not addressed the problem of specialization. The fact that white-collar crimes often demand special skills and particular organizational positions might lead to the assumption that white-collar criminals will specialize in white-collar type crimes. Although the Wheeler et al. data do not allow a precise tracking of the form of a criminal career, they do identify offenders who have some white-collar criminality in their pasts.[9]

Only about a third of the chronic offenders have prior white-collar crime arrests. Least likely to evidence this type of specialization are bribery offenders and bank embezzlers; most likely are mail fraud and securities violators. In the latter case almost half of the chronic offenders, as we defined them, had at least one prior white-collar crime arrest. Although these data do not allow us to disentangle the complicated issues surrounding specialization, they do challenge the idea that there is much greater specialization in white-collar crime than in other types of offending.

We suspect that there are various types of criminal careers for those involved in white-collar crime. For some, like many of the securities violators in the Wheeler et al. sample, the skills needed to carry out an offense and the complexity of the crime scenarios involved may lead to a relatively late onset of criminality, a low frequency of offending, and a relatively high degree of specialization. For others, white-collar crime, often of a relatively trivial type,[10] represents only one part of a mixed bag of criminal activities. Such offenders are likely to begin offending much earlier in life and commit crimes (often not white-collar in nature) with much greater frequency. These scenarios represent perhaps the extremes of criminal "careers" in a white-collar crime sample and illustrate the diversity of offenders who are prosecuted under white-collar crime statutes.

⬛ Conclusions

Contrary to common assumptions, we found in a sample of offenders convicted of federal white-collar crimes that white-collar criminals are often repeat offenders. This fact led us to begin analyzing the criminal careers of such offenders, an effort that we are now continuing in the context of a National Institute of Justice-supported follow-up study of the Wheeler et al. sample.[11] Our initial findings suggest that white-collar criminals' "careers" begin later and evidence lower frequency of offending than do those of street criminals. They also challenge the assumption that such careers will be highly specialized.

The fact that white-collar criminals are often repeat offenders raises the question of whether it is useful to develop criminal justice policies for white-collar crime, like those for common crime (e.g., see Greenwood 1985), that focus upon high-rate criminals. That many white-collar offenders commit crimes of a non-white-collar type appears to support those who argue that there is little use in making research or policy distinctions between white-collar criminals and other offenders (e.g., see Hirschi and Gottfredson 1987).

The social backgrounds of offenders that fall within a white-collar crime sample appear to make them particularly susceptible to criminal justice intervention. As Zimring and Hawkins (1973, p. 128) note, those with the most to lose in a society are also those who place the most at risk when they commit crimes (see also Benson and Cullen 1988; Geis 1977). Given the fact that white-collar crimes are assumed to be instrumental, rather than expressive (see Chambliss 1984), we might expect that the threat of sanctions would be particularly salient for white-collar criminals. Accordingly, we believe there is good reason to focus research and policy on the problem of reducing individual recidivism among such offenders. What is less clear, however, is how different sanctions will affect higher status criminals. In fact, there is reason to suspect that simple assumptions linking harsher sanctions to greater deterrence will not apply for white-collar crime (e.g., see Benson and Cullen 1988).[12]

Turning to the more general problem of whether it is useful to develop special policies for those who commit white-collar crimes, we think it is important to place our findings in the context of a more general understanding of the nature of white-collar criminality prosecuted in the federal courts. Weisburd et al. (forthcoming) suggest that such crimes are most often committed by those who fall in the middle classes of our society. These are not those upper-class or elite criminals ordinarily associated with white-collar crime. But neither are they similar to the street criminals who have received the bulk of criminological attention. Clearly, we must reevaluate criminal justice policy with these offenders in mind.

⊠ Notes

1. Although this forms the primary sample in the Wheeler et al. study, they also collected information on all SEC and antitrust offenders convicted in the three-year period they examined.

2. Prior to the offense which led to their inclusion in the Wheeler el al. study.

3. We operationalized this by identifying those people who had at least one of the following characteristics: an occupational title of doctor, judge, lawyer, accountant, or clergyman; a social class of manager, owner or officer; and assets of at least $500,000. The management class included government managers and inspectors. Of the sample, 370 individuals fit this definition of white-collar social class. Again, following Katz, those who did not use their occupations to commit their offenses were then eliminated, leaving 319 offenders in the sample.

4. We use the term "career" in reference to the crime patterns evidenced by offenders in the sample. We find it useful to use dimensions of offending identified with criminal career research, but we recognize that the criminal career paradigm may be especially problematic in the case of white-collar crime (see Gottfredson and Hirschi 1988, for a more general critique of criminal career research).

5. This sample was made up of 210 individuals convicted of postal theft or postal fraud in the same districts and time period from which the Wheeler et al. white-collar sample was drawn. Postal theft cases generally involve thefts of government-issued checks for welfare or social security benefits, often from mail boxes on the day they arrive. The primary distinction between postal theft and postal forgery is simply whether the defendant is caught at the time of the theft or when he or she tries to cash the check by forging the endorsement of the recipient.

6. For example, in a probability sample of defendants arrested for various felony crimes in New York City in 1971, almost two thirds of the defendants had prior arrest records, and one third had prior felony convictions (Vera Institute of Justice 1977, p. 21).

7. As we will discuss later, those convicted of white-collar crimes often have non-white-collar offenses in their criminal histories.

8. We included here the arrest that led to their inclusion in the Wheeler et al. sample, and thus for practical purposes a chronic offender was defined as any member of the sample with two or more prior arrests for any type of crime. As Tillman notes there is no agreement on what constitutes a chronic offender (1987, p. 574). His definition is based on a comparison of arrest and police contact statistics, and attempts to find an arrest criterion equivalent to the five or more police contacts threshold used by Wolfgang, Figlio, and Sellin (1972, p. 219).

9. For this variable, all tax, business or personal frauds, other business violations (e.g., criminal violations of fair labor laws, health and safety laws of antitrust regulations), embezzlements, briberies and mail frauds, whether under state or federal statutes, were considered white-collar crimes.

10. Such as lying on credit card applications.

11. This study uses various criminal justice system data bases to track the post-sanctioning criminal careers of these defendants.

12. It is often suggested that more punitive sanctions will result in a greater deterrent influence on the offender (e.g., see Cook 1980). But in the case of white-collar crime there is strong reason to suspect that sanctions may also "backfire." In particular, we suspect that dramatic losses of prestige or status may reduce the cost of future criminality for white-collar offenders, thus increasing rather than decreasing recidivism.

 # References

Benson, M. L. 1985. "White Collar Offenders Under Community Supervision." *Justice Quarterly* 2:429-438.

Benson, M. L. and F. T. Cullen. 1988. "The Special Sensitivity of White-Collar Offenders to Prison: A Critique and Research Agenda." *Journal of Criminal Justice* 16:207-215.

Blumstein, A. and J. Cohen with P. Hseih. 1982, *The Duration of Adult Criminal Careers*. Washington, DC: National Institute of Justice.

Blumstein, A., J. Cohen, J. A. Roth, and C. A. Visher, eds. 1986. *Criminal Careers and "Career Criminals."* Washington, DC: National Academy Press.

Braithwaite, J. and G. Geis. 1982. "On Theory and Action for Corporate Crime Control." Pp. 189-210 in *On White Collar Crime,* edited by G. Geis. Lexington, MA: D. C. Heath.

Chambliss, W. J. 1984. "Types of Deviance and the Effectiveness of Legal Sanctions." Pp. 398-407 in *Criminal Law in Action.* 2nd ed., edited by W. J. Chambliss. New York: Wiley.

Cook, P. J. 1980. "Research in Criminal Deterrence: Laying the Groundwork for the Second Decade." Pp. 211-268 in *Crime and Justice: An Annual Review of Research,* edited by N. Morris and M. Tonry. Chicago: University of Chicago Press.

Edelhertz, H. and T. D. Overcast, eds. 1982. *White Collar Crime: An Agenda for Research.* Lexington, MA: D. C. Heath.

Geis, G. A. 1977. "The Heavy Electrical Equipment Antitrust Case of 1961." Pp. 117-132 in *White Collar Crime: Offenses in Business, Politics, and the Professions,* edited by G. Geis and R. F. Meier. New York: Free Press.

Greenwood, P. 1985. "The Incapacitative/Deterrent Role of Increased Criminal Penalties." *Proceedings of the Attorney-General's Crime Conference 85.* Sacramento, CA: California Department of Justice.

Gottfredson, M. and T. Hirschi. 1988. "Science, Public Policy and the Career Paradigm." *Criminology* 26:37-55.

Hirschi, T. and M. Gottfredson. 1987. "Causes of White Collar Crime." *Criminology* 25:949-974.

Katz, J. 1979. "Legality and Equality: Plea-Bargaining in the Prosecution of White-Collar and Common Crime." *Law and Society Review* 13:431-459.

Mann, K. 1989. "Sanctioning White Collar Offenders." Paper presented to the School of Criminal Justice, Rutgers the State University of New Jersey, February.

Shapiro, S. P. 1980. *Thinking About White Collar Crime: Matters of Conceptualization and Research.* Washington, DC: National Institute of Justice.

Sviridoff, M. and J. E. McElroy. 1985. *Employment and Crime: A Summary Report.* New York: Vera Institute of Justice.

Tillman, R. 1987. "The Size of the 'Criminal Population': The Prevalence and Incidence of Adult Arrest." *Criminology* 25:561-580.

U.S. Bureau of the Census. 1972. *Public Use Samples of Basic Records from the 1970 Census: Description and Technical Documentation.* Washington, DC: Government Printing Office.

Vera Institute of Justice. 1977. *Felony Arrests: Their Prosecution and Disposition in New York City Courts.* New York: Author.

Weisburd, D., S. Wheeler, E. Waring, and N. Bode. Forthcoming. *Crimes of the Middle Classes.* New Haven: Yale University Press.

Wheeler, S., K. Mann, and A. Sarat. 1988. *Sitting in Judgment: The Sentencing of White Collar Offenders.* New Haven: Yale University Press.

Wheeler, S., D. Weisburd, and N. Bode. 1982. "Sentencing the White Collar Offender: Rhetoric and Reality." *American Sociological Review* 47:641-659.

——. 1988. *Study of Convicted Federal White-Collar Crime Defendants.* National Archives of Criminal Justice Data. The Inter-University Consortium for Political and Social Research. Ann Arbor: University of Michigan.

Wheeler, S., D. Weisburd, E. Waring, and N. Bode. 1988. "White Collar Crimes and Criminals." *American Criminal Law Review.* 25:331-357.

Wolfgang, M. E., R. M. Figlio, and T. Sellin. 1972. *Delinquency in a Birth Cohort.* Chicago: University of Chicago Press.

Zimring, F. E. and G. J. Hawkins. 1973. *Deterrence: The Legal Threat in Crime Control.* Chicago: University of Chicago Press.

DISCUSSION QUESTIONS

1. What are the implications of these findings for supervising white-collar offenders in prison?

2. Which criminological theories best explain the finding that many white-collar offenders have criminal histories?

Glossary

Academic dishonesty: intellectual theft.

Academic incest: consensual "student-faculty relationships in which both participants are from the same department but not necessarily in a student-teacher relationship" (Skinner et al., 1995, p. 139).

Administrative proceedings: these proceedings are not designed to punish but are designed to control certain future actions.

Advanced fee fraud: occurs when financial consultants or other individuals charge fees in advance of helping homeowners address their financial problems.

Airbag fraud: When mechanics fraudulently repair airbags and charge customer for repair.

Allocution: refers to the part of the trial process where individuals are permitted to address the court prior to sentencing.

Alternative sanctions argument: suggests the use of less costly civil and administrative procedures to respond to misconduct.

Annuities fraud: when insurance agents misrepresent the types of returns that their clients would get from investing in annuities.

Antitrust laws: designed to promote and protect competition among businesses and corporations.

Apolitical white-collar crime: situations where politicians get in to trouble for doing things that are outside of the scope of politics but are violations of the public trust.

Appeal to higher loyalties: a neutralization where offenders justify their wrongdoing by suggesting that the misbehavior was done for the good of a larger group.

Applied general systems theory: Society is composed of a number of different types of systems and these systems operate independently, and in conjunction with, other systems.

Appraisal fraud: occurs when appraisers misrepresent the actual value of a home.

Archival research: studies that use some form of record (or archive) as a database in the study.

Attorney-client privilege: a doctrine that protects confidential information shared by defendant to attorney.

Audits: conducted by forensic accountants to identify financial fraud.

Auto insurance fraud: when mechanics dupe the insurance company into paying for unnecessary or nonexistent repairs.

Auto repair fraud: billing for services not provided, unnecessary repairs, airbag fraud, and insurance fraud.

Automotive sales fraud: A variety of actions including turning an odometer back, selling unsafe cars, and selling stolen cars.

Awareness strategies: increasing awareness among employees about various issues related to employee theft.

Bait and switch practices: instances when customers are lured into a store with the promise of a sale item that does not exist, or is not available in an appropriate amount.

Bid rigging: occurs when competitors conspire to set specific bids for goods or services they would supply in response to a request for bids; also known as collusion.

Bid rotation: occurs when competitors take turns submitting the lowest bid on a series of bids.

Bid suppression: refers to instances where competitors agree not to submit a bid for a particular job on the understanding that a specific competitor will likely be selected for that job.

Billing for nonexistent prescriptions: when pharmacists bill for prescriptions that do not exist.

Billing for services not provided: when auto mechanics bill customers for services not provided.

Boundary maintenance: individuals learn the rules of the workplace when some individuals are caught breaking those rules.

Breadth of victimization: when one single corporate offense could harm thousands, if not millions, of individuals.

Broker embezzlement: when brokers take money that is supposed to be in an investment account and use it for their own personal use.

Broker fraud: when stock brokers fail to meet their legal obligations to investors.

Builder bailout schemes: occurs when builders offer buyers "excessive incentives" but hide those offers from the mortgage company to make it appear that the property is worth more than it is actually worth.

Builder-initiated mortgage frauds: occur when builders or developers engage in behaviors that are designed to defraud the lender or the buyer.

Campaign finance laws: place restrictions on the way political campaigns are financed, with specific attention given to contributions and expenditures.

Case records: official records that are housed in an agency that has formal social control duties.

Case studies: entail researchers selecting a particular crime, criminal, event, or other phenomena and studying features surrounding the causes and consequences of those phenomena.

Celebrity bashing: refers to instances where celebrity offenders are attacked by inmates seeking fame and notoriety.

Censure: when officials may withdraw support or withhold information.

Character witnesses: individuals who share information about the defendant that demonstrates that it is not like the defendant's character to engage in wrongdoing.

Chunking: occurs when investors buy several properties without telling the bank about the properties other than the one the bank is financing.

Churning: excessive selling of the same property for the purpose of generating fees and commissions.

Civil justice system: the system of justice where individuals seek recourse for offenses by way of a civil lawsuit.

Civil proceedings: occur when an individual or government representative, referred to as a plaintiff, files civil charges against an individual or business.

Class action lawsuits: used to address corporate wrongdoing; refers to situations where a group of victims jointly sue a business or corporation for the harm caused by the corporation.

Class bias: refers to bias implicit throughout the entire judicial processing of white-collar cases that includes the hiring of high powered defense attorneys, the complacency of criminal justice officials adjudicating the cases, the disparate treatment of corporations, and inadequate laws that all work to protect the powerful and weaken the minority.

Clean sheeting: when agents sign clients' names on documents and forms and benefit financially from the deception.

Client-oriented defense: the client is the one directing how the attorney is defending the case.

Collective embezzlement: occurs when a crime is committed by the organization against the organization.

Commodities: raw materials such as natural gas, oil, gold, agricultural products, and other tangible products sold in bulk form.

Commodities fraud: the "fraudulent sale of commodities investments" (FBI, 2009b).

Community integration: Groups of individuals, who otherwise would not have become acquainted with one another, come together in their response to white-collar crime.

Community service: refers to situations where offenders are told to perform a certain number of hours or days of services for the community.

Community-based sanctions: refer to instances where offenders are sentenced to probation or parole after their incarceration.

Compensatory damages: awards made to plaintiffs that the defendants are ordered to pay in order to compensate victims for their victimization experience.

Complementary bidding: occurs when competitors submit bids with artificially high estimates or specific demands that cannot be met so that a specific competitor with a lower price or without the demands is selected; also known as "cover" and "courtesy" bidding.

Compliance program: "organizational system aimed at comprehensively detecting and preventing corporate criminality" (Goldsmith & King, 1997, p. 9).

Comprehensive Environmental Response Compensation and Liability Act: also known as the Superfund Act, it was passed in 1980 to fund the clean-up of earlier environmental damage.

Computer crime: a range of computer-related behaviors that are criminally illegal or otherwise harmful.

Conceptual ambiguity: vaguely and loosely defined terms.

Condemnation of condemners: a neutralization where offenders blame the criminal justice and social control systems for their misdeeds.

Conflict theorists: focus on the way that those with power exert influence in order to use the law to their advantage as an instrument of power.

Conspiracy appraisal frauds: occur when appraisers work with other offenders as part of broader mortgage schemes.

Contract lawsuits: refer to allegations between buyers and sellers and/or lenders and borrowers that involve fraud, employment discrimination, tortuous interference, or allegations of unfulfilled agreements.

Control theory: suggests that individuals' bonds to society keep them from engaging in criminal behavior.

Cooperating witnesses: refers to witnesses who are cooperating with the prosecution as a result of some involvement they had in the case.

Co-pay waivers: when providers waive the patient's co-pay but still bill the insurance company.

Corporate crime: illegal behavior that is committed by employees of a corporation to benefit the corporation, company, or business.

Corporate crime liability: this occurs when a corporation is held liable and criminally prosecuted.

Corporate system: businesses and corporations that carry out business activity as part of our capitalist society.

Counterfeiting software crimes: when individuals make counterfeit copies of particular software programs.

Coupon stuffing: when employees steal coupons and use them later.

Crackers: individuals who crack into computer systems "with [the intent] to sabotage and cause chaos to [the] corporation" (Wiggins, 2002, p. 20).

Credits for nonexistent returns: when employees give credit for returns to collaborators.

Crime Victims Rights Act: permits victims of all types of federal offenses to participate in the allocution process.

Criminal fines: monetary penalty awarded by the judge after an offender has been convicted of a crime.

Criminal justice system: the system of justice where violations of the criminal law are handled.

Criminal proceedings: occur when criminal charges are filed against the defendant; sanctions could include imprisonment, fines, probation, community service, and restitution.

Criminaloid concept: engaging in harmful acts behind a mask of respectability.

Culpable conduct: not quite intent, but includes a history of misconduct, deliberate misconduct, concealing misconduct, tampering with monitoring equipment, and practicing business without a license.

Damage control argument: this orientation emphasizes the importance of restoring the public's confidence by means of public prosecutions.

Deceptive sales: illicit sales practices that are driven by corporate policies and directives.

Deferred prosecution agreement (DPA): refers to instances where the prosecutor agrees not to prosecute the corporation if the corporation agrees to certain conditions to be completed over a probationary period.

Defiance: when officials block any efforts toward change.

Definitions socially constructed by businesses: behaviors defined by a particular company or business as improper.

Deflated appraisals: occur when appraisers underestimate the value of the home in order to force the seller to lower the home's price.

Delivery of a controlled substance: when the pharmacist wrongfully provides a controlled substance to a customer.

Denial of responsibility: refers to situations where offenders neutralize their behaviors by suggesting that they are not responsible for their misconduct.

Denial of victim: refers to situations where offenders convince themselves that victims deserve the harm they experience.

Determinism: behavior is caused or influenced by preceding events or factors.

Deterrence theory: based on the assumption that punishment can stop individuals from offending if it is certain, swift, and severe.

Deviant misuse of the justice process: refers to situations where offenders misuse the justice process in a way that gains them some sort of advantage.

Differential association theory: assumes individuals learn to commit crime from their peers through a process in which they learn how to commit crimes, why to commit those crimes, and why laws restricting those crimes are inappropriate.

Discovery-oriented defense: this particular defense strategy is dictated by the characteristics of the charges, with no set formula used to respond to the cases.

Disintegrative shaming: focuses on the bad act and embarrasses offenders, causes anger, and potentially leads to additional harm.

Double billing: when two or more parties are billed for the same procedure or service.

Dual settlement statements fraud: occurs when settlement agents send a settlement statement with a higher price to the bank and a different statement with the actual sales price to the seller.

Due diligence defense: argues that the corporation did everything it could do, in good faith, to abide by the law.

Economic system: the system that drives our economy.

Educational system: white-collar careers typically develop here because this system provides opportunities to increase the understanding of white-collar crime.

Elder abuse: "any criminal, physical, or emotional harm or unethical taking advantage that negatively affects the physical, financial, or general well being of an elderly person" (Payne, Berg, & Byars, 1999, p. 81).

Elder financial abuse: when workers steal money or property from older persons in their care.

Elder neglect: when workers fail to provide the appropriate level of care required by the patient.

Elder physical abuse: instances where workers hit, slap, kick, or otherwise physically harm an older person for whom they are being paid to provide care.

Elder sexual abuse: when workers have inappropriate and harmful sexual contact with older persons in their care.

Election law violations: situations where political officials violate rules guiding the way that elections are supposed to be conducted.

Electronic and software piracy: the theft of copyright protected electronic information including software, electronic programs, and electronic files such as movies and music.

Embezzlement: when employees steal money from an account to which they have access.

Emotional consequences: experiences such as stress, violation of trust, and damage of public morale that victims of white-collar crime and all members of society are exposed to.

Empirical ambiguity: a concept that only minimally reflects reality.

Enemy civilian social system crimes: crimes against residents of countries in which the U.S. military is fighting.

Entertainment service system: settings where customers consume or purchase various forms of services designed at least partially for entertainment or pleasure.

Environmental Protection Agency (EPA): enforces criminal and civil laws as an agency aiming to protect public health and deter future misconduct as well as to facilitate fund generation and cost savings.

Environmental racism: a term used to describe the heightened risk of victimization for minorities.

Environmental state crimes: refers to criminal or deviant behaviors by a governmental representative(s) that result in individuals and/or the environment being harmed by pollutants and chemicals.

Equity fraud: occurs when the investor does not pay the equity loan or the mortgage, resulting in the homeowner losing his or her home to foreclosure; or when offenders steal the equity of a home by forging a homeowner's signature on equity loan forms and then directing the funds from the equity loan to the offenders' bank account.

Equity skimming: occurs when investors convince financially distressed homeowners to use their home equity to "hire" the investor to buy the home, or part of the home, from the homeowner and rent it back to the homeowner.

Experimental group: the group that receives the independent variable (or the treatment).

Experiments: studies in which researchers examine how the presence of one variable produces an outcome.

Expert witnesses: witnesses who share their professional insight and interpretation of the evidence used in a case.

Exploitation: refers to situations where businesses take advantage of their workers.

External audits: refers to audits conducted by consultants hired by the corporation.

External whistleblowers: term for individuals who share damaging information regarding their employer with outside organizations like law enforcement agencies or the media.

Extra-occupational crimes: crimes committed against the American civilian social system.

Faculty double billing: When professors bill multiple sources for the same effort of work or reimbursement.

Faculty embezzlement: when faculty members or college/university staff steal funds from an account to which they have access to.

Failure to report: when workers in the health care field fail to report suspected cases of abuse.

False advertising: occurs when businesses make inaccurate statements about their products or services in order to facilitate the sale of those items/services.

False Statements Act and False Claims Act: govern against the submission of fraudulent claims or bills for services; guard against situations where individuals try to defraud the government.

Falsifying account information: when agents or brokers change account information without the client's knowledge.

Falsifying records: when providers change medical forms in an effort to be reimbursed from the insurance provider.

Fear mongering: when officials create fear to "overshadow" real issues.

Federal Water Pollution Control Act: this act requires companies to self-disclose to the EPA instances when they have discharged potentially harmful substances into navigable waters.

Field research: Strategies where researchers enter a particular setting to gather data through their observations in that setting.

Financial Crimes Section (FCS): located in the FBI's Criminal Investigations Division, this entity investigates cases of white-collar crime.

Flipping: occurs when scammers buy and resell properties with inflated prices.

Foreclosure rescue scams: various illicit activities that use impending foreclosures or a homeowner's financial distress as an element of the offense.

Foreign exchange fraud: when brokers or other officials convince "victims to invest in the foreign currency exchange market" (FBI, 2009b) through illegitimate and fraudulent practices.

Foreign friendly civilian crimes: crimes committed against citizens of another country.

Forensic accountants: they review financial records and work schedules, read e-mails, interview workers and bosses, gather and review other available evidence, and develop a report detailing their conclusions about the presence of fraud in a business.

Fraud audits: identify control mechanisms and weaknesses in a business that place the business at risk for fraud, and identify those with access who have taken advantage of the weaknesses.

Fraud-for-housing: occurs when borrowers lie about their qualifying information in order to secure a mortgage so they can purchase a home.

Fraud-for-profit: occurs when offenders commit the fraud in order to reap a monetary benefit from the mortgage transaction.

Fraudulent loan origination: scams where professionals help buyers qualify for loans for which the buyers are not actually qualified.

Front running: when "a broker takes advantage of the special knowledge about a pending custom order and trades on his or her own account before executing that order" (Schlegel, 1993, p. 63).

Futures contracts: "agreement[s] to buy or sell a given unit of a commodity at some future date" (Schlegel, 1993, p. 60).

Futures trading fraud: fraud occurring in the trading of futures contracts and options on the futures trading market.

Ganging: situations where providers bill for multiple family members though they treat only one of them.

Gender harassment: sexist remarks and behavior.

General deterrence: suggests that offenders should be punished in order to keep other potential offenders from engaging in misconduct.

General strain theory: a social-psychological approach to explaining how crime is an adaptation to stress and frustration.

Generic drug substitution: when pharmacists give the customer a generic drug, but bill the insurance company for the more expensive brand-name drug.

Ghostwriting: situations where professors or researchers have their work written by someone else, but only the professor's name appears on the work.

Good faith defense: argues that the defendant lacked knowledge and intent and therefore did not know the crime was being committed.

Government definitions: those illegal acts characterized by deceit, concealment, or violation of trust and that are not dependent upon the application or threat of physical force or violence; individuals and organizations commit these acts to obtain money, property, or services, or to secure personal or business advantage.

Government witnesses: this category of witnesses includes police officers, investigators, auditors, and other officials who developed the case as part of the investigation process.

Grades for sex: professors use the power of grading in order to solicit sexual favors from students.

Group boycotts: situations where competitors agree not to do business with specific customers or clients.

Harmful consumer products: goods that enter the marketplace that cause significant harm to consumers.

Harmful treatment of consumers: refers to situations where businesses either intentionally or unintentionally put consumers who are using their services at risk of harm.

Health Insurance Portability Act of 1996: made health care fraud a federal offense, with penalties ranging from 10 years to life in prison.

Hedge fund fraud: fraudulent acts perpetrated in hedge fund systems.

Hedge fund system: "private investment partnership[s] . . . [with] high net worth clients" (FBI, 2009b).

High yield investment schemes: these promise investor low risk or even no risk investment strategies when in fact the funds are not actually invested.

Home health care: the provision of health care services at the patient's home.

Home improvement scams: agents or investors conceal problems with homes that should be disclosed to potential buyers.

Home repair fraud: contractors and repair persons rip off individuals for various types of repairs.

Horizontal price fixing: competitors agree to set prices at a certain level.

House arrest: refers to instances where offenders are told that they must be at home either all of the time or when they are not at work, the doctor's office, or a religious service.

Ignorance defense: refers to situations where the defendant argues that he or she did not know that the criminal acts were occurring.

Illegal dumping: refers to situations where employees or businesses dump products they no longer need in sites that are not recognized as legal dump sites.

Illegal emissions: refers to situations where companies or businesses illegally allow pollutants to enter the environment.

Illegally buying prescriptions: when a pharmacist buys prescriptions from patients, and then bills the insurance company without filling the prescription.

Individual economic losses: the losses that individual victims or businesses incur due to white-collar crimes.

Inflated appraisals: the intentional over-estimation of the value of a home in order to allow the home to be sold at an inflated price.

Innovators: accept the goal of financial success but replace legitimate means with illegitimate means.

Insider trading: when individuals share or steal information that is "material in nature" (Leap, 2007) for future investments.

Institutional anomie: occurs because society promotes values related to financial success but fails to promote values that are consistent with using legitimate means to attain financial success.

Internal audits: audits conducted by the organization's accounting department.

Internal strategies: policies and practices performed within the retail setting in an effort to prevent employee theft.

Internal whistleblowers: individuals who share information with officials within the organization where the employee works, often reporting the misconduct to the company's security program.

International environmental crimes: environmental offenses that cross borders of at least two different countries or occur in internationally protected areas.

Internet crimes: a range of offenses committed through the use of the Internet.

Inter-occupational crimes: phrase Bryant (1979) uses to describe situations where members of the military criminally victimize the enemy.

Intra-occupational crimes: phrase Bryant (1979) uses to describe instances where military officials commit criminal acts against the American military system.

Investment fraud: when investments made by consumers are managed or influenced fraudulently by stock brokers or other officials in the economic system.

Iran-Contra affair: in the mid-1980s, U.S. political officials authorized the sale of weapons to Iran as a part of covert efforts to trade arms for hostages.

Isolated occurrence defense: argues that the misconduct was a rare event done by a single employee and not part of any systematic criminal activity.

Jailstripe crimes: a term for criminal acts that offenders commit while incarcerated.

Just deserts: a punishment orientation that suggests that offenders should be punished for one primary reason: because they deserve it.

Kickbacks: when providers direct patients to other providers in exchange for pecuniary response from the other provider.

Knowing endangerment: refers to situations where individuals or businesses intentionally mishandle hazardous wastes or pollutants that pose risks to their workers or to community members.

Labeling theory: focuses on the way that individuals develop criminal labels; suggests that the act of labeling individuals can result in behaviors consistent with those labels.

Lack of fraudulent intent defense: argues that the defendant did not intend to commit a criminal act.

Lay witnesses: individuals who have some relevant information to share about the white-collar crime case based on something they saw or experienced.

Learning theories: body of theories that suggest that criminal behavior is learned.

Liar loans: situations where investors lie about loans they have or are trying to get.

Life course theory: uses a social psychological orientation to identify how events early in one's life course shape experiences later in one's life.

Loss prevention strategies: efforts that businesses use to keep employees from stealing from the business.

Mail fraud statutes: prohibit the use of the U.S. mail service to commit crimes.

Market allocation: when competitors agree to divide markets according to territories, products, goods, or some other service.

Market manipulation: situations where executives or other officials do things to artificially inflate trading volume and subsequently affect the price of the commodity or security.

Media reports: news articles, press reports, and television depictions of white-collar crimes that help demonstrate what kind of information members of the public receive about white-collar crime, and to uncover possible patterns guiding white-collar offenses that may not be studied through other means.

Medicaid: a state-level program that serves the poor.

Medical fraud: intentional criminal behaviors by physicians.

Medical malpractice: situations where health care providers "accidently" injure patients while delivering health care.

Medical snowballing: when providers bill for several related services though only one service was provided.

Medicare: a federally funded program that serves the elderly population.

Medication errors: when health care providers deliver or prescribe the wrong medications to patients.

Meeting competition defense: argues that a business's price discriminations were done in good faith in order to stop undesirable actions of a competitor.

Misdirection: when officials feign interest but change the subject.

Mislabeling drugs: when pharmacists label drugs incorrectly in an effort to hide that they did not provide the prescription drug to the patient.

Misrepresentation: deliberately misinforming the customer about the coverage of an insurance policy.

Monetary penalties: include criminal fines, restitution, civil settlements, and compensatory and punitive damages awarded in civil trials.

Mortgage fraud: when a real estate or bank representative intentionally provides false information to a financial institution in order to secure a loan.

Multiplicity of indictment defense: argues that the offender is being charged for one single offense on several different counts in the indictment.

Natural law: behaviors or activities that are defined as wrong because they violate the ethical principles of a particular culture, subculture, or group.

Neutralization theory: assumes juveniles understand right from wrong and that before delinquents commit delinquent acts they neutralize or rationalize their behavior as appropriate.

Non-prosecution agreement (NPA): refers to instances where the prosecutor indicates that the prosecution will not occur, based on the corporation's agreement to certain conditions.

Objectivity: researchers must be value-free in doing their research.

Occupational crime: phrase used by Clinard and Quinney (1973) to describe crimes committed in any type of legal occupation.

Occupational system: the system where the bulk of professionals are found.

Organization misconduct: refers to instances where laws, rules, or administrative regulations are violated by an individual or group of individuals in an organization who, in their organizational role, act or fail to act in ways that further the attainment of organizational goals.

Organizational advantage argument: this explanation for why prosecutors choose not to prosecute suggests that "organizational structure may serve as a buffer between the white-collar offender and social control mechanisms" (Tillman et al., 1997, p. 55).

Organizational culture strategies: strategies to promote a sense of organizational culture that inhibits theft.

Organizational probation: refers to cases where corporations can be sentenced to a term of probation.

Overcharging: when employees charge customers more than they should.

Over-ordering supplies: when employees' order more supplies than are needed and keep the supplies that were not needed.

Pacification: a form of elder physical abuse where a worker over-medicates an elder.

Parallel proceedings: instances where a specific white-collar crime is heard in more than one court simultaneously.

Parsimony: researchers and scientists should keep their levels of explanation as simple as possible.

Pecuniary-based offenses: misbehaviors that are ultimately done for the economic gain that comes along with the commission of the offenses.

Phantom treatment: when providers bill Medicare, Medicaid, or other insurance agencies for services they never provided.

Physical harm: a possible consequence of white-collar crime (e.g., physical or sexual patient abuse, death, or serious physical injury).

Pingponging: when patients are unnecessarily referred to other providers, or "bounced around" to various medical providers.

Plausible deniability: when officials conceal actions to make behavior seem appropriate.

Plea bargains: this is a stage of adjudication where the prosecutors decide whether to allow a defendant to plead guilty in exchange for a reduced sentence or some other incentive.

Police corruption: when police officers violate the trust they have been given and abuse their law enforcement authority.

Police sexual misconduct: "Any behavior by a police officer, whereby an officer takes advantage of his or her unique position in law enforcement to misuse his or her authority and power to commit a sexually violent act or to initiate or respond to some sexually motivated cure for the purpose of personal gratification" (Maher, 2003, p. 355).

Political extortion/bribery: political officials use their power to shape outcomes of various processes.

Political system: defines laws and regulations describing all forms of crime.

Ponzi schemes: these scam investors by paying them from future investors' payments into the offender's scheme.

Prearranged trading: when "brokers, or brokers and local brokers, first agree on a price and then act out the trade as a piece of fiction in the pit, thereby excluding other potential bidders from the offering" (Schlegel, 1993, p. 63).

Prescription fraud: schemes where pharmacists work with drug addicts to carry out an offense.

Pre-sentence reports: reports developed by probation officers that include a wealth of information about offenders, their life histories, their criminal careers, and the sentence they receive.

Price discrimination: refers to practices where different prices are charged simply to restrict competition between competitors.

Price fixing: occurs when competitors agree on a price at which goods or services should be sold.

Price gouging: refers to situations where businesses conspire to set artificially high prices on goods and services.

Proactive strategies: refer to situations where the police develop criminal cases in an active way.

Process-oriented defense: this refers to instances when the attorneys process these cases the same way, independent of case or offender characteristics.

Professional-disciplinary proceedings: these proceedings are administered through the state bar association where professional boards review allegations of wrongdoing.

Promissory note fraud: when agents get clients to invest in promissory notes that are scams.

Provision of unnecessary services: when health care providers perform and bill for tests or procedures that are not needed.

Punitive damages: awarded when the defendant's conduct exceeds the legal criteria for mere or gross negligence.

Qualifications fraud: refers to situations where professionals lie about a buyer's qualifications in order to secure a mortgage and allow the buyer to purchase the home.

Quasi-experimental designs: Studies that mimic experimental methods but lack certain elements of the classical experimental design.

Questionable Doctors: A report and database, published by the nonprofit group Public Citizen, that collects data on physicians involved in misconduct.

Qui tam lawsuits: situations where an individual sues a corporation or company on behalf of the government.

Racketeer Influenced and Corrupt Organizations (RICO) Act: found in Title IX of the Organized Crime Control Act, targets criminal groups by legislating against extortion, violence, and fraud.

Rational choice theory: considers the limits of human rationality while still considering humans as rational; suggests that offenders will consider the benefits of offending and weigh those benefits against possible negative consequences that arise from misconduct.

Reactive strategies: situations where the police respond to reports of criminal incidents.

Real estate agent/investor fraud: a variety of scams committed by agents and investors, including home improvement scams, fraudulent loan origination, chunking, liar loans, and churning.

Rebels: workers who reject the goals and means of society and replace the societal-prescribed goals and means with their own goals and means.

Record reviews: occur when white-collar crime investigators review an assortment of records such as financial records, banking records, sales records, e-mail correspondence, phone records, property deeds, loan applications, and any other records that are relevant to the case under investigation.

Recreational path: when pharmacists initially begin using illegal street drugs, and then expand their drug use to include prescription drugs once they enter pharmacy training.

Redirection: When officials feign interest, but change the subject.

Regulatory agencies: governmental agencies responsible for making sure that regulations are followed in industries and businesses across the United States; exist to make sure that businesses and their workers are abiding by laws and regulations.

Regulatory system: consists of local, state, and federal agencies charged with regulating various businesses.

Rehabilitation: a philosophy of punishment that suggests that offenders are brought into the justice process so that the government can play a role in treating whatever issues the offenders have that may have contributed to their wrongdoing.

Reintegrative shaming: focuses on the bad act and communicates messages of disapproval that are followed by efforts to reintegrate the offender back into the community.

Relativism: All things are related.

Reliance on the advice of counsel defense: legal defense where defendants argue that their attorneys advised them to perform the action in question.

Religious system deception: situations where church leaders lie to their congregants in an effort to promote an appearance of "holier than thou."

Relying on self-righteousness: when officials minimize allegations.

Resale fraud: refers to instances where used items are sold as new.

Research definitions: when researchers define white-collar crime through studying and gathering data that allow them to reliably and validly measure the behavior.

Research misconduct: a range of behaviors that center around researchers engaging in various forms of wrongdoing during the course of their research.

Restitution: a monetary penalty that offenders are ordered to pay to victims for their suffering.

Retail system: setting where consumers purchase various types of products.

Retaliation: when corporate or business officials target advocates exposing the wrongdoing.

Retreatist: a white-collar worker who accepts neither the goals of society nor the means to attain those goals.

Retribution: a philosophy of punishment that suggests offenders should be punished to satisfy societal demands.

Reverse mortgage fraud: situations where fraudulent activities occur as part of the reverse mortgage transaction.

Ritualist: white-collar worker who does not accept the goals of society but goes through the motions of engaging in the means prescribed by society.

Robinson-Patman Act: makes price discrimination illegal if it is done to lessen competition.

Rogue employee defense: argues that the corporate misconduct was the result of an individual employee and not the result of any corporate activities.

Rolling over: persuading the customer to cancel an old insurance policy and replace it with a more expensive, "better" policy.

Routine activities theory: assumes that crime occurs because of the presence of motivated offenders, the absence of capable guardians, and the availability of suitable targets that all exist at the same time and place.

Sales-directed crimes: occur against consumers when agents or brokers steal from consumers by using fraudulent sales tactics.

Sales/service system: businesses that sell basic goods and services to customers.

Scapegoating: refers to excuses where offenders blame others for their wrongdoing.

Seductive behavior: inappropriate sexual advance.

Self-control theory: assumes all types of crime are caused by the presence of low self-control.

Self-policing: refers to efforts by companies and businesses to develop their own policing responses to white-collar crime.

Self-policing audits: refers to audits done either as part of routine procedures or that may be initiated out of concern that fraud is occurring in the organization.

Sexual abuse: hands-on offenses where the offender inappropriately touches victims, hands-off offenses such as voyeurism and exhibitionism, and/or harmful genital practices where genital contact is made between the offender and the victim.

Sexual bribery: offering rewards for sex.

Sexual coercion: threatening punishment to get sex.

Sexual contact with students: instances where professors have some form of direct contact of a sexual nature with students in their classes or under their supervision.

Sexual harassment: a range of behaviors where employees perform sexually inappropriate actions against their colleagues or consumers.

Sexualized behavior: goes beyond comments and includes actual activities of a sexual nature committed by the offending party.

Sexualized comments: when individuals make comments to others that are of a sexual nature.

Shaming: an alternative sanction strategy that promotes shaming and stigmatization.

Sherman Antitrust Act: in general, this act makes it illegal for competitors to engage in activities that restrict competition.

Short counting: when pharmacists dispense fewer pills than prescribed, but bill the insurance company as if they had dispensed all of the pills.

Short sale fraud: lending institutions allow homes to be sold for amounts that are lower than what the homeowner owed on the home's mortgage.

Shortchanging: when employees do not give customers all of their change and pocket the difference.

Significant environmental harm: this type of harm includes actual environmental harm, threat of environmental harm, failure to report potentially environmentally harmful activities, and the possibility that the behavior will escalate if it is not handled criminally.

Skepticism: social scientists must question and re-question their findings.

Sliding: when agents include insurance coverage that was not requested by the customer.

Slumlord: landlords who profit from renting run-down apartments that are not maintained by the property owner.

Smoking gun: indisputable evidence that substantiates that a crime has been committed.

Social change: those who survive white-collar crime victimization become stronger.

Social disorganization theory: suggests that a neighborhood's crime rate is shaped by the ability of its members to agree upon and work toward a common goal, such as crime control.

Social harm: workplace behaviors that might not be illegal or deviant, but might actually create forms of harm for various individuals.

Social services system: the numerous agencies involved in providing services to members of the public.

Social system: a setting where individuals have various needs fulfilled and learn how to do certain things, as well as why to do those behaviors.

Societal economic losses: the total amount of losses incurred by society from white-collar crime.

Software crimes: situations when computer software is central to the offense.

Specific deterrence: suggests that punishment should occur in order to stop the punished offender from engaging in future wrongdoing.

Stacking: persuading persons to buy more insurance policies than are needed.

State crimes: situations where governments, or their representatives, commit crime on behalf of the government.

State-corporate crime: crimes and misconduct committed by employees of government agencies.

Strain theory: traces the source of strain to interactions between the social and economic structures; assumes strain is caused by the failure to achieve economically valued goals.

Straw buyer fraud: individuals who do not plan on living in or even owning a house purchase it and then deed it over to the person who will live there.

Subcontracting: when competitors hire one another on subcontracts after the winning bid has been selected.

Substitute providers: employees who perform medical services though they are not authorized to do so.

Sweetheart deals: employees give friends and family members unauthorized discounts.

Switching: when a sales person switches the customer's policy so that the coverage and the premiums are different from what the victim was told.

System capacity argument: this explanation for why prosecutors do not prosecute points to the difficulties officials face in responding to these crimes.

Systems theory: assumes all systems are interrelated and focuses on the interconnections between various societal systems and the way that various systems influence white-collar wrongdoing.

Technological strategies: the use of various forms of technology to prevent employee theft in retail settings.

Technological system: societal system that includes structures and agencies involved in developing and promoting technology.

Textbook fraud: when faculties sell complimentary textbooks that they received from publishers to book dealers who resell the books.

Theft crimes against consumers: occur when workers or employers steal directly from clients or customers.

Theft of credit card information: when employees steal the customer's credit card information.

Theft of goods: when employees steal the items the retail setting is trying to sell.

Theft of money from the cash register: when employees take money out of the register.

Theft of production supplies and raw materials: when employees steal items used to produce goods for retail settings.

Theft of software: when workers steal computer software that their company owns, and use it for their personal use.

Tort lawsuit: refers to situations where someone claims loss, injury, or damage from the negligence or intent of another.

Unauthorized access: when individuals break into various computer databases to which they do not have legitimate access.

Unbundling: when providers bill separately for tests and procedures that are supposed to be billed as a single procedure.

Unfair labor practices: corporate violations where workers are subjected to unethical treatment by their bosses and corporate leaders.

Uniform Residential Landlord and Tenant Act (URLTA): this act is a federal law stipulating that homes must be habitable, up to code, safe, and capable of providing the necessary utilities.

Unnecessary auto repairs: when mechanics perform repairs that were not necessary and bill the customer for those services.

U.S. Sentencing Commission: the entity responsible for developing strategies to promote fairer sentencing at the federal level through the development of sentencing guidelines.

Vertical price fixing: refers to situations where parties from different levels of the production and distribution chain agree to set prices at a certain level.

Viatical settlement fraud: when insurance agents conceal information on viatical settlement policies allowing individuals to invest in other people's life insurance policies.

Victimization surveys: surveys that sample residents and estimate the extent of victimization from the survey findings.

Violations of criminal law: white-collar crimes defined as criminally illegal behaviors committed by upper-class individuals during the course of their occupation.

Violations-of-occupation crimes: "violations that occur during the course of occupational activity and are related to employment" (Robin, 1974).

Violations of regulatory law: workplace misdeeds that might not violate criminal or civil laws, but that violate a particular occupation's laws.

Violations of trust: when white-collar offenders use their positions of trust to promote misconduct.

Warning light syndrome: outbreaks of white-collar crime could potentially send a message to individuals, businesses, or communities that something is wrong in a particular workplace system.

Whistleblowers: individuals who notify authorities about wrongdoing in their organization.

White-collar crime: any violations of criminal, civil, or regulatory law—or deviant, harmful, or unethical actions—committed during the course of employment in various occupational systems.

White-collar crime victims: individuals, businesses, nongovernmental institutions, or the "government as a buyer, giver, and protector-gatekeeper" (Edelhertz, 1983, p. 117).

White-collar environmental crimes: situations where individuals or businesses illegally pollute or destroy the environment as part of an occupational activity.

White-collar gangs: a gang is "a self-formed association of peers, bound together by mutual interests, with identifiable leadership, well-developed lines of authority, and other organizational features, who act in concert to achieve a specific purpose or purposes which generally include the conduct of illegal activity and control over a particular territory, facility, or type of enterprise" (Miller, 1975, p. 121); the phrase white-collar gang suggests that whiter-collar workers often commit their crimes in groups.

White-collar undercover investigations: typically occur when white-collar crime investigators already have evidence of wrongdoing by the suspect or the corporation.

Windshield appraisal fraud: occurs when appraisers fail to even go into the home to determine its value; home's value determined by appraisers looking through the windshield of their automobile.

Withdrawal from conspiracy defense: used in antitrust offenses to argue that the defendant withdrew his or her involvement from the misconduct before the illegal actions occurred.

Workplace deviance: broader definition of white-collar crime that includes all of those workplace acts that violate the norms or standards of the workplace, regardless of whether they are formally defined as illegal or not.

Workplace interview: conducted in internal investigations to gather information about any wrongdoing.

Workplace-disciplinary proceedings: allegations of wrongdoing are reviewed through a company's equal opportunity office or human resources department.

References

Accused dentist claims breast rubs appropriate. (2007, October 16). Retrieved July 30, 2011 from http://www.msnbc.msn.com/id/21325760/wid/11915773?GT1=10514

Accused of plagiarizing dissertation, tenured professor resigns at Kean U. (2007, March 14). *Chronicle of Higher Education.* Retrieved July 30, 2011, from http://chronicle.com/article/Accused-of-Plagiarizing/38363

Ackerman, J. (2001, January 16). Massachusetts regulators take action against two securities dealers. *Boston Globe.*

Ackman, D. (2001). *Tire trouble.* Forbes.com. Retrieved July 30, 2011, from http://www.forbes.com/2001/06/20/tireindex.html

Adam, A. (2008). Fraud big time variable annuities—the gimmick—Targeting the seniors. Retrieved July 21, 2011, from http://www.sec.gov/comments/s7-14-08/s71408-306.htm

Adams, B., & Guyette, J. E. (2009, March). Dummy proof. *Automotive Body Repair News, 48*(3), p. 56.

Adams, K. (2009, July 2). Notorious white collar criminals: Where are they now? *Financial Edge.* Retrieved January 19, 2011, from http://financialedge.investopedia.com/financial-edge/0709/Notorious-White-Collar-Criminals-Where-Are-They-Now.aspx

Adams, M. (2010, May 8). Is Gulf oil rig disaster far worse than we're being told? *NaturalNews.com.* Retrieved August 10, 2010, from http://www.naturalnews.com/028749_Gulf_of_Mexico_oil_spill.html

Agnew, R. (1985). A revised strain theory of delinquency. *Social Forces, 64,* 151–167.

Agnew, R. (1992). Foundation for a general strain theory of crime and delinquency. *Criminology, 30,* 47–88.

Albanese, J. S. (1984). Corporate criminology: Explaining deviance of business and political organizations. *Journal of Criminal Justice, 12,* 11–19.

Albonetti, C. A. (1999). The avoidance of punishment: A legal-bureaucratic model of suspended sentencing in federal white-collar cases prior to federal sentencing guidelines. *Social Forces, 78*(1), 303–329.

Albrecht, W. S., & Searcy, D. J. (2001). Top 10 reasons why fraud is increasing in the U.S. *Strategic Finance, 82,* 58.

Albright, M. (2007, December 8). Retail thieves these days are often technically savvy and organized. *McClatchy-Tribune Business News.*

Alschuler, A. W. (1972). Courtroom misconduct by prosecutors and trial judges. *Texas Law Review, 50*(4), 629–667.

Alshuler, M., Creekpaum, J. K., & Fang, J. (2008). Health care fraud. *American Criminal Law Review, 45*(2), 607–664.

Aluede, O., Omoregie, E. O., & Osa-Edoh, G. I. (2006). Academic dishonesty as a contemporary problem in higher education: How academic advisers can help. *Reading Improvement, 43*(2), 97–106.

Alvesalo, A. (2009). Economic crime investigators at work. *Policing and Society, 13*(2), 115–138.

Alvesalo, A., & Whyte, D. (2007). Eyes wide shut: The police investigation of safety crimes. *Crime, Law, and Social Change, 48,* 57–72.

Anderman, E. M., Cupp, P. K., & Lane, D. (2010). Impulsivity and academic cheating. *Journal of Experimental Education, 78,* 135–150.

Anderson, C. (2010, January 2). '09, the year of the Ponzi scam; schemes that collapsed quadrupled this year; Investors lost $16.5 B., not counting Madoff case. *Newsday,* p. A27.

Anderson, G., Hussey, P., Frogner, B., & Waters, H. (2005). Health spending in the United States and the rest of the industrialized world. *Health Affairs, 24,* 903–914.

Anderson, J. C. (2010, June 18). Arizona mortgage-fraud prosecutions. Retrieved June 21, 2010, from http://www.azcentral.com/12news/news/articles/2010/06/18/20100618arizona-mortgage-fraud-indictments.html

Anderson, K., (2010, September 10). More harsh criticism of EPA at D.C. forum. *Brownfield AG News for America.* Retrieved from http://brownfieldagnews.com/index.php?s=More+harsh+criticism+of+EPA+at+D.C.+forum

Anderson, K. B. (2004, August). *Consumer fraud in the United States: An FTC survey.* Washington, DC: Government Printing Office.

Anderson, T. (2007, October). Retail workers don't plan thefts. *Security Management, 51*(10), p. 38.

Andsager, J., Bailey, J. L., & Nagy, J. (1997). Sexual advances as manifestations of power in graduate programs. *Journalism & Mass Communication Educator, 52*(2), 33–42.

Angel, J., & McCabe, D. M. (2009). The ethics of speculation. *Journal of Business Ethics, 90,* 277–286.

Anonymous. (1991). Sexual harassment: A female counseling student's experience. *Journal of Counseling & Development, 69*(2), 502–506.

Appelbaum, B., Hilzenrath, D., & Paley, A. R. (2008, December 13). "All just one big lie"; Bernard Madoff was a Wall Street whiz with a golden reputation. Investors, including Jewish charities, entrusted him with billions. It's gone. *Washington Post* (Suburban ed.), p. D01.

Appin, R., & O'Connor, C. M. (2003, May 5). Market rises as spectre of corporate fraud fades. *High Yield Report.* Retrieved July 30, 2011, from http://www.highbeam.com/doc/1G1-101171551.html.

Argust, C. P., Litvack, D. E., & Martin, B. W. (2010). Racketeer influenced and corrupt organizations. *American Criminal Law Review, 47*(2), 961–1013.

Armsworth, M. (1989). Therapy for incest survivors. *Child Abuse and Neglect, 13,* 549–562.

Arnold, B. L., & Hagan, J. (1992). Careers of misconduct: The structure of prosecuted professional deviance among lawyers. *American Sociological Review, 57*(6), 771–780.

Attorney General Holder announces civil lawsuit regarding Deepwater Horizon oil spill. (2010). *Justice News.* Retrieved July 29, 2011, from www.justice.gov/iso/opa/ag/speeches/2010/ag-speech-101215.html

Austin, Z., Simpson, S., & Reynen, E. (2005). "The fault lies not in our students, but in ourselves": Academic honesty and moral development in health professions education—Results of a pilot study in Canadian pharmacy. *Teaching in Higher Education, 10*(2), 143–156.

Aycock, E. B., & Hutton, M. F. (2010). Election law violators. *American Criminal Law Review, 47*, 363–400.

Ayers, K., & Frank, J. (1987). Deciding to prosecute white collar crime: A national survey of state attorneys general. *Justice Quarterly, 4*(3), 425–439.

Baldston, K. (1979). Hooker Chemical's nightmarish pollution record. *Business and Society Review, 30,* 25.

Banerjee, N., & Goodstein, L. (2006, November 5). Church board dismisses pastor for "sexually immoral conduct." *New York Times.* Retrieved July 6, 2011, from http://www.nytimes.com/2006/11/05/us/05haggard.html?scp=1&sq=Church%20board%20dismisses%20pastor%20for%20%E2%80%98sexually%20immoral%20conduct%st=cse

Barboza, D., & Lohr, S. (2007, July 25). F.B.I. and Chinese seize $500 million of counterfeit software. *New York Times.* Retrieved July 30, 2011, from http://www.nytimes.com/2007/07/25/business/worldbusiness/25soft.html

Barker, T. (2002). Ethical police behavior. In K. Lersch (Ed.), *Policing and misconduct* (pp. 1–25). Upper Saddle River, NJ: Prentice Hall.

Barker, T., & Roebucks, J. (1973). *Empirical typology of police corruption-A study in organizational deviance.* Springfield, IL: Charles C Thomas.

Barnard, J. (2002). Allocation for victims of economic crimes. *Notre Dame Law Review, 39,* 40–76

Barnard, J. W. (2001). Allocution for victims of economic crimes. *Notre Dame Law Review, 77*(1), 39.

Barnard, R., (2009, July 2). Madoff case: Act gives fraud victims a voice. *Richmond Times-Dispatch.* Retrieved from http://www2.timesdispatch.com/search/?source=all&query=%22madoff+case%3A+act+gives+fraud+victims+a+voice%22

Barnes, W., & Kozar, J. M. (2008). The exploitation of pregnant workers in apparel production. *Journal of Fashion Marketing and Management, 12,* 285–293.

Barnett, C. (n.d.). The measurement of white-collar crime using uniform crime reporting (UCR) data. Federal Bureau of Investigation, U.S. Department of Justice. Retrieved from http://www.fbi.gov/about-us/cjis/ucr/nibrs/nibrs_wcc.pdf

Barnett, H. (1999). The land ethic and environmental crime. *Criminal Justice Policy Review, 10*(2), 161–191.

Barnett, H. C. (1981). Corporate capitalism, corporate crime. *Crime and Delinquency, 27*(1), 4–23.

Barnett, H. C. (1993). Crimes against the environment: Superfund enforcement at last. *American Academy of Social Science, 525,* 119–133.

Barrows, C. W., & Powers, T. (2009). *Introduction to management in the hospitality industry* (9th ed.). Hoboken, NJ: John Wiley.

Basken, P. (2009, September 10). Medical "ghostwriting" is still a common practice, study shows. *Chronicle of Higher Education.* Retrieved June 4, 2010, from http://chronicle.com/article/Medical-Ghostwriting-Is-a/48347/

Bassnett, S. (2006, September 29). Hands off my bottom, mister! *The Times Higher Education Supplement.* Retrieved June 7, 2010, from http://www.timeshighereducation.co.uk/story.asp?storyCode=205661&sectioncode=26

Beare, M. (2002). Organized corporate criminality: Tobacco smuggling between Canada and the US. *Crime, Law, and Social Change, 37,* 225–243.

Beck, D. G. (1981). The Federal Water Pollution Control Act's self reporting requirement and the privilege against self incrimination: Civil or criminal proceeding and penalties? United States v. Ward. *Brigham Young University Law Review, (4)*983.

Beck, E. (1979). The Love Canal tragedy. *EPA Journal.* Retrieved December 10, 2010, from http://www.epa.gov/aboutepa/history/topics/lovecanal/01.html

Behrmann, N. (2005, September 19). Collapse of US fund exposes global debt scam: Bayou seen caught in fraudsters' trap while trying to recoup losses. *The Business Times Singapore.* Retrieved June 1, 2010, from http://www.aussiestockforums.com/forums/archive/index.php/t-1993.html

Belser, A. (2008, January 1).Be careful with thieving workers. *Pittsburgh Post Gazette.* Retrieved March 2, 2010, from http://wwww.postgazette.com/pg/08021/850539-28.stm

Bennett, W. F. (2007). Real estate scam emerges. *North County Times.* Retrieved July 6, 2011, from http://www.nctimes.com/news/local/article_897f29dd-0903-53af-bbfc-7029267ac1d3.html

Bensinger, K., & Vartabedian, R. (2009, October 25). New details in crash that prompted Toyota recall. *Los Angeles Times.*

Benson, M. L. (1985a). Denying the guilty mind: Accounting for involvement in a white-collar crime. *Criminology, 23*(4), 583–607.

Benson, M. L. (1985b). White collar offenders under community supervision. *Justice Quarterly, 2*(3) 429–436.

Benson, M. L. (1989). The influence of class position on the formal and informal sanctioning of white-collar offenders. *Sociological Quarterly, 30*(3), 465–479.

Benson, M. L. (1990). Emotions and adjudication: Status degradation among white-collar criminals. *Justice Quarterly, 73*(3), 515.

Benson, M. L., & Cullen, F. T. (1988). The special sensitivity of white-collar offenders to prison: A critique and research agenda. *Journal of Criminal Justice, 16,* 207–215.

Benson, M. L., & Cullen, F. T. (1998). *Combating corporate crime: Local prosecutors at work.* Boston: Northeastern University Press.

Benson, M. L., Cullen, F. T., & Maakestad, W. J. (1988). *Local prosecutors and white-collar crime: Final report.* Washington, DC: U.S. Department of Justice, National Institute Justice.

Benson, M. L., Cullen, F. T., & Maakestad, W. J. (1990). Local prosecutors and corporate crime. *Crime and Delinquency, 36*(3), 356–372.

Benson, M. L., & Kerley, K. (2001). Life course theory and white-collar crime. In H. Pontell & D. Shichor (Eds.), *Contemporary issues in criminology and criminal justice: Essays in honor of Gilbert Geis* (pp. 121–136). Upper Saddle River, NJ: Prentice Hall.

Benson, M. L., & Moore, E. (1992). Are white-collar and common offenders the same? An empirical and theoretical critique of a recently proposed general theory of crime. *Journal of Research in Crime and Delinquency, 29*, 251–272.

Berg, B. L. (2009). *Qualitative research methods for the social sciences* (7th ed.). Boston: Allyn & Bacon.

Berkman, S., Boswell, N. Z., Bruner, F. H., Gough, M., McCormick, J. T., Egens, P., Ugaz, J., & Zimmermann, S. (2008). The fight against corruption: International organizations at a crossroads. *Journal of Financial Crime, 15*(2), 124.

Bernard, T. S. (2010, July 19). Need a mortgage? Don't get pregnant. *New York Times*. Retrieved from http://www.nytimes.com/2010/07/20/your-money/mortgages/20mortgage.html

Bertrand, D. (2003, August 14). Auto fixer in scam jam: 6 at shop busted in insure fraud. *New York Daily News*, Suburban, p. 1.

Bharara, P. (2007). Cry uncle and their employees cry foul: Rethinking prosecutorial pressure on corporate defendants. *American Criminal Law Review, 44*(1), 53–114.

Bierstedt, R. (1970). *The social order* (3rd ed.). Bombay and New Delhi: Tata McGraw-Hill.

Bilimoria, D. (1995). Corporate control, crime, and compensation: An empirical examination. *Human Relations, 48*(8), 891–908.

Black, A. (2005, October 7). Unnecessary surgery exposed! Why 60% of all surgeries are medically unjustified and how surgeons exploit patients to generate profits. *Health*. Retrieved July 6, 2011, from http://www.naturalnews.com/012291.html

Block, A. A. (1996). American corruption and the decline of the Progressive ethos. *Journal of Law & Society, 23*(1), 18–35.

Bloomquist, L. (2006, December 21). Workers walk off jobs at Days Inn. *Knight Ridder Tribune Business News*, p. 1.

Bohm, R. M., & Vogel, B. L. (2011). *A primer on crime and delinquency theory* (3rd ed.). Belmont, CA: Wadsworth, Cengage Learning.

Bolitho, J. (2009, November 2). Two CMU math faculty members violate integrity policy: University returns $619,489 in grant money. *Central Michigan Life*. Retrieved January 29, 2010, from http://www.cm-life.com/2009/11/02/two-cmu-math-faculty-members-violate-integrity-policy-university-returns-619489-in-grant-money/

Botsko, C. A., & Wells, R. C. (1994) Government whistleblowers: Crime's hidden victims. *FBI Law Enforcement Bulletin, 63*(7), 17–21.

Bradley, D. (2008). Real estate fraud. *FBI Law Enforcement Bulletin, 77*(9), 1–7.

Brainard, J. (2008, August 29). Scientists who cheated had mentors who failed to supervise them. *Chronicle of Higher Education*. Retrieved June 4, 2010, from http://chronicle.com/article/Scientists-Who-Cheated-Had/1112

Braithwaite, J. (1982). Challenging just deserts: Punishing white-collar criminals. *Journal of Criminal Law and Criminology, 73*(2), 723–763.

Braithwaite, J. (1989a). *Crime, shame, and reintegration*. New York: Cambridge University Press.

Braithwaite, J. (1989b). Criminological theory and organized crime. *Justice Quarterly, 6*(3), 333.

Braithwaite, J. (1991). Poverty, power, white-collar crime and the paradoxes of criminological theory. *Australian and New Zealand Journal of Criminology, 24*(1), 40–48.

Braithwaite, J. (1993). The nursing home industry. In M. H. Tonry & A. J. Reiss (Eds.), *Beyond the law: Crime in complex organizations* (pp. 11–54). Chicago: University of Chicago Press.

Brasner, S. (2010, April 23). In brief: Florida agent hit with fraud charge. *Wall Street Journal Abstracts*, p. 3.

Brawley, O. (2009). Prostate cancer screening: Is this a teachable moment. *Journal of the National Cancer Institute, 101*, 19, 1295–1297.

Bredemeier, K. (2002, May 16). Memo warned of Enron's Calif. strategy: West Coast senators complain about market manipulation during power crisis. *Washington Post*, p. A04.

Brickey, K. F. (2006). In Enron's wake: Corporate executives on trial. *Journal of Criminal Law & Criminology, 96*(2), 397–433.

Brickner, D. B., Mahoney, L. S., Moore, S. J. (2010). Providing an applied-learning exercise in teaching fraud detection: A case of academic partnering with IRS criminal investigation. *Issues in Accounting Education, 25*(4), 695–719.

Brinkley, J. (1994, January 23). The nation: The cover-up that worked: A look back. *The New York Times*. Retrieved July 29, 2011, from http://www.nytimes.com/1994/01/23/weekinreview/the-nation-the-cover-up-that-worked-a-look-back.html?scp=1&sq=The%20nation:%20The%20cover-up%20that%20worked:%20A%20look%20back&st=cse

Brown, E. (2004, December 4). Can for-profit schools pass an ethics test? *New York Times*. Retrieved July 6, 2011, from http://query.nytimes.com/gst/fullpage.html?res=9907E3D81131F931A25751C1A9629C8B63&pagewanted=all

Brown, E. (2008, February 20). City throws slumlord in jail (for nine days). *New York Observer*, Retrieved June 29, 2010, from http://www.observer.com/2008/hpd-throws-apparent-slumlord-jail-9-days

Brown, W. (1995, December 9). It's getting tougher. *Thrifty Herald*, p. 21.

Bryant, C. (1979). *Khaki-collar crime*. New York: Free Press.

Buckhoff, T., Higgins, L., & Sinclair, D. (2010). A fraud audit: Do you need one? *Journal of Applied Business Research, 26*(5), 29.

Bucy, P. H. (1988). Fraud by fright: White collar crime by health care providers. *North Carolina Law Review, 67*, 855–937.

Buell, M., Layman, E., McCampbell, S. W., & Smith, B. V. (2003). Addressing sexual misconduct in community corrections. *Perspectives, 27*(2), 26–37.

Buell, M., & McCampbell, S. W. (2003). Preventing staff misconduct in the community correction setting. *Corrections Today, 65*(1), 90–91.

Burdeau, C. (2010, December 2). Judge: Deal to fix homes with Chinese drywall going well. *Business Week*. Retrieved June 1, 2010 from http://www.businessweek.com/ap/financialnews/D9JS1TIG0.htm

Bureau of Justice Statistics. (2006). *Compendium of federal justice statistics, 2004*. Washington, DC: U.S. Department of Justice.

Bureau of Justice Statistics. (2011). *State and federal prisoners and prison facilities*. Washington, DC: U.S. Department of Justice.

Bureau of Labor Statistics. (2010). *Nonfatal occupational injuries and illnesses requiring days away from work, 2009*. News release, November 9, U.S. Department of Labor. Retrieved February 1, 2011, from http://www.bls.gov/news.release/osh2.nr0.htm

Burns, R. G., & Lynch, M. J. (2004). *Environmental crime: A sourcebook*. New York: LFB Scholarly.

Burns, R. G., & Orrick, L. (2002). Assessing newspaper coverage of corporate violence: The dance hall fire in Goteborg, Sweden. *Critical Criminology, 11*, 137–150.

Burns, S. (2006, May 15). China rocked by "sandpaper" chip fraud. Retrieved July 30, 2011, from http://www.v3.co.uk/vnunet/news/2156106/china-shocked-chip-fraud

Burnstein, J. (2008a, November 18). Oakland Park man arrested again on construction-related theft charges. *Sun Sentinel*, p. 7.

Burnstein, J. (2008b, November 19). Man arrested in Delray Beach on remodeling fraud charges; he's already awaiting trial in Broward: Awaiting trial in Broward, he's arrested in Delray Beach over 4 jobs never completed. *Sun Sentinel*, p. 6.

Burton, D., Erdman, E., Hamilton, G., & Muse, K. (1999). *Women in prison: Sexual misconduct by correctional staff* (GAO/GGD-99-104). Washington, DC: U.S. Government Accounting Office.

Byars, K., & Payne, B. K. (2000). Physicians' and medical students' attitudes about Medicaid. *Journal of Health and Human Services Administration, 15*(4), 242–250.

Calavita, K., & Pontell, H. N. (1991). Other people's money revisited: Collective embezzlement in the savings and loan and insurance industries. *Social Problems, 38,* 94–112.

Calavita, K., & Pontell, H. N. (1994). The state and white-collar crime: Saving the savings and loans. *Law & Society Review, 28*(2), 297–324.

Calavita, K., Pontell, H. N., & Tillman, R. H. (1997). *Big money crime: Fraud and politics in the savings and loan crisis.* Berkeley: University of California Press.

California Department of Real Estate. (2009). Advances fees for loan modifications are now illegal in California. *DRE California.* Retrieved February 1, 2010, from http://www.dre.ca.gov/pdf_docs/FraudWarnings CaDRE03_2009.pdf

California Environmental Protection Agency. (2005, September 28). *Criminal investigation detects major illegal waste disposal operation in the Antelope Valley.* Retrieved July 29, 2011, from http://www.dtsc.ca.gov/pressroom/upload/NEWS_2005-T-50-05.pdf

Campbell, J. (2009). Mother of all swindles. *Sunday Herald Sun*, p. 70.

Canada, J., Kuhn, J. R., & Sutton, S. G. (2008). Accidentally in the public interest: The perfect storm that yielded the Sarbanes-Oxley Act. *Critical Perspectives in Accounting, 7,* 987–1003.

Carden, A. (2008). Beliefs, bias, and regime uncertainty after Hurricane Katrina. *International Journal of Social Economics, 35*(7), 531–545.

Carlson, D. (2009). Guy who sued Facebook joins Facebook. Gawker.com. Retrieved July 6, 2011, from http://gawker.com/5053748/?tag=valleywag

Carlson, N. (2010, May 13). *Well, these new Zuckerberg IMs won't help Facebook's privacy problems.* Retrieved July 6, 2011, from http://www.businessinsider.com/well-these-new-zuckerberg-ims-wont-help-facebooks-privacy-problems-2010-5#ixzz0rswuPzMH

Carter, D. L., & Katz, A. J. (1996). Computer crime: An emerging challenge for law enforcement. *FBI Law Enforcement Bulletin, 65*(12), 1.

Carter, T. S. (1999). Ascent of the corporate model in environmental-organized crime. *Crime, Law, and Social Change, 31*(1), 1–30.

Casten, J. A., & Payne, B. K. (2008). The influence of perceptions of social disorder and victimization on business owners' decisions to use guardianship strategies. *Journal of Criminal Justice, 36*(5), 396–402.

Castillo, F. (2007). *Real estate closing fees kickback fraud.* Retrieved June 22, 2010, from http://ezinearticles.com/?Real-Estate-Closing-Fees-Kickback-Fraud&id=597525

Castleberry, S. B. (2007). Prison field trips: Can white-collar criminals positively affect the ethical and legal behavior of Marketing and MBA students? *Journal of Marketing Research, 29*(5), 5–17.

Cauley, L. (2007, August 6). Rigas tells his side of the Adelphia story; on his way to prison, former cable mogul describes the scandal from his point of view. *USA Today*, p. 1B.

Center for Medicare and Medicaid Services. (2011). National health expenditure fact sheet. Retrieved July 30, 2011, from http://www.cms.gov/NationalHealthExpendData/25_NHE_Fact_Sheet.asp#TopOfPage

Centers for Disease Control. (2009). *Centers for Disease Control and Prevention investigation update: Outbreak of Salmonella typhimurium infections.* Retrieved July 6, 2011, from http://www.cdc.gov/salmonella/typhimurium/update.html

Cheit, R. E., & Davis, Z. R. (2010). Magazine coverage of child sexual abuse. *Journal of Child Abuse, 19*(1), 99–117.

Chien, E., & Kleiner, B. H. (1999). Sex discrimination in hiring. *Equal Opportunities International, 18*(5/6), 32.

Chinese goods scare prods regulators. (2007). Oxford Analytica Daily Briefing Service. Retrieved July 6, 2011, from http://www.oxan.com/display.aspx?ItemID=DB137125

Chittum, M. (2003, December 20). USDA to investigate Natural Bridge Zoo bears. *Roanoke Times and World News.* Retrieved July 30, 2011, from http://www.highbeam.com/doc/1P2-12671138.html

Chong, J. (2007, July 24). Study data at UCLA falsified. *Los Angeles Times.* Retrieved July 30, 2011, from http://articles.latimes.com/2007/jul/24/local/me-researcher24

Clarey, R. L. (1978). Prosecution of consumer fraud—New York's new approach. *Criminal Law Bulletin, 14*(3), 197–202.

Clarke, R. V., & Cornish, D. B. (1985). Modeling offenders' decisions. In M. Tonry & N. Morris (Eds.), *Crime and justice* (Vol. 6). Chicago: University of Chicago Press.

Clayton, C. (2010). Lincoln calls hearing on EPA impact on farmers. *Progressive Farmer.* Retrieved July 30, 2011, from http://www.dtnprogressivefarmer.com/dtnag/view/ag/printablePage.do?ID=BLOG_PRINTABLE_PAGE&bypassCache=true&pageLayout=v4&blogHandle=policy&blogEntryId=8a82c0bc2a8c8730012b351b985a0825&articleTitle=Lincoln+Calls+Hearing+on+EPA+Impact+on+Farmers&editionName=DTNAgFreeSiteOnline

Clinard, M., & Quinney, R. (1973). *Criminal behavior systems: A typology* (2nd ed.). New York: Holt, Rinehart & Winston.

Clinard, M. B., & Yeager, P. C. (1980). *Corporate crime.* New York: Free Press.

Coburn, N. F. (2006). Corporate investigations. *Journal of Financial Crime, 13*(3), 348–368.

Coffee, J. C. (1980). Corporate crime and punishment: A non-Chicago view of the economics of criminal sanctions. *American Criminal Law Review, 17*(4), 419–476.

Coffey, L. T. (2000, January 23). Beware of door-to-door scams. *St. Petersburg Times*, p. 3H.

Cohen, L. E., & Felson, M. (1979). Social change and crime rate trends: A routine activities approach. *American Sociological Review, 44,* 588–608.

Cohen, M. A. (1989). Corporate crime and punishment: A study of social harm and sentencing practice in the federal courts, 1984–1987. *American Criminal Law Review, 26*(3), 605–660.

Cohen, M. A. (1992). Environmental crime and punishment: Legal/economic theory and empirical evidence on enforcement of federal environmental statutes. *Journal of Criminal Law and Criminology, 82*(4), 1054–1108.

Cohen, T. H. (2005, August). Federal tort trials and verdicts, 2002–03 (Bureau of Justice Statistics). Washington, DC: Department of Justice.

Cohen, T. H. (2009). Tort bench and jury trials in state courts, 2005. U.S. Department of Justice. Retrieved July 11, 2011, from http://bjs.ojp.usdoj.gov/content/pub/pdf/tbjtsc05.pdf

Cohen, T. H., & Hughes, K. A. (2007). *Bureau of Justice Statistics special report: Medical malpractice insurance claims in seven states, 2000–2004.* Retrieved July 6, 2011, from http://bjs.ojp.usdoj.gov/content/pub/pdf/mmicss04.pdf

Coleman, J. (1982). *The asymmetric society.* Syracuse, NY: Syracuse University Press.

Coleman, J. (1994). *The criminal elite: The sociology of white-collar crime.* New York: St. Martin's.

Coleman, J. W. (1987). Toward an integrated theory of white-collar crime. *American Journal of Sociology, 93*(2), 406–439.

Collin, B. C. (2001). *The future of cyberterrorism: Where the physical and virtual worlds converge.* 11th Annual International Symposium on Criminal Justice Issues. Retrieved July 29, 2011, from http://afgen.com/terrorism1.html

Collins, H. (2010, October 11). Former KB Home CEO escapes jail time. *Daily Finance.* Retrieved July 30, 2011, from http://www.dailyfinance.com/2010/11/11/former-kb-home-ceo-escapes-jail-sentence/

Colvin, G. (2004, July 26). White-collar crooks have no idea what they're in for. *Fortune Magazine.* Retrieved July 11, 2011, from http://money.cnn.com/magazines/fortune/fortune_archive/2004/07/26/377147/index.htm

Comte, F. (2006). Environmental crime and the police in Europe: A panorama and possible paths for future action. *European Environmental Law Review, 15*(7), 190–231.

Condon, S. (2010, May 3). How much does BP owe for Gulf oil spill? Political Hotsheet. CBS News. Retrieved July 6, 2011, from http://www.cbsnews.com/8301-503544_162-20004034-503544.html

Congressman resigns over affair with female aide; "I have sinned." (2010, May 10). *National Post.* Retrieved December 10, 2010, from http://www.nationalpost.com/news/world/story.html?id=3045823

Conley, J. (2007, October 18). Natural Bridge Zoo faces penalties. *Roanoke Times and World News.* Retrieved July 30, 2011, from http://www.roanoke.com/news/roanoke/wb/136282

Cooper, A. (2009, October 30). Obama rules over false US ads in the Wild West. *Campaign,* p. 19.

Copes, H., & Vieraitis, L. M. (2009). Understanding identity theft: Offenders' accounts of their lives and crimes. *Criminal Justice Review, 33,* 329–349.

Coutts, H. (2009). Enrollment abuse allegations plague University of Phoenix [Electronic version]. *The Nation.* Retrieved July 6, 2011, from http://www.thenation.com/article/enrollment-abuse-allegations-plague-university-phoenix

Cox, L. (2010). The "July effect": Worst month for fatal errors, study says. ABC World News.Com. Retrieved July 6, 2011, from http://abcnews.go.com/WN/WellnessNews/july-month-fatal-hospital-errors-study-finds/story?id=10819652

Coyle, P. (1995). Bench stress. *ABA Journal, 81,* 60–63.

Cramm, P. D. (2009, May 26). The perils of prosecutorial misconduct. *FindLaw.* Retrieved July 6, 2011, from http://knowledgebase.findlaw.com/kb/2009/May/1208577_1.html

Cressey, D. R. (1953). *Other people's money: A study in the social psychology of embezzlement.* Glencoe, IL: Free Press.

Creswell, J. (2007, May 21). Mortgage fraud is up, but not in their backyards. *New York Times.* Retrieved July 6, 2011, from http://www.nytimes.com/2007/05/21/business/21fraud.html?scp=1&sq=Mortgage%20fraud%20is%20up,%20but%20not%20in%20their%20backyards.%20&st=cse http://www.nytimes.com

Croall, H. (1989). Who is the white-collar criminal? *British Journal of Criminology, 29*(2), 157–174.

Croall, H. (1993). Business offenders in the criminal justice process. *Crime, Law, and Social Change, 20*(4), 359–372.

Crofts, P. (2003). White collar punters: Stealing from the boss to gamble. *Current Issues in Criminal Justice, 15*(1), 40–52.

Crumb, D. J., & Jennings, K. (1998, February). Incidents of patient abuse in health care facilities are becoming more and more commonplace. *Dispute Resolution Journal,* pp. 37–43.

Cullen, F. T., Clark, G. A., Mathers, R. A., & Cullen, J. B. (1983). Public support for punishing white-collar crime: Blaming the victim revisited? *Journal of Criminal Justice, 11,* 481–493.

Cullen, F. T., Link, B. G., & Polanzi, C. W. (1982). The seriousness of crime revisited: How attitudes toward white-collar crime changed? *Criminology, 20*(1), 83–102.

Cullen, F. T., Maakestad, W. J., & Cavender, G. (1987). *Corporate crime under attack: The Ford Pinto case and beyond.* Cincinnati, OH: Anderson.

Culpepper, D., & Block, W. (2008). Price gouging in the Katrina aftermath: Free markets at work. *International Journal of Social Economics, 35*(7), 512–520.

Curry, P. (2007). *Common forms of mortgage fraud.* Retrieved June 21, 2010, from http://www.bankrate.com/brm/news/real-estate/reminiguide07/mortgage-fraud-most-common-a1.asp

Dabney, D. (1995). Neutralization and deviance in the workplace: Theft of supplies and medicines by hospital nurses. *Deviant Behavior, 16,* 313–331.

Dabney, D. (2001). Onset of illegal use of mind-altering or potentially addictive prescription drugs among pharmacists. *Journal of American Pharmaceutical Association, 41,* 392–400.

Dabney, D., & Hollinger, R. C. (1999). Illicit prescription drug use among pharmacists: Evidence of a paradox of familiarity. *Work and Occupations, 26*(1), 77–106.

Dabney, D., & Hollinger, R. C. (2002). Drugged druggists: The convergence of two criminal career trajectories. *Justice Quarterly, 19*(1), 181–213.

Daly, K. (1989). Gender and varieties of white-collar crime. *Criminology, 27*(4), 769–794.

Danner, M. J. E. (1998). Three strikes and it's *women* who are out: The hidden consequences for women of criminal justice reforms. In S. L. Miller (ed.), *Crime control and women: Feminist implications of criminal justice policy* (pp. 1–14). Thousand Oaks, CA: Sage.

Danner, P. (2009, July 14). BRIEF: Weston man charged with running $14M commodities fraud. *Fort Lauderdale Criminal Attorneys Blog,* Retrieved July 30, 2011, from http://www.fortlauderdalecriminalattorneyblog.com/2009/07/weston_man_charged_with_operat.html#more

Davies, K. R. (2003, December). Broken trust: Employee stealing. *Dealernews, 39*(12), p. 22.

Davies, P. A. (2003). Is economic crime a man's game? *Feminist Theory, 4,* 283–303.

Davila, M., Marquart, J. W., & Mullings, J. L. (2005). Beyond mother nature: Contractor fraud in the wake of natural disasters. *Deviant Behavior, 26*(3), 271–293.

Debusmann, B., Jr. (2010). *Madoff aide's arcade games, off-road vehicles up for auction.* Reuters. Retrieved from http://www.reuters.com/article/2010/06/25/us-madoff-auction-idUSTRE65O0CJ20100625

DeJesus, N. (2007, November 13). Student workers caught stealing from campus bookstore. College Media Network. Retrieved July 30, 2011, from http://webcache.googleusercontent.com/search?q=cache:WheYZe7Xp_sJ:www.mesapress.com/home/index.cfm%3Fevent%3DdisplayArticlePrinterFriendly%26uStory_id%3D8de28f34-7155-42aa-87d4-19273af5941f+%E2%80%9CIt%E2%80%99s+always+shocking+when+someone+you+trust+steals+from+you%E2%80%9D&cd=1&hl=en&ct=clnk&gl=us&source=www.google.com

Delaney, E. (1994). *The exercise of investigative discretion.* Washington, DC: U.S. Environmental Protection Agency.

Denzin, N. K. (1983). A note on emotionality, self, and interaction. *American Journal of Sociology, 89*(2), 402–409.

Dey, A. (2010). The chilling effect of Sarbanes-Oxley. *Journal of Accounting and Economics, 49,* 53–57.

Dey, I. (2009, June 28). The final curtain falls for Madoff: US prosecutors demand 150 years in jail for the $65Bn fraudster, writes Iain Dey. *The Sunday Times* (1st ed.), p. 10.

Dhami, M. K. (2007). White-collar prisoners' perceptions of audience reaction. *Deviant Behavior, 28*(1), 57–77.

DiGabriele, J. A. (2008). An empirical investigation of the relevant skills of forensic accountants. *Journal of Education for Business, 83*(6), 331–338.

Disaster in the Gulf: 107 days and counting. (2010, August 4). *FOX News.* Retrieved July 29, 2011, from http://www.foxnews.com/politics/2010/05/28/disaster-gulf-days-counting

Doctor "threatened to withhold drugs from patient if she refused to have sex." (2009, August 24). *Telegraph.* Retrieved June 17, 2010, from www.telegraph.co.uk

Donahue, K. (2004). Statement of Kenneth Donohue, Inspector General Department of Housing and Urban Development. Statement before the House of Representatives Subcommittee on Housing and Community Opportunity Committee on Financial Services. Retrieved July 30, 2011, from www.hud.gov/offices/oig/data/DonohueTestify10-7.doc

Donsanto, C. C., & Simmons, N. (2007). *Federal prosecutions of elected officials* (7th ed.) Washington, DC: U.S. Department of Justice.

Dorn, N., Van Daele, S., & Vander Beken, T. (2007). Reducing vulnerabilities to crime of the European waste management industry: The research base and the prospects for policy. *European Journal of Crime, Criminal Law, and Criminal Justice, 15*(1), 23–36.

Doughman, A. (2010, May 21). Judge says UW can fire assistant research professor. *Seattle Times.* Retrieved July 30, 2011, from http://seattletimes.nwsource.com/html/localnews/2011924401_aprikyan22m.html

Dreese, J. J. (1998). Priest child molesters disgrace the Catholic priesthood. In B. Leone & B. Stalcup (Eds.), *Child sexual abuse* (pp. 68–73). San Diego, CA: Greenhaven Press.

Duke University. (2010). Southern Center on Environmentally-Driven Disparities in Birth Outcomes. *Children's Environmental Health Initiative.* Retrieved July 30, 2011, from http://cehi.env.duke.edu/sceddbo/projecta.html

Dyer, S. (2004, May 6). False transcripts add to Southern University grade-changing scandal. *Diverse Issues in Higher Education.* Retrieved February 1, 2011, from http://diverseeducation.com/article/3667/

Edelhertz, H. (1983). White-collar and professional crime: The challenge for the 1980s. *American Behavioral Scientist, 27,* 109–128.

Edinboro University graduate claims professor sexually harassed him. (2009, October 5). Retrieved December 15, 2010, from http://www.pennlive.com/midstate/index.ssf/2009/10/edinboro_university_graduate_c.html

Efrati, A. (2009, May 7). Madoff relatives got millions, court filing says; disgraced financier's long-time secretary says she believes he isn't cooperating with investigators in order to protect others. *Wall Street Journal,* p. B11.

Elis, L. A., & Simpson, S. S. (1995). Informal sanction threats and corporate crime: Additive versus multiplicative models. *Crime and Delinquency, 32*(4), 399.

Elofson, M. (2010, January 19). Troy criminal justice professor indicted. *Dothan Eagle.* Retrieved June 7, 2010, from http://www.gulfeast.com/dothaneagle/dea/news/crime_courts/article/criminal_justice_professor_indicted/123781/

Epstein, J. (2011, February 10). Tom Delay lawyers seek a retrial. *Politico.* Retrieved February 23, 2011, from http://www.politico.com/news/stories/0211/49224.html

Equal Employment Opportunity Commission. (2010). Job bias charges approach record high in fiscal year 2009, EEOC reports. Retrieved July 30, 2011, from http://www1.eeoc.gov//eeoc/newsroom/release/1-6-10.cfm?renderforprint=1

Ericson, R., & Doyle, A. (2006). The institutionalization of deceptive sales in life insurance. *British Journal of Criminology, 46,* 993–1010.

Erickson, B. E. (2010). Drug safety reform. *Chemical and Engineering News, 88*(25), 22.

Ermann, M. D., & Lundman, R. (1978). *Corporate and governmental deviance: Problems of organizational behavior in contemporary society.* New York: Oxford University Press.

Ermann, M. D., & Lundman, R. (2002). *Corporate and governmental deviance* (6th ed.). New York: Oxford University Press.

Euben, D., & Lee, B. (2005). *Faculty misconduct and discipline.* Paper presented at the National Conference on Law and Higher Education, Stetson University College of Law. Retrieved June 15, 2010 from http://www.aaup.org/AAUP/programs/legal/topics/misconduct–discp.htm

Evans, R. D., & Porche, D. A. (2005). The nature and frequency of Medicare/Medicaid fraud and neutralization techniques among speech, occupational, and physical therapists. *Deviant Behavior, 26,* 253–270.

Evans, S. S., & Scott, J. E. (1984). Effects of item order on the perceived seriousness of crime: A reexamination. *Journal of Research in Crime and Delinquency, 21,* 139–151.

Ex-Ernst & Young partners get jail sentences. (2010, March 23). Accounting Today. Retrieved July 6, 2011, from http://www.accountingtoday.com/news/Ex-Ernst-Young-Partners-Get-Jail-Sentences-53067-1.html

Ex-mayor in "jail-sex" row. (1992, January 6). *Daily Telegraph,* p. 3.

Ex-pastor testifies in embezzlement trial. (2010, September 2). WBNS-10TV. Retrieved December 10, 2010, from http://www.10tv.com/live/content/local/stories/2010/09/02/story-columbus-ex-pastor-testifies-embezzlement-trial.html?sid=102

Ex U.S. mortgage executive charged with huge fraud. (2010). Retrieved July 30, 2011, from http://in.mobile.reuters.com/article/businessNews/idUSN1614313320100616

Falkenberg, K. (2008). Time off for bad behavior: White-collar offenders can get a year off their terms for doing rehab. *Forbes.* Retrieved July 11, 2011, from http://www.forbes.com/2008/12/20/prison-crime-waksal-biz-beltway-cz_kf_1222prison.html

Fannie Mae. (2007). Mortgage fraud overview. Retrieved July 30, 2011, from www.efanniemae.com/utility/legal/pdf/mtgfraudoverview.pdf

Faragher, J. (2007, December 4). Shut out. *Personnel Today,* 22–23.

Farole, D. J. (2009). Problem solving and the American bench: A national survey of trial court judges. *Justice System Journal, 30*(1), 50–69.

Fatal crash spurs review of Toyota floor mats. (2009, September 15). Associated press. Retrieved July 30, 2011, from at http://beta2.tbo.com/business/breaking-news-business/2009/sep/15/fatal-crash-spurs-review-toyota-floor-mats-ar-74585/

Fattah, E., & Sacco, V. (1989). *Crime and victimization of the elderly.* New York: Springer.

FDA: Georgia plant knowingly sold peanut butter tainted with salmonella. (2009). Retrieved August 31, 2010 from http://articles.nydailynews.com/2009-02-06/news/17916106_1_private-lab-tests-peanut-butter-usda

Fearn, H. (2008, May 22). Sex and the university. *The Times Higher Education Supplement.* Retrieved June 7, 2010, from http://www.lexisnexis.com

Federal Bureau of Investigation. (2005). Mortgage fraud operation "quick flip." Retrieved June 21, 2010, from http://www.fbi.gov/pressrel/pressrel05/quickflip121405.htm

Federal Bureau of Investigation. (2009a). Crime in the United States: Robbery. U.S. Department of Justice. Retrieved from http://www2.fbi.gov/ucr/cius2009/offenses/violent_crime/robbery.html

Federal Bureau of Investigation. (2009b). *Financial crimes report to the public: Fiscal year 2008.* Retrieved July 29, 2011, from http://www.fbi.gov/stats-services/publications/fcs_report2008

Federal Bureau of Investigation. (2009c). *2008 financial crimes report.* http://www.fbi.gov/stats-services/publications/fcs_report2008

Federal Bureau of Investigation. (2010a, January 11). *Hedge fund manager who bilked relatives out of $25 million sentenced to over 10 years in federal prison.* Retrieved July 29, 2011, from http://www.fbi.gov/losangeles/press-releases/2010/la011110a.htm

Federal Bureau of Investigation. (2010b). *2009 financial crimes report.* Retrieved January 5, 2011, from http://www.fbi.gov/stats-services/publications/financial-crimes-report-2009

Federal Deposit Insurance Corporation. (2007). *Staying alert to mortgage fraud.* Retrieved July 29, 2011, from http://www.fdic.gov/regulations/examinations/supervisory/insights/sisum07/article02_staying-alert.html

Federal Trade Commission. (2001). *Advertising FAQs: A guide for small businesses.* Retrieved August 3, 2010 from http://business.ftc.gov/documents/bus35-advertising-faqs-guide-small-business.pdf

Federal Trade Commission. (2004). KFC's claims that fried chicken is a way to eat better don't fly. Press release. Available online. Retrieved August 1, 2010, from http://www.ftc.gov/opa/2004/06/kfccorp.shtm

Federal Trade Commission. (2010a). *FTC investigation of ad claims that Rice Krispies benefits children's immunity leads to stronger order against Kellogg.* Retrieved July 30, 2011, from http://www.ftc.gov/opa/2010/06/kellogg.shtm

Federal Trade Commission. (2010b). *Price discrimination among buyers: Robinson Patman violations.* Retrieved June 30, 2010, from http://www.ftc.gov/bc/antitrust/price_discrimination.shtm

Federal Trade Commission. (n.d.). *Guide to antitrust laws.* Retrieved August 2, 2010, from http://www.ftc.gov/bc/antitrust/index.shtm

Feldman, S. (2009, April 30). Dangerous liaisons. *The Times Higher Education Supplement.* Retrieved June 17, 2010, from http://www.timeshighereducation.co.uk/story.asp?storyCode=406375&sectioncode=26

Financial Crimes Enforcement Network. (2009). Mortgage loan fraud connections with other financial crime. Retrieved July 29, 2011, from http://www.fincen.gov/news_room/rp/files/mortgage_fraud.pdf

Financial Crimes Enforcement Network. (2010a, April 27). FINCEN warns lenders to guard against home equity conversion mortgage fraud schemes. Retrieved July 29, 2011, from http://www.fincen.gov/news_room/nr/pdf/20100427.pdf

Financial Crimes Enforcement Network. (2010b, May). Mortgage loan fraud. Loan modification and foreclosure rescue scams. http://www.fincen.gov/news_room/rp/files/MLFLoanMODForeclosure.pdf

Financial Crimes Enforcement Network. (2010c, October). The SAR activity review: Trends, tips, and issues. Retrieved July 29, 2011, from http://www.fincen.gov/news_room/rp/files/sar_tti_18.pdf

Financial Crimes Enforcement Network. (2010d, December 14). Mortgage fraud suspicious activity reports rise 7 percent. Retrieved July 29, 2011, from http://www.fincen.gov/news_room/nr/pdf/20101214.pdf

Fischer, A., & Sheppard, J. (2008). Financial institutions fraud. *American Criminal Law Review, 45,* 531–559.

Fisher, L. M. (1992, June 23). Sears Auto Centers halt commissions after flap. *New York Times.* Retrieved July 30, 2011 from http://www.nytimes.com/1992/06/23/business/sears-auto-centers-halt-commissions-after-flap.html

Fisse, B. (1991). Introduction: Corporate and white-collar crime. *Current Issues in Criminal Justice, 3*(1), 7–8.

Fitzgerald, J. D., & Cox, S. M. (1994). *Research methods in criminal justice.* Belmont, CA: Cengage.

Fitzgerald, L. F. (1990). Sexual harassment: The measurement of a construct. In M. Paludi (Ed.), *Ivory power: Sexual harassment on campus,* New York: State University of New York Press.

Florida student arrested for passing gas. (2008, November 22). *North Country Gazette.* Retrieved July 31, 2011, from http://www.northcountrygazette.org/2008/11/22/criminal_gas/

Foo, L. J. (1994). The vulnerable and exploitable immigrant workforce and the need for strengthening worker protective legislation. *Yale Law Journal, 103*(8), 2179–2212.

Former Entellium CEO gets 3-year jail sentence for fraud. (2009, April 2). *Mercer Island Reporter.* Retrieved July 30, 2011, from http://www.pnwlocalnews.com/east_king/mir/news/42350327.html

Fox, M. F. (1994). Scientific misconduct and editorial and peer review processes. *Journal of Higher Education, 65*(3), 298–309.

Frank, N. (1984). Policing corporate crime: A typology of enforcement styles. *Justice Quarterly, 1*(2), 235–251.

Frank, N. (1993). Maiming and killing: *Occupational health crimes. Annals of Political and Social Science, 525,* 107–118.

Frank, N. K., & Lynch, M. J. (1992). *Corporate crime, corporate violence: A primer.* Albany, NY: Harrow and Heston.

Frankel, T. (2006). *Trust and honesty: America's business culture at a crossroad.* New York: Oxford University Press.

Frean, A., & Lea, R. (2010, February 3). Toyota recall: Last words from a family killed as Lexus crashed. *The Times.* Retrieved on October 19, 2010, from http://www.timesonline.co.uk/tol/news/world/us_and_americas/article7012913.ece

Friedman, M. (2009, September 28). Retailers report "shrinkage" of inventory on the rise. *Arkansas Business, 26*(39), p. 17.

Friedrichs, D. (2004). Enron et al.: Paradigmatic white collar crime cases for the new century. *Critical Criminology, 12,* 113–132.

Friedrichs, D. O. (1997). The downsizing of America: A neglected dimension of the white collar crime problem. *Crime, Law & Social Change, 26,* 351–366.

Friedrichs, D. O. (2002). Occupational crime, occupational deviance, and workplace crime: Sorting out the difference. *Criminology and Criminal Justice, 2,* 243–256.

Fugitive phony doctor nabbed. (October 12, 2004). *Reuters.* Retrieved July 30, 2011, from http://www.sysopt.com/forum/showthread.php?t=171184

Futty, J. (2010, July 16). Man sentenced for illegal tire dumping. *Columbus Dispatch.* Retrieved July 29, 2011, from http://www.dispatch.com/live/content/local_news/stories/2010/07/16/tire_dumping.html

Fyfe, J. J., & Kane, R. (2005). *Bad cops: A study of career-ending misconduct among New York City police officers.* Rockville, MD: National Institute of Justice.

Galbraith, J. K. (2005). Introduction: Control fraud and economic criminology [Editorial]. *Journal of Socioeconomics, 34,* 731–733.

Garoupa, N. (2005). The economics of business crime: Theory and public policy. *Security Journal, 18*(1), 24–41.

Gathright, A. (2008). Bill to safeguard renters from slumlords advances. Retrieved June 29, 2010, from http://blogs.rockymountainnews.com

Gauthier, D. K. (2001). Professional lapses: Occupational deviance and neutralization techniques in veterinary medical practice. *Deviant Behavior, 22*(6), 467–490.

Geis, G. (1976). Defrauding the elderly. In J. Goldsmith & S. Goldsmith (Eds.), *Crime and the elderly* (pp. 7–19). Lexington, MA: D. C. Heath.

Geis, G. (1978). White-collar crime. *Crime and Delinquency, 24,* 89–90.

Geis, G. (2000). On the absence of self-control as the basis for a general theory of crime: A critique. *Theoretical Criminology, 4,* 35–53.

Geis, G., & Dimento, J. (1995). Should we prosecute corporations and/or individuals? In F. Pearce & L. Snider (Eds.), *Corporate crime: Contemporary debates* (pp. 72–90). Toronto, Ontario, Canada: University of Toronto press.

Georgia State University Faculty Handbook. (2010). Retrieved July 29, 2011, from http://www2.gsu.edu/~wwwfhb/fhb.html

Gerber, J. (1994). "Club Fed" in Japan? Incarceration experiences of Japanese embezzlers. *International Journal of Offender Therapy and Comparative Criminology, 38*(2), 163–174.

Gerber, J., Jensen, E. L., & Fritsch, E. J. (1996). Politics and white collar crime: Explaining government intervention in the savings and loan scandal. *Critical Criminology, 7*(2), 59–73.

Gershman, B. (1999). Judicial misconduct during jury deliberations. In L. Stolzenberg & S. J. D'Alessio (Eds.), *Criminal courts for the 21st century* (pp. 291–314). Upper Saddle River, NJ: Prentice Hall.

Gershman, B. L. (1982). Abscam, the judiciary, and the ethics of entrapment. *Yale Law Journal, 91*(8), 1565–1591.

Ghiselli, R., & Ismail, J. A. (1998). Employee theft and efficacy of certain control procedures in commercial food service operations. *Journal of Hospitality & Tourism Research, 22,* 174–187.

Gibson, K. (2000). Excuses, excuses: Moral slippage in the workplace. *Business Horizons, 43,* 65–85.

Gill, M. (2005). *Learning from fraudsters.* London: Protiviti.

Ginsberg, B., & Shefter, M. (1995). Ethics probes as political weapons. *Journal of Law and Politics, 11,* 497–511.

Glasberg, D. S., & Skidmore, D. (1998a). The dialectics of white-collar crime: The anatomy of the savings and loan crisis and the case of Silverado Banking, Savings, and Loan Association. *American Journal of Economics and Sociology, 57*(4), 423–449.

Glasberg, D. S., & Skidmore, D. L. (1998b). The role of the state in the criminogenesis of corporate crime: A case study of the savings and loan crisis. *Social Science Quarterly, 79*(1), 110–128.

Glazer, M. (1983, December). Ten whistleblowers and how they fared. *Hastings Center Report,* pp. 33–41.

Glen, D. (2010, May 17). Former U. of Louisiana dean is sentenced to more than 5 years. *Chronicle of Higher Education.* Retrieved July 30, 2011, from http://chronicle.com/article/Former-U-of-Louisville-Dean/65603/

Glink, I. (2009). Mortgage fraud v. 2009. Retrieved June 21, 2010, from http://moneywatch.bnet.com/saving-money/blog/home-equity/mortgage-fraud-v2009/715/

Glink, R. I., & Tamkin, S. J. (2008, April 5). The two types of mortgage fraud, plus a primer on tax sales. *Washington Post.* Retrieved June 21, 2010, from http://www.washingtonpost.com/wp-dyn/content/article/2008/04/04/AR2008040401789.html

Glor, J. (2010, January 29). Toyota recall costing the automaker dearly. *CBS News.* Retrieved October 19, 2010, from http://www.cbsnews.com/stories/2010/01/29/business/main6153710.shtml

Glovin, D. (2009a, March 17). Madoff property is subject to forfeiture, U.S. says. *The Globe and Mail,* p. B13.

Glovin, D. (2009b, April 4). Mum's the word; Madoff's secret say nothing about methods. *The Gazette,* p. C4.

Glovin D., & Hurtado, P. (2010, May 22). New Castle's Kurland gets 27 months in first Galleon sentence. *Bloomberg.* Retrieved July 30, 2011, from http://www.bloomberg.com/news/2010-05-21/new-castle-s-kurland-given-27-month-term-in-galleon-insider-trading-case.html

Goldman, B. M., Gutek, B. A., Stein, J. H., & Lewis, K. (2006). Employment discrimination in organizations: Antecedents and consequences. *Journal of Management, 32,* 786–830.

Goldsmith, M., & King, C. W. (1997). Policing corporate crime: The dilemma of internal compliance programs. *Vanderbilt Law Review, 50*(1), 1–47.

Goldstein, J. (2008, October 14). NIH suspends Emory grant amid questions over Pharma payments. *Wall Street Journal.* Retrieved July 30, 2011, from http://blogs.wsj.com/health/2008/10/14/nih-suspends-emory-psych-grant-amid-questions-over-pharma-payments/

Goodchild, J. (2008, December 1). Criminology professor Hollinger on forthcoming results from the National Retail Security Survey and trends in retail shrinkage. *CSO Online.* Retrieved June 30, 2011, from http://www.csoonline.com/article/461365/richard-hollinger-on-shoplifting-and-retail-shrink

Gordon, R. A., Michels, J. L., & Nelson, C. L. (1996). Majority group perceptions of criminal behavior: The accuracy of race-related crime stereotypes. *Journal of Applied Social Psychology, 26,* 148–159.

Gottfredson, M. R., & Hirschi, T. (1990). *A general theory of crime.* Stanford, CA: Stanford University Press.

Grabosky, P., & Gant, F. (2000). *Improving environmental performance, preventing environmental crime.* Canberra, Australia: Australian Institute of Criminology.

Grady, T. (2003, December). Repairers balk at study citing 42 percent fraud rate. *Automotive Body Repair News, 42*(12), p. 1.

Grasmick, H. G., Tittle, C. R., Bursik, R. J., Jr., & Arneklev, B. J. (1993). Testing the core empirical implications of Gottfredson and Hirschi's general theory of crime. *Journal of Research in Crime and Delinquency, 30,* 5–29.

Gray, C. (2004). The line between legal error and judicial misconduct: Balancing judicial independence and accountability. *Hofstra Final, 32,* 1245–1269.

Great White band manager faces relatives. (2006, May 9). Retrieved December 15, 2010, from http://www.foxnews.com/story/0,2933,194658,00.html

Green, G., & Bodapati, M. (1999). The "deterrence trap" in the federal fining of organizations: A research note. *Criminal Justice Policy Review, 10*(4), 547–559.

Green, S. (2007, December 11). Washing toilets for 12 cents an hour; Florida jail won't be Disney World. *Toronto Sun,* p. 4.

Green, G. S. (1990). *Occupational crime.* Chicago: Nelson-Hall.

Green, G. S. (1993). White-collar crime and the study of embezzlement. *ANNALS of the American Academy of Political and Social Science, 525,* 95–106.

Green, S. J., (2005, April). Auto wrecker facing another illegal waste-dumping case. *Seattle Times.* Retrieved July 30, 2011, from http://community.seattletimes.nwsource.com/archive/?date=20050409&slug=dump09m

Hackett, E. J. (1993). A new perspective on scientific medicine. *Academic Medicine, 68*(9) (supplement*),* S72–S76.

Hagan, J. (1982.) The corporate advantage: A study of the involvement of corporate and individual victims in a criminal justice system. *Social Forces, 60*(4), 993–1022.

Hagan, J., Negal, I., & Albonetti, C. (1980). The differential sentencing of white collar offenders in ten federal district courts. *American Sociological Review, 48,* 802–820.

Hagan, J., & Palloni, A. (1986). Club Fed and the sentencing of white-collar offenders before and after Watergate. *Criminology, 24*(4), 603–621.

Hagan, J., & Parker, P. (1985). White-collar crime and punishment: The class structure and legal sanctioning of securities violations. *American Sociological Association, 50*(3) 302–316.

Haiken, M. (2011). Annuities may not be a good choice for your parents. *Your Guide to Better Living.* Retrieved July 29, 2011, from http://www.betterliving.com/1153/beware-annuities-may-not-be-a-good-choice-for-your-aging-parents/?pa=2&tc=pg

Hale, C. (2002). Cybercrime: Facts & figures concerning this global dilemma. *Crime and Justice International, 18*(65), 5–26.

Hall, J., & Brajer, V. (2008). *Benefits of meeting federal clean air standards in the South Coast and San Joaquin Valley Air Basins.* Fullerton: California State University. Retrieved July 30, 2011 from http://business.fullerton.edu/centers/iees/reports/Benefits%20of%20Meeting%20Clean%20Air%20Standards.pdf

Halsey, M. (1997). The wood for the paper. *Australian and New Zealand Journal of Criminology, 30,* 121–148.

Halsey, M. (2004). Against "green' criminology. *British Journal of Criminology, 44*(6), 833–853.

Halsey, M., & White, R. (1998). Crime, ecophilosophy, and environmental harm. *Theoretical Criminology, 2*(3), 345–371.

Halverson, R. (1992). Sears nixes commission pay in light of fraud charges. *Discount Store News,* July 6. Retrieved July 29, 2011, from http://findarticles.com/p/articles/mi_m3092/is_n13_v31/ai_12466021/

Hamermesh, D. (2009, November 6). Charity won't contain this secondary market. Retrieved July 30, 2011, from http://www.freakonomics.com/2009/11/06/charity-wont-contain-this-secondary-market/

Hamm, M. S. (2007). "High crimes and misdemeanors": George W. Bush and the sins of Abu Ghraib. *Crime, Media, & Culture, 3*(3), 259–284.

Hammett, T. M., & Epstein, J. (1993). *Local prosecution of environmental crime* (Technical Report). Washington D.C.: National Institute of Justice.

Hansard, S. (2007, June 18). Judges cracking down on securities fraud; states report more convictions, longer sentences. *Investment News, 25.* Retrieved June 8, 2011, from http://www.investmentnews.com/article/20070618/FREE/70614017

Harden, M. (2010, February 6). Philanthropist, swindler Vilar sentenced to 9 years in prison. *Denver Business Journal.* Retrieved July 29, 2011, from http://denver.bizjournals.com/denver/stories/2010/02/01/daily77.html

Harris, A. (1989, October 25). Jim Baker gets 45-year sentence; Televangelist fined $500,000; Eligible for parole in 10 years. *Washington Post.* Retrieved July 30, 2011, from http://www.highbeam.com/doc/1P2-1219165.html

Harris, D., & Benson, M. (1996). Nursing home theft: An overlooked form of elder abuse. In R. Cibik, R. Edwards, G. C. Graber, & F. H. Marsh (Eds.), *Advances in bioethics* (Vol. 1, pp. 171–188). Greenwich, CT: JAI Press.

Harris, D. K., & Benson, M. L. (1999). Theft in nursing homes: An overlooked form of elder abuse. *Journal of Elder Abuse & Neglect, 11*(3), 73–90.

Harris, G. (2008, October 3). Top psychiatrist didn't report drug makers' pay. *New York Times.* Retrieved July 30, 2011 from http://www.nytimes.com/2008/10/04/health/policy/04drug.html

Harris, G. (2009, March 10). Doctors' pain studies were fabricated, hospital says. *New York Times.* Retrieved June 4, 2010, from http://www.nytimes.com/2009/03/11/health/research/11pain.html?_r=2&adxnnl=1&ref=us&adxnnlx=1312053446-quDa4FtMaqjedJ592V8caA

Hay, K. (2010, October 19). Asbestos disposal draws fine; waste illegally put in dumpster. *Albuquerque Journal.* Retrieved October 24, 2010 from http://www.abqjournal.com/biz/192154380471biz10-19-10Htm#ixzz1A1bqBKd0

Hayman, G., & Brack, D. (2002). *International environmental crime: The nature and control of environmental black markets: Workshop report.* London, UK: Royal Institute of International Affairs, Sustainable Development Programme.

Hazard, G. (1991). The future of legal ethics. *Yale Law Journal, 100,* 1239–1250.

He made his own bed: Crooked investment banker gets 3 years in the pokey. (2006). *Wall Street Folly.* Retrieved July 30, 2011, from http://files.wallstreetfolly.com/wordpress/2006/05/he-made-his-own-bed-crooked-investment-banker-gets-3-years-in-the-pokey/

Health Care Fraud and Abuse Program. (2010). *Annual report for FY 2009.* Washington, DC: U.S. Department of Health and Human Services and U.S. Department of Justice.

Healy, B. (2009a, February 12). Madoff's wife pulled $15.5 m from account withdrawals in weeks before husband's arrest. *Boston Globe* (3rd ed.), p. A1.

Healy, B. (2009b, June, 23). Broker aided Madoff, US says; Jaffe's profits called fraudulent; SEC seeks return of investor money. *Boston Globe,* p. 1.

Healy, B., & Mandell, H. (2009, March 13). An apologetic Madoff goes to jail; admits to massive Ponzi scheme, awaits many-years sentence. *Boston Globe,* p. A1.

Heath, B., & Morrison, B. (2009, July 26). EPA study: 2.2M live in areas where air poses cancer risk. *USA Today.* Retrieved from http://www.usatoday.com/news/nation/environment/2009-06-23-epa-study_N.htm

Healy, B., & Syre, S. (2008, December 13). Boston donors bilked out of millions—Trader accused of $50 billion con game—One nonprofit closes; others may suffer. *Boston Globe,* p. A1.

Heenan, P. T., Klarfeld, J. L., Roussis, M. A., & Walsh, J. K. (2010). Securities fraud. *American Criminal Law Review, 47*(2), 1015–1087.

Heires, K. (2010, February 12). Ex-Goldman programmer indicted: Fleeting value of trading code may be key to case. *Security Industry News.* Retrieved July 29, 2011, from http://www.securitiesindustry.com/news/-24683-1.html

Hemraj, M. B. (2002). The detection of financial irregularities in the US corporations. *Journal of Financial Crime, 10*(1), 85–90.

Henning, P. J. (2010, March 25). When legal bills become a cause for dispute. *New York Times.* Retrieved July 29, 2011, from http://dealbook.blogs.nytimes.com/2010/02/01/when-legal-bills-become-an-item-of-dispute/

Herman, K., Sunshine, P., Fisher, M., Zwolenik, J., & Herz, J. (1994). Investigating misconduct in science. *Journal of Higher Education, 65,* 384–400.

Hernandez, J. C. (2010, April 2). U.S. urges homeowners to remove Chinese drywall. *New York Times.* Retrieved July 30, 2011, from http://www.nytimes.com/2010/04/03/business/03drywall.html

Heslop, G. (2007). Fraud at the Top. *Internal Auditor, 64*(2), 87–89.

Higgins, G. E. (2007). Digital piracy: An examination of low self control and motivation using short-term longitudinal data. *CyberPyschology and Behavior, 10*(4), 523–529.

Higgins, G. E., Fell, B. D., & Wilson, A. L. (2006). Digital piracy: Assessing the contributions of an integrated self-control theory and social learning theory using structural equation modeling. *Criminal Justice Studies, 19*(1), 3–22.

Hill, T. J., & Lozell, S. B. (2010). Antitrust violations. *American Criminal Law Review, 47*(2), 245–285.

Hinduja, S. (2001). Correlates of Internet software piracy. *Journal of Contemporary Criminal Justice, 17,* 369–382.

Hippensteele, S. K., Adams, A. K., & Chesney, M. L. (1992). Sexual harassment in academia: Students' reactions to unprofessional behavior. *Journal of Criminal Justice Education,, 3*(2), 315–330.

Hirschi, T. (1969). *Causes of delinquency.* Berkley: University of Berkley Press.

Hirschi, T., & Gottfredson, M. (1987). Causes of white-collar crime. *Criminology, 25*(4), 949–972.

Hoffman, D. E. (2008). Treating pain versus reducing drug diversion and abuse. *St. Louis University Journal of Health Law and Policy, 1,* 233–311.

Hohn, D. A., Muftic, L. R., & Wolf, K. (2006). Swashbuckling students: An exploratory study of Internet policy. *Security Journal, 19,* 110–127.

Hollinger, R. C., & Lanza-Kaduce, L. (1988). The process of criminalization: The case of computer crime laws. *Criminology, 26*(1), 101.

Hollinger, R. C., Slora, K. B., & Terris, W. (1992). Deviance in the fast-food restaurant: Correlates of employee theft, altruism, and counterproductivity. *Deviant Behavior, 13*(2), 155–184.

Holtfreter, K. (2004). Fraud in US organizations: An examination of control mechanisms. *Journal of Financial Crime, 12*(1), 88–95.

Holtfreter, K. (2005). Is occupational fraud "typical" white collar crime? A comparison of individual and organizational characteristics. *Journal of Criminal Justice, 33,* 353–365.

Holtfreter, K., Reisig, M. D., & Pratt, T. C. (2008). Low self-control, routine activities, and fraud victimization. *Criminology, 46*(1), 189–220.

Holtfreter, K., Van Slyke, S., Bratton, J., & Gertz, M. (2008). Public perceptions of white-collar crime and punishment. *Journal of Criminal Justice, 36,* 50–60.

Holtz, D. (2009, March 21). Confections disappear, employee nabbed. *McClatchy-Tribune Business News.* Retrieved July 30, 2011, from ABI/INFORM Complete. (Document ID: 1664682411)

Hopey, D., & Templeton, D. (2010, December 13). What you can't see. *Pittsburgh Post-Gazette.* Retrieved July 29, 2011, from http://www.post-gazette.com/pg/10347/1109199-114.stm

Hours before arrest, Barry gave anti-drug sermon. Mayor preached against drugs to teens just hours before arrest. (2010, January 20). *Baltimore Evening Sun.* Retrieved July 31, 2011 from http://articles.sun-sentinel.com/1990-01-20/news/9001200236_1_mayor-barry-cocaine-sting-fbi-agents-arrest

Howe, L. K. (1977). *Pink collar workers.* New York: Avon.

Huber, N. (2010). Take the risk out of hiring. *Caterer & Hotelkeeper, 200,* 40.

Huckabee, C. (2009, March 15). Professor whose article was retracted resigns from Harvard Medical School. *Chronicle of Higher Education.* Retrieved July 30, 2011, from http://chronicle.com/article/Professor-Whose-Article-Was/42521

Hundley, K. (2010, June 29). Whistle-blower case details allegations of massive fraud at WellCare. *Tampa Bay.Com,* Retrieved July 30, 2011, from http://www.tampabay.com/news/business/whistle-blower-case-details-allegations-of-massive-fraud-at-wellcare/1105487

Hunter, R. D. (1999). Officer opinions on police misconduct. *Journal of Contemporary Criminal Justice, 15,* 155–170.

Huntington Park insurance agent arrested on grand theft charges. (2009, December 28). *Claims Journal.* Retrieved July 29, 2011, from http://www.claimsjournal.com/news/west/2009/12/28/106246.htm

Hutchins, C. (2010). Henry McMaster: Slumlord millionaire? Retrieved June 29, 2010, from http://www.free-times.com/index.php?cat=1992912064227409&ShowArticle_ID=11012505101683172

Illinois Environmental Protection Agency. (2010). *Open dumps.* Retrieved July 30, 2011, from http://www.epa.state.il.us/land/illegal-dumping/open-dumps.

Inmate ran identity theft ring from inside prison: Judge sentences him to 14.5 more years behind bars. (2011, January 22). *Consumer Affairs.* Retrieved July 6, 2011, from http://www.consumeraffairs.com/news04/2011/01/inmate-ran-identity-theft-ring-from-inside-prison.html

Insurance agent accused of scam. (2007, September 19). *St. Petersburg Times,* p. 1.

Insurers' recent success a milestone in a year of Chinese drywall litigation. (2010). *Insurance Journal.* Retrieved July 30, 2011, from http://www.insurancejournal.com/news/southcentral/2010/12/23/115924.htm

Interlandi, J. (2006, October 22). An unwelcome discovery. *New York Times.* Retrieved June 4, 2010, from http://www.nytimes.com/2006/10/22/magazine/22sciencefraud.html?pagewanted=1

Internal Revenue Service. (2010). Examples of mortgage and real estate fraud investigations—fiscal year 2010. Retrieved July 29, 2011, from http://www.irs.gov/compliance/enforcement/article/0,,id=230291,00.html

Is Martha Stewart truly a changed woman? (2005, March 7). *Msnbc.com.* Retrieved January 19, 2011, from http://www.msnbc.msn.com/id/7112803/ns/business-us_business

Isely, P. J., Isely, P., Freiburger, J., & McMackin, R. (2008). In their own voices: A qualitative study of men abused as children by Catholic clergy. *Journal of Child Sexual Abuse, 17*(3/4), 201–215.

Ivancevich, J., Konopaske, R., & Gilbert, J. (2008). Formally shaming white-collar criminals. *Business Horizons, 51,* 401–410.

Iyer, R., & Eastman, J. K. (2006). Academic dishonesty: Are business students different from other college students? *Journal of Education for Business, 82*(2), 101–110.

Jacobsen, R. A., Jr., Seat, K. L., Shugarman, K. D., & Gildea, A. J. (1991). United States. International Financial Law Review: Supplement, 57. Retrieved July 30, 2011, from ABI/INFORM Global (Document ID: 1385266)

Jacobson, J. (2005, October 28). MIT dismisses biology professor for faking data. *Chronicle of Higher Education.* Retrieved July 30, 2011, from http://chronicle.com/article/MIT-Dismisses-Biology/121430/

Jacobson, S. (2009, September 7). Ex-pastor delivers apology: Haggard omits details of sex scandal in tour of churches with wife. *Dallas Morning News.* Retrieved July 30, 2011, from http://nl.newsbank.com/nl-search/we/Archives?p_product=DM&p_theme=dm&p_action=search&p_maxdocs=200&s_hidethis=no&s_dispstring=ex-pastor%20and%20haggard&p_field_advanced-0=&p_text_advanced-0=(ex-pastor%20and%20haggard)&xcal_numdocs=20&p_perpage=10&p_sort=YMD_date:D&xcal_useweights=no

Jarrell, M. L. (2007). *Environmental crime and the media: News coverage of petroleum refining industry violations.* New York: LFB Scholarly Publishing.

Jayasuriya, D., & Sharp, C. (2006). Auditors in a changing regulatory environment. *Journal of Financial Crime, 13*(1), 51–55.

Jenkins, A., & Braithwaite, J. (1993). Profits, pressure and corporate lawbreaking. *Crime, Law, and Social Change, 20,* 221–232.

Jenkins, C. (2008, October 7). Seniors share stories of fraud. *St. Petersburg Times,* p. 3B.

Jennings, M. (2008). *Business ethics* (6th ed.). Mason, OH: Southwestern Cengage.

Jesilow, P., Geis, G., & O'Brien, M. J. (1985). "Is my battery any good?" A field test of fraud in the auto repair business. *Journal of Crime and Justice, 8,* 1–20.

Jesilow, P., Geis, G., & O'Brien, M. J. (1986). Experimental evidence that publicity has no effect in suppressing auto repair fraud. *Sociology and Social Research, 70*(3), 222–223.

Jesilow, P., Pontell, H. N., & Geis, G. (1985). Medical criminals: Physicians and white-collar offenses. *Justice Quarterly, 2,* 149–165.

Joel Tenenbaum fined. (2009). Joel Tenenbaum fined $675,000 for illegally downloading music. *SodaHead Opinions.* Retrieved July 29, 2011, from http://www.sodahead.com/living/joel-tenenbaum-fined-675k-for-illegally-downloading-music-does-the-punishment-fit-the-crime/question-538253/

Johnson, H. (2010, May 31). And off to jail they go: Disney duo nabbed by SEC. *Investment News,* p. 0050.

Johnson, K. (2009, July 15). White collar cons as the pros: The tab for prison prep: Up to $20K. *USA Today,* p. 1A.

Johnstone, P. (1999). Serious white collar fraud: Historical and contemporary perspectives. *Crime, Law, and Social Change, 30,* 107–130.

Jones, A. (2008, April 4). Ex-tech professors put a family member on payroll. *Atlanta Journal Constitution.* Retrieved July 31, 2011, from http://www.ajc.com/metro/content/metro/stories/2008/04/23/tech0423.html?cxntlid=inform_artr

Jones, B. R. (2007). Comment: Virtual neighborhood watch: Open source software and community policing against cybercrime. *Journal of Criminal Law and Criminology, 97*(2), 601–629.

Judge not: Fall from honor. How Sol Watchler went from esteemed chief judge of New York to shamed prison inmate. (1997). *Psychology Today.*

Kane, J., & Wall, A. D. (2006). *The 2005 National Public Survey on White Collar Crime.* Fairmont, WV: National White Collar Crime Center.

Kane, P., & Cillizza, C. (2009, June 17). Sen. Ensign acknowledges an extramarital affair. *Washington Post.* Retrieved July 30, 2011 from http://www.washingtonpost.com/wp-dyn/content/article/2009/06/16/AR2009061602746.html

Kane, R. J. (2002). Social ecology of police misconduct. *Criminology, 40*(4), 867–896.

Karpoff, J. M., Lee, D. S., & Martin, J. S. (2008). The consequences to managers for financial misrepresentation. *Journal of Financial Economics, 88*(2), 193–215.

Kass, J. (2009, August 21). From Quinn on down, all were on her side. *Chicago Tribune.* Retrieved July 30, 2011, from http://articles.chicagotribune.com/2009-08-21/news/0908200904_1_towns-home-politicians-deacon

Katz, I. (2007, March 13). South Florida a hot spot for commodities fraud. *McClatchy-Tribune Business News,* p. 1.

Kaufman, J. (1988, March 7). The fall of Jimmy Swaggart [Electronic version]. *People, 29*(9). Retrieved February 22, 2011 from http://www.people.com/people/archive/article/0,,20098413,00.html

Kazan-Allen, L. (2007). U.S. Senate hearing: ADAO leadership testifies before U.S. Senate. Retrieved July 29, 2011, from http://asbestosdiseaseawareness.org/

Keane, A. G., & Kitamura, M. (2009, November 25). Toyota's recalls test promise to make "better cars" (update 1). *Bloomberg News.* Retrieved July 1, 2010, from http://www.bloomberg.com/apps/news?pid=newsarchive&sid=ayG_dQWAhAp0

Keenan, C. E., Brown, G. C., Pontell, H. N., & Geis, G. (1985). Medical students' attitudes of physician fraud and abuse in the Medicare and Medicaid programs. *Academic Medicine, 60*(3), 167–173.

Kell, J. (2010, October 8). Former "CHIPS" actor Wilcox faces charges. *Wall Street Journal.* Retrieved July 30, 2011, from http://online.wsj.com/article/SB10001424052748704696304575538461638198690.html

Kelly, C. (2009, August 29). Going to the big house? Let us plan your stay; A growing U.S. industry coaches criminals on how to prepare for, and survive, life behind bars. *Toronto Star,* p. IN01.

Kelly, M. L., & Parsons, B. (2000). Sexual harassment in the 1990s: A university-wide survey of female faculty, administration, staff, and students. *Journal of Higher Education, 71*(5), 548–568.

Kerbs, J. J., & Jolley, J. M. (2007). The joy of violence: What about violence is fun in middle-school. *American Journal of Criminal Justice, 32*(1), 12–29.

Kerley, K. R., & Copes, H. (2004). The effects of criminal justice contact on employment stability for white-collar and street-level offenders. *International Journal of Offender Therapy and Comparative Criminology, 48,* 65–84.

Kimball, P. (2005). *Syndi-Court justice: Judge Judy and exploitation of arbitration.* Retrieved June 24, 2010, from http://www.ananet.org/dispute/essaycomp.html

"Kingpin of commodities fraud" gets 17 1/2 years: Florida telemarketer even offered clients high-interest loans to buy his non-existent products. (2006, June 23). *Edmonton Journal,* p. E2.

Kinnaird, B. A. (2007). Exploring liability profiles: A proximate cause analysis of police misconduct: Part II. *International Journal of Police Science and Management, 9*(3), 201–213.

Kintisch, E. (2006, June 28). Poehlman sentenced to 1 year of prison. *ScienceNow*. Retrieved June 4, 2010, from http://news.scienceno.org/sciencenow/2006/06/28-01.html

Kline, P. M., McMackin, R., & Lezotte, E. (2008). Impact of the clergy abuse scandal on parish communities. *Journal of Child Sexual Abuse, 17*(3/4), 290–300.

Knight, J. (1995, November 17). The misuse of mandatory counseling. *Chronicle of Higher Education*, p. B1.

Knopp, J., Jr. (1966). Branding and the Robinson-Patman Act. *Journal of Business, 39*(1), 24.

Knottnerus, J. D., Ulsperger, J. S., Cummins, S., & Osteen, E. (2006). Exposing Enron: Media representations of ritualized deviance in corporate culture. *Crime, Media & Culture, 2*, 177–195.

Knox, N. (1997, September 7). Broker fraud sanctions hit a record high. *Chicago Sun-Times*, p. 56.

Knox, N. (2000, June 2). Task force scours for note fraud: 4,600 investors fell victim to promissory note scam. *USA Today*, p. 1B.

Konigsmark, A. R. (2006, October 24). Crooked builders hit storm victims. *USA Today*, p. 3A.

Kopel, J. (2008). New law requires rental units to be habitable. *The Colorado Statesman*. Retrieved July 29, 2011, from http://www.coloradostatesman.com/kopel/new-law-requires-rental-units-be-habitable

Kopperud, S. (2010, September 24). *Senate Ag panel spanks EPA*. Retrieved July 29, 2011, from http://brownfieldagnews.com/2010/09/24/senate-ag-panel-spanks-epa/

Korolishin, J. (2003, September). Store employees remain largest source of shrink. *Stores, 85*(9), p. LP24.

Kovaleski, S. F. (2002, January 12). Monitoring device sought for slumlord; D.C. wants to make sure man lives in his building. *Washington Post*, p. B03.

Kramer, R. C. (1984). Is corporate crime serious crime? Criminal justice and corporate crime control. *Journal of Contemporary Criminal Justice, 2*, 7–10.

Kramer, R. C., Michalowski, R. J., & Kauzlarich, D. (2002). The origins and development of the concept and theory of state corporate crime. *Crime and Delinquency, 48*(2), 263–282.

Kreps, D. (2010, January 8). Settlements near for victims of 2003 Great White night club fire. *Rolling Stone*. Retrieved July 30, 2011, from http://www.rollingstone.com/music/news/settlements-near-for-victims-of-2003-great-white-nightclub-fire-20100108

Kresevich, M. (2007, February) Using culture to cure theft. *Security Management, 51*(2), p. 46.

La, J. (2005, March 30). Altered grades lead to student's arrest: Campus computer experts say security measures detected unauthorized access. *Daily Nexus, 94*(85), p. 1.

LA County Division of Consumer Affairs. (2010). False advertising. Retrieved July 31, 2011, from http://dca.lacounty.gov/tsFalseAdvertising.htm. Available online

Landlord jailed for inhuman conditions in Bronx buildings. (2008). New York City Department of Housing and Preservation. Retrieved July 29, 2011, from http://www.nyc.gov/html/hpd/html/pr2008/pr-02-20-08.shtml

Langton, L., & Cohen, T. H. (2008). Civil bench and jury trials in state courts, 2005. *Bureau of Justice Statistics*. Washington, DC: U.S. Department of Justice, Office of Justice Programs.

Langton, L., & Piquero, N. L. (2007). Can general strain theory explain white-collar crime? A preliminary investigation of the relationship between strain and select white-collar offenses. *Journal of Criminal Justice, 35*(1), 1–15.

Larsson, P. (2006). International police co-operation: A Norwegian perspective. *Journal of Financial Crime, 13*(4), 456–466.

Lasley, J. R. (1988). Toward a control theory of white-collar offending. *Journal of Quantitative Criminology, 4*(4), 347–362.

Latimer, P. (2002). Reporting suspicions of money laundering and "whistleblowing": The legal and other implications for intermediaries and their advisers. *Journal of Financial Crime, 10*(1), 23–29.

Lawless, J. F. (1988). The white collar defendant. *Trial, 24*(9), 42.

Layman, E., McCampbell, S., & Moss, A. (2000). Sexual misconduct in corrections. *American Jails, 14*(5), 23–35.

Layton, L. (2009, October 13). Under Obama, regulatory agencies step up enforcement. Retrieved July 31, 2011, from http://www.washingtonpost.com/wp-dyn/content/article/2009/10/12/AR2009101202554.html

Leap, T. L. (2007). *Dishonest dollars: The dynamics of white-collar crime.* Ithaca, NY: ILR Press.

Lederman, D. (2009, September 11). The game of ghost writing. *Inside Higher Ed.* Retrieved July 29, 2011, from http://www.insidehighered.com/news/2009/09/11/ghostwrite

Lee, D. E. (2009). Cheating in the classroom: Beyond policing. *The Clearing House, 82*(4), 171–174.

Lee, J. (2010, November 12). *What were you thinking? Criminal justice students and their social networking sites.* Paper presented at a meeting of the Georgia Political Science Associations, Savannah, GA.

Lee, M. S. (1998). United States v. Nippon Paper Industries Co.: Extending the criminal provisions of the Sherman Act to foreign conduct producing a substantial intended effect in the Untied States. *Wake Forest Law Review, 33*(1), 189–217.

Lee, M. T., & Lundman, R. (1999). Pinto "madness" as a flawed landmark narrative. Social Problems, 46, 30–47.

Leegin Creative Leather Products, Inc. v. PSKS, Inc., 127 S.Ct. 2705 (2007).

Lehr, J. (2010, March 23). Joplin dentist granted probation in Medicaid fraud. *All Business.* Retrieved July 29, 2011, from http://www.allbusiness.com/government/government-bodies-offices-regional/14166639-1.html

Leonning, C. D. (2001, December 14). Slumlord gets 60 days—in his building: D.C. man who denied tenants heat, hot water agrees to unusual sentence. *Washington Post*, p. B01.

Leto, J. L., Pogrebin, M. R., & Stretesky, P. B. (2007). Defending the indigent white-collar criminal: Federal public defender defense strategies for post-indictment representation. *Journal of Crime and Justice, 30*(2), 79.

Levi, M. (2006). Media construction of financial white-collar crimes. *British Journal of Criminology, 46*(6), 1037–1057.

Levin, M. (1984). Corporate probation conditions. *Fordham Law Review, 52*, 637–662.

Levine, J. P. (1983). Using jury verdict forecasts in criminal defense strategy. *Judicature, 66*(10), 448.

Lewis, C. A. (1983). Judicial misconduct in California. *San Fernando Valley Law Review, 11*, 43–69.

Lim, H. A. (2002). Women doctors and crime: A review of California physician sanctioning data 1990–1994. *Justice Professional, 15*(2), 149–167.

Litton, R. (1998). Fraud and the insurance industry: Why don't they do something about it, then? *International Journal of Risk and Crime Prevention, 3*(3), 193–205.

Loane, S. (2000, December). White collar criminals suffer a bad case of jailhouse blues. *Sydney Morning Herald.* Retrieved July 30, 2011 from http://www.sheilas.com.au/sheilas-articles/2000/12/11/whitecollar-criminals-suffer-a-bad-case-of-jailhouse-blues/

Locker, J. P., & Godfrey, B. (2006). Ontological boundaries and temporal watersheds in the development of white-collar crime. *British Journal of Criminology, 46,* 976–992.

Lofquist, W. S. (1993). Organizational probation and the U.S. Sentencing Commission. *Annals of American Academy of Political and Social Science, 525,* 157.

Londoño, E. (2007, August 19). Gaithersburg man admits to equity-skimming scam. *Washington Post.* Retrieved July 29, 2011, from http://www.washing tonpost.com/wp-dyn/content/article/2007/08/18/AR2007081801136.html?nav=emailpage

Longshore, D., & Turner, S. (1998). Self-control and criminal opportunity: Cross-sectional test of the general theory of crime. *Criminal Justice and Behavior, 25*(1), 81–98.

Lopez, R. J. (2010, February 10). Former Redondo Beach police officer accused of embezzling money pleads guilty. *Los Angeles Times.* Retrieved July 29, 2011, from http://latimesblogs.latimes.com/lanow/2010/02/redondo-beach-embezzlement-case.html

Loughran, S. (2004, August 9). In hospital deaths from medical errors at 195,000 per year USA. *Medical News Today.* Retrieved July 29, 2011, from http://www.medicalnewstoday.com/articles/11856.php

Lucchetti, A. (1996, August 19). Used-car sales soar, fueling mileage scams. *Wall Street Journal,* p. B1.

Lyman, F. (2003a). *Anger builds over EPA's 9/11 report.* Retrieved July 30, 2011, http://www.msnbc.msn.com/id/3076626/ns/health-your_environ ment/t/anger-builds-over-epas-report/

Lyman, F. (2003b). *Messages in the dust: What are the lessons of the environmental health response to the terrorist attacks of September 11?* National Environmental Health Association. Retrieved July 30, 2011, from http://www.neha.org/pdf/messages_in_the_dust.pdf

Lynch, M. J., McGurrin, D., & Fenwick, M. (2004). Disappearing act: The representation of corporate crime research in criminology journals and textbooks. *Journal of Criminal Justice, 32,* 389–398.

Lynch, M. J., Stretesky, P., & Hammond, P. (2000). Media coverage of chemical crimes, Hillsborough County, Florida, 1987–97. *British Journal of Criminology, 40,* 112–126.

Madoff's victims. (2009). *Wall Street Journal.* Retrieved July 29, 2011, from http://s.wsj.net/public/resources/documents/st_madoff_victims_ 20081215.html

Maher, T. M. (2003). Police sexual misconduct: Officers' perceptions of its extent and causality. *Criminal Justice Review, 28*(2), 355–381.

Makkai, T., & Braithwaite, J. (1991). Criminological theories and regulatory compliance. *Criminology, 29*(2), 191–217.

Makkai, T., & Braithwaite, J. (1994). Reintegrative shaming and compliance with regulatory standards. *Criminology, 32*(3), 361–385.

Malos, S. (2007). Appearance-based sex discrimination and stereotyping in the workplace: Whose conduct should we regulate? *Employment Responses Rights, 19,* 95–111.

Manhattan U.S. attorney charges 14 defendants with more than $20 million in insider trading. (2009, November 5). *Justice Department Documents and Publications.* Retrieved July 31, 2011, from http://www.fbi.gov/newyork/press-releases/2009/nyfo110509.htm

Mann, K. (1985). *Defending white-collar crime: A portrait of attorneys at work.* New Haven, CT: Yale University Press.

Mann, K., Wheeler, S., & Sarat, A. (1980). Sentencing the white-collar offender. *American Criminal Law Review, 17,* 479–500.

Mannheim, H. (1949). Sutherland, Edwin, H.: White-collar crime. *ANNALS of the American Academy of Political and Social Science, 266,* 243–244.

Marcotte, D. (2008). Role of social factors in the sexual misconduct of Roman Catholic clergy: A second look at the John Jay data. *Sexual Addiction & Compulsivity, 15*(1), 23–38.

The Marquet report on embezzlement: A study of major embezzlement cases active in the U.S. in 2009. (2009, January 14). *Marquet International.* Retrieved July 30, 2011, from http://www.marquetinternational.com/pdf/Report%20On%20Major%20Embezzlements%202009.pdf

Mars, G. (1983). *Cheats at work: An anthropology of workplace crime.* London: Allen and Unwin.

Martha Stewart reads a statement outside Manhattan federal court Friday after she was sentenced to five months in prison. (2004, July 17). *Associated Press.* Retrieved June 6, 2010 from http://nl.newsbank.com/nl-search/we/Archives?p_product=APAB&p_theme=apab&p_action=search&p_maxdocs=200&s_dispstring=martha%20stewart%20statement&p_field_advanced-0=&p_text_advanced-0=&%28%22martha%20stewart%20statement%22%29&xcal_numdocs=20&p_perpage=10&p_sort=YMD_date:D&xcal_useweights=no

Martin, R., Mutchnick, R., & Austin, W. T. (1990). *Pioneers in criminological thought.* New York: Macmillan.

Martin, S. (2007). A rule of reason for vertical price fixing. The Metropolitan Corporate Counsel. Retrieved July 29, 2011, from http://www.metrocor pcounsel.com/current.php?artType=view&artMonth=June&artYear=2011&EntryNo=7284

Martin, S. L., Coyne-Beasley, T., Hoehn, M., Mathew, M., Runyan, C. W., Orton, S., & Royster, L. A. (2009). Primary prevention of violence against women: Training needs of violence practitioners. *Violence Against Women, 15*(1), 44–56.

Martin, V. (2004). Detection and prevention of mortgage loan fraud. *RMA Journal.* Retrieved July 29, 2011, from http://findarticles.com/p/arti cles/mi_m0ITW/is_1_87/ai_n14897572/

Martinelli, T. J. (2007). Minimizing risk by defining off-duty police misconduct. *Police Chief, 74*(6), 40–45.

Marx, G. T. (1982). Who really gets stung? Some issues raised by the new police undercover work. *Crime & Delinquency, 28*(2), 165–200.

Maryland contractor fined $1.2 million for asbestos violations. (2010, June 7). *Mesothelioma News.* Retrieved July 29, 2011, from http://www.meso theliomanews.com/2010/06/07/maryland-contractor-fined/

Mason, K. A. (2007). Punishment and paperwork: White-collar offenders under community supervision. *American Journal of Criminal Justice, 31*(2), 23–36.

Mason, K. A., & Benson, M. L. (1996). The effect of social support on fraud victims' reporting behavior: A research note. *Justice Quarterly, 13*(3), 511–524.

Mass, A. (1986). U.S. prosecution of state and local officials for political corruption: Is the bureaucracy out of control in the high-stakes operation involving the constitutional system? *Publius: Journal of Federalism,* 17(3), 195–230.

Matza, D. (1964). *Delinquency and drift.* New York: John Wiley.

May, D. C., & Wood, P. B. (2005). What influences offenders' willingness to serve alternative sanctions. *The Prison Journal, 85*(2), 145.

Mazur, T. (2001, April 16). Culture beats internal theft. *DSN Retailing Today, 40*(8), p. 14.

McAllister, L. (2008). On environmental enforcement and compliance: A reply to Professor Crawford's review of making law matter: Environmental protection and legal institutions in Brazil. *George Washington International Law Review, 40*(3), 649–685.

Mcardle, J., & Nelson, G. (2010, December 16). Environmental justice activist urges EPA chief to "roll up your sleeves" at tense W.H. forum. *New York Times.* Retrieved July 29, 2011, from http://www.nytimes.com/gwire/2010/12/16/16greenwire-environmental-justice-activist-urges-epa-chief-24157.html

McBarnet, D. (1991). Whiter than white-collar crime. *British Journal of Sociology, 42,* 323–344.

McCarthy, B. (2011, January 12). *Crime and punishment: Judge orders book written as community service.* Retrieved from http://www.walletpop.com/2011/01/12/judge-orders-book-as-community-service/

McCarthy, B. J. (1981). *Exploratory study of corruption in corrections.* Unpublished doctoral dissertation, Florida State University.

McCormack, A. (1985). The sexual harassment of students by teachers: The case of students in science. *Sex Roles, 13*(1 & 2), pp. 21–32.

McCoy, K. (2009, June 30). Appeal of Madoff's 150 year sentence wouldn't matter. *USA Today.* Retrieved January 20, 2011, from http://abcnews.go.com/Business/story?id=7973772&page=1

McCready, B., & Tinley, J. (2009, December 16). Alleged embezzler in FBI custody. *New Haven Register.* Retrieved July 30, 2011, from http://www.nhregister.com/articles/2009/12/16/news/milford/al—embezzle_1216.txt

McDade, R. J., & O'Donnell, K. (1992). Parallel civil and criminal proceedings. *American Criminal Law Review, 29*(2), 697–738.

McDonald's "wrong" to fire worker over cheese slice. (2010, January 26). *The Telegraph.* Retrieved July 31, 2011, from http://www.telegraph.co.uk/foodanddrink/foodanddrinknews/7080767/McDonalds-wrong-to-fire-worker-over-cheese-slice.html

McGurrin, D., & Kappeler, V. E. (2002). Media accounts of police sexual violence: Rotten apples or state supported violence? In K. M. Lersch (Ed.), *Policing and misconduct* (pp. 121–142). Upper Saddle River, NJ: Prentice Hall.

McIntosh, A. (2008, June 19). State cracks down on unregistered car dealers. *McClatchy-Tribune Business News.* Retrieved July 30, 2011, from ABI/INFORM Complete. (Document ID: 1497556761)

McKay, B. (2006, July 6). Coke employee faces charges in plot to sell secrets. *Wall Street Journal,* p. B6.

Mclaughlin, T. (2010, April 15). BRIEF: Destin man gets 5 years for fraud: Owen collected $2.2 million for Oasis futures business. *Northwest Florida Daily New,* p. B1.

McMullan, J. L., & Perrier, D. C. (2007). Controlling cyber-crime and gambling: Problems and paradoxes in the mediation of law and criminal organization. *Police Practice and Research, 8*(5), 431–444.

McNamara, M. (2006, May 23). *FTC head opposes anti-gouging law: Says regulation would be hard to enforce and could cause fuel shortages. CBS News.* Retrieved July 29, 2011, from http://www.cbsnews.com/stories/2006/05/22/business/main1639514.shtml

McNeill, B. (2010, May 28). UV fights inquiry by Cuccinelli. *Charlottesville Daily Progress.* Retrieved July 29, 2011, from http://www2.dailyprogress.com/cdp/news/local/education/article/uva_fights_inquiry_by_cuccinelli/56663/

McNulty, P. (n.d.). *Principles of federal prosecution of business organizations.* Washington, DC: U.S. Department of Justice.

McShane, L. (2009, July 31). Hoboken mayor Peter Cammarano resigns after arrest in sweeping corruption probe. *NY Daily News.* Retrieved July 29, 2011, from http://www.nydailynews.com/news/ny_crime/2009/07/31/2009-07-31_hoboken_mayor_peter_cammarano_resigns_after_arrest_in_sweeping_corruption_probe.html

Meddling at EPA? Activists point to survey. (2008, April 23, 2010). Retrieved December 15, 2010 from http://wapedia.mobi/en/United_States_Environmental_Protection_Agency?t=9

Medicaid Fraud Reports. (1991, March). Washington, DC: National Association of Attorneys General.

Medicaid Fraud Reports. (1994, March). Washington, DC: National Association of Attorneys General.

Medicaid Fraud Reports. (1995, July). Washington, DC: National Association of Attorneys General.

Medicaid Fraud Reports. (1995, September). Washington, DC: National Association of Attorneys General.

Medicaid Fraud Reports. (1996, March). Washington, DC: National Association of Attorneys General.

Medicaid Fraud Reports. (1998, September). Washington, DC: National Association of Attorneys General.

Medicaid Fraud Reports (2006, November). Washington, DC: National Association of Attorneys General.

Medicaid Fraud Reports. (2009). Washington, DC: National Association of Attorneys General.

Medicare.Gov. (2008). *Nursing homes: About nursing home inspections.* Retrieved July 29, 2011, from http://www.medicare.gov/nursing/aboutinspections.asp?PrinterFriendly=true

Meier, K. J., & Holbrook, T. M. (1992). "I seen my opportunities and I took 'em": Political corruption in the American states. *Journal of Politics, 54*(1), 135–155.

Meincke, P. (2009, June 12). *Chicago owner loses home in mortgage scam.* Retrieved June 29, 2010, from http://abclocal.go.com/wls/story?section=news/local&id=6862674

Melenyzer, L. (1999). Double jeopardy protection from civil sanctions after Hudson v. United States. *Journal of Criminal Law and Criminology, 89*(3), 1007.

Mercado, C. C., Tallon, J. A., & Terry, K. J. (2008). Persistent sexual abusers in the Catholic Church: An examination of characteristics and offenses patterns. *Criminal Justice and Behavior, 35,* 629–642.

Merton, R. K. (1938). Social structure and anomie. *American Sociological Review, 3,* 672–682.

Messner, S., & Rosenfeld, R. (2007). *Crime and the American dream* (4th ed.). Belmont, CA: Wadsworth.

Meyer, P. (2011, January 11). Tom DeLay is sentenced to three years. *Los Angeles Times.* Retrieved from http://articles.latimes.com/2011/jan/11/nation/la-na-tom-delay-20110111

Microsoft. (2010). *What is counterfeiting?* Retrieved July, 29, 2011, from http://www.microsoft.com/resources/howtotell/en/counterfeit.mspx

Middlemiss, A. D., & Gupta, N. (2007). US interagency law enforcement cooperation since September 11, 2001: Improvements and results. *Journal of Financial Crime, 14*(2), 138–149.

Miller, G. (1993). White-collar criminals share one trait—Greed. *Corrections Today, 55*(3), 22–24.

Miller, W. (1975). *Violence by youth gangs and youth groups as a crime problem in major American cities* (Final Report). Washington, DC: National Institute for Juvenile.

Millspaugh, P. E. (2001, Winter). Can corporations be incarcerated? *Business and Society Review, 72*, pp. 48–51.

Minkel, W. (2002). Sniffing out the cheaters. *School Library Journal, 48*(6), 25.

Minkes, J. (1990). Crimes of the rich. *Probation Journal, 37*, 127–130.

Minor, W. W. (1981). Techniques of neutralization: A reconceptualization and empirical examination. *Journal of Research in Crime and Delinquency, 18*(2), 295–318.

Mishra, B. K., & Prasad, A. (2006). Minimizing retail shrinkage due to employee theft. *International Journal of Retail and Distribution Management, 34*(11), p. 817.

Mohr, H., Pritchard, J., & Lush, T. (2010, June 9). BP spill response plans severely flawed. *MSNBC.com.* Retrieved October 20, 2010 from http://www.msnbc.msn.com/id/37599810/

Mokhiber, R. (no date). Top 100 corporate criminals of the decade. *Corporate Crime Reporter.* Retrieved July 29, 2011, from http://www.corporatecrimereporter.com/top100.html

Mon, W. (2002). Casual factors of corporate crime in Taiwan: Qualitative and quantitative findings. *International Journal of Offender Therapy and Comparative Criminology, 46*(2), 183–205.

Montano, E. (2001, June 21–22). *Technologies of electronic crime.* Paper presented at the 4th National Outlook Symposium on Crime, Canberra, Australia.

Montell, G. (2009). President of University of Texas-Pan American, accused of plagiarism, will retire. *Chronicle of Higher Education.* Retrieved June 10, 2010, from http://chronicle.com/blogs/onhiring/president-of-u-of-texas-pan-american-accused-of-plagiarism-will-retire/826

Montgomery, W. D., Baron, R. A., & Weisskopf, M. K. (2007). Potential effects of proposed price gouging legislation on the cost and severity of gasoline supply interruptions. *Journal of Competition Law & Economics, 3*(3), 357–397.

Moore, E., & Mills, M. (1990). The neglected victims and unexamined costs of white-collar crime. *Crime and Delinquency, 36*, 408–418.

Moorhead, M. (2011, January 20). Dade County pastor gets 30 months for embezzling funds. *St. Petersburg Times.* Retrieved July 11, 2011, from http://www.tampabay.com/news/courts/criminal/dade-city-pastor-gets-30-months-for-embezzling-funds/1146104

Morgan, T. (1995). Sanctions and remedies for attorney misconduct. *Southern Illinois University Law Journal, 19*, 343–370.

Morris, J. (1999). Big hairy pile of whoa! Heroin, Pinochet, ABBA—oh my! Retrieved July 29, 2011, from http://www.gettingit.com/article/261

Morris, J. (2010). America's asbestos age. *The Center for Public Integrity.* Retrieved July 29, 2011, from http://www.publicintegrity.org/investigations/asbestos/articles/entry/2184/

Morris, R. G., & Blackburn, A. G. (2009). Cracking the code: An empirical exploration of social learning theory and computer crime. *Journal of Crime and Justice, 32*(1), 1–34.

Mortgage Asset Research Institute. (2010). *12th periodic mortgage fraud case report.* Retrieved July 29, 2011, from http://www.lexisnexis.com/risk/downloads/literature/MortgageFraudReport-12thEdition.pdf

Mortgage Bankers Association. (2007). Mortgage fraud: Strengthening federal and state mortgage fraud prevention efforts. Retrieved July 31, 2011, from http://www.mbaa.org/files/News/InternalResource/57274_Study.pdf

Moyer, L. (2009a, March 12). Bernie behind bars. *Forbes.com.* Retrieved July 30, 2011, from http://www.forbes.com/2009/03/12/madoff-white-collar-crime-fraud-business-wall-street-prisons.html

Moyer, L. (2009b, June 29). A history of long prison sentences. *Forbes.com.* Retrieved January 19, 2011, from http://www.cbc.ca/money/story/2009/06/25/f-forbes-madoff-prison-sentences.html

Moyer, W. (2010, December, 18). *Love Canal: A city built on a toxic dump.* Retrieved July 29, 2011, from http://ezinearticles.com/?Love-Canal---A-City-Built-On-A-Toxic-Dump&id=5578148

Mueller, G. (1996). An essay on environmental criminality. In S. Edwards, T. Edwards, & C. Fields (Eds.), *Environmental crime and criminality* (pp. 1–34). New York: Garland.

Mullen, F. (1999, January 25). Six steps to stopping internal theft. *Discount Store News, 38*(2), p. 12.

Mullins, C., & Rothe, D. (2007). The forgotten ones. *Critical Criminology, 15,* 135–158.

Mundy, L. (2008, October 5). When Michelle met Barack. *Washington Post.* Retrieved July 29, 2011, from http://www.washingtonpost.com/wp-dyn/content/story/2008/10/03/ST2008100302144.html

Munroe, T. (1992, July 22). Senate panel hears about fraud, deception in auto-repair industry. *Washington Times,* p. C3.

Murray, A. (2009a, June 25). Lax enforcement keeps slumlords from cleaning up act. Retrieved June 29, 2010, from http://www.laprogressive.com/rankism/social-justice/lax-enforcement-keeps-slumlords-from-cleaning-up-act/

Murray, A. (2009b, December 17). Slumlord pays tenants $3.3 million to settle inner city law center lawsuit. Retrieved June 29, 2010, from http://www.tenantstogether.org/article.php?id=1156

My dad is not a slumlord. (2010). *Columbia's Free Weekly Free Times*, Issue 23.22. Retrieved July 30, 2011, from http://www.free-times.com/index.php?cat=1992912063981076&ShowArticle_ID=11010106101677999

Nahra, K. J. (1999, October). Handling the double-edged sword: Insurers and the fight against health care fraud. *Health Law, 12,* 12–17.

Nakayama, G. (n.d.). *Transmittal of final OECA parallel proceedings policy.* Washington, DC: Office of Enforcement and Compliance Assurance.

Nammour, M. (2009, November 1). Two former hotel guards jailed for stealing guests' belongings. *McClatchy-Tribune Business News.* Retrieved July 30, 2011, from ABI/INFORM Complete. (Document ID: 1890524941)

Nardo, M. (2004). Mapping the trails of financial crime. *Journal of Financial Crime, 12*(2), 139–143.

Nath, L., & Lovaglia, M. (2008). Cheating on multiple-choice exams: Monitoring, assessment, and an optional assignment. *College Teaching, 57*(1), 3–8.

National Center on Elder Abuse. (2008). *Major types of elder abuse.* Retrieved July 30, 2011, from http://www.ncea.aoa.gov/NCEAroot/Main_Site/FAQ/Basics/Types_Of_Abuse.aspx

National Commission on Urban Problems. (1972). *Building the American city.* Washington, DC: Government Printing Office.

National Health Care Anti Fraud Association (2010). The problem of health care fraud. Retrieved September 18, 2011, from http://www.nhcaa.org/web/dynamicPage.aspx?webcode=anti_fraud_resource_centr&wpscode=TheProblemofHCFraud

National Oceanic and Atmospheric Administration. (2010). New federal rule allows NOAA to deny port entry to illegal fishing vessels: Press release. Retrieved July 30, 2011, from http://www.noaanews.noaa.gov/stories2010/20101013_fishing.html

National White Collar Crime Center. (2009). Welcome. Retrieved July 30, 2011, from http://www.nw3c.org/

NC man sentenced in Virginia for mortgage fraud. (2010, June 21). *Bloomberg Businessweek*. Retrieved July 5, 2010, from http://www.businessweek.com/ap/financialnews/D9GFR1E00.htm

Near, J. P., & Miceli, M. P. (2008). Wrongdoing, whistle-blowing, and retaliation in the U.S. government: What have researchers learned from the merit systems protection board (MSPB) results? *Review of Public Personnel Administration, 28*(3), 263–281.

Neil, M. (2009, September 2). Pfizer whistle-blower's $51.5M payday could spark more qui tam suits. *American Bar Association Journal*. Retrieved July 31, 2011, from http://www.abajournal.com/news/article/pfizer_whistleblowers_51.5m_payday_could_spark_more_qui_tam_suits/

Nelson, J. (2010, February 5). Supervisor Biane spent $50,000 to hire white-collar criminal lawyer. *Daily Bulletin*. Retrieved July 31, 2011, from http://inlandpolitics.com/blog/2010/02/06/dailybulletin-supervisor-biane-spent-50000-to-hire-white-collar-criminal-lawyer/

Nestle subsidiary to settle FTC false advertising charges: Will drop deceptive health claims for BOOST kid essentials: Case involving drink for kids is agency's first challenging deceptive probiotic advertising. (2010, July 14). *PR Newswire*. Retrieved July 30, 2011, from ABI/INFORM Complete. (Document ID: 2080992161)

Nestor, S. (2004). The impact of changing corporate governance norms on economic crime. *Journal of Financial Crime, 11*(4), 347–352.

Neumeister, L., & Hays, T. (2009). Madoff to plead guilty to eleven counts. *HuffingtonPost.com*. Retrieved July 29, 2011, from http://www.huffingtonpost.com/2009/03/10/bernard-madoff-expected-t_n_173424.html

Newbold, G., & Ivory, R. (1993). Policing serious fraud in New Zealand. *Crime, Law, and Social Change, 20*, 233–248.

Newman, M. (2010, March 8). No misconduct by professor who used student's work in paper. Retrieved June 1, 2010 from http://www.timeshigereducation.co.uk/story.asp?storycode=410686

Nibert, D., Cooper, S., & Crossmaker, M. (1989). Assaults against residents of a psychiatric institution. *Journal of Interpersonal Violence, 4*(3), 342–349.

Ninemsn staff. (2010, January 18). *Doctor convicted over lemon juice antiseptic*. Retrieved July 29, 2011, from http://news.ninemsn.com.au/world/1001073/doctor-convicted-over-lemon-juice-antiseptic

Norman, D. (2009, September 12). Real estate investor convicted on 19 counts for his involvement in a mortgage fraud conspiracy. *Real Estate Industry News*. Retrieved July 29, 2011, from http://www.realestateindustrynews.com/special-posts/real-estate-investor-convicted-on-19-counts-for-his-involvement-in-a-mortgage-fraud-conspiracy/

Nuckols, B. (2010, February 4). Baltimore mayor resigns, gets probation in scandal. *Associated Press*. Retrieved July 30, 2011, from http://www.usatoday.com/news/nation/2010-02-04-baltimore-mayor-replaced_N.htm

O'Connor, T. (1991, November). *Workplace violence in the fast food domain*. Paper presented at the annual meetings of the American Society of Criminology, Baltimore, MD.

O'Donnell, J. (2004, March 18). State time or federal prison? *USA Today*. Retrieved January 19, 2011, from http://www.usatoday.com/money/companies/2004-03-18-statetime_x.htm

O'Donnell, J., & Willing, R. (2003, May 11). Prison time gets harder for white-collar crooks. *USA Today*. Retrieved January 19, 2011, from http://www.usatoday.com/money/companies/management/2003-05-11-bighouse_x.htm

O'Hear, M. M. (2004). Sentencing the green collar offender: Punishment, culpability, and environmental crime. *Journal of Criminal Law and Criminology, 95*(1), 133–276.

O'Sullivan, S. (2011, February 3). Delaware crime: Wilmington pastor charged with embezzlement. *News Journal*. Retrieved March 10, 2011, from http://www.delawareonline.com/article/20110203/NEWS01/102030351/Delaware-crime-Wilmington-pastor-charged-embezzlement

OC lawyer arrested for defrauding 400 homeowners-DA presses criminal charges. (2010). Retrieved July 29, 2011, from http://mandelman.ml-implode.com/2010/01/oc-lawyer-arrested-for-defrauding-400-home-owners-with-promises-of-loan-modifications-%E2%80%93-da-presses-criminal-charges-against-three-accused-%E2%80%9Cscammers%E2%80%9D/

Occupational Safety and Health Administration. (2006). All about OSHA. Retrieved July 29, 2011, from http://www.osha.gov/Publications/3302-06N-2006-English.html

Occupational Safety and Health Administration. (2010a). OSHA frequently asked questions. Retrieved December 17, 2010, from http://osha.gov/osha_faqs.html

Occupational Safety and Health Administration. (2010b). The whistleblower protection program. Retrieved December 17, 2010, from http://www.whistleblowers.gov/index.html

Office of New York State Attorney General. (2010). Cuomo announces charges against former UB researcher for hiring actors to testify during misconduct hearing and attempting to siphon $4 million in taxpayer funds. Retrieved June 10, 2010, from http://www.ag.ny.gov/media_center/2010/feb/feb16a_10.html

Office of Research Integrity. (2010a). About ORI. Retrieved July 30, 2011, from http://ori.hhs.gov/about/

Office of Research Integrity. (2010b). Case summary—Scott J. Brodie. Retrieved July 29, 2011, from http://ori.hhs.gov/misconduct/cases/Brodie_Scott.shtml

Office of the Governor Rick Perry. (2010). Statement by Gov. Rick Perry on EPA's efforts to take over Texas' air permitting program. Retrieved July 30, 2011, from http://governor.state.tx.us/news/press-release/14677/

Olick, D. (2010, January 15). Big banks accused of short sale fraud. *CNBC*, Retrieved June 22, 2010, from http://www.cnbc.com/id/34877347/Big_Banks_Acussed_of_Short_Sale_Fraud

Oliphant, B. J., & Oliphant, G. C. (2001). Using a behavior-based method to identify and reduce employee theft. *International Journal of Retail and Distribution Management, 29*(10), 442.

Olivarez-Giles, N. (2010, January 26). Owner of 22 Midas auto shops settles fraud claims. *Los Angeles Times*, Business, Part B, p. 7.

Oppel, R., Jr. (2003, March 27). Panel finds manipulation by energy companies. *New York Times*, p. A14.

Orland, L. (1980). Reflections on corporate crime: Law in search of theory and scholarship. *American Criminal Law Review, 17*, 501–520.

Owens, J.B. (2000, June). Have we no shame?: Thoughts on shaming, "white-collar" criminals, and the Federal Sentencing Guidelines. *American University Law Review, 49*, 1047–1058.

Pacini, C., Qiu, L. H., & Sinason, D. (2007). Qui tam actions: Fighting fraud against the government. *Journal of Financial Crime, 14*(1), 64–78.

Page, R., Savage, A., Stitt, K., & Umhoffer, R. (1999). Environmental crimes. *American Criminal Law Review, 36*(3), 515–592.

Parker, W. (2009). *A gynecologist's second opinion.* New York: Penguin Group.

Passas, N. (2001). False accounts: Why do company statements often offer a true and a fair view of virtual reality? *European Journal on Criminal Policy and Research, 9*(2), 117–135.

Passas, N. (2004). Law enforcement challenges in Hawala-related investigations. *Journal of Financial Crime, 12*(2), 112–119.

Passas, N. (2005). Lawful but awful: "Legal corporate crimes." *Journal of Socio-Economics, 34*, 771–786.

Paul, T. (2006). Five reverse home mortgage scams to watch out for. Retrieved July 29, 2011, from http://ezinearticles.com/?five-Home-Mortgage-Scams-to-Watch-Out-For&id=273604

Payne, B. K. (1995). Medicaid fraud. *Criminal Justice Policy Review, 7*, 61–74.

Payne, B. K. (2003a). *Crime in the home health care field.* Springfield, IL: Charles C Thomas.

Payne, B. K. (2003b). *Incarcerating white-collar offenders.* Springfield, IL: Charles C Thomas.

Payne, B. K. (2005). *Crime and elder abuse: An integrated perspective* (2nd ed.). Springfield, IL: Charles C Thomas.

Payne, B. K. (2006). Problems controlling fraud and abuse in the home health care field: Voices of fraud control unit directors. *Journal of Financial Crime, 13*(1), 77–92.

Payne, B. K. (2010). Understanding elder sexual abuse and criminal justice system's response: Comparisons to elder physical abuse. *Justice Quarterly, 27*(2), 206–224.

Payne, B. K. (2011). *Crime and elder abuse: An integrated perspective* (3rd ed.). Springfield, IL: Charles C Thomas.

Payne, B. K. (in press). Failure to report elder abuse and criminal penalties. *Crime and Delinquency.*

Payne, B. K., & Berg, B. L. (1997). Looking for fraud in all the wrong places. *The Police Journal: A Quarterly Review for the Police of the World, 70*, 220–230.

Payne, B. K., & Berg, B. L. (1999). Perceptions of nursing home workers, police chiefs, and college students regarding crime against the elderly. *American Journal of Criminal Justice, 24*, 139–149.

Payne, B. K., Berg, B. L., & Byars, K. (1999). A qualitative examination of the similarities and differences of elder abuse definitions among four groups: Nursing home directors, nursing home employees, police chiefs and students. *Journal of Elder Abuse & Neglect, 10*(3/4), 63–86.

Payne, B. K., & Burke-Fletcher, L. B. (2005). Elder abuse in nursing homes: Prevention and resolution strategies and barriers. *Journal of Criminal Justice, 33*(2), 119–125.

Payne, B. K., & Cikovic, R. (1995). An empirical examination of the characteristics, consequences, and causes of elder abuse in nursing homes. *Journal of Elder Abuse & Neglect, 7*(4), 61–74.

Payne, B. K., & Dabney, D. (1997). Prescription fraud: Characteristics, causes, and consequences. *Journal of Drug Issues, 27*(4), 807–820.

Payne, B. K., & Gainey, R. (1998). The electronic monitoring of offenders released from jail or prison: Safety, control, and comparisons to the incarcerated experience. *Prison Journal, 84*, 413.

Payne, B. K., & Gainey, R. (2004). Social and governmental altruism, deterrence theory, and nursing home regulatory violations: A state-level analysis. *Journal of Crime and Justice, 72*(2), 59–78.

Payne, B. K., & Gainey, R. (2006). The criminal justice response to elder abuse in nursing homes: A routine activities perspective. *Western Criminology Review, 7*(3), 67–81.

Payne, B. K., & Gainey, R. (2009). *Family violence and criminal justice.* Cincinnati, OH: Anderson.

Payne, B. K., & Gray, C. (2001). Fraud by home health care workers and the criminal justice response. *Criminal Justice Review, 26*, 209–232.

Payne, B. K., & Stevens, E. D. (1999). An examination of recent professional sanctions imposed on Alabama lawyers.. *Justice Professional, 12*, 17–43.

Payne, B. K., & Strasser, S. M. (2010). *Financial exploitation of nursing home residents: Comparisons to physical abuse and the justice system's response.* Unpublished manuscript. [Available from Brian K. Payne, PhD, Department of Criminal Justice, Georgia State University, Atlanta, GA]

Payne, B. K., Time, V., & Raper, S. (2005). Regulating legal misconduct in the Commonwealth of Virginia. *Women and Criminal Justice, 15*(3), 81–95.

Peck, C. (2010, May 24). *U.S. EPA files complaint against Nevada businessman for solid and hazardous waste violations in Indian country.* Retrieved July 29, 2011, from http://yosemite.epa.gov/opa/admpress.nsf/93f5831f40fc943685257359003f5346/4ebeb82b9379a601852577270056dd73!OpenDocument

Pelofsky, J. (2010, June 17). Authorities reveal mortgage fraud crackdown, 485 arrests. *Reuters.* Retrieved July 31, 2011, from http://www.reuters.com/article/2010/06/17/us-mortgage-fraud-idUSTRE65F3E620100617

Pendlebury, R. (2010, June 18). Special investigation: Why is BP taking all the blame? *Daily Mail.* Retrieved September 12, 2010, from http://www.dailymail.co.uk/news/article-1287226/GULF-OIL-SPILL-Whys-BP-taking-blame.html

People v. Eubanks, 927 F.2d 310 (Cal. 1996).

Peterson, B. K. (2004). Education as a new approach to fighting financial crime in USA. *Journal of Financial Crime, 11*(3), 262–267.

Petress, K. C. (2003). Academic dishonesty: A plague on our profession. *Education, 123*(3), 624–627.

Pfiefer, W. (2010, April 12). Bruce Karatz brings in star witness. *LA Times.* Retrieved July 31, 2011, from http://articles.latimes.com/2010/apr/02/business/la-fi-karatz2-2010apr02

Pillemer, K., & Moore, D. (1990). Highlights from a study of abuse of patients in nursing homes. *Journal of Elder Abuse & Neglect, 2*, 5–29.

Pimentel, D., Cooperstein, S., Randell, H., Filiberto, D., Sorrentino, S., Kaye, B., Nicklin, C., Yagi, J., Brian, J., & O'Hern, J. (2007). Ecology of increasing diseases: Population growth and environmental degradation. *Human Ecology, 35*(6), 653–668.

Pino, N. W., & Smith, W. L. (2003). College students and academic dishonesty. *College Student Journal, 37*(4), 490–500.

Piquero, A. R., Piquero, N., Terry, K. J., Youstin, T., & Nobles, M. (2008). Uncollaring the criminal: Understanding criminal careers of criminal clerics. *Criminal Justice and Behavior, 35*, 583–599.

Piquero, N. L., & Benson, M. L. (2004). White-collar crime and criminal careers: Specifying a trajectory of punctuated situational offending. *Journal of Contemporary Criminal Justice, 20*(2), 148–165.

Piquero, N. L., Carmichael, S., & Piquero, A. R. (2008). Research note: Assessing the perceived seriousness of white-collar and street crime. *Crime and Delinquency, 54,* 291–312.

Piquero, N. L., & Davis, J. (2004). Extralegal factors and the sentencing of organizational defendants: An examination of the federal sentencing guidelines. *Journal of Criminal Justice, 32*(6), 643–654.

Piquero, N. L., Exum, M. L., & Simpson, S. S. (2005). Integrating the desire-for-control and rational choice in a corporate crime context. *Justice Quarterly, 22*(2), 252–280.

Piquero, N. L., Schoepfer, A., & Langton, L. (2010). Completely out of control or the desire to be in complete control? How low self-control and the desire for control relate to corporate offending. *Crime & Delinquency, 56*(4), 627–647.

Piquero, N. L., Tibbetts, S. G., & Blankenship, M. B. (2005). Examining the role of differential association and techniques of neutralization in explaining corporate crime. *Deviant Behavior, 26,* 159–188.

Pirrong, C. (2010). Energy market manipulation: Definition, diagnosis, and deterrence. *Energy Law Journal, 31*(1), 1–20.

Plimton, E. A., & Walsh, D. (2010). Corporate criminal liability. *American Criminal Law Review, 47,* 331–343.

Plushnick-Masti, R. (2010, December 30). Rick Perry, Texas continue to wage battle against EPA as fight over regulations grows fierce. Retrieved July 31, 2011, from http://www.huffingtonpost.com/2010/12/30/rick-perry-texas-epa_n_802643.html

Podgor, E. S. (2007). The challenge of white collar sentencing. *Journal of Criminal Law and Criminology, 97*(3), 731–759.

Pollack, H., & Smith, A. B. (1983). White-collar v. street crime sentencing disparity: How judges see the problem. *Judicature,* 67(4), 175–182.

Pollock, J. (2004). *Ethics in crime and justice* (4th ed.). Belmont, CA: Wadsworth.

Pontell, H., Jesilow, P., & Geis, G. (1984). Practitioner fraud and abuse in medical benefit programs. *Law and Policy, 6,* 405–424.

Pontell, H. N. (2005). White-collar crime or just risky business? The role of fraud in major financial debacles. *Crime, Law & Social Change, 42,* 309–324.

Pontell, H. N, Jesilow, P., & Geis, G. (1982). Policing physicians: Practitioner fraud and abuse in a government medical program. *Social Problems, 30*(1), 117–125.

A Ponzi nation. (2009, December 29). *New Zealand Herald.* Retrieved June 15, 2011, from http://www.nzinvestors.com/business-news/15831-ponzi-nation.html

Posner, R. (1980). Retribution and related concepts of punishment. *Journal of Legal Studies, 9*(1), 71–92.

Poveda, T. G. (1992). White-collar crime and the justice department: The institutionalization of a concept. *Crime, Law and Social Change, 17,* 235–252.

Powell, S. M. (2010, December 5). *Perry taking his rebellion national: States' rights crusade will begin with EPA battle.* Retrieved July 30, 2011, from http://www.chron.com/disp/story.mpl/metropolitan/7324941

Power, L. G. (2009). University students' perceptions of plagiarism. *Journal of Higher Education, 80*(6), 643–662.

PR Newswire. (2007, August 9). *Profnet wire: Government & law: Safety of imported products.* Retrieved July 29, 2011, from http://www.smart-brief.com/news/aaaa/industryPR-detail.jsp?id=24DF678E-43D9-453F-AD14-D0EFFF2F9015

Pratt, M. K. (2001, November 23). Retailers take steps to combat employee-theft epidemic. *Boston Business Journal, 21*(42), 37.

Presier, S. E., & Swisher, C. C., III (1988). Representing the white-collar defendant. *Trial, 24*(10), 72.

Price Waterhouse v. Hopkins, 490 U.S. 228 (1989).

Pulkkinen, L. (2010, May 25). State: UW doctor traded addict drugs for sex. Retrieved June 17, 2010, from http://www.katu.com/news/94853414.html

Punch, M. (2000). Suite violence: Why managers murder and corporations kill. *Crime, Law, and Social Change, 33,* 243–280.

Punch, M. (2008). The organization did it: Individuals, corporations, and crime. In J. Minkes & L. Minkes (Eds.), *Corporate and white-collar crime* (pp. 102–121). Thousand Oaks, CA: Sage.

Punch, M. (2009). *Police corruption: Deviance, accountability, and reform in policing.* Portland, OR: Willan Publishing.

Pusey, I. (2007). The role of the regulator in combating financial crimes: A Caribbean perspective. *Journal of Financial Crime, 14*(3), 299–319.

Quinney, R. (1974). *The social reality of crime.* Boston: Little, Brown.

R[X] for the "Ratlord": Live in your own slums. (1987, July 27). *Newsweek,* p. 54.

Rackmill, S. J. (1992). Understanding and sanctioning the white collar offender. *Federal Probation, 56*(2), 26–34.

Rakovski, C. C., & Levy, E. S. (2007). Academic dishonesty: Perceptions of business students. *College Student Journal, 41*(2), 466–481.

Raloff, J. (2010, June 2). *July: When not to go to the hospital.* Science News, Retrieved July 29, 2011, from http://www.sciencenews.org/view/generic/id/59865

Ramsey-Klawsnik, H. (1999). *Elder sexual abuse: Workshop handouts.* Presented at a workshop of the Virginia Coalition for the Prevention of Elder Abuse.

Randall, D. (2010, May 9). Million gallons of oil a day gush into Gulf of Mexico. *The Independent.* Retrieved July 29, 2011, from http://www.independent.co.uk/news/world/americas/million-gallons-of-oil-a-day-gush-into-gulf-of-mexico.1969472.html

Rasmussen, D. G., & Leauanae, J. L. (2004). Expert witness qualifications and selection. *Journal of Financial Crime, 12*(2), 165–171.

Rataj, T. (2001). Cybercrime causes chaos. *Law and Order, 49*(5), 43–46.

Rawkowski, J. J. (2004). Does the consumer have an obligation to cooperate with price discrimination. *Business Ethics Quarterly, 14*(2), 263–274.

Record number of shoplifters and dishonest employees apprehended by US retailers according to 20th Annual Theft Survey by Jack L. Hayes International. (2008, October 1). *Business Wire.* Retrieved July 31, 2011, from http://www.businesswire.com/news/home/20090901005013/en/Shoplifters-Dishonest-Employees-Apprehended-Record-Numbers-Retailers

Reed, G. E., & Yeager, P. C. (1996). Organizational offending and neoclassical criminology: Challenging the reach of a general theory of crime. *Criminology, 34*(3), 357–382.

Reilly, C. (2011, January 1). Raunchy videos starring Enterprise skipper come to light. *The Virginian-Pilot.* Retrieved February 22, 2011, from http://www.hamptonroads.com/2010/12/raunchy-videos-starring-enterprise-skipper-come-light

Reilly, M., Lott, B., & Gallogly, S. (1986). Sexual harassment of university students. *Sex Roles, 15,* 333–358.

Reiss, A. J., & Biderman, A. D. (1980). *Data sources on white-collar lawbreaking.* Rockford, MD: National Institute of Justice.

Rejesus, R. M., Little, B. B., & Lovell, A. C. (2004). Using data mining to detect crop insurance fraud: Is there a role for social scientists? *Journal of Financial Crime, 12*(1), 24–32.

Restaurant closed briefly after dead deer found in kitchen. (2010, October 27). *USA Today.* Retrieved July 29, 2011, from www.usatoday.com/news/2008-10-27-2714710309_x.htm

Ria, C. (2009, October 27). Product liability. *Finance Alley.* Retrieved July 29, 2011, from http://www.financealley.com/article_1200710_18.html

Richardson, H. (2010). WVU tackles white-collar crime in forensic accounting program. *The State Journal, 26*(27), 10.

Richardson, R. (2008). *CSI computer crime & security survey.* Retrieved June 29, 2010, from http://gocsi.com/survey

Richburg, K. B. (2009, July 24). Rabbis, politicians snared in FBI sting: Corruption probe brings 44 arrests in N.J. and N.Y. *Washington Post.* Retrieved March 19, 2011, from http://www.washingtonpost.com/wp-dyn/content/article/2009/07/23/AR2009072301449.html

Richter, M. (2010). Reporting slumlords and landlords. Retrieved June 29, 2010, from http://www.whow.com/way_5399687_reporting-slumlords.html

Riggs, A. (2007, August 20). Beware of post-storm home repair scams. *Knight Ridder Tribune Business News.* Retrieved July 31, 2011, from ABI/INFORM Complete. (Document ID: 1322672341)

Roberts, C. (2007). Rarer than rabies: The legacy of Michael Nifong. Retrieved July 30, 2011, from http://www.freerepublic.com/focus/f-news/1871830/posts

Robie, C., Kidwell, R., & King, J. (2003). The ethics of professorial book selling. *Journal of Business Ethics, 47,* 61–76.

Robin, G. D. (1974). White-collar crime and employee theft. *Crime and Delinquency, 20,* 251–262.

Robinson, M., & Murphy, D. (2009*). Greed is good: Maximization and elite deviance in America.* Lanham, MD: Rowman & Littlefield.

Rogers, D. (2002). Eye of the storm: Cybercrime poses a threat to national security, but is the threat overblown or underestimated? *Law Enforcement Technology, 29*(11), 60–62, 64–65.

Rosenbaum, P. (2009, April). Loss prevention. *AFP Exchange, 29*(3), 40.

Rosenmerkel, S. P. (2001). Wrongfulness and harmfulness as components of seriousness of white-collar offenses. *Journal of Contemporary Criminal Justice, 17,* 308–327.

Rosoff, S. M. (1989). Physicians as criminal defendants. *Law and Human Behavior, 13*(2), 231–236.

Ross, E. A., (1907). *Sin and society: An analysis of latter-day iniquity.* Boston: Houghton Mifflin.

Ross, J., & Rothe, D. (2008). Ironies of controlling state crime. *International Journal of Law, Crime, and Justice, 36,* 196–210.

Rossetti, S. J. (1995). Impact of child abuse on attitudes toward God and the Catholic Church. *Child Abuse & Neglect, 19*(12), 13.

Rothe, D. (2009). Beyond the law: The Reagan administration and Nicaragua. *Critical Criminology, 17*(1), 39–67.

Rothe, D., & Friedrichs, D. (2006). The state of the criminology of crimes by the state. *Social Justice, 33,* 147–161.

Rothe, D., Muzzatti, S., & Mullins, C. (2006). Crime on the high seas. *Critical Criminology, 14,* 159–180.

Rothe, D., & Ross, J. (2008). The marginalization of state crime in introductory textbooks on criminology. *Critical Sociology, 34,* 741–752.

Rudra, A. (2010). What is title insurance & how you can use it to protect your home. Retrieved June 22, 2010, from http://www.investingthesis.com

Ruggiero, V. (2007). It's the economy, stupid! Classifying power crimes. *International Journal of the Sociology of Law, 35,* 163–177.

Ruiz, M. (2010). Where is Bernie Madoff still a hero? *AOL News.* Retrieved July 29, 2011, from http://www.aolnews.com/2010/06/06/where-is-bernie-madoff-still-a-hero-prison/

Rutledge, G. P. (2006). Disclosure and sharing of sensitive information: A US securities regulatory perspective. *Journal of Financial Crime, 13*(3), 339–347.

Ryan-Boyle, C., Simon, J., & Yebler, J. (1991). Sentencing of organizations. *American Criminal Law Review, 29,* 762–770.

Sack, K. (2010, December 23). Doctor arrested in whistle-blowing case. *New York Times.* Retrieved July 29, 2011, from http://www.nytimes.com/2010/12/23/us/23nurses.html

Sambides, N., Jr.(2009, June 24). Police charge contractor with Lincoln paving scam. *McClatchy-Tribune Business News.* Retrieved July 31, 2011, from ABI/INFORM Complete. (Document ID: 1758884291)

Sayre, K. (2011, January 13). Developer who pleaded guilty to harboring stolen antiques gets 3 years probation. Al.com. Retrieved July 11, 2011, from http://blog.al.com/live/2011/01/matt_walker_sentenced_to_three.html

Scallan, E., Hoekstra, R. M., Angulo, F. J., Tauxe, R. V., Widdowson, M. A., & Roy, S. L. (2011). *Foodborne illness acquired in the United States—major pathogens: Emerging infectious diseases.* Retrieved July 31, 2011, from http://www.cdc.gov/eid/content/17/1/7.htm

Scannell, K. (2007, May 7). Insider trading: It's back with a vengeance. *Wall Street Journal.* p. B1.

Schaefer, H. (2003, August 21). One theft charge remains in Whitetail Inn case. *Rhinelander Daily News,* p. A1.

Schanzenbach, M., & Yaeger, M. L. (2006). Prison time, fines, and federal white collar criminals: The anatomy of a racial disparity. *Journal of Criminal Law and Criminology, 96*(2), 757–793.

Schapiro, R. (2009, July 19). Shanks for the advice: White-collar crooks learn jail survival from ex-con. *New York Daily News.* Retrieved July 31, 2011, from http://articles.nydailynews.com/2009-07-19/news/17927418_1_white-collar-jailhouse-mutual-respect

Schemo, D. (2001, December 2). William & Marry? Not if she's his student. *New York Times.* Retrieved July 31, 2011, from http://www.nytimes.com/2001/12/02/us/william-mary-not-if-she-s-his-student.html

Schiff, M. B., & Kramer, L. C. (2004). Conducting internal investigations of employee theft and other misconduct. *The Brief, 33*(3), 63.

Schlegel, K. (1993). Crime in the pits. *Annals of the American Academy of Political and Social Science, 525,* 59-70.

Schmidt, P. (2003, September 19). Reports allege misconduct at UConn. *Chronicle of Higher Education, 50*(4),A26.

Schneider, C. (2004). *Dirty air, dirty power: Mortality and health damage due to air pollution from power plants.* Boston: Clean Air Task Force.

Schoenfeld, H. (2005). Violated trust: Conceptualizing prosecutorial misconduct. *Journal of Contemporary Criminal Justice, 21*(3), 250–271.

Schoepfer, A., Carmichael, S., & Piquero, N. L. (2007). Do perceptions of punishment vary between white-collar and street crime? *Journal of Criminal Justice, 35,* 151–163.

Schoepfer, A., & Piquero, N. L. (2006). Exploring white-collar crime and the American dream: A partial test of institutional anomie theory. *Journal of Criminal Justice, 34*(3), 227–235.

Schrager, L. S., & Short, J. F. (1978). Toward a sociology of organizational crime. *Social Problems, 25,* 407–419.

Schudson, M. (2004). Notes on scandal and the Watergate legacy. *American Behavioral Scientist, 47*(9), 1231–1238.

Schwemberger, J., Mosby, J., Doa, M., Jacobs, D., Ahsley, P., Brody, D., Brown, M., Jones, R, & Homa, D., et al. (2005). Blood lead levels: United States, 1999–2002. *Mortality Weekly Report, 54*(20), 513–516.

Sci Tech Blog. (2009, August 5). *Student arrested for "modding" Xbox consoles.* July 31, 2011, from http://scitech.blogs.cnn.com/2009/08/05/student-arrested-for-modding-xbox-consoles/

Scott, M. B., & Lyman, S. (1968). Accounts. *American Sociological Review, 33,* 46–62.

Searcey, D. (2010, October 20). BP claims process moves forward, but not without grumbling. *Wall Street Journal.* Available online. Retrieved July 31, 2011, from http://blogs.wsj.com/law/2010/10/20/bp-claims-process-moves-forward-but-not-without-grumbling/

Searcey, D., & Efrati, A. (2011, March 18). Madoff beaten in prison: Ponzi schemer was assaulted by another inmate in December; officials deny incident. *Wall Street Journal.* Retrieved January 19, 2011, from http://online.wsj.com/article/SB10001424052748704743404575128031143424928.html

Secretary charged with embezzling from employer. (2010, February 12). *St. Louis Business Journal.* Retrieved July 31, 2011, from http://www.bizjournals.com/stlouis/stories/2010/02/08/daily66.html

Securities and Exchange Commission. (2009a). Ponzi schemes—Frequently asked questions. Retrieved July 29, 2011, from http://www.sec.gov/answers/ponzi.htm#PonziVsPyramid

Securities and Exchange Commission. (2009b, April 30). *SEC charges Wall Street investment banker and seven others in widespread insider trading scheme.* Retrieved July 29, 2011, from http://www.sec.gov/news/press/2009/2009-99.htm

Securities and Exchange Commission. (2009c, November 5). SEC charges Wall Street ring that made over $20 million serially trading on acquisition information tipped by attorney at international law firm. Retrieved July 29, 2011, from http://www.sec.gov/litigation/litreleases/2009/lr21283.htm

Securities and Exchange Commission. (2010). Investigation of the failure of the SEC to uncover Bernard Madoff's Ponzi scheme. Retrieved July 31, 2011 from http://www.sec.gov/news/studies/2009/oig-509.pdf

Securities and Exchange Commission, Division of Enforcement (2010). *Securities and Exchange Commission enforcement manual.* Retrieved July 29, 2011, from http://www.sec.gov/divisions/enforce/enforcementmanual.pdf

Seibel, J. (2009, June 11). Warrant accuses auto repair shop of fraud. *Journal Sentinel, Inc.* Retrieved July 31, 2011, from http://www.jsonline.com/news/waukesha/47881922.html

Shapiro, R. (2009, July 19). Shanks for the advice: White-collar crooks learn jail survival from ex-con. *New York Daily News.* Retrieved July 29, 2011, from http://articles.nydailynews.com/2009-07-19/news/17927418_1_white-collar-jailhouse-mutual-respect

Shapiro, S. (1985). The road not taken: The elusive path to criminal prosecution for white-collar offenders. *Law and Society Review, 12,* 179–218.

Shapiro, S. P. (1990). Collaring the crime, not the criminal: Reconsidering the concept of white-collar crime. *American Sociological Review, 55*(3), 346–365.

Shea, D. J. (2008). Effects of sexual abuse by Catholic priests on adults victimized as children. *Sexual Addiction and Compulsivity, 15*(3), 250–268.

Shelman, J. (2008a, April 22). *U has questions on prof's e-mail claims.* Retrieved June 17, 2010, from http://www.startribune.com/local/18028664.html

Shelman, J. (2008b, April 29). U profs' pay cut as probe continues. Retrieved June 17, 2010, from http://www.startribune.com/local/18340159.html

Shepherd, J. (2005, November 4). List of research fraud grows as MIT star is fired for faking data. *The Times Higher Education Supplement.* Retrieved July 31, 2011, from http://www.timeshighereducation.co.uk/story.asp?storyCode=199479&sectioncode=26

Sherman, N. I. (2005, January 12). Yale professor ousted for misconduct. *Harvard Crimson.* Retrieved June 17, 2010, from http://www.thecrimson.com/article/2005/1/12/yale-professor-ousted-for-misconduct-following/?print=1

Sheuya, S. (2008). Improving the health and lives of people living in slums. *Annals of the New York Academy of Sciences, 1136,* 298–306.

Shichor, D. (1989). Corporate deviance and corporate victimization: A review and some elaborations. *International Review of Victimology, 1*(1), 67–88.

Shover, N., Fox, G., & Mills, M. (1994). Long term consequences of victimization by white-collar crime. *Justice Quarterly, 11,* 75–98.

Shover, N., & Routhe, A. (2005). Environmental crime. *Crime and Justice, 32,* 321–371.

Simon, D. (2006). *Elite deviance* (8th ed.). New York: Random House.

Simon, D. R. (2000). Corporate environmental crimes and social inequality: New directions for environmental justice research. *American Behavioral Scientist, 43*(4), 633–645.

Simon, D. R., & Swart, S. L. (1984). The Justice Department focuses on white-collar crime: Promises and pitfalls. *Crime and Delinquency, 30*(1), 107–119.

Simpson, S. S., & Koper, C. S. (1992). Deterring corporate crime. *Criminology, 30*(3), 347–375.

Simpson, S. S., & Koper, C. S. (1997). The changing of the guard: Top management characteristics, organizational strain, and antitrust offending. *Journal of Quantitative Criminology, 13*(4), 373–404.

Simpson, S. S., & Piquero, N. L. (2002). Low self-control, organizational theory, and corporate crime. *Law & Society Review, 36*(3), 509–547.

Sims, B. (2009, July 8). UAB animal transplant studies by two researchers found falsified. *Birmingham News.* Retrieved July 30, 2011, from http://blog.al.com/spotnews/2009/07/uab_animal_transplant_studies.html

Sims, R. L. (1993). The relationship between academic dishonesty and unethical business practices. *Journal of Education for Business, 68*(4), 207–211.

Singer, R. (1999). Slumlord legislation on the agenda. *The Inquirer: Philly.com.* Retrieved July 30, 2011, from http://articles.philly.com/1999-11-15/news/25495020_1_slumlords-blight-manufacturing-exemption

Singletary, M. (2000, June 7). Promissory scams leave many broke. *Washington Post,* p. H01.

Sinrod, E. J., & Reilly, W. P. (2000). Cyber-crimes: A practical approach to the application of federal computer crime laws. *Santa Clara Computer and High Technology Law Journal, 16*, 1–53.

Sipes, D. D. (1988). Legal and ethical perspectives of selling complimentary copies of the college textbook. *Journal of Law and Education, 17*(3), 355–373.

Sizemore, B. (2011, January 6). Ex-del Hamilton charged with bribery, extortion for ODU job. *The Virginian-Pilot.* Retrieved from http://hampton roads.com/2011/01/exdel-hamilton-charged-bribery-extortion-odu-job

Skinner, L., Giles, M. K., Griffith, S. E., Sonntag, M. E., Berry, K. K., & Beck, R. (1995). Academic sexual intimacy violations: Ethicality and occurrence reports from undergraduates. *Journal of Sex Research, 32*(2), 131–143.

Skinner, W. F., & Fream, A. M. (1997). A social learning theory analysis of computer crime among college students. *Journal of Research in Crime and Delinquency, 34*(4), 495–518.

Slapper, G. (1993). Corporate manslaughter: An examination of the determinants of prosecutorial policy. *Social and Legal Studies, 2,* 423–443.

Smallwood, S. (2005a). Former scientist at University of Vermont to plead guilty to vast research fraud. *Chronicle of Higher Education.* Retrieved July 29, 2011, from http://www.chroniclecareers.com/article/Former-Scientist-at-U-of/119713/

Smallwoood, S. (2005b, April 1). U. of Colorado will investigate allegations of misconduct against controversial professor. *Chronicle of Higher Education, 51*(30), A36.

Smietana, B. (2005). New interfaith report focuses on pastors who steal from unsuspecting congregations. *Religion News Service.* Retrieved February 22, 2011 from http://www.adventistreview.org/2005-1508/story5.html

Smith, B. (2006, October 2). D.C.'s "Pathetic record" in housing enforcement. *National Law Journal.* Retrieved July 21, 2011, from http://www.law .com/jsp/nlj/legaltimes/PubArticleLT.jsp?id=1159347927230

Smith, B. V., & Yarussi, J. M. (2007*). Breaking the code of silence: Correctional officers' handbook on identifying and addressing sexual misconduct with offenders.* Washington, DC: National Institute of Corrections.

Smith, C. (2011, February 16). Heiress to testify in Edwards inquiry. *Pittsburgh Tribune-Review.* Retrieved February 23, 2011 from http://www.pitts burghlive.com/x/pittsburghtrib/news/pittsburgh/s_723051.html

Smith, M. L., Rengifo, A. F., & Vollman, B. K. (2008). Trajectories of abuse and disclosure: Child abuse by Catholic priests. *Criminal Justice and Behavior, 35*(5), 13.

Smith, R. (1997, December). Some used car dealers may be dishonest. *Credit Management,* p. 16.

Smith, R. (2006). Research misconduct: The poisoning of the well. *Royal Society of Medicine, 99,* 232–237.

Smith, T. R. (2004). Low self-control, staged opportunity, and subsequent fraudulent behavior. *Criminal Justice and Behavior, 31*(5), 542–563.

Snider, L. (1990). Cooperative models and corporate crime: Panacea or cop-out? *Crime and Delinquency, 36*(3), 373–390.

Snyder, E. A. (1989). New insights into the decline of antitrust enforcement. *Contemporary Policy Issues, 7*(4), 1.

Snyder, E. A. (1990). The effect of higher criminal penalties on antitrust enforcement. *Journal of Law and Economics, 33*(2), 439.

Solomon, C. M. (1992, July). Keeping hate out of the workplace. *Personnel Journal, 71*(7), 30.

Sorensen, P. T. (2009). The failure of *Sprint v. Mendelsohn* and what courts should do now. *Labor Law Journal, 60,* 185–195.

Sorkin, M. (2008). Watchdog group blasts agency over child safety. *St. Louis Post Dispatch.* Retrieved July 29, 2011, from http://business.highbeam .com/435553/article-1G1-174735507/watchdog-group-blasts-agency-over-child-safety

Souryal, S. S. (2009). Deterring corruption by prison personnel: A principle-based perspective. *Prison Journal, 89*(1), 21–45.

Sowa, T. (2010, March 20). GU joins police to fight fraud: Accountant teams help solve small-scale crime. *Spokesman Review.* Retrieved July 31, 2011, from http://www.spokesman.com/stories/2010/mar/20/gu-joins-police-to-fight-fraud/

Sowinski, G. (2009, April 10). Virtual car dealer faces charges. *McClatchy-Tribune Business News.* Retrieved July 31, 2011, from ProQuest Newsstand. (Document ID: 1676674681)

Spahr, L. L., & Alison, L. J. (2004). US savings and loan fraud: Implications for general and criminal culture theories of crime. *Crime, Law & Social Change, 41,* 95–106.

Spalek, B. (2001). White-collar crime victims and the issue of trust. *British Society of Criminology,* Volume 4. Retrieved July 31, 2011, from http:// www.britsoccrim.org/volume4/003.pdf

Speaks, G. E. (1997). Documenting inadequate care in the nursing home: The story of an undercover agent. *Journal of Elder Abuse & Neglect, 8*(3), 37–45.

Speer, D. L. (2000). Redefining borders: The challenges of cybercrime. *Crime, Law, and Social Change, 34*(3), 259–273.

Spivack, P., & Raman, S. (2008). Regulating the "new regulators": Current trends in deferred prosecution agreements. *American Criminal Law Review, 45*(2), 159–193.

Spurgeon, W. A., & Fagan, T. P. (1981). Criminal liability for life-endangering corporate conduct. *Journal of Criminal Law and Criminology, 72*(2), 400.

Sramcik, T. (2004, January 1). San Diego shop chain latest to be accused of fraud. ABRN News. Retrieved July 29, 2011, from http://www.search-autoparts .com/searchautoparts/Industry+News/San-Diego-shop-chain-latest-to-be-accused-of-fraud/ArticleStandard/Article/detail/88775

St. Louis Police Department. (2006) *Home repair fraud.* Retrieved July 29, 2011, from http://ww5.stlouisco.com/police/PDFDIR/Brochures/Repair_ Fraud.pdf

Stanko, E. A. (1992). Intimidating education: Sexual harassment in criminology. *Journal of Criminal Justice Education, 3*(2), 331–340.

Stannard, C. I. (1973). Old folks and dirty work: The social conditions for patient abuse in a nursing home. *Social Problems, 20,* 329–342.

State of California Commission on Judicial Performance. (2010). 2009 Annual report. Retrieved July 31, 2011, from http://cjp.ca.gov/res/docs/ Annual_Reports/2009_Annual_Report(1).pdf

Stempel, J., & Plumb, C. (2008, December 13). Billions "gone to money heaven"; Friends, high-profile firms among those who invested with alleged fraudster Bernie Madoff. *Toronto Star,* p. B04.

Stenzel, P. L. (2011). Resource Conservation and Recovery Act. In *Encyclopedia of Business* (2nd ed.). Retrieved from http://www.refer enceforbusiness.com/encyclopedia/Res-Sec/Resource-Conservation-and-Recovery-Act.html

Stephenson-Burton, A. (1995). Public images of white collar crime. In D. Kidd-Hewitt & R. Osborne (Eds.), *Crime and the media: The post-modern spectacle.* London: Pluto.

Stevens, E., & Payne, B. K. (1999). Applying deterrence theory in the context of corporate wrongdoing: Limitations on punitive damages. *Journal of Criminal Justice, 27*(3), 195–207.

Stinson, P. M. (2009). *Police crime: A newsmaking criminology study of sworn law enforcement officers arrested, 2005–2007.* Unpublished doctoral dissertation, Indiana University of Pennsylvania.

Strom, P., & Strom, R. (2007). Cheating in middle school and high school. *Educational Forum, 71*(2), 104–116.

Stuart, D. (1995). Punishing corporate criminals with restraint. *Criminal Law Forum, 6*(2), 219–256.

Sullivan, B. (2011). Tom Delay: Arrogance is not a crime. Foxnews.Com. Retrieved July 29, 2011, from http://politics.blogs.foxnews.com/2011/01/15/tom-delay-arrogance-not-crime

Summerford, R. Q. (2002). Expert witnessing. The White Paper: Topical Issues on White-Collar Crime. *Association of Certified Fraud Examiners.* Retrieved July 30, 2011, from http://www.forensicstrategic.com/Articles/Expert%20Witnessing%20The%20Changing%20Landscape.pdf

Sutherland, E. (1939). *Principles of criminology* (3rd ed.). Philadelphia: Lippincott.

Sutherland, E. (1949). *White-collar crime.* Holt, Rinehart & Winston.

Sutherland, E. H. (1934). *Principles of criminology* (2nd ed.). Philadelphia, PA: Lippincott.

Sutherland, E. H. (1940). White-collar criminality. *American Sociological Review, 5,* 1–12.

Sutherland, E. H. (1941). Crime and business. *ANNALS of the American Academy of Political and Social Science, 217,* 112–118.

Sutter, J. D. (2010, August 9). Gulf oil spill is stopped, but true story of damage will be long in coming, scientists say. *Cleveland.com.* Retrieved July 31, 2011, from http://www.cleveland.com/science/index.ssf/2010/08/gulf_oil_spill_is_stopped_but.html

Sykes, G. (1958). *A society of captives.* Princeton, NJ: Princeton University Press.

Sykes, G., & Matza, D. (1957). Techniques of neutralization. *American Sociological Review, 22,* 664–670.

Tappan, P. (1960). *Crime, justice, and correction.* New York: McGraw-Hill.

Tappan, P. D. (1947). Who is the criminal? *American Sociological Review, 12,* 96–102.

Taub, S. (2006, December 20). Four former Enterasys execs convicted. *CFO.com.* Retrieved July 31, 2011, from http://www.cfo.com/article.cfm/8466560/c_8465548?f=todayinfinance_next

Taylor, M. (2001). Fraud control central. *Modern Healthcare, 31*(19), 22–23.

Teacher accused of putting hit on student. (2010, April 7). *WSBTV.com News.* Retrieved June 10, 2010 from http://www.wsbtv.com/news/21631567/detail.html

Tergesen, A. (2009, August 27). Mortgage fraud: A classic crime's latest twist. *As reverse loans grow more popular, scams put older adults at risk.* Retrieved July 31, 2011, from http://online.wsj.com/article/SB10001424052970204044204574362641338197748.html

Terry, K. J., & Ackerman, A. (2008). Child sexual abuse in the Catholic Church: How situational crime prevention strategies can help to create safe environments. *Criminal Justice and Behavior, 35*(5), 15.

Terry, T. (2010, November 18). School audit leads to arrest. *WAGT News.* Retrieved July 29, 2011, from http://www2.wagt.com/news/2010/nov/18/school-audit-leads-arrest-ar-1107039/

"There's no brakes . . . hold on and pray": Last words of man before he and his family died in Toyota Lexus crash. (2010, February 3). *Daily Mail.* Retrieved October 19, 2010, from http://www.dailymail.co.uk/news/worldnews/article-1248177/Toyota-recall-Last-words-father-family-died-Lexus-crash.html#ixzz12kCksE2z

Thomas, M. (2005). A victim over the slumlords. *ShelterforceOnline,* 142. Retrieved June 29, 2010, from http://www.nhi.org/online/issues/142/organize.html

Thomas, O. (2010, May 19). Facebook CEO's latest woe: Accusations of securities fraud. VentureBeat, Retrieved July 31, 2011, from http://venturebeat.com/2010/05/19/facebook-connectu-securities-fraud/

Thomsen, L. C. (2006). Testimony concerning insider trading before the Senate Judiciary Committee, December 5. Retrieved July 29, 2011, from http://www.sec.gov/news/testimony/2006/ts120506lct.pdf

Thrall, R., III. (2003). "Study" a fraud. *Automotive Body Repair News, 42*(12), 6.

Tillman, R., Calavita, K., & Pontell, H. (1997). Criminalizing white-collar misconduct: Determinants of prosecution in savings and loan fraud cases. *Crime Law and Social Change, 26*(1), 53–76.

Tillman, R., & Pontell, H. (1992). Is justice "collar blind"?: Punishing Medicaid provider fraud. *Criminology, 30*(4), 547–574.

Tillman, R., & Pontell, H. (1995). Organizations and fraud in the savings and loan industry. *Social Forces, 73*(4), 1439–1463.

Tomasic, R. (2011). The financial crisis and the haphazard pursuit of financial crime. *Journal of Financial Crime, 18*(1), 7.

Tombs, S. (2008). Corporations and health safety. In J. Minkes & L. Minkes (Eds.), *Corporate and white-collar crime* (pp. 18–38). Thousand Oaks, CA: Sage.

Trahan, A., Marquart, J. W., & Mullings, J. (2005). Fraud and the American dream: Toward an understanding of fraud victimization. *Deviant Behavior, 26*(6), 601–620.

Traub, S. H. (1996). Battling employee crime: A review of corporate strategies and programs. *Crime and Delinquency, 42*(2), 244–256.

Triplett, R. (1993). The conflict perspective, symbolic interactionism and the status characteristics hypothesis. *Justice Quarterly, 10,* 541–558.

Trischitta, L. (2001, March 8). Three south Florida restaurants briefly closed by state inspectors. *Sun Sentinel.* Retrieved July 29, 2011, from http://articles.sun-sentinel.com/keyword/inspector/recent/2

Troy criminal justice professor indicated on rape charge involving 21-year-old student. (2010, January 20). *Press-Register.* Retrieved June 7, 2010, from http://blog.al.com/live/2010/01/troy_criminal_justice_professo.html

Trumka, R. (2008). Employment-related crimes. *American Criminal Law Review, 45*(2), 341–380.

24 arrested for mortgage fraud schemes. (2009). *Chicago Breaking News Center.* (2009). Retrieved July 6, 2011, from http://archive.chicagobreakingnews.com/2009/03/fbi-makes-arrests-in-mortgage-fraud-probe.html

Two Miami doctors convicted of Medicare, Medicaid fraud. (2009). Federal Bureau of Investigation. *Press Release.* Retrieved July 29, 2011, from http://www.fbi.gov/miami/press-releases/2009/mm081709b.htm

U.S. Attorney's Office Middle District of Pennsylvania. (2011). York county consultant gets prison for $1.5m scheme. Retrieved July 30, 2011, from http://www.justice.gov/usao/pam/news/2011/Cochran_Bossi_1_21_2011.htm

U.S. Consumer Product Safety Commission. (2010a). *2010 performance and accountability report.* Washington, DC: Author.

U.S. Consumer Product Safety Commission. (2010b). *Imported drywall and health: A guide for health care professionals.* Washington, DC: Author.

U.S. Consumer Product Safety Commission. (2010c). *Investigation of imported drywall: Status update, September 2010.* Retrieved July 31, 2011, from http://www.cpsc.gov/info/drywall/sep2010status.pdf

U.S. Consumer Product Safety Commission. (2010d). *Toy memo: Toy-related deaths and injuries, calendar year 2009.* Available online. Retrieved July 31, 2011, from http://www.cpsc.gov/library/toymemo09.pdf

U.S. Department of Health and Human Services. (2010). *Office of Inspector General semiannual report to Congress.* Washington, DC: Health and Human Services.

U.S. Department of Justice. (1994). *Environmental justice strategy.* Washington, DC: U.S. Department of Justice.

U.S. Department of Justice. (2009). Eli Lilly and Company agrees to pay 1.415 billion for off label promotion of Zyprexa. Retrieved June 30, 2011, from http://www.justice.gov/usao/pae/News/2009/jan/lillyrelease.pdf

U.S. Department of Justice. (2010a, May 14). Arlington security guard, who hacked into hospital's computer system, pleads guilty to federal charges. [Press release]. Retrieved July 30, 2011, from http://www.justice.gov/usao/txn/PressRel10/mcgraw_ple_pr.html

U.S. Department of Justice. (2010b, November 4). [News release]. Retrieved June 10, 2010 from http://www.justice.gov/criminal/cybercrime/frostSent.pdf

U.S. Department of Justice. (2010c). Report to Congress on the activities and operations of the Public Integrity Section for 2009. Retrieved July 29, 2011, from http://www.justice.gov/criminal/pin/docs/arpt-2009.pdf

U.S. Department of Justice. (2011, January 12). *Medical device manufacturer sentenced for failure to report defibrillator safety problems to FDA.* U.S. Department of Justice: Washington, D.C. Retrieved July 11, 2011, from http://www.justice.gov/opa/pr/2011/January/11-civ-035.html

U.S. Department of Justice. (n.d.). *Preventing and detecting bid rigging, price fixing, and market allocation in post-disaster rebuilding projects: An antitrust primer for agents and procurement officials.* Washington, DC: U.S. Department of Justice. Retrieved June 27, 2011, from http://www.justice.gov/atr/public/guidelines/disaster_primer.htm

U.S. Department of Justice, Environment and Natural Resources Division. (2010). *Summary of litigation accomplishments, fiscal year 2009.* Washington, DC: U.S. Department of Justice.

U.S. Department of Justice, Federal Bureau of Investigation. (1989). *White collar crime: A report to the public.* Washington, DC: Government Printing Office.

U.S. Environmental Protection Agency. (1998). *Illegal dumping prevention guidebook.* Chicago: USA Region 5.

U.S. Environmental Protection Agency. (2008, October 3). *Minnetonka man sentenced for violating Clean Water Act.* Retrieved from http://www.epa.gov/compliance/resources/cases/criminal/highlights/2009/rosenblum-keith-10-03-08.pdf

U.S. Environmental Protection Agency. (2010a). *Beazer Homes USA, Inc.* Retrieved July 30, 2011, from http://www.epa.gov/compliance/resources/cases/civil/cwa/beazer.html

U.S. Environmental Protection Agency. (2010b). *Environmental justice.* Retrieved December 17, 2010 from http://www.epa.gov/osw/wyl/envjustice.html

U.S. Environmental Protection Agency. (2010c). *Laws that we administer.* Retrieved on December 17, 2010 from http://www.epa.gov/lawsregs/laws/index.html

U.S. Environmental Protection Agency. (2010d). Research Development Office of Research Development. About the Office of. Retrieved July 30, 2011, from http://www.epa.gov/aboutepa/ord.html

U.S. Environmental Protection Agency. (2010e). *What is an environmental crime?* Retrieved on December 17, 2010 from http://www.epa.gov/compliance/criminal/investigations/environmentalcrime.html

U.S. Environmental Protection Agency. (2010, October 8). *Doe Run Resources Corporation settlement.* Retrieved November 14, 2010, from http://www.epa.gov/compliance/resources/cases/civil/mm/doerun.html

U.S. Government Accountability Office. (2003). *Medicaid: A program highly vulnerable to fraud.* Washington, DC: USGAO.

U.S. Government Accountability Office. (2005). *Mutual fund trading abuses: Lesson can be learned.* Washington, DC: Government Printing Office.

U.S. Government Accountability Office. (2009). *Corporate crime: DOJ has taken steps to better track its use of deferred and non-prosecution agreements, but should evaluate effectiveness.* Washington D.C.: USGAO.

U.S. Government Accountability Office. (2010). *For-profit colleges: Undercover testing finds colleges encouraged fraud and engaged in deceptive and questionable marketing practices.* Washington, DC: General Accountability Office.

U.S. Office of Inspector General. (1999). *Criminal calls: A review of the Bureau of Prisons' management of inmate telephone privileges.* Retrieved July 29, 2011, from http://www.justice.gov/oig/special/9908/index.htm

U.S. Office of Inspector General. (2008). *An investigation of allegations of politicized hiring and other improper personnel actions in the Civil Rights Division.* Washington, DC: U.S. Department of Justice.

U.S. Sentencing Commission. (1996). *Adequacy of federal sentencing guideline penalties for computer fraud and vandalism offenses: Report to Congress.* Washington, DC: U.S. Sentencing Commission.

Ugrin, J. C., & Odom, M. D. (2010). Exploring Sarbanes-Oxley's effect on attitude. Perceptions of norms, and intentions to commit financial statement fraud from a general deterrence perspective. *Journal of Accounting and Public Policy, 29*(5), 439–458.

Ulrich, L. (2000). Music on the Internet: Is there an upside to downloading? Hearing before the Committee on the Judiciary, United States Senate, July 11, 2000. Retrieved July 29, 2011, from http://www.gpo.gov/fdsys/pkg/CHRG-106shrg74728/html/CHRG-106shrg74728.htm

Union of Concerned Scientists. (2008). *Interference at the EPA: Science and politics at the U.S. Environmental Protection Agency.* Cambridge, MA: Author.

United States Conference of Catholic Bishops. (2011). The nature and scope of the problem of sexual abuse of minors by Catholic priests and deacons in the United States: A research study conducted by the John Jay College of Criminal Justice. Retrieved July 30, 2011, from http://www.usccb.org/nrb/johnjaystudy/

University of Colorado Investigative Committee Report. (2007). Report of the Investigative Committee on the standing committee on research misconduct at the University of Colorado at Boulder concerning allegations of academic misconduct against Professor Ward Churchill.

Retrieved July 29, 2011, from http://www.colorado.edu/news/reports/churchill/download/WardChurchillReport.pdf

University of Phoenix parent guilty of fraud. (2008, January 16). *Associated Press.* Retrieved July 29, 2011, from http://www.azcentral.com/business/articles/0116biz-apollogroupsuit16-ON.html

Unnever, J. D., Benson, M. L., & Cullen, F. T. (2008). Public support for getting tough on corporate crime: Racial and political divides. *Journal of Research in Crime and Delinquency, 45*(2), 163–190.

Vakkur, N., McAfee, R., & Kipperman, F. (2010). The unintended effects of the Sarbanes-Oxley Act of 2002. *Research in Accounting Regulation, 22,* 18–20.

Van Cleef, C. R., Silets, H. M., & Motz, P. (2004). Does the punishment fit the crime? *Journal of Financial Crime, 12*(1), 56–65.

Van den Berg, E. A. I. M., & Eshuis, R. J. (1996). *Major investigations of environmental crimes.* Arnheim, Netherlands: Gouda Quint.

Van Wyk, J. A., Benson, M. L., & Harris, D. K. (2000). A test of strain and self-control theories: Occupational crime in nursing homes. *Journal of Crime and Justice, 23*(2), 27–44.

Varian, B. (2000, February 3). Former insurance agent guilty of fraud. *St. Petersburg Times,* p. 1.

Vaughn, D. (1992). The macro-micro connection in white-collar crime theory. In K. Schlegel & D. Weisburd (Eds.), *White-collar crime reconsidered.* Boston: Northeastern University Press.

Vaughan, D. (2001). Sensational cases, flawed theories. In H. N. Pontell & D. Shichor (Eds.), *Contemporary issues in crime and criminal justice: Essays in honor of Gilbert Geis* (pp. 45–66). Upper Saddle River, NJ: Prentice Hall.

Vaughan, D., & Carlo, G. (1975). The appliance repairman: A study of victim responsiveness and fraud. *Journal of Research in Crime and Delinquency, 12,* 153–161.

Vickers, M. (2007). Are you at risk for mortgage fraud? *Fortune.* Retrieved June 21, 2010, from http://www.moneycnn.com/popups/2006/fortune/fraud/index.html

Vinten, G. (1994). Asset protection through whistleblowing. *Journal of Asset Protection and Financial Crime, 2*(2), 121–131.

Volunteer Lawyers Program Community Legal Services. (2009). *Arizona tenants' rights and responsibilities handbook.* Phoenix, AZ: Legal Services Corporation.

Voyles, K. (2011, January 19). Day care owner guilty of white-collar crime; must repay $75K. *Gainseville.com.* Retrieved July 11, 2011, from http://www.gainesville.com/article/20110119/ARTICLES/110119370

Wahl, A. (2009, November 23). Toy safety still a crapshoot. *Canadian Business, 82*(20), 16.

Waldfogel, J. (1995). Are fines and prison terms used efficiently? Evidence on federal fraud offenders. *Journal of Law and Economics, 38*(1), 107–139.

Walker, J. (2010, May 19). Academics fight Cuccinelli's call for climate-change records. *The Virginian-Pilot.* Retrieved from http://hamptonroads.com/2010/academics-fight-cuccinellis-call-climatechange-records

Walker, S., & Alpert, G. P. (2002). Early warning systems as risk management for police. In K. M. Lersch (Ed.), *Policing and misconduct* (pp. 219–230). Upper Saddle River, NJ: Prentice Hall.

Waller, M. (2007, December 29). Even in prison Martha Stewart could not resist breaking the rules. *The Times* (London). Retrieved July 31, 2011, from http://business.timesonline.co.uk/tol/business/columnists/article3105406.ece

Walters, R. (2007). Food crime, regulation, and the biotech harvest. *European Journal of Criminology, 4*(2), 217–235.

Washington, E. (2006). The impact of banking and fringe banking regulation on the number of unbanked Americans. *Journal of Human Resources, 41*(1), 106–137.

Wear, D., Aultman, J. M., & Borges, N. J. (2007). Retheorizing sexual harassment in medical education: Women students' perceptions at five U.S. medical schools. *Teaching and Learning in Medicine, 19*(1), 20–29.

Webb, T., & Pilkington, E. (2010, June 20). Gulf oil spill: BP accused of lying to Congress. *The Guardian.* Retrieved October 20, 2010, from http://www.guardian.co.uk/environment/2010/jun/20/gulf-oil-spill-bp-lying

Weber, J., Kurke, L. B., & Pentico, D. W. (2003). Why do employees steal?: Assessing differences in ethical and unethical employee behavior using ethical work climates. *Business Society, 42,* 359–380.

Weisburd, D., Chayet, E. F., & Waring, E. (1990). White-collar crime and criminal careers: Some preliminary findings. *Crime and Delinquency, 36,* 342–355.

Weisburd, D., Waring, E., & Chayet, E. (1995). Specific deterrence in a sample of offenders convicted of white-collar crimes. *Criminology, 33,* 587–607.

Weisburd, D., Waring, E., & Wheeler, S. (1990). Class, status, and the punishment of white-collar criminals. *Law and Social Inquiry, 15*(2), 223–243.

Weisburd, D., Wheeler, S., Waring, E., & Bode, N. (1991*). Crimes of the middle class: White-collar offenders in the federal courts.* New Haven, CT: Yale University Press.

Welch, H. (2008, February 5). Avoiding scams: 20,700 Americans fall for these investment schemes every year. *Jacksonville.Com,* Retrieved July 21, 2011 from http://jacksonville.com/tu-online/stories/020508/bus_243662551.shtml

Welch, M. (2009). Fragmented power and state-corporate killings: A critique of Blackwater in Iraq. *Crime, Law, and Social Change, 51,* 351–364.

Wells, J. T. (2003a). Follow the greenback road. *Journal of Accountancy, 196*(5), 84–87.

Wells, J. T. (2003b). The fraud examiners. *Journal of Accountancy, 196*(4), 76–79.

Wells, J. T. (2010). Ponzis and pyramids. *CPA Journal, 80*(2), 6.

Wheeler, S., Mann, K., & Sarat, A. (1988). *Sitting in judgment: The sentencing of white-collar criminals.* New Haven, CT: Yale University Press.

Wheeler, S., Weisburd, D., & Bode, N. (1982). Sentencing the white collar offender: Rhetoric and reality. *American Sociological Review, 47*(5), 641–659.

Wheeler, S., Weisburd, D., & Bode, N. (1988). *Nature and sanctioning of white collar crime.* Rockville, MD: National Institute of Justice.

Wheeler, S., Weisburd, D., & Bode, N. (2000). Nature and sanctioning of white collar crime, 1976–1978: Federal judicial districts. *Inter-university Consortium of Political and social Research,* Ann Arbor, MI.

Wheeler, S., Weisburd, D., Waring, E., & Bode, N. (1987–1988). White-collar crimes and criminals. *American Criminal Law Review, 25,* 331–358.

White, G., & Schneider, C. (2008, October 14). Depression expert at Emory pulls out of research projects. *Atlanta Journal Constitution,* p. A1.

White, J. B., Power, S., & Aeppel, T. (2001, June 20). Agency to comment on Ford tire safety, while inquiry into Explorer is considered. *Wall Street Journal,* p. A.3.

White, M. D., & Terry, K. J. (2008). Child sexual abuse in the Catholic Church: Revisiting the rotten apples explanation. *Criminal Justice and Behavior, 35*(5), 658–678.

White, R. (2008). Depleted uranium, state crime, and the politics of knowing. *Theoretical Criminology, 12*(1), 31–54.

White-collar crime rising. (2003, December 23). *Desert News.* Retrieved January 19, 2011, from http://findarticles.com/p/articles/mi_qn4188/is_20031223/ai_n11419131/?tag=rbxcra.2.a.11

Wiggins, L. M. (2002). Corporate computer crime: Collaborative power in numbers. *Federal Probation, 66*(3), 19–29.

Wiggins, O. (2009, June 12). Insurance agent accused of defrauding seniors of $280,000. *Washington Post*, p. B02.

Wilkins, L. (1965). *Social deviance.* Englewood Cliffs, NJ: Prentice Hall.

Williams, F. P., & McShane, M. D. (2008). *Criminological theory* (5th ed.). Upper Saddle River, NJ: Prentice Hall.

Williams, J. W. (2005). Governmentability matters: The private policing of economic crime and the challenge of democratic governance. *Policing and Society: An International Journal of Research and Policy, 15*(2), 187–211.

Williams, J. W. (2008). Out of place and out of line: Positioning the police in the regulation of financial markets. *Law and Policy, 30*(3), 306–355.

Wilson, J. Q., & Kelling, G. L. (1982). Broken windows: The police and neighborhood safety. *Atlantic Monthly, 249*, 29–38.

Wilson, P. R., Lincoln, R., Chappell, D., & Fraser, S. (1986). Physician fraud and abuse in Canada: A preliminary examination. *Criminology, 28*, 129–143

Wilson, R. (2003, September 19). Research-fraud investigation leads to departures from Northern Kentucky University. *Chronicle of Higher Education, 50*(4), A18.

Wislar, J., Flanagin, A., Fontanarosa, P., & Dangelis, C. D. (2010). Prevalence of honorary and ghost authorship in six general medical journals, 2009. *Peer Review Congress.* Retrieved July 29, 2011, from http://www.ama-assn.org/public/peer/abstracts-0910.pdf

Wolfe, S. M., Kahn, R., & Resnevic, K. (2010, April 5). *Ranking of state medical boards' serious disciplinary actions: 2007–2009. Public Citizen.* Retrieved July 29, 2011, from http://www.citizen.org/page.aspx?pid=3168

Worcester, B. A. (1998, July 6). Summer staffs open to scrutiny. *Hotel and Motel Management, 213*(12), 7.

World Health Organization. (2005). *The environment and health for children and their mothers. Fact sheet.* Retrieved July 29, 2011, from http://www.who.int/mediacentre/factsheets/fs284/en/index.html

World Health Organization. (2008). *Air quality and health. Fact sheet.* Retrieved July 29, 2011, from http://www.who.int/mediacentre/factsheets/fs313/en/index.html

Wright, D. E, Titus, S. L., & Cornelison, J. B. (2008). Mentoring and research misconduct: An analysis of research mentoring in closed ORI cases. *Science and Engineering Ethics, 14*(3), 323–336.

Wright, J., Cullen, F., & Blankenship, M. (1995). The social construction of corporate violence. *Crime and Delinquency, 41,* 20–36.

Wright, R. (2006). Why (some) fraud prosecutions fail. *Journal of Financial Crime, 13*(2), 177–182.

Yakovlev, P., & Sobel, R. (2010). Occupational safety and profit maximization: Friends or foes. *Journal of Socio-Economics, 39,* 429–435.

Yaniv, O., & Moore, T. (2008, February 21). Surrender deadline today for Bronx slumlord. *Daily News*, p. 18.

Yar, M. (2006). *Cybercrime and society.* Thousand Oaks, CA: Sage.

Yeager, P. (1986). Analyzing corporate offenses. In J. E. Post (Ed.), *Research on corporate social performance and policy.* Greenwich, CT: JAI Press.

Yohay, S. C., & Dodge, G. E. (1987). Criminal prosecutions for occupational injuries: An issue of growing concern. *Employee Relations Law Journal, 13*(2), 197–223.

Yoskowitz, A. (2007, April 5). 2/3 of students don't care about illegal downloading says survey. Retrieved July 31, 2011, http://www.afterdawn.com/news/article.cfm/2007/04/06/2_3_of_students_don_t_care_about_illegal_downloading_says_survey

Young, J. R. (2008). Judge rules plagiarism-detection tool falls under "fair use." *Chronicle of Higher Education, 54*(30), A13.

Yu, O. & Zhang, L. (2006). Does acceptance of corporate wrongdoing begin on the "training ground" of professional managers? *Journal of Criminal Justice, 34,* 185–194.

Zachariah, H., & Johnson, A. (2010, May 27). *Dairy-farm worker fired, arrested over video: Owner blasts brutality, is silent on his actions.* Retrieved July 29, 2011, from www.dispatch.com/live/content/local_news/stories/2010/05/27/dairy-farm-worker-fired-arrested-over-video.html

Zambito, T., Martinez, J. & Siemaszko, C. (2009, June 29). Bye, bye Bernie: Ponzi king Madoff sentenced to 150 years. *New York Daily News.* Retrieved July 11, 2011, from http://articles.nydailynews.com/2009-06-29/news/17924560_1_ruth-madoff-ira-sorkin-bernie-madoff

Zane, P. C. (2003). The price fixer's dilemma: Applying game theory to the decision of whether to plead guilty to antitrust crimes. *Antitrust Bulletin, 48*(1), 1–31.

Zeman, N., & Howard, L. (1992, June 22). Trading places. *Newsweek*, p. 8.

Zernike, K. (2003, September 20). Students shall not download. Yeah, sure. *New York Times.* Retrieved July 31, 2011 from http://www.nytimes.com/2003/09/20/technology/20COLL.html

Zuckoff, M. (2005). *Ponzi's scheme.* New York: Random House.

Zwolinski, M. (2008). The ethics of price gouging. *Business Ethics Quarterly, 18*(3), 347–378.

Credits and Sources

Section I. Introduction and Overview of White-Collar Crime

Photo 1.1: Fletcher6 (http://commons.wikimedia.org/wiki/File:Wall_Street_%26_Broadway.JPG)

Photo 1.2: Casey Deshong (FEMA Photo Library, http://www.fema.gov/photolibrary/photo_details.do?id=42030)

Photo 1.3: Elliot P. (http://www.flickr.com/photos/pesut/364905354/sizes/l/)

Photo 1.4: Digital Vision/Thinkstock

Table 1.1: Adapted from Payne, Brian K. (2005) *Crime and elder abuse: An integrated perspective.* 2nd ed. Springfield, IL: Charles C Thomas.

Section II. Understanding White-Collar Crime

Table 2.2: Uniform Crime Reports (2010).

Photo 2.1: Leif Skoogfors/FEMA (http://www.fema.gov/photolibrary/photo_details.do?id=38844)

Table 2.3: Adapted from Kane, J., & Wall, A. (2005). *The national public survey on white collar crime.* Fairmont, WV: National White Collar Crime Center.

Table 2.4: Adapted from National White Collar Crime Center. (2005). *The national public survey on white collar crime.* Fairmont, WV: National White Collar Crime Center.

Figure 2.2: Adapted from Federal Trade Commission Staff Report. (2004). *Consumer fraud in the United States: An FTC survey.* Washington, DC: Federal Trade Commission.

Photo 2.2: U.S. Coast Guard (http://cgvi.uscg.mil/media/main.php?g2_itemId=498425)

Photo 2.3: Iamwisesun (http://en.wikipedia.org/wiki/File:Conan_O'Brien_performing.jpg)

Section III. Crimes in Sales-Related Occupations

Photo 3.1: Greg Gorman/U.S. Customs and Border Protection, Dept. of Homeland Security (http://www.cbp.gov/xp/cgov/newsroom/multimedia/photo_gallery/afc/mp_disney/disneymp_27.xml)

In Focus Box 3.1: National Association of Attorneys Generals. (2009). Top 10 Consumer Complaints Made to State Attorney Generals. Available online at http://www.naag.org/top-10-list-of-consumer-complaints-for-2008-aug.-31-2009.php

Photo 3.2: Marvin Nauman/FEMA (http://www.fema.gov/photolibrary/photo_details.do?id=23015)

Photo 3.3: Photographer's Mate 3rd Class Todd Frantom (http://www.navy.mil/view_single.asp?id=14885)

Section IV. Crimes in the Health Care System

Photo 4.1: U.S. National Archives/White House Photographic Office

In Focus Box 4.1: National Association of Attorneys Generals. (2009). Medicaid Fraud Reports. Available from http://www.namfcu.net/resources/medicaid-fraud-reports-newsletters/2009-publications/09NovDec.pdf

Figure 4.1: Adapted from Payne, B. K. (1995). Medicaid fraud. *Criminal Justice Policy Review, 7,* 61–74.

Figure 4.2: Adapted from Payne, B. K. (1995). Medicaid fraud. *Criminal Justice Policy Review, 7,* 61–74.

In Focus Box 4.2: National Association of Attorneys Generals. (2009). Medicaid Fraud Reports. Available from http://www.namfcu.net/resources/medicaid-fraud-reports-newsletters/2009-publications/09MayJune.pdf

Photo 4.2: National Institutes of Health (http://www.media.nih.gov/imagebank/display.aspx?ID=39)

Photo 4.3: Comstock/Thinkstock

Table 4.1: Cohen, T. H. (2005). Federal tort trials and verdicts, 2002-2003. Bureau of Justice Statistics Bulletin. Washington, DC: U.S. Department of Justice.

In Focus Box 4.3: Cohen, T., & Hughes, K. (2007). *Medical malpractice insurance claims in seven states, 2000-2004.* Bureau of Justice Statistics, U.S. Department of Justice: Washington D.C.

Table 4.2: Cohen, T. & Hughes, K. (2007). Medical malpractice insurance claims in seven states, 2000-2004. Bureau of Justice Statistics. Washington, DC: U.S. Department of Justice.

Section V. Crime in Systems of Social Control

Figure 5.1: Adapted from Payne, B. K., Time, V., & Raper, S. (2005). Regulating legal misconduct by lawyers in the Commonwealth of Virginia: The gender influence. *Women and Criminal Justice, 15,* 81-96; and Payne, B. K., & Stevens, E. H. (1999). An examination of recent professional sanctions imposed on Alabama lawyers. *The Justice Professional, 12,* 17-43.

Photo 5.1: Susan Roberts (Wikimedia)

Figure 5.2: Adapted from State of California Commission on Judicial Performance. (2010). *2009 Annual Report.*

In Focus Box 5.1: State of California Commission on Judicial Performance. (2002). Available from http://cip.ca.gov/userfiles/file/Censures/Block12-09-02.pdf

Photo 5.2: Ildar Sagdejev (http://commons.wikimedia.org/wiki/File:2009-03-20_610_N_Buchanan_Blvd_in_Durham.jpg)

Table 5.1: U.S. Department of Justice. (2010). Report to Congress on the activities and operations of the public integrity section for 2009. Washington, DC: U.S. Department of Justice.

Photo 5.3: U.S. Congress

Photo 5.4: U.S. Military

Figure 5.3: Adapted from John Jay College of Criminal Justice. (n.d.). The nature and scope of the problem of sexual abuse of minors by catholic priests and deacons in the United States. In *A Research Study Conducted by the John Jay College of Criminal Justice.* Available from http://www.nccbuscc.org/nrb/johnjaystudy/

Figure 5.4: Adapted from John Jay College of Criminal Justice. (n.d.). The nature and scope of the problem of sexual abuse of minors by Catholic priests and deacons in the United States. In *A research study conducted by the John Jay College of Criminal Justice.* Available from http://www.nccbuscc.org/nrb/johnjaystudy/

Section VI. Crimes in the Educational System

Photo 6.1: Jrcla2 (http://commons.wikimedia.org/wiki/File:Wren_front.jpg)

Photo 6.2: James Gathany/Centers for Disease Control and Prevention

Figure 6.1: Adapted from Wislar, J., Flanagin A., Fontanarosa, P., & DeAngelis, C. (2009). Prevalence of honorary and ghost authorship in 6 general medical journals, 2009. *Peer Review Congress.* Available from http://www.ama-assn.org/public/peer/abstracts-0910.pdf

Photo 6.3: dbking (Wikimedia)

In Focus Box 6.1: Office of Research Integrity. (2009). Washington, DC: U.S. Department of Justice. Available from http://ori.dhhs.gov/misconduct/cases/press_release_poehlman.shtml

Table 6.1: Adapted from Euben, D. & Lee, B. (2005). Faculty misconduct and discipline. In Presentation to National Conference on Law and Higher Education, February 22, 2005. Available from http://www.aaup.org/AAUP/programs/legal/topics/misconduct-discp.html

Section VII. Crime in the Economic and Technological Systems

Photo 7.1: Pete Souza (http://en.wikipedia.org/wiki/File:Zuckerberg_meets_Obama.jpg)

In Focus Box 7.1: Initial decision release no. 396 administrative proceeding file no. 3-13280 United States of America before the Securities and Exchange Commission Washington, D.C. 20549 In the Matter of Don Warner Reinhard Supplemental Initial Decision June 1, 2010. Available online at http://www.sec.gov/litigation/aljdec/2010/id396cff.pdf

Photo 7.2: David Shankbone (http://en.wikipedia.org/wiki/File:Martha_Stewart_2_Shankbone_Metropolitan_Opera_2009.jpg)

Photo 7.3: Carlos Cruz (http://commons.wikimedia.org/wiki/File:Cindyrella%27s_Castle_@_Magic_Kingdom.jpg)

Table 7.1: Available from http://www.sec.gov/answers/ponzi.html

Figure 7.1: Adapted from McCoy (2009).

Photo 7.4: U.S. Department of Justice (http://commons.wikimedia.org/wiki/File:BernardMadoff.jpg)

Table 7.2: Information from various news and governmental sources including Associated Press ("Martha Stewart Reads," 2004), Associated Press ("Accused Dentist," 2007), Cosgrove-Mather, 2003, Crawford (2005), Hays (2006), Johnson (2005), Johnson (2006), Kolker (2009), Masters (2005), U.S. Securities and Exchange Commission (n.d.), White (2005).

Table 7.3: Adapted from Richardson. (2008). CSI Computer Crime & Security Survey. Available from http://www.gocsi.com/survey

In Focus Box 7.2: Press release from the U.S. Department of Justice (2010, June 6)

Table 7.4: 2009 Internet Crime Report. (n.d.). Fairmont, WV: National White Collar Crime Center.

Table 7.5: Richardson. (2008). CSI Computer Crime & Security Survey. Available from http://www.gocsi.com/survey

Photo 7.5: Kreepin Deth (http://commons.wikimedia.org/wiki/File:Metallica_at_The_O2_Arena_London_2008.jpg)

Section VIII. Crimes in the Housing System

Photo 8.1: Nate Cull (http://commons.wikimedia.org/wiki/File:Favela-Nova_Friburgo.jpg)

Figure 8.1: Financial Crimes Enforcement Network. (2009). *The SAR activity review: Trends, tips, and issues.* Washington, DC: U.S. Department of Treasury.

In Focus Box 8.1: United States Attorneys Office. (2010).

Figure 8.2: Adapted from Donahue, K. (2004, October 7). "Statement of Kenneth Donuhue, Inspector General Department of Housing and Urban Development." Before the United States House of Representatives Subcommittee on Housing and Community Opportunity Committee on Financial Services.

In Focus Box 8.2: Federal Deposit Insurance Corporation. (2007). Available from http://www.fdic.gov/regulations/examinations/supervisory/insights/sisum07/aritcle02_staying-alert.html

Table 8.1: U.S. Department of Treasury. (2010). Financial Enforcement Crime Network. Available from http://www.fincen.gov/news_room/nr/html/20100617.html

Photo 8.2: Craig Crawford, Department of Justice.

Section IX. Crimes by the Corporate System

Table 9.1: Antitrust enforcement and the consumer. (n.d.) In U.S. Department of Justice.

Table 9.2: Adapted from Mokhiber, R. (n.d.). Top 100 Corporate Criminals of the Decade. In *Corporate Crime Reporter.*

Table 9.3: U.S. Government Accountability Office. (2010).

Table 9.4: EEOC. (2010). In Charge Statistics. Available from http://www.eeoc.gov/eeoc/statistics/enforcement/charges.cfm

Figure 9.2: Bureau of Labor Statistics. (2010). In *2009 Nonfatal occupational injuries and illnesses: Private industry, state government, and local government. Table 9.5:* Bureau of Labor Statistics. (2010). Table 2.

Table 9.6: Occupational Safety and Health Administration (OSHA), United States Department of Labor. (2010b). Employer rights and responsibilities following an OSHA inspection. Available from http://www.osha.gov/Publications/osha3000.html

In Focus Box 9.1: OSHA. (n.d.). Available from http://www.osha.gov/Publications/teen_worker_brochure.html

Table 9.7: U.S. Consumer Product Safety Commission. (2010). In Toy Memo.

Photo 9.2: Photo by Kathleen Payne.

In Focus Box 9.2: House Committee on Oversight and Reform. (n.d.).

Figure 9.3: Adapted from Lynch, M. J., McGurrin, D., & Fenwick, M. (2004). "Disappearing act: The representation of corporate crime research in criminology journals and textbooks." *Journal of Criminal Justice*, 32(5), 389-398.

Section X. Environmental Crime

Photo 10.1: U. S. Coast Guard photo (http://cgvi.uscg.mil/media/main.php?g2_itemId=1031998)

Photo 10.2: U. S. Coast Guard photo by Petty Officer 2nd Class Rob Simpson (http://cgvi.uscg.mil/media/main.php?g2_itemId=1031998)

In Focus Box 10.1: http://www.epa.gov/history/topics/lovecanal/03.htm

Photo 10.3: Photo by Kathleen Payne

In Focus Box 10.2: Reprinted from: Career Opportunities for Students. http://www.epa.gov/careers/stuopp.html#coll

Figure 10.1: Data compiled from EPA Office of Enforcement and Compliance. (n.d.). In *Annual Reports.*

Figure 10.2: U.S. Environmental Protection Agency. (n.d.). Available from http://www.epa.gov/compliance/criminal/fugitives/posters/beltran-08-wanted-poster.pdf

Table 10.1: EPA Office of Enforcement and Compliance. (2010 Oct 8). In Doe Run Resources Corporation Settlement.

Table 10.2: EPA Office of Enforcement and Compliance. (2010). Available from http://www.epa.gov/compliance/resources/reports/nets/nets-f2-penalties.pdf

Photo 10.4: James Tourtellotte (http://www.cbp.gov/xp/cgov/newsroom/multimedia/photo_gallery/afc/world_trade_center/wtc_16.xml)

Photo 10.5: Jim Watson/AFP/Getty Images

Table 10.3: Adapted from Mueller, G. (1996). An essay on environmental criminality, pp. 3-32. In Edwards, S. M., Edwards, T. D., & Fields, C., *Environmental crime and criminality.* New York: Garland.

Section XI. Explaining White-Collar Crime

In Focus Box 11.1: Excerpt from Merton. (1938). Social structure and anomie. *American Sociological Review, 3*(5), 672-682.

Photo 11.1: Rolls Press/Popperfoto/Getty Images

In Focus Box 11.2: Excerpt from Sutherland. (1939). *Principles of criminology,* 3. Philadelphia: J. B. Lippincott.

Table 11.2: Evans & Porche. (2005). Adapted from *Deviant Behavior.* Taylor & Francis.

Photo 11.2: Delphi234 (http://commons.wikimedia.org/wiki/File:NYPD_Security_Camera.jpg)

Photo 11.3: Photo Courtesy of ICE

Section XII. Policing White-Collar Crime

Photo 12.1: Courtesy of the FBI

Table 12.2: F.B.I. (2010, 2009). In Financial Crimes Report. Available from http://www.fbi.gov/stats-services/publications/financial-crimes-report-2009/financial-crimes-report-2009#forensic

Figure 12.2: Adapted from FBI (2010). 2009 Financial Crimes Annual Report.

In Focus Box 12.1: F.B.I. (2009). In 2008 Mortgage Fraud Report. Available from http://www.fbi.gov/stats-services/publications/mortgage-fraud-2008

Photo 12.2: Gerald L. Nino

Table 12.5: Adapted from Securities and Exchange Commission, Division of Criminal Enforcement. (2010). In *Enforcement Manual.* Available from http://www.sec.gov/divisions/enforce/enforcementmanual.pdf

Photo 12.3: Photo by Kathleen Payne

Photo 12.4: Photo by Kathleen Payne

Photo 12.5: Photo by Kathleen Payne

Section XIII. Judicial Proceedings and White-Collar Crime

Photo 13.1: Sue Kim (http://commons.wikimedia.org/wiki/File:Denny_Chin.jpg)

Photo 13.2: Comstock/Thinkstock

In Focus Box 13.1: U.S. Code. (n.d.).

Table 13.1: McNulty. (n.d.). *Principles of Federal Prosecution of Business Organizations.* U.S. Department of Justice: Office of Deputy Attorney General.

Table 13.2: Adapted from U.S. Government Accountability Office. (2009). In DOJ's *Use of Deferred and Non-Prosecution Agreements,* p. 16.

In Focus Box 13.2: Adapted from Stewart, M. (2004 July 15). In Martha Stewart's letter to Judge Cedarbaum.

Table 13.3: Adapted from Cohen, T. (2009). Tort bench and jury trials in state courts, 2005. In U.S. Department of Justice: Office of Justice Programs; and Farole, D. (2009). Contract bench and jury trials in state courts, 2005. In U.S. Department of Justice: Office of Justice Programs.

Table 13.4: Adapted from Cohen, T. (2009). Tort bench and jury trials in state courts, 2005. In U.S. Department of Justice: Office of Justice Programs; and Farole, D. (2009). Contract bench and jury trials in state courts, 2005. In U.S. Department of Justice: Office of Justice Programs.

Table 13.5: Nakayama, G. (n.d.). Transmittal of Final OECA Parallel Proceedings Policy. Environmental Protection Agency.

Section XIV. The Corrections Sub-System and White-Collar Crime

Figure 14.1: Bureau of Justice Statistics. (2006). *Compendium of federal justice statistics, 2004.* Washington, DC: U.S. Department of Justice.

Table 14.1: Bureau of Justice Statistics. (2006). *Compendium of Federal Justice Statistics, 2004.* Washington, DC: U.S. Department of Justice.

Photo 14.1: U.S. Navy photo by Photographer's Mate 2nd Class Samuel J. Price

Photo 14.2: Patrick Denker (http://commons.wikimedia.org/wiki/File:Modern_chain_gang.jpg)

Photo 14.3: Sam Beebe (http://www.flickr.com/photos/sbeebe/3468562591/)

Figure 14.2: Langton, L., & Cohen, T. H. (2008). Civil bench and jury trials in state courts, 2005. *Bureau of Justice Statistics.* Available from http://www.usdoj.gov/bjs/pub/pdf/cbjitsc05.pdf

Table 14.2: Langton, L., & Cohen, T. H. (2008). Civil bench and jury trials in state courts, 2005. *Bureau of Justice Statistics.* Washington, DC: U.S. Department of Justice: Office of Justice Programs. Available from http://www.usdoj.gov/bjs/pub/pdf/cbjitsc05.pdf

Table 14.3: Adapted from Langton, L. & Cohen, T. (2008). Civil bench and jury trials in state courts, 2005. *Bureau of Justice Statistics.* Washington, DC: U.S. Department of Justice: Office of Justice Programs.

Table 14.4: Adapted from Cohen, T. H. (2005). Punitive damage awards in large counties, 2001. In *Bureau of Justice Statistics.*

Table 14.5: Payne, B. (2003). *Incarcerating white-collar offenders: The prison experience and beyond.* Springfield, IL: Charles C Thomas.

Table 14.6: Lofquist, W. (1993). Organizational probation and the U.S. sentencing commission. *Annals of the American Academy of Political and Social Science, 525,* 157-169.

Index

About the Author

Brian K. Payne is Chair and Professor of the Department of Criminal Justice at Georgia State University. His research interests include family violence and criminal justice, elder abuse, electronic monitoring, and white-collar crime. He has published six books, including *Incarcerating White-Collar Criminals: The Prison Experience and Beyond* (2003) and *Family Violence and Criminal Justice* (3e) (2009). He has also published a number of journal articles and presented at many professional meetings.

SAGE Research Methods Online

The essential tool for researchers

Sign up now at
www.sagepub.com/srmo
for more information.

An expert research tool

- An **expertly designed taxonomy** with more than 1,400 unique terms for social and behavioral science research methods

- **Visual and hierarchical search tools** to help you discover material and link to related methods

- Easy-to-use navigation tools
- Content organized by complexity
- Tools for citing, printing, and downloading content with ease
- Regularly updated content and features

A wealth of essential content

- The most comprehensive picture of quantitative, qualitative, and mixed methods available today

- More than **100,000 pages of SAGE book and reference material** on research methods as well as editorially selected material from SAGE journals

- More than **600 books** available in their entirety online

Launching 2011!

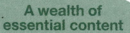 **SAGE** research methods online